MW01101128

Modern American Colloquialisms

美国口语词典

[美]Edward G. Seidensticker 主编

[美]John G. McCaleb
[日]安田一郎　　编

张文华　　编译

外语教学与研究出版社

(京)新登字 155 号

责任编辑:黎　云

本词典的录音带由海文音像出版社出版发行

Modern American Colloquialisms
美国口语词典
MEIGUO KOUYU CIDIAN
[美]Edward G. Seidensticker 主编
张文华编译
*　*　*
外语教学与研究出版社出版发行
(北京市西三环北路十九号)
本社编辑部计算机室排版
机械工业出版社印刷厂激光照排中心制版
北京第二新华印刷厂印刷
新华书店总店北京发行所经销
开本 787×1092　1/32　29.5 印张　1204 千字
1990 年 12 月第 1 版　1995 年 4 月第 3 次印刷
印数:60 001—75 000 册
*　*　*
ISBN 7—5600—0809—7/H·365
定价:28.80 元

目　录

编译者的话

本书是一部独特的词典。它不仅收录当前美国使用频率较高的大量口语，而且对这些口语的来龙去脉、字面意义、比喻意义、使用方法、注意事项、同义语、反义语等，做了极为确切的解释和说明。每一条都有足够的例句，而这些例句并不是一般英语教科书中的语法模式，也不是会话课本里的简单杂谈，而是从美国的小说、报刊、广播、电视、甚至连环画的文字部分摘录出来的。光是这几万条例句，就可以看出原著者的苦心和本书的可贵了。

本书既是一部良好的美国口语词典，也是一部非常实用的美国口语教科书，不但适于作为学习课本，而且适于自修。每条自成体系，可以说开卷有益。所注的发音不是一般词典里的发音，而是美国人在实际谈话中的发音。也就是说，如能按本书各条的注音正确讲出，自然会掌握地道的美国口语。这是靠一般词典或工具书得不到的东西。另外，本书所收各条美国口语，不仅是当前美国社会最常用的，而且是比较文雅的，正如原著者在序言中所说，美国的下流话、肮脏话一概不录。这一点可能正适合我国广大读者的口味。

美国英语与英国英语不同，正如广东话与北京话不同一样。本书在许多条中，都用具体的实例说明这一点。凡是弄不清两者的区别的读者，通过本书会得到比较明确的概念。特别是，同样为美国英语，正式文章与日常说话又有显著的差异。本书对这种差异也有明确的解释。而且，例句不是单调的、死板的，而是自然的、灵活的。讲的人有男也有女，有老人也有儿童，有干各类工作的人，包括强盗、囚徒，并有种种不同的话题。可以这样说，这部词典不仅告诉你怎样正确地运用美国口语，而且向你讲述了美国人在想些什么和干些什么，也就是反映了当前美国社会的真实动态。

编译者珍视这部词典，因为编译者一生从事翻译工作，学习了多种外语，当然会与各式各样的词典打交道，说老实话，还没遇到过这样一部可人心意的著作。对于原著者来说,美国口语是他的母语,精通自不必说,但是,如果他对语言学没有认真研究,不积累大量实际材料,去芜存菁,是编不出这样一部好书来的。编译者有幸把它翻译出来,愿与热心学习美国口语的各位读者共同欣赏。万一有的地方解释错误,决非原著之过,应该打编译者的屁股。

外语教学与研究出版社总编辑靳平妥同志应允出这部书,并给与亲切的指导,特此致谢。另外,责任编辑黎云同志精细地审读,提出许多非常宝贵的意见;外文翻译社副社长洪英同志、中国大百科全书出版社钱振鹏同志和尤国宏同志,始终给与技术上的帮助,使本书能够早日脱稿;在此,编译者表示深深的谢意。

最后,希望阅读本书的读者先看《体例说明》。

张文华

1991年6月

体例说明

(一)中心条目和条头

中心条目:本词典用大号黑正体排印中心条目,中心条目下收录美国当前常用的英语表达法(即条头)四千余条。中心条目一律按英语字母顺序排列。中心条目一般由一个词构成,亦有两个以上词构成的固有名词或固定习语。

条头:条头用小号黑正体排印,列在中心条目下面。条头在中心条目内按英语字母顺序排列。

条头按以下原则安排在有关中心条目之下:

条头中如只有一个名词,则该条头列在该名词作为中心条目的条目中。如:

(as) ugly as sin

shut *one's* **eyes to** *something*

条头如为"名词+名词"的形式,则该条头列在后一个名词作为中心条目的条目中。如:

crocodile tears

a flea trap

条头中如有两个或两个以上名词,则该条头一般列在第一个名词作为中心条目的条目中。如:

the lay of the land

the rank and file

条头中如有"好象……似的"的意思的 like 或 of 时,则该条头列在 like 或 of 后的名词作为中心条目的条目中。如:

have a mind like a sponge

the patience of Job

条头中如前一个名词为所有格时,则该条头列在后一个名词作为中心条目的条目中。如:

(as) scarce as hen's teeth

条头中如没有名词,则该条头列在其关键词(动词、形容词、

副词、介词等)作为中心条目的条目中。如:

tie *someone* **down**

go easy on *something*

How come?

get with it

中心条目原则上用一个单词,但有两个以上单词构成的固有名词或者固定习语时,不在此限,如:

John Q. Public

the Big Apple

poli sci

条头中的 *something, someone, one's* 等,在会话中用相应的名词或代词替换。( )内的词可省略。( )内再需用圆括号时为避免重复用<　>代替。[ ]内的词可代换它前边的词。开头的 a, an, the, be 是必要的附加词。在实际运用时,be 动词要作相应的变化。

(二)释义和解说

有少数条头的译文是固定的,如 crocodile tears (鳄鱼的眼泪),a Stetson (牛仔帽),the Windy City (芝加哥市)等。但大多数条头不但可以有不同译法,而且实际上也包含着几种意义,往往在字面意义之外,另有比喻意义。根据原著精神,本书条头的释义一般只选取最主要的、有代表性的、可以灵活运用的意义,不罗列,不喧宾夺主。

本书所收录的美国口语,大致可分四类,均在释义前注明:

[口]指虽然是一般口语,但在比较正式的文章中也可以使用。

[话]指主要在讲话时使用。在通俗杂志里可以见到,但正式文章中以不用为好。

[俗]指粗俗的口语,在使用时要考虑说话对象和场所,不能随便乱说。

[谚]指在日常会话中经常使用的谚语。

本书各条最后多有◇符号，表示◇后面的文字可以在各例句中代换条头，意义相同。

→符号主要有两种用法：一是在解说中指示参见条；一是指示主条头。

凡是(( ))内的文字都是附加说明或提示，供参考用。如 **a nobody** 一条中：

◇ an unimportant person ((just→very))

在这里，(( ))中的文字可以适当代换，即本条例句 I′m just a nobody. 就可以改换说：I′m a **very** unimportant person.

凡是小大写均指所要检索的中心条目。

(三)注音与说明

读音用国际音标，紧接条头注出，置于方括号中间。重音点在音节左上角，次重音点在音节左下角。

条头第一个单词如为 be，因 be 有不规则屈折变化，不注音。用圆括号括起的附带性词语，如 (for *something*), (with *something*) 等，不注音。

属于替换性的词，主要有 *one's, oneself, someone, something, someone's, do something, doing something, one* 等，在注音中用～符号，表明代入后要发音。

音标例解：

＜单元音＞

[i]	easy [ˈi(ː)zi]	[ʌ]	cut [kʌt]
[ɪ]	chicken [ˈtʃɪkən]	[ɑ]	dot [dɑt]
[e]	belt [belt]	[ɔ]	call [kɔ(ː)l]
[æ]	catch [kætʃ]	[o]	shadow [ˈʃæ(ː)do]
[ə]	above [əˈbʌ(ː)v]	[u]	pull [pul]
	custom [ˈkʌstəm]	[uː]	booze [buːz]

＜双元音＞

[eɪ]	cake [keɪk]	[aɪ]	night [naɪt]
[ou]	dough [dou]	[ər]	heard [hə(ː)rd]

[au]	down [daun]	[ɑr]	hard [hɑ(ː)rd]
[ɔɪ]	boy [bɔɪ]	[ɔr]	horse [hɔ(ː)rs]
[ɪr]	peer [pɪ(ː)r]	[or]	score [sko(ː)r]
[er]	pair [pe(ː)r]	[ur]	sure [ʃu(ː)r]

＜辅音＞

[p]	penny ['peni]	[θ]	thick [θɪk]
[b]	beef [bi(ː)f]	[ð]	this [ðɪs]
[t]	time [taɪm]	[h]	home [houm]
[d]	dime [daɪm]	[tʃ]	chow [tʃau]
[k]	kick [kɪk]	[dʒ]	pledge [ple(ː)dʒ]
[g]	goat [gout]	[l]	loin [lɔɪn]
[f]	face [feɪs]	[m]	mail [meɪl]
[v]	vine [vaɪn]	[n]	nest [nest]
[s]	slip [slɪp]	[ŋ]	ring [rɪŋ]
[z]	zip [zɪp]	[j]	yes [jes]
[ʃ]	shut [ʃʌt]	[w]	wet [wet]
[ʒ]	treasure ['treʒər]	[r]	rail [reɪl]

在美国口语中，最主要的发音现象是一种“连锁”现象，即以强音节为中心，吸引前后的弱音节形成一个音组，如：

come apart at the seams [ˌkʌmə'pɑrdətðə 'siːmz]

其中，apart 中的 part 是强音节，以它为中心，此一条头在发音上形成 comeapartatthe seams 这样的“连锁”。

在连锁中，冠词 an 一定要分成 a 和 n，作 [ə n]。这是因为实际会话中如此，务请读者注意。例如：

(as) slippery as an eel [əz 'slɪpəri əzə 'niːl]

an ace in the hole [ə ˌneɪsənðə 'houl]

在发音方面，另一个特别值得注意的现象，是音的“弱化”。常见的词如 am [æm], have [hæv], 在连锁中往往发音为 am [əm] [m], have [həv] [əv] [v]。特别是 and [ænd], 在连锁中常“弱化”为 [ənd] [ən] [n], 如：

fight like cats and dogs [ˌfaɪt laɪˈkːæ(ː)tsənˈdɔːgz]

go at *something* **hammer and tongs** [goʊət ～ ˈhæmərən ˈtɔːŋz]

在“强元音+t+弱元音”的场合，t 音一般转成 d 音，如：

be in hot water [in ˌhɑt ˈwɔ(ː)dər]

hit the bottle [ˌhɪtðə ˈbɑ(ː)dl]

Come and get it! [ˈkʌmənˈgedət]

A

from A to Z [frəˈmeɪdə ˈziː] [口] **(从最初到最末)全部** 因为在英语字母表中,A是最初的字母,Z是最后的字母,所以“从A到Z”意为“自始至终”、“彻头彻尾”、“完全”。注意:美国口语Z的发音不是[zed],而是[ziː]。*Roy knows Japanese history from A to Z.* 罗伊对日本的历史了解得很透彻。*I've read all of Poe's works from A to Z.* 爱伦·坡的全部作品,从头到尾我都读过了。*He's mastered his field from A to Z.* 他精通自己的专业。◇ in its [their] entirety / completely

aback

be taken aback [ˈteɪkən əˌbæ(ː)k] [口] **吃惊;吓一跳** 原为海上用语,指游艇等正在扬帆行驶时,风向突然改变,帆从正面受到强风的袭击而“被吹翻过来”。在一瞬间,整个船猛烈震动,令人产生急刹车的感觉。有时桅杆折断,船体破损,是很危险的现象。*The entire ship paused and shuddered as the sails were taken aback by a sudden strong head wind.* 由于一阵强烈的顶头风突然把帆吹翻过来,船一下子停住了,不断震动。作为比喻,一般用以表示“(面临令人震惊的事件而)吓一大跳”、“(一瞬之间)畏缩不前”的意思;但也常用以表示“(面临意外的事情,一瞬之间)不知所措”、“(一瞬之间)为难”之类轻一些的意思。*I was taken aback when I glanced up and saw the look of utter hatred in her eyes.* 我抬头一看到她眼睛里充满极端憎恶的神情时,不禁吓了一大跳。*Most foreigners are taken aback by the prices the first time they eat in a Japanese restaurant.* 第一次到日本饭店就餐的外国人,一见那价码,大多数都为之咋舌。在下面两个例句中则表示“惊慌”、“不知所措”的意思。*Kermit was obviously taken aback at the huge number of people who had turned out to meet his plane.* 克米特见到有那么多人来迎接他的飞机,显然张皇失措了。*I was taken aback at your being taken aback at my being here. I had thought that you were expecting me to come.* 你知道我在这里而显得很惊慌,这真出我的意外。我原来还以为你盼望我来呐。也常有如下列例句那样表示“(由于恐怖而)惊慌失措”的场合。*Lois was momentarily taken aback at the sight of the two strange men in her apartment, but she quickly recovered her composure and demanded to know why they were there.* 洛伊丝见到有两个陌生人在她的公寓里,一瞬之间惊慌失措,但是她很快就镇静下来,质问他们为什么会在那儿。如以上所示,大多是被动语态,但也使用take *someone* aback (使人吓一跳)这样的主动语态。*The filth and squalor of the family's home took us aback.* 那一家的屋子里的污秽肮脏,简直把我们吓了一大跳。*The sight of the masked gunman took me momentarily aback. It must have been at least half a minute before I found the presence of mind to step back into the shadows.* 当见到一个蒙面持枪的歹徒时,在一时之间把我吓得魂飞魄散。至少过了有半分钟,我才恢复知觉,隐蔽起来。◇ be dumbfounded [startled, shocked]

about

be not about to *do something* [ˌnɑdəˈbauˈtːə ~] [话] **完全没有去做……的意图** 注意:这一条不单单是 be about to *do something* 的否定形式。肯定形式的意思是“现在马上去做……”,否定形式的意思并不是“现在不马上去做……”,而是加强 about 的发音,表达强烈反对的意志:“完全没有去做……的意图”。例如:*I'm about to tell you the answer to that.* 我现在正要回答你的那个问题。但是它的否定形式并不意味着“我现在不马上回答你的那个问题”,而是“我完全没有回答那个问题的打算”。*I don't care when the deadline is. I'm not about to stay up all night working on this.* 我不管什么时候是截止期限。我根本不打算彻夜干这种工作。*I'm not about to sit around the house doing nothing when I have the chance to go skiing.* 既然有去滑雪的好机会,我决不打算在家里闲呆着。*I'm not about to go out shopping in all this rain.* 老这样下雨,我根本不打算出去买东西。◇ be certainly not going to *do something*

be up and about [around] → UP

abracadabra

abracadabra [ˌæ(ː)brəkəˈdæːbrə] [口] **啊,真不可思议!** 此词源出公元1—2世纪的古代宗教符咒,其本身没有特定意义。最常使用它的是魔术师,在变戏法时表示“啊,真不可思议!”另外是当人念咒时,表示“天灵灵,地灵灵”的意思。*The moment the magician said “abracadabra” the egg turned into a pigeon.* 魔术师嘴里说“啊,真不可思议!”的一刹那,鸡蛋变成了鸽子。当小孩子受点轻伤的时候,大人有时说:*Abracadabra. Now all the hurt is gone.* 天灵灵,地灵灵,我的宝宝全不痛。由于此词是“魔术师所使用的莫明其妙的话”,又转义为“无法理解”。*I don't know if he will compromise with us or not. I talked to his lawyer but all I got was a string of legalistic abracadabra.* 我不知道他是否会跟我们和解。我跟他的律师谈过了,但是我所得到的只是一大串没法理解的法律术语。◇ Look, (it's) magic! / jargon

absence

Absence makes the heart grow fonder. [ˈæ(ː)bsənts ˌmeɪksðə ˈhɑrt ˌgrouˈfɑːndər] [谚] **久别情深** 贝利(James Haynes Bayly) 19世纪初期为一首别离歌《很久很久以前》(Long, Long Ago) 作曲,以此知名。本条是别离歌中的一句,为人们普遍应用。直译为“(对方)不在,会更增强思念的心情”。现在被作为谚语。一般指男女间的爱情。*Don't worry about your boy friend's being away for a few months. Absence makes the heart grow fonder, you know.* 你的男朋友远行三两个月,你用不着担心。俗话说,久别情深嘛。*They say that absence makes the heart grow fonder, but I wonder. I'm afraid if I'm away too long Sally will forget all about me.* 人们都说久别情深,不过我有所怀疑。我害怕我走得太久了,萨莉会把我忘得一干二净。意义相反的谚语有 Out of SIGHT, out of mind. 即“久别情疏”。◇ Separation increases one's love.

account

pad *someone's* **account** (with *something*) [ˌpæ(ː)d ~ əˈkaunt] [口] **虚报帐目** 这个 pad 与 pad the BILL (with *something*) (→) 中的 pad 相同。account 是“(交易的)帐目”。*The ABC Company is padding our account with extra charges.* ABC公司在写花帐,给我们增添一些额外的费用。与 pad the bill (with *something*) 的不同点在于:pad the bill 是“(每当开帐单时) 多算钱”,而本条的意义是“(在老主顾帐目上)写花帐”。*Do you think they are padding our account?* 你以为他们在给我们写花帐吗? → pad *one's* expense ACCOUNT ◇ purposely enter more into the accounting books than *someone* should pay

pad *one's* **expense account** [ˌpæ(ː)d ~ ɪksˈpents əˌkaunt] [口] **虚报必要费用** 这个 pad 与 pad the BILL(with *something*)(→) 中的 pad 相同。expense account 是资方给报销的“(交际费、交通费等)必要费用的结算”。如果公司职员、顾问以及合同工等在报销时申请的钱数超过实际的花费,就说:*He is padding his expense account.* 他报花帐啦。*The lawyer we engaged appears to have been padding his expense account.* 我们所委

托的律师似乎多报销必要的费用啦。→ pad *someone's* ACCOUNT(with *something*) ◇ claim returnable expenses which *one* has not incurred

doctor the accounts [ˌdɑktərðɪ ˈəkaunts] [口] **伪造帐目** 这里的 doctor 是动词，本义为"诊疗"、"医治"。本条如果直译则为"对帐簿做处理"，但要注意：这种表达法必须带有"不正当地"的意味。*The defendant, John Bell, was found guilty of doctoring the accounts to cover up his brother's embezzlement.* 被告约翰·贝尔由于伪造帐目掩盖他弟弟侵吞的款项而被宣告有罪。例句中的 the 有时用 *one's*, these, those 代替。*It seems that some doctors doctor their accounts in order to avoid paying taxes.* 好象有些医生为了偷税漏税而篡改帐目。也常使用被动语态，如 *These accounts have been doctored.* 这几笔帐已经被篡改了。也说 doctor the books。◇ falsify the [*one's*, these, etc.] financial records

ace

an ace in the hole [ə ˌneɪsənðə ˈhoul] [话] **备用的王牌** 此语源出四明一暗扑克牌游戏(stud poker)。只将最初一张牌扣起，亮出其余四张。扣起的牌为 the card in the hole，如果这张牌是最强的牌 A(ace)，那就成为 an ace in the hole 了。*I felt I had won the game unless Luke had an ace in the hole.* 这是按字面的使用方法，意为"如果卢克扣着的牌不是 A，我觉得我已经赢了这一局了。"作为比喻，则用于表示"不了解对方"、"有厉害手段"之类的场合。比较起来，人们对这一习用语主要采取比喻用法。*What are we waiting for? What good is an ace in the hole if we don't use it?* 我们还等什么呀？手里既有备用的王牌，如果不用不是白糟塌了吗？如这一例句所示，动词多用 be。也可以用 *one's* ace 代替 an ace。*We're not going to put our best pitcher in first. He's our ace in the hole.* 我们最初不叫我们最好的投球员上场，他是我们备用的王牌。*Don't tell them that we have that information. That's our ace in the hole.* 不要告诉他们我们获得了那份情报，那是我们备用的王牌。*George seems awfully confident. He must have an ace in the hole.* 乔治似乎非常有信心，他必然有一张备用的王牌。*I haven't given up yet. I still have one more ace in the hole.* 我还没有认输，我还有一张备用的王牌呐。◇ a (powerful) secret stratagem [weapon]

come within an ace of *doing something* [ˈkʌm wɪˌðɪn əˈneɪsəv ～] [话] **差一点就要……** 本条中的 ace 原意为扑克中的 A 或骰子中的么，亦即在各种游戏用具中代表"一点"，因而在这一习用语中有"仅(差)一点点"的意义。整个习用语具有"(只差一点点)就要……"的意味。多用于表示不佳的情况，但如 *We came within an ace of winning.* 我们因差一点点而没有取得胜利。也用于表示好的意思。*Although Lew was highly favored, he came within an ace of losing the match.* 虽然人们对卢的评价很高，但他在比赛中差一点就要输掉了。*I came within an ace of disclosing our plans to that guy.* 我差一点儿没把我们的计划泄露给那个家伙。*I came within an ace of being hit by a car.* 我差一点没被汽车撞上。◇ come very close to *doing something* / almost *do something*

have an ace up *one's* **sleeve** [ˌhævə ˈneɪˌsʌp ～ ˌsli(:)v] [口] **藏有备用的王牌** up *one's* sleeve 字面意义为"袖口上方"。本条的表达法原指在玩扑克牌时，采取欺骗手段，把最大的牌 A 藏到衣袖里。*The gambler was accused of having an ace up his sleeve.* 人们指责那个赌徒把一张 A 藏到袖子里了。这是完全按照字面的使用方法。作为比喻，是"藏有备用的王牌"之意。根据上下文的脉络也可能产生"这是狡猾的行为"的感觉，但这种场合毕竟很少。*I don't think Virgil has told us all he knows. I suspect he's still got an ace up his sleeve.* 我认为弗吉尔并没有把他所知道的情况全都告诉我们。我猜测他还隐藏着最重要的情报。*The other team in the negotiations shows more confidence than the situation* *would seem to warrant. They must have an ace up their sleeve somewhere.* 根据情况来判断，谈判的对方不应该有那么大的自信心。他们肯定在什么地方藏有取胜的王牌。一般使用 have，但有时改用其他动词。*The new secret weapon gave the Allies an ace up their sleeve, but they bided their time, waiting for the most opportune moment to play it.* 那种新的秘密武器，对于同盟国来说，是一张宝贵的王牌。但是，他们不急不躁，等待着最好的时机去使用它。在"备用的王牌"这同一的意义上，另有 an ACEin the hole 的说法。在这一习用语中完全不存在 an ace up *one's* sleeve 偶尔带有的"狡猾的"含义。◇ be concealing a powerful [an important] piece of information [resource, etc.] / have an undisclosed strategy [plan, resource, etc.]

acid

acid [ˈæ(ː)səd] [话] **LSD** → an acid HEAD

an acid freak [ə ˈnæ(ː)səd ˌfri(ː)k] [话] **常服麻醉药 LSD 的人** → an acid HEAD

an acid head → HEAD

pop acid [ˌpɑˈpæːsəd] [话] **服用 LSD** 这里的 pop 意为"把(糖块、丸药等)一下子扔进嘴里"。acid 是 LSD 的暗语(LSD 是一种麻醉剂，学名 lysergic acid diethylamide [麦角酸二乙基酰胺]，美国贩毒吸毒者的黑话称之为 acid)。*Have you ever popped acid?* 你服用过 *LSD* 吗？也可以说 drop acid。 → an acid HEAD◇ take LSD

acquaintance

have a nodding acquaintance (with *someone*) [ˌhævə ˈnɑːdɪŋ əkˈweɪntənts] [口] **点头之交** nod 是"点头"、"打招呼"；acquaintance 是"相识"、"见过面"。因此，逐字翻译就是"(与某人)见面认识，只是点点头打招呼的程度"。在实际上，一般用于表达"不大熟悉的对手"的意味。*I don't know her very well. We have only a nodding acquaintance.* 我对她的情况不很了解。我们只是见过面、点点头而已。*I have a nodding acquaintance with him because we often eat at the same restaurant, but I don't know him well enough to introduce you.* 我与他有点头之交，因为我们常在一个饭馆里吃饭，但是对他还不够熟悉，没有达到介绍给你的程度。另外，a nodding acquaintance 也指"有点头之交的人"本身。*He's a nodding acquaintance, but I don't know where he lives.* 他是一位与我有点头之交的人，但是我不知道他住在什么地方。其次，也有在 have a nodding acquaintance 后边不接 with *someone* 而接 with *something* 形成 have a nodding acquaintance with *something* 的情况。在这种场合，acquaintance 意为"(关于 *something* 的)知识、能力"。with *something* 的场合也与 with *someone* 的场合一样，很少表示"多少知道一些"，大多表示"不大熟悉"、"不大会"的意味，当然也可能包含着谦逊成分。*I have only a nodding acquaintance with French literature.* 我不大熟悉法国文学。*Even after ten years in America she appears to have little more than a nodding acquaintance with English.* 她虽然在美国已经呆了十年，但是看起来不大会英语。另外，这种情况虽然极少，但有用 bowing (bow 是"鞠躬"之意)代替 nodding 而说 have a bowing acquaintance 的时候。◇ know *someone* [each other] slightly

acquired

an acquired taste → TASTE

act

act up [ˌæ(ː)kˈtʌ(ː)p] [口] **偏离正确方向的行动或作用** act 意为"行动"、"动"。这里的 up 是增添"恣意"、"逆反"意味的副词。简单地说，act up 的形象化翻译就是"乱暴"，而"乱暴"的主体大致可分为以下四类：1. 儿童、饲养的动物(等违反教养、训练)；2. 机械类；3. (一度就医或应该痊愈的)病、伤；4. (气候[天气]、海、火山等)自然物。以下按主体的类别举一些例句。1. 儿童、动物 *The children acted up in class.* 孩子们在上课时间乱闹起来了。*The horses are acting up because of the storm.* 由于狂风暴雨，马在乱跳乱蹦。2. 机械类 *The car has started acting up again. We'll have to get it fixed.* 汽车又开始出毛病啦。我们必须把它送去修理了。*Our television acts up every time an airplane flies over the neighborhood.* 每当飞机从附近飞过,我们家的电视机就出毛病。3. 病,伤 *My cold is acting up again.* 我的感冒又发作啦。再有一点应该特别注意:在病、伤场合的用法中,多半不是用病、伤本身作主语,而是用受该病、伤影响的患部作主语。例如,一般都说 My lungs(肺)are acting up again. 而并不说 My tuberculosis(肺结核)is acting up again. *He says his back is acting up again.* 他说他的后背又疼起来了。4. 自然 *Nature often acts up in autumn.* 一到秋天,大自然常有狂暴的现象。*The weather [sea] has really been acting up for the past three days.* 最近三天,天气[海]的确是够狂暴的。*Mt. Vesuvius has begun acting up again.* 维苏威火山又开始爆发了。◇ behave abnormally

read (*someone*) **the riot act** [ˌriːdðə ˈraɪəˌdæ(ː)kt] [口] **严厉叱责** The Riot Act (《暴乱取缔条例》)是 1715 年英国发布的一项法律,《条例》规定:凡有 12 人以上具骚扰意图而集会者,可命令其集会解散。read 是"宣读(该条例)"。本条习用语的本来意义是"(向参加集会的人宣读条例)命令解散"。但是,现在在会话中并不用这一意义。*When Smedley had been late for work three days in a row, the boss called him into his office and read the riot act.* 当斯梅德利连续三天上班迟到以后,老板把他叫到自己的办公室,狠狠批评了一顿。如此例所示,这一表达法用于发怒的场合,相当于"严厉叱责"。在使用的时候,大多不是指三言两语,而是指相当长时间的说教;从本来的意义出发,其内容一般包含着严厉的警告。乍看起来似乎文词生硬,但这是个一般性的表达法,在会话中也是经常出现的。*The students have been behaving better ever since the principal read the riot act last week.* 自从上个礼拜被校长严厉批评之后,学生们老实多了。在强调的场合,常加添 really 一词。*My father really read me the riot act for getting home so late last night.* 昨天夜里我回家太晚了,父亲把我狠狠地训了一大阵。◇ reprimand *someone* severely

actions

Actions speak louder than words. [ˈæ(ː)kʃənz ˌspi(ː)k ˌlaudərðn ˈwəːrdz] [谚] **行动胜于雄辩** 直译为:"行动的说话声音比言语高。"与"不言实行"的意义相近,但是严格地讲,并不一定是不要"言"。其意义的内涵是:"用嘴说也可以,但是更重要的是用行动(做表率、显诚意等等)"。这一谚语多被用作父母、老师等的行动准则,或者作为父母、长辈对子女或部下的教导。*In training children, young parents must realize that actions speak louder than words and always set an example of good behavior.* 在教育孩子的时候,年轻的父母必须领悟行动胜于雄辩这句话,永远树立良好行为的模范。*If you expect to get a raise, you have to show that you deserve it. After all, actions speak louder than words.* 如果你期望工资提级,那你就必须有值得提级的表现。归根结底,行动胜于雄辩嘛。◇ What one does is more important than what one says.

Adam

not know *someone* **from Adam** [nɑt ˌnou ~ frə ˈmæːdəm] [话] **完全不知道(他是什么人)** 据《圣经》所载,Adam (亚当)是人类的鼻祖。没有什么人会见到过他。因此,"不知道他与亚当有什么区别"这句话的意思就是"完全不知道他是什么人"。*Why should I stick out my neck for this Mr. Brown? I don't know him from Adam.* 为什么我要为这个布朗先生铤而走险呢?我根本不知道他是个什么人呀。*I'm afraid an introduction to Mr. Jones from me wouldn't help you much. He doesn't know me from Adam.* 我给琼斯先生写一封介绍信,恐怕也帮不了你什么大忙。因为他完全不知道我是老几呀。*When I met her again a few days later, it appeared that she didn't know me* *from Adam.* 当我几天后再遇见她的时候，她似乎完全不知道我姓甚名谁了。◇ not know *someone* at all

add

add up [ˌæːˈdʌp] [话] **合乎逻辑** add+副词 up 这一词形，根据 add 是及物动词还是不及物动词而意义有所不同。在及物动词的场合，如 *Add up the figures.* 请把数字加起来。这是“合计”的意思；如果是不及物动词，则是“计算相符”的意思。*The figures add up perfectly.* 计算完全相符。*The figures don't add up.* 数字有出入。把这个作为不及物动词词组的 add up 用于比喻，那就有“合乎逻辑”的意味了。*Henry's story adds up. He seems to be telling the truth.* 亨利所讲的合乎逻辑。他似乎在说真实情况。*You'd better think up another story. That one doesn't add up.* 你最好另编一套瞎话吧。现在所讲的驴唇不对马嘴。除了象以上的例句用于表示“说话合情合理”而外，也用于表示“人的行动(事物)的合情合理”等等。*Don't you see? It all adds up. He left the key in the car because he wanted it to be stolen.* 你还不明白吗？那完全合乎逻辑呀。由于他希望人家偷车，才把钥匙放在车里的。*How did the money disappear from the safe if the safe was locked? It just doesn't add up.* 如果保险柜锁着，钱怎么会从保险柜里不翼而飞呢？这完全不合乎逻辑。从最后这两个例句也可以看出，肯定句是用 all、否定句是用 just 来加强语气的。→ ADD up to *something* ◇ be logically consistent / make sense

add up to *something* [ˌæːˈdʌptə ~] [话] **结果是……** 按照字面意义，就是“合计为……”。*It adds up to three hundred fifty.* 总共为三百五十。*The bill added up to ten and a quarter.* 结帐一共 10 元 25 分。也转用于数字以外，意为“(把说话、事实等种种因素都考虑在内)结果成为……”。*No matter how you slice it, his story adds up to a pack of lies.* 不管你怎样分析，他所讲的话毕竟是一堆谎言。为了加强语气，常增添 all。*A: What do you think it all adds up to? B: It adds up to the fact that we've been cheated.* 甲：经过全盘考虑，你到底怎样认为？乙：总地来说就是这样一个事实，我们受骗啦。→ ADD up ◇ indicate [mean] *something*

addict

a work addict [ə ˌwəːr ˈkæ(ː) dɪkt] [口] **工作迷** → a WORKAHOLIC

affair

have an affair (with *someone*) [ˌhævə ˈnəfeːr] [口] **(与异性)有暧昧关系** 仅 an affair 一词就相当于“不正当的男女关系”，因此，have an affair 也是指与正经恋爱有点不同的、比较轻浮的、多少带有不道德情调的男女关系。*Mary is always having an affair with a different man.* 玛丽经常与不同的男人有暧昧关系。根据上下文的语气，有时用“通奸”、“轧姘头”等字样解释最为贴切。*George got fired for having an affair with the boss's wife.* 乔治由于跟老板的婆娘通奸而被开除了。*I hear Bill is having another affair.* 我听说比尔又跟另一个女人姘上啦。◇ pursue a romantic relationship

affairs

mind *one's* **own affairs** [ˈmaɪnd ~ ˌou nəˈfeːrz] [口] **不管他人瓦上霜** → mind *one's* OWN BUSINESS

afire

like a house afire → HOUSE

aftertaste

have a bad aftertaste [ˌhævə ˌbæː ˈdæːftər.teɪst] [口] **余味不佳、不良印象** → leave a bad TASTE in *someone's* mouth

age

act *one's* **age** [ˌækt ~ ˈeɪdʒ] [口] **行动与年龄相适应** 正象父母训斥孩子时所说的 *Act your age!* 看看你多大啦！那样，常用命令式。而当子孙见到老太太打扮得过分花梢或者象年轻人一样打打闹闹、蹦蹦跳跳的时候，就用较和缓的口气说

You should act your age. 你该考虑考虑自己的年纪。*If he had acted his age, he wouldn't have gotten hurt.* 如果他的行动与年龄相适应，他就不会受伤啦。◇ behave in accordance with what is expected of someone *one's* age

a coon's age [ə 'kuːn.zeɪdʒ] [话] **极长时间** coon 是 raccoon (浣熊)的省略。本条是因浣熊活的时间长而产生的习用语，强调 a long time。有点乡下佬开玩笑的味道。*How have you been, Ralph? I haven't seen you in a coon's age.* 你一向咋样啊，拉尔夫？我有老长时间没瞧见你啦。*I wonder how Mr. Badger is getting along? I haven't seen him for a coon's age.* 巴杰先生现在怎么样？我好长好长时间没有见到他啦。如以上两个例句所示，本条的表达法一般是在否定句中使用。虽然说经常用于人久别重逢等时刻，但并非以此为限。*I'm from Virginia but I haven't been back there in a coon's age.* 我虽然来自弗吉尼亚州，但是好长好长时间没有回去过了。*She's been sick for a coon's age.* 她很长时期卧病在床。*It's been a coon's age since the Socialists were last in power.* 社会党上次取得政权以后，时间已经很久了。◇ (for) a long(, long) time

agrees

something **agrees with** *someone* [~ ə'griːz wɪð ~] [口] **(食物、气候、生活等)适合身体[性情]** agree 一般是"(意见)相合"的意思，但在本条则是"(食物、饮料等)适合身体"、"(生活、工作等)适合性情"的意思。*The climate in Hawaii agrees with me.* 夏威夷的气候对我很合适。这是用于肯定句。但大多使用 not agree 或 disagree 等构成否定句。*Canada's harsh winters don't agree with me.* 加拿大的严冬不适合我的体质。*Life in the city has never agreed with him.* 都市生活从来都不适合他的性情。在讲食物、饮料的时候，也是同样。*Spices don't agree with me.* 调味料不适合我的体质。*This salad doesn't agree with me.* 这种色拉对我的身体不合适。在食物[饮料]偶尔破坏身体正常状态的场合，也常用这一否定式。*The fish I ate last night didn't agree with me.* 我昨天夜里吃鱼中毒了。无论如何，在谈到饮食而说 not agree 的时候，是指吃坏了肚子、吃了不好受或者发生变态反应，决没有所谓"不合口味"的意义，这一点务请注意。◇ *something* suits *someone's* constitution [temperament]

air

an air rifle [ə 'ne(ː).raɪfl] [口] **气枪** → a BB GUN

an air shuttle → SHUTTLE

disappear into thin air [dɪsə.pɪr ɪntə .θɪ'neːr] [口] **(忽然)消失** → vanish into thin AIR

be full of hot air [.fuləv.hɑ(ː)'deːr] [话] **(所说的话)毫无价值** → be full of BEANS[2]

give *someone* **the air** [.gɪv ~ ðɪ 'eːr] [话] **(把情人等)甩开** 这里的 air 不是"空气"，而是"(人的)气氛[样子、态度等]"。the 是"那个"。因此，按字面直译就是"给与某人那个态度"，而实际意思则为"(由于要离开某人)而冷淡对待"。*A: I thought you were dating Sally these days. B: Naw. She gave me the air.* 甲：我以为这些天你正与萨莉幽会呢。乙：没有没有。她已经把我甩了。这是在情侣关系中，一方断绝来往的情况。*The girl I met at the party last night seemed very friendly, but when I asked her for a date, she gave me the air.* 昨天晚上在社交聚会中遇到的姑娘，似乎对我非常怀有好感，但是当我请她定一个约会日子的时候，她却干脆拒绝了。这是"拒绝"来求交往的异性的场合。不管哪一种情况，一般来说，这一习用语是表达异性之间的"拒绝"或"被甩"，但亦可如下列例句那样应用于朋友关系。*I don't know what happened. We had been the closest of friends for many years when suddenly he gave me the air.* 我不知道究竟发生了什么事情。我们多年以来是最亲密的朋友，而他突然跟我绝交了。get the air (from *someone*) 则是"被甩"。*I hear Sam got the air from Lisa.* 我听说莉萨把萨姆甩了。*A: Did you get the date?*

B: *No, I got the air.* 甲:你得到对方约期幽会了吗?乙:没有。我被甩啦。另外, give *someone* the air 有"(将某人)开除"的意思, get the air 则是"被开除"。然而,这是令人感到极为陈腐的表达法,所以现在几乎不在这个意义上使用。◇ jilt *someone* / (begin to) treat *someone* coldly

on the air [ˌɔ(ː)nðɪ ˈeːr] [口] **正在广播** 这是广播电台的用语,或是在 *You can't go in the studio. They're on the air now.* 你不能进播音室,他们现在正在广播[放映]。这样的话中使用,或者作为播音室外指示灯上的文字表示"禁止入内"的意思。在日常会话中,如 *His English program is on the air three times a day.* 他的英语节目一天广播三次。*That program was on the air for five years.* 那个节目已经放映五年了。也常常用以表示"正在播放"的意思。另外, on air (没有 the) 不是正确的英语。◇ broadcasting / broadcast

out of thin air [ˌaudəv ˌθɪˈneːr] [口] **从无中……** thin air (薄的空气)意味着"无"。相关的动词有 make, create, appear 等,即"从无中"make, create, appear 什么东西。因此,如 *The boss seems to think I can make customers appear out of thin air.* 老板似乎认为我能从子虚乌有中变出新的顾客来。这一句话所示,是用以表示认为"毫无道理"或"莫名其妙"的心情。*If you want me to write this report for you, you'll have to give me all the data. I can't create something out of thin air, you know.* 如果你想叫我给你写这份报告书,你必须向我提供全部资料,因为我不能凭空创作什么呀。*The magician waved his wand and a rabbit appeared out of thin air.* 魔术师把他的小棒一挥,一只兔子突然出现了。◇ (as if) by magic

vanish into thin air [ˌvæ(ː)nəʃ ɪntə ˌθɪˈneːr] [口] **(忽然)消失** thin air (薄的空气)意为"无",是加强 vanish (消失)的词组。air 是透明的,什么东西即便被它包围也被会看见,尤其是 thin air,就更没有看不见的道理。这一习用语则或多或少地表示不断感到莫名其妙、"到底是怎么回事呢?"的疑问心情。*I saw the man I was chasing run into a side street, but when I reached there, he had vanished into thin air.* 我明明见到我所追赶的那个人跑进了一条胡同,可是当我到达那儿的时候,他竟然无影无踪了。为了加强语气,往往增添 just 或 simply,或两者的结合体 just simply。*Where in the world are my glasses? They couldn't have just simply vanished into thin air.* 我的眼镜究竟到哪里去了呢?它总不能一下子就无影无踪了吧。*I haven't seen Kirk for over two weeks. He seems to have just vanished into thin air.* 我已经有两个多礼拜没有看见柯克啦。他好象一下子就钻到了地缝里似的。*The magician waved his wand and the rabbit suddenly vanished into thin air.* 魔术师把他手里的小棒一挥,兔子就突然不见影儿了。也用 disappear into thin air。◇ completely disappear

walk on air [ˌwɔːkɔ(ː) ˈneːr] [口] **(由于高兴而)飘飘然** 直译是"在空气上走路"。表示由于高兴而飘飘然的心情。一般用进行时。*Todd is walking on air this week. He just found that he passed his college entrance exams.* 这个星期,托德高兴得手舞足蹈,因为他刚刚考上大学。*When the handsome movie star spoke to Betty, she felt as if she were walking on air.* 当英俊的电影明星向贝蒂说话的时候,她心里有些飘飘然了。偶尔也有不是进行时的场合,但显得太生硬,会话中很少使用。*After hearing the good news, Charles walked on air [was walking on air].* 听到这个好消息以后,查尔斯乐得手舞足蹈。另外还有以 tread 代替 walk 形成 tread on air 的表达法,但这主要是英国的英语。◇ be extremely happy [elated] / be happy as never before ((无进行时))

airs

assume airs [əˌsuː ˈmeːrz] [口] **装模作样** → put on AIRS

give *oneself* airs [ˌgɪv ~ ˈeːrz] [口] **装模**

作样 → put on AIRS

put on airs [pu.dəː 'neːrz] [口] **装模作样** 在这里,air 是"气氛"、"心情"的意思,与 *There was an air of sadness about him.* 他怀着一种忧郁的心情。中的用法相同。put on 是"做出……的样子"、"假装"。本条直译为"装出种种气氛"。换个说法就是 assume airs,但 assume airs 令人感到很生硬,因而在日常会话中不大使用。*I don't like Jane. She's always putting on airs.* 我不喜欢简。她总是装腔作势。put on airs 的使用面比较窄,常指"显示超出本人以上的架势",而且仅限于引起对方不快的言行。*As soon as the Joneses acquired some money, they began to put on airs.* 琼斯一家捞到一些钱之后,马上就开始神气十足了。put on airs with *someone* 是"对某人装腔作势"。*Don't try to put on airs with me. I knew you when you were only a drugstore clerk.* 甭想在我面前摆臭架子。你在杂货店当店员的时候,我就认识你。give *oneself* airs 也是同义,但比 put on airs 显得生硬一点。*No sooner had she become friends with the boss's wife than she began to give herself airs.* 她刚刚跟老板的妻子交上朋友,就神气活现起来了。airs 的前面有时加形容词。*It's disgusting the ridiculous airs she gives herself! You'd think she was a royal princess or something!* 她那滑稽可笑的装腔作势的样子实在令人作呕!你会以为她是个公主之类的人物哪! ◇ pretend *one* is better than *one* is / act above *one's* station

aisles

have *someone* **rolling in the aisles** [.hæv ~ 'roulɪŋɪnðɪ 'aɪlz] [话] **捧腹大笑** aisles 是"(剧场等的)座位之间的通道"。本条的原意是:演员的动作或台词过分滑稽,使得观众"捧着肚子在通道上打转"。*someone* 的部分大致有十分之九是用意味着 audience (听众)的 them 代入。*The latest Broadway comedy has them rolling in the aisles.* 最近出台的百老汇喜剧使得观众捧腹大笑。也有用 audience 代替 them 的情况。*The comedian had the audience rolling in the aisles.* 这位喜剧演员使得观众捧腹大笑。也有使用动词 be 的说法,例如 *We were rolling in the aisles.* 简直把我们笑破了肚皮。也有省略 rolling 的形式,在这种场合,多半用 lay 代替 have。*Jackie Gleason's new act laid [had] them in the aisles.* 杰基·格里逊的新节目令观众捧腹大笑。从以上的例句可以看得很清楚,这一表达法通常应用于剧场内的职业演员的演技或演出节目,但对社交聚会或一般游艺会也有使用的时候。*Joe's imitation of famous politicians had us rolling in the aisles.* 乔模仿著名政治家的即兴表演使得我们捧腹大笑。◇ make *someone* laugh uncontrollably

aleck

a smart aleck [ə 'smɑ(ː)r.dælɪk] [话] **骄傲自大的人** → a wise GUY

alive

be alive and kicking [ə'laɪvən 'kɪkən] [话] **生气勃勃** alive 是"活着"。这里的 kicking 是"(象被捉住的兔子那样)乱蹦乱跳"。 也就是说,这一习用语不仅具有"(身体)健康"的意义,而且含有"活蹦乱跳地动转"的意味。表达比较通俗,也常作为寒暄的词句使用。*I haven't seen Ben in a long time. I wonder if he's still alive and kicking.* 我好久没有见到本了,不晓得他是否依然精力旺盛。*Mr. Spry is an amazing old man, still alive and kicking at ninety-five.* 斯普赖先生是一位令人惊异的老汉,九十五岁还那么生气勃勃。*A: Hi, Lem. How are you these days? B: Alive and kicking.* 甲:嘿,列姆。最近怎么样啊?乙:很精神。◇ be well and active

skin *someone* **alive** → SKIN

alky

an alky [ə 'næ(ː)lki] [话] **酒精中毒(的人)** 本条是这样构成的:把 an alcoholic ("酒精中毒者"一词的正式说法)中的-oholic 去掉,为了发音方便把 c 改成 k,再加上指小词-y (如果是 alcy,也可能发音为 ['æ(ː)lsi],容易混淆)。这是一个相当通俗的习用语。*If that guy keeps on drinking like this every night, he's going to become an alky.* 如果那家伙象这样每天晚上继续喝下去的话，他会成为酒精中毒者的。◇ an alcoholic

all

be all in [ˌɔː ˈlɪ(ː)n] [话] **精疲力尽** all 是"完全"之意的强调表达。in 具有(caved) in 的情调。caved in 是"(洞窟等的顶棚、墙壁)塌下来"。因此，应用到人类的身上，就成为"肉体有垮台的感觉"，亦即"精疲力竭"。另外，这一习用语除本条的意义外，也可能具有"全都参加"的意味。究竟一句话中的 be all in 是使用的哪一种意义，那只能根据上下文来判断。*After trying to find our way into the cave for three hours, we were all in.* 我们寻找洞窟的入口长达三小时之久，因而弄得精疲力尽。be all in 的变形最多，除了动词 be 外，也可以用 look、seem 等。*They looked all in.* 他们显出非常疲劳的样子。*What in the world have you been doing? You seem all in.* 你究竟干什么来着？你好象已经精疲力尽了似的。另有 be beat, be tuckered out (→ TUCKER *someone* out) 等，大致同义。◇ be exhausted

all in all [ˌɔ(ː)lɪˈnɔːl] [口] **从整体看** 这一表达法给人的印象是："虽然不完美，但从各方面考虑，总的结果是……。" *It may use a bit of gas, but all in all it's a very good car.* 它可能多费一点儿汽油，但是从整体来看，却是一辆很好的汽车。*All in all, I think it was a successful party.* 从整体来看，我认为这是一次成功的社交聚会。◇ all points considered (together)

one's **all in all** [~ ˈɔː lɪˈnɔːl] [口] **(精神上)不可代替的东西[人]** 按字直译是"(某人的)一切中的一切"。意为"极为喜爱的、没有就活不成的、成为人生最大精神支柱的东西[人]"。*Literature is his all in all.* 对于他来说，文学是最宝贵的东西。*She was his all in all.* 她是他的一切的一切。如两例所示，这一习用语主要与动词 be 一同使用。◇ what *one* lives for

look all over (for *something* [*someone*]) [ˌlukɔː ˈlovər] [话] **到处搜寻** → look HIGH and low (for *something* [*someone*]) (for) **once and for all** → ONCE

alley

be right down *someone's* **alley** [ˌraɪtˌdaun ~ ˈæ(ː)li] [话] **(正是某人的)特长** → be right up *someone's* ALLEY

be right up *someone's* **alley** [ˌraɪˌdʌp ~ ˈæ(ː)li] [话] **(正是某人的)特长** alley 是"小巷"。这里的 up 是相当于 *My house is up this street.* 我家正在顺这条街走上去的地方。中的"走上去的地方"的表达法。从而把这个短语全部直译，就成为"正在顺着(某某居住的)胡同走上去"了。从"自己所住的地方是非常熟悉而且关心的地方"这一想法出发，"(自己所住的)胡同"便出现比喻的意义，演绎为"正是自己所能并关心的东西"、"拿手好戏"。这一成语的原形没有 right，而是 be up *someone's* alley。原形不大使用，即便使用，也是象 *Tennis isn't up my alley.* 网球不是我的爱好[特长]。这样，几乎只限于否定句。在肯定句的场合，添加强调的 right，则大多可以认为是不能缺少的零件。"保龄球场"一词在英语中叫做(bowling) alley，因此，Bowling is right up my alley. 这句话就带有诙谐的味道了。不过，这一表达法并不局限于体育运动，几乎在任何场合都可以使用，十分方便。*Let's put Bill in charge of our new product. Sales is right up his alley.* 叫比尔负责我们的新产品吧。他对推销的确有一手。*Math is right up my alley.* 数学是我的拿手。用 down 代替 up，意思相同。*If it's a book on mushrooms, why not get Mr. Whitestone to write it? That'd be right down his alley.* 如果想要一本谈蘑菇的书，为什么不请怀特斯通先生执笔呢？那正是他拿手的呀。附带说一句：在英国的英语中，也说 be right up [down] *someone's* street。◇ be exactly in the area of *someone's* interest and ability / be *someone's* forte / exactly match *someone's* talents

alligator

make like an alligator [ˌmeɪkˌlaɪkə ˈnæləˌgeɪdər] [话] **急走** 直译"象钝吻鳄一样行动",这没有什么速度感。其实,这乃是习用语 drag ass [ˈdræː ˈgæːs] 的委婉的说法。这里的 drag 是从具有"加速竞走"意义的 a drag RACE 借用的词,因而在感觉上是相当快的。为了避免不雅的词 ass (屁股),就由 drag ass 的字面意义"拖着屁股"而想象到"鳄鱼行走的样子",于是产生本条头的表达法,意思是"走"或"离开",但特别用于匆忙的场合。主要是十几岁的少年或男大学生的用语,虽然有点陈旧,但现在仍然可以常常听到。*Let's make like an alligator.* 我们赶紧去吧! 请注意:如这一例句所示,主语即使是复数,alligator 依然是单数。*I made like an alligator over to the store.* 我急急忙忙到商店去了。*They made like an alligator out of there when they saw the teacher coming.* 当他们看见老师来了的时候,赶紧从那儿逃走了。◇ go (quickly)

alone

leave well enough alone → LEAVE

let alone → LET

along

all along [ˌɔ(ː)ləˈlɔːŋ] [口] **从最初起(一直)** *There were policemen all along the wall.* 沿着墙一直布满了警察。在这类句子中,all along 是表示"沿着……一直"这样空间概念的前置词短语,但是把它一转,便成为亦可用于表示"从最初起一直"这样时间概念的副词短语了。*We knew all along that Jones was the culprit, but we didn't have any proof.* 我们从最初就了解琼斯是罪犯,但是我们没有掌握任何证据。*That's what I said all along. Why didn't you believe me?* 关于那件事情,我从最初起就一直讲。你为什么不相信我呢? ◇ from the (very) beginning

altogether

the altogether [ðɪ ˈɔːltəˈgeðər] [话] **赤裸裸** 把 altogether nude [naked] (全部裸体的)中的 nude [naked] 去掉,加 the 而成。在过去,naked 或 nude 属于下流话,是禁忌语。本条的表达法是那个时代的遗物,原来是作为一种委婉的说法而使用的。现在已经没有那样的感觉,是日常会话中习用的短语。主要以 in the altogether 的形式使用。*When I opened the door, she was standing there in the altogether.* 我打开门的时候,她正一丝不挂地站在那里。另外,象在 strip down to the altogether (把衣服全部脱光,一丝不挂)这样的短语中,也与 to 一起使用。*We had to strip down to the altogether for our physicals.* 为了身体检查,我们必须全部脱光,一丝不挂。◇ the nude / complete nudity

amscray

amscray [ˈæ(ː)mˌskreɪ] [话] **(立即)走开** → SCRAM

anchor

weigh anchor [ˌweɪ ˈæ(ː)ŋkər] [口] **起锚 / 出航** → get under WAY

ands

No ifs, ands or buts. → IFS

Angels

The City of the Angels [ðə ˌsɪdi əvðɪ ˈeɪndʒəlz] [口] **洛杉矶市** → L.A.

ants

have ants in *one's* pants [hæˈvæ(ː)ntsɪn ~ ˌpæ(ː)nts] [话] **坐立不安** 指好象"蚂蚁进入裤子(pants)中"那样不镇静,身体乱动、站也不是坐也不是的神情。在"想要做什么事情"或者"(怀着焦虑或期望而)等待什么[什么人]"的场合使用。*When the man who had promised to bring the money at lunch time hadn't appeared by one-thirty, we all had ants in our pants.* 那个人约定在午饭时间把钱拿来,等到一点半他还不见影儿,我们大家都象热锅上的蚂蚁稳不住神儿了。*Congratulations on your success in the negotiations. The boss has had ants in his pants all morning waiting for your report.* 恭贺你谈判成功。老板整个上午

都坐立不安地等待你的汇报。另外,象 *Husbands often get ants in their pants while their wives are getting ready to go out.* 当妻子在外出前梳洗打扮的时候,她们的丈夫总是等得不耐烦,坐立不安。这一例句一样,也常使用 get ants in *one's* pants (等得不耐烦,坐立不安)的表达法。*Let's eat. The children are starting to get ants in their pants.* 我们坐下吃饭吧。孩子们等得不耐烦,已经坐立不安啦。◇ be restless

anybody

everybody who's anybody → EVERYBODY

anyhoo

anyhoo [ˈeni.huː] [话] **无论如何** anyhow 的变形,诙谐的说法。最近已有陈旧之感,但在 1945–1955 年间曾经流行一时。在一般的词典中查不到。然而,即便在现在,四十岁以上的人口头上常用它,有时在小说中、在《润滑油》之类的历史影片中也会出现。另外,anyhow 具有种种不同的意义,而 anyhoo 只用于表示其意义之一"无论如何"的场合。也就是说,*Anyhoo, let's get started.* 不管怎样,咱们开始吧! 这一用法是正确的,但在说 *Who are you anyhow?* 你究竟是谁? 的时候,不能把 anyhow 说成 anyhoo。◇ anyhow

anyplace

not get anyplace [.nɑt geˈdeni.plèɪs] [话] **不发迹** → GO PLACES

anything

like anything [.laɪ ˈkeniθɪŋ] [话] **势头很猛** 直译应为"好象什么似的"。是强调行为、动作激烈的表达法。最初创出这一习用语,大概是由于想要形容激烈的程度而又找不到适当的词汇,姑且来个"好象什么似的"再说。这一说法略有孩子的稚气,一般用于对当事人不相宜或者不好的事情。可以形容人,也可以形容自然现象。*As a child, Doris was very shy. If a stranger so much as looked at her, she would start to cry like anything.* 多丽丝在小的时候非常腼腆。如果有陌生人瞧上她两眼,她就会哇哇地哭起来。*By the time the fire engine arrived, the house was burning like anything.* 当消防车开到的时候,房子的火势已经很猛了。也常用于形容大雨、暴雪的激烈程度。*We set out under a cold, overcast sky, and by five o'clock it was snowing like anything.* 我们是在天气寒冷、阴云低垂的情况下出发的,到了五点钟左右,天下起大雪来了。◇ very hard / fiercely

anywhere

not get anywhere [.nɑt geˈdeni.*h*we(ː)r] [话] **不发迹** → GO PLACES

ape

go ape (over *something* [*someone*]) [.gou ˈeɪp] [话] **狂热起来** go ape 的意思是"象无尾猿那样反应",但作为具体的形象,你这样想会得到一个清晰的概念:"有人给猴子香蕉之类的东西,猴子兴奋起来,一边狂叫,一边来回乱跳乱蹦"。从下面的例句可以看到,根据用法或情况的不同,这一习用语会有各种各样的译法,但是,不论哪一种译法,总是以上述的形象为基础的。其次,这一表达法在 go ape 的后面有时伴有、有时不伴有前置词+*something* [*someone*]。在伴有的场合,正如条头所示,前置词以 over 占压倒的多数,但随着意思的变化,偶尔也有用 about 或 for 的时候(以下,说明以 over 为代表)。在前一场合,也就是在 go ape over *something* [*someone*]的场合,常常形成这样的意义:"由于喜爱上 over 后面的物[人]而大闹起来",亦即"对 over 后面的物[人]发生激情,狂热起来"。*Everyone these days seems to be going ape over science fiction movies.* 最近,似乎每个人都热衷于科幻影片。*Ned's friends all went ape over his new sports car. Everybody wants to drive it.* 内德的朋友们全都疯狂地爱上了他的新赛车,每个人都想要驾驶它。这是"对于物发生狂热"的例句。下面是"对于人发生狂热"的例句:*Our new English teacher is very handsome. All the girls are going ape over him.* 我们新来的英语老师非常英俊。所有的女生都对他狂热起来。*Sue has gone ape for that new boy in school.* 苏完全迷上了那个新转学来的男孩子。至于没有 over *something [someone]*的形式，也就是单单 go ape 的场合，意义分为两样。一样是与上面的 go ape over *something [someone]*相同，具有“极度狂热起来”的意味。首先“物”的场合——*Carl liked your painting. As soon as he saw it he went ape.* 卡尔爱上了你所画的画。他一见到就完全倾倒了。其次是“人”的场合——*Every time Bud sees your sister he practically goes ape. He's got it pretty bad.* 巴德每次见到你的妹妹都为之神魂颠倒，相思病十分严重。在这一场合，如果直译就是“与(给与香蕉的)猴子一模一样”。巴德为朋友的妹妹神魂颠倒，一见了她就意马心猿，仿佛在不断地指手划脚，对旁边的什么人说：“喂，你瞧瞧她呀，真是个尤物啊！”等等，这情景真是跃然纸上。只是 go ape 的场合，还有另外一个意义，即“(失去自控能力)发起狂来”或者“失去理智而大吵大闹”。在“极度兴奋”这一点上与头一个意义相似，但是这第二个意义并非特指“喜爱上物或人，头脑发热兴奋起来”。正如 *As soon as I arrived I knew something was wrong. Everyone was running around as if they'd gone ape.* 我一到达，马上就知道发生了什么不对头的事情。每个人都在那里来回乱跑，仿佛疯了似的。这一例句所示，有发生什么事故而“仿佛疯了似的”的场合，也有象下一例句那样，由于极度愤怒而“疯狂起来”或者“失去本来面目”的场合。*Lynn was so angry I thought she'd go ape.* 林恩怒气冲冲，我简直以为她疯了。最后再谈一点：另有一种表达方式，即用 be 代替 go 而说 be ape over [about] *something [someone]*。这一习用语表示状态，所以可以解释为“非常热心”。“物”的场合——*I'm not against your plan, but I can't say that I'm ape about it either.* 我不反对你的计划，但是我也不能说对它很有好感。“人”的场合——*At one time, all the young people were ape over the Beatles.* 一时之间，所有的青年人都热中于甲壳虫乐队。有时也使用 ape 极端喜爱的“香蕉”，而说 go bananas (over *something[someone]*)，其语感与 go ape 相同。以上的例句全部可以用这一表达法代入。◇ become wildly excited (about *something [someone]*)

apology

a poor apology for *something* [ə ˌpu(ː)rə ˈpɑ(ː)ləʤi fər ～] [口] **有名无实** 这里的 apology 意味着“不是正牌货，而是粗糙的代用品”，再加上 poor (劣质)一词，就十足地表现出不满意的感情了。for *something* 是“代替正牌货”的意思。*That restaurant has a nice atmosphere, but they serve a poor apology for a meal.* 那家饭店气氛很不错，不过上的菜却有名无实了。在谈到人时也使用。*That guy may have graduated from a first-rate university, but still he's a poor apology for an engineer.* 那家伙可能是从一所一流大学毕业的，但是依然是一个有名无实的工程师。另外，a poor apology for an excuse 本来意为“不成为辩解的拙劣的辩解”，但是麻烦在于有时使用 a poor excuse for ～这一表达法作为 a poor apology for ～的同义语。也就是说把 apology 与 excuse 调换一下，而说 a poor excuse for an apology，这就成为“不成为谢罪的拙劣的谢罪”的意思了。务请注意不要弄错。两者都是口头上常用的老套子。再有，由于语调不好，不能说 a poor apology for an apology，a poor excuse for an excuse，但在除此以外的场合 apology 与 excuse 还是可以调换使用的。◇ a very inferior [unacceptable] *something*

appearance

make an appearance (at *something*) [ˌmeɪkə nʌˈpɪ(ː)rəntˢ] [口] **1. 出席；2. 演出** 动词 appear 除“露面”、“出现”的意义外，还有“演出”的意思。*Frank Sinatra will appear at the Sands Hotel on Saturday.* 本星期六，弗兰克·西纳特拉将在山德斯饭店演出。由此，make an appearance 也具有“出席”、“演出”的双重意义。前者的场合，用法与 put in an

APPEARANCE (at *something*) 相同。*I have to make an appearance at the meeting tonight.* 今天晚上的会议我非出席不可。在"演出"的意义上,用法与本条第一个例句中的 appear 相同。*I have made many appearances on this stage.* 我在这个舞台上演出过许多次了。另外,象 *The famous newscaster Edward R. Murrow made his first appearance on television in 1948.* 著名的新闻播音员爱德华·*R*·默罗是 *1948* 年在电视上第一次露面的。这句话里一样使用 first, last, only, greatest 等形容词的场合, an appearance 的 an 一般改用人称物称代词的所有格。◇ attend (*something*) / perform [appear] (at [on] *something*)

put in an appearance (at *something*) [ˌpudɪnə nʌˈpɪ(:)rən*t*s] [口] **露面** 直译就成为"把出现插入"。一般来说比 attend (出席)的意义轻,特别是在"(礼仪性的)稍一露面"的场合多有使用。*I wonder where Ernie is. He said he'd put in an appearance.* 不知厄尼跑到哪里去了,他说他会露露面的。另外如 *I'd like to have a drink with you, but I have to put in an appearance at a reception tonight.* 我很愿意跟你一块喝上一杯,但是我今天晚上必须出席一个招待会。常与具有 must 意义的 have to 一起使用。也用 make an APPEARANCE (at *something*) 的表达法。◇ attend (*something*)

appetite

sharpen *someone's* **appetite** [ˌʃɑ(:)rpən ~ ˈæ(:)pəˌtaɪt] [口] **吊起胃口** → whet *someone's* APPETITE (for *something*)

whet *someone's* **appetite** (for *something*) [ˌhwet ~ ˈæ(:)pəˌtaɪt] [口] **激起欲望** whet 本来是"(用磨石)磨(刀、剑等)"的意思。appetite 是"食欲"。把两者合在一起,就成为"刺激食欲"了。*The walk through the park whetted my appetite.* 在公园里一散步,我的食欲就上来了。这一表达法也转用于其他的各种"欲望",但在转用时, whet *someone's* appetite 后面常伴有 for more (更加),如: *My first readings in philosophy whetted my appetite for more.* 我开始读哲学书籍,更加引起我对哲学的兴趣。*I had thought that my son's getting lost in the mountains would cool his ardor for camping, but it only served to whet his appetite for more.* 我原以为我的儿子在山中迷路会冷却他对露营的热情,哪知道结果有如火上浇油一样。*The worsening traffic congestion has done nothing to whet my appetite for driving.* 由于交通堵塞情况的严重,我驾车出去的兴趣越来越淡薄了。另外,也可以用与 whet 同义的 sharpen 构成 sharpen *someone's* appetite,但按字面意义使用的倾向比较强。◇ make *someone* want (to do) *something*

apple

be the apple of *someone's* **eye** [ðɪ ˈæ:pl əv ~ ˈaɪ] [口] **掌上明珠** 源出圣经《旧约》的一节的表达法。《申命记》(Deuteronomy) 第 32 章第 10 节有这样一段话: He found him in a desert land, and in the howling waste of the wilderness; he encircled him, he cared for him, he kept him as the apple of his eye。(耶和华遇见他在旷野荒凉野兽吼叫之地,就环绕他、看顾他、保护他如同保护眼中的瞳仁。) 就象这样,在古代, the apple of *someone's* eye 是"瞳孔"的意思。古代人以为瞳孔是球形,就把它比做 apple (苹果)。现在人们则用作比喻,表示"(对于某人来说,象眼球一样)宝贵的东西、不能代替的东西、掌上明珠似的东西"的意义,根本没有人使用原来的"瞳孔"的意义了。"瞳孔"的英文是 pupil。*Mr. Grant dotes on his granddaughter. She's the apple of his eye.* 格兰特先生很溺爱他的小孙女。她是他的掌中珠。*That dog is the apple of our son's eye.* 那条狗是我们儿子的心爱之物。象以上两个例句所示,百分之九十用于指"人"或人饲养的猫、狗等,但也有指"物"的情况。*Fred's new car is the apple of his eye. He's always polishing and tuning it.* 弗雷德的新车是他心爱的宝贝,他经常擦亮和修整它。◇ be the most cherished thing in *someone's* life

an apple polisher [ə ˈnæ(:)pl ˌpɑ(:)plɪʃər] [口] **拍马屁** → polish the APPLE

a bad apple [ə ˈbæ: ˈdæ:pl] [口] **坏蛋** 有这样一条谚语: One bad apple spoils the barrel. (一个坏苹果烂一筐。) 这是从古拉丁语移入英语的,谚语本身现在已经不大为人们使用,但其中的 bad apple (烂苹果)部分却在日常会话中广泛流行。虽然说是"苹果",但经常作比喻用,指的是"人",指的是"有他一个人存在就会把周围所有人带坏的人"或者"由于他的原因给周围引起麻烦的人"。*Stay away from Pete. He's a bad apple.* 不要接近皮特,他是一个坏蛋。*Ralph's brother has always been a bad apple. Wherever he goes, you can be sure there's going to be trouble.* 拉尔夫的弟弟始终是一个不良分子。不论走到什么地方,他必定惹事生非。*It's easy to see who the bad apple is. Not a single party member in that faction had ever taken a bribe until that guy joined it.* 谁是祸根,那是很容易找出来的。在那个家伙参加该派以前,收受贿赂的党员连一个也没有。◇ (a bad person who is) a bad influence

the Big Apple → BIG APPLE

polish the apple [ˌpɑlɪʃ ðɪˈæ:pl] [口] **阿谀奉承** 指"讨人喜欢"。通常多指为谋求私利而"大拍马屁"。汉语俗语叫"舔油屁眼子"。过去,美国学生为了讨好老师而把擦得闪闪发光的苹果给老师送去。这一习用语即从此种风俗而来。*The chief hasn't accepted our plan yet. I guess I'd better go in and polish the apple a bit.* 头头还没有批准我们的计划。我看,也许去一趟拍拍马屁会好些吧。在会话时,有在 apple 之前加 old、在 apple 之后加 or two 等词的情况,但是,那只是为了调整语调,别无意义。*Let's get Ruben to talk to him. He's good at polishing the old apple.* 我们叫鲁宾去跟他谈吧。因为他是善于阿谀奉承的人。*That guy is a pushover for flattery. If you want him to help you, all you have to do is polish an apple or two.* 那个家伙一被恭维就晕头转向。如果你想求他帮助你,你只要去拍拍马屁就行啦。在会话中也采取 do some [a little, a bit of, a lot of, etc.] apple-polishing 的形式。在这种场合,必须有 some 或 a little 之类的形容词。*The boss heard that you were criticizing him yesterday. You'd better go do some apple-polishing.* 老板已经听到你昨天批评他的话啦。你还是去拍几下马屁为好。也有把 apple-polishing 当作名词单独使用的情况。*It was easy. All it took was a little apple-polishing.* 很简单哟!只不过稍微拍一下马屁,就万事亨通了。an apple polisher 是"拍马者(马屁精)"。*The kids don't like Carl much. He's the biggest apple polisher in our class.* 同学们不大喜欢卡尔,因为他是我们班里最大的马屁精。另外,在辞典一类的书里载有 apple-polish 这一动词,但在实际会话中几乎完全不使用。◇ flatter *someone* / use flattery

applecart

upset the [*someone's*] **applecart** [ʌpˌsetðɪ ˈæ(:)plkɑrt] [口] **(过去的成绩、努力、计划等)全都付诸流水** applecart 是"运苹果的手推车"。upset 是"弄翻"。an apple man (卖苹果的人),象中国卖烤白薯的人那样,推着 applecart,在街头边走边卖。从卓别林的影片开始,这种 applecart 常在美国的喜剧片中出现。——在路上,蛮不讲理的人[车]从前边跑过来,撞到卖苹果人的 applecart 上,装得整整齐齐的一车苹果咕噜咕噜地滚到马路上……。卖苹果的人一边嘟哝着骂娘,一边拼命地去拾苹果,刚巧在把最后一个苹果装到车上的时候,又来个残酷无情的家伙,把那 applecart 推个底朝天。——本条的表达法就令人联想上述的场面。这一表达法使用于事业、体育运动等大有可为的项目,在计划、企图以及过去积累的成绩等中途受挫而付诸流水的场合。*Don't tell anyone about our plan until we are ready to act or you may upset the applecart.* 在我们做好实行的准备之前,不要把我们的计划对任何人讲,否则也许会付诸流水的。*Our new* *company was just about to turn the corner and show a profit for the first time when a recession came along to upset the applecart.* 当我们的新公司刚刚度过难关，第一次盈利的时候，工商业萧条起来，一切都完蛋了。*With the score already eleven to one in the fourth inning, the game was all but in the bag when a heavy downpour upset the applecart.* 在第四回合，得分已经是 *11* 比 *1*，比赛简直是稳操胜券了，偏偏这时候来了一场倾盆大雨，全都给搅黄了。applecart 前边也可以加形容词。*Heavy gains by the Republicans in the last election almost upset the Democrat's political applecart.* 在最近的选举中，共和党人取得压倒的胜利，民主党的政治营垒几乎完全被摧毁了。在这个例句中，所谓 the Democrat's political applecart 的具体意义是"民主党过去所获得的议席"等等。也可以把 the 换成 *someone's*，而说 upset *someone's* applecart。*So he thinks he's going to be the next president, does he? Well, we'll just have to upset his little applecart*。他在打算当下任的总裁，是不是？那么，我们就非打破他的如意算盘不可啦。这一例句中的 little 不是"小"的意思，而是表示轻蔑的语气。◇ ruin *someone's* plans [the situation]

apple-pie

in apple-pie order → ORDER

apron

be tied to *one's* **mother's apron strings** → STRINGS

ardor

cool *someone's* **ardor** (for *something*) [ˌku(ː)l ～ ˈɑ(ː)rdər] [口] **给(人的)热情泼冷水** ardor 是"热情"。cool 是"使冷却"。*Jack used to go skiing almost every week, but the crowded condition of the slopes these days seems to have cooled his ardor.* 杰克过去几乎每个星期都去滑雪，可是最近滑雪场地拥挤不堪，似乎使他的热情冷却下来了。*A: I thought you were going to try to get a date with Sally. B: Yeah, I was planning to until I met her boy friend the other day. His size cooled my ardor.* 甲：我想你正在向萨莉求爱，约期幽会哪。乙：嗯，我倒有这个打算，但是，前几天我碰到她的男朋友了，那个大块头使我的心凉了半截。如以上例句所示，本来的意义是"使热情冷却"；但是，在根本谈不上什么"热情"的场合，也用于表达"使人失去那种心情"这样轻松的意味。例如，一个人过去由于业务上的关系，在出差时常常乘坐飞机，但在报纸上频繁出现飞机失事的新闻时，他说：*The recent spate of plane accidents has cooled my ardor for flying*。最近出现大量的飞机事故，我不大想坐飞机了。◇ cause *someone* to lose his enthusiasm

area

an area code → CODE

arm

a shot in the arm → SHOT

twist *someone's* **arm** [ˌtwɪst ～ ˈɑ(ː)rm] [口] **(为了迫使某人就范而)采取强制手段** 按字面讲，是"拧某人的胳膊"。*A: Why did you hit Billy? B: Because he twisted my arm.* 甲：你为什么打比利？乙：因为他拧我的胳膊。转用于比喻。*He'll do it for us, but I may have to twist his arm a bit.* 他会给我们干的，不过，我也许必须给他施加点压力。*The dean had to twist the arms of some of the faculty members before he finally got his way.* 院长在最终达到他的要求之前，不得不对几位教授采取了强制手段。*The President had to twist a few arms in order to get the bill passed.* 总统为了法案的通过，对少数几个人采取了强制手段。另外还有名词形式的 arm-twisting，如说 do some arm-twisting。在这一场合，也可以用 a little, a bit of 等代替 some。*A little arm-twisting should do the trick.* 施加一点压力会达到目的。*Sometimes you have to do some arm-twisting to get things done around here.* 在这儿，为了达到目的，有时候你必须采取一些强制手段。◇ apply (some, a bit of, etc.) pressure (to *someone*)

would give *one's* **right arm** [wud ˌgɪv ～ ˈraɪ ˈdɑ(:)rm] [话] **(要是有[能]……)该多么好** 直译为"(为了……)豁出右胳膊都可以",表示对很难实现的事情或很难人手的东西的强烈愿望。而难以实现的事情或难以人手的东西的具体内容,通常多以 for *something*, to have *something*, to (be able to) *do something*, to be *something* [*someplace*] 等形式表达。*I'd give my right arm to have a car like that [for a car like that].* 我要是有那样一辆汽车该多么好。*I'd give my right arm to be able to sing like Sally.* 我要是能象萨莉那样唱歌该多么好。*I'd give my right arm to (be able to) pitch a no-hitter against the Giants.* 我要[能够]在投球时使巨人队始终无安打,就是死也甘心。*I'd give my right arm to be a movie actor.* 我要是当一个电影演员该多么好。*I'd give my right arm to be in Paris tonight.* 我今天晚上要是能去巴黎该多么好。would give anything 或 would give *one's* EYETEETH 亦同义。◇ would be extremely happy

armor

a chink in *one's* **armor** → CHINK

arm's

keep *someone* **at arm's length** → LENGTH

arms

take up arms (against *someone*) [ˌteɪ ˌkʌ(:) ˈpɑ(:)rmz] [口] **(群众等)拿起武器** → be up in ARMS

be up in arms [ˌʌpɪˈnɑ(:)rmz] [口] **满腔怒火** 这里的 arms 是"武器",本条原意是"(群众等)拿起武器",但是,这种字面意义现在通常用 take up arms (against *someone*) 来表达。当前,在一般人的感觉中,已经形成这样一种印象,即:这里的 arms 的含义由"武器"转为"手",本条的含义则为"(由于满腔怒火)挥起两只拳头"。主要用于群众对某件事极为愤慨而表示猛烈反对的场合。也有应用于某一个人的时候。在这种场合,如说 *Pop is up in arms because you used the car without his permission.* 爸爸大动肝火,因为你未经他的许可而使用他的汽车。多用于单单表示"猛烈愤怒"的意思。另外,在特别要指出"反对(什么)"的文句中,一般在最后补加～over *something*。*Parents are up in arms over the new school curriculum.* 家长们对学校新安排的课程极为愤怒。*Perhaps you'd better rethink your plan to increase taxes, Governor. The people are up in arms.* 州长,您最好重新考虑一下您的增税方案。老百姓在猛烈反对哪。也用 get up in arms,意为"极为愤怒[猛烈反对]"。*Residents are getting up in arms over the government's plan to build a new airport.* 居民们猛烈反对政府建造新机场的计划。有时也可在后边续加～ about *something*。*The boss is up in arms about the company's poor sales record last month.* 由于公司上个月的销售额不佳,老板正在大动肝火。◇ be extremely angry (about *something*)

around

have been around [hæv ˌbɪnəˈraund] [话] **社会经验丰富** around 是"到处"。因此,have been around 的本来意思是"(来到某个场所)到处转悠[在房间等出出进进]"。*A: Has Bob come to work today? B: Yes, he's been around since about ten o'clock.* 甲:今天鲍勃上班了吗? 乙:是呀,他从十点左右就在转悠哪。也就是说"(已经看见)鲍勃在公司中到处活动"了。不过,这个 have been around 并不是仅仅具体地表示"(来到某个场所)到处转悠",在很多场合也作比喻,具有"(来到这个世界上时间很长)到处活动"的意思。其涵义为"踏遍社会各个角落,积累了种种的经验"。*I won't say you shouldn't date him. But as your friend, I should warn you that he's really been around.* 我不是说你不要跟他约会。不过,作为你的朋友,我要提醒你,他可是个情场老手啊。当然,在这句话里暗示着"他善于勾引女人"和"专门玩弄女性"的意思。*Be careful what kind of people you introduce my little brother to. He* *hasn't been around much, you know.* 你把我弟弟介绍给别人时，请注意对方是什么样的人。你要知道，他涉世未深啊。"社会经验丰富"这一习用语，如果换一个表达法，有时可以说"不是小孩子"。*You can't pull the wool over my eyes. I've been around, you know.* 你不要在我面前打马虎眼，我又不是个三岁小孩子。◇ have a lot of experience

be up and about [around] → UP

artist

a con artist [ə ˌkɑːˈnɑrdəst] [话] **大骗子手** con 是 confidence (信用)的省略语。使人相信而加以欺骗的行为叫做 a confidence game (欺诈)，欺骗人的家伙叫做 a confidence man。用通俗的说法，这两个词分别是 a con GAME, a con man。在 con man 中手段特别巧妙的骗子手就是 a con artist。但请注意：不用 a confidence artist 的说法。*Al is a con artist who specializes in tricking widows out of their savings.* 阿尔是一个大骗子手，他专门欺骗寡妇，弄走她们的存款。*Take care. This city is full of con artists.* 多加小心。这个城里有很多很多大骗子手。另外单独用 con 时，它是动词，具有"欺骗"之意，如 *You wouldn't be trying to con me, would you?* 你不是打算欺骗我吧，是不是？ → CON *someone* into [out of] *doing something* ◇ an expert swindler

ask

ask away [ˌæ(ː)skəˈweɪ] [话] **连珠炮似地(进行质问等)** → FIRE away

ask for it [ˈæ(ː)skfərɪt] [话] **自找……** → ask for TROUBLE

attendance

dance attendance on *someone* [ˌdænːtsə ˈtendənt.sə(ː)n ~] [口] **大献殷勤** 出典：莎士比亚的《亨利八世》第五幕第二场 To dance attendance on their lordships' pleasures. (百般殷勤，博取爵爷高兴。) 这一表达法给人的印象是："在听吩咐的时候，好象跳舞一样来回走动。" *Just because Peter comes from a rich family, he seems to think everyone ought to dance attendance on him.* 正因为彼得是财主家庭出身，他仿佛以为每一个人都应该向他大献殷勤哪。*I'd like to get a date with Susan but how can I? She has half the fellows in school dancing attendance on her.* 我倒很想跟苏珊约会一下，但是办不到呀！学校里的男生有一半都在向她大献殷勤啊。*I don't mind working late once in a while, but the boss seems to expect me to dance attendance on him till nine or ten every night.* 一回半回加点班，这我倒不在乎，可是老板似乎想叫我每天晚上呆到九、十点钟，给他干这干那呢。*someone* 有时不直接表示"人"，而形成 the whim(s) of *someone*, the pleasure of *someone*, 或者 *someone's* whim, *someone's* pleasure 的形式。*That congressman doesn't seem to have a mind of his own. He spends most of his time dancing attendance on the whims of pressure groups from his election district.* 那位议员好象自己没有什么见解。他消耗自己的大部分时间去迎合本选区的有势力集团的意见。◇ give *someone* all *one's* attention

Aussie

an Aussie [əˈnɔːsi] [话] **澳洲佬** 把 Australian 的 Aus-加上指小词 -(s)ie 而成。是给"澳大利亚人"起的绰号，但丝毫没有轻蔑的意味，可以放心使用。*Our boss is an Aussie.* 我们的老板是个澳洲佬。此外，Aussie 也作为形容词使用，表示"澳大利亚(人)的"。*Is that an Aussie custom?* 那是澳洲的习惯吗？此外，在英国英语中，这个 Aussie 偶尔也用以表示"澳大利亚"的国名，但在美国英语中，完全没有这一意义。◇ an Australian

autograph

an autograph hound → HOUND

aversion

***one's* pet aversion** [~ ˌpedə ˈvəːrʒən] [口] **最讨厌的事情(东西)** → *one's* pet PEEVE

awakening

a rude awakening [ə ˌruːdə ˈweɪkənɪŋ] [口]

如梦初醒 原来出自 rudely awaken 一语，即“(在睡梦中)被人粗暴地弄醒”的意思。但 rude awakening 只作为比喻使用，表示“对迄今没有注意到的不愉快事情，忽然间醒悟过来”。*Tom thought he was the boss's favorite employee, but he had a rude awakening when he was passed over for promotion.* 汤姆过去一直认为他是老板垂青的雇员，但是当别人都先后被提升的时候，他有如大梦初醒。特别是在会话中，常常形成 be in for a rude awakening 的形式。直译是“rude awakening 在等待着”，亦即“明白了严峻的现实”的意思。*I had been confident that my partner was honest, but I was in for a rude awakening.* 我过去一直认为我的伙伴很诚实，但是我明白现实是多么残酷了。*If Sam thinks he can trick me and get away with it, he's in for a rude awakening.* 如果萨姆认为他能欺骗我而蒙混过关，那就大错特错了。◇ (being [going to be] made) aware of an uncomfortable fact

away

do away with *something* [*someone*] → DO

ax

get the ax(e) (from *someone* for *something*) [ˌgetðɪ æ(ː)ks] [话] **被切断(与……的)关系** 按照字面解释是“挨斧头”，但作为比喻则具有“被切断关系”的意义。与 give *someone* the AX(E) (for *something*) 的场合一样，其内容主要分下列三种情况：①被解除雇佣关系 *If Roy doesn't start coming to work on time, he's soon going to get the ax.* 如果罗伊不开始按时上班，他很快就会被解雇的。②被解除当学生的资格 *Biff got the ax for painting the dean's car pink.* 比弗由于把院长的汽车涂成淡红色被勒令退学了。③被断绝与情人的关系 *Mary got the ax from Jack.* 玛丽被杰克甩了。在以上三种情况的任何一种，当添加“被断绝关系”的理由时，都象②的例句那样，采取 for ～的形式。◇ ①get [be] fired ② get [be] expelled (from school) ③ get [be] thrown over ((三种情况皆用 from *someone* → by *someone*))

give *someone* **the ax(e)** (for *something*) [ˌgɪv ～ ðɪ ˈæ(ː)ks] [话] **断绝与……的关系** ax(e) 是“斧子”。因此，本条的字面意义是“给……一斧子”。作为比喻，则是从“用斧子(把……的脑袋)一下子砍掉”的构思出发，而用于表示“与……断绝关系”的意义。至于“断绝关系”的内容，主要有下列三种情况。①断绝雇佣关系 *The boss gave Dennis the ax yesterday.* 老板昨天把丹尼斯解雇了。②开除学籍 *The dean gave Greg the ax for cheating on midterms.* 由于在期中考试中作弊，克雷格被院长勒令退学了。③断绝恋爱关系 *Jennie gave Oliver the ax.* 珍妮把奥利弗甩了。在以上任何一种情况，当添加“断绝关系”的理由时，都象②的例句那样，采取 for ～的形式。另外，讲“被断绝与……的关系”时，象 *Oliver was given the ax by Jennie.* 奥利弗被珍妮甩了。这样的被动式也不是不能使用，但一般来说，采取象 *Oliver got the ax from Jennie.* 这一句中的 get the ax 的形式。→ get the AX(E) (from *someone* for *something*) ◇ ① fire *someone* ② expel *someone* (from school) ③ throw *someone* over

have an ax(e) to grind [ˌhævə ˈnæ(ː)kstə ˌgraɪnd] [口] **心怀叵测** 直译为“有一把斧子要磨”。由美国政治家本杰明·富兰克林 (Benjamin Franklin, 1706—1790) 少年时代的逸话产生的、历史比较浅的成语。据说，一天来了一个男子，他想磨斧子，但是不懂得 grindstone (研磨盘)的使用方法，于是，少年富兰克林便用尽自己的力量，把重达一百公斤以上的 grindstone 推转了好多次。其间，那个男子连连夸奖少年。可是斧子刚一磨好，他就嘲笑少年说：“这是我故意叫你研磨的骗局啊！”然后扭头就走了。“有一把斧子要磨”转成“心怀叵测”，就是由此而来。*It seems kind of Mr. Goodface to offer to help us, but we'd better be careful. He usually has an ax to grind.* 古德费斯先生好象很亲切，说要支援我们，但是我们还是多加小心为妙。他一向是没有好心眼儿的。*I'm sure Roger is* *really doing what he thinks is best. He's not the type to have an ax to grind.* 我认为罗杰的确是怀着满腔的诚意在干的。他不是那种居心不良的人。ax 前面也可加形容词。*To all appearances, Miss Primlips' testimony seems to be entirely objective, but as the defendant's ex-fiancée she may have some personal ax to grind.* 从表面上来看，普林利波斯小姐的证词似乎全是很客观的，但是作为被告过去的未婚妻，她也许有一些个人的意图。此外，也常使用 with an ax(e) to grind 的形式。*You shouldn't be upset by that guy's behavior. The world is full of people with axes to grind.* 你不要为那个家伙的行为而感到不快。世界上到处都有心怀叵测的人。◇ have an ulterior motive

B

babe

(like) a babe in the woods [(laɪk)ə ˈbeɪ bɪnðə ˈwuːdz] [口] **(简直)一无所知** 意为“(好象)在森林中的一个婴儿”,是在谈到没经验的人、世故浅的人时强调其危险性的习用语。这一表达法源出 1600 年左右英国的一首歌“The Children in the Wood”(《孩子们在森林中》)。在美国,“森林”作 woods,一般用复数形式;但在英国,至今仍使用单数形式。*Our son would be like a babe in the woods in New York. If he goes to school there, we don't want him to live alone.* 我们的儿子在纽约人生地疏,一定什么也不了解。如果在那里上学,我们不希望他单独住宿。为了加强语气,往往象以下的例句那样给 babe 加上 just 或 real,请注意它的位置。*When I started in this business, I was just a babe in the woods. I was lucky to have done so well.* 当我开始干这个买卖的时候,我是擀面杖吹火,一窍不通。我能够搞得这样兴隆,全凭运气呀。*When it comes to traveling abroad, my wife is a real babe in the woods. She's never even ridden in an airplane before.* 一谈去外国旅行,我的妻子简直是丈二和尚,摸不着头脑. 她过去连一次飞机都没坐过呢。*The professor may be an expert in political science, but he's obviously just a babe in the woods when it comes to the real dog-eat-dog world of politics.* 那位教授可能是个政治学专家,但是当谈到狗咬狗的实际政局时,他显然是茫无所知。◇ as helpless as a baby

baby

burp the baby [ˌbə(ː)rpðə ˈbeɪbi] [口] **使婴儿打嗝** → a BURP

throw out the baby with the bath [ˌθrou ˌautðə ˈbeɪbi wɪðːə ˈbæːθ] [话] **把婴儿连同洗澡水一起倒掉** 这里的 bath 意为 bath water (洗澡水),有时也说 throw out the baby with the bath water。原义“把婴儿放在盆子里洗过之后,连水带婴儿都泼掉”,亦即“为了除去多余的东西(洗过的水)而把宝贵的东西(婴儿)也抛开”的意思。*It's understandable that you're angry at their proposals, but if you break off negotiations with them completely, you'll be throwing out the baby with the bath.* 你对他们提出的条件很生气,这是可以理解的,但是,如果完全停止与他们的谈判,你就会因噎废食啊。 这一表达法也多用于因本末倒置而一无所获的场合。*The power of a government to rule is based on the nation's Constitution. Therefore any government which attempts to weaken the Constitution in order to increase its own power is throwing out the baby with the bath.* 一个政府的统治权是以国家宪法为基础的。因此,任何政府为了增加它自己的权力而试图削弱宪法,必然如镜花水月,希望落空。 throw out ～的形式占压倒多数,极少用 throw away。*If we try to smoke the rats out of the barn and the barn burns down, we'll be throwing away the baby with the bath.* 如果我们为了用烟把老鼠熏出谷仓而烧掉了谷仓,那可是不但没赚着钱连本儿也赔了。 ◇ gain *one's* objective in a way that renders the objective meaningless

(as) weak as a baby [ə ˈzwi(ː)kəzə ˈbeɪbi] [口] **虚弱无力** → (as) weak as a KITTEN

baby-sit

baby-sit [ˈbeɪbiˌsɪt] [口] **看孩子** “父母外出而由保姆看孩子”的情况很多,但不一定指“由保姆看孩子”,也有“祖母在儿子[女儿]夫妇外出时看孙子或外孙”的场合。当保姆的很多是高中女学生,在附近住的夫妇二人外出时,按一小时多少钱受雇,到对方的家里去看孩子。*Hello, Jane. Can you baby-sit for us about four hours tonight?* 哈罗,简。你今天晚上能替我们看孩子吗?大约四个钟头。如这一例句所示,讲"替(孩子的父母)"时用 for ~的形式。如果象 *I'm going to baby-sit my grandchildren tomorrow.* 明天我要照看孙子。这样有动作对象存在,baby-sit 一般作为及物动词使用,但也有时伴有前置词 with,采取 baby-sit with ~的形式。a baby-sitter [ˈbeɪbiˌsɪdər] 则为"看孩子的人"。*I have to find a baby-sitter for Wednesday night.* 我必须找一个人在星期三的夜里看孩子。另外,baby-sit 也能从"看孩子"的意义转用于在笑谈中或腻烦的情绪下讲"照料(新来的工作人员)"或"接待顾客"的场合。*I'm baby-sitting some new employees this week.* 我这个礼拜在照顾几个新来的工作人员。*I'll be late tonight. I've got to baby-sit some visiting firemen.* 今天夜里我要弄得很晚。我必得接待几位远来的客人。◇ take care of *someone's* child(ren)

baby-sitter

a baby-sitter [ə ˈbeɪbiˌsɪdər] [口] **看孩子的人** → BABY-SIT

bachelor

a bachelor dinner [ə ˈbæ(:)tʃələr ˈdɪnər] [口] **告别独身晚宴** → a bachelor PARTY

a bachelor girl → GIRL

a bachelor party → PARTY

back

back talk [ˈbæ(:)kˌtɔ(:)k] [话] **顶嘴** → TALK back (to *someone*)

behind *someone's* **back** [bəˌhaɪnd ~ ˈbæ:k] [口] **背后** 字面意义为"在某人的背后",即"在某人听不见的地方"、"在某人看不见的地方"。*I have no confidence in myself. I always feel that people are laughing at me behind my back.* 我没有自信心,我总觉得人们在背地里耻笑我。*Here after, always discuss your plans with me beforehand. I won't have you sneaking around doing things behind my back.* 今后,你有什么计划必须先跟我商量。我不允许你在背地里偷偷摸摸地搞鬼。以上,可以考虑是与 when *someone's* BACK is turned 大致同义,其反义语为 to *someone's* FACE。*If he criticizes you to your face, you can't expect him to say nice things behind your back.* 如果他当面批评你,你别指望他在背地里说你的好话。◇ in *someone's* absence

get off *someone's* **back** [geˌdɔ(:)f ~ ˈbæ(:)k] [话] **停止罗嗦** 按字面意义是"从某人的背上下来",但这一习用语给人的感觉是"停止(站在背后)越过肩膀说三道四"。至于"说三道四"的内容,正如 *Get off my back, will ya? I told you I'd do it when I got the time.* 别罗嗦了好不好?我已经告诉你了,我有时间就干。这一例句所示,是"不满的意见"或"说教"、"指示"等使对方极为腻烦的东西。*Why don't you get off the poor fellow's back? Can't you see that he's doing his best?* 你对那个可怜的家伙别再罗嗦了好不好?你没看见他在尽最大的努力吗? *Yes, yes, I know that my report is late, but if you don't get off my back I'll never get it done.* 是的,是的,我知道我的报告写晚了,但是,如果你不停止唠唠叨叨,我永远也完不成呀。get 也可以用 keep 或 stay 替代。两者都是"控制住一向的罗嗦"的意思,在实际使用的场合,可以考虑它们与 get 大致同义。*I wish the boss would keep off my back. I'll be a nervous wreck before this project is over.* 但愿老板不再唠叨我了。不等这项工作干完,我会神经错乱了。*You'd better tell that guy to stay off my back. One of these days I'm going to come out swinging.* 你最好告诉那个家伙别再罗嗦我。说不上哪一天我会打他一个耳光的。get *someone* off *one's* back 是"使某人停止唠叨(纠缠)"的意思。*We've got to think of some way to get our creditors off our backs.* 我们得想个什么办法别叫债主纠缠我们。在这一场合,也可以用 keep 或 stay 代替 get。*Mr. Loophole hired a* *first-class tax accountant in hopes of keeping the tax office off his back.* 路普霍尔先生为了不受税务局的刁难,雇用了一位第一流的理税员。 → get on *someone's* BACK (about *something*) ◇ stop pestering *someone*

get on *someone's* **back** (about *something*) [ˌgedɔ(ː)n ~ ˈbæ(ː)k] [话] **唠叨** 直译是"骑在(某人)背上"。具体形象是"从他人背后唠唠叨叨指点要做这个做那个",使听话的人怀有"讨厌"、"还罗嗦什么"的心情。表示说教、叱责、牢骚、指令等等,在日常会话中频繁使用。*That guy's always getting on my back about something or other.* 那个家伙对我总是这个那个地唠叨没完。*Do you have to get on poor Charles's back every time he makes a simple mistake?* 可怜的查尔斯每一次犯一点小错误,你就非唠叨个没完不可吗?以下是催促乃至不满的场合。*The translation is already a week overdue. You'd better get on Mr. Summer's back about it.* 翻译的期限已经过一个礼拜啦。你最好对萨默先生提出不满的意见。 以下是指令乃至多嘴多舌。*If Carl gets on my back one more time about the way I do my work, I'm going to lose my temper.* 卡尔如果再一次对我的工作方法多嘴多舌,我就要发脾气啦。 如果用动词 be 代替 get,意为"哓哓不休"。*Dewey's on my back again about that money he claims I owe him.* 杜威硬说他借给我钱了,他又在为这件事哓哓不休。 另外也有 have *someone* on *one's* back 的说法,意为"受人责难"。*I'll have the boss on my back if I don't finish this on time.* 这个我不按时完工,就得受老板的批评。 with *someone* on one's back 大致是"受人苛责"。*How can I get anything done with you on my back all the time?* 我老是受你的苛责,怎么能干出什么事情呢?另外, get on *someone's* back 的反义语是 get off *someone's* BACK。 ◇ harass [hound] *someone* / get after *someone*

give *someone* **the shirt off** *one's* back → SHIRT

have a monkey on *one's* **back** → MONKEY

have *one's* **back to the wall** [hæv ~ ˌbæ(ː)k təðə ˈwɔːl] [口] **进退维谷** 字面意义为"背后是墙",原来表示"被人追赶到墙壁那里,既不能前进也不能后退"的状态。*The tunnel through which I had been running suddenly came to a dead end, and I could hear my pursuers coming closer. I literally had my back to the wall.* 我从隧道逃跑,突然到了死葫芦头,而且听到追赶我的人越来越近,毫不夸张地讲我真是进退维谷了。 也转作比喻使用。*In 1940, with the Nazi army just across the English Channel and supplies growing short. England had its back to the wall.* 1940年,纳粹军队进抵英吉利海峡的一侧,这时英国供应日益困难,陷入了山穷水尽的地步。 也可以用 back 作主语而讲 *one's* back is to the wall。*Our creditors are demanding payment and the banks are refusing to lend us any more money. I'm afraid our backs are to the wall.* 我们的债主要求还账,而各银行又拒绝再借给我们更多的钱。这可真把我们逼得走投无路啦。 ◇ be in a desperate position

have *someone* **on** *one's* **back** [ˌhæv ~ ɔːn ~ ˈbæ(ː)k] [话] **被人缠磨** → get on *someone's* BACK (about *something*)

know *someplace* **like the back of** *one's* **hand** [ˌnou ~ laɪkðə ˌbækəv ~ ˈhæ(ː)nd] [口] **了如指掌** 原意是"(对那个地区或场所)象对自己的手背一样熟悉"。*Jerry knows New York like the back of his hand.* 杰里对纽约是了如指掌。 *I'll have no trouble finding your house. I know that area like the back of my hand.* 我找你的家不会发生什么困难,因为我对那个地区了如指掌。 *someplace* 也有时指大厦(内部)。在这一场合,就是说详细了解某一办事处(商店、房间等)在大厦内的什么地方。*Doris knows that building like the back of her hand.* 多丽丝对那个大厦了如指掌。 ◇ be extremely familiar with *someplace*

(roll off *someone***) like water off a duck's back** → WATER

be no skin off *someone's* **back** → SKIN

stab *someone* **in the back** (by *doing something*) [ˌstæ(ː)b ~ ɪnðə ˈbæ(ː)k] [话] **背信弃义** 字面意义是“背后捅人一刀”。*The murderer stabbed him in the back.* 杀人凶手从背后捅了他一刀。转用于比喻,有“冷不防”的意味,往往相当于“暗下毒手”的意思。*That guy really stabbed me in the back. He quit his job with me and went to work for my strongest competitor.* 那小子简直是从背后捅了我一刀。他不在我这里了,竟跑到我最厉害的竞争对手那里去工作。*I wouldn't trust Mr. Oily. He'll stab you in the back the first chance he gets.* 我不信任奥利先生,他一有机会就会背信弃义的。◇ betray *someone's* trust

take a back seat (**to** *someone*) → SEAT

turn *one's* **back on** *someone* [ˌtə(ː)rn ~ ˈbæ(ː)kɔ(ː)n ~] [口] **(对某人)不理睬** 字面意义是“(由于轻蔑或愤怒)转过身去以后背对着某人”。*I greeted him at the reception, but he merely turned his back on me and began speaking to someone else.* 在招待会上我向他问好,但他转过身去不理睬我,跟另一个人交谈去了。转作比喻使用,有“(对发生困难的亲戚朋友以及在道义上理应伸手搭救的人)视而不见,采取不关心的态度”的意思。*Jerry is a true friend. He never turned his back on me even when I was accused of stealing the company's money.* 杰里是一位真正的朋友。即使在我被指控偷窃公司的钱款的时候,他也没有不理睬我。*You've got to help me. We've been friends for a long time, haven't we? Don't turn your back on me now.* 你要帮我一下。咱们是多年的老朋友啦,是不是?现在你不要抛弃我哟。*After all the support I've given the boss, it was a great shock to have him turn his back on me when I needed his support.* 我曾经卖很大力气支持老板,而当我需要他来援助的时候,他却毫不理睬,这真令人大为震惊。*The world must not turn its back on the Southeast Asian refugees.* 全世界的人都不应该对东南亚的难民弃而不顾。另外也偶尔用以表示“(为了到别处去开始新生活、谋求新出路而将老朋友、老同伴)抛弃”的意思。→ turn *one's* BACK on *something* ◇ ignore *someone's* plight

turn *one's* **back on** *something* [ˌtə(ː)rn ~ ˈbæ(ː)kɔ(ː)n ~] [口] **丢开(旧有的生活方式、习惯等)** 当谈到人时,即前条 turn *one's* BACK on *someone*,有“(因忽视、采取不关心的态度而)抛弃不管”的意思。就“以背相向”这一点来说,与本条虽然相同,但本条的英语中并无“不关心”的含义。*When the ex-convict was offered an honest job, he decided to turn his back on his old way of life and try to make something of himself.* 当那个有前科的罪犯得到一个正经的工作时,他下决心抛弃自己过去的生活方式,努力重作新人。*Even though the people of a primitive culture may adopt the benefits of modern civilization, it is difficult for them to turn their backs on the old ways of doing things.* 原始文化的人们即使能够接受现代文明的恩泽,他们也很难放弃旧有的生活方式。在下一例句中,all my grammar books 并不仅仅是“我的一切文法书”,应该解释为“过去依赖文法书死记硬背的习惯”。*I realized that if I really wanted to become fluent in English, I would have to turn my back on all my grammar books and start again from scratch.* 我已经体会到,如果我真想把英语说得很流畅,我就得完全丢开依赖文法书死记硬背的老习惯,重打鼓另开张。另外,如果讲实际动作的“以背向着(墙壁等)”用 turn *one's* back to (the wall, etc.),不能说 on the wall。◇ abandon *something*

turn *one's* **back to** *something* [ˌtə(ː)rn ~ ˈbæ(ː)ktə ~] [口] **以背向着……** → turn *one's* BACK on *something*

when *someone's* **back is turned** [*h*wen ~ ˈbæːkɪz ˌtəːrnd] [口] **背地里** 字面意义是“当(某人)把背转过去的时候”。在一般辞典中很少收录,但它与 behind *someone's* BACK 大致同义,是一个普遍使用的固定词组。when 根据场合的不同可以变换，使用 whenever, every time, as soon as, once, the minute 等。*I want to trust Jack, but whenever my back is turned he cuts the ground from under my feet.* 我倒很想信任杰克，但是只要我一转身，他就下绊子摔倒我。*You say you are my friend, yet when my back is turned you go around spreading stories about me.* 你说你是我的朋友，但是在背地里却到处散布给我编造的瞎话。*Is this what you do to a friend when his back is turned?* 这就是当一个朋友不在的时候你对他采取的行动吗？"背地里"一语应用于经常干坏事的人时，则有"只要眼睛一离开"的意味。*The boys always promise to be good, but as soon as my back is turned they begin fighting again.* 男孩子们总保证说要当好孩子，但是只要我的眼睛一离开，他们马上就开始打架。*That restaurant will pad your bill when your back is turned.* 那个饭店，只要你一马虎大意，就会给你开花账。有时也使用 when [whenever, every time, as soon as, once, the minute, etc.] *someone* turns *his* back 这样的主动语态。*Is that what you say about me when I turn my back?* 当我不在的时候，你就是那样地议论我吗？*Every time I turn my back that child is into mischief again.* 我只要眼睛一离开，那孩子就又开始淘气了。◇ when *someone* is not there / when *someone* is not watching [careful]

when *someone* **turns** *his* **back** [*h*wen ～ ˌtə(ː)rnz ～ ˈbæ(ː)k] [口] **暗中** → when *someone's* BACK is turned

back-seat

a back-seat driver → DRIVER

backward

bend over backward (to *do something*) [ˌbendovər ˈbæ(ː)kwərd] [话] **费尽力气(去做某事)** 原意"把身体向后弯"。这是一个相当别致的表达法。其意味也许不易捉摸，但只要了解原来的构思是"(为了做某事而)采取不合道理的姿势"、"蛮干"，就容易领会了。backward 也可以加-s，用 backwards 代替。或是象 *I don't understand why she is angry with me. I've bent over backward to be nice to her.* 我不理解她为什么生我的气，我一向对她是极力体贴的。这样，多用于对人有所奉献的场合；或是象 *The principal bends over backward to be fair to all the students.* 校长竭力公平对待所有的学生。这样，多用于并非一时地、而是不断采取某一姿态的场合。*I'm not about to bend over backward to help that guy. What has he ever done for me?* 我完全没有费尽力气去帮助那个家伙的意思。他过去对我究竟干了些什么呀？有时也用 lean over backward(s)。*Mr. Allen has leaned over backwards to meet our demands. The least we can do is to defer to his wishes on this one point.* 艾伦先生为了满足我们的要求而花了很大力气。我们起码能够做到的事情，是在这一点上不辜负他的期望。◇ make a special effort (to *do something*)

lean over backward (to *do something*) [ˌliːnovər ˈbæ(ː)kwərd] [话] **拼命(去做某事)** → bend over BACKWARD (to *do something*)

bacon

bring home the bacon [ˌbrɪŋ ˌhoumðə ˈbeɪkən] [话] **持奖赏[成果]而归** 直译"拿着熏猪肉回家"。古时，在地方的庙会等场合，有过一种娱乐活动，即把猪的全身都涂上油，然后放开，谁能抓住它谁就可以拿走。猪身上滑溜溜的，肯定不好抓。在这种 greased-pig contest (抓涂油猪竞赛)中取胜的人，"带着猪得意洋洋地回家"。这已成为本条习用语来源的定论。本来应该是 bring home the pig，不知为什么不用 pig 而用 bacon 一词。大概是由于得到了 pig 以后，可以把它熏制而吃香喷喷的 bacon 的缘故吧。实际上使用于在比赛或竞赛中取得优胜得奖而归的场合，以及更广泛地使用于就所委托的事情或工作等，取得一定成果而归[做贡献]的场合。*The basketball team set out for the tournament with high hopes of bringing home* *the bacon.* 篮球队怀着要捧冠而归的气吞山河的心情前去参加比赛了。*Michael practiced hard for the English speaking contest, but his speech failed to bring home the bacon.* 迈克尔为了参加英语辩论比赛会进行了刻苦的练习,但是他的讲话未能使他获奖而归。象下面例句这样作为比喻使用的时候也很多。*John has gone to the bank to try to secure a loan. Let's just hope he is able to bring home the bacon.* 约翰到银行去了,试图获得一笔贷款。我们但愿他能够取得成果而归。*Kerry is one of this newspaper's top reporters. You can always depend on him to bring home the bacon.* 克里是这家报纸的一流记者之一。他能够永远不负所望,采访来极好的素材。这一场合的 bring home the bacon 是"(在采访中)取得某些成果而归"的意思。也可以有象下面例句这样有点过时的表达法:*The contract negotiations broke down, and our representative was forced to return home without the bacon.* 合同的谈判破裂了,我们的代表不得不空手而还。此外还用以表达"(按期)挣来生活费"的意思。*Most women want to marry steady, reliable men who will always bring home the bacon.* 绝大多数女子都愿意嫁给永远能按时挣来生活费的坚实可靠的男人。*After a year of free-lancing, I had to find another job. My writing just didn't bring home the bacon.* 当了一年自由作家之后,我不得不找另外的工作了。我只靠写作不能够糊口。◇ secure the championship [prize, etc.] / achieve what *one* has set out to accomplish / earn a living

bad

a bad apple → APPLE
bad blood → BLOOD
a bad guy → GUY
bad news → NEWS
be a bad scene → SCENE

go from bad to worse [ˌgou frəmˈbæːdtə ˈwəːrs] [口] **越来越坏** 字面意义是"从坏走向更坏"。大体上可以认为是强调了 become [get] worse 的表达法。在经济、人际关系、成绩等方面广泛使用。*We were hoping to recover our losses the following year, but when the oil shock came, things went from bad to worse.* 我们曾经指望在下一年度弥补上我们的亏损,可是发生了石油危机,事态越来越恶化了。常使用进行时。*A: How are things between Lyle and his wife these days? B: Going from bad to worse, I hear.* 甲:莱尔和他的夫人之间的关系最近如何?乙:我听说越来越糟啊。*Since our son went out for the baseball team, his grades have been going from bad to worse.* 我们的儿子自从参加棒球队以后,他的学习成绩越来越差了。◇ get increasingly worse

have it bad (for *someone*) [ˌhævət ˈbæːd] [话] **害了严重相思病** 在讲"病名"时使用 have a bad case of ~ (得了严重的……病),本条是由此创出的表达法。it 是所谓的"状况的 it",在这里可以笼统地认为是指疾病或恋爱的症状。bad 与 badly 相同,意为"严重地"。在十多年以前有一首名为"I've Got It Bad and That Ain't Good"的布鲁斯爵士乐,这也是使用 have it bad 的一个例子,意思是"迷醉郎君愁煞人"。*A: I hear Joan can't go to the party because she has poison ivy. B: Yeah. I'm afraid she's got it bad.* 甲:我听说琼由于野葛中毒,出了斑疹,不能出席社交晚会了。乙:是啊!她的病似乎很重哪!这是按字面意义的用法。*A: I think I'll fly up to Bangor and see Betty this weekend. B: Sounds like you've got it bad.* 甲:我打算这个周末乘飞机到班戈去看贝蒂。乙:看起来,你的相思病相当严重哪!为了加强说话的语气,常在 it 与 bad 之间加个 pretty。*From the looks of things, Kirk has it pretty bad for your sister.* 看样子,柯克对你妹妹十分着迷哪。*A: I hear Joe is dating Lucy almost every night lately. B: Yeah. I'm afraid he's got it pretty bad.* 甲:我听说乔最近几乎每天夜里都与露西幽会哪。乙:是啊。他似乎病入膏肓啦。◇ be very much in love

(with *someone*)

bad-mouth

bad-mouth *someone* [*something*] [ˈbæːd-ˌmauθ ～] [话] **(背地里)说坏话** bad-mouth 不用于"(当面)说不中听的话"的时候,在后一场合,一般讲 criticize *someone* to his face,等等。有的词典把 bad-mouth 解释为"一贬到底",其实"贬"则贬矣,却不是一定非达到"到底"的程度不可,勿宁说在本条的习用语中往往飘荡着"多么卑鄙"的气息。*Sue's always bad-mouthing people she doesn't like.* 苏对她所不喜欢的人,总是在背地里说坏话。*I can't believe that Carl would bad-mouth me like that.* 我简直不敢相信卡尔竟是那样在背地里说我的坏话呀。"说坏话"的对象不仅限于"人"。*He's bad-mouthing our plan just because he wasn't invited to take part in it.* 他一味贬低我们的计划,只不过因为他没被邀请参加而已。另外,象 bad-mouthing 这样加 -ing 的时候,发音也可以为 [ˈbæ(ː)dˌmauθɪŋ], 但一般作 [ˈbæ(ː)dˌmauðɪŋ]。◇ say malicious things about *someone* [*something*]

badger

the badger game → GAME

bag

be all but in the bag [ˌɔːlbədɪnðə ˈbæːg] [话] **十拿九稳** → be in the BAG

be *someone's* **bag** [～ ˈbæːg] [话] **爱好[拿手]** bag 怎么会具有这一意义,不大清楚。不过,也有人说原来是"(爵士音乐家所属的)流派"。这是一个新表达法,特别是青年人常挂在口头上。从"爱好"、"趣味"起,直至"拿手"、"专长",意义相当广泛。*I'm a jazz fan. Classical music just isn't my bag.* 我是爵士乐的热烈爱好者。至于古典音乐,我一点儿也不喜欢。*Drugs aren't Stu's bag. He always sticks to whiskey.* 司徒对麻醉药不感兴趣。他专门喝威士忌。也有"爱好"与"拿手"各半、二者混合的场合。*I tried teaching school for a couple of years, but I found it wasn't really my bag.* 我在学校里试教了两年书,但是发现我不是干这一行的材料。象以上所举的例子,多半用于否定句。但并不是非如此不可。*Words are my bag. I'm a dictionary editor.* 语言是我的专长。我是一个词典编纂者。*Words are my bag. I love to work crossword puzzles.* 我对语言有兴趣。我非常喜欢搞纵横字谜。◇ be *someone's* taste [interest, forte]

a bag of bones → BONES

have *something* **in the bag** [ˌhæv ～ ɪnðə ˈbæːg] [话] **稳操胜券** → be in the BAG

be in the bag [ɪnðə ˈbæːg] [话] **必胜无疑** "(猎物等)已经入于袋中",亦即"必胜无疑"之意。与汉语俗语"手拿把掐"的思路相似。就体育比赛来说,如果讲 This (game) is in the bag. 那就是"已经稳拿了"。*When Mr. Bigstuff suddenly became very friendly with me, I knew the contract was in the bag.* 当比格斯塔夫先生突然对我表示非常友好时,我确信那项合同已经毫无问题了。也有这样的表达法:在 be 与 in the bag 之间插入具有"实际上"的意义的 all but, 构成 be all but in the bag, 意为"十拿九稳"。*After our team hit a home run with the bases loaded in the top of the ninth, the game was all but in the bag.* 我们队在第九次积分表上来了个满垒打,这次棒球比赛的胜利已经是十拿九稳了。也有 have *something* (all but) in the bag 这样的说法。*The Democratic candidate has the election all but in the bag.* 在选举中,民主党候选人已经稳操左券了。*By the fiftieth lap, it was clear that Petty had the race in the bag.* 在赛跑中,佩蒂跑到第五十圈就显然会夺魁了。◇ be virtually won

leave *someone* **holding the bag** [ˌli(ː)v ～ ˌhouldɪŋðə ˈbæːg] [话] **转嫁(某人),逃避罪责** 直译为"叫某人拿着袋子,自己扬长而去"。语源不详。在这里,the bag 是"责任"或"讨厌的任务"的意思。本条意为"把责任(讨厌的任务)加在某人身上,自己走开",一般指有意识的行为,但也有本来无意识而结果却形成逃避罪责的场合。从被转嫁责任的一方来看,就属于"倒霉"了。*Let's go back and tell the teacher that we broke the window, too. We can't leave Jimmy holding the bag.* 我们要回去告诉老师,我们也是打碎窗户玻璃的人。我们不能逃之夭夭,叫吉米一个人承担全部责任呀。*When the police arrived, the other bank robbers ran off with the money, leaving Louie holding the bag.* 当警察到达的时候,抢劫银行的其他罪犯都携款跑掉,只剩下路易一个人当倒霉鬼了。也常使用被动语态。*Everyone said that they would share the responsibility, but when the time came, I was left holding the bag.* 大家都说分担责任,但是一到时候,只留下我一个人当倒霉鬼了。也可以去掉 leave 而只使用 hold the bag。*After my partner ran up a lot of big debts he died, and there I was, (left) holding the bag.* 我的伙伴借了大批的债以后就死了,剩下我一个人必须负全部责任。◇ make *someone* take [leave *someone* to take] all the blame [responsibility] (for *something*)

let the cat out of the bag → CAT

bail

bail *someone* [*something*] **out** [ˌbeɪl ～ ˈaut] [口] **(从困境中)救出** bail 作为名词是"保释金",作为动词是"交保释金"的意思。*Mike's friends raised enough money to bail him out of jail.* 迈克的朋友凑足了保释金营救他出狱。这是按字面意义的用法。可以用作比喻。*Unless a fairy godmother comes along soon to bail us out, this company is going under.* 除非有一位福神马上前来拯救我们,否则,这个公司就要倒闭啦。如这一例句所示,经常使用于表示"从经济的困境中救出",但是,并不仅限于"经济的困境"。*Every time my brother has gotten into trouble I've bailed him out, but this is absolutely the last time.* 我的弟弟每次惹事生非的时候,我都为他解除困难,可是,这是绝对的最后一回了。*You've got to bail me out. The boss thinks I went to a baseball game yesterday.* 你想法救救我吧。老板以为我昨天去看棒球比赛啦。也可以象下面例句这样改变词的顺序:*The bank bailed out the company with a timely loan.* 银行的及时贷款使公司摆脱了困境。◇ save [rescue] *someone*

bait

rise to the bait [ˌraɪztəðə ˈbeɪt] [口] **上钩** 字面意义是"(从水底)浮上来、到有食饵的地方"。可以按照本来的意义使用,如 *I could see the fish on the bottom of the river, but none of them would rise to the bait.* 我能够看见河底的鱼,但是没有一条浮上来吃食饵。但也使用于比喻,如 *The police put a notice in the paper that the fugitive's mother was sick. They are now waiting to see if he will rise to the bait.* 警察叫报纸刊登一条消息说,那个逃犯的母亲病了。他们现在正等待着,看逃犯是否会自动上钩。*The lawyer for the prosecution asked the defendant a number of leading questions, but he refused to rise to the bait.* 负责起诉的律师向被告提出一系列诱导口供的问题,但是他始终不落入圈套。*We tried to trick Tom by telling him that Sally had called to invite him to dinner tonight, but he wouldn't rise to the bait.* 我们试图对汤姆来个恶作剧,告诉他萨莉来电话请他今天晚上去吃饭,可是他没有上这个当。也可以用 take 或 swallow 代替 rise to,而说 take the bait (吃食饵)、swallow the bait (吞食饵)。作为比喻时尽管在意义上有一点差别,但用法则完全一样,因此可以与 rise to 互换。◇ react as *someone* hopes / fall into the trap

swallow the bait [ˌswɑləðə ˈbeɪt] [口] **吞食饵(上当)** → rise to the BAIT

take the bait [ˌteɪkðə ˈbeɪt] [口] **吃食饵(受骗)** → rise to the BAIT

bald

(as) bald as a billiard → BILLIARD

(as) bald as a coot → COOT

(as) bald as a billiard ball [əz ˈbɔːl dəzə ˈbɪljərd ˌbɔːl] [话] **亮光光的秃头** → (as) bald as a BILLIARD

ball

be a ball [ə 'bɔːl] [话] **极为愉快** → have a BALL

one's **ball and chain** [~ 'bɔː lən'tʃeɪn] [话] **老婆** ball and chain 的本义为“带有重铁球的脚镣子”。过去，叫犯人在户外劳动时，为防止他们逃跑而带上这种刑具。现在，在漫画中还经常出现。*The prisoner, wearing a ball and chain, was breaking rocks with a sledge hammer.* 那个囚犯戴着有重铁球的脚镣，用长柄大铁锤在破碎石块。从“简直把丈夫当作犯人似地束缚起来”这一构思出发，转用于在笑谈中指“老婆”。*Yes, I'm going to the party tonight, but I'll have to drag along my ball and chain.* 是呀，我要参加今天的社交晚会，但是，我必须带着我家的母老虎。◇ *one's* wife

the ball is in *someone's* **court** [ðə 'bɔːləzɪn ~ 'ko(ː)rt] [话] **应该(某人)做出反应** 直译为“球在某人的场地上”，这意味着“球回到自己一边的场地上，应该打回去了”。这是从网球而来的习用语。*This is our final proposal. The ball is now in your court.* 这是我们最后的提案。现在轮到你发言啦！*If they accept our conditions, the will be in our court. We have to decide how to react.* 如果他们接受我们的条件，就轮到我们回话啦 。怎样应付，我们必须决定啊。*They had refuted all my arguments. I knew that the ball was now in my court, but I wasn't sure how best to return it.* 他们驳倒了我的所有论点。我知道现在该我进行反驳了，但是我不知如何措词最好。*Frank had lured the man out of his hotel room. Now the ball was in Joe's court. He had to get into the room and search it without being discovered.* 弗兰克已经把那个人引诱出他所住的旅馆房间了。这回该轮到乔行动了。他必须进入室内搜查，而不留下任何痕迹。◇ (it) is *someone's* turn to act [react]

a ball of fire [ə ˌbɔ(ː)ləv'faɪr] [话] **精力充沛的活动家** 直译“一团火”，汉语也有“干工作象一团火似地”的说法，英语的形象大致一样。这一习用语令人在眼前浮现出一刻不停地猛烈活动的姿态，在体育运动、工作、学习等方面广泛使用。语意不仅仅是“猛烈”，而含有“巧妙”、“高明”的意思。用另外的英语说，有 a human dynamo。*Lyle is not a good student, but on the basketball court he's a ball of fire.* 莱尔不是一个勤奋用功的学生，但是一到篮球场上，他却是生龙活虎一般。*As a salesman, Stu is no ball of fire.* 作为一个推销员，司徒没有什么了不起的地方。一般使用 real 加强语气。*Frank is a good reporter. He may appear lazy, but send him out on an assignment and he becomes a real ball of fire.* 弗兰克是一位优秀的新闻记者。乍看起来，他好象很懒，但是一派他出去进行采访，他就真正象一团火似地猛干了。◇ an outstandingly energetic performer ((强调的场合 outstandingly → amazingly))

be behind the eight ball [bəˌhaɪn*d*ðɪ 'eɪtˌbɔːl] [话] **陷入窘境** 字面意义是“(白球)在黑球的后边”。在台球游戏中，使用白球把其他十五个球打入桌角的袋中。但是，在某一种游戏法中，规定最后打入十五个球当中的黑球，在此以前，不但不许打它入袋，而且不许白球碰到它。因此，在打球的时候，如果白球正“在黑球的后边”，黑球另一侧(即以黑球为中心而在白球相反方向)是要去打的球，由于黑球的阻碍，就非常难打了。*I couldn't get a clear shot because my cue ball was behind the eight ball.* 我的白球正在黑球的后边，所以就非常难打了。可转作比喻使用。*If I don't pass my finals, I'm going to be behind the eight ball.* 如果我学期考试不及格，我就要陷入窘境了。往往用 really 加强语气。*Our company is really behind the eight ball. We have a huge debt to pay but can't borrow any more money.* 我们公司的确是一筹莫展了。我们有大批债务非还不可，但是连一点贷款也弄不到手。*I need my car for my job, so when I lost my license for speeding I was really behind the eight ball.* 为了工作方便，我需要有汽车。因此，当我由于行车超速而失去驾驶证的时候，我的确非常为难了。如果象 be behind the eight ball with *someone* 这样后边带有 with *someone*，则为“与某人关系不佳”的意思。*I'm behind the eight ball with my boss.* 我与老板之间的关系很不好。也有 put *someone* behind the eight ball 的说法，即“逼人绝境”的意思。*Mr. Smith's refusal to see me put me behind the eight ball.* 史密斯先生拒绝接见我，弄得我非常为难。另外，find *oneself* behind the eight ball 也是一个定型的表达法，意思是“感到为难”。*When Ralph couldn't come up with the money, we found ourselves behind the eight ball.* 当拉尔夫筹措不到钱款的时候，我们感到非常窘迫了。◇ be in a difficult position / be in trouble

get on the ball [gɔ.dɔ(ː)nðə ˈbɔːl] [话] **紧张起来** → be on the BALL

get the ball rolling [ˌgetðə ˈbɔːl ˈrouliŋ] [话] **使(会议、社交晚会、工作等)顺利开始** 字面意义为“使球转动”，是把“会议”、“社交晚会”、“工作”等比拟为“球”(ball) 的表达法。为了使 ball 能够 get rolling，是需要努力一番的，因而多用于充当主语的人“发动”、“带头”的情况。*I agree that the project is a good idea, but we won't be able to get the ball rolling unless we get some more money.* 我承认那个计划是一个好的方案，但是，如果我们筹措不到更多的资金，那是不能付诸实现的。象这一例句所示，并不仅限于在“(把停止的球)开始(转动)”的场合使用。又如 *Negotiations were stalled until we got the ball rolling again with a compromise proposal.* 谈判陷入停顿状态，直到我们提出一个妥协方案，才又顺利进行下去。也用于“(把一度停止的球)中途(再转动起来)”的场合。*Jim, since this is the first meeting of the year, would you get the ball rolling by giving a brief review of last year's activities?* 吉姆，这是今年的第一次会议，你能不能打头炮，先简单扼要地讲一讲去年的业务情况呢？*Most of the people at the party were strangers to each other, so the hostess tried to get the ball rolling by introducing each guest to everyone.* 参加社交晚会的人大多都互不相识，因此，女主人为了使晚会开得活泼有趣，就把客人一一向大家介绍。动词也使用 start, set 等代替 get。另外，ball 之前也可以加适当的形容词。*A good way to start the conversational ball rolling is to ask a person about his hometown.* 使谈话顺利开始的一种良好方法就是向对方询问他故乡的事情。the ball gets rolling 意为“顺利[正式]地开始”。*It won't make much difference if you're a little late to the meeting. The ball won't get rolling for an hour or so.* 你出席会议晚一点也没有多大关系，反正得过上一个钟头左右才能进入正题。也可以用 really 加强语气。*You shouldn't have left the party so early. The ball really got rolling about then o'clock.* 你不该那么早就离开社交晚会。到了十点钟左右，晚会才真正热闹起来啊。→ keep the BALL rolling ◇ get things moving / begin (the activities [procedures, process, conversation, etc.])

have a ball [ˌhævə ˈbɔːl] [话] **度过非常愉快的时光** 字面意义是“开舞会”。但在现代不大使用这一意义，开舞会一般都说 hold a ball 或者 give a ball。当然，在最初的时候，have a ball 也作“开舞会”解。不过，ball 比学生主办的 school dance 或个人家庭的 dance party 等豪华得多，规模大得多，给人以上流社会娱乐活动的印象，因此，作为比喻，have a ball 就具有“度过非常愉快的时光”的意味了。而且，可以认为，随着人们频繁使用这一比喻意义，本来意义的使用方法也就逐渐消声匿迹了。*We had a ball at the dance last night.* 昨天夜里，我们在舞会上度过了非常愉快的时光。*A: How was your vacation? B: We had a ball.* 甲：假期过得如何？乙：愉快极啦！实际上，在“内心极为凄苦”的场合，也常以讽刺的口吻使用 have a ball。*Why didn't you help us fix the road yesterday? We had a real ball.* 昨天你们为什么没有帮助我们修路呢？哎，我们甭提多高兴啦！如这一例句所示，在作为讽刺话使用时，常以

real 加强语气。但不能说只要一加 real 就带有讽刺意味。*Tom says he had a real ball at the beach last week.* 汤姆说,上个星期他在海滨度过了非常愉快的时光。另外,有时也用 be a ball (非常愉快)这一表达法。*You should come to the party tonight. It'll be a ball.* 今天夜里,您务必来参加社交晚会啊!一定会非常愉快的。这一句型也可以用于说讽刺话。*A: How was your math exam? B: It was a real ball.* 甲:你的数学考得怎样?乙:哎呀,甭提多惨啦! ◇ have a wonderful time

have a lot on the ball [hævə ˌludɔ(ː)nðə ˈbɔːl] [话] **非常有能力** "在球上有很多东西"的意义是"(投球手)能投变化多端的球",原是打棒球的用语。*The pitcher had a lot on the ball during the early innings, but he seems to be getting tired now.* 投球手在最初几局投的球变化多端,但是看起来他现在已经累啦。转义是"能力很强"、"(工作、学习等)成绩很好"。*Al has a lot on the ball, but I'm not sure he's completely honest.* 阿尔非常有能力,但是我不了解他是否十分诚实。*Frank should do well in his new job. He appears to have a lot on the ball.* 弗兰克在他的新工作中一定很有成绩。他显然是很有能力的。象以上的例句所示,在 have 与 on the ball 之间加 a lot 的情况最多,但也偶尔有加 much, more, very little, something, anything, what (*someone* has) 等的时候。另外,在加强语气时常常使用 really。*Most of the students are good at math, but I'm afraid they don't really have much on the ball when it comes to English.* 大多数学生的数学都很不错,但是据我看,他们在英语方面可就不那么擅长啦。*Let's put the new players on the field and see what they have on the ball.* 让我们把新选手拉到场地上去,看看他们的能力究竟如何。另外,如果在这最后的例句中,用 mound (投球手的踏板)去代替 field,那就不是比喻的意义,而要按字面意义解释为"看看他们能投出怎样的球"了。◇ be very capable

keep the ball rolling [ˌki(ː)pðə ˈbɔːl ˈroulɪŋ] [话] **使(会议、晚会、工作等)不停顿** 字面意义是"保持球在转动的状态",亦即"使转动的球不停顿"。根据上下文,也可以具有"使不迟滞"或"使不松懈"的意味。*I have to leave the meeting for about thirty minutes. Try to keep the ball rolling until I get back.* 我必须离开会议约半个钟头。在我回来之前,请照常开下去。*Keep the ball rolling. We have to finish this work by tonight.* 不要停下,今天晚上我们必须完成这个工作。*As the party flagged, John tried to keep the ball rolling by telling tall stories.* 由于社交晚会开得越来越不起劲,约翰大吹牛皮,试图使它不停顿下来。如下一例句所示,ball 之前也可以加形容词。*The American President worked hard to keep the diplomatic ball rolling between Egypt and Israel.* 美国总统拼命使埃及与以色列不断绝外交关系。→ get the BALL rolling ◇ keep things [the activities, the procedures, the process, the conversation, etc.] going [moving]

be on the ball [ˌɔ(ː)nðə ˈbɔːl] [话] **全神贯注** 字面意义"站在球上",亦即"当心不要掉下来"。因此,广泛用以表示"精神紧张"的意思。*As a salesman, Green needs more experience. If he had been on the ball, he wouldn't have let that customer escape.* 作为一个推销员,格林还需要有更多的经验。如果他精神高度集中,是不会让那位顾客跑掉的。*Hubie is a good player. He's just not always on the ball.* 胡比是一位好选手。只不过他的精神常不集中。在这一表达法中,除动词 be 而外,也使用 get, stay, keep 等动词。get on the ball 是"集中精神"。*If you don't get on the ball and start studying harder, you're going to flunk.* 如果你不集中精神,更加努力地学习,你就会名落孙山了。*Get on the ball, you guys. We have to finish before the chief gets back.* 大家加把油啊!在头头回来以前,咱们非干完不可。stay [keep] on the ball 意为"全神贯注"。*Prof. Withers is a tough teacher. You've got to stay on* *the ball in his classes.* 威瑟斯教授是一位严厉的老师。在他上课的时候，你必须全神贯注。*In a tiring job like this, it's hard to keep on the ball every minute of the day.* 在象这样一种容易疲劳的工作中，很难每时每刻都集中精神。*If you want to succeed in this job, you've got to get on the ball and stay there.* 你如果想在这一工作中有所成就，你必须全神贯注，坚持不懈。keep *someone* on the ball 是"使某人精神振奋"。*A good coach tries hard to keep his players constantly on the ball.* 一个优秀的教练极力使他的选手们经常保持高昂的士气。◇ be alert

play ball (with *someone*) [ˌpleɪ ˈbɔːl] [话] **(与某人)合作** 字面意义为"(与某人)一道玩球"。原来的含义是："为了一道玩球，就不能不相互合作"。附带说一下：字面意义的 play ball 不限于棒球，也包括其他各种球戏，连儿童们玩小球都算在内，应用幅度很宽。一个人"玩球"则为 play with a ball。作为比喻，使用方法如下：*You had better play ball with us or you'll be sorry.* 你最好跟我们合作，否则你会后悔的。*The Congress is refusing to play ball with the President on this bill.* 关于这项法案，国会拒绝与总统合作。with 以下常省略：*We had hoped to get their help on this project, but they refused to play ball.* 对于这一规划，我们曾经希望得到他们的协助，但是他们拒绝合作。*We need a big loan in order to expand, but the bank won't play ball.* 为了扩展业务，我们需要一笔贷款，但是银行不肯合作。◇ cooperate

put *someone* **behind the eight ball** [ˌput ~ bəˌhaɪndðɪ ˈeɪtˌbɔːl] [话] **逼人走投无路** → be behind the eight BALL

put *someone* **in the ball park** → PARK

put the ball in *someone's* **court** [ˌputðə ˈbɔːlɪn ˈ~ ˈko(ː)rt] [话] **逼上梁山** 字面意义是"(在网球比赛中)把球打入对方的场地"。"被打到自己场地的球，不管愿意不愿意，也必须打回去"——从这一构思出发，就在比喻中用以表示"以某种行为(或言语)使得对方站在不得不转向下一个行动的立场"的意义。在对方来说，一般怀有"如何是好"或"总得想个办法"的被逼无奈的心情。*I thought I had all but won the debate, but Jim's clever argument put the ball back in my court.* 我以为我在这次辩论中稳操胜券了，但是吉姆的巧妙的论点使得我不得不重战几个回合。*I had often been critical of the boss for being too conservative in his thinking, but his agreeing to let me try my latest idea had put the ball in my court.* 我常常指责老板的思想过于保守，可是，由于他同意叫我试搞我最近提出的方案，这回逼得我不能不想主意了。*Ted's critical questions keep me on the defensive at almost every meeting. I've got to think of some way to put the ball in his court for a change.* 特德的批评性的质问使我几乎在每一次会议上都处于防守的地位。我必须设法改变一下局面，把球打回去。象 put the ball squarely in *someone's* court 这样，可以用 squarely 加强语气。squarely 的字面意义是"规规矩矩"，在讲网球比赛时也使用。*Egypt's latest proposal has put the ball squarely in Israel's court.* 埃及最近的建议逼得以色列不得不想办法应付了。有时也可以用 place 代替 put。*My younger opponent's amazing speed in the slalom has placed the ball in my court. I have to better his time or lose face.* 在障碍滑雪中，比我年轻的对手的惊人的速度真把我逼上梁山了。我在时间上不超过他，就无法回去见江东父老了。◇ put [place] *someone* in the position of having to respond [act, perform (well)]

stay [keep] on the ball [ˌsteɪ / ˌki(ː)pɔ(ː)nðə ˈbɔːl] [话] **全神贯注** → be on the BALL

balloon

go over like a lead balloon [gouˌouvər laɪkə ˌle(ː)dbəˈluːn] [话] **(笑谈、建议等)完全不受欢迎** go over 是"越过"。这一习用语的构思是：听笑谈、建议等的人有一个标准，而且要"越过"那个标准。like a lead balloon 是"象一个铅的气球"。

"铅的气球"很重,不能飘上天空,根本谈不上"越过"什么。换言之,就是"简直不能越过"。所谓"(笑谈、建议等)简直不能超越对方的标准",即意味着"(笑谈、建议等)完全不受欢迎"。*Fred's joke went over like a lead balloon.* 弗雷德的笑谈没有引起一丁点儿反应。*I'm afraid my proposal to the committee will go over like a lead balloon.* 我给委员会提的建议,大概是完全不会被接受的。除笑谈、建议外,也用于开音乐会、戏剧演出等。*A: How did the PTA like the jazz concert? B: It went over like a lead balloon.* 甲:学生家长与教师联谊会对爵士音乐会的反应如何?乙:简直不受欢迎!进一步发展,也可以单独使用 a lead balloon 表示"一点趣味也没有"的意思。但是,这种表达法很少使用。*That guy's jokes are all lead balloons.* 那个家伙所讲的笑话没有一个令人发笑的。◇ be an utter failure / be very poorly received

ball-park

ball-park ['bɔːl 'pɑ(ː)rk] [话] **大概情况** → put *someone* in the ball PARK

balls

Great balls of fire! ['greɪt 'bɔːlzə ˌfaɪr] [话] ((表示极度惊异、否定等)) **怎么!** → Great SCOTT!

baloney

baloney [bə'louni] [话] **胡说八道** baloney 原指 Bologna sausage (博洛尼亚香肠)。这是一种价格低廉的大香肠,据说最初产于意大利的博洛尼亚,除猪牛肉外还加入其他各种原料,一般给人以低级品的印象。因此,也就用于表示"靠不住的话"、"没有内容的空谈"之类的意思。baloney 偶尔缀字为 boloney。*He says he doesn't have enough money? That's a lot of baloney. He's got more than all the rest of us put together.* 他说他没有多少钱?简直是瞎话连篇!把咱们大家的钱都加在一起也没有他的多。作为口实或辩解而"说瞎话"的场合,一般形成 give *someone* a lot of [a bunch of, some, that, etc.] baloney 的形式。*When I asked him why he hadn't finished the work, he gave me a bunch of baloney about having been sick.* 当我问他为什么没把活儿干完的时候,他瞎话连篇,说是他病了。*You're too busy to help? Don't give me that baloney. I saw you playing tennis yesterday afternoon.* 你说你太忙,不能搭把手?不要对我说这种瞎话吧!我看见你昨天下午还打网球呢。也可以象下面这样,作为独立的感叹词使用。*Baloney! I don't believe it.* 胡说八道!我不信有那样的事。另有 malarkey [mə'lɑ(ː)rki] (又缀为 marlarky) 一词,意义和用法与 baloney 完全相同,以上例句皆可代入。◇ nonsense

bananas

go bananas (over *something* [*someone*]) [ˌgou bə'næ(ː)nəz] [话] **如疯似狂** → go APE (over *something* [*someone*])

band

to beat the band [tə ˌbi(ː)tðə 'bæːnd] [话] **势头猛烈** 这一 beat 的意义,有如 *I can beat you to the station.* 我会比你先走到车站。这句话中的 beat,是"先到达"。band 是"乐队"之意。本条意为"(孩子们猛烈地)跑到军乐队的前边"。下面一句是按字面的用法:*When the children heard the parade coming, they ran to beat the band to the corner.* 当孩子们听到游行队伍前来的声音时;他们向前跑去,要比乐队先到达马路口。从"象孩子们拼命奔跑似地"这一意味一转,就成为广义的、表示"势头"凶猛的习用语了,如:*The two men were arguing to beat the band.* 那两个人吵得很凶。*Suddenly it began raining to beat the band.* 突然下起了倾盆大雨。*When the music began, everyone started dancing to beat the band.* 音乐一开始,大家都精力十足地跳起舞来了。*Ever since the 1950's, Japanese industry has been growing to beat the band.* 20 世纪 50 年代以来,日本工业突飞猛进地发展起来。◇ very vigorously [hard, rapidly, etc.]

bandit

a one-armed bandit [ə ˌwʌ.nɑrmd ˈbæ(ː)ndɪt] [话] **吃角子老虎** 正式名称为 a slot machine [ˈslɑ(ː)t məˌʃiːn] (发音请注意)。slot 为 coin slot (硬币投入口),与投入的 coin 数相比,命中率很低,因此戏称之为"独臂强盗"(a one-armed bandit)。*Even the airport terminal in Las Vegas is full of one-armed bandits*。甚至在拉斯维加斯的航空终点站,都有大批的吃角子老虎。另外,在有些辞典里把这种赌具译成"自动售货机"(a vending machine),但在使用中绝无此义。◇ a slot machine

bandwagon

climb on the bandwagon [ˌklaɪmɔ(ː)nðə ˈbæːnd.wæːgən] [口] **赶浪头** 按字面意义,bandwagon 是"乐队所乘的马车",climb on 是"爬上去"。过去在选举中,竞选者乘 bandwagon 到处游说。每当游说的时候,人们登上自己中意的竞选者的马车,向大家表明"我也拥护这个人呀!"在群众当中,也有不少登上马车的"支持者"是谋求在该竞选者当选以后得到有形或无形的利益。因此也常发生这样的现象:被认为稳操胜券的竞选者的马车,会有大批的人争先恐后一拥而上。这一习用语现在也常应用于选举,有时表示"抛开劣势的阵营而转入优势的阵营",也有时表示"过去一直不表态,而在看准谁占优势之后倒向那一边"的意思。*When it became apparent that Reagan was going to win the election, everybody began climbing on the bandwagon*. 当里根已经显然赢得选举胜利的时候,大家都开始倒向他的一边了。后来,在非选举的场合也常使用起来了。*No one seemed prepared to accept my idea at first, but when I gained the support of several famous people, suddenly everyone wanted to climb on the bandwagon*. 最初似乎没有一个人肯接受我的方案,可是,在我得到几位著名人物的支持时,大家都愿意倒向我这一边了。也可以用 get, jump, hop, be 等动词代替 climb。get 与 climb 大致相同,jump, hop 的场合则具有"猛力跳上车去"的感觉。be on the bandwagon 是"正在倒向某人一边",表示状态。*Don't worry about people supporting our movement. Once we get started, a lot of people will be happy to hop on the bandwagon*. 不必担心人们是否支持我们的运动。一旦走上轨道,有大量的人会高高兴兴前来参加的。如果用 off 代替 on 而说 climb [get, jump, hop] off the bandwagon,那就成为"脱离某人一边"、"离开……阵营"了。*Late in the election campaign, when Kennedy's popularity began to sag, there was a great scramble to hop off the bandwagon*. 选举运动的最后阶段,当肯尼迪的声望开始下降的时候,有大批的人争先恐后地离开他的阵营。bandwagon 的前面也可以加形容词。*When Japanese cars began selling well in the U.S., American automobile manufacturers were anxious to get on the small-car bandwagon*. 当日本汽车开始在美国畅销的时候,美国的汽车厂家争先恐后地改制小型车辆。the bandwagon 偶尔采用 *someone's* bandwagon 的形式。*Unless we get more support, people will hesitate to climb on our bandwagon*. 我们如果得不到更多的支持,群众会裹足不前,不来投奔我们的阵营。◇ give *one's* support to *someone* / side with *someone*

bane

the bane of *one's* **existence** [ðə ˈbeɪnəv ~ ɪgˌzɪstənts] [口] **讨债鬼** bane 源出古盎格鲁撒克逊语 *bana*(杀人者),意为"破灭的根源"。本条的字面意义是"毁灭某人生存的罪魁祸首"。在硬性文章中,也有象 *Gambling was the bane of his existence*. 赌博是毁灭他的根源。这样一板一眼的用法,但在日常会话中,一般用于表示说某人是"讨债鬼"这样轻快的调子。在这一场合,多以"人"为主语,但也有例外。*That guy's always showing up at awkward times. He's the bane of my existence*. 那家伙总是在艰难的时刻出现。他真是要我命的讨债鬼。bane 的前面加 great,语气更强。*His wife's* *spendthrift ways were the great bane of his existence.* 他的老婆挥霍无度，是要他命的大讨债鬼。◇ (what) makes my [his] life difficult

bang

bang *something* **up** [ˌbæ(:)ŋ ～ ˈʌp] [话] **(由于碰撞而)伤痕累累** 这里的 bang 是"砰地一下撞上"，bang ～ up 与表明"撞坏"的 smash ～ up 或 bust ～ up 不同，指从外观上看坑洼不平、伤痕累累，但一般还能使用的状态。*The movers banged up our new table.* 搬家工人把我们的新桌子撞得满处是伤。*Jack banged his car up in an automobile accident.* 杰克在一次汽车事故中把他的车撞得伤痕累累。常插入 all 加强语气。*Jill fell down on the ice and banged her face all up.* 吉尔在冰上摔倒了，弄得她满脸是伤。get banged up 是"被造成许多伤"的意思。*This table got banged up when we were moving.* 在我们搬家的时候，这个桌子被撞得到处是伤了。*My suitcase got pretty banged up on our trip.* 在我们这次旅行中，我的手提箱被弄得伤痕累累。◇ damage *something* (here and there)

get a bang out of *something* [*someone*] [ˌgedə ˈbæ(:)ŋ audəv～] [话] **开心** bang 本来是相当于"砰"、"乓"之类的拟音词，后来发展为种种不同的意义。在本条中意为"(使人快活的)刺激"，是在接触有趣的或出奇的事物而内心浮动时使用的表达法。语气要轻松自如。*I get a bang out of meeting new people.* 我会见一些新朋友，心里十分高兴。在加强语气时插入 big。*Everybody gets a big bang out of Charlie. He's full of funny stories.* 只要有查理，大家就快活得了不得。他有一肚子有趣的故事。*I got a bang out of that funny hat Jill was wearing at the party last night.* 吉尔在昨天的社交晚会上戴的那顶滑稽的帽子，使我特别开心。◇ enjoy *something* ((big → very much))

banged

get banged up [get ˌbæ(:)ŋ ˈdʌp] [话] **撞得到处是伤** → BANG *something* up

bang-up

bang-up [ˈbæ(:)ŋˈʌp] [话] **顶呱呱** → do a bang-up JOB

bank

bank on *someone* [*something*] [ˈbæ(:)ŋ kɔ(:)n ～] [话] **(多少怀有不安的心情)指望** bank on 一般译为"指望"，被认为与 count on 完全同义，但两者之间具有细微的差别，使用方法自然也就有所不同了。请比较以下两个例句：① *Please come quickly. I'm counting on your helping me.* 请你快来哟！我正指望你帮助我哪！② *Please come quickly. I'm banking on your helping me.* 请你快来哟！我正期望你帮助我哪！①的 count on 是含有把对方"估计在内"的意味的"指望"，这是极普通的表达法。与此相比，②的 bank on 在使用时听起来就不自然，原因是：这一场合的 bank 原为名词，意思是"(在赌博中)存放在庄家那里的本钱"。从 make bank on *something* (为赌……而凑钱)这一表达法中，可以见到蛛丝马迹。动词词组 bank on 是由名词 bank 的这一用法发展而来，虽然同是"指望"，但与 count on 不一样，是"(认为对能够指望的事情可以下赌注的那样的)指望"，令人觉得说话人的内心里多少有一些象在赌博时的不安和紧张的感觉。因此，如上边的例句所示，在由对方的自由意志决定的事情上，势必要避免直接向对方使用这一表达法。在其他的场合，如 *I'm banking [counting] on his helping me.* 我在指望得到他的帮助。可以认为两者的用法大致相同，但在 bank on 方面，依然是在"指望"的心情中具有若干不安的成份。*I'm banking on John's arriving before ten o'clock.* 但愿约翰十点钟以前能够到达。这句话也是表示"我想约翰十点以前会到达的(但多少有些不安)"。与此相对，如果使用 count on，那就具有"十点以前肯定到达，大致不会有错"的意味了。*A: Why are you including Mr. Waver among your list of supporters at the meeting? He has said he wouldn't attend. B: I know, but I'm bank-*

ing on his changing his mind. 甲：你为什么把韦佛先生也计算在在会议中支持你的人之内呢？他说他不打算参加会议。乙：那我晓得。但是，我在期望他改变主意哪！这里的“在期望他改变主意”中也是多少带有不安的成份。*Abe is an honest man. Whatever he says, you can bank on its being true.* 阿贝是一个诚实的人。凡是他所说的话，你全可以相信，没错。在这一例句中，象 can bank on (下赌注也可以)这样使用 can，是在强调“信得过”的意思，因此可以认为 bank on 与 count on 大致相同。*A: Do you think the bank will lend us some more money? B: I wouldn't bank on it.* 甲：你认为银行会借给我们比这更多的钱吗？乙：我看指望不得。这与 count on 完全一样。象这样构成否定形式的时候，两者之间的差异全都消失。◇ depend on *someone* [*something*]

barf

barf ['bɑːrf] [俗] **吐出(吃了的东西)** 拟音词，主要为学生用语。*He barfed on the front lawn.* 他在庭前的草地上吐了。飞机坐席后背的口袋中常备一种卫生袋，叫做 an airsickness bag，人们也戏称为 a barf bag ['bɑ(ː)rf ˌbæːg]。*Quick! Where's a barf bag! Jimmy's sick.* 快！卫生袋在哪里！吉米病啦。→ lose *one's* DINNER ◇ vomit

bar-hopping

go bar-hopping [ˌgou 'bɑːrˌhɑ(ː)pɪŋ] [话] **出入酒肆** hop 是“蹦跳”。本条给人的印象是：好象蝗虫一样，从一个 bar 向另一个 bar 蹦跳而去。喜欢串酒馆的酒徒的姿影通过这一表达法历历如在眼前。虽然有 barhop 这一动词，但极少使用。*The young bachelors in my office seem to go bar-hopping almost every night.* 我们单位的年轻的单身汉，似乎每天夜里都去串酒馆。*I used to go bar-hopping a lot when I was younger, but now I'd rather go home early and curl up with a good book.* 我在年轻的时候常常出入酒肆，但是现在我宁愿早早回家，以读好书为乐。也有时用 go 以外的动词。*My husband isn't home tonight. He's probably out bar-hopping with some of his friends.* 我丈夫今天晚上不在家。多半是跟几个朋友一起去串酒吧了。也有象下列例句一样不伴有动词而单独使用的时候。*Bar-hopping seems to be Reginald's favorite sport.* 串酒馆仿佛是雷金纳德所喜好的运动。顺便提一下：在英国英语中 bar-hopping 作 pub-crawl(ing)。那里不是蹦着去，而是爬行 (crawl) 着去。◇ go drinking from bar to bar

bark

Someone's **bark is worse than** *his* **bite.**

[～ 'bɑrkɪz ˌwə(ː)rsðən ～ 'baɪt] [口] **嘴上凶，不可怕** 直译为“(狗)吠比咬还厉害”，也就是“吠的声音很凶，(即便咬上也)没什么了不起”。人们也往往按照字面的意义来使用。但是，正如在 *Don't mind Fido. His bark is worse than his bite.* 不必对费多提心吊胆。它常吠，但不咬人。这一例句中那样，一般是用以表示为了使对方安心而讲“(自己的狗)完全不咬人”的意味。如果用在人的身上，就意味着“嘴上虽然很严厉，却并不那么可怕”或者“虽然嘴上唠唠叨叨，实际上并不那么厉害”。当同事由于被老板之流严厉叱责而垂头丧气的时候，常使用这一习用语进行安慰。*Don't worry about what the boss said. His bark is worse than his bite.* 老板说的那些话你不要往心里去。他嘴上很凶，但不是那么可怕的人。*Most new students are afraid of Professor Jones at first, but they soon learn that his bark is worse than his bite.* 新学生最初都害怕琼斯教授，但是他们不久就明白了，他说话虽然很严厉，人并不那么可怕。◇ *Someone* is not as frightening [ill-tempered, strict, etc.] as *he* sounds [as one might judge from *his* speech].

barn

go around Robin Hood's barn [ˌgouəˌraund 'rɑbən ˌhudz 'bɑ(ː)rn] [话] **意想不到地绕远** 字面意义是“绕着罗宾汉的堆房走”。barn 是“存放农

耕用家畜、干草、谷物、农具之类的大棚子”，比东方的“堆房”概念大得多。关于这一习用语的来源，有如下的说法：罗宾汉在 Sherwood Forest (谢尔伍德森林)境内到处奔跑，没有固定的住所、田地等。因此，也不会有什么“堆房”。由于“绕着 Robin Hood's barn 走”是根本不会有的事情，也就用这句话来表达“意想不到地绕远”了。此说真伪程度如何且莫管它，至少可以帮助大家记忆这一习用语吧。*Sorry we're late. The rain had washed a bridge away, so we had to go around Robin Hood's barn to get here.* 我们来迟了，真对不起。大雨把桥给冲走了，因此兜了一个大圈子才走到这儿。*It's frustrating to listen to the chief's explanations. He always goes around Robin Hood's barn to get to the point.* 听头头的说明真叫人起急。他在点题之前总是兜个大圈子。常用 all the way (远远地)加强语气。*Frank has a terrible sense of direction. Whenever he drives, we end up going all the way around Robin Hood's barn to get anywhere.* 弗兰克不会辨别方向到了惊人的程度。每逢他驾驶车的时候，不管到什么地方去，都会叫我们兜个远远的大圈子。另外，有时不用 go 而说 take *someone* (带着去)；前置词也不用 around，而以 by way of (经由)代替。*You have to be careful of the taxi drivers in this city. If you don't give them precise directions, they'll take you by way of Robin Hood's barn to reach your destination.* 在这个城市里，你必须留心出租汽车的司机们。你如果不把要去的地址对他们说得一清二楚，他们会打马虎眼，领你兜很大的圈子才把你送到地方。另外，一些词典(包括大词典在内)几乎全未收录这一固定词组，但是，这是无论如何要记住的表达法之一。◇ go a great way out of *one's* way / make a great detour

barrel

barrel [ˈbæ(ː)rəl] [话] **(车子等)飞驰** 一说到 barrel，首先浮现在头脑里的是“木桶”，但是另外作为名词，此语还有“气缸”(cylinder) 之类的意义。这个具有“气缸”意义的 barrel 动词化后，就产生本条的中文释义了。也就是从“充分利用气缸”转到“(车子等)飞驰”，当然，在“(人)快跑”的场合是不大使用的。语法上的特征是：不单独使用，经常要伴有 along, down, over, up, through 之类的副词或前置词。又如 *They were barreling along at a hundred kilometers per hour.* 他们的车以每小时一百公里的速度在飞驰。这一例句所示，常使用进行时；另外与 come 或 go 结合，使用 come barreling, go barreling 形式的场合也很多。*A big foreign car came barreling up the street.* 一辆大型外国汽车飞驰到街上来了。除车子外，有时在讲到船、飞机等的时候也使用。*A Coast Guard patrol boat went barreling out of the harbor.* 海岸警戒部队的一只巡逻艇飞速开出了港口。*A light plane came barreling down from the skies.* 一架小型飞机从空中以高速俯冲下来。◇ move [travel] (at high speed)

have a of fun → FUN

have *someone* **over a barrel** [ˌhæv ~ ˌouvərə ˈbæ(ː)rəl] [话] **使其处于一筹莫展的状态** → be over a BARREL

lock, stock and barrel → LOCK

more fun than a barrel of monkeys → FUN

be over a barrel [ˌouvərə ˈbæ(ː)rəl] [话] **一筹莫展** 在英美来说，桶(barrel) 是能装约 120 公升的大容器。“(身休)被按在(横放着的)大桶上”即是“身子不能动转”的意思。这一表达法专作比喻使用，指被逼入绝境，一筹莫展。有时是被他人(或自己的行为)逼到这样的地步，也有时是大势所趋，只好如此。*If we don't get a bank loan by next week, we'll be over a barrel.* 我们到下个星期如果得不到银行的贷款，我们就要一筹莫展了。常用 really 一词加强语气。*A taxi driver who loses his license for drunken driving is really over a barrel.* 一个由于酒后开车而失去驾驶证的出租汽车司机，简直如虎落平阳一样。另外还常有一种说法，即用 have 代替动词 be，形成 have *someone* over a barrel (使某人处于一筹莫展的状态)。在这一场合,"穷追猛赶"的主语一般是人,而且在使用时多半令人产生"他掌握生杀予夺的大权"的感觉。*He has us over a barrel. If we do the work the way he says to, we'll go in the red. If we don't, he can sue us for breach of contract.* 他逼得我们走投无路。如果我们依照他所说的办法去干,我们就会赔本。如果我们不听他的,他有可能控告我们不履行合同。*Don't worry. He'll come across with the money. We've got him over a barrel.* 你甭担心。他会来付款的。我们已经把他逼上梁山,叫他没有别的路可走。◇ be in a helpless position

scrape the bottom of the barrel [ˌskreɪpðə ˈbɑ(ː)dəməðə ˈbæ(ː)rəl] [口] **搜集残羹剩饭** 字面意义是"(为了得到最后残余的东西而)刮桶底"。这一意义虽然不是绝对不使用,但本条是专用于比喻的表达法。使用较多的情况是形容"优秀的人已经用尽"或"好的东西已经被拿光",因而"不得不如此如此"。*Near the end of the war, all the best men had been recruited. The army had to scrape the bottom of the barrel, taking teenagers and old men in order to get enough soldiers.* 在战争快要结束的时候,所有的壮丁都已经应征入伍了。军队为了补充兵额,不得不把十几岁的孩子和老头都搜罗一空。*The biggest publishers acquire most of the best foreign books. The others are often forced to scrape the bottom of the barrel.* 大多数的外国好书都叫各大出版社弄去了。其他出版社往往只能去捞一点残羹剩饭。*That guy is a terrible salesman. They must have been scraping the bottom of the barrel when they hired him.* 那个家伙是一个最糟糕的推销员。在他们雇用他的时候,他肯定是被打扫的剩货。另外,有时去掉 the bottom of,而说 scrape the barrel,意义相同,可以自由替换,但语气略微缓和一些。◇ take what is left (after the best has already been taken)

base

not get to first base (with *something* [*someone*]) [nɑt ˌgetːə ˌfəːrstˈbeɪs] [话] **毫无成效** 从 first base 可以了解,这本来是棒球用语。按字面意义可以这样使用:*Dave has been at bat three times tonight, but he still hasn't gotten to first base.* 戴夫今天晚上已经击球三次了,但是他还没能到一垒。作为比喻,在"劝说"、"执行计划"、"男女关系"等问题上,用于虽然努力但进行得不顺利的场合。在词典上大多以 get to first base 的形式出现,但请注意:在实际使用时,通常用以构成否定句。*I'm trying to persuade the dean to hire another English teacher, but so far I haven't gotten to first base.* 我试图说服院长再聘请一位英语老师,可是至今还不见一点成效。*If you want to make a lot of money, you'd better try something else. You'll never even get to first base with that plan.* 如果你想发大财,最好去干点别的事情。按照那个计划,你永远会两手空空,毫无所得。*I've asked Betty for a date any number of times and even sent her flowers, but still I can't get to first base with her.* 我曾多次向贝蒂提出约会,甚至送给她鲜花,可是至今仍然是镜花水月,好梦难成。有时也说 not reach first base。◇ have no success

basket

put all *one's* **eggs in one basket** → EGGS

bass

a bass fiddle [ə ˈbeɪs ˈfɪdl] [口] **低音提琴** → a bull FIDDLE

bat

be (as) blind as a bat [əz ˈblaɪndəzə ˈbæ(ː)t] [话] **跟瞎子一样** 字面意义是"象蝙蝠一样瞎"。可以用以强调眼睛看不见这一点,如说 *I had been talking to the old man for nearly ten minutes, when suddenly I realized he was as blind as a bat.* 我跟老人谈话将近十分钟,才突然注意到他的眼睛完全看不见。但是在普通的文句中,这一习用语并不意味着 completely blind (完全看不见),而是增强 not able to see well(不能很好地看见)

的意义。*Without my glasses I'm blind as a bat.* 我一不戴眼镜，就跟睁眼瞎一样。*There is a huge road sign on the corner. Any one who missed it would have to be as blind as a bat.* 那拐角处有一个巨大的道路标志。谁要是没有看到它，那简直等于睁眼瞎子。又，在实际上，blind 一词不只具有"眼睛看不见"或"眼睛不能很好地看见"的意义，另外还有"不明白"、"意识不到"等比喻的意义，在后一场合，也用本条的表达法加强语气。*If you don't see what she means, you're as blind as a bat.* 如果你不明白她的话的意思，你简直是个大糊涂虫。根据上下文，bat 也有时用复数。*When it comes to their own faults, most people are as blind as bats.* 一涉及到自己的缺点，大多数人跟瞎子一样。◇ have very poor eyesight / be completely blind

go to bat for *someone*[ˌgoudə ˈbæ(ː)tfər～] [话] **(为某人)积极辩护、(对某人)积极支援** 这里的 bat 是"(用球拍子)打"。本条整体意义为"代替(某人)去打球"。单是 bat for ～意为"(为某人)代打"，而加上 go to，则有"积极地去干"的感觉。转用于"自愿去帮助有困难者"的场合。*During the time I was sick, my neighbors went to bat for me by preparing meals and taking care of my children.* 在我有病期间，我的邻居们又给我做饭，又替我照看孩子，积极地来帮助我。象这一例句所示，可以用于不是以口头、而是以具体行动照顾他人的场合，不过，这一用法是比较罕见的。一般来说，如以下的例句所示，是在用言语帮助人的场合使用。*Phil went to bat for me when I was accused of overstepping my authority.* 当我被谴责有越权行为的时候，菲尔曾积极地替我辩护。例如，*When I needed a raise, he went to bat for me.* 也是"当我有必要提高工资时，他到头头那儿给我美言了几句。"的意思，不能望文生义，解释为"给予物质援助"，如"借给钱"之类。此句的前半部也可以换个说法，作 When I wanted a raise, ～，但是在英文来说，还是用 needed 自然，因为令人直接产生"正在为难"的感觉。*I've got to help Charlie. He went to bat for me when I needed it.* 我不能不去帮助查理。当我困难的时候，他为我卖过很大力气。*When a big-time gangster gets into trouble with the law, he always has a whole slew of lawyers to go to bat for him.* 当一个巨匪目无法纪、为非作歹的时候，总有一大批律师出来为他效劳。*When the coach began talking of dropping Jim from the team, all his teammates went to bat for him.* 当教练员开始谈到要叫吉姆退队的时候，所有的队友都为他说情。◇ lend *someone* (*one's*) support / defend [help] *someone*

bath

(a) full bath [(ə) ˈful ˌbæːθ] [口] **带澡盆的卫生间** → the BATHROOM

(a) half bath [(ə) ˈhæ(ː)f ˌbæːθ] [口] **(没有澡盆的)卫生间** → the BATHROOM

throw out the baby with the bath → BABY

bathroom

the bathroom [ðə ˈbæːθ.ruːm] [话] **卫生间**

字面意义是"浴室"，但在英语中几乎完全不用这一意义。"浴室在那里？"和"我想要洗个澡。"分别是 Where's the bath? 和 I'd like to take a bath. 决不说 bathroom。在美国的住宅中，浴室包括洗澡盆、淋浴器、洗脸台、便桶，一应俱全，因此，the bathroom 只用以委婉地指"卫生间"。例如，在乘车的时候想要撒尿，也是同样说 *I'd like to go to the bathroom.* 就行了。在人家的家里要去厕所时，说 *May I use the bathroom?* 比较委婉的说法是 *May I wash my hands?* 或者是 *I'd like to wash my hands.* 等等。回答如：*The bathroom is just down the hall to your left.* 卫生间在门厅的左侧。不是私人住宅的卫生间叫做 restroom。*Where is the restroom?* 卫生间在哪儿？顺便提一下：在美国的房地产广告中，(a) full bath 意味着"澡盆、淋浴、洗脸台、便器"一应俱全；(a) half bath 则指只有"便器、洗脸台"。◇ the toilet

bats

have bats in *one's* **belfry** [hæv ˈbæ(ː)tsən

～ 'belfri] [话] **头脑有些奇怪** bat 本来是"蝙蝠", belfry 是"(教会的)钟楼", 但在这里是作为比喻使用, 前者比做"思考", 后者比做"头脑"。本条是一个比喻表达法, 也就是把"钟声一响, 受惊的蝙蝠在钟楼内来回乱飞乱撞"的样子比做"思想在头脑中乱跑乱转"。*If you think I'm going to spend the night in that haunted house, you've got bats in your belfry.* 如果你以为我打算在那个闹鬼的房子里过夜, 你的头脑可就有点奇怪啦。*That whole family is a little strange, if you ask me. The daughter appears to be the only one who doesn't have bats in her belfry.* 如果你叫我说的话, 那一家人全都有点反常。似乎只有小姐一个人的头脑没有什么变态。另外, 这一习用语也用于表示真正"头脑有病", 意思是"精神不正常"、"得了精神病", 但在这一场合, *one's* belfry 的 *one's* 常改用 the。*Her father had bats in the belfry and had to be put away.* 她的父亲精神失常, 已经被隔离了。◇ be strange in the head / be crazy

battle

fight the battle of the bulge [ˌfaɪtðə 'bæ(ː)dl əvðə 'bʌ(ː)ldʒ] [话] **努力减轻体重** bulge 一般是"膨胀"的意思。作为军事用语, 意为"战线的突出部分"。第二次世界大战期间, 德军在欧洲进行总反攻作战的时候(1944 年 12 月 16 日～1945 年 1 月 16 日), 在德军的进攻之下, 比利时南部阿登地区(Ardennes) 的战线的盟国占领地区失陷一大块, 德军深入在比利时北部与东部的盟军阵地。因此, 人们称这次大反攻为 the Battle of the Bulge (突出之战)。*The Nazis' last great counter-attack of World War II is called the Battle of the Bulge because it caused a great bulge in the battle line of the Allied armies.* 第二次世界大战期间纳粹最后一次大反攻被称为"突出之战", 因为它使德军战线突出很大一块。本条习用语就是由此而来, 把"减轻体重"戏称为"减少腰围膨胀之战", 亦即"突出之战"。这种说法令人产生诙谐的感觉, 多用 be fighting the battle of the bulge 这样的进行式。*My husband is always fighting the battle of the bulge.* 我的丈夫永远在努力减轻体重。*No dessert for me, thanks. I'm fighting the battle of the bulge.* 谢谢, 请不要给我上甜食了。我正在努力减轻体重。如果采取 fighting the ～这样的动名词形式, 有时可省略 fighting。*I was always slim when I was young. Little did I think I would ever have to worry about (fighting) the battle of the bulge.* 我年轻的时候, 身体一直是很苗条的。从来没有为努力减轻体重而费过心思啊! 有时不但没有能够减轻体重, 反而胖了起来, 这种情况叫 lose the battle of the bulge。这也是诙谐的说法。*I'm afraid I'm losing the battle of the bulge.* 恐怕我努力减肥的战斗要失败了。◇ struggle with a weight problem

be half the battle [ˌhæ(ː)fðə 'bæːdl] [口] **等于胜了一半** 这一表达法来自谚语 The first blow is half the battle. (先来一拳, 胜了一半。) 本条字面意义是"为战斗的(要素的)一半"。*Our opponents for this game may be strong, but we have a chance if we show that we're not afraid of them. That'll be half the battle.* 在这次比赛中, 我们的对手肯定很强, 但是, 如果我们显示出我们并不害怕他们, 那我们还是有取胜机会的。这样就等于胜了一半。如此例句所示, 对于实际的比赛或战斗, 中文可用"胜了"二字, 在其他场合, 则有必要选择与"胜了"相当的字眼儿。例如, *Don't worry about your entrance exams. You are good in English and that's half the battle.* 就可译为你不必担心入学考试。你的英语很棒, 那就等于有一半录取的把握。*I'm sure Derek will succeed in this work. He has enthusiasm and that's half the battle.* 我相信德里克在这个工作中会成功的。他有热情, 这就等于完成了工作的一半。*In boxing, a fighting spirit is half the battle.* 在拳击比赛中, 斗志旺盛是取胜的重要因素。◇ be the most important thing

battlewagon

a battlewagon [ə ˈbæ(ː)dl.wæ(ː)gən] [话] **战舰** 原为海军用语,但一般人现在也普遍使用。*There were three battlewagons moored in the harbor.* 港口曾有三艘战舰停泊。 ◇ a battleship

bawl

bawl *someone* **out** [.bɔːl ~ ˈaut] [话] **(大叫大嚷地) 斥责** → CHEW *someone* out / SCOLD *someone* (for *something*)

bay

a bay window → WINDOW

bring *something* [*someone*] **to bay** [.brɪŋ ~ təˈbeɪ] [口] **穷追不舍** bay 是"狗用拖长的、低低的声音叫",在这里是"(狩猎中,狗把猎物追得无处可逃时的)吠声"。整个习用语意为"穷追不舍,把(某物或某人)逼到被群狗围上乱叫的状态"。一般含有在穷追不舍之后"团团围住使其不能动转"的意味。可以照字面意义使用,如 *The dogs brought the wounded stag to bay.* 群狗穷追受伤的雄鹿,使其无处可逃。但是在狩猎之外,也象以下的例句那样广泛应用。*After a long chase, the zoo keepers brought the escaped lion to bay in a cul-de-sac.* 经过长时间的追赶以后,动物园的饲养员们终于把逃走的狮子追进了一个死胡同。当然,也可以在谈到"人"的时候使用。*The police finally brought the kidnappers to bay.* 警察终于捕获了那些绑架匪徒。*I realized that if I continued running toward the cliff, my pursuers would soon bring me to bay.* 我心里已经明白,如果我继续向着悬崖跑去,追赶我的人马上就会使我上天无路,入地无门。→ have *something* [*someone*] at BAY / hold *something* [*someone*] at BAY / keep *something* [*someone*] at BAY ◇ (run down and) corner *something* [*someone*] / drive *something* [*someone*] into an-inescap able position

have *something* [*someone*] **at bay** [.hæv ~ətˈbeɪ] [口] **(追上以后)使其不能动转** bay 是"(猎犬把猎物追得无处可逃时的)吠声"。这一表达法是 bring *something* [*someone*] to BAY(→) 亦即"穷追不舍"的下一阶段,表示"使其处于走投无路"的"状态"。*The dogs, having caught up with the stag, now have it at bay.* 群狗追上了雄鹿以后,使其连一动也动不了。这是从追赶者的立场说话,一般使用主动语态。*I had run till I could run no farther. My pursuers now had me at bay with my back to the sea.* 我一直在跑,现在无路可逃了。追赶我的人把我逼到海边,使我不能动转了。*I'm afraid our creditors have us at bay. We have no choice but to declare bankruptcy.* 我看债主已经把我们逼得走投无路了。我们除了宣告破产没有另外的办法。→ keep *something* [*someone*] at BAY ◇ have *something* [*someone*] cornered / have *something* [*someone*] in an inescapable position

hold *something* [*someone*] **at bay** [.hould ~ ətˈbeɪ] [口] ① **(追获后)使其不能动转** ② **(被追获者使对方)不得近身** 这里的 bay 与 bring *something* [*someone*] to BAY(→) 相同,是"(狩猎中,狗把猎物追得无处可逃时的)吠声"。整个表达法在使用时分为两种意义:①是从追者的立场来讲,指"使(某物或某人)处于群狗(围上)狂吠的状态"。这一表达法与 have *something* [*someone*] at BAY 相似,但是 have 仅仅表示"使其如此"的状态,而 hold 则充满"积极的姿态",因而本条的说法意为"令其如此",强制性溢于言表。②则是站在相反的立场,从被追赶者方面来讲,指"不让(追来者)接近己身",结果与 keep *something* [*someone*] at BAY(→) 意义相同。下面两个例句属于①的场合。*The dogs surrounded the stag and held it at bay until the hunters arrived.* 那几条狗把雄鹿团团围住,不许它动地方,一直等到猎人们来临。这是本来的使用方法,当然,也可以用于狩猎以外的事情。*Two of the policemen held the escaped convict at bay while another circled around behind him.* 当一名警察从逃犯身后包抄的时候,另两名警察已把那个犯人捉获,使其不能动转。下面两个例句属于②的场合。*The stag used its antlers to hold the dogs at bay while the does escaped.* 在几只雌鹿逃走的时候，一只雄鹿用它的角为武器，使那些狗不能近身。*I'll hold the gunmen at bay while you run and notify the police.* 我不叫那几个持枪匪徒靠近，你快跑去报告警察。◇ ① keep *something* [*someone*] cornered / keep *something* [*someone*] in an inescapable position ② → keep *something* [*someone*] at BAY

keep *something* [*someone*] **at bay** [ˌki(ː)p ~ ətˈbeɪ] [口] **(被追赶者)不让对方靠近** bay 与 bring *something* [*someone*] to BAY (→) 相同，为"(狗把猎物追得无处可逃时的)吠声"。如果说："保持狗仅仅狂吠的状态"，那意思就是"狗来到身边狂吠，但阻止它进一步扑上身来"。*The cornered stag used its antlers to keep the dogs at bay.* 那只被逼入困境的雄鹿用它的角阻止群狗扑上身来。可转用于比喻。*The Allies' strategy in World War II was to attack Germany while keeping Japan at bay.* 盟军在第二次世界大战中的战略，是在不让日本插足的期间袭击德国。*We are having difficulty keeping our creditors at bay.* 我们正在费尽心机防止债主逼债。*This medicine will not cure the disease, but it will keep it at bay.* 这种药治不好那种病，但是可以防止它进一步恶化。→ have *something* [*someone*] at BAY ◇ prevent *something* [*someone*] from encroaching (farther) / keep *something* [*someone*] at a distance / prevent *a disease* from spreading

BB

a BB gun → GUN

bead

take a bead on *something* [ˌteɪkə ˈbiːˌdɔ(ː)n ~] [话] **瞄准** → set *one's* SIGHTS on (doing) *something*

beam

be broad in the beam [ˈbrɔːdənðə ˈbiːm] [话] **屁股大** beam 原指"船体最宽的部分"。*She's a good ship, but too broad in the beam to make much speed.* 这句话是按照原来的用法表示 那是一只好船，不过船体太宽，给不出速度。的意思。由于"船"的代词是 she，水手们就用 beam 表示"女子屁股"的意义。这就是转义的来源。现在依然如此，首先联想到的是"女性"，但如最后的例句所示，在谈到男性时也可以使用。这是个诙谐的说法，但没有下流的感觉，勿宁是一种委婉的表达法。*She's a nice girl, but too broad in the beam for my taste.* 她是一位很漂亮的姑娘，但是根据我的审美观点，臀部过大了。*Mabel is built like a pyramid—narrow in the shoulders and broad in the beam.* 梅布尔的体形好象一座金字塔，两肩很窄，屁股很大。get [become] broad in the beam 是"屁股长肉"。*I'm going to have to go on a diet. I'm getting a bit broad in the beam.* 我非节制饮食不可啦。我的屁股上有点长肉了。*Men who do desk work all day tend to become broad in the beam.* 整天趴办公桌的人们，屁股容易长肉。◇ be wide in the hips [buttocks, bottom]

off the beam [ˌɔ(ː)fðə ˈbiːm] [口] **道路[方向、思想]弄错** beam 是飞机的"指示航路的电波"。因此，本条的字面意义是"偏离航路"。*For some reason, the plane appears to be several degrees off the beam.* 不知什么原因，这架飞机似乎脱离航向好几度。在反映脱离道德或伦理的"正道"的上下文中经常使用本条的表达法。*Man's conscience is designed to tell him when he is off the beam.* 一个人在走邪门歪道的时候，良心会向他指明所犯的错误。*Many juvenile delinquents are raised in good homes but somehow get off the beam during their teen years.* 许多少年犯都是由良好家庭养育大的，可是不知为什么，他们在十几岁的时候就误入歧途了。如下一例句那样，也有"思考的方向错了"的场合。*Our recent experiments in nuclear physics have not been very successful. Somewhere we seem to have strayed completely off the beam.* 我们最近的核物理学试验不太成

功。说不上什么地方，我们的思路似乎完全错了。除了 completely 外，也可以象下面的例句那样用 way 加强语气。*A: Did you get that math problem right? B: No. I was way off the beam.* 甲：那道数学题你已经做好了吗？乙：没有，我完全解答错了。反义语是 on the BEAM。◇ (go) astray / off (the proper) course / (completely) mistaken

on the beam [ˌɔ(ː)nðə ˈbiːm] [口] **(思想、计划、行动等)方向正确** 字面意义是"飞机按照指示航路的电波正确飞行"，所表示的意味与 off the BEAM 恰好相反。*Our instruments indicate that our plane is on the beam.* 我们的仪表指明，我们的飞机航向是完全正确的。也转用于比喻。*The police knew they were on the beam when they learned that the two suspects had once worked in the same place.* 当警察了解到两个嫌疑犯曾经在一个单位工作过，他们知道他们的搜查方向是正确的了。以下翻译所用的词句有变化，但基本上都是"方向正确"的意思。*A: How are your plans going for establishing the new department? B: Right on the beam.* 甲：你要设立一个新的部的计划怎么样啦？乙：正在稳妥地进行啊！也就是按照计划、"沿着正确的方向"在进行中。另外，正如这一例句所示，往往用 right 来加强语气。*Most rock groups lose popularity very quickly, but the Beatles stayed on the beam for many years.* 大部分摇滚乐团都很快就不受人欢迎了，但是甲壳虫乐队却多年以来一直博得人们的青睐。在这一场合，也是投大众的所好，"沿着正确的方向"继续前进的意思。*My son tends to be a bit wild at times, but fortunately the influence of his teachers has kept him on the beam.* 我的儿子动不动就想胡作非为，幸亏有老师的教导，使他一直品行端正，恪守校规。◇ on the (proper) course / moving in the right direction

bean

a bean pole [ə ˈbiːn ˌpoul] [口] **细高挑儿** → a string BEAM

a string bean [ə ˌstrɪŋ ˈbiːn] [话] **细高挑儿** 字面意义是"扁豆"。扁豆因背上有一条好似细绳(string)的筋，故名 string bean。在美国，煮 string beans 之前，先把豆角折成两段，去掉筋。在这种场合，以 string 为动词，而说 string the beans。*We're going to have string beans tonight. Would you string them for me, please?* 今天晚上我们吃豆角。你能不能给摘一下筋呀？string bean 的另一个意义是"身材高而很瘦的人"，也就是俗语的"细高挑儿"，这当然是由扁豆的细长姿态而来。*Lew may be a string bean, but he can really hit the ball.* 不错，卢是个细高挑儿，但他是个击球的能手啊。有时也说 a bean pole (豆角蔓的支柱)，意义相同。◇ (a) tall and skinny (person)

beans

be full of beans① [ˌfuləvˈbiːnz] [话] **精神饱满** 本来的意义是"(马吃了许多豆子)精神旺盛"。*Our children seldom get sick. They're always full of beans.* 我们家的孩子很少生病。他们总是活蹦乱跳的。*I've never known a boy to be so full of beans. He runs around laughing and playing all day long.* 我从来没见过一个如此精神饱满的男孩子。他整天不停地来回跑，一边笑，一边玩。正如这两个例子所示，本条的表达法多用于指孩子们或年轻人，但是，也不是不能指老年人。如下例：*Grandpa shouldn't be going mountain climbing with the kids. Sometimes I think he's too full of beans for his own good.* 爷爷不该跟小孩子们一起去爬山。有时候我想，他精神头儿太足了对自己的身体未必有利。◇ be full of energy / be energetic

be full of beans② [ˌfuləvˈbiːnz] [话] **(所说的话)非常无聊** 直译为"充满了豆子"。原来是一种委婉说法，为"爱放屁"的意思。在美国，人们认为 beans (豆)是"放屁的根源"，吃多了就爱放屁。然而现在，be full of beans 已经失去那种意义，而与 be full of hot air 同义，也就是在谈论夸大的话、脱离实际的话、吹牛的话等等时用以表示"(这话)无聊之极"的意味。*I don't believe it. You're full of beans.* 我不相信那种事。你的话太无聊啦！*When Galileo insisted that the earth revolved around the sun, everybody said that he was full of beans.* 当伽利略坚持地球绕太阳转的理论的时候，人人都说他是在胡言乱语，信口开河。*Talk about being full of beans! George just told me that he met an old man who claimed his son was the oldest man in the world.* 即使信口开河，也得有个边儿呀！乔治竟告诉我说，他碰到一位老头硬说他的儿子是世界上年纪最大的寿星。也有时相当于说某人"是个大傻瓜"。*If he said that, it only proves he's full of beans.* 如果他是那样说的，那只能证明他是个大傻瓜。*That guy's so full of beans, he doesn't know up from down.* 那个家伙完全是个大傻瓜，他连上与下都区别不开。另外，有时根据同样的思考方法使用 prunes (洋李脯)一词，讲 be full of prunes。◇ not know what *one* is talking about / be full of foolish talk / foolish

not amount to a hill of beans [nɑdəˌmauntuə ˌhɪləˈbiːnz] [话] **(都加在一起也)没什么了不起** 直译是"都加在一起，也没有豆子的山那么大"。a bean 是举个例子，用以代表"没有价值的东西"。原来的思路是："没有价值的东西不管拼凑多少，结果也不会具有价值"。*I'm not sure what Hal's income is, but I'm sure it doesn't amount to a hill of beans.* 我不知道哈尔的收入究竟有多少，但是我敢肯定不会是个了不起的数目。*If you measured the sincerity of all the politicians in the world, it wouldn't amount to a hill of beans.* 如果你测量一下全世界政治家的诚意，就算都加在一起，也实在少得可怜。另有一个说法是 be not worth a hill of beans。它与数量的多少无关，而是"没有任何价值"的意思。*Let him say whatever he likes. His opinion isn't worth a hill of beans as far as I'm concerned.* 他爱说什么就让他说好啦。他的意见对于我来说一点儿价值都没有。*As a mathematics text, that book isn't worth a hill of beans.* 作为数学教科书，那本著作一点儿价值都没有。◇ be not very much / not come to [total] very much

not know beans about *something* [nɑtˌnou ˈbiːnzəˌbaut ~] [话] **一窍不通** beans (豆)是无价值的东西、极微小的东西的象征。在这里是"一丁点儿"的意思。整个条头意为 not have any knowledge of *something* (对于某件事没有任何知识)，在使用时一般含有若干轻蔑的味道。*Don't listen to Ned. He doesn't know beans about fixing a car.* 你不要听内德的话。他对于修理汽车是一窍不通。*How can I sell life insurance? I don't know beans about the insurance business.* 我怎么能当人寿保险的推销员呢？我对于保险业务是一窍不通啊。偶尔有省略 about 以下部分的情况。*No use asking him about it. That guy doesn't know beans.* 关于那件事，问他没用处。那家伙什么也不知道。◇ not know anything about *something*

be not worth a hill of beans [nɑtˌwə(ː)rθə ˌhɪləˈbiːnz] [话] **毫无价值** → not amount to a hill of BEANS

spill the beans [ˌspɪlðə ˈbiːnz] [话] **泄露秘密** 字面意义是"不留神弄洒了豆子"。spill 一词原含有"不经心"的意味。*We'll have to eat corn tonight. Jean spilled the beans.* 我们今天晚上只好吃玉米了。琼把豆子全都洒了。然而，作为比喻这一习用语表示"泄露秘密"的意思时，不仅在"不经心(泄露秘密)"的场合使用，在"有意地"或者"不知其为秘密地"泄密的场合同样常常使用。例如，在 *I was hoping to surprise Martha with the good news when I met her tonight* (我原想在今天晚上会见马莎的时候告诉她那个好消息，以便使她大吃一惊)，*but unfortunately someone had already spilled the beans.* 这一例句中，but 以下①可以解释为"但是很遗憾，有个人(明明知道在我亲口对马莎讲之前要对她保密而)不经心地泄露给她了"；②可以认为是"(尽管知道我要对她保密的事情而)故意泄露给她了"，③也可以考虑为"(并不知情而)讲了出去"。总而言之，对于这个 spill the beans，三种解释全都成立。在这一场合，究竟应该是哪一种解释，没有前后关系是无法断定的。也就是说，是"不经心"呢？是"故意地"呢？还是"不知其为秘密地"呢？这可以由上下文确定。*I'm sorry I inadvertently spilled the beans about your plan.* 我无意中泄露了你们的计划，真对不起。在这一例句中，如果没有 inadvertently (无意中)，也同样弄不清究竟相当于上述三种解释中的哪一种。*Don't tell David about our plans. He's sure to spill the beans.* 别把咱们的计划告诉戴维。他肯定会泄密的。假定戴维不是一个太坏的人，也不是不可能产生"不经心"的感觉，但是，也可能是"故意地"。*If we don't do as he says, he may spill the beans to the cops.* 如果我们不照他所说的去做，他也许要向警察告密的。这是一个显然"故意地"的例子。*Pretend you don't know me. If you even speak to me, that would spill the beans to a sharp man like my father.* 你要假装不认识我。你只要跟我一说话，在我父亲那样眼光锐利的人面前，咱们的事就会完全暴露了。这是显然"不经心"的例子。大概是情侣之类不让父亲了解两人间的关系吧。另外，如这一例句所示，也可以不以"人"作主语，而以"动作"、"神态"等作主语。"(动作、神态等)泄漏秘密"也就是"(根据动作、神态等)人家了解了秘密"的意思。◇ tell *someone* / let slip the news (of *something*) / inform *someone*

bear

a bear [ə 'beːr] [话] **非常难的课程** 学生用语。bear 是"熊"，但是如果说 This course is a bear. 这句话给人的感觉是："这是一门非常难的课程，不以与熊摔跤的心情艰苦奋斗就不可能及格"。另外，也有时用 bear 指"难对付的先生"。*Professor Jones is a real bear.* 琼斯教授是一位极难对付的老师。反义语为 a snap COURSE。◇ (a) very difficult (course)

grin and bear it → GRIN

bearings

find *one's* **bearings** [ˌfaɪnd ~ 'be(ː)rɪŋz] [口] **知道自己的位置[方位、方向]** → get *one's* BEARINGS

get *one's* **bearings** [ˌget ~ 'be(ː)rɪŋz] [口] **知道自己的位置[方位、方向]** bearing 原为海上用语，指"(以星、月、日等为目标物，自己的相对)位置"。所以用 bearings 这一复数形式，是因为船的"位置"是由经度和纬度二者来表示的。*The navigator took the ship's bearings.* 领航员测定了船现在的位置。也可以转用于"(人的)位置[方位]"，多以 get *one's* bearings 的形式出现。*Having waked up in a strange bed, it took me several minutes to get my bearings.* 我睡醒时发现是躺在一张陌生的床上，经过好几分钟才明白自己是在什么地方。*I stepped from the darkened church into the sunshine. The light was so bright that at first I couldn't get my bearings.* 我跨出幽暗的教堂的大门，踏进灿烂的阳光中。由于日光太强，我最初不了解自己在什么方位。"需要一段时间"去"了解(自己的)位置[方位]"的场合，动词除 get 外，也使用 find。*When one moves to a new city, it usually takes him several weeks to completely get [find] his bearings.* 当搬到一个新城市的时候，通常要过几个星期才能完全熟悉周围的情况。另外，这个 bearings 可以考虑是指"地理的状况"，也可以认为是 his bearings in the social and business world，亦即"他在社交界和商业界的状况"。再有，当 bearings 不是以地理的、物理的意味而是象以下的例句那样以比喻的、抽象的意味使用时，重点并非"(自己所处的)位置"，而多半在于"(今后应该进取的)方向、出路、目标"。*For a long time I couldn't decide what to do with my life. I had been out of school for several years before I finally found [got] my bearings.* 有很长一个时期我决定不了人生应该走什么道路。从学校出来又过了好几年，我才终于确定了自己前进的方向。*Many young soldiers returning from the battlefield to civilian life have difficulty getting their bearings again.* 从战场返回市民生活的青年士兵，有许多

人费很大力气去确定生活的目标。反义语是 lose *one's* BEARINGS. ◇ comprehend where *one* is / gain a sense of direction / become familiar with the situation / decide the direction *one* should take

lose *one's* **bearings** [ˌlu:z ~ ˈbe(:)rɪŋz] [口] **迷失位置[方位]** 与反义语 get *one's* BEARINGS(→) 相同，这是使用 bearings 的又一个定型的表达法。*The ship lost its bearings in the storm.* 是按照正解的使用方法，意为 在暴风雨中，船迷失了方位。由正解发展，如 *After I turned the corner I lost my bearings for a moment.* 转过角落之后，我一时之间不知道自己的方位了。这一例句所示，从字面意义的"迷失方位"一直扩大到抽象意义的"迷失前进的方向"。*Since the former president died, our company seems to have lost its bearings.* 自从前任总裁去世以后，我们公司似乎已经迷失了前进的方向。*So many young people these days have lost their bearings in life.* 近来，有非常多的青年人迷失了人生道路的方向。◇ lose *one's* sense of direction

beast

be a disgrace to man and beast → DISGRACE

beat

beat [ˈbiːt] [话] **精疲力尽** → BUSHED

beat it [ˈbi(:)dɪt] [话] **(马上)走开** 19 世纪初开始流行。是轻松的口语。一般在亲密的朋友之间、对待晚辈或者孩子们相互间使用。*Beat it. I'm busy now.* 快走开！我现在正忙哪。*Beat it, kid. You're too young to hang around here.* 小家伙，赶快走开吧！象你这样年纪轻轻的，可不能在这种地方转悠啊。如这两个例句所示，多用语气很强的命令式。但是，也不一定非这样不可。*We'd better beat it before the teacher gets here.* 我们还是在老师来到这儿以前走开为好。*When we heard someone coming, we beat it out of there.* 当我们听到有人来的脚步声，我们立即离开了那个地方。另有 SCRAM 一词意义相同，使用方法相同，以上各例句中的 beat it 全都可以用 scram(med) 代替。但是，在最后的例句中可不能说 scram out of there，只说 we scrammed 就行了。◇ go away / leave [get out of *someplace*] (in a hurry)

beat *someone* **up** [ˌbi(:)t ~ ˈʌ(:)p] [口] **狠揍** beat 是"打"，up 是"彻底地"的意思。有时也许用棒子或者拿脚踢，但一般用于用手殴打或狠揍的场合。*He called me a liar so I beat him up.* 他管我叫说谎者，因此我把他狠揍了一顿。*Three men ganged up on him and beat him up.* 三个男子结成一伙对付他，把他痛打了一顿。*We were beaten up by a group of strangers.* 我们被一群不认识的人痛打了一顿。◇ give *someone* a thorough beating

beats

something **beats me** [~ ˌbi(:)tsˈmiː] [话] **(我)一点儿也不懂** 直译为"某件事战胜我"，换句话说就是"对于某件事情，我简直理解不了"。*This math problem beats me. I've worked for over an hour on it and I still can't get it.* 这道数学题把我完全蒙住了。我已经作了一个多小时，仍然没有能够解开。*That guy's attitude beats me. Sometimes he acts as if he doesn't want any friends.* 我对那个家伙的态度一点儿也不明白。有时候他那神情好象不需要任何的朋友。如上面的例句所示，主语一般是人以外的事物。*That girl beats me. Some days she's very nice to me and other days she won't even give me the time of day.* 那个姑娘[的态度]使我捉摸不透。她有几天对我很甜，而另外的日子则对我连理也不理。这一例句也是同样，从语法上说，主语是"那个姑娘"本身，但是从意义上说，勿宁应该认为是她的"态度"或"举止"。另外，也常用代词 it 作主语。*It beats me. You'll just have to figure it out for yourself.* 我一点儿也不懂。你非自己解答不可啦。*It beats me how you think you can get into college without studying.* 我真弄不懂你怎么会以为不努力用功也能上大学。除这个 it 外，有时也用 that 作主

语。*A: How often should I take this medicine? B: That beats me. Why don't you call the doctor and find out?* 甲：这个药，我一天得吃多少次呢？乙：这我可不知道。你打个电话问一下大夫如何？也有象下面的例句那样完全省略主语的情况。*A: How in the world are we going to find any gas in the middle of the desert like this? B: Beats me. maybe we should try digging for it.* 甲：在这样的沙漠正中间，我们怎样做才能找到一些汽油呢？乙：我也弄不清。我们试掘一下看看如何？◇ I just don't understand [know] (*something*).

beauty

Beauty is in the eye of the beholder. ['bju(:)di ɪ.zɪnðɪ .aɪəvðə bə'houldər] [口] **美是主观的问题** behold 是"看"，beholder 是"看的人"，本条直译为"美在看的人的眼睛里"。这是一个谚语性的固定说法，对诉诸视觉的东西使用。*Beauty is in the eye of the beholder. That's why different kinds of art appeal to different people.* 美是主观的问题。正因为如此，不同类的美术作品会打动不同人的心灵。*Steven seems to think his wife is beautiful. It all goes to show that beauty is in the eye of the beholder.* 史蒂文似乎认为他的妻子很美。这就叫做情人眼里出西施嘛。◇ Beauty is a subjective thing.

Beauty is only skin deep. ['bju(:)di zonli .skɪn'diːp] [谚] **容貌不能衡量人** 直译"美人不过皮一层"，意思是"容貌好看，不一定内心也美"。这是古已有之的表达法，原形是 Beauty's but skin deep. 出自英国赫列福德的约翰·戴维斯(John Davies of Hereford) 1616 年所著的剧本。在美国也曾长期使用这一形式，但现今，is only 的形式是普遍的，只应用于女性。*I'll admit that Martha is a beautiful woman, but beauty is only skin deep.* 我承认马莎是个美人儿，但是容貌不能衡量人呀。*When I was young, I wanted to marry a beautiful woman. I had many sad experiences before I learned that beauty is only skin deep.* 当我年轻的时候，我曾希望与一个美人儿结婚。在我懂得容貌不能衡量人之前，我有过许多可悲的经验。*His wife is extremely homely but she's a beautiful person. It all goes to show that beauty's only skin deep.* 他的妻子长得极不好看，但是她是一个大好人。正如谚语所说，容貌不能衡量人啊！◇ You can't judge a woman by her beauty.

beaver

an eager beaver [ə .ni(:)gər 'biːvər] [话] **干劲十足的人** beaver (海狸)经常转动，是有名的"勤劳动物"。再加上 eager (热心的)这样一个褒义词，合在一起成为"什么工作都肯干、而且一心一意、满怀热情地去做的人"的意思。在某种情况下，一个人过分紧张往往会引起周围的同事们为难和讨厌，但是在这一习用语本身并不含有那种不愉快的情调。*Most new employees are eager beavers for the first six months or so.* 大多数新来的工作人员在最初的六个月左右都是勤勤恳恳、埋头苦干的。常用 real 加强语气。*Let's give that job to Edgar. He's a real eager beaver.* 我们把那个工作交给埃德加吧。他是一个干劲十足的人。*Frank would be more popular among his fellow students if he weren't such an eager beaver.* 弗兰克如果不是那样一个干劲十足的人，他的同学们会更欢迎他的。◇ an eager worker

bed

get out of bed on the wrong side [ge.daudə 'bedənðə .rɔːŋ 'saɪd] [话] **大清早起来就不顺心** 字面意义是"从床的另一侧起来"，常用于毫无理由而心绪不佳的时候，或者作为心绪不佳的辩解，等等。一般习惯是附加 this morning 或 today，有时附加 that day 等。*I'm sorry I snapped at you. I guess I got out of bed on the wrong side this morning.* 我冲你嚷叫了，真对不起。我大清早起来就觉得心里不顺当。*The boss has been in a bad mood all day today. He must have gotten out of bed on the wrong side this morning.* 老板

今天一天都闷闷不乐。他一定是有什么事很不顺心。也可以说 get up (有时用 out) on the wrong side of the bed。*I decided it best not to show my father my report card today. He got up on the wrong side of the bed this morning.* 我想，今天不让父亲看学生成绩通知书是上策。他大清早起来似乎就不顺心。◇ be in a bad temper (since *one* got up this morning)

go to bed [ˌgoudə ˈbe(ː)d] [口] **(上床)就寝** → SLEEP

go to bed with the chickens [godəˌbed wɪðə ˈtʃɪkənz] [话] **睡得非常早** 直译"与鸡一同上床"，即"与鸡在同一时刻开始睡觉"，意思是"晚上就寝的时间非常早"。*Dick always goes to bed with the chickens. He has to catch the six-thirty train every morning.* 迪克就寝的时间永远特别早。他每天早晨必须赶六点半的火车。◇ go to bed very early

be no bed of roses [ˌnou ˌbedəv ˈrouzəz] [口] **(生活、境遇等)并不轻松** bed of roses 是"铺满玫瑰花的床"，转义"安乐窝"。*I had thought that marriage would be a bed of roses, but mine seems to have more thorns than blossoms.* 我原来以为结婚一定非常美好，但是我的婚姻却是痛苦多于快乐。如此例所示，也能用于肯定句，但是可以说，这是例外的表达法。一般皆如以下的例句那样在否定句中使用而含有"不象外表那么好看"的意思。*This job is no bed of roses. The pay is good but my boss is a real Simon Legree.* 这个工作并不轻松。工资虽然高，但是我的老板却是一个地道的冷酷无情的人。如果把这句话说成 This job isn't a bed of roses.，意思当然也通，但是一般不这样讲，而采取 no ～的形式。*Having to support one's family by working at two jobs is no bed of roses.* 干两份工作养家，可不是轻松的事情。但是，如果为了加强语气而使用 exactly，反而 it's not [it isn't] exactly a bed of roses 成为定型。*Life in Japan is fine, but for people who don't speak Japanese it's not exactly a bed of roses.* 日本的生活是美好的，但是对于不会说日语的人也并不十分轻松。◇ be not (an) easy (situation)

bedpost

between you and me and the bedpost [bətwi(ː)ˌnjuː ənˌmiː ənðə ˈbedˌpoust] [话] **讲个悄悄话** → between you and me and the GATEPOST

bee

be (as) busy as a bee [əz ˈbɪzi əzə ˈbiː] [话] **忙得不可开交** 直译为"象蜜蜂一样忙"，表示"象不停地飞舞的蜜蜂一样忙得团团转"的样子。主要应用于妇女和儿童，有点"令人愉快"的味道。*Mother's been as busy as a bee all week getting ready for Christmas and New Year's.* 母亲为了准备过圣诞节和新年，整整一个星期忙得不可开交。*The little girls were busy as bees, making mud pies and dressing their dolls.* 小女孩们用泥做馅饼，给洋娃娃穿衣服，简直忙得不可开交。◇ be very busy

have a bee in *one's* bonnet (about *something*) [ˌhævə ˈbiːən ～ ˌbɑ(ː)nət] [话] **心迷一窍** 从 15 世纪就已经存在的古老的表达法。直译为"在自己的帽子中有一只蜜峰"。原来的思路是："某一思想象蜜蜂一样在帽子(＝头脑)中嗡嗡地飞旋，不肯离去"。这一表达法的原形可能是过去的习用语 have bees in the head 或者 have a head full of bees。两者都用以表达"头脑古怪"的意思。而这个 head 变成了 bonnet，语意也从"头脑古怪"变成了"心迷一窍"。从说话者来看，多半意味着"奇妙的想法"、"脱离实际的想法"甚至"毫无根据的想法"，并不一定只限于从客观上看、说是"古怪的念头"。这一习用语的重点不在于思想内容的本身，而在于"心迷一窍"的自体。例如，*Our son has a bee in his bonnet about becoming a doctor.* 我们家的儿子心迷一窍，非要当个医生不可。在这句话里，从客观上看，"要当个医生"本身也许完全不是"古怪的念头"，但对于儿子的父母来说，总是一个多多少少有违命之感的"想法"。*My husband has a bee* *in his bonnet about buying an island to live on.* 我的丈夫有一个古怪的念头，一心要买个岛屿居住。a bee 也可使用 another bee 或 bees 的形式。*Here comes Mrs. Apiary again. From the looks of her, she's got another bee in her bonnet.* 瞧，爱匹阿里夫人又来啦。从她那样子来看，她又有什么离奇古怪的想法了。象以上所述，一般是在指古怪的思想或欲望，但也可以具体地指人或物。在这一场合，大多伴有"一味认定"的意思。*Mrs. Locket's got a bee in her bonnet about burglars. She's suspicious of every new face in the neighborhood.* 洛基特夫人对强盗的警惕性特别强。附近一出现新面孔，她都怀疑是强盗。有时也用以表达"头脑古怪"的意思。如 have bees in *one's* bonnet 那样，bee 多用复数形式。这意思就是说，心迷一窍就够受的了，竟然"满脑子千奇百怪的思想"。*The old woman obviously has bees in her bonnet, but everyone loves her anyway.* 那位老太太显然一脑子千奇百怪的思想，尽管如此，每个人都喜欢她。也往往见到 with a bee in *one's* bonnet 的形式。*Every generation is full of young people with bees in their bonnets about how to improve the world overnight.* 在任何一代人中，都会有许许多多的青年怀抱着如何在一夜之间改造世界的空思遐想。如果是 put a bee in *someone's* bonnet，意为"向(某人)灌输怪思想"。*What?! Grandpa wants to go back to school? Who in the world put that bee in his bonnet?* 什么?! 爷爷想再进小学读书? 谁给他灌输了这个莫明其妙的怪思想? ◇ be obsessed with the idea of (*doing*) *something* [with a strange idea] / be slightly daft

put a bee in *someone's* **bonnet** [ˌpudəˈbiːən ~ ˌbɑ(ː)nət] [话] **向(某人)灌输怪思想** → have a BEE in *one's* bonnet (about *something*)

beef

beef (about *something*) [ˈbiːf] [话] **发牢骚** 发音、缀字皆与"牛肉"的 beef 相同。这一表达法是由过去的黑社会中的用语 cut a beef (发牢骚)而来。但是，这个 beef 却完全没有匪帮专用语的气氛，已经成为极其普通的俚语了。*I don't like to beef, but this time I feel I have a legitimate reason to do so.* 我不喜欢发牢骚，但是这一回，我认为我有表示不满的正当理由。*That guy is always beefing about something.* 那个家伙总是一肚子牢骚。也有作为名词使用的情况，表示"不平"、"不满"、"牢骚"、"意见"等意思。请注意：在这一场合，它与"牛肉"的 beef 不同，而是动名词了。特别是 have a beef (with *someone* about *something*) 为一固定的说法，如 *I have a beef about that.* 我对那件事有意见。*I have a beef with Doris about the way she spends money.* 我对于多丽丝花钱的方式不满意。*We're getting too many beefs from our customers.* 顾客们对我们的意见太多啦。*What's your beef?* 你有什么苦水? ◇ complain

have a beef (with *someone* about *something*) [ˌhævəˈbiːf] [话] **有不满** → BEEF (about *something*)

beeline

make a beeline for *someplace* [ˌmeɪkəˈbiːˌlaɪn fər ~] [话] **循直线走向(某处)** beeline 的意思是"(蜜蜂归巢时的)最短距离的一直线"。由此转用于人或其他动物，在表示"沿最短路线急走"的场合，说 make a beeline for *someplace*。这里的 for 是"前往(目的地)某处"的意思。也可以说 ~ to *someplace*，但有点不自然。然而，根据上下文，有不用 for 而代入其他前置词的情况。例如，*He made a beeline up the mountain.* 他径直地登上山去。*The dog made a beeline across the yard.* 狗经直穿过了庭院。不论是哪一种场合，除"急走"的意义外，一般含有"不顾一切、一心一意"的意义。*When the final bell rang, all the children in the classroom made a beeline for the door.* 下课铃声一响，教室里的孩子们全都径直向门口冲去。*Our son loves to eat. Whenever he gets home he makes a beeline for the refrigerator.* 我们家的儿

子喜欢吃。他刚一进家门就径直向冰箱跑去。有时以 beeline 作为动词表示同样的意义,说 beeline it for *someplace*,但这一表达法较少使用。*As soon as I heard the news of my father's accident, I beelined it [made a beeline] for the hospital.* 我听到爸爸发生事故的消息后,立即径直向医院跑去。◇ rush straight to *someplace*

beer

a beer bust → BUST

draft beer [ˈdræft ˈbɪ(:)r] [口] **生啤酒** draft 是"从桶类容器倒出液体"的意思,因而 draft beer 为"从桶里直接倒入杯子的啤酒"。有些国家卖的瓶装或罐装啤酒常标有 draft beer 的字样,就英语来说,这是不正确的。再有,美国的酒馆、餐厅等常有写着"Beer on Draft"或"Beer on Tap"(→ have *something* on TAP<for *something*>)的招牌,意思是"有生啤酒",这些字样完全是招牌用语,在日常会话中,"生啤酒"只能用 draft beer。*There's nothing like a mug of cold draft beer on a hot summer day.* 在夏季的大热天里,喝上一杯冷的生啤酒比什么都强啊。◇ beer from the keg

be small beer [ˌsmɔ(:)l ˈbɪ:r] [话] **(规模、资格等)微不足道** 本来 small beer 在英国指"弱啤酒",在美国是"少量啤酒"的意思。使用方法例如别人家里请吃饭,人家问 *Anything to drink?* 喝点儿什么?你可以回答说:*I'll have a small beer.* 我喝一点儿啤酒吧。但是,以上所讲只是使用字面意义的场合,如下面的例句所示,人们也经常把它作为比喻使用。*Ours is not a small company, but it's pretty small beer beside a giant like General Motor.* 我们的公司不算很小,但与通用汽车公司等巨型企业比起来,则是小巫见大巫了。另外,这一表达法既然是"(与……比起来)小巫见大巫"的意思,那就必然用于与其他做比较的场合,这时,既有象上面例句中的 General Motor 那样直接举出比较对象的情况,也有象下面例句那样不举出比较对象的情况。*As a military operation, the 1812 British invasion of America was small beer.* 作为军事作战来说,*1812* 年英国入侵美洲是微不足道的。在说这句话的时候,头脑里会浮现出诺曼底作战以及其他历史上著名的军事作战,相互比较之后,才讲出"微不足道",只不过没在表面上提出比较对象罢了。除比规模外,也有比资格的场合。*He is obviously a smart scientist, but small beer compared to someone like Einstein.* 他显然是一位优秀的科学家,但与象爱因斯坦那样的人相比,却是小巫见大巫了。*Why do you bother messing around with him? He's very small beer.* 你为什么跟他打交道呢?他是个非常微不足道的家伙。这多半讲的是谈判一方的代表小材大用了,对方不出更高级的人物是不行的。有时也使用 small-beer 这一复合词的形式。*You shouldn't sell your book to a small-beer publishing company like that.* 你不应该把你的著作卖给那样一家微不足道的出版社啊。另外,be small beer 是从英国传入美国的表达法,但美国也有 be small potatoes 这样独创的习用语。两者意义完全相同,但后者在使用上没有任何限制。◇ (very) small scale(d)

bees

the birds and the bees → BIRDS

have bees in *one's* **bonnet** [ˌhæv ˈbi:zən ~ ˌbɑ(:)nət] [话] **头脑古怪** have a BEE in *one's* **bonnet** (about *something*)

beggars

Beggars can't be choosers. [ˈbe(:)gərz ˌkæntbi ˈtʃu:zərz] [谚] **讨饭不能嫌饭馊** 在英国诗人约翰·海伍德(John Heywood)所编的《格言集》(*Proverbs*, 1546)中,有一条为 Beggars should be no choosers. 当初这似乎是一种普遍的说法。另外的说法还有 Beggars must be no choosers.或 Beggars mustn't be choosers. 以及 Beggars shouldn't be choosers. 等等。现在最常使用的是本条条头的形式。字面意义是"乞丐不能成为挑肥拣瘦的人",但是,并不只限于象乞丐那样"向人家讨东西"的场合,作为比喻也广泛地使用。*I was hoping for* *a cold glass of beer, but when the old woman kindly brought me a hot cup of tea I accepted it gratefully. After all, beggars can't be choosers.* 我本来想喝一杯冷啤酒，但是当老太太亲切地端来一碗热茶时，我很感谢她的美意。接过来喝了。毕竟是讨饭不能嫌饭馊啊！*No, I won't lend you my new dress. You'll have to be satisfied with this old one. Beggars can't be choosers, you know.* 不，我不想把我的新衣服借给你。你凑合着穿这件旧的吧。要知道，讨饭不能嫌饭馊呀。*I didn't like the job he offered me, but beggars can't be choosers.* 我不喜欢他给我的那个工作，但是，讨饭不能嫌饭馊啊！◇ People who receive favors are in no position to complain about what they receive.

behavior

be on *one's* **best behavior** [ɔ(:)n ～ ˌbesɪbəˈheɪvjər] [口] **谨言慎行** → mind *one's* P's and q's

behind

the behind [ðə bəˈhaɪnd] [话] **(人的)屁股** 单是 behind 为"在后、向后"，加定冠词 the 即成为名词，意为"屁股"。*The ball hit me in the behind.* 球打在我的屁股上了。也可以用 my, your, her 等所有格代替 the。*I fell on my behind.* 我摔了个屁股蹲儿。→ the BOTTOM ◇ the buttocks

belch

a belch [ə ˈbe(:)ltʃ] [口] **打嗝** → a BURP

belfry

have bats in *one's* **belfry** → BATS

bell

something **rings a bell** [～ ˌrɪŋzə ˈbe(:)l] [话] **总算想了起来** 最初创造这一习用语的设想是："刺激头脑中存在的铃，使它隐约作响"，也就是"刺激记忆力，使人总算想了起来"。几乎在所有的场合，*something* 的地方(＝主语)是人名、地名之类的名称，但也有时用其他的词。*The stranger's name rang a bell. I was sure I had met him somewhere before, but I couldn't remember where.* 那个陌生人的名字，我总算想了起来。过去我的确在什么地方见过他，不过我记不起究竟是在哪儿了。*The name of the town rang a bell. Where had I heard it before?* 那个城镇的名字我忽然想起来了。过去我是在哪儿听到的哪？*Wait! What did you just say? That rings a bell somewhere.* 等一下！你刚才说什么来的？那对我很有启发啊！◇ arouse an indistinct memory / sound familiar

belly

a belly buster [ə ˈbeli.bʌstər] [话] **拙笨跳水，肚皮先下** → a belly FLOP

a belly button → BUTTON

a belly flop → FLOP

a belly whop [ə ˈbeli.*h*wɑ(:)p] [话] **拙笨跳水，肚皮先落** → a belly FLOP

go belly up [gou ˌbeliˈʌ(:)p] [话] **倒闭** 字面意义是"肚子向上"。*Hundreds of fish were floating belly up in the water.* 意为几百条鱼肚子向上飘浮在水中。本条的表达法是从鱼死的状态联想而来。*A record number of companies went belly up last year.* 去年倒闭公司的数目达到空前的水平。如此例所示，专用于表示"(在经济上)达到无可挽救的状态"、"破产倒闭"的意思。这是一个比较新的词汇，常见于最近的报刊杂志。*If we don't get some new orders soon, we're going to go belly up.* 如果不马上有一些新的订货，我们就要破产倒闭了。*When government subsidies were cut off, the museum went belly up.* 政府停止了补贴之后，博物馆关门大吉了。动词也可以用 turn 代替 go，但一般是用 go。*The giant trading company, unable to meet its financial obligations, turned belly up.* 由于负债累累，无法偿还，那家大型贸易公司倒闭了。◇ go bankrupt

make a belly landing [ˌmeɪkə ˈbeli ˌlændɪŋ] [话] **机身着陆** → make a pancake LANDING

bellyache

bellyache (about *something*) ['beli.eɪk] [话] **满腹牢骚** bellyache 意为"肚子痛",一般作为名词使用。*He had a bellyache from eating too many persimmons.* 他由于吃柿子太多,把肚子吃坏了。可以认为这是 a stomachache 的轻松的说法。然而,如果把 bellyache 作为动词使用,意义就不是"肚子痛",而是"满腹牢骚"或"发泄不满"了。*Don't pay any attention to Charlie. He's always bellyaching about something.* 根本不要去理查理。他永远是满腹牢骚的。*Stop your bellyaching. We all have to work just as hard as you do.* 你不要净发牢骚啦。我们大家也跟你一样,不拼命干活是不行的。另外,在这一意义上的 bellyache,多为男性使用,但这并不是绝对的。*Norah's a funny girl. She always bellyaches about the amount of homework we have, but she makes the best grades in the class.* 诺拉是一个有趣的女孩。她总抱怨说我们的家庭作业太多,可是她在班上的成绩却最好。也有时作为具有"牢骚"、"不满"意味的名词使用。*What's your bellyache?* 你发什么牢骚哪?从上面的各例句也可以看出,这一表达法与 complain 相似。实际上,上边的例句全部都可以将 complain 代入。从译文"满腹牢骚"也可以了解,bellyache 含有"谈论发了牢骚也没用处的事情"的意味。因此,例如某甲在说 *He's always bellyaching about something.* 的时候,某甲的话中包含着对 he 批评的意味。意思是说:"他的牢骚不满没有什么根据,缺乏说服力。因此,一点也不值得同情。可以置之不理。"另外一点是:bellyache 含有"净谈子虚乌有的事"或者"总讲怎么说也没有用处的事"的情绪。因此,多与 always, still 等一起使用。与此相反,complain 只是"抱怨"、"诉苦",至于"所怨"、"所诉"是否有事实根据,那与此词无关,而且也不含有"净"呀、"总"呀之类的意味。总而言之,它是一个没有内涵的词。另外,bellyache 的派生词有 a bellyacher,是"爱发牢骚的人"。*People would like you more if you weren't such a bellyacher.* 如果你不是那样一个爱发牢骚的人,大家会更欢迎你的。◇ complain

belt

have *something* **under** *one's* **belt** [.hæv '~ ʌndər ~ .belt] [话]**富有(经验、成果等)** under *one's* belt (在腰带下边)意味着"胃"。整个条头的原意是"肚子里装有食物"。*I can't work well unless I have a good breakfast under my belt.* 我的肚子吃不上象样的早饭,我就不能很好地工作。如此例所示,也有用本来意义的时候。作为比喻,用法如下:*Joan loves to travel. She already has three trips to Japan under her belt.* 琼喜欢旅行,她已经到过日本三次了。*The champion has over thirty ring victories under his belt.* 冠军已经取得三十多次的胜利。*Now that I have the necessary capital under my belt, I can put my ideas to work.* 现在我有了必要的资金,可以实现我的理想了。*something* 处代入"经验"、"成果"等,把这些东西"装在肚子里",那就是"持有"的意思了。常有使用 with *something* under *one's* belt 这一形式的情况,如下例:*There are few reporters with two Pulitzer Prizes under their belt.* 只有极少数的新闻记者得过两次普利策奖。◇ have *something* to *one's* credit / have secured [experienced] *something*

hit below the belt [.hɪt bə.louðə 'belt] [话] **卑鄙** 拳击手对准比赛对手的腰带下方打去,口语说 *X hits Y below the belt.* 当然这是犯规。后来发展为比喻用法,指不正大光明,如:*That's hitting below the belt.* 那太卑鄙了!*You'd better do things right or you'll find that I can hit below the belt, too.* 你干事情最好还是要正大光明,否则的话,我会叫你明白我也能够给人下毒手的。*I welcome healthy criticism, but that reporter hits below the belt.* 我欢迎健康的批评,但是那位记者所写的太卑鄙啦。◇ use unfair tactics

tighten *one's* **belt** [ˌtaɪtn ～ ˈbelt] [口] **勒紧裤带** 字面意义是"把腰带勒紧",原意是"勒紧腰带以解除饥饿",亦即"忍耐饥饿",多少带有笑谈的味道。 *After our canoe sank in the river with all our food, we had no choice but to tighten our belts and start hiking.* 自从我们的独木舟连同全部口粮在河里沉没以后,我们就只好饿着肚皮,开始用两只脚走。用作比喻,是"压缩生活"、"削减经费"的意思。最初的构想是:"要忍耐不得不挨饿的苦难生活"。 *During the Great Depression, almost everyone was forced to tighten his belt.* 在大萧条时期,几乎人人都不得不勒紧裤带。 *The whole nation was urged to tighten its belt for the war effort.* 为了进行战争,全国人民要勒紧裤带。 *Most export companies were forced to start tightening their belts because of the rapid weakening of the dollar.* 由于美元的暴跌,大多数出口公司不得不开始压缩经费。由于是 belt,因而有时用 notch (腰带的窟窿眼)来加强语气。也就是说,依靠增加 a [another] notch (or two) 或 a few more notches 来表达"更加"或"更进一步"的意思。 *Every time my father lost his job, we just sighed and tightened our belts another notch.* 父亲每一次失业,我们都只好叹口气,更加勒紧我们的裤带。也有 belt-tightening 的形式,作为名词或形容词使用。 *Last year our company had to do some drastic belt-tightening.* 去年,我们的公司不得不大幅度地削减经费。 *If things don't get better soon, we'll have to commence belt-tightening operations.* 假若情况不迅速好转的话,我们就不得不采取削减经费的措施了。偶然也有 pull in *one's* belt a [another] notch (or two) 之类的说法。意思是"再把腰带勒紧一些"。 *If the economic situation gets any worse, everyone will have to pull in their belts a few more notches.* 如果经济形势继续恶化的话,每一个人都必须把裤带勒得更紧一些。◇ practice frugality / economize

berry

(as) brown as a berry [əz ˈbraunəzə ˈbe(ː)ri] [话] **晒得黝黑** 直译为"象 berry 一样的棕色"。但是,这个 berry 并不是"(草莓一类的)浆果",一般是被称为 beans 的可可豆或咖啡豆的别名。这一表达法只在形容"日晒"的样子时使用,特别用于儿童或青年女性,带有"很好玩"的含义。从"日晒"的程度来说,这已经是"最高程度的日晒"了,因而与中文"晒得黝黑"一语相近,但是,一般来说,东方人比西洋人黑的程度高,所以在肤色浓淡本身构成问题的场面或上下文中,可考虑本条的意义相当于日本人的说法"晒得象小麦一样颜色",这样比较合乎实际。 *After a week at the beach, Sue was as brown as a berry.* 在海边呆了一个星期之后,苏晒得黑黝黝的。 *The children get brown as berries every summer.* 孩子们每年夏天都晒得黝黑黝黑的。◇ very suntanned

berth

give *someone* [*something*] **(a) wide berth** [ˌgɪv ～ (ə)ˌwaɪd ˈbəːrθ] [口] **回避** berth 原为海上用语,意为"回旋余地",亦即"在船与船之间、船与岸之间留有行船必要的余地"。因而,就本来的意义说,give a wide berth 也是"(为了有行船的余地,在与其他船只或海岸之间)留下安全的距离"。古时不说 wide berth 而说 good [clear] berth,但现代则专用 wide。 *The waters are pretty shallow here. We'd better give the coast a wide berth.* 这一带水太浅。我们最好离岸更远一些。也转作比喻使用。 *Here comes Mrs. Tonguewagger. We'd better give her a wide berth if we don't want to listen to her talk about her son for the next hour or so.* 通格维加夫人到这儿来啦。如果我们不愿意费一个多小时去听她谈论自己的儿子,最好还是躲开她吧。 *I'd give wide berth to that guy if I were you.* 如果我是你,我就对那个家伙敬而远之。"敬而远之"、"回避"的对象不仅限于"人"。 *My wife used to like to ride horses, but she's given them wide berth since she fell off one and broke her leg.* 我老婆过去总好骑马,但是自从她打马

上摔下来、腿部骨折以后,她对马就敬而远之了。*I've always given mathematics wide berth.* 我对数学总是敬而远之。另外,在美国一般的词典中,这一习用语均写作 give ~ a wide berth,但是实际情况是,如以上的例句所示,大多省去 a wide berth 中的 a。◇ avoid *someone* [*something*] / stay away from someone [*something*]

beside

be beside *oneself* **with** *something* [bə'saɪd ~ wɪð ~] [口] **(由于喜怒哀乐而)发狂** 这个 beside 是"在旁边"。本条全部直译,意为"由于某种原因,自己的精神脱离肉体,存在于自己的旁边",亦即"由于某种原因失去自己平日的冷静"。*something* 处由表示"喜怒哀乐"的名词代入,一般为 joy (喜)、anger (怒),而用 joy 者最多。例如: *When we learned that Dad had survived the plane crash, we were beside ourselves with joy.* 当我们听说爸爸在飞机事故中得以生还,我们简直欣喜若狂。*I've never seen the boss as beside himself with rage as when Ralph got drunk and insulted our biggest client.* 当拉尔夫喝醉了酒,侮辱我们最大的主顾时,老板勃然大怒,我还从来没有见过他动那样大的肝火。*Am I happy?! I'm beside myself with joy.* 你问我是不是快乐?! 我高兴得简直要发狂啊! 此外,something 处可以代入 pride (骄傲)、pity (怜悯)、admiration (称赞)等,不过使用得不太多。*Mrs. Brown was beside herself with pride when she learned that her son had passed his entrance exams.* 布朗夫人知道她的儿子已经考取大学的时候,她趾高气扬,狂得了不得。*We were all beside ourselves with pity at the sight of the starving children.* 当见到那些饥饿的孩子们时,我们大家都怀着无限的同情。*We're all beside ourselves with admiration for you.* 我们大家对你佩服得五体投地。◇ be delirious (with joy) / be furious (with rage) / be puffed up with pride / be full of joy [rage, anger, pride, pity, admiration]

best

make the best of *something* [ˌmeɪkðə 'bestəv ~] [口] **(在不利的条件下)顽强奋斗** 意思是"承认失败或倒霉是不得已的事情,为此而尽最大的努力"。乍看起来,与 make the MOST of *something*(→)的形式非常相似,但请注意,两者的意义不同。*There's no use crying over spilt milk. We'll just have to accept our failure and make the best of it.* 已经完蛋的事情,后悔也没有用。我们只能承认失败,然后努力奋斗。*Jimmy is not one to let small setbacks bother him. He just accepts the fact that such things happen and makes the best of them.* 吉米不是一个由于小小的挫折而灰心丧气的人。他承认发生那种事情的必然性,而能够妥善处理。*Since we forgot to take the rice on our camping trip, we just had to make the best of things without it.* 我们去野营,却忘了带米,结果不得不精心策划,采取应变措施。◇ manage as well as *one* can

put *one's* **best foot forward** → FOOT

bet

one's **best bet** [~ 'best͵bet] [话] **(达到目的的)最好方法** bet 是"赌注",所以 best bet 是"最好的赌注",亦即"最有赢的希望的赌注"。*My best bet was on Sharp Boy in the third race.* 我赢得最痛快的是在第三轮竞赛中押到"快小伙"身上的赌注。但是,象这样按照字面意义使用的情况极少,而按照本条中文释义使用的情况则占绝大多数。不过,即使在这种场合,由于使用 bet 一词,仍然具有"赌博"的因素,亦即经常缠绕着"(用那个最好的方法)不知究竟能否成功"这样一种惴惴不安的感觉。典型的句子是从 if 开始,采取"如果想要……的话,最好的方法是……"的形式。*If you want to get to the airport on time, your best bet would be to take a taxi.* 如果你想要及时赶到机场,最好的方法是乘出租汽车。如这一例句所示,经常应用于比较轻微的事态。但是,在非研究"重大策略"不可的场合也是使用的,例如: *If we are going* to avoid bankruptcy, our best bet would be to cut down on production. 如果我们想要避免破产，最好的方法是压缩生产。总起来说，就是经常要从若干 choice (抉择)中选取 the best，因此也可以使用定冠词，用 the best bet 代替 *one's* best bet。以上各例句中的 *one's* 也全都可以换成 the。另外，如果在 *one's* 或 the 与 best bet 之间插入 next (其次的)而形成 *one's* [the] next best bet ['neks*t* ˌbes*t* ˌbet] 的话，就是"次好的解决办法"了。 *I haven't got enough money to take a taxi that far. What's the next best bet?* 我没有足够的钱乘出租车到那么远的地方。其次的好办法是什么呢？ ◇ *one's* best chance of success / the best method

one's **next best bet** [~ 'neks*t* ˌbes*t* ˌbet] [话]**次好的解决办法** → *one's* best BET

better

be all better ['ɔːl 'bedər] [话] **(全)好啦** 儿童用语，相当于大人所说的 be completely well 或 be fully recovered (完全康复了)。从重病到擦伤，广泛使用。 *I've got the mumps now, but the doctor says I'll be all better soon if I stay in bed.* 我现在得了流行性腮腺炎，但是大夫说，只要我卧床休息，马上就会好的。 *My finger is all better now.* 我的手指头全好啦。◇ be completely well

one's **better half** → HALF

think better of *doing something* → THINK

think better of *something* [*someone*] → THINK

between

between you and me [bətwi(ː)ˌnjuː ən'miː] [话] **只是咱们私下里说说** → between you and me and the GATEPOST

bid

make a [*one's*] **bid for** *something* ['meɪkə 'bɪ(ː)dfər' ~] [口] **(为获得……而)斗争** 原来是"投标"的意思，现在多用作比喻。 *We made a bid for that house but someone else got it.* 我们对那所房子投了标，可是叫别的什么人弄到手了。也有这样使用的情况，但可以说这是极罕见的例句。"投标"，一般用 bid for [on] *something* 或者 put in a bid (for [on] *something*)。本条的英语，如果只取其意义，则与 try 大致相同，但是，它经常含有"窥伺机会"的意思，从这一点看，可以说是一个比较有戏剧性感觉的表达法。 *We made a bid for freedom, but we were arrested at the border.* 我们曾为获得自由铤而走险，但是在国境被逮捕了。 *The President decided against making a bid for re-election.* 总统已经死了心，决定不竞选连任了。for *something* 有时也用 to *do something*。 *The ex-king made a bid to recover his throne.* 前国王为恢复他的王位而进行了斗争。*one's* bid 的场合常含有这样的意味："如果放过这个机会，就没有进行斗争的可能了"，也就是说"这是最后的机会"。 *I've made my bid for fame and fortune. I'm too old now to try again.* 我曾经为获得名声和财富而努力奋斗。但是现在年纪太大了，无法再去奔啦。*one's* bid 的形式也可以省略 for *something* 或者 to *do something* 以下的部分。 *If you want to become dean of the department, now's the time to make your bid.* 如果你想当系主任，现在是你争取的时候了。◇ make an attempt to achieve *something*

big

a big brother → BROTHER

a big cheese → CHEESE

Big deal. → DEAL

a big eater [ə ˌbɪ(ː)'gi(ː)dər] [话] **大肚子汉** → eat like a HORSE

a big gun → GUN

the big house → HOUSE

a big shot → SHOT

a big sister → SISTER

a big wheel → WHEEL

make it big → MAKE

the Big Apple [ðə ˌbɪ'gæːpl] [话] **纽约市** "大苹果"怎么是"纽约市"呢？正确的来源不明。在有上下文可以判断的场合，也有指"纽约市"以外的某大都市或其中心地区的情况，但极罕见。 *I just got back from the Big Apple.* 我刚刚从纽约

市回来。*I love the Big Apple.* 我很喜欢纽约市。◇ New York City

the Big Pond [ðə ˌbɪg ˈpɑ(ː)nd] [话]**大西洋** → the big POND

big-time

big-time [ˈbɪg ˈtaɪm] [话] **最高级的** → the big TIME

bigwig

a bigwig [ə ˈbɪg.wɪ(ː)g] [话] **大人物** 特指"政治或官僚阶级的要人",但可广泛称任何部门的"大人物"。古时的大人物戴最大号的假发 (wig),本条习用语即由此而来。*The question was decided by a group of Senate bigwigs.* 参议院的几位大人物已经解决了那个问题。*Mr. Foster is one of the town bigwigs.* 福斯特先生是镇内的大人物之一。*A bigwig from the home office is coming tomorrow.* 明天有一位总公司的要员前来。◇ an important person

bill

bill and coo [ˌbɪlənˈkuː] [口] **谈情说爱** 这一英语没有贴切的译文,勉强翻译的话,大概最为近似的是"谈情说爱"。bill 一般为名词"鸟嘴",但在这里是动词"(鸟)把嘴碰在一起",coo 也是动词"(鸟) 咕咕地叫"。相爱的鸟 (love birds) 或是把嘴合在一起,或是咕咕地对语,永远和睦相处。本条的表达法由此而来,指一对恋人或是轻轻接吻、或是喁喁私语的样子。从旁边来看,令人产生愉快的感觉。*Come on, you love birds. It's time to go.* 喂,你们二位,该走啦! 如此例所示,对情意绵绵的一对也有时称为 love birds。*Jack and Jill sat at their table all during the dance billing and cooing like a pair of love birds.* 在舞会中,杰克和吉尔始终坐在桌子那里,象一对野鸳鸯似地谈情说爱。*If you two will stop billing and cooing for a few minutes, I have something I'd like to say.* 如果你们俩能够停止几分钟谈情说爱,我有点儿话想说一下。◇ act like (a pair of) love birds

fill the bill [ˌfɪlðə ˈbɪ(ː)l] [话] **凑合** bill 一般作"帐单"解。但本条的表达法是由剧院用语而来,bill 指"文娱节目"。fill the bill 本来的意思是"凑足文娱节目"。按照字面意义的使用方法,如 *His may not be a great performance, but at least it will fill the bill.* 他的表演也许不十分好,但是至少可以凑合顶一个节目啊。多半是表达这样的感情:"如果高要求的话,这不是完全令人满意的表演,但是在演技方面大致具备必要的条件,所以还是可以上场的"。因此,在作为比喻使用时,也就成为"满足必要条件"的意义。在这一场合,同样不是说"毫无意见"、"完全满意",而是意味着"这个也算凑合啦"。*I need a larger wrench, but I think this one will fill the bill.* 我需要一把更大的扳手,可是我想这一把也能凑合用。如此例所示,多用于"作为……的代用品也凑合了"的句子类型。*I'd rather have a steak, but pork chops will fill the bill.* 我是想吃牛排,但是猪排也凑合。*As a whodunit, the author's latest book doesn't quite fill the bill.* 作为推理小说,这位作家的最新作品不十分理想。*My son was originally aiming to get into Stanford, but now he's decided that the state university will fill the bill.* 我的儿子原来的志愿是进斯坦福大学,但是现在他考虑进州立大学就行了。以上所举的例句无一不是贯穿着这样的意思:"满足于比最高级次一等的状况"。但是,使用这一表达法并非不能表示"完全令人满意",但在这一场合,为了表示出"满意"的意味,常添加 completely 或 perfectly 以增强语气,构成 completely fill the bill 或者 fill the perfectly 的说法。*This will fill the bill perfectly.* 这个正合适。◇ be sufficient to meet *someone's* [the] requirements

foot the bill (for *something*) [ˌfutðə ˈbɪ(ː)l] [口] **负责付钱** 这个 foot 原来仅一个字就意味着"合计 (数字)"。现在,当用它表示同一意义的时候,必须加个 up,而以 foot up the bill 的说法代替 add up the bill。*Thank you very much, sir. Just a moment while I foot up the bill.* 先生,多谢您光顾。请稍等一下,我算算

帐。本条条头的表达法即由此种用法发展而来,原来的构想是:“既有算帐者,必有付款人”。换句话说,可以考虑它与 pay the bill 相同,不过在含义上多少有一点差别。两者全都是“付钱”,但 pay the bill 除字面意义外别无他意,而 foot the bill 则含有“承担付款责任”的意味。例如在餐厅里,如果说“由我付钱”,用 I'll pay the bill. 或者用 I'll foot the bill. 全都可以,但是说“我去付钱”,须用 I'll go pay the bill.,用 foot 就不自然。因为“责任”与 go 不吻合。*Order whatever you need to finish the work. I'll foot the bill.* 凡是完成任务所需要的东西,你都可以定购。由我付钱。*Who in the world do you expect to foot the bill for all this stuff?* 你究竟想要让谁来为所有这些付钱哪?如以上两个例句所示,一般是按照字面意义使用,实际上与金钱有瓜葛。但也有作比喻使用的时候,表示“承担他人或者共同造成灾难等等的责任”的意思,例如:*The politicians start the wars, but it is the young men of the nation who have to foot the bill.* 发动战争的是政治家们,但是要由国家的青年人去付出代价。另外,宾语不限定是 bill,也可以用 rent, cost, expense 等,例如:*Can you foot the monthly rent for a big house like that?* 象那么大一所房子,你付得起每月的租金吗? ◇ pay

give *someone* **a clean bill of health** [ˌgɪv ~ əkˌli(ː)nˌbɪləv ˈhe(ː)lθ] [口] **(医生)保证健康** 一般美国人虽然使用,但并不知道语源。这一习用语原指“在船出航的港口,当局发给船长一张健康证,证明在出船的时刻,全船人员或货物均无传染病的嫌疑”,是由 The port authorities gave the ship a clean bill of health. (港口当局发给该船一张健康证。) 这一说法发展而来。一般不是在“书面”保证的场合、而是在“口头”保证的场合使用。*My doctor gave me a clean bill of health at my annual physical check-up last week.* 上个星期,在每年一度的身体检查时,医生保证说我身体健康。*My father's heart attack was a great shock to us. He had just been given a clean bill of health by his doctor.* 父亲的心脏病发作对我们震动很大。医生刚刚保证说他身体健康啊。也可以用 completely 加强语气。*I'm sorry, Mr. Kent, I can't give you a completely clean bill of health unless you let me take a few X-rays.* 对不起,肯特先生,除非你让我给你做一下 *X* 光检查,我不能完全保证你是健康的。get [receive] a clean bill of health 是“(由医生)保证说身体健康”。*I'm sure there's nothing wrong with me. I got a clean bill of health from my doctor just last month.* 我敢肯定我的身体没有任何问题。上个月刚刚得到医生的保证,他说我身体健康。这个表达法也可以脱离“健康”的意义而用作比喻,表示“(经调查)认为无缺陷、没有不正行为”。*After two days of questioning, the Senate investigating committee gave the new nominee to the post of FBI Director a clean bill of health.* 经过两天的质询,参议院调查委员会批准了对新联邦调查局局长的任命。*Our company was investigated by the tax authorities this year, but fortunately we received a clean bill of health.* 今年我们公司受到税务局的调查,但是很幸运,他们承认我们是照章纳税的。另外,顺便提一下,“健康证明书”不是 a bill of health, 而是叫做 a health certificate。 ◇ pronounce *someone* perfectly healthy

pad the bill (with *something*) [ˌpæ(ː)ðə ˈbɪ(ː)l] [口] **虚报帐目** pad 的字面意义是“塞入棉花、破布条子、衬垫等使之膨胀”。转作比喻,是“(增加没有关系的东西、不必要的东西)使之比原来大”的意思。这一习用语中的 bill 是“帐单”。*You have to be careful when dealing with that company. They often pad the bill with unnecessary charges.* 跟那个公司做生意的时候,你必须提高警惕。他们常常开花帐,增添一些不必要的费用。*That restaurant padded our bill.* 那家饭店开花帐,多算我们的钱了。如此例所示,也可以使用所有格代替 the。→ pad *someone's* ACCOUNT (with *something*) ◇ purposely overcharge

sell *someone* **a bill of goods** [ˌsel ~ əˌbɪləv ˈguːdz] [话] **上当受骗** 这一表达法过去只用于表示"买假商品上当受骗"的意思。a bill of goods 原意为"制造商把一次订货或委托贩卖的商品发送到商店"。这种交易通常是不先看货，专凭信用。因此，常有"假货"泛滥。在这一 a bill of goods 前边加上 sell *someone* 作为比喻使用，便是由上述情况而来。*That cup doesn't look like real silver to me. I'd say someone sold you a bill of goods.* 依我看，那个杯子不象是真银的。你大概上当受骗啦。可是现在已经从"买假商品上当受骗"进一步发展到"被荒唐的说明、解释、议论等欺骗了"、也就是"相信了假话"的意义，而为人们普遍应用。至于使用方法，则如下面的例句那样，多采取 sell *someone* a bill of goods about ~的形式。*Frank tried to sell me a bill of goods about how I'd become rich overnight If I invested in his new company.* 弗兰克鬼话连篇，他骗我说只要我向他那新成立的公司投资，一夜之间就会发财。sell *someone* a bill of goods 虽然意为"被假话欺骗"，但是也会有这样的情况："说话"一方并不一定认为自己是在"骗人"，而"听话"一方的主观上有"可能是胡说八道"的感觉。例如在上边的例句中就是如此，弗兰克也许真的相信"只要听我的话，一夜就可以变成富翁"。也就是说，在 sell *someone* a bill of goods 中不一定含有"打算欺骗"的意图。不过，象以下的场合，则显然是有意图的。*You say you saw Leonard at the baseball game? Why that guy sold me a bill of goods about how he had to go and visit his sick mother in the hospital today.* 什么？你说你在棒球场上见到伦纳德啦？不知为什么这家伙要跟我讲瞎话，说他今天非到医院去看生病的母亲不可。另外，虽然说在现代不常用"买假商品上当受骗"这一意义，一般使用的是"被假话欺骗"的意义，但也偶尔可以见到过去的使用方法的影子。*Until we were married, I thought my wife was a beautiful woman. Then when I saw her without her makeup the first time, I realized I had been sold a bill of goods.* 结婚以前，我总以为我的妻子是个美人儿。后来，当我第一次看到她那没化妆的面孔，我才明白自己上当受骗了。◇ trick *someone* (into believing that ~)

billiard

(as) bald as a billiard [əz ˈbɔːl dəzə ˈbɪljərd] [话] **亮光光的秃头** 强调"秃"的说法。billiard 是 billiard ball (台球)的略语，有时就说 (as) bald as a billiard ball。*When our daughter was born, she was bald as a billiard.* 我家的女儿出生的时候，脑袋亮光光的。*Our teacher is as bald as a billiard.* 我们的老师是亮光光的秃头。◇ completely bald

billy

a silly billy [ə ˈsɪli ˈbɪli] [话] **傻瓜** silly 是比较柔和的说法，意思是"缺乏常识的"、"稀里糊涂的"。Billy 为男人名 William 的爱称，billy 即由此而来。原来，Silly Billy 是英国国王威廉四世 (William IV, 1765–1837) 的绰号。本条主要是女性用语，语调轻松，令人有亲切的感觉。*You silly billy. Of course I remember today's your birthday.* 你这个小傻瓜。我当然记得今天是你的生日呀！也写作 a silly Billy。 → a DUMBHEAD ◇ a stupid person

bin

a loony bin [ə ˈlu(ː)ni ˌbɪ(ː)n] [话] **精神病院** loony 是"疯子"、"狂人"的意思。将 lunatic [lunətɪk] (狂人)的 lun 加 -y 而制成的俚语，也有时缀作 luny。bin 原意为"大贮藏箱"。两者合在一起，就成为"装精神失常的人们的大贮藏箱"亦即"疯人院(精神病院)"了。*His father's in a loony bin someplace.* 他的父亲在某个地方的疯人院里。这是正经的用法，但在表示这一意义时多用笑谈的口气。*That guy and his crazy ideas. He ought to be put in the loony bin.* 那个家伙总是一脑子千奇百怪的思想，应该把他送进精神病院啦。◇ an insane asylum

binge

go on a binge [ˌgouɔ(:)nə ˈbɪ(:)ndʒ] [口] **纵酒** binge 意为"(毫无顾忌地、过度地)浸沉在……中",按一般的上下文,系指"泡在酒里"。有的是一个人坐在家里静静地独饮,也有的是一大群人到外边吵吵闹闹地去痛饮,但是中心意义则是"喝酒喝到非常愚蠢的程度"。因此,一般带有"不好"乃至批评的意味。go on a binge 包含着"喝起来就没完"、"不能控制自己"的感觉。另外,人们常把 spree 作为此词的同义语,表面上虽然相似,但意义有所不同,这一点请注意。spree 是"(由于着迷而)大手大脚地(有时过度地)去做……"的意思,用于喝酒的场合,go on a SPREE 这一说法不是指"非常愚蠢"或"控制不住",而是强调开怀大饮的乐趣。而 go on a binge 则不同,即便是讲自己、说 We went on a binge. 的时候,也与 We went on a spree. 的意义有差别,多半含有一半反省的心情。可用 real 加强语气。 *Jack doesn't drink much, but every once in a while he goes on a real binge.* 杰克不大喝酒,但是偶尔也暴饮一顿。为了表示 binge 时间之长,可以说 an all- night binge, a two- day binge, a week-long binge 等等。*They went on an all-night binge last night and were all late to work this morning.* 昨天晚上他们灌了一夜猫尿,今天早晨上班全都迟到了。*Dick and Harry went on a two-day binge over the weekend.* 迪克和哈里在周末足足喝了两天酒。另外,与酒没有关系,也用于表示"埋头于……"的意思。在这一场合,一般伴有表示内容的形容词。*Sometimes I go on a whodunit binge for weeks on end.* 有时候,我一连几个星期埋头看推理小说。 *Once in a while my wife goes on a shopping binge.* 有时候,我的妻子如疯似狂地出去买东西。◇ indulge in too much drinking / indulge *oneself* in unrestrained ~ reading (etc.) [in unrestrained ~ing]

bird

(a) bird colonel → COLONEL

A bird in hand is worth two in the bush. [ə ˌbəːrdnˈhæːnd ɪzwə(:)rθ ˌtu(:)ɪnðəˈbu(:)ʃ] [谚] **天上的仙鹤不如手中的麻雀** 直译为"手中的一只鸟,其价值与树丛中的两只鸟相等"。古时,英格兰也有一条谚语: Better one bird in hand than ten in the wood. 本条的提法,据云源出塞万提斯 (Cervantes) 的《堂吉诃德》(*Don Quixote*, 1605) 一书的英译本。*I think we should accept their offer. It's true that we might get higher bids later, but a bird in hand is worth two in the bush.* 我认为我们应该接受他们的条件。的确,我们以后也许会卖上更高的价钱,但是天上的仙鹤不如手中的麻雀啊。hand 也可以加定冠词作 in the hand。*Mr. Lyot may not be a prince charming, but I'd accept his offer of marriage if I were you. After all, you're not getting any younger, and a bird in the hand is worth two in the bush.* 李奥先生可能不是一个理想的心上人,但是如果我是你的话,我会同意跟他结婚的。不管怎样,你的年纪已经不太小啦,天上的仙鹤不如手中的麻雀啊! 如下面的例句所示,也可以采取非正规的形式,将 bird 变换成其他的名词。*I've decided to enter the Ohio State University. After all, a degree in hand from there is worth two or three top-ranked university degrees in the bush.* 我已经决定入俄亥俄州立大学啦。不管怎样,从那里得一个学位总比妄想从一流大学得两三个学位有把握。◇ It is better to accept less than one may hope for now rather than risk getting nothing later.

an early bird [ə ˈnəːrli ˌbəːrd] [话] **早起、早来或早干活的人** → The early BIRD catches the worm.

The early bird catches the worm. [ðɪ ˌəːrliˈbəːrd ˌkætʃəzðə ˈwəːrm] [谚] **早起必有三分利** 这是一条谚语,原意"早起的鸟可以捉住虫子"。在英语中多少含有一些竞争意识,即"不早早起来前去,所想要的东西就会被别人拿走"。*I always get up at five-thirty. I believe in the old saying, "The early bird catches the worm."* 我每天都是在五点半钟起床。我相信古老的格言"早起必有三分利"。在

英语方面,使用方法也比较广泛,不仅指“早起的人”,也可以指“开会、上班等比规定时刻来得早的人”或“在工作、生意中比别人先下手、行动快的人”。在这一场合,含有“先下手为强”或“先发制人”的意味。*My appointment isn't until three, but I plan to get there an hour early. The early bird catches the worm, you know.* 约会是三点钟,但是我打算提前一小时到达那里,这叫做先发制人嘛。在会话中,也常用 gets the worm 代替 catches the worm。 *A: How come you got such good seats? B: Haven't you heard? The early bird gets the worm.* 甲:你怎么弄到那么好的席位呢? 乙:你没听说过吗? 这叫做捷足先登啊! 也有下面这样的变形。*I realize that March may seem a bit early to start looking for a summer job, but it's always the early bird that gets the worm.* 我明白,三月就开始找夏季的工作,这也许早了一些,但是不论什么时候总是先下手为强啊! 也可以单独使用 early bird, 意指“早起的人”、“早来[干]的人”。*My husband is an early bird. He's always up by six.* 我的丈夫是个早起的人。他总是在六点钟左右起床。 *Our office doesn't open till ten, but Bert is an early bird. He's always there by nine-thirty.* 我们公司十点钟才开始营业,可是伯特来得早。他每天总是九点半必到。◇ The person who gets up [arrives, acts] early is the one who meets with success.

eat like a bird [ˌiːtlaɪkə ˈbəːrd] [口] **饭量极小** 实际上按照体重的比例,(小鸟)吃食可谓狼吞虎咽,但是,如果我们说 eat like a bird, 那就意味着“一个人的饭量竟和小鸟吃的东西一样多”了。这一习用语具有“惯常”的语意,因而一般不用于仅仅一天没有胃口的场合。*Sally eats like a bird.* 萨莉的饭量极小。 *I'm worried about Mr. Wrenn. He's been eating like a bird recently.* 我很为雷恩先生担忧,他最近总吃不下饭。◇ eat very little

be (as) free as a bird [əz ˈfri(ː)əzə ˈbəːrd] [话] **象小鸟一样自由** 字面意义是“象小鸟一样完全自由自在”,一般表示“好象从笼子里放了出来似地,摆脱某种束缚”的状态。*After having spent almost a year in detention during his trial, Jed could hardly believe that now he was as free as a bird.* 杰德在受审期间被拘留将近一年,他几乎不敢相信自己现在已经象小鸟一样自由了。 *My divorce became final last week. Now I'm free as a bird.* 上个星期,我的离婚终于办好啦。现在我象小鸟一样自由了。如果要表达精神解放的感觉,则用 feel (as) free as a bird。 *Having finally paid off the last of my debts, I felt as free as a bird.* 刚刚还完了最后的债,我觉得如释重负,一身轻松。 *When I finished my entrance exams, I felt as free as a bird.* 当结束了入学考试的时候,我感到无比的轻松。◇ be completely free

birds

the birds and the bees [ðə ˈbəːrdznðə ˈbiːz] [口] **性的知识** 在向孩子们说明性行为或与此有关的生理现象时使用的委婉的说法。因人们常以“鸟”和“蜂”作例子来谈性的知识,故云。成年人在开玩笑或转弯抹角地说话时也使用。*Come here, Timmy. It's about time I told you about the birds and the bees.* 到这儿来,蒂米。我该向你讲一讲有关性的知识啦。 *I didn't know anything about the birds and the bees until I got married.* 结婚以前,我对性的知识是一无所知呀。◇ sex

be for the birds [fərðə ˈbəːrdz] [话] **无聊得很** 这一表达法原来的构思是“这个东西(=主语)也许能够满足忽东忽西飞翔的小鸟,对于人来说,那就差得太远了”。常含有轻蔑的意味。*History is for the birds.* 历史太没有意思啦。 *Marriage is for the birds, if you ask me. I plan to stay single all my life.* 如果你叫我说的话,结婚简直无聊得很。我打算一生保持独身。 *That guy is for the birds. He's* *always coming up with "great" ideas that never work.* 那个家伙实在无聊极了。他总是怀有"伟大的"思想,却没有一个顶用。 *That writer's novels are for the birds.* 那位作家所写的小说简直无聊透顶。◇ be not worthy of serious consideration

kill two birds with one stone [ˌkɪl ˌtuːˈbəːrdz wɪð ˌwʌnˈstoun] [口] **一举两得** 直译是"用一块石头打下来两只鸟",与汉语成语"一箭双雕"的概念相同。 *If I go to New York on Friday, I can kill two birds with one stone. I can go to the doctor's and visit my mother all on the same day.* 如果我在星期五去纽约,就能一举两得,既能去看医生,又能在同一天去看望我的母亲。◇ accomplish two things at the same time [with only one effort]

birthday

in *one's* **birthday suit** → SUIT

biscuit

a biscuit [ə ˈbɪskət] [口] **热松饼** → a horse BISCUIT

a dog biscuit [ə ˈdɔːg ˌbɪskət] [口] **犬用饼** → a horse BISCUIT

a horse biscuit [əˈhɔ(ː)rs ˌbɪskət] [话] **马粪** biscuit 在英国英语中是"饼干",但在美国英语中,"饼干"叫做 cookie, 而 biscuit 则为加黄油、猪油等脂肪烤制的一种卷面包。"马粪"称为 horse biscuit 是由其形状而来,即"马制作的卷面包"的意思。这是个诙谐的说法,但也是一种婉曲的表达。*In the age before automobiles, horse biscuits were a big urban pollution problem.* 在汽车出现之前的时代,马粪是城市污染的一大问题。顺便提一下,如果说 a dog biscuit, 那可不是"狗粪",而是为了喂狗而把谷物、肉、骨头等的粉末混在一起烤制的硬饼,特请注意。◇ (a piece of) horse dung

bit

champ at the bit [ˌtʃæ(ː)mpətðə ˈbɪ(ː)t] [口] **(因行动受制约而)焦急** bit 是马具"嚼子"。直译为"(马振奋起来)咬嚼子"。骑马用语。按字面意义可以这样使用: *After a full night's rest, the horses were champing at the bit to be on the way again.* 充分休息了一晚上之后,那些马又振奋起来,准备重赴征程了。在作比喻使用的场合,多以人为主语。就象马愿意早早出发而主人不骑它跑的情况一样,在"(被什么东西压制而)心急如焚"的场合使用。多用进行时。*Let's leave for the beach early today. The children are already champing at the bit.* 今天咱们早点儿到海滨去吧。孩子们已经急得不耐烦啦。 *After three postponements of the space flight, the astronauts were champing at the bit.* 宇宙飞行已经推迟三次了,宇航员们心急如焚。 *The sales manager is champing at the bit because the boss hasn't approved his plan to enlarge the sales campaign.* 由于总经理还没有批准他的扩大推销活动的计划,销售经理急得象热锅上的蚂蚁一样。◇ be impatient (to *do something*)

bite

Someone's **bark is worse than** *his* **bite.** → BARK

bite off more than *one* **can chew** [ˈbaɪˈdɔːf morðən ~ kənˈtʃuː] [口] **力不胜任** 字面意义是"要嚼比所能嚼碎的更多的东西"。bite 是用前齿"往下咬", chew 是用后齿"嚼"。请从下面的例句体会这一习用语的意思吧。*I advise you not to try to work at a full-time job and go to school at the same time. You'll be biting off more than you can chew.* 我劝你不要干全天的工作同时又上学。这你会疲于奔命的。 *In trying to build a house by myself, I bit off more than I could chew.* 我试图自己动手盖一所房子,结果是力不胜任啦。 *Lou was successful as a small-time criminal, but when he got involved with the Mafia, he found he had bitten off more than he could chew.* 卢干个小偷小摸之类是很顺手的,但是当他跟黑手党搞在一起的时候,他感到自己已经力不从心了。*Don't mess with me, buddy. You're biting off more than you can chew.* 你不要对我指手划脚,小兄

第。你还差得远着哪! ◇ attempt more than *one* can handle

I'll bite. ['aɪl .baɪt] [话] **(对于质问、丝毫不加考虑地回答)不明白** 在这里，bite 是"鱼去吃食饵"。本条直译为"我象鱼去吃食饵那样去做"。也就是这样的构思："(对于急着叫人听答案的人说)我满足你的希望,洗耳恭听你的答案"。多用于猜迷以及回避无聊的、轻浮的质问的场合。 *A: Do you know what one strawberry said to the other? B: I'll bite. What? A: If you hadn't been so fresh, we wouldn't be in this jam.* 甲:你知道一个草莓对另一个草莓说了什么? 乙:不知道呀。说了什么? 甲:如果你不是那么新鲜,我们也不会这样成为果酱了。这是一种俏皮话,甲的回答包含着可以称之为"谜底"的东西,别有意义。原来 fresh (新鲜)另有一义是"莽撞", jam (果酱)另有一义是"窘境",因此,全句的意义可以解释为:如果你不是那么莽撞,我们还不至于陷入这样的窘境哪! 不管是谜语也好,或是普通的质问也好,回答的人常有"认真考虑太无聊啦"或者"考虑这个太费劲啦"的心情。 *She: Do you know where I think we should go on our vacation this summer, dear? He: All right, I'll bite. Where?* 她:亲爱的,今年的暑假,你知道我想咱们到哪里去吗? 他:哎呀,我不知道。哪里? 特别是对下面这样无聊的质问, I'll bite. 可能是最恰当的回答。 *A: Do you know what I'd do if I had a million dollars? B: I'll bite. What would you do if you had a million dollars?* 甲:如果我有了一百万美金,你知道我要干什么? 乙:我不知道。如果你有了一百万美金,你要干什么呢? ◇ I don't know. / Tell me.

put the bite on *someone* (for *something*) [.putðə 'baɪ.dɔ(:)n ~] [话] **叫(某人)出钱** bite 是"咬"。本条字面意义是"为了得到(某物)而咬(某人)"。例如,象下面这样使用: *Don't worry about the money. I'll put the bite on my old man.* 不要担心钱。我会叫我爸爸出的。 *I tried to put the bite on my brother for part of the bill, but he didn't have any money, either.* 我想叫我弟弟付一部分钱,但是他也没带着什么钱。虽然同样是叫对方出钱,但这一习用语在使用时,根据上下文而有意义上的差别,既可以是"借钱"、"强制叫人出钱",也可以是"用威胁手段抢钱"或"敲竹杠"。究竟应该如何解释,一切只能根据上下文判断,别无他法。 *That guy's always trying to put the bite on me for carfare home.* 那个家伙每次回家都要向我借钱付汽车费。 *Don't let Bill put the bite on you. He'll never pay you back.* 你不要把钱借给比尔。他是绝对不会还你的。下面可以说是"强制叫人出钱"的例句。 *The government is planning to put the bite on the taxpayers for twenty billion more in taxes.* 政府正在计划叫纳税人多交纳二百亿美元的税。下面是"敲竹杠"。 *When the gang discovered Mr. Edon's dark past, they began to put the bite on him for a thousand dollars a month.* 那帮家伙发现艾顿先生有见不得人的历史,就开始每个月敲他一千美元的竹杠。 ◇ get *someone* to pay (*something*) / borrow [extort] (*something*) from *someone*

bitter

be a bitter pill (for *someone*) **to swallow** → PILL

blab

blab ['blæ:b] [口] **泄漏(秘密等)** 有故意泄漏的场合,也有由于轻率或不注意而泄露的场合。因此,当说 *Carl is blabbing your secret to everyone in the office.* 卡尔正在向单位的每个人泄漏你的秘密哪! 的时候,只凭这句话不能判断卡尔究竟是由于怀恨在心而故意讲的呢,还是只因轻率而随便云云呢? 象下边这个例句: *He must be taking revenge on you for insulting him last week.* 一定是由于上个礼拜你侮辱了他,他在进行报复哪。有了来龙去脉,才明白是故意干的。如果是轻率或不注意的结果,就会形成这样的句子: *He should know better than to be so indiscreet.* 他应该知道一个人不能那么轻率啊。 *Don't tell Olivia. She'll blab it all over town.* 不要告诉奥莉维亚。她会向全城的人乱讲的。奥莉维亚究竟是故意地散布呢,还是她仅仅是一位喜欢东家长西家短乱说的人呢?只凭这个句子是不能了解的。下面两个例句,可以了解显然是故意的。*If the police catch Frankie, he's sure to blab.* 如果警察抓住弗兰基,他一定会坦白交待的。 *You'd better not blab to the teacher about what we did.* 你千万不要向老师汇报我们所干的事情。blab 的人是 a blabber ['blæːbər],多用于表示"故意地"而不是"轻率地"讲不相宜的话的人。*Better not tell my little brother about it. He's a real blabber.* 这件事最好不要对我弟弟讲。他马上会传出去的。◇ tell (*something* to *someone*) / talk / tell (*someone*)

a blabber [ə 'blæːbər] [口] **泄漏秘密等的人** → BLAB

blabber ['blæ(ː)bər] [口] **说话不知所云** 原意是"(婴儿)咿咿呀呀",如 *The baby lay in its crib, blabbering away to itself.* 婴儿躺在摇篮里,咿咿呀呀自言自语。后来转用到成年人身上。*Don't listen to Joe. He's always blabbering about something he doesn't know anything about.* 不要听乔讲话。他总是对自己丝毫也不了解的事情信口开河,瞎白乎一顿。*Let's not invite that guy to make a speech. He'll just blabber on and on about how Democracy is the hope of the world.* 咱们不要请那个家伙来讲演吧。他总是不知所云地讲什么只有民主才能拯救世界之类的话,絮絮叨叨没完。如这两个例句所示,一般是就讲话的内容而言。但也有象下面例句那样用于说话方式的场合。*Caught off guard by his question, I was barely able to blabber out a reply.* 抽冷子被他一问,我竭尽全力胡乱地回答了一番。有时 blabber 作为名词使用,意为"不知所云的话"。*I can't stand that woman's blabber.* 我忍受不了那个女人絮絮叨叨的话。◇ talk (incoherently) / stutter [mutter]

blabbermouth

a blabbermouth [ə 'blæ(ː)bərˌmauθ] [话] **多嘴多舌的人** 从语源上说是动词 BLABBER 与 mouth 的复合词,但从意义上说则是动词 BLAB (→) + mouth,这样考虑比较容易理解。一般指"由于爱说话而漫不经心地泄漏了秘密的人",不大用于表示"故意散布秘密的人"的意思。*You blabbermouth! Didn't I tell you it was a secret!* 你这个多嘴多舌的家伙!我没告诉你那是个秘密吗! *Don't tell that blabbermouth anything you don't want everyone in town to know.* 凡是你不愿意弄得满城风雨的事情,千万不要告诉那个多嘴多舌的家伙。有时象下一例句那样,与秘密毫无关系,仅用于表示"爱说话的人"的意思。*I'll admit that Rich can keep a secret. But he's still a blabbermouth.* 我承认里奇能够保密。尽管如此,他的确是一个爱说话的人。◇ talk too much / a(n indiscreet) talker

black

the black sheep of the family → SHEEP

give *someone* [*something*] **a black eye** → EYE

in black and white [ɪn 'blæ(ː)kən'*h*waɪt] [口]**白纸黑字** 字面意义是"以黑与白"。"黑"表示"墨","白"表示"纸"。换句话说,就是"规规矩矩写出",大多用于表示"(不只口头上,而)写成正式字据"的意思。*You shouldn't pay any money until you get the contract in black and white.* 在你得到白纸黑字的合同之前,你连一分钱也不要付。put *something* (down) in black and white 是一个固定的说法,意思是"写成正式字据"。down 的用处是调整语调,有时加、有时不加。*I agree that their offer is too good to be true. I won't believe it until they put it (down) in black and white.* 我也是认为他们提出的条件太好了,不写成白纸黑字,我是不敢相信的。同样,see it (down) in black and white 也是固定了的形式,意思是"见到写成正式字据"。*Yes, their offer is very good, but tell them I want to see it (down) in black and white.* 是的,他们所提出的条件非常好,但是,请转告他们要写成白纸黑字,我是不见兔子不撒鹰的。除了"写成正式字据"的意义外,还

有以下的使用方法。*Of course it's true. Look at the morning paper. It's right there in black and white.* 当然那是真的。你看看早上的报纸呀！白纸黑字写得一清二楚。*It was too good to be true, but there it was in black and white. We had won ten million dollars in the lottery.* 事情太好啦，简直不敢相信是真的。可是，白纸黑字印得很清楚啊，我们买的彩票中了一千万美元的奖。另外，in black and white 还有一个"用单色"的意义。*Most movies used to be in black and white.* 过去的电影片大部分是黑白片。*Was that movie in color or black and white?* 那部影片是彩色的还是黑白的？◇ (clearly) in writing

Black Maria

a Black Maria [ə ˌblæk məˈraɪə] [话] 囚车 → a paddy WAGON

blank

draw a blank [ˌdrɔ(:)ə ˈblæ(:)ŋk] [口] **落空** 字面意义是"抽个空签"。*I had hoped to win something in the lottery, but I drew a blank.* 我曾希望买彩票捞点什么，可是我抽了空签。转作比喻使用，意思是"做某事原指望如何如何，结果却等于零[被否定]。" *I've asked Mary three times for a date, but each time I've drawn a blank.* 我已经向玛丽提出三回约期幽会了，但是每一次都落了空。在"找东西落了空"的场合也常使用，亦即"找不到"的意思。*I looked all over the house for the book, but I drew a blank.* 我找那本书，在屋子里都翻遍了，可是没有找到。下面的例句是"在记忆中搜寻，但是落了空"，亦即"想不出来"的意思。*I should remember his name, but I just draw a blank.* 我应该记得他的名字，但是怎么也想不起来了。◇ obtain a negative result

blanket

throw a wet blanket on *something* [ˌθrouə ˌwetˈblæ(:)ŋkəˌdɔ(:)n ~] [话] **泼冷水** 字面意义是"把湿毛毯扔到某物上。" *He threw a wet blanket on the fire to put it out.* 他为了扑灭火，把一条湿毛毯扔了上去。用作比喻的时候，在美国人的头脑里首先想到的是 throw a wet blanket on a party (向社交集会泼冷水)，也就是 on 的后面代入 party 一词。*Olivia threw a wet blanket on the party when she said she was going home if the boys didn't watch their language.* 奥莉维亚说，如果男青年们说话不检点，她就要告辞回家了，这使社交集会大为扫兴。不过，这一表达法的使用面很广，除上述用法外，在谈到如 plan (计划)，enthusiasm (热忱)，atmosphere (气氛)，hope (希望) 等等时也可以使用。*I'm afraid the weatherman has thrown a wet blanket on our plans to go hiking tomorrow.* 我看，天气预报员使我们明天出去远足的计划告吹了。*My father's negative attitude threw a wet blanket on our enthusiasm.* 父亲的否定态度给我们的热情泼了一瓢冷水。此外，还有一个意味着"给……泼冷水"的动词 wet-blanket，实际上几乎完全没人使用。*The boss's sour mood wet- blanketed the atmosphere of the meeting.* 老板的一脸官司降低了会议的气氛。象这样的用法不能说是没有，但是，即便在这一场合，一般也是使用 throw a wet blanket on ～的形式。◇ put a damper on *something*

a wet blanket [ə ˈwet ˈblæ(:)ŋkət] [话] **使大家扫兴的人** 这一表达法的来源是：当发生火灾的时候，为了把火扑灭，用水浸湿毛毯 (wet blanket) 盖到火上。给人的印象是："把呼啦一下子着起来的火立即扑灭"。wet blanket 的基本意义是："当一个集会的气氛正在不断热烈起来的时候，以言语行动去泼冷水而使大家扫兴的人"。指在社交晚会等热闹场中愁眉苦脸的人、早早退席的人、以及在游戏时有同伴相约也不参加甚至泼冷水的人，等等。实际上，指这几类人而言的场合占压倒多数。*I'm sorry to be such a wet blanket, but I'm afraid I have to go home now.* 我使大家扫兴，实在太对不起了。不过，我现在必须回家啦。*Let's not invite Doris to the party. She's such a wet blanket.* 不要请多丽丝参加社交晚会，她总爱使大家扫兴。关于邀请不去的人，使用方法如下：*Don't be a wet blanket, Sid. Everyone else is going. Why won't you?* 锡德，不要扫大家的兴吧。其他的人全去，你为什么不去呢？ *C'mon, Ralph. Everyone else is drinking. Why be a wet blanket?* 来一杯，拉尔夫。除了你，人人都在开怀痛饮，你干嘛扫大家的兴呢？从以上的例句可以看出，同 be 动词一起使用的时候多，当然也有单独使用的场合。 *Let's not invite that wet blanket.* 咱们不要邀请那个扫人兴的家伙。意思相近的习用语有 a party-pooper [ˈpɑ(ː)rdi.pu(ː)pər]。这个词的原意为"在社交晚会中最先退席，给晚会的热烈气氛泼冷水的人"，但在现在几乎与 wet blanket 的意义同样广泛，所有场合大致都能代换。 *Don't be a party-pooper [wet blanket], Jim. It's still only ten o'clock.* 不要扫大家的兴吧，吉姆。刚刚十点钟，还早着哪！ → a KILLJOY ◇ a party dampener

bleed

bleed *someone* **white** → WHITE

blessing

a blessing in disguise [ə .blesɪŋ ɪndəsˈgaɪz] [口] **因祸得福** blessing 的意思是"应该祝福"、"应该高兴"、"应该感谢"等等。in disguise 的字面意义是"伪装"，也就是"只从外表看不明白"。把二者加在一起，就成为"本来是应该祝福的事情，但是只从外表看不明白"，无论从原来的构思或使用的情况来讲，都与汉语成语的"因祸得福"或"塞翁失马焉知非福"十分相似。*Our son's automobile accident turned out to be a blessing in disguise. The man who ran into him was a company president who offered him a good job.* 我们的儿子发生汽车事故，结果却因祸得福了。撞他的人是一位公司总裁，他给了他一份很好的工作。 *The doctor says that my husband's broken leg should be looked on as a blessing in disguise since it will force him to take a long-needed rest.* 据医生说，我的丈夫的腿骨骨折实在值得庆幸，因为这迫使他不得不做好久以前就有必要的休息了。◇ a fortuitous calamity

blind

be (as) blind as a bat → BAT

a blind date → DATE

blink

be on the blink [ɔ(ː)nðə ˈblɪŋk] [话] **发生故障** blink 是个动词，意为"眨眼"或是"(电灯)一明一灭"。把它当名词，再加上 on the ～，就成为处于那种状态了，也就是"不是连续地顺利运转、有时停止不动"的意思。原义为"不能很好地动"或"动作不顺利"，现在则与 broken 或者 not working 等同样，也使用于"完全失去机能"的场合，或者使用于"动动停停、多少有点毛病"的场合。*Our refrigerator is on the blink. The motor has completely stopped.* 我家的冰箱发生故障了。马达完全不转啦。 *My TV is on the blink. Some days it works fine, but others I can only get three stations.* 我的电视机出毛病了。有几天完全正常，但又有几天我只能收到三个台。如以上的例句所示，经常在谈到机械之类的东西时使用，但也有时用于身体的情况，特别是胃的舒适与否。*My stomach is on the blink today. Must be something I ate.* 今天我的胃很难受。一定是吃什么东西吃坏啦。另外，也用 go on the blink 表示"发生故障"、"出了毛病"的意思。*The generator went on the blink again.* 发电机又出毛病啦。◇ not work (properly) / be upset

bliss

wedded bliss [ˈwedəd ˈblɪs] [口] **极端幸福的婚姻生活** wedded 是"结婚"之意。bliss 是"天堂幸福"、"神赐天福"等含有宗教意味的表达法，为一般所常用。但是在 wedded bliss 的场合，bliss 并没有宗教的色彩，仅仅是"无比幸福"的意思。两个词合在一起，便成为"极端幸福的婚姻生活"。然而，不可否认，这一表达法有夸张的调子和陈腐之感，因而，如 *Their home is a picture of wedded bliss.* 他们的家庭是一幅美满姻缘的图景。这一例句所示,也有认真按照“极端幸福的婚姻生活”的意思使用的情况,但一般来说,以诙谐的、讽刺的口气使用的时候比较多。*My wife and I have enjoyed twelve years of wedded bliss interspersed with fights just about every other day.* 我们两口子享受了十二年极端幸福的婚姻生活,中间点缀着几乎每隔一天就要有一次的争吵。◇ an extremely happy married life

block

a chip off the old block → CHIP

knock *someone's* **block off** [ˌnɑ(:)k ~ ˈblɑ(:)ˌkɔ:f] [话] **敲脑袋** block 为俗语,意思是“脑袋”。整个条头的意味的是“把脑袋一下子打掉”。*If you call me names again, I'll knock your block off.* 如果你再说我的坏话,我要敲你的脑袋。*A: Did he hit you hard? B: I'll say! He almost knocked my block off.* 甲:他打你打得很厉害吗? 乙:还不厉害哪?! 他简直要把我的脑袋敲掉啦! 如以上两例所示,这是儿童们常用的表达法。大人说也是可以的,不过略微显得幼稚。有时用“人”以外的东西作主语。*A flower pot fell out of the window and pretty near knocked my block off.* 一个花盆从窗台上掉了下来,差一点儿没敲掉我的脑袋。◇ hit *someone* so hard *he* feels *his* head has come off

blockhead

a blockhead [ə ˈblɑ(:)kˌhe(:)d] [话] **笨蛋** block 是“(用木、石、混凝土等制成的)立方体”,在这里具有“木块”的感觉,也就是说:不是脑子,而是“用木块制成的头”。汉语俗语也说“木头脑袋”,意思相同。比起 a DUMBHEAD (→)来语气更强。*You blockhead! Now you've ruined all our carefully laid plans!* 你这大笨蛋! 你现在把我们精心制定的计划全都给毁啦! 如此例所示,特别是在当面骂人笨蛋的时候使用得多。◇ a stupid person

blood

bad blood [ˈbæ:dˈblʌ(:)d] [口] **消除不掉的恶感** 多用于以前有过纠纷、相互不睦、长期耿耿于怀的状况。从深恶痛绝直到略感不快,“恶感”的程度有种种的不同,但是,就此种感情“一直耿耿于怀”这一点来说,则经常是共通的,亦即在感情上有用大道理难以消除的疙瘩。除了作“恶感”解外,根据上下文,还分别会有与“讨厌”、“怨恨”、“憎恶”等相近的含义。多使用 there is bad blood between [among] ~的形式。如果用 among,当然是三人以上的场合了。*You'll never get those two men to cooperate. There's too much bad blood between them.* 你永远也没办法使那两个家伙合作。他们之间的积怨太深,无法消除。*For some reason, there has been bad blood between Ted and Dick ever since they were small children.* 不知怎么回事,特德和迪克从很小的时候起就互相不睦,积怨难除。还有一个 *they* have bad blood between [among] ~的形式。*Jane and Mary have had bad blood between them ever since last year when Tom threw Mary over for Jane.* 自从去年汤姆甩了玛丽而与简要好以来,简与玛丽就相互憎恨起来了。也常有结合 make for 或 cause 使用的情况。*The disagreement made for [caused] a lot of bad blood among them.* 由于意见不合,他们之间产生了相当多的恶感。还有 bad blood with *someone* (与某人之间的恶感)的形式。*The last thing I need is bad blood with my wife's father.* 我可不想跟我的岳父闹翻。◇ bad feelings ((is → are / has → have / too much → too many))

Blood is thicker than water. [ˈblʌdəz ˌθɪkərðən ˈwɔ:dər] [谚] **血浓于水** 17 世纪产生于英国、随后不久即在美洲广为流传的格言。*Why shouldn't Dad hire Cousin Jed instead of some stranger? The stranger may have better qualifications, but blood is thicker than water, you know.* 爸爸为什么不雇用表哥杰德,而用外人呢? 外人的条件也许更好一些,但是俗话说得好:胳膊总是向里弯啊。*I'll tell you why you shouldn't take sides with Ralph against your own brother.*

Because blood is thicker than water, that's why. 我告诉你为什么你不该站在拉尔夫一边反对你自己的哥哥。原因就是:自家人总得向着自家人呀。*I realize you don't care much for your uncle, but he needs your help now more than Mr. Smith does. And, after all, blood is thicker than water.* 我了解你不大喜欢你的叔叔,不过,他现在比史密斯先生更需要你的帮助。无论如何,自家人应该向着自家人嘛。◇ Blood relations are more important than outsiders.

something **gets in (to)** *someone's* **blood** [～ˌgetsən(tə)～ ˈblʌ(:)d] [口] **上瘾** 字面意义是:"某种东西进入某人的血液"。比"热心去干"、"已经着迷"更进一步,而是"成为自己身体的一部分",因此,这是一个带有"离不开"的感觉的表达法。也有讲"一次经验"的场合,但一般来说,是用于"反复多次"的场合。究竟用 into 还是用 in,要根据说话的语调来确定,但在日常会话中用 in 的时候多。*It's all right to gamble once in a while, but you mustn't let it get in your blood.* 偶然赌博一次也没有什么坏处,但是你可不能迷上它啊。*Once sailing gets into a man's blood he can never get it out.* 玩帆船一旦上了瘾,就欲罢不能了。把条头的形式变化一下,也可以使用 get *something* in(to) *one's* blood, be something that gets in(to) *someone's* blood, 或 have *something* in *one's* blood 等形式。*He got skiing in his blood at a very early age.* 他从很年轻的时候起就迷上滑雪运动了。*Mountain climbing is something that gets in your blood.* 爬山成了习惯,是欲罢不能的。*My husband loves newspaper work. He's got it in his blood.* 我的丈夫热爱新闻工作,他乐此不疲。下面的例句不是讲继续不辍,而是谈到现在已经中断的事情。*I haven't been skin diving for a long time, but I plan to return to it someday. I've got it in my blood.* 我好久没有穿潜水服潜泳了,但是我计划哪一天还要去潜泳。我对此已经入迷啦。◇ become obsessed with [captivated by] *something* ((never get it out → never give it up))

make *someone's* **blood boil** [ˌmeɪk ～ ˈblʌd ˌbɔɪl] [话] **使人大为恼火** 字面意义是"使某人的血沸腾",但这不是"由于兴奋而兴高采烈",而是"由于恼怒而怒火中烧"。有的词典把它译成"使激怒",但这一表达法并非表示怒形于色的状态,而是以反映内在感情、心理现象为重点。*Mr. Shakaleg's dancing for hours with all the pretty girls made his wife's blood boil.* 沙卡雷格先生一连几小时总跟漂亮的姑娘跳舞,这使他的夫人连肺都气炸了。*The thought of that guy's becoming a millionaire by selling my invention makes my blood boil.* 一想到那个家伙靠出卖我的发明而变成百万富翁,我简直连肺都气炸了。*Seeing politicians ride around in big cars while there are people without enough to eat makes my blood boil.* 我一看到政治家们坐着豪华的汽车到处转,而有很多人连饭都吃不饱,心里就感到非常气愤。◇ make *someone* extremely angry

make *someone's* **blood run cold** [ˌmeɪk～ ˈblʌˌrʌ(:)n ˌkould] [口] **令人毛骨悚然** 逐字翻译是"(恐怖等)使人血冷下来",这种感觉是容易体会的。"令人毛骨悚然"的主体有的是"听了可怕的声音或故事",例如:*The sound of footsteps behind me in the darkened hallway made my blood run cold.* 在黑暗的门厅里,身后的脚步声使我毛骨悚然。*Mrs. Frost is a cruel woman. The way she talks about her invalid grandfather makes my blood run cold.* 弗罗斯特太太是一个残酷的女人。我听到她怎样谈论她那已经瘫痪的祖父的时候,简直起了一身鸡皮疙瘩。也有的如下边的例句那样,是"见了可怕的情景"。另外,在强调表达"恐怖"的程度时,也可以根据情况,译成"吓死我了"之类的比较贴切的口语。*Seeing the body on the floor with a knife in its back made my blood run cold.* 见到地上的尸体,背上插进一把刀子,这简直把我吓得魂都出了窍。◇ be terrifying [gruesome]

sweat blood [ˌswet ˈblʌ(ː)d] [话] **苦得要命** 直译:“使出血汗”。主要意义是“(为了做什么而)非常劳苦”,但其中常多少含有“忧虑”的意味。有人说这一表达法源出《圣经·新约》中的《路加传》(Luke)第22章44节: And being in an agony he prayed more earnestly; and his sweat became great drops of blood falling down upon the ground. (耶稣极其伤痛,祷告更加恳切;汗珠如大血点,滴在地上。) *I sweat blood in order to finish that report in time for today's meeting.* 为了赶上今天的会议,我忙着写那份报告,简直叫人苦死了。*I sweat blood helping that guy get a job, and he didn't even thank me.* 我千辛万苦去给那小子找工作,而他连一个谢字都不说。如以上例句所示,在表示“苦得要命”的意义时,多采取 sweat blood +不定式(或动名词)的形式,但如下例的说法也很自然。 *You spend too much time sweating blood for money. Don't you know that the best things in life are free?* 你为了捞钱千辛万苦,浪费了太多的时间。难道你不晓得人生中最宝贵的东西是不能用金钱买到的吗? sweat blood 也有象下面例句那样,使用于因有所担心而焦急等待的情况。在这一场合就不是“苦得要命”,仅仅是 be extremely anxious (即“由于惦念而坐立不安”)的意思而已。*What do you mean, I don't care whether you live or die! I sweat blood while you were in that operating room.* 你说我不关心你的死活,这简直是胡说八道! 当你在手术室里的时候,我一直在担心,坐不稳站不安啊。*After one engine stopped, we all sweat blood until the plane landed safely.* 有一个发动机不转的时候,我们在飞机安全降落以前,人人都焦急得坐立不安。◇ work extremely hard / be filled with anxiety

bloody

bloody but unbowed [ˈblʌdi bəˌdʌnˈbaud] [口] **决不屈服** W. E. Henry 因肺结核住医院时曾作诗“Invictus”(1888年),其中有一句是 Under the bludgeoning of chance, my head is bloody but unbowed. (命运的大棒打得我头破血出,但是我决不屈服。) 本条即源于此。在当时,这首诗曾经脍炙人口,一个世纪过去了, bloody but unbowed 作为习用语,依然非常流行。*At the last round, the challenger advanced to the middle of the ring, bloody but unbowed.* 在最后一轮比赛,挑战者虽然鲜血淋淋也决不屈服,毅然走进拳击场的中央。如这一例句所示,有按照字面意义用以表示“血迹斑斑”的场合,但一般来说,与上边引用的诗句一样,是作为比喻使用的。*After being struck by the union for ten weeks, management was bloody but unbowed.* 工会进行了十个星期的罢工,资方虽然受到沉重打击,但是没有屈服。近年以来,诙谐的使用方法也多了起来。*My fight with my wife last night left me bloody but unbowed.* 昨天夜里我跟老婆打架,虽然血染战场,但是我并未投降。◇ hurting [weakened, damaged] but refusing to give up

yell bloody murder → MURDER

bloomer

a late bloomer [əˌleɪt ˈbluːmər] [口] **大器晚成** 按照字面意义,如果说 *This flower is a late bloomer.* 那就是 此花在开花季节终了时开。亦即“迟开的花”的意思。这一表达法可以与汉语成语“大器晚成”相对应,但也有一点差别。也就是说,“大器晚成”是指人生几十年的光阴,而 a late bloomer 指的时期比较短,最多五、六年的程度,主要应用于儿童或青年。当然,根据上下文,也有与汉语成语极其相似的用法,如: *Mr. Dally proved to be a late bloomer. No one ever dreamed that he would ever end up as president of the company.* 达利先生可算得上是大器晚成。任何人做梦也没有想到他会当上公司的总裁呀。下面是一般的用例: *Ann was a late bloomer. When she first entered school she did very poorly, but now she makes straight A's.* 安的智能发挥得比较晚。她刚进学校的时候,成绩非常不好,但是现在,她各门课程都是 A。 *Paul was such a slow worker* *at first that we almost fired him, but he proved to be a late bloomer. Now he's one of our most capable men.* 保罗初来的时候是一个非常迟钝的工作人员，我们几乎要开除他，但是他很有潜力，现在成为我们单位最能干的人员之一。◇ (a person who is) late in exhibiting his [her] potential

blotto

blotto ['blɑ(:)dou] [话] **酩酊大醉** 本来是英国英语，在美国并不十分流行，但也有所闻。注意：英国人发音作 ['blɔtəu]。blotto 比 stinking DRUNK 或 STINKO 强烈，具有"直到不省人事"的意味。在这一场合，美国人多使用 dead DRUNK 或 STONED 等。*Fred's blotto. We'd better leave him in the car.* 弗雷德已经酩酊大醉了。我们还是把他留在车里好。虽然是形容词，但只作表语使用。◇ completely drunk

blow

blow (*someplace*) ['blou] [话] **溜之大吉** blow (*someplace*) 的 blow 是一种非常随便的使用方法。形象与 The wind blows. (风吹)的 blow 相近，表示"象风一样走开"的意思。一般使用于因某个场所"没有意思"、"腻了"、"有危险性"而离去的场合。既可作不及物动词，亦可作及物动词。*This is a boring party. Let's blow.* 这个晚会实在叫人腻烦。咱们溜之大吉吧。*When we heard the police sirens approaching, we blew.* 当我们听到警车的警笛越来越近时，我们撒鸭子跑掉了。*Let's blow this place. Maybe there's a better hotel a little farther on.* 我们赶快离开这个地方吧。也许往前走几步会有比较好的旅馆。*It seems the suspects blew town a couple of days ago.* 嫌疑犯似乎两天前就从这个镇溜走了。◇ leave (in a hurry)

blow *money* (on *something*) [ˌblou ~] [话] **挥金如土** 形象是"狂风把钞票刮跑"。是或者为了玩乐，或者为了买自己想要的东西，大手大脚使用金钱时的表达法。专指挥霍、乱花钱。*Martin blew ten thousand dollars on the races yesterday.* 昨天在赛马场，马丁挥霍了一万美元。*You're foolish to blow all your money on a girl.* 你把自己所有的钱都花在一个姑娘身上，真够愚蠢的啦。条头中 *money* 的部分，可用与"钱"划等号的东西代入，如 pay (工资)、savings (储蓄)、inheritance (遗产)等等。*We blew six month's pay on a vacation in Europe last year.* 去年我们在欧洲休假，花掉了半年的工资。*I blew all my savings on this house, but I don't regret it.* 我把所有积蓄的钱都花在这所房子上了，但是我并不后悔。*Jack blew his inheritance on wine, women and song.* 杰克把他所得的遗产全都花在吃喝嫖赌上了。也有 blow *someone* to *something* 的说法，是"毫不吝惜地请客"的意思。这一表达法是 treat (请客)一词的夸大。*C'mon. I'll blow you to a drink.* 来！我豁出钱，咱们喝上一杯吧！如果说 blow *oneself* to *something*，那是"自己请自己"，有"豁出钱来豪华一番"的感觉。*I think I'll blow myself to a steak dinner tonight.* 今天晚上我豁出去了，晚饭来个牛排。◇ spend [squander] money

blow *something* ['blou ~] [话] **化为泡影** *something* 处能代入的是"机会"、"计划"等等。也就是说，本条的字面意义是"把机会等刮跑了"。*Joe blew the whole project by losing the plans on his way to meet our client.* 乔在前去会见我们的主顾时，在半路上把图纸丢了，整个计划全都化为泡影啦。如这一例句所示，一般用于因本人的失败、失误而"使计划告吹"、"使机会白白错过"的场合。*This is your big opportunity to make good. Don't blow it.* 这是你能得到成功的大好机会。可不要白白丢掉。*A: Did you get a date with Betty? B: No, I blew it. I was alone with her for ten minutes, but I couldn't get up the nerve to ask her.* 甲：你向贝蒂约好幽会的事了吗？乙：没有，我自己弄砸了。我跟她单独在一起有十来分钟，但是我没有向她提出来的勇气。*Our team had three great chances to make a touchdown and blew them all.* 我们橄榄球队有三次触地得分的大好机

会,但是都白白地丢掉了。*something* 处代入 *one's* lines (台词)则意为"说错台词",是一个固定的说法。*Just at the most exciting part of the play, Marilyn blew her lines.* 戏正演到最激动人心的场面,玛里琳竟说错了台词。◇ ruin *something* / fail to take advantage of the opportunity

blow *someone* **to** *something* [ˌblou ～ tə' ～] [话] **为某人挥霍一下** → BLOW *money* (on *something*)

b. l. t.

a b. l. t. [ə ˌbi(:)ˌel'ti:] [话] **咸肉、莴苣、番茄夹心面包** b. l. t. 分别是 bacon, lettuce, tomato 三个字的字头。原来是快餐馆等处服务员向厨师传达客人所点的食品时使用的略语,后来客人也使用起来,直至成为一般用语。*I'll have a b. l. t. and a cup of java.* 我要一份"肉茄包"和一杯咖啡。*I got hungry, so I went to the fridge and fixed myself a b. l. t.* 我饿了,所以到冰箱去拿东西,自己制作了一份"肉茄包"。◇ a bacon, lettuce and tomato sandwich

blubber

blubber ['blʌbər] [口] **呜呜地哭** 语源是中世纪英语 blubren (起泡)。*When the boss told Simon he was fired, he suddenly sat down and started blubbering.* 当老板告诉西蒙他已被解雇的时候,西蒙突然坐了下来,开始呜呜哭起来。*I can't get this engagement ring on your finger with you blubbering like that, honey.* 宝贝儿,你这样呜呜地哭,我无法把这订婚戒指给你戴到指头上呀。有时也具有"一边啼泣一边说"的意思。*The lost child blubbered his name.* 迷路的孩子一边呜呜地哭,一边说出自己的名字。◇ cry (loudly)

a tub of blubber [ə ˌtʌbə'blʌbər] [话] **肥粗胖大** tub 是"大桶", blubber 是"鲸鱼油"。本条的构思与 a tub of LARD 相同,是"胖得象一篓油似的"的意思。*Tim is real tub of blubber. A little more and he won't be able to get through the door.* 蒂姆简直肥得象一篓油。再胖一点儿,连房门都走不过去了。◇ (an) obese (person) ((real → really))

blubberhead

a blubberhead [ə 'blʌbərˌhe(:)d] [话] **糊涂虫** 这里的 blubber 是"鲸鱼油"。本条的构思与 a FATHEAD 相同,亦即"(用鲸鱼油塞满脑袋的)糊涂虫"的意思。*You blubberhead! Now you've ruined all our plans.* 你这个糊涂虫! 现在你把我们的计划全都破坏啦! → a DUMBHEAD ◇ a stupid person

blue

a blue movie → MOVIE

a bolt from the blue → BOLT

once in a blue moon → MOON

out of the blue [ˌaudəðə 'blu:] [口] **突如其来** → out of a clear blue SKY

till *one* **is blue in the face** → FACE

blues

sing the blues (about *something*) [ˌsɪŋðə 'blu:z] [话] **悲叹** *Ella Fitzgerald is good at singing the blues.* 埃拉·菲茨杰拉德善于演唱布鲁斯。正如这一例句所示, blues 是一种爵士乐的风格,是伤感的歌。本条的字面意义就是"唱悲伤的歌"。转用于一般表示"悲叹"的意义。虽然同样是"悲叹",但这一表达法仅用于表示"因为感到不满而叹息"、"由于该做而没有做,结果长吁短叹"等的场合,不用于"为人死而悲痛"这样深沉的场合。根据上下文,也常含有近似"发牢骚" (complain) 而使他人见了"讨厌"的感觉。由于有 sing 这一动词在,所以专用于从口头说出的场合。用进行时的时候较多。*George is always singing the blues about how much money his wife spends.* 乔治总是叹息他的老婆用钱过多。*You'll be singing the blues next year if you don't study harder for your entrance exams.* 你如果不更刻苦用功准备入学考试,明年你就该唉声叹气了。*Stop singing the blues about having to get up at five o'clock every morning. We're all in the same boat, you know.* 你不要为了每天早晨五点钟起床而怨天怨

地吧,论辛苦,咱们大家全是一样啊。◇ lament / be sorry

blush

at first blush [ət'fə(:)rst 'blʌʃ] [口] **乍看起来** blush 在现代英语中是"脸红"的意思,但在数百年以前,也与 glance ['glæ(:)nts] (一见)作为同义词使用。本条的 at first blush (有时也作 on first blush)是当今仍沿用 blush 的古代意义的唯一习用语。*At first blush the work seemed difficult, but I soon mastered it.* 乍看起来,那工作好象很不容易,但是我很快就掌握啦。*Arabic is much easier than may seem at first blush.* 阿拉伯语比刚一接触时的印象容易得多。◇ at first glance

board

go by the board [.gou.baɪðə 'bo:rd] [口] **化为泡影** 指决心、努力、计划等落空。这里的 board 是"船舷"。本条原义是"桅杆等落到船外,顺水流走"。了解这一意义,头脑里自然会反映出本条习用语的具体内容。在表达有明确的原因或是失败、或是白费的场合使用。*When the oil shock came, all our efforts to save our struggling company went by the board.* 石油危机一出现,我们为挽救风雨飘摇的公司所做的一切努力都化为泡影了。*I always intend to be very cool with her, but every time she looks up at me and smiles, all my resolve goes by the board and I become like a blushing, tongue-tied teenager.* 我总打算对她表示非常冷淡,但是,每当她望着我微笑的时候,我的一切决心都风流云散,我好象变成一个憋得满脸通红、连话也说不出来的初出茅庐的娃娃了。*When the ship began to sink, pride and dignity went by the board as everyone scrambled for the lifeboats.* 当船开始下沉的时候,什么骄傲,什么威严,全都不见影儿了,所有的人都争先恐后地抢着上救生艇。board 也偶而使用复数的形式 boards。◇ come to nothing / disappear

sweep the board [.swi(:)pðə 'bo:rd] [口] **大获全胜** 这里的 board 是 playing board, 亦即"赌博的桌子"。sweep 是"一扫而光"。因此,本条的原来意义是"把桌上的赌注一扫而光",赌场术语叫"扫盘子"。*If I had had one more ace I could have swept the board.* 当时我要多有一张 *A*,我就能扫盘子了。从这一意义发展起来,就变成"(在各种比赛中)囊括全部奖赏[锦标]"的意义了。*That movie practically swept the board, winning every Oscar but one.* 那个影片实际上等于囊括了所有奥斯卡金奖,只有一项没有得到。*In badminton, China is expected to sweep the board.* 在羽毛球比赛中,中国可望囊括全部金牌。也可以象下面的例句那样加 clean 以强调意义。*In swimming, America swept the board clean.* 在游泳比赛中,美国队大获全胜。◇ take all the prizes [medals, etc.]

boardinghouse

a boardinghouse reach → REACH

boat

be in the same boat [ɪnðə .seɪm'bout] [话] **风雨同舟** 在大海里飘浮的小船上,不论怎样向同船的人叫苦,结果会碰到这样的回答: *Stop complaining. We're all in the same boat.* 不要再抱怨啦! 咱们大家是风雨同舟啊! 本条习用语就是从这一构思而来。这里的 boat 指"困难的状况"、"不好的境遇"等等,不用于顺利的事情。*When it comes to having to commute long distances, most Tokyo workers are in the same boat.* 在必须远距离上下班这一点上,东京的大多数职工是患难相同的。两人的场合常加 both, 三人以上常加 all。*I was hoping that Henry would lend me some money, but it seems we're both in the same boat. He's broke, too.* 我曾指望亨利能借给我几个钱,但是看起来我们是难兄难弟啊。他也是一文不名。*I wish you would stop complaining about high prices. We're all in the same boat, you know.* 我希望你不要再为物价高发牢骚了。你要知道,咱们的状况全都一样糟。◇ be in the same situation

miss the boat (on *something*)① [.mɪsðə ˈbout] [话] **坐失良机** 字面意义是"误了上船"。等到想起上船，为时已晚。这一习用语即用于表示"白白地放过大好机会"的意思。放过机会的原因多半是决定过迟或行动过慢。*We missed the boat when we didn't buy that house last year. The new owner has just sold it for twice the price he paid for it.* 去年我们没买那所房子，真是坐失良机。现在新房主以买价的两倍价钱把它卖出去啦。*Mary's a very popular and talented girl. If you don't ask her to marry you soon, you're going to miss the boat.* 玛丽是一个很有人缘、又有才能的姑娘。如果你不赶快向她求婚，你就会坐失良机啦！如下面例句所示，也有由于判断错误的场合。*We missed the boat on that contract by bidding too high.* 由于报价过高，我们失掉了签订那份合同的机会。boat 可用 bus (公共汽车)代换。意义与用法完全相同，但两相比较，一般都用 boat。*If you were hoping to apply for that job, I'm afraid you've missed the bus. The deadline for applications closed yesterday.* 如果你打算应聘去干那份工作，很遗憾，你已经错过机会了。因为征聘是到昨天截止的。◇ miss *one's* chance

miss the boat (on *something*)② [.mɪsðə ˈbout] [话] **未能抓住要点** 与上一条的 miss the BOAT (on *something*)① 的意义似乎完全不同，但也有相通之处，即"失去充分理解对方所说的话的机会"。"未能抓住要点"的原因，不论是由于头脑迟钝，还是心不在焉，责任都在听的人身上。即使责任显然在说话人的说话方式的场合，如果使用这一表达法，也是表示"真对不起，我没有注意听"这样的谦逊口吻。*I'm afraid I missed the boat on that explanation. Would you mind running through it once again?* 对不起，你的解释我没有注意听清楚。能不能请你再说一遍？这一表达法不是用于漏听一个单词或一个短语的场合，而是用于对整个讲话全不理解的场合。*Professor Kneedeep is a very subtle speaker. If you don't listen very carefully to every nuance, you may miss the boat.* 倪德普教授讲话令人非常难以捉摸。你如果不非常认真地听他每个词句的意味，就得不到其中的三昧。另外，在用以表示这一意义时，不能象 miss the BOAT(on *something*)① 那样说 miss the bus。◇ not grasp the meaning

rock the boat [.rɑ(:)kðə ˈbout] [话] **无意中把事情闹大** 常按照字面意义"使小船摇动"使用。也有故意的场合，但比较少。*Hey! Don't rock the boat! I can't swim.* 喂，不要把船弄得直晃荡！我可不会游泳呀。作为比喻，用以表示"把本来挺好的[安定的]状态搞乱"的意思。一般用于不是蓄意的、而是不小心地干出这样事情的场合。*Management had almost reached agreement with the union when the personnel department rocked the boat by threatening to fire three union members.* 厂方与工会已经快要达成协议了，人事部门偏偏在这时候威胁要开除三个工会会员，结果把风波闹大了。*The bank seems willing to give us a loan. Don't rock the boat by mentioning that sales are down this month.* 银行似乎有意向我们贷款。千万不要顺嘴说出本月销售额下降，以免把事情搞砸了。也偶尔有主语不是"人"的场合。*Just when the political situation was growing more stable, increased terrorist activity began to rock the boat.* 正当政局日益稳定的时候，恐怖分子活动的猖獗开始把一切都搞乱了。◇ disturb the situation

body

over *someone's* **dead body** [.ovər ˈ~ ˈde:d ˈbɑ:di] [话] **就是死也不同意** *someone* 处代人说话的人或成为话题的人。主语是他的对手或者是对手想要做的事情。占压倒多数的句子结构是 You [He, She, etc.] will (have to) *do something* over my dead body. / it will (have to) be over my dead body."越过某人的死尸去干什么"这一习用语原来的构思是："你如果想要做什么的话，不杀掉某人，跨过他的尸体，就绝对不容许你去做"，它表示"哪怕死也不让你去做"

这样顽固到底的意志。*Father to son: You'll study music over my dead body! You're going to be a doctor just like your father!* 父亲对儿子说:你要学音乐,我死也不答应!你要子继父业,当医生!这一表达法一定用于表示猛烈反对什么事情的场合,因而多半与汉语的"只要我还有一口气,就不准……"相当。*If my son wants to marry that woman it'll be over my dead body!* 只要我还有一口气,就不准我的儿子跟那个娘儿们结婚! *I'm sure that if the city builds a road through Mr. Smith's property, it'll be over his dead body.* 如果我市要在筑路时穿过史密斯先生的地产,必须首先粉碎他的猛烈反对才行。*A: Your son told me he's going to buy a motorbike. B: Over my dead body he will! Those things are too dangerous.* 甲:你的儿子跟我说,他准备买一辆摩托车。乙:我死也不会答应的。那种玩艺儿太危险啦!在这一例句中,he will 放在最后,这是加强语气、表示强烈意志时经常使用的造句方法。说 He will over my dead body. 当然也可以,但是语气弱得多。◇ *someone* will never permit *someone* to *do something* / over *someone's* strongest protest

bogged

be bogged down (on *something*) [ˌbɑ(ː)gː ˈdaun] [口] **陷入困境** → be STUCK(on *something*)

get bogged down (*on something*) [get ˌbɑ(ː)gːˈdaun] [口] **遇到麻烦** → be STUCK (on *something*)

boggle

boggle the mind → MIND

boilermaker

a boilermaker [ə ˈbɔɪlərˌmeɪkər] [话] **啤酒兑威士忌** 字面意义是"制造锅炉的东西"。也就是说,"啤酒兑威士忌,如果长期饮用,是使胃象锅炉一样坚硬、不管如何敲打也丝毫不受影响的饮料"。当然,起码条件是胃没有破碎,人没有死。*I'll have a boilermaker.* 给我来一杯啤酒兑威士忌。*Joe says that water rusts your pipes so he always drinks boilermakers.* 乔说水会使内脏生锈,所以他老是喝啤酒兑威士忌。◇ whiskey in beer

bolt

a bolt from the blue [ə ˈbɔlt frəmðə ˈbluː] [口] **晴天霹雳** a bolt 就是 a bolt of lightning (一条闪电)。the blue 是诗歌用语,意为"碧蓝的天空"。*Their daughter's elopement was a bolt from the blue.* 对他们来说,女儿的私奔有如晴天霹雳。如此例所示,这一习用语可以作为表语使用,直接连接 be 动词,但是较多的使用方法是在它的前边先加个 as 或者 like,特别是会话中要冠以 like。*The decision to close down the plant was like a bolt from the blue.* 工厂关闭的决定有如晴天霹雳一样。除 be 动词外,常用 come。*The news of his death came like a bolt from the blue.* 他去世的消息好象晴天打了一个霹雳。如以上的例句所示,主要是在发生不愉快或者不幸的事情时使用,但并不以此为限。*My promotion to vice-president came as a bolt from the blue.* 我能升任副总裁,简直是突如其来,连做梦也没有想到。另外,特别是在会话中,也常用 out of 代替 from。*My husband's demand for a divorce was like a bolt out of the blue.* 我的丈夫提出离婚要求,这好象晴天霹雳一样。◇ a completely unexpected shock ((be like → be / come like → come as))

shoot *one's* **bolt** [ˌʃu(ː)t ~ ˈboult] [口] **把所有力量都用光了** shoot 是"发射",bolt 是"(crossbow 的)矢"。所谓 crossbow 是中世纪欧洲人使用的弓,如字面所示,为十字形,比普通的弓射程远,命中率高。那样子很象在现在的步枪的托架上安装一个与之成直角的大弓,也和步枪一样装有引发机。搭到弓上的箭,亦即 bolt,也比普通的箭粗,力量非常强大,只要一被射中,大抵是致命伤。但是也有相反的一面,搭箭拉弓的操作需要时间,因此在使用时必须慎重。如果一次射出的箭没能给敌人造成致命伤,在搭第二支箭之前,就很容易遭到敌人的反击。谚语 A fool's bolt is soon shot. (愚兵乱射箭。)就是由这种情况产生的。本条的 shoot *one's* bolt 可以认为是由此谚语派生出来的。有些词典把这一习用语译作:“竭尽全力”,但在实际上,一般是用以表达“(由于竭尽全力,结果)已经没有余力”、“把所有力量都用光了”的意思。*Naval historians say that Japan shot her bolt at the Battle of Midway. After that she traveled a downhill road to certain defeat.* 海军历史学家们说,日本在中途岛海战中把最后的力量使光了。从那以后,它向着必然败北的道路滑下去了。总之,“发射 bolt”→“拿出最后一着”→“竭尽全力”→“把所有的力量都用光了”——这就是 shoot *one's* bolt 的意义发展的构图,在实际使用时,一般以“竭尽全力”的意味为隐在后边的背景,正面出现的则是“把所有的力量都用光了”。*Margaret Mitchell was a very talented writer, but she evidently shot her bolt with Gone With the Wind, which was the only novel she ever wrote.* 玛格丽特·米切尔是一位非常有才华的作家。但是在写了《飘》之后,这位才女显然已经才尽如江郎,使这部小说成为了她唯一的作品。*By the time of World War II, the British Empire had already shot its bolt.* 第二次世界大战时期,大英帝国已经日落西山,失去了它昔日的威风。另外,上述的谚语 A fool's bolt is soon shot. 在现代几乎已经无人使用。至于本条的 shoot *one's* bolt, 也是一个自古就有的表达法,例如以《格利佛游记》(*Gulliver's Travels*) 而享有盛名的斯威夫特 (Jonathan Swift) 在 1738 年就说过:“因为没有新鲜味,我不使用。”不过,它迄今仍为人们喜闻乐道。→ shoot *one's* WAD ◇ use up [expend] (all [most of]) *one's* fire power [resources, energies, etc.]

bolts

a bucket of bolts [ə ˌbʌkədə ˈbolts] [话] **破旧的车** 字面意义是“满满一桶螺栓”。把“车身”比做“洋铁桶”的表达法。原来的构思是:“车子一跑起来,本来应该拧得很紧的各个螺栓,就好象乱扔到洋铁桶里边似的,于是车身咯嗒咯嗒地响”。*We've got to get rid of this bucket of bolts and buy a new car.* 咱们非处理掉这辆老爷车、再买一辆新车不可了。也有时应用于汽车以外的带发动机的交通工具,如飞机、轮船等。*I wouldn't fly in Ned's plane if I were you. It's nothing but a bucket of bolts.* 如果我是你,我可不坐内德的飞机。那是一架破旧不堪的老爷飞机。◇ an old, worn-out car [plane, boat, etc.]

bone

a bone of contention (between *them*) [əˌbounəvkənˈtentʃən] [口] **相争的原因** contention 是“相争”。本条直译为“成为相争根源的一块骨头”。请读者想一下两条狗为一块骨头在咬架的样子。由于同一构思,另有 have a BONE to pick with *someone* 这样一个表达法。*Both our sons always want to use the car. It's often a bone of contention between them.* 我家的两个儿子总是都想用汽车。这汽车常常成为他们相争的原因。*What time to have breakfast is a bone of contention between my wife and me. She's a night owl and I'm an early riser.* 要在几点钟吃早饭成为我们俩口子争执的原因。她是个夜游神,而我却早起惯了。也可以使用于表示争执虽然尚未发生,但“可能成为引起争执的事物”。*Why don't we settle the exact boundary between our property for once and for all? If we don't, it'll always be a bone of contention between us.* 我们精确划定一下两家地产之间的界线,来个一劳永逸好不好?如果不这样做,它将永远成为双方争执的原因。◇ a point of argument [disagreement]

bone up (on *something*) [ˌbou ˈnʌp] [话] **突击学习** 这一表达法来自 H. G. Bohn [ˈboun] 其人的姓氏。Bohn 搜集各国在历史、科学、哲学、文学等方面已有定论的一流学者、思想家的著作,编成《鲍恩古典文库》,从 1846 年开始在英国出版,廉价出售。这在当时美国学生中间大受欢迎,作为应付考试的学习参考书使用。Bohn 这一姓氏本身便成为“自习参考书”的代名词了。后来进一步演变,又具有“刻苦用功的学生”的意义,直至作为动词使用,意为“刻苦用功”。在这一过程中,原来的使用方法被扬弃了,它的来历也被人忘记了,Bohn 不知不觉地变成了同音的 bone。现在附加上具有“充分”、“非常”意义的 up,成为 bone up 的形式,专作动词使用。一般指具有特殊目的的短期突击学习,但也用于学习新的学科的场合以及复习已经忘掉一半的课程或事项等的场合。这一表达法多用于应付学校考试的学习,但除此之外,在为开会、谈判、会见、到国外旅行等进行各种各样的“预备学习”时也可以使用。例如,如果说 *Mr. Swift is boning up on American geography.*,那意思就是斯威夫特先生已经确定去美国出差或办其他事情,一有功夫就研究美国的地理。因为含有“迫切需要”的意味,所以象 *I have to bone up on Canadian immigration procedures.* 我必须抓紧研究加拿大的移民手续。这样,在使用时多与 have to [hæ(:)ftə] 或者 (have) got to [gɑ(:)də] 结合起来 。如果连学习的目的也要说出的时候,这与 study 的场合相同,用前置词 for 接续。*I have to bone up on next year's sales program for the board of directors meeting tomorrow.* 为了明天召开的董事会,我对来年度的销售计划必须再认真审核一番。根据上下文已经了解研究的对象的场合,一般省掉 on ~的部分。*I have to bone up for my Friday math test.* 为了星期五的数学考试,我必须抓紧复习。◇ study up / study (*something*)

one's **crazy bone** [~ ˈkreɪzi ˌboun] [话] **(受触时发麻的)肘部尺骨端** → *one's* funny BONE

be (as) dry as a bone [əz ˈdraɪ əzə ˈboun] [话] **完全干涸** 字面意义为“象骨头一样干”,是强调 dry (干了的) 的说法。在使用时,大致可以区分为三种意义。但不论是哪一种场合,全都含有表示“本来干了不行的地方偏偏 dry”这样一种无可奈何的心情的意味。在三种意义当中,最有代表性的是“(场所、容器等)完全干了”。另外,动词一般用 be 动词,有时也使用 become 或 get 等。*After four months with no rain, even the riverbed became as dry as a bone.* 由于一连四个月没下雨,连河床都完全干涸了。*We were only halfway across the desert when the gas tank got as dry as a bone.* 我们横穿沙漠才走了一半,油箱就完全干了。第二种意义是“嗓子干渴”。*Let's stop for a drink. I'm as dry as a bone.* 咱们停下喝点什么吧,我的嗓子渴得直冒烟。第三种意义是“绝对禁酒”。也就是说,dry 有“禁酒的”的意味。*I'm sorry, but you can't buy a drink here. This town is as dry as a bone.* 对不起,这里买不到带酒精的饮料。这个城镇是绝对禁酒的。在这一场合,只说 This town is dry. 当然也行,但是由于加上 as a bone,就变成了会话调子,而且使意味加强一些。另外还有一个形容词 bone-dry,它也与 dry as a bone 同样,三种意义通用。*The well is bone-dry.* 水井已经完全干涸了。*My throat is bone-dry.* 我的嗓子干得直冒烟。*This county is bone-dry.* 这个县绝对禁酒。请注意:这一形容词只能用作表语,没有 bone-dry + 名词这样作为定语的用法。◇ be completely dry

one's **funny bone** [~ ˈfʌni ˌboun] [话] **(一碰就发麻的)肘端骨** 肘端的内侧部分一不留神碰到桌子角或其他什么东西上的时候,手腕会产生一种麻酥酥的感觉。这实际上不是骨的作用,而是上腕骨与尺骨之间的粗神经的活动所致。在英语中,把这一部分称为 funny bone,在日常会话以及其他场面中频频出现,所以有必要牢牢记住它的意义。funny 是“好玩”的意思,也就是用 funny 一词来形容那种麻酥酥的“奇异的”感觉。*A: What's the matter? B: I hit my funny bone on the corner of the table.* 甲:怎么啦?乙:我的肘端骨碰到桌子角上了。*Just as the speaker stood up to address the audience, he struck his funny bone on the arm of his chair and grimaced with pain.* 正当讲演者站起来要向听众开讲的时候,由于胳臂肘碰到椅子扶手上,他痛得直皱眉头。代替 *one's* funny bone

使用的有 *one's* crazy bone。这一 crazy 也表示同样的感觉。*Nothing feels worse than banging your crazy bone on something.* 没有比把胳臂肘撞到什么东西上让人感到更难受的了。另外还有一个实际上很少使用的定型的表达法,即 tickle *someone's* funny bone。tickle 是"胳肢使发痒",但是这里的 funny bone 却与"肘端骨"没有关系,美国人听了这一习用语也联想不到"肘端骨"。这是"身体某一部分有一根能引起笑的骨头,胳肢它使其发痒"的形象概念的表达。也就是说,这一场合的 funny bone 与 sense of humor 的意味近似,而 tickle *someone's* funny bone 换一说法就是 appeal to *someone's* sense of humor。*Here's a story that will tickle your funny bone.* 我可有一个会使你发笑的故事。◇ the nerve in *one's* elbow / *one's* sense of humor

have a bone in *one's* **leg** [ˌhævə ˈbounɪn ~ ˌle(ː)g] [话] **不知为什么不想去[不想干]** 逐字翻译是"腿中有一块骨头",但这是在"到什么地方去"或"做什么"的时候用以表示"没有兴趣"的心情的一种诙谐的说法。*I'm not going on the picnic today. I'm afraid I've got a bone in my leg.* 今天我不去郊游啦。不知为什么,我不想去。*Why won't you help us clean the tennis court? And don't tell me you've got a bone in your leg.* 你为什么不帮助我们打扫网球场呢?你别跟我说你不知为什么不想干啦。从上边的例句也可以看出,英语的"腿中有骨头(因而不去[不干])"是作为"不去"或"不干"的口实使用的,但是,只要是人类,"腿中有骨头"乃是天经地义,这一点不能成为口实。把不能作为口实的事情作为口实,以表达"没有确实理由,只是不知为什么不想去[不想干]"这样一种心情,便是本条习用语的幽默、趣味所在。也有用 get 代替 have 的说法,即 get a bone in *one's* leg,但这一说法的释义应为"不知为什么不想去[干]了"。*Guy's not coming to your party, Amy. He says to tell you he suddenly got a bone in his leg.* 艾米,盖伊不来参加你的社交晚会啦。他叫我告诉你,他不知为什么突然不想参加了。◇ have some nonsensical excuse / really not want to

have a bone to pick with *someone* [ˌhævə ˈbountə ˌpɪkwɪð ~] [话] **有点意见** 字面意义是"有一块与人同啃的骨头"。最初的构思为两条狗在一起而只有一根骨头的情景。*I've got a bone to pick with you. How come you didn't come to my party last night?* 我对你可有点儿意见。昨天晚上我开社交集会,你怎么竟然不来呀?如这一例句所示,一般就是如此轻松地使用,至于就严重问题而"大有不满"的场合,则不能用这一表达法。因此,象上边例句那样,直接向对手讲的情况居多。*Jan says she has a bone to pick with you about your always snitching pencils from her desk.* 简说她对你有点儿意见,因为你总爱从她的书桌里拿铅笔。对于与自己的利害没有直接关系的事情,也可以使用这一表达法。*I enjoyed reading your article on inflation, but I have a bone to pick with you over your interpretation of the economic situation.* 我很有兴趣地拜读了你谈论通货膨胀的文章,但是对于你对经济形势的分析,我却有点小小的意见。下面的例句是对这一表达法的应用。*Please don't misunderstand me. I have no bone to pick with this committee. I came here tonight only to make sure I have all the facts correct.* 请不要误解我的意思。我对这个委员会没有一点儿意见。我今天晚上前来,只是要核对一下我所掌握的事实是不是完全正确的。◇ have a complaint to settle with *someone* / have a difference of opinion (*one* would like to discuss) with *someone*

tickle *someone's* **funny bone** [ˌtɪkl ~ ˈfʌni ˌboun] [话] **逗人发笑** → *one's* funny BONE

work *one's* **fingers to the bone** → FINGERS

bone-dry

bone-dry [ˈbounˈdraɪ] [话] **完全干涸** → be (as) dry as a BONE

bonehead

a bonehead [ə ˈboun.he(ː)d] [话] **呆头呆脑的人** 字面意义是“只用骨头做出来的脑袋”,也就是“没有脑筋的脑袋”,指“头脑不灵活的人”。 *The head of our department is a real bonehead.* 我们部的头头是十足呆头呆脑的人。此词的原形即可成为形容词,特别在 a bonehead mistake (愚蠢的错误) 或 a bonehead play (〈运动员等的〉拙笨的失误)之类的说法中常常使用。 *A bonehead play by the shortstop cost us the game.* 由于游击手拙笨的失误,我们输掉了这场棒球。亦作 boneheaded。 *How could you make such a bonehead(ed) mistake?* 你怎么会犯如此愚蠢的错误哪? → pull a BONER / a DUMBHEAD ◇ a stupid person

a bonehead mistake [ə ˈbounˈhe(ː)d məsteɪk] [话] **愚蠢的错误** → pull a BONER

a bonehead play [ə ˈbounˈhe(ː)d ˈpleɪ] [话] **拙笨的失误** → pull a BONER

boner

pull a boner [ˌpulə ˈbounər] [话] **犯大错误** a boner 是把 a bonehead [boneheaded] mistake 压缩成一个词的表达法,在意义上两者完全相同。例如 *Another bonehead mistake like that and you're fired.* 你再犯那么愚蠢的错误,就开除你。改说 *Another boner like that and you're fired.* 也可以。bonehead(ed) 原来的构思是“脑袋全部是骨头构成的”,也就是“没有脑筋”,由此发展成“愚蠢(的)”的意思。 *You bonehead. That's not the way to do it!* 你这糊涂虫!那样干不行!后来又演变出 a bonehead(ed) mistake 或者在体育运动、比赛中常用的 a bonehead(ed) play 等说法。pull 在这里是与 make 具有同一意味的。常用 real 加强语气。 *I pulled a real boner yesterday. I asked Sally to go to the movies with me, forgetting that I already had a date with Sue.* 昨天我犯了个天大的错误。我忘记已经跟苏有约会,而约萨莉一同去看电影了。也可以不用动词陪伴而单独使用。 *Sid doesn't often make mistakes, but when he does, it's usually a real boner.* 锡德不常有过失,但是当他犯错误的时候,通常是愚蠢透顶的错误。另外, bonehead(ed) mistake 或 bonehead(ed) play 不用 pull, 一般用 make。 *We would have won if the pitcher hadn't made that bonehead play.* 如果不是投手来那么个拙笨的失误,我们棒球队就打赢啦。◇ make a stupid mistake

bones

a bag of bones [ə ˌbæ(ː)gə ˈbounz] [话] **瘦得皮包骨** 把瘦的人或动物的身体比做“装骨头的口袋”的表达法。口袋里没有肉只有骨头,也就是汉语俗语所说的“皮包骨”。常常使用 just 加强语气。 *You'd better eat more if you don't want to become just a bag of bones.* 如果你不想变成只剩下一把骨头的瘦猴,最好还是多吃点东西。 *Ned came back from the war he was just a bag of bones.* 内德从战场回来的时候,他简直就剩下皮包骨了。在动物方面,多用于谈到马或狗的场合。 *That horse is just a bag of bones.* 那匹马瘦得简直就剩皮包骨了。但是,在谈到马或狗时,也有象下一例句那样,指的是“瘦的身体”本身,在这一场合,把它解释作“瘦马”或“瘦狗”比较贴切。 *It's getting about time to get rid of this bag of bones and get a new horse.* 现在该把这匹瘦马处理掉,再弄一匹新马了。skin and bones 也是“瘦得皮包骨”,This horse is skin and bones. 与 This horse is a bag of bones. 在意义上几乎完全相同。但是请读者注意: skin and bones 只能当作形容词使用,不能指“瘦的身体”本身,因此,在上面的例句中,~ get rid of this bag of bones 的 bag of bones 不能换成 skin and bones。 → be only SKIN and bones ◇ extremely thin

feel it in *one's* bones [ˌfɪ(ː)lɪtn ~ ˈbounz] [话] **有直觉** 直译是“在骨头中感到”,也就是“(不是用头脑[理性])在身体的某个部分感觉到”的意思。在理由不清楚、但总感觉是那样的场合使用。至于感觉的内容,有好的场合,也有坏的场合。 *I'm going to win big at the races* *today. I can feel it in my bones.* 在今天的赛马中，我一定会大赢。我有这样的直觉。it 也可以用短句 (feel in *one's* bones) that ～来代替。*He had long felt in his bones that no matter how hard he studied he would never get into a top-flight university.* 他从很久以前就有一种直觉：无论怎样拼命用功，也永远进不了一所一流大学。如以上的例句所示，主要是针对未来的事情而言，但也有象下边这样的场合。 *A: How do you know he's lying? B: I don't. But I feel it in my bones.* 甲：你怎么知道他是在说谎哪？乙：我并不知道。但是我有这样的感觉呀。◇ feel it intuitively / feel intuitively that ～

make no bones about (*doing*) *something* [ˌmeɪkˌnou ˈbounzəbaut ～] [口] **不当作一回事 (毫不介意、满不在乎、毫不含糊、毫不掩饰)** make no bones 原是"明明有骨头，并不把它当作骨头"，也就是"在肉汤或炖肉中虽然有骨头，也不当作一回事，照样大吃特吃"的意思。 about 后边一定接某种"不相宜"的事情，但是，根据某人对他人的不当言行究竟怎样"不当作一回事"的具体情况，这一表达法的使用方法可以分成下面的四大类：① *That guy makes no bones about cheating on exams. He does it all the time.* 那家伙对于在考试中作弊不当作一回事，每逢考试他都那样干。② *That guy makes no bones about (his) cheating on exams. He tells everyone about it.* 那家伙对于自己的考试作弊满不在乎，他对谁都讲。③ *The principal makes no bones about (his attitude toward) cheating on exams. He fails anyone who is caught.* 校长对于考试中作弊的态度是毫不含糊的。不管是哪个学生，一抓住就给不及格。④ *The principal makes no bones about cheating on exams. Boys will be boys, he says.* 校长认为考试中作弊一事没什么了不起。他说，孩子总归是孩子，难免干点糊涂事嘛。这就是说，①是"本人不把自己的不端行为当作一回事，满不在乎地去干"；②是"本人对自己或自家人的不端行为不当作一回事，满不在乎地向别人讲"。我们可以这样讲：这个①和②乃是 make no bones 的最典型的使用方法。其次，③是"对于他人的不端行为，毫不客气地表明自己认为干坏事就不行的明确态度 (也就是不把其他各种想法当一回事)；④是"认为别人的不端行为不足以当作问题"。在上边的例句中，为了说明的方便，完全以"不端行为"作为"不当作一回事"的对象了，在实际上当然并不仅限于此。例如 ① *I make no bones about it. If I need something I ask for it, even from a stranger.* 我对这种事情是不在乎的。如果我需要什么东西，哪怕是个陌生人，我也管他要。② *My son makes no bones about his dislike for studying.* 我的儿子毫不掩饰他对学习的厌烦。在这里，①的对象是"一般人会踌躇的事情"，②的对象是"讨厌的心情"，其他还有种种事物可以当作"不当作一回事"的对象。 make no bones 后边的前置词一般用 about，但也有时用 of。 *He makes no bones of [about] the fact that he helps his wife with the dishes.* 他毫不掩饰他帮助妻子刷盘子的事实。另外，make no bones 也可以按语法的规范，有时采取 not make any bones 的形式。甚至偶尔会使用 make bones 这样的肯定形。*It's foolish to make bones about [of] such trifles.* 把那种小事搁在心上，真太愚蠢了。◇ ① have no compunction about (*doing*) *something* ② make no secret of (*doing*) *something* ③ be forthright about (*doing*) *something* ④ not consider *something* to be a problem

be only skin and bones → SKIN

bonnet

have a bee in *one's* **bonnet** (about *something*) → BEE

have bees in *one's* **bonnet** [ˌhæv ˈbiːzən ～ ˌbɑ(ː)nət] [话] **一脑子奇怪念头** → have a BEE in *one's* bonnet (about *something*)

put a bee in *someone's* **bonnet** [ˌpudə ˈbiːən ～ ˌbɑ(ː)nət] [话] **向他人灌输怪思想** → have a BEE in *one's* bonnet

(about *something*)

boob

a boob [ə ˈbu:b] [话] **傻瓜** 原意是"头脑不足的人",但在语感上,"缺乏常识,容易上当"的意味强。与 a SIMPLETON 的意思大致一样。原来作 a booby [ˈbu:bi],现在则多用 boob。*That boob just cost us our biggest customer.* 那个傻瓜把我们的最大主顾给弄没了。→ a booby HATCH / a DUMBHEAD ◇ a stupid person

a boob tube → TUBE

boobies

boobies [ˈbu(:)ˌbi(:)z] [俗] **乳房** → BOOBS

boo-boo

make a boo-boo [ˌmeɪkə ˈbu(:)ˌbu:] [话] **失误** 语源不详,可能是具有"傻瓜"意义的 BOOB 与哭泣的象声词 boo-hoo 相结合的产物。喜剧演员杰利·刘易斯(Jerry Lewis) 在电影中以此为口头禅,随后普遍流行起来。一般在有小的失误、犯幼稚的错误时使用。*I made a slight boo-boo, dear. I put salt in the pie instead of sugar.* 亲爱的,我闹了个小小的差错。我在甜馅饼里没放糖,而加了盐。如这一例句所示,常在自己有失误时使用。在体育运动中有过失的场合,也常使用。*We were only five yards away from a touchdown when the quarterback made a real boo-boo. He handed the ball off to a member of the other team.* 我们在橄榄球比赛中,离触地得分只剩下五码了,这时候四分卫失了手,他竟把球递给对方的一个队员了。boo-boo 亦可单独使用。*Charlie left ten thousand dollars in a taxi yesterday. Another boo-boo like that and we'll be out of business.* 查理昨天把一万元美金丢在出租汽车里了。如果再来这样的失误,我们就得关张大吉了。也有时把动词改用 pull,而说 pull a boo-boo,这大概是与 pull a BONER 相混淆的表达法。*How could you pull a boo-boo like that?* 你怎么会犯那样的错误?◇ make a (stupid) blunder

boobs

boobs [ˈbu:bz] [俗] **乳房** 原来是 bubbies [ˈbʌˌbi(:)z],后来变成 boobies [ˈbu(:)ˌbɪ(:)z],而现在则多使用 boobs。虽然也有单数形式 a booby,但这种形式很少使用。男人之间的用语。*She has a nice set of boobs.* 她那对乳房挺不错呀。◇ breasts

booby

a booby [ə ˈbu:bi] [话] **傻瓜** → a BOOB

a booby hatch → HATCH

a booby prize → PRIZE

book

book learning → LEARNING

crack a book [ˌkrækə ˈbu(:)k] [话] **啃书本** 字面意义是"把书撕裂"。crack 原意为"(把核桃等) 砸开"。后来转用于表示"(为了使内容[内里所装的东西]归自己所有而把……) 打开"的意思。除本条外,还可以在 crack a SAFE 等条见到 crack 的这一用法。crack a book 为学生用语,book 是教科书。这一表达法一般用于否定句,如 *I haven't cracked a book for over a week.* 我已经有一个多礼拜没啃书本啦。*That guy makes good grades without hardly ever cracking a book.* 那家伙几乎一点也不啃书本,分数却很高。◇ study

curl up with a good book [ˌkə(:)rˈlʌp wɪðə ˌgudˈbu(:)k] [口] **悠然自在看闲书** curl up 是"蜷着身子",后边加上 with a good book,就使人在头脑里出现这样的形象:"(手里拿本书,在沙发或安乐椅上) 横坐着,把身子一窝"。其实,与这种形象风马牛不相及,身体是什么架势都没有关系,本条仅仅用于表达"悠然自在地看书"的意思。*When I'm home alone at night, I like to curl up with a good book.* 当夜里只有我一个人在家的时候,我喜欢悠然自在地看点闲书。虽然并不象本条这样是一种定型的说法,但也有讲"悠然自在听音乐"的场合。*Sue was curled up in an easy chair listening to music.* 苏听着音乐,悠然自在地横坐在安乐椅上。当然,也可以单独使用 curl up,只表示"(为了睡眠而) 蜷着身子"的意思。

When I got home, the children were curled up on the sofa asleep. 当我回到家里的时候,孩子们已经蜷着身子在沙发上睡着了。*Our cat likes to curl up on my lap.* 我家的猫喜欢蜷着身子卧在我的膝盖上。◇ relax and read / relax by reading

in *one's* **book** [ɪn ˈ~ ˌbu(:)k] [话] **在(某人)看来** 这里的 book 的本来意义不是"书",而是 list (名簿),是"自己所喜欢的人物的名簿",古时说 He's in my book. 乃是"我喜欢他。"的意思。现在,由这一使用方法进一步发展,在对善恶问题发表自己的意见时,用以表示"依(谁)说"、"依(谁)看"的意思。*That woman is not to be trusted in my book.* 依我看,那个女人不可靠。但是,在"善"与"恶"二者之间多用于"善"的场合,如 *In my book, there's no better man for the job.* 依我说,没有任何人比他更适合于那个工作啦。*Jimmy says that in his book, there's no finer engineer anywhere than Jack.* 吉米说,在他看来,任何地方也没有象杰克那样优秀的工程师。如以上的例句所示,一般的使用方法是就"人"而言,但也有用于其他事物的情况。*That's the best school in the country in my book.* 在我看来,那所学校是全国第一。◇ in *one's* opinion

throw the book at *someone* [ˌθrouðə ˈbu(:)kæt ~] [话] **(对某人)判最重刑** 这里的 book 是"载有法律条文的书"。这一表达法的实际意思并不是从那条文规定的刑罚中挑出一种进行处罚,而是"课以书中所载的全部刑罚",亦即"把书本身整个都抛过去"。 我们可以说, 这是"(对某罪犯)处以最重刑"意义的夸张说法。这一说法源出黑社会。*When the defendant proved to be unrepentant, the judge threw the book at him.* 当审判员了解到被告怙恶不悛以后,就对他判了最重的刑罚。*Luke has already been to prison twice. If he is caught again, they'll throw the book at him.* 卢克已经进过两次监狱了。如果他再被抓住,他们会判他最重的刑罚。除象这样使用于真正的罪犯而外,也可以转用于日常生活,表示"加重处罚"的意味。*The principal threw the book at us for cutting class.* 校长以我们怠课为理由而给了我们严重的处罚。*My father is very strict. If he finds I've used the car without his permission, he'll throw the book at me.* 我父亲是非常严厉的。如果他发现我未经他许可而擅自用汽车,他会狠狠处罚我的。◇ give *someone* the heaviest possible sentence / punish *someone* severely

books

doctor the books [ˌdɑktərðə ˈbu(:)ks] [话] **造假帐** → doctor the ACCOUNTS

hit the books [ˌhɪtðə ˈbu(:)ks] [话] **(加油)学习** hit 一词是"打",特别使用于"猛力地[狠狠地]打"的场合。hit the books 或 hit the BOTTLE(酗酒) 等的 hit 则与本来的意义无关,只借用其"猛力"的形象,再与暗示特定行为的名词组合到一起,用以表示"加油干"、"大张旗鼓地干"的意思。hit the books 的 books 是"教科书"。这主要是大学生或高中生的用语。*Finals start next week. I've gotta start hitting the books tonight.* 下星期就开始期终考试了。我从今天晚上起不加油准备不行啦。但是近年以来,在学生中间显然出现一种倾向,即:"加油"的韵味已经没有了,只用它表示"学习"的意义。*I think maybe I'll hit the books for an hour or so before I turn in.* 我想在上床以前复习一个来钟头吧。◇ study (hard)

be one for the books [ˌwʌnfərðə ˈbu(:)ks] [话] **妙极了、棒极了、惨极了** 这里的 book 是 record book (记录本)。本条的字面意义是"可以写入记录本的一件了不起的事情"。这一习用语是在谈到极端有趣的事件、非常惨痛的经历、令人难以相信的失误等等时,被人用以表达"这简直是最高纪录啦!"的意味。是把"吃惊"、"愕然"、"钦佩"等心情表露于外的一种说法。*Bill's act in the amateur show was one for the books. I've never laughed so hard in my life.* 在业余表演会上,比尔的演技简直棒极了。我有生以来还是第一次象那样笑破肚皮呢。可用 really 加强语气。*The look on her face when I told her who my friend was, was really one for the books.* 当我告诉她我的男朋友是谁的时候，她脸上的表情简直妙不可言。根据上下文，有时译作“惨极了”、“简直糟糕透顶”更为贴切。*Our trip through the mountains was one for the books. We had two flat tires, Joe fell into the river with our lunch, and then we got lost trying to find our way back to the car.* 我们的山中旅行惨极了。两次轮胎放炮，乔连同大家的午饭掉到河里去了，而我们回头去找汽车的时候，又迷了路。*You have made a lot of stupid mistakes since you've been working here, but this is one for the books.* 你到这里工作以后，犯过一系列愚蠢的错误。但是这一回，简直是糟糕透顶啦！还有一个 be something for the books 的形式，在以不可数的名词作主语时常常使用。*His stupidity is something for the books.* 他简直是愚蠢透顶啦！也有象下面例句那样，用以代替见面寒喧的情况。*This rain is really something for the books, isn't it?* 这雨下得真够大的啦，是吧？◇ be something extraordinary

boom

lower the boom (on *someone* [*something*]) [ˌlouərðə ˈbuːm] [话] **采取极端严厉的措施** 由海上用语而来的说法。这里的 boom 是“从货船起重机底部斜着伸出的臂膀”，依靠这一臂膀的上下移动装卸货物。lower 是“降下”。也就是说，lower the boom 本来的意思是“(为了卸货而)降下 boom”。从这一形象进一步发展，形成如下的想法：如果“把 boom 降到人的身上”，人所受的打击一定是非常沉重的。于是，本条的表达法就作为比喻广泛地流行起来。*Before I could react, he lowered the boom on me with a right to the jaw.* 没等我来得及躲闪，他已经狠狠地用右勾拳击中了我的下颚。这是在肉体上 lower the boom。但是，这种“迎头痛击”的韵味，从下面的例句中可以看到，是在任何场合都存在的，其语感与汉语成语“当头一棒”大有相似之处。*The police are lowering the boom on drunken drivers.* 警察对喝醉酒的汽车司机采取极端严厉的措施。lower the boom 的对象不仅限于“人”。在上面的例句中，把 drunken drivers 改换成 drunken driving 也可以。*Our teacher lowered the boom today because so many students hadn't done their homework. Over half the class had to stay after school.* 因为不完成家庭作业的学生太多，今天我们老师进行了严厉的惩处。全班有半数以上的人放学后不准回家。*The plant manager finally lowered the boom on absenteeism: anyone missing a day's work without authorization would be docked two days' pay.* 工场的场长对于旷工现象终于采取了严厉措施：凡是不经批准就不上班者，缺勤一天就扣两天工资。在以上的例句中，或是“放学后不准回家”，或是“扣工资”，全都揭示了处罚的内容。但是，并不是非如此不可。*The boss told me today that he's going to lower the boom if we don't ease up on entertainment expenses.* 老板今天对我说，大家如果不缩减交际费，他就要采取强硬手段啦。*My father really lowered the boom on me last night for getting home so late.* 昨天夜里我回家太晚，被老子狠狠训了一大顿。◇ adopt a very severe attitude (toward *someone* [*something*]) / take very strict measures (with *someone* [vis-à-vis *something*])

boondocks

the boondocks [ðə ˈbuːnˌdɑ(ː)ks] [话] **乡下**
→ the BOONIES

boonies

the boonies [ðə ˈbuːˌni(ː)z] [话] **乡下** 这一英语源出菲律宾他加禄语 *bundok*。*bundok* 是“山”的意思，美军占领菲律宾的时候，把它变成 the boondocks [ˈbuːnˌdɑ(ː)ks]，作为俗语使用。此词的省略形式是 the boonies，最近象 the boondocks 一样在美国人的日常会话中频频出现。两者均加定冠词和用复数形式。也有时指实际的“山沟”、“僻壤”，而一般则是先以某个大都市为前提，指相对的“乡下”。不论如何，the boondocks 也好，the boonies 也好，全都是诙谐的、半开玩笑的说法，而且在以下的例句中，两者全都可以相互调换使用。*I wish we could go to New York sometime. Every time Dad has a vacation, he wants to head for the boonies.* 我希望，咱们什么时候去纽约一趟。爸爸每次到了假期，总是要往乡下跑。在这样的场合，the boonies 可以是外地的“小城市”，也可以是真正的“山沟”。 *Ours wasn't a very famous band. We spent most of our time playing in the boonies.* 我们的乐队不是一个非常著名的乐队，大部分时间是在外地演出。这构成所谓“巡回演出”的形象。*I've never heard of that town. It must be someplace out in the boonies.* 我从来没有听到过那个城镇的名字。一定在很偏僻的地方吧。美国纽约人认为纽约以外地方的所有人都是乡下佬，纽约人的“城里人”意识相当强。*People in New York often refer even to Los Angeles as the boonies.* 纽约人在口头上，连洛杉矶都常常被称为乡下。另外，the sticks 也与 the boonies 作同一意义使用。本来 stick 是“小茎”、“小木片”，但在伐木工人的俚语中则意味着“(一棵)树”，由此，在人们的日常会话中，它就以 the sticks 的形式变成“长着树的地方”→“乡下”了。这是与 the boonies 意义完全相同的词，代入以上例句也会产生同样的感觉。◇ the country / the hinterlands

boot

boot *someone* **out** [ˌbu(ː)t ~ ˈaut] [话] **轰出去** → KICK *someone* out

get the boot [ˌgetðə ˈbuːt] [话] **被赶走** → give *someone* the BOOT

give *someone* **the boot** [ˌgɪv ~ ðəˈbuːt] [话] **(从公司、组织、俱乐部等处)赶走** boot 是“长靴”。本条是一个压倒具有同样意味的 KICK *someone* out 的、相当幽默的说法。*Larry was absent from work so many times that I finally gave him the boot.* 拉里旷工的次数太多，我终于把他赶走了。*It ain't fair. No matter how healthy you are, as soon as you reach sixty-five they give you the boot.* 太不合理啦！不管你身体多么健康，只要一到六十五岁，他们就会把你赶出去。这一表达法一般用于工作问题，但也有如下例所示用于“交际圈”或“俱乐部”的场合。*He used to belong to that club, but he got into a fight with another member one night so they gave him the boot.* 他一向是属于那个俱乐部的，但是有一天晚上他跟俱乐部的另一个成员打架，人家把他给赶走啦。get the boot 则是“被赶走”。*I don't have a job anymore. I got the boot last week.* 我现在已经失业了，我上个星期被开除啦。◇ fire [dismiss] *someone* / take away *someone's* membership

to boot [təˈbuːt] [口] **而且** 这个 boot 与“靴子”的 boot 毫无关系，古语作 bot，中世英语作 bote，原意为“利益”或“有利”。在莎士比亚的戏剧里，有 a bootless errand 一语，这不是“光着脚的差使”，而是“跑腿徒劳无功”。在现代，只用 to boot 的形式，意思是“加上利益”，作连词“而且”、“况且”、“加之”等等使用。*The union is asking not only for a raise in wages but for new workers to boot.* 工会不仅要求提高工资，而且要求增加工人。*Helen is rich, talented and beautiful to boot.* 海伦不但有钱，有才，而且长的好看。儿童们也常使用这一表达法。*If you give me your catcher's mask, I'll give you my bat and throw in this football to boot.* 你要是把接球面罩给我，我就给你球棒，外搭上这个足球。不只用于好的意味，也有如下边例句那样用于不好意味的情况。*I can't eat this food. It tastes terrible and it's cold to boot.* 这东西我吃不下去。不但味道糟极了，而且冰凉冰凉的。◇ too

bootleg

bootleg whiskey → WHISKEY

bootlicker

a bootlicker [ə ˈbu(ː)t.lɪkər] [话] **拍马屁的**

人 → lick *someone's* BOOTS

boots

die with *one's* **boots on** [ˈdaɪ wɪð ～ ˈbuːt.sɔːn] [口] **在战斗中死去** 字面意义是"穿着靴子死去"。 *He was a brave soldier who died with his boots on.* 他是一位勇敢的士兵，在作战中壮烈牺牲了。正如这一例句所示，原来是只用于士兵的一种表达法。现在勿宁是把工作等等看作是战斗，一般用于表示"在执行任务中死去"的意思。有时与 die in HARNESS(在工作中死去)相同，仅表示"在未退职的期间死去"的意思。然而，即使在这一场合，也仍然保留着本来的"战斗"的影子，而刻画出"在勤勤恳恳工作中"、"在玩强奋斗中"英勇死去的形象。 *Many cowboys in the old West died with their boots on.* 在过去的美国西部，有许多牛仔在与环境的搏斗中死去。 *I'm sure the mayor will not let his age prevent him from running for re-election. He's determined to die with his boots on.* 据我看，市长绝对不会因为上了年纪而不竞选连任，他是决心干到死的。在涉及警察、消防队员等有"战斗"形象的职业时，也会具有与 be killed in the line of duty (殉职)相类似的意义。 *Being a policeman is not as dangerous as most people think. Less than one percent actually die with their boots on.* 当警察并不象一般人所想的那么危险。实际上殉职的人数不到百分之一。◇ die fighting

one's **heart is in** *one's* **boots** [ˈhɑːrtɪzɪn ～ ˈbuːts] [口] **意气消沉** → *one's* HEART sinks

lick *someone's* **boots** [.lɪk ～ ˈbuːts] [话] **拍马屁** 字面意义为"舔别人的靴子"，是对"阿谀奉承"行为的低贱加以夸张的表达法。一般含有非常轻蔑的意味，但根据具体情况，也用于"奉承"、"讨好"之类比较轻的"献殷勤"的场合。 *Gary always stays after class and licks the teacher's boots awhile. He says it's his only hope of passing this course.* 加里在下课后总要留下向老师讨一阵好。据他说，这是他能使这门课程及格的唯一的希望。 *She expects all her boy friends to lick her boots.* 她以为她的所有男朋友都会向她献殷勤的。 *Don't waste your time licking the boss's boots. He doesn't like bootlickers.* 你不要白费时间去拍头头的马屁。他不喜欢马屁精。如这一例句所示，"拍马屁的人"叫做 a bootlicker [ˈbu(ː)t.lɪkər]。这一说法比 an apple polisher (讨好者)等在语气上要强烈得多。(→ polish the APPLE)。另外，有的词典也收录 lick *someone's* shoes 一语，但这在美国口语中是不使用的。◇ behave in a servile manner toward *someone*

bootstraps

pull *oneself* **up by** *one's* **own bootstraps** [.pul ～ ˈʌpbaɪ ～ .oun ˈbu(ː)t.stræ(ː)ps] [口] **完全靠自己的艰苦奋斗起家** bootstrap 是"(男靴后面或两侧附带的)拔靴带"。这一表达法的字面意义是：拉拔靴带，穿上靴子；穿上以后再拉，"用自己的靴子上的靴带，把自己往上拉"。只要一考虑，就知道这是完全办不到的事情。但是，归根到底，它表示"(不借他人的力量)自己把自己拉上去"的意义。作为比喻，它意味着"靠自己的力量白手起家"。各种词典中也有"独力完成"、"不借他人帮助自己干"等释义，但这样是有点不够的。这一表达法只能在极有限的场合使用，它表示在人生大道上，首先确定职业的目标，白手起家，经过千辛万苦，以自己的力量建立了经济的、社会的或者政治的地位。特别是在谈到那些下决心刻苦奋斗终于功成名就的人们的生平故事时，此习用语是常常出现的。例如，林肯从绗年起就备尝辛苦的故事是世人皆知的，如果说 *Abraham Lincoln pulled himself up by his own bootstraps.* 那就恰如其分。 *Felix pulled himself up by his own bootstraps. Although he had only four years of schooling when he started to work as a copyboy, he worked hard and rose to become the publisher of the city's largest newspaper.* 费利克斯是靠着自己努力奋斗获得他的地位的。他只上了四年学，就开始到报馆当取送稿件的小鬼，可是一直努力工作，最后成为市内最大报纸的发行人。不过，发迹的程度有种种不同，一切要根据其人的具体情况和志向来衡量，因此，即使他最后获得的地位并不十分显赫，也可以使用这一表达法。*Though a penniless orphan, he pulled himself up by his own bootstraps and became the respected owner of a small restaurant.* 他原来是个一文不名的孤儿，但是他倚靠自己的力量艰苦奋斗，终于成为一家小餐厅的令人尊敬的店主。另外，也可以使用其他具有"使上升"意味的动词如 raise ～ (up)、lift ～ (up) 等等来代替 pull ～ up。◇ make a success of *oneself* through *one's* own efforts

booze

booze ['bu:z] [话] **酒** 中古英语 bousen (狂饮)是它的语源。只要是含有酒精的饮料，不论是哪一种，一概都算 booze，但是，它一般不指葡萄酒、啤酒之类的淡酒，而是特指威士忌、杜松子酒等酒精成分高的 hard liquor 类。但是，这是一个相当亲昵的说法。*You got any booze?* 你有酒吗？*Shall I bring a bottle of booze to the party tonight?* 今天的社交晚会，我带瓶好酒去吧？虽然多作为名词使用，但有时具有"饮酒"的意义。而且，在这一场合，经常伴有"接着喝"、"大量喝"的意味。*Graham boozed until day break and then slept all day.* 格雷厄姆一直喝到天亮，然后大睡一天。◇ liquor

a booze hound → HOUND

booze it up [.bu:zə'dʌp] [话] **痛饮** BOOZE 是"饮酒"。it up 接在 booze 或 live 等动词后边，增添"大大地"、"豪华地"之类的意味 (live it up 意为"边喝边闹，大为高兴")。请注意：这里的 it 在语法上称为 situational "it" (状况的 it)，并不特指什么东西。*OK, everybody, let's booze it up tonight.* 喂，咱们大家今天晚上痛痛快快喝它一夜吧！*We boozed it up all over town last night.* 昨天晚上，我们喝遍了全城的酒馆。◇ drink a lot

hit the booze [.hɪtðə 'bu:z] [话] **酗酒** → hit the BOTTLE

boozed

boozed up [.bu:z'dʌ(:)p] [话] **喝醉了** 换句话说，就是 filled up with booze (装满了酒)的意思 (→ BOOZE)。*Let me call a taxi. You can't drive home boozed up like this.* 我给你叫辆出租汽车吧。你醉得这个样子，不能开车回家啦。*We all got boozed up last night.* 昨天晚上，我们全都喝得酩酊大醉。常加 all 增强语气。*We'd better call the station master. That fellow staggering along the edge of the platform is all boozed up.* 咱们最好是叫一下站长。在月台边上摇摇晃晃的那个人准是喝醉了。◇ drunk

bore

bore *someone* **to death** [.bo(:)r ～ tə'de(:)θ] [口] **使人憋闷得要死** → bore *someone* to TEARS

bore *someone* **to tears** → TEARS

born

a born loser → LOSER

bottle

hit the bottle [.hɪtðə 'bɑ(:)dl] [话] **酗酒** 这里的 hit 与 hit the BOOKS(→) (拼命用功)的使用方法相同，具有"加油干"、"大干特干"的意味。这一场合的 the bottle 表示"(用酒瓶) 喝酒"。本条习用语一般不使用于一次饮酒，而使用于天天的、形成习惯的大喝特喝的场合。*Stan was a good worker until his wife died and he began to hit the bottle.* 斯坦在他由于妻子去世而开始酗酒之前，本是一位很勤恳的工人。*Doug is an alcoholic. He's all right as long as he's on the wagon, but recently he's been hitting the bottle again.* 道格是个酒鬼。只要他戒酒，一切都很正常，但是最近他又大喝特喝起来了。如下一例句所示，用于一次饮酒的情况不是绝对没有，但这可以算作例外的使用方法了。*You were really hitting the bottle last night, weren't you?* 昨天晚上你可是喝了不少啊，是吧？ the bottle 可以换用 the sauce 或 the booze。sauce, booze 都是"酒"的意思的诙谐说法。*Poor Sam. His wife has started hitting the sauce again.* 萨姆真够可怜的。他的老婆又开始大喝猫尿啦。

◇ drink a lot

play spin the bottle [ˌpleɪ ˌspɪnðə ˈbɑ(ː)dl] [口]**搞转瓶游戏** spin the bottle 是"转瓶(游戏)"的意思,可当作一个名词。在美国的家庭晚会中,中、小学生大小的孩子们常搞的一种游戏。在游戏时,男孩子们和女孩子们围成一个圆圈,其中一个人进入圈内,把瓶子横放,并使其旋转。瓶子停下以后,瓶口对着的异性要吻转瓶人的面颊,而转瓶人也可以吻那个异性的面颊。如果瓶口指向同性,一般要重转一次,要不然就预先规定由右邻或左邻的异性吻面颊。 *Talk about unlucky! We played spin the bottle at Tom's party and every time I spun, it ended up pointing at that butterball Suzie Hogg.* 甭提多倒霉啦! 我们在汤姆家的晚会上玩转瓶游戏,每次我转,瓶口总是对着那个大胖墩苏吉·霍格。◇ play a kissing game

a thermos bottle [ə ˈθəːrməs ˌbɑ(ː)dl] [口]**暖瓶** 原是商品名称,因而有时把 t 字母大写,作 Thermos。正式说法是 a vacuum bottle [ˈvæ(ː)kjuəm ˌbɑ(ː)dl] (真空瓶),但在会话中几乎不使用。 *Joanne said she'd bring a thermos bottle of coffee.* 乔安妮说,她把咖啡装到暖瓶里拿来。有时把 bottle 省略而只说 a thermos。 *I forgot and left my thermos at school.* 我把暖瓶忘在学校里了。◇ a vacuum bottle

bottom

bet *one's* **bottom dollar** → DOLLAR

the bottom [ðə ˈbɑ(ː)dəm] [话] **(人的)屁股** 原来的构思是"(人的)底部"。这是表示"屁股"的最广泛使用的语言。有正式说法,医生等就好用 the buttocks [ðə ˈbʌdəks],但这种说法文绉绉的,在会话中很少使用。顺便提一下,把 buttocks 省略成 butt,在会话中倒是使用,但这一说法俗不可耐,用时必须考虑对方是谁。另外还有一个 ass [ˈæːs],很下流。bottom 或 the BEHIND 则均可安心使用。 *The boy's mother spanked him on the bottom.* 母亲打儿子的屁股。 *Jane has a fat bottom.* 简的屁股很大。the 或 a 也可以用物主代词代替。 *My bottom hurts.* 我的屁股痛。◇ the buttocks

get to the bottom of *something* [ˌgetːəðə ˈbɑ(ː)dəməv ～] [口] **查明真相[原因]等** 这里的 bottom 由"底部"转义为"原因"。 get to ～一语具有"设法达到"的韵味。 *something* 处一般代人 mystery 或 problem。 *The murder seemed inexplicable, but Miss Marple was determined to get to the bottom of it.* 那一杀人案件令人摸不着头脑,但是玛普小姐下决心要使真相大白。 *If we just discuss it calmly together, I'm sure we can get to the bottom of this problem.* 如果我们心平气和地一起来商讨的话,我相信,我们能够查明这一问题的原因所在。◇ discover the facts [cause] of *something*

scrape the bottom of the barrel → BARREL

Bottoms

Bottoms up. [ˈbɑdəmˈzʌ(ː)p] [话] **干杯** 字面意义是把 bottoms (底) 来个 up (朝上),亦即"一饮而尽"。 *Bottoms up, gentlemen. It's time to hit the road.* 先生们,把杯里的酒全喝光了吧! 到出发的时间啦! 如此例所示,是"把杯中残余的酒最后喝光"的意思。但这一习用语一般用以表示"干杯!" *Bottoms up!* 干杯! *Has everyone been served? All right, then, bottoms up!* 大家都有酒了吗? 好,那末,干杯! 不过,这是一种亲昵的说法,因此,在正式场合(比如结婚宴会上)不能使用。 *To a long and lasting relationship between our two companies. Bottoms up!* 为了我们两个公司长期保持始终不渝的友谊,干杯! 这个场面也不会是在正式宴会上,可能是在正式宴会后的第二次小会或便餐席上。另外,Cheers. 一词也是"干杯!"的意思,在亲昵的关系中使用。Cheers! (干杯!)还有一个更随便的说法是 Here's mud in your eye. 这句话与 Bottoms up. 或 Cheers. 不同,即便是朋友相聚之类的非正式集会,只要人数多了(如同学会),就不能使用它。这是极少数亲密的朋友在酒吧间或俱乐部里开始喝酒时说的一句话,相当于"来,干杯吧!"或"来,喝吧!"最后,我们讲一讲在正式的场面用什么说法来表达"干杯"的意思。说法也是多种多样，下面且举几个具有代表性的例子。首先是 I propose a toast to ～的形式。to 以后说应该成为"干杯"对象的人物、事情等等。 *I propose a toast to the happy couple.* 为两位新人的幸福干杯！ *I propose a toast to the continued success of our venture.* 为我们事业的继续繁荣昌盛干杯！ 另外还有 May I propose a toast? 或 I would like to propose a toast. 等等说法。而且，在使用这些表达法时，如 May I propose a toast (to the happy couple)? 或 I would like to propose a toast (to the continued success of our venture). 所示，加不加 to ～都可以。再有，在某种场合，只说 To the happy couple. 或者 To the continued success of our venture. 就表示"干杯"了。◇ Let's drink (to ～).

bouncer

a check bouncer [ə 'tʃek ˌbauntsər] [话] **常开空头支票的人** → bounce a CHECK

bout

throw a bout [ˌθrouə 'baut] [口] **(拳击等)在假比赛中输了** → THROW a race [game, etc.]

bow

bow and scrape ['bauən'skreɪp] [口] **点头哈腰** 这里的 scrape 是"搔(地面、地板等)"。本条整体的字面意义是描述古代的风俗"一边鞠躬，一边把右脚向后撤"、"毕恭毕敬地行礼"。 *When the gang boss came out of the prison, at least a hundred flunkies were lined up bowing and scraping on both sides of the gates.* 当流氓团伙的头子出狱的时候，至少有一百个歹徒排列在大门的两侧，毕恭毕敬地向他行礼。转义为"点头哈腰"。在会话中一般使用这一意义。含有搓着两手的低三下四的韵味。 *Look at that guy over there. From the way people around him are bowing and scraping he must be a pretty big wheel.* 你瞧对面那个家伙。从他周围那帮人点头哈腰的样子来看，他肯定还是相当大的人物哪。 *I can't stand that guy. Just because he became captain of the basketball team he expects everybody to bow and scrape to him.* 我不能容忍那个家伙。他认为当上了篮球队长，所有的人都得向他点头哈腰呢。◇ kowtow

box

go home in a box [goˌhoumɪnə 'bɑ(:)ks] [话] **(在外边)亡故** 这里的 box 是"棺材"。字面意义是"进了棺材回家"。 *If the boss doesn't give more thought to his health, he'll go home someday in a box.* 老板如果不多注意一下他的身体，说不上哪天会一命呜呼的。 *Hand over the money, or you'll go home in a box.* 快把钱拿出来，不然马上叫你见阎王。◇ die (away from home)

an idiot box [ə 'nɪdiət ˌbɑ(:)ks] [话] **电视机** an IDIOT 原为心理学用语，意为"只具有两岁以下思维能力的人"。转用于一般会话，表示"糊涂虫"、"傻瓜"、"低能儿"的意味。idiot box 这一说法则令人产生"使糊涂虫喜欢的箱子"、"低能儿的游戏箱"之类的联想。 *Turn off that idiot box. Can't you see I'm trying to study?* 把电视机关上。你看不见我要学习吗？◇ a television (set)

boxcars

boxcars ['bɑ(:)kˌskɑ(:)rz] [话] **双六点** a boxcar 是铁路的"有盖货车"。由于骰子的两个六点并在一起很象这种货车，所以有了本条的表达法。原来是叫做"掷双骰子"(craps)的一种赌博的用语，现在不论什么游戏，只要出两个 6，人们就好用 boxcars 一词。在玩 craps 的时候，只限于第一次掷的时候说 boxcars，而在其他游戏中则没有这样的惯例，只要一齐出两个 6，永远可以说 boxcars。 *Dave rolled boxcars three times in a row.* 戴夫一连出了三次双六点。如此例所示，多用 roll boxcars 这一短语。→ snake EYES ◇ double sixes

boy

a mama's boy [ə 'mɑ(:)məz ˌbɔɪ] [话] **离不开母亲的娇儿** 指不问"妈妈"就什么也不会干的"男孩子"、不问是非总爱牺牲妻子而偏袒“母亲”的“男士”等,他们即使还没有达到“恋母情结”,但已经离这种症状只有咫尺之遥了。*Jimmy's a mama's boy. He has to ask his mother before he can do anything.* 吉米是个离不开母亲的娇儿。他不管要做什么事情,都必须先去问他母亲。*Come on, Bill, don't be such a mama's boy. Nobody's ever gonna know we went swimming in the river.* 来,比尔,不要什么事都得先问妈妈。咱们到河里去游泳,谁也不会知道的。*One of the greatest mistakes a woman can make is to marry a mama's boy.* 在女人会犯的最大错误中,有一条就是嫁给一个离不开娘的窝囊废。◇ a mother-dominated boy [man]

boys

separate the men from the boys → MEN

bracelets

bracelets ['breɪsləts] [话] **手铐** bracelet 当然一般指“手镯”。但是,在作“手镯”解时,单数、复数皆能使用,而在作“手铐”解时,经常用复数。作“手铐”解的 bracelets 主要是警察或黑社会人的用语,在推理小说以及以盗匪为题材的影片中常常出现。*Slap the bracelets on this punk, Joe. We're taking him to the station.* 乔,快给这个小流氓戴上手铐。我们把他送到派出所去。◇ handcuffs

brag

be nothing to brag about [ˌnʌθəntə 'bræːgəbaut] [口] **没有什么了不起** 直译是“没有什么可夸耀的”,在有些场合,按照直译的意思使用就可以了。不过在语感上,它多半具有“没有什么了不起”的韵味。*Our sales have been better this year, but they're still nothing to brag about.* 今年我们的销路好了一些,但还没有大幅度的提高。强调的时候常加 certainly。*His pitching is certainly nothing to brag about.* 他的投球简直没有什么了不起。比几乎同义的 be nothing to CROW about 使用率高。◇ be not worth bragging about / be not so outstanding

brain

a brain [ə 'breɪn] [话] **有才华的人** 原意“头脑(好的人)”。*Bill is a brain. He gets all A's in math without much studying.* 比尔头脑聪明。他不大钻研,数学却总是 A。*I can never hope to be at the top of my class. There are too many brains in there.* 我永远没有在我们班里拔尖儿的希望,因为班里有才华的人太多了。常用 real 加强语气。*That guy is a real brain. He developed an entirely new type of computer program when he was only nineteen.* 那个人真是富有才华。当他仅仅十九岁的时候,就研制出一种完全新型的计算机程序。*Those two are the brains in our class.* 那两个学生是我们班里的尖子。另外,如最后的例句所示,根据上下文,也可以使用 the brains 的形式。但这一形式常具有其他的意义。→ the BRAINS (of [behind] *something*) ◇ a genius / a bright person

brain *someone* ['breɪn ~] [话] **打(某人)头部** 名词 brain (脑)的动词化。字面意义是“使溅出脑浆”、“杀人”,但在实际上几乎完全不使用这一解释,美国人听了这一表达法也联想不到那么凄惨的场面。一般是用这一说法强调“猛打(脑袋)”的意思。*My little brother brained me with a wooden sword.* 弟弟用木刀猛打了我的头部一下。如此例所示,不是用“手”打,通常是用“石头”、“棒子”之类的东西。也有象下面例句那样的场合,是由于“事故”或出于“偶然”。*A flower pot fell out of the window and brained me.* 一个花盆从窗台上掉下来,砸到我的脑袋上了。常用被动语态 be brained, 或 get brained。*The policeman was brained by a rock thrown by a demonstrator.* 警察的脑袋被示威者扔的石块砸上了。*A: What happened to your head? B: I got brained by a baseball bat in yesterday's game.* 甲:你的头部是怎么啦? 乙:昨天棒球比赛的时候,我的脑袋挨了一球棒。◇ hit *someone* over [on] the head

one's **brain child** → CHILD

cudgel *one's* **brain**[ˌkʌdʒəl ～ 'breɪn] [口] **绞尽脑汁** → rack *one's* BRAIN

have *something* **on the brain** [hæv ~ ˌɔ(:)nðə ˈbreɪn] [口] **脑子里只有……** 字面意义是"脑子里有某物"。*something* 的部分添入动名词,普通名词。*I can't get my husband to take me anywhere but to restaurants. He's got eating on the brain.* 除了餐厅而外,任何地方丈夫都不带我去。 他的脑子里只有一个吃字。 *Don't pay any attention to Bart. He's got boats on the brain.* 用不着去关心巴特的事情。 他的脑子里只有船。可以用 nothing but 加强语气。 *We can't get Tony to do his social studies homework. He's got nothing but mastering French on the brain.* 叫托尼搞社会科学的家庭作业是办不到的。他一心一意地要掌握好法语。 也可以说 get *something* on the brain,直译为"某种事情进入脑袋里了",有点"鬼迷心窍"的味道。 *Once Joan gets something on the brain, she talks of nothing else.* 一旦琼对什么事情入了迷,她嘴里就没有别的任何东西了。 ◇ think about nothing but *something*

rack *one's* **brain** [ˌræ(:)k ~ ˈbreɪn] [口] **绞尽脑汁** rack 在这里是"送上拷问台"。本条的意思就是"对脑子进行拷问"。使用方法如: *I've racked my brain, but I have yet to come up with any solution to the problem.* 我已经绞尽了脑汁,但是还没有给那个问题找到任何答案。*I racked my brain for a suitable topic of conversation with my taciturn visitor.* 面对沉默寡言的客人,我绞尽脑汁寻求适当的话题。在努力回想什么事情的场合也常常使用,例如: *Sue racked her brain, trying to remember where she had left her pocketbook.* 苏左思右想,试图回忆她在哪儿丢掉了手袋。也有时用复数形式作 rack *one's* brains。 *Mary racked her brains, trying to guess who could have sent her such an expensive present.* 玛丽绞尽脑汁,考虑究竟是谁会送给她那么值钱的一件礼物。也可以使用作"用棍棒打"解的 cudgel [ˈkʌdʒəl],而说 cudgel *one's* brain(s),虽然没有象 rack *one's* brain(s) 那样普遍使用,但是意义相同。◇ stretch *one's* mental ability to the limit / think very hard (, trying to find [remember, guess, etc.] *something*)

brains

beat *one's* **brains out** [ˌbi(:)t ~ ˈbreɪnˌzaut] [话] **拚命绞脑汁** 这一表达法给人的印象是拚命思考,达到"要把脑浆敲出来"的程度,是强调"竭尽全力"的一种说法。 *I beat my brains out all night working on that math problem before I finally got the answer.* 我整整一个晚上拚命绞脑汁解那道数学题,最后总算找到了答案。*I beat my brains out for a whole week drawing up this plan, and what does the boss do? He turns it down without even reading it.* 我整整一个星期拚命绞脑汁起草这份计划,可是,你猜老板怎么着? 他连看都不看一眼,就把它否决了。 *I've beat my brains out, but I just can't remember where I've met that man before.* 我拚命地思索过去在什么地方见过那个男人,但是我怎么也记不起来。这一表达法本来是只有一点点"拚命"的含意,但有时候却不以"绞脑汁"为重点,而把重点放在"拚命"这一含意上。 *I've beat my brains out trying to make my husband happy, but he doesn't seem to appreciate anything I do.* 我拚命想讨丈夫的喜欢,但是他好象完全不理解我的一切苦心。◇ stretch *one's* mental ability to the limit / struggle [work, think] very hard / try and try

beat *someone's* **brains out** [ˌbi(:)t ~ ˈbreɪnˌzaut] [话] **打得个屁滚尿流** 字面意义是"把某人的脑浆敲出来",但是"敲"的地方并不一定非"头"不可。这是一个非常幽默的说法,表达"饱以老拳"的形象。*The school bully said that if he caught you he was going to beat your brains out.* 学校的霸王说,如果他抓住你,他要把你打得个屁滚尿流。 *You stay away from my girl or I'll beat your brains out.* 你不要勾搭我的女朋友,否则我会把你砸个稀巴烂。根据语调,也可以加 almost, just about。 *I had thought I* *was stronger than that guy, but he almost beat my brains out.* 我一直认为我比那个家伙有劲儿,结果我却被他打了个落花流水。◇ give *someone* a good thrashing ((不能插入 almost))

the brains (of [behind] *something*) [ðə ˈbreɪnz] [口] **实权人物** 虽然是复数形式,但作单数使用。指"机构、组织中推动工作的中枢人物",这种人不仅能出谋画策,而且拥有付诸实行的绝对权力。因此,一般来说,总是一个单位的领导集团的成员。*The president of the company is Mr. Dolittle, but Joe, the junior partner, is actually the brains of the outfit.* 公司的董事长是多里特尔先生,但是实权却掌握在一位普通董事乔的手里。*Who is the brains of that organization?* 那个组织的实权人物是谁? the brains of ~的 of 改为 behind,就成为"在背后有实权的人"亦即"后台老板"的意思了。*Who is the brains behind that organization?* 那个组织的后台老板是谁? *We don't want to make any arrests until we find out who the brains behind the gang is.* 在弄清楚那个帮派的后台老板究竟是谁之前,我们一个人也不打算逮捕。下面是没有 of [behind] ~的形式。*We caught two of the conspirators but they were only underlings. We haven't caught the brains yet.* 我们抓住了两个阴谋分子,但是,他们只不过是小卒而已。首谋者还没有抓到呢。如以上的例句所示,一般用于指"一个组织的指挥者",但也有时用于表示"拟定并推行计划的人"的意思。在这一场合,前置词常用 behind,采取 the brains behind the plan [plot, scheme] 的形式。*Who was the brains behind the assassination plot?* 暗杀计划的首谋者是谁? 另外,brains 偶尔用单数形式,作 the brain。◇ the chief organizer / the supreme planner / the boss (of *something*)

brainstorm

a brainstorm [ə ˈbreɪn.stɔ(ː)rm] [话] **突然计上心头** 这一表达法原来的构思是"脑子里来了暴风雨"。常与 have、get 等动词一起使用。几乎在所有的场合可与 an inspiration (灵感)代换。*I've just had a brainstorm as to how we can get the money we need.* 关于我们怎样能够弄到我们所需要的那笔钱,我刚刚想出来一条妙计。如此例所示,一般使用这一表达法时,在"突然计上心头"的本人来说,含有"妙"的意味;但由他人看来,则多半不是如此。*There's no stopping the boss when he gets one of his brainstorms.* 老板一有了个什么鬼点子,他就不会中止的。*Oh no! Not another one of your crazy brainstorms.* 得啦得啦! 别再出你那种馊主意啦! 另外,在英国,brainstorm 具有"精神错乱"的意味,但在美国人的会话中,这种意味是绝对不存在的。顺便提一下,与美国的 a brainstorm 相当的英国英语是 a brain wave。◇ a (sudden) inspiration [idea]

brainstorming

a brainstorming session → SESSION

brand-new

brand- new [ˌbræ(ː)ˈnːjuː] [口] **崭新** → spanking NEW

brass

get down to brass tacks → TACKS

bread

bread [ˈbre(ː)d] [话] **钱** 比较新的用语。原为爵士乐师的行话。现在,特别是在青年人的会话中常常出现。earn *one's* daily bread (挣一天的面色)与 earn money 结合到一起,结果便成了 bread = money。因此,*I hate this job. But I've got to earn my bread somehow.* 这句话既可以解释为"我讨厌这个工作。但是,我总得混碗饭吃呀。"也可以解释为"我讨厌这个工作。但是我总得挣几个钱啊。" *You got any bread? I'm a little short.* 你手里有钱吗? 我正缺点钱。*I think I'll get a part-time job this summer vacation. I've got to make a little bread.* 今年暑假我想找个临时工作干。我必须挣几个钱。另外,一百多年以前就开始有个习用语 the long green,也是"钱"的意思。这一说法的来源,是由于美元纸币背面为"绿色"。特别在黑社会里通行。*Let's invite Duke to become a partner in our next venture. He's got lots of the long green.* 我们邀请杜克参加我们下次搞的事业吧。他有大量的钞票。同样由于从"绿色"的联想,在美国的俚语中,青菜中的 lettuce (莴苣)、cabbage (卷心菜)、spinach (菠菜)等也意味着"钱"。这几种说法全都比 bread 的历史早,其中 lettuce 的应用最广泛。这一表达法原为杂技团人员的隐语。*I wish I knew a quick way to get my hands on a little lettuce.* 我要是知道用什么简便方法弄到点钞票,那多好啊! 另外还有一个 scratch。动词 scratch 是"挠"。象鸡挠地面找食一样,人靠辛辛苦苦劳动挣钱。这一说法便是由此种构思产生的。*I've got to find some work soon. I'm getting low on scratch.* 我得赶快找点工作干了。我几乎没有一点儿钱啦。→ DOUGH ◇ money

one's **bread and butter** [~ ˌbredn-ˈbʌ(ː)dər] [话] **饭碗** 直译是"(某人的)面包和黄油"。如下面的三个例句所示,"面包和黄油"意味着 *one* 的"生活手段"。按照三个例句的顺序,成为"饭碗"的分别是 hands (手), teaching (教书)和 I (我)。*A professional pianist has to take extremely good care of his hands. They're his bread and butter.* 一个职业钢琴家必须极端注意保护他的手。手就是他的饭碗。*I prefer writing to teaching, but I can't quit until my works begin to sell. I'd be giving up my bread and butter.* 我喜欢写作而不喜欢教书,但是在我的作品能够卖出去以前,我不能放弃教书,因为那就等于丢掉我的饭碗了。*I know I owe a lot of my success in boxing to my manager, but I still expect him to treat me with respect. After all, I'm his bread and butter.* 我知道我在拳击中的成功有经纪人很大的功劳,但是我仍然希望他尊敬我。归根结底,我是他的饭碗。除"饭碗"的意义外,虽然极为少见,但有象下边的例句那样只意味着"生活"的情况。*You shouldn't place too many demands on Harry. He's got his bread and butter to think of too, you know.* 你不能苛求哈里,给他加太多的负担。你要知道,他还得考虑他自己的生活哪。◇ *one's* means of making a living

know which side *one's* **bread is buttered on** [ˌnou ˌhwitʃˈsaɪd ~ ˌbre(ː)dɪzˈbʌdər-ˌdɔːn] [话] **了解什么对自己有利** 字面意义是"了解面包是哪一面抹黄油",也就是"知道自己的面包哪一面香"。当然只作为比喻使用。*Big business supports the conservative party and unions support the progressive party because each knows which side their bread is buttered on.* 大企业支持保守党,工会则支持进步党,因为各自都知道哪一方对自己有利。本条大多用于表示"依靠或支持哪一边有利"的意味,但并不是只限于此。*If you know which side your bread is buttered on, you'll give up the idea of marrying a girl your father doesn't approve of.* 如果你明白怎样做对自己有利,你就会放弃与你父亲所不同意的姑娘结婚的意图了。on 也可以放在 which 以前,但语气变得生硬了。*If Sue gets in trouble, she'll come to me first. She knows on which side her bread is buttered.* 如果苏发生麻烦问题,她会首先到我这儿来。她知道怎样做对自己有利。另外,在英国英语中,有时省略 on,但在美国英语中不加不行。◇ know whom it is in *one's* best interests to serve [support, obey, turn to, etc.]

bread-and-butter

a bread-and-butter letter → LETTER

breadbasket

the breadbasket[ðə ˈbre(ː)dˌbæ(ː)skət] [话] **肚子** 直译"装面包的篮子",转义为"(装面包[食物])的胃"。一般用于说"(肚子上)受到了打击"、"(肚子)痛了"的场合。虽然是孩子们常用的说法,但是成年人也用,特别是在体育运动等活动中。*Jimmy hit me in the breadbasket.* 吉米用拳头打我的肚子了。*I wasn't looking when the ball was thrown, and it hit me in the breadbasket.* 由于投球的时候我没注

意看,球打到我的肚子上了。*The champ gave the challenger a hard left to the breadbasket.* 冠军用左勾拳猛力一击,打中了挑战者的腹部。也可以用 *one's* breadbasket 的形式。*I fell on my breadbasket.* 我摔了个大马趴。另外用于比喻,也有"(主要的)粮食产地"的意思。*The Midwest is America's breadbasket.* 中西部是美国的谷仓。◇ stomach

breadwinner

a breadwinner [ə ˈbre(ː)dˌwɪnər] [口] **挣钱养家的人** 这里的 winner 是"获得者",不是"胜利者"。这是在以面包为主食的国家才会出现的表达法,如果在中国,就应该说"大米(或馒头)的获得者"了。*Who is the breadwinner in your family?* 府上是谁挣钱养家? *With the increase in the number of working wives, more and more families are coming to have two breadwinners.* 由于家庭妇女就业人数的增加,越来越多的家庭有两个人挣钱养家了。另外,常与"养家"的意思无关,仅用以表示和 wage earner (挣工资的人)相同的意思。*Most New York breadwinners must commute more than an hour to work.* 纽约的职工上班大多需要坐一个多小时的车。◇ a wage earner (of a family)

break

break *something* **to** *someone* **gently** [ˌbreɪk ~ tə ~ ˈdʒentli] [话] **用婉转的方式向某人报告坏消息** break 是"(把对方完全不知道的事情突然)说出、揭明"的意思。*something* 处代人与"坏消息"相当的词句。这里的 gently 是"用尽可能婉转不使人大为震惊的口吻"的意思。*Knowing that the old man had a weak heart, I tried to break the news of his son's death to him gently.* 由于知道老人的心脏有病,我尽可能婉转地说出他的儿子已经死去的消息。*No matter how gently I may try to break it to him, I know my husband will take it very hard.* 不管我怎样努力委婉地对他说,我知道我的丈夫一定会非常难受的。*There's no way to break this to you gently, Harris. You just haven't been doing your job, so we're going to have to let you go.* 哈里斯,这件事我没有办法对你说出而不伤你的心。你未能很好地去干你的工作,所以我们决定辞退你了。◇ tell *someone something* in such a way as to lessen the shock

breast

make a clean breast of *something* [ˌmeɪkə ˈkliːn ˈbrestəv ~] [口] **彻底坦白** 字面意义为"用(某物)做一个干净的胸脯"。正如霍桑(Nathaniel Hawthorne)的小说《红字》(*The Scarlet Letter*) 所写,过去有在犯人胸前打上烙印的惯例。因此,本条习用语原是"除去胸前的烙印"意思,但是现在的用法不同了,如果完全敞开胸怀,就说 clean breast (干净的胸怀)。*something* 的部分多用 it 或 everything 代入。坦白的内容不是烦恼、不满之类,而是坏的事情,从儿童的恶作剧直至人们的犯罪,广泛使用这一表达法。*When Ted's superior accused him of misusing company funds, he broke down and made a clean breast of it.* 当上级指责特德挪用公司钱款的时候,特德知道无法隐瞒,便坦白交待了。*I'm not willing to stick my neck out to help you unless you make a clean breast of everything.* 只要你不一一坦白交待,我决不想冒着风险去帮助你。*You'll feel better if you make a clean breast of it to your father.* 你如果把这件事情向你父亲合盘托出,你的心情会轻松愉快的。*The suspect made a clean breast of everything.* 嫌疑犯把全部事实都坦白交待了。◇ confess all [everything] / tell *someone* everything

breath

save *one's* **breath** [ˌseɪv ~ ˈbre(ː)θ] [口] **保持沉默** 直译为"节约气息",亦即"不说无用的话"的意思。但是,不是用于闲话连篇、喋喋不休等场合,而是用于在谈正经事或者大家议论的时候,由于不必要说而闭口无言的场合。*Save your breath. There's no use arguing with John. He's made up his mind.* 甭费唇舌啦。跟约翰辩论是没有一点用处的,他已经铁了心。*A: Kurt wants to talk to you. B: Tell him to save his breath. The matter's already been decided.* 甲:库尔特想跟你谈一谈。乙:你告诉他,不必白费口舌啦,那件事已经决定了。*You may as well save your breath, Steve. I'm not going and that's final.* 史蒂夫,你别白费口舌了。我说不去,就是不去。*I soon saw that he wasn't going to change his mind, so I decided to save my breath.* 我跟他谈了几句,就看出他决不打算改变自己的主意,所以我就保持沉默了。→ waste *one's* BREATH ◇ it is futile to talk about it

take *someone's* **breath away** [ˌteɪk ~ ˈbre(ː)θəˌweɪ] [口] **令人激动得喘不出气来** 字面意义是"把(某人的)气息取走",乍看起来,与汉语的"令人惊叹"、"叹观止矣"相类似。例如:*The beauty of the scene below took our breath away.* 眼底的美景令我们惊叹不已。但是,这一表达法在英语中的使用非常广泛,不能译为"令人惊叹"的时候是很多的。在面临各个例句的时候,有必要一个一个地琢磨。*The intensity of the noise that greeted his ears when he opened the door of the factory took his breath away.* 当他打开工厂的门的时候,那巨大的噪音向他的耳朵猛烈袭来,使他大吃一惊。象这种地方,没有译成"令人惊叹"的必要,倒可以译为"吓了一大跳"或"吓得缩成一团"等等。*The blast of cold air that hit me when I stepped outside took my breath away.* 我刚走出门外,一阵冷风向我吹来,使我连气都喘不出来了。*I was quite impressed with Mr. Smoothy. His charm and easy flow of words practically took my breath away.* 斯穆塞先生给我留下了非常深刻的印象。他的魅力和对答如流的口才实在使我为之倾倒。另外,take *someone's* breath away 也可以用 take away *someone's* breath 的形式。还有一个把 take 和 breath 用连接号连接起来的形容词 breath-taking,此词专用于形容 beauty (美丽)或 splendor (壮丽)等名词,因此大多可译为"令人惊叹"。*She is a woman of breath-taking beauty.* 她是一位美貌惊人的女子。*The view from the mountain was breath-taking.* 从山上往下一看,那景色实在美得惊人。◇ be overpowering

waste *one's* **breath** [ˌweɪst ~ ˈbre(ː)θ] [话] **怎么说也没用** 字面意义是"浪费气息"。这一习用语表示与 save *one's* BREATH 完全相反的概念。在使用方法上,不论从正面说 You're wasting your breath. 或是用打消的口气说 Don't be wasting your breath. 或 Don't waste your breath. 结果意义全都一样。*You're wasting your breath. No matter what you say, I won't change my mind.* 你白浪费你的口舌。不管你说什么,我也不会改变自己的主意。*Don't waste your breath talking to that guy. He's as stubborn as a mule.* 你不必浪费口舌跟那个家伙谈。他是个顽固透顶的人。*I'm not going to waste my breath on that guy any more.* 我再也不跟那个家伙白费口舌啦。*You haven't been listening to me all evening, have you. Well, you can just solve your own problems. I'm tired of wasting my breath on you.* 我今天晚上一直跟你谈,你连一句也没有听。那么,你自己的问题就自己去解决好啦。我已经厌烦了,不想对你多费一点口舌了。◇ waste *one's* time (talking to *someone*)

breather

take a breather [ˌteɪkə ˈbriːðər] [话] **歇口气** breather 是"(为了喘口气而)休息一下"、"喘息时间",take a breather 就成为"略微休息一下"的意思了。*I'm beat. Let's take a breather.* 我累极了。咱们歇口气吧。*This kind of work is very tiring. It's best to take a breather every once in a while.* 这种活儿太累人。最好是干一会儿歇一会儿。另外,take a breather 是个普通的形式,根据不同情况,有时也可以用其他动词代替 take。*I need a breather. Let's knock off for a few minutes.* 我需要喘口气啦。咱们休息两三分钟吧。再有,"歇口气"时间的长短是相对的,既有象上边例句中的短时间,也

有象下一例句中的长时间。*After working for almost three months without a day off, I needed a breather.* 干了将近三个月，一天也没有休息，我需要歇口气了。这大概需要几天的功夫。◇ take a short rest

breath-taking

breath-taking [ˈbreθ.teɪkɪŋ] [口] **令人惊叹(的 FS** → **take** *someone's* BREATH away

breeze

bat the breeze [.bætðə ˈbriːz] [话] **闲聊天** → shoot the BREEZE

fan the breeze [.fæ(ː)nðə ˈbriːz] [话] **闲聊天** → shoot the BREEZE

shoot the breeze [.ʃu(ː)tðə ˈbriːz] [话] **闲聊天** 直译是"(用语言)射击微风"，这是毫无意义的举动。因此，这一表达法具有"东家长西家短"、"山南海北胡侃"、"闲聊大天"的意味。*Joe and I went over to Mr. Surrey's house last night and shot the breeze over a few beers.* 乔和我昨天晚上到萨里先生家里去，一边喝啤酒一边聊大天儿。*We aren't talking about anything especially important — just shootin' the breeze.* 我们并不是在谈什么特别重要的事情，只不过是闲聊天而已。这种闲聊往往加油加醋，夸大其词，因此，根据上下文，有时具有"信口开河"的意味。*Don't take what he says seriously. He was only shooting the breeze.* 对他说的话不必认真，他只是信口开河而已。又如 *The typist is out shooting the breeze with the driver again.* 打字员又磨洋工，找司机闲聊天去了。这是"放下工作不干去闲聊天"，即"软磨硬泡、偷懒耍滑"的意思。也有时说 bat the breeze，或者用 fan the breeze，意义均相同。◇ talk (idly)

bricks

like a ton of bricks [laɪkə ˈtʌnəv ˈbrɪ(ː)ks] [话] **势头凶猛** 直译为"象一吨砖似的"。照字面使用，是强调东西落下或人倒下时其势之猛的一种表达法，与 fall (倒、落)、hit (打、击)、come down (落下来) 等动词结合在一起，专用于表示物理的意义，亦即"(象一吨砖掉下来似的) 咕咚一声"或"(象一吨砖倒下来似的) 轰隆一声"的感觉。*Someone hit me from behind and I fell like a ton of bricks.* 有人从我背后猛然一击，我咕咚一声倒下去了。*The ceiling came down on me like a ton of bricks.* 天棚轰隆一声从我上边落下来了。作为比喻，一般常与 FALL for *something* (上圈套)、以及 hit *someone* (忽然发现)、come down on *someone* (叱责) 等动词词组结合起来使用。虽然意思不一样了，但与原来的使用方法同样，仍然与 fall, hit, come down 等动词 (词组) 结合，这是本条习用语的特征。fall for *something* like a ton of bricks 是"上了个大圈套"，与 swallow *something* hook, line and sinker (→ swallow *someone's* LINE)的意义大致相同。这一表达法的 like 以下可用 hook, line and sinker 代换。*He fell for Jack's trick like a ton of bricks.* 他大大地中了杰克的阴谋诡计。*She fell for his line like a ton of bricks.* 他的花言巧语，使她大受欺骗。但是，由于"吞"与"砖"的结合是很奇怪的事情，所以作为比喻，根本没有 swallow *something* like a ton of bricks 的说法。FALL for *someone* (爱慕<异性>)与 like a ton of bricks 结合起来，是"一心迷恋"的意思了。*He fell for her like a ton of bricks.* 他一心迷恋上她了。其次，hit *someone* like a ton of bricks 是一个几乎定型的说法。这里的 hit *someone* 是"想到了(答案等)"或"明白了(真相等)"的意思。like a ton of bricks 则具有"(一瞬间) 突然"的感觉。*I had been wondering what to do for several days when, just like that, the answer hit me like a ton of bricks.* 我考虑了好几天究竟怎么办才好，结果在一瞬间，头脑里突然出现了答案。*When I saw Alan walking with Alice in the park, it suddenly hit me like a ton of bricks. They had been lying to me all along.* 当我看到艾伦同艾丽丝一道在公园里散步的时候，我突然醒悟过来了。他们原来一直跟我撒谎呀。hit *someone* 也可以象下面的例

句那样表示“受到震动”的意思。*The unusual beauty of the place hit me like a ton of bricks.* 那异常绮丽的风光使我大吃一惊。come down on *someone* like a ton of bricks 是 come down hard on *someone* 这一习用语的更加强烈的说法,也是一个习用语。意思是“气势汹汹地叱责”。*When the boss found me goofing off, he came down on me like a ton of bricks.* 当老板发现我偷懒耍滑的时候,他气势汹汹地训斥了我一大顿。*A: What did your father say about your bad report card? B: He came down on me like a ton of bricks.* 甲:你父亲见了你那不好的成绩单,他说什么来着? 乙:他暴跳如雷,把我狠狠训斥了一大顿。另外,偶然也有用 a pile 或 a load 等代替 a ton 的场合,意思不变。◇ completely / with great force

bridge

water under the bridge → WATER

bridges

burn *one's* **bridges (behind** *one***)** [.bə(:)rn ~ 'bri(:)dʒəz .bə(:)rn ~ .brɪ(:)dʒəz bə'haɪnd ~] [口] **背水而战**原意是“(在战争时)走过一座桥烧一座桥”。如果按照字面使用,就是表示“绝对不退却一步”的坚强意志,与“布背水阵”的意义相近。*In order to prevent his soldiers from retreating, the general ordered that all bridges behind them be burnt.* 为了防止士兵后退,将军下令烧掉他们走过去的所有的桥。但是,在作为比喻使用的时候,就不只是表示坚强的意志了,一般用于这样的场合:为了达到一个目的,“毫不在乎地”或者“毫无办法地”使自己处于不能折回的境地,结果断绝自己的退路,放弃求援的指望。*There's no returning home now. You burnt your bridges when you married against your father's wishes.* 现在已经回不了家啦。你违背父亲的意愿而结婚,已经把回家的路堵死了。*If you quit your present job before you find another, you'll be foolishly burning your bridges behind you.* 如果你没找到另外的工作就先辞去当前的工作,那太愚蠢了,弄得自己连条后路都堵死了。bridges 根据上下文也可以用单数形式。*It was too late to change his mind now. By attacking his guard and fleeing from the embassy he had burnt his last bridge behind him. He had no choice but to defect.* 现在要改变他的主意已经太迟了。他袭击门卫,逃出大使馆,业已堵死了自己的后路。他没有另外的办法,只好远走高飞。◇ (do something to) prevent *oneself* from turning back

bring

bring *something* **off** [.brɪŋ ~ 'ɔ:f] [话] **完成** 这一习用语除用于“困难工作”、“技艺”等外,也用于“坏事”。译作“完成”,大致可以概括它的意义。*It's an extremely difficult assignment, but if anyone can bring it off I'm sure Phil can.* 这是一个非常困难的任务,如果说有谁可以完成的话,我敢肯定菲尔能行。*It's going to be hard to convince the committee to accept our plan. Do you think you can bring it off?* 使委员会接受我们的计划是一件很困难的事情。你认为你能够完成这个任务吗? *The Chinese skating team brought off the intricate maneuver very beautifully.* 中国滑冰队非常漂亮地完成了复杂的技巧动作。*That gang brought off two daytime bank robberies at downtown banks in one week.* 那群歹徒一个星期之内,在光天化日下,竟两次抢劫了闹市区的银行。◇ manage *something* / succeed (at *something*) / (manage to) *do something* successfully

briny

the briny [ðə 'braɪni] [话] **海** briny 原为 brine (高浓度的盐水)的形容词,意为“(象 brine 一样)咸”。最初用作诗的用语 the deep (海)的修饰语,后来 the briny deep 成为诗中的固定词组,它也随着流传下来。1900 年左右开始,在口语中,这个 the briny deep 中的 deep 脱落了,只剩下 the briny 表示“海”,人们在亲切的交谈中使用这一表达法。*A* *plane suddenly dropped from the clouds and disappeared into the briny.* 一架飞机突然从云彩中间掉下来，消失到大海里了。◇ the ocean

britches

be too big for *one's* **britches** [ˌtu(:) ˌbɪ(:)gfər ~ ˈbrɪtʃəz] [话] **狂妄自大** britches 为"裤子"，是比 pants 或 trousers 更随意的说法。正式缀字为 breeches (发音相同)，但有陈腐之感，现在一般均从实际发音写作 britches。本条全部直译为"对自己的裤子来说过大了"。作为比喻，常用于一个人妄自尊大的场合。*I can't abide that guy. He's too big for his britches.* 我不能容忍那个家伙。他太狂妄自大啦。grow [get] too big for *one's* britches 是"变得趾高气扬"。*People who become rich suddenly often grow too big for their britches.* 凡是穷人乍富，往往腆腰凸肚。*Don't get too big for your britches. Somebody may take you down a notch or two.* 你不要那么趾高气扬。有人会挫败你的傲气的。同一意义还有一个说法是 too big for *one's* boots，但把它作为英国英语考虑为宜。有的词典把 too big for *one's* pants 列为本条习用语的类语，但是务请读者注意：它只能按照字面意义使用，如：*Jimmy has gotten too big for his pants. We'll have to buy him another pair.* 吉米长大了，他的裤子显得小了。我们得给他另买一条啦。◇ think too highly of *one's* own importance

broad

be (about) as broad as it is long [(əˌbaud)əz ˈbrɔːdəzədɪz ˈlɔːŋ] [口] **背着抱着一样沉** 字面意义是"长和宽(大致)相同"，亦即"square (正方形)"的意思。*This table looks about as broad as it is long.* 这张桌子看起来长和宽差不多。也转用于比喻。*A: Which way do you think we should go? B: Well, it's about as broad as it is long. The road over the mountain is much shorter, but the road around the mountain is much better.* 甲：你认为我们应该走哪条路？乙：嗯，背着抱着一样沉啊。穿山而行距离短，绕山而行道路平。如以上例句所示，多加 about 以及 just about 等，但根据说话时的口气，也有不加的时候。*As far as the cost is concerned, it's as broad as it is long. If we buy the cheaper machine, it will cost a lot to have it installed. If we buy the more expensive one, installation is free.* 关于费用的问题，是背着抱着一样沉。我们如果买便宜点的机器，要付大量的安装费；我们如果买贵一些的机器，安装就不要钱。◇ it doesn't (really) make any [much] difference / it's (about) the same either way

a broad [ə ˈbrɔːd] [俗] **女人** a bawd [ˈbɔːd] (1700 年左右开始，指"妓院的老鸨"；后指"妓女") 一词的变形。但一般来说，broad 一词本身并不具有令人联想到卖淫的意味。尽管如此，它却成为对女性的蔑称 (一般指十九岁以上)，使用时需要慎重。亲密男性朋友之间常挂在嘴上。*Will there be any broads at the party?* 社交晚会有女的吗？*She's just a dumb broad.* 她简直是一个蠢货。另外，弗兰克·西纳托拉(Frank Sinatra)在电视中把这个词当作口头禅，大家认为这是他卖弄说话技巧的一个小道具。◇ a woman

broke

be broke [ˈbrouk] [话] **一文不名** break 除"破坏"的意义外，还有"使人把钱耗尽"、"使人破产"的意味。在后一意味的场合，不是使用 broken，而是使用 break 的旧的过去分词 broke。这是一种轻松的表达法。*I'm broke tonight. How about you?* 我今天晚上一文不名。你怎么样？这一例句表示"(一时) 手里没钱"。除此而外，也用于"总没有钱"的场合。*I'd like to have my own house, but I'm broke.* 我想自己有一所房子，但是一点儿钱也没有。在加强语气时，除 completely (完全地) 而外，还常使用同义词

stone 或 flat 等。*I want to go to college, but my old man's stone [flat] broke.* 我很想上大学，可是我的老子一贫如洗。如以上的例句所示，多用于谈论个人的经济情况，除此而外，在谈论公司之类的机构的经济情况时，也常常使用。*If sales don't improve soon, this company's going to be broke.* 如果销售额不马上增加，这个公司就要破产了。也常改变动词，说 go broke。*If you keep spending money like this, you're going to go broke.* 你如果总象这样大把花钱，很快就会一文不名的。如这一例句所示，可以用于个人的情况，但是，实际上多半用于谈论公司之类的机构。*Thirty companies went broke in New York alone last month.* 上个月，仅纽约一个地方就有三十家公司倒闭了。◇ not have any money

go broke [.gou 'brouk] [话] **破产** → be BROKE

go for broke [.goufər 'brouk] [话] **豁出去** broke 是 break 的过去分词的古老形式，指"一文不名"的状态。go for broke 原是赌博场的隐语之一，意为"把所有的钱都押到一把牌或掷一次骰子上"。*When I was dealt a third ace, I decided to go for broke.* 当我得到第三个 *A* 的时候，我决定孤注一掷了。这种说法不只赌博中使用，作为比喻，在一般场合也广泛使用起来。*I'm against going for broke on this one project. If it doesn't succeed, the company's finished.* 我反对孤注一掷，把一切都押在这个方案上。如果不成功，公司就完蛋了。*The enemy has us outnumbered and surrounded. If we're going to get out of here, we'll have to go for broke. Put every man into the charge.* 敌军人数比我们多，而且把我们包围了。如果我们要从这里突围，就得完全豁出去，每一个人都投入战斗。象下面的例句那样，就不意味着"豁出去"，仅意味着"竭尽全力"，这是一种轻快的使用方法。*We went for broke to meet the deadline.* 为了不误限期，我们竭尽了所有力量。◇ gamble everything on one try

brokenhearted

brokenhearted [.broukən'hɑ(:)rdəd] [口] **肝肠欲断** → break *someone's* HEART

Bronx

a Bronx cheer → CHEER

broth

Too many cooks spoil the broth. → COOKS

brother

a big brother [ə 'bɪg 'brʌðər] [口] **哥哥** 有时见到人们把这一习用语译作"身体大的弟兄"。其实，这个 big 与 older [elder] 完全同义。在会话中，特别是谈到小孩子或者青少年的哥哥时，一般不说 older [elder] brother, 而说 big brother。这一说法不论年龄大小均常使用，不仅如此，它比 older [elder] brother 令人感到一种亲热的味道。与身体的实际大小毫无关系。*My big brother got married last week.* 我哥哥上个星期结婚了。*Betty has two big brothers and one little sister.* 贝蒂有两个哥哥和一个妹妹。顺便提一下：乔治·奥威尔 (George Orwell) 曾在他的小说《一九八四年》中使用这一表达法，自从那部小说问世 (1949 年) 以来，big brother (无冠词，一般字头大写，作 Big Brother) 就具有另外一种意义了，或指"(一个国家的) 统治阶级"，或戏指"头头"。*Be careful of what you say. Big Brother may be listening.* 说话要当心些。也许头头在听着哪！→ a little BROTHER ◇ an older brother

a little brother [ə 'lɪdl 'brʌðər] [口] **弟弟** 这里的 little 与 younger 完全同义。本条与意味着"哥哥"的 a big BROTHER 相对应。因此，完全没有"身体小的弟兄"的意思。在会话中，little brother 是比 younger brother 更富有人情味的说法，不论年龄大小，人们均喜欢使用。*My little brother will be twenty years old next week.* 我弟弟下星期就二十岁了。*I never dreamed I'd have a little brother who'd become President someday!* 我从来没有梦想过我有一个弟弟将来在哪一天当上总统！→ a big BROTHER ◇ a younger brother

brotherly

The City of Brotherly Love [ðə ˈsɪdiəv ˈbrʌðərli ˈlʌ(:)v] [口] **费城** → PHILLY

brown

(as) brown as a berry → BERRY

brown-bag

brown-bag it [ˈbraun.bæ(:)gət] [话] **自带午饭** 一般指学生、教师、职工等中午不到外边吃饭,自带简单的食物。美国人所带的食物几乎全是三明治,装入纸袋。因纸袋多为棕色,故称 brown-bag。但体力劳动者自带饭食时,一般不使用这一表达法。*I always brown-bag it.* 我永远是自带午饭的。*Joe says he won't go out for lunch with us. He's brown-bagging it today.* 乔说他不跟咱们一起出去吃午饭啦。他今天自带午饭了。名词形式为 brown-bagging。*Brown-bagging has become popular among young office workers.* 在公司的青年职工中间,很流行自带午饭。"总是自带午饭的人"叫做 a brown-bagger。*Roy never eats out at lunch. He's a brown-bagger.* 罗伊中午决不到外边去吃饭。他总是自带三明治的。另外,美国有些地方的大餐厅、夜总会除啤酒、葡萄酒外,不卖其他酒精饮料。因此,就有人用纸袋装威士忌一类的小酒瓶带进去,这种行动也叫做 brown-bag it。*Have a drink on me. I'm brown-bagging it tonight.* 我请你喝一杯。今天晚上我自带威士忌啦。◇ take [bring] *one's* lunch (in a paper bag)

brown-bagger

a brown-bagger [ə ˈbraun.bæ(:)gər] [话] **总是自带午饭的人** → BROWN-BAG it

brunch

brunch [ˈbrʌntʃ] [口] **早午饭** breakfast (早饭)的 br-与 lunch (午饭)的 -unch 的合成语。时间是在 10~11 点钟左右,吃的东西大多是早饭的内容。如果时间再迟一点,吃的又不是早饭的内容,那就不是 brunch,而是 early lunch 了。*We usually get up late on Sunday and have brunch about eleven.* 星期日我们总是晚起床,十一点钟左右吃早饭兼午饭。另外,这个 brunch 也可以作为不及物动词使用,但使用频率极低。如上一例句所示,一般采取 have brunch 的形式。◇ a combination of breakfast and lunch

brush

brush *someone* **off** [.brʌʃ ~ ˈɔ:f] [话] **干脆打发走** → give *someone* the BRUSH-OFF

brush-off

give *someone* **the brush-off** [.gɪv ~ ðə ˈbrʌ(:).ʃɔ:f] [话] **痛痛快快打发走** 如果把 brush *something* off (用刷子刷掉<衣服上的尘土之类>)应用到人身上,将 *something* 换成 *someone*, 就成为 brush *someone* off, 意为"(象掸掉衣服上的尘土一样)赶快把人撵走"、"痛痛快快地打发走"。*There's some guy waiting to see me. As soon as I brush him off, let's go to dinner.* 有一个人在等着见我。我赶快把他打发走,咱们就去吃晚饭。把这个 brush 和 off 用连字符连接起来,加以名词化,就是 give *someone* the brush-off 的 brush-off 了。意思是"断然拒绝",与 brush *someone* off 大致同义,但使用频率高。在拒绝申请或委托、断绝来往等场合使用。就表面态度来说,有的严若冰霜,有的则彬彬有礼。*A: Have you gotten a date with Sue yet? B: No. She always gives me the brush-off.* 甲:你已经跟苏约期幽会了吗? 乙:没有。她总是断然拒绝啊。*If you think you can give me the brush-off so easily, you've got another think coming.* 如果你以为你能够那么轻而易举地把我甩掉,那可是白日做梦。*Once he became famous, he began giving all his old friends the brush-off.* 他一旦成了名,就开始与所有的老朋友断绝来往。*I tried to make an appointment to see the vice-president, but his secretary gave me the brush-off.* 我企图得到副总裁的约见,但是他的秘书断然拒绝了。

get the brush-off 与被动语态的 be given the brush-off 同样是"遭到断然拒绝"的意思，但比 be given ~更常为人们所使用。*A: How did your meeting with Mr. Shortshrift go? B: I got [was given] the brush-off. He says he's not interested in my proposal.* 甲：你跟肖特什里夫特先生会见的结果如何？乙：我遭到他完全的拒绝啦。他说，他对我的建议毫无兴趣。brush-off 也可以加形容词。*A: Would the boss talk to you about a raise? B: No. I got the same old brush-off.* 甲：老板跟你谈关于提高工资的问题了吗？乙：没有。我照旧遭到他的断然拒绝。◇ get rid of *someone* / treat *someone* very coldly

buck

make a fast buck [ˌmeɪkə ˈfæ(ː)st ˈbʌk] [话] **迅速赚钱** → make a quick BUCK

make a quick buck [ˌmeɪkə ˈkwɪk ˈbʌk] [话] **忙活着捞钞票** buck 是"一美元的钞票"。本条直译是"做一张快的一美元钞票"。这个"做"是"赚"的意思。*There are fewer steady workers these days. Too many people are just out to make a quick buck.* 近来，踏踏实实工作的人少起来了。忙活着捞钞票的人可是太多啦。*I'm not really all that interested in making a quick buck. What I'd like is a good, steady job.* 说老实话，我对于忙着捞钱并没有多大兴趣。我喜欢的是一个良好的、稳定的工作。另外，有时用 fast (快) 代替 quick，而说 make a fast buck。◇ make money in a hurry

pass the buck (to *someone*) [ˈpæːsðə ˈbʌ(ː)k] [话] **逃避责任** 这里的 buck 是"(玩扑克牌的)庄家的标志"。本条习用语原意为"(在扑克牌游戏中)把庄家往下轮"。杜鲁门总统有一段著名的趣闻：他曾模仿这一表达法，把写有 The buck stops here. 字样的木牌置放到自己的案头。这一格言的意义是"庄家标志在这里停住"，亦即"全部责任在我身上"。*Don't expect Carl to assume responsibility for making a decision. He's famous for passing the buck.* 不要期待卡尔负做决定的责任。他是以逃避责任而著名的。*The seasoned bureaucrat's greatest talent is that of passing the buck.* 官场老油子的最大才能就是善于逃避责任。象下一例句那样加 to *someone* 的场合，是"把责任推诿于人"的意思。*When Jimmy was blamed for breaking the window, he tried to pass the buck to Joe.* 当吉米由于打碎窗户玻璃而受责备的时候，他企图嫁祸于乔。◇ shift responsibility to someone else / shift the responsibility to *someone*

bucket

a bucket of bolts → BOLTS

be a drop in the bucket → DROP

kick the bucket [ˌkɪkðə ˈbʌkət] [话] **死** 字面意义是"踢水桶"。关于这一表达法的来源，有一种说法是：企图上吊自杀的人先挂好绳子，然后往往站到倒放的水桶上，最后是"踢水桶"。此说正确与否不明。不管来源如何，这是一个相当幽默的说法。*It's been some ten years since grandpa kicked the bucket.* 我爷爷去世已经有十年左右了。*Those guys are just waiting for their old man to kick the bucket so they can get his money.* 那些不孝的孩子正在等待他们的老子一命呜呼，以便瓜分他的财产。◇ die

buckle

buckle down (to *something*) [ˌbʌkl ˈdaun] [口] **鼓足干劲** 字面意义是"把皮带的扣子扣紧"。有"下定决心"的意思。在工作、学习、体育运动等方面使用。*If we don't buckle down, we won't meet the deadline.* 我们不鼓足干劲，就不能按期完成啦。*After her teacher warned her that she might fail, Sue began to buckle down to her studies.* 自从老师警告她可能留级之后，苏开始努力学习了。也常用 buckle down and *do something* 的说法。Buckle down and get to work! 是"加油干吧！"的意思。也可以说 knuckle [ˌnʌkl] down (to *something*), knuckle down (and *do something*)，意思相同。◇ (begin to) apply *oneself* diligently

bud

nip *something* **in the bud** [.nɪp ～ ɪnðə ˈbʌ(:)d] [口] **防微杜渐** 字面意义是"在萌芽时摘取"。按字面意义使用的场合,可以说 nip [pick, clip, cut off, etc.] the bud (before it blooms)。这一表达法专用比喻的意义。 nip *something* in the bud 的 *something*, 指事件,计划,策略等。整个习用语的意思是"防患于未然"、"消灭于萌芽状态中"。*Through a tip from an informant, the police were able to nip the planned bank robbery in the bud.* 由于情报员的秘密通报,警察得以粉碎了抢劫银行的阴谋计划。*Our plan to cut classes was nipped in the bud when the principal saw us sneaking down the hall.* 由于校长发现我们偷偷溜出大厅,我们的逃课计划告吹了。◇ prevent *something* from happening / stop *something* in its beginning stages

bug

a camera bug [ə ˈkæ(:)mrə .bʌ(:)g] [话] **照相迷** → a SHUTTERBUG

put a bug in *someone's* **ear** [.pudə ˈbʌ(:)gən ～ .ɪ(:)r] [话] **透露情况** 最初的构思是:虫子 (bug) 飞进耳朵 (ear) 里,令人坐立不安。bug 的内容一般是对听者本人或第三者有好处的事情。通常用于希望对方听到情报后采取某种行动的场合。 *I know you want to be transferred to the sales department. I'll put a bug in the boss's ear for you.* 我知道你想调到销售部去。我给你往老板的耳朵里吹吹风。 *A: How did you know I wanted a watch? B: Your little sister put a bug in my ear.* 甲:你怎么知道我想要一块手表呢? 乙:你妹妹向我透露情况啦。*George didn't know there was a job opening in that office until I put a bug in his ear.* 在我向他透露情况之前,乔治不了解那个单位有一个人员空额。◇ mention it [*something*] to *someone* / tell *someone*

bughunter

a bughunter [ə ˈbʌ(:)g.hʌntər] [话] **昆虫学者** 直译为"狩猎虫子的人"。一种幽默的说法。 *George's grandfather was a well-known bughunter.* 乔治的祖父是一位著名的昆虫学家。也说 a bugologist [.bʌˈgɑlədʒɪst] (→ BUGOLOGY)。◇ an entomologist

bugology

bugology [.bʌˈgɑ(:)lədʒi] [话] **昆虫学** 分解则为: bug (虫) + -o- (连结元音)+ -logy (～ 的研究), 相当于 entomology [.entəˈmɑlədʒi] (昆虫学)。一种诙谐的说法。 *Howard is a specialist in bugology.* 霍华德是一位昆虫学专家。如果说"昆虫学家",将 -gy 变成具有"某学家"意义的 -gist, 就成为 bugologist [.bʌˈgɑ(:)lədʒɪst]了。 *Roy's dad is a bugologist at the state museum.* 罗伊的爸爸是州立博物馆的一位昆虫学家。另外,在学生用语中,也用这两个名词分别指"生物学"(biology) 和 "生物学家"(biologist)。 *I have to take two years of bugology.* 我必须选修二年生物学。◇ entomology

bulge

fight the battle of the bulge → BATTLE

bull

a bull fiddle → FIDDLE

(like) a bull in a china shop [(laɪk)ə .bu(:)lɪnə ˈtʃaɪnə .ʃɑ(:)p] [话] **粗心人** china shop 是"瓷器店"。本条的字面意义是"(好象)一头在瓷器店里的公牛",令人会想到"无法制服的狂暴分子"的形象。在一般的词典中也都译作"乱暴者",但这不正确。因为实际上并不是指"乱暴者",而是指"(在平常的举动中就会毁坏物品的)粗心人",或者"(不懂世故人情的) 粗心人"。下一例句中的 John 也不是由于狂暴而毁坏物品,而是由于动作不留神才搞得一塌糊涂。 *John is like a bull in a china shop. The last time he visited our home, he fell into the Christmas tree and broke most of the ornaments and then accidentally knocked three dishes off the dining room table.* 约翰是一个粗心人。上次来我家的时候,他跌倒在圣诞树上,弄坏了树上的大部分装饰品，然后又无意中把饭厅的桌子上的碟子碰掉地下三个。下面例句中的George 和 Pete 是"粗鲁的人"。*George is very rich, but when it comes to the social graces he's like a bull in a china shop. He's forever saying the wrong thing at the wrong time and offending people with his crude behavior.* 乔治很有钱，但是在社交方面，他却是个鲁男子。他总是在不相宜的时间说不对头的话，以粗野的行为激怒别人。*I'll admit that Pete has the required technical know-how, but I still don't think we should take him with us. In delicate negotiations like these, he's too much of a bull in a china shop.* 我承认皮特具有所需要的技术知识，但是我依然不认为我们应该带他一块儿去。在这种非常细致的谈判中，他的线条实在过于粗了。这一表达法一般应用于男性，但也并非不能用到女人身上。*That Mrs. Sharptongue has about as much tact as a bull in a china shop.* 那位夏普汤格太太愚蠢得出奇，跟闯进瓷器店的公牛差不多。◇ very clumsy [inadept]

(as) headstrong as a bull [əz ˌhedsˌtrɔ(ː)ŋəzə ˈbu(ː)l] [口] **死顽固** → (as) stubborn as a MULE

take the bull by the horns [ˌteɪkðə ˈbu(ː)l baɪ ðə ˈhɔ(ː)rnz] [话] **(面对困难)挺身而出** 具体形象是："雄牛 (bull) 狂暴起来，乱闹不止，因而人只好采取最后手段，鼓起勇气，直接扭住它的角(take ~ by the horns)，努力将它制服"。*The bullfighter, having lost his cape and sword, took the bull by the horns and tried to wrestle it to the ground.* 斗牛士失掉了他的披肩和剑，抓住公牛的角，试图把它按倒在地上。这是按字面意义使用的例子。转作比喻使用。在这一场合，也是经常在"作为最后的手段"的上下文中使用。*When most of his officers proved to be inept, the general took the bull by the horns and led the charge himself.* 当他手下的大多数军官都表现出无能的时候，将军挺身而出，亲自指挥战斗。既有象这样使用于直接关系到生死存亡的严重场面的时候，也有使用于比这轻松得多的状况的时候。*It's time to take the bull by the horns. I'm going to demand a raise even though it may mean risking my job.* 到了该豁出去的时候啦。我要冒着砸了饭碗的危险去要求增加工资。*If my go-between can't get permission for me to marry her, I guess I'll have to take the bull by the horns and go to see her father myself.* 如果媒人说不妥我与她结婚的事情，我看就只好大着胆子，自己直接去见她的父亲了。◇ take resolute action / adopt a resolute course of action

bullet

bite the bullet (and *do something*) [ˌbaɪtðə ˈbulət] [口] **下定决心** 字面意义是"咬子弹"。在没有麻药的时代，给在战场上受伤的士兵做手术时，要叫他咬一颗子弹忍耐疼痛。这是本条习用语的来源。可能由于受语源的拘束吧，一般的英汉词典中仅仅译为"忍受痛苦"、"忍气吞声"等等，但这是英国英语。在美国英语中，这一表达法使用于不管是多么讨厌、多么辛苦的事情，只要非干不可，就拿出勇气去干的场合。在实际上，多采取"下定决心去做……"的形式。*After pussyfooting around for several months, Hal decided to bite the bullet and ask his boss for a raise.* 哈尔经过几个月的犹疑不决之后，终于下定决心去请求老板给他提高工资了。如这一例句所示，典型的说法是用 and ~接续。*The nation cannot overcome inflation unless Congress bites the bullet and slashes welfare spending.* 除非议会下定决心大幅度削减福利开支，国家是无法克服通货膨胀的。*When faced with an unavoidable task— no matter how unpleasant— a real man doesn't waste time worrying about it. He bites the bullet and does it.* 当面临一种非完成不可的工作任务时，哪怕这个任务是多么令人讨厌，一个真正的人也不会为此而烦恼，白白浪费时间。他会下定决心，咬着牙去干的。*I hear you're getting married. When did you decide to bite the* *bullet?* 听说你要结婚啦。你什么时候下定决心的啊？也有象下一例句那样，专用被动语态表示“忍受”、“忍耐”的意思，但这是极为罕见的实例。*Bill is a very gentle fellow. When he is treated unfairly he never complains. He just bites the bullet.* 比尔是一个非常老实的人。别人对待他不公正，他也从无怨言。什么事情他都是忍耐着。另外，在英国英语中常加 on, 说 bite on the bullet; 但在美国英语中，总不加 on, 而采取 bite the bullet 的形式。◇ overcome *one's* irresolution / act with fortitude / step manfully forth / bear it patiently

bum

a bum [ə ˈbʌ(ː)m] [口] **无业游民、懒汉** → BUM *something* (off *someone*)

bum *something* (off *someone*) [ˌbʌm ˈ~] [话] **乞讨** 动词 bum 的基本意义是“央求他人，白要一点东西”。“白要的东西”一般是零钱、纸烟，以及点烟的火等等。也可以用 from 代替 off。 *That guy's always bumming cigarettes off [from] me.* 那个家伙总是向我讨纸烟抽。*Lemme bum a light, will ya?* 借火点点烟好吗？如此例所示，bum 在许多句子里相当于汉语的“借”或“请借给我”，但是这种“借”一般没有“还”的意思，因而是一种“乞讨”。例如，*Can I bum a dollar off you, Bill?* 比尔，能借给我一美元吗？这在英语中的意味是：“还不还不知道，但是多半是不会还的”。因此，如果把这一表达法应用于金钱时，从常识上来判断，最多不过两三美元而已。“白要的东西”不仅仅是以上所说的零钱或物品。也有象下面例句所示“白要劳力”的情况。*I bummed a ride with Charlie as far as New York.* 我白搭查理的车，一直到达纽约。如果查理去纽约没有事情，特意为搭车人办事而开车送他前去纽约，就不能使用这一习用语。查理有事，已经确定开车前去，而“我”分文不出，白搭他的车，讨点便宜——这才是 bum 一词的根本意义所在。如以上的例句所示，bum 的人通常以熟人为多，但有时也可以是完全陌生的人、二流子、乞丐等等。*Can I bum a light, friend?* 朋友，借个火使使好吗？ *A man dressed in rags tried to bum a dollar off me.* 一个衣服褴褛的人向我讨一美元。另外，如果追溯 bum 一词的语源，在 19 世纪淘金热的时代，旧金山曾经流行 bummer 一语。据一般的说法，bummer 源出德语的 *Bummler* (懒汉)，当时系指“吊儿郎当的人”或“自己什么也不干、专门向他人乞讨的人”；但从南北战争时期开始，就意味着“到处乱串、掠夺老百姓食物的逃兵”了。打那以后，这个 bummer 中的 -mer 脱落了，出现 bum 这样一个名词，直到现在，人们仍然常常用它来表示“无业游民”、“懒汉”等意思，例如：*A couple of bums were camped by the side of the road.* 两个流浪汉露宿在大路的旁边。*That bum never does any work.* 那个懒汉什么也不干。本条条头的 bum 是这一名词的动词化。→ a bum STEER / a bum RAP ◇ cadge *something* (from *someone*)

a bum rap → RAP

a bum steer → STEER

bump

bump *someone* **off** [ˌbʌmp ~ ˈɔːf] [话] **杀掉** → KNOCK *someone* off

bumpkin

a bumpkin [ə ˈbʌmpkən] **乡下佬** → a country BUMPKIN / a country HICK

a country bumpkin [ə ˈkʌntri ˈbʌmpkən] [口] **乡下佬** country 在这里当然是“乡村的”的意思。bumpkin 的语源被认为是荷兰语的 *Boomken*(小树)或者 *Bommekijn* (小木桶)。古时，此词为英国人对荷兰人的蔑称。后来逐渐变成“乡下佬”的意味。因此，不加 country, bumpkin 单独就是“乡下佬”，不过在习惯上多半与 country 构成一个词组使用。*I always stay home on Saturday nights. That's when all the country bumpkins come to town.* 每个星期六的晚间我都呆在家里，因为那正是所有的乡下佬拥进城里的时候。*Don't let Mr. Cather fool you. He may look like a country bumpkin, but actually he's a very shrewd lawyer.* 你可不要上卡瑟先生的

当。他看起来活象个乡下佬,其实是一个非常精明的律师啊。另外,还有许多相当于“乡下佬”的表达法,如 a country HICK, a hayseed, a yokel, a clodhopper 之类。这些表达法在原则上是能够相互变换使用的,但多多少少有一点细微的差别。country hick 是 a city SLICKER 的反义语, gullible (容易受骗)的意味比较强烈,与此相反,本条的 a country bumpkin 则给人以“动作等 awkward (迟缓、不灵活)”的深刻印象。换句话说 country bumpkin 是以表达眼睛所见的感觉为中心的说法。至于其他三个表达法, hayseed 和 yokel 与 country hick 相近, clodhopper 则与 country bumpkin 相近。但是,比起 clodhopper 来,人们更多地使用 country bumpkin。→ CLODHOPPERS ◇a gawky, country-bred person

bumps

goose bumps [ˈgu(:)s ˌbʌmps] [话] **鸡皮疙瘩** goose 是“鹅”, bump 是“突出物”。本条直译即为“鹅的皮肤上的小疙瘩”。与 goose PIMPLES(→)同样,是一个常用的表达法,特别是青年人喜欢使用。*The movie was so scary it gave me goose bumps.* 影片非常恐怖,把我吓得起了一身鸡皮疙瘩。

bunch

a bunch [ə ˈbʌntʃ] [话] **许多** 在 a bunch of flowers, a bunch of grapes (一束花,一串葡萄)中的 bunch,是一般的使用方法。但是根据上下文,此词成为相当于“许多”的一种幽默说法。例如, I've got a bunch of papers to grade. 中的 bunch of papers 就不是“一束文件”,而是“(须批阅打分的)许多作文[论文、答卷等]”。原来, bunch 作为“束”解时不能与 paper(s) 一起使用,大束(文件)是 bundle,小束(文件)为 packet。如果说 There's a bunch of people to see you. 那意思是“有很多人来见你”。也常常与加强语气的 whole 一道使用。 *We had a whole bunch of food left over after the party.* 社交晚会开过以后,我们剩下的食品简直堆积如山。另外,女人们常用这一表达法代替 very much,而说 Thanks a bunch. (多谢多谢。)或者 I love you a whole bunch. (我非常非常爱你。)男人只在诙谐或讽刺的场合使用。◇ a lot

bundle

a bundle [ə ˈbʌndl] [话] **很多很多** 一般来说, bundle 可作“束”、“包”解,如 a bundle of hay (一捆干草), two or three bundles of laundry (两三包要洗涤的衣服), bundles from the department store (百货公司寄来的包裹)等。但是,根据上下文,以及根据重音的位置,此词也是强调“多”的一种表达法。例如,如果说 There's a bundle of people here. 作“这儿有一束人”讲就有点儿费解,因此,你可以放心大胆地解释为“这儿有很多很多的人。”然而, There's a bundle of letters for you. 究竟作何解释呢?是“一束信件”呢?还是“大批信件”呢?这只要洗耳静听,也是不会弄错的,因为当 bundle 表示“很多很多”的意味时,重音就在此词的上边。也就是说,作“一束”解为 a bundle of ˈletters,而作“很多很多”解时则为 a ˈbundle of letters,根据这一重音位置,上边的例句就是“你来了大批的信件。”的意思了。另外,在以“很多很多”的意味使用的场合,不仅象上面所讲那样,在 of 以下加 people 或 letters 之类的具体名词,也可以象下一例句那样加抽象名词。 *I've got a bundle of troubles.* 我有大堆大堆的烦恼啊。为了更进一步加强语气,又往往把 whole 放在 bundle 的前边,如说 *A whole bundle of new houses have been built.* 建造了大批大批的新房子。再有,如果 bundle 的后边不带 of ~,则往往是“大量金钱”的意思。 *Ten thousand dollars? Wow! That's quite a bundle!* 一万美元?嗬!那可是很大的数目啊! → make a BUNDLE / make *one's* BUNDLE ◇ a tremendous number [amount]

make a bundle [ˌmeɪkə ˈbʌndl] [话] **赚大钱** 字面意义是“制作一束”。这是个省略的说法,原句为 make a bundle of money。这里的 bundle 指“(很多)钱”

(→ a BUNDLE)。 *Jack made a bundle on the commodities market last year.* 杰克去年在商品市场上赚了一大笔钱。如此例句所示,多半后接 on ~或 in ~,以表示赚钱的方法。这一表达法不仅限于个人,在谈到公司等等时也可以使用。*If this succeeds, our firm will make a bundle.* 如果这个搞成的话,我们公司将赚一笔大钱。赚钱方法不论,哪怕是赌博也可以使用此习用语。*Whitey Rock made a bundle on the races.* 怀特·罗克在赛马中赚了大钱。→ make *one's* BUNDLE ◇ make a lot of money

make *one's* **bundle** [ˌmeɪk ~ ˈbʌndl] [话] **发大财** 乍一看,这一表达法与 make a BUNDLE(赚大钱) (→)完全相同;但是,a 和 *one's* 一调换,意思则大不一样了。在"赚大钱"这一点上,两者是相同的,然而,make *one's* bundle 是"创造一生享用不尽的财富"的意思。因此,论钱的数目,往往要够得上"一笔财产",而且大多具有"经过长时期的积累"的意义。与此相比,make a bundle 的金额只是个相对的数目,而且多用于"成败在于一举"的场合。另外,如果说 make a bundle,个人、公司、组织等均可作为主语;而 make *one's* bundle 的主语仅限于个人或一个家族。*When I make my bundle, I think I'll retire to Florida.* 等我发了大财,我想辞退工作,到佛罗里达去过安闲日子。*Mr. Jones made his bundle in international trade.* 琼斯先生从事国际贸易成了大富翁。◇ become rich

bunny

a dumb bunny [ə ˈdʌ(ː)m ˈbʌni] [话] **傻瓜** dumb 是"愚蠢的",bunny 是对人们认为最傻的动物"兔子"的爱称。本条的说法虽然与 a FOOL 同义,但没有那么严重,毋宁说令人产生一种亲切的感觉。在使用时大多含有疼爱对方的口气,仿佛说"你这个小傻瓜哟!"、"你这人真叫人没办法呀!"。*Has that dumb bunny messed things up again?* 那个傻瓜又把事情搞糟了吗? *You dumb bunny. Why didn't you say from the beginning that you wanted to go, too?* 你这个傻瓜哟!为什么你一开始不说你也要去呢? → a DUMBHEAD ◇ a stupid person

burn

burn *someone* **up** [ˌbəːrn ~ ˈʌ(ː)p] [话] **令人生气** burn *something* up 是"烧光"的意思。*The fire burned all his books up.* 由于失火,他的藏书全被烧光了。把 *something* 换成 *someone*,意思与 make *someone* mad 大致相同,是"令人生气"。从语感上说,是"使人大怒",但在实际上,根据讲话的前后关系,从"使人勃然大怒"直到"使人有点发火",应用的范围很宽。*someone* 的地方代入 me 的场合占绝大多数。*It burns me up the way people throw trash on the street.* 人们往大街上扔垃圾,真叫我生气。*That burns me up. After promising he would be here for sure, Jimmy just called me to say he couldn't make it.* 真叫我火冒三丈!吉米原来约定一定到这儿来,可是刚才却给我来电话,说他来不了啦。*That guy burns me up. He's always trying to show how smart he is.* 那家伙真叫我生气。他总是要显示他的头脑多么聪明。*That sort of thing always burns my husband up.* 我的丈夫对于那类事情总是非常气愤的。也有时采取 be burned up (在生气)或者 get burned up (发怒) 的形式。*What are you so burned up about? It was partly your fault.* 你为什么要发那么大的火呢?这里也有你的失误啊! *That was a terrible thing for him to do. I get burned up every time I think about it.* 他竟做出那样无法无天的事情来了。我一想起来就怒不可遏。◇ make *someone* mad

have *something* **to burn** [ˌhæv ~ təˈbəːrn] [话] **绰绰有余** → have MONEY to burn

burner

put *something* **on the back burner** [ˌput ~ ɔ(ː)nðə ˈbæ(ː)k ˈbəːrnər] [口] **(一时地)束之高阁** 这里的 burner 是做饭用的"煤气[电]灶"。back burner 是"里侧的灶具"。在美国,厨房的灶具一般分成前后两列,每列两具,总共四具。前列的两

具用于当前有必要加酌料或者搅和的饭菜,后列的灶具则用于仅仅不叫它凉的饭菜或者是以微火长时间去炖的饭菜。back burner 可以说是一种备用灶具,把锅放到那上面,就意味着当前先搁一搁再说。因此,在作为比喻使用时,也就具有"把正在进行的事情暂时停下,留待以后处理"的意味了。但是,尽管是"束之高阁",却并不是在此期间完全不过问这一问题,而是继续进行研究和调查,只不过将全面进行的时间延缓而已。本条的英语大多是在这样的场合使用。*He says he has put all his other projects on the back burner for a while until he finishes writing his new novel.* 他说,在他的新长篇小说脱稿之前,他把其他的一切事情都束之高阁了。在这一场合,也并不是完全放弃 other projects, 在写 new novel 的余暇,比如说,总是会跟人见面聊天、叫人代为搜集资料、做些简单易行的事情的。*The government has decided to put the question of a tax increase on the back burner for another year or so.* 关于增税问题,政府已经决定再搁上一、二年再说了。从这一例句的内容也可以考虑到:政府在这一、二年之间肯定会对"增税问题"继续进行调查研究的。虽然不实行,但是在做准备工作。下面的例句也是如此。*Inflation has forced us to put our plans to buy a new house on the back burner for the time being.* 由于通货膨胀,我们买一所新房子的计划当前只好束之高阁了。keep *something* on the back burner 是"(暂时)不进行"。be on the back burner 也是同义。与 put *something* on the back burner 相比,这两个习用语在大多数场合都具有更强烈的"现在为实现某一目标正做一些工作"的意味。因此,根据上下文,有时与"正在继续研究"的意思十分相近。*The President is apparently keeping his inflation-fighting plan on the back burner while he gauges the public's reaction to it.* 总统在观察群众的反应期间,显然把他的与通货膨胀做斗争的计划暂时搁置下来。*We haven't given up the project yet. It's still on the back burner.* 我们并没有放弃那个计划。现在正继续研究中。◇ set *something* aside (for the time being)

burp

a burp [ə ˈbə(ː)rp] [话] **打嗝** 象声词。*Someone at the next table let out a big burp.* 在旁边那个桌子,有人打了一个大嗝。如这一例句所示,打嗝的"打",英语叫做 let out (让它出来)。另外,burp 也常作不及物动词使用,如说 *Someone burped.* 有人打嗝了。作为及物动词使用,只限于说 burp the baby (使婴儿打嗝)。与 burp 相当的"正式"说法,是 belch [ˈbe(ː)ltʃ]。有些词典在 burp 一词的后边标上 ((俗)) 或 ((卑)) 的字样。但在实际上,burp 听起来比 belch 更为悦耳,在会话中占压倒的多数。"使婴儿打嗝"这句话,在正式书写的场合也不使用 belch,经常作 burp the baby。顺便提一下:由于"打嗝"的发射音,在军用俚语中称"手提式机枪"、特别是第二次世界大战中德军使用的那种"机关手枪"(machine pistol) 为 a burp gun。◇ a belch

a burp gun [ə ˈbə(ː)rp ˌgʌ(ː)n] [话] **机关手枪** → a BURP

bus

miss the bus (on *something*) [ˌmɪsðə ˈbʌ(ː)s] [话] **坐失良机** → miss the BOAT (on *something*)①

a rubberneck bus [ə ˈrʌbərnek ˈbʌ(ː)s] [话] **旅游汽车** → RUBBERNECK at *something*

a shuttle bus [ə ˈʃʌtl ˌbʌs] [口] **两个地点间近距离往返公共汽车** → an air SHUTTLE

bush

beat around the bush [ˌbi(ː)də ˌraundðə ˈbu(ː)ʃ] [口] **说话兜圈子** 特别是在英国英语中,有用 about 代替 around 的情况。本条的字面意义是"在灌木丛周围敲"。这是一个比喻性的成语:为了查明猎物在什么地方,不是直接进入灌木丛,而是采取在树丛周围敲打、将猎物撵出来的方法。我们见到有人把这一习用语译为"刺探"、"旁敲侧击"等等,这是不正确的。不错，这一表达法也有在具有上述意义的上下文中使用的情况，但它本身并没有直接去“探”、“敲”的意味。它仅仅表示“由于一语道破不合适，或者由于缺乏这样做的勇气，因而拐弯抹角地说”而已。*Stop beating around the bush and come to the point. I'm a busy man.* 你别兜圈子了，快说正题吧。我很忙。◇ talk around the subject (without coming to the point)

bushed

bushed [ˈbu(ː)ʃt] [话] **累极了** 与 tired 或 weary 等不同，它只表示“身体的疲劳”，不用于“精神疲惫”的场合。另外，如 I'm [I feel] bushed. 或 You look bushed. 这样的话所示，经常作为表语使用，不能放在名词前边当定语。*You look bushed. Why don't you got to bed early?* 你似乎太累了。怎么不早点儿上床睡觉？加强语气时多用 completely。*After working all day in the yard, I was completely bushed.* 我在院子里干了一整天活儿，简直累死啦。另外，人们又常使用同义词 beat，用法也一样。◇ exhausted

bushel

hide *one's* **light under a bushel** → LIGHT

bushes

beat the bushes (for *something*) [ˌbi(ː)tðə ˈbuʃəz] [话] **拚命搜寻** 字面意义是“(为寻求某物而)敲灌木丛”。这是由狩猎而来的一个表达法。现在在谈到狩猎时也是使用的，如 *The hunters spent all day out beating the bushes for quail, but didn't find a single one.* 猎人们费了一整天功夫到处拚命搜寻鹌鹑，但是连一只也没有找到。即便在这一场合，也没有“敲灌木丛”的意味。*As soon as the Pacific War started, the American government began beating the bushes for qualified Japanese teachers.* 太平洋战争刚一爆发，美国政府就开始拚命搜罗合格的日语教师。*You have to beat the bushes these days if you want to find a doctor who will make house-calls.* 最近一个时期，如果想请一位到家来出诊的大夫，就必须拚命去到处搜寻。如以上两个例句所示，一般使用时都包含着“千辛万苦地”或者“跑遍所有地方”的意味。在强调的场合，常添加 really。*They don't make this model of car anymore. I really have to beat the bushes to get spare parts for it.* 这种型号的汽车已经不再制造了。为了得到零件，我必须拚命地到处去搜寻。◇ search far and wide

business

do a land-office business (in *something*) [duə ˌlæ(ː)nˌdɔ(ː)fəs ˈbɪznəs] [口] **生意大为兴隆** do business 是“做生意”；land office 是“国有地管理局的办事处”。1862 年，美国实施 The Homestead Act (宅地法案)的时候，把国有地无偿分给一般市民，因此，有大批的人涌入各个地方的 land office。也就是说，land office “大大兴隆”了。do a land-office business 源出于此，意思是“做 land office 式的买卖”，亦即“生意兴隆通四海，财源茂盛达三江”了。*The manufacturers of electronic games have done a land-office business this year.* 今年制作电子游戏的厂家生意大为兴隆。*That real estate company is doing a land-office business in one-room apartments.* 那家房地产公司由于搞单间房的公寓，生意大为兴隆。*We're not exactly doing a land-office business, but sales have risen a bit over the past year.* 我们店的生意还谈不到大为兴隆，但是在过去一年里，销售额却是逐步上升的。◇ do a rapid and thriving business

mean business [ˌmiːnˈbɪznəs] [话] **动真格的** 直译是“并非游戏，而是生意”。这一说法拿 business 与 play 作对比，强调多么严肃认真。*Before, I've let you off with simply a warning, but this time I mean business!* 以前，我只是警告一下就放过了你，但是这一次我可动真格的啦！*If you don't do as I say I'll disown you. And I mean business!* 如果你不按照我的话去做，我就把你赶出家门。我说的可是真话，你别当耳旁风！*I wasn't prepared to argue with the man. He had a gun and as far as I could judge, he* *meant business.* 我没打算跟那个人争辩。他拿着枪，而且根据我的判断，他是在动真格的。◇ be (completely) serious

mind *one's* **own business** [ˌmaɪnd ~ oun ˈbɪznəs] [口] **少管闲事** 原意为“管理自己的生意”。*He would make more money if he would stop trying to help other people and mind his own business more carefully.* 如果他不竭力去帮助别人，多注意经营自己的生意，本来还会更加发财的。有象这样按照本来的意义使用的情况。但是，一般是作为比喻使用。在这一场合，*one's* business 与 *one's* affairs 同义，指“自己的事情”，亦即“一心自扫门前雪”→“莫管他人瓦上霜”。*Mind your own business.* 你管你自己好啦！ *Why don't you mind your own business?* 不要多管闲事好吗？ *I wish that woman would mind her own business for a change.* 但愿那个女人也改变一下作风，少管他人的闲事。*It generally takes people a long time to learn that they'd be better off minding their own business.* 一般来说，一个人需要很长时间才会了解少管闲事为妙。如以上的例句所示，这一表达法一般是指他人的干扰，但也有象下一例句那样用作自戒的格言。*Every time I try to help someone, it seems they end up depending on me completely. I should learn to mind my own business.* 每一次我要去帮助人，结果，他们就完全依赖上我。我必须切记莫管他人瓦上霜啊。另外还有一个表达法 mind *one's* own affairs，略嫌生硬。◇ not bother with other people's affairs

bust

a beer bust [ə ˈbɪ(ː)r ˌbʌ(ː)st] [话] **啤酒晚会** 大学生用语。bust 为美国俚语，指“狂欢的酒会”。*Going to the beer bust this Friday? I hear it's only five dollars stag or drag.* 本星期五的啤酒晚会你去吗？不管单人去还是带女朋友去，听说只要五美元。◇ a beer party

bust *something* **up** [ˌbʌst ~ ˈʌ(ː)p] [话] **破坏** → BANG *something* up

buster

a belly buster [ə ˈbeliˌbʌstər] [话] **拙笨跳水，肚皮先下** → a belly FLOP

busy

be (as) busy as a bee → BEE

buts

No ifs, ands or buts. → IFS

butt

the butt [ðə ˈbʌt] [俗] **(人的)屁股** → the BOTTOM

butter

one's **bread and butter** → BREAD

butter *someone* **up** [ˌbʌdər ~ ˈʌ(ː)p] [话] **有求于人而大拍马屁** 动词 butter ~与 put butter on ~同样，常在 *Please butter the toast.* 请在烤面包片上抹黄油。之类的句子中使用。但是，具有“大量”意义的 up 却不大按照字面意义使用。一般说 put a lot of butter on ~。然而在用作比喻的场合，却有 butter *someone* up 的说法。也就是为了利用对方达到某种目的而“给人抹上厚厚的一层黄油”。一般可以作“阿谀奉承”解，不过，由于包括一些动作在内，比如为了取悦对方而划火柴点烟，给对方去取来什么东西等等，也有不能用“阿谀奉承”几个字完全概括的场合。这一表达法与 flatter 或者 polish the APPLE 不同，经常含有很明确的目的，此点务请读者注意。*Don't pay any attention to his flattery. He's only buttering you up in hopes of getting you to help him.* 你不要听他那套奉承话。他只是为了得到你的帮助才大拍马屁的。*Phil is buttering up the boss in hopes of getting a raise.* 菲尔希望增加工资，正拍老板的马屁哪。当然，如果态度过于明显，被人一眼看穿，多半会遭到严词拒绝。*There's no use trying to butter me up. The answer is still no.* 你拍我的马屁也没有用处。不行还是不行。◇ use flattery on *someone*

butter-and-egg

a big butter-and-egg man → MAN

butterball

a butterball [ə ˈbʌdərˌbɔːl] [话] **大胖子** 关

于 butterball 一词,大家可以这样想象:比如在大餐厅中,在上面包时会附带球状的黄油,如果把这黄油球进一步加大,就会成为象小皮球大小的东西了。古时,西方人在家庭里自制黄油,就是把它做成小皮球大的 butterball。"象黄油球一样圆乎乎的人"的构思就是由此而来。另外,如 a tub of LARD 等等,还有各种各样表示"胖子"意义的英语单词或词组,但是 butterball 却与它们不同,而具有"胖得好玩儿"的意味。*The Jones family are all butterballs.* 琼斯一家子全都胖乎乎的。*My wife used to be very chic, but recently she has become quite a butterball.* 我的妻子一向非常窈窕,但是最近却变成个大胖子了。孩子们在打招呼时,也常常使用。*Hey, butterball. You wanna play baseball with us?* 喂,胖墩儿! 跟我们一起打棒球好吗? ◇ a fat person

butterfingers

(a) butterfingers [(ə) ˈbʌdər.fiŋgərz] [话] **常拿不住东西的人[手指]** 字面意义是"黄油手指",亦即"好象抹了黄油似的、滑溜溜的、常常掉落东西的手指头"。使用方法如: *He has butterfingers.* 他常从手中掉落东西。或者说 *a person with butterfingers* 从手中常掉落东西的人。*No one who has butterfingers like John should ever have become a camera salesman.* 象约翰那样常常从手中掉落东西的人,就不应该当照像机的售货员。现在词义有所变化,大多不是指的"手指"本身,而是指"有那样手指的人"。请注意:在这种场合,即使是一个人,也用复数形式,作 a butterfingers。加强语气时,加 real。*My wife is a real butterfingers. She breaks three or four dishes every week.* 我老婆真没办法,手里总拿不住东西。她每个星期都摔坏三、四个盘子。有时也作呼词使用。*Watch out, butterfingers! You almost dropped that bowling ball on my foot.* 当心,你这个笨手笨脚的人! 你滚的那个木球差一点没砸了我的脚。有形容词 butterfingered。*That man is nothing but a butterfingered buffoon.* 那个人简直是一个笨手笨脚的小丑。◇ (a person with) a tendency to drop things

butterflies

have butterflies in *one's* **stomach** [hæv ˈbʌdər.flaɪzɪn ~ .stʌmək] [话] **忐忑不安** 请大家想象一下"蝴蝶 (butterflies) 在胃(stomach)中来回飞翔"的滋味吧。这一习用语表达不安、紧张之类的感觉,汉语俗语说"好象怀里揣个小兔子"或"心里塞兔子"。*Sam had butterflies in his stomach as he went to the boss's office to ask for a raise.* 萨姆到经理办公室去要求增加工资的时候,他的心扑通扑通直跳。动词 have 换成 get,就成为"心跳起来"了。*I get butterflies in my stomach just thinking of making a speech before a large group of people.* 我只要一想到面对那么一大群人做报告,我的心就扑通扑通地跳了起来。有时省略 in *one's* stomach。*All the actors had butterflies just before the curtain went up.* 大幕就要拉开的时候,所有的演员都感到忐忑不安。◇ be extremely nervous

butterfly

a butterfly kiss → KISS

a social butterfly [ə .souʃəl ˈbʌdər.flaɪ] [口] **交际花** 从字面就可以想象到,本条是指"象穿花的蝴蝶一样在社交界大肆活动的女子"。不能说没有"轻佻的人"的感觉,但这一表达法本身并无轻蔑的、批判的味道。*Miss Smith is quite a social butterfly. She attends at least one dinner or dance every week.* 史密斯小姐是一个非常爱交际的人,她每星期至少参加一次晚宴或舞会。*Mrs. Whirl is such a social butterfly it makes me tired just watching her flit from party to party.* 怀尔夫人是一位大交际花,我只看到她从这个社交晚会到那个社交晚会奔忙的样子,就已经疲惫不堪了。◇ (a woman who) spends (quite) a lot of [so much] time attending social gatherings

button

a belly button [ə ˈbeli .bʌtn] [俗] **肚脐** 字面意义是"肚子的钮扣"。这是一个人们

常用的说法,但是偶尔也有讨厌它的人,因此,本书姑且把它分在[俗]的一类。*I have a pain around my belly button.* 我的肚脐周围疼。 顺便提一下:"肚脐凸出(的人)"叫做 a goes-outer [ˌgoˈzaudər],"肚脐凹入(的人)"叫做 a goes-inner [ˌgoˈzɪnər]。*Are you a goes-outer or a goes-inner?* 你是鼓肚脐,还是凹肚脐? ◇ a navel

hit the panic button [ˌhɪtðə ˈpæ(ː)nɪk ˌbʌtn] [话] **惊慌失措** → push the panic BUTTON

on the button [ˌɔ(ː)nðə ˈbʌtn] [话] **非常准确** 直译"在钮扣的上方",是"击中目标"的意思。钮扣的上方是"下颌",在拳击中打中下颌表明打得准确。多用 right 加强语气。 *A: Did I hit the target? B: Right on the button.* 甲:我打中目标了吗? 乙:非常准确。*A: Did he arrive on time? B: On the button.* 甲:他准时到达了吗? 乙:非常准时。*A: I hope I didn't say the wrong thing. B: No, your remarks were right on the button.* 甲:我希望我的话不太离谱儿。乙:不不,你的发言正中要害。另外,在应用于时间上时,与 on the DOT 同义。◇ right in the center [on time, to the point, etc.]

push the panic button [ˌpuʃðə ˈpæ(ː)nɪk ˌbʌtn] [话] **惊慌失措** 第二次世界大战期间,飞机遇有紧急情况时,驾驶员按电钮命令飞机上的军人空降。人们戏称这一电钮为"the panic button" (惊慌的按钮)。本条源出于此。这是一个相当幽默的说法。*I don't know what happened next. When I heard the explosion, I pushed the panic button and ran.* 后来发生了什么事情我不知道,当我一听到爆炸的声音时,就手忙脚乱地逃走了。*There's no need to push the panic button. You probably simply left your passport at the travel agency.* 不要惊慌失措嘛。恐怕你只是把护照忘到旅行社啦。也可以用 hit 代替 push。*Now don't go hitting the panic button. I'm sure we can solve this problem with a little rational thought.* 喂,用不着惊慌失措嘛。我们只要稍微动一下脑筋,肯定会解决这个问题的。但是,一般英语词典收录的 press the panic button 却是一个极不搭配的词组。虽然同样是"按",与 push 相比,press 一词略嫌生硬,只限于表达"冷静地、不慌不忙地按"的意味,因此,把它塞入这一习用语,总是有点格格不入的感觉。另外,有种种不同的"钮"被人戏称为 panic button。*This is my "panic button". When a caller overstays his welcome, I push it and my secretary rushes in to tell me that I have an important call from overseas.* 这是我的"紧急电钮"。当一位来客坐的时间过长的时候,我就按它一下,秘书就会跑来报告说从国外来了重要的电话。◇ panic / get hysterical

buttonhole

buttonhole *someone* [ˈbʌtnˌhoul ~] [口] **抓住别人闲聊** buttonhole 的字面意义是"抓住别人的钮扣眼儿"。这一表达法原义是"为了闲聊而抓住对方的西服钮扣或钮扣眼儿",过去专用于表示"拉住别人进行长谈"的意思。*Don't let Mr. Windy buttonhole you. He's the biggest bore in town.* 千万别叫温狄先生拉住你闲聊。他是全镇最大的讨厌鬼。*There's nothing worse than to be buttonholed by a gossip like Mrs. Bird.* 天下没有比被伯德夫人之流拉住瞎三话四更糟糕的事情了。但是现在呢,越来越多的人不是用它来表示"长谈",而是表示"为了想要与很忙的人物谈话,而看准时机抓住片刻的空闲"的意思。*The reporters buttonholed each person as he emerged from the meeting.* 新闻记者们在会议结束时,拉住每一位从会场走出来的人,跟他谈上几句。*The boss has a full schedule today, but perhaps you can buttonhole him for a few minutes when he comes out for lunch.* 总经理今天的日程表排得满满的,不过,当他出来去吃午饭的时候,你也许会堵住他谈三两分钟。*I'll try to buttonhole Jack after church tomorrow and get his opinion on this.* 明天在教堂做完礼拜之后,我去抓住杰克,听取他对这一问题的意见。◇ detain *someone* in conversation / detain *someone* (for a few minutes' talk)

buttons

have a few buttons missing [hævə ˌfju(ː) ˈbʌtnz ˌmɪsɪŋ] [话] **头脑有点儿不正常** 是从 have all *one's* BUTTONS 演绎出来的表达法。带有"有点古怪"的感觉,与 have ROCKSin *one's* head, have a SCREW loose 等同义。 *No, I wouldn't say he's crazy, though he certainly does seem to have a few buttons missing.* 不,我不能说他已经疯了,但是他的头脑确实有点不正常。 *Anyone who would make a statement like that must have a few buttons missing.* 能做那样发言的人,肯定头脑有一些不正常。另外,也有 be missing a few buttons 或者 be missing a few marbles 的说法,可能由于语感不佳,很少说 have a few marbles missing。 *The union must be missing a few buttons [marbles] if they think we'll agree to such a steep pay raise.* 工会如果认为我们会答应那样大幅度提高工资,他们的头脑肯定有点不正常。在以上的几种表达法中,有时均可用 some, several, one or two 代替 a few。◇ be a little strange in the head

have all *one's* **buttons** [hæˌvɔ(ː)l ~ ˈbʌtnz] [话] **头脑健全** 这里的 button 是"控制机械的电钮"。这一表达法的构思是:"如果电钮齐备,人和机器同样,也会正常运转(=正常的思考力和判断力进行活动)"。主要使用疑问、假定、否定等形式。 *Bill's a strange fellow. I sometimes wonder if he has all his buttons.* 比尔是一个奇怪的家伙。我有时怀疑他的头脑是否健全。 *If I had all my buttons, I wouldn't be in this business.* 我要是头脑清醒,就不会做这个生意啦。另外,也可以使用 marbles(儿童游戏弹的玻璃球),而说 have all *one's* marbles。 *Anyone who would try to ride a bicycle on the freeway doesn't have all his marbles.* 要到高速公路上去骑自行车的人,他的头脑不会健全。→ have a few BUTTONS missing ◇ be completely normal

buy

ˈbuy *something* [ˈbaɪ ~ / ˌbaɪ ˈ~] [话] **理解(对方所说的话)** 这个 buy 不是"购买东西"的"买",而是"承认"、"认可"、"同意"、"采纳(他人意见)"、"理解"等等的意思。其构思与汉语"不买他的账"的"买"大致相同。 *I'm sorry, but I'm afraid I just can't buy that explanation. It just won't wash.* 很抱歉,我对那种解释怎么也理解不了。不合逻辑嘛。 *You say you lost my money on the way to the racetrack? You don't really expect me to buy that cock-and-bull story, do you?* 你说在去赛马场的路上把我的钱丢啦?你不会真地以为我会相信那种无稽之谈吧? *I know he's your friend and you want me to accept his explanation, but I just don't buy it.* 我知道他是你的朋友,你希望我相信他的解释,但是我怎么也接受不了啊。 *The court refused to buy Tony's story about self-defense.* 法院拒绝接受托尼的正当自卫的说法。 *A: We'll repay the first half of the loan by the end of next month. B: O.K., I'll buy that, but on the condition that the entire loan is returned by the end of April.* 甲:在下月底以前,我们将还上一半贷款。乙:很好,我同意。但是有个条件,到四月底,全部贷款必须还清。◇ accept *something* / believe *something*

Buzz

Buzz off. [ˈbʌːˈzɔːf] [话] **走开!** 在英国英语中,有"走"、"离去"、"切断电话"等多种意义;但在美国口语中,一般为"走开!"、"滚出去!"的意思。buzz 是象声词,意为"嗡嗡叫"。这一表达法是把对方比做"讨厌的苍蝇"、"烦人的虫子"。 *Buzz off! Can't you see we're busy?* 走开吧!你没看见我们很忙吗?如此例所示,在说这句话时多用充满"讨厌"情绪的命令式。 *Buzz off. You're too little to go with us.* 走开!你太小,不能跟我们一起去。 *That guy's a pest. Tell him to buzz off.* 那个家伙是个讨厌鬼。你告诉他,叫他走开!另外,在美国口语中,也偶尔使用"离去"的意义,与 CUT out 等的用法相同。 *I'm tired of this place. Let's buzz off.* 我对这个地方已经厌倦了。咱们离开这里吧！ ◇ Go away. / leave

give *someone* **a buzz** [ˌgɪv ~ əˈbʌ(ː)z] [话] **(给某人)打电话** buzz 是"嗡、嗡"的叫声，这里指叫电话的声音。因此，如果直译的话，就是"对某人嗡、嗡一下"。直到最近为止，电话都是发出"铃、铃"的响声，因此有了 give *someone* a RING(对某人铃、铃一下)的说法。自从"嗡、嗡"叫的电话机问世以来，就出现 give ~ a buzz 这一新语了。 *I'll give you a buzz about two tomorrow.* 明天下午两点来钟我给你打电话。也可以说 give *someone* a call。 ◇ call *someone* (on the telephone)

have a buzz on [ˌhævə ˈbʌːˌzɔːn] [话] **微醉** buzz 是相当于"嗡嗡"的象声词。have ~ on 是"带在身上"。本条指由于酒喝多了，"脑袋有些嗡嗡响"或者"身上有些麻酥酥"的"微醉状态"。 *The man accused me of being drunk, but I'd had only one bottle of beer. I didn't even have a buzz on.* 那个人指责我喝醉了，但是我只喝了一瓶啤酒，就连微醉都够不上。为了加强语气，buzz 的前面常加 good。 *I'm not drunk, but I've got a good buzz on.* 我没有酩酊大醉，但是也颇有点醉意了。还有个 get a (good) buzz on 的形式，是"已经微醉"的意思。 *Why do you want to leave so soon? I haven't even gotten a good buzz on yet.* 你干吗这么早就想走？我还没喝多少，连点儿醉意都没有哪。◇ be feeling mellow

bygones

let bygones be bygones [let ˈbaɪˌgɔːnz biˈbaɪˌgɔːnz] [口] **过去的事让它过去吧** bygones 是 things that have gone by, 亦即"过去的事"。本条的字面意义是"过去的事就让它过去吧"，指"将过去的不和、争吵等一笔勾销"，在打算言归于好的时候常常使用。相当于汉语成语"捐弃前嫌"、"冤仇宜解不宜结"等。 *Let's forget our differences and let bygones be bygones.* 让我们忘掉相互间的不和，过去的事叫它过去好了。 *I had been in a rage when my brother refused to lend me money, but when he went bankrupt and came to me for a job, I decided to let bygones be bygones.* 当我哥哥不肯借给我钱的时候，我十分愤慨；但是当他破了产而来求我找工作的时候，我决心捐弃前嫌了。◇ lay our grudges aside / forgive and forget

C

cab

a cab [ə ˈkæːb] [话] **出租汽车** 在美国,“出租汽车”的正式名称是 a taxicab, 条头的 cab 为略语。顺便提一下:这个 taxicab 原是把 a taximeter cab 短缩了的,而其中的 taximeter 则由法语 *taxi*(车费)+*metre*(计量器)而来。cab 的情况比较复杂,据说是 cabriolet [ˌkæbriəˈleɪ] (有篷双轮轻便马车) 的略语。在英语中,当把一个词缩短的时候,一般作法总是把该词从中间一刀两断,留下一半,扔掉一半。可是,在 taxicab 的场合,不但留下了前半部分的 taxi, 而且留下了后半部分的 cab, 出现一种异常的现象。也就是说,在美国,不但同样使用 taxi 和 cab 这两个词,就连它们的祖师爷 taxicab 也是常挂在嘴边上。因此,如果说“叫辆出租汽车去吧”,不论是 Let's take a taxi. 也好, Let's take a cab. 也好,或者是 Let's take a taxicab. 也好,全都是极其自然的说法。◇ a taxicab

cabbage

cabbage [ˈkæ(ː)bɪdʒ] [话] **钞票** → BREAD

cabbie

a cabbie [ə ˈkæ(ː)bi] [俗] **出租车司机** 在意味着“出租汽车”的 a CAB 后面加上指小词 -ie, 为了发音方便重复一个 b。*Ask the cabbie if he'll take us to Washington.* 问一下司机,能不能把咱们送到华盛顿。但是,由于有些司机不喜欢人们用这个名词直接招呼他,在叫车的时候,一般用 driver (司机)是稳妥的。◇ a (taxi) driver

Caddy

a Caddy [ə ˈkæ(ː)di] [话] **卡迪拉克牌轿车** 把 Cadillac [ˈkædəˌlæ(ː)k] 中的 Cad-加指小词 -y,由于发音关系,习惯上重复一个 d。这是 GM (美国通用汽车公司)制造的最高级轿车的爱称。又可缀为 Caddie (-ie 也是指小词)。 *Mr. Jones always drives a Caddy. He must have plenty of money.* 琼斯先生总是驾驶一辆卡迪拉克牌轿车。他肯定是个大财主。有时去掉 -dy 只称 a Cad [ˈkæːd]。◇ a Cadillac

Caesar's

Great Caesar's ghost! [ˈgreɪt ˈsiːzərz ˈgoust] [话] **哎呀呀!** ((表示惊愕、否定等)) → Great SCOTT!

Cain

raise Cain (with *someone*) [ˌreɪz ˈkeɪn] [话] **大发脾气[大吵大闹]** 字面意义是“把该隐叫起来”。可能是作为 raise the DEVIL(→) 的委婉表达法而产生的。据说,古代的人们相信:只要嘴里一说 devil, 就会招来恶魔,因而用 Cain 一词来代替。Cain 是《圣经·旧约》的《创世纪》(Genesis) 中出现的人物。他是亚当和夏娃的长子,曾杀死其弟亚伯。由于他给人以“性情狂暴,容易发怒”的印象,所以便成了 the devil 的代称。另外, raise the devil 是“带有行动的暴怒[吵闹]方式”,而 raise Cain 则主要是强调“吵闹”的一种说法,往往相当于汉语的“怒吼”、“大发脾气”、“喧嚣”、“大叫大嚷”等等。*Your father will raise Cain if he finds out you didn't go to school today.* 如果你父亲发现你今天没有上学,他会大发脾气的。*The boss raised Cain with me for not finishing my work on time.* 由于我没有按时完成任务,老板大动肝火了。下面是“大吵大闹”的例子。*The plan is for our friends to raise enough Cain outside to cover our escape.* 计划是这样:叫我们的朋友们在外面大吵大叫,我们趁这个机会逃走。不仅使用于人,动物“吵闹”的场合也一样使用。*Just as I was sneaking out of the back gate, the dog next door started raising Cain.* 正当我偷偷溜出后门的时候，邻家的狗就汪汪狂吠起来了。再者，“吵闹”有种种的不同。在“尽情狂欢”、“对酒歌唱”的场合，也可以使用这一表达法。在这种场合，Cain 前边常加 a lot of 或 a little 等形容词。*We used to raise a lot of Cain on the weekends when we were students.* 我们在学校念书的时候，每到周末都要尽情热闹一番。*I feel like going out and raising a little Cain tonight.* 今天晚上，我很想出去快活一番哪。◇ become very angry / make (a lot of) noise / have boisterous fun

cake

have *one's* **cake and eat it, too** [ˌhæv ~ ˈkeɪk əˌni(:)dɪˈtːuː] [话] **二者兼得** 这一表达法来自英国的 You can't eat your cake and have it. 一语。在美国，把 eat 和 have 互调位置，再加上个 too，一般采取 You can't have your cake and eat it, too. 的形式。这两句话都是谚语，意思是“又要吃糕饼，又要收藏起来，二者不能兼顾”，与汉语俗语“好绫罗，尽头短”，“不能两全其美”同义。在否定句中，大多使用 can't，而且只表示比喻的意味。*You've got to either give up the idea of going to college or quit the tennis team and start studying harder. It's about time you realized that you can't have your cake and eat it, too.* 你或者是放弃上大学的想法，或者是脱离网球队而开始拚命用功，二者不可得兼，现在你该明白这个道理了。*You may spend my bonus on a new coat, or we can use it for a vacation, but not both. My bonus is just not big enough to let us have our cake and eat it, too.* 你可以用我的奖金买一件新外衣，或者我们用这笔钱休假，但是不能兼顾。因为我的奖金数量不多，达不到又要鱼又要肉的程度。虽然如以上的例句所示，多使用于否定句，但也有在肯定句中使用的情况，例如：*We used to often be torn between going to the movies and watching our favorite program on TV, but now that we've bought a video tape recorder we are able to have our cake and eat it, too.* 是去看电影呢？还是在家看喜爱的电视节目呢？过去我们常常为此而烦恼，现在可好了，我们已经买了一台录像机，可以二者兼得了。汉语俗语说：“馒头糕饼一齐吃”。本条的表达法不一定非“一齐”(同时) 不可，也有象下面这样的说法：*Many workers spend all their salary as they get it and still hope to retire comfortably, but they can't have their cake and eat it, too.* 有许多工人领到工资就花得一干二净，却仍然希望过舒服的退休生活，但是，二者是不可能兼得的。◇ pursue [do, enjoy] two mutually exclusive activities [things]

be a piece of cake [ə ˌpi(:)səv ˈkeɪk] [话] **易如反掌** 这一表达法的来历十分有趣。它原来是在美国产生的，战争时期传入英国后才开始流行起来。后来又反输入美国，最近在它的故土已经常被人们使用了。不过，在美国人听起来，依然还有点“英国英语”的味道。本条直译为“是一片糕饼”，意思是“与吃一片糕饼同样地简单”，强调轻而易举。除“易如反掌”之外，根据上下文，也可以译作“不费吹灰之力”、“容易极了”等等。*A: Are you sure you have all your instructions down pat? B: Don't worry. This'll be a piece of cake.* 甲：所有的操作规程你确实都记住了吗？乙：你放心吧，这不是易如反掌嘛！ *A: How was your exam? B: A piece of cake.* 甲：你考试怎么样？乙：没费劲就过关了。*I thought this job was going to be a piece of cake, but actually I've never worked so hard in my life.* 我原以为这个工作容易极了，但是在实际上，我有生以来还没有干过这样费劲的活儿。也有指人本身而言的时候。*A: Do you think you can handle the challenger tomorrow, champ? B: Sure. He'll be a piece of cake.* 甲：冠军，你认为你明天能够击败挑战的人吗？乙：当然啦。他算不了一回事。◇ very easy (to handle)

take the cake [ˌteɪkðə ˈkeɪk] [话] **好冒尖啦！** 字面意义是“拿糕饼”。过去，在美国南部黑人的社交晚会上，常举行“走步比赛”。他们把糕饼放在正中央，一对对的舞伴形成一个圆圈走步。走步最优美的一对舞伴可以获得那块糕饼,作为奖赏。因此,take the cake 曾经一度有"得奖"的意思,在一般的英汉辞典里也有"得第一名"、"得一等奖"之类的译法。但在实际上,这一意义的使用早已是凤毛麟角了。现代使用的意义是"顶好"、"最高",但其中十之八九是用于挖苦、讽刺的场合,所谓"好冒尖啦!"的真正意义是"糟糕透了!" *I've heard some ridiculous excuses for being late, but yours takes the cake.* 我听到过几个人为迟到辩解,理由都很可笑,而你的理由简直是滑稽透顶了。*The world may be full of stupid people, but you certainly take the cake.* 社会上有许许多多的愚人,而你可以说是稳拿第一啦。*As a poor dancer, Steve takes the cake. My shoes are ruined.* 论跳舞技术之糟,史蒂夫简直拔尖儿了。他把我的鞋全踩破啦。也有按照本来的意义(亦即 be the best 的意义)使用的时候,不过,这种情况极为稀少。*Everyone told some very funny stories, but Tom's took the cake.* 大家都讲了些非常有趣的故事,其中汤姆的最为生动。◇ be the worst

cakes

sell like hot cakes [.sel:aɪk 'hɑt.keɪks] [话] **卖得飞快** 不论怎样考虑,现在也无法把烤饼(hot cake)跟"卖得飞快的货物"联系到一起。这一习用语是 18 世纪末出现的,它的来源可能是这样:在"汉堡包"、"热狗"等产生之前的时代,烤饼在市集、庙会上的销路大概很好,由此把"卖得飞快"、"非常抢手"就说成"卖得象烤饼一样"了。*That book is selling like hot cakes.* 那部书卖得飞快。*The lots in that new subdivision sold like hot cakes.* 那一片新的分小块出售的地皮卖得飞快。另外也说 go like hot cakes, 它的使用范围要比 sell ～广,即便不是实际商品的场合也能使用。*Everyone loves my mother's rolls. They always go like hot cakes.* 人人都喜欢我母亲烤的面包卷,总是把它抢吃光了。顺便提一下:"烤饼"的实物现在多不称 hot cake, 而叫做 pancake 了。*Our shop's pancakes sell [go] like hot cakes.* 我们铺子的烤饼不胫而走。◇ sell [go] very fast

calaboose

the calaboose [ðə 'kæ(:)lə.bu:s] [话] **拘留所** → the HOOSEGOW

call

give *someone* **a call** [.gɪv ～ ə'kɔ:l] [话] **(给某人)打电话** → give *someone* a BUZZ

have a close call [.hævə .klous'kɔ:l] [话] **千钧一发** → have a close SHAVE

calling

miss *one's* **calling** [.mɪs ～ 'kɔ:lɪŋ] [口] **选错职业** calling 一般译作"神的感召",在这里指"能够发挥才能的工作"、"理想的职业"亦即"天职"。miss 是"失落"、"没有拿到"。条头的意思是"未能走上最适合自己才能的职业的道路"。*My father is an English teacher, but recently he has become so good at photography that he feels he may have missed his calling.* 我的父亲是一位英语教师,但是最近在摄影方面大有成绩,因此他感到自己可能选错了职业。在极力奉承或者开玩笑的时候也常常使用。*I didn't know you could sing so beautifully. You missed your calling.* 我真不知道你的歌会唱得这么好听,你浪费了你的天才啦。常用 really 加强语气。*My section chief really missed his calling. He should have been a slave driver.* 我那个科的科长的确选错了职业。他应该是一个奴隶的监工。◇ enter the wrong profession

camel's

the straw that broke the camel's back → STRAW

camera

a camera bug [ə 'kæ(:)mrə .bʌ(:)g] [话] **照相迷** → a SHUTTERBUG

can

can *someone* ['kæ(:)n ～] [话] **开除** 这个 can 是俗语"屁股"的意思。有 throw *someone* out on *his* can 的说法,意为"把某人狠狠抛出去,摔个大屁股蹲

儿”。can *someone* 就是由此转化而来。Tell the guy at table number three not to make so much noise. If he gives you any trouble, can him. 的意思是“你告诉三号桌子那个家伙不要吵得那么凶。如果他不老实,就揪住他,把他硬撵出去。”虽然有象这一例句使用“抛出去”的意义的场合,但是现在,如下边的例句所示,一般使用“解雇”、“勒令退学”的意义。最初只用于“被学校开除”(throw *someone* out of school),如:*Yousa Poni got canned for cheating on her final exams.* 尤萨·邦妮由于在期终考试时作弊,被学校开除了。如今则多用“从工作岗位被开除”的意义。*The company canned three fellows for drinking on the job.* 公司开除了三个人,因为他们在上班时间喝酒。这是用主动语态。但一般都是用被动语态,如 *Three fellows were [got] canned for drinking on the job.* 有三个人因为在上班时间饮酒而被开除了。*George was canned during the recession.* 乔治在生意萧条期间被开除了。*A: I thought you were working at the Trout Drugstore. B: I was, but I got canned last week.* 甲:我记得你不是在特劳特杂货店上班吗? 乙:是的。但是我上个星期被解雇了。◇ fire *someone*

one's **can** [~ 'kæ(:)n] [俗] **屁股** 这个称呼有些不雅。一般是男人使用,指的也是男人的屁股。这一表达法大致只用于“摔[或被人摔]个屁股蹲儿”的时候,或者“坐着不动窝儿”的时候。*I slipped and fell on my can.* 我滑倒了,摔了个屁股蹲儿。在把人从屋子里赶出去的场合也常常使用。在下面的例句中,threw him out on his can 直译应为“把他扔出去,叫他摔个屁股蹲儿”,但是在这句话里,on his can 是否真摔了屁股蹲儿并不重要,只不过是强调狠狠抛出去的含义的一种说法罢了。*When he got drunk and shouted abuse at the manager, they threw him out on his can.* 他喝醉了酒而辱骂经理的时候,人们揪住他,硬把他撵了出去。以下两个例句,是屁股太沉坐着不动窝儿的场合。*Get off your big fat can and help us, will you?* 你抬一抬你那大肥屁股,帮我们一把好不好? *The chief never does any work. He just sits there on his can all day reading the racing news.* 头头从来不干任何工作。他整天连屁股也不抬,净看赛马新闻。◇ *one's* buttocks [rear end, behind]

the can [ðə 'kæ(:)n] [俗] **厕所** 名词 can 除“罐”的意义外,还作“厕所”解。在使用这一意义时,必须象条头那样加定冠词。古时有用“罐子”作 commode (便器)的习惯,因而在最初的时候,can 意味着“便器”。现在也有时使用这一意义。*I was sitting on the can when the earthquake struck.* 当地震袭来的时候,我正坐在马桶上。不久前,除“便器”的意义外,又加上了“厕所”的意义。在世界大战中,美军使用“厕所”一义特别普遍,因而在群众中也流行起来。尽管如此,这是一个非常庸俗的说法,主要的使用者是男性。*Mike is in the can.* 迈克上厕所啦。*Where's the can?* 厕所在哪儿? *Be back in a minute. I gotta go to the can.* 我马上就回来。憋不住啦,不上趟厕所不行。除此而外,还有作“拘留所”和“监狱”解的时候,但是使用频率很低。这两种意义相比较,作“拘留所”解的场合多。*When I couldn't pay the fine, they threw me in the can.* 由于付不出罚金,他们把我关进了拘留所。◇ the toilet

Can it. ['kæːnɪt] [话] **别出声啦!** 这里的 can 是动词,意为“装成罐头”。it 不是代表一个固定的名词,而是根据情况,表示 the noise (喧闹)、the talk (谈论)等意味。也就是说,这一表达法的最初的构思是:“那种 noise 或者 talk 现在不合适,先把它封到罐里,等以后再打开吧。”多为男性使用。*Can it, you guys. I'm trying to study now.* 你们别吵啦,我现在要学习啦。*Can it! Here comes the prof.* 别说话啦。老师来啦。*Can it for a while.* 这话先别提啦! 也有用 the+名词代替 it 的情况。*Can the noise, will you? Dad's still in bed.* 你们安静点好不好? 爸爸还在睡觉哪。*Can the cheap talk. There are ladies present.* 别说下流话啦。有女士们在座啊。◇ Stop the talk [noise, etc.].

cancer

a cancer stick → STICK

candle

burn the candle at both ends [ˌbə(ː)rnðə ˈkæ(ː)ndl ətˌbou*ˈ*θeːndz] [话] **拚命工作、玩乐** 按照字面解释，这一表达法意为“从蜡烛的两头点火”。实际上，美国人也几乎全都这样理解。不过，原来的说法是 burn the candle at both ends of the day(早晨和晚上都点蜡烛)，后来把 of the day 省略了，变成现在这种形式。原来的意思是“干活一直干到深夜，早晨起来还得接着干”。现在一般解释为“从两头点火”，用法也变成表示“一天之中，白天晚上都使用体力”了。多半用于白天工作、夜里玩乐的场合。*I used to work hard all day and play hard all night, but now that I'm older, I find I no longer have the energy to burn the candle at both ends.* 我过去一直整天拚命劳动，整夜拚命玩乐，但是现在年纪大了，我发现再也没有两头消耗的精神头儿了。也有用于白天晚上都干工作的场合，但在这种场合，一般不是指同一的工作，而是指两个以上不相同的工作。*I want you to either reduce your class load at the university or give up your evening job. You can't go on like this, burning the candle at both ends.* 我希望你或是减少在大学中的课程负担，或是放弃晚间的工作，你这样两头奔忙，身体受不了啊！ *In addition to his regular job, Ralph is also serving as a consultant to several government agencies and helping to set up his brother in business. I just don't know how long his health will permit him to go on burning the candle at both ends like this.* 除了他的正规工作而外，拉尔夫还在几个政府机关中担任顾问，并且协助他的弟弟做生意。我简直不知道他这样八面兼顾，身体健康会维持多久。◇ work and play [work, play] so hard

can't hold a candle to *someone* [ˌkæ(ː)nt ˌhouldə ˈkæːndl tə ～] [口] **望尘莫及** 古时，在英国还没有路灯的时代，有钱的老爷太太从饭店或戏院出来之后，要雇一个男孩拿着蜡烛 (hold a candle)，照亮暗黑的道路，送他们回家。这种“持烛人”叫做 a linkboy，充当 linkboy 的绝大多数是社会最下层的人。条头的 can't hold a candle to *someone* 的字面意义是“连给某人持烛的资格都没有”，亦即汉语俗语所说“连给人提鞋都不要”。这一表达法专用于强调“相差悬殊”的心情。*I'm fairly good at tennis, but I can't hold a candle to Kim.* 我的网球算打得很不错了，但根本无法和金相提并论。*It used to be that no ball team could hold a candle to the Giants.* 在过去，没有一个球队能够与巨人队相比。如以上的例句所示，助动词一般都用 can，但并不是限定如此。 *Sally may be pretty, but she doesn't [can't] hold a candle to Ruth.* 萨莉也许算作美人，但比起鲁丝来，可就有天壤之别了。有时也用 be not fit to hold a candle to *someone* 的说法。 *Why does she want to marry a guy like that? He's not fit to hold a candle to her.* 她为什么想跟那样一个男人结婚呢？简直是把一朵鲜花插到牛粪上了。也用于人与人、组织与组织以外的比较。*Mt. Fuji is certainly a high mountain, but it doesn't hold a candle to Mt. Everest.* 富士山的确是一座高山，但与珠穆朗玛峰一比可就小巫见大巫了。◇ be no match for *someone* / be not in the same class as *someone* [*something*]

canned

canned music → MUSIC

canoe

go paddle *one's* **own canoe** [ˈgou ˈpæ(ː)dl ～ ˌouŋkəˈnuː] [话] **不管他人瓦上霜** → paddle *one's* own CANOE

paddle *one's* **own canoe** [ˌpæ(ː)dl ～ ˌouŋkəˈnuː] [话] **自力更生** 字面意义是“自己划自己的独木舟”，换句话说就是：“不用他人的帮助，完全依靠自己的力量进行”。 *Ben's been paddling his own canoe ever since he was just a kid.* 本从很小的时候起就自食其力。*Though the work was complicated, I applied myself* *diligently to learning my new job, and in six months I was able to paddle my own canoe.* 虽然那个活儿很复杂，但是我勤勤恳恳努力钻研新的工作，只用六个月就能够独当一面了。另外，paddle *one's* own canoe 除“自力更生”的意义外，还可以作为 mind *one's* own BUSINESS(少管闲事)的同义语使用。在这一场合，paddle 的前面常加 go。 *I tried to help him but he told me to go paddle my own canoe.* 我想去帮助他，可是他对我说：请不必劳神。顺便提一下：paddle *one's* own canoe 这一表达法由于林肯总统使用过而脍炙人口。1844 年，它最初见于一篇题名为 *Settlers in Canada* (《加拿大的开拓者》)的小说中。1854 年 5 月号 *Harper's Magazine*(《哈珀斯杂志》)发表的一篇诗中又使用了它，从此便流行起来，直至今日。◇ fend for *oneself* / mind *one's* own affairs

cap

have *one's* **cap set for** *someone* [ˌhæv ~ ˈkæ(:)p ˌsetfər ~] [口] **追求男人** 字面意义是“为某人而调整帽子”。英国在维多利亚时代，女人在家里也戴帽子。当有自己对之有好感的男子前来拜访时，为了给人留下良好的印象，就换上最漂亮、最相宜的帽子。这一习用语就是由此种风俗习惯产生的。美国人对此语的历史来源知者甚少，他们的头脑中很自然地固定了这样一种观念：“女性为了获得男性，下定决心，重新整理一下头上的帽子”。在这时候，“获得男性”的目的有两个：一是“作为情侣”，一是“作为结婚对象”。另外，一般的词典都将这一习用语写作 set *one's* cap for *someone*，但在实际上，象本条条头的形式 have *one's* cap set for *someone* 的使用率要高千倍万倍。例如，*Sally has set her cap for the new boy in school.* 萨莉在追求新入学的男生。这句话说了也不算错，但是一般都说 Sally has her cap set for ～. 例如，*Betty had her cap set for Jack for many years before she finally got him to pop the question.* 贝蒂追求杰克好多年了，她终于使他来求婚了。 *Watch out for Doris. She seems to have her cap set for you.* 你注意一下多丽丝。她似乎在追你哪！ ◇ be trying to win [attract] a boy [man]

put on *one's* **thinking cap** [ˌpuˈdɔ(:)n ~ ˈθɪŋkənˌkæ(:)p] [话] **琢磨** 直译是“戴上用于思想的帽子”。 *It may seem difficult, but just put on your thinking cap. I'm sure you'll come up with a good idea.* 这个问题看起来似乎很难，但是，你仔细琢磨琢磨。你肯定会有好主意的。 *George is not much help when he's busy, but once he sits down and puts on his thinking cap he fairly bubbles with good suggestions.* 乔治在忙的时候用处不大，但是，只要他一坐下来，开动脑筋，锦囊妙计便会一个接一个地出现。也可以说 have on *one's* thinking cap。 *We all had on our thinking caps, but we weren't producing any fresh ideas.* 我们大家全都开动脑筋了，但是没有想出任何的新点子。◇ think hard [carefully]

set *one's* **caDp for** *someone* [ˌset ~ ˈkæ(:)pˈfər ~] [口] **女人追男人** → have *one's* CAP set for *someone*

card

a card [ə ˈkɑːrd] [话] **非常有趣的人** card 本来是“扑克牌”的意思，但也可以应用于人。 *Ralph is a real card. He's full of jokes and pranks.* 拉尔夫实在是个非常有趣的人。他满肚子是笑话，竟搞鬼把戏。从这一例句也可以了解，这种人有点“奇特”，但并不是“怪人”，他只是为了使别人高兴而故意耍些花招而已。多用以指男性。但这不是绝对的。另外，如上面的例句所示，最高级的强调是加 real，其他强调用词还有 quite(相当的)等。 *I think you'll like Fay. She's quite a card.* 我想你会喜欢费的。她是一个相当有趣的女人。再有，与“有趣的人”正相反的词是“讨厌鬼”，人们在讽刺时也称“讨厌鬼”为 a card，特别是最近时期，这种倾向很强烈。 *A: You'd better be careful. I can mop up the floor with you any day. B: You're quite a card, aren't you.* 甲：你最好加点儿小心吧。不管哪一天，我都可以把你打得个屁滚尿流。

乙：哎呀，你这人可相当有意思啊。*A: Jack's quite a card, isn't he. B: Yeah, he ought to be shuffled and dealt with.* 甲：杰克这个人很有点儿意思，是吧？乙：嗯，该狠狠教训他一顿啦。在最后这一例句中，甲是真心说"有意思"还是说的讽刺话，仅从文字是弄不清楚的，但乙是当作讽刺话听的，因而那样回答。shuffle and deal 按字面是"用粗暴方法处置"，亦即"狠揍一顿"的意思。同时，在扑克牌游戏中，shuffle 是"洗牌"，deal 是"配牌"的意思。在这里是语意双关，特别是中学生以下的孩子们常用来相互逗趣。◇ an amusing person

a face card [ə ˈfeɪsˌkɑ(ː)rd] [口] **带人像的牌(扑克牌)** "带人像的牌"可以直译为 picture card。这种说法不是没有，然而很少有人使用。face card 一语的来源是：扑克牌中的几张带人像的牌分别画着 Jack(杰克)、Queen(女王)、King (国王)的面部。*In this game, all face cards count ten points each.* 在这种打法中，所有带人像的牌每张按十分计算。顺便提一下：在中国，常简称几张大牌为 J, Q, K, A(或么)，但在英语中是不行的，必须称 jack, queen, king, ace。◇ a picture card

cards

have the cards stacked against *one* [ˌhævðə ˈkɑ(ː)rdz ˌstækt ə ˈgenst ～] [口] **处于不利状态** → stack the CARDS

have the cards stacked in *one's* **favor** [ˌhævðə ˈkɑ(ː)rdz ˌstæktɪn ～ ˈfeɪvər] [口] **处于有利状态** → stack the CARDS

a house of cards → HOUSE

be in the cards [ˌɪnðə ˈkɑːrdz] [话] **命中注定** 原意是"在用扑克牌占卜时，出现于牌上"。相当于中国旧时代所说"算命算出来的"。*You are going to meet a tall, handsome man. It's in the cards.* 你要见到一位身材很高的美男子。这是牌上说的。如例句所示，可以按照字面意义使用，但这是占卜师信口雌黄的特殊场合。一般的用法与扑克牌无关，只是表示"似乎肯定如此"的意义。*Given George's drive and talent, it was in the cards that he would become president some day.* 按乔治的干劲和才能来说，早晚有一天他会当董事长的。*I'd hoped to go to Europe last year, but I guess it just wasn't in the cards.* 去年我本想去一趟欧洲，但命中注定没有去成。这句话暗含"没交上这样的好运"的意思。这是 be in the cards 的典型的使用方法之一。*I'm sure marriage isn't in the cards for me. I've never been popular with boys.* 我是命中注定结不了婚的。在小伙子们面前，我从来就不受欢迎。*Following the big scandal, everyone knew that a reorganization of the company was definitely in the cards.* 发生大丑闻之后，人人都觉得公司肯定非改组不行。另外，在英国英语中，前置词改为 on 而作 be on the cards，但在美国英语中不这样说。◇ be (virtually) destined (to ～)

lay *one's* **cards on the table** [ˌleɪ ～ ˈkɑ(ː)rdˌzɔnðə ˈteɪbl] [口] **打开天窗说亮话** 原为扑克牌游戏用语，即"摊牌"的意思。*With a smile, the gambler laid his cards on the table.* 赌徒微微一笑，把他的牌在桌上摊开了。这是按照字面意义使用的例子。虽然可以转作比喻使用，但在下一例句中，按字面意义和按比喻意义解释都行，如果没有上下文作参考，仅凭这一句话是无法断定的。*He laid his cards on the table and told me that as a matter of fact he didn't have any money.* 他把手里的牌往桌子上一摊[他打开天窗说亮话]，告诉我他实际上连一分钱也没有了。以下是用作比喻的例子。*I'm sick and tired of beating around the bush with them. I've decided to lay my cards on the table.* 我已经厌烦跟他们互相摸底了。我下决心向他们挑明了。强调时多用 all。*If you want our cooperation, you are going to have to lay all your cards on the table.* 如果你想叫我们跟你合作，那你非把内心的打算合盘托出不可。也可以把 lay 换成 put，而说 put *one's* cards on the table。以上例句中的 lay 虽然全可以用 put 代替，但人们大多使用带 lay 的句型。◇ tell *someone* openly of *one's* intentions [plans, resources, etc.] / frankly admit the truth

play *one's* **cards close to the chest** [ˌpleɪ ~ ˈkɑ(:)rdz ˌkloustəðə ˈtʃe(:)st] [口] **竭力不动声色** → play *one's* CARDS close to the vest

play *one's* **cards close to the vest** [ˌpleɪ ~ ˈkɑ(:)rdz ˌkloustəðə ˈve(:)st] [口] **竭力不动声色** vest是西服"背心"。本条直译为"贴着背心摆弄自己的牌"。这一表达法是从扑克牌游戏而来,即"为了不让他人看见自己的牌,要贴近自己的前胸来调配"的意思。*We'd better play our cards close to the vest. There are plenty of people who would try hard to stop us if they knew what we were going to do.* 我们要竭力不动声色为妙。如果他们了解我们要干什么,有很多很多人会千方百计地来阻止我们。常在close的前面加副词。*It's difficult to know what the boss is planning next. He always plays his cards fairly close to the vest.* 很难知道老板的下一步计划是什么。他总是丝毫不动声色。如以下所述,这一表达法在形式上有种种细小的变异。首先,*one's* cards可用it来表达: *I'm playing it close to the vest this time. I failed the last time because too many people learned of my plans before I was ready to act.* 这回我可是守口如瓶啦。上回所以失败,是因为在我还没有准备好行动之前,许多人就知道了我的计划。把vest改为chest,意思完全不变。原来,在英国英语中,vest意为"贴身内衣"(undershirt),所以只能使用chest一词。cards亦可加形容词。*That country always plays its diplomatic cards close to the chest.* 那个国家在外交方面是永远不动声色的。*Play it close to the chest. Our success depends on maintaining the utmost secrecy.* 不要透露一点风声。我们成功与否全看能不能绝对保密。有时不用play而用keep或hold替换。在这一场合,是"保持不外露"的意思,大多用be keeping [holding]的形式。*We haven't found out what Bob's plans are yet. He's keeping [holding] his cards too close to the chest.* 我们还没有识破鲍勃的计划是什么。他简直是守口如瓶啊。另外,也可以说to *one's* vest,但不太普遍。*Let's play it close to our vests. There's no sense in taking unnecessary risks.* 竭力不要露相。冒不必要的危险是毫无意义的。也有从这种用法进一步发展而表示"不冒不必要的危险"的意味的场合,不过,这种情况极罕见。*Graham always plays his cards close to the vest. I'm sure he'd never put all his money into one venture.* 格雷厄姆永远不冒不必要的风险。我敢肯定,他绝对不会把所有的钱都投入到一个事业中。◇ be close-mouthed [secretive] about *one's* plans ((always 永远在be动词后边))

play *one's* **cards right** [ˌpleɪ ~ ˈkɑ(:)rdz ˌraɪt] [话] **搞得不错** 字面意义是"对于自己手中的(扑克)牌正确处理"。*I had a good hand. I knew if I played my cards right I could win the game.* 我的手气不错。我明白,如果我搞得好,我肯定会赢这一局。在用作比喻的场合,也多采取if ~的形式。*If we play our cards right, we can make a lot of money out of this deal.* 如果搞得好的话,这笔生意我们可以捞很多的钱啊。*The old man isn't easy to convince, but if you play your cards right, I think he'll go along with you.* 那个老头是不容易被说服的,但是如果你搞得好,我想他是会协助你的。*Of course we'll succeed. It may look hard, but it's just a matter of playing our cards right.* 我们当然是会成功的。事情看起来似乎很难,但是只不过是会搞不会搞的问题而已。有时用well代替right。*We can trust Wylie to do a good job in the negotiations. He always plays his cards well.* 我们可以派怀利去办好交涉,他总是搞得不错的。play *one's* cards wrong意思相反,是"搞得不好"。也可以说badly,但一般使用right的反义词wrong。*I'm afraid we played our cards wrong. We shouldn't have sent the letter until the outcome was clear.* 依我看,我们大概把事情搞糟了。在没弄清楚结果之前,我们不该发信。◇ do things in the right way

play *one's* **cards wrong** [ˌpleɪ ～ ˈkɑ(ː)rdz ˌrɔ(ː)ŋ] [话] **搞得不好** → play *one's* CARDS right

put *one's* **cards on the table** [put ～ ˈkɑ(ː)rˌdzɔnðə ˈteɪbl] [口] **开诚布公** → lay *one's* CARDS on the table

stack the cards [ˌstæ(ː)kðə ˈkɑ(ː)rdz] [口] **耍花招** 按字面意义,stack 是"(在打扑克时为了自己来好牌而)洗牌作弊"的意思。 *Be careful when you play poker with that guy. They say he stacks the cards.* 跟那个家伙玩扑克的时候,你可要当心! 据说他洗牌作弊。这是本来的用法。然而,在作比喻使用的场合,仅表示"于己有利",究竟这样做是否"正当",那与此语无关。常在后边添加 in *one's* favor 或 against *someone*。 *I should have known better than to try to negotiate with that outfit. They had stacked the cards (in their favor) even before we started talking.* 跟那帮家伙简直没法打交道。在会谈开始之前,他们就为了占便宜而大耍花招啦。 *After my third failure, I couldn't but feel that fortune had stacked the cards (against me).* 在我第三次失败之后,不能不感到命运之神是在耍弄我了。也可以使用被动语态,而说 the cards are stacked。但是,在这一场合,有时与"花招"无直接关系,只表示"被置于不利的状态"的意思。 *I knew the cards were stacked against me, but I had no choice but to try to escape.* 我知道情况对我很不利,但是我除了设法逃走之外毫无其他办法。 *Why did you try it? You knew the cards were stacked before you started.* 你为什么要干那个呢? 你明明知道在你开始之前早已有人做了手脚啦。 have the cards stacked against *one* [in *one's* favor] 是"处于不利[有利]地位"的意思。 *Anyone born in the slums has the cards stacked against him from the beginning.* 出生在贫民窟的人,从呱呱坠地那一天起就处于不利的地位。 *John decided to try to enter medical school. Since his father was a wealthy doctor, he had the cards stacked in his favor.* 约翰决心投考医大了。由于他父亲是位富裕的医生,他处于很有利的地位。另外,亦可使用 deck (扑克牌的一组)一词,以 stack the deck 代替 stack the cards, 两者意思相同。◇ arrange things unfairly

carpet

call *someone* **on the carpet** (for *something*) [ˌkɔːl ～ ˌɔ(ː)nðə ˈkɑ(ː)rpət] [口] **批评** 原来的意思是"主人为了叱责仆人,把他叫进自己的书房之类铺着地毯的房间"。现在,广泛用于长辈对晚辈的过失、上级对下属的工作错误等进行指责的场合,也包括原义所指的场合在内。特别是公司中常常使用,但不是非如此不可。实际上有叫来申斥的情况,但这一表达法与叫来与否并无直接关系。 *The chief called us on the carpet for spending too much on entertainment.* 由于花的交际费太多,头头把我们批评了一顿。象这样使用主动语态的情况不少,但一般来说,还是用被动语态的时候为多。 *The salesman was called on the carpet for losing three customers in one month.* 那个推销员由于一个月内失去三家客户而受到了批评。 *Three students were called on the carpet for cheating.* 三名学生由于考试作弊而受到了批评。 *That guy is always being called on the carpet.* 那个家伙经常不断挨批评。◇ reprimand *someone*

carrot

the carrot and the stick [ðə ˈkærətnðə ˈstɪk] [口] **胡萝卜加大棒** 来源不明。一说最初是在根据美国作家哈米特 (Dashiell Hammett) 的名著《马耳他的猎鹰》(*The Maltese Falcon*)改编的同名电影(1941 年)中出现的。那部影片中有一段对白是这样: Bogart: Why should I do this? Greenstreet: For the same reason a donkey with a carrot in front and a stick in back goes forward instead of backward. Bogart: (*after a pause*) Tell me about the carrot. (博加特: 我为什么非干这个不可? 格林斯特里特: 正如一条驴,前边有胡罗卜,后边有大棒子,只

会向前走，不会往后退。道理就是这样。博加特(稍停一下)：给我讲讲胡萝卜吧！）这一习用语的基本内容与汉语俗语“打一巴掌，给个甜枣吃”差不多。例如：*If you want prison birds to do their best, you have to use both the carrot and the stick.* 如果你想叫那些囚犯好好干活儿，胡萝卜加大棒缺一不可。*I promise you that you will not leave here until you have told us what we want to know. I am willing to use either the carrot or the stick. The choice is up to you.* 我明告诉你，你不对我们讲我们所要知道的事情，就甭想从这儿走出去。我可以打一巴掌，也可以给个甜枣。何去何从，任你选择。下一个例句是这一表达法的变形应用。*We prefer to get our students to do their best by offering them carrots, but sometimes we have to use the stick as well.* 我们主要用鼓励的方法促使学生们尽到最大的努力，但是有时候也不能不给一点惩罚。可以把两个名词用连字符结合到一起，形成 carrot-and-stick，当作修饰名词的形容词使用。*My father believed in the carrot-and-stick approach with us, but the carrots were usually pretty scarce.* 我父亲对我们采取胡萝卜加大棒式的教育方法，但是通常极少给胡萝卜。◇ reward(s) and punishment(s) / kindness and [or] force

carrot-top

a carrot-top [ə ˈkæ(ː)rə,tɑ(ː)p] [话] **红毛(人)** 直译为“胡萝卜色的头”，即“胡萝卜色的头发”，意为“鲜橙色的头发”。但这一表达法不是限定纯粹的“胡萝卜色”，也指一般的“红毛”。所谓“红毛”，其范围很广，包括深棕色在内。如果说 carrot-top，一般认为“胡萝卜色”以及与之相近的“红毛”就可以了。另外，carrot-top 可以指“头发”本身，如 *He has a real carrot-top.* 他的头发是真正的胡萝卜色。也可以指“头发的主人”，如 *He's a real carrot-top.* 他真是个红毛儿。*Hey, carrot-top! Ya wanna go swimming with us?* 喂！红毛儿！你不跟我们游泳去吗？ *All of the Jones children are carrot-tops.* 琼斯家的孩子们全都是红毛儿。在以上的例句中，没有必要一定是“胡萝卜色”，但在以下的例句中，根据上下文，则肯定是“胡萝卜色”无疑。 *There are a lot of red-haired people in the world, but you seldom see a carrot-top like Biggs.* 世界上有许许多多红头发的人，但是很少见到象比格一家人那样的胡萝卜色的头发。◇ a red-head(ed person)

cart

put the cart before the horse [ˌputðə ˈkɑ(ː)rt bəˌforðə ˈhɔ(ː)rs] [口] **本末倒置** 字面意义是“把运货车 (cart)放在拉车的马的前边”。这是英语中最古老的成语之一。据说古罗马政治家西塞罗(Cicero)在公元前 61 年写的一篇文章中就使用过这句当时已经流传很久的格言。虽然可以说 *Don't put the cart before the horse.* 不要本末倒置吧！ 等等，但主要是用进行时或动名词短语，采取 putting ～的形式，如 *You're putting the cart before the horse.* 你那是本末倒置呀！ *What do you mean by billing me before you deliver the merchandise? That's putting the cart before the horse.* 你的东西还没有送到就叫我开帐单，这是什么意思？简直是本末倒置啊。用 get 代替 put 的情况也很多。 *Wait a minute. Let's not get the cart before the horse.* 等一下。不要把事情的前后顺序颠倒了。*You're getting the cart before the horse.* 你那是本末颠倒呀。另外还有 set the cart before the horse 的说法，但在美国口语中是决不使用的。◇ do [get] things backward

Casanova

a Casanova [əˌkæ(ː)zə ˈnouvə / ˌkæsəˈnouvə] [口] **花花公子** Casanova (卡萨诺瓦) 和 Don Juan [ˌdɑ(ː)n ˈwɑːn] (唐璜)都是以勾引女人的天才而闻名的人物。唐璜是虚构的或传说的人物，但卡萨诺瓦 (1725-1798)却实有其人，是意大利的作家。18 世纪，他在风雷激荡的欧洲东奔西走，以冒险和渔色度过自己的一生。他的全名为 Giovanni Jacopo Casanova de Seingalt (塞因加特的乔凡尼·雅各布·卡萨诺瓦)。*Been seeing other women behind my back, have you? I never want to see you again, you Casanova!* 你背着我又勾搭其他的女人去了,是不是?我永远不想再见到你,你这个色鬼!实际上就这样使用。如果一概译为"色鬼"、"色狼",所反映的是完全丑恶的形象;但在英语中,使用此词时多半具有比较轻松的语气。因此,根据上下文,译为"浪荡公子"、"花花公子"等会更贴切。*I always warn the new girls about Jim. He's the office Casanova.* 我常警告新来的姑娘们,说吉姆在我们公司是最爱乱搞男女关系的人。在下面的句子里,语气就更轻快了。*You'll never get Dennis to go steady with you. He's too much of a Casanova.* 你想叫丹尼斯跟你确定关系,那是绝对办不到的。他简直比花花公子还要花哪!另外,在美国口语中,Don Juan 所表示的意义与 Casanova 大致相同,但 Don Juan 最多只能译作"浪荡公子",不象 Casanova 也具有"色鬼"的意味。◇ a philanderer

case

case the joint → JOINT

make a federal case out of it [ˌmeɪkə ˈfedərəl ˌkeɪ ˌsaudəvɪt] [话] **大肆渲染** federal case 是"联邦调查局(＝FBI)的案件"的意思。这一表达法最初的构思是"本来是地方警察该管的事情,偏偏交到联邦调查局处理。与此同样,本来事情(it)不大,却故意起哄,大肆鼓噪起来"。*O.K., O.K. So I got drunk at a party and embarrassed you in front of your friends. I said I was sorry, didn't I? There's no need to make a federal case out of it.* 明白啦,明白啦。只不过是我在一次社交晚会上喝醉了酒,当着你的朋友们的面使你难堪了。我不是已经道歉了吗?没有必要大肆渲染,小题大作吧。*Ned's too touchy. Every time somebody says something he doesn't like, he thinks he has to make a federal case out of it.* 内德是个大神经病。每当有人说了他不喜欢的事情,他就觉得非把这件事情添油加醋、大肆渲染一番不可。另外,这一表达法也可以按照字面的意义使用,例如:*Because the city police were slow in solving the kidnapping, the mayor wanted to make a federal case out of it.* 因为市里的警察办事缓慢,没有迅速解决绑架事件,市长想把它移交联邦调查局处理了。但是,在这一场合,一般惯用的表达法是 ～ the mayor wanted to call in the FBI. ◇ blow it completely out of proportion / get overly [so] excited (about it)

cash

be strapped for cash [ˌstræpːfər ˈkæːʃ] [口] **缺钱** → be strapped for MONEY

cat

the cat has *someone's* **tongue** [ðə ˈkæ(ː)t hæz ～ ˌtʌ(ː)ŋ] [话] **舌头不好使** 最初的构思是:"猫把(孩子的)舌头叼走了"。汉语俗话不是用"猫",而是说"舌头叫狗咬去了"。一般是大人对"舌头不好使"的孩子使用,或者在大人相互谈到"舌头不好使"的孩子时使用。*Why don't you thank Mr. Jones for the nice present, Jimmy? Has the cat got your tongue?* 琼斯伯伯送给你那么好的礼物,吉米,你怎么也不谢谢?舌头不好使啦?*I'm sorry my daughter wouldn't talk to you. For some reason the cat seems to have her tongue today.* 请原谅,我的女儿不能跟您谈话。不知为什么,今天她好象舌头不好使啦。"舌头不好使"的原因一般是"羞怯",但也有时是"出了毛病"。*I asked you what you did with the money. Surely the cat hasn't got your tongue.* 我问你那笔钱怎么的了?莫不是你真的哑巴啦?动词除了 have (got),也用 get,意思是"说不出话来"。*She is a very shy little girl. Every time a stranger speaks to her, the cat gets her tongue.* 她是一个非常怕羞的小姑娘。每当生人对她说话的时候,她总是启不了口。另外,大人相互谈话,不是谈论孩子,也有使用这一表达法的情况。在这种场合含有讽刺的意味。*I'll ask you once more. If you* *bought this ring rather than stealing it, where is the receipt? Surely the cat hasn't got your tongue.* 我再问你一次。如果这戒指不是偷的而是你买的,发票在哪里呀?你的舌头还没有叫狗咬去吧? → lose *one's* TONGUE ◇ *someone* is too shy to speak (the cat seems → it seems) / *someone* can't speak [talk]

Curiosity killed the cat. → CURIOSITY

a ′fraidy cat [ə ′freɪdi ˌkæ(:)t] [话] **胆小鬼** ′fraidy 是把 afraid (害怕)一词的 a-去掉而加 -y 所构成的作定语用的形容词。cat (猫)的形象是一种胆小的动物,有点动静立即发抖。本条是儿童用语,小学五、六年级以下的孩子们常常使用。*Joanie is a ′fraidy cat.* 乔尼是个胆小鬼。*Don't be such a ′fraidy cat.* 用不着那么害怕。也可以不用撇号,而写作 fraidy cat, fraidy-cat 或者 fraidycat。还有 fraidcat 的说法,但人们不使用它。→ a ′scairdy CAT ◇ (a person who is) easily frightened (such →so)

let the cat out of the bag [ˌletðə ′kæ(:)daudəðə ˌbæ:g] [口] **漫不经心泄露秘密** 古时,在农村市场上有把小猪装入布袋出售的习惯。为了欺骗买主,农民常把猫装入布袋冒充小猪。可是这个重要的"商品"却钻了出来,买卖不得不告吹。本条的表达法就是由这一故事而来。the cat 转义指"秘密",一般用于"漫不经心"泄漏机密的场合。本来是指"欺骗性的"行为,现在的使用方法大多不是指这种情况。*The look on my companion's face told me I had said too much—I had let the out of the bag.* 从我的同伴的表情可以看出,我已经说走嘴了,泄漏了不该泄漏的秘密。*Stu let the cat out of the bag while he was drunk.* 司徒在喝醉的时候泄漏了秘密。不仅限于"言语","动作"也可以泄密。*I hadn't known where the loot was hidden, but the suspect's glance at the fireplace let the cat out of the bag.* 我不晓得赃物藏在哪里,但是嫌疑犯向壁炉那里一瞥,使我知道地方了。也有并非本人"漫不经心"、而是由不知其为秘密的他人泄漏的场合。*I was planning to surprise my wife by taking her to the theater tomorrow, but my secretary let the cat out of the bag by calling my home to say that the tickets were ready.* 我本来计划使我的妻子吃一惊,明天带她去看戏,但是我的秘书往家里打电话说票子已经买好,把秘密给泄漏了。有的时候也采取 the cat is out of the bag 的形式,意为"极力保守秘密,结果还是泄漏了"。*Well, the cat is out of the bag. A newspaper reporter has discovered that we are planning a merger with the XYZ Company.* 真糟糕,秘密已经泄漏啦。我们打算与 *XYZ* 公司合并的计划已经被一个新闻记者探听去了。◇ (inadvertently) reveal the secret

look like something the cat dragged in [ˌluk ˌlaɪk ˌsʌ-m ðə′kæ(:)t ˌdræ(:)g ˌdɪn] [话] **好象阴沟里的老鼠** 这一表达法是把"人的外观"比做"猫从外边拖到家里来的东西"。通常以"人"为主语,表明对这个人的全部印象。除了"服装"而外,还包括"容貌",如呆呆的眼神,蓬乱的头发,胡子拉碴等等。*What in the world have you been doing to get your clothes so filthy? You look like something the cat dragged in.* 你把衣服弄得那么脏,简直象个泥猴似的,究竟干什么来着? *After getting drunk and sleeping in his clothes on a park bench last night, Stu arrived at the office looking like something the cat had dragged in.* 司徒昨天晚上喝醉了,穿着衣服在公园的长凳上睡觉,今天来上班,简直象个叫花子一样难看。◇ look terrible

not room (in *someplace*) **to swing a cat**→ ROOM

a ′scairdy cat [ə ′ske(:)rdi ˌkæ(:)t] [话] **胆小鬼** ′scairdy 是给 scared 加上 -y 所构成的用作定语的形容词。本条条头可以缀作 scaredy cat, scaredy- cat 或 scaredycat,但通常是把 -are-部分改作 -air-,最前面加个撇号,书写形式与同义语 a ′fraidy CAT 相似。意思是"象猫一样马上会逃走的胆小的人"。与 ′fraidy cat 同样,是小学五、六年级以下的儿童们的用语。*Jimmy is such a ′scairdy cat.* 吉米真是胆小如鼠。◇ (a person who is) easily frightened ((such → so))

a scaredy cat [ə ˈske(ː)rdi ˌkæ(ː)t] [话] **胆小的人** → a ˈscairdy CAT

There's more than one way to skin a cat. → WAY

catch

catch at straws [ˌkætʃət ˈstrɔːz] [话] **抓把稻草不放** → catch at a STRAW

catch it (from *someone* for *something*) [ˈkæ(ː)ˌtʃɪt] [话] **挨批** 一讲 catch it, 首先联想到的是"抓住球"、"抓住狗"之类的"抓住它"的意义,但是根据上下文,也有"受申斥"的意味。有人不喜欢用 catch hell,而采取这一委婉的说法 (→ catch HELL <from *someone* for *something*>)。这里的 it 指"长辈或上级的恼怒"。儿童们最常使用这一表达法,但成年人也有时使用。*You're going to catch it (from the teacher).* (老师)会批你的哟! 常用 really 加强语气。*I really caught it from the boss for missing the departmental meeting yesterday.* 由于昨天没出席部门的会议,我被部长狠狠批了一顿。◇ be reprimanded (by *someone* for *something*)

play catch [ˌpleɪ ˈkæ(ː)tʃ] [口] **投球接球练习** 体育运动用语。例如说: *Let's play catch.* 咱们练习投球接球吧! play catch 的球不限于棒球,任何球类运动的球都可以。如果在会话时要说出球的种类,用 with 接续,如: ~ with a baseball, ~ with a tennis ball 等。◇ toss a ball back and forth

cathouse

a cathouse [ə ˈkæ(ː)tˌhaus] [俗] **妓馆** 字面意义是"猫的房子",但没有人使用这一意义。美国人一般认为此词所指为下等妓院,但实际上并非绝对如此,如说: *That woman works in the city's most elegant cathouse.* 那个女人在本市最豪华的妓馆中混事儿。◇ a brothel

catnap

a catnap [ə ˈkæ(ː)tˌnæ(ː)p] [话] **假寐** 将此词加以分解,则 cat 是"猫", nap 是"小睡"。合起来就是"象猫那样不论时间地点打个盹儿",白天也行,晚上也行,有时横卧到地板上,也有时就坐在椅子上。总而言之,"不是正式上床睡觉,而是打个盹儿"。但是,一般来说,此词不是指"本人无意识地昏昏沉沉地打瞌睡",而是指"自己积极地要休息片刻,来个假寐"。例如 *I was up late last night so I had several quick catnaps at my desk today.* 我昨天夜里很晚才睡,所以今天趴在桌子上偷偷打了几次小盹儿。这句话决不能解释为"终于有好几次不知不觉地迷糊过去了"。如果想说"不知不觉地迷糊过去",英语的表达法有 ~ so I dozed [fell asleep] several times at my desk today 等。另外,也可以分写作 a cat nap。再有,catnap 可以作为动词使用。*The boss caught me catnapping at my desk.* 我正趴在桌子上假寐,被头头抓住啦。◇ a light nap

cat's

the cat's meow → MEOW

the cat's pajamas [ðə ˌkæ(ː)ts pəˈdʒɑːməz] [话] **最好(的东西[人])** → the cat's MEOW

the cat's whiskers [ðə ˌkæ(ː)ts ˈhwɪskərz] [话] **最好(的东西[人])** → the cat's MEOW

cats

fight like cats and dogs [ˌfaɪt laɪˈkːæ(ː)tsənˈdɔːgz] [话] **经常气势汹汹地打架** 字面意义是"象猫与狗那样打架"。西方人认为猫和狗是"死对头",所以产生了 fight like cats and dogs 这一表达法。美国人一听到这句话,脑际就会浮现出人们激烈吵架、相互殴打、相互扔东西打之类的场面。另外,cats and dogs 虽然是复数形式,但一般多指一对一的打架。*The couple next door fight like cats and dogs. It's a wonder that they're still married.* 隔壁那两口子三天两头儿打架。奇怪的是,他们依然在同居。如这一例句所示,多用于"三天两头儿"、"一年到头儿"的场合。但也有例外。*Within an hour after they had met, they were fighting like cats and dogs.* 他们相见还不到一个钟头,两个人就象疯狗似地掐起来了。顺便提一下:在英国英语中,cat 和 dog 都作单数,说 fight like cat and dog。◇ be always [furiously] fighting [quarreling]

Holy cats! ['houli 'kæ(:)ts] [话] **哎呀,我的天哪!** → Holy cow!

rain cats and dogs [.reɪŋ'kæ(:)tsn'dɔ:gz] [话] **倾盆大雨** → rain PITCHFORKS

cause

be a lost cause [ə 'lɔ(:)st'kɔ:z] [口] **没有实现的可能性** be 也可以用 become 代替,意义当然也就变为"失去希望"。cause 是"以某种信念为基础的奋斗目标",lost 则是"这一目标越来越渺茫,不管如何努力奋斗,也没有达到的可能性"。*Peace became a lost cause when President Roosevelt cut off Japan's supply of oil.* 当罗斯福总统下令停止向日本供应石油时,和平已经毫无实现的希望了。本来这一习用语是用于大是大非、主义、运动等方面的,但是,也有象下边例句那样用于日常琐事,表示"没有指望"的意思。这是一种极其轻松的使用方法。*When the opposite team hit back-to-back home runs, our hopes of winning became a lost cause.* 当对方球队连续本垒打的时候,我们就没有得胜的希望了。*I'm afraid your contact lenses are a lost cause. We'll never find them in this dark theater.* 依我看,你那隐形眼镜片算丢定了。在这么黑暗的剧院里,你是绝对摸不到的啊。◇ be (a goal) doomed to failure / be hopeless

caution

throw caution to the winds [.θrou 'kɔ(:)ʃəntəðə 'wɪ(:)ndz] [口] **不顾一切** 字面意义是"把小心谨慎(caution)扔到风里去"。用于"豁出去干(什么事情)"的场合。*The road was dangerously slick with ice, but when I saw the last train was about to leave, I threw caution to the winds and broke into a run.* 道路上结了冰,非常滑,一不小心就会摔倒,但是当我看见最后一趟车已经快要开了的时候,就不顾一切,撒腿向它跑去。可以在 caution 前边添加表示强调的 all。*I knew the man might be a shyster, but I wanted to trust him. Throwing all caution to the winds, I handed him the money.* 我知道那个人可能很狡猾,但是我愿意信赖他。我不管三七二十一,把钱交给他了。可以象下一例句那样,用 modesty (羞怯)、prudence (慎重)词代替 caution,但是使用率最高的是条头的 caution。*Seeing no one else on the beach, the girl threw all modesty to the winds and flung off her bathing suit before running into the water.* 那个姑娘见到海岸上没有另外的任何人,就不顾羞怯,把游泳衣也脱了,光着身子向海中跑去。同样,也可以用动词 fling 或 cast 代换 throw。特别是在用 fling 的时候,"豁出去"的感觉更加强了。不过,一般还是用 throw。*I wasn't sure whether Mary loved me or not, but she was leaving— perhaps for good. I decided to fling caution to the winds and ask her to marry me.* 我不能确定玛丽是不是爱我。但是她要走了,也许是一去不回头了。我决定豁出去向她求婚。◇ abandon all caution [modesty, etc.]

ceiling

hit the ceiling [.hɪtðə 'si:lɪŋ] [话] **暴跳如雷** ceiling 是"天花板"。本条的最初构思是:"把身子跳起来,脑袋撞到天花板上"——一个人的恼怒达到如此激烈程度。*The boss'll hit the ceiling when he finds that we've overrun the budget.* 老板如果知道我们超出预算,他会暴跳如雷的。也可以用 roof (屋顶)代替 ceiling,而说 hit the roof。◇ (suddenly) become very angry

celeb

a celeb [ə sə'le:b] [话] **有名人物** celeb 是 a celebrity [sə'lebrəti]的略语。主要是文艺界、文艺杂志等的用语。但不一定专指文艺界人士。是个相当随便的说法。*The Secretary of State was among the celebs at the party held at the Park Hotel.* 在出席公园饭店的晚会的著名人物中有国务卿。◇ a celebrity

cent

cut *someone* **off without a cent** [ˌkʌt ～ ˈɔ(ː)f wɪˌðaudə ˈse(ː)nt] [口] **一分钱遗产也不给** 直译是"把某人(从遗产中)切掉,一分钱也没有"。美国人是根据遗嘱(will)处理财产,不是把全部财产都给与家属。本条条头就是在这种场合使用的表达法。一般词典常译成"断绝父子关系"、"废嫡"等,这是实质性错误,务请注意。这一表达法仅仅是有关遗产的经济措施而已。顺便提一下:英国人也许宽厚一些,也许是喜欢幽默的缘故,他们在这一场合,总是说只给一先令遗产,即 cut *someone* off with a shilling。*Mr. Green cut his profligate son off without a cent.* 格林先生没有留给他那个浪荡公子一分钱遗产。在强调时,可以说 cut *someone* off without a red cent 或者 ～ *someone* ～ without one red cent。*If my son doesn't do as I say, I'll cut him off without a red cent.* 如果我的儿子不照我所说的话去做,我连一分钱的遗产也不给他留下。当然,也可以说 cut off *someone* ～。*He cut off his relatives without a cent.* 他没有留给亲属一分钱遗产。也说 cut *someone* out of *one's* will。◇ leave *someone* no inheritance ((强调的 red → absolutely))

cents

one's **two cents worth** [～ ˌtuː ˈse(ː)nts ˌwɔːrθ] [话] **一文不值的意见** 字面意义是"(某人的)两分钱的价值"。这一表达法省略了后边的 of opinion,专用于"意见"、"发言"、"忠告"等。two cents 是"只值两分钱"、"毫不足取"的意味。*Well, that's my two cents, for what it's worth.* 好啦,这是我的一点儿刍荛之见,也许没有什么用处。正如这一例句所示,一般用以表示谦逊,或者含有一点轻蔑、嘲讽的味道。*If you'll listen for a moment, I'd like to put in my two cents worth.* 如果你能够听一下的话,我愿意陈述我的小小的意见。*The meeting took a long time because every man jack wanted to get in his two cents worth.* 因为不管张三李四都要发表不值一文钱的意见,所以会议开了很长时间。如以上两个例句所示,动词多用 put in, 或 get in。*Samantha always seems to feel she has to put in her two cents worth, even when she obviously doesn't know what she's talking about.* 萨曼莎这个人甚至当她连自己都显然不知道她在说什么的时候,都觉得非讲讲她那一文不值的臭意见不可。*Will you please be quiet. When I want your two cents worth, I'll ask for it.* 请安静一下吧。当我想听你的高见的时候,我会去求教的。◇ (offer) *one's* opinion

chaff

separate the wheat from the chaff → WHEAT

chain

one's **ball and chain** → BALL

chain-smoke

chain-smoke [ˈtʃeɪnˌsmouk] [口] **连续吸烟** 字面意义是"连锁吸烟",也就是"用前边抽剩的烟头点火,一支又一支接连不断地吸下去"。虽然可以按照字面意义使用,但是在大多数的场合是与用不用前边抽剩的烟头点火无关,仅仅强调吸烟支数之多,具有"连续不断地吸烟"乃至"吸大量的烟"的意味。*Harry chain-smoked two packs of cigarettes in today's conference.* 在今天的会议中,哈里一连吸了两包香烟。chain-smoke 的人是 a chain smoker。*I didn't know Harry was such a chain smoker.* 我过去不知道哈里是那样大量吸烟的一个人。◇ smoke one cigarette after another

chair

get the chair [ˌgetðə ˈtʃeːr] [话] **坐电椅** → FRY

champ

a champ [ə ˈtʃæ(ː)mp] [话] **(拳击、摔交等的)冠军** champion 的缩略形式。*The champ's record is now twenty-one wins against three losses.* 冠军现在的纪录是 21 胜 3 败。有时用此词戏称不是"冠军"的人,轻松地打招呼。*Hiya, champ. How's business?* 喂,老兄,你好吗? ◇ a champion

chance

Fat chance! [ˈfæ(:)tˈtʃæ(:)nts] [话] **天晓得!** fat chance 的字面意义是"肥机会",与 good chance 相同;但在实际上却是 almost no chance (几乎没有希望)的意思。常作反语使用。另外,惊叹号"!"也有时改用句点。 *A: Jimmy says he's going to go to Harvard University. B: Fat chance! He'll be lucky to get into college at all.* 甲:吉米说他打算进哈佛大学。乙:天晓得! 他能进个什么普通大学就算万幸啦。 *A: Greg says he can beat you easily at tennis. B: Ha! Fat chance!* 甲:格雷格说在网球比赛中,他很容易就能打败你。乙:哼! 天晓得! 如以上的例句所示,fat chance 作为会话中的答话,多采取 Fat chance! 的形式。除此而外,还有 A fat chance *someone* has of *doing something*(某人几乎没有做某事的可能性)这样一个形式可以使用。在这形式中,fat chance 也是在句子一开头就出现,但与 Fat chance! 的场合不同,一般加冠词。*A fat chance I have of getting a vacation this summer. The boss has just decided that we should all double our sales by September.* 今年夏天我几乎没有得到休假的可能性了。老板刚刚决定:到九月为止,我们所有的店员都必须把销售额提高一倍。不过,根据说话的调子,冠词可从略。◇ Impossible!

be itching for a chance to *do something* [ˈɪ(:)tʃɪŋfərə ˈtʃæ(:)ntstə ˈ~] [话] **跃跃欲试** be itching to *do something* 是表示"想要做什么,急得心里发痒"的意思的固定说法。中间插入 for a chance (寻找机会),便形成本条的表达法。这个 itching 原本是"发痒"的意思。 *Why don't you put Joe Green in charge of this project? He's itching for a chance to show you that he's got what it takes.* 你叫乔·格林负责这项工程好不好? 他跃跃欲试,想向你显示一下他有足够的能力哪。为了加强语气,常加 just。 *Hollywood is full of would-be movie actors who are just itching for a chance to prove themselves in front of the camera.* 好莱坞充满了想要当电影演员的人,他们跃跃欲试,想得到在摄影机前显示自己才能的机会。也有象下一例句那样用作反语,或表示讽刺的意味。*Anyone who drives like that must be itching for a chance to get killed.* 象那样开车的人,肯定是心里发痒,急着找死呢! ◇ ((不加 just)) be hoping very much for an opportunity to *do something* / want very much to *do something*

not stand a chance [nɑt ˌstændə ˈtʃæ(:)nts] [话] **无望** → not have a PRAYER(of *something*)

an outside chance [ə ˌnautsaɪd ˈtʃæ(:)nts] [口] **一线希望** 直译为"外侧的可能性"。但这里的 outside 具有"远离"或"离开"的感觉。本条的意思是"可能性或机会在远远的一边"。可以用于肯定,表示"虽然少,但是有";也可以用于否定,表示"只有那么一点点"。两者相比,用于肯定面的时候居多。下面三个例句都是肯定的用法。 *It's too early to give up yet. We still have an outside chance of winning.* 现在就认输可太早啦。我们还有一线得胜的希望哪。 *My husband is feeling very good today. He was told that he has an outside chance of being elected next president of the company.* 我丈夫今天情绪非常好。他听人家说,虽然只是一线希望,但有当选公司下届董事长的可能性。 *Don't start celebrating yet. There's still an outside chance that we may lose the election.* 不要高兴得太早。我们在选举中失败的可能性虽然很小,但有还是有的啊。下面两个例句是从否定的观点使用的。在这一场合,必须加上限定的词 only 或 just 等。 *Though at first given only an outside chance of defeating the incumbent, the Republican candidate came through with flying colors.* 虽然在最初击败现有候选人的可能性微乎其微,但是共和党的候选人却大获全胜了。 *I decided not to present my proposal. There was only an outside chance of its being accepted anyway.* 我

决定不提出我的建议了。无论如何,被采纳的可能性是微乎其微的。用 possibility 代替 chance,意义相同。但请注意,在这一场合动词不能用 have。*A: Do you think you will be transferred overseas this year? B: It's an outside possibility.* 甲:你认为你今年会调到国外去工作吗? 乙:这种可能性不能说完全没有。◇ a slight [slim] possibility ((*one* has → there is))

change

for a change [fərə ˈtʃeɪndʒ] [话] **偶尔改变一下** 直译是"为了变化"乃至"追求变化"。多用于对当前的倾向或趋势不满而企图改变潮流的场合,或者希望有所改变的场合。不仅涉及人的行动方式,也可以涉及自然现象或社会现象。这一表达法要轻松地使用,反映"偶尔变一变不好吗?"的希求心情。*Must you always be bumming cigarettes off me? Why don't you buy your own for a change?* 你非总向我讨烟吸不可吗? 为什么不自己买上一回半回呢? *You've been going out too many evenings recently. It's about time you stayed home and studied for a change.* 你最近晚间往外跑的次数太多了。你该收一收心,在家里学习啦! 下面例句是谈到游山玩水的,在这一场合,意思与"换个地方"或"换换空气"相近。*I'm getting tired of taking our vacation at the beach every year. This summer, why don't we go to the mountains for a change?* 每年都是去海滨度假,我已经有点腻了。今年夏天,我们换个地方到山上去吧! 以下是使用于自然现象或社会现象的场合。*I'm tired of all this rainy weather. I wish the sun would come out for a change.* 这样接连不断地下雨,我腻烦死啦。但愿太阳公公偶尔出来露一露面啊! 在象下面这样所希求的变化已经发生或者正要发生的场合,则具有"这回总算……"或"好容易才……"的意味。*I'm glad to see that taxes are finally going to come down for a change.* 令人高兴的是,税金这回总算是要往下降了。for a change 与 instead 大致相同,因此常有用 instead (代替)替换 for a change 的情况。但是,instead 本身并不含有"改变当前的倾向"或"当前的倾向在改变"的意味。也就是说,与 for a change 相比,instead 是一个缺乏内涵的、中庸的表达法。◇ once in a while / instead (of *doing something*)

have a change of heart [ˌhævə ˌtʃeɪndʒəv ˈhɑ(ː)rt] [口] **改变心情** 字面意义是"有心情[心]的变化"。请注意它与 change *one's* mind 的不同点。*Of course I haven't had a change of heart. I've just changed my mind, that's all.* 当然,我并没有改变我的心情。我只不过改变了一下想法而已。按照美国人的思想,heart 在胸,为感情所寄居的地方;mind 在头,为理性所寄居的地方;二者相比,heart 是根本的东西,因此,如果"改变 heart",当然"mind 也改变";而 heart 保持不变、只改变 mind 也是可能的。也就是说,从英语的角度来看,"改变 heart"是了不起的大事,而"改变 mind"则轻而易举。因此,本条条头的 have a change of heart (不能说 change *one's* heart) 一般使用于"通过打动心灵的经验"或"依据深刻的反省"这一类的上下文。*After seeing his poverty, I've had a change of heart. I've decided to give him the job after all.* 看见他那贫穷的状况,我的心情改变了。结果,我决定叫他干那个工作。*Upon reflecting on how badly he had been treating his wife, George had a change of heart about demanding a divorce.* 乔治反省自己对待妻子如何恶劣,他回心转意,不要求离婚了。也可以用 undergo, suffer 等动词代替 have,而说 undergo [suffer] a change of heart, 意义大致相同。*Scott used to be prejudiced against Blacks, but since he has had a Black roommate at college, he has undergone a change of heart.* 斯科特对黑人一向抱有偏见。但是自从他在大学中有了一位黑人室友之后,他的心情发生了变化。另外,还可以使用 cause 或 bring about 之类的动词,采取 cause [bring about] *someone's* change of heart 的形式。意思是"使(某人)改变心情"。*I* *thought you had decided not to go to college. What's caused your change of heart?* 我以为你已经决定不上大学啦。是什么原因使你的心情发生了变化呢? ◇ experience a change in *one's* feelings

changeable

(as) changeable as the weather→ WEATHER

charley

a charley horse → HORSE

charm

turn on the charm [ˌtə(:)rˌnɔ(:)nðə ˈtʃɑ:rm] [话] **施展魅力** 意思是"作为达到目的的一种手段,有意识地施展自己的魅力"。在这里,charm 是广义的"魅力",包括人品、惹人喜爱、娇媚、善于应酬等等,因人而异,因男女而有不同。这一表达法给人的感觉是:"自己知道自己的魅力,在必要时把开关一按 (turn on),将这个武器打出去。" *It's difficult to refuse Betty's requests when she turns on the charm.* 贝蒂一撒娇,你就很难拒绝她的要求。*Jack is good at getting people to do what he wants. He knows when to get angry and when to turn on the charm.* 杰克善于使人听命于他。他知道什么时候来硬的一手,什么时候来软的一手。*It's no use turning on the charm, baby. The answer is "No."* 小姐,你施展魅力也没有用处。回答是"不行"。◇ (consciously) exhibit the attractive points of *one's* personality

charmed

lead a charmed life → LIFE

chase

lead *someone* **a merry chase** [ˌli:d ~ əˌmeri ˈtʃeɪs] [口] **使追者疲于奔命** 这里的 merry 是反语,意思不是"愉快"、"高兴",而是"达到讨厌的程度"、"狼狈不堪"。lead *someone* a chase 是"被追的人反而成了带头人,使追者紧追猛赶",加上个 merry, 就成为"使追者到处追赶,疲于奔命"了。*The bank robbers led the police a merry chase through three states before they were caught.* 银行抢劫犯使警察疲于奔命,跑了三个州才把他们追捕到手。*Our canary got out of its cage yesterday and led us a merry chase all over the neighbor hood.* 昨天,我家的金丝雀从笼子里飞走了,害得我们在附近到处搜寻,疲惫不堪。*Nancy is leading Ned a merry chase, but in the end I think she'll marry him.* 南希使得内德神魂颠倒,苦苦追求,但是到最后,我想她是会跟他结婚的。◇ make *someone* work hard chasing *one*

a wild-goose chase [ə ˌwaɪldˈgu:s ˌtʃeɪs] [口]**徒劳的追求** 古时候有一种竞赛,叫做 wild-goose chase。在竞赛中,一群骑马的人互相争着跑在前面,并没有固定的终点。不过,跑在前头的人有选择到什么地方去的权利,为了享受这种一马当先的快感,并不确定目标,东西南北来回转,争取跑在前面。在竞赛中,马群的 formation(队形)跟 wild-goose(雁)成群飞翔时的队形(V 字型)相似,所以称这种竞赛为 wild-goose chase。由于这种竞赛在表面上具有"毫无目标地到处来回转"的性质,本条在用作比喻时,就成为"没头的苍蝇,乱撞"或者"瞎子点灯,白费蜡"的意思了。*When the policeman told us that the street we were looking for didn't exist, we realized that the man had sent us on a wild-goose chase.* 当警察告诉我们说我们所寻找的街道根本就不存在的时候,我们才明白那个人是叫我们白白跑腿了。在这一例句里,找的对象是物。*I'll try to find your daughter for you, but it may turn out to be a wild-goose chase. There are thousands of Mary Smiths in America, and besides, she may well have changed her name or gotten married.* 我试试看,寻找一下你的女儿。但是也可能瞎子点灯,白费蜡。在美国,有成千上万个叫玛丽·史密斯的人,另外,她也许改名换姓,或者跟人结了婚。在这一例句中,找的对象是人。◇ a hopeless quest

chaser

a skirt chaser [ə ˈskə(:)rtˌtʃeɪsər] [俗] **色鬼** → a SKIRT

a woman chaser [ə ˈwumənˌtʃeɪsər] [话]好

色的男人 → a SKIRT

chatter

chatter ['tʃæ(ː)dər] [口] **喋喋不休** 原是"吱吱"、"唧唧"之类的小动物鸣叫声的象声词。 *We could hear the squirrels [monkeys] chattering in the trees.* 我们听到松鼠[猴子]在树林里吱吱地叫。这是本来的使用方法。机枪的发射声也用 chatter 来形容。 *Machine guns began to chatter off to my right.* 机枪在我的右方嗒嗒嗒地响起来了。本条是把这一象声词转用于人的多嘴多舌。这一表达法以音响为重点,令人感到是一种刺激神经的高亢的声音,因而常用以描述儿童或女人的说话方式。例如: *The yard was full of children, yelling and chattering away.* 院子里全是孩子,唧唧喳喳,又说又叫。 *I wish my secretary would make her typewriter chatter the way she does her mouth.* 但愿我的秘书能使她的打字机也象她的嘴那样,一天到晚嗒嗒嗒地不闲着。可以用固定的词组 chatter like a magpie (象喜鹊一样唧唧喳喳)来加强语气。 *Whenever my sisters get together, they chatter like a bunch of magpies.* 每当我的姐姐妹妹们凑在一起的时候,她们总是唧唧喳喳,说个没完。作为名词, chatter 是"闲聊的话"的意思。 *I've had enough of that woman's chatter.* 那个女人闲聊的一套话,我已经听腻了。 a chatterbox, a chatterer 都是"饶舌者"的意思,但在会话中多使用前者。 *Let's not invite Mrs. Peshak. She's too much of a chatterbox.* 咱们别请佩莎克太太吧。她是个最爱饶舌的人啊! *My daughter doesn't talk much, but my little boy is a real chatterer.* 我的女儿不爱多说话,可是我的小儿子的嘴简直闲不住。◇ talk (fast and rhythmically)

chatterbox

a chatterbox [ə 'tʃæ(ː)dər.bɑ(ː)ks] [口] **饶舌者** → CHATTER

cheapskate

a cheapskate [ə 'tʃiːp.skeɪt] [话] **吝啬鬼** cheap 是"吝啬的"的意思。skate 在这一场合与 fellow 或 chap 相同,是"人"或"家伙"的意思。这是个古老的词,在这一意味上,很少单独使用。本条条头是由 cheap 与 skate 合成的,本来是两个词。主要指在金钱方面吝啬,不肯掏腰包。 *That cheapskate! After all the things I've bought for him, he won't even lend me one yuan!* 那个吝啬鬼! 我给他买过那么多的东西,而他连一块钱也不借给我! 大家在一起吃吃喝喝的时候,有的人爱钻空子,总是避免分担所花的费用。条头的表达法也完全适用于这样的场合。 *That cheapskate never helps to pay for our meals together.* 我们大家在一起吃饭的时候,那个吝啬鬼绝对不掏自己的腰包。吝啬的男子不受欢迎,这似乎是四海皆然。如下一例句所示,美国的女郎也常在背后发牢骚。 *I'm never going to date that cheapskate again! He took me to dinner at a fried chicken stand and then let me walk home!* 我永远也不再跟那个吝啬鬼约会啦! 他请我吃饭,只在小摊上来了个炸鸡,然后又叫我步行回家! 也有用于不是借贷金钱、而是借贷东西的情况。 *My sister's a real cheapskate. She'll never lend me any of her clothes.* 我姐姐是个地地道道的吝啬鬼。她绝对不肯把她的任何一件衣服借给我。◇ a miser / a stingy fellow [person]

cheat

cheat on *someone* ['tʃiː .dɔ(ː)n ~] [话] **(有配偶者)与人私通** → TWO-TIME *someone* (with *someone*)

cheaters

cheaters ['tʃiːdərz] [话] **眼镜** 单数形式 a cheater 只能按字面意义使用,指"骗子手"、"捣鬼的人"、"舞弊者"。复数形式不知为什么具有"眼镜"的意义。一种诙谐的说法。与 glasses 同样,可加 a pair of。 *The culprit was wearing (a pair of) cheaters.* 犯人戴着(一付)眼镜。◇ glasses

check

bounce a check [.bauntsə 'tʃe(ː)k] [话] **开空头支票** 字面意义是"使支票跳回

来”。在美国，不论是个人还是公司，当付钱的时候，除了信用卡以外，普遍利用支票。每个人或单位都根据自己在银行的存款开支票，如果存款不足，所开的支票就不能兑换现金，而“跳回来”(bounce)。“使支票跳回来”就是“开空头支票”的意思。由于漫不经心而开空头支票的情况比较多，如果故意这样做，自然得到警察局吃官司了。*If you bounce a check, you are not allowed to maintain a bank account for six months.* 如果开空头支票，银行户头六个月不能使用。*I bounced two checks last month, but fortunately both of them had been written to friends of mine.* 上个月我开出两张空头支票，幸好这两张全都是开给自己朋友的。bounce 可作不及物动词使用，如说 *A check bounces.* 支票兑不了现金。*I wrote a check for the rent, but I didn't have enough money in my account so it bounced.* 我开了张支票付房租，但是由于我的户头存款不足，没有兑现。另外，如果说 a check bouncer, 那意思是“好开空头支票的人”。*My wife is a check bouncer. She's forever writing rubber checks.* 我的妻子是个好开空头支票的人。她经常开空头支票。这位太太也许只是由于漫不经心而已；但是，check bouncer 也具有专干这种勾当的惯犯的意味。→ a paper HANGER ◇ issue a bad check

a check bouncer [ə ˈtʃek ˌbauntsər] [话] **好开空头支票的人** → bounce a CHECK

give *someone* **a rain check** [ˌgɪv ～ əˈreɪnˌtʃe(:)k] [话] **下次再请吧** → take a rain CHECK

pass a bad check [ˌpæsə ˌbæ(:)d ˈtʃe(:)k] [话] **(故意)开空头支票** → a paper HANGER

a rubber check [ə ˈrʌ(:)bər ˈtʃe(:)k] [话] **空头支票** 直译是“橡皮的支票”。由 bounce a CHECK(开空头支票)这一表达法类推出来的一种说法。bounce a check 的构思是：由于 bounce 是“(球一类的东西)弹回来”，那么，bounce a check 就是支票不能兑现而“跳着跑回自己的手里来了”。既然能跳着跑回来，支票也肯定是象皮球一样用橡皮 (rubber) 制作的东西。这就是 rubber check 一语产生的来源。*Rubber checks always bounce.* 空头支票永远是被银行拒付而退回的。*The man had left town before I realized that he had given me a rubber check.* 等我发现那个人给我开的是一张空头支票，他已经离开这个镇了。也可以使 rubber 和 check 两个词分开，如下面的说法：*All of my wife's checks seem to be made of rubber. She never remembers how much money she has in the bank, so they often bounce.* 我老婆开的支票似乎全都是空头的。她从来不记得她在银行里存了多少钱，所以常常被拒付退回。◇ a check backed by insufficient funds

take a rain check [ˌteɪkə ˈreɪnˌtʃe(:)k] [话] **下一次吧** rain check 本来是在户外举行棒球之类比赛或运动会时因雨中止而由主办者向观众发出的“顺延入场券”。*It started pouring during the third inning, so we all got rain checks.* 在第三局时开始下大雨了，所以我们都得到了雨天顺延入场券。由此转用于比喻，意思是“以后有机会再领盛情”(指他人邀请吃饭等)。动词使用 get 不如使用 take 普遍。这一表达法包含着“本来想去，可是很遗憾，有事去不成”的抱歉心情。在辞谢的话后边加上这么一句，可以使对方不至于心里不舒服。这是一种社交辞令，多用于与内心无关而随便说说的场合。*I'm sorry I won't be able to go to your house for dinner tonight. I'll have to take a rain check.* 很抱歉，我今天晚上不能去府上吃晚饭。等下一次吧。*A: How's about a quick one after work tonight? B: I'm afraid I'll have to take a rain check. I've got a meeting at six.* 甲：今天晚上下班后，咱们喝一杯怎么样？乙：真对不起，我得下次再领盛情啦。六点钟我有个会议要参加。*I'm sorry I can't join you tomorrow. Can I take a rain check?* 真对不起，我明天不能参加啦。咱们下一次好吗？take 可用 have 代替，有时也用 get 代替。*Thanks for the invitation, but I'm really beat. Can I* *have [get] a rain check?* 谢谢你的邀请。但是,我实在累极了。咱们下一次好不好? 还有 give *someone* a rain check 的形式。Can [Will, Would] you give me a rain check? 这样的句子构造,在会话中与 Can I take a rain check? 的意义相同。有时也用 I'll give you a rain check. 的说法。*Can you give me a rain check on our date tonight? I'm afraid I've caught the flu.* 今天晚上我们的约会改到下一次好不好? 我大概传染上流感啦。*You can't make it? That's too bad. But I'll give you a rain check.* 你不能来? 那太遗憾了。不过,下一次我还请你的。◇ (ask *someone* to let *one*) make [do] it [join *him*] another time [night, day, etc.]

checkup

a medical checkup [ə ˈmedəkl ˈtʃeˌkʌ(ː)p] [口] **身体检查** → a PHYSICAL

a physical checkup [ə ˌfɪzəkl ˈtʃeˌkʌp] [口] **身体检查** → a PHYSICAL

cheek

turn the other cheek [ˌtə(ː)rnðɪ ˌʌðər ˈtʃiːk] [口] **宽容大度** 由《圣经》中的话转成的习用语。依照耶稣的说法,不要 an EYE for an eye and a tooth for a tooth(以眼还眼,以牙还牙)(→),有人打你的右脸,连左脸也转过来由他打,这样一来,自己的形象会更高大。*When someone strikes you, it is difficult to turn the other cheek.* 当别人打你的时候,要宽容大度是很难的。这句话可以按照字面解释为"有人打你",也可以作为比喻解释为"受到侮辱"。*We refuse to turn the other cheek.* 我们决不把左脸也转过来由他打。这是珍珠港遭到日军袭击后,当时的美国总统罗斯福的一句名言,意思是"不雪此耻,决不罢休。" *Your forceful means of persuasion will not work against my brother. He will simply turn the other cheek.* 你苦口婆心地劝说我哥哥也没有用处,他只会俯首听命。*Don't expect me to turn the other cheek every time someone takes advantage of me.* 不要认为我象条顺毛驴似的,老是叫人家骑。◇ offer unresisting forgiveness

cheer

a Bronx cheer [ə ˈbrɑ(ː)ŋks / ˈbrɔ(ː)ŋks ˈtʃɪ(ː)r] [话] **嘘嘘声** 稍微详细说明一下就是:把舌头伸在两唇之间,使唇和舌一起振动发出的声音。Bronx,用不着说,就是"纽约市的布朗克斯区",cheer 一般是"喝采"的意思。本条的字面意义为"布朗克斯式的喝采",实际上是指"嘘嘘"的声音。*When the batter struck out, a Bronx cheer arose from the stands.* 当击球员由于三次未打中而出局的时候,看台上响起一片嘘嘘声。*No sooner had the teacher turned his back than someone in the back of the classroom gave a Bronx cheer.* 老师刚刚转过脸去,教室的后排就有人发出了嘘嘘的声音。如这一例句所示,"发出嘘嘘声"用 give a Bronx cheer 就可以。但是,如果 give 有间接宾语,则必须把不定冠词改为定冠词,作 give *someone* the Bronx cheer。这一点务请注意。*The fans don't like that player. No matter how well he does, they always give him the Bronx cheer.* 球迷们不喜欢那个运动员。不管他打的多么好,他们总是对他发出嘘嘘声。另外,"被人嘘嘘"是 get the [a] Bronx cheer, 用定冠词和不定冠词均可。但是,在这一场合,如用 get the Bronx cheer from *someone* 的形式,在后边加 from *someone*,就必须用定冠词。*The foreman got the Bronx cheer when he asked the workers to put in more overtime.* 工头又要求工人们加班时,引起了一片嘘嘘声。关于这一表达法的来源,一般的美国人认为是由于在体育运动(特别是棒球比赛)中,布朗克斯区的居民喜欢发出嘘嘘的声音。但是,正确的说法是:是由于布朗克斯区有一家 the National Theater (国家剧院),观众用这样嘘嘘的方式对待他们不喜欢的演员。顺便提一下:地名一般是不加冠词的,但是 Bronx 却是极少数的例外之一,如 *I live in the Bronx.* 我住在布朗克斯区。这一例句所示,须加 the。最初,有一个名叫 Jonas Bronks 的丹麦人率领他的同族在这个地方定居，the Bronks 就是“布朗克斯一族”的意思，后来作为地名使用，以迄于今。在缀字方面，Bronks 变成了 Bronx。◇ a sound of derision

cheering

be all over but the cheering [ˈɔː ˈlouvər bətðə ˈtʃɪrɪŋ] [话] **人多势众** → be all over but the SHOUTING

cheers

Cheers. [ˈtʃɪːrz] [话] **干杯** → BOTTOMS up.

cheese

a big cheese [ə ˌbɪg ˈtʃiːz] [话] **大人物** 这里的 cheese 与“食用的干酪”没有关系，原为印地语 *chiz*(意思是“物”)，在过去的殖民时代，住在印度的英国人开始把它当作英语一样使用。以前单独使用，意为“重要人物”、“有权势者”，现在一般都添加 big。是一种相当亲密的说法。*Her old man is a big cheese in New York.* 她的老子在纽约是个了不起的人物。如果把 a 换成 the，就成为“领袖”、“首长”、“总经理”之类“最有权势的人物”了。*Who's the big cheese around here?* 这一带的头面人物是谁？另外，过去曾用 the cheese 或 the real cheese 表示“(人们认为)最高级的东西”，如说 *Talkies're the cheese.* 有声片是最高级的东西。但现在除在历史影片中，平时是见不到这种用法的。◇ an important person

chest

play *one's* cards close to the chest [ˌpleɪ ~ ˈkɑ(ː)rdz ˌkloustəðə ˈtʃe(ː)st] [口] **竭力不动声色** → play *one's* CARDS close to the vest

play it close to the chest [ˌpleɪ ɪt ˌkloustəðə ˈtʃe(ː)st] [口] **竭力不动声色** → play *one's* CARDS close to the vest

chestnut

an old chestnut [ə ˌnould ˈtʃestˌnʌ(ː)t] [口] **老掉牙的笑话[故事、音乐]** 为什么把“陈旧的栗子”用做这一意义，不了解。这一表达法包含着“现在还听这一套太没意思了”或者“那种玩意儿谁都知道”的意思。在使用于唱歌、音乐等的时候，又多一层“已经过时”的意思。*My uncle is full of jokes and stories, but unfortunately they're all chestnuts.* 我的伯父有一肚子笑话和故事，遗憾的是，全是老掉牙的东西。如这一例句所示，chestnut 原来是单独使用的，可能是由于感到劲头不足，在会话中多半都加上个 old。*A: Have you heard the story about the salesman and the farmer's daughter? B: Oh, no! Not that old chestnut.* 甲：你听到过推销员与农民女儿的故事吗？乙：得啦得啦，别提那老掉牙的故事啦！ *My father says that the music I like gives him headaches. He's always listening to the old chestnuts he liked when he was young.* 我爸爸说他听了我所喜好的音乐就头疼。他永远听他年轻时候所喜好的那些老掉牙的东西。◇ an old, stale joke [story, song, etc.]

Chevy

a Chevy [ə ˈʃe(ː)vi] [话] **雪佛兰牌轿车** Chevrolet [ˌʃevrəˈleɪ] 的 Chev-加上指小词 -y 形成的新语，为 GM (美国通用汽车公司)生产的最便宜的小轿车的爱称。*Although Mr. Smith is the richest man in town, he always buys a Chevy.* 虽然史密斯先生是镇上最有钱的人，但是他总是购买雪佛兰车。偶尔脱落 -y 而说 a Chev [ˈʃeːv]。◇ a Chevrolet

chew

bite off more than *one* can chew → BITE

chew *someone* out [ˌtʃuː ~ ˈaut] [话] **狠狠斥责** chew 是“咀嚼”。原来的构思是：“长辈对晚辈象要嚼碎似地狠狠申斥”。在这里，“嚼碎”相当于汉语的“咬牙切齿”。这是为了纠正对方的错误而采取的一种“激烈”而且“时间长”的批评方式，有时带有“罗嗦”的味道。*The boss chewed me out for being late to the meeting.* 由于我开会来晚了，头头把我狠狠批评了一大顿。*The sergeant chews his men out for something almost every day.* 中士几乎天天找碴儿狠狠批评他的部下。强调时加 really。*The teacher really chewed Jimmy out for breaking the window.* 吉米打碎了窗户玻璃，老师对他大大地训斥了一顿。还有 give *someone* a chewing out 的说法。在这一表达法中，强调时多用 good 代替 really，有时为了进一步加强语气，二者并用，如：*Ed's father (really) gave him a good chewing out for using the car without permission.* 埃德由于未经许可就用车，被他父亲狠狠地训斥了一大顿。◇ reprimand *someone* severely

chewing

give *someone* **a chewing out** [ˌgɪv ～ ə ˌtʃu(ː)əˈnaut] [话] **狠狠批评** → CHEW *someone* out

chicken

be chicken [ˈtʃɪ(ː)kən] [话] **畏惧** 指象鸡那样胆小。这一表达法特别使用于一个人面临危险的事情、可能招人恼怒的事情等，在有必要拿出勇气的时刻，看看到底有没有斗争精神的场合。*Don't be chicken. Go ahead and dive in.* 不要怕嘛！赶快往水里跳。*I told him he should ask the boss, but he's too chicken.* 我对他说，他应该去求求老板，但是他太胆小啦。可用 turn [get, become] chicken 表示"害起怕来"、"胆怯起来"的意味。*He turned chicken and backed out.* 他害起怕来，不干了。另外，偶尔加 a 当作名词使用，如 *He's a chicken.* 他是个胆小鬼。→ CHICKEN out ◇ be timid

(a) chicken colonel [(ə) ˈtʃɪkən ˈkə(ː)rnl] [俗]**上校** → (a) bird COLONEL

chicken feed → FEED

chicken out [ˌtʃɪkəˈnaut] [话] **由于胆怯而作罢** 这是把 turn chicken (胆怯)与 back out (作罢[退下]) 合在一起的说法 (→ be CHICKEN)。*At the last minute, Harry chickened out.* 到了紧急关头，哈里胆怯不干了。*When I saw the size of my opponent, I just about chickened out.* 我一看到对手那么大的块头，就胆怯起来，简直想弃权了。◇ lose courage and back out

be no spring chicken [ˌnou ˌsprɪŋ ˈtʃɪkən] [话] **不那么年轻** spring chicken 是"童子鸡(特别指不超过十个月的肉嫩的笋鸡)"的意思。这一表达法的来源是：在古时候，不是春天 (spring)就很难得到这样的鸡。转义指"年轻人"。但是经常只在否定句中强调中年以上的人已经不那么年轻的场合使用。*I don't know how old Mr. Moe is, but he's no spring chicken.* 我不知道莫先生多大岁数，但是他年纪不轻了。*Mrs. Gray may not be a granny, but she's certainly no spring chicken.* 格雷夫人也许还算不上老太太，但是她的年纪肯定不小啦。◇ be far from young

run around like a chicken with its head cut off [ˌrʌnəˌraund laɪkə ˈtʃɪkən wɪðəts ˈhed ˌkʌdɔːf] [话] **慌里慌张急得来回转** 请读者想一下"被割掉头的鸡乱蹦乱跳的样子"吧。汉语俗语说："东一头西一头地象被掐了脑袋的苍蝇一样"，正是这个意思。典型的应用场合，如：幼小的孩子不见了，母亲慌张起来，急得要命；本来以为人家委托的工作还有几天日子，但是忽然想起明天就到期了，急得乱转。*When the mother realized her little girl was gone, she began running around like a chicken with its head cut off.* 当母亲发现她的小女孩不见影儿的时候，她开始东一头西一头地乱跑，好象没头的苍蝇一样。主语如果是复数，chicken 一般也用复数。*Ever since the office staff learned this morning that the boss was coming back a week early, they've been running around like chickens with their heads cut off.* 当办事处的工作人员们今天早晨听说头头提前一个星期回来的时候，大家都慌手慌脚，急得乱转。◇ rush about in a great flurry

turn chicken [ˌtə(ː)rn ˈtʃɪkən] [话] **胆怯** → be CHICKEN

chickens

count *one's* **chickens before they hatch** [ˌkaunt ～ˈtʃɪkənz ˌbəforðeɪ ˈhæ(ː)tʃ] [口]**如意算盘打得太早** 直译是"鸡还没孵出来，先数有几只鸡"。意思是"高兴得太早啦"。*Do you really think you* *can find a job as easily as that? If you ask me, you're counting your chickens before they hatch.* 你真认为你能那么轻而易举地找到工作吗？叫我说，你的如算盘打得太早啦！另外，虽然也常见到 ～ before they are hatched 的形式，但是在会话中，～ before they hatch 的使用频率高。◇ depend on the benefit to be derived from a still uncertain source

go to bed with the chickens → BED

child

one's **brain child** [～ ˈbreɪn ˌtʃaɪld] [口] **(某人)头脑的产物** 原来的构思是："某人头脑生的孩子"。一般来说，即 *one's* soriginal idea [plan, etc.]。在谈到主意、计划、发现等时常常使用。*We can't vote down this plan. It's the boss's brain child.* 我们对这个计划不能投反对票，它是咱们老板的心血呀。也常使用 the brain child of *someone* 的形式。*The idea of talking over a wire was the brain child of Alexander Graham Bell.* 通过一根电线讲话这个主意，是亚历山大·格列阿姆·贝尔想出来的。也有指具体的"物"的场合。*This rocket is the brain child of Dr. Strangeduck.* 这种火箭是斯特兰吉达克博士发明的。在复数的场合，当然要把 child 改为 children。*Most of the scientific inventions of the eighteenth century were the brain children of the leisured class.* 18 世纪的科学发明，大部分是有闲阶级头脑的产物。◇ *one's* (original) idea / (something that was) (originally) conceived by *someone*

child's

child's play → PLAY

chimney

smoke like a chimney [ˌsmoukl aɪkə ˈtʃɪmni] [话] **纸烟不离嘴** 这里的 smoke 具有双重意义：一是"冒烟"，一是"吸烟"。like a chimney 是"象烟囱一样"。本条的意思是"纸烟一根接着一根吸，简直象烟囱一样在冒烟"。这是表示"吸烟太多"的一种夸张说法。*I used to smoke like a chimney until my doctor made me quit.* 在医生禁止我吸烟之前，我总是纸烟不离嘴。*Mr. Gander smokes like a chimney.* 甘德先生简直象个烟囱，总不断冒烟。◇ smoke incessantly

chin

chin music → MUSIC

Chin up! [ˌtʃɪˈnʌp] [话] **振作起精神来！** → keep *one's* CHIN up

keep *one's* **chin up** [ˌki(:)p ～ ˈtʃɪˌnʌ(:)p] [口] **保持精神旺盛** 直译为"保持下巴(chin)朝上"，用不着说，这是"保持精神旺盛"的象征性的行动。作为这种行动的前提，经常是容易令人垂头丧气的事情。也就是说，本条习用语在使用时往往近似"下定决心，排除万难"的意味。在鼓励人的时候，常说 *Chin up!* 振作起精神来！这是 Keep your chin up!的短缩形式。*After my husband lost his job, we had great difficulty keeping our chins up for a while.* 我丈夫失业以后，在最初一个阶段，我们费了很大劲努力保持振作的精神。*I'm afraid we're lost. But keep your chin up. We'll find our way out of these mountains somehow.* 我们似乎迷路了。但是，振作起精神来！我们总会找到一条路走出这些山的。*Mrs. Smith managed to keep her chin up despite the rumor that her husband was involved in a scandal.* 史密斯夫人虽然听说她的丈夫与一项丑闻有关，但是她仍然保持住了坚定的态度。◇ maintain *one's* courage

take it on the chin [ˌteɪkɪdɔ(:)nðə ˈtʃɪ(:)n] [话] **蒙受重大打击** 原为拳击比赛用语，意思是"下巴狠狠挨了一拳"。it 指"猛烈的拳击"。*The challenger tried to dodge the champion's punch but he took it on the chin.* 挑战者试图躲开冠军的一拳，但是正迎面打在下巴上了。转作比喻使用。*The world's economy took it on the chin when the OPEC nations suddenly raised the price of oil.* 当石油输出国组织的国家突然提高石油价格的时候，世界经济蒙受了重大的打击。在强调这一表达法时可加个

really。 *Our company really took it on the chin during the recent recession. We barely managed to survive by laying off half the staff.* 在最近的经济衰退中，我们公司的确受到了严重的打击。我们解雇了一半工作人员，才算勉强度过难关。 *A self-confident person can take it on the chin without becoming discouraged.* 一个有自信心的人即使受到严重的打击也不会气馁。原意本来是"从正面挨了一拳"，现在又有发展，可以用于表示"挨了很多拳，被打得落花流水"以及"遭到粗暴对待"的意味了。*Our team really took it on the chin in today's game. The opposing team scored a run in every inning.* 在今天的棒球比赛中，我们队简直被打得个落花流水。对方的球队每一局都得了分。*I'm always taking it on the chin from that guy.* 我总是挨那个家伙的狠揍。 *The Prime Minister has really been taking it on the chin in the newspapers recently.* 在最近，首相受到报纸极为严厉的批评。另外，关于这个表达法，英文词典中常解释为 endure punishment。但是，这里的 punishment 并不是"惩罚"的意思，而是 rough treatment (粗暴对待)的意思，与以下两个例句中的 punishment 的用法一样。*Our team endured a lot of punishment at the hands of our opponents.* 我们队被对手打得够惨的。 *This car has taken a lot of punishment.* 这辆汽车被用得够苦的。此外，endure 也不是普通场合的"忍耐"、"克制"的意思，而是与 undergo 或 experience 相同，意为"经验"。原来，如果仅仅是 take it 的话，则常作"能忍耐"解，但是在它后面一加上 on the chin，就几乎完全没有那样的意思了。◇ experience a hard blow [rough treatment]

china

(like) a bull in a china shop → BULL

chink

a chink in ***one's*** **armor** [ə ˈtʃɪnkɪn ～ ˈɑr(ː)mər] [口] **(强人的)弱点** chink 是"裂缝"。本条原来的构思是：西方古代的甲 (armor)虽然遮护全身，但某个地方必有使剑能够刺进去的 chink。现在指有权势的、了不起的人物的"弱点"、"疼处"。这是一个成语式的说法，在千方百计寻找对方的弱点加以攻击的场合使用。 *He must have a chink in his armor somewhere. It we could only find it!* 他肯定在什么地方有弱点。我们能找到它就好啦！如果是特定的"弱点"，冠词 a 当然改作 the。 *His love of drink is the chink in his armor. Get him drunk and I'm sure he'll talk.* 贪杯是他的弱点。把他灌醉了，他肯定会说出来的。◇ a point where *one* can be easily attacked / *one's* weak point

chip

a chip off the old block [ə ˈtʃɪ.pɔ(ː)fðɪ ˌould ˈblɑ(ː)k] [话] **与父亲一模一样的儿子** 这里的 chip 是"碎片"。block 是"木块"。本条的字面意义是"旧木块的碎片"。最初的构思是把 family tree 当做一种 block，而 chip 是它的"碎片"。因而，偶尔也有按照本来的意义使用的场合，例如：*I learned that old Mr. Smith was the illegitimate son of my great grandfather and thus also a chip off the old block.* 我已经知道老史密斯先生是我曾祖父的私生子，因此他也是我们家族的一员。但是，现在一般只在谈到"父子关系"的时候使用，多指"酷似老人的孩子"。严密地讲，这个"老人"仅指"父亲"，这个"孩子"仅指"儿子"。*Mr. Oak was always a solid, reliable man, and his son is a chip off the old block.* 欧克先生一向严肃认真，是一个很可靠的人，他的儿子也跟他一模一样。如这一例句所示，一般在赞美别人的儿子或夸奖自己的儿子时使用。*He's not a bad boy, but not exactly a chip off the old block.* 他不是一个坏孩子，但是跟他父亲不完全一样。孩子们爱说这样一句开玩笑的话：*He's a chip off the old block, but the block was rotten.* 他倒跟他的老子一模一样，但是他的老子可糟透啦！这句话已经成为一个固定的用语。虽然属于例外，但也有如下一例句那样使用本条的表达法贬低他人的儿子的场合。*Mr.*

Tightpurse is as stingy as they come, and I'm afraid his son is a chip off the old block. 泰特波斯先生是一个极端吝啬的人,遗憾得很,他的儿子跟他一模一样。另外,在过去不是用 off 而是用 of,常说 a chip of the old block,但是现在已经不用这种表达法了。◇ just like his father

have a chip on *one's* **shoulder** [ˌhævə ˈtʃɪpɔn ~ ˌʃouldər] [话] **叫阵** 这一表达法来自孩子们选拔头目的一种方式:一个孩子把木片(chip)放到肩(shoulder)上,说 I dare you to knock it off. (我看,谁也不敢把它碰掉。)这是向对方叫阵。如果有人接受挑战,把木片打掉,两个人就要武斗,决一胜负。本条习用语转用于指当别人说话时采取针锋相对的态度。 *How come you have such a chip on your shoulder today?* 你今天怎么象吃了枪药似的? 也可以说 carry a chip ~,意义相同。*That fellow always seems to carry a chip on his shoulder.* 那个家伙总摆出要武斗的架势。*He went through life with a chip on his shoulder.* 他这一辈子不论遇见什么事情都采取斗争的态度。如此例所示,也常使用 with a chip on *one's* shoulder 的形式。◇ be always [so] ready to quarrel

chips

cash in *one's* **chips** [ˌkæ(:)ʃɪn ~ ˈtʃɪ(:)ps] [话] **死** 字面意义是"把筹码换成现金"。 *It's getting late. I think I'll cash in my chips.* 时间不早啦。我想,我得把筹码换现金,离开赌场啦。本条的表达法是把人生比做打扑克之类的赌博。"把筹码换现金"就是"最后结算输赢多少",拿人生来说,也就是"死亡"。这是一个十分委婉的说法。*Too bad about Frank. He was awfully young to cash in his chips.* 弗兰克实在太不幸了。他那么年轻就离开人世啦。*I'm an old man. I'll soon be cashing in my chips.* 我年纪大了。我很快就得去见阎王啦。另外,除这一意义而外,有时还用以表示如下的意义:为了确保已经得到的利益,或者为了不受更大的损失,"中途停止一笔生意"、"卖掉股票,退出某一公司"。*If there's a buyer for my share of the business, I'd like to cash in my chips.* 如果有买主,我愿意把手中的股票卖掉,与公司脱离关系。◇ die

be in the chips [ˌɪnðə ˈtʃɪ(:)ps] [话] **钱多得很** 这里的 chips 原为 poker chips,即"打扑克用的筹码",与"钱"大致同义。这一表达法来自赌场的一种具体形象:在打扑克时大胜,筹码堆积如山。*If this deal goes through, we'll be in the chips.* 如果这笔生意搞好了,我们就会有大批的钱到手了。*My father always dreamed of someday being in the chips, but nothing he ever tried seemed to succeed.* 我爸爸总是梦想有朝一日发大财,但是他搞的生意就没有一样似乎能成功的。如以上的例句所示,这一习用语多半是用于表示"钱多得很,今后一生都不愁没钱花"的意思。但是,也用于表示钱数虽不多,而精神上似乎成了财主的场合。*I'm in the chips tonight. I won a thousand dollars at the races.* 我今天晚上是大财主。在赛马中我赢了一千美元。一般只在谈到"人"的时候使用,但也可以用于谈到"公司"等的场合,意思是"生意兴隆,财源茂盛"。*That company has been in the chips ever since it started selling electronic games.* 那个公司自从销售电子游戏机之后,财源滚滚,可赚了不少钱。另外有一个意义相似的表达法是 be in the money,使用方法与 be in the chips 完全相同。*We're in the money! I won a thousand dollars at the races today.* 咱们发了大财啦! 今天在赛马中,我赢了一千美元。◇ be rich / have lots of money / make great profits

when the chips are down [ˌhwenðə ˈtʃɪpsər ˌdaun] [话] **在关键时刻** 从扑克牌游戏而来的表达法。chip 是赌钱的"筹码"。这一习用语给人的感觉是:"一旦摆上筹码,就不能再抽回来"。在用作比喻时,也是"已经到了无法后退的紧急关头"的意思。*Jimmy may appear to be lazy and undependable, but he always comes through when the chips are down.* 乍看起来,吉米似乎很懒,也很不可靠,但是每当关键时刻,他总是踏踏实实完成任务。在体育运动等方面也常使用。*Let's send in Lefty as a pinch hitter. He's always good for a hit or two when the chips are down.* 现在情况紧急，咱们派左撇子去替换击球员吧。每当关键时刻，他都会稳稳当当来一两个安打的。◇ when the situation is urgent

choosers

Beggars can't be choosers. → BEGGARS

chopper

a chopper[1] [ə ˈtʃɑ(:)pər] [话] **直升机** 在美国人听起来，直升机飞的时候发出 chop-chop-chop [ˈtʃɑp ˈtʃɑp ˈtʃɑp] 的声音。本条的表达法即来源于此。-er 为词尾，表示"干什么的人或物"。最初是朝鲜战争期间美军中使用的俚语。是一种亲昵的说法。*Did you hear? A chopper crashed in the woods outside of town this morning.* 你听到了吗？今天早晨有一架直升机在城外的树林子里坠毁了。又称 a WHIRLYBIRD, an EGGBEATER。◇ a helicopter

a chopper[2] [ə ˈtʃɑ(:)pər] [话] **(小型)机枪** chop 是"(用斧子)劈木头"。这一表达法原来的构思就是："把人砍倒的工具"。特指 a Tommy GUN(汤姆逊式 45 口径的机枪)。但是，凡是手提式机枪皆可称为 chopper。黑社会用语，常在强盗影片或武侠小说中出现。在军队中，除说俏皮话时而外，几乎完全不用。*Hand me the chopper, Louie. I'll show these cops how to shoot.* 路易，把机枪递给我。我要叫这些老警看看我的枪法。◇ a submachine gun

chops

lick *one's* **chops** [ˌlɪk ~ ˈtʃɑ(:)ps] [话] **馋涎欲滴** chops 是"颚"或"嘴的四周"。这一表达法可按照字面意义"舐嘴的四周"使用，也可按照比喻意义"高兴地等待"使用。*The dog began licking his chops as soon as he saw the meat.* 狗一看见了肉，就开始用舌头舐嘴的四周。*Will dinner be ready soon? It smells so good that everyone is already licking their chops.* 饭快好了吗？味道太香了，大家已经馋涎欲滴啦。*The relatives are already licking their chops over the old man's money.* 对于那位老人的钱，亲属们已经馋涎欲滴了。◇ wait in pleasurable anticipation ((over → of receiving))

chow

chow [ˈtʃau] [话] **饭** chow 来自汉语，这一点确实无疑。但是，原来的汉语究竟是什么？对这个问题有好几种说法：①是 *ch'ao*(炒)，②是 *chiao*(饺子)，③是 *chow-chow*(中国的泡菜)这一洋泾浜英语的短缩形式。另外，英语采用这一词汇是 19 世纪后半叶的事情，这一点是肯定的；但是，关于怎样传入的问题，人们调查研究的结果并不一样。归纳起来，说法有两大类：①是作为船上用语，最初变成了英国英语；②是在美国西部修筑铁路的时候，有大批中国人在那里做工，因而最初纳入了美国英语。这两类说法究竟哪个可以作为定论，现在几乎不可能解决。是男性轻松的语言，特别是小伙子们相互间使用。*This is good chow.* 这饭很好吃。*How's about some chow?* 吃点饭怎么样？ *Have you had chow yet?* 你已经吃饭了吗？使用 chow 的表达法有 CHOW down, a chow HALL, a chow HOUND, a chow LINE, chow TIME。请参阅各条。◇ food / dinner [breakfast, lunch, supper]

chow down [ˌtʃau ˈdaun] [话] **吃饭** 这里的 CHOW(→) 是由意为"饭"的名词转化而来的动词，加上 down 就是"把饭往下送到肚子里去"，也就是汉语文言所说"纳入腹中"。原为军用俚语。*Let's chow down before we go.* 咱们出发前填饱肚子。*Hey, everybody. Let's chow down.* 喂，大家全都来吃饭。◇ eat (dinner [breakfast, lunch, supper])

a chow hall → HALL

a chow hound → HOUND

a chow line → LINE

chow time → TIME

chowhound

a chowhound [ə ˈtʃauˌhaund] [话] **馋鬼** → a chow HOUND

chowtime

chowtime [ˈtʃau.taɪm] [话] **开饭时间** → chow TIME

Christmas

be lit up like a Christmas tree → TREE

(as) slow as Christmas [əzˈslouəz ˈkrɪsməs] [话] **太慢了** 美国的孩子们日夜盼望的不是元旦，而是圣诞节的来临。因此，在形容"迟"、"费时间"的时候，就说"象圣诞节一样慢"。一般与 be 动词一起使用。*Haven't you finished your homework yet? You're as slow as Christmas.* 家庭作业还没搞完吗？你可太慢啦。这主要是儿童用语，一般是孩子对孩子或者大人对孩子在会话中使用。*Do you think they could've gotten lost? They're sure slow as Christmas getting here.* 你看，他们是不是迷了路啊？他们还没有到这儿，实在太慢啦。as ～ as 中的前一个 as，为了语调关系，往往省略。*You're slow as Christmas. If you don't walk faster we'll miss the train.* 你可太慢了。如果你不快走一点儿，咱们就赶不上火车啦。◇ very [so] slow

Christ's

for Christ's sake [fər ˈkraɪˈsːeɪk] [俗] **无论如何** → for Pete's SAKE

Chubby

Chubby [ˈtʃʌ(ː)bi] [俗] **胖子** → FATSO

chug-a-lug

chug-a-lug [ˈtʃʌgə.lʌ(ː)g] [话] **咕嘟咕嘟地喝** 象声词。在美国人听起来，大量液体通过喉咙时，作"恰格·哦·拉格"的声音。汉语作"咕嘟咕嘟"。*I was so thirsty I chug-a-lugged three glasses of water.* 我渴极了，一连咕嘟咕嘟地喝了三杯水。如此例所示，在喝水时可以用这个象声词。但是，一般是用于形容喝啤酒的样子。多数场合是指"一口气喝下去"，但不一定非"一饮而尽"不可。这一说法主要是强调豪饮的雄壮气氛。*Stu can chug-a-lug a whole liter of beer without taking a breath.* 司徒能够一口气喝整整一升啤酒。*Don't chug-a-lug your beer. We don't have any more money.* 不要使劲喝啤酒吧。咱们已经没钱啦。a chug-a-lug contest 是大学学生喜欢搞的"喝啤酒比赛"。*Our club is having a chug-a-lug contest tonight.* 今天晚上，我们的俱乐部举行一场喝啤酒比赛。◇ gulp down

church

a church key → KEY

(as) poor as a church mouse → MOUSE

cinch

a cinch [ə ˈsɪ(ː)ntʃ] [话] **轻而易举** 字面意义是"使马鞍固定的肚带"。原是美国的牛仔们从墨西哥人的西班牙语 cincha 借用而来。本条的最初构思是："要拴肚带，只要穿过扣环一拉就行，十分简单"。因此，就用此词表示"不费事"、"很容易"的意思。*A: Can you do it? B: Sure. It's a cinch.* 甲：你干得了吗？乙：当然干得了。那太容易了。*Climbing a small mountain like that is a cinch.* 登那么一座小山，轻而易举。*A: How can you learn all this English before the test tomorrow? B: It's a cinch. I'll just put my English text book under my pillow before I go to sleep.* 甲：在明天考试以前，你怎么能记得住这么多的英语呢？乙：那太容易啦。我只要在睡觉以前把我的英语课本放到枕头底下就行了。如以上的例句所示，美国人见到或听到 cinch 一词首先联想到的是"极其简单"的意思。但由此发展，还使用它表示另外一个意义。他们想："既然极其简单，结果就必然不出所料"。所以，此词也就具有"不会有错"、"肯定如此"的意味。例如 It's a cinch that she'll win. 这句话，它的含义是："由于在她来说，得胜是轻而易举的事，因此，她必胜无疑。"可以根据上下文或者句子结构区分这两种意义。在这里，句子结构有三种基本形式：① It's a cinch (that) she'll win. 这句话是在 cinch 的后边接续 (that) ～ will ～，一般来说，表示"确定无疑"。如果把这里的 that ～换成 for *someone* to ～，而说 ② It's a cinch for her to win. 那就变成"轻而易举"的意思了。如果象 ③ She's a cinch to win. 这样采取"主语 + be 动词 +

cinch + to 带动词不定式”的形式，两种意义都可能成立。也就是说，根据上下文的关系，句 ③既可以换成 ① It's a cinch that she'll win. (她必胜无疑。) 也可以换成 ② It's a cinch for her to win. (在她来说，取胜易如反掌。) ◇ (very) easy / a foregone conclusion

circular

the circular file → FILE

city

a city slicker → SLICKER

The City of Brotherly Love [ðə ˈsɪdiəv ˈbrʌðərli ˈlʌ(:)v] [口] **费城** → PHILLY

The City of the Angels [ðə ˌsɪdi əvðɪ ˈeɪndʒəlz] [口] **洛杉矶市** → L. A.

civ

Western civ → WESTERN CIV

civil

keep a civil tongue in *one's* head → TONGUE

clam

a clam [ə ˈklæ:m] [话] **不爱说话的人** → CLAM up

clam up [ˌklæ: ˈmʌ(:)p] [话] **保持沉默** 这一表达法是把 clam (蛤蜊)加上个表示“完全地”的意味的 up，形成动词。汉语的说法是“守口如瓶”。*When the suspicious-looking stranger learned that my companion was a policeman, he clammed up.* 当那个看起来很可疑的陌生人知道我的同伴是位警察的时候，他沉默不语了。如此例所示，一般用于原来正在交谈、由于某种原因忽然闭口不讲的场合。*Every time I ask about the money, he clams up.* 我一问到那钱的事，他就沉默不语了。*C'mon, Charlie. Don't clam up on me. Just tell me why you're leaving.* 你说呀，查理。不要对我守口如瓶。你只告诉我你为什么要走就行。但是，也有象下一例句的场合，不是本人坚决不肯开口，而是想说却说不出来，因而保持沉默。*My students are quick to answer questions in Chinese, but whenever I ask something in English they all clam up.* 我用汉语提问，我的学生们对答如流，但是当我用英语提问的时候，他们全都不吭声了。a clam 是“不爱说话的人”。*Archie is a real clam. I'll bet he never says a dozen words a day.* 阿尔奇是一个真正不爱说话的人。我敢肯定，他一天连十句话也说不到。◇ turn [fall] silent

clams

clams [ˈklæ:mz] [话] **美元** clam 的一般意义是“蛤蜊”，但常用以指“美元”。这是一种轻松的说法。究竟是哪一种意义，可以根据上下文判断。例如说 We're having clams tonight. 这是“我们今天晚饭吃蛤蜊。”的意思；如果说 He paid me fifty clams. 则肯定是“他付给我五十美元。”但是，当 clam 作“美元”解时，一般用以表达“钱数相当多，超出想象之外”的心情(当然也就不采取 a clam 的单数形式了)，因此，当我们说 That guy wants three hundred clams for that car. 这句话时，就不仅仅意味着“那家伙的汽车想卖三百美元”，而是意味着“那样一辆破车，那家伙索价高达三百美元”。同样，前边的例句 He paid me fifty clams. 如果译成“他居然付给我五十美元之多。”就更传神了。另外还有个 smackers [ˈsmækərz]，此词与作为“美元”解的 clam 意义完全相同，两者可以互相替换使用。◇ dollars

class

cut class [ˌkʌt ˈklæ(:)s] [口] **逃学** → GOOF off

clay

feet of clay → FEET

clean

come clean [ˌkʌm ˈkli:n] [话] **坦白交待** 直译是“干干净净地来”。最初的构思是“隐瞒真实情况是肮脏的”。因此，“老实说出真实情况就干净了”。相当于汉语的“坦白交待”，经常含有“不管问什么，都要毫不隐瞒地说出”的意味。主要是警察在涉及犯罪问题时使用。*You'd better come clean. We know you stole the money. Where is it?* 你最好是坦白交待。我们知道你偷了钱。藏在什么地方啦？*If you come clean now, you may get a reduced sentence.* 你现在如果坦白交待，也许会得到减刑。偶尔用于犯罪以外的事情。例如一个孩子说：*Come clean, little brother. What did you do with my baseball glove?* 你说老实话，小弟弟。你拿我的棒球皮手套干什么来着？在这一场合，如果译成"坦白交待"就有点过分严重了，只能译"说老实话"、"说真的"等等。◇ confess

give *someone* **a clean bill of health** → BILL

make a clean breast of *something* → BREAST

One's **nose is clean.**[~ ˌnouzəz ˈkliːn] [话] **清白** → keep *one's* NOSE clean

cleaners

take *someone* **to the cleaners** [ˌteɪk ~ təðə ˈkliːnərz] [话] **使人囊空如洗** 字面意义是"(把某人)带到洗衣店里"，也就是说"象在洗衣店里把衣袋掏空一样，将对手的钱弄得精光"。*Some strangers took Joe to the cleaners in a crap game.* 在一场双骰子赌博中，几个陌生人使乔输得个精光。*Don't do business with that guy unless you have an iron- clad contract. He'll take you to the cleaners if you give him half a chance.* 如果没有牢不可破的合同，你千万别跟那个家伙做买卖。只要你给他半点儿机会，他就会使你囊空如洗。也常用被动语态。*I got taken to the cleaners in a poker game last night.* 昨天夜里玩扑克，我被人家赢得个精光。◇ take all the money *someone* has

clear

(as) clear as day [əzˌklɪ(ː)rəz ˈdeɪ] [口] **一清二楚** → (as) clear as DAYLIGHT

(as) clear as daylight → DAYLIGHT

(as) clear as mud → MUD

clerk

a desk clerk [ə ˈdes(ː)ˌklə(ː)rk] [口] **旅馆服务台的工作人员** → the front DESK

cliff-hanger

a cliff-hanger [ə ˈklɪfˌhæ(ː)ŋər] [口] **扣人心弦的作品** 直译是"吊在悬崖的人"。原指冒险式、悬念式的影片和小说，以及情节剧，亦即扣人心弦的作品。在以 Batman (巴特曼)或 Tarzan (泰山)为代表的过去的惊险系列影片中，每一集结尾时，多半是片中主角仅用手指吊在悬崖绝壁上的令人毛骨悚然的场面。孩子们很高兴地等待演下一集的周末。由于联想到那种可怕的场面，人们就把这一类影片和小说都称之为 cliff-hanger 了。*When I was a kid, I always enjoyed those weekend cliff-hangers at the movies. You know, those serials with Batman, Superman and Dick Tracy.* 我小的时候，每当周末总是很高兴地看扣人心弦的电影。你知道，就是有巴特曼、超人和狄克·特雷西的那一些系列片。*All of Alistair MacLean's novels are cliff-hangers.* 阿里斯泰尔·麦克莱恩的小说全都是扣人心弦的作品。现在，这一表达法不仅用于电影或小说，而且广泛使用于一切扣人心弦的东西和"且听下回分解"的故事。特别是在体育运动中常常使用。*The marathon was quite a cliff- hanger. Three runners crossed the finish line within five seconds of each other.* 那次马拉松的确是一场扣人心弦的比赛。有三个运动员几乎一齐到达终点线，互相之间的差距都在五秒以内。*Talk about a cliff- hanger! The score changed hands at least ten times, and the game-winning basket was made after the final whistle blew.* 这场球赛真够扣人心弦的啊！比分高低至少变换了有十次，而决定胜负的一个球是在吹结束哨以后进篮的。在如下的情况也可以使用：*I think we have enough fuel to make it to the airport, but it's going to be a real cliff-hanger.* 我本来以为我们有足够的燃料飞到机场，但是没多少油了，真叫人胆战心惊。◇ (a very) suspenseful (adventure [movie, novel, race, game, etc.])

climber

a social climber [ə ˈsouʃəl ˌklaɪmər] [口] 向

上流社会爬的人 *Social climbers are people who are unable to rise socially on their own merits.* 所谓向上爬的人,就是那些不能以自己的实力提高社会地位的人。从上面的例句可以了解:这一表达法在使用时几乎完全带有批判的味道。在美国的社会中,一切都要靠实际的本领,一个人只要有能力,自然会取得较高的社会地位。因此,利用人事关系向上爬的人就变成被轻蔑的对象了。*Mrs. Ivy is a nice woman, but she's too much of a social climber for my taste.* 艾维太太是一个很好的女人,但是叫我看,她太好出风头,总想往上爬。*Most important people avoid accepting invitations from the Joneses. They have a reputation for being social climbers.* 大多数有名望的人都谢绝琼斯夫妇的邀请,因为谁都知道他们俩喜欢拉关系向上爬。◇ (people who are) (too) socially ambitious

clinging

a clinging vine → VINE

clink

the clink [ðə 'klɪŋk] [话] **拘留所** clink 一般指"当啷"声。有许多美国人也认为: clink 所以具有"拘留所"的意义,是由于拘留所的门"当啷"一声关上。但是,实际上并非如此。从前英国有个监狱,叫做 Clink Prison (Clink 是地名),人们把这个 Clink (克林克) 普通名词化,用以表示"监狱"的意义。后来传到美国,则主要指"拘留所"但是,这是一个非常随便的说法,如果把 jail 当作"拘留所"的正式称呼,那么 clink 就有"小狗窝"的意味了。*I'm not going to pay his fine for him. A couple of days in the clink will be good for him—make him think.* 我不打算代他付罚款。叫他在拘留所里呆上三两天,对他会有好处的,这可以使他反省。另外,如果不加冠词,只作 in clink,这是英国英语的用法;在美国,必须如上面的例句所示,在使用时加上定冠词。这是因为每个市镇的警察局都附设拘留所, clink 是固定存在的单位,在会话中一般指的是"那个市镇"的 clink,而不是泛指各个拘留所。实际上也常有在 clink 的前边加 town 的情况。*The town clink always gets filled with drunks on Saturday night.* 每到星期六的夜里,镇拘留所总是装满了喝醉酒的人。the clink 除用以表示"警察局的拘留所" (偶尔指"监狱")外,还有"军队的禁闭室"一义。*Pvt. Jones spent a week in the clink for going AWOL.* 二等兵琼斯由于未请假外出而蹲了一个星期的禁闭。除 the clink 外,最近人们也常使用 the slammer 表示"拘留所"的意思。slam 是"砰地一下关上", slammer 是它的派生词。这个词才是真正由拘留所关门声音而来的象声词。但是, slammer 要比 clink 更多地用以表示"监狱"的意义。◇ jail / guardhouse ((军队的))

clip

a clip joint → JOINT

clock

a clock watcher → WATCHER

fight the clock [ˌfaɪtðə 'klɑ(ː)k] [口] **与时间赛跑** 直译是"与钟表战斗",亦即"与时间战斗"。意思是:"为了按时完成什么任务,加紧进行"。从字面给人的印象是"不住地看钟表";但在实际上是不是真看钟表,那要根据情况来决定。多在讲干工作的场合使用。但本条的应用范围很广,如一天之中有极多的约会时,急忙前往某个地方时,搞急救时等等,全都可以使用它。*We'll have to fight the clock in order to finish this job on time.* 为了按期完成这项工作,我们非抓紧时间、争分夺秒不可。*Newspaper people spend their lives fighting the clock.* 搞新闻工作的人一辈子都与时间赛跑。work against the clock 也表示同样的意义,但这一表达法主要用于讲干工作的场合。*The professors were working against the clock to finish grading the entrance exams by Monday.* 教授们争分夺秒地评阅入学考试的卷子,要在星期一以前评完。有一点请读者注意: work against the clock 如果与表示"必须"的 must 或 have to 一起使用,就会产生不大自然的感觉,这一点跟 fight the clock 大不相同。◇ work as fast as possible (in order to finish on [in] time)

have a face that would stop a clock → FACE

work against the clock [ˌwə(ː)rk əˌgenstðə ˈklɑ(ː)k] [口] **争分夺秒** → fight the CLOCK

clodhopper

a clodhopper [ə ˈklɑ(ː)dˌhɑ(ː)pər] [话] **乡下佬** → a country BUMPKIN / a country HICK

clodhoppers [ˈklɑ(ː)dˌhɑpərz] [话] **农民的劳动鞋** 把 clodhopper 分解开来, clod 是"土块", hopper 是"跳跃的东西", 二者加在一起就是"适于在土块上跳跃的鞋"。一般指农民下田时所穿的高及踝骨的 high-top shoes, 皮子厚, 分量重, 很结实。另外, 这一表达法还有"土里土气"的含义, 因此在去鞋店的时候, 最好不要说"我要 clodhoppers", 免得麻烦。*A good pair of clodhoppers is necessary for working in the fields.* 在田地里干活, 需要有一双结实的劳动鞋。*Every geologist has to have a strong pair of clodhoppers.* 每一位地质学家都必须有一双结实的劳动鞋。这种 clodhoppers 在青年中间也成为一种时髦的东西。*College students have recently taken to wearing clodhoppers and overalls.* 最近, 大学生们都喜欢穿劳动鞋和工作裤。有时戏指一般的鞋。*Get your dirty clodhoppers off my desk!* 不要把你那穿着肮脏鞋子的脚放在我的书桌上! 再有, 如果使用单数的形式作 a clodhopper, 那是"在土块上跳跃的人", 意为"乡下佬"(→ a country BUMPKIN)。◇ heavy, high-top work shoes

close

have a close call [ˌhævə ˌklousˈkɔːl] [话] **死里逃生** → have a close SHAVE

have a close shave → SHAVE

closet

a skeleton in the closet → SKELETON

clotheshorse

a clotheshorse [ə ˈklouzˌhɔ(ː)rs] [口] **讲究穿戴的人** 原义"晒衣服的衣架", 但不大用这一解释。本条的构思是: 人体本身就是"活的衣裳架子"。专指最注意服装的人, 而且服装必须"高级"、"有最新流行的样式"。虽然同样喜欢打扮, 但是上穿 T 恤衫、下着牛仔裤式粗线条的装束, 不能说是 clotheshorse。*I hate Jenny's cocktail parties. Most of her guests are just clotheshorses who blabber on forever about the latest fashions.* 我对詹妮的鸡尾酒会讨厌透了。她的大部分客人都是非常讲究穿戴的人, 他们总是喋喋不休地谈论最时髦的式样。如这一例句所示, 在会话中常含有一种批判的意味, 即: "外表打扮得多么好, 肚子里却是大草包"。不过, 在最近, 这种批判的意味已经淡薄, 单指"讲究穿戴的人"而广泛使用的倾向强烈起来。*Jimmy is a real clotheshorse. He must spend over half his salary on his wardrobe.* 吉米是一个非常讲究穿戴的人。他肯定把工资的一半以上都花到衣服上了。*Since Jim moved to New York, he's become quite a clotheshorse.* 吉姆自从搬到纽约去以后, 变成一个非常讲究穿戴的人了。◇ a person who dresses to show off his [her] sense of style (and who～) / a fashionable dresser

clothing

a wolf in sheep's clothing → WOLF

cloud

Every cloud has a silver lining. [ˌevri ˈklaud ˌhæzə ˌsɪlvər ˈlaɪnɪŋ] [谚] **黑暗中总有一线光明** 这是西方的一句谚语。汉语叫"否极泰来"。字面意义为"每一片云彩都有银色的衬里", 亦即"从地面上看是一片乌云, 但乌云的背面有太阳照耀, 闪着银光"。这一谚语含有鼓励人的意味: "即便遇到不幸或灾难也不要失望, 因为否极泰来, 还会有好运来临的"。*Don't be so downcast. Every cloud has a silver lining. If you look hard enough, I'm sure you'll find it.* 不要那样垂头丧气。黑暗中总有一线光明的。你如果拼命去搜索, 肯定会找到它的。既有这样直接引用的场合, 也有象下边例句那样改变一下说法的情况。*The clouds kept piling* *over my life and I had yet to find one silver lining*. 在我的生活中，坏事儿是一桩接着一桩，好运却总不见来临。下一例句也可以看作是一种变形。*Sure, you're discouraged, but don't give up yet. That silver lining is up there somewhere*. 的确，你会大失所望的。不过，还不要灰心。正如谚语所说，前途仍有一线光明。这句话中 That silver lining 的 that 指"谚语中所说的那个……"。◇ Every bad situation has something good about it.

be on cloud nine [ɔ(:)ŋ'klaud'naɪn] [话] **高兴得坐不住** 字面意义是"在九重云上"。*Sally's on cloud nine because her favorite rock star spoke to her*. 萨莉高兴得坐不稳站不安，因为她所喜欢的摇滚乐明星对她说话了。*Is he happy? He's on cloud nine*. 你问他是不是快乐？他好象坐在云彩上，飘飘然了。现在讲一讲这一习用语形成的过程。原来的说法并不是 be on cloud nine, 而是 be on cloud seven (如今还偶尔可以听到人们说 seven)。据推测，这个 be on cloud seven 是 be in seventh HEAVEN(→) 与漫画上的"死人坐在云彩上边弹竖琴"的情景结合到一起的产物。另一方面，在美国气象局的术语中，有 cloud nine 一词。在气象学中，云分九类，此词即指第九类的云(具体地说，就是夏季的积雨云)。从数字上说，cloud nine 比 cloud seven 大，因此，飞行员们就习惯用 on cloud nine 代替 on cloud seven 了。后来在群众中推广，形成象今日这样的一个定型的用语。◇ be very, very happy

be on cloud seven [ɔ(:)ŋ'klaud'sevən] [话] **高兴极了** → be on CLOUD nine

be under a cloud [ˌʌndərə 'klaud] [口] **受怀疑[谴责]** 直译是"在云彩下边"，如果解释为"被云彩的 shadow 遮住"，就更容易理解了。原来的构思是："被人怀疑或谴责，处于见不得人的立场"。*Rolf says he can't go back to his own country. It seems he is under a cloud there because of some missing stock certificates*. 罗尔夫说他不能返回自己的祖国。似乎由于丢失一些股票，他受到了怀疑。*I've been under a cloud at the office ever since my careless comments caused a customer to cancel a big contract*. 因为我不留神说的几句话，一位主顾取消了一笔大合同，从那以后，公司里的人都以谴责的目光看我。under a cloud 有时可与 be 以外的动词结合。*Mr. Verbal is an ex-English teacher who left school under a cloud after getting drunk and insulting the president of the PTA*. 维尔巴尔先生原来是一位英语教师，由于喝醉了酒侮辱学生家长与教师联谊会会长而受谴责，辞职不干了。另外，be under a cloud 可以用于表示 be depressed (沮丧[闷闷不乐])的意义，但这一用法不普遍。*Old Mr. Melon has been under a cloud ever since his beloved collie died*. 自从他所喜爱的柯利牧羊犬死了以后，梅隆老先生一直闷闷不乐。◇ be under suspicion [in disfavor]

clouds

have *one's* **head in the clouds** → HEAD

clout

clout ['klaut] [口] **(政治的、经济的)影响力** 此词除一般熟知的"敲"、"击"的意义外，可用于表示本条条头的释义。换句话说，它与 pull 相当，只不过略有差异而已。pull 是"利用人事关系等产生的影响力"，而 clout 则是"依靠本人的实力所产生的影响力"。所以有这样的差异，是因为前者由主要意义"拉"派生而来，后者则由"击"的意义派生而来。*It's difficult to sell airplanes in Japan unless you have clout in the political world*. 除非你在政界有影响力，否则在日本是很难销售飞机的。如此例所示，一般与动词 have 一道使用。*Let's ask James to help us. He has a lot of clout with the boss*. 我们去向詹姆斯求援吧。他对老板是很有影响力的。*A big organization like that has a tremendous amount of economic clout*. 那样一个大企业在经济方面的影响力极为巨大。◇ influence / power

clover

be in the clover [ˌɪnðə 'klouvər] [话] **生活富裕** 原来的构思是："在牛羊最爱吃的

三叶草生长的地方”。这是一个比喻的表达法，强调“拥有大量金银财宝，生活极为舒适”的意思。*We're in the clover! Our number won the national lottery!* 我们就要过舒适的生活啦！我们买的国家彩票中奖了。如此例所示，多用于“就要……啦”这样一种表达方式。但并不是必须如此。*Don't be chicken. All we have to do is rob one bank and we'll be in the clover.* 不要胆怯嘛。我们只要抢劫一家银行，一辈子就会过舒服日子啦。主语不一定非“人”不可。*Our company was in the clover until the oil shock came along.* 在发生石油危机以前，我们公司是很富足的。另外，有时省略 the，作 be in clover。◇ be rich / can live in luxury / be doing extremely well

cluck

a dumb cluck [ə 'dʌ(:)m ˌklʌk] [话] **愚人** dumb 是“愚笨的”，cluck 是表示母鸡叫声的象声词。人们把母鸡当作傻动物的典型。*You want to marry John Smith?! I wouldn't let you marry that dumb cluck if he were the last man on earth!* 你说你想要跟约翰·史密斯结婚?! 即使他是地球上的最后一个男人，我也不允许你嫁给那样一个大傻瓜！→ a DUMBHEAD ◇ a stupid person

clutch

clutch up [ˌklʌ(:)'tʃʌ(:)p] [话] **呆若木鸡** clutch up 表示“由于紧张、恐怖等，身体变得僵直，听不清别人的话”的样子，近似汉语的“呆若木鸡”、“缩成一团”。有时用于实际上“身体僵直”的场合，也有时用于心理上“发怵”、“畏缩”的场合。*When he finally had the man he'd vowed to kill in his sights, he clutched up and couldn't pull the trigger.* 当他终于瞄准他发誓非杀死不可的那个男人的时候，他的身子僵直起来，未能勾动扳机。*A: How did you do on your orals? B: Not too well. When I saw all those stern-looking professors, I clutched up.* 甲：你的口试怎么样？乙：不太好。当我看到所有那些教授都板着面孔的时候，心里发怵，连话都说不出来了。*Jamie obviously clutched up when the border guards started shooting. We looked back and saw him standing as stiff as a board right in the middle of no-man's-land.* 当边防军人开枪射击的时候，杰米显然吓得呆若木鸡了。我们回头一看，他好象一块木头广告牌子，笔直地插在无人地带的正中央。◇ become (too) tense

C-note

a C-note [ə 'siːˌnout] [俗] **一百美元钞票** 原为黑社会用语。C 是 century 的缩写。century 一般指“一百年”，但在这里是“一百个”的意思。note 是“纸币”。也就是说，C-note 为“包含有一百个美元的纸币”。另外，这一表达法至今仍没有完全失去黑社会的臭味，因此在银行的窗口使用是不太合适的。*Did you see that guy? He's got a whole wallet full of C-notes.* 你看见那个家伙了吗？他的皮夹子塞满了一百美元的钞票。*Can you break a C-note?* 你能把一百美元的钞票换成零的吗？◇ a hundred-dollar bill

coal

pour on the coal [ˌpɔrɔnðə 'koul] [话] **最大限度加快速度** 字面意义是“往里加煤”。这是自有火车以后就有的表达法。现在不仅对于火车，对于电车、汽车、自行车、马车、飞机、船、甚至人，凡是能够“跑[飞]”的东西，全都可以使用。*“Stagecoach robbers! Pour on the coal!” yelled the guard to the old man holding the reins.* 警卫员对手执缰绳的老头儿大喊道：“驿马车强盗！加快速度！”*When the pilot realized he was coming in too low, he poured on the coal.* 当飞机驾驶员发现着陆高度过低的时候，他把减速柄拉到最大限度。*When the goal line came in sight, all the marathon runners in the lead began to pour on the coal.* 当已经看得见终点线的时候，跑在最前边的马拉松选手们，全都加快速度，开始了最后的冲刺。有时作为比喻，用于“跑[飞]”以外的行动。*We've got to pour on the coal if we're to finish this work by the deadline.* 要想在限期以前完成这个工作，我们就必须加把油。◇ go faster / increase the speed (to the maximum)

coals

drag *someone* **over the coals** (for *something*) [ˌdræ(ː)g ~ ˌovərðə ˈkoulz] [口] **斥责** → rake *someone* over the COALS (for *something*)

haul *someone* **over the coals** (for *something*) [ˌhɔːl ~ ˌovərðə ˈkoulz] [口] **申斥** → rake *someone* over the COALS (for *something*)

rake *someone* **over the coals** (for *something*) [ˌreɪk ~ ˌovərðə ˈkoulz] [口] **责备** coals 是"(煤、柴等的) 旺火"。本条直译是"把人放在熊熊烈火上,用耙子去耙",这是古代的刑讯方法之一。多用于表示"狠狠教训"的意味。主要用于长辈申斥晚辈、上级指责下级的场合,但并不绝对如此,平辈或同事之间也可以使用。 *Joe's girl friend really raked him over the coals for forgetting her party.* 乔由于忘记出席女朋友的社交晚会,被她狠狠地责备了一顿。如这一例句所示,常用 really 加强语气。又如下一例句,也常使用被动语态: *John was [got] raked over the coals for being late for school every morning this week.* 约翰在这个星期每天早上都上学迟到,受到了严厉的批评。也可以用具有"拉"的意义的 haul 或 drag 代替 rake, 而说 haul [drag] *someone* over the coals。 ◇ berate *someone* severely

coast

the coast is clear [ðə ˌkoustəz ˈklɪːr] [话] **无人阻碍** 原是海上走私者的暗语,使用如下: *Make sure that the coast is clear before coming in. The coast guard's been patrolling every night recently.* 在上岸之前,先要弄清楚海滨是不是晴朗。最近每天夜里都有海岸警卫队巡逻。"海滨晴朗"是一句暗语,意思是"没有一个人",后来被人们广泛使用了。一般用于最怕被人看见的场合,例如: *Wait till the coast is clear, then climb over the fence and run for the car.* 等到没有人的时候,跳过围墙,向汽车那里快跑。又如: *We'll be hiding behind the shed. As soon as the coast is clear, bring us something to eat.* 我们隐藏在小棚子的后边。只要一没有人,就赶快给我们送点吃的东西来。这都是按照原来意思的用法。有人灵活运用这个习用语,编成下面的小幽默故事。题目姑且叫做《傻丈夫》。*"Who was the phone call from, dear?" "I dunno. It must have been some sailor calling the wrong number. He wanted to know if the coast was clear again tonight."* "亲爱的,是谁来的电话?""我不晓得是谁。多半是某个水手叫错号码了,因为他问今天夜里海滨是不是还很晴朗。"(实际上是妻子的情夫来电话,问今天晚上家里有人没有。)这一表达法也有例外的使用法,与怕人看见的意义毫无关系。下一例句是汽车从狭窄的道路走上大道或跨上高速公路的场合。*"The coast is clear on this side," said Frank as I pulled up to the stop sign.* 当我见到"暂停"的牌子而把汽车停下的时候,弗兰克说:"走这边没问题。"本条条头的英语有种种变化的形式,例如可以这样说: *We can't leave yet. We're waiting for the coast to clear.* 我们现在还不能离开。我们要等到没有一个人的时候再走。 ◇ no one is around

coaster

a roller coaster [ə ˈroulər ˌkoustər] [口] **游乐园的滚动飞车** roller 与 roller skate (四轮滑冰鞋)中的 roller 一样,是"象车轮似的滚动的东西"。 coast 是象自行车下坡时不蹬也走的情况一样,意为"惯性滑行"。因此,本条直译为"依靠滚动的惯性滑行"。 *Lois is chicken. She's afraid to ride the roller coaster.* 洛伊丝胆小如鼠。她不敢乘滚动飞车。人们在形容各种事物激烈变动的样子时,常用 roller coaster 作比喻。 *Miriam's moods change so often that living with her is like riding on a roller coaster.* 米莉亚姆是一个心情变化太快的人,跟她生活在一起,就象坐滚动飞车一样,永远安定不下来。*The price of gold has been on a real roller coaster recently.* 最近,黄金

的价格忽上忽下,变动很大。

cock

the cock of the walk [ðə ˌkɑ(:)kəðə ˈwɔ:k] [话] **大头头** cock 是"雄鸡"。walk 在这里是"为了放鸡吃食而用篱笆围上的场地",通常与鸡窝连在一起。这块场地现在一般叫做 a chicken run,过去则称为 a chicken walk。本条的字面意义是"在围上的场地中的雄鸡"。这一表达法活生生地描绘出雄鸡率领一群母鸡,大摇大摆地走着,威风凛凛,大有国王的架势。由于它是场地中最趾高气扬的鸡,所以要加定冠词,作 the cock。*I was glad to see the mayor get his comeuppance in the last election. He's been the cock of the walk so long around here he seems to think he owns the place.* 我看到市长在这次选举中失败,得到他应有的惩罚,心里十分高兴。他在这里当大头头好长时间了,似乎以为这块地方归他私人所有。cock 前边的 the 也有省略的时候。 *Prof. Witherspoon is accepted as cock of the walk among the would-be intellectuals in this town. All the old hens are always cackling over him.* 维瑟斯彭教授在本镇的自命为知识分子的人们中间,被认为是群龙之首。所有的老太婆总是对他恭而敬之,曲意奉承。如此例所示,在使用这一表达法时,常含有若干轻蔑的意味。但是,象下一例句那样,丝毫没有轻蔑的口吻,只表示"某一领域公认的大人物"的意思。这种情况也很不少。*Ali was cock of the walk for many years in boxing circles.* 在很多年间,阿里是拳击界的霸主。◇ the most powerful [influential] person

a cock-and-bull

a cock-and-bull story → STORY

cocktail

a Molotov cocktail [ə ˌmɑlə.tɑf ˈkɑk.teɪl] [口] **火焰瓶** 这一表达法是由前苏联外交部长 V. M. Molotov 的姓氏构成的。直译为"给莫洛托夫预备的鸡尾酒"。最初使用这种武器的大概是 1939 年抵抗入侵苏军的芬兰人民。现在作为"火焰瓶"的通称广泛使用。*The demonstrating students began throwing Molotov cocktails at the riot police.* 示威的学生们开始向特种警察机动队投掷火焰瓶。有人把 Molotov 的发音作 [ˈmɑlə.tɑ:v] 或者 [ˈmolo.tɔf]。◇ a glass-bottle grenade

code

an area code [ə ˈne(:)rɪə ˌkoud] [口] **(电话)地区号码** 在美国,各电话区 (telephone area) 大多与各州是一致的,但也有与州不一致的电话区。各电话区都有自己的三位数的地区号码。在一般的上下文中,多伴有定冠词或所有格。*By using the area code, you can dial anyplace in the country.* 只要拨地区号码,你可以打电话到全国的任何地方。*What's your area code?* 你的地区号码是多少? ◇ the long-distance number

a zip code [ə ˈzɪp ˌkoud] [口] **邮政编码** 请注意:"邮政编码"不能说 post(al) code (英国英语) 或者 postal number。正式名称是 zip code number,但在会话中,几乎在所有的场合都省掉 number,只说 zip code。这个 zip 的来源是:原美国邮政部(1971 年 7 月改组为邮政公用事业局)在决定邮政编码的称呼时,采取 (Postal) Zone Improvement Program (邮区改革计划)的每个词的头一个字母,合在一起就成了 zip。zip 本来有意义,为子弹在空中飞时的"尖啸声",这与"书信早早到达"的意愿是完全吻合的。在美国,邮政编码是五位数,前三位表示州和投递区,后两位表示邮区。号码从东海岸开始直到西海岸,依次增大。在普通的上下文中,多使用定冠词或所有格。 *Letters are often delivered as much as a day earlier if you use the zip code.* 如果你写上邮政编码,信件通常要早到一天。*Do you know her zip code?* 你知道她的邮政编码吗? ◇ a post office delivery zone number

coffin

a coffin nail → NAIL

coin

pay *someone* **back in** *his* **own coin** [ˌpeɪ

～ 'bæ(:)kın ～ ˌoun'kɔın] [口] **以其人之道还治其人之身** 这里的 coin 不是“硬币”，而是“一个国家的通货”的意思。pay *someone* back 的字面意义是“还钱”。因此，本条整体直译为“支付与借钱的时候用相同的通货”，也就是“如果借的是美元，就用美元还”、“如果借的是法郎，就用法郎还”的意思。作为比喻，相当于汉语成语“以其人之道还治其人之身”的意思，在使用时常常带有恶劣的情绪。只说 pay *someone* back，作为比喻，也表示“反击[报复]”的意思，但在这一场合，并不包含“以其人之道”的韵味。 *A: Why did you do that? B: I was just paying him back for what he did to me.* 甲：你为什么做那样的事情？乙：他对我使坏，我只不过报复一下而已。pay *someone* back in *his* own coin 的使用方法如下：*A: You shouldn't spread stories about Hal like that. B: Why not? I'm only paying him back in his won coin after the terrible things he's said about me.* 甲：你不应该象那样给哈尔散布流言飞语啊。乙：为什么不应该呢？他既然给我造了很多可怕的谣言，我只不过是以其人之道还治其人之身罢了。*The woman was terribly rude to you. You should have paid her back in her own coin.* 那个女人对你太粗暴无礼啦。你应当以其人之道还治其人之身呀。*You can't complain if he turns a deaf ear to your pleas for help. He's only paying you back in your own coin for your refusing to help him when he needed you.* 如果在你请求他帮忙的时候他根本不理睬，这你可不能抱怨啊。因为他过去曾经需要你帮助，而你拒绝了，现在他只不过是以其人之道还治其人之身而已。*Any country who places restrictions on imports can expect to be paid back in its own coin.* 任何国家限制进口，别的国家也必然会采取同样的措施进行回击。◇ treat *someone* [make *someone* suffer] in like manner

cold

blow hot and cold → HOT

be cold ['kould] [话] **远离目标、远未猜中** → be WARM

get cold feet → FEET

know *something* **cold** [ˌnou ～ 'kould] [话] **完全熟悉** 这里的 cold 不是“冰冷地”，而是“完全地”的意思，比 completely 或 perfectly 更进一步加强语气。 *I know this lesson cold.* 这一课我完全记住了。如此例所示，这一表达法是在表示“完全背会”、“(把事实等) 完全放入脑中”的场合使用。*I don't think he's an impostor. I asked him a lot of questions about his background, and he knew the answers cold.* 我不认为他是一个冒牌货。关于他的经历，我提出一大堆的问题，而他的回答是天衣无缝的。*Ask me anything you want from this book. I know it cold.* 关于这本书的内容，你可以随便向我提问。因为我已经背得滚瓜烂熟。know *something* cold 虽然已经成为一个固定的说法，但是 cold 在作“完全地”解时，也可以同其他的动词搭配使用。 *The bullet stopped him cold.* 那颗子弹使他完全不能动弹了。*He turned me [the proposal] down cold.* 他完全拒绝了我［那个建议］。◇ know *something* perfectly [thoroughly]

leave *someone* **cold** [ˌli(:)v ～ 'kould] [话] **不感兴趣** 字面意义是“使人寒冷”，换句话说就是“使人不发生兴趣”。用以表示“不大赞成”、“实在不敢苟同”的意味。 *That guy leaves me cold.* 我不喜欢那个家伙。这一例句是以人为主语，但也有不以人为主语的场合。 *The government's policies leave me cold.* 我不赞成政府的一些政策。*That singer may be popular, but his style leaves me cold.* 那位歌手可能很红，但是我对他的风格不感兴趣。◇ not move [impress] *someone*

quit (*something*) **cold turkey** → TURKEY

stop *someone* **cold** [ˌstɑp ～ 'kould] [话] **使人一动也不能动** → know *something* COLD

turn *someone* [*something*] **down cold** [ˌtə(:)rn ～ ˌdaun 'kould] [话] **完全拒绝** → know *something* COLD

cold-shoulder

cold-shoulder *someone* ['kould'ʃouldər ~] [口] **对人冷冰冰地** → give *someone* the cold SHOULDER

collar

get hot under the collar [,get 'hɑ(:)dʌndərðə 'kɑ(:)lər] [话] **怒气冲天** 这里的 collar 是"衣领"。本条的字面意义是"衣领下边发热"。汉语讲"怒火中烧"、"压不住心头的怒火",热的是"心头",而美国人热的地方则是"脖子根"(衣领遮住的部位)。*Don't get so hot under the collar. I said I was sorry, didn't I?* 你不要那么恼火吧。我不是已经向你道歉了吗? *Jane had no right to laugh at my new hairdo. I get hot under the collar every time I think about it.* 简没有对我的新发式发笑的权利。我一想到这件事就怒气冲天。为了加强语气,可以添加 all。*Phil got all hot under the collar just because I danced a couple of times with his girl.* 我跟菲尔的女朋友跳了几次舞,仅仅为了这个,菲尔就怒气冲天了。如下一例句所示,这一表达法有时不是用于表示"愤怒"、而是表示"兴奋"的意思,务请读者注意。*Every time I think of a girl like Irma, I get hot under the collar.* 我每次想到象爱尔玛那样的姑娘,就感到很兴奋。be hot under the collar 是"正在发怒",而 make *someone* hot under the collar 则是"使人发怒"。*What are you so hot under the collar about?* 你干吗发那么大的火? *Don't make disparaging remarks about women's lib in front of Sally. It makes her hot under the collar.* 不要当着萨莉的面大肆诬蔑妇女解放运动吧,那会使她大为恼火的。◇ get angry

college

a cow college [ə 'kau ,kɑlədʒ] [话] **牛圈大学** 既然称"牛圈大学",当然是一种带有轻蔑意味的说法,系指不出名的乡下大学。*If you don't study harder you'll end up having to go to some little cow college that nobody's ever heard of before.* 如果你不加紧学习,结果就会进入某个没人听说过的牛圈大学了。即使校址在大都市,只要是三流大学,照样可以称为 cow college。*I don't care if Podunk University is in New York. I still say it's a cow college.* 我不管波丹克大学是不是在纽约,我仍然认为它是一所乡下的牛圈大学。cow college 也可以专指"农业大学"。在这一场合,不包含那种轻蔑的意味。*My sister went to a cow college out West and became a farmer's wife.* 我妹妹去西部上农业大学,而且嫁给了一个农民。◇ a(n unknown) college of no distinction

give it the old college try → TRY

colonel

(a) bird colonel [(ə) 'bəːrd 'kə(:)rnl] [话] **上校** 原为军队俚语。在美国的陆军(the army)、空军 (the air force)、海军陆战队 (the marines) 中,按正式名称,"上校"称 colonel,"中校"称 lieutenant colonel (但一般不加 lieutenant,只称 colonel)。由于上校的肩章有鹫的图案,所以俗称 bird colonel (海军和海岸警卫队的"上校"称 captain,不在此例)。另外,bird colonel 一词也与 colonel 或 (lieutenant) colonel 同样,在指"人"的场合必须加冠词,在指"上校职称"的场合不要冠词。*He's a bird colonel.* 他是一个上校。*Lieutenant Colonel Smith was promoted to bird colonel.* 史密斯中校晋升上校了。比 bird colonel 再稍微轻松一点儿的说法是 (a) chicken colonel。这个 chicken 是名词,意为"鸡",所以只不过是掉换一下上述的 bird 的说法而已。但是,根据重音的不同,它又可以作为形容词使用,意为"胆小的"。因此,在实际会话的场合,千万注意不要说错了。也就是说,如果发音为 ['tʃɪkən 'kə(:)rnl],这毫无问题仅指"上校";如果漫不经心的发音为 [,tʃɪkən 'kə(:)rnl],那就成为"胆小的上校[中校]"了。→ be CHICKEN ◇ (a) full colonel

(a) chicken colonel [(ə) 'tʃɪkən 'kə(:)rnl] [俗] **上校** → (a) bird COLONEL

color

(that's) a horse of another color → HORSE

colors

come through with flying colors [ˌkʌm ˌθruː wɪθ ˈflaɪɪŋ ˈkʌlərz] [口] **干得出色** 原来的形式是 come off with flying colors。come off 是 come off the battlefield (离开战场)的意思，with flying colors 是"打着胜利的旗帜"的意思。*The victorious army came off the battlefield with flying colors.* 得胜的军队离开了战场，旗帜迎风飘扬。在转作比喻使用时，come off 的部分改变成 come through 的情况占压倒的多数。through 具有"突破(战场)"的感觉，常用于表达"排除万难"的意思。*We were worried whether our team could win, but they came through [won] with flying colors.* 我们曾经担心我们队是不是能够打赢，但是队员们大胜而归。如此例所示，本条习用语在使用时几乎与 win (取得胜利)同义。此外，如以下的例句所示，也可以用于表示与 pass (合格)、succeed (成功)等词大致相同的意义，而且与 win 的场合一样，均能与 come through 掉换使用。*A: How did Jane do on her final exams? B: She came through [passed] with flying colors.* 甲：简的期终考试怎么样？乙：她考的成绩很不错呀。*A: Did you succeed in getting the contract? B: Yes. We came through [succeeded] with flying colors.* 甲：合同已经签订了吗？乙：是的。我们已经高奏凯歌了。◇ succeed [win, pass, etc.] magnificently

nail *one's* **colors to the mast** [ˌneɪl ~ ˌkʌlərz tәðә ˈmæːst] [口] **表明决不屈服的态度** 字面意义是"把旗子钉在桅杆上"。严密地讲，colors (旗)在海军中意味着"国旗"、"军队旗"、"军舰旗"三种，在这一场合特指"国旗"。在过去的时代，开战前要把国旗钉在桅杆上，表示绝对不向敌人屈服的坚决意志(降旗意味着投降)。*It is said that Lord Nelson often nailed his colors to the mast of every ship before entering a battle.* 据说，纳尔逊爵士在会战之前，总是把国旗钉在他的舰队的每只军舰的桅杆上。这是按照字面意义使用的场合。以下是按照比喻意义使用的例句。*My wife has nailed her colors to the mast. If I don't give in, she is going to demand a divorce.* 我的妻子已经表明决不屈服的态度。如果我不让步，她就要求离婚。*I had been hoping to be able to reach a compromise with Roger, but his recent statements make it clear that he has nailed his colors to the mast. There is no choice but to fight him in court.* 我曾经希望能够与罗杰达成妥协，但是他最近的言论已经很清楚地表明他要坚持到底的决心。除了到法庭上与他进行斗争外，没有选择的余地了。其次，也可以不照葫芦画瓢地说 nail *one's* colors to the mast，而采取 to the mast of ~的形式。例如：*In his latest book, Adam Mint nailed his colors to the mast of liberal socialism.* 亚当·敏特在他最近的著作中高举自由社会主义的旗帜，表明斗争到底的坚决意志。另外，nail *one's* colors to the mast (of ~)有时采取 nail *one's* flag to the mast 的形式。◇ take an uncompromising position

reveal *someone* **in** *his* **true colors** [rәˌviːl ~ ɪn ~ ˌtruː ˈkʌlərz] [口] **原形毕露** → show *someone* in his true COLORS

reveal *one's* **true colors** [rәˌviːl ~ ˈtruː ˈkʌlərz] [口] **露出庐山真面目** → show *one's* true COLORS

sail under false colors [ˈseɪˌlʌndər ˈfɔːls ˈkʌlərz] [口] **伪装起来** 这里的 colors 指"旗子"(→ nail *one's* COLORS to the mast)。本条直译是"打着假旗子航行"。原来的意思就是："海贼或者敌人的船只挂着假的国旗，冒充他国船只航行"。*The enemy destroyer succeeded in sinking many of our cargo ships by sailing under false colors.* 敌人的驱逐舰伪装他国船只航行，击沉了我国的许多货船。作为比喻，一般用于隐蔽自己的敌人身份、充当间谍以及有什么内疚的场合，但也有对对方没有恶劣意图的场合。一种情况是掩饰真实的面目和来历，一种情况是不暴露自己的真正心情。*When the gang was arrested, they were astounded to learn that one of their* *members was a police spy sailing under false colors.* 当那个匪帮被捕并得知他们的成员之一是伪装了的警方侦探时，他们不免大吃一惊。*He says he supports us, but I suspect him of sailing under false colors. I'm sure his sympathies are with our rivals.* 他说他支持我们，但是我怀疑他没有暴露自己的真正心情。他肯定是同情我们的对手的。*I decided to sail under false colors for the time being by pretending to be Mrs. Franklin's long-lost brother.* 我决定冒充富兰克林夫人的久已失踪的弟弟，把自己的来历掩盖一个时期。在下两个例句中，既可以理解为隐瞒身份，也可以理解为不暴露"真心"。*I suspect Lou of sailing under false colors.* 我怀疑卢隐瞒了自己的身份［真正想法］。*We found that Bill was sailing under false colors. All the while he was pretending to be our friend, he was actually in league with our rivals.* 我们发现比尔在隐瞒自己的真实想法［身份］。他一直伪装成我们的朋友，而在实际上，他与我们的对手是沆瀣一气的。◇ act under [assume] a false identity / act under false pretenses / only pretend (to be what *one* appears to be [to believe what *one* espouses])

show *one's* **colors** [ˌʃou ～ ˈkʌlərz] [口] **表明态度[立场]** 这里的 colors 是"旗子"、特别是"国旗"的意思(→ nail *one's* COLORS to the mast)。本条原来的意思是：以前没有挂国旗的船只，现在"出示 *one's* colors (本国的国旗)，表明国籍"。*We don't know what country the ship was from. It refused to show its colors.* 我们不晓得那只船是哪个国家的。它拒绝表明国籍。作为比喻，用法如下：*I don't know if Mr. Green will help us against our rivals or not. So far he hasn't shown his colors.* 我不了解格林先生是否会帮助我们反对我们的竞争者。直到如今他还没有表明态度。*We know you are sympathetic to our cause, but sympathy alone will not help us. We ask that you stand up and show your colors.* 我们明白你同情我们的事业，但是仅仅同情对我们是没有帮助的。我们请求你旗帜鲜明地表明自己的态度。在谈到国家时也可以应用这一表达法。*Until 1940 England was standing alone against Germany while America sat on the fence, refusing to show its colors.* 直到 1940 年，英国一直单独对抗德国，而美国则抱骑墙态度，不肯表明自己的立场。◇ reveal [make clear] *one's* position

show *someone* **in** *his* **true colors** [ˌʃou ～ ɪn ～ ˌtruː ˈkʌlərz] [口] **暴露出真实嘴脸** 最初的构思与 show *one's* true COLORS (→)相同，但用法迥异，务请读者注意。这一表达法常用于坏的事情。例如：*Hugh claimed to care nothing about his fiances money, but his refusal to marry her when her father went bankrupt showed him in his true colors.* 休曾声称他不在乎未婚妻的钱，但是当未婚妻的父亲破产之后，他马上拒绝同她结婚，暴露出他的真实嘴脸。因此，比起 show *one's* true colors 来，这一表达法的使用范围有一定的限制。这里的 colors 原意为"旗子"(→ nail *one's* COLORS to the mast)，但由于加前置词 in，就不是"旗子"，而是具有"变色龙式的人的颜色"的含义了。一般用 *something* 作主语。*Outwardly, Henry appears to be a kind and tolerant man, but his occasional beating of his wife shows him in his true colors.* 从外表上看，亨利似乎是一个和善而温厚的人，但是他有时动手殴打他的妻子，这就暴露出他的真实嘴脸了。也可以用 reveal 代替 show。*That country claims to be a peace-loving nation, but its attack on its smaller neighbor revealed it in its true colors.* 那个国家虽然号称爱好和平，但是它袭击比它小的邻邦，这就暴露出它的真实嘴脸了。◇ reveal what *someone* is really like / reveal *someone's* true character

show *one's* **true colors** [ˌʃou ～ ˈtruː ˈkʌlərz] [口] **露出真面目** 关于 colors 一词，请参阅 nail *one's* COLORS to the mast 条。本条的字面意义是："原来打着假旗子航行的船显示出自己的真旗

子”(→ sail under false COLORS)。*When the pirate ship had tricked the freighter into the range of its guns, it suddenly ran down the flag it had been flying and showed its true colors.* 当海盗船巧妙地欺骗一艘货轮进入其射程距离的时候，它突然降下所悬挂的国旗，把带有骷髅图案的真实旗子挑了起来。转作比喻使用。在这一场合，多应用于坏的事情，但并不绝对如此。*I had been pretending to be Mrs. Franklin's long-lost brother, but when her real brother suddenly showed up one day, I was forced to show my true colors.* 我曾经冒称是富兰克林夫人的失踪多年的弟弟，但是，当她真正的弟弟有一天突然出现时，我不得不露出了真面目。 *That country claims to be a peace-loving nation, but it showed its true when it attacked its smaller neighbor.* 那个国家口口声声说自己是一个爱好和平的国家，可是当它进攻比它小的邻国时，就露出了庐山真面目。动词可用 reveal (展现，暴露)代替 show。 *They tricked the spy into revealing his true colors.* 他们用巧妙的手法使那个间谍暴露了他的真实面目。*Outwardly, Henry appears to be a kind and tolerant man, but once in a while he reveals his true colors by beating his wife.* 从表面上看，亨利似乎是一个和善而温厚的人，但是也有个别的时候由于殴打妻子而暴露他的本质。→ show *one's* COLORS ◇ reveal *one's* true identity [true character]

strike *one's* **colors** [ˌstraɪk ～ˈkʌlərz] [口] **放弃斗争** 这里的 strike 意为“把(旗子之类) 降下”，colors 是“旗子”(→ nail *one's* COLORSto the mast)。正在战斗的时候把军旗降下来，这意味着“投降”。*Cease fire! The enemy has struck his colors!* 停止射击！ 敌人投降啦！ 这是按字面意义的用法。作为比喻，用以表示“放弃斗争”的意味，但这种说法不太柔和。*We may have lost half our games so far this season, but it's too early to strike our colors. We still have a chance for the pennant.* 这个季节，我们的比赛可能要输掉一半，但是放弃战斗还为时过早啦。我们还有争取三角锦旗的机会。*As the leading candidate gained in strength, his rivals began one after another to strike their colors.* 由于居第一位的候选人势力增大，他的竞争者一个接一个放弃竞选活动了。另外，如果把条头中的 *one's* 换成 the，作 strike the colors，那就不具有比喻的意义，只具有“降下旗子”的字面意义了。 *We always strike the colors at nightfall.* 我们总要在天刚一黑的时候把旗子降下来。◇ give up the fight

strike the colors [ˌstraɪkðə ˈkʌlərz] [口] **降旗** → strike *one's* COLORS

come

be as *something* **as they come** [əz ˌ～ əzðeɪ ˈkʌ(ː)m] [话] **最高的** 为了说明这一表达法怎么会具有“最高的”的意义，需要多说几句。首先举个例子来分析一下。 *I'm sorry, sir, but we don't have any larger screws. This is as large as they come. If you need something larger, you'll have to use a bolt.* 对不起，先生，可是我们没有比这更大的螺丝钉。现在工厂制造的螺丝钉，这一种是最大号的。如果你要用更大一些的，那就只好用螺栓了。如此例所示，*something* 的地方一般使用形容词。they 的地方经常是 they，没有特指某物的名词，在这一例句中，它在意义上与 screws (螺丝钉)相同。as ～ as 的形式与我们说 This winter is as cold as we have ever had. (很少有这样寒冷的冬天。) 这句话时的 as ～ as 完全一样，意为“在……当中是最突出者之一”。成问题的是 come 的意味。如果你头脑里考虑它的后边省略了 from the factory (从工厂里)，那就容易明白了。“从工厂里来的”也就是“工厂里制作的”的意思，这个 come 与 be made (被制造) 完全相同。*This toothpaste comes in three sizes.* 这种牙膏的生产有三种型号。通过以上的说明，就可以把 be as *something* as they come 直译为“在工厂的出品中，这是最……的”。本条内的第一个例句，就是按照字面意义使用的。常转作比喻使用，表示“最高的"或者"出类拔萃的"的意思。*I'm very happy that Bill has agreed to help us. As a lawyer, he's as sharp as they come.* 比尔同意来帮助我们,我实在太高兴啦。作为律师,他是一位出类拔萃的人物。*Mr. Flint is as stingy as they come. He invited me to dinner at a restaurant and then asked me to pay half the bill.* 象弗林特先生那样的吝啬鬼真是绝无仅有。他邀请我到饭店里去吃饭,最后算帐时却要我付一半钱。常如下一例句那样,用 (just) about 调整语调。 *Alaskan winters are about as cold as they come.* 阿拉斯加的冬天真是寒冷到了极点。*I don't think I can get into that university. Their entrance exams are just about as hard as they come.* 我估计自己根本进不了那所大学。它的入学考试难度最高。◇ be the largest [smallest, sharpest, most difficult, etc.] there is (anywhere) / no one [nothing] is stingier [colder, etc.] than *someone* [*something*]

Come again? [.kʌmə'gen] [话] **你说什么?** 未听清对方的话或者未理解对方的话时反问的用语。有些词典作 Please come again. (请再说一遍。)但是,几乎没人使用这种形式。因为如果加上 Please 的话,一般来说,就得按字面意义解释为"请再光临"了。Come again? 把尾音向上挑,作反问用,这已经是习惯成自然的说法。如果用别的语调说这句话,那就不构成反问了。 *A: Please come again. B: Come again? A: I said, "Please come again." B: Oh, thank you very much.* 甲:请再光临。 乙:你说什么? 甲:我说"请你再来"。乙:哦,非常感谢你 。 *A: His name is John Jacob Jinglehammer Smith. B: Come again?* 甲:他的名字是约翰·雅各·金勒哈默·史密斯。乙:你说什么? ◇ What did you say?

Come and get it! ['kʌmən'gedət] [话] **吃饭喽!** 字面意义是"来拿吧!"。it 常指"已经做好的饭菜"。也就是说,本条的意思是:"饭已经做好了,请来吃饭吧!"在说这句话时多半是提高嗓门,喊叫 Co—me'n ge—dit! ['kʌ::mən'ge::dət]。典型的例子如:母亲从厨房里呼喊正在二楼的孩子们;牧场的厨师走出房门,一边按铃,一边大声呼喊牛仔们回来吃饭;等等。◇ Dinner [Breakfast, Lunch, Supper] is ready!

come by (*someplace*) [.kʌm'baɪ] [口] **顺便到……[从……经过]** → COME by (*something*)

come by (*something*) [.kʌm'baɪ] [话] **到手** 换个说法就是 come to have (获得)。*Pictures by this artist are hard to come by.* 这位画家的作品是很难弄到手的。如此例所示,这一表达法最常用于很难弄到手的场合。但并不绝对如此。*How did you happen to come by this Chinese scroll painting?* 这幅中国的挂轴,你是怎样弄到手的? *Ralph came by that old house when his grandfather died.* 拉尔夫在他祖父去世的时候得到了那所老房子。在以下的例句中虽然不一定非译成"得到"、"弄到手"不可,但是这一表达法的本来意义 come to have [possess] 并没有变,在英语的构思方面与上面所举的例句完全相同。例如: *When my father was young, a college education wasn't so easy to come by.* 当我父亲年轻的时候,受大学教育不是那么简单的事情。这在英语的构思中,仍然是"得到大学教育"的意思。*A good date is hard to come by at Spring Prom time.* 在春季舞会时期,很难找到一个很好的舞伴。*If Jack was born in America, how did he come by that English accent?* 如果杰克是出生在美国,他怎么满口英国人的口音? *Where did you come by an idea like that?* 你怎么会有那样的想法呢? *How did you come by that black eye?* 你的眼眶青肿,那是怎么搞的?另外,如果把 *something* 换成 *someplace*,作 come by (*someplace*),是"顺便到……"、"从……经过"的意思,务请读者注意。*I came by his office on the way here.* 我在前来这里的路上,顺便到他那个公司去了一趟[从他的公司门前经过]。◇ come into the possession of *something* / get

come down on *someone* [.kʌm 'daunɔ(:)n ~] [口] **申斥** → like a ton of BRICKS

come off it [ˈkʌˌmɔːfɪt] [话] **别胡扯啦!** 使用命令式的时候居多。 *A: The governor never fails to send me a Christmas card every year. B: Oh, come off it, George. The governor doesn't know you from Adam.* 甲:州长年年都给我寄圣诞卡来。乙:嘀,乔治,你别胡扯啦! 州长根本就不知道您老儿贵姓。 *A: How should I know what horses won yesterday? I told you I was in bed with a fever. B: Come off it, Stu. We all know you went to the races yesterday.* 甲:我怎么能知道昨天哪些马跑赢了呢? 我跟你们说过啦,我因为发烧,一直躺在床上。乙:司徒,你别胡扯啦! 我们大家全都知道昨天你去赛马场了。命令式以外的使用方法如下例: *When he said that he couldn't show us his Italian sports car because it was in the garage for repairs, I told him to come off it and admit that he only had a motorcycle.* 他说他不能给我们看他的意大利制造的赛车,因为车正在汽车修配厂修理,我于是叫他不要胡说八道,坦白承认他只有一辆摩托车而已。◇ stop pretending

come up with *something* [ˌkʌˈmʌpwɪð ~] [口] **找到、想出** 这一表达法的具体形象是"把藏在什么地方的东西拿上来"。基本上与 produce 或 supply 同义,是"把某种东西拿出来[筹划出来],使他人或自己能够看到或使用"的意思。在"拿出来"当中,包含有"找出来"、"想出来"等等。 *The man reached into his pocket and came up with a dollar.* 那个男人把手伸进衣袋,掏出来一美元。 *The librarian came up with the missing book.* 图书馆员找到了那本遗失的书。 *I have to come up with a thousand dollars by Friday.* 我在星期五以前必须筹措出一千美元。"找出来[筹划出来]"的地点,不一定非是外边的某处不可。特别是想法、主意之类,多半是在"自身之中找出来[筹划出来]",亦即"自己想出来"。 *Progress on my new novel is slow. I need to come up with some new ideas for plot development.* 我写这部新的长篇小说进度很慢。为了情节的发展,我需要有一些新的构思。 *I can't seem to come up with any good ideas recently.* 最近以来,我的头脑似乎想不出任何的好主意来。以上两个句子,从常识上判断,可以作为"自己想出来"的实例。但是,也有"由别处找出来"的思考和主意。下一个例句既可以理解为自己想出来,也可以当作是由别处找出来。 *The boss asked me to come up with some new ideas for tomorrow's meeting.* 头头叫我给明天的会议带来一些新计划。下一个例句就更暧昧了。 *Tom came up with a new idea at yesterday's meeting.* 根据上面的说明,这个句子可以有两种解释: ①汤姆在昨天的会议上想出了新的方案。②汤姆给昨天的会议带来了一个新的方案。在②的场合,既可理解为"汤姆提出了自己想出来的方案",也可以理解为"汤姆提出了他从什么地方弄来的方案"。另外,除以上所讲外,偶尔还有 come up with ~与 catch up with ~ (赶上)表示同一意义的情况。 *We came up with their boat just as it was leaving the harbor.* 正当船要从码头驶出的时候,我们赶上了他们的船。◇ produce [bring forth, find, supply] *something*

Easy come, easy go. → EASY

How come? → HOW

comeuppance

get *one's* **comeuppance** [ˌget ~ ˌkʌˈmʌpəns] [话] **应得的惩罚** comeuppance 意为"当然的报酬",分解开是 come + up + -ance (构成名词的词尾)。这一表达法具有"该来的东西来了"的意味,在本人来说,会感受到这种报应;而他人见了,又无不称快。除基本意义"应得的惩罚"外,根据上下文,也有"人家给颜色看"、"自作自受,大吃苦头"的意味。 *That man is always insulting people. I'd like to see him get his comeuppance.* 那个人总好侮辱别人。我真想看一看他怎样受到应得的惩罚。 *The neighborhood bully finally got his comeuppance at the hands of a younger boy.* 邻居那个爱欺负人的孩子,终于被另一个比他小的少年狠狠地教训了一顿。 *The arrogant* *foreman got his comeuppance when the boss bawled him out in front of the workers.* 当老板在工人们面前大声训斥工头的时候，那个傲慢的工头大大丢丑。也可以说 give *someone his* comeuppance, 即"给与应得的惩罚"。*Pete has often bragged about cheating on his wife behind her back, but she finally gave him his comeuppance by demanding a divorce.* 皮特常常吹牛，说他背着自己的老婆怎样玩女人，结果他老婆要求离婚，给他点儿颜色看看。另外，偶尔去掉一个 p，而缀为 comeupance。◇ get *one's* just deserts

coming

have it coming (to *one*) → HAVE

con

a con [ə 'kɑːn] [话] **囚犯** → an EX-CON

a con artist → ARTIST

a con game → GAME

con *someone* **into [out of]** *doing something* [ˌkɑ(ː)n ~ ˌɪntə / ˌaudəv ~] [话] **哄骗** con 原是 confidence (信任)的缩略，因而从 a confidence game (骗局)简化为 a con GAME，而又把其中的 con 作为动词使用。con *someone* into *doing something* 是"用甜言蜜语哄骗他人去干某种事情"的意思。*A man who pretended to be from a reputable store conned my wife into paying a thousand dollars for a piece of worthless imitation jewelry.* 一个假冒从某个著名商店来的人用花言巧语欺骗了我的妻子，使她付出一千美元买了一块不值几文钱的仿造宝石。*The fellow conned me into following him into a building. The next thing I knew, I woke up with a lump on my head and an empty wallet.* 那个家伙骗我跟着他走进一座大楼。这以后我就什么也不知道了。等我清醒过来，发现头上肿个大包，钱包已经空了。这一表达法不仅使用于犯罪，也可以用以表示比犯罪轻的"用花言巧语使人同意"、"巧妙地说服"的意味。另外，有时对方并没有特意"欺骗"之心，但在我方来看却有"上当了"的感觉，也用这一表达法强调此种心情。*I don't know why I let my wife con me into going to such an expensive place for our vacation.* 我不知道我怎么会上了老婆的当，竟到那样一个花销很大的地方去度假。*I won't be able to go fishing with you. My brother has conned me into helping him paint his house this weekend.* 我不能跟你一道去钓鱼了。我哥哥说了不少好听的话让我这个周末去帮助他油漆屋子。con *someone* out of *doing something*(骗人不做某事) 与 con *someone* into *doing something* (骗人做某事) 一样，既可用于犯罪之类的严重的情况，也可用于表示很轻的意味。*The thief, who claimed to be a detective, conned me out of checking his identity.* 那个小偷自称是个侦探，骗我不去调查他的身份。*You're wasting your breath. I've made up my mind to play golf tomorrow, and nobody is going to con me out of (doing) it.* 你是白费唇舌。我决心明天去打高尔夫球，不管谁说什么好听的话，都不能阻止我前去。另外，也可以用 con *someone* out of *something* 的说法表示"骗取什么东西"的意味。*A man who called himself a real estate agent conned us out of all our savings.* 一个自称是房地产商的人把我们的积蓄全都骗走了。*My big brother tried to con me out of my allowance so he could take his girl friend to the movies.* 我哥哥为了要带女朋友去看电影，花言巧语把我的零花钱弄走了。◇ trick [dupe, talk] *someone* into [out of] *doing something*[out of *something*]

conclusions

jump to conclusions [ˌdʒʌmptə kən'kluːʒənz] [口] **贸然下结论** 直译是"跳到结论去"，具有"在未弄清情况之前"的意味。哪怕"结论"只是一个，conclusion 一般是复数形式。*Stu never thinks things through carefully. He's always jumping to conclusions.* 司徒从来不认真考虑各种事情，他永远是贸然地下结论。*Let's not jump to conclusions. Just because a man has blood on his* *hands doesn't mean he's guilty*. 咱们不要贸然地下结论。不能因为一个人手上有血,就马上断定他是罪犯。但是,如果 conclusion 前边加形容词,则大多使用单数形式。例如: *It seems I jumped to a faulty conclusion*. 我好象贸然得出一个错误的结论。再有,在象 jump to the conclusion that ~这样引出同位的 that clause 的场合,当然要用定冠词。*When I saw a strange man drive off in our car, I jumped to the conclusion that he had stolen it. I didn't know that he was a friend of my husband's*. 我见到一个陌生人开走我们的汽车,我就贸易下结论说他是偷车贼,哪知道他原来是我丈夫的朋友。也有用 leap (跳)代替 jump 的说法,作 leap to conclusions,但略嫌生硬。◇ arrive at a hasty conclusion (without ascertaining all the facts)

leap to conclusions [ˌli(ː)ptə kənˈkluːʒənz] [口] **过早下结论** → jump to CONCLUSIONS

confidence

(be) brimming with confidence [ˈbrɪmɪŋ wɪð ˈkɑ(ː)nfədəntsˌ] [口] **充满信心** 这里的 confidence 与 self-confidence 同义,是"自信"。brim 作为名词是"容器、杯子等的边",作为动词则是"液体在容器里装得满满的,几乎要溢出来"的意思。本条的具体形象是:"充满信心,几乎要从里边溢出来"。请注意:经常用进行时。*Having studied a full month for the exam, Jack was brimming with confidence*. 杰克为了考试已经努力学习了整整一个月,他充满了信心。*Susan set out for New York, brimming with confidence*. 苏珊信心十足地前往纽约去了。◇ (be) full of self-confidence

a confidence game [ə ˈkɑnfədənts ˌgeɪm] [话] **骗局** → a con GAME

a confidence man [ə ˈkɑnfədənts ˌmæ(ː)n] [话] **骗子手** → a con ARTIST

conniption

have a conniption [ˈhævə kəˈnɪpʃən] [话] **大发雷霆** conniption 意为"暴怒"、"歇斯底里(的发作)"。加上 have 就意为"大动肝火,简直歇斯底里快要发作起来了",也就是"大发雷霆"。*My dad is gonna have a conniption when he sees what I did to the car*. 我爸爸如果看见我把汽车弄成这个样子,他一定要大发雷霆的。也说 throw a conniption (大叫大闹)。*My mother threw a conniption when she saw I had painted the walls of my room purple*. 我母亲见到我把自己住室的墙油漆成紫色,如疯似狂地叫嚷起来了。正如以上的例句所示,本条多用于发怒的场合,但也有时用以表达其他的感情,如"担心"、"困窘"等等。*Where in the world have you been till two o'clock in the morning? Your mother has been so worried she's about to have a conniption*. 直到后半夜两点钟,你究竟在哪儿来着?你母亲为你担心,几乎要发疯了。另外,还可以用 have [throw] a fit 表示同一的意味,不论在哪种场合都能与 have [throw] a conniption 相互替换。◇ by very angry

throw a conniption [ˌθrouə kəˈnɪpʃən] [话] **大叫大闹** → have a CONNIPTION

conscience

weigh on *someone's* **conscience** [ˌweɪɔ(ː)n ~ˈkɑ(ː)ntʃənts] [口] **良心不安** 这一习用语来自如下的说法: *The pack weighed heavily on my back*. 包袱沉重地压在我的背上。作为比喻表示良心受到谴责,不论是深感内疚还是略有歉意,均可使用。*Having had Fred pay the entire cost weighed on my conscience*. 弗雷德付了全部费用,这使我内心很不安。*It weighs on my conscience that I haven't repaid the old man for his kindness*. 对于老人的好意没有报答,我深感内疚。也可以用 upon 代替 on,只是稍微生硬一些。*It weighed upon my conscience that I hadn't informed the police that I was at least partly to blame for the boy's death*. 对于那个少年的死,我至少也有一部分责任,这一点我没有向警察报告,所以良心上是不安的。与按字面意义使用的场合一样,以 heavily 加强语气。*Be sure you make the right decision. If you don't,* *the consequences will weigh heavily on your conscience for many years.* 你必须做出正确的决定。不然的话，你会在以后的很多年受到良心的严厉谴责。◇ bother *someone* (considerably) ((heavily → deeply))

content

to *one's* **heart's content** [tə ~ ˈhɑ(:)rts kənˈtent] [口] **心满意足地** 直译为"一直达到心的满足"。 *American school children are not given homework for the summer vacation. They are able to play to their heart's content.* 在暑假期间，美国的小学不给学生留家庭作业。因此，学生们能够玩个痛快。 *You'd better get up and study. After finals you can sleep to your heart's content.* 你最好是起来念念功课。等过了期末考试，你可以随心所欲地睡大觉了。 *You can talk to your heart's content, but it won't make a bit of difference. I've already made up my mind.* 你可以尽情地讲你的话，不过，讲不讲都不起一丁点儿作用，因为我已经下定决心了。◇ as long [much] as *one* likes

contention

a bone of contention (between *them*) → BONE

contest

a greased- pig contest [ə ˌgri:zdˈpɪg ˌkɑ(:)ntest] [口] **追涂油猪竞赛** → bring home the BACON

conversation

a conversation piece → PIECE

convictions

have the courage of *one's* **convictions** → COURAGE

coo

bill and coo → BILL

cookies

toss *one's* **cookies** [ˌtɔ(:)s ~ ˈkuki(:)z] [俗] **呕吐** 直译为"把(吃下去的)甜饼干(从嘴里)抛出"。主要是学生等年轻人使用的一种轻松的、委婉的说法。 *The man tossed his cookies on the floor.* 那个男子呕吐了一地。→ lose *one's* DINNER ◇ vomit

cooking

What's cooking? → WHAT'S

cooks

Too many cooks spoil the broth. [ˌtu(:)ˌmeni ˈkuks ˌspɔɪlðə ˈbrɔ:θ] [谚] **厨师太多烧坏汤** 字面意义为"太多的厨师损害肉汤"。汉语中这类谚语很多，如"人多砌倒墙"、"三个和尚没水吃"等等。有时也说 Too many cooks spoil the soup. 但实际上使用于 soup (汤)的情况极少。 *You folks get out of the kitchen while I fix dinner. Too many cooks spoil the broth.* 我做饭的时候你们请离开厨房，人多了碍事。如此例所示，家庭主妇倒是常用这一谚语表示"请不要妨碍做饭"的意思。再举一个其他方面的用例：*This plan will never succeed if everyone tries to put his own ideas into it. Too many cooks spoil the broth.* 如果每个人都想塞入自己的意见，这个计划是永远不能成功的。厨师太多烧坏汤嘛。因为这是一个妇孺皆知的谚语，所以只说其中的一部分，人们也会马上理解。 *There are just too many cooks in this office.* 这个衙门的厨师就是太多啦。◇ Too many people trying to have a voice in something spoil the result.

Too many cooks spoil the soup. [ˌtu(:)ˌmeni ˈkuks ˌspɔɪlðə ˈsu:p] [谚] **厨师多了烧坏汤** → Too many COOKS spoil the broth.

cool

blow *one's* **cool** [ˌblou ~ˈku:l] [话] **沉不住气** → lose *one's* COOL

(as) cool as a cucumber → CUCUMBER

keep *one's* **cool** [ˌki(:)p ~ ˈku:l] [话] **沉着** 这里的 cool 是名词，意为"冷静"。年轻人特别喜欢使用这一表达法。年纪大一点的人喜欢 keep cool, stay cool 或者 keep *one's* HEAD 等具有同样意义的说法。 *Fred's a sharp negotiator. He always keeps his cool under pressure.* 弗雷

德是一位谈判专家。不论遇到什么紧急情况,他都镇定自若。*If a policeman stops you, keep your cool. Just pretend you're a tourist.* 如果有警察拦住你,你要沉住气,假装是个旅游者就行了。反义语为 lose *one's* COOL ◇ remain calm

lose *one's* **cool** [ˌlu(ː)z ~ ˈkuːl] [话] **沉不住气** cool是名词,意为“冷静”。青年人特别喜欢使用这一表达法。上了岁数的人则常用 lose *one's* HEAD,意思大致相同。*The challenger was winning until about the eighth round, when he began to lose his cool.* 一直到第八回合,挑战者都占有优势,但是以后他沉不住气了。*I shouldn't have gotten angry, but when he started insulting me I lost my cool.* 我本来不应该动怒,但是当他开始侮辱我的时候,我沉不住气了。如果用稍微轻松一点的说法,就使用 blow (吹),而讲 blow *one's* cool。*Don't blow your cool.* 不要着慌嘛。反义语是 keep *one's* COOL。◇ become excited [flustered, nervous, etc.]

play it cool (with *someone*) [ˌpleɪət ˈkuːl] [话] **不露声色** 比较新的用语。1955年左右开始由青年人使用,在嬉皮士中间流行,后来普遍化了。非常轻松的说法。意思是:“不论内心如何焦急、兴奋或不安,不在言语和行动中表现出来,采取悠然自得的态度”。特别是在向对方要什么、叫对方干什么或者想接近对方的时候使用。*We'd better play it cool. If they realize how badly we need their business, they may try to lower our fee.* 我们最好不露声色。如果他们了解我们多么需要他们这笔生意,他们就可能降低我们的手续费了。*You have to play it cool with a girl like Betty. If she thinks a boy really likes her, she starts playing hard to get.* 你对待贝蒂那样一位姑娘必须采取不即不离的态度。如果她认为一个男孩子真正爱上了她,她会摆起架子来的。*Play it cool, man. Don't let them see your weakness.* 喂,你要从容一些,别叫他们看出你的弱点来。◇ show a nonchalant attitude

coon's

a coon's age → AGE

coop

fly the coop [ˌflaɪðə ˈkuːp] [话] **开小差** coop本来意为“鸡舍”,俚语也作“监狱”解。因此,fly the coop 过去有“越狱潜逃”的意思。但是现在,几乎完全不作这一意义使用,多指“犯罪者或内心有愧的人从当前所住的地方偷偷逃走”。这是一种轻松的表达法。*The robbery suspect flew the coop despite police surveillance.* 在警察的监视下,抢劫嫌疑犯竟偷偷地溜走了。*We mustn't let him know we suspect him. If he learns that we're looking for him, he's sure to fly the coop.* 千万不要叫他知道我们在怀疑他。如果他了解到我们正在寻找他,他肯定会溜之乎也的。把此义一转,完全与犯罪者无关,只表示“再呆下去不合适,感到局促得很,所以从这个地方不告而别”,这种用法也非常多。*As soon as the teacher turned his back, the boys all flew the coop.* 老师刚一转过身去。男孩子们就一溜烟似地跑掉了。*When I returned to the tree under which I had left the young girls, they had flown the coop.* 我把女孩子留在大树底下,但是当我回来的时候,她们全都溜走了。◇ escape / run away

coot

(as) bald as a coot [əz ˈbɔːl dəzə ˈkuːt] [话] **光秃秃** coot是一种水鸟,学名蹼鸡,属秧鸡科。喙短,覆以一个延伸到额的扁平肉质盾,看起来光秃秃的,因此,美国人也称这种水鸟为 bald coot。本条习用语一般对完全秃头的人和剃光头的孩子们使用。是一种有点戏谑成份的说法。*The old man was bald as a coot.* 那位老人的脑袋已经光秃秃的。*Our son came back from the barber shop as bald as a coot.* 我们的儿子从理发店回来,头发已经全剃光了。◇ completely bald

cop

cop out [ˌkɑ(ː)ˈpaut] [话] **放弃、逃避** 在

过去的时代,这一表达法曾用以表示种种的意义,如"坦白"、"现行犯就擒"、"死亡"、"失败"等等。*After three hours of grilling by the police, I finally copped out.* 经过警察一连三小时的严厉审讯,我终于坦白交代了。*He copped out robbing a store.* 他抢劫一家商店时被捕了。*The day after he entered the hospital, he copped out.* 他入医院第二天就去世了。*A: Did you get the job? B: No, I copped out.* 你找到工作了吗? 乙:不,已经吹了。虽然作"坦白"解的用法在侦探小说中还常常出现,但是,在现在的日常会话中,以上的几种意义几乎全都不用了。现在主要用于表示比较新的意味,如"放弃"、"逃避"等。在使用"逃避"一义的场合,大多略带轻蔑的口吻,而且言外总含有若干卑怯、背叛的意味。主要是青年人好用这一表达法。在讲许诺的对象时,后边加 on *someone*。另外,这一表达法一般用于下列两种场合:一是不论明确与否,反正是有某种"许诺"存在,例如:*You promised you would help us. Don't cop out on us now.* 你曾经答应前来帮助我们。现在可不能撒手不管我们呀。一是本人正式参与某种事情,却中途脱逃,例如:*He copped out after helping us for only one day.* 他只帮助我们一天就甩手不干了。*A: Isn't Cal coming with us? B: Naw, he copped out. He said he had to study or something.* 甲:卡尔不跟我们一道去吗? 乙:不,他溜掉了。他说他必须去学习或者去干什么事情。*After all the planning the three of us did to start a surfing shop when we got out of high school, Sid copped out and went to college.* 我们三个人从高中毕业以后,就百般筹划开一个冲浪运动用具商店,可是锡德甩手不干,进大学了。*Don't expect the President to keep all his campaign promises. He'll cop out just like all the others.* 你不要期待总统会遵守他在竞选时提出的一切诺言。他也会跟其他所有的总统一样把一切诺言都丢到脖子后边去的。*A: I thought Locke was a Republican. B: He was, but he copped out and joined the Navy.* 甲:我过去以为洛克是个共和党员呐。乙:他过去是。但是他已经脱党参加海军了。*James used to be active in the radical movement, but he copped out and went to work for a big trading company.* 詹姆斯过去一直是激进运动的积极分子,可是他不再从事活动,到一家大贸易公司去工作了。但是,也可能有这样的场合,即与"许诺"并无直接关系,从第三者来看是"当然应该做的事情"。例如:*A: Did the Prime Minister answer all the reporter's questions? B: No, he copped out as usual.* 甲:首相回答记者提出的所有问题了吗? 乙:没有,他照例是回避了。名词 a cop-out 是"遁辞"、"口实"的意思。*A: Did he really have to study? B: No. That was just a cop-out.* 甲:他真的非去学习不可吗? 乙:不是。那只不过是个口实而已。*Management's insistence on discussing company morale in its negotiations with the union is a cop-out. It merely wants to avoid talking about its promised "forward-looking stance" on wages and benefits.* 资方在与工会进行谈判时,咬住职工的干劲问题不放,这是一个借口。他们只是想要避而不谈他们所保证的工资和福利"向前看的姿态"罢了。◇ back out / renege / withdraw

copacetic

be copacetic [.kopə'sedɪk] [话] **好极了**

语源不详,一说来自意第绪(Yiddish)语,一说 20 世纪 10 年代美国文艺界开始流行,究竟哪一个说法正确,无法肯定。在寒暄时,一方说:"How're you today?"(你好吗?)另一方回答:"Copacetic, copacetic."(很好,很好。)也就是说,这是 fine 的轻松的说法。虽然略嫌陈旧,但现在仍然可以听到。条头虽然译为"好极了",但在实际使用时,根据表达方法的不同,也可以译为"万事如意"、"顺利"、"称心"等等。*A: Hello, Ned. How's the world treating you these days? B: Everything is copacetic.* 甲:哈罗,内德。你最近的情况怎么样? 乙:万事如意啊。*Store manager: Any problems while I was out? Clerk: No, sir. Everything is copacetic.* 商店经理：我不在的期间有什么问题吗？店员：没有，老板。一切事情都很顺利。*Everything was copacetic with me all day long.* 在整个一天中，我一切事情都称心如意。另外，也可以缀作 copecetic, copasetic, copesetic, kopacetic, kopasetic, kopecetic, kopesetic，但发音完全一样。现在，用 k 开头的缀法极为罕见。◇ be fine

cop-out

a cop-out [ə ˈkɑː.paut] [话] **口实** → COP OUT

copycat

a copycat [ə ˈkɑ(ː)pi.kæ(ː)t] [话] **模仿者** 字面意义是"模仿的猫"。基本意思是"模仿别人的人"。但主要为儿童用语，指学其他儿童的说话和动作的孩子。*Jimmy's a copycat. He always draws the same pictures I do in school.* 吉米竟模仿别人。在学校里我画什么画他也画什么画。*Don't be such a copycat. If you don't stop copying everything I do, I'm going to tell Mama.* 你不要那样学别人的样。如果我干什么你总学我干什么，我就要告诉妈妈去啦。下面是成年人以戏谑的口吻使用的例子。*The new toy manufacturer was accused by its rivals of being a copycat.* 新上市的玩具的制造者被竞争的同行指责剽窃他人的模型。偶尔有用作动词以代替 copy 的情况。*I don't like Tommy Jones. He copies [copycats] everything I say.* 我不喜欢汤米·琼斯。我说什么，他学什么。◇ a copier / an imitator

core

be rotten to the core [.rɑ(ː)tntəðə ˈkoːr] [口] **坏透了** core 是"果实的心"。本条可以按字面意义使用，如：*This apple is rotten to the core.* 这个苹果已经连心儿都烂了。作为比喻，常指人坏透了，如说：*That boy is going to end up in jail someday. He's rotten to the core.* 那个小子早晚有一天得进监狱。他简直坏透了。不仅用于"个人"，也可以用于由人集合起来的"组织"，以形容它的腐败。*There's no use trying to reform the state's government. It's rotten to the core.* 试图改革州政府是白费心机，因为它已经腐败透顶了。也可以说 be rotten through and through。有的词典说这一习用语与 be rotten at the core 完全同义，这是不正确的，因为前者不能作"果实的心腐烂了"解。◇ be completely rotten

corn

be pure corn [ˈpju(ː)r ˈkɔ(ː)rn] [话] **一点意思也没有** → CORNY

corner

paint *oneself* **into a corner** [ˈpeɪnt ～ɪntuə ˈkɔ(ː)rnər] [口] **使自己陷入困境** 原来的构思是"在油漆地板的时候，到最后一看，把自己堵在墙的一角，想出也出不来了"。普通词典似乎不见这一习用语，但它在会话中却是经常出现的。例如：*We don't want to make too many promises to them or else we may find we've painted ourselves into a corner.* 我们不愿意对他们许诺太多，否则的话，我们就很可能使自己陷入困境。这是用于八方许诺结果寸步难行的场合。又如：*The suspect told so many lies to the police that he finally painted himself into a corner.* 嫌疑犯向警察说了太多的谎话，结果不能自圆其说了。这是用于自己的话相互矛盾因而作茧自缚的场合。有时代入 *oneself* 的词与主语并不直接一致，但是，即便在这一场合，内容还是同样的。例如在下一例句中，management (经营部门) 和 company (公司) 虽然词义不同，但结果还是指的一回事。另外，corner 的前边常加 financial, difficult, embarrassing 之类的形容词。*Management painted the company into a financial corner through overly rapid expansion.* 经理们由于过分迅速扩展业务，使公司在经济方面陷入了困境。也有条头表达法的反义说法，例如：tiptoe [sneak, creep, etc.] out of the corner。tiptoe 是"踮着脚走"。这一说法的意思是"想办法摆脱困境"，但并不是一条习用语。*The Presi-*

dent was having great difficulty tiptoeing out of the embarrassing corner into which he had painted himself when he said that he would never institute price controls to fight inflation. 总统说他决不用控制物价的方法对付通货膨胀，这使他自己陷入了困境，他费了九牛二虎之力才从困境中摆脱出来。◇ maneuver *oneself* into an uncomfortable [untenable, difficult, etc.] position

turn the corner [.tə(ː)rnðə 'kɔ(ː)rnər] [口] **情况好转** 字面意义是“转角”。*The car turned the corner.* 汽车转过了街角。作为比喻，主要用于生病、生意萧条等场合，意思是“从坏的情况恢复到好的情况”，即“有所好转”。*Your husband's operation was successful, but he won't turn the corner for at least forty-eight hours.* 给你丈夫做的手术很成功，不过，至少得四十八个小时他才能脱离危险。*The Secretary of the Treasury predicted that the nation's economy would turn the corner next spring.* 财政部长预言说，国家的经济情况到明年春天会有所好转。*Raising our sales volume by ten percent will enable us to turn the corner.* 如果把销售额提高百分之十，我们就能渡过难关。◇ begin to improve / start on the road to recovery

cut corners [.kʌt'kɔ(ː)rnərz] [口] **偷工减料** “把角 (corner) 切去(cut)”的意思是“不沿着街角去转弯，而是斜穿过去”。也就是说，这一表达法本来的意思是“抄近路”。corners 作复数形式，当然是“处处抄近路”的意思了。*Several marathoners were disqualified for cutting corners.* 有几名马拉松选手由于抄近路而被取消了资格。转作比喻，用以表示“千方百计压缩时间、劳力、经费等”的意思。在这一场合，多带有“依靠降低质量”的意味。因此，本条的意思是“偷工减料”，如下面的例句所示，多用于各类的工作。*In this business, we can't afford to cut corners. Everything depends on our reputation.* 我们这种买卖不容许偷工减料，因为信用第一嘛。*Recent innovations in our production line have allowed us to reduce expenditures without cutting corners.* 最近在生产线上的技术革新，使我们用不着偷工减料就可以减少开支了。除各类工作而外，有时也用于伙食“偷工减料”的场合，例如：*At times we have to cut a corner or two on our meals in order to make ends meet.* 有时候，为了生活费不超支，我家的伙食必须有几顿要简单一点。另外，正如这一例句所示，corners 有时可以变换一下形式，作 a corner or two; 也有时象下一例句那样，在前边加 a few 等修饰语。*We can't possibly finish the work on time unless we cut a few corners.* 如果我们不偷点工减点料，这活儿是不能如期完成的。以上全都是“降低质量”的例子，但是 cut corners 并不一定非以“质量低下”为前提不可。请根据下边的例句自己仔细体会这一点。*The boss often praised the foreman for his ability to cut corners without sacrificing product quality.* 厂长经常称赞工长，说他能够在不牺牲产品质量的情况下压缩生产成本。*Young housewives must learn to cut corners if they are to manage their households efficiently.* 年轻的主妇们要使家庭的日子过得好，就必须学会如何精打细算。◇ economize / sacrifice quality

corny

corny ['kɔ(ː)rni] [话] **枯燥无味** 这一表达法本来是 corn-fed (吃玉米长大的)一词的缩略形式，最初意为“乡巴佬喜好的”，为专用以修饰名词 joke 的形容词。现在除 joke 外，还可以修饰 music, drama, talk, design 等。在意义方面，现仍残留一点“乡巴佬喜好的”的含义，但主要是用以强烈地表达“由于缺乏新的 sense 而产生的枯燥无味[没有意思、非常无聊]的感觉”。特别是青年人，他们在谈 drama 或 music 时，也用这一表达法表示“情调太感伤、无聊得很、旋律太陈腐、枯燥无味”的意思。当然，不论是哪种场合，都含有轻蔑的心情。*My father likes that music of thirty years ago.* 我父亲喜欢三十年前那种老掉牙的音乐。*Talk about corny! The dialogue in that movie* *was so old and trite it should've had whiskers.* 没有比那再枯燥无味的啦！那部影片的对白全是老生常谈，简直陈腐得快发霉了。corny 的强调说法是 (be) pure corn。*His jokes are all pure corn.* 他说的笑话全都枯燥极了，一点儿意思也没有。*That music is pure corn.* 那个音乐枯燥已极，没有一点儿新鲜气氛。◇ old and trite / overly sentimental

counsel

keep *one's* **own counsel** [ˌki(:)p ~ ˌoun ˈkauntsəl] [口] **不露心计** 这里的 counsel 是"意图"、"计划"，keep 是"藏而不露"的意思。在不公开自己的意见或计划以及不与人商谈的场合使用。一般认为，只有强人才能够 keep *one's* own counsel。这一表达法既没有褒的意味，除特殊情况外，也没有贬的意味。是比较高尚的用语。*Though everyone around her was full of suggestions about how to deal with her problem, Mrs. Smith kept her own counsel.* 虽然关于怎样处理她的问题，史密斯夫人周围的每一个人都提出了一大堆建议，可是她本人却把自己的想法藏在心里，毫不外露。*Many people asked me what my decision was on the matter, but I decided that for the moment I would keep my own counsel.* 对于那件事情，许多人都问我做出了怎样的结论，但是我决定在一时之间不说出自己的看法。◇ not reveal *one's* thoughts

count

count on *someone* [*something*] [ˈkaun dɔ(:)n ~] [口] **指望** → BANK on *someone* [*something*]

take a head count [ˌteɪkə ˈhedˌkaunt] [话] **计算头数** → count NOSES

country

a country bumpkin → BUMPKIN

a country hick → HICK

countryside

scour the countryside (for *something* [*someone*]) [ˌskaurðə ˈkʌntrisaɪd] [口] **到处搜索** scour 是"哪里都搜索到"的意思。the countryside 指"广大的农村"。这一表达法使用于在广大的地方到处搜索的场合。有时实际上是 countryside，也有时略为夸大，仅指附近场所或大厦以内而已。*We scoured the countryside before we finally found the house we wanted.* 我们东奔西跑，到处去找房子，总算找到了一所合意的。*The search party scoured the countryside for three days but still could not find the lost child.* 一群搜寻的人东奔西跑地找了三天，但是还没有发现失踪的孩子。*Where have you been all morning? I've been scouring the countryside for you.* 你一上午到哪儿去啦？我到处找你。◇ search all over the entire area / look everywhere

courage

call forth sufficient courage (to *do something*) [ˌkɔ(:)l ˌforθ səˌfɪʃənt ˈkəːrɪdʒ] [口] **鼓足勇气** → get up the NERVE (to *do something*)

gather sufficient courage (to *do something*) [ˌgæ(:)ðər səˌfɪʃənt ˈkəːrɪdʒ] [口] **鼓足勇气** → get up the NERVE (to *do something*)

have the courage of *one's* **convictions** [ˌhævðə ˈkəːrɪdʒəv ~ kənˈvɪkʃənz] [口] **坚持自己的信念** 在人的一生中，会碰到各种各样困难的局面。每当碰到这种局面时，最主要的是坚持自己的信念，不屈不挠，勇往直前。本条的表达法便是从这一思想出发，格调相当高。*Sid showed that he had the courage of his convictions when he refused to help his classmate cheat on the exam.* 锡德拒绝帮助他的同班学友在考试中作弊，这表明他是一个能够坚持自己的信念的少年。*The problem with young people today is that many do not have the courage of their convictions.* 现代青年的问题是：有许多人不坚持自己的信念。*I should have spoken up at the time, but I'm afraid I didn't have the courage of my convictions.* 当时我应该把话讲清楚，但是很遗憾，我没有坚持自己的信念。◇ (be strong enough to) act according to what *one* believes is right

screw up *one's* **courage** [ˌskru(ː)ˌʌp～ˈkəːrɪdʒ] [话] **鼓起勇气** 这一表达法原来的形式是 screw up *one's* courage to the sticking point。screw up 是"拧紧(弦乐器的弦)", to the sticking point 是"达到固定不动的程度"。因此,整条意为"把勇气鼓到不能再鼓的地步"。现在,一般省略 to the sticking point。*This was undoubtedly going to be a difficult interview. I stood outside the door for a few moments screwing up my courage before I went in.* 这肯定是一次困难的会谈。我鼓起勇气走进房间之前,在门外停了一会儿。*Jeff finally screwed up his courage, but just as he opened his mouth to ask Sarah to marry him the doorbell rang.* 杰夫终于鼓起了自己的勇气。但是,正当他要启口向萨拉求婚的时候,门铃却响起来了。可以象下面的例句那样加上 to the sticking point。但这种例句极为罕见。*Sure, it's difficult. But just screw up your courage to the sticking point. I'm sure you'll do a good job.* 那的确是困难的事情。但是,你要鼓足勇气。我相信你一定会干得很好。在说"干……的勇气"时,把 *one's* courage 改为 the courage。*I stood for a long time looking at the dark water far below, screwing up the courage to take the plunge.* 我望着在远远下方的暗黑的水面,站了好久,然后才鼓起勇气跳进去。◇ (force *oneself* to) gather *one's* courage

course

be par for the course → PAR

a required course [ə rəˈkwaɪrd ˈko(ː)rs] [口] **必修课** → an ELECTIVE

a snap course [ə ˈsnæ(ː)p ˈko(ː)rs] [话] **极容易的课程** 这里的 snap 是从 snap *one's* fingers 而来的形容词,意思是"象弹手指那样容易的"(→ snap *one's* FINGERS at *something*)。course 是"课程"。本条习用语指用不着怎么钻研便能得到学分的课程。用不着说,这是学生用语。*You should take Introduction to Geology. That's a snap course.* 你应该选修地质学概论。那是一门极容易的课程。也可以说: *That course is a snap.* 那门课程容易极了。另外,有时称讲授 a snap course 的老师为 a snap teacher。*I take all of Mr. Jones' courses I can. He's a snap teacher.* 我尽可能地选修琼斯先生的各种课程。这位老师的学分最容易拿到手。a snap course 的反义词是 a BEAR。◇ a very easy course

court

the ball is in *someone's* **court** → BALL

put the ball in *someone's* **court** → BALL

cover

under separate cover [ˌʌndər ˌsepərət ˈkʌvər] [口] **另外邮寄** separate 是"另外的"。这里的 cover 是"信封"、"包装"的意思。这一表达法是书信中的习用语,但在口头上也常常使用。请注意: separate cover 不加冠词。*We are sending under separate cover the merchandise you ordered.* 您所订购商品另邮奉上。这是信函。下面是口语: *O. K., Jim. I'll write you next week. The book I borrowed I'll send you under separate cover.* 好啦,再见吧,吉姆。我下个星期给你写信。我借你的书,另外寄给你。◇ in a separate envelope [parcel] / separately

cow

a cow college → COLLEGE

cow juice → JUICE

a cow pie → PIE

Holy cow! [ˈhouli ˈkau] [话] **天哪!** Holy Christ! 的委婉的说法。这里的 cow (牛)没有特别的意思,只是代替 Christ (基督)一词使用而已。除 Christ 外,如 Jesus, God 等对上帝的称呼,以及有关上帝的神圣名词,在使用其本来意义以外的意味时,一般用完全无关的词汇代替。这样可以避免存在亵渎神明的心情。*Holy cow! Someone just fell out of that airplane!* 天哪! 刚刚有人从那架飞机上掉下来啦。*Holy cow! Did you see that shot? He just made a basket from the far end of the court!* 我的天哪! 你看见那一下投篮了吗? 他竟从球场最远的一端一下子投进去了。cow 也可以用 cats, smoke, mackerel, Moses 等词代换,如果直译,它们分别是"圣猫"、"圣烟"、"圣鲭"、"圣摩西"。*Holy cats! It's already a quarter to six. The boss'll be back in only fifteen minutes!* 我的天哪!已经差一刻到六点啦。再有十五分钟老板就要回来了。*Holy smoke! That car must be going over a hundred miles an hour!* 我的天哪! 那辆飞奔的汽车,时速肯定在一百英里以上! *Holy mackerel! This trash box is full of hundred-dollar bills!* 我的天哪! 这个字纸篓里竟塞满了一百美元的钞票! *Holy Moses! The dam just broke!* 我的天哪! 水坝刚刚崩溃啦!

a sacred cow [ə ˌseɪkrəd ˈkau] [口] **不可冒犯的人(或物)** 字面意义是"神牛"。印度教把牛看作神圣不可侵犯的东西。这一表达法即由此而来。cow 的内容包括偶像化的人以及不能批评或攻击的政策、思想、习俗、制度等,加上 sacred (神圣的)则含有讽刺的意味。*That new reporter was called on the carpet for writing an article critical of mayor. The poor fellow didn't know that the mayor is a sacred cow around here.* 新来的记者由于写了一篇批评市长的文章而遭到严厉的叱责。这个可怜的人不知道市长是当地神圣不可侵犯的大人物。*The government won't change its policy toward England. That's one of the President's sacred cows.* 政府不会改变对英国的政策,那是总统的不可冒犯的原则之一。*The President will never succeed in dismantling the social security system. It's one of the Democrats' most sacred cows.* 总统即使想要废除社会保障制度,他也绝对办不到,因为那是民主党人最不可冒犯的政策之一。◇ (a person) held to be immune to criticism / an untouchable policy [institution, etc.]

cowpoke

a cowpoke [ə ˈkauˈpouk] [话] **牛仔** → a COWPUNCHER

cowpuncher

a cowpuncher [ə ˈkauˌpʌntʃər] [话] **牛仔** 意思是"对牛 (cow) 用棒子捅的人 (puncher)"。从美国开发西部时代起,此词即为 cowboy 的轻松的说法。*Nowadays, cowpunchers often use trucks and airplanes instead of horses.* 现在的牛仔们不骑马牧牛了,他们经常使用卡车和飞机。另外,又用表示"用棒子捅"的意义的 poke 构成 a cowpoke 的说法。◇ a cowboy

cows

till the cows come home [ˌtɪlðə ˈkauz ˌkʌmˌhoum] [话] **直到驴年马月** till the cows come home 的后边有 by themselves 没说出来。本条原来的意思是:"只要不去赶,牛就不会自己回到棚子里来",也就是"它们永远站在原来的地方不动"。forever 一词除了"永久"外,还有"长时间"的意味,对于本条习用语也可作同样的考虑。*If you're waiting for me to lend you the money, you can wait till the cows come home. You haven't paid me back the thousand yuan I lent you last time.* 如果你等着我借给你钱,那你就永远等下去好啦。上次我借给你一千块钱,你还没还哪。*Let's go on ahead. Jane's always late. If we wait for her, we'll be here till the cows come home.* 咱们先走吧! 简永远是迟到的。如果我们等她,我们得在这儿呆到驴年马月了。*Don't ask Mrs. Gibbet how she's feeling. Once she starts explaining her ailments, she'll talk till the cows come home.* 不要问吉伯特夫人身体如何。她一旦讲起自己哪儿不舒服,话匣子一开就永远没个完。◇ forever

crack

crack a book → BOOK

crack a joke → JOKE

crack a safe → SAFE

crack up [ˌkræ(:)ˈkʌ(:)p] [话] **大笑** crack 原为"破裂"的意思。*The plane came in too low and cracked up at the end of the runway.* 那架飞机飞进机场时太低了,在跑道的尽头撞个粉碎。有时用以表示"人的神经坏了",如:*The emotional* *strain became too much for him and he eventually cracked up.* 他因为情绪过于紧张，精神终于崩溃了。也有时用以表示“疯狂”的意思，如：*First he began to laugh and then he began to cry. I was afraid he had cracked up.* 他先是哈哈大笑，然后又哭了起来。我想他大概是疯了。本条习用语原来就是这样表示“因控制不住感情而疯狂地笑或哭”的意思，但现在主要用于表示“笑”。也常有实际并不怎么笑、而在外表上故意装着 crack up 的情况。 *One look at the outlandish outfit Sid was wearing and we all cracked up.* 我们一见到锡德穿的那套奇装异服，全都哈哈大笑起来了。*All the students cracked up when the big dog jumped onto the teacher's desk and began to lick him in the face.* 当大狗跳上老师的讲台、开始舐他的脸的时候，学生们哄堂大笑起来了。为了加强语气，常在前边加 almost 或 just about。*The announcer's pants fell down and the audience almost cracked up.* 报幕员的裤子掉了下来，引起观众的哄堂大笑。在这一场合，almost cracked up 不是“差一点儿大笑起来”，而是“差一点儿疯了似地大笑起来”。*I just about cracked up when I saw the stunned look on their faces.* 我看到他们那种目瞪口呆的样子，几乎发疯似地大笑起来了。有时也使用 crack *someone* up 的形式。 *His jokes always crack me up.* 他讲的笑话总是使我哈哈大笑。◇ burst into uncontrollable laughter

have a crack at (*doing*) *something* [ˌhævə ˈkræ(ː)kət ～] [话] **有自信去试试看** → take a CRACK at (*doing*) *something*

not crack a smile → SMILE

take a crack at (*doing*) *something* [ˌteɪkə ˈkræ(ː)kət ～] [话] **有自信去试试看** 与 take a STAB at (*doing*) *something* 意义大致相同，但语感却不一样。这里的 crack 与 stab 相同，也是“试图”的意思，但比 stab 更有积极性，多用以表达“只要去干，必能成功”的心情。换句话说，take a stab at ～是没有多大自信的说法，而 take a crack at ～则是充满信心的说法。在表达比较强烈情绪的上下文中，具有“只要是我就毫无问题”的意味。因此，它与 take a stab at ～不同，在以失败而告终的“试试看”的场合很少使用。无论如何，这是一个表明男子大丈夫气概的说法。 *He took a crack at convinc-ing the chief, and sure enough he succeeded.* 他试着去说服科长，果不出所料，他成功了。*That's not the way to do it. Here, let me take a crack at it.* 不是那样做法。来，让我试试看。如此例所示，*something* 处可代入 it，请注意：其发音则由 [ət] 变为[æt]。*I'll take a crack at fixing your bicycle tomorrow.* 明天，我试试修理你的自行车。有时说 have a crack at (*doing*) *something*，同义。→ have a TRY (at <*doing*> *something*) / give *something* a TRY ◇ try *doing something*

cracked

be not the *something* **it's cracked up to be** [ˌnɑtðə ～ ɪts ˌkræ(ː)kˈtʌp təˌbiː] [话] **名不符实** 二、三百年以前，crack 有“自大”、“自夸”的意味。但在现代，只有地方方言使用 crack 的这一意义。在美国通用的表达法中，至今还残存着这一意义的，大概就是本条的习用语中出现的 crack 了。本条的英语直译为“没有达到自吹自擂那样的程度”。但是，be cracked 从“被自吹自擂”又进一步发展，一般用于表示“大有名声”的意思。*This book isn't the great novel it's up to be.* 这本书虽然很有名，但并不是一部那么了不起的小说。*Being a test pilot is all right, but it's not the job it's cracked up to be.* 当试飞员是很不坏的，但并不是象一般人认为的那么了不起的工作。也有应用于“人”的场合，例如：*The new Prime Minister turned out not to be the great leader he was cracked up to be.* 现在看起来，新首相名不副实，他不是那么一位杰出的领导人。*I don't think that guy's the great singer he's cracked up to be.* 我觉得那个家伙名不副实，他不是那么一位优秀的歌手。除 the *something* 外，也可以用关系词 what 或代名词 all，两者都是“名不副实者”的意思。同样，既可应用于"物"，亦可应用于"人"。*This job isn't what it's cracked up to be.* 这种工作不是象人们认为的那样好。*That guy isn't all he's cracked up to be.* 那个家伙名实难符。◇ be not the *something* it's [he's] supposed [reputed] to be／ be not the *something* that people say [think] it [he, they, etc.] is [are]

cracking

get cracking (on *something*) [get'kræ(:)kən] [话] **精神饱满地开始去干** 这一表达法源出现在已成废语的 crack on (高速度前进)。get cracking 的 get 是"开始去……", cracking 是"精神十足地前进", 因此, 严密地说, 本条整个的意思是"精神饱满地投入前进的状态"。这一表达法广泛使用于"工作"、"学习"、"出发(旅行)等"。是具有意气冲天的男子气概的语言。*OK. Let's get cracking.* 好啦, 咱们开始！ *If we don't get cracking soon, it'll be dark before we get there.* 如果咱们不赶快出发, 天黑以前就到不了那里了。表示"开始干……"的时候用 on, 要说 get cracking on *something*. *Get cracking on those books.* 赶快开始念那些书吧！有时不是表示"从头开始", 而是表示"开始认真去干已经在做的事情"。*We've got to get cracking on this project or we'll get increasingly behind.* 如果我们不加把劲儿去干这项工作, 就要越来越落后了。◇ get started / start working in earnest

cradle

rob the cradle [ˌrɑ(:)bðə 'kreɪdl] [话] **与年纪小得多的异性交往** rob 与具有"偷窃"意味的 steal 不同, 是"盗取……里边的东西或……持有的东西", 因此, rob the cradle 是"夺走摇篮里的婴儿"的意思。转作比喻, 则是"与年纪小得多的异性交往"的意味。五十岁的男子与二十来岁的女性交往, 就说 He's robbing the cradle. 如果女方五十岁, 男方二十来岁, 那就要说 She's robbing the cradle. 了。少男少女也常使用这一表达法, 在这一场合, 小上两三岁也可以说 rob the cradle。*Jane likes to go out with younger men. She's been famous for robbing the cradle ever since she was in high school.* 简喜欢跟年纪小些的男孩子一起出去玩。自从她入高中以来, 她就是以与年纪小的男孩子交往出了名的。不过, 这一表达法多用于戏谑的场合, 在严肃的情况下, 比如一个四十岁的男子勾搭十六岁的姑娘, 姑娘的父亲大怒, 恫吓说: "你别勾搭我家的女儿!"在这种场合, 是不大使用 You're robbing the cradle. 的。这时候, 一般是使用 You're much too old for my daughter. 之类的说法。也可以用于"与年纪小得多的异性结婚"的场合, 但极罕见。*Bluebeard must have liked to rob the cradle. All six of his wives were young maidens.* 蓝胡子肯定是喜欢与年纪小得多的女性结婚。他的六个妻子全都是十几岁的姑娘。另外, "与年纪小得多的异性交往的人"可以称之为 a cradle-robber, 但一般使用由动词 snatch (抢夺、窃取)而来的 snatcher, 称为 a cradle-snatcher。*Better not introduce your little sister to James. He's a notorious cradle-snatcher.* 你最好不要把你妹妹介绍给詹姆斯。他专找年纪小得多的异性交朋友, 已经臭名昭著了。◇ date [marry] *someone* much younger than *oneself*

cradle-snatcher

a cradle-snatcher [ə 'kreɪdl ˌsnæ(:)tʃər] [话] **专找年纪小得多的异性交朋友的人** → rob the CRADLE

crash

crash the gate [party] → GATE

a crash wagon → WAGON

crate

a crate [ə 'kreɪt] [话] **破旧的汽车[飞机、轮船]** crate 原为运货用的木箱, 一般是很粗糙的制品。因此, 人们就用此词泛指破旧的交通工具, 形容坐在里边好象被装到粗制的木箱中摇摇晃晃一样。通过以下的例句可以了解, 此词常常被用以夸大其词。*Why don't we get a new car, Dad? We've had this old crate over ten years now.* 爸爸, 咱们买辆新车不好吗?

咱们这辆老破车已经坐了十多年啦。*Mr. Jones has plenty of money. I don't see why he insists on driving that same old crate year after year.* 琼斯先生有的是钱,我真不明白他为什么一年又一年老开那辆破旧的汽车。*The bus we took was a broken-down crate that barely wheezed up the mountain.* 我们乘坐的是一辆破旧不堪的公共汽车,它呼哧呼哧喘着气,好容易才爬上山。*Is everybody aboard? Now, let's see if I can get this crate off the ground.* 全都上飞机了吗?好啦,现在该我试试这个破旧货能不能起飞了。*If you think this ship is bad, you should have seen the rusty crate I went to Europe in last summer.* 如果你以为这只船不好,我倒真想叫你看看我去年夏天去欧洲时乘坐的那艘生满了锈的破船。也可以作为反义词,在谈到新买的漂亮交通工具时,故意戏谑地说 crate。例如:*Have you seen Ned's new sports car? It's quite a crate.* 你见到内德的新赛车了吗?简直漂亮极啦!另外,象摩托车之类人体露在外边的交通工具,不能使用 crate 一词。道理很简单:因为原义是"木箱",只能限定把人能够整个装到里边的东西。◇ a(n old broken-down) car [bus, plane, ship, etc.]

craw

stick in *someone's* **craw** [.stɪkɪn ~ 'krɔː] [话] **非常不顺心** → stick in *someone's* GIZZARD

crazy

be crazy about *something* [*someone*] ['kreɪzi ə.baut ~] [话] **喜欢极了** crazy 是"发狂",be crazy about ~意为"对……喜欢得发狂"。这是一个夸张的表达法。大多降低程度,作"非常喜欢"的意味使用。对象不论,东西、人、动物、行为等皆可。使用范围极广,因而在译成中文时,可有种种不同的译法,不必拘泥一格。例如:*Jane is crazy about cats.* 简极喜欢猫。*Norman is crazy about Chinese food.* 诺曼非常爱吃中国餐。*Jack is crazy about Betty.* 杰克对贝蒂爱得发疯。*Francis is crazy about going to the movies.* 弗朗西斯是个电影迷。*I'm crazy about her.* 我被她弄得神魂颠倒。也说 be wild about ~ ['waɪl dəbaut ~]。◇ have an intense liking for *something* [*someone*]

one's **crazy bone** [~ 'kreɪzi .boun] [话] **一敲就发麻的肘端骨** → *one's* funny BONE

a crazy house → HOUSE

crazy like a fox → FOX

go stir crazy [.gou 'stəːr .kreɪzi] [话] **因长期坐牢而发痴** → in [out of] STIR

cream

a cream puff → PUFF

creek

be up the creek (without a paddle) [.ʌpðə 'kriːk (wɪ.ðaudə 'pæːdl)] [话] **陷入窘境** creek 是"小河",paddle 是"桨"。本条的字面意义是"在小河的上游 (没有桨)"。意思是:"应该坐船返回,但是没有桨,无可奈何"。例如:*I had lost my paddle, and my canoe was drifting toward the falls.* 我的桨已经丢掉了,河水把我的小船推向瀑布。请读者在头脑里思索一下这样的情况,对于本条的含义就容易理解了。作为比喻,在陷入窘境不知怎么办好的时候使用,有点儿"束手无策"的味道。*Talk about being up the creek.* 这算不了什么困难啊!*I'm going to be up the creek if my girl friend finds out that I took Sally to the movies last night.* 如果我的女朋友知道我昨天晚上带萨莉去看电影,那我就要非常尴尬了。*I had a job that was to start the week after graduation, so when I flunked my final exams I was really up the creek.* 我找到了一份工作,毕业后一个星期就开始上班,因此,当我期末考试不及格的时候,我完全陷入窘境了。加上 without a paddle 就更增强语气。*We don't have a spare tire. If we have a flat on this mountain road, we'll be up the creek without a paddle.* 我们没有带备用轮胎。我们的车如果在这山路上放炮,那我们就叫天天不应、叫地地不灵了。◇ be in a very difficult position [situation]

creeps

give *someone* **the creeps** [ˌgɪv ~ ðə ˈkrɪːps] [话] **令人毛骨悚然** creeps 是动词 creep (爬) 的名词化,意思是"毛虫等在皮肤上爬时的感觉"。主语随意,东西、声音、地点、人等全都可以。*Let's get out of here. This place gives me the creeps.* 咱们快离开这儿吧,这种地方令我毛骨悚然。*That guy gives me the creeps.* 那个家伙讨厌极了。另外,常使用形容词 creepy 而说 a creepy sound, a creepy sight, a creepy place 等。*Just as I was going to sleep, a creepy sound came from the stairs.* 我正要上床睡觉,楼梯那儿传来令人毛骨悚然的声音。*What creepy music!* 这是多么悲怆的音乐,听了叫人不寒而栗。◇ give *someone* a weird feeling

creepy

creepy [ˈkrɪːpi] [话] **令人毛骨悚然的** → give *someone* the CREEPS

crimp

put a crimp in *something* [ˌpudə ˈkrɪmpɪn ~] [话] **打乱计划** a crimp 是"铁、铝等固体东西的褶皱"。本条的整个意思是"在某种东西上弄出褶皱"。这一表达法可以按字面意义使用,例如: *The workman used a pair of pliers to crimp [put a crimp] in the edge of the sheet of metal.* 工人用钳子使白铁皮卷边。在笔直的东西上弄出褶皱,这意思就是说"破坏了原来的笔直的状态"。因此,作为比喻,这一表达法就具有"打乱计划"、"扰乱"、"妨碍"的意思了。*The weather put a crimp in our plans to go to the beach.* 我们要去海滨,天气却打乱了我们的计划。请读者注意:并不是"完全破坏了计划",而是"使计划不能顺利进行"。*The boss put a crimp in my schedule when he called a meeting for this afternoon.* 老板说今天下午开会,这打乱了我的日程。*The drop in the value of the dollar put a crimp in our company's export sales.* 美元贬值使我们公司的出口销售额受到损害。*The accident put a crimp in the rush hour traffic.* 那次事故阻碍了上下班高峰时间的交通运输。put a crimp in *someone's* style 是个定型的说法,与 cramp *someone's* STYLE 大致相同。一般使用时,略具诙谐的语气。例如: *I'd like to go out more often but my low salary puts a crimp in my style.* 我倒是喜欢常出去玩,可是工资太低,难以如愿啊。◇ hamper [dislocate] *something*

cripes

Cripes. [ˈkraɪps] [话] **妈的!** 在不便使用 Christ 一词的场合,用这一委婉的表达法。有轻轻地骂娘的味道。*Oh, cripes. We're out of gas.* 哼,妈的,又没煤气啦。这表示失望的心情。*Cripes, what a mess we're in!* 妈的,这多么麻烦呀! *Cripes, it's cold!* 妈的,天冷啦! 另外,如果使用惊叹号,例如: *Cripes! How many of these things did you buy, anyway?* 什么? 这种东西你到底买了多少哇? 这时, cripes 具有"什么!"、"怎么!"的意味,重点不是骂娘,而是"惊愕"。*Cripes! You didn't tell him the truth, did you?* 怎么! 你没有对他说真实情况嘛?

croak

croak [ˈkrouk] [话] **咽气** 原义是"青蛙等低哑的鸣声"。最初的构思是:当人被杀死的时候,会发出象青蛙一样的叫声。原来意为"杀死",现在不用这一意义。虽然有常在"人被杀"时使用的倾向,但并不以此为限,自然死的场合也可以使用。*The old fellow croaked before he could tell us who shot him.* 那个老头没等告诉我们是谁向他放的枪就咽气了。◇ die

crock

a crock [ə ˈkrɑ(:)k] [话] **胡说八道** crock 本来的意义是"陶制的壶"。陶制的壶怎么会有了"胡说八道"的意思呢? 原来有人买壶,可是商店无货,商人对他说:对不起,这有 a crock of shit (一把便壶)。本条条头是省略了 of shit 的表达法。在省略下面的 of shit 之后,仍然保持着强调 crock 中装满粪便的意义。这一表达法只在男人们的会话中出现,虽然省略的形式已经比较委婉,但一般不能在女人面前使用。*Did you see that crock in the paper about politicians being the most honest people in the country?* 你看见报纸上那篇胡说什么政治家是国家最诚实的人的文章了吗？如以下的两个例句所示，以 That's a crock. 的形式使用的情况，在日常会话中占绝对的多数。意思是："无聊得很"、"一派胡言"、"别开玩笑啦"等。*That's a crock. I don't believe a word of it.* 简直是一派胡言［无聊得很］。我连一句也不相信。*That's a crock and you know it. Why would I swipe your sweater?* 别开玩笑啦。你心里明白，我怎么会偷你的毛衣？有时也指"胡说八道的人"。*You're a crock. I never said anything like that.* 你真是一个胡说八道的家伙。我从来没有说过那种话。◇ a ridiculous article [story, accusation, etc.] / a lie

crocked

crocked ['krɑ(:)kt] [话] **醉醺醺地** → half CROCKED

half crocked [ˌhæ(:)f 'krɑ(:)kt] [话] **有几分醉意** 既然有 half crocked，当然也有 crocked (醉醺醺地)的说法。crocked 不是 completely drunk (酩酊大醉)，而是指"醉眼朦胧"的状态。*You don't know what you're saying. You're crocked.* 你自己不知道你在说什么话。你已经喝醉了。但在实际会话中，绝大多数使用本条条头 half crocked 的形式。*We started drinking early, and we were half crocked by the time the guests arrived.* 我们很早就开始喝酒，等到客人们来临的时候，我们已经有几分醉意了。*Ted's not a strong drinker. A bottle of beer and he's half crocked.* 特德没有酒量。只要一瓶啤酒，他就喝个半醉。*I don't remember what happened. I was half crocked.* 我不记得发生了什么事情。当时我已经喝得个半醉了。如以上的例句所示，多用 half crocked 作谓语，但也有时加一连字符，作 half-crocked ['hæ(:)f'krɑ(:)kt] 的形式，用于名词之前。*On the station platform were some half-crocked college students.* 在车站的站台上，有几个喝得半醉的大学生。crocked 是具有"使无用[变得无用]"意义的 crock 的过去分词，过去曾用以表示"没用了"、"垮台了"(= broken down) 的意思；现在，在会话中几乎完全不使用这一意义的 crock，只是偶然在书刊上见到而已。*The horse crocked before the race was half over.* 那匹马在比赛中还没跑到一半就垮掉了。◇ half drunk

crocodile

crocodile tears → TEARS

crook

by hook or crook → HOOK

crooked

go crooked [ˌgou 'krukəd] [口] **为非作歹** → turn CROOKED

turn crooked [ˌtə(:)rn 'krukəd] [口] **作奸犯科** crooked 从"弯曲的"的意思进一步发展为"不正的"、"不正直的"的意思。因此，本条最初的构思是"离开正道，向不正的 (crooked) 方面转过去 (turn)"。一般在谈到职业犯罪分子时使用。*Jason used to be an honest businessman, but for some reason he turned crooked.* 贾森一向是一个诚实的买卖人，但是由于某种原因，他走上犯罪的道路了。*Children of Mafia families don't turn crooked; they are trained to be crooked from an early age.* 黑手党人家里的孩子们并不是误入歧途；他们从很小的时候起就受到作奸犯科的训练。turn crooked 的反义词是 go STRAIGHT。*Jake went straight for many years, but he turned crooked again after he met an old friend from prison.* 多年以来，杰克一直规规矩矩，但是自从遇见一个从监狱出来的老朋友之后，他又走上了犯罪的道路。另外，turn crooked 也有时作 go crooked。◇ become dishonest / turn to a dishonest life

crow

as the crow flies [əzðə 'krou ˌflaɪz] [口] **直线距离** 字面意义是"象乌鸦飞一样"。最初的构思为"不管地形上的障碍物，也不管人所修筑的道路，象乌鸦从上空飞过那样一段距离”,也就是“直线距离”。不一定非“乌鸦”不可,是“鸟”就如此,只是用“乌鸦”作代表而已。*I suppose Johnstown is about twenty-five miles from here as the crow flies.* 从这里到约翰斯顿的直线距离大约25英里。*It seems like a long way because of the winding road, but it's only about ten kilometers as the crow flies.* 由于道路曲折,好象路程很远,但是直线距离只有十公里左右。◇ (if one were to go) in a straight line

eat crow [.i(:)t 'krou] [口] **深自愧恨** 在英国英语中有一个同样的表达法,就是 eat humble PIE。本条习用语则纯粹是美国货,这是因为它源出如下的一段小插曲:在1812年的英美战争中,有一个美国兵进入英国人占领区去打乌鸦,被英国兵缴了械,并被强迫把那只乌鸦一口吞下去。那个美国兵马上取回枪,来个投桃报李,强迫英国兵把剩下的乌鸦全都吞下去。*Jim was forced to eat crow when, after bragging about how smart he was, he failed the exam.* 吉姆自吹自擂,说他的头脑如何聪明,当他考试失败的时候,不能不感到羞愧难当了。如此例所示,这一说法用于过去枉自尊大、现在始知其非的场合。一般来说,不仅指本人感到耻辱的心情,而且伴有使他承认失败或错误的具体的“行动”。*I wouldn't be too hasty to act if I were you. You may end up having to eat crow.* 如果我是你的话,我不急急忙忙采取行动。万一弄不好,很可能会深自愧恨的。如此例所示,多与 have to ~,或者 make *someone* ~ 的形式结合起来使用。*That guy is not satisfied just to make me eat crow. Now he's trying to get me fired from my job.* 那家伙使我受到屈辱还不满足,现在又企图使我失掉工作。*Let them brag all they want before the game. They'll be eating crow when it's over.* 让他们在比赛之前爱怎么吹就怎么吹吧。等比赛结束的时候,他们就会感到丢脸了。◇ (humiliatingly) admit *one* was wrong / be humiliated (by having to admit *one* was wrong)

be nothing to crow about [.nʌθəntə 'krouəbaut] [话] **没有什么了不起** crow 原指“雄鸡报晓的啼鸣”。由于雄鸡叫时大摇大摆、神气十足,此词就转用于表示“摆臭架子”、“高唱凯歌”等意思。也就是说,本条的整个意义应为“不到摆臭架子的程度”,但在实际会话中,多用以表示“没有什么了不起”的意味。*Our victory today was nothing to crow about. Our opponents have lost every game this season.* 我们今天的胜利没有什么了不起。在这个赛季里,对方每次比赛都是大败而归。*The author's writing style is nothing to crow about.* 这位作家的写作风格没有什么特殊的。与 be nothing to BRAGabout 意义大致相同,但语气稍强。◇ be not worth bragging about / be not so outstanding

crush

have a crush on *someone* [.hævə 'krʌ(:).ʃɔ(:)n ~] [口] **迷恋上异性** crush 一般作“压碎”解。在这一表达法中,指“一见钟情”,即对异性一下子产生了强烈的爱情。年轻人的用语,是一种比较幼稚的说法。使用者年纪最大的是高中学生。成年人也是在谈到高中以下的年轻人时使用。*Billy has a crush on Suzy.* 比利迷恋上了苏吉。*Sally's got a crush on Mr. Kennedy, our English lit teacher.* 萨莉迷恋上了我们的英国文学教师肯尼迪先生。get a crush on *someone* 是“热爱”。*When I was in elementary school, I got a crush on a different boy every year.* 我上小学的时候,每年热爱上一个不同的男孩子。*someone's* crush 是“所迷恋上的人”。*Who's Dizzy's latest crush?* 迪齐最近迷恋上什么人啦? ◇ be infatuated with *someone*

cry

be a far cry from *something* [ə 'fɑːr 'kraɪ frəm ~] [话] **差远啦** 直译为“远离……的叫声”。原来的构思是:“大声喊叫也传不到那么遥远”。然而,现在极少使用“距离远”的意味,下面是一个非常罕见的例子:*His house is a far cry from town.* 他的家离镇上很远。一般的使用方法如下: *Our hotel accommodations were a far cry from what we had expected.* 我们使用的旅馆设备可比我们所期望的差远了。*I'm afraid my painting is a far cry from real art.* 我的画恐怕离真正的艺术太远了。在比较人的优劣或物的好坏时,具有"望尘莫及"或"远远赶不上"的意味。*He's an excellent novelist but still a far cry from Tolstoy.* 他是一位优秀的小说家,但与托尔斯泰相比却是望尘莫及。*A: How do you like Boston? B: Boston's all right. But it's a far cry from New York.* 甲:波士顿怎么样? 乙:波士顿很不错,但是远远赶不上纽约呀。◇ be a long way [very different] from *something*

cucumber

(as) cool as a cucumber [əz ˌkuːl əzə ˈkju(ː)ˌkʌmbər] [话] **非常沉着** 字面意义是"象黄瓜一样冷静"。cucumber(黄瓜)有凉的感觉。cool (冷静)的第一义是"清凉"。这一表达法是两者的谐意。*Lieutenant Smith is as cool as a cucumber even under fire.* 史密斯中尉即便在炮火下也是非常沉着的。*Despite the fact that one of the engines was on fire and the plane was fast losing altitude, the pilot appeared to be as cool as a cucumber.* 尽管一个发动机着火,飞机迅速往下沉落,可是驾驶员大有稳如泰山的样子。*Even when the demonstrators began shouting threats, the governor remained as cool as a cucumber.* 甚至在示威群众开始大嚷大叫、进行威胁的时候,州长依然是镇定自若。◇ extremely self-composed / completely unruffled

cud

chew the cud [ˌtʃuːðə ˈkʌ(ː)d] [话] **慢慢考虑** 原意是牛之类的反刍动物 (a ruminant) "把吃下去的东西从胃返回口中再咀嚼",亦即"反刍"(ruminate)。chew 是"咀嚼",cud 是"从胃中返回的食物"。这一表达法的原意和使用方法与 ruminate 大致相同,但可以说更具会话的气氛。按字面意义应用于动物的场合,the cud 也可以换用 its [her, his, etc.] cud。*No matter how hard I pulled on her rope, the old bossy refused to budge. She just stood there calmly gazing at me and chewing her cud.* 不管我怎样用劲拉缰绳,那条老母牛一点儿也不动窝。它只是站在那儿,静静地望着我,嘴里咀嚼从胃里返回的东西。由于把某种思考比做 cud,使其"在脑袋里反刍",所以在作比喻使用的场合,常含有"不慌不忙"、"悠然自得"的意味。这一表达法在冥思苦想、认真考虑的场合不能使用。后边一般接 on 或 about (关于……),但偶尔有接 of ~的场合。不过,of ~的说法有点生硬,在会话中很少听见。*I can't give you my answer right away. Let me chew the cud on it for a few days.* 我不能马上答复你。容我慢慢地考虑几天。常用于回顾过去而进行反思的场合。*While I was in the hospital, I had plenty of time to chew the cud about what I should and shouldn't have done in the past.* 当我住在医院的时候,我有充分的时间去慢慢地考虑过去哪些事情是该做的、哪些事情是不该做的。也有回顾过去漫谈往事的场合,令人感到好象"在脑袋里对一桩桩往事进行反刍"。*The old men liked to sit around the stove, chewing the cud of their lost youth.* 老人们喜欢围坐在火炉边,漫谈他们已经逝去的青春时代。偶尔用以表示"嚼烟块"的意思。*In the old days, most baseball pitchers liked to chew the cud on the mound.* 在早先,大多数棒球投手都喜欢在踏板上嚼烟块。◇ ruminate

cuff

on the cuff [ˌɔ(ː)nðə ˈkʌ(ː)f] [话] **赊欠** cuff 是"衬衫的袖口"。这一表达法的来源是:在过去,酒吧服务员把客人吃喝的钱数记在袖口上 (on the cuff),日后再去讨帐。如下面例句所示,常用 put *something* on the cuff 的形式表示"记帐"的意味。*Put our drinks on the cuff, Charlie. I'll pay you next week.* 查理,把我们喝的酒钱先记上吧。我下个星期付钱。*Give me a hundred dollars down and we'll put the rest on the cuff.* 你先交一百美元定

钱，其余可以赊欠。这一表达法主要用以表示"赊欠"的意思，但也有时用以委婉地表示"白给"的意思。究竟应作何解释，只能根据上下文来判断。例如 *The owner of that restaurant is very kind. He often gives meals to poor people on the cuff.* 餐厅的主人是非常和善的。他常给穷人饭吃，不收钱。这句话的意思明白无误，但是象下面的一句话就不好肯定了：*I don't have much money on me, but I know a little restaurant where we can eat on the cuff.* 我口袋里没有多少钱，但是我认识一家小饭馆，咱们到那里吃饭可以赊欠[不给钱]。这句话可以解释为"不给钱白吃"，因为那家饭馆也许是亲戚朋友开的。另外，on the cuff 是美国特有的英语，在英国英语中，"赊欠"不说 on the cuff, 而说 on the slate ['sleɪt], 但后者没有"白给"的意义。◇ on credit / free

speak off the cuff [ˌspi(:)ˌkɔ(:)fðə 'kʌ(:)f] [口] **即席讲话** cuff 是"衬衫的袖口"。在人前讲话时，一般总是预先准备一篇讲演稿。但过去常有这样的情况：由于未能做好准备，当场把讲话的要点写在袖口上，象学生在考试时作弊一样，一边偷看袖口上的字迹，一边用嘴去说。本条习用语即来源于此。按照字面，speak off the cuff 是"从袖口上看着字去说"的意思，也就是毫无准备的"即席讲话"。也许有人会想：只要讲一次话，袖口就完蛋了。这请不要担心。因为过去西服衬衫的袖口是可以摘下来的，而且有一层很厚的糨糊，只要一下水，写的字就会随糨糊而被去掉了。动词一般用 speak, 但也可以用 tell (*someone*), say (*something*), give (*something*) 等代换。*Ben hadn't prepared a speech, so he had to speak off the cuff.* 本没有准备演说，因此他不得不临时抱佛脚来个即席讲话了。*Ben forgot to bring his prepared speech, so he had to speak off the cuff.* 本忘了带准备好的讲稿，因此不得不来了个即席演说。*If you want me to make a speech, let me know ahead of time. I'm not about to speak off the cuff.* 如果你想要我做一次演说，请预先通知我。我可不来即席讲话。如以上三个例句所示，一般用于在"群众面前"或"开大会"讲话的场合。但在两个人单独对话时，也是可以使用的，例如：*I'm giving you this strictly off the cuff, George, so I'm not sure all the facts are absolutely correct.* 乔治，我现在向你讲的这些话全凭自己的记忆，因此我不敢保证所有事实都绝对正确。这一表达法也可以用以表示"非正式"的意味，也就是由"不是做正式准备的演说，而是做即席的、非正式的讲话"这一意义发展而来。*After the department chief had presented his company's official position on the question, he said off the cuff that actually the company would be willing to compromise on several points.* 公司的部长对该问题表明了本公司的正式立场，然后，他又私下讲：在几点上，公司实际上是愿意妥协的。如此例所示，在用以表示"非正式"的意味的场合，由于讲话内容大多不便公开，所以常带有"说悄悄话"的味道。加上连字符，off-the-cuff 可作为形容词使用。*I haven't prepared a speech, but I'd like to make a few off-the-cuff remarks to you.* 我没有准备来讲演，不过，我向大家随便谈几句话吧。◇ speak extemporaneously

cup

be *someone's* **cup of tea** [～ˌkʌpəv'ti:] [话] **爱好，拿手** 本来的意义是"自己的一杯茶"。这是由英国人喜欢喝茶而产生的一个表达法。现在，在美国也常常使用。*Whodunits are not my cup of tea.* 我不爱好侦探小说之类的东西。在否定句中使用的倾向比较强烈，但也用于肯定句。*If you want to go and see a movie, how about a good shoot-'em-up Western? Now that's my cup of tea.* 如果你想去看电影，看一部精采的西部武打片如何？现在我最喜欢这种东西。常用 just 加强语气。*Let's not invite Frank. No doubt he's a nice fellow, but he's just not my cup of tea.* 咱们不要邀请弗兰克吧。毫无疑问，他是一个很好的人，但是我怎么也不喜欢他。虽然可以用于表示"拿手"

的意味，但有一个特点：在这一场合，也总是包含着“爱好”的情调。思路是：“由于爱好，所以搞得好”。*We're going to offer Mark the role of the murderer in our new play. It should be just his cup of tea.* 在这次要排的戏里，我们打算叫马克演杀人者的角色。他演这个角色一定很拿手。*From what you've told me, this should be your cup of tea. It's an editing job in a publishing house.* 依照你所说，这个工作应该是你的拿手好戏了。是在出版社里当编辑。另外还有一个说法是 be *someone's* dish of tea, 不过在美国很少有人使用。◇ be exactly what [the kind] *someone* likes [does] best

curiosity

Curiosity killed the cat. [ˌkjuriˈɑsədi ˌkɪldðə ˈkæ(:)t] [话] **好奇也要有分寸** 直译是“好奇心把猫杀死了”。西方人把猫当作好奇心的象征。这一表达法最初的构思是：由于好奇心的驱使，有时会冒风险而丧了性命。不过，有人把它译为“好奇使人丧命”，却是过分一点儿了。当然，在以盗匪为题材的电影或小说中，作为威胁的话来使用时，这样翻译也未为不可。但一般来说，这是一个委婉的表达法，在有不愿对人讲述或害怕别人听去的事情时，用它来柔和地回绝对方，意思等于 Don't be so nosy. (不要那么刨根问底吧!)或 It's none of your business. (少管闲事吧!) *Why do you want to know how much money he makes? Curiosity kill-ed the cat, you know.* 你为什么想要知道他挣多少钱？俗话说，好奇也要有分寸呀。*A: What are you going to give me for Christmas? B: Curiosity killed the cat.* 甲：圣诞节你给我什么礼物？乙：告诉你就没有意思啦。◇ You shouldn't be so curious.

curl

curl up with a good book → BOOK

customer

an ugly customer [ə ˌnʌgli ˈkʌstəmər] [话] **粗暴的人** ugly 是 ugly behavior (行为丑恶) 的意思，指使用暴力，威胁他人，向人纠缠，死乞白赖地追逐女人等等。customer 原义为“顾客”，转用于表示“一沾边就会惹麻烦的人”的意思。ugly customer 一般在谈到男人时使用。*When he starts drinking, he can become an ugly customer.* 他一喝上酒，就会大吵大闹，令人毫无办法。*You'd better not tangle with him. He's an ugly customer.* 你最好别跟他发生纠纷。他这个人软硬不吃，很难对付。*That pro wrestler looks like an ugly customer.* 那个职业拳击手看样子非常吓人。还有一个说法是 an ugly- looking customer。*The leader of the group was flanked by a pair of ugly-looking customers wearing guns.* 在那个集团头目的两侧，各有一名面目狞狰的持枪的男人。另外，这一表达法不仅用于“人”，有时也可以用于“动物”。例如：*Gorillas are generally very gentle creatures, but once they feel threatened they can become very ugly customers.* 大猩猩平时是非常温顺的动物，但是，当它们一旦感到受威胁时，就狂暴起来难以制伏了。◇ a dangerous and difficult- to- handle fellow [animal] ((ugly-looking → seemingly ugly))

cut

can cut it [kəŋˈkʌ(:)dət] [话] **搞下去** 比较新的表达法。语气轻松，特别是青年人喜欢使用。但 can cut it 怎么会变成这样的意义则不详。具体形象是：“用刀子把硬的东西咔嚓一下子切开”。多用于否定句。*This work is too hard for me. I just can't cut it*[ˌkæːŋˈkʌdət]. 对我来说，这个工作太难了。我怎么也搞不下去。*Rick wasn't able to cut it as a race driver.* 里克当赛马手，没能够长期搞下去。如以上的例句所示，一般是在未能持续干某种事情的场合使用。但是，也可以用于一时之间的事情。*This is a very difficult trumpet solo. Do you think you can cut it?* 这是一首很难的小号独奏曲。你认为你能搞得了吗？即便在这一场合，质问者的意图也是垂询能否毫无阻碍地、顺顺当当地吹奏到底，所以也包含着一直搞下去的意味。可以认为，这一点与其它例句是完全相同的。◇ can do [play, etc.] it / can succeed

cut and run [ˌkʌtn'rʌ(:)n] [话] **抛开一切仓皇逃走** 原意是"在紧急情况下,船割断锚索开走"。*When the English armada appeared, the Spanish ships cut and ran.* 当英国舰队出现的时候,西班牙的舰艇割断锚索,赶紧逃走了。在作为比喻使用的时候,也不仅仅是"急忙逃走"(leave in a hurry)。*When the principal appeared in the hallway, the students cut and ran.* 当校长在走廊中出现的时候,学生们仓皇逃窜了。*If the police begin to suspect our little game, be sure to let me know before you cut and run.* 如果警察开始怀疑我们的小把戏,你在逃走之前一定要告诉我。如以上两个例句所示,这一表达法是在"马上停止正在干的事情"的场合使用;或者如下例所示,在"马上断绝已往的关系"的场合使用。*My marriage is a complete failure. If it weren't for the children, I think I'd just cut and run.* 我的婚姻是一次完全的失败。如果不是为了孩子,我早就想抛开一切、逃之大吉了。*I'm sick and tired of my job. I'd like to quit, but I can't just cut and run. My partner depends on me too much.* 我对这个工作厌烦极了。我很想甩手不干,但是我不能不管不顾、逃之夭夭呀。我的伙伴是非常依重我的。◇ (cut all ties [drop everything] and) run away

cut it out [ˌkʌdɪ'daut] [话] **停止妨碍他人的事情** it 代表某种状况,这里指讨厌的话、恶作剧、扰乱他人的行动等。本条习用语多用命令式。*Cut it out, you guys. Can't you see I'm trying to study?* 你们别闹啦!你们没看见我正努力用功吗?*Cut it out. You're hurting my arm.* 别弄啦!我的胳臂快叫你折断啦!*A: Why did you hit him? B: He was teasing me. I told him to cut it out, but he wouldn't listen.* 甲:你为什么打他呢?乙:他戏弄我来着的。我叫他不要闹,他不听嘛。还有一个 cut out (the) *something* 的形式,特别是在"停止不良行为、习惯等"时使用。在这一场合,如果代入 *something* 的是一个表示某一特定行为的词,一般要加定冠词 the;如果是一个表示习惯的词,一般不加冠词。*Cut out the smoking. This is a no-smoking area.* 不要抽烟啦!这里禁止吸烟。*You could save some more money if you cut out smoking.* 如果戒掉吸烟的习惯,你会多攒下一些钱。◇ stop (it)

cut out [ˌkʌ'daut] [话] **溜走** 主要是年轻人使用。一种轻松的表达法。有的词典解释为 leave quickly, suddenly, secretly and / or permanently (迅速地、突然地、悄悄地或永久地离去),但是可以认为:这一习用语与 permanently 没有直接关系。从以下的例句可以看出,它与汉语俗语的"溜之大吉"、"溜之乎也"、"开小差"等的意味十分相近。*This party is no fun. Let's cut out.* 这个社交晚会没啥意思,咱们溜之大吉吧。*We'd better cut out before the fuzz starts snooping around.* 我们最好是在警察开始巡逻之前溜走。*There's no chance of finding work in this town. Why don't we cut out?* 在这个城镇里,没有找到工作的机会,咱们为什么不赶快离开呢?*A: Where's Al? B: I dunno. He cut out a while ago.* 甲:阿尔在哪里?乙:我不晓得。几分钟之前,他不见影儿了。*I don't know what happened after that. When the other kids started popping acid, we cut out.* 那以后的情况,我就不知道了。当别的孩子们开始服 *LSD*(致幻药)的时候,我们就溜走了。◇ leave

cut out (the) *something* [ˌkʌ'daut(ðə)~] [话] **戒除不良行为、习惯** → CUT it out

be cut out for [to be] *something* [ˌkʌ'dautfər ~ / ˌkʌ'dautːəbi ~] [话] **天性适合做某种事情** 逐字直译是"为适合某种事物而切割出来的"。原意为"裁缝按照一定的样式剪裁衣料"。把这一意义套用在人身上,就是"能力、才干、天性等适合于某种职业或生活方式",也就是"有干那个的素质"或"天生是干那个的材料"。*If you really think that's the kind of work you're cut out for, why don't you try it?* 如果你真的认为自己生性适合那种工作,为什么不试试看呢?但是,在实际应用时,这一表达法多用否定形式，亦即表示“天生不适合”的意思。*I'm just not cut out for life in the city. I've decided to go back and work on my father's farm.* 我天生就不适合过城市生活。我已经决定回父亲的农场干活去了。*I guess I'm just not cut out to be a salesman. I'm not aggressive enough.* 看起来，我天生就不适合当推销员。我没有足够的死乞白赖的劲头。◇ have the talent [inclination, temperament] for [to be] *something*

'cuz

'cuz [kəz] [话] **因为** 在会话中，because 的 be-脱落，而剩下的 -cause 听起来是 'cuz 的声音。这一形式常在漫画、小说中出现。*I'm going 'cuz I want to.* 我所以去，是因为我愿意去。在书写时，有时不用撇号(')。◇ because

D

dagger

look daggers at *someone* [.luk 'dæ:gərzət ~] [话] **怒目而视** dagger 是投掷特用的、有柄两刃的"短剑"。在这一习用语中,表示瞪着眼看对方时的"锐利的目光"。本条的整个意思是"用锐利的目光去看某人"。常在当着别人的面不好意思直接批评对方的言行或表示不满的情况下使用。在美国的连环画中,我们常常可以看到怒目而视的人的视线被画成一排小的 dagger,其来源就在于有本条这样一个表达法。*Mrs. Dirk looked daggers at her husband when he mentioned her age to their guests.* 当她的丈夫对客人们提到她的年龄的时候,德克夫人怒目望着他。*Mary looked daggers at her boy friend when he asked Helen to dance.* 当自己的男朋友邀海伦跳舞时,玛丽向他投去恼怒的目光。*Everyone looked daggers at Bill for cutting in at the front of the line.* 比尔加塞儿到队伍的前列,每个人都对他怒目而视。◇ glare angrily at *someone*

Dagwood

a Dagwood sandwich → SANDWICH

daily

the daily grind → GRIND

daisies

be pushing up daisies [.puʃənʌp 'deɪzi(:)z] [话] **进棺材** daisy 是在美国各地都生长的"雏菊"。本条直译为"把雏菊推上去"。乍看起来,简直令人莫名其妙。其实很简单:由于这种植物常在坟头生长,所以就产生了埋在它下边亦即"死"的意义了。这是一种很随便的说法。特别是歹徒们在进行威胁时常常使用。*The last man who crossed me is pushing up daisies.* 上回和我作对的那个家伙已经进棺材啦。但是,这不是唯一的用法。人们也常以诙谐的口吻说这句话,如:*If I keep exercising at this rate, I'll be pushing up daisies in another week.* 如果我照这样坚持操练下去,过一星期就得进棺材啦。◇ be dead and buried

daisy

(as) fresh as a daisy [əz 'freʃəzə 'deɪzi] [话] **精神十足** daisy 有好几种,在英国多指"英国雏菊",在美国则称"牛眼菊"(oxeye daisy)。本条的字面意义是"象雏菊那样新鲜"。*After my nap, I felt as fresh as a daisy.* 午睡以后,我感到精神头很足。虽然可以这样说,但是本条习用语多半是在"经过重劳动、激烈运动、拚命学习后,依然毫不疲倦、精神十足"的场合使用。另外,虽然主要与 be 动词一起使用,但也可以如上面的例句那样,伴以 feel, 或者 look, seem 等。*Pete is in top condition. He was as fresh as a daisy even after climbing Mt. Taishan.* 皮特的身体状况极佳,他登泰山之后还丝毫没有倦容。*It's hard to believe you stayed up all night studying. You look fresh as a daisy.* 你学习了一整夜,真令人几乎难以相信。看起来,你还是精神十足嘛。在强打精神的场合也常使用,例如:*Me tired? Whaddya mean? I'm fresh as a daisy.* 你说我疲倦了? 别瞎说啦! 我精神头儿很足啊。◇ completely refreshed [fresh]

dam

water over the dam → WATER

damn

damn (*something* [*someone*]) **with faint praise** → PRAISE

damned

I'll be damned. ['aɪlbi 'dæ:md] [俗] **万万没有想到** → I'll be HORNSWOGGLED.

dance

dance attendance on *someone* → ATTENDANCE

give *someone* **a song and dance** (about *something*) → SONG

dark

be (completely) in the dark [(kəm'plitli) ɪnðə 'dɑ(:)rk] [口] **(完全)不知道** 原意是:"对情况毫无所知,如在黑暗之中"。但是,这一表达法丝毫没有急切地想要从黑暗当中走出来的意思。只是在某种事情、计划等没有得到通知的场合使用。在会话中常说 *I'm still in the dark on that point.* 关于这一点,我还不了解[还没有人通知我]。但更多的场合是用 completely 加强语气。*I'm completely in the dark as to his thinking at present.* 目前我对他的想法完全不了解[没有被告知]。另外,除 be 动词外,还常用 keep 构成 keep *someone* (completely) in the dark 的说法。意思是:"(完全)不叫某人知道",因而更强烈地表现出"把某人装到闷葫芦里"的感觉。*They keep me in the dark about that.* 关于那件事情,他们对我是完全保密的。*They're being kept completely in the dark concerning her movements.* 关于她的活动情况,他们完全被蒙在鼓里了。◇ be (completely) uninformed

keep *someone* **(completely) in the dark** [.ki(:)p ~ ɪnðə 'dɑ(:)rk] [口] **(完全)不叫某人知道** → be (completely) in the DARK

a shot in the dark → SHOT

whistle in the dark [.hwɪsl ɪnðə 'dɑ(:)rk] [口] **嘴上逞强** 这一表达法最初的构思是:一个人在漆黑的地方行走,心里本来很害怕,但是竭力不露出害怕的样子,硬要"在黑暗中吹口哨"。一般用进行时。*A: Why should I be afraid of a haunted house? B: There you go again—whistling in the dark.* 甲:我怎么会害怕闹鬼的房子呢? 乙:你又来了,净嘴上逞强。原来只在谈到恐怖的时候使用,但是现在,如下面的例句所示,可用于自己担心的事情以及其他各种状况。为了加强语气,常加 just 或 only。*Mac says he could beat me with one hand tied behind his back? Don't worry. He's just whistling in the dark.* 麦克说他把一只手绑在身后也能打败我吗? 你不用担心。他只是嘴巴逞能而已。*Jim is only whistling in the dark when he says his company can outsell ours.* 吉姆说他那个公司的销售额会超过我们,那只是嘴上逞强而已。◇ try to sound brave [confident] / say that [*something*] in order to hide *one's* fears

darned

I'll be darned. ['aɪlbi 'dɑːrnd] [话] **简直意想不到** → I'll be HORNSWOGGLED.

date

ask *someone* **for a date** [.æsk ~ fərə 'deɪt] [口] **(男性)提出约会** → make a DATE (with *someone*)

a bilnd date [ə .blaɪn(:)'deɪt] [口] **由介绍人安排的男女初次会面** 直译为"盲目的约会"。男女双方互不相识,由第三者(媒人)介绍会面。中国过去叫做"相看"或"相亲"。虽然从媒人口里听到一些预备知识,但是不到会面现场,双方是互不相识的,所以叫作 blind date。*I've got a blind date tonight with my roommate's sister.* 今天晚上我与同屋住的朋友的妹妹经人介绍初次会面。*I arranged a blind date for my cousin who is visiting me this weekend.* 这个周末我的表妹前来看望我,我为她安排了一次"相亲"。*I met my wife on a blind date.* 我是由媒人介绍"相亲",跟我妻子认识的。这一表达法除"相亲"的意义外,又指"相亲的对象"。*My blind date was so ugly that I wished for a moment that I were blind, too.* 我相看的对象长得实在太丑了,我简直希望在那一瞬间我的眼睛什么也看不见。◇ a sight-unseen date

get a date (with *someone*) [.gedə 'deɪt] [口] **(男性)得到约会的承诺** → make a DATE (with *someone*)

have a date (with *someone*) [.hævə 'deɪt] [口] **有约会** → make a DATE (with *someone*)

a heavy date [ə ˌhevi ˈdeɪt] [话] **重要的约会** heavy 一词有 heavy petting (热烈地拥抱)、heavy necking (热烈地搂脖子)等用法,但在这里只表示 important (重要),并没有"热烈"的意味。 *Can I borrow your new suit tonight? I've got a heavy date.* 今天晚上你的那套新衣服借给我好吗? 我有重要的约会。 *No use talking to Dick about going to the baseball game. He has a heavy date with Ophelia Bumps.* 你跟迪克说去看棒球比赛也没用。他跟奥菲莉亚·班普斯有重要的约会。 *Necrophyle is so unpopular, any date he gets he considers a heavy date.* 内克罗菲尔太不招人喜欢了,因此,对于他来说,任何一个约会都是重要的约会。如以上的例句所示,这一说法一般代表男性的观点,但偶尔也可以由女性说出来,例如: *Hortense has a heavy date with Fatty Doughbutt.* 霍腾斯跟法提·杜巴特有重要的约会。◇ an important [a big] date

make a date (with *someone*) [ˌmeɪkə ˈdeɪt] [口] **约定日期** 许多人把 make a date 理解为"男女约定幽会"或"约定幽会日期",这是错误的。date 原为"日期"的意思,后来发展为"决定与人相见的日期",又发展为"定期与人相见"和"相见的约定",一般是按照这些意义使用。这个 date 根据所结合的动词的不同,而使"约见"对象的种类发生变化。首先,我们先举几个例子说明本条条头的 make a date 吧。 *I've got to make a date with my dentist. I've got a bad toothache.* 我得和牙科大夫预约看病了。我的牙疼得很厉害。 *I made a date with my lawyer to discuss the matter.* 我跟律师已经约定日期讨论那个问题了。 *Mrs. Jones says she hopes to make a date with her usual hairdresser.* 琼斯夫人说她希望跟一向为她做头发的理发师预约个日期。如以上的例句所示,一般来说,make a date 是在"与医生、律师、理发师等专业人员约会"的场合,也就是在"为了与专业人员见面而预约"的场合使用。即便用错了,也不会构成"男女约定幽会"的意思。这是因为 make 一词具有的意味是:"由于是办事情或处理事务,只要一打招呼,对方当然是会接见的"。顺便提一下,本条的 make a date 与 make an appointment 大致相同。如果硬要指出它们的不同之处,那就是 appointment 具有较强的事务性的意味。如上所述,从 make a date 首先联想到的是专业人员,但根据不同的情况,也可以应用于亲戚、熟人、朋友等(如为朋友,则多用于女性)。但是,即使在这种场合,这一表达法也具有"要办某种事情或事务"的味道,因此,为了表明"为什么相见",一般都伴有 to+不定式动词(为了……)或者前置词 for (为了……)。 *My wife has made a date to have [for] lunch with her aunt.* 我的妻子约她的婶娘一起吃午饭。在这一句里的 to have lunch 也可以作广义解释为"有事情"。其次。如果是 ask *someone* for a date 或 get a date (with *someone*),那就是以"异性"为对象了。前者是"男性提出约会",后者是"男性得到约会的承诺"。不过,前者的对象虽然是"异性",但一般不包括情人,只限于"未确定关系的对手",理由很简单: ask 一词含有"恳求允许"的意味,如果是关系比较稳定,相会是当然的事情,使用这一表达法就不自然了。 *I think I'll ask Betty for a date.* 我想跟贝蒂约会。 *Did you get a date with Sally for the dance?* 你已经同萨莉约好去跳舞了吗? 最后,还有一个 have (got) a date (with *someone*)。对方是专业人员也好,亲戚、熟人、朋友也好,比较固定的对象也好,全都可以使用。另外,男性可以使用,女性使用也无妨。下面且举两个例句,可略见一斑。 *I have a date with the dentist tomorrow.* 我跟牙科医生预约明天去看病。 *I have a date with Sue [Sam] tomorrow night.* 我和苏[萨姆]明天晚上有个约会。◇ make an appointment

day

call it a day [ˌkɔːlɪdə ˈdeɪ] [话] **今天就到这儿吧** 根据上下文,偶尔也可以作"这就叫一天"解释,但是通常意为"一天(的工作)到此结束",在使用时采取 *Let's call it a day.* 咱们今天就到此结束。的形式。因为在英语中 finish 是“结束”的意思，所以常听到有人在本来应该说 Let's call it a day. 的时候却说 Let's finish。但是，大家必须注意：后者的意思是“现在手头的工作不要停止，一直到干完为止”、“一定要完成它”。 *I'm tired. Let's call it a day.* 我累了。今天就到这儿吧。 *I'm afraid we'll have to call it a day. I have an important meeting this evening.* 我看，咱们只好到此为止啦。今天晚上我要参加一个重要的会议。 *When it got dark we were forced to call it a day.* 天都黑了，咱们必须停止工作了。同义的表达法还有 call it quits (for the day) (→ call it QUITS)。 *I'm tired. Let's call it quits (for the day).* 我累了。工作就到此为止吧。另外，根据上下文，call it a day 也可以用于表示“全天不干工作睡大觉”的意思。 *I'm sleepy. I think I'll call it a day.* 我太困啦，今天干脆睡大觉吧。◇ quit for the day

(as) clear as day [əz.klɪ(:)rəz 'deɪ] [口] **显而易见** → (as) clear as DAYLIGHT

day after day ['deɪæftər 'deɪ] [口] **天天** → DAY in and day out

day in and day out [.deɪ'ɪnən .deɪ'aut] [口] **每天每日** 这是在强调“每天每日总是老一套”的时候使用的表达法，一般不用于谈论使自己满意或高兴的事情的场合。 *It must be monotonous for bank tellers, counting other people's money day in and day out.* 银行的出纳员每天每日点别人的钞票，一定是枯燥无味的。 *You've been playing day in and day out for over a week now. It's about time you began thinking about studying as well.* 你这样每天每日地玩也有一个多星期啦，应该考虑一下学习的事情了。另外，有时省略 and 而说 day in、day out。又，day after day 的表达法也常用于同样的场合，但语气弱一些。 *It rained day after day during our trip.* 在我们旅行期间，天天下雨。◇ all day long every day

a day off [ə .deɪ 'ɔ:f] [口] **休息日** → an off DAY

Great day. ['greɪt'deɪ] [话] **哎呀呀** → Good NIGHT.

(as) honest as the day is long [ə'zɑnəstəzðə .deɪ .ɪz 'lɔ:ŋ] [口] **非常正直** 字面意义是“象天长那么正直”。特别是在推荐、保举、夸奖人的时候常常使用。 *Your money will be completely safe with Mr. Rightchange. He's as honest as the day is long.* 你把钱存在莱特钱吉先生那里是绝对可靠的，他是一个非常正直的人。 *My son is as honest as the day is long. He would never have stolen your watch.* 我的儿子是一个非常正直的人，他绝对不可能偷你的手表。◇ extremely honest

be late in the day for *something* [.leɪtnðə 'deɪfər ～] [口] **为时过晚** 这一表达法如果没有 for *something* 的部分，只是 (be) late in the day，那就意味着“白天当中晚的时刻”，例如： *We arrived there rather late in the day.* 我们下午很晚的时候到达那里。也就是说，这个 day 不是“一天”，而是与 night (夜) 相对的 day (日)。如果象本条条头那样加上 for *something*，那就是 be too late to be opportune or effective (早已贻误大好时机或有效期)的意思了。在这一场合，in the day 表示“在整个过程中”的意思。 *A: I've decided to try for university after all, Dad. B: Rather late in the day for a decision like that, don't you think? Entrance exams are only about three months away now.* 甲：爸爸，我还是决定考一下大学。乙：难道你不认为现在才下这个决心未免太晚了吗？入学考试离现在只有三个来月的时间啦。如此例所示，late 前多加副词 rather, 以及 too, somewhat, a little 等。另外，在 be late in the day 的后边，除 for *something* 外，可采取 to *do something* 或者 for *someone* to *do something* 的形式。 *This project has to be finished by next week. It's too late in the day to change the basic plans.* 这个设计到下个星期必须完成。改变基本计划已经为时过晚了。 *A: Why don't you take up skiing, Grandpa? B: I'm afraid it's somewhat late in the day for an old man like me to do that. Perhaps I'll try bowling.* 甲：爷爷，你怎

么不滑雪呀？乙：象我这样一个上了年纪的老头，做那种运动怕是为时过晚啦。我还是试试滚木球吧。*I told my husband that it's a little late in the day to be talking about not having any children, seeing as how I'm already over three months pregnant.* 我告诉我的丈夫说，现在讲不要孩子为时有点晚了，我怀孕已经三个多月了。◇ be too late

not give *someone* **the time of day** → TIME

not stand the light of day → LIGHT

an off day [ə ˌnɔːf 'deɪ] [话] **不走运的日子**　这里的 off 是"脱离正轨"的意思。所谓 off day，也就是"无论干什么都不顺当或者老是失败的日子"、"倒霉的日子"。*I'm having an off day today. Nothing seems to go right.* 今天是个不走运的日子，我似乎干什么都不顺利。*Something must be wrong with me. I'm having so many off days recently.* 我一定有点失常了，最近是一连串倒霉的日子。*Everyone suffers from an off day once in a while.* 月有阴晴圆缺，人有旦夕祸福。另外，有些词典把 off day 解释为"休息日"、"不值班的日子"，但是，除极特殊的场合外，本条并不用以表示这种意义。这可能是与表示"休息日"、"不值班的日子"的最普通的用语 a day off 弄混了吧。*You should have a day off. You've been working too hard recently.* 你该休息一天啦。最近你的工作太累了。◇ a day in which everything seems to go wrong

pass the time of day (with *someone*) → TIME

a red-letter day [ə ˌred'ledər ˌdeɪ] [口] **值得纪念的日子**　这一表达法的来源是：古时候，天主教会用红色的文字把节日和祝圣的日子写到日程表上。一般的词典译为"节日"，至少说现在不使用这一意义。*It's a great honor for us to meet you, Mr. President. This is a red-letter day for us that we'll remember all our lives.* 总统阁下，我们能够见到您，感到非常荣幸，这是一个值得我们永生纪念的日子。如此例所示，本条习用语是"对于个人或机关有重要意义的、值得纪念的日子"的意思。*September the twenty-first has always been a red-letter day for us. That was the day in 1945 that our son, who had been reported missing in action, returned from the war.* 9月21日永远是我们值得纪念的日子。我们的儿子据传在作战时下落不明，1945年的那一天却从前线回来了。*April 1st seems to have been some kind of red-letter day for my uncle, but I can't recall exactly why.* 4月1日是我叔父的一个什么值得纪念的日子，但是我想不起来究竟是怎么一回事了。◇ a memorable day [occasion]

save (*something*) **for a rainy day** [ˌseɪv fərə ˌreɪni 'deɪ] [口] **有所储备以防万一**　a rainy day 是"下雨的日子"，指"真有必要的时候"、"困难的时候"。save for 是"为……做储备"的意思。*We never spend my husband's bonus. We always save it for a rainy day.* 我们从来不动我丈夫的奖金。我们总是把它储蓄起来，以备万一急需。*We'd better not spend all our money now. We should save something for a rainy day.* 我们现在最好不要把所有的钱都用光了。我们要有所储备，以防万一。如以上两个例句所示，一般是在谈到钱的时候使用。但也有象下一例句那样，使用于钱以外的东西，特别是"饮料和食品"。*We didn't eat all the canned goods you gave us. We decided to save some of them for a rainy day.* 你给我们的罐头，我们没有全都吃掉。我们决定存上几听，以备万一的时候使用。在讲一般节约的场合，通常省略代入 *something* 的词句。例如：*You spend your money too freely. You should learn to save for a rainy day.* 你花钱太随便啦。你必须学会节约，以备万一。◇ save (*something*) for a time when *it* is really needed

That'll be the day! ['ðæːdlbiðə ˌdeɪ] [话] **那样的事永远等不来**　这里的 the day 是"大好的日子"。本条的字面意义是"那一定是个大好日子吧！"*Only one more year until I get out of the army. Ahh, that'll be the day!* 我只剩一年就要从军

队复员了。啊,真盼着那一天! 如此例所示,按照本来的意义,可以用于确实能够实现的事情。但是,这一表达法表示如此肯定的场合却是极少的。一般如: *A: Jimmy says he's decided to get up at five o'clock every morning and study English. B: Hah! That'll be the day!* 甲:吉米说他决定每天早晨五点钟起床学习英语。乙:哼! 等太阳从西边出来吧! 象这样作为反语使用,表示"那样的日子永远等不来",带有极大的讽刺意味。*A: Maybe the boss will give you a big raise. B: Ha! That'll be the day!* 甲:老板也许会把你的工资提高一大截呢。乙:哼! 太阳不会从西边出来。*A: I hear that France is going to lift all import restrictions. B: That'll be the day!* 甲:我听说法国要废除有关进口的一切限制。乙:决不会有那样的事。◇ I'll believe that only when I see it [when it happens]. / It'll never happen. / Impossible!

daylight

(as) clear as daylight [əz'klı(:)rəz 'deı,laıt] [口] **昭然若揭** 逐字翻译为"象日光一样清楚",相当于汉语的"昭然若揭"、"一清二楚"、"显而易见"等。*It's clear as daylight. She just wants to marry you for your money.* 那不是明摆着吗? 她是为了钱才想嫁给你。*How can you be so dense? The solution is as clear as daylight.* 你的脑子怎么那么笨? 答案是非常清楚的。有时用 day 代替 daylight,意味相同。*Of course! Don't you see? The answer was right before our eyes all the time, as clear as day.* 啊,对啦! 你还不明白? 答案始终摆在我们的眼前,简直是昭然若揭呀。◇ perfectly obvious

day's

be all in a day's work → WORK

days

have seen [known] better days [hæv ,si(:)n / ,noun ,bedər'deız] [口] **今非昔比** 使用范围极广,包括个人的经济和健康情况,公司的生意好坏,人与人的关系,地区或环境的好坏,等等。这一说法是把"令人不满意的(或者过于平淡无奇的)不今"与"比较良好的(或者繁荣昌盛的)昔"做对比,基本的意思是:"过去有过比现在好的时期"。有时把重点放在"过去",用于表示"好时候也有过呀"的怀旧心情;也有时仅仅用于强调现在的不怎么好的状态。正因为如此,根据上下文的不同,这一表达法会具有种种不同的意义,相互之间差异很大。用 seen 或用 known,意义不变。但比较起来,一般都用 seen。*He has seen better days.* 他也有过黄金时代。*The shabbily dressed old man sitting on the park bench was obviously a gentleman who had known better days.* 在公园的长凳上坐着的那位衣衫褴褛的老人显然是个有过美好日子的绅士。*Our company is not doing too badly, though I'll admit that it has seen better days.* 我们公司现在的状况不算太坏,但是过去比现在的确强得多。也用于表达身体的健康情况和精神的饱满状态。*A: How are you? B: Well, I've seen better days.* 甲:你身体好吗? 乙:唉,比过去差多啦。下面是应用于人际关系的例子: *Our marriage has seen better days.* 我们的婚姻过去曾经是很甜蜜的。可以应用于地区或环境,下面的例句是对当地居民的生活水平做今昔的对比: *One could tell at a glance that the neighborhood, while still respectable, had known better days.* 那一带不算太坏,不过一眼就可以看出,过去比现在要好得多。也常用这一表达法来谈论"物",如破车、旧鞋、老狗等等,表示"旧了"、"老了"的意思。原来是个戏谑的用语。*These shoes have seen better days. I guess I'd better buy a new pair.* 这双鞋已经破旧不堪了,我看还是买一双新的为好。*This old dog has seen better day.* 这条狗已经老态龙钟了。◇ experienced better [more affluent] times

D.C.

D.C. ['di:'si:] [话] **华盛顿市** 美国人常常把 the District of Columbia (哥伦比亚特区)的缩略 D.C. 作为美国首都

Washington 的同义词使用。D.C. = Washington 这一用法之所以产生，当然是由于 Washington 在 the District of Columbia，而前者占有后者的全部面积，亦即两者在地理上是完全同一的区域。顺便说一下：美国独立以后，各州(当时为 13 个州)都想把首都放在自己的州内。各州领导人为了避免争执，达成一项协议：由维吉尼亚州和马里兰州各让出少许土地，成立一个特别区，定名为 the District of Columbia，归联邦政府直接管辖。也可以这样说：在美国脱离英国而独立之后，美国政府又脱离美国(各州)而独立了。◇ Washington

dead

(as) dead as a doornail → DOORNAIL
dead drunk → DRUNK
a dead duck → DUCK
a dead giveaway → GIVEAWAY
a dead heat → HEAT
a dead marine → MARINE
be dead on *one's* feet → FEET
a dead pigeon [ə ˌde(ː)d ˈpɪdʒən] [话] **注定要完蛋的人[或事物]** → a dead DUCK
be a dead ringer → RINGER
a dead soldier → SOLDIER
be dead tired [ˈde(ː)d ˈtaɪrd] [口] **筋疲力尽** → be dead on *one's* FEET
be dead to the world → WORLD
over *someone's* dead body → BODY

deaf

fall on deaf ears → EARS

deal

a big deal [ə ˌbɪg ˈdi(ː)l] [话] **大人物** → Big DEAL.

Big deal. [ˈbɪ(ː)g ˈdiːl] [话] (讽刺口气)了不起呀！ 请注意：开头大写，最后打句点。如果只是 big deal，首要意义为"大生意"。*Our company just completed a big deal with a German trading company.* 我们公司刚刚与一家德国贸易公司做成了一笔大生意。从这一意义发展，形成一个比喻意义，即指在商业、社交、体育运动等方面的"重大的[豪华的、杰出的]事项"。*I hear they're having some big deal at the Great Wall Hotel tonight with lots of singers and movie stars.* 听说今天晚上有大批歌唱家和电影明星云集长城饭店，推出一些精采的节目。这个比喻意义的 big deal，如果在会话中以 Big deal. 的形式单独使用，就变成象条头那样讽刺的意味："了不起呀！"或者"阔气得很呀！" *So after all the noise the union made, they finally got us a five dollars a week raise. Big deal!* 工会大嚷大叫了半天，终于给我们争来了工资的提高，每周五美元整。真了不起呀！ *A: Did you know that your ex-girl friend has become engaged to a millionaire? B: Yeah. Big deal. Now her nose will be so high in the air she'll probably suffer from oxygen starvation.* 甲：你知道你过去的女朋友跟一位百万富翁订婚了吗？ 乙：嗯，阔得很啊！ 现在她的鼻子会抬得老高老高的，好象得了氧气缺乏病一样。另外，以上的所有 big deal 都指"人以外的东西"。但也可以应用于"人"，意思是"了不起的人物"、"大人物"。在这一场合，big deal 本身并不含有什么讽刺的意味。 *Ted thinks he's a big deal since he got that Italian sportscar.* 特德自从买了那辆意大利赛车之后，就以为自己是个了不起的人物啦。 *A: Who's that guy with the boss? B: I dunno. Some big deal from New York.* 甲：跟老板在一起的那个家伙是谁？ 乙：我不知道。听说是从纽约来的大人物。◇ I'm unimpressed.

the deal falls through [ðəˈdi(ː)l ˌfɔ(ː)lzˈθruː] [口] **交易失败** 商业界常用的表达法。deal 是 transaction (交易)的轻松的说法；fall through 是 collapse (崩溃、垮台)的意思。主语有时也用其他的词，例如 plan (计划)，negotiations (交涉)等，但最常被用到的是 deal。 *Despite all our efforts, the deal fell through.* 虽然我们尽了所有的努力，那笔交易终于没有做成。the deal 中的 the 有时用 this, that, *one's* 来代替。 *You have made your last mistake in this company. If this deal falls through, you're fired.* 在这个公司，你上次所犯的错误是最后一次了。如果这笔生意又以失败而

告终，就解雇你。*That deal wouldn't have fallen through if we had made more careful preparations.* 如果我们更细致地做好准备，那笔买卖是不会做不成功的。反义语为 the DEAL goes through。→ *one's* PLANS fall through ◇ the transaction is not successfully completed [fails]

the deal goes through [ðə'di(:)l .gouz'θru:] [口] **交易顺利进行** 这里的 deal 是 transaction (交易)的轻松说法。go through 是"通过(交易的终点)"亦即"(交易)顺利进行"。这是商业界特别常用的表达法，除"合同进展顺利"、"签订合同"的场合外，也使用于"按照合同交易已经完成"的场合。*The deal went through without a hitch.* 交易进行得非常顺利。go through 本身就含有"顺利"的意思，但在这一场合，按照英语的语调，需要加 without a hitch (毫无阻碍地、轻轻快快地)。如以下的例句所示，the deal 中的 the，根据具体情况，可改变为 this 或 that。*If this deal doesn't go through, we'll have to try another approach.* 如果这笔交易进展不顺利，我们必须采取其他的方法试试看。*If that deal had gone through, we'd have been in the chips right now.* 如果那笔交易进行得很顺利的话，我们现在就已经发大财啦。反义语是 the DEAL falls through。◇ the transaction is successfully completed [is successful]

deal *someone* **in** (on *something*) ['di(:)l ~ 'ɪ(:)n] [话] **让(某人)入伙** 原为扑克牌游戏用语，deal 是"分牌"的意思。*If you're going to play poker, deal me in.* 如果你们玩扑克的话，也分给我一份牌。也就是"我也想玩，算我一个"的意思。转用于比喻，表示"参加做买卖、旅行、娱乐及其他规划"的意思。*John says that if we need someone else to put up money for our new company we can deal him in.* 约翰说，如果我们的新公司还需要有人投资的话，他也可以入股。一般使用 deal *someone* in 的形式，有时后边加上个 on *something*。但请注意，deal *someone* in on *something* 中 *something* 的前置词必须用 on，决不能够说 in *something*。*Frank wants us to deal him in on the trip to Hawaii.* 弗兰克希望跟我们一起到夏威夷去旅行。反义语为 DEAL *someone* out (on *something*)。◇ include *someone* (in *something*)

deal *someone* **out** (on *something*) [.di(:)l ~ 'aut] [话] **让(某人)退出一伙** 原为扑克牌游戏用语，意思是：一个人对他的牌友说"这一次[从今天起]不分给我牌了"。*Hey, how come you're dealing me out?* 喂，你们怎么不分给我牌呀？象这样说的场合是有的。但是，一般都用命令式，在由于本人的意志而"脱离伙伴"的时候使用，如：*Deal me out on the next hand. I have to make a telephone call.* 下一把牌别算我。我必须去打一个电话。转作比喻，表示"脱离做生意、旅行、娱乐、及其他规划的伙伴"的意思。在这一场合，仍然多用命令式，而且是根据本人的意志"退出"。*I'd like to go to Hawaii with you guys, but if you're going to go by boat, deal me out. I get seasick.* 我很愿意跟你们这些人一道去夏威夷，但是如果你们坐船去，就别算上我啦，因为我晕船。另外，当说明退出什么具体活动时，在英语中采取 deal *someone* out on *something* 的形式，务请注意：前置词用 on 而不用 from。*Deal me out on the hike next week. I have something else I've go to do.* 下个星期的远足不要算上我啦。我有别的事情非做不可。反义语为 DEAL *someone* in (on *something*)。◇ not include *someone* (in *something*)

Dear

a Dear John letter → LETTER

death

bore *someone* **to death** [.bo(:)r ~ tə'de(:)θ] [口] **使人烦得要死** → bore *someone* to TEARS

be death on *something* [*someone*][①] ['de(:)-.θɔ(:)n ~] [话] **巧妙处理** 字面意义是"……对于某事(某人)来说是死亡"。这当然是一个比喻的表达法。根据立场的不同，可能有两种解释。例如说 A is death on B. ① 从 A 的立场来看，"B 是很好对付的人，一下子就可以把他打死"；②从B的立场来看，"A是一个极为可怕的人，简直可以叫人死"。本条讲的是①的意义。至于②的意义，见下一条 be DEATH on *something* [*someone*]②。所谓"B是很好对付的人"，也就是"能很巧妙地处理B"，汉语俗语叫"一物降一物"。*That batter is death on fast balls.* 那位击球员能够很巧妙地对付快球。*Be careful when you play tennis with Lee. He's death on baseline shots.* 你跟李打网球的时候千万多加小心。他特别善于抽底线球。*Our cat is death on rats.* 我家的猫是抓耗子的好手。on的后边绝大多数是接 *something*，但也有时接 *someone*。*The Red Baron was death on inexperienced enemy pilots.* 对于初上战场的敌方飞行员，红男爵有如猫捉老鼠一般。The Red Baron是第一次世界大战期间德国著名的飞机驾驶员里希特豪芬男爵(Baron von Richthofen)的绰号。在以上的例句中，A(主语)是人；在下面的例句中，主语是没有生命的。意思是："A对B特别有效"。*Dr. Pauling claims that vitamin C is death on colds.* 波林博士声称，维生素C对感冒特别有效。*This powder is death on cockroaches.* 这种粉剂治蟑螂效果特别好。*This missile is death on fighter planes.* 这种导弹对战斗机有巨大威力。◇ handle *something* very easily / be expert at disposing of *something* [*someone*] / be very effective against *something*

be death on *something someone*]② [ˈde(ː)ˌθɔ(ː)n ～] [话] **严厉对待** 按最初的构思，"对……来说是死"的意思就是"要求严格，达到使其死的程度"。它表示主语对on以下的东西[人]极端厌恶、不能忍受的心情。*Our English teacher is death on sloppy writing.* 我们的英语老师对于写字潦草是严厉对待的。*My grandfather is death on smoking.* 我的祖父极端厌恶吸烟。对于人也常使用。*My husband is death on unruly children.* 我的丈夫对于不规矩的孩子是非常严厉的。*The new department head is death on lazy employees.* 新的部长对待懒惰的部下是非常严厉的。→ be DEATH on *something* [*someone*]① ◇ be very strict with *something* [*someone*] / be very opposed to *something*

be embarrassed to death [emˈbæ(ː)rəstəˈde(ː)θ] [话] **羞愧得要死** → *one* could have DIED

the kiss of death → KISS

deck

clear the deck (for action) [ˈklɪ(ː)rðəˈde(ː)k (fəˈræːkʃən)] [话] **清除障碍(便于行动)** 本来是海军用语，意思是："清理甲板，准备战斗"。*Enemy ship sighted! Clear the deck for action!* 发现敌舰！清理甲板，准备战斗！这是按照字面的用法。作为比喻，一般用于表示"搬开东西"的意思。如：*Let's clear the deck for action. We've got to get this work finished today.* 咱们把障碍物统统搬开。这件工作，咱们今天非干完不可。*Clear the deck for action. All of these New Year's cards must be addressed and mailed by this evening.* 把妨碍工作的东西全搬开。今天傍晚以前，所有这些贺年片都必须写好姓名住址并且寄走。可以用 of *something* 代替 for action。在这一场合，不限于"物"，在谈到"问题"等时也可以使用。*Let's clear the deck of all old business prior to bringing any new questions before the meeting.* 在向会议提出任何新的问题之前，先把残留的事情全部处理干净吧。*Once the deck has been cleared of the old foreign exchange law and all its attendant problems, foreign trade will develop much more smoothly.* 一旦废除旧的外汇法并解决附带的所有问题，对外贸易会非常顺利地发展下去。除"物"或"问题"外，这一表达法也可以应用于"人"。*Clear the deck, everyone! Let the ambulance through!* 大家赶快躲开！让救护车开过去。如此例所示，在应用于"人"时用命令式，表示"躲开！躲开！"的意思，一般省略 for action。*O.K., everybody, clear the deck. Your father is going to show you how spring housecleaning should* *really be done.* 喂，大家都躲开啦！躲开啦！爸爸要叫你们看看春季大扫除应该怎么搞。*Clear the deck! We're coming through!* 躲开！躲开！我们要走过去！另外，也可以用复数 decks；但在美国英语中，一般用单数。◇ get everything *one* doesn't need [get *something*] out of the way / finish (up) [get rid of] *something* / get out of the way

deck *someone* [ˈde(ː)k ～] [话] **击倒** 来自海军俚语的表达法。这里的 deck 意为"把对手击倒在 deck(甲板)上"。主要用于在拳击比赛中把人击倒的场合。*The man decked me with one blow.* 那个人一拳就把我击倒了。*The challenger decked the champion twice in the first round.* 在第一回合，挑战者两次把冠军击倒。虽然并不普遍，但也有用于在拳击以外的情况下把人击倒的场合。*A burst from an enemy machine gun decked two men on my right.* 敌人机关枪的一阵连发射击，把我右边的两个人打倒了。◇ knock *someone* down

deck *oneself* **out in** *something* [ˌdek ～ ˈaudɪn ～] [话] **打扮起来** deck 有"装饰"的意义，加上 out 就产生了"充分地"、"漂亮地"的感觉。本条可以理解为"把自己漂漂亮亮地打扮起来"，但这是一个相当轻松的表达法，因而有时完全与汉语俗语"穷打扮"吻合。为了加强语气，可加 all，作 deck *oneself* all out～。*For the party, Joan decked herself out in a red evening gown, a double rope of pearls, high heels and a fur cape.* 为了参加社交晚会，琼把自己打扮了起来，她穿上红色的夜礼服，戴上一串双层的珍珠项链，蹬上高跟鞋，披上毛皮披肩。在讲"打扮"的状态的时候，使用 be (all) decked out (in *something*)的形式。*What are you all decked out for?* 你有什么事，打扮得这样漂亮？*Ralph arrived at the office decked out in morning clothes.* 垃尔夫穿着晨礼服到公司来了。另外，特别是 be decked out 的场合，不仅用于人，也用于物。*The room was all decked out for Christmas.* 为了过圣诞节，房间完全装饰起来了。◇ dress *oneself* up in *something*

hit the deck[1] [ˌhɪtðə ˈde(ː)k] [话] **卧倒(隐蔽)** 源出海军用语。直译为"打甲板"，意思是"把自己的身体投到甲板上"，亦即"俯卧到甲板上"。多在受敌机攻击时作为口令使用。*Hit the deck! Here comes an enemy plane!* 卧倒！敌机来袭！后来进一步推广，意义变为"在受到攻击时，把身体赶快伏在地板或地面上"。*When we realized someone was shooting at us, we all hit the deck.* 当我们发现有人在向我们射击的时候，大家全都立即卧倒了。*When the angry old woman began swinging her mop, all the men hit the deck.* 当愤怒的老太太开始挥舞她的拖把的时候，所有的男人都赶忙卧倒了。也可以用以表示"突然倒下"或者"被打翻在地"的意思，例如：*One blow from the big man's fist and Shane hit the deck.* 沙恩吃了大汉一拳，马上倒在地上了。◇ throw *oneself* down (on the ground, floor, etc.) / fall down

hit the deck[2] [ˌhɪtðə ˈde(ː)k] [话] **迅速起床** 与 hit the deck[1]同样，原为海军用语。但是，这一表达法是 hit the deck with *one's* feet (用脚敲甲板)，也就是从床上一跳起来，脚就落到甲板上了。当然，现在已经不限于海军，普通人也广泛使用，但有一点请读者注意：这一表达法经常带有"生气勃勃，有如生龙活虎一般"的含义。*O.K., you guys, hit the deck. It's after seven o'clock.* 好啦，你们赶快起床，已经过七点啦。*When I heard someone yell "Fire!" I hit the deck running.* 当我听到有人喊叫"失火啦！"的时候，立即跳下床跑了出去。*The nights seem too short. No sooner than I hit the sack, it's time to hit the deck again.* 夜似乎太短了，我刚一上床睡觉，马上又到了起床的时间。◇ get up [out of bed]

play against a stacked deck [ˌpleɪ əˌgenstə ˌstækːˈde(ː)k] [口] **人家预先做了手脚，自己必输** → play with a stacked DECK

play with a stacked deck [ˌpleɪ wɪðə ˌstækːˈde(ː)k] [口] **自己预先做了手脚，必然取胜[有利]** a deck 是"一副扑克牌"，a stacked deck 是由扑克牌游戏用

语 stack the deck 产生的表达法。stack the deck 与 stack the CARDS 相同，原意为“以不正当洗牌方式，使好牌到自己的手中来”。因此，条头 play with a stacked deck 的字面意义就是“以不正当的洗牌方式玩扑克牌”。但请读者注意，可没有 play with stacked cards 的说法。 *The gambler was caught playing with a stacked deck.* 那个赌徒洗牌作弊，被人抓住了。转作比喻使用，意思是“在开始前，预先做好手脚，使自己获得胜利[有利]”，也就是某人所干的事情全是为自己取胜[有利]而预先摆好了圈套。 *Whatever you do, don't get involved with the Mafia. They play with a stacked deck.* 你不管做什么事情，都不要跟黑手党打交道。他们的所作所为，总是为自己得利而预先摆好圈套。 *You can try negotiating with them if you want, but you can't win. They always play with a stacked deck.* 如果你愿意的话，你可以跟他们交涉一下看。但是，你是不可能取胜的。他们总是事先做好对自己有利的安排。另外还有一个表达法是 play against a stacked deck，把 with 改成了 against，这也是一个习用语，意思是“玩扑克的对手持有以不正当洗牌方式弄到的好牌”，也就是“对方预先做了手脚，自己玩下去必输无疑”。不过，play with a stacked deck 显然带有人为的意味，而 play against a stacked deck 则表示社会或事情本身就对自己不利，多半具有客观性。 *Developing nations complain that in dealing with the advanced countries, they're always playing against a stacked deck.* 发展中国家抱怨说，在与发达国家打交道时，他们永远处于先天的不利地位。 *Anyone who tries to start in this business without connections is playing against a stacked deck.* 任何人企图不通过人事关系来搞这个买卖，他从一开始就处于不利的地位。◇ operate with things arranged to *one's* own advantage

stack the deck [ˌstæ(ː)kðə ˈde(ː)k] [口] **玩弄花招** → stack the CARDS

deejay

a deejay [ə ˈdiːˈdʒeɪ] [话] **流行音乐唱片节目的播音员** 取 disc jockey 的第一个字母 d 和 j，按照发音缀成的习用语。 *Who is your favorite deejay?* 你最喜欢的流行音乐播音员是谁？也可以写作 dee-jay 或 DJ。 → a disc JOCKEY ◇ an announcer who plays records on the radio

deep

give *something* **the deep six** [ˌgɪv ～ ðə ˌdi(ː)pˈsɪ(ː)ks] [话] **抛弃……** → DEEP SIX *something*

go off the deep end → END

deep-six

deep-six *something* [ˈdiːpˈsɪks ～] [话] **丢弃废物** 本来是海上用语，意思是“沉入六寻的海底”。后来在口语中作为名词使用，意为“水葬”。又进一步发展成为动词，具“丢弃”的意味。 *My room is getting pretty crowded. I think I'll deep-six these old books.* 我房间里的东西太多了，我想把这些旧书扔掉。如此例所示，只用于表示“丢掉无用之物”的意思。但是，自从水门事件以后，也常常使用于把见不得人的东西“偷偷丢掉”的场合。 *The Watergate conspirators planned to deep-six an incriminating file in the Potomac River.* 水门事件的同谋者计划把成为罪证的文件扔到波托马克河里去。 *The criminals succeeded in deep-sixing the evidence just before the police arrived.* 罪犯们赶在警察到来之前把证据都消毁了。 *Before Tom got married, he deep-sixed all the pictures of his old girl friends.* 汤姆在结婚之前，把他过去的女朋友们的照片全都扔掉了。也用 give *something* the deep six 的形式，但这一表达法中不包含“偷偷地”的意味。例如： *This desk is getting pretty old. Why don't we give it the deep six?* 这个书桌太旧了，咱们把它扔了吧。另外，在以上的例句中，抛弃的对象全都是具体的“物”，但也可以用于“计划”等，例如： *We deep-sixed that plan. [We gave that plan the deep six.]* 我们没有采纳那个计

划。◇ dispose of *something*

degree

give *someone* **the third degree** [ˌgɪv ~ ðə ˌθə(ː)rdːə'griː] [话] **严厉讯问** third degree 的字面意义是"第三级"。古时,the Freemasons (共济会员)有三个阶层,即:徒弟、工匠和师傅。师傅会员(master mason) 的阶层称为 the third degree (第三级)。在升为师傅的时候,要进行测验,而测验的一个项目就是"严厉讯问",亦即"升入 the third degree 必须通过严格口试"。后来进一步发展,the third degree 本身竟被人们用来表示"严厉讯问"的意思了。*The police gave the suspect the third degree in an effort to trip him up and make him confess.* 警察严厉讯问那个嫌疑犯,努力找出他话中的漏洞,使他坦白交待。如此例所示,最初使用的意义是"警察长时间的、集中火力的严厉讯问",后来转用于其他事情,而且广泛流行。*The boss gave me the third degree about that mix-up in the orders we sent out yesterday.* 老板为了昨天发出订货时搞错了的事对我严厉盘问。*So I didn't get the job. So what? You don't have to give me the third degree about it.* 我没有得到那个工作。你问为什么?关于这件事,你没有必要严厉责问我。如以上的例句所示,经常同 give 一起使用。get the third degree (from *someone*) 也是一个定型的说法,意思是"受到严厉的询问"。 *I got the third degree from my dad about getting home so late last night.* 昨天夜里我回家太晚了,受到爸爸的严厉责问。另外,也可以与 put *someone* through 或者 subject *someone* to 之类的动词短语一起使用。 *Mr. Lemon is a tough man to see. His secretary really put me through [subjected me to] the third degree before she let me in his office.* 想见到莱蒙先生可不容易。在我进入他的办公室之前,那位女秘书刨根问底,把我问了个底朝天。也有象 third-degree *someone* 这样作为动词的用法,但使用的频率不怎么高。 *You can count on the chief's third-degreeing anyone who overspends on entertainment.* 不论谁超支交际费,必然要受到科长的严厉询问。◇ subject *someone* to intensive questioning / question *someone* (very [so]) closely

delish

delish [də'lɪːʃ] [话] **好吃** 将 delicious 缩短并按发音缀字的习用语。如果前一个元音 [i] 也是重音和长音,作 ['diː'lɪːʃ] 或 ['diːː'lɪːʃ],那是强调"好吃极啦!"的表达法。在这一场合,缀法一般是 deelish 或 dee-lish。但是请注意:它的用法与 delicious 不同,只能作表语。 *These rolls are delish.* 这些面包圈很好吃。*Her pies are deelish.* 她制作的馅饼好吃极啦。*I've never eaten anything so dee-lish.* 我从来没吃过这么好吃的东西。◇ delicious

demote

demote *someone* [də'mout ~] [口] **降低(某人的)地位** → kick *someone* UPSTAIRS

Denmark

Something is rotten in the state of Denmark. [ˌsʌmθɪŋɪz 'rɑ(ː)tn ɪnðə ˌsteɪtəv'denˌmɑ(ː)rk] [口] **有点奇怪** 从莎士比亚 (Shakespeare) 名剧《哈姆雷特》(*Hamlet*) 的对白中借用来的表达法。在第一幕第四场,哈姆雷特由于与国王的幽灵对话,叫部下退下,部下马塞拉斯 (Marcellus)说了这样一句话。原来的意思是:"在丹麦这个国家里,有什么东西正在腐烂。"人们在不能理解或觉得可疑的时候,心里会想"有人在搞什么名堂"或者"他在搞歪门斜道哪"等等,而用这一表达法来表示"有些可疑"、"有点奇怪"、"气味不对"的意思。是一个调子比较轻松的说法。*Upon hearing so many different stories as to how the accident happened, I began to suspect that something was rotten in the state of Denmark.* 关于事故的发生原因,我听到了种种不同的说法,我心里开始感到有点奇怪啦。*No matter how many times I do the accounts, the figures don't add up. If you ask me, something is rotten in the* *state of Denmark*. 我虽然计算了好多次,但是帐目总对不上茬。如果叫我说的话,这里边有点可疑。另外也使用 There is something rotten in the state of Denmark. 的形式,虽与莎翁原作不同,意义则是一样的。*My girl friend canceled our date, saying that she was sick, but when I called her house she was out. There's something rotten in the state of Denmark*. 我的女朋友说是病了,取消了我们的约会,可是当我给她打电话的时候,她却不在家。这真有点可疑。偶尔省略 the state。例如: *Something is rotten in Denmark. The telephone number he gave me doesn't exist*. 真有点奇怪,他给我的电话号码根本不存在。◇ Something suspicious [strange] is going on.

dense

dense ['de(:)nts] [口] **头脑愚钝** → THICK-HEADED

depth

be beyond *one's* **depth** [bi.ɑ(:)nd ~ 'de(:)pθ] [口] **力所不及** → be out of *one's* DEPTH

be out of *one's* **depth** [.audəv~'de(:)pθ] [口] **力所不及** *one's* depth 是"有自己身高那么深的地方"。本条整体的字面意义是"处于身子站不住的地方"。*The river suddenly grew deeper, and the little boy, who couldn't swim, was soon out of his depth*. 河水突然深了起来,那个不会游泳的少年立即陷入了过深的水中。作为比喻,使用方法如下: *I never should have tried to enter that college. The moment I saw the entrance exam I knew I was out of my depth*. 我根本不应该要进那所大学。我一见到入学考试的题目,马上明白自己是力所不及啊。常用 completely 或 entirely 加强语气。*We can't compete with a big company like that. We'd be completely out of our depth*. 我们不能与那样一个大公司竞争,我们根本没有那么大的力量。也常用 beyond 代替 out of。*I thought I was pretty good in math, but I'm beyond my depth in that class*. 我原来以为我的数学很不错,但是在那个班里,我的实力差远啦。另外,也可把这一表达法倒过来,说成 *something* is out of [beyond] *someone's* depth,如最后一个例句的后半部,可以改为 ~ but that class is beyond [out of] my depth. 意思不变。还有两个说法,一是 get out of [beyond] *one's* depth, 一是 go beyond *one's* depth。在要做力所不及[不自量力]的事情时使用。*The murdered man was a small-time gangster who got out of [beyond] his depth when he tried to negotiate with the Mafia*. 被杀的人是一个微不足道的歹徒,他竟不知天高地厚,企图跟黑手党打交道。◇ ((主语 it [*something*])) be too difficult (for *someone*) / be beyond *someone's* competence [ability]

derrière

a derrière [ə .deri'eːr] [话] **(人的)屁股** 从法语直接移植的词,作为一种委婉的、戏谑的表达法使用。*Sweet mother nature appears to have endowed Mrs. Horsey with a rather large derrière*. 大自然是一位温柔的母亲,她似乎赐给霍西夫人一个相当大的臀部。*I slipped and fell on my derrière*. 我脚下一滑,摔了个大屁股墩儿。◇ buttocks

designs

harbor designs on *something* [*someone*] [.hɑ(:)rbər də'zaınzɔ(:)n ~][口] **怀有目的** → have DESIGNS on *something* [*someone*]

have designs on *something* [*someone*] [.hæv də'z aınzɔ(:)n ~] [口] **有所企图** designs 在这里是"(要把某种东西据为己有的)企图、阴谋"的意味,必须加 -s。整个表达法的含义是"为了把某种东西据为己有而在心里给它加上自己的图案(=自己的标记)"。如以下的例句所示,使用范围很广。*You'd better not borrow money from that guy. He has designs on your land*. 你最好不要向那个家伙借钱。他企图把你的土地弄到手。*Be careful. That company has designs on* *two or three of your best employees.* 请你留神。那个公司企图挖走你的两三个优秀职工。本条在企图夺取人命的场合也使用。*Mike learned that the gang had designs on his life.* 迈克了解到歹徒们要阴谋杀害他。也用于表示渔色。*Jack appears to have designs on Mr. Smith's wife.* 杰克似乎对史密斯先生的老婆有不良企图。可以用具有"怀抱"意义的 harbor ['hɑ(:)rbər] 构成 harbor designs on ~,也可以用 upon 代替 on,但二者均略有生硬的感觉。另外,put designs on ~在形式上虽然相似,但它只有"制图"的意义,请不要弄混。◇ have an intention to take *something*

desk

a desk clerk [ə 'des(:),klə(:)rk] [口] **(旅馆的)服务台值勤员** → the front DESK

a desk jockey → JOCKEY

the front desk [ðə ,frʌnt'de(:)sk] [口] **服务台** 指旅馆等的"服务台"。省略 front,只说 desk 也可以懂。*Please call the front desk and ask the check-out time.* 请给服务台打个电话,问一问结帐离开的时间。另有 the registration desk, the registration counter, the check-in counter 等说法。在 the front desk 值勤的工作人员叫做 a desk clerk。*The desk clerk asked Mr. Clark to fill out a registration card.* 服务台值勤员请克拉克先生填写住宿登记卡。◇ the registration desk [counter]

deuce

a deuce [ə 'dju:s] [话] **(扑克牌中的)2** 拉丁语的"2"为 *duŌs*,传入古代法语作 *deus*,又经由法语传入中古英语,形成本条的表达法。在骰子中也使用这一意义("两点"),但在美国人的头脑里,只要一说 deuce,一般都是首先想到扑克牌中的2。在扑克牌游戏中,这一表达法的使用频率与 two 相等。*I held two deuces and a queen.* 我手里有两张 2,一张 Q。*Jack played the deuce of clubs to my trey of hearts.* 我出红心 3,杰克出了梅花 2。◇ a two

devices

leave *someone* **to** *his* **own devices** [,li(:)v ~ tə ~ ,oundə'vaɪsəz] [口] **听其自便** 这里的 device 不是"技巧"、"策略"或"装置",而是相当于 will (意志), desire (欲望), inclination (意向)等词的意义。但是,device 被人们普遍使用表达以上各词的意义已经是过去的事情了,在现代,只残留在本条条头的习用语中,而且经常是复数形式。这一表达法直译为"随他本人的意志[欲望、意向]",换句话说就是"不给与指导或援助,他爱怎么就怎么吧"。*I'm fed up with the way he keeps changing his mind. From now on I'm leaving him to his own devices.* 他的心思一天三变,我已经腻烦透了。从今以后,随他自己去吧。*You can't leave the students to their own devices. Every time you take your eyes off them, order declines.* 你不能对学生们放任不管。只要眼睛一离开,秩序就会乱。另外,象下边的两个例句那样,在句子的开头采取 Left to *one's* own devices 的形式。可以认为,头一个例句是省略了 Having been,第二个例句是省略了 If I had been. *Left to my own devices, I wandered about the town enjoying the warm, spring sun.* 由于有了空闲,我沐浴着春日温暖的阳光,在城镇的街头漫步。*Left to my own devices, I would have signed the contract right away, but the boss insisted on another round of negotiations.* 如果按照我的意思,我马上就签订合同了,可是老板硬是主张再谈判一次。除以上的用法外,当一个人要离开某个地方的时候,向过去呆在一起的人(只限于同辈或晚辈)告别,常以轻松的口吻使用这一表达法。在这一场合,"任其自便"的本来意义已经非常淡薄,仅表示"你们慢慢玩吧"或"以后请多关照"之类的意味而已。*Well, I'll leave you two young folks to your own devices. I have to get back to work.* 好啦,两位年轻的伙伴,你们慢慢玩吧。我必须回去干活啦。另外,由于把 leave *someone* to *his* own devices 中的 device 误解为"技巧"、"策略",现代英语竟产生了如下的使用方法。*When* *the enemy cut our lines of communication and supply, we were suddenly left to our own devices.* 当敌人切断我方的交通网和补给线的时候,我们立即要靠自己的机智进行活动了。◇ let *someone* do as *he* wishes

devil

between the devil and the deep blue sea [bə.twi(:)nðə ˈdevələnðə ˈdi(:)pˈblu:ˈsi:] [口] **进退两难** 直译为"在恶魔与蓝色的深海之间"。关于语源,一般的说法是: devil 一词过去有"船的龙骨两侧、贴近水面的船板的缝隙"的意思。在给这种缝隙涂沥青的时候,水手必须冒着生命危险。据说本条习用语即由此而来。不过,这条习用语中的 devil 也与 be the DEVIL to pay 中的 devil 同样,作"恶魔"解释比较顺理成章。这一表达法多半是来自基督在死海 (the Dead Sea) 附近受到恶魔 (the Devil)诱惑的故事(《新约全书》)。在 1721 年出版的詹姆士·凯陵 (James Kelling)编的《苏格兰格言全集》(*Complete Collection of Scottish Proverbs*)中,刊载有 between the devil and the Dead Sea 这一表达法,据介绍为古苏格兰的格言。"在恶魔与死海之间",也就是"无处可逃"的意思。不知什么时候,这个 Dead Sea 变成了 deep sea, 又为了调整语调而加个 blue, 结果便形成 deep blue sea 了。作为比喻是"进退维谷"的意思,但是多用于表示在二者之中做选择"顾此必失彼"的状况。 *The doctors are between the devil and the deep blue sea. The only medicine that will save the patient's life produces an allergic reaction.* 医生们正进退两难,只有一种药能够救活那个病人,但是它会引起过敏反应。 *America finds herself between the devil and the deep blue sea. If she supports the Arabs, she will make an enemy of Israel, but if she sides with Israel, the Arabs may cut off her oil supply.* 美国正在左右为难。如果支持阿拉伯人,它就会使以色列成为敌人;但是,如果站在以色列一边,阿拉伯人就可能不供给它石油。 *I'm caught between the devil and the deep blue sea. We're having guests for dinner tonight, but I've got to finish this work before I leave the office. If I go home early, I'll be in Dutch with the boss; but if I don't, I'll be in the doghouse with my wife.* 我现在是左右为难。今天晚上我家里有一些客人来吃饭,但是,我必须在下班之前完成这个工作。如果我早些回家,就得不到老板的欢心;如果不早些回家,就要惹老婆发脾气。本条不一定非是"顾此必失彼"的状况不可。在"左也不好,右也不妙"的上下文中,也可以使用这一表达法。 *The Arabs' growing military strength and America's refusal to cooperate has put Israel between the devil and the deep blue sea.* 阿拉伯人的军事力量日益强大,而美国又拒绝给与援助,以色列已经陷入进退维谷的绝境了。另外,如下面的例句所示,也可以用以表示"后面危险逼近,实际无处可逃"的意思。这是与本来的意味相似的一种使用方法。 *With my pursuers on one side and a yawning chasm on the other, I was caught between the devil and the deep blue sea.* 后边是追兵,前边是张着大口的峡谷,我已经完全无处可逃了。◇ facing two undesirable options / in a serious predicament

be the devil to pay [ðə ˈdevəltə.peɪ] [话] **那可不得了** 翻翻词典,查一下语源,大多是这样说明的:这句英语原来的形式是 the devil to pay and no pitch hot; 在过去, devil 有"(船的龙骨两侧或吃水线附近很不容易涂沥青的)船外板与外板之间的缝隙"的意味 (→ between the DEVIL and the deep blue sea)。pitch 是"沥青", pay 是"涂沥青之类的防水材料"。整个意思是:"为了防止漏水,必须把船外板的缝隙涂上沥青,可是偏偏没有热的沥青",所以"那可不得了"。乍一看,你会觉得这种说明的确言之有理,但是作为稳妥的语源论来说,其中存在着许许多多的疑问。西方自古以来就有这样的传说:如果欠恶魔的债,最后它会取走你的灵魂。把条头的 devil 直接理解为"恶魔",因为是"向恶魔借了债",所以"那可不得了"——这样解释是更为稳妥的。确实devil有“船外板的缝隙”之意，但那是船员们使用的专门术语。事实大概是这样：船员们借用自古以来就有的习用语be the devil to pay中的devil，为了讲得俏皮，又加上了 and no pitch hot。*There'll be the devil to pay if the boss learns I took the day off today.* 老板如果知道我今天没上班，那可不得了。*I've got to go see my mother. There'd be the devil to pay if she heard I'd been in town without contacting her.* 我现在必须去看我的母亲。如果她听说我来过这个镇而又不同她打招呼，那可不得了哇。常用 very 加强语气。*Most people are still behind the President, but if inflation gets much worse, there's going to be the very devil to pay.* 大多数人仍然是支持总统的，但是，如果通货膨胀进一步加剧的话，那就要有极大的麻烦了。如下例所示，也可以用于过去的事情。*When I got home late after wrecking my father's new car, there was the very devil to pay.* 当我毁坏了我父亲的新汽车而很晚才回家的时候，那可真倒了一次大霉。◇ ((very → a tremendous amount)) be a lot of trouble / be a lot to answer for

have the luck of the devil [ˌhævðə ˈlʌkəvðə ˈde(ː)vəl] [话] **大走红运** → have the devil's own LUCK

like the devil [ˌlaɪkðə ˈdevəl] [话] **猛烈地** 字面意义是“象恶魔一样”。更正确地说，就是 with the violence or force attributed to the devil (象恶魔那样凶猛)。这是表示猛烈程度的一个副词短语。*My hand hurts like the devil.* 我的手痛得厉害。*We worked like the devil to finish on time.* 为了按时完成任务，我们拚命干了好一阵。*Do you like the strong-smell-ing preserved bean curd? It stinks like the devil, but it's very good.* 你喜欢臭豆腐吗？它闻起来臭得了不得，但是很好吃。另外有个like hell，意义与之相似，但非常庸俗，是一个轻松的表达法。一般用于亲密的朋友之间，语调自如。女性通常不大用这种说法。例如 My husband hates like the devil to spend money. (我的丈夫非常讨厌花钱。) 这句话，如果用 like hell 代替 like the devil，语气就带有极强烈的感情。用汉语来表达，就是：“我家的老头子是个吝啬鬼，一个铜板都舍不得花。”◇ extremely (hard, bad, much, etc.)

play the devil with *something* [ˌpleɪðə ˈdevəlwɪð ～] [话] **搞坏** play the devil 直译为“扮演恶魔的角色”，意思是“造成象恶魔的恶作剧所引起的那种事态”。*The train strike has played the devil with our travel plans.* 铁路罢工完全打乱了我们的旅游计划。多用 very 加强 devil 的语气。*This steep inflation is playing the very devil with my pocketbook.* 这样猛烈的通货膨胀把我的经济状况完全搞坏了。当然，“搞坏”的对象不仅仅是“计划”或“钱包”，如说 play the devil with *someone's* nerves，“神经”也是其中之一。*I know our daughter's piano lessons are good for her, but her constant practicing plays the devil with my nerves.* 我知道钢琴课对我女儿是大有好处的，但是她经常练习，我的神经可受不了啊。另外，有时受 raise the DEVIL 这一说法的影响，而形成 raise the devil with *something* 的表达法，意思相同。◇ be very detrimental to *something*

raise the devil [ˌreɪzðə ˈdevəl] [话] **大吵大闹** 这里的 raise 是“把睡眠者叫起来”的意思。本条表达法的最初构思是：“把恶魔叫起来，就引起意外的吵闹”。一般来说，可以认为与 raise Cain 完全同义，但是两者之间仍有一点点区别。简单地说，raise the devil 等于“raise Cain +使对方[周围]困惑的行动”，这样考虑就容易明白了。所以，本条的表达法无论在意义方面还是用法方面都有一定的局限性 (→ raise CAIN <with *someone*>)。例如：*My father warned me that he would raise the devil if my grades didn't get better.* 我父亲警告我说，如果我的成绩没有进步，他会大为恼火的。在说这句话的时候，raise the devil 不仅表达“大发雷霆”、“暴跳如雷”之类的具体形象，而且包含着“采取使人困惑的行动”(给与惩罚等)。*The local residents raised the very devil when they learned that a* *new airport was to be built in Los Angeles.* 当地居民听说又要在洛杉矶建一个新飞机场的时候,他们气势汹汹地大闹起来了。在这一场合,含义不仅是"一片愤怒声",而且伴有集会、示威、到官府请愿等各种激烈的抗议行动。另外,这句话中的 very 是加强语气。*Every year some minor property damage is caused by kids who go out and raise the devil on Halloween.* 每年在万圣节前夕,孩子们都兴高采烈地出去玩耍,结果总使家财受一点点损害。这句话一看就明白,含义不仅是"兴高采烈地玩耍",而是伴有损害家财之类的"使周围困惑的行动"。再有,有时想说 play the /DEVIL with *something*, 而采取了 raise the devil with *something* 的表达法。◇ take vociferous action / complain loudly / have boisterous [destructive] fun

speak of the devil [ˌspi(ː)kəvðə ˈdevəl] [话] **说到曹操,曹操就到** 原形是英国英语的谚语 Talk of the devil and he's sure to appear. 意思是:"一谈到恶魔,恶魔必定出现。" 在美国英语中,本条表达法的后边有时加 and he's sure to appear。例如: *Well, well, speak of the devil and he's sure to appear! We were just talking about you, Charlie.* 哎呀呀,真是说到曹操,曹操就到哇! 查理! 我们刚刚谈到你。但是,如下两个例句所示,在下边连有语句的场合,一般省掉 and ~。*Speak of the devil, here comes Marsha now!* 真是说到曹操,曹操就到。看,玛莎来啦! *Speak of the devil, if it isn't Jimmy. I was just saying that we ought to get together with you sometime soon.* 真是说到曹操,曹操就到啊。那不是吉米吗? 我们正在谈着最近应该见你一面呢。◇ Well, well, (speaking of Charlie [Marsha, etc.])

devil's

have the devil's own luck → LUCK

dew

mountain dew [ˌmauntnˈdjuː] [话] **玉米威士忌酒** 直译为"山露"。由于在深山酿造而产生的表达法。与 MOONSHINE(→) 虽然同义,但本条为一轻松的表达法。*Them what refuse mountain dew are few.* 不饮"山露"的人绝无仅有。◇ homemade (corn) whiskey

dibs

dibs [ˈdɪ(ː)bz] [话] **小额金钱** → have DIBS on *something* [*someone*]

have dibs on *something* [*someone*] [ˌhæv ˈdɪb.zɔ(ː)n ~] [话] **享有优先权** 语源有两种说法。一说来自 dibstones (略作 dibs) 一词,此词指英国儿童用羊骨与球玩耍的游戏。另一说法是:这个 dibs 是名词 divvy (分配) 的复数形式 divvies 的音变。DIVVY up *something* 是"分某种东西", have first divvies on ~ 则意为"对……有优先权"。把这个 divvies 变为 dibs 的表达法便是 have first dibs on ~。*I have first dibs on using the skateboard.* 的意思是 我有优先使用这个滑板的权利。根据此说,则条头是脱落了上述表达法中的 first。如果省略 first,那就意为"这个滑板归我所有",没有借给对方的意思了。这一表达法在表示"对……有优先权"的意义上,大人也有使用者,但是最常挂在口头上的是孩子们。*I have dibs on that piece of cake.* 那块蛋糕是我的呀! *I've got dibs on Sally Ann for the next dance.* 下一轮是我跟萨莉·安跳舞啦。*None of us will get to go to that convention in New York. The section chief has dibs on that trip.* 我们谁都不能出席在纽约召开的那个会议。科长有优先权嘛。另外,虽然不大使用,但 dibs 有"小额金钱"的意思。这显然是来自 dibstones 的表达法。◇ have priority on *something* [*someone*]

dice

load the dice against *someone* [**in** *one's* **favor**] [ˌloudðə ˈdaɪs əˈgenst ~ / ɪn ˌ~ ˈfeɪvər] [话] **使(某人的)处境不利[有利]** load 是"灌上",load the dice 是在赌博中为了出自己所希望的点子而"给骰子灌上铅"。*The loser of the game claimed that the casino had loaded the dice.* 输了的赌徒声称,赌场给骰子灌了铅。在以比喻的意义使用的场合,一般

要伴有 against *someone*(使……不利)或者 in *one's* favor (与己有利),二者必居其一。 *He used his influence to load the dice against us.* 他利用自己的势力使我们处于不利的境地。*I had thought I had a chance to become president of this company, but Jim has loaded the dice in his favor by marrying the boss's daughter.* 我本来以为自己有机会当上这家公司的总经理,但是吉姆与老板的女儿结婚,他取得了有利的地位。不但可以用 in *one's* favor, 也有用 in *someone's* favor 的场合,即"使某人处于有利的处境"。 *He used his influence to load the dice in our favor.* 他运用自己的权势,使我们处于有利的地位。在使用被动语态的时侯,意思是"处境(情况)不利[有利]",从客观上看的感觉很强。*The dice are loaded against us. Even if we succeed in getting the door open, we'll never get past the guard.* 情况对我们很不利,即使我们能够把门打开,也绝对突破不了守卫的一关。另外,dice 是 die (骰子)的复数形式,也就是经常作为复数处理,这一点务请注意。还有一个 with the dice loaded (against [in favor of] *one*)的形式,意思是"处于(不利的[有利的]) 条件[情况、立场])"。*A person with no education goes through life with the dice loaded against him.* 一个没受教育的人,在人生的道路上处于不利的地位。◇ put *someone* in an unfavorable [*one* in a favorable] position

no dice ['nou'daɪs] [话] **不行** dice 是 die (骰子)的复数形式。可以这样使用: *There are no dice in this room.* 这个房间里没有骰子。但本条所要讲的自然是作为习用语的 no dice 了。原为赌场用语,在双骰子赌博中,当掷出输掉赌注的点子(craps)时,庄家向其他正要掷骰子的赌徒要求暂停,就喊 no dice,意思是"不要掷骰子!"、"等一下!"后来转作比喻使用。 *No dice. You can beg until you're blue in the face, but I still won't lend you the money.* 不行。你就是说到舌敝唇焦,我也是不借给你钱。*No dice. I didn't get the job.* 吹啦! 那份工作我没弄到手。如上面的例句所示,no dice 多半放在句子的最前端,而且单独使用。但有时采取 it is [was] no dice 的形式。*It's no dice. The car just won't start.* 不行。这车怎么也开动不了。*I asked him to help us but it was no dice.* 我曾去求他帮助我们,但是他没有答应。*The hero fell in love with his friend's little sister early in the novel, but it was no dice.* 在小说的开头,男主人公与他的朋友的妹妹相爱,但是后来并没有成为眷属。此外,这一表达法与 no SOAP (→) 十分相似,但用法有一些差异。◇ the answer is no / (it is) no use [futile]

play with loaded dice [ˌpleɪwɪð ˌloudə'dːaɪs] [话] **在交易中事先做手脚** loaded dice 是"为了出特定的点子而灌铅的骰子"。 *After I lost a lot of money in that crap game, I learned that they had been playing with loaded dice.* 我在双骰子赌博中输了很多钱之后,才明白他们用的骰子是灌了铅的。这是按字面意义的使用方法。作为比喻,如以下的例句所示,是在"交涉"、"交易"等场合常常使用的一个表达法。由于 loaded dice 是存心骗人的,所以奥妙的所在并不容易识破。 *Never do business with a Mafia-related enterprise. They play with loaded dice.* 永远不要与黑手党参加的企业做生意。他们总是做好手脚,始终对自己有利。*It's best to be chary in negotiating with that country. Its leaders have a habit of playing with loaded dice.* 跟那个国家搞交涉必须万分谨慎。他们的领导人有一个习惯,就是一开始就做好手脚,使事情对他们自己有利。下面是这一表达法的变形。*I don't think we should do business with that guy. He seldom plays unless the dice are loaded.* 我认为我们不应该跟那个家伙谈生意。他不先做好手脚,是不会达成交易的。◇ deal from an unfairly arranged position

dick

a dick [ə 'dɪ(ː)k] [俗] **侦探** detective 的缩略变形。原为黑社会用语,后受盗匪影片的影响,在社会中普遍使用。如果单独使用，一般指"便衣警察"。加上形容词，意义就发生变化。a private dick (private detective)是"私人侦探"，而 a house dick (house detective) 则是旅馆、百货商店等的"便衣警卫"。这是个相当没有礼貌的说法，以 detective 为职业的人都讨厌这个字眼。顺便提一下："便衣警察"又称 a plainclothesman [ə 'pleɪn'klouzmən], a plainclothes (police) officer, a plainclothes policeman。*Watch out for that guy. He may be a dick*.注意那个家伙，他可能是个侦探。*There was a private dick nosing around here yesterday*. 昨天有一个私人侦探在这一带打探。*There's a shoplifter! Call the house dick!* 有扒手！快叫警卫！◇ a detective

every Tom, Dick and Harry → TOM

a house dick [ə 'haus.dɪ(:)k] [俗] **(旅馆、百货店等处的)便衣警卫** → a DICK

a private dick [ə .praɪvət'dɪ(:)k] [俗] **私人侦探** → a DICK

die

one **thought (that)** *one* **would die (of embarrassment)** [~ .θɔ(:)t (ðət) ~ wu'dːaɪ (əv em'bæ(:)rəsmənt)] [话] **羞愧得无地自容** → *one* could have DIED

died

one **could have died** [~ .kudəv'daɪd] [话] **难堪已及** 这句英语是 *one* could have died of embarrassment 的省略说法，也可以添加 of embarrassment 使用。实际上几乎要死的场合一般说 might have died, 不能与 could have died 混同。使用者多为女性。*I could have died (of embarrassment) when the steak I was trying to cut flew off my plate and landed in my hostess's lap*. 当我去切牛排的时候，这块牛排从盘子里飞了出去，落到女主人的腿上，我简直羞愧死了。*My husband insulted me right in front of the ambassador. I could have died!* 我的丈夫竟当着大使的面侮辱我，我简直难堪极了。*The preacher's wife said she could have died when her husband's false teeth fell out of his mouth as he was preaching*. 牧师的妻子说，当她的丈夫正在布道的时候假牙从嘴里掉了出来，她简直感到难堪极了。过去，曾如英国英语那样，说 *one* thought (that) *one* should die (of embarrassment)，现在也说 ~ *one* would die (of embarrassment)。另外还有个 be embarrassed to death 的表达法。◇ be unutterably embarrassed

dig

dig *something* [*someone*]① ['dɪ(:)g ~] [话] **理解** 这里的 dig 是动词，在 19 世纪中叶，人们用它来表示" study a subject diligently"的意思，也就是"对某一学科(subject) 刻苦钻研"。最初的构思是：象"挖洞"一样对 a subject"往下挖"。后来进一步发展，就具有现在这样的"充分理解[明白]"的意义了。是青年人喜欢用的表达法，主要用于否定句和疑问句。*I don't dig this algebra problem. It doesn't seem to fit the formula in the book*. 我弄不懂这道代数题，它好象跟教科书里的公式套不上。*I told you to stay away from my girl. You dig?* 我告诉你不要接近我的女朋友。你听懂了吗？常用 just 加强语气。*How come our class gets so much more homework than yours? I just don't dig it*. 我们班留的家庭作业怎么比你们班多得多？我简直一点儿也不明白。在应用于"人"时，说法如下：*I just don't dig that guy. He invites me to his party, and then when I show up he gives me the cold shoulder*. 我觉得那个人简直莫名其妙。他请我参加他的社交晚会，但是我去了以后，他对我却冷若冰霜。◇ understand *something* [*someone*]

dig *something* [*someone*]② ['dɪ(:)g ~] [话] **喜好** 按照历史的顺序，dig 一词的意义的发展情况是："挖掘"→"钻研"→"理解[明白]"，这在上边的 DIG *something* [*someone*]①中已经讲过了。但是到了 20 世纪 30 年代，又增添了一个新的意义，即"喜好"。最初开始使用这一意义的是爵士乐爱好者，特别是在谈到音乐时使用；后来一般的人，特别是在青年人中间，也普遍使用起来，而且使用范围扩大到音乐以外的领域。在意味上与 appreciate (欣赏)相近,但是 dig 具有爵士乐用语的本色,是偏重感觉的表达法。如果说 appreciate 是"用头脑理解",则 dig 就是"用身体理解"了。 *I dig classical music. I could listen to it all day long and not get tired of it.* 我喜好古典音乐,就是听上一整天我也不腻烦。 *Rollie seems to dig China. He says it's a wonderful place to live.* 罗利似乎很喜欢中国。他说这是一个极好的居住地方。常用 really 加强语气。 *I really dig Doris. She's a great girl.* 我非常喜欢多丽丝,她是一位出类拔萃的姑娘。 *My brother really digs Chinese food. He goes to a Chinese restaurant almost every week.* 我的哥哥特别喜欢吃中国饭,他几乎每个星期都去一次中国餐馆。◇ like *something* [*someone*]

dig *something* [*someone*][3] ['dɪ(:)g ~] [话] **(兴致勃勃地)看[听]** 动词 dig 最新的使用方法。 *Dig that guy over there with the purple coat and orange pants.* 你瞧瞧在那边儿的那个穿紫色上衣和橙黄色裤子的家伙。如此例所示,在"看见"出人意外的事物或"听到"难以相信的事情的场合使用。 *Did you dig that blond that just walked by? What I wouldn't give to have a date with her?* 你看见刚才走过去的那个金发碧眼的姑娘了吗?如果能跟她约会,那该多么好啊! 可以象这样采取疑问句的形式,但是一般来说,是在肯定式的命令句中使用。 *Dig this guy. He says this year's Miss America once had the hots for him.* 你听听这个家伙在说什么! 他说今年的美国小姐过去曾经跟他打得火热。 *Hey, dig this! It says here in the paper that that new rock group is coming to town.* 喂,你听听这个大好消息! 报纸上说,那个新的摇滚乐团要到我们镇上来了。在这个意义上的 dig 也多少带有 DIG*something* [*someone*][2] 的用法的 appreciate (欣赏)的气氛。在下一例句中,这一气氛十分显著。 *We were sitting around digging some old rock records when a rock came sailing through the window.* 我们正听一些旧的摇滚乐唱片入神的时候,一块石头从窗外飞了进来。◇ look at [see, listen to] *something* [*someone*]

digger

a gold digger [ə 'goul.dɪːgər] [话] **以色相骗取男子财物的女人** 有些词典译作"掘金者"或"淘金狂",但是几乎没有按照这种字面意义使用的情况。"掘金者"是 a (gold) prospector, 现在在西部剧中还常出现。prospector 是"试掘的人"的意思。a gold digger 指不仅为了骗取金钱,而且为了得到贵重的礼物,参加花费很大的娱乐而与男子交往的女人。当然啦,这种女人一般具美人的形象。 *Sure, she's a beautiful woman, but beware. She's also a gold digger.* 的确,她是个美人儿,但是,你要多加小心。她可是一个为了财物而与男子交往的女人啊。不管长得多么漂亮,只要是为了钱财而欺骗男子,当然会受到社会的轻视。因此,常常在这一表达法的前边加上 little 甚至表示更强烈的侮辱性的 cheap little 之类的定语。例如: *That little gold digger took Jason for every last penny he had.* 那个小妖精勾搭贾森,把他的钱包弄个精光。再有,这种女人当中也包括"以金钱为目的而结婚的人"。在下面的例句中,real 是加强语气。 *That Mrs. Lovegems must be a real gold digger. I see in the paper where she's just snared her fourth millionaire husband.* 那位拉维杰姆斯夫人肯定是个专为金钱而跟男子结婚的女人。我看见报纸上说,她现在第四次嫁给百万富翁啦。◇ a money-seeking woman

diggity

Hot diggity! ['hɑt:.dɪgɪdi] [话] **太棒啦!** → Hot DOG!

digs

digs ['dɪ(:)gz] [话] **宿舍** diggings 的缩略形式。diggings 在英国英语中原为"住处"的意思。dig 是"挖掘",因此最初的构思是:象鼹鼠那样的动物,挖个洞在里边居住。这一表达法多指学生或单身汉所居住的公寓中的一室。也有"鸡窝"、"鸟巢"的含义。 *I got some new digs* *nearer the university campus.* 我搬到离大学校园更近一些的另一个宿舍了。*Harvey must like to move. He's changed his digs four or five times since he came to New York.* 哈维必定是爱好搬家。自从来纽约之后,他已经换过四、五次宿舍了。因为 digs 本来有"鸡窝"、"鸟巢"的含义,如果用以指一所独立的住宅或者豪华的府第,那就多少有一些滑稽之感了。*I've got to find some suitable digs for my growing family.* 我家人口不断增加,得找一个适当的窝了。在这一场合,一般要用 house 或者 residence, 但讲话的人故意用开玩笑的口吻说 digs, 表示谦逊。下面的例句则是完全戏谑地使用这一表达法。*There are some pretty fancy digs on this street. Mostly rich people live around here.* 这条街上很有一些非常漂亮的鸡窝。在这儿住的大部分都是腰缠万贯的人。◇ a place to live

dilemma

be in a dilemma [ɪnə də'lemə] [口] **处于进退两难的境地** → on the HORNS of a dilemma

on the horns of a dilemma → HORNS

dime

be a dime a dozen [ə'daɪm ə'dʌ(:)zn] [话] **不稀罕** dime 是"十分钱的硬币"。本条的字面意义是"一打十分钱",如说 *These candy drops are a dime a dozen.* 这种糖球十分钱买 12 块。既然十分钱可以买一打,这种东西必然"到处都有","马上就可以到手"。*Books like that are a dime a dozen.* 那种书太不稀罕啦。*Caddies are a dime a dozen around here.* 在这一带,卡迪拉克牌小轿车有的是。也可以用以指"人"。*Good-looking girls in New York are a dime a dozen.* 纽约美女如云。◇ can be found anywhere

a dime store [ə 'daɪm ˌsto(:)r] [话] **大众百货店** → a FIVE-AND-TEN

stop on a dime [ˌstɑ(:)pɒnə 'daɪm] [话] **刹车特别灵** dime 是"十美分的硬币",在美国的货币当中体积最小。本条 stop on a dime 的意思是:"当汽车从那小小的十美分的硬币上通过的时候,即便踩制动器,汽车也不会从十美分的硬币上滑脱出去,而是完全停在它的上面。"也就是说"刹车非常灵"。这是一种夸张的表达法,多在吹嘘自己的车(特别是汽车)的时候使用。*My new car will stop on a dime.* 我的新汽车刹车特别灵。*A: You shouldn't follow the car in front so close. B: Don't worry. This car'll stop on a dime.* 甲:你不要和前边的车离得太近呀。乙:甭担心。这辆车的刹车特别灵。stop on a dime 中的 stop 如果换成 turn, 那意思就是"在十美分的硬币上也能转",即"旋转半径小"(have a small turning radius),可以绕极小的圈。*You should see Ned's new sportscar. It'll turn on a dime.* 你去看看内德的新赛车,它能绕极小的圈。以上所讲都是以车为主语,但也有以人为主语的表达法,即 stop [turn] *something* on a dime。例如可以说:*I can stop this car on a dime.* 我能够把这辆汽车立即刹住。换句话说就是"这辆汽车的刹车特别灵。"结果跟以汽车为主语的表达法 *This car'll stop on a dime.* 意思完全一样。◇ brake to a stop in an extremely short distance

turn on a dime [ˌtə(:)rnɒnə 'daɪm] [话] **能绕极小的圈** → stop on a DIME

dimple

a tummy dimple [ə 'tʌmi ˌdɪmpl] [话] **肚脐** 直译是"肚子的酒窝"。幼儿语。女人们相互间也使用。*Your tummy dimple is showing.* 你的肚脐露出来啦。◇ a navel

dimwit

a dimwit [ə 'dɪ(:)m.wɪt] [口] **傻瓜** dim 是"昏暗",wit 是"智力",两者合在一起意为"头脑不清晰的人"亦即"愚钝的人"。*Better not ask Tom to do it. That dimwit would forget his head if it weren't screwed on.* 不要叫汤姆去干那件事吧。如果脑袋不是牢牢地长在他的身上,他这个笨蛋连脑袋都会忘记的。dim 与 wit 之间加个连字符,后面再加 -ted, 就构成形容词 dim-witted ['dɪ(:)m.wɪdɪd]。*Of all the dim-witted ideas!* 多么愚蠢的想法啊! → a DUMBHEAD ◇ a stupid person

dim-witted

dim-witted ['dɪ(:)m.wɪdɪd] [口] **愚笨的** → a DIMWIT / THICK-HEADED

dinner

a bachelor dinner [ə 'bæ(:)tʃələr 'dɪnər] [口] **告别独身宴会** → a bachelor PARTY

lose *one's* **dinner** [.lu(:)z ~ 'dɪnər] [话] **呕吐食物** 直译为"丢失吃的饭",换句话说就是"呕吐"的意思。这是一个轻松的表达法。与正式的说法 vomit ['vɑ(:)mət] 为同义语。vomit 一词给人的印象过于明显,因此在日常会话中不大使用。为了避免说这个词,常常使用具有同一意义的 be sick, throw up [.θrou'ʌ(:)p], upchuck ['ʌp.tʃʌk], lose *one's* dinner 等。其中最委婉的是 be sick,其次为 throw up 和 upchuck。 lose *one's* dinner 比前面的三个说法调子轻松,在一般会话中经常出现。*Jimmy lost his dinner [threw up, upchucked, was sick] on the train.* 吉米在火车上呕吐了。更随便一些的说法有 BARF 和 toss *one's* COOKIES,主要是青年人相互间使用。还有一个听了就令人难受的最庸俗的表达法,即 PUKE。 ◇ vomit

a potluck dinner [ə .pɑt.lʌk 'dɪnər] [口] **各自带来菜饭的晚宴** potluck 是"现成的菜饭", potluck dinner 本来也是同样的意思。*I didn't have time to go shopping today, so we'll just have a potluck dinner.* 今天我没有时间出去买东西,咱们晚饭只好吃现有的饭菜啦。但是,在现在,这种用法已经极为罕见了。*My club is going to have a potluck dinner tonight, and I have been asked to bring a meat dish.* 我们俱乐部今天晚上开自带饭菜的宴会,叫我带一盘肉去。在这一例句中,已经不是指"现成的菜饭",而是指各自带不同的菜、大家凑起来吃的宴会。这种用法已很普遍。*Once a year the people in our neighborhood get together for a potluck dinner.* 每年我们左邻右舍都自带饭菜聚餐一顿。也可以用 supper, lunch, meal 等词代替 dinner。*Our church is having a potluck supper tonight.* 在我们教堂,今天晚上举行自带菜饭的宴会。另外,虽然用的是 dinner 一词,但不一定是在黄昏或夜里举行,也可以指白天举行的宴会。*The company wives are sponsoring a potluck dinner at noon tomorrow.* 公司职工的妻子们明天中午举行一次自带菜饭的宴会。◇ a dinner to which everyone brings food

What's for dinner? [.*h*wʌtsfər 'dɪnər] [话] **今天吃什么菜?** → WHAT'S cooking?

dip

a dip [ə 'dɪ(:)p] [话] **扒手** 原为黑社会用语,为 a pickpocket 的轻松说法。dip 本来是"(在水一类的液体中)浸一下"的意思。最初的构思是:"象把手浸入水中那样,将手伸入他人衣袋中的人" (a person who dips his hand into other people's pockets)。*Danny has worked as a dip for twenty years.* 丹尼当扒手已经有二十年了。另外,在黑社会中,有用此词作为绰号的情况。*Danny the Dip has lifted thousands of wallets during the past twenty years.* 扒手丹尼在过去的二十年间偷了几千个钱包。◇ a pickpocket

take a dip [.teɪkə 'dɪ(:)p] [口] **游一会儿泳** 字面意义是"(把自己)泡一下"。与 go swimming (前去游泳)不同,take a dip 是到达游泳池、海边等游泳场所以后专用的台词。*"I think I'll take a dip," said Nancy as she put on her bathing cap.* 南希一边戴上她的游泳帽,一边说:"我想去游一会儿泳。" *"Me, too," answered Ned. "Let's all take another dip before we go home."* "我也去。"内德回答说:"在回家之前,我们大家都再游一会儿泳吧。"如果是说"游上一小会儿",则常用 take a quick dip。◇ have a short swim

diploma

a diploma mill → MILL

dirt

dish the dirt (about *someone* [*something*]) [.dɪʃðə 'də(:)rt] [话] **说人家的闲话** dish 的意思是"把做好的菜用勺盛到盘子里"。the dirt 是"泥土"。本条直译为"把泥土盛到盘子里"。这一表达法是把言语比做做好的菜,意为"说玷污他人的话"。用法如下:*Our wives are in the* *next room dishing the dirt about somebody or other.* 我们的妻子正在隔壁的房间里东家长西家短地说闲话呢。*Whew! How that Mrs. Soilpot dishes the dirt! The ears of half the people in town must be burning.* 嘿！索伊尔波特太太的闲话简直满天飞！本城有一半人会由于她的闲话而感到耳根子发烧。"说人家的闲话"并不限于女性。对于男人，这一习用语当然也可以使用。*That guy is always dishing the dirt about someone else's mistakes.* 那小子总是爱讲别人的失误。也可以插入 up 而作 dish up the dirt，意思完全一样。*The way that woman dishes up the dirt you'd think she doesn't know anything good about anyone.* 你听那个女人说闲话的调儿，会以为她对别人的好事简直连一点儿也不知道。最近，偶尔有人仅用 dish 一个词表示"闲谈"、"瞎聊"的意味。*The neighborhood wives get together one morning a week just to dish over a cup of coffee.* 附近的娘儿们每星期有一个早晨聚会到一起，边喝咖啡边闲聊天。◇ gossip (maliciously)

do *someone* **dirt** [ˌdu(:) ~ ˈdə(:)rt] [话] **辜负对方的信任而干卑鄙的勾当** 字面意义是"玷污(某人)"。另有 do *someone* dirty 的说法，但极少使用。在不是很深的情谊，只是极其普遍的人际关系中，也可以使用这一习用语表示"本来从常识上讲可以期待的事情，对方竟倒行逆施了"的意味。*That guy did me dirt. After I asked him for advice on my new invention, he patented it in his own name.* 那个家伙干了对不起我的勾当。我本来请他对我的新发明提点意见，而他却用自己的名字申请了专利权。*I wouldn't trust that Harry too far. He has a reputation for doing people dirt.* 对那个哈里是不能够太信任的。他背叛别人而干卑鄙的勾当已经臭名昭著了。可用 really 加强这一表达法的语气。*Frankie really did Sarah dirt. After promising to marry her, he dropped her for another woman.* 弗兰基对萨拉的行为实在太卑鄙了。他答应跟她结婚，却又把她甩掉而找另一个女人去啦。◇ subject *someone* to underhanded treatment

eat dirt [ˌi(:)tˈdə(:)rt] [话] **含垢忍辱** 字面意义是"吃泥土"。最初的构思是："采取过分的低姿态，泥土进入嘴里"。*Mr. Hoity may be a great man, but I refuse to eat dirt for anyone.* 霍伊提先生可能是一位了不起的人物，但是不论对方是谁，我决不含垢忍辱。*When I was in the army, my sergeant made me eat dirt.* 当我在军队的时候，我们班的军士侮辱我，使我忍气吞声。*The president of that company pays his employees a lot of money, but they have to eat dirt to get it.* 那个公司的总经理付给职工很高的工资，但是他们必须低三下四，含垢忍辱。◇ grovel / take a lot of verbal abuse (from *someone*)

hit pay dirt [ˌhɪt ˈpeɪˌdə(:)rt] [话] **碰到所追求的东西** hit 是"侥幸挖到[碰上]"的意思。pay dirt 是"有采掘价值的金矿等"。因此，本条习用语的原意是"挖到有希望的矿脉"。*After digging here and there for many years, the old prospector finally hit pay dirt.* 经过多年的到处试掘，老勘探师终于碰到了有开采价值的矿苗。也转作比喻使用。*Many of our recent products haven't sold very well, but we finally hit pay dirt with our latest item.* 我们厂最近的产品销路不大好，但是我们最新的一项产品终于大大走俏了。*The new singer hit pay dirt with her first song.* 那位新歌手唱了第一支歌就红了起来。并不一定仅用于有利可图的事情。*The detectives had to search long and hard for a clue to the murder before they hit pay dirt.* 便衣警察经过长期的拚命侦察，才摸到了杀人犯的线索。*Because I didn't know Smith's first name, I started calling all the Smiths in the phone book. Luckily, I hit pay dirt on the third call.* 由于我只知道对方姓史密斯，不知道他叫什么名字，所以我就按照电话簿上的次序，开始一个一个叫姓史密斯的人的电话，幸好叫到第三回就碰对了。另外，在美式橄榄球中，用 hit pay dirt 表示 make a touchdown (触地得分)的意思。*The opposing team hit pay dirt* *with a long pass.* 对方球队来一个长距离传球，在我方界内触地得分了。可以用 strike 代替 hit，而说 strike pay dirt，意义相同，在以上的例句中，都可以用 strike 替换。不过，一般使用 hit pay dirt。◇ succeed / see *one's* efforts rewarded

hit the dirt [ˌhɪtðə ˈdə(ː)rt] [话] **为躲避攻击而向地面迅速卧倒** 字面意义是"投身泥土中"。原为陆军用语，从下面的说法而来。*An artillery shell came whistling overhead and all the soldiers hit the dirt.* 一颗炮弹从头顶上呼啸而来，所有的士兵都卧倒了。*Hit the dirt! There's a sniper in that tree.* 卧倒！那颗树上有狙击手。后来就不限于"战斗"，而广泛用于表示为了躲避"危险"而"卧倒"的意思。*When someone opened the front door, we hit the dirt and began easing back into the bushes.* 当有人打开大门的时候，我们赶快卧倒，开始悄手悄脚地后退到灌木丛中。*As soon as I saw the low-flying plane was going to crash, I hit the dirt.* 当我看见一架低空飞行的飞机正要坠毁的时候，我赶紧卧倒了。◇ throw *oneself* down (on the ground)

strike pay dirt [ˌstraɪk ˈpeɪˌdə(ː)rt] [话] **碰到所寻求的东西** → hit pay DIRT

disagrees

something **disagrees with** *someone* [~ ˌdɪsəˈgriːz wɪð ~] [口] **(食物、气候等)对身体不适宜** → *something* AGREES with *someone*

disc

a disc jockey → JOCKEY

disease

foot-in-mouth disease [ˌfutnˈmauθ dəˌziːz] [话] **拙语症** → put *one's* FOOT in *one's* mouth

disgrace

a disgrace to *one's* **family** [ə dəsˌgreɪs tə ~ ˈfæ(ː)məli] [口] **使全家丢脸的人** → be a DISGRACE to man and beast

be a disgrace to man and beast [ə dəsˌgreɪs təˈmæːnənˈbiːst] [话] **禽兽不如** 直译为"不论对于人还是对于动物，都是可耻的存在"。这一表达法包含着"连动物都不会干那种事"的意味。语气极为强烈，有时可以译作"下流坯子"、"人间败类"、"衣冠禽兽"等。*That man is a disgrace to man and beast. He comes home drunk every night, insults his neighbors, and then has the nerve to try to borrow money from us.* 那个人真是一个有耻于人类的家伙。他每天夜里喝醉了酒才回家，辱骂街坊，还厚着脸皮要向我们借钱。*After what you've done, I'm ashamed to call you my son. You're a disgrace to man and beast.* 你竟做出那样的事情，连我都以有你这个儿子感到耻辱。你简直还不如禽兽哪！顺便说一下：在做了什么坏事使家人丢脸的时候，常常讲 a (pure) disgrace to *one's* family (简直是有辱门楣)。◇ *one's* conduct is extremely disgraceful / be guilty of extremely disgraceful conduct

disguise

a blessing in disguise → BLESSING

dish

a dish [ə ˈdɪ(ː)ʃ] [话] **美人** dish 除"盘子"外，还有"一盘菜"的意思。*How many dishes do you plan to serve at the dinner?* 宴会上你计划上几道菜？本条的表达法便是用这个 dish 比做女性。这是一个极其轻松的、日常的使用方法。最初的构思是："美得几乎叫人想要一口吞下去"或者"简直是男人的美味佳肴"。不是指 cute (聪明伶俐) 的女子，而是指 beautiful (好看)、sexy (富有性感)、charming (迷人)的女子。*You should meet Ron's little sister. She's quite a dish.* 你应该见见罗恩的妹妹，那简直是个尤物。*Vera's not much of a dish, but she has great gams.* 薇拉算不上个大美人，但是她的大腿好看极了。如果是 *one's* dish，则与 *one's* cup of tea 同义 (→ be *someone's* CUP of tea)。*Litera-*

ture is not my dish. 我对文学没有兴趣。◇ a beauty

dish [ˈdɪ(ː)ʃ] [话] **聊天** → dish the DIRT (about *someone* [*something*])

dish it out [ˌdɪʃɪˈdaut] [话] **严惩、痛斥** 这一表达法的原形是 dish out the food, 意思是"把盘子里的食品拿出来分"。*Amy, you dish out the beans while I cut the meat.* 艾米,我切肉这功夫,你把盘子里的豆子分一下。后来,这个原形发展成两个形式,一是 dish out the *something*, 一是本条条头的 dish it out。前者是在 food 的部分改用其他名词,如 flattery (奉承)、praise (称赞)、punishment (惩罚)等。原形 dish out the food 有"大量地"、"满满地"的含义。在 dish out the *something* 中,这种含义依然百分之百地存在,令人感到"把 *something* 盛得满满的"。这一表达法的意思是"大量地做某事",例如 dish out the flattery 就是"百般奉承", dish out the punishment 就是"大加惩罚"。*The chief was really dishing out the praise at today's department meeting.* 部长在今天的职工大会上说了一大套表扬的话。*Our English teacher likes to dish out the homework.* 我们的英语老师喜欢留大量的家庭作业。dish out 常常象在下一例句中那样与 take it 前后呼应地使用。这是来源于本来的使用方法,即 dish out 为"从盘子里往外分",而 take it 则是"接受分的东西"。另外,有时也用 a lot [bit, etc.] of 等代替 the。*The challenger dished out a lot of punishment, but the champ was able to take it.* 挑战者的拳头进行了多次的痛击,但是冠军还是招架得很好。现在言归正传。本条条头的 dish it out 虽然也具有"大量地"的意思,但是这一表达法的用途只限于表示"严惩"或"痛斥"的意思。请注意:由于在 dish 与 out 之间加了词义含糊的、表示状况的 it, 用法发生了变化。*The chief must have really been angry with you. You could hear him dishing it out from all the way across the hall.* 头头对你一定是大动肝火啦,从走廊的对面都能听见他猛烈批评你的声音。下面的例句也是 dish out 与 take it 对应使用的。*There's no reason to get angry just because someone criticizes you a little. The trouble with you is that you can dish it out but you can't take it.* 天下哪有这种道理,人家稍微批评你几句你就大动肝火。你的最大缺点是:只许你教训别人,不许人家动你一根毫毛。*I wouldn't want to get in a fight with Doug. He can really dish it out.* 我不愿意跟道格交手,他会把我打得头破血流的。另外,尽管用的是 dish it out 的形式,如果在句子中,it 为具体表明前后文中某个词的代词,那就不一定是"严惩"或"痛斥"的意味了。例如:*When it comes to flattery, you can really dish it out, can't you.* 如果说奉承话,你会象连珠炮似地往外放,要多少有多少。在这一场合,it 是前边的 flattery 的代词。◇ berate *someone* / give out a lot of criticism [punishment, it, etc.]

dish out the *something* [ˌdɪˈʃautðə ~] [话] **大量地做某事** → DISH it out

disheartened

become disheartened [bəˌkʌm dɪsˈhɑ(ː)rtnd] [口] **灰心丧气** → lose HEART

dive

make a dive for *something* [ˌmeɪkə ˈdaɪvfər ~] [话] **朝着(某物)扑去** 直译为"跳入水中"。这一表达法使人联想到在游泳时头先入水的跳水姿态。可以用于一个人的场合,如:*I made a dive for the gun.* 我向前扑过去取枪。如果是两个人以上向某种东西扑,多半带有"争先恐后"的含义。*Spotting the gun on the floor at the same time, both men made a dive for it.* 两个人同时发现地板上有一支枪,他们争先恐后地扑了过去。*The quarterback fumbled, and everyone made a dive for the loose football.* 后卫接球失误,球员们一齐向那个在地上滚动的足球扑了过去。不仅如这些例句所示在"要取东西"的场合使用,也可以用以表示"为了逃脱或躲避而向某处飞奔[冲击、涌去]"的意思。*Hearing footsteps behind him, he made a dive for the* *bushes.* 听到身后有脚步声,他急忙向灌木丛中奔去。*When the fire alarm went off, we all made a dive for the doorway.* 当火灾警报响起的时候,我们全都向门口冲去了。◇ rush headlong to get *something* [for *something*]

divvy

a divvy [ə'dɪvi] [话] **分得的一份** → DIVVY up *something*

divvy up *something* [ˌdɪvi'ʌ(ː)p ~] [话] **瓜分** divvy 是取名词 dividend ['dɪvəˌdend] (红利) 的 div- 加上指小词 -y,为了发音的方便又重复一个 v 而构成的。原为名词,是表示"分得的一份"之意的轻松的表达法。*Harry says his divvy is too small.* 哈里说,他分得的那一份太少啦。但是,在现代英语中,很少作为名词使用,大多是用作动词。有时省略 up,例如:*Let's divvy the loot and make tracks outa here.* 咱们把赃物一分,赶紧从这儿溜走吧。但是,一般采取 divvy up 的形式。*The relatives are still fighting over how to divvy up the inheritance.* 亲属们还在争吵怎么瓜分遗产呢。*The three boys divvied the marbles up evenly among themselves.* 三个小男孩把玻璃球平均瓜分了。◇ divide *something*

DJ

a DJ [ə 'diː'dʒeɪ] [话] **流行音乐唱片节目的播音员** → a DEEJAY

do

do away with *something* [*someone*] [ˌduə 'weɪ wɪð ~] [口] **处理掉** 字面意义是"把……去掉",因此有"除去"、"结束"、"废止"、"处理"等意味,不论是哪种意味,其中心意思总归是"处理掉"。*Our old refrigerator was making so much noise that we finally did away with it and bought a new one.* 我们的旧电冰箱噪音太大,因此,我们终于把它处理掉,买了一台新的。*Society must do away with racial discrimination.* 社会必须废除种族歧视。do away with the need for *something* 的形式也是一个定型的说法,意思是"不再有……的必要"。*This new machine does away with the need for weekly lubrication.* 这台新机器用不着每个星期注油一次。如果 with 后面是"人",这一表达法意为"杀死",也就是"把人处理掉"。*Mr. Bluebeard is suspected of having done away with his first wife.* 布鲁伯德先生有杀害他的第一个妻子的嫌疑。*Having learned that the police suspect the truth, I determined to do away with myself.* 当我了解到警察已经怀疑事情的真相,我就决心自杀了。◇ dispose of *something* [*someone*] / get rid of [obviate] *something* / kill *someone*

make do with *something* [*someone*] → MAKE

make do without *something* [*someone*] → MAKE

D. O. A.

D. O. A. ['diː'ou'eɪ] [话] **送到(医院)已经死亡** 由 dead on arrival 的每一个单词的第一个字母构成。是医院、警察的用语。在侦探小说中经常出现。*I'm afraid the victim was D. O. A., doctor.* 大夫,很遗憾,我想被害者被送到这里时已经死了。*Chief, there's been a bad accident on the freeway. Four people involved. They're all alive now, but it looks as if a couple of them may be D. O. A.'s.* 局长,高速公路上发生了一起重大的事故。当事人四名。他们现在全都活着,但是看起来有两名等不到被送入医院就得死亡。◇ dead on arrival (at the hospital)

dodge

a tax dodge [ə 'tæ(ː)ks ˌdɑːdʒ] [口] **逃税花招** 原来 dodge 一词与 dodge ball (躲球游戏) 中的 dodge 相同,是"闪开身子"的意思。tax dodge 是为了不纳税而巧妙地"闪开身子"的窍门,但不一定是"偷税漏税"(tax evasion)。*The rich often use many clever tax dodges to reduce their taxable income.* 有钱人常常玩弄许多巧妙的逃税花招,以减少应该课税的收入额。*Mr. Green had his lawyer set up the Green Foundation as a tax dodge.* 格林

先生玩弄逃税的花招，叫他的律师成立格林基金会。◇ a method of avoiding taxes

dog

a dog biscuit [ə 'dɔːg ˌbɪskət] [口] **犬用小甜饼** → a horse BISCUIT

a dog in the manger [ə ˌdɔ(ː)g ɪnðə 'meɪndʒər] [口] **占着茅坑不拉屎的人** manger 是"牛槽"。条头的字面意义为"牛槽中的狗"。这一表达法来自《伊索寓言》(Aesop's Fables) 中的一个故事：有一条狗进入牛棚，向牛狂吠，咬牛，它根本不吃干草，可是也不叫牛吃。*That guy is a dog in the manger. It's been ten years since he quit playing tennis, but still he refuses to lend me his racket.* 那个家伙简直是占着茅坑不拉屎。他已经十年不打网球了，可是他还是不肯把他的球拍借给我。大多应用于"物"，但也有应用于"人"的场合。*Don't be a dog in the manger. You've broken up with Sally. Why won't you introduce her to me?* 你不要占着茅坑不拉屎啦。你已经跟萨莉吹了，为什么不把她介绍给我呢？另外，也使用于自己干不了或不愿意干而又不叫愿意干的人去干的场合。不论哪一种场合，在加强语气时都常使用 real。*My brother's a real dog in the manger. Just because he doesn't like to go sightseeing, he doesn't want us to go either.* 我的哥哥简直是一只占着牛槽的狗，他自己不想出去旅游，也不愿意让我们去。◇ a person who refuses to let others have [do] things which *he himself* does not want [want to do] (real etc. → absolutely)

Hot diggity dog! ['hɑtː'dɪgɪdi 'dɔːg] [话] **棒极啦!** → Hot DOG!

Hot dog! ['hɑt(ː)ˌdɔːg] [话] **太棒啦!** 本条音调响亮，富有现代感。但是，这是自本世纪初就有的古老的表达法。具有一些童稚的意味。男人、尤其是男孩子们常常使用。*"Hot dog!" said Jimmy when he saw his father bringing home a new bike.* 当吉米看见他父亲买来一辆新自行车时说："太棒啦！"正如这一例句所示，这一表达法并不是在"达到目的"或"大功告成"时的欢呼声，而是在意想不到的幸运来临时表示的单纯的喜悦。*Hot dog! The radio just announced that because of this heavy snow there'll be no school tomorrow!* 太棒啦！刚刚电台广播说，由于这场大雪，明天学校停课！*The war's over? Hot dog! That means we'll be home for Christmas!* 战争结束啦？太棒啦！这就是说，咱们可以回家过圣诞节啦。有时说 Hot diggity dog! ['hɑtː'dɪgɪdi 'dɔːg]，加个 diggity 是为了加强语气，因此译为"棒极啦！"*Hot diggity dog! Look at this. We've just won one thousand dollars in the lottery!* 棒极啦！你看看呀！我们中了彩票，一千美元！也可以省略 dog，如：*Hot diggity! Steak for supper!* 棒极啦！晚饭吃牛排！◇ Hooray!

put on the dog [puˌdɔ(ː)nðə 'dɔːg] [话] **大摆阔气** 这一场合的 put on 是"装腔作势"或"故作姿态"的意思，the dog 没有特定的意义。这一表达法原是小说家巴格(L. H. Bagg) 创造出来的，最初见于他所写的小说《在耶鲁的四年间》(*Four Years at Yale*, 1871) 中。在那本书里，作者用这一说法表示"浓妆艳抹"的意思，至于他怎么会想出这样的词句，对此我们一无所知。不论如何，这句话在当时曾经大为流行，后来又从"浓妆艳抹"的意义进一步发展，现在普遍用于表示 make an ostentatious display of elegance, wealth or culture (极力显示典雅、有钱、有教养)的意义了。*Hitler tried to achieve international acceptance of the Nazi party by putting on the dog at the 1936 Olympics.* 希特勒为了使纳粹党得到国际的承认，在 *1936* 年的奥林匹克运动会上拚命炫耀了一番。可用 really 加强语气。*When the Hunts give a party they don't do things halfway. They really put on the dog.* 当亨特家举行社交集会的时候，他们的确尽一切力量把它搞得热火朝天，决不半途而废。在下面的句子里，意义与"装门面"相近。*Will you lend me your new suit and fifty dollars? I want to put on the dog for my new girl* *tonight*. 你能借给我你那套新衣服和五十美元吗？我想今天晚上在新女朋友面前装装门面。在下一例句中，只是"装腔作势"的意味。*Dr. Dolittle isn't just putting on the dog when he uses all those big words. That's the way he talks all the time*. 多利特尔博士大量使用那些难懂的字眼儿，并不是为了装腔作势，那是他讲话时的老毛病。◇ put on an ostentatious display / show off

work like a dog [ˌwə(ː)rklaɪkə ˈdɔːg] [话] **卖命** 直译为"象狗一样劳动"。这里的"狗"指"没有自由，只是听从命令，象奴隶一样拚命干活的动物"。因此，work like a dog 含有"如此拚命劳动却得不到一点表扬或报酬"、"实在悲惨得很"的意味。*I work like a dog for that company and what thanks do I get? I haven't had a raise for almost two years now*. 我给那个公司卖命，得到什么报酬啦？现在快两年了，连一分钱的工资也没有增加。*I work like a dog to make my wife happy and still all she does is nag, nag, nag*. 我为了使妻子幸福而卖命劳动，可是她依然是唠叨、唠叨，唠叨个没完。以上的例句是应用于日常的劳动。但也可以应用于仅仅一次的工作或劳动，如：*Jim worked like a dog to finish that report on time. The least you can do is thank him for it*. 吉姆大卖力气，按时写完了那份报告。你至少应该向他道一声谢。另外有一个说法是 work *one's* FINGERS to the bone，意思大致相同，但多为女人使用。与此相对，work like a dog 则可以说是男性的专用语。◇ work extremely hard

doggoned

I'll be doggoned. [ˈaɪlbi ˈdɔ(ː)ˈgɔːn*d*] [话] **真他妈的！** → I'll be HORNSWOGGLED.

doghouse

be in the doghouse (with *someone*) [ɪnðə ˈdɔːgˌhaus] [话] **关系不妙** 直译为"进人犬舍"。丈夫得罪了妻子，不得走进家门，只好"进入犬舍"。如果想象一下这样的场面，就可以理解本条习用语的意味了。*I'm in the doghouse with my wife for forgetting her birthday yesterday*. 我忘记了昨天是妻子的生日，因此跟她关系很不妙。如此例所示，多以丈夫为主语，应用于夫妻关系上。但是，也可以应用于其他的人际关系。*Ralph is in the doghouse with his girl because he stood her up last night*. 拉尔夫昨天晚上对他的女朋友失约，因此弄得与她的关系很不妙。*Don't tell the boss I was late today. I'm already in the doghouse as it is*. 不要告诉老板我今天上班迟到，本来他对我已经没好印象了。另外有个 put *someone* in the doghouse 的表达法。*Your mentioning to my wife that I wasn't working last night really put me in the doghouse*. 你对我的老婆说昨天晚上我并没有加班，惹得她对我大发脾气。还可以说 get *someone* in(to) the doghouse。*My failure to turn in my report on time got me in the doghouse with my section chief*. 由于我未能按期限交出报告，惹得科长大为恼火。◇ be in trouble

dogs

Barking dogs seldom bite. [ˈbɑrkɪŋ ˈdɔːgz ˌseldəm ˈbaɪt] [谚] **吠犬不咬人** *Our neighbor's dog is very noisy, but I don't think it's dangerous. After all, barking dogs seldom bite*. 邻居的狗虽然叫得很凶，但是我觉得它没有危险。俗话说得好，吠犬不咬人嘛。*You wouldn't worry about your landlord's threats. Barking dogs seldom bite*. 你不必害怕房东的恫吓。俗话说，吠犬不咬人。*Sure they're angry, but let them yell. After all, barking dogs seldom bite*. 他们的确是怒了，但是，让他们叫嚷去吧。毕竟是吠犬不咬人啊。有象下面这样的变形：*When I saw the screaming mob coming toward me, I could only pray that what they say about barking dogs was true*. 当我看到一群人一边呐喊一边向我涌来的时候，我只能默默地祈祷，希望"吠犬不咬人"这句谚语是灵验的。也有时作 A barking dog seldom bites. dog 用单数形式。→ *Someone's* BARK is worse than *his* bite. ◇ People who use a lot of angry words seldom take action.

One's **dogs are barking.** [~ ˈdɔːgzər ˈbɑrkən] [话] **脚走累了** 这里的 dogs 不是"犬",在俚语中指"脚(踝骨以下部分)"。因此,本条的英语不是"犬在吠",正确的解释为"脚在发牢骚"。 *I hiked for twenty kilometers today. My dogs are really barking.* 今天我徒步旅行走了二十公里,我的两只脚实在太累啦。◇ *One's* feet are tired.

fight like cats and dogs → CATS

go to the dogs [ˌgoudəðə ˈdɔːgz] [话] **衰落** 字面意义是"到狗那里去"。原来的意味是:"一度繁荣的城镇完全衰落了,一群群的狗大摇大摆地在街道上走",亦即"城镇已经成了狗的世界"。主要指"一度经济繁荣,但是日趋衰败",但也用于"士气不振,道德水平下降"的场合。*That used to be a very fashionable area, but since the rich people have all moved out, it has gone to the dogs.* 在过去,那是一个非常高级的住宅区,但是自从有钱人都搬走了以后,已经衰败不堪了。*Mr. Beagle used to be a very successful company president, but since he started drinking heavily, both he and his company have gone to the dogs.* 比格尔先生过去是一位很有成就的公司总经理,但是自从他酗酒以来,不但他个人日益颓废,公司的营业也一蹶不振了。*According to the newspapers, crime and juvenile delinquency are increasing rapidly. If something is not done soon, the whole country will go to the dogs.* 据报纸上说,成年人犯罪和少年犯罪都在迅速增长。如果不赶快采取措施,整个国家的前途堪忧啊。◇ fall into a ruinous condition

lead a dog's life → LIFE

let sleeping dogs lie [let ˌsli(ː)pɪŋ ˌdɔːgz ˈlaɪ] [话] **不要惹事生非** 字面意义是"叫睡着的狗躺在那里好啦"。可以照字面意义使用,但一般用作比喻,表示"不要招灾惹祸,没事找事"的意思。*My son got bit when he tried to pet a strange dog lying in the street. He hasn't learned that he should let sleeping dogs lie.* 我的儿子去爱抚一只陌生的卧在街头的狗,结果被狗咬了一口。他还不懂得,狗在躺着睡觉的时候最好不要去动它。这是按照字面意义使用的场合,但是说话者显然意识到这一习用语的比喻意义了。*I know the tax office owes us a small refund, but if we apply for it they may look at our tax returns more closely. We'd best let sleeping dogs lie.* 我知道税务局欠我们一点儿余额,但是如果去要的话,他们就会更仔细地审查我们的报税单。我们最好不要去惹麻烦。*I was a fool to ask why I suddenly got an unexpected raise. I should have let sleeping dogs lie.* 我真傻,竟去质问为什么突然给我增加工资。我不该去没事找事啊。◇ not risk unfavorable results by disturbing the status quo

rain cats and dogs [ˌreɪŋˈkæ(ː)tsnˈdɔːgz] [话] **倾盆大雨** → rain PITCHFORKS

doing

take a lot of doing [ˌteɪkə ˌlɑ(ː)də ˈdu(ː)ən] [话] **很费事** 意思是"为了达到目的,要花费相当的时间和劳力",一般伴有"真够人呛"的意思。 *It took a lot of doing but I finally arranged for my wife to accompany me on my trip abroad.* 我费了九牛二虎之力,总算办好了我妻子随我出国旅行的一切手续。*It will take a lot of doing to be ready to leave by tomorrow.* 预备明天动身,还有许多事要办哪。可用 some, a bit of 等代替 a lot of。*It may take some [a bit of] doing, but I think I can convince the boss to go along with our idea.* 可能要费一些[一点儿]周折,但是我相信,我能够说服老板采纳咱们的意见。◇ require a lot of time and effort

doll

a doll [ə ˈdɑːl] [话] **美人** 美国人听到 doll 一词,一般来说,首先想到的当然是"玩具娃娃"。*The little girl has a new doll.* 那个小姑娘有个新玩具娃娃。但在现代,除了上述的意义外,这一表达法已经具有了多种多样的意义了。首先,在男性使用的场合与在女性使用的场合,意义就不一样。在男性使用的场合,第一个意义就是条头的译文“美人”。原指象商店橱窗里的假人那样的仅仅好看而没有头脑的美人,现在已不存在“没有头脑”的意思,单纯指“美人”而言了。*Get a load of that doll over there. I wonder what her name is.* 你瞧瞧在那边的那个美人哟! 不知道她叫什么名字。*Have you met Fred's fiancée? She's a living doll.* 你见到弗雷德的未婚妻了吗? 那可真是一个极漂亮的美人呀! 这里的 living 是形容 doll 的最高级的强调表达法,另外还可以用 a real doll 或 really a doll 的说法表示强调。其次, doll 又有“女人(泛指)”的意味。这是男性把女性看作东西的用法,妇女解放运动家们听了一定会生气的。*What do those dolls out in the hall want?* 走廊里来的那些女的要求什么? 以上是男性对女性,下面讲一下女性对男性怎样使用 doll 这个名词。首先,女性把 doll 的男性用法翻版,用以表示“有魅力的英俊男子(外表好看的男人)”的意义。*Isn't the captain of the baseball team a doll?* 棒球队长不是一个英俊的青年吗? 其次,女性在谈到儿童时使用 doll 一词,这是“多可爱的孩子”的意思。*Look at that little boy and girl over there. Aren't they dolls?* 你瞧瞧那边的那个小男孩和小女孩,真可爱,是不是? 最后,正如男性用 doll 一词形容女性的美一样,女性在谈到女人本身时也用这一表达法来形容她或她们的漂亮。不过,在这一场合,意思并不一样, doll 所指不是“男人眼睛里的美人”,而是近似“可爱的姑娘”。*My brother's new girl friend is a doll.* 我弟弟新近交的女朋友是个挺可爱的姑娘。另外,象以上这样使用 doll 的女性,以高中生、大学生等年轻人居多。→ be a DOLL ◇ a beautiful girl ((living → very / extremely))

be a doll [ə ˈdɑːl] [话] **好心肠(的人)** doll 除“玩具娃娃”或“美人”的意义外,还指“好心肠的人”。但在使用这一意义的场合,常伴有 be 动词。主要是女性对男性或孩子们使用的话。*Be a doll and let me use your car today, will you?* 今天请你把车让我用一下好吗? 只在关系密切的人们中间使用。至于母亲委托孩子去干什么的时候,常用如下的表达法。*Be a doll and wash these vegetables for me.* 好乖乖,来帮我洗洗菜。在象这样使用命令式的场合,实际上是在求人帮忙时开头的一个口头语,等于汉语“你行行好”的意味。相反,在别人给干了什么之后,也常用这一表达法表示轻轻的谢意。*A: Your husband was a real doll to help me yesterday. B: Don't mention it.* 甲:你丈夫昨天帮我的忙,他真是一位好心肠的人。乙:哪里哪里,那算不了什么。*Thank you for being so kind to my mother. You're a doll.* 感谢你对我母亲的关心,你的心肠真好。偶尔也有男性对女性使用的情况。*Linda, be a doll and type these letters for me, will you?* 琳达,请你把这信给我打一下好吗? → a DOLL ◇ be (very) sweet [kind]

dollar

bet *one's* **bottom dollar (that [on]～)** [ˌbet ～ ˈbɑ(ː)dəm ˈdɑ(ː)lər] [话] **绝对有把握** bet 是“赌”, bottom dollar 是“最后的一美元”,整个意思是“连最后的一块钱也赌上”,也就是“非常有信心”、“坚决地相信”。用英语换句话说,即 be absolutely certain (绝对有把握)。当然,这要比 *I'll bet that he'll succeed.* 他一定会成功的。之类没有 *one's* bottom dollar 的形式具有更强烈的确信程度。*Football is my favorite sport. Whenever there is a home game, you can bet your bottom dollar that I'll be there.* 足球是我最喜爱的运动。当地一有比赛,我是绝对参加的。*Fred says he's sure his nephew didn't steal the money, but I'll bet he wouldn't bet his bottom dollar on it.* 弗雷德说他认为偷钱的人不会是他的外甥,但是我认为他说这话并没有绝对的把握。◇ you can be sure (that～) / be absolutely sure (that ～)

dollars

dollars to doughnuts [ˈdɑ(ː)lərztə ˈdouˌnʌ(ː)ts] [话] **十拿九稳** 同样构思的表达法有 ten to one。在赌博中讲“十对

一",就是九成能赢,输的机会只有一成,因此有"十之八九"的意思。如果把条头的 dollars (美元)看作 ten, doughnuts (炸面圈)看作 one,那就容易掌握这一表达法的意义了。也就是说把一个"有价值"的东西与一个"无价值"(炸面圈是最廉价的小吃)的东西做对比。*I'll bet you dollars to doughnuts there'll be a recession before the end of the year.* 可以十拿九稳地说,年底以前会有一次经济衰退。如此例所示,I'll bet you dollars to doughnuts ~. 是基本形式。本条条头是省略了前半部分 I'll bet you。*It's dollars to doughnuts that she isn't expecting us tonight.* 她肯定不会想到我们今天晚上要去啊。*Dollars to doughnuts they've forgotten about their appointment with us this afternoon.* 他们肯定已经忘记今天下午和我们的约会了。◇ it's almost certain / I'm sure

feel like a million dollars [ˌfi(:)laɪkə ˈmɪljənˈdɑ(:)lərz] [话] **自我感觉良好** 直译为"感到象一百万美元那样"。在这里,a million dollars 是形象化的语言,意为"好极了",与 a million-dollar smile (一百万美元的微笑)用法相同。美国人经常用"一百万美元"来强调"好"的程度。*I had been in poor health for a long time, but I came back from my Florida vacation feeling like a million dollars.* 我曾经长期有病,但是自从到佛罗里达州休假归来以后,自我感觉极佳。*Since I started jogging every day I feel like a million dollars.* 自从每天慢跑以后,我的自我感觉好极了。另有 look like a million dollars 的表达法。意思是"看起来非常健康"。这一表达法用于从他人来看的场合,不能用于自己讲自己。*Phil had been in poor health for a long time, but he came back from his Florida vacation looking like a million dollars.* 长期以来,菲尔一直身体不大好,但是自从他从佛罗里达州休假归来以后,看样子健康极了。特别用于爱打扮的女性,表示"漂亮极了"的意味。*With her new evening dress and upswept hair style, June looked like a million dollars.* 琼穿上新的晚礼服,把头发梳成向上的式样,看起来漂亮极啦。另外,feel like a million dollars 的表达法有省略 dollars 的时候。例如:*Whenever I get to bed early, I wake up feeling like a million.* 凡是我晚上早睡的时候,第二天起床就自我感觉良好。◇ feel wonderful [extremely healthy]

dome

a dome [ə ˈdoum] [话] **(人的)脑袋** dome 是"圆屋顶",用它来比喻人的脑袋的形状。是一个轻松的表达法。*I sometimes wonder what's going on in his dome.* 我有时不明白他的脑子里在想什么。*Have you ever seen a dome as bald as that?* 你看见过象那样的大秃头吗? ◇ a head

Don

a Don Juan [ə ˌdɑ(:)n ˈwɑːn] [口] **勾引女子的男人** → a CASANOVA

doodad

a doodad [ə ˈdu(:)ˌdæ(:)d] [话] **叫不出名称的小玩意儿** → a THINGAMABOB

doohickey

a doohickey [əˈdu(:)ˌhɪki] [话] **叫不出名目的小玩意儿** → a THINGAMABOB

door

keep the wolf from the door → WOLF

show *someone* the door [ˌʃou ~ ðəˈdo(:)r] [话] **下逐客令** 字面意义是"对某人指着门(叫他出去)"。但在实际使用的时候,这一表达法完全不表示"指着门"的动作,仅仅是"撵走"的意思。也就是说,show *someone* the door 只有比喻的用法。例如:*She showed me the door.* 她撵我走。在这句话里,根本不表示她是不是指着门,如果译为"她指着门叫我走",那就大错特错了。当然,在现实生活中,当撵人走的时候,也常有指着门的动作。例如说:她一边指着门一边说:"这是出口,请你出去。"在这种场合,"指着门"在英语中一般用 point to the door 来表达。上面的整句话可以译为 *"There is the door. Please leave," she said, pointing to the door.* 请通过下面的实例体会 show *someone* the door 的意味和使用方法。*If that guy comes around here bothering you again, just call me. I'll show him the door in a hurry.* 如果那个家伙再到这儿来打扰你，你叫我好啦。我会马上把他撵走的。*Rich women must be hard to please. That's the fifth husband she's shown the door.* 有钱的女人一定是难以取悦的。她现在撵出去的已经是她的第五个丈夫了。如果在 *someone* 与 the door 之间加个 to，成为 show *someone* to the door，那意思就完全不同了，是"把某人送到门口"。*Though a very busy man, Mr. Dorman is unfailingly courteous. He always personally shows his callers to the door.* 多尔曼先生虽然是一位大忙人，但是他决不失礼，总是亲自把客人们送到门口。◇ get rid of *someone* / have *someone* leave

show *someone* **to the door** [ˌʃou ~ təðə ˈdo(:)r] [口] **(把某人)送到门口** → show *someone* the DOOR

doormat

use *someone* **for a doormat** [ˌju(:)z ~ fərə ˈdo(:)rˌmæ(:)t] [话] **拿人当小菜碟** 直译是"拿人当作门前擦鞋垫使用"。意思是"象踩门前的擦鞋垫一样，任意地对待他人"。这一表达法是从 WALK all over *someone*(踩在他人身上走路)联想而来。比如我们说 *He tries to walk all over me.* 他总骑着我的脖子拉屎。实际上与 *He tries to use me for a doormat.* 他总拿我当小菜碟儿。具有同样的意味。不仅用于颐指气使的场合，在胡说八道、拿人不当人等等不同的场合均能使用。*You have to stand up to the boss once in a while or he'll start using you for a doormat.* 你应该顶撞老板一回半回的，否则的话，他就拿你当小菜碟儿啦。在体育运动中也常使用。*We'll use their team for a doormat.* 我们要把他们那个队打个落花流水。偶尔用 as 代替 for，虽然略微生硬一些，但意思完全不变。*Mr. Milquetoast ought to stand up for his rights and stop letting everyone use him as a doormat.* 米克托斯特先生应该维护自己的权利，不再让任何人骑在自己的脖子上拉屎撒尿。a doormat 也可以单独使用，意思是"听人呵斥的、任人摆布的、甘受屈辱的可怜虫"。*How that doormat ever got to be a department head I'll never know.* 我简直不明白，那个唯唯诺诺、逆来顺受的家伙怎么会当上了部长。◇ treat *someone* however one likes

doornail

(as) dead as a doornail [əz ˈde(:)dəzə ˈdo(:)rˌneɪl] [话] **完全死了** doornail 是"门上使用的大头钉"。这是一个历史悠久的表达法，莎士比亚曾经使用过。"象大头钉那样"怎么会是"完全地"的意思呢？一般美国人也弄不清楚。原来在木匠的行话中有 dead-nailing 一词，动词作 deaden the nail，意思是将钉子打进去一半，然后把未打进的一半扭弯，使其牢固。也就是说，木匠用 dead 一词表示钉子横着倒下的状态。本条的表达法即由此发展而来。*A: The woman is still alive. How about the man? B: As dead as a doornail.* 甲：女的还活着。那个男的怎么样？乙：完全没气儿啦。as ~ as 中的前一个 as 常因说话的语调而脱落。*Be careful with that bottle. It's cyanide. One swallow of that and you'd be dead as a doornail.* 可要当心那个瓶子，那是氰化物。只要喝上一口，你便会一命呜呼啦。不仅限于"肉体的死亡"，也可以作为比喻使用，表示希望、计划等完全破灭或告吹。*After my long illness, any hopes I might have had of going to college next year were as dead as a doornail.* 由于长期患病，我明年要上大学的一切希望全都破灭了。◇ completely dead [gone]

dope

a dope [ə ˈdoup] [话] **笨蛋** dope 本来的意思是"麻醉剂"。如说 *He takes dope.* 他经常吸毒。后来进一步发展，又用于表示"头脑不灵、仿佛吸了毒的人"的意思。一般伴有"缺乏常识"的内涵。语调轻松，多用于具有戏谑、亲昵的气氛的场合。*What can you do with a dope like that? No matter how much you explain, he still gets it all wrong.* 你对那样一个笨

蛋有什么办法呢？你就是磨破嘴皮子向他解释，他也仍然给你搞个乱七八糟。加 -y 可以变成形容词。*I've never heard of such a dopey plan.* 我从来没有听到过象那样愚蠢的计划。→ a DUMBHEAD ◇ a stupid person

a dope sheet [ə 'doup.ʃi(:)t] [话] **赛马快报** → a racing FORM

dopey

dopey ['doupi] [话] **愚笨的** → a DOPE

Dora

a dumb Dora [ə 'dʌ(:)m 'do(:)rə] [口] **笨女人** 这里的 dumb 是"无知"、"愚钝"、"死心眼"的意义。Dora (多拉)是女人的名字，但由于与 dumb 语音谐调，就产生了本条的表达法，"单纯"的意义很强，近似汉语的"痴"字。请注意：是"笨"而不是"蠢"。*Why are so many beautiful women such dumb Doras?* 为什么十个美人九个痴呢？偶尔 Dora 小写，作 a dumb dora。→ a DUMBHEAD ◇ a stupid woman [girl]

do-re-mi

do-re-mi ['dou 'reɪ 'mi:] [话] **钱** 美国俚语 DOUGH['dou]意为"钱"(money)，与大音阶的第一个音 do 谐音，再加 re 和 mi 调整语调，便构成这一滑稽的表达法。唱歌的"多—来—米"变成了"现金"和"财产"的意味。*Did you bring any do- re-mi?* 你带着钱吗？*The Joneses seem to have plenty of do-re-mi.* 琼斯家似乎有很多财产。◇ money

dose

give *someone* **a dose of** *his* **own medicine** [.gɪv ~ ə.dousəv ~ .oun'medəsn] [口] **以其人之道还治其人之身** → give *someone* a taste of *his* OWN MEDICINE

dot

on the dot [ɔ(:)nðə 'dɑ(:)t] [话] **准时地** 这里的 dot (点)指"钟表上的刻度"。本条的字面意义是"表针正在刻度上边"，也就是"按照时间，分秒不差"的意思。常用 right 加强语气。*A: What time did you leave home? B: It was ten o'clock on the dot.* 甲：你什么时间从家里出来的？乙：十点整。*I was afraid Jake might be late, but he arrived on the dot.* 我还担心杰克会迟到呢，可是他准时到达了。*Jack is never late in repaying his debts. He always pays right on the dot.* 杰克在还债时从来不过期，他永远是准时付款。→ on the BUTTON ◇ exactly (on time [at ~ o'clock])

double

a double [ə 'dʌ(:)bl] [口] **二垒打 [棒球]** → a FOUR-BAGGER

on the double [.ɔ(:)nðə 'dʌ(:)bl] [话] **急忙** 这是由陆军用语 in double time 产生出来的表达法。in double time 意为"步调加快一倍"，即标准行进步调每分钟为 90 步，加倍为每分钟 180 步。 on the double 原来也是用于表示"步调加快一倍"的意味，但后来发展成为"急忙"、"赶快"的意思，而且在一般人中间广泛使用起来。*When we heard about the accident, we went home on the double.* 我们听到发生事故的消息，就急忙回家了。*Get in here! On the double!* 到这里来！赶快！◇ (very) quick(ly)

double-cross

double-cross *someone* [.dʌbl 'krɔ(:)s ~] [话] **欺骗** betray *someone* [*something*] 也有"欺骗"的意思，但 betray 一词意义广泛，用中文解释，有"出卖"、"背叛"、"叛变"、"辜负"等多种说法。它的性质是一般的。本条的 double-cross 在使用方法上有一定的限制，它仅指"不遵守信义或誓约而欺骗对方"。假定我们说"辜负世人的期待"，由于并没有同世人预先订过具体的誓约，那就根本谈不上什么"违约"，因而在译成英语时不能用 double-cross，而用 betray 就恰如其分了。另外，double-cross 这一表达法语气有些粗野，一般人虽然不是不能使用，但典型的使用者多半是匪帮，见于他们相互之间的对话。在侦探小说、情节影片中也常出现。*That guy double-crossed me. He was supposed to let me beat him up in front of my girl friend, but instead he made me look like a fool.* 那个家伙欺骗了我。本来说定了他让我在我的女朋友面前狠揍他一番，但是他说话不算话，反而把我弄得好象个小丑了。*Louie double-crossed the rest of the gang by making off with all the loot himself.* 路易欺骗他的同伙，把偷的钱全部拐走了。*You double-cross me and you're dead.* 你要是欺骗我，小心你的狗头！double-cross 的名词是 a double-cross，词形不变，但请注意发音：重音和次重音位置互换，作 ['dʌbl ˌkrɔːs]。*It looks like a double-cross.* 看起来上了一次当。还有一个使用 double-cross 的习用语 pull a double-cross (on *someone*)，意义与动词的 double-cross 完全一样。*If you try to pull a double-cross on me, you'll never live to tell about it.* 如果你要欺骗我，你就甭想活在世上。另外，"double-cross 的人"叫做 a double-crosser [ˌdʌbl 'krɔːsər]。*You double-crosser! I'll get you for this!* 你这个叛徒！我决饶不了你！◇ betray [trick] *someone*

pull a double-cross (on *someone*) [ˌpulə 'dʌbl ˌkrɔ(ː)s] [话] **欺骗(对方)** → DOUBLE-CROSS *someone*

double-crosser

a double-crosser [ə ˌdʌbl 'krɔːsər] [话] **背信弃义的人** → DOUBLE-CROSS *someone*

double-date

double-date ['dʌbl 'deɪt] [口] **参加两对男女的约会** 意思是"两对男女一起约会"。*Bill and Jim are double-dating two sisters tonight.* 今天晚上，比尔和吉姆与姊妹俩一起约会。*George and I are double-dating with Tom and Mary for the dance.* 乔治和我，汤姆和玛丽，我们一起参加舞会。这一表达法改成名词为 a double date 或者 double-dating。*Let's have [go on] a double date. [Let's double-date.]* 咱们来个双双约会[赴会]吧。*Double-dating is very popular among high school students.* 双双约会在高中学生中间是很盛行的。另外，也有"三对男女一起约会"的活动，这叫做 triple-date ['trɪpl 'deɪt]，名词为 a triple date 或者 triple-dating。◇ go on a date together as two couples

doubting

a doubting Thomas → THOMAS

dough

dough ['dou] [话] **金钱** 字面意义是"制面包的生面团"。最近，由于青年人开始用 BREAD 一词表示"金钱"，本条的表达法略有衰退的趋势。但是，直至今日，它作为表示"金钱"意义的俚语，依然被人民群众广泛地使用。这一表达法寿命很长，已有一百多年的历史，最初是"由贿赂得到的钱"，"用不正当方法得到的钱"的意思，然而后来进一步发展，变成"一般的金钱"，现在已经完全失去"不正当"的意思了。*How much dough have you got on you?* 你带着多少钱？*A house like that costs a lot of dough.* 那样一所房子价钱很高。*I'd like to buy a new car, but I haven't got the dough.* 我想买辆新汽车，但是没有那笔钱。◇ money

doughnuts

dollars to doughnuts → DOLLARS

down

be down and out [ˌdau nə'naut] [话] **一败涂地** 来自拳击用语。原是形容这样的状态："拳击手倒下了，裁判员数到十还是起不来"，亦即"被打倒在地，再也站不起来了"。后作为比喻使用。*By the time the Allied Armies reached the outskirts of Berlin, Nazi Germany was completely down and out.* 当盟国军队直叩柏林城下的时候，纳粹德国便彻底垮台了。也可以说 leave *someone* down and out。*The Great Depression of 1929 left many former rich men down and out.* 1929 年的大萧条使许多过去的有钱人彻底破产了。还有一个从本条派生出来的名词，即 a down-and-outer。这是"穷困潦倒的人"或"落伍者"的意思。*Every evening the down-and-outers line up here for a free meal from the Salvation Army.* 每天傍晚，许多穷人在这儿排队，领取救世军施舍的饭。另外，用动词 feel 代替 be，构成 feel down and out 的说法，一般

表示健康状态,即“完全没有精神”或“身上一点力气都没有”的意思。*I've been feeling down and out ever since I started taking that new medicine the doctor gave me.* 自从我开始吃医生给我的那种新药以后,我连一丁点儿精神都没有了。be down and out 有个变形的表达法,即 be down but not out。意思是:“虽然失利,但不举手投降”。*After losing his first two primary campaigns, the candidate told reporters that he was down but not out.* 候选人在最初两轮预选中失败了之后,对新闻记者们说:他虽然失利,但并不会一败到底。◇ be hopelessly poor [incapacitated]

be down but not out [ˈdaun bət.nɑ(ː)ˈdaut] [话] **虽然失利,但不举手投降** → be DOWN and out

be down in the mouth → MOUTH

feel down and out [.fi(ː)l .dau nəˈnaut] [话] **完全没有精神** → be DOWN and out

get *someone* **down** → GET

down-and-outer

a down-and-outer [ə .dau nəˈnaudər] [话] **穷困潦倒的人** → be DOWN and out

down-at-the-heels

down-at-the-heels [ˈdaunətðə ˈhi(ː)lz] [口] **褴褛的** → down at the HEELS

downstairs

kick *someone* **downstairs** [.kɪk ~ .daunˈsteːrz] [话] **降(某人)的级** → kick *someone* UPSTAIRS

Down Under

Down Under [.dau ˈnʌndər] [话] **(在、往)澳大利亚[新西兰]** Down Under 一般指澳大利亚,但有时也指新西兰。从英美人的角度看,澳大利亚和新西兰在地球的下侧 (under),因而产生这一爱称。*Meet a friend of mine from Down Under.* 我给你介绍一下我的澳大利亚朋友。*Hi, Dave, How were things Down Under?* 哦,戴夫。澳大利亚怎么样? *We do it differently Down Under.* 我们澳大利亚人不那样干。当然,在以上的例句中,“澳大利亚”均可改作“新西兰”。在英美的词典里,都用小字母,写作 down under。但在书信中,第一个字母大写的人居多。◇ (in [to, from]) Australia [New Zealand]

dozen

be a dime a dozen → DIME

be six of one and half a dozen of the other → SIX

draft

draft beer → BEER

drag

drag [ˈdræ(ː)g] [话] **减重短程高速汽车比赛** → a drag RACE

a drag race → RACE

a drag strip [ə ˈdræ(ː)g .strɪp] [口] **减重短程高速汽车赛车道** → a drag RACE

the main drag [ðə ˈmeɪnˈdræ(ː)g] [话] **繁华的大街** 听到 drag 一词,一般来说,美国人首先联想到的是“拖”(动词)。但在本条,它是“街道”的意思。开始使用 drag 作“街道”解的是过去的美国的流浪汉,但语源不明。可以设想把“街道”称为 drag 是由于它是“流浪汉拖着脚走的场所”,也可以设想 drag 一词是“高大马车”的意思,因而把这种交通工具来往的场所也称为 drag。不论来源如何,在现代,把它与 main (主要的) 结合起来,就变成了一个轻松的表达法,意思是“比一般街道宽而且往来的车多的大路”,亦即“主要的大街”、“繁华的大街”。*Two sports cars came barreling down the main drag.* 两辆赛车沿着大马路疾驰而来。◇ the principal street

stag or drag → STAG

dragster

a dragster [ə ˈdræ(ː)gstər] [话] **减重高速汽车** → a drag RACE

draw

beat *someone* **to the draw** [.bi(ː)t ~ təðə ˈdrɔː] [话] **(比对方)抢先行动** beat 常用于表示“比对方先下手[走]”的意味。本条直译为“比对方先拔出手枪或宝剑”。按照字面意义使用如下: *There is no cowboy in this territory who can beat*

Shane to the draw. 在这个地区的牛仔中，论拔手枪之快，没有一个能赶上沙恩的。作为比喻，广泛使用于男女往来、工作等。*I was planning to ask Betty to the prom, but Jack beat me to the draw.* 我本来打算请贝蒂参加学校的舞会，可是叫杰克抢先了。· *We didn't get the contract with ABC Corporation. One of our rivals beat us to the draw.* 我们没有能够与ABC公司签订合同，有一家竞争的对手抢先了。另外还有一个 beat *someone* to the punch 的说法，字面意义为"抢先痛击对方一拳"，作为比喻使用的时候与 beat *someone* to the draw 同义。*I was planning to pay for the dinner, but Jeff beat me to the punch.* 我本来打算付晚饭钱，可是杰夫抢先付了。◇ act more quickly than *someone*

be quick on the draw [ˌkwɪkɔ(ː)nðə ˈdrɔː] [话] **反应快** 本来的意思是"拔手枪的速度快"。*In the old West a sheriff had to be quick on the draw.* 在过去的西部，如果不能拔枪速射，就当不了县保安官。*In this business you have to be quick on the draw. Even a day's delay in reading the situation can cost many customers.* 干这种生意，必须反应快。对情况的了解哪怕晚一天，就会失去许多顾客。如此例所示，常用作比喻，表示"反应快"的意味。*Whenever a pretty new girl came to town, Fred was always the first one to get a date with her. None of the rest of the fellows were ever quick enough on the draw.* 每当镇上新来一个漂亮的姑娘时，弗雷德总是第一个跟她约会的人。其他的小伙子没有一个象他那样反应快。*Ronald is very quick on the draw. He is ready to answer most questions even before the asker finishes talking.* 罗纳德反应非常快。不等提问的人把话说完，他就对大部分问题准备好了答案。quick 的反义词是 slow，因此我们可以用 be slow on the draw 表示"反应慢"的意思。*You should have popped the question earlier. You lost her to someone else because you were too slow on the draw.* 你早点儿求婚就好啦。由于你的反应太慢，结果叫别人把她弄到手了。◇ react quickly

be slow on the draw [ˌslouɔ(ː)nðə ˈdrɔː] [话] **反应慢** → be quick on the DRAW

dress

dress *someone* **down** [ˌdres ~ ˈdaun] [口] **痛斥** → give *someone* a DRESSING down

dressed

be dressed up fit to kill → KILL

dressing

give *someone* **a dressing down** (for *something*) [ˌgɪv ~ əˌdresɪŋ ˈdaun] [口] **严加训斥** 在长辈对晚辈、上级对下级严厉叱责的场合使用。这里的 dressing 来自具有"纠正"意义的动词 dress。现在，它单独一词已不具"纠正"的意义，但与 down 结合在一起，就意味着"为了纠正他人的言行而严加训斥"了。*Bill's teacher dressed him down for eating in class.* 比尔在上课时吃东西，老师把他狠狠批评了一顿。但是，在实际上用 dress *someone* down 这一表达法的时候并不多，一般是把 dress down 动名词化，说 give *someone* a dressing down。虽然不是专门的军队用语，但在军官批评部下的场合常常使用。即便不是这样的场合，这一表达法也令人产生"以军人那样严厉的态度和口气"的感觉。另外，这种批评不是三言两语，多半是指较长时间的"耐心"教育。*The captain gave the lieutenant a dressing down for not being in proper uniform.* 中尉军容不整，上尉给予了严厉的批评。使用被动语态 be given a dressing down (by *someone* for *something*)表示"受到严厉批评"的意思的情况比较多。还有 get a dressing down (from *someone* for *something*) 这一表达法，意义相同。不论以上的哪一种形式，为了加强语气，常常在 dressing down 之前添加形容词 good。*Allen was given [got] a good dressing down by [from] his father for neglecting his studies.* 艾伦由于不用功而被他父亲狠狠地训斥了一大顿。另外，在英国英语中，这一表达法包括体罚在内，但在美国口语

中,仅指口头的批评。◇ reprimand *someone* severely

drink

the drink [ðə ˈdrɪ(:)ŋk] [话] **海[湖,池,川等]** 字面意义是"那个饮料"。这一表达法主要在人或物落入水中的场合使用。海是具有代表性的,但只要是比落下去的人或物大的"水体",不论什么都可以。当然,这是一个轻松的表达法。*The plane went into the drink.* 飞机掉到海里了。*As I was crossing the board which lay across the creek, my foot slipped and I fell in the drink.* 当我从小溪上搭着的木板上走过的时候,脚下一滑,掉到水里去了。◇ the ocean [lake, pond, river, etc.]

I'll drink to that. [ˈaɪl ˌdrɪnktə ˈðæ(:)t] [话] **我赞成** 直译为"我为那个喝酒"。"那个"(that)指对方所说的话。最初是在社交晚会的酒宴中,为了向谈话的对手表示赞同,一边举起酒杯一边说 I'll drink to that. 即"你说的很对,我为此喝一杯"的意思。现在,在与酒无关的场面也广泛使用。*A: He was the best Prime Minister England ever had. B: I'll drink to that.* 甲:在历代英国首相中,他是最好的。乙:我同意你的看法。*A: What say we go on a spree tonight? B: I'll drink to that.* 甲:今天晚上咱们狂欢一下怎么样? 乙:很不错呀。*A: Marriage is a bad scene. B: I'll drink to that.* 甲:结婚最没意思啦。乙:的确是这样。◇ I agree completely. / That's a very good idea.

be *someone's* **meat and drink** → MEAT

You can lead a horse to water, but you can't makehim drink. → HORSE

driver

a back- seat driver [ə ˌbæ(:)kˌsi(:)t ˈdraɪvər] [话] **不在权限或职责范围内而指手划脚的人** 直译是"坐在汽车后座上的驾驶员"。原指"坐在汽车后座上而向开车者唠唠叨叨、指手划脚的人"。常按照字面意义使用,但就怎样驾驶而指手划脚者不限定坐在后座上的人,坐在助手位置的人也可以。*It's not pleasant to ride in the same car with Mrs. Jones. She's a terrible back-seat driver.* 跟琼斯夫人乘一辆汽车是很不愉快的,她总是坐在后座瞎指挥,唠叨个没完。从这个用法一转,广泛用于表示"不在权限或职责之内而妄自指手划脚的人"的意思。*This company has too many back- seat drivers.* 在这个公司,指手划脚的幕后参谋太多了。*Whenever I'm designing a new piece of merchandise, some back- seat driver from the sales department comes and tries to tell me how to do my job.* 每当我设计一项新商品的时候,销售部总有什么人前来指手划脚,要告诉我怎样干我的工作。另外,没有 back-seat drive 这样的动词,但有动名词 back-seat driving,按字面意义和作为比喻均常使用。*That's enough! I'm tired of your back-seat driving.* 够了够了! 我对你的指手划脚已经烦死啦! ◇ a person who give unwanted advice on things that don't concern *him*

a slave driver [ə ˈsleɪv ˌdraɪvər] [口] **冷酷无情的雇主[上司、老师等]** → a SIMON LEGREE

a Sunday driver [ə ˌsʌndi ˈdraɪvər] [话] **危险的司机** 直译为"星期日的驾驶员",指缺乏驾驶技术而猛开车的司机。当司机胡乱开车的时候,乘车人胆战心惊,常常喊叫: Hey, Sunday driver! 意思是:"喂,好好开呀!" *The roads seem full of Sunday drivers these days.* 最近,马路上似乎满是胡乱开车的人。*Sorry I'm late. I got stuck behind a Sunday driver for most of the way.* 对不起,我来晚了。在一路上,前边是个胡乱开车的家伙,我怎么也超越不过来。◇ an erratic driver

drop

at the drop of a hat [ətðə ˈdrɑ(:)pəvə ˈhæ(:)t] [口] **马上** 字面意义是"帽子一落下"。在美国开发西部的时代,每当决斗(斗殴)的时候,证明人把帽子往下一扔,就是开始的信号。这一表达法便是由此种风习而来。也就是"帽子往下一落,马上就厮杀起来"的意思。现在,只保留"马上"的部分,专作比喻使用。

Jane is desperate to be popular. She'll date any boy at the drop of a hat. 简妍命要出风头。任何男孩子跟她约会，她都马上就答应。这仿佛是在叙述客观的事实，但多含有批判的意味。*Many people get divorces these days at he drop of a hat.* 最近，有许多人一说离婚马上就离。*The Government raises taxes at the drop of a hat.* 政府一说增税马上就增加税额。这一表达法相当频繁地与 be ready to + 不定式(准备……) 的形式结合使用。*I never know when the chief will send me somewhere on business. I have to be ready to go at the drop of a hat.* 为了生意上的事情，我从来不知道老板什么时候派我到什么地方去。我必须做好准备，一有命令立即出发。*My wife loves to travel. She's ready to go anywhere at the drop of a hat.* 我的妻子非常喜欢旅游。她做好了准备，不论去什么地方，马上可以出发。◇ without urging at the slightest pretext / at a moment's notice

be a drop in the bucket [ə ˌdrɑ(ː)pənðə ˈbʌkət] [口] **沧海一粟** a drop in the bucket 出自《圣经·旧约》，在《以赛亚书》(Isaiah) 第 40 章 15 节有这样一句话: Behold, the nations are as a drop of a bucket, and are counted as the small dust of the balance. (看哪，万民都象水桶的一滴，又算如天平上的微尘。) 但在现代，已不用 ~ of a bucket 的形式，而常说 a drop in the bucket 了。按字面意义是"在水桶里的一滴水"。从这一意义也可以了解，本条的表达法经常含有"与全体相比，只不过一点点"的意思。因此，在实际使用的时候，多与表示比较的词组如 (as) compared to ~等结合到一起。*You've accomplished a lot, but it's only a drop in the bucket (as) compared to what lies ahead.* 你完成了不少工作，但与摆在面前的任务相比，只不过是一点点罢了。*Man's knowledge of the universe is just a drop in the bucket compared to all there is to know.* 人类对于宇宙的知识，与所有尚待探求的知识相比，只不过是沧海一粟罢了。不使用 compared to 这一说法，意味也不变。*We've managed to save ten thousand yuan, but that's a mere drop in the bucket when you think of the cost of a new house these days.* 我们省吃俭用储蓄了一万块钱，可是按最近的房价，要买所新房子还是杯水车薪啊。另外，从上面的例子可以了解，一般来说，a drop in the bucket 用 only, just, mere 等加强语气。◇ a very small amount / very little

drop out (of *something*) [ˌdrɑ(ː) ˈpaut] [口] **中途停止** → fall by the WAYSIDE

get the drop on *someone* (by *doing something*) [ˌgetðə ˈdrɑ(ː)pɔ(ː)n ~] [话] **捷足先登** get the drop on *someone* 原来意为"抢先拔出手枪瞄准某人"。这里的 the drop 是"枪口往下"，就是"按照眼睛——照尺——照星——目标成一直线的角度把枪口下移"的意思。谁先这样瞄准，他就比对方占有绝对的优势。本条的表达法即来源于此。*I didn't have a chance to draw. He got the drop on me by coming up from behind.* 当时我没有拔手枪的机会。他出现在我的背后，先用枪口对准了我。转作比喻是"一步领先"的意思。但请注意它与 get the JUMP on *someone* (by *doing something*) 的不同点。一般来说，二者都是"抢先一步，占据优势"的意思。但是，get the jump on 这一表达法的重点在前半部分，亦即"抢先一步"，而 get the drop on 则"占据优势"的涵义很强。*I'm afraid we let our rivals get the drop on us. They applied for the patent needed to conclude the contract with ABC Corporation just two days before we did.* 看起来，我们的竞争对手已经捷足先登了。他们比我们早两天申请了与 *ABC* 公司签订合同所需要的专利权。*Nixon got the drop on the other would-be Republican candidates for President by securing the backing of party bigwigs before the campaign started.* 尼克松在选举运动开始之前就取得党内头面人物的支持，比共和党其他企图得到总统候选提名的人占有优势。have the drop on *someone* 也是人们常常使用的一个定型的表达法，当然是表示"抢先一步"或者"占据优势"的状态

了。*Graduates of that university have the drop on their rivals for government jobs.* 那个大学的毕业生比他们的竞争对手在政府机关就业的机会多。◇ gain the advantage on [over] *someone*

drown

drown *one's* **troubles [sorrows]** (in *drink*) → drown *one's* TROUBLES (in *drink*)

drug

a drug on the market [ə ˌdrʌ(ː)gɔnðə ˈmɑ(ː)rkət] [口] **滞销的商品** 关于语源，说法有二。一是解释为“对市场的 drug”。这里的 drug 是“麻醉剂”，即“使市场麻痹的东西”。另一个解释是“非有处方不可、因而很难卖出市场的 drug (药)”。究竟哪一个解释正确，现无定论。*This used to be one of our best selling products, but since many of our rivals have copied it, it's gotten to be somewhat of a drug on the market.* 这种产品一向是我们的畅销品之一，但是自从我们的许多竞争对手仿制以来，在市场上成了一种滞销品啦。如此例所示，一般用于因“供过于求”而滞销的场合。*Art lovers are very fickle. This painter's works once sold for very high prices, but now they're just a drug on the market.* 艺术爱好者的兴趣是变幻莫测的。这位画家的作品有一度卖很高的价钱，但是现在在市场上却无人问津了。也可以不用于物，而用于人，例如：*I'd hoped to teach history in high school, but by the time I graduated from college, history teachers had become a drug on the market.* 我本来希望到高中去教历史，但是到我从大学毕业的时候，历史教师已经多如过江之鲫了。另外，条头中的前置词 on 有时用 in 代换。◇ something [someone] nobody wants (to buy [hire])

drunk

dead drunk [ˈde(ː)d ˈdrʌ(ː)ŋk] [口] **烂醉如泥** 直译为“象死过去一样喝醉了”，用于形容“醉成一摊泥，人事不省”的状态。*The driver of the wrecked car was dead drunk.* 发生事故的汽车的司机是个烂醉如泥的家伙。*Leave him alone. He's dead drunk.* 甭管他啦，他已经喝得烂醉如泥啦。这个 dead 是用作副词的。另有 He's a dead drunk. (他是大醉鬼。)的说法，所以在讲话时请注意有无冠词。◇ completely drunk

(as) drunk as a lord → LORD

stinking drunk [ˈstɪŋkən ˈdrʌ(ː)ŋk] [话] **酩酊大醉** stinking 一般是具有“臭”、“讨厌”意思的形容词，但在这里却是副词，意思是“达到臭的程度”，即“不得了”、“非常地”。是个很轻松的说法。同类的用法有 stinking RICH (非常有钱的) 等。在这种表达法中，令人产生“酒香扑鼻”、“铜臭熏人”的感觉。*We got stinking drunk last night.* 昨天晚上我们喝得酩酊大醉。另外，请不要把 He's stinking drunk. (他已经酩酊大醉了。) 与 He's a stinking drunk. (他真是一个讨厌的醉鬼。) 弄混了。◇ very drunk

druthers

druthers [ˈdrʌðə(ː)rz] [话] **选择、愿望** I would rather (我宁可……)的缩略。I'd rather ～发音为 [aɪ ˈdræðər]，在方言中发音为 [ə ˈdrʌðər]。这个 [ə ˈdrʌðər]脱落了 [ə]，再加上表示复数的 [-z]，依照发音标记，就是本条条头的 druthers。这是一个相当随便的说法，但是，在日常会话中广泛使用。特别是 If I had my druthers, I'd ～.的形式，人们使用得较多。*If I had my druthers, I'd stay home today.* 如果按照我本人的愿望，今天我宁可留在家里。以下再举几个用例。*I thought I'd order our dinner brought in tonight. Do you have any druthers?* 今天晚饭，我想从饭馆叫菜。你点什么菜呀？*Well, those are your three choices. Name your druthers.* 好啦，你要从这三个中挑选一个。说你要哪个吧。*My husband never asks me my druthers.* 我的丈夫从来不问我的愿望如何。◇ a [*one's*] preference

dry

be (as) dry as a bone → BONE

(as) dry as dust → DUST

be dry behind the ears → EARS

Dry up. [ˌdraɪˈʌ(:)p] [话] **快住口吧!** 字面意义为“完全弄干吧!”。这一表达法是把滔滔不断的谈话比做河里的流水。“叫河水干吧!”的转意就是“不要再说下去了。” *Dry up, will you? I'm tired of hearing your constant complaining.* 闭上你的嘴巴好不好?你老是不断发牢骚,我实在听腻啦。正如这一例句所示,多使用命令式:Dry up, will you? 或者 Oh, dry up. 这一表达法虽然与 Shut up.(住口!) 同义,但是它的特点是专用于滔滔不绝的谈话或牢骚。也偶尔有不用命令式的场合。 *Joe finally dried up after he saw how fed up we had become with his endless talk.* 乔看出我们对他的没完没了的谈话已经腻烦透了之后,终于不再说下去了。◇ Be quiet. / Stop (*one's* endless) talking.

leave *someone* **high and dry** → HIGH

dry-as-dust

dry-as-dust [ˈdraɪəzˈdʌ(:)st] [口] **非常干燥无味的** → (as) dry as DUST

dry-gulch

dry-gulch *someone* [ˈdraɪˌgʌltʃ ~] [话] **伏击** a dry gulch 指美国沙漠地带为数很多的、雨季以外没有水的、深而险峻的小峡谷。过去,印第安人常在这样的地方设下埋伏,袭击白种人。后将这一名词变为动词,形成条头的表达法。中埋伏的也许是一个人或几个人,而袭击者一般总是人多势众,因此,这一表达法多伴有“太卑怯了”的意思。通常具有杀意,但并不绝对如此。 *The Indians dry-gulched the hunting party.* 印第安人设下埋伏,袭击了一群狩猎者。 *The Confederate troops were dry-gulched by the Yankees.* 南军遭到了北军的伏击。 *We were dry-gulched by a bunch of robbers.* 我们受到一群强盗的伏击。◇ attack *someone* from ambush

duck

a dead duck [ə ˌde(:)ˈdːʌk] [话] **注定要完蛋的人[物]** “死鸭子”为什么会有这样的意义,不详。 *Our pursuers have guns. If they catch up with us, we're dead ducks.* 追的人拿着枪哪。如果他们追上我们,我们就完蛋啦。如此例所示,在使用这一表达法时,总包含着作为句子主语的人现在虽然活蹦乱跳、但命中注定要死亡的意味。 *Mr. O'Walley has been fighting bankruptcy for many months. Now that the tax office has found he cheated on taxes, his company is a dead duck.* 欧瓦利先生为了摆脱破产的危机一直奋斗了好几个月。现在税务局又发现他偷税漏税,他的公司已经无法挽救了。 *The boss has threatened to fire you before. When he finds out you've been entertaining your friends on your expense account, you're a dead duck.* 老板早就说过要解雇你。如果他发现你用交际费请你的朋友们大吃二喝,你肯定就得卷行李啦。 *Unless the government can get some support from the opposition, its energy bill is a dead duck.* 政府如果得不到反对党的若干支持,它的能源法案肯定是通不过的。也可以用 pigeon (鸽子)代替 duck (鸭子),而说 a dead pigeon。另外,在英国英语中,这一表达法具有“已经无用之物”、“已经毫无价值之物”等意义,但一般美国人不会这样理解。◇ doomed (to die [to fail, to face severe punishment, etc.]) / finished

be duck soup → SOUP

take to *something* **like a duck to water** [ˌteɪktə ~ laɪkə ˈdʌktə ˈwɔ(:)dər] [话] **天生喜好** 尽管是第一次入水,小鸭子马上会适应环境,不但毫无困难,而且对水非常喜欢。这一表达法表示对某一事物天生就喜爱的意思。 *Darrell takes to life in China like a duck to water.* 达雷尔非常喜欢在中国生活,这合乎他的天性。 *I never did well in arithmetic, but our son seems to take to it like a duck to water.* 我的算数从来没有得过好分数,但是我们的儿子似乎天生就喜欢算术。如果讲的是特别需要技术的事情,这一表达法还含有“也有这样的才能”的意味。例如: *Jack took to tennis like a duck to water.* 杰克天生喜爱网球,他也有这方面的才能。也可以把省略的 takes 加上,作 take to *something* like a duck takes to water。*From the first day of school, Johnny took to reading like a duck takes to water.* 从上学的第一天起，琼尼就自然而然地爱好上了读书。◇ take to *something* very naturally / be instinctively good at *something* / take an instinctive liking to *something* (from the very beginning)

duck's

(roll of *someone*) **like water off a duck's back** → WATER

ducks

(go) teach *one's* **grandmother** (how) **to milk ducks**[ˌ(gou)ˌtiːtʃ ~ ˈgræ(ː)nˌmʌðər (hau)dəˌmɪlkˈdʌks] [话] **班门弄斧** → (go) teach *one's* GRANDMOTHER (how) to suck eggs

duds

duds [ˈdʌ(ː)dz] [话] **衣服** 此词来自具有同一意义的中古英语 dudde。现在与 clothes 一样只用复数的形式。也用于表示"个人所有物"的意思，但极罕见。可以把这一表达法当作 clothes 的俚语看待。*I gotta buy some new duds.* 我得买点新衣服了。*I thought we'd only be here for two days, so I only brought one change of duds.* 我原来以为我们在这儿仅呆两天，所以只带了一套换的衣服。◇ clothes

dumb

dumb [ˈdʌ(ː)m] [话] **愚笨的** 此词本来是"不能说话的"的意思。原来的使用方法如：*Dumb people are called mutes.* 不能说话的人叫做哑巴。*Be kind to dumb animals.* 要爱护不会说话的动物。在日常会话中，用以表示"愚笨的"或"愚蠢的"的意义的频率极高，等于 stupid。*What a dumb thing to do!* 你干了多么愚蠢的事情！*It takes a pretty dumb guy to do a thing like that.* 不是一个十足的大笨蛋，决干不出那样的事情来。◇ stupid / foolish

a dumb bunny → BUNNY

a dumb cluck → CLUCK

a dumb Dora → DORA

a dumb ox [ə ˈdʌ(ː)ˈmɑːks] [话] **(身材高大的)拙笨的人** → a LUMMOX

play dumb (with *someone*) [ˌpleɪ ˈdʌ(ː)m] [话] **装聋作哑** DUMB 原义"不能说话的"，在俚语中变成"愚笨的"或"愚蠢的"的意思。本条习用语显然具有俚语的意味，play dumb 直译就是"装糊涂"。*He says he doesn't know where she is, but he's just playing dumb.* 他说不知道她住在什么地方，那只是瞪着眼睛说瞎话罢了。*Don't play dumb with me or you'll be sorry.* 甭跟我装傻，有你后悔的日子。◇ feign ignorance

dumbbell

a dumbbell [ə ˈdʌ(ː)mˌbe(ː)l] [话] **笨蛋** 按照字面意义，dumbbell 是体操用具"哑铃"。例如说：*Frank exercises every day with dumbbells.* 弗兰克每天做哑铃操。如果把此词拆开来看，dumb 是"不能说话的"，bell 是"铃"，合起来则为"不能出声的铃"，这与 DUMB (→) 的另一意义"愚笨的"是息息相通的。在会话中常用于表示"愚笨的"、"头脑迟钝的"之类的意味。*You dumbbell! Can't you do anything right!* 你这个笨蛋！你就不能干好一件事情吗？ *Me? Marry a dumbbell like May Detigh? You're out of your mind!* 我？你叫我跟梅·德泰那样一个笨女人结婚？你莫不是发疯啦！→ a DUMBHEAD ◇ a stupid person

dumbhead

a dumbhead [ə ˈdʌ(ː)mˌhe(ː)d] [话] **傻瓜** 字面意义是"愚笨的脑袋"。在具有"傻瓜"、"呆子"、"糊涂虫"、"笨蛋"、"愚人"等意味的英语中，这一表达法最有代表性（关于 dumb 的来源，请参阅 DUMB 条）。与 a FOOL 比，语气轻松得多。*That dumbhead. He should have told us he was going alone.* 那个傻瓜。他应该告诉我们他要一个人去。除 dumbhead 以外，在本书中收录的表示"傻瓜"或近似意味的词有（冠词省略）：blockhead, blubberhead, bonehead, boob, booby, dimwit, dope, dumb bunny, dumb cluck, dumb Dora, dumb ox, dumbbell, dum-dum, dummkopf, dummy, fathead, fool, half- wit, idiot, imbecile, lame- brain, lummox, moron, nincompoop, ninny, nitwit, numbskull, sap, silly billy, simpleton。以上这些用语在意义上都差不多,但使用方法有一定的差别。现大致分类如下,供读者参考。最严厉的说法是 fool, 只在真正动怒时使用。次一级严厉的是 nincompoop, 但与 fool 不同,常以开玩笑的口吻使用。imbecile, moron, idiot 虽然在使用时大多表达说者的真心思想,但没有 fool 那种破口骂人的味道。至于其他的一些表达法,一般来说,都有一定程度的戏谑成分,即使说者动怒,其中也含有亲密的感情。在数量上,带 dumb 的词 (dumbhead, dumbbell, dumb cluck 等) 显然多一些。dumb ox 和 lummox 指男性,而 dumb Dora 则指女性。dumb bunny 最柔和,几乎永远伴有"可爱"的意味。dum-dum 可以认为是年轻人的专用语。silly billy 包含着亲密的感情,专由女性使用。dimwit, numbskull (或者 numskull), fathead, bonehead, blockhead, dummkopf 强烈地表示"不论如何思索,头脑总不开窍"的意思。nitwit, lame-brain, half-wit 主要指"智力本身有缺陷、无可奈何的人"。dope, sap, simpleton, boob (或者 booby) 大多指"没有常识,听了别人的话就信以为真的人"。simpleton 是个有点生硬的表达法。ninny 虽然也指"缺乏经验,屡遭失败的人",但与 sap 等词不同,含有"只要久经锻炼,必将通达事理"的意味。dope, sap, simpleton, boob 与 ninny 完全相反,指"即便有了失败经历,也不能吸取教训,直至地老天荒也改正不了"。另外,还有很多类似 fool 的词,如 dolt, dullard, dunce 等等。这些说法不是陈旧,就是比较生硬,因而在现今的会话中很少使用,本书也不一一列举了。◇ a stupid person

dum-dum

a dum-dum [ə 'dʌ(:)m.dʌ(:)m] [话] **傻瓜** 将 DUMB 重叠并按发音缀字的表达法。主要是青年人使用,含有亲密的感情。*George, you're a real dum-dum.* 乔治,你真是个傻瓜哟! → a DUMBHEAD ◇ a stupid person

dummkopf

a dummkopf [ə 'du(:)m.kɔ:f] [话] **死脑瓜骨** 完全照搬德语 *Dummkopf* ['dumkɔpf] 的表达法。此词相当于英语的 a DUMBHEAD, 但比 dumbhead 劲头强烈一些,语调倒很接近 a BLOCKHEAD。主要在呼唤傻瓜时使用。*You dummkopf! How many times do I have to tell you to knock before you enter.* 你这死脑瓜骨!进来以前一定要敲门,我得跟你说多少次你才能记住呀? ◇ a stupid person

dummy

a dummy [ə 'dʌmi] [话] **笨人** 原为 DUMB 加 -y,按发音缀字的表达法。自 16 世纪起作"哑巴"解。但是现在很少使用这一意义,一般用以表示"笨人"的意味。在英语中,相当于"笨蛋"、"傻瓜"的词非常多(→ a DUMBHEAD),但在大量的同义词中,dummy 语气比较柔和,有时对被称为"笨人"者具有亲密的情感。例如: *Don't tell me that dummy is lost again.* 那个笨家伙莫不是又迷路啦。*You dummy. You know I like you better than Mary.* 你这个小傻瓜呀!你明明知道我喜欢你胜过喜欢玛丽啊。顺便提一下: dummy 一词另外还有很多意义,最常用的意义是"人体模型"。这一意义是 19 世纪产生的,思路仍然是"不能说话的人或类似人的东西"。*I wonder how come most Chinese department store dummies have foreign faces.* 真奇怪,中国百货商店橱窗中的假人为什么大多是外国脸儿。◇ a stupid person

dump

dump on *someone* ['dʌm.pɔ(:)n ~] [话] **倾吐衷肠** 在 dump 与 on 之间仿佛有 *one's* troubles (烦恼) 存在。dump 是"把重的东西猛地扔下[抛出]"。本条表达法的最初构思是"把成为沉重负担的烦恼猛地抛到对方的身上"。但是,实际并不是单方面抛出,对方 (关系密切的朋友或同伴) 总是会细心倾听的。所以,这一表达法是以对方的同情为前提的。*Whenever she has a fight with her boy* *friend, she always goes over and dumps on Alice.* 每当她跟自己的男朋友吵架的时候，她总是跑到艾丽斯那里去倾诉一肚子的委曲。 *Bob is a good friend. He always lets me dump on him.* 鲍勃真是一个好朋友。我有什么烦恼的事情，他总是听我向他倾诉。*You can dump on me if you want.* 如果你需要的话，我愿意倾听你的一肚子烦恼。本条是一个比较新的表达法。◇ tell *someone one's* troubles

dumps

be down in the dumps [ˌdaunɪnðə ˈdʌ(ː)mps] [话] **垂头丧气** 在莎士比亚时代，dump 的意思是"慢速的哀歌或舞蹈"。现在，此解早已明日黄花，只留下"伤心"、"郁闷"这样一点余韵而已。不过，仅仅是 dump 一个词还不行，如今必须使用 be down in the dumps 的形式，既要加 the，本身又是复数。如果一不留神，把 -s 给漏掉了，那就不是"心情沮丧"，而变成"下到垃圾堆"这样一句莫名其妙的话了，这一点务请读者注意。这一表达法与 be down in the MOUTH 相似，但语气强烈一些。*George is down in the dumps because he lost his pay envelope.* 乔治由于丢失装着工资的封筒而垂头丧气。常用 feel, look, seem 等代替动词 be。 *I feel down in the dumps today.* 我今天打不起精神来。*John has seemed down in the dumps ever since he came home from Paris.* 约翰自从巴黎归来以后，似乎闷闷不乐。有时省略 down。 *Is anything wrong? You look in the dumps.* 出什么事儿啦？看起来你的精神很不好。◇ be depressed

be in the dumps [ɪnðə ˈdʌ(ː)mps] [话] **精神不振** → be down in the DUMPS

dunno

dunno [dəˈnou] [话] **不了解、不知道** don't know 音变后，按发音缀成的表达法。也就是说，在轻松的日常会话中，don't know 发音作 [dəˈnou]。在漫画、小说等的会话部分经常可以见到。*A: What time is it now? B: I dunno. I haven't got a watch.* 甲：现在几点钟？乙：不晓得，我没带表。*I dunno if they're coming or not.* 我不知道他们到底来不来。顺便提一下：在日常会话中，doesn't know 和 didn't know 也与 don't know 同样常有发生音变的情况，但不知为什么，并没有象 dunno 这样定型的表记法。另外，doesn't know 一般发音为 [ˌdʌdˈn(ː)ou]，didn't know 一般发音为 [ˌdɪdˈn(ː)ou]，但有时进一步简化，分别发音作 [ˌdʌˈnːou] 和 [ˌdɪˈnːou]。如果只是 didn't，特别是在漫画、小说等的儿童会话部分，有时表记作 din't 或 dint，发音均为 [ˈdɪn(ː)t]。◇ don't know

dust

bite the dust [ˌbaɪtðə ˈdʌ(ː)st] [话] **在战斗中被击毙** dust 是"尘土"。本条的字面意义是"咬地面的土"。这是从美国西部开发时代的各种战斗中产生的一个表达法。 *Soldiers were biting the dust all around me.* 我周围的士兵全都被打死了。*The sheriff let off one round and the thief bit the dust.* 县保安官放了一枪，小偷应声倒毙了。有时不管是否打死，仅表示"被击倒"的意思。*Go and see if those three who bit the dust are still alive.* 你去看看那三个被击倒的人是不是还活着。后来，把这个"被击毙[倒]"的意思一转，又成为"死亡"一词的轻松的表达法。*Two of the cholera patients have already bitten the dust.* 两个霍乱病患者已经死了。现在更进一步作为比喻使用，表示"在竞争中失败"，包括"比赛输了"、"企业倒闭"等，范围很广。*Our team bit the dust today.* 我们队今天输啦。*The present business depression has caused many companies to bite the dust.* 当前的生意萧条使许多公司都倒闭了。◇ be shot to death / fall dead / fall (after being shot) / die / lose / fail

(as) dry as dust [əz ˈdraɪəz ˈdʌ(ː)st] [口] **非常枯燥无味** 直译为"象尘埃一样干燥"。是强调枯燥无味、沉闷已极的表达法。 *I hate to have to listen to the boss's speeches. They're always dry as dust.* 我最讨厌听老板的报告，他的报告永远是枯燥无味的。*I couldn't finish that book*

Hal gave me. I found it as dry as dust. 我没能读完哈尔送给我的那本书，我觉得它太枯燥无味了。在直接形容名词的场合，或是用连字符连起来作 dry-as-dust，或是构成一个词作 dryasdust。*The book John recommended that I read turned out to be a dry-as-dust treatise on economics.* 约翰推荐叫我读的那本书，原来是一部非常枯燥无味的经济论著。在极为罕见的场合，有用 a dryasdust 表示“无聊极了的人”的情况。在这种场合，第一个字母有时大写，作 Dryasdust。来源是：司各脱 (Sir Walter Scott, 1771–1832)经常在自己所著小说的卷头写上“呈献 Dr. Jonas Dryasdust”的字样。Dr. Jonas Dryasdust 当然是个虚构的人物。司各脱的意思是说：“我的书枯燥无味，非常无聊，只有 Dr. Dryasdust (枯燥无味博士)可能感到有趣，爱不释手。”这是司各脱的自我解嘲，也是一种幽默。*Dr. Dewey may be a great scholar, but as a speaker he's just another dryasdust.* 杜威博士可能是一位伟大的学者，但是他的讲话却是枯燥无味，简直无聊极了。◇ very dull [uninteresting]

make the dust fly [ˌmeɪkðə ˈdʌ(:)st.flaɪ] [话] **干得起劲** 直译为“使尘土飞扬”，原来可能是形容“热火朝天地打扫卫生”的表达法。实际上，现在也多用于打扫卫生的场合，例如：*I've never seen anyone clean house as fast as Mrs. Dartabout. She really makes the dust fly.* 我没见过任何人象达特包特夫人那样飞快地打扫屋子。她干得实在起劲啊。如以下的例句所示，也常用以形容干工作的样子。这一表达法的具体形象是：速度快，干劲大，动作麻利，有条不紊。*Talk about making the dust fly! The carpenters who fixed our roof were finished in less than an hour.* 要说那干劲，可真够热火朝天的！给咱们家修理房顶的几位木工师傅，不到一个小时就把活儿干完啦。在 see 之类的动词后边，有时省略句子中的 (*someone*) make，例如：*If you want to see (someone make) the dust fly, ask Johnny to help you. He's the fastest worker I've ever seen.* 如果你想看一看干活起劲的样子，可以去请琼尼帮助你。我没见过比他手脚更麻利的工人。◇ clean [work] at a fast pace

Watch *someone's* **dust.** [ˈwɑtʃ ~ ˈdʌ(:)st] [话] **转瞬之间走去(到达)** → watch *someone's* SMOKE

Dutch

go Dutch [ˌgou ˈdʌ(:)tʃ] [话] **分摊** 自古就有的表达法，意思是：“按照荷兰人的方式办”。过去，英国人认为荷兰人吝啬。这一表达法便是由此种偏见产生的。在历史上，英国与荷兰曾经长期处于敌对关系。结果，在英语中就出现了许许多多用 Dutch 一词表示轻蔑意义的习用语，go Dutch 是其中具有代表性的一个。但是，这一表达法现在已经完全没有过去那种轻蔑的意味，普通的美国人根本弄不清楚为什么会有 go Dutch 这样一个说法。*Let's go Dutch tonight.* 今天晚上咱们分摊付钱吧。*Recently there are many girls who, even when out on a date, prefer to go Dutch in order to show their independence.* 最近有许多姑娘为了表示自己的独立性，甚至在与男朋友约会的时候，都宁愿各自付各自的钱。◇ (each) pay *one's* own way

be in Dutch with *someone* [ɪnˈdʌtʃ wɪð ~] [话] **与某人关系不妙** 字面意义是“与某人的关系就象与荷兰人的关系一样”。关于这一表达法的来源，最有力的说法是：17 世纪以后，在国际政治和贸易等方面，英国与荷兰激烈竞争，两国一直互相仇视。*I'm in Dutch with the boss [my wife].* 我与老板[我妻子]的关系不妙。*He is often in Dutch with his superiors.* 他常冒犯自己的上司。如以上的例句所示，这一表达法在与长辈、上司、有权干涉自己行动的人、具有密切利害关系的人“一时关系恶化”的场合使用。用 for ~的形式表达“恶化的理由”。*He's in Dutch with his wife for forgetting her birthday.* 他由于忘记妻子的生日，跟她的关系很不妙。用 get 代替动词 be，就变成“搞糟关系”的意思。在这一场合，多用 by ～的形式而不是 for～的形式表达"恶化的理由"。 *I got in Dutch with Frank by not attending the meeting.* 我由于没有出席会议，搞糟了与弗兰克的关系。也可以说 get *someone* in Dutch with *someone*，把 get 作为及物动词使用。在这一场合，大多不以"人"为主语，而是以"使关系恶化的理由"为主语。*His temper often gets him in Dutch with people.* 他的火暴脾气常常使他与别人关系紧张。作为及物动词，还可以使用 put。 *His back talk put him in Dutch with his teacher.* 他爱顶嘴，搞糟了他与老师之间的关系。◇ be in trouble with *someone*

dyed-in-the-wool

dyed-in-the-wool [ˈdaɪdɪnðə ˈwu(ː)l] [口] **彻头彻尾的** 字面意义是"在毛线未织成呢绒前染了颜色"。在织成呢绒以后染色，容易褪色；但在毛线的阶段染色，颜色就不容易掉。本条的表达法就是由这一情况产生的。专作比喻使用。*You'll never get your father to vote for a Communist candidate. He's a dyed-in-the-wool conservative.* 你想叫你父亲投共产党候选人的票，那是绝对办不到的。他是一个玩固透顶的保守分子。*The government will never be able to close the race tracks. There are too many dyed-in-the-wool gamblers among the voters.* 政府永远也不会取缔赛马。在选民当中，积习已久的赌徒太多啦。*That guy is more than stupid. He's a dyed-in-the-wool ignoramus.* 那个家伙不是愚笨，而是无知到了极点。◇ thoroughgoing / complete

dynamo

a human dynamo [ə ˌhjumən ˈdaɪnəˌmou] [口] **精力充沛的人** → a BALL of fire

E

eager

an eager beaver → BEAVER

ear

bend *someone's* **ear** [ˌbend ～ ˈɪ(ː)r] [话] **喋喋不休** 直译为"使某人的耳朵弯曲"。用于表示"唠叨没完,使对方的耳朵都疲倦得耷拉下来"的意思。虽然不直接包含"达到令人讨厌的程度"的意味,但多用于表示这样的状态。例如: *Paul bent my ear about his troubles last night until I thought I would scream.* 保罗昨天晚上向我喋喋不休地谈他的烦恼,使得我简直都要喊叫起来了。也可以采取 bend *someone's* ear till it falls off 的形式。添加上 till it falls off (直至掉下来),"厌烦"的感情就昭然若揭了。 *Stay away from Mrs. Flapjaw. She'll bend your ear till it falls off.* 不要接近弗拉普焦夫人。她会向你喋喋不休地说东道西,腻烦死你的。下面的例句是作为说笑的表达法。 *Something important has come up. Mind if I bend your ear for a moment?* 有点重要的事情。能扰一下您的清听吗? ◇ talk on and on / speak to *someone*

go in one ear and out the other [ˌgoɪn ˈwʌˌnɪ(ː)r əˌnautðɪ ˈʌðər] [话] **左耳进右耳出** 直译是"这一个耳朵进,那一个耳朵出"。多用于对他人的规劝、忠告、提醒等一概不听的场合,但并不以此为限,也可以用于因心不在焉而把他人的话当耳旁风的场合。根据上下文,有时与汉语成语"马耳东风"、"对牛弹琴"相当。但请读者注意:这句英语中丝毫没有"不知恩情"的意味。为了加强语气,多与 just 一起使用。 *I'm always telling the students that they have to study harder, but it just seems to go in one ear and out the other.* 我总是对学生们讲要加强学习,可是这似乎是马耳东风。 *Why don't you ever pay attention? Everything I say to you goes in one ear and out the other.* 你怎么总不注意听呢? 不管我说什么,你都是左耳进右耳出。 *Almost all the students failed the test. It seems my lectures just went in one ear and out the other.* 在考试中,几乎全班学生都不及格。看起来,我的讲义他们一点也没听进去啊。这是从结果来考虑,表示"没有留下任何印象"的意思。◇ not penetrate *someone's* mind / have no effect

have a tin ear [ˌhævə ˈtɪ(ː)ˈnɪ(ː)r] [话] **音盲** tin ear 是"马口铁的耳朵"。条头意思是"用马口铁的耳朵,分不清微妙的音阶"。 *Horatio has a tin ear. He can't tell one song from another.* 霍雷肖是个音盲。他区别不开这支歌与那支歌的不同。 *I have such a terrible tin ear that even opera sounds like so much caterwauling to me.* 我是一个非常严重的音盲。就连歌剧,我听着也象猫叫一般。也常使用 with a tin ear 的形式。 *No one with a tin ear like hers should ever have taken piano lessons in the first place.* 象她这样一个音盲,根本就不应该学习钢琴的课程。be tone-deaf (音盲)的意义也完全相同。 "唱不了歌"的英语是 can't carry a tune。 如果强调自己五音不全,就说 I can't even carry a tune in a bucket. (直译:我简直不能用水桶提曲调。) 这是一种诙谐的说法,把 a tune (曲调) 比做 water (水)。 *You don't want me to sing in the choir. I can't carry a tune.* 你甭想叫我到唱诗班去唱歌,我五音不全啊。◇ be tone-deaf

keep an ear to the ground [ˌki(ː)pə ˈnɪ(ː)rtəðə ˌgraund] [话] **注意信息** 在过去出门骑马的时代,如果要了解对方的动向,就把耳朵贴到地面上。这一表达法即由此而来。但在按字面意义使用的场合,一般不用 keep ～,而用 put an [*one's*] ear to the ground (把一只[自己的]耳朵贴到地面上)。*The Indian put his ear to the ground to listen for any approaching horses.* 印第安人把他的耳朵贴到地面,倾听是否有马匹前来。作为比喻,指对于自己所关心的事情、有关自己业务或工作的事情等,千方百计地搜集情报。这是一个定型的说法,颇有"支起耳朵"的味道。*If you want to succeed in this business, you have to make lots of friends and keep an ear to the ground.* 如果你想在这种事业上取得成功,就必须广交朋友,时时刻刻注意信息。*Politicians soon learn the importance of keeping an ear to the ground.* 政治家们很快就懂得注意信息的重要性。也可以说 keep *one's* ear ~。*I don't know of any job of the type you're looking for, but I'll keep my ear to the ground.* 我不知道有没有你想找的那种工作。不过,我可以注意探听一下。也使用 have an [*one's*] ear to the ground 的形式。*Ben is the man to ask about any forthcoming changes in rules concerning government contracts. He always has his ear to the ground.* 关于与政府签订合同的规定,如果你要打听今后会有什么变化,最好是去向本求教。他经常注意这方面的信息。◇ keep abreast of the latest information [the current situation]

make a silk purse out of a sow's ear → PURSE

play (*something*) **by ear** [ˌpleɪ ~ baɪ ˈɪ(ː)r] [口] **凭耳朵听弹奏** 直译是"用耳朵弹奏"。意思是"能把听来的乐曲进行弹奏"。如果有乐谱而头脑里记熟,"不看乐谱弹奏",那叫做 play (*something*) from memory。不论是"凭耳朵听弹奏"或者"不看乐谱弹奏",假如所讲的是一般音乐,*something* 处不用代入任何词,只说 *Can you play by ear?* 你能凭耳朵听弹奏吗?在指个别音乐的场合,如说"那个曲子你听了能弹奏吗?",*something* 处自然要用相应的词代入:*Can you play it [that song, etc.] by ear?* 你能凭耳朵听弹它[那支歌等]吗?这一表达法主要用于钢琴,但讲任何乐器都可以。*Few musicians are able to play by ear.* 只凭耳朵听就能弹奏的音乐家是少有的。*Let's ask Jack to play piano for the party. He plays by ear.* 开社交晚会时,咱们请杰克弹钢琴吧。他凭耳朵听就能演奏。*Oscar Peterson is a great jazz pianist. He can't read music, but he can play any number by ear after hearing it only once.* 奥斯卡·彼得森是一位伟大的爵士乐钢琴家。他不会读乐谱,但是不论什么曲子,他只要听一遍就能够弹奏。请读者注意:如果采取 play it by EAR (→) 的形式,也有"毫无准备,临时去干"的意思。" ◇ play music [*something*] by having only heard it

play it by ear [ˌpleɪɪt ˌbaɪ ˈɪ(ː)r] [话] **毫无准备,临时去干** 这一表达法来自类似的习用语 play (*something*) by EAR(凭耳朵听弹奏)。具体形象是:听了一支陌生的曲子,当场就能全部记牢,很熟练地演奏出来。一般用以表示"不需准备,直接去干"的意味。也就是说,由于没有开会讨论或接见面谈的时间,或者由于没有任何可靠的信息,毫无准备地当机立断处理某种事务。*I didn't know what was expected of me at the meeting, so I had no choice but to play it by ear.* 我不了解在会议上需要我去干什么,因此我除了盲人瞎马地去干而外,没有别的办法。*I have no idea how far the union is willing to compromise on their demands. We'll just have to play it by ear.* 我毫不知道工会希望在什么样的要求上达成妥协。因此,我们只能根据情况的发展即时进行应付。*Leave the negotiations to Dave. He's very good at playing it by ear.* 叫戴夫去谈判吧。他善于随机应变,灵活应付。另外,也使用这一表达法表示在做什么事情的时候,由于没有计划或经验,只是根据具体情况,凭着直感去干的意味。*Since I had absolutely no experience in that kind of work, for the first six months or so I had to play it by ear.* 由于我对那种工作完全没有经验,在最初的半年左右,我不能不凭着直感摸索着去干。◇ improvise (according to circumstances)

pound *one's* **ear** [ˌpaund ～ ˈɪ(ː)r] [话] **睡觉** 最初的构思是:"用枕头连续地敲耳朵"。从原来的意义出发,就不能用于"坐着假寐"的场合。一般指躺在床上睡觉,但是只要是躺下"正式入寝",在沙发上或在睡袋中也是可以的。*A: Where's John? B: He's in the next room pounding his ear.* 甲:约翰在什么地方? 乙:他在隔壁的房间里睡大觉哪。◇ sleep

put a bug in *someone's* **ear** → BUG

talk *someone's* **ear off** [ˌtɔ(ː)k ～ ˈɪ(ː)ˌrɔːf] [话] **唠叨没完没了** 原来的构思是:"对方罗罗嗦嗦说的话太长,简直象绞索套在耳朵上,要把它勒掉了"。*I don't like to go out with Fred. He'll sit in the same place for hours on end talking your ear off.* 我不喜欢跟弗雷德一起出去。他总是一连几个小时坐在一个地方,唠唠叨叨说个没完没了的。*Don't get cornered by Mrs. Flapjaw. She'll talk your ear off.* 千万别叫弗拉普焦夫人纠缠住你。她会向你唠叨个没完没了的。可以添加 almost 调整语调。*Mr. Proudpop almost talked my ear off last night about his son's exploits in the army.* 昨天晚上,普劳德波普先生对我大谈他的儿子在军队中的英勇事迹,唠叨个没完没了。另外,常常可以听到人们讲具有同一意义的表达法 talk *someone's* head off,但在一些词典中往往收录的 talk *someone's* arm [leg] off 却极少使用。◇ tire *someone* with endless talk ((不能加 almost 等词))

turn a deaf ear (to *something*) [ˌtə(ː)rnə ˈde(ː) ˈfɪ(ː)r] [口] **置之不理** 直译为"把一只聋耳朵转向……",指"对要求、请愿等完全不听"。*I begged him to help us, but he turned a deaf ear to all my pleas.* 我请他帮咱们一下,可是怎么恳求他都是置之不理。*He is very generous in giving money to the needy, but when it comes to any request for a loan he always turns a deaf ear.* 他对贫困的人捐款是非常慷慨的,可是如果你要向他借债,他一概置之不理。*The people have largely turned a deaf ear to the government's request for energy conservation.* 政府号召避免浪费能源,大多数人都不响应。◇ refuse to listen ((to all my pleas → to any of my pleas))

early

an early bird [ɔː ˈnəːrli ˌbəːrd] [话] **早起的人、早来的人、早干的人** → The early BIRD catches the worm.

ears

be all ears [ˈɔː ˈlɪːrz] [话] **洗而恭听** 直译为"全身都成为耳朵"。这一表达法令人产生非常渴望去听的感觉。从轻松的会话直到严肃的演说,在各种情况下广泛地使用。*Tell me about it. I'm all ears.* 你告诉我呀,我很想听一听。*The world was all ears to hear about the explorers' adventures on Mars.* 整个世界都在注意倾听火星探险家的冒险故事。*Whenever their counselor told them a ghost story, the usually rowdy campers were all ears.* 当夏令营辅导员向孩子们讲一个幽灵的故事的时候,平常那些爱吵闹的孩子全都鸦雀无声地听起来了。◇ want very much to hear [know] / listen with all *one's* attention

be dry behind the ears [ˌdraɪ bəˌhaɪnðə ˈɪːrz] [话] **富有经验,独当一面** 由于刚生下的婴儿的耳朵里侧是湿的,就产生了 be wet behind the EARS 的说法,意思是"是个乳臭未干的毛孩子"。把其中的 wet 改换成 dry,就变成本条的表达法了。必须注意的是:这一表达法的否定形式 be not dry behind the ears (没见过世面的)与 be wet behind the ears 虽然意义相同,但语气是不一样的。也就是说,be wet ～带有相当大的瞧不起的口气,而 be not dry ～则是口气比较缓和的说法。*It's true that Chet makes a lot of mistakes, but don't be too hard on him. He's just not dry behind the ears yet.* 的确,切特犯了很多的错误,但是不要过于责难他。他初出茅庐,涉世还未深啊。*Who does that guy think he is, trying to tell me how to do my job. I was dry behind the ears long before he was born.* 那家伙不知道自己吃几碗饭,竟想要指导我怎样干工作。在他还没生下来之前,

我早就独当一面了。常用 completely 加强语气。*It takes new graduates a bit of time on the job before they are completely dry behind the ears.* 新的大学毕业生需要有一段时期才能在工作中完全独当一面。◇ be experienced

one's **ears burn** [~ ˈɪ(ː)rz ˌbəːrn] [口] **耳朵发热** 指由于被人议论而耳朵发热或脸上发烧。这是自古以来就存在的表达法,在 14 世纪英国作家乔叟(Geoffrey Chaucer)的作品中就可以看到。*My ears are burning. Someone must be talking about me.* 我的耳朵发热,一定有人在议论我。这是一个人们经常使用的定型的说法。本条的表达法只用于"议论"、"闲言"等,如果实际上耳朵发烧(发热),要说 My ears are [feel] hot. *Your ears must have been burning yesterday. We were all talking about you.* 你昨天一定耳朵发烧了吧,我们大家都谈论你来着。一般用于自己不在时被人"议论"的场合,但也有"偷听"的情况。例如:*My ears began to burn when I overheard what they were saying about me.* 当我偷听到他们议论我的话时,我脸上开始发烧了。

fall on deaf ears [ˌfɔ(ː)lɔn ˈde(ː) ˈfiːrz] [口] **被人置若罔闻** 直译是"话落到聋的耳朵上"。这一表达法用于"不管怎么说,人家也不听"的场合。充当主语的主要是"忠言"、"警告"、"要求"、"训诫"、"恳求"等。*I have told him any number of times that if he wants to get into a good college he will have to study harder, but all of my words fall on deaf ears.* 我对他不知说多少遍了,如果他想要进入一所好的大学,他就必须加强学习,可是他把我的话全都当作耳旁风了。*I know my advice is probably falling on deaf ears, but I think you are unwise to take action without consulting your father.* 我知道你大概不会听我的忠告,不过我认为你不跟自己的父亲商量就采取行动是不明智的呀。*The government's call for energy conservation has largely fallen on deaf ears.* 政府号召节约能源,可是大多数人都置若罔闻。◇ go unheeded

Little pitchers have big ears. → PITCHERS

be music to *someone's* **ears** → MUSIC

pin *someone's* **ears back** [ˌpɪn ~ ˈɪːrz ˌbæ(ː)k] [话] **猛揍** 字面意义是"把两个耳朵钉到脑袋上"。一般指"用拳头猛揍",特别是在威胁的话里常常使用。*You say that once more and I'll pin your ears back.* 你敢再说一遍,我就叫你鼻青脸肿。*Wait till I catch that guy. I'm gonna pin his ears back.* 你等我抓住那小子,我会狠狠地揍他一顿。*Jimmy pinned Bobby's ears back for snitching on him to the teacher.* 吉米由于博比到老师那里反映他的情况,把博比狠狠揍了一顿。也可以作为比喻使用,表示"彻底打垮"的意思。*The Giants may have won today's game, but tomorrow we'll pin their ears back.* 在今天的比赛中,巨人队算是获胜了,但是明天我们一定把他们彻底打垮。◇ give *someone* a good pummeling / defeat *someone* roundly

be up to *one's* **ears** (in *something*) [ˌʌptə ~ ˈɪːrz] [话] **深深陷入,不能动转** → be up to *one's* NECK (in *something*)

be wet behind the ears [ˌwet bəˌhaɪnðə ˈɪːrz] [话] **乳臭未干** 字面意义是"象刚生下来的孩子一样,耳朵里侧还是湿的",指没有练达成人,对世事非常无知。与反义习用语 be dry behind the EARS (→) 的否定形式具有同样的意思,但 be wet ~这一表达法直截了当,在对他人使用时显然带有轻蔑的语气。*That sergeant considers all second lieutenants to be wet behind the ears.* 那个军士认为所有的少尉都是黄口小儿。在稍微强调时,多半加 still。*In those days I was a cub reporter and still wet behind the ears.* 在那个时期,我是个初出茅庐的记者,乳臭还没有干哪。*When it comes to girls, Henry is still wet behind the ears.* 关于交女朋友的事,亨利还嫩着哪。◇ have no experience / be a beginner

earshot

beyond earshot [ˌbiɑnˈdɪːr.ʃɑ(ː)t] [口] **声音所及范围之外** → within EARSHOT

out of earshot [ˌaudəˈvɪːrˌʃɑ(ː)t] [口] **超出声音所及的范围** → within EARSHOT

within earshot [wɪˌðɪ(ː)n ˈɪːrˌʃɑ(ː)t] [口] **听力所及距离以内** shot 有枪弹、导弹、球等的"飞的距离"的意思。earshot 直译为"耳朵达到的距离"。加上 within，就意味着"在声音达到耳朵的范围以内"，亦即"听力所及的范围内"。多半用于大声呼喊的场合，但并不以此为限，普通的声音可以，其他声音也行。*I called for help, but there was no one within earshot.* 我曾经呼救，但是没有人能够听得到我的声音。*It's easy to get lost in this forest. Be sure to stay within earshot.* 在这个森林中是很容易迷失的。你一定要保持声音可以被人听到的距离。反义语是 out of [beyond] earshot。*I called to them, but they were already out of earshot.* 我曾经呼喊他们，可是他们已经走远，根本听不见了。*I didn't hear the gun go off. I guess I was beyond earshot.* 我没有听到枪声，大概我超出了听力所及的距离。也可以使用具有同一意义的 range (所及范围)，说 within [out of, beyond] hearing range。但是，hearing range 另有一义，指无线电周波多少可以被听到的"范围"。*The hearing range of dogs extends higher than that of man.* 狗的听觉范围超出人的听觉范围。◇ within a distance at which *one* [*someone*] can hear

earth

bring *someone* **down to earth** [ˌbrɪŋ ～ ˌdauntə ˈəːrθ] [口] **使(某人)回到现实中来** 原来的构思是："当人象鸟一样在空中飞翔的时候，把他拉回地面上来"。earth (地球) 指"现实世界"、"实际生活"。*Jed arrived at his office in high spirits, but his boss's harsh words quickly brought him down to earth.* 杰德兴致勃勃地来到公司上班，但是老板那些刺耳的话马上使他从幻想中清醒过来了。*Even optimistic Americans were brought down to earth by the stock-market crash of 1929.* 即使是乐观的美国人，在 1929 年股票市场的暴跌中也从大梦中清醒过来了。这一表达法也可以作 bring *someone* back [back down] to earth。*I guess I've had my head in the clouds, haven't I. I suppose I should thank you for bringing me back down to earth.* 那时我的头脑总象腾云驾雾一般，是吧？我应该感谢你使我大梦初醒，回到现实中来。*The unexpectedly poor election results brought the majority party back to earth.* 选举结果糟糕到出人意料的地步，这使多数党从幻想中清醒过来了。另有 come [get] down [back, back down] to earth 的说法，意思是"回到现实中来"。*If you expect to succeed in this office, you'd better come down to earth and start working harder.* 你要打算在这个公司里取得成功，只有回到现实中来，更拚命地工作。*It was difficult to get back down to earth after our marvelous vacation at the beach.* 我们在海滨度过美好的假期以后，很难回到日常的生活中来。◇ return *someone* to reality

come (back) down to earth [ˌkʌm (ˌbæ(ː)k) ˌdauntə ˈəːrθ] [口] **从梦中回到现实世界** → bring *someone* down to EARTH

get back (down) to earth [ˌget ˌbæ(ː)k (ˌdaun)tə ˈəːrθ] [口] **从幻想中清醒过来** → bring *someone* down to EARTH

move heaven and earth (to *do something*) → HEAVEN

run *someone* [*something*] **to earth** [ˌrʌn ～tuˈəːrθ] [口] **查明所在的地方** run ～ to earth 的具体形象是"追捕狮子之类的猎物，把它打倒在地面上"。原指在狩猎时"把狐狸之类的动物追入穴中"。后来，"穴中"的意味消失，对于任何狩猎全都可以使用了。*The hunters ran the bear to earth in the meadow.* 猎人们在草地上把熊追住了。也用于"抓人"。*The police finally ran the prison escapee to earth in the next state.* 警察终于在邻近的州内把越狱的犯人逮住了。这是按照常识的解释。但是，根据实际情况，这一句话也可以解释为："警察已经查明越狱的犯人在邻近的州内。"也就是说，run *someone* [*something*] to earth 从"追得无处可逃"的意思进一步发展,又具有"查明所在之处"的意味了。现在,一般使用后一意义。至于"查明"的方法,通常是"自已前去",但也有"到处打电话,委托他人前去寻找"的情况。不论哪种情况,总伴有"费尽九牛二虎之力"的意味。*We searched for the packet of letters for over an hour before we ran them to earth in an old desk in the basement.* 我们费了一个多小时的功夫寻找那一沓子信,才在地下室的旧桌子中发现它们。*After trying to contact Mr. Footloose all day, I finally ran him to earth at the barber shop.* 我一整天都试图与富特卢思先生取得联系,后来终于查明他在理发馆里。另有一个表达法是 run *someone* [*something*] to ground, 意思相同。*Since Mr. Cramer is a traveling salesman, he's often difficult to run to ground.* 因为克拉默先生是在各地巡游的推销员,所以常常难以弄清他正在什么地方。◇ find *someone* [*something*]

the salt of the earth → SALT

easier

Easier said than done. [ˌiːziər ˌsedðən ˈdʌ(ː)n] [口] **说时容易做时难** 这一表达法是 That [It] is easier said than done. 的省略形式。也常常带有 That [It] is。虽然是一句格言,但在英语中完全没有"告诫"的意思。一般的使用方法是:一个人听了对方的话,回答说"你说的倒很容易,要做起来可很难啊!"而且不是泛泛地说"难",总有具体的理由。我们举几个例句研究一下。*A: If you study six hours every day after school, you should be able to get into that university. B: I'm afraid that's easier said than done.* 甲:如果你在每天放学以后,再学习六个小时,你准能考上那所大学。乙:遗憾的很,你说得倒容易,可是实际上办不到啊。在这一例句中,乙所指的"实际上办不到"并不是"原来有这个意思,可是自已意志不够坚强,所以坚持不下来"这样精神上的问题,而是由于有别的工作或者其他具体的理由,"挤不出六个小时来"。以下的例句也是一样,并不是一般的"说起来容易做起来难",这一点务请读者注意。*We'd like to build a new house, but with prices as high as they are these days, that's easier said than done.* 我们很想建造一所新居,但是最近物价这么高,真是说时容易做时难啊。*A: What would you say to taking a vacation in Europe? B: I'd say "Easier said than done."* 甲:你看到欧洲去休假怎么样? 乙:俗话说"说时容易做时难"呀。另外,与"言易行难"相当的说法是 That's easy enough (for *someone*) to say. 美国人常使用。◇ That's (easy to say but) not so easy to do.

easy

(as) easy as falling off a log → LOG

(as) easy as (apple) pie [ə ˈzi(ː)ziəz (ˌæpl) ˈpaɪ] [话] **极简单** → (as) easy as falling off a LOG

Easy come, easy go. [ˌiːzi ˈkʌ(ː)m ˌiːzi ˈgou] [话] **(钱)来得容易去得快** easy 是 easy money (不义之财)中的 easy。本条的整个意思是"钱来得容易,去得也容易"。*After Jack won five hundred dollars on the first race and lost it all on the second, he just laughed and said, "Easy come, easy go."* 杰克在第一轮赛马中赢了五百美元,但在第二轮中他又全都输掉了。然后,他只是哈哈一笑说:"钱来得容易去得快嘛。" *Louis believes in easy come, easy go. The hundred thousand dollars he inherited when his uncle died was all spent before the year was out.* 路易斯相信俗话所说钱来得容易守不住。他的叔父去世时给他留下十万美元,在不到一年的时间里,他就花得个一干二净。也可以应用于金钱以外的事情。在这种场合,多带有讽刺的口吻。*A: I hear your girl jilted you. Too bad. B: Well, easy come, easy go.* 甲:听说你的女朋友把你甩了。太不幸啦。乙:没什么,来得容易去得快嘛。◇ Money easily gained is easy to spend [lose].

Easy does it. [ˌiːzi ˈdʌzɪt] [话] **多加小心** 意思是"干活[行走]要注意,别慌手慌脚"。主要是在叫人拿易碎物品、重要物品、沉重物品时多多注意、谨慎从事的场合使用。在发音方面,头一个音节,即 [.i:zi ～] 的 [i:]往往拉长,作 [i::] 或者 [i:::]。*"Easy does it," said the doctor as the ambulance drivers lowered the injured man to the ground.* 当急救车的人员把受伤者从车上抬下来的时候,大夫说:"轻一点啊!" *Easy does it. Don't bump the door with the edge of the table.* 小心点儿,不要叫桌子边撞到门上。在添加所拿物品的场合,一般用 with ～接续。*Easy does it with that box of china-ware!* 那个瓷器箱子可要轻拿轻放呀! 不仅在搬运东西时使用,也常用于在山路上驾驶汽车、取除炸弹的雷管等场合。*Easy does it. The roads are slick with ice.* 开车小心点儿,路上满是冰。*Easy does it when you pull back on the joy stick.* 当你拉飞机的操纵杆的时候,可要多加小心啊。◇ Gently. / Be careful.

go easy on *someone* [.gou 'i:ziɔn ～] [口] **酌情处理** *I know he's been a bad boy, but I hope you will go easy on him.* 我知道那孩子干了坏事,但是我希望你能够酌情处理。*Sure, he made a mistake, but I think we should go easy on him. After all, this is his first year on the job.* 他确实犯了错误,但是我认为对他应该宽大处理。无论如何,他是头一年干这个工作啊。如以上的例句所示,这一表达法常用于责备"失败"或"过错"的场合。但也有象下一例句那样,用于表示"对新手留点情"的意思。*Go easy on me. I've never played tennis before.* 对我可要手下留情啊,我过去从来没有打过网球。也可以使用动词 be 而采取 be easy on *someone* 的形式,意义和用法与用 go 完全一样。*The judge was easy on him because he was a first offender.* 由于他是初犯,法官对他从宽处理了。◇ be lenient with *someone*

go easy on *something* [.gou 'i:ziɔn ～] [口] **有节制地使用** 当金钱或饮食由于数量有限而不得不节约的时候,常常使用这一表达法。*Better go easy on the entertaining this month. The boss is on the warpath because of budget overruns.* 这个月的招待费最好省着用。由于预算超支,老板正在大发雷霆哪。*Go easy on the bread. That's the last of it.* 面包要省着点吃。吃完那个就没有啦。on 的后边也可以用动名词。*We'd better go easy on buying new clothes. We haven't got much money left.* 我们最好少买新衣服吧,剩下的钱可不多了。也有动机与"节约"无关的场合。*My doctor told me to go easy on rich foods.* 医生叫我少吃味道太浓的食品。在命令句中,省略 go。*Easy on the wine. That's our last bottle.* 葡萄酒要省着点喝。那是我们最后的一瓶了。◇ practice restraint in *doing something* not eat [drink, etc.] too much (of) *something*

be on easy street → STREET

take it [things] easy [.teɪkɪt 'i:zi / .teɪk .θɪŋz ～] [口] **轻松地干** 这一表达法的使用范围非常广泛。在这里,take 具有"干"、"采取什么态度"、"思考"等意味。easy 的基本意义是"不费力地"、"悠闲地",也就是"轻松地"。根据上下文,可以译成"缓慢地"、"小心地"、"悄悄地"、"逍遥自在地"、"悠然自得地"等多种多样的副词。it 是所谓的"状况的 it",没有特定的指示物,只是含糊其词地表示"那种事物"的意味,至于"那种事物"究竟是什么,就不明确了。请根据以下的例句进行体会吧。多用于命令句。*Take it easy. There's no need to get angry.* 缓和点哟! 用不着发火嘛。*You'd better take it easy on this road. There are a lot of sharp curves.* 在这条公路上,急转弯太多,还是慢着点开车为好。*Take it easy when you carry this table upstairs or else you'll scar the walls.* 你把这个桌子往楼上搬的时候,要小心点儿,不要碰坏了墙。如果谈到具体的东西的时候,用 take it easy on *something* 的形式。*Ow! Take it easy on my sore arm.* 哎哟! 轻着点儿,我的胳膊疼得厉害。在用于饮食的场合,是"省着点吃[喝]"的意思。*Take it easy on the bread. That's the last of it.* 面包省着点儿吃吧,那是最后的了。"轻松地干[思考]"如果不明确指定特有的对象,则多半说 take things easy。这个 things 依然是含糊其词地指

"一切事物"。在大多数场合,把 things 换成 it 也几乎意思完全不变。*I'm not going to get another job right away. I'm going to take things [it] easy for a while.* 我不打算马上去找新的工作。先逍遥自在它几天再说。*Just stay here and take things [it] easy for a couple of hours. I'll be back as soon as possible.* 你在这儿悠闲自在地呆上两个小时。我尽可能早点儿回来。*I caught a bad cold and had to take things [it] easy for two or three day.* 我得了重感冒,不得不休息了两三天。如果按照 things 的字面意义概括地讲一般的"事物",那么,这一 things 不能用 it 置换。例如: *You should give more thought to your responsibilities. There's such a thing as taking things too easy, you know.* 你应该更认真地考虑你的责任。常有这样的事情,人们把事情想得过于轻松啦。在这个句子里,如果把 things 改作 it,那就不是"想得过于轻松",而是含糊其词的"轻松地干"的意味了。最近,这一表达法又在分手时作为轻松的寒暄语使用,具有"请便吧"、"那么"的意味。内在的涵义是"悠悠闲闲,不要着急"。在这一场合是定型的说法,不能把 it 换成 things。*Take it easy. I'll see you tomorrow.* 那么,明天见。◇ relax / go slow / be careful / be easygoing

eat

eat *someone* **out of house and home** → HOUSE

eater

a big eater [ə ˌbɪ(ː)ˈgi(ː)dər] [话] **饭量大的人** → eat like a HORSE

eating

be eating *someone* [ˈi(ː)tn ˌ~ / ˌi(ː)tn ˈ~] [话] **有不高兴的事情** 这里的 eat 具有"吃某人的心"、"侵蚀某人的感情"的意义。常用进行时。*What's eating that guy? I asked him for the time and he almost took my head off.* 那个家伙吃什么耗子药啦?我只向他打听一下时间,他就气势汹汹地几乎揪掉我的脑袋。如此例所示,这一表达法是对不了解为什么正在"大不高兴"、"怒气冲冲"的人使用的,因此不能够说 The problem is eating him. 之类的话。 *Something seems to be eating the boss. Aren't the contract negotiations going well?* 不知为什么,老板似乎很不高兴。莫非是合同没有谈妥吧? *What's eating you? You've been in a bad mood all day.* 你究竟怎么啦?整天情绪都不佳啊。除人而外,可以用于动物。*I wonder what's eating the dog. He's been running around and barking all day.* 我家的狗不知道为什么那么烦躁。一整天狂吠不停,到处乱转。◇ be bothering *someone* / be putting *someone* in a bad mood

ec

home ec → HOME EC

econ

econ [ˈiːˌkɑːn] [话] **大学的经济学课程** economics 一词的缩略。学生用语。*I hate econ.* 我非常讨厌经济学课程。*Amy is majoring in econ.* 艾米的专业是经济学。也可以当作形容词使用。*Tomorrow we have an econ test [a test in econ].* 明天我们有经济学的测验。◇ economics

ed

phys ed → PHYS ED

edge

put an edge on *something* [ˌpudə ˈneːdʒɔ(ː)n ~] [口] **增加(欲望、尖锐程度等)** 这里的 edge 是"刀口"。本条原意为"使刀有刃"。 *I used an old leather strap to put an edge on my knife.* 我用一条旧皮带磨小刀的刃。作为比喻,用于表示食欲、知识欲、热情等等"增加"的意味。例如: *The hike through the woods put an edge on my appetite.* 穿越森林的徒步旅行使我的食欲增加了。*The many Chinese students I rubbed elbows with at school put an edge on my thirst to know more about their country.* 在学校中同许多中国学生的交往,增强了我进一步了解中国的愿望。在应用于"语言"的场合,具有"增加尖刻程度"的意味。*The* *old man's harsh voice seemed to put an edge on his words that he probably did not intend.* 老人刺耳的声音似乎增加了他一字一句的尖刻程度，而他大概并没有这种意图。edge 的前边可加 increasing, sharp, sharper, further 等形容词。*The letters from my father put an increasing edge on my desire to return home as soon as possible.* 父亲的一封封来信使我的归家之心越来越迫切。◇ sharpen *something* (in a way that ～)

set *someone's* **nerves on edge** → NERVES

set *someone's* **teeth on edge** → TEETH

take the edge off *something* [ˌteɪkðɪ ˈeːdʒɔ(ː)f ～] [口] **使势头减弱** 与 put an edge on *something* 相反，按字面是"使刀的刃变钝"的意思。*Chopping hard wood like that takes the edge off an ax.* 砍那样坚硬的木头会弄钝斧刃。这意思就是说，虽然没有 edge，也并不是完全不能够砍。因此，在作为比喻使用的场合，"欲望"、"尖锐性"、"势头"也只是减弱了，仍然有所残余。*The apple that I ate took the edge off my appetite, but I still felt hungry.* 如果直译，这句话的前半部是我吃的苹果减弱了我的食欲。整句话的意思是：我肚子饿得厉害，吃苹果好了一点，可是仍然觉得饿。*The piles of homework soon took the edge off my enthusiasm for math.* 家庭作业堆积如山，很快使我降低了对数字的兴趣。*A sudden downpour took the edge off the enemy attack.* 一阵暴雨使敌人的攻势减弱了。◇ dull *something*

eel

(as) slippery as an eel [əz ˈslɪpəri əzə ˈniːl] [口] **油滑** 字面意义是"象鳝鱼一样滑"。*I couldn't hold on to the rope. It was covered with ice and slippery as an eel.* 我未能紧握绳子停住不动。绳子上满是冰，简直象鳝鱼一样滑。如此例所示，对于 rope, cable (钢索)、hose (软管) 等类似鳝鱼形状的东西，可以按照字面意义使用。但是，一般作比喻使用，指人的"滑头滑脑"。*I don't trust the head of their negotiating team. He's slippery as an eel.* 我不信任对方参加谈判的代表团团长，那是个大滑头。*Talk about slippery as an eel! I tried for three hours to get a definite answer from him but I just couldn't pin him down.* 这样的大滑头简直天下少有！我费了三小时的唇舌打算得到他明确的答复，可是结果瞎子点灯——白费蜡。除以上这样"令人摸不清真实意图"的场合而外，也用于"隐蔽身份"、"隐蔽住处"的场合。*The police have tried to arrest the culprit any number of times, but he always gets away. He's as slippery as an eel.* 警察曾经多次要逮捕那个犯人，可是每一次他都逃脱了。这家伙真是隐身有术啊。*That guy's as slippery as an eel. I've tried to contact him I don't know how many times but he always manages to avoid me.* 那家伙真是狡兔三窟呀。我不知道有多少次要跟他取得联系，可是他始终设法躲开了我。◇ very skilled at evasion

egg

egg *someone* **on** (to <*do*> *something*) [ˌe(ː)g ～ ˈɔːn] [口] **怂恿** 这里的 egg 与"蛋"完全没有关系。它与 edge 属于同一语源。egg 和 edge 均来自古代斯堪的纳维亚语 (Old Norse) 的 *egg* (刀的刃或尖端)。在 Old Norse 中，*eggja* 一词的意义是"用刀尖顶着使人前进"，后又作为比喻，用以表示"给与刺激"→"唆使"的意味。此词以 eggian 的形式进入古代英语 (公元 700～1100 年)，只作比喻使用，意义与原词大致相同，而且一直流传到现在。不过，eggian 变成了 egg on。16 世纪起又采取了 egg *someone* on 的形式。顺便提一下：此后，edge 的意义有所扩大，作为动词是"(给刀具) 开刃"、"引起(食欲)"；作为名词就不仅指"刀口"了，一般用于表示东西或场所的边、缘、沿、边际、边界等的意思。然而，egg 却始终只有这一个使用方法。edge *someone* on 虽然与 egg *someone* on 长期共存表示同一意义，但在一百年左右以前成为废语，现在只剩下 egg *someone* on 一枝独秀了。*When Frank began to fail, his friends egged* *him on to greater efforts.* 当弗兰克眼看着要降班的时候，朋友们鼓励他再加一把劲学习。如此例所示，可以用于"劝人学好"的场合，但是一般指"怂恿别人干坏事"。*Leroy egged his friend on to swipe a watch.* 勒鲁伊怂恿朋友去偷手表。*I didn't really want to do it, but the guys just kept egging me on.* 我本来不想去干那件事，可是同伴们非叫我去干不可。◇ incite [encourage] *someone*

a good egg [ə ˌgu(ː)ˈdeːg] [话] **好人** 直译是"好的蛋"。但这里的 egg 原为孩子们互相间使用的俚语，意思是"什么也不懂的小毛孩子"。但是，在 good egg 一词中，egg 失去"毛孩子"或"年纪轻"的意味，单指"人"而言了。本条的表达法含有亲密、夸奖的成份，语气很轻松，但也有一丁点儿小看对方的口吻。大多用于男性，偶尔也用于女性。*Ralph is a good egg. I'm sure you'll like him once you get to know him.* 拉尔夫是个好人。如果你跟他混熟了，肯定会喜欢他。*Jim is really a good egg. If only he didn't have such a short fuse.* 吉姆的确是个好人，如果他不那么容易发火就好啦。→ a good GUY① ◇ a nice person

a goose egg [ə ˈgu(ː)ˌse(ː)g] [话] **零** 在各国语言中，都根据"蛋"的形状而用它表示"零"的意味。汉语说"鸭蛋"，得零分叫"吃鸭蛋"。英国自古以来在板球运动中一直使用 duck's egg (鸭蛋)一词。美国在开始盛行棒球运动的时候，也曾借用这个词。然而，不知为什么(可能由于美国人感觉 a duck's egg 太小) 把它改为 goose egg (鹅蛋)了。从那以后，不仅在棒球运动中使用，在其他体育运动中也使用起来。甚至在学校中，也普遍用它表示学生成绩的"零分"。*It was a tie game. Both teams ended up with goose eggs.* 这场比赛打个平局，两队比分是零比零。*I got a goose egg on my math test.* 在数学测验中，我得了个大鸭蛋。有时把 goose egg 作为动词使用，例如说：*Our opponents goose-egged us.* 对方让我们吃了大鸭蛋。顺便提一下：在网球比赛中意味着"零分"的 love，大概来自法语中的网球用语 *l'oeuf* (蛋)。◇ a zero

lay an egg [ˌleɪə ˈneːg] [话] **彻底失败** 根据字面意义"生蛋"，很难理解这是指什么而言。这里是把"蛋"比做数字的"零"。也就是说，只要了解"生零"是怎么回事，就容易掌握本条条头的意味了。这一表达法的原来形式是 19 世纪中叶英国板球用语 achieve a duck's egg (一分未得)。传入美国以后，achieve 改成了 lay, a duck's egg 变成了 a goose EGG。因此，在 19 世纪后半叶的美国英语中就有这样的说法：*A: Did you win? B: No, we laid a goose egg.* 甲：你们胜啦？乙：没有，我们吃了大鸭蛋。现在，特别是在体育运动中，goose egg 依然代表"零分"的意义。*We were lucky to win. We had nothing but goose eggs until the ninth inning.* 我们得胜完全是侥幸。在第九局以前，我们吃了大鸭蛋，一分都没有。自从这一表达法用以表示"(艺人)失败"的意味以来，就省略了 goose，使用范围也逐渐扩大了，直至今日。这一表达法的重点并不是演出、演技、作品等"搞得不好"，而是"完全不受欢迎"。也就是说，即使同样是"以失败而告终"，这一表达法是指不合观众的口味。虽然是同一的演出或作品，由于观众的口味，既可能 lay an egg，也可能大受欢迎。这一表达法现在仍然是大多应用于艺术界。例如：*The new million-dollar Broadway musical laid an egg.* 耗资百万美元的百老汇的新歌舞剧完全不受欢迎。*As a movie director he is generally very successful, but he sure laid an egg this time.* 作为电影导演，他一向是非常成功的，可是这一回他砸锅了。*Joni is a very good singer, but every time she tries to be funny she lays an egg.* 琼妮是一位非常好的歌手，但是她每次想搞个噱头，都完全不受观众的欢迎。*That author must be losing his touch. He's laid several eggs since his last best seller.* 那位作家一定是江郎才尽。自从上次的畅销书以后，他出的几部作品全都失败了。这一表达法也常用于"玩笑"。*That guy's jokes are terrible. He laid eggs all over the stage last night.* 那个家伙的笑话太过分了，昨天晚间他所讲的那些完全不受人欢迎。

◇ be a failure / produce an inferior work / be poorly received / tell a flat joke

eggbeater

an eggbeater [ə 'ne(:)g.bi(:)dər] [话] **直升机** 字面意义是指厨房使用的"搅蛋器"。现在几乎全是电动的,但直至不久以前还是手摇式。*We bought Mother an electric mixer, but she seems to prefer her old eggbeater.* 我们给妈妈买了一个电动搅拌机,可是她似乎爱用那个旧的手摇搅蛋器。由于手摇式搅蛋器的形状和声音类似直升机,它的名称开始被作为直升机的轻松的代用词了。*Fred pilots an eggbeater for an oil company.* 弗雷德在一家石油公司当直升机驾驶员。直升机俗语又称 a CHOPPER, a WHIRLYBIRD。◇ a helicopter

egghead

an egghead [ə 'ne(:)g.he(:)d] [话] **知识分子** 在很久以前的俚语中,egghead (蛋的上端) 指"秃头的人"。到 20 世纪初,可能由于人们认为秃头的人脑瓜灵,此词便用以表示"知识分子"的意味了。后来,这一用法日趋衰落。1952 年民主党人史蒂文森 (Adlai Stevenson) 竞选总统,他是一个秃头的知识分子,于是大家又用 egghead 一词指支持他的知识阶层的人们。从此,作为表示"知识分子"意味的俚语,此词再度普遍流行起来。*I'm sure Foster will know the answer. He's a real egghead.* 福斯特肯定能回答这个问题。他是一位真正有知识的人。如此例所示,这一表达法可以仅指"知识渊博的人"、"智力杰出的人",但是在很多场合有弦外之音,包含着"虽然知道的东西不少,然而没有常识,或者缺乏应用能力"的意味。*Stevenson wasn't elected because most Americans don't trust eggheads.* 史蒂文森所以没有当选为总统,是因为大多数美国人不信任知识分子。*There are too many university eggheads advising the government.* 在政府的顾问中,大学教授级的知识分子太多了。◇ an intellectual

eggs

kill the goose that laid the golden eggs → GOOSE

put all *one's* eggs in one basket [pu.dɔ(:)l ~ 'eːgzən .wʌn'bæːskɪt] [口] **孤注一掷** 字面意义是"把自己所有的蛋放在一个筐里"。一般用于否定句,表示否定的意思,包含着"一旦掉到地上,全都摔坏了,什么都完了"的意味。当然,这是一个比喻的表达法。eggs 一般象征着金钱 (投资)、努力、消遣等,而 basket 则象征着所寄托的事业、人、团体、方法、计划等等。*We should spread our investments over several companies. It wouldn't be wise to put all our eggs in one basket.* 我们应该把我们的资金投入几个公司,孤注一掷是很不明智的事情。也可以用 into 代替 in,但语调略嫌生硬。*Jimmy was so confident of getting into the university of his choice that he took only one entrance exam. He should've known better than to put all his eggs into one basket.* 吉米自信绝对能进入他所选定的大学,所以只参加了一个学校的入学考试。他应该知道孤注一掷是愚不可及的。如果把动词由 put 改成 have,作 have all *one's* eggs in one basket,则表示"已经全部装进 one basket"的危险状态。*With only one good pitcher this season, I'm afraid we have all our eggs in one basket.* 在这个季节里,我们队只有一名好投球手,胜败如何,全在他一个人身上了。◇ risk everything on a single venture [person, group, method, plan, etc.]

(go) teach *one's* grandmother (how) to suck eggs → GRANDMOTHER

ego

an ego trip → TRIP

eight

be behind the eight ball → BALL

put *someone* behind the eight ball [.put ~ bə.haɪndðɪ 'eɪt.bɔːl] [话] **使 (某人) 陷入困境** → be behind the eight BALL

elbow

bend the elbow [.benːðɪ 'el.bou] [话] **喝酒**

直译为"弯肘部"。因为喝酒举杯,总要使肘部弯曲,所以产生这一表达法。*Let's stop somewhere on the way home and bend the elbow.* 在回家的路上,咱们顺便到什么地方喝上一杯。*He likes to bend the elbow.* 他很喜欢喝酒。◇ drink / have a drink

be no skin off *someone's* elbow [nou ˌskɪˌnɔ(ː)f ˈ~ ˌelbou] [话] **无关痛痒** → be no SKIN off *someone's* back

use elbow grease → GREASE

elbows

rub elbows (with *someone*) [ˌrʌˈbe(ː)l bouz] [口] **交往** rub 是"擦",elbow 是"肘"。具体形象是:在社交场所、俱乐部、教会、集会等处,与邻近的人相互碰胳膊肘。因此,这一表达法就有了"与人交往"的意味。*You must have come up in the world recently, Jay. I hear you've been rubbing elbows with the Rockefellers.* 杰伊,看起来你最近爬上去啦。听说你跟洛克菲勒家的人们有交往了。如此例所示,多用于"与著名人物交往"的场合,但并不是非这样不可。*The International Youth Conference was great. We enjoyed being able to rub elbows with other young people from all over the world.* 国际青年会议开得好极啦。我们在会议期间能够与从全世界各个地区前来的青年人畅叙友情。*I don't know Mr. Grant very intimately, though we have been rubbing elbows at various social occasions over the years.* 这些年来,虽然我与格兰特先生常在社交场所碰头,但是和他并没有很深的交情。另外,可以用 shoulders (肩)代替 elbows,而说 rub shoulders with *someone*,意义和用法完全相同。◇ mix [associate] (casually) with *someone*

elective

an elective [ə nəˈlectɪv] [话] **选修(课程)** 一般来说,elective 是形容词,意思是"可以选择的"。在这里是大学和高中学生用语。他们把具有"选修课程"意义的 an elective course 中的 course 省略掉,将 elective 作为名词使用,表示未省略之前的整个短语。*How many electives are you taking this semester?* 这一学期你选修了几门课程? *Is calculus an elective?* 微积分是选修课吗?顺便提一下:an elective (course) 的反义语为 a required course (必修课程),没有缩略的说法。◇ an elective course

elephant

An elephant never forgets. [ə ˈneləfənt ˌnevər fərˈgets] [谚] **大象永远不会忘** → have a memory like an ELEPHANT

have a memory like an elephant [ˌhævə ˌmeməri laɪkə ˈneləfənt] [话] **记忆力特别好** 字面意义为"记忆力跟大象一样"。是强调 have a good memory (记忆力好) 的表达法。自古以来,西方人士就认为象是记忆力极佳的动物。据说有人猎象,象受伤后逃走。几年后,这个人又与那只象相遇,当然他已经不认得是自己伤害过的那一只了。可是那只象却记得曾经袭击过它的敌人,向他猛扑过来。由此,就产生了 An elephant never forgets. (大象永远不会忘记。)这一条谚语,又在谚语的基础上产生了本条的习用语 have a memory like an elephant。从以上所述就可以想象到,这一表达法一般用于表示"对不利于自己的事情记忆力特别好"的意思。但是,即便在这样的场合,说话的内容也达不到大象报仇雪恨那样强烈的程度。*Don't make any loose promises to Jane. She's got a memory like an elephant.* 可不要随随便便对简许下什么愿。她的记性特别好。这一表达法也可以用于夸奖或表示佩服的场合,如:*John always does well in history because he has a memory like an elephant.* 因为约翰的记忆力特别强,所以他的历史课总是学得很好。不过,这种用法不是很普遍的。特别是在学习的场合,一般不是用 have a memory like an elephant,而是常讲 have a mind like a SPONGE。◇ never forget anything

a white elephant [ə ˌhwaɪˈdeləfənt] [口] **无用的长物** 这一表达法来自古时泰国国王以白象 (white elephant) 赏赐失宠的家臣的故事。因为是国王赏赐的象,既不能杀，也不能给人，只能耗费金钱去饲养它。结果，受赏的家臣必然倾家荡产。这一表达法使用于虽然毫无用处但又不能任意处理、并且需要金钱或劳力去管理和维护的东西。*The house I inherited turned out to be a white elephant. It's too big for our needs or our pocketbooks, but we can't find anyone who wants to buy it.* 我继承了一所房子，结果是个无用的长物。对于我们的需要来说，它太大了，而且过于费钱，可是我们又找不到一个买主。常用 real 加强语气。*That expensive new machine we had installed in order to increase productivity is a real white elephant. It keeps breaking down, and even on rare occasions when it runs smoothly it is very costly to maintain.* 为了提高生产率，我们花费很大代价安装了一台新机器，可是这台机器完全是无用的长物。它总是发生故障，即使偶尔顺调运转，也需要极高的维修费。有时也应用于虽然不需要维持费（劳力），但是无用而又不能丢掉的东西。*The furniture in the old house was a menagerie of white elephants left over from the Victorian Period.* 那所旧房子中的家具全是维多利亚时代遗留下来的无用的长物。a white elephant sale 是"拍卖不用的物品"。*The women's society of the church is planning to hold a white elephant sale.* 教会的妇女会正在计划举办一次不用物品的拍卖。◇ a useless (and costly) thing

embarrassed

be embarrassed to death [emˈbæ(ː)rəstə ˈde(ː)θ] [话] **羞愧得要死** → *one* could have DIED

embarrassment

one **thought (that)** *one* **would die (of embarrassment)** [～ ˌθɔ(ː)t (ðət) ～ wuˈdːaɪ (əv emˈbæ(ː)rəsmənt)] [话] **曾经羞愧得要死** → *one* could have DIED

emcee

an emcee [ə ˌnemˈsiː] [话] **司仪、节目主持人** emcee 是 master of ceremonies（字面意义为"仪式长"）中的 master 和 ceremonies 的第一字母合成 mc，然后按读音缀成的。有时写作 M.C. 或者 MC。与 master of ceremonies 同样，一般指广播或电视中座谈、猜谜、流行歌曲等轻松节目的"主持人"，也指宴会、社交晚会等笑语风生的盛大集会的"司仪"。*David Frost is a popular emcee on TV.* 戴维·弗罗斯特是一位很受欢迎的电视节目主持人。另外，这个 emcee 与 master of ceremonies 不同，可以作为动词使用。*Loy is going to emcee our wedding reception.* 洛伊给我们的结婚宴会当司仪。顺便提一下：学术会议等正式会议的主持人或主席称 a moderator 或者 a chairman。◇ a master of ceremonies

end

be at the end of *one's* **tether** [ətðɪ ˌendəv ～ˈteðər] [口] **山穷水尽** end 是"尽头"，tether 是拴牛、马、羊、狗的"系绳"。这些动物只能在系绳"尽头"所达到的范围内活动。因此，这一表达法在作为比喻使用的时候具有"界限"的意味。*With our food gone, our snowmobile wrecked and a snowstorm closing in, we were at the end of our tether.* 我们吃的东西没有了，摩托雪车出故障了，又是满天的暴风雪，真是到了山穷水尽的地步了。*After a series of physical and economic setbacks, I was at the end of my tether.* 由于身体不断有病，经济上屡遭波折，我到了山穷水尽的地步。*I'm afraid he may not live much longer. He's just about at the end of his tether.* 我看他不会活多久了，他已经是奄奄一息啦。以上例句中所讲的是办法、体力、财力、生命力等的界限。在讲"忍耐(克制)的界限"时，常常在后边加 with *someone*。*I'm at the end of my tether with that boy. He absolutely refuses to do anything I say.* 我对那个男孩子已经忍无可忍了。不管我说什么，他连一句也不听。tether 的前边可加形容词。*I'm at the end of my financial tether.* 我的经济情况困难到了极点。另外一个非常普遍使用的形式是 come to [reach] the end of *one's* tether（达到山穷水尽的地步）。*I am afraid,* *gentlemen, that we have come to [reached] the end of our tether. The company's financial resources are depleted and the banks refuse to lend us any more money.* 先生们，很遗憾，我们已经达到了山穷水尽的地步。公司的资金耗尽了，各银行拒绝再向我们贷款。*You try to talk some sense into our son. I've come to [reached] the end of my tether (with him).* 你跟我们的儿子说道说道吧。我对他再也忍耐不下去了。还有一说法是 bring *someone* to the end of *his* tether (把某人逼到山穷水尽的地步)。*The long drought has just about brought the farmers of this district to the end of their tether.* 长期的干旱几乎把这个地区的农民们逼到山穷水尽的地步了。再有，用 rope (绳索) 代替 tether 可以构成 the end of *one's* rope 这一表达法。它在"力量、办法等的界限"的意义上，使用方法与 the end of *one's* tether 完全相同，两者可以互相替换。但是在"忍耐(克制) 的界限"这一意义上，一般不使用这一表达法。◇ have reached the limits of *one's* resources [endurance]

be at *one's* **wits' end** [ət ～ˈwɪts ˈe(:)nd] [口] **不知如何是好** 这里的 wit 不是"幽默的机智"，而是"知识的力量 (intellectual power)"。wits' end 是"知识力量的界限"。本条的整个意思是："达到了思考能力的界限"。这一表达法源出《圣经 · 旧约》中的《诗篇》(Psalms) 第 107 篇 27 节：They reel to and fro, and stagger like a drunken man, and are at their wits' end. (他们摇摇晃晃、东倒西歪，好象酒醉的人。他们的智慧无法可施。) 一般词典译法作"不知如何是好"。在绝大多数的场合，这种译法是适当的。但是严格地讲，译文与英语的意思是貌合而神离的。"不知如何是好"给人的第一个印象是"发愣"，而 be at *one's* wits' end 一般具有"着急"、"心里火烧火燎"的内涵。例如：*When my husband hadn't returned home for three days, I was at my wits' end.* 当我丈夫三天没有回家的时候，我不知如何是好了。在这一场合，那位太太给人的印象决不是"发愣"，而是"焦急不安"。*George is at his wits' end. He says that if he can't borrow a large sum of money by Monday his company will go broke.* 乔治正在不知如何是好哪。他说到星期一为止他如果借不来一大笔款，他的公司就要破产了。这句话里的乔治也令人感到正在苦思对策，心急如焚。*No matter what I say, my son refuses to study, and recently he has been getting into trouble outside of school. I'm absolutely at my wits' end with him.* 不论我说什么，我的儿子也不肯用功学习，最近他又在学校外边惹是生非。这真叫我对他不知如何是好啦。be at *one's* wits' end 的 *one's* 可以省略。*If I don't finish this work on time I may get fired. I'm just about at wits' end.* 如果我不按期完成这项工作，很可能要被解雇。我简直不知如何是好。◇ be desperate to know what to do

the end of *one's* **rope** [ðɪ ˌendəv ～ˈroup] [口] **力量、办法等的界限** → be at the END of *one's* tether

go off the deep end [ˌgouˈɔ(:)fðə dɪːˈpe(:)nd] [话] **贸然行事** go off 是"从跳台上跳入水中"。the deep end 即 the deep end of the (swimming) pool，意为"游泳池的深端"，可以认为前边有 at 或 into。但是，在实际上，如果是"从跳台上向游泳池的深端跳"，英语一般作 go in at the deep end，决不用本条条头的 go off the deep end。这一表达法从"不考虑自己会不会游泳就往深处跳"的具体形象进一步发展，专作比喻使用，表示"自己控制不住自己，或是胡来，或是冒进"的样子。*I'm afraid Charles isn't patient enough to succeed. Every time he gets a new idea, he goes off the deep end with it.* 我总觉得查尔斯对于成功缺乏足够的韧性。每当他有一个新想法的时候，他便不管三七二十一，胡来一阵。*Since Ned's brother cheated him out of his inheritance, he goes off the deep end at the very mention of his name.* 内德由于哥哥把应该属于他的遗产骗走了，他一听到哥哥的名字就控制不住自己，火冒三丈。*When her husband died, she* *went off the deep end. She stopped seeing all her old friends and began hitting the bottle.* 当她的丈夫去世后，她控制不住自己了。她不与一切老朋友见面，开始酗酒。也可以用否定式表示忠告，例如：*Don't go off the deep end. Let's make sure of the facts before you act.* 不要胡来嘛。在行动之前，先要弄清楚事实。◇ become so excited [upset, distraught, etc.] as to lose perspective

see beyond the end of *one'* **nose** → NOSE

ends

be at loose ends [ət ˌluː ˈse(ː)ndz] [口] **无事可干，心里没着没落** 表示没有事干、不知如何是好的心情。在想干点什么却没有什么可干，呆得心里起急，六神无主的场合使用。时间的幅度很广，仅仅一天呆着没事也好，一年以上没有工作也好，全都可以使用这一表达法。*Jim has been at loose ends ever since he lost his job.* 吉姆自从失业以后，心里一直没着没落。*Having studied so hard for the past few years, my son was at loose ends after passing his entrance exam.* 我的儿子在过去几年非常刻苦用功，自从考上大学以来，呆得不知如何是好了。常常用 feel 代替动词 be，而说 feel at loose ends。例如：*I was planning to work in the yard today, but now that it has started raining I feel at loose ends.* 我本来打算今天在庭院中工作，但是刚刚又下起雨来，心里没着落了，不知如何是好。◇ be restless and unsettled

make (both) ends meet [meɪˌke(ː)ndz ˈmiːt / meɪk ˌbouˌθe(ː)ndz ～] [口] **使收支相抵** 关于这一表达法的来源，有两种说法。一种说法是：它的原形是 19 世纪的簿记用语 make ends mete。ends 是"收入和支出"，而 mete (发音同 meet) 是"相等 (equal)"的意思。这一表达法原来的意思是"收入与支出平衡"。另一种说法是：这一表达法是 make ends of the year meet 省略了其中的 of the year，原意为"农民把收获物从这一个收获期保持到下一个收获期"。究竟哪个说法正确，现在没有定论。本条条头直译为"使两端合起来"，美国人一般也这样解释。*With three sons in college, we are having difficulty making both ends meet.* 我家有三个儿子上大学，费尽九牛二虎之力才能使收支相抵。如此例所示，一般用于家庭生活，公司、机关等是很少使用的。both 不论有无，意思不变。*Unless my wife and I both work, we can't possibly make ends meet.* 除非妻子和我全都出去工作，我家的收支是不可能平衡的。*The recession has caused many families to just about give up trying to make ends meet.* 经济萧条使许许多多家庭都几乎放弃了对收支平衡的精打细算。◇ make income match expenses

tie up the loose ends [ˌtaɪˈʌpðə ˌluːˈse(ː)ndz] [口] **最后完成** loose ends 意为"细绳之类下垂的端"。作为比喻，意思是"工作等未完成的部分"。tie up 是"结上"。本条的字面意义是"把下垂的绳头结上"，也就是说"把未完成的工作完成"。这是一个定型的表达法。*We've almost finished. Let's call it quits for the day. We can tie up the loose ends on Monday.* 我们快完成了，今天收工，我们到星期一把活儿干完就行。常用 some, several, a few, two or three 等形容词代替 the。*We'll be finished with this work as soon as we tie up some loose ends.* 我们干完一些收尾的活儿，这项工作就完事大吉了。为表示"还剩下一些收尾工作"的意味，常用 have some [a few, several, two or three, etc.] loose ends to tie up 的说法。在这一场合，极少使用 the loose ends 的说法。*The negotiations are almost finished. We just have a few loose ends to tie up.* 谈判快结束啦，只剩下很少的几个零星问题有待解决。◇ complete the final details

enemy

be *one's* **own worst enemy** [～ ˌoun ˌwə(ː)rst ˈenəmi] [口] **自己害自己** 容易看见他人的缺点，自己的缺点却总看不到；然而，恰恰是自己注意不到的缺点损害了自己，所以说"最大的敌人是自己"，这就是本条表达法的意义。*Ralph is his own worst enemy. His lack of manners* *always rubs people the wrong way*. 拉尔夫是自己害自己。他没有礼貌,总是引起别人发脾气。*I've made so many mistakes today that I'm beginning to think I'm my own worst enemy*. 我今天犯了很多错误,使我开始想到我是自己在害自己。如以上的例句所示,主语大多是说话人本身。但也有以他人的言行、态度、性格等为主语的场合,说法是 *one's something* is *one's* own worst enemy。*People often blame their failures on others, not realizing that such an attitude is their own worst enemy*. 人们往往把自己的失败归罪于别人,不晓得正是这种态度损害了自己。◇ be the one that harms *oneself* the most

engine

gun *one's* **engine** [.gʌn ~ 'endʒən] [口] **加大油门** 初期飞机的速度控制杆类似枪的板机,因而称速度控制器(the throttle) 为枪 (the gun)。后来,把 gun 作为动词,意为"拉控制杆",于是就产生了本条的表达法。这一表达法与 give her the GUN 极相似,两者的不同点是:后者意味着"挂档加快速度",而 gun *one's* engine 只是"加大油门",与挂不挂档没有关系。究竟指的是哪一种场合,要由上下文来决定。飞机、汽艇等只要是有引擎的交通工具,全都可以使用,但现在多用于汽车或摩托车。*All the drivers were gunning their engines, impatient for the start of the race*. 所有驾驶车的人都加大了油门,急切地等待比赛的开始。*I wonder how much gasoline is wasted every year by people who gun their engines while waiting at stoplights*. 由于人们在信号灯前停车的时间也加大油门,每年真不知道浪费多少汽油。*The man gunned his engine and drove off in a tremendous burst of speed*. 那个人加大油门,以猛烈的速度把车开走了。在特别考虑汽车本身的场合,要说 gun the engine。*Gunning the engine on a cold morning is bad for a car*. 在寒冷的早晨加大油门,对汽车是不利的。◇ (repeatedly) press on *one's* accelerator

English

English ['ɪŋglɪʃ] [口] **侧旋(球)** English 作为形容词是"英国(人)的"、"英语的",作为名词是"英语"、"英国人"等。除此而外,还有"侧旋" (名词) 一解。在使用这一意义时,有时将第一个字母小写,作 english。人们可以说这样的笑话:"虽然完全不会说英语,English 却非常棒"。这一表达法原为台球用语,指用台球杆去击台球 (a cue ball) 正中心以外的地方时所产生的 spin (旋转)。后来就不限于台球,也转用于棒球、网球、排球等的球技,表示使球出现的"侧旋"的意思。在实际使用时,为了加强语气,前面往往加上 a lot of, plenty, a little, some, any 等。*He really puts a lot of English on the ball when he serves [a lot of English on his serves]*. 他在发球的时候,使球侧旋得非常厉害。*Put a little more English on it*. 再多来点侧旋。如以上的例句所示,put English on ~表示"使球侧旋"的意思。人们也常说 give ~ some English,意思一样。*Give it some English*. 来点侧旋吧。另外有 ~ has English on it 或者 there is English on ~的说法,意思是"这球是侧旋的"。*That ball didn't have any English on it*. 刚才这个球一点也不带侧旋。*There was too much English on that ball for me*. 刚才这个球侧旋太厉害,我对付不了。另外,只有美国人把 English 作"侧旋"解;在英国英语中,一般使用 side 表示同一的意义。◇ spin

envy

be green with envy ['gri:nwɪð 'envi] [话] **羡慕极了** 古代的人似乎认为心里一嫉妒,脸色就发绿。有些词典译作"非常怨恨",但是这一表达法并不用于表示那么强烈的意味。*Wait till you see my new dress, Sue. You're going to be absolutely green with envy*. 苏,你等着看我的新衣服吧,准叫你馋得不得了。从这一例句也可以了解,在形式上好象强调 be envious, 但在实际上却是使语调更柔和了。这一表达法一般用轻松的口吻。*We were all green with envy when we learned that Tom had gotten a date with* *the most beautiful girl on the campus.* 当我们知道汤姆跟我们大学的校花约会以后，我们全都羡慕极了。也可以把这一习用语拆开，象下面这样说：*You shouldn't let your envy show like that, Becky. Green doesn't go very well with that dress you're wearing.* 贝基，你不要暴露出那么羡慕的样子。那种神情可跟你现在穿的新装完全不相符呀。◇ be extremely envious

equalizer

an equalizer [ə ˈni(ː)kwəˌlaɪzər] [话] **枪** 字面意义是"使人平等的东西"。这一表达法的最初构思是：对方不论是多大的人物，只要我手中有枪，就会和他势均力敌。黑社会用语，常在强盗影片中使用。特别指手枪；也有指步枪、匕首、棍棒等其他武器的场合，但极罕见。侦探小说中常常出现这样的对白：*Don't move! I've got an equalizer here in my pocket.* 不许动！我衣袋里有枪。◇ a gun

erase

erase *someone* [əˈreɪs ～] [话] **干掉（某人）** erase 的字面意义是"用橡皮擦去"。后来用以表示"把碍事的人杀死"的意思。原为黑社会用语，常在强盗影片、侦探小说的会话中出现。*Erase that guy.* 把那个家伙干掉！"用橡皮擦去"的英语为 rub out。有时也用 rub *someone* out 的表达法表示"把某人消灭掉"的意思。*The gang rubbed him out.* 匪徒们把他干掉了。◇ kill *someone*

Eskimo

an Eskimo kiss → KISS

essence

be of the essence [əvðɪ ˈesənts] [口] **绝对不可少的** essence 是"最宝贵的东西"。这一表达法最常应用于"时间"。在会话中，Time is of the essence. 已经是定型的说法，意思是"一寸光阴一寸金"。*In this kind of operation, time is of the essence.* 在这类手术中，时间是成败的关键。*Take me to the hospital—and step on it! Time is of the essence.* 把我送医院去，赶快！我挺不了多长时间啦。以下是以 time 以外的东西为主语的例句。*In training wild animals, cool nerves are of the essence.* 在训练野生动物时，头脑冷静是绝对必要的。*If you want to master English, constant practice is of the essence.* 如果你想掌握英语，不断练习是绝对不可少的。也可以使用否定式，如：*His financial backing would be helpful, but it's not of the essence.* 他的经济支援很有用处，但并不是绝对不可缺少的东西。◇ be the most important thing [factor]

even

call it even [ˌkɔ(ː)lət ˈiːvən] [口] **借贷两讫** → call it SQUARE

get even with *someone* (for *something*) [ˌgeˈdiːvən wɪð ～] [口] **报复** → GET back at *someone* (for *something*)

even-steven

be even-steven [ˈiːvənˈstiːvən] [话] **不相上下** steven 是与 even 押韵的俏皮话，没有特别意义。美国俚语的制造方法之一是添加合辙押韵但是毫无意义的词构成新语，如 a thriller-diller (惊险小说、影片等)、a silly BILLY (傻瓜)、rootin'-tootin' (怒气冲冲)等。也就是说，steven 意义和用法与 be even 完全一样，只不过是多少增强一些语气而已。这一表达法一般用于在借贷关系中两人处于同样立场的场合，例如：*Here's the five dollars I owe you. Now we're even-steven.* 喂，这是我借你的那五美元。咱们现在谁也不欠谁啦。*After playing poker for more than two hours, Charlie and I were still even-steven.* 查理和我玩了两个多小时扑克牌，双方依然不见输赢。*A: Hey! How come you hit me? B: That's for the lick you gave me yesterday. That makes us even-steven.* 甲：嘿！你为什么打我呀？乙：你昨天打我，我是还你一下。现在咱们谁也不欠谁啦。另外，由于 Steven [Stephen] 是男子的姓，所以有时将 S 大写，作 even-Steven；也有时拼写为 even-stephen [even-Stephen]，拚法虽有改变，发音却一样。◇ be (completely) even

everybody

everybody who's anybody ['e(:)vri.bɑdi hu'ze(:)ni.bɑdi] [话] **所有名流** 直译为“个个有身份的人”。who's 当然是 who is 的省略形式。这里的 anybody 与 (a) SOMEBODY (→)相同，意思是“某一地区或社会中有身份的人”。这一表达法的前一个重音最强，一般作 EVErybody，“一个不剩”的意味十分突出。 *You should join that club, dear. Everybody who's anybody belongs to it.* 亲爱的，你应该加入那个俱乐部。所有名流全都加入了。另外，因为这是一个定型的说法，所以 who's 的 is 一般不受主句时态的影响。 *It was an important occasion. Everybody who's anybody was present.* 那是一个重要的集会，所有名流全都出席了。 *I'll have to buy a new dress for the party. Everybody who's anybody will be there.* 为了出席社交晚会，我必须买一套新衣服了。所有名流全都要参加的。◇ all the important people

exam

an exam [ə nɪg'zæ(:)m] [口] **(学校的主要)考试** an examination 的缩略。在教育领域，主要指中学以上(直至研究生院)的主要测验。与 test 同义，但一般指比 test 更重要的考试，时间也比较长。适用于入学考试 (an entrance exam)，期中考试 (a midterm exam)，期末考试 (a final exam)，对其他的考试几乎完全不能使用。 *We have our final exam in history tomorrow.* 明天我们有历史课期末考试。另外，exam 最初只是学校用语，但现在作为广义的 examination 的缩略形式，在其他领域也常常使用，如说 a physical EXAM(身体检查)。→ a QUIZ ◇ an examination

make up an exam [.meɪ'kʌpə nɪg'zæ:m] [口] **补考** → a MAKE-UP

a make-up exam [ə 'meɪkʌp ɪg.zæ:m] [口] **补考** → a MAKE-UP

a medical exam [ə 'medəkl ɪg.zæ:m] [话] **身体检查／医学试验** → a PHYSICAL

a physical exam [ə .fɪzəkl ɪg'zæ:m] [话] **身体检查** → a PHYSICAL

ex-con

an ex-con [ə .neks'kɑ:n] [话] **以前判过刑的人** ex-为前缀，意思是“前任的”、“以前的”。con 是 convict 的缩略，意思是“囚犯”。二者合起来为“以前的囚犯”，亦即“过去判过刑的人”。 *Nobody will give a job to an ex-con like me.* 象我这样过去被判过刑的人，谁也不会雇用我的。 *He looks and talks like a tough ex- con, but actually he's a very soft-hearted family man.* 他那长相和说话很象一个桀骜不驯的过去被判过刑的人，但是实际上他是一个心地善良、热爱妻子儿女的人。在本条开头已经说明，con 是“囚犯”的意思，但在根据前后关系可以判断的场合，能与 ex-con 按同一意义使用。 *You shouldn't be dating that guy. Don't you know he's a con?* 你不要跟那个小子约会，你不知道他是一个过去被判过刑的人吗？尽管如此，在表示“以前判过刑的人”的意义时，一般还是使用 ex-con。◇ a former convict

excuse

a poor excuse for *something* [ə .pu(:)r ɪks'kju(:)s fər ～] [口] **蹩脚货** → a poor APOLOGY for *something*

exhibition

make an exhibition of *oneself* (by *doing something*) [.meɪkən .eksə'bɪʃənəv ～] [口] **出洋相** 直译为“使自己成为展览品”。这里的 exhibition 是“难看的[可怜的]情景”的意思。本条的整个意思是“自己硬要做出难看的、可怜的或者滑稽的样子当众出丑”。 *I'm very poor at public speaking. I refuse to make an exhibition of myself by trying to make a speech before hundreds of people.* 我不善于在众人面前讲话。我拒绝向几百个人作演说，免得当众出丑。如此例所示，有本人自觉怕出洋相的场合。但是，多数场合是本人不自觉地硬要出洋相。这一表达法常用于形容喝醉了酒而手舞足蹈的人、穿不相称的服装而满不在乎的人等等。 *I don't like to go to parties with*

Stu. Every time he gets drunk he makes an exhibition of himself. 我不愿意跟司徒一道参加社交晚会。他每一次喝醉了都出洋相。为了加强语气，常加含有讽刺意味的形容词 regular。也就是说，a regular exhibition 并不是"司空见惯的展览会"，而是有参观价值的、规模很大的、"琳琅满目的展览会"。因此，本条意思便是"大大地出洋相"、"出很大很大的丑"。 *Mrs. Mureeda should act her age. She makes a regular exhibition of herself by wearing young people's fashions.* 穆理达太太应该根据自己的年纪办事啊。她居然穿年轻人的新潮服装，真是大出洋相。另外有一个表达法是用 spectacle ['spektəkl] (奇观)代替 exhibition 而构成的 make a spectacle of *oneself*，意义和用法完全一样。◇ make *oneself* look like a fool

existence

lead a hand-to-mouth existence [.li(:)də 'hæ(:)ntə.mauθ ɪg'zɪstən*t*s] [口] **勉强维持生活** → live from HAND to mouth

expense

pad *one's* **expense account** → ACCOUNT

expressway

an expressway [ə nəks'pres.weɪ] [口] **首都高速公路** → a HIGHWAY

extra

go the extra mile → MILE

eye

be the apple of *someone's* **eye** → APPLE

Beauty is in the eye of the beholder. → BEAUTY

an eye for an eye and a tooth for a tooth [ə 'naɪfərə 'naɪ ənd*ə* 'tu:θfər*ə* 'tu:θ] [口] **以眼还眼，以牙还牙** 原为《圣经》中的文句，后成为习用语。据《圣经·旧约》中的《出埃及记》(Exodus) 第 21 章 24 节，上帝命令以色列人民"以眼还眼，以牙还牙，以手还手……以打伤还打伤"。在《圣经·新约》中，耶稣根据上帝的这一命令，于《马太福音》(Matthew) 第 5 章 38–41 节的《山上垂训》(The Sermon on the Mount) 中做了如下的教诲：You have heard that it was said, "An eye for an eye and a tooth for a tooth." But I say to you, do not resist one who is evil. If anyone strikes you on the right cheek, turn to him the other also; and if anyone would sue you and take your coat, let him have your cloak as well; and if anyone forces you to go one mile, go with him two miles. (你们听见有话说："以眼还眼，以牙还牙。"只是我告诉你们，不要与恶人作对；有人打你的右脸，连左脸也转过来由他打。有人想要告你，要拿你的里衣，连外衣也由他拿去。有人强逼你走一里路，你就同他走二里。) 这里引用的部分是耶稣的特别著名的语录，人们常常作为习用语使用的，除 an eye for an eye 外，还有 turn the other CHEEK 和 go the extra MILE。*Under ancient law, if someone put out your eye or cut off one of your hands, you were permitted to do the same to him. This was known as the rule of an eye for an eye.* 在古代的法律中，如果有人弄瞎你的一只眼睛，或者砍掉你的一只手，也允许你对那个人做相同的处置。这就是所谓的以眼还眼法则。如此例所示，有省略 ～ and a tooth for a tooth 的场合。但是，一般情况是不省略的。 *Since Israel does not accept the New Testament, it still follows the old law of an eye for an eye and a tooth for a tooth.* 由于以色列不接受《新约》，至今仍然遵循以眼还眼和以牙还牙的古代律法。*There are many people who believe that if nations do not give up the idea of an eye for an eye and a tooth for a tooth, the world will eventually be destroyed.* 许多人都相信：如果各国不放弃以眼还眼和以牙还牙的想法，世界总有一天要毁灭的。◇ revenge by the same means used by one's adversary

give *someone* [*something*] **a black eye** [.gɪv ～ ə.blæ(:)'kaɪ] [口] **败坏名声** black eye 是"在打架时被人打出来的青肿眼眶"。 *The bully gave Jimmy a black eye.* 吉米被流氓打得鼻青眼肿。

这是按照字面意义使用的场合。这个 black eye 正是干了“打架”之类不体面的事情的证据。因此，give *someone* [*something*] a black eye 在作为比喻使用时，就具有“使人失去体面”、“败坏他人名声”或“把某人或某一事物搞臭”的意味了。*The rumors that he has been friendly with underworld figures has given the candidate a black eye.* 关于那位候选人与黑社会人物交往密切的流言把他的名声搞臭了。*Rioting and unruly behavior by its supporters gave the anti-war movement a black eye.* 反战运动的支持者由于搞暴乱和不法行动而败坏了这一运动的名声。动词多用 give，但不以此为限。*The term "capitalism" has a black eye in this country.* 在这个国家里，“资本主义”一词臭不可闻。◇ give *someone* [*something*] a bad reputation

Here's mud in your eye. [ˌhɪrz ˈmʌ(ː)dnjər ˌaɪ] [话] **干杯** → BOTTOMS up

in the public eye [ɪnðə ˌpʌblɪˈkaɪ] [口] **常在公开场合出现** 直译为“在公众的眼睛里”。这一表达法仅指“被人看见”的状态，即使根据上下文有“引人注目”、“当众出丑”之类的意味，也与它本身无关。特别在谈到政治家或著名人物时常常使用。*The President's job keeps him in the public eye.* 总统由于职务关系，经常在公开场合露面。*In order to get re-elected, a politician has to remain in the public eye.* 为了能够再次当选，政治家必须经常在公开场合出现。*That new singer is much in the public eye these days.* 那位新歌手最近经常登台演唱。◇ in (the) people's awareness

keep an eye open (for *something* [*someone*]) [ˌki(ː)pə ˈnaɪˌopən] [口] **密切注意** → keep an EYE out (for *something* [*someone*])

keep an eye out (for *something* [*someone*]) [ˌki(ː)pə ˈnaɪ ˌaut] [口] **十分留心** 直译为“把一只眼睛放在外边”。在一心注视着目标出现或人前来的场合使用。用法与同义的习用语 keep *one's* EYES peeled 几乎一样，但具有从容不迫的感觉，不象后者那样令人感到十分紧张。*We're getting a little low on gas. Better keep an eye out for a filling station.* 我们的车没多少油啦，注意点哪儿有加油站。*My mother always keeps an eye out for bargains at the supermarket.* 我母亲总是十分留心超级市场的特价商品。*You're looking for a part-time job? I don't know of any good ones right now, but I'll keep an eye out (for one) for you.* 你在找兼职的工作吗？我现在不知道有什么适当的地方，但是我会留心给你寻找的。*Keep an eye out for Fred. I'd like to see him before he goes home.* 你看看弗雷德在哪儿，我想在他下班以前见见他。另外，可以用 open 替换 out 而讲 keep an eye open (for *something* [*someone*])，意义相同，上面的例句均可用这一表达法代换。◇ watch (out)

~ my eye! [~ ˈmaɪ ˈaɪ] [话] **别瞎说啦!** → ~ my FOOT!

not bat an eye [nɑt ˌbædə ˈnaɪ] [话] **泰然自若** bat 是“眨眼”。直译是“眼睛连一眨都不眨”，与汉语的表达法完全一致。*The defendant did not bat an eye when the judge handed down a life sentence.* 当法官宣判他无期徒刑的时候，被告泰然自若，眼睛连眨都没眨。*No matter how much we threatened him, he never batted an eye.* 不管我们怎样威胁他，他始终连眼睛都不眨。常以 without batting an eye 的形式作状语使用。*Mr. Price must be a very rich man. He paid the outrageous bill without batting an eye.* 普赖斯先生一定是个非常有钱的人。人家漫天要价，他也照样付钱，连眼睛眨都不眨。有时用 eyelash (睫毛) 或 eyelid (眼皮) 代替 eye。特别是 eyelash 的场合，语气稍微加强了一些。*A: What was the suspect's reaction when you confronted him with the evidence? B: Didn't bat an eyelash.* 甲：当你把证据摆在那个嫌疑犯的面前的时候，他有什么反应？乙：简直连眼睛眨都没有眨一下啊。另外，一般词典译作“连个盹也没打”或者“没有合眼，一会儿也没睡”，但与此相当的英语是 spend a sleepless night 或者 not sleep a wink, 本条的表达法决不能作这一意义使用。◇ show (absolutely) no sign of emotion [fear, surprise, etc.]

a private eye [ə ˌpraɪvəˈdaɪ] [话] **私人侦探** 字面意义是"非正式的眼睛"。从语感上讲，这里的 private (私人的、私立的) 接近"非正式的(侦探)"、"秘密的 (观察)"。原来是苏格兰警察局的便衣警察平克顿 (Pinkerton) 于 1850 年在芝加哥市设立了美国第一家 private detective agency (私立侦探事务所)，由于接二连三侦破许多大案件而赫赫有名。这个 Pinkerton Agency 现在也是美国屈指可数的私立侦探事务所之一。由于自创立以来就以"人的一个眼睛"为商标，所以人们就把 private detective 也叫做 private eye 了。 *Frank's father used to be a special investigator for the New York Police Department, but now he's a private eye.* 弗兰克的父亲原为纽约警察局的特别调查员，但是现在当私人侦探了。◇ a private detective

see eye to eye (with *someone* on *something*) [ˌsiː ˈaɪdəˈaɪ / ˈaɪtuˈaɪ] [口] **意见完全一致** 字面意义是"使眼睛看眼睛"。出典为《圣经·旧约》中的《以赛亚书》(Isaiah) 第 52 章 8 节: Thy watchmen shall lift up the voice; with the voice together shall they sing; for they shall see eye to eye, when the Lord shall bring again Zion. (听啊，你守望之人的声音。他们扬起声来，一同歌唱。因为耶和华回归锡安的时候，他们必亲眼看见。) 不过，现在已经舍弃原来的意义，而用以表示"意见完全一致"了。*I see eye to eye with Bill on this question.* 关于这个问题，我与比尔的意见完全一致。相当于 with *someone* 的实体可以转成主语，例如: *My brother and I are very close, but we've never seen eye to eye on politics.* 弟弟跟我感情极好，但是对于政治，我们的看法从来没有一致过。*Though we don't quite see eye to eye (with each other) on this, our thinking is very close.* 对于这件事情，虽然我们 (相互间) 的意见不完全一致，但是我们的想法却是非常接近的。◇ agree (completely)

there is more to *something* [*someone*] **than meets the eye** [ðərəz ˈmo(ː)rdə ~ ðən ˌmi(ː)tsðɪ ˈaɪ] [口] **只从表面上看不出来** 字面意义是"有比眼睛看到的还要多的东西"。多用现在时。可以用于"事"，如: *There must be more to this case than meets the eye.* 这个案件肯定内情很复杂。也可以用于"人"，如: *She may appear a bit spaced out, but there's more to her than meets the eye.* 她似乎有点不对头，但是光从表面看不出她究竟是怎么了。因为这一表达法只表示"仅从外观不能判断"的意思，所以不论是表面看起来好的场合，还是表面看起来不好的场合，全都可以应用。*Don't be too quick to accept his proposal. I'm sure there is more to it than meets the eye.* 不要太匆忙地接受他的建议。这里面肯定会大有文章的。*The problem seemed simple enough at first glance, but I soon realized that there was more to it than met the eye.* 那个问题乍看起来似乎太简单了，但是我很快就明白它的内涵是很复杂的。可以用 here 或者 there 来代替 to *something* [*someone*]，也偶尔地仅讲 there is more than meets the eye。 *I wouldn't be too confident of quick success. There's more there than meets the eye.* 我不能狂妄地自信很快就能成功。事情并不象表面上那么简单啊。*With a girl like that, there's more than meets the eye.* 象那样一个姑娘，仅从表面上看是不行的。◇ there is more to *something* [*someone*] than is at first noticeable

turn a blind eye (to *something*) [ˌtə(ː)rnə ˌblaɪnˈdaɪ] [口] **装作看不见** 字面意义是"把一只眼睛闭上，用闭上的那只眼睛去看"。汉语俗语叫做: 睁一个眼睛，闭一个眼睛；明明看到却假装没看见。*As long as Hank was winning, his wife turned a blind eye to his gambling.* 只要汉克赢钱，他的老婆对他参加赌博就装作看不见。 *The government seems willing to turn a blind eye to graft in high places as long as the public remains unaware of it.* 只要公众还没有发觉，政

府对于高级官员贪污似乎愿意睁一只眼闭一只眼。*Parents who criticize other people's children often turn a blind eye when it comes to faults in their own.* 喜欢批评别人孩子的父母，当自己的子女犯错误时，往往装作看不见。◇ pretend not to see (*something*)

with fire in *one's* **eye** → FIRE

eyeballs

be up to *one's* **eyeballs** (in *something*) [ˌʌptə ~ ˈaɪˌbɔːlz] [话] **水一直泡到脖子，身子动转不了** → be up to *one's* NECK (in *something*)

eyebrows

be up to *one's* **eyebrows** (in *something*) [ˌʌptə ~ ˈaɪˌbrauz] [话] **水没脖子，身子动弹不了** → be up to *one's* NECK (in *something*)

eyelash

not bat an eyelash [nɑt ˌbædə ˈnaɪˌlæ(ː)ʃ] [话] **眼睛连眨也不眨** → not bat an EYE

eyelid

not bat an eyelid [nɑt ˌbædə ˈnaɪˌlɪd] [话] **眼睑眨都不眨一下** → not bat an EYE

eyes

before *someone's* **very eyes** [bəˌfor ~ ˈveri ˈaɪz] [口] **就在（某人）眼前** 同样的表达法有 under *someone's* very NOSE。两者的不同点是：under ~ nose 不一定非在眼前不可，而且原则上用于本人没有注意到的场合；而本条的表达法一定是在眼前，而且通常在本人亲眼看到的场合使用。*The murder took place before the policeman's very eyes.* 谋杀是在警察的眼皮底下进行的。这一表达法是变戏法的常套用语，例如：*Watch closely, ladies and gentlemen. I will now, before your very eyes, turn this rabbit into a snake.* 女士们，先生们，请仔细观看。就在诸位的眼前，我要把这只兔子变成一条蛇。用以加强语气的 very 可用 right 替换，例如：*The teacher caught the student cheating right before his eyes.* 老师抓住了一个就在他眼皮底下作弊的学生。请读者注意：在这一场合，位置也改变了。另外，在进一步加强语气的时候，very 和 right 也可以并用，例如：*When I opened the door to the apartment, there, right before my very eyes, was the lost painting.* 当我打开公寓房间的门的时候，哎呀，丢失的那幅画竟然出现在我的眼前。◇ right in front of *someone* / right within *someone's* view

close *one's* **eyes to** *something* [ˌklouz ~ ˈaɪztə ~] [口] **闭眼不看** → shut *one's* EYES to *something*

cry *one's* **eyes out** [ˌkraɪ ~ ˈaɪˌzaut] [话] **痛哭不止** 直译为“哭得把眼球都掉出去”。同样的表达法 cry *one's* HEARTout 强调“悲哀”的心情，本条习用语则强调“哭泣”的行动。例如，我们可以说：*Stop crying your eyes out!* 不要老哭个没完！但是，如果象下列的说法就有些不自然：Stop crying your heart out! (不要悲伤个没完！）因为，提出这样的要求是不恰当的。本条的表达法一般在“号啕大哭”的场合使用。*When Jennie's dog died, she cried her eyes out all afternoon.* 当珍妮的狗死了的时候，她痛哭了一个下午。如果把 all afternoon 说成 for many days, 那就不自然了。因为一连好多天大哭不止，这是不可能有的事情。*You can cry your eyes out all day, but you'll get no sympathy from me.* 你可以大哭上一整天，但是我决不会同情你的。*There's no use crying your eyes out. What's happened has happened.* 总哭也没有用。发生的事情已经发生啦。可以用 weep 代替 cry，但有点文学的味道，在会话中很少使用。◇ cry ceaselessly [so much]

one's **eyes are bigger than** *one's* **stomach** [~ ˈaɪzər ˌbɪgərðən ~ ˈstʌmək] [话] **眼睛大肚皮小** 这一表达法与汉语俗语完全一致。在美国的家庭中，每当吃饭的时候，不是把做好的菜按人数分盛在盘子里，而是放在一个大容器里。每个人按自己想吃的多少从那个容器中取出，然后依照顺序将大容器传给别人。根据饭桌上的礼仪，自己所取的一份必须全都吃完，不能有残余。可是，如果遇到特

别好吃的菜或者自己爱吃的菜,往往有取出过多而吃不完的情况。本条的表达法就是从这种情况产生出来的。因为不知自己能吃多少而取出过量的菜的多半是小孩子们,所以这一表达法常用作对儿童们的警告。例如: *Don't take so much at once. Your eyes are always bigger than your stomach.* 一次不要取那么多。你总是眼睛大肚子小。成年人也有由于判断错误而吃剩下的时候,在这种场合,要用过去时,并加上道歉的话。例如: *I'm sorry I couldn't eat everything. I guess my eyes were bigger than my stomach.* 实在对不起,我没有全吃干净。我真是眼睛大肚子小啊。◇ *one* thinks *one* can eat more than *one* actually can

feast *one's* **eyes on** *something* [ˈfiːst ~ ˈaɪzɔn ~] [话] **一饱眼福** 一般来说, feast 作为名词是"盛宴"的意思;作为动词,以 feast on *something* 的形式,则为"饱餐"的意思。*In Hawaii we feasted on roast pig and pineapple.* 在夏威夷,我们饱餐了烤猪肉和菠萝。如此例所示,饱餐总是用嘴来进行的。但是,本条的表达法的构思则是"用自己的眼睛饱餐一顿"。汉语叫做"饱眼福",与英语的构思完全相同。不过在英语中还有一个"养目"的意思。*Phil doesn't like to swim. He goes to the beach to feast his eyes on all the beautiful girls there.* 菲尔并不喜好游泳。他到海滨去是为了去看云集在那里的漂亮姑娘,一饱眼福。*Having lived in the desert for six months, we feasted our eyes on the beautiful green grass and trees.* 在沙漠里居住了半年之后,我们尽情地欣赏美丽的青草和树木。也常用命令式。在这一场合,根据上下文可以有种种不同的译法,但万变不离其宗,归根结底还是"饱眼福"的意思。*Feast your eyes on this. It's a plan I've drawn up for making a million dollars.* 你瞧瞧这个吧。这是我拟定的赚一百万美元的计划啊。*Feast your eyes on this emerald ring. Isn't it gorgeous?* 叫你开开眼,你瞧这个翡翠戒指!怎么样,够好看的吧? ◇ (greatly) enjoy looking at *something* / Look at *something*!

keep *one's* **eyes peeled** (for *something* [*someone*]) [ˌki(ː)p ~ ˈaɪz ˌpi(ː)ld] [话] **留神** 字面意义是"保持眼睛瞪着"。这一表达法表示毫不疏忽地张望着的状态,多半带有一定程度的紧迫感。*We're almost out of gas. Keep your eyes peeled for a filling station.* 我们的汽油眼看就没有了。留点神,看哪里有加油站。*Keep your eyes peeled. I think the man we're looking for lives in this neighborhood.* 你多留点神。我们找的那个人大概就住在这附近。*I don't think there are any poisonous snakes in this area, but you'd better keep your eyes peeled just in case.* 我认为这个地区没有什么毒蛇,但是你最好多留点神,以防万一。另外,也可以用 peel 的同类词 skin 构成 keep *one's* eyes skinned (for *something* [*someone*]) 的说法,意义和用法完全一样,但没有条头的表达法使用频率高。还有一个类似的说法是 keep an EYE out (for *something*[*someone*]) (→)。◇ stay on the alert

keep *one's* **eyes skinned** (for *something* [*someone*]) [ˌki(ː)p ~ ˈaɪz ˌskɪ(ː)nd] [话] **注意观看** → keep *one's* EYES peeled (for *something* [*someone*])

make eyes at *someone* [ˌmeɪ ˈkaɪzət ~] [口] **漫送秋波** make eyes 的构思是"特意做出眼神",即向异性"漫送秋波"。*Why don't you ask Sally for a dance? She's been making eyes at you all night.* 你怎么不请萨莉跳舞呢?她整个晚上都在向你送秋波哪。*Ralph thinks he's a great lover. He makes eyes at practically every girl that he passes on the street.* 拉尔夫认为自己是个很了不起的情人。当他走在街上的时候,几乎对碰见的每一个姑娘飞眼。这一表达法也在男女相互间眉目传情的场合使用。*Jack and Jill must really be in love. They spend all their time making eyes at each other.* 杰克和吉尔一定是真地相爱了。他们总是含情脉脉地你看着我,我看着你。◇ cast amorous glances at *someone* / look amorously into each other's eyes

pull the wool over *someone's* **eyes** →

WOOL

shut *one's* **eyes to** *something* [ˌʃʌt ～ ˈaɪztə ～] [口] **佯装不知** 字面意义是"闭上眼睛不看"。当然可以按这一意义使用，如：*Shut your eyes and try to go to sleep.* 你闭上眼睛睡觉好啦。作为比喻，表示虽然看见但是假装没看见的意思。汉语俗语是"睁一只眼闭一只眼"。*As long as Hank was winning, his wife shut her eyes to his gambling.* 汉克只要是赢钱，他的老婆就佯装不知道他去赌博。*If you will return the money you stole from me, I am willing to shut my eyes to your indiscretion.* 如果你把偷我的钱还给我，我就假装不知道你的轻率行为。*Mt. Fuji is a beautiful mountain if you shut your eyes to the litter.* 如果你闭眼不看那些乱丢的垃圾，富士山是一座很美的山。也可以说 close *one's* eyes (to *something*)。◇ disregard [ignore] *something*

be a sight for sore eyes → SIGHT

snake eyes [ˈsneɪˌkaɪz] [话] **双么** 直译为"蛇的眼睛"。因为掷两个骰子时出两个么，很象蛇的两只眼睛，所以有这样一个表达法。原是双骰子赌博戏 craps [ˈkræ(ː)ps] 的专用语，现在凡是使用骰子的任何赌博都可以使用。*Jerry rolled snake eyes three times in a row.* 杰里一连三次掷出了双么。如此例所示，多与动词 roll (滚动)配套使用。→ BOXCARS ◇ two ones

eyeteeth

cut *one's* **eyeteeth** [ˌkʌt ～ ˈaɪˌtiːθ] [口] **通达人情世故** eyetooth 是"上犬齿"。因为在眼睛 (eye) 的正下方，故英语中有此名称。cut 在这里不是"切割"，而是"出(牙)"的意思。本条的表达法直译为"生出成年人的上犬齿"。专用于比喻。在这一场合，eyeteeth 的年龄不是指生理学的生上犬齿的实际年龄，一般是指十八、九岁能够自立的青年人。意义是"积累各种经验，通达世故人情，为步入成年做好准备"。*Having grown up in the harsh environment of the slums, I cut my eyeteeth at a very early age.* 我是在贫民窟的艰苦环境中长大的，因此年纪很小的时候就已经积累了各种各样的生活经验。*Karl didn't have the advantages of most children. By the time he was ready to cut his eyeteeth, his mother and father were both dead.* 卡尔没有大多数儿童所具有的优越条件。当他快到通达世故人情的年龄时，父母都已经去世了。有时加上 on *something*，则与 cut *one's* TEETH on *something* 一样，表示"开始某种工作或爱好"。*When I first met Mr. Updike, he had barely begun to cut his eyeteeth as a writer.* 当我第一次见到厄普代克先生的时候，他刚刚开始写作的生涯。*Many pilots of my age cut their eyeteeth on that airplane.* 跟我年纪相同的许多飞行员都是用那架飞机开始训练的。◇ gain experience (of the world)

would give *one's* **eyeteeth** [wud ˌgɪv ～ ˈaɪˌtiːθ] [话] **如果那样该多么好** would 是假定式。an eyetooth 是最难脱落的"上犬齿"，在英语中一般称 a canine <tooth>[ˈkeɪˌnaɪn]。因此，按照字面意义，本条的表达法仿佛在表示一种坚强的决心，既然"连难以脱落的上犬齿都可以给"，那便是"豁出去了"。可是，实际上并不是这样。这一表达法所表示的乃是一种强烈的愿望。例如：*I'd give my eyeteeth for that job.* 我若是干上那个工作该多么好啊。这一例句的句型是 would give *one's* eyeteeth for *something*，如果用 to have 代替 for，意思也一样。*You shouldn't envy Perry his bachelor's life. He'd give his eyeteeth to have [for] a wife like yours.* 你用不着羡慕佩里的独身生活。他还认为如果有你太太那样一个妻子该多么好哪。另外，也可以采取 to (be able to) *do something* 或者 to be *something* [*someplace*]的形式。*I'd give my eyeteeth to be able to afford a car like that.* 我要能有那样一辆小汽车该多好啊。*Lou says he'd give his eyeteeth to be a professional baseball player.* 卢说他如果当上职业棒球运动员该多么好啊。还有一个表达法是用 right arm (右臂)代替 eyeteeth，即

would give *one's* right ARM, 意义、用法两者完全一样。因此，上面各例句中的 eyeteeth 均可用 right arm 代入。不过，使用 right arm 的表达法语调轻松，近年以来在会话中越来越频繁出现。◇ would sacrifice anything (to ~) / would exchange anything (for ~)

F

face

cut off *one's* **nose to spite** *one's* **face** → NOSE

a face card → CARD

fall flat on *one's* **face** [ˌfɔːl ˈflædən ～ ˈfeɪs] [话] **完全失败** 字面意义是"脸朝下直挺挺地倒下"。在人体摔倒的姿态中,这是最糟糕的一种。作为比喻,在做某种事情完全以失败而告终的时候使用。具体形象是:"在群众面前正表演难度很大的技艺(舞蹈、唱歌、魔术等均可)时,突然被什么东西绊倒,来个大马趴"。实际上也经常用于在表演节目时彻底失败的场合。*Because I hadn't practiced it for many years, when I tried to show the children some magic tricks I fell flat on my face.* 当我给孩子们表演魔术的时候,由于好多年没有练习过,结果完全失败了。*I'm a born loser. Every time I try anything new, I always fall flat on my face.* 我天生就是个不中用的人。每一次我尝试点新的东西,总是以彻底失败而告终。*Louis started a new company, but his inexperience caused him to fall flat on his face.* 路易斯开办了一家新公司,但是由于毫无经验而完全失败了。另外,具有"直挺挺地"的意味的flat本来是为了加强语气而添加的,而且已经习惯成自然了。如果省略这个副词,而说 fall on *one's* face, 意思也无变化。◇ fail completely

feed *one's* **face** [ˌfi(ː)d ～ˈfeɪs] [话] **吃饭** 直译是"填饱脸"。这一表达法使人产生的感觉是:"不是往胃里吃饭,而是给脸吃饭,因此,不管吃多少也没有吃饱的时候"。它具有"不论是否饥饿,也不论味道如何,只是为了吃而吃"的意味。特别是在开玩笑或者吃惊的场合常常使用。*All that guy thinks about is feeding his face.* 那个家伙心里所想的只有一个吃字。*We can't leave yet. Fatso's still feeding his face.* 我们还不能启程。胖子还没吃完饭哪。◇ eat

have a face that would stop a clock [ˌhævə ˈfeɪs ðədəd ˌstɑpə ˈklɑ(ː)k] [话] **奇丑的嘴脸** 在英语中,clock(挂钟、坐钟等)的字盘 (dial) 又称 face。这一表达法最初的构思是:"在人的脸与钟的面相遇的时候,由于人脸的奇丑,钟大吃一惊,连针都停下了"。造句法为虚拟语气形式。在这一表达法中,不知是何道理,只能用 clock (钟)而不能用 watch (表)。一般词典很少收录,但这是一个经常使用的表达法。*Mr. Dial is the kindest man you'll ever meet, but he has a face that would stop a clock.* 戴尔先生是世间少有的一位最和蔼可亲的人,但是他的脸可难看极了。这是用于男性。但对女性也是同样可以使用的。*Talk about ugly! She has a face that would stop a clock.* 别提多么难看啦!她长得简直三分象人,七分象鬼。有时改换一下句型出现,例如:*When you have a face of the clock- stopping variety like mine, you have to work hard to develop at least a good personality.* 一个人如果长得象我一样丑陋,他至少需要努力去培养良好的性格。如果将 have 变成 with, 则可构成形容词语句。*When I opened the door, there stood a man with a face that would stop a clock.* 我一打开门,外边站着一个相貌极为丑陋的男子。最后,还有一个变形是 *someone's* face would stop a clock。*Her face probably wouldn't stop a clock, but it would certainly never win the owner a beauty contest.* 她的脸也许算不上非常难看,但是可以肯定,她在选美竞赛中是不会榜上题名的。◇ have a very [an unbelievably] ugly face

help *someone* **save face** [ˌhelp ～

ˌseɪv'feɪs] [口] **帮助某人保全面子** → save FACE

keep a straight face [ˌki(:)pə ˌstreɪt'feɪs] [口] **板着脸** straight face 的字面意义是"笔直的脸",换句话说就是"把脸绷着";亦即"神情严肃,没有笑容"的意思。因此,straight face 常用于表示与"笑脸"恰恰相反的意义。把这个 straight face 加以 keep (保持),那就是"经常板着脸,不露一丝笑意"的意思了。 *When the president's pants fell down at the board meeting, it was all everyone could do to keep a straight face.* 当总经理在董事会议席上掉了裤子的时候,大家总算保持住严肃的神情,没有笑出声来。 *I know I shouldn't have laughed at his piano playing, but I just couldn't keep a straight face.* 我知道在他演奏钢琴的时候我不应该笑,但是我怎么也未能绷住自己的脸。straight face 加前置词 with,可以构成副词短语,意思是"以严肃的神情"。 *He looked at me with a straight face, but I wasn't sure whether he was serious or not.* 他以严肃的神情望着我,但我弄不清楚他是否当真如此。另外,还常使用 perfectly 加强语气,例如: *Of course he wasn't joking. He told me with a perfectly straight face that he wouldn't be able to pay back the money he owes us.* 当然,他不是在说笑话。他以非常认真的神情对我讲,他还不上他向我们借的那笔钱。 ◇ keep (*oneself*) from laughing [smiling]

keep face [ˌki(:)p'feɪs] [口] **保全面子** → save FACE

keep *someone* **from losing face** [ˌki(:)p ~ frəm ˌlu:zɪŋ 'feɪs] [口] **不使(某人)丢面子** → save FACE

lose face [ˌlu(:)z'feɪs] [口] **失面子** 字面意义即为"丢脸"。是 save FACE 的反义语。这一表达法证明英美人士虽然不象中国人那样爱面子,但是也注意他人或社会上对自己的评价。 *You'll lose face if you don't keep your promise.* 如果你不遵守自己的诺言,那会失面子的。 *I'll lose face if I can't repay my debts.* 如果我还不上债,就会失面子。 *Mrs. Redding lost face when her husband got angry and refused to attend her party.* 雷丁太太的丈夫生了气,不参加她的社交晚会,使她丢了面子。为了加强语气,在 lose 与 face 之间可加入 a lot of 或 a good bit of 等。 *The school principal lost a lot of face when his son was caught cheating on his exam.* 校长的儿子在考试时作弊,被人抓住了,使得校长非常丢面子。如果进一步加强语气,则使用 completely。 *I completely lost face when the man I recommended embezzled company funds.* 由于我所荐举的那个人盗用公司资金,我完全失了面子。 ◇ suffer humiliation [disgrace]

maintain face [ˌmeɪn.teɪn'feɪs] [口] **维护脸面** → save FACE

preserve face [prəˌsə(:)rv'feɪs] [口] **保持面子** → save FACE

save face [ˌseɪv'feɪs] [口] **保全面子** 字面意义是"拯救脸"。在欧美各国,本来没有用"脸"这个词表示他人对自己的评价或自己在他人心目中的威望的习惯,face 作"脸面"、"面子"解的表达法是从中国输入的。动词除 save 外,有时用 keep (保持)以及略嫌生硬的 maintain 或 preserve (两词均是"维持"的意思),但是 save 具代表性。 *Gil bragged that he knew the governor quite well. Now that the governor is going to visit our school, Gil is hoping to save face by pretending to be sick.* 吉尔曾经吹嘘说州长是他的老相识。这回,那位州长要到我们学校来参观了,吉尔假称有病,希望借此保住他的面子。 *When the mayor was caught taking bribes, he tried to save face by pretending they were political contributions.* 市长受贿的情况暴露以后,他为了保全面子,伪称那是政治捐款。save face 的反义语是 lose FACE。顺便提一下:在英语中没有表示"保持他人的脸面"的习用语。因此,就利用以上列举的有关"面子"的表达法,构成 help *someone* (to) save [keep, etc.] face (帮助某人保全面子)或者 keep [prevent] *someone* from losing face (使某人不失面子)之类的语句。 *You've got to help me save* *face. If you won't lend me the money, I'll go bankrupt.* 你来帮助我保全脸面吧。如果你不借给我钱,我就得破产啦。另外,从 save face 进一步发展,又出现 face-saving 这样一个形容词,意思是"为了保全面子的"。*I'm in trouble. I need a quick face-saving idea.* 我正在陷入窘境。我需要有一个能够马上保全面子的好主意。*The government's announcement was considered a mere face-saving maneuver.* 大家认为,政府的通告只不过是一个为了保全面子的招数而已。◇ avoid humiliation

till *one* **is blue in the face** [ˌtɪl ～ ɪzˌblu(ː) ɪnðə ˈfeɪs] [话] **舌敝唇焦** 直译为"直至脸色发青"。最初的构思是:"由于嘴里不断说话,没有吸气的功夫,脸色因缺氧而发青"。是一种夸张的表达法。一般用于无论费多少唇舌也得不到对方相应的反响或答复的场合。有的词典释义为"由于狂怒或紧张而精疲力竭,嘴也说不出话来",实际上根本没有这样的用法。因为这一表达法专指说话而言,所以常与动词 talk, argue, complain, scream 等一起使用。*I've talked to the boss till I'm blue in the face, but he absolutely refuses to change his method of hiring people.* 我向老板讲了又讲,直至舌敝唇焦,可是他绝对不肯改变用人的方法。*You can argue till you're blue in the face; I still won't go.* 不论你怎样苦口婆心地劝说,我也是绝对不会去的。till 是口头语,但也可以用 until。*I've complained to the paper boy until I'm blue in the face but he still won't deliver the paper before seven.* 我向送报的少年提意见,嘴唇都快磨破了,可是他照旧不在七点钟以前把报送来。◇ until *one* is tired of talking [arguing, etc.]

to *someone's* **face** [tə ～ ˈfeɪs] [口] **当面** 常与 say, tell 等表示"说"的意味的动词一起使用。*If you have something to say to me, say it to my face. Don't go sneaking around talking behind my back.* 你有什么话要向我讲,就请当面讲,不要偷偷在背后说闲话。*He called me a liar, did he? I'll bet he wouldn't call me that to my face.* 他称我是说谎大王,是吗? 我敢打赌,他当着我的面绝对不会这样称呼我。*A: I think you should tell him frankly how you feel about him. B: Oh, no! I couldn't tell him to his face!* 甲:我觉得你应该坦率地讲出你对他的看法。乙:不行不行! 我当着他的面说不出口呀! 反义语是 behind *someone's* BACK。◇ (<to> *someone*) directly

face-saving

face-saving [ˈfeɪˌsːeɪvɪŋ] [口] **为了保全面子的** → save FACE

fag

a fag① [əˈfæːg] [话] **香烟** 俚语,由 a fag end (绳索的散端)省略 end 而成。20 世纪 40 年代,世间流行用 a fag 表示"搞男性同性恋者"的意思 (→ a QUEER),因而作"香烟"解的使用频率日益降低,但至今仍然可以常常听到。*Hey, Joe. Lemme have a fag, will ya?* 喂,乔。给我一支香烟好吗? ◇ a cigarette

a fag② [ə ˈfæːg] [俗] **搞男性同性恋者** → a QUEER

fair

All's fair in love and war. → LOVE

by fair means or foul [ˌbaɪ ˈfeːr ˈmiːnzər ˈfaul] [口] **不择手段地** → by HOOK or crook

fair game → GAME

the fair sex → SEX

fair to middling [ˈfeːrdə ˈmɪdələn] [话] **还可以** → SO-SO

Turnabout is fair play. → TURNABOUT

fair-weather

a fair-weather friend → FRIEND

fairy

a fairy [ə ˈfe(ː)ri] [俗] **(男性) 同性恋者** → a QUEER

fake

fake *someone* **out** [ˌfeɪk ～ ˈaut] [话] **以假动作欺骗(某人)** fake 一词具有"伪装"、"假装"、"在体育比赛中以假动作迷惑对方"等意义。*The ball carrier eluded his* *would-be tackler by faking to the left and then cutting back to the right.* 持球人假装向左，躲开拦截他的人，然后从右方长驱直入。fake *someone* out 仍具有“迷惑对方”的固有意义，“欺骗”的手段则是“弄虚作假”。这里的 out 有“排除干扰而取得成功”的意味。从下边的例句可以看出：这一表达法是在与对手要花招、搞竞争的场合使用，而不能用于单纯撒谎进行欺骗(比如说“我头疼，得早走一步”)的场合。*George faked me out. He told me he wasn't going to the dance, so that he could gain time to ask Nancy before I did.* 乔治用欺骗手段迷惑了我。他告诉我说他不打算去跳舞，这样就能够赢得时间在我之前约请南希。*When the ball carrier runs at you and then feints to the side, you've got to learn not to follow him with your whole body. You're always too easy to fake out.* 当持球人跑到你身边，然后假装向旁边一闪的时候，你千万不要用自己的整个身体去阻挡他，因为这样永远是极容易被他晃过的。在具体叙明“欺骗的手段”时，用 by ～承续。*The driver behind me faked me out by yelling and pointing to one of my back tires. When I pulled over to check, he roared past me laughing.* 我的车后边那辆车的司机用虚假的方式欺骗了我，他一边喊叫，一边指着我的汽车的一个后轮胎。当我停下车去检查的时候，他哈哈大笑，从我的身边开着车飞驰而去了。*A: How come you sold your manuscript to the publisher so cheaply? B: He faked me out by pretending he was only buying it as a favor to me.* 甲：你为什么把稿子那么便宜地卖给出版社啦？乙：出版商欺骗我，他假装买我的稿子是对我的特殊照顾。也可以省略 out，只使用 fake *someone*。在这一场合，可以认为与 bluff (以假象骗人)大致同义。*You wouldn't be trying to fake [bluff] me, would you?* 你是不是要哄骗我呀？◇ trick [fool] *someone*

fall

fall all over *someone* [ˌfɔ(:) ˌɔ(:) ˈlouvər ～] [话] **过度地表示感激或钦佩的心情** 西方人在向对方表达自己的喜悦心情时，往往拥抱、接吻、握手。由于非常感激，有时超越常规，想将全身压到对方身上 (fall all over)。这就是本条习用语的来源。在表达感激或钦佩的心情时，根据上下文，可以有种种不同的解释。最主要的是仔细体会句子的内容。*My aunt fell all over the man who returned her lost ring, causing him to flee in embarrassment.* 我的伯母欣喜若狂地扑向那个送还她丢失的戒指的男人，那个人不知所措，撒腿就跑了。*Mrs. White falls all over her son every time he makes a good grade on a test.* 每当儿子在考试中获得高分数时，怀特太太就欣喜若狂地对儿子大肆夸奖一番。这一表达法如果去掉 all，那就要按字面意义解释，即“跌到某人身上”，请读者注意不要在这一点上搞错了。◇ display an excess of thanks [admiration]

fall down on the job (of *doing something*) → JOB

fall flat → FLAT

fall for *someone* [ˈfɔ:lfər ～] [话] **对异性迷恋** 专用于男女关系。有“向对方拜倒”的意味。*Della is a beautiful and talented girl. I'm not surprised that you've fallen for her.* 迪拉是一位才貌双全的姑娘。你迷恋上她，那是不足为奇的。*Thank you for the beautiful bracelet, Tim. You sure know how to make a girl fall for you, don't you.* 蒂姆，谢谢你给我的漂亮的手镯。你的确了解怎样使一个姑娘倾心于你呢。此外还有许多反映恋爱心情的表达法，如 fall in love with *someone*, be STUCK on *someone*, have a CRUSH on *someone* 等，但它们各有细微的差别。如果按认真的程度排列，则顺序如下：fall in love with＞ fall for＞ be stuck on＞ have a crush on。fall in love with 可以说是真正的恋爱，be stuck on 和 have a crush on 不过是一时的倾心。因此，I fell in love with [fell for] her, so I married her. 这句话是正常的，而 I was stuck [had a crush] on her, so I married her. 则有些不自然了。原因是：be stuck on, have a crush on 过于轻飘,在印象上根本与结婚联系不上。再有,为了加强语气,常常使用 fall for *someone* in a big way 或者 like a ton of BRICKS, 例如: *She fell for him in a big way.* 或 *She fell for him like a ton of bricks.* 她从内心里热爱他。◇ fall in love with *someone*

fall for *something* ['fɔːlfər ~] [话] **受骗、上当** 比 be cheated (被人欺骗)之类更为轻松的表达法,言外有"太糊涂了"的意味。*Don't tell me you fell for that old trick.* 我不相信你会中那老一套的骗局。这是单独使用 fall for 的例子。另外,为了增强意味,常与 like a ton of BRICKS 或 HOOK, line and sinker 等配合在一起使用。例如: *A: Did he believe your story? B: He fell for it like a ton of bricks.* 甲:他相信你的瞎话了吗? 乙:他完全信以为真啦。*A: You mean he handed you that old line about his wife not understanding him? B: Yeah. And I was stupid enough to fall for it, hook, line and sinker.* 甲:你的意思是说,他又向你卖弄那老一套,说他的妻子不理解他吗? 乙:是的。我太愚蠢啦,上了他的大当。如果逐字翻译的话, like a ton of bricks 的意思是"象一吨砖那样"。hook, line and sinker 是"鱼钩、鱼竿上的线以及线的前端的坠子",亦即"一般鱼只是咬钩,现在却连钩带线以及坠子全吞下去"的意思。总起来说,两者都是强调上了大当的比喻表达法。◇ be deceived by *something* / accept *something*

fall over each other [ˌfɔ(ː) ˈlouvərˌɪtʃˌʌðər] [话] **争先恐后** → FALL over one another

fall over one another [ˌfɔ(ː) ˈlouvər ˌwʌnəˌnʌðər] [话] **争先恐后** 这一表达法形容争先恐后、互相抢夺什么东西的样子。按字面意义,有"互相要骑到对方身上"的意味。根据上下文,有时可以译为"抢着干……"。*The reporters fell over one another in their attempts to interview the Prime Minister.* 新闻记者们争先恐后地要对首相进行采访。也可以把 one another 换成 each other, 而说 fall over each other。*The town officials fell over each other in their eagerness to show the President he was welcome.* 城镇的官员们争先恐后地向总统表示欢迎的热忱。常用 all 加强语气。*The children were very good today. They fell all over themselves in trying to be helpful.* 今天孩子们表现得非常好,他们争先恐后地要帮助我干活儿。◇ strive with one another to be first (in *doing something*)

one's **plans fall through** → PLANS

be riding for a fall [ˌraɪdnfərə ˈfɔːl] [话] **自讨苦吃** 直译为"为了从马上跌落 (fall) 而骑马"。最初的构思是:"骑马的方式过于胡来,简直是为了从马上掉下来而骑马"。一般是针对随意乱来的人而言,带有"等着瞧吧,一定会吃苦头的"的心情。为从现在的状态预测未来的结果的表达法。*That guy thinks he's a Don Juan, but he's riding for a fall if he keeps on dating a different girl every week. He'll soon find no one will date him at all.* 那个家伙认为自己是一个风流才子,但是,如果他继续不断地每周与一个不同的姑娘约会,他会自讨苦吃的。用不了多少时候,就没有任何一个姑娘跟他约会了。常用 only 或 really 加强语气。*This company is only riding for a fall if we continue to borrow money without securing any more long-term contracts.* 如果我们不能签订更多的长期合同而继续贷款的话,这个公司马上就会遇到严重的后果。*That guy is really riding for a fall. He seems to think he can lord it over us just because his father is a friend of the boss.* 那个家伙简直是在自讨苦吃。只不过由于他的父亲是老板的朋友,他就认为自己可以对咱们指手划脚了。也可以用于威胁的语句,例如: *Shut your mouth, buddy. You're riding for a fall, and I'm just the one who can give it to you.* 老弟,闭上你的嘴吧! 你是自讨没趣,我马上就能给你颜色看看。也有明知"自讨苦吃"而决心去干某种事情的场合。*I knew I was probably riding for a fall, but I had no choice but to demand that justice be done.* 我知道会自讨苦吃,但是我除了主持正义没有另

外的抉择。如以上的例句所示,这一表达法一般作为比喻使用,但也有按字面意义使用的情况。*George had better slow his horse a bit. He's riding for a fall.* 乔治应该把马放慢一些。他那样骑马会从马上摔下来的。◇ be on a course that will lead to unfortunate results

falls

the deal falls through → DEAL

false

act under false pretenses → PRETENSES

family

a family skeleton [ə ˌfæməli ˈskelətən] [口] **不可外扬的家丑** → a SKELETON in the closet

be in the family way → WAY

fancy

a fancy price → PRICE

take a fancy to *someone* [*something*] [ˌteɪkə ˈfæ(ː)n*t*sitə ~] [口] **爱上** → take a SHINE to *someone*

fanny

one's **fanny** [~ˈfæ(ː)ni] [话] **屁股** 轻松的说法。*She has a big fanny.* 她的屁股大。我们可以这样说,但主要与所有格一起使用。*He sat around on his fanny all day yesterday.* 昨天他坐了一整天。*I fell on my fanny.* 我摔个屁股蹲儿。顺便提一下,在英国英语中,fanny 是对"女性生殖器"的粗俗称呼,因此在使用时必须弄清上下文。◇ *one's* buttocks

fantastic

trip the light fantastic [ˌtrɪpðə ˌlaɪtˌfænˈtæ(ː)stɪk] [话] **跳舞** 这里的 trip 是"用轻快的步子边走边跳"的意思。the light fantastic 有"轻快幻想曲"的意味。1632 年,英国诗人米尔顿 (John Milton) 在他所写的《快活的人》("L'Allegro")中有这样的词句:"... trip it... on the light fantastic toe"(用轻快的、梦一般的脚步……来跳它……)。这就是本条习用语的来源。现在,只有在文学作品中使用米尔顿原诗的表达法。在会话中,本条习用语主要用于男女一起参加舞会的场合以及在舞会上男性约请女性起舞的场合。这是一个轻松的、有些诙谐的说法。*Shall we trip the light fantastic?* 我们跳一曲好吗? *My wife is always wanting to go out and trip the light fantastic.* 我老婆总是爱出去跳舞。◇ dance

far

Far be it from me to *do something*. [ˈfɑ(ː)rˌbiɪtfrəm(ː)ˈiːdə ~] [话] **丝毫没有……的打算** 逐字翻译为"我离做这种事情远得很"。意思是"不持这种观点"或"没有这种意图"。*Far be it from me to stop you from going.* 我根本没有阻止你前去的念头。*Far be it from me to disagree with you.* 我丝毫没有反对你的意见的打算。这是单独使用的例子。如下面的例句所示,常有用 but ~接续的情况。在这一例句中,前半句是将 I don't want to tell you ~的说法进一步加强,而 but 以下部分则是缓和语气的委婉陈述。从例句开头用大写 F 可以了解,这一表达法几乎完全用于句子的前端。另外,不定式 to ~多用与"说"字有关的动词。*Far be it from me to tell you what to do, but I feel you are being unwise.* 我丝毫没有告诉你怎样做的打算,不过,我觉得你很不明智。在这一场合,省略 but 以下部分也是可以讲得通的,然而,听的人难以确定"丝毫没有告诉你怎样做的打算"这话是否出于真心,言外是否还有 but 以下部分的含义。*Far be it from me to say that he can't go to American to study, but he mustn't expect me to furnish the money.* 我决不是说他不能去美国留学,不过他不应当指望我提供学费。*Far be it from me to interfere, but I certainly think you should try to make her change her mind.* 我决不想多管闲事,不过,我确实在想你应当努力使她回心转意。虽然这是一个委婉的表达法,但有时用于表示极大的讽刺。*Far be it from me to complain, but you are standing on my foot.* 我丝毫没有埋怨你的意图,不过,尊足站到敝脚上了。◇ I have (absolutely) no intention of *doing something*

be a far cry from *something* → CRY

far-sighted

far-sighted[1] ['fɑ(:)rˌsaɪdəd] [口] **远视的** 例如说 *a far-sighted person* 一个远视的人, *I'm far-sighted.* 我是远视眼。有时与 long-sighted ['lɔ(:)ŋˌsaɪdəd]同义使用。反义词为 NEAR-SIGHTED(近视的)。*I'm far-sighted, but two of my brothers are near-sighted.* 我是远视眼,但是我的两个兄弟是近视眼。顺便提一下:"老花眼"也是一种 far-sightedness,不过,在英语中,除医学名词 presbyopia [ˌprez'biopiə] 而外,没有相应的词汇。一般人对这个医学名词是听不懂的。如果硬要译成英语,可以讲 far-sightedness due to age。例如:我的父亲是老花眼。这句话可以译成 *My father is far-sighted due to age*. 另外,far-sighted 一词最近常去掉连字符,作 farsighted。→ far-sighted[2] ◇ able to see only distant objects clearly

far-sighted[2] ['fɑ(:)r'saɪdəd] [口] **有先见之明** 请参见前一条目 FAR-SIGHTED[1]。由"远视的"转义为"有先见之明",但第二音节的重音不一样,务请注意。例如,在写成文字的时候,"有远见的人"英语作 a far-sighted person; "他有先见之明"英语作 He is far-sighted. 但在说话的场合,由于重音强弱的差别,二者分别具有"有远见的人"和"他是远视眼"的意味。顺便说一下:前者也可以说 a person with foresight ['fo(:)rˌsaɪt], 后者则可以说 He has foresight. 另外,在表示"有先见之明"的意思时,有时也使用上一条目中提到的 long-sighted (但为两个重音 ['lɔ(:)ŋ'saɪdəd])。反义词为"鼠目寸光" short-sighted (→ SHORT-SIGHTED[2])。*What this country needs are more far-sighted leaders.* 这个国家需要更富有远见的领导人。不仅形容人,也可以形容 policy, plans, thinking 等。*The government was criticized for its lack of far-sighted policies.* 政府由于缺乏长治久安的政策而受到批评。与前一条目同样, far-sighted 也可以去掉连字符,作 farsighted。◇ (*someone*) able to discern (and plan for) future trends / (*something*) based on wide, long-term considerations

fast

play fast and loose with *something* [*someone*] [ˌpleɪ 'fæ(:)stən'lu:s wɪð ～] [口] **敷衍了事** fast and loose 是古时江湖艺人在 fair (定期集市)上玩弄的戏法之一。他把一条腰带卷起来,在正中间做个环,一看好象扣眼似的。然后,把腰带放到桌子上。他叫看热闹的人在那个环的中间钉个钉子,然后哧溜一下子把腰带拉开,向钉钉子的人讨钱。这是在扣眼的地方弄虚作假的戏法,它的妙处是:由观众看起来,无论怎样拉,在钉子的阻碍下,腰带是拉不掉的。这就是"看起来很牢 (fast),实际上很松 (loose)"的意思。因此,过去一直用这一表达法表示"使对方感到你非常可靠,而你却悄悄溜走并不守约"的意思。现在使用范围极广,可以表示"敷衍了事"、"不当作一回事"、"不予重视"等等的意味。常用于男女关系,表示"苟苟且且"、"玩弄感情"的意思。*She's not a woman you can play fast and loose with. With her it's all or nothing.* 她不是一个你玩玩就可以扔掉的女人。跟她交往,必须百分之百地认真。*I wouldn't get emotionally involved with him if I were you. He's famous for playing fast and loose with girls' affections.* 如果我是你的话,我跟他是不会动真心的。他好玩弄女孩子的感情,这已经是人人皆知的事情。以下,根据上下文,意思有细微的差别。*I'm tired of your playing fast and loose with my money.* 你任意挥霍我的钱,我已经感到厌烦啦。*He's not really an out-and-out liar, but he does tend to play fast and loose with the truth at times.* 他的确不是一个彻头彻尾的说谎大王,但是他有时竟然把真实当作可有可无的事情。*He was deported for trying to play fast and loose with China's foreign exchange laws.* 他由于违反中国的外汇管理法,企图暗中捣鬼,而被驱逐出境了。◇ treat *something* [*someone*] however *one* pleases

pull a fast one (on *someone*) [ˌpulə ˈfæ(ː)stwən] [话] **骗人** → PUT one over on *someone*

fat

chew the fat [ˌtʃuːðə ˈfæ(ː)t] [话] **闲聊** → chew the RAG

Fat chance! → CHANCE

the fat is in the fire [ðə ˈfæ(ː)tsɪnðə ˈfaɪr] [话] **欲罢不能** 把脂肪(fat)放到火上,一下子就燃烧起来,即使取出脂肪,火势也不会减弱。本条的表达法就是从这一构思而来。在做出决定或采取行动后已经欲罢不能的场合使用。多半带有危机感。*The Japanese people didn't really want to go to war with America, but once Japanese Navy had bombed Pearl Harbor the fat was in the fire.* 日本人民的确不希望跟美国打仗,但是日本海军一经轰炸珍珠港,事情就欲罢不能了。*There is still time to change our minds now. However, once the final decision is made to put our plan into action, the fat will be in the fire.* 现在还有时间改变我们的想法。不过,一旦最后决定把我们的计划变成行动,那就不能打退堂鼓啦。*Perhaps I shouldn't have told her the truth, but it's too late now. The fat's already in the fire.* 也许我不应该向她讲述真实的情况,不过,现在为时已晚啦。一言既出,驷马难追啊。◇ there is no turning back

fathead

a fathead [ə ˈfæt.he(ː)d] [话] **笨蛋** fat 是"脂肪"。本条的意思是"脑袋里充满脂肪的傻瓜"。与 a BLUBBERHEAD 虽然同义,但使用频率高得多。*If I never see that fathead again it'll be too soon.* 我永远不愿意再见到那样一个笨蛋了。有时作为形容词使用。在这一场合,如果作为定语,可以用原形 fathead, 也可以加 -ed 构成 fatheaded,但作为谓语时则必须使用后者。*How could you make a fathead(ed) mistake like that?* 你怎么会犯那样愚蠢的错误呢? *He's unbelievably fatheaded.* 他是一个令人难以相信的大笨蛋。→ a DUMBHEAD ◇ a stupid person

Fats

Fats [ˈfæ(ː)ts] [俗] **胖子** → FATSO

Fatso

Fatso [ˈfæ(ː)tsou] [俗] **大胖子** 胖人的绰号。以前有 Fats [ˈfæ(ː)ts] 的名称,为了调整语调,后边加了个 -o。Fats 一词现仍存在,但一般使用 Fatso。*His name is Bill, but everybody calls him Fatso.* 他叫比尔,但是人人管他叫胖墩儿。这是对一个人固定了的爱称。但主要是向胖人打招呼时使用,含有戏谑或轻蔑的成份。作为爱称,一般指男性;作为呼词,对女性亦可使用。青少年间使用的特别多。*What's the matter, Fatso? Why, you've eaten only five hamburgers.* 怎么回事呀,大胖子?你怎么才吃五个汉堡包啊? *Hey, Fatso! What's your name?* 喂,胖子!你叫什么名字啊?除了 Fatso 和 Fats 而外,同义词还有 Fatty [ˈfæ(ː)di], Pudgy [ˈpʌ(ː)dʒi], Tubby [ˈtʌ(ː)bi], Chubby [ˈtʃʌ(ː)bi]等。在这许多同义词中间,作为打招呼的用语,Fatso 是最尖酸刻薄的,很容易伤害对方的感情。大致说起来,按照以上排列的顺序,越往后就越柔和,因此,作为固定的爱称使用频率最高的是倒数第一个的 Chubby。从后边往前,作为爱称的使用率一个比一个低。另外,除 Fatso 和 Fats 而外,均可将第一个字母小写,作形容词使用。

fatty

Fatty [ˈfæ(ː)di] [俗] **胖子** → FATSO

fault

to a fault [tuə ˈfɔːlt] [口] **过分地** 字面意义是"达到成为缺点的程度"。这一表达法经常接在形容词表语的后边。*Phil is kind to a fault. He spends half the day helping other people.* 菲尔过分好心,他每天要用一半的时间去帮助别人。*My wife is neat to a fault. If I drop a single ash on the rug, she comes running with the vacuum cleaner.* 我的妻子是一个过分爱干净的人。只要我把一点点烟灰落到地毯上,她就拿着吸尘器急忙跑来

了。*Sue is conscientious to a fault. She does her work extremely well, but it takes her twice as long as anyone else.* 苏这个人过于认真。她干的工作极为出色,但是要比别人多用一倍的时间。◇ to excess / excessively ~

favorite

favorite ['feɪvərət] [口] **最喜欢的** favorite 常常有人译为"特别喜爱的"、"特别受喜爱的"等。有时这样翻译也过得去。但是,此词的正确意义是"最喜欢的"。因此,从意义上讲,这已经是最高级,more favorite 或 most favorite 的说法欠妥。请读者通过以下的例句体会英美人对 favorite 一词所怀有的概念。*My favorite kind of pie is cherry.* 我最喜欢的馅饼是樱桃馅饼。这句话等于说:I like cherry pie best of all pies. (在所有各种馅饼中,我最喜欢樱桃馅饼。) *Chow-chow is his favorite Chinese food.* 什锦蜜饯是他最喜爱的中国食品。*Miss Thelma is my favorite teacher.* 西尔玛小姐是我最喜欢的老师。另外有一个表达形式是"one of *one's* favorite + 名词(复数)",意思是"有好多最喜欢的东西,而这是其中之一"。*Poe is one of her favorite authors.* 爱伦·坡是她最喜欢的作家之一。这句话等于说:Poe is one of her best-liked authors. (她最喜欢的作家有很多,爱伦·坡是其中的一位。) *One of my favorite books is Gone With the Wind.*《飘》是我最喜爱的读物之一。*Politics is one of his favorite topics.* 政治是他最喜欢的话题之一。作为名词,favorite 的意思是"最喜欢的东西[人]"。*Of all foreign cities, Paris is our favorite.* 在所有的外国城市中,我们最喜爱的是巴黎。也有复数形式。*I really can't say what author I like best. I have many favorites.* 我实在说不上来我最喜欢的是哪一位作家。我最喜欢的作家有很多位。*This dish is one of my favorites.* 这道菜是我最喜欢吃的菜之一。*Sinatra songs have been great favorites in America for many years.* 许多年间,西纳特拉的歌在美国最受人欢迎。*Bill is a great favorite with the ladies.* 比尔是最受女人们欢迎的一个男子。在上级与部下、老师与学生的关系间使用时,特别具有"最倚重的心腹"、"最得意的门生"的意味。*Ron is the boss's favorite.* 罗恩是老板最大的红人。*He was a favorite of the king.* 他是国王最信赖的宠臣之一。如果用于赛马,则指"由于可能获胜而最受欢迎的马",即所谓的"热门马"。*Slowpoke is the favorite horse in the first race.* 斯洛波克是第一轮比赛最有希望获胜的马。应用到运动员身上,也具有同样的意味。*In this golf tournament, Alex is the favorite.* 在这场高尔夫球锦标赛中,亚历克斯最有希望获胜。◇ most preferred

play the favorite [ˌpleɪðə 'feɪvərət] [话] **把赌注押到热门马身上** → play the FIELD

favorites

play favorites (with *someone*) [ˌpleɪ 'feɪvərəts] [口] **有偏心眼儿** 许多词典都没有收录这一表达法,但是这是一个在会话中经常使用的固定词组。这里的 favorite 等于 pet,亦即"最得意的门生"、"最宠信的部下"的意思。这一表达法常用复数形式。*Nobody likes that teacher. She is always playing favorites.* 谁也不喜欢那位老师。她总是偏心眼儿。*You must learn not to show your likes and dislikes for people. A good leader cannot afford to play favorites.* 你必须学会不显露对人的好恶。一个良好的领导者不能偏袒张三、打击李四。下面举一个后接 with *someone* 的句型的例子:*Parents should never play favorites with their children.* 父母绝对不要偏疼子女。另外,favorite 还有"最有希望获胜的马"的意思,如果在 play 与 favorite 之间加个 the 而构成 play the favorite,便是"把赌注押到热门马身上"(→ play the FIELD)。*I've decided to play the favorite.* 我决心把赌注押到热门马身上了。◇ treat *someone* [a child (etc.)] with more favor than others [another]

faze

not faze *someone* [nɑt 'feɪz ~] [话] **丝毫**

也不惊恐 这里的 faze 为动词，源出方言 feeze(赶走)，意思是"使惊慌"、"使胆怯"。在会话中经常使用本条的习用语，但除戏谑的场合外绝对不用于肯定句。*The bullets whizzing past him didn't seem to faze the policeman at all. He just kept running toward the man with the gun.* 子弹从耳边嗖嗖飞过，那个警察却好象丝毫也不惊恐。他照直向持枪的人奔去。*His accusation didn't faze me. I knew he was only groping in the dark.* 我对他的指控丝毫也不感到惊恐。我知道他完全是在捏造。*None of my threats fazed him.* 不管我怎么吓唬他，他一点儿也不害怕。◇ not bother *someone*

feast

feast on *something* ['fi:stɔn ～] [口] **享口福** → feast *one's* EYES on *something*

feather

You could have knocked me over with a feather. [jə.kudəv 'nɑktmi.ouvər wɪðə 'fe(:)ðər] [话] **大吃一惊** knock *someone* over 是"(把某人)击倒"。本条直译为"用一根羽毛就能把我击倒"，意思是"由于过分吃惊，碰到一根羽毛都会栽个大跟头"。是对极度惊恐的夸张表达法，相当于汉语"把人吓晕过去了"。*I had thought that Lynn barely knew who I was, so when he told me he loved me, you could have knocked me over with a feather.* 我原来以为林恩对我一无所知，所以当他说他很爱我的时候，我实在大吃一惊啊。*When I heard that I had been selected to represent China in the All-Asia English Speech Contest, you could have knocked me over with a feather.* 当我得知自己被选拔为出席亚洲英语讲演比赛大会的中国代表时，实在大吃一惊。有时 knocked me over 作 knocked me down。*A: How did you feel when the Prime Minister called to ask your opinion? B: You could have knocked me down with a feather.* 甲：当首相打电话来征求您的意见的时候，您是什么心情啊？乙：我简直大吃一惊啊。◇ I was completely dumbfounded.

fed

be fed up (with *something*) [.fed'ʌ(:)p] [口] **腻味透了** 字面意义是"吃的东西一直堵到嗓子眼"，即指"已经太多了"、"厌烦极了"、"腻味透了"。*I'm fed up with your constant complaining.* 我对你经常不断地发牢骚实在腻味透啦。如此例所示，with 以下是所厌烦的事情的具体内容。这一表达法使用范围极广，可以用于各种各样的事情。下面举几个例子：*I'm fed up with this weather. We haven't seen the sun for over a week now.* 这个天气真腻味死人，我们现在已经一个多星期没见过太阳啦。*I'm fed up with my wife's cooking.* 老婆做的菜，我实在吃腻了。*Let's go. I'm fed up with waiting for that guy.* 咱们走吧！我等那小子实在等腻啦。在加强语气时，常增添 completely。*I had thought that living in the country would be pleasant, but after three months I was completely fed up.* 我原来以为在农村生活一定是很愉快的，但是过了三个月，我已经完全感到厌倦了。◇ have had (just about) enough (of *something*) / be utterly bored

federal

make a federal case out of it → CASE

feed

chicken feed ['tʃɪkən .fi:d] [话] **很少量的钱** 直译为"鸡食"。最初的构思是："只有象鸡的饲料那么一丁点儿价值的钱"。*The money we got today is chicken feed. After we knock over that bank next week, we'll be in the clover.* 今天我们弄来的钱还不够打壶酒哪。等我们下个星期抢劫那家银行，就可以花天酒地一番啦。往往用 only 加强语气。例如：*My salary is only chicken feed.* 我的工资只够给鸡买一把米。与 PEANUTS 为同义语。◇ a very small amount (of money)

feedbag

put on the feedbag [.pudənðə 'fi:d.bæ:g] [话] **吃饭** put on 是"穿上(衣服)"、"戴上(眼镜)"的意思。feedbag 是"挂在马脖子上的饲料袋"。本条习用语直译为"给

马挂上饲料袋”。这是把人比做马的轻松的表达法。*I'm getting hungry. Let's stop in at that restaurant and put on the feedbag.* 我饿啦，咱们到那家饭馆吃点饭吧。◇ eat (a meal)

feel

feel *someone* **out** [.fi(:)l ～ 'aut] [口] **试探** 这里的 feel 是“探索”、“摸索”。本条的表达法直译为“摸索出”，亦即“试探对方的意见、想法、心情等”的意思。这是面对面地直接探听，不是“向周围的人们询问”。*I'll feel Sid out to see if he'd be interested in joining us in this venture.* 我要向锡德试探一下，看他有没有跟咱们一起搞这项事业的兴趣。*The final decision hinges on the chief's opinion. I'm going to have dinner with him tomorrow night. I'll feel him out then.* 最后的决定完全取决于头头的意见。明天晚上我和他在一起吃饭的时候，向他探听一下。*We'd better feel out all the neighbors before we act.* 我们开始搞之前，最好先打听一下所有邻居的意见。另外有一个表达法是 feel *something* out, *something* 处大多是用 situation (情况), feelings 或 sentiments (感情) 等词代入。*I don't know whether we should set up manufacturing facilities in America or not. I'll try to feel the situation out when I'm in New York next week.* 我不知道咱们是否应该在美国建立工厂。等下个星期我去纽约的时候摸一下情况。*I'm going to feel out the sentiments of the other members about changing the club rules.* 关于改变俱乐部的章程一事，我打算先征求一下其他成员的意见。类似的习用语有 SOUND*someone* out, 但它没有“向对方婉转地说”的意思。因此，在一般的语句中，feel you out 的说法就很不自然，而经常讲 sound you out。*I wanted to sound you out on this first.* 关于这件事，我曾想首先听听你的意见。◇ (indirectly) probe *someone's* feelings

feeler

put out a feeler [.pu.daudə 'fi:lər] [口] **试探** feeler 是昆虫类的“触角”，即动物学名词 antenna 的通俗说法。但不能说 put out an antenna。这一表达法直译为“伸出触角”，含意很容易体会。*I don't know if they will consider our company for the project or not, but it won't hurt to put out a feeler.* 我不知道他们是否考虑叫我们公司承包那项工程，但是试探一下没有什么坏处。*When Shig had dinner with the boss, he put out a feeler to test the boss's reaction to his idea.* 西格在与老板共进晚餐的时候，他试探老板对他的计划的反应。如以上的例句所示，这一表达法是在探听对方的意见或反应的场合使用。可以用复数形式 feelers, 也可以在 feeler 之前添加形容词。*The presidential hopeful put out feelers to see if his candidacy would be accepted by the party.* 那位可望当选总统的人多方面进行试探，看看本党是否会批准由他做候选人。*Tired of fighting a senseless war, both countries began to put out peace feelers.* 两国对于打一场毫无意义的战争都厌倦了，都开始试探媾和。◇ make a roundabout inquiry

feet

cut the ground from under *someone's* **feet**
→ GROUND

be dead on *one's* **feet** [.de(:)dən ～'fi:t] [口] **精疲力尽** 直译为“站着 (on *one's* feet) 死掉”，表示“极度疲劳”的样子。*After walking ten kilometers over the mountain, I was dead on my feet.* 走了二十里山路，我已经精疲力尽。*I had sat up studying for two nights in a row. By the time of the exam, I was dead on my feet.* 我一连两个整夜温习功课，没有睡一点觉，到考试的时候已经精疲力尽了。常用 literally 加强语气。*My wife has been working very late recently at the office. When she gets home at night, she is literally dead on her feet.* 我的妻子最近在公司加班，每天都干到很晚。当她夜里到家时，简直累得象一摊稀泥了。be dead tired 也是强调“疲倦”的表达法，在以上的全部例句中都可以用它替换。但比较起来，be dead on *one's* feet

的语气还是强一些。◇ be exhausted

fall on *one's* **feet** [ˌfɔːlɔn ~ ˈfiːt] [口] **安然摆脱困境** → land on *one's* FEET

feet of clay [ˌfi(ː)dəv ˈkleɪ] [口] **致命的弱点** 这一表达法源出《圣经·旧约》中《但以理书》(Daniel) 第 2 章关于巴比伦国王尼布甲尼撒做梦的故事。国王梦见一个巨大的形象:头是金,胸和臂是银,躯干是黄铜,腿是铁,而下边是两只泥足。希伯来先知但以理解释这个梦说:巨人的样子十分雄伟,但脚是用松软的泥土制成的,所以很容易摔倒。也就是说,他预言这个梦是暗示国王的灭亡。由于有这样的典故,have feet of clay 便意味着"无论多么有权有势的伟大人物也存在着致命的弱点"了。一般用于表示大人物的弱点。*Great men are often found to have feet of clay.* 伟大的人物往往有致命的弱点。*Most small boys see their fathers as perfect. Only later do they learn that even fathers are ordinary men with feet of clay.* 绝大多数小男孩都认为他们的父亲是完美无缺的。直到后来,他们才了解父亲也是具有弱点的普通人。◇ human weaknesses

get back on *one's* **feet** [get ˌbækɔn ~ ˈfiːt] [口] **复原** → put *someone* back on *his* FEET

get cold feet [ˌget ˌkould ˈfiːt] [话] **胆怯** 字面意义是"脚冷",可以按照这一意义使用。但一般用于"原来计划干什么事情,一旦要开始的时候,却又害怕起来,失去信心,不想去干了"的场合。*I had agreed to give a speech, but as the time approached, I began to get cold feet.* 我已经答应进行一次演说,但是随着时间迫近,我开始胆怯了。*John wanted to ask Mary to marry him, but he got cold feet and couldn't go through with it.* 约翰本想向玛丽求婚,但是他胆怯了,始终未能出口。*Sue likes mountain climbing, but when she thought about climbing Mount Everest she got cold feet.* 苏喜好登山,但是她一想到攀登珠穆朗玛峰,心里就怯生生的了。在表示"正在发怵"、"勇气正在消失"的状态的场合,讲 have cold feet。*Don't tell me you have cold feet.* 你不可能是胆怯吧。顺便提一下:字面意义的"脚冷",在英语中一般说 *one's* feet get cold。◇ lose *one's* nerve

have the world at *one's* **feet** → WORLD

land on both feet [ˌlæ(ː)ndɔn ˌbouθ ˈfiːt] [口] **安然脱离困境** → land on *one's* FEET

land on *one's* **feet** [ˌlæ(ː)ndɔn ~ ˈfiːt] [口] **安然摆脱困境** 原意是:"象猫一样,掉在地上也会脚先着地"。*The child wasn't hurt in his fall from the window because, fortunately, he landed on his feet.* 孩子从窗户上掉下去了,幸好他两脚先落地,没有受伤。这是按本来的意味使用的例子。转用于表示"虽然陷入困境,但是顺利脱险"的意味,使用范围极广。*For some reason Rollo has led a charmed life. Despite his many misfortunes, he has always managed to land on his feet.* 不知为什么,罗洛的生命似乎有魔法在保护着。他多次逢凶化吉,安然无恙。*We were very lucky. A wonderful new job offer right after my husband's company went bankrupt allowed us to land on our feet.* 我们是非常幸运的。我丈夫的公司破产以后,马上有人请他去干一个极好的新工作,这样就使我们安然脱离了困境。另外,动词一般使用 land,有时也说 fall on *one's* feet。*Don't worry about what's in the past. It's all over now and we fell on our feet, didn't we?* 不要总惦记着过去的事情。现在,一切都风流云散啦,我们不是已经安然摆脱困境了吗?是吧?有时用 on both feet 代替 on *one's* feet。*We've got to be more careful about how we invest our money in the future. We can't expect to land on both feet like this every time.* 今后我们投资需要更加谨慎。我们不能指望每一次都象这次一样逢凶化吉啊。◇ escape undue hardship [harm, etc.]

not let the grass grow under *one's* **feet** → GRASS

pull the rug out from under *someone's* **feet** [ˌpulðə ˈrʌ(ː) ˌgautfrəˌmʌndər ~ ˈfiːt] [口] **拆台** → pull the RUG out from under *someone*

put *someone* **back on** *his* **feet** [ˌput ～ ˌbækɔn ～ ˈfiːt] [口] **使恢复原状** 直译"把人象原来那样放在他的脚上",意为"使栽倒的人重新站起来"。*The father picked up his little boy and set him back on his feet.* 那个父亲把他的小男孩抱起来,让小男孩恢复站立的姿势。这是按着字面意义使用的例子。这一表达法广泛用作比喻。另外,如上面的例句所示,在按照字面意义使用的场合,动词是用 set,讲 set *someone* back on *his* feet,而很少使用 put。但在作为比喻使用的场合,则多半要用 put。*Leslie had been an out- and- out alcoholic, but Alcoholics Anonymous put him back on his feet.* 莱斯利过去是一个嗜酒如命的家伙,但是参加戒酒会以后,他重新做人了。有时不用 back,而在 on *someone's* feet 后边加个 again,意思完全相同。例如:*Mr. Smiley has put many ex- cons on their feet again by giving them jobs when they got out of prison.* 斯迈利先生对许多刑满释放的人给予工作,使他们自力更生,重新做人。back 和 again 也有同时并用的情况。 *A timely bank loan helped put the company back on its feet again.* 由于有一项银行贷款救急,这家公司又转危为安了。在这一例句中,put 的宾语不是 *someone* 而是 *something*,这是拟人化的一种。也可以用于表示"使人恢复健康状态",例如: *That new medicine the doctor gave me put me back on my feet in a hurry.* 医生新给我的药使我迅速恢复了健康。如前所述,动词有时用 set。*Government aid set many people back on their feet following the depression.* 在萧条之后,由于政府的援助,许多人都恢复了原来的状况。"使恢复原状"的主体及其对象(即主语与宾语)具有同一利害关系的场合,动词常使用 get。*We worked hard to get the company back on its feet again.* 我们努力奋斗,使公司站稳了脚跟。在这一例句中,we 究竟是这一公司的工作人员还是向这一公司发放贷款的银行,这一点是不明确的,但是不论是什么人,总是与 the company 具有共同的利害关系。以上所用的动词全是及物动词,但是也有作为不及物动词的用法,即 get back on *one's* feet (again), 意思是"恢复原状"。*We struggled many years to get back on our feet after our house burned down.* 自从我家的房子惨遭回禄之后,我们为了重建旧居奋斗了许多年。◇ allow *someone* to recover (financially [socially, physically, etc.])

stand on *one's* **own feet** [ˈstæ(ː)ndɔn ～ ˌounˈfiːt] [口] **自立** 字面意义是"站在自己的脚上"。*It was six months after my accident before I was able to stand on my own feet again.* 我发生意外事故之后,过了半年才能靠自己的力量站了起来。如此例所示,即便使用本来的意义,事情也可以说得通。不过,在这一场合,说 stand without help 比较自然。可以认为,本条条头是专门作为比喻使用的表达法。 *I don't care if he is my son, I can't support him forever. He's got to learn to stand on his own feet.* 不能因为他是我的儿子,我就得养活他一辈子,他也必须学会自立才行。*At first the subsidiary received unreserved aid from the parent company, but by the end of the second year it was standing on its own feet.* 最初,下属公司要得到总公司的全面援助,但到第二年终了时,它能够自力更生了。*Some of the newly independent countries of the world have had difficulty standing on their own feet.* 世界上有一些新独立的国家自力更生是很困难的。为了加强语气,有时加 two 作 *one's* own two feet。*I don't want your help. I'm perfectly capable of standing on my own two feet.* 我不需要你的帮助,我完全能够自立啦。◇ make *one's* own way (independently)

sweep *someone* **off** *his* **feet** [ˌswi(ː)p ～ ɔ(ː)f ～ ˈfiːt] [口] **给与深刻的印象** 字面意义是"刷足"。可以这样说: *The huge wave swept me off my feet.* 巨浪冲刷着我的脚。作为比喻,意思是:"巨浪冲过脚面,以凶猛的力量压倒一切"。用于"一个人的言语、行动、品德给与他人极强烈的印象"的场合。*Their tremendous welcome swept me off my feet.* 他们的热

烈欢迎给与我极深刻的印象。*Mr. Arnold's personality is so strong that he sweeps people off their feet when they first meet him.* 阿诺德先生的个性极强，人们第一次见到他就会留下极深刻的印象。在男性对女性有意识地给与强烈印象的场合，使用这一表达法特别多。*Ralph swept Mary off her feet by giving her presents and taking her out to expensive restaurants every night.* 拉尔夫又是送礼，又是每天请玛丽到高级餐厅吃晚饭，弄得玛丽倾心不已。◇ make a tremendous impression on *someone*

take a load off *one's* **feet** → LOAD

fell

at one fell swoop → SWOOP

feller

a feller [ə 'felər] [话] **男人** 原为 a fellow 的方言，但城市人常作为戏谑语使用。*Them city fellers ain't got no manners. [Those city fellows don't have any manners.]* 那些城里长大的家伙什么礼节也不懂。*You fellers want to see my sheepskin?* 你们这些小子想看我的毕业证书吗？也可以戏谑地用以指“情郎”。下面的例句究竟是方言还是欢谑的表达法，只能根据上下文来决定。不过，在这样的场合，多用所有格，而且不能以 fellow 替换。*Have you met Jane's new feller?* 你见过简新交的男朋友(情郎)吗？◇ a fellow / a [*one's*] boy friend

feminist

a feminist [ə 'femənəst] [口] **男女平等主义者** 又译“女权运动者”。既包括争取女权的妇女本身，也包括参加这一运动的男性。*Mary is a dyed-in-the-wool feminist. Given half a chance, she'll talk your ear off about women's rights.* 玛丽是一个彻头彻尾的男女平等主义者。只要有一丁点儿机会，她就会向你滔滔不绝地讲述妇女的权利。*The feminist movement in America is spreading year by year.* 在美国，女权运动的声势一年比一年扩大。◇ a women's rights advocate

fence

The grass is always greener on the other side of the fence. → GRASS

sit on the fence [ˌsɪdə(ː)nðə 'fe(ː)nts] [口] **保持中立** 直译为“坐在篱笆上”，汉语叫“骑在墙头上”。有人译作“采取机会主义态度”、“观看形势”等等，根据上下文似乎很通顺，但本条习用语本身并没有这样的意味，它所指的只是不表示赞成与否而保持中立的态度。一般用于在面临重大问题、纠纷、严峻事态时决定不了向右、向左还是一直保持中立为好的场合。*Our country can't afford to sit on the fence on such an important international question.* 我国对于这样一个重大的国际问题，不能采取不左不右的态度。*We'd better sit on the fence and watch the situation for a while.* 我们最好是先不表示态度，暂时观望形势的发展。另外有 be on the fence, remain on the fence, straddle (骑) the fence 等说法。*It's difficult to remain on the fence when you are under pressure from both sides.* 当两边都向你施加压力的时候，是很难保持中立的。*We'd better straddle the fence on this question.* 对于这个问题，最好是不置可否。如果改变为名词，则为 a fence-sitter。一般来说，sit on the fence 是一时的状态，而 fence-sitter 则完全相反，主要指有这种习惯的人，因而大多伴有“狡猾”、“意志薄弱”等不良的意味。根据上下文关系和会话的内容，具“机会主义者”或“见风使舵者”的意义。*That country is a traditional fence-sitter.* 那个国家一向采取机会主义的态度。◇ maintain a neutral attitude

straddle the fence [ˌstræ(ː)dlðə 'fe(ː)nts] [口] **骑墙态度** → sit on the FENCE

fence-sitter

a fence-sitter [ə 'fentˌsɪːdər] [口] **机会主义者** → sit on the FENCE

fiddle

a bass fiddle [ə 'beɪs 'fɪdl] [话] **低音提琴** → a bull FIDDLE

a bull fiddle [ə 'bul 'fɪdl] [口] **低音提琴**

这一表达法是借用体大而声音低沉的 bullfrog (牛蛙) 一词前半部分的 bull (公牛), 后加小提琴的别名 FIDDLE (→)而构成。虽然是轻松的说法, 但为此种乐器的通称。fiddle 一词有时带轻蔑的含义, 而 bull fiddle 并不如此。*Can you play a bull fiddle?* 你能拉低音提琴吗? 正式名称应为 double bass ['dʌbl 'beɪs], contrabass ['kɑntrə.beɪs] 或者 bass viol ['beɪs 'vaɪl], 但这些名称主要是在古典音乐中使用。在爵士乐中, 一般称 bass fiddle ['beɪs 'fɪdl], string bass ['strɪŋ 'beɪs] 或者简称 bass。*Tony plays bass (fiddle) in a jazz band.* 托尼在一个爵士乐队中拉低音提琴。◇ a double bass

a fiddle [ə 'fɪdl] [口] **小提琴** violin 的俗称。管弦乐团演奏古典音乐时使用的一般称为 violin。在乡村与西部音乐中使用的通常叫做 fiddle。*My uncle loves to play the fiddle at square dances.* 我的伯父喜欢为四人对舞拉小提琴。有时对古典音乐用的 violin 随意称为 fiddle, 但根据上下文, 可能含有轻蔑的意味, 这一点务请读者注意。例如, 如果对一个爱用 violin 拉古典音乐的人当面称他为 a fiddle player, 他不会给你好颜色看的。另外, a fiddle player 也可以用 a fiddler [ə 'fɪdlər]代替。*A: Craig is a good fiddle player. B: Is he a fiddler in a hillbilly band?* 甲: 克雷格是一个很不错的小提琴手。乙: 他是在牛仔乐团里拉小提琴的吗? ◇ a violin

(as) fit as a fiddle [əz 'fɪdəzə 'fɪdl] [话] **十分健康** fiddle 是一种轻松的说法, 与 violin 同义。有人说: 在古时候, 人们普遍认为 fiddle 是最美好的、无可非议的乐器, 因此产生了"身体象 fiddle 一样 fit (健康)"的表达法。但这不是定论。另外, 有的词典作为同义语收录有 (as) fit as a flea, 但这是英国英语, 在美国是不用的。*What do you mean I'm too sick to work? I'm as fit as a fiddle.* 你说我病情很重不能工作, 这是什么意思? 我健壮如牛啊。*The doctor pronounced my husband fit as a fiddle.* 医生断言我丈夫十分健康。→ a FIDDLE ◇ very healthy

play second fiddle to *someone* [*something*] [.pleɪ .sekənd'fɪdltə ~] [话] **当二把手** fiddle 就是 violin (小提琴)。本条直译为"演奏第二提琴"。在管弦乐团中, 第二提琴在 first violin 的次位, 负责伴奏。因此就产生了本条的表达法。意思是"充当二把手"、"当副手"。大多在谈到工作时使用。*I don't mind playing second fiddle to a talented person like Lynn.* 给林恩那样一位有才能的人当二把手, 我没有什么意见。*I'm going to quit. The new president obviously doesn't know how to run a company, and I refuse to play second fiddle to a guy like that for the rest of my life.* 我要辞职不干啦。新来的总经理显然不懂得怎么经营一个公司, 我下半辈子决不给这样一个人当二把手。*I'm sick and tired of playing second fiddle to that guy.* 我给那个家伙当二把手, 实在头疼死啦。有时用于表示"被放到次要地位"、"成为牺牲品"的意味。*In a country like that, the consumer always plays second fiddle to the needs of the army.* 在那样一个国家里, 总是军需第一, 消费者被放到次要地位。*Ann didn't realize when she married that she would have to play second fiddle to her husband's job.* 安在结婚的时候没有认识到她的丈夫把工作放在第一位, 而把她放到次要地位。◇ take a secondary position to *someone* [*something*]

field

play the field [.pleɪðə 'fi:ld] [话] **广泛活动** 原为赛马用语。the field 意为"一次赛马中出场的全部马匹", play 意为"赌"。合起来为 play the field, 它与 play the favorite (对热门马下赌注)相对, 是"对热门马以外的所有马下赌注"的意思。*I'll play the favorite and you play the field. That way one of us is sure to win.* 我买热门马票, 你买其他马的票, 这样一来, 你我必有一个会赢钱的。作为比喻使用时, 并不是"热心干一件事", 而是"对各种各样的事情都要去试试看"的意思。从"工作关系"一直到"男女交往", 这一表达法使用范围极广。*Because of* *the wide fluctuations in wholesale prices, I don't think we should make an exclusive contract with any one maker. For the time being, it would be wiser to play the field.* 由于批发价格变动太大，我认为我们不能与任何一个厂家签订专销合同。在目前这个时候，广泛销售多家厂商的产品是比较明智的。*Ed is a consultant whose services are so sought after that he can afford to play the field.* 埃德是一位大红大紫的顾问，所以他能广泛联络，四处活动。在男女关系上特别频繁使用。*You'll never get Juan to go steady with you. He likes to play the field.* 你跟胡安永远也确定不了关系，他喜欢到处勾搭女人。◇ maintain open access to all possibilities / operate over a wide range / date many different girls

fierce

something fierce [ˌsʌ-m ˈfɪ(:)rs] [话] **猛烈的(地)** 非常轻松的说法。fierce 的意思是"猛烈的"、"激烈的"。本条直译为"有点什么猛烈的东西"。可作为形容词和副词使用。先举作为形容词使用的例子。*Don't ever go into the publishing business. The competition is something fierce.* 千万不要去搞出版业，因为竞争是很激烈的。*I made the mistake of crossing swords with Mrs. Razortongue. Whew! That woman has a temper something fierce.* 我犯个错误，跟雷佐汤谷太太发生了口角。哎呀，那个婆娘的脾气可真够火暴的。作为副词，是"猛烈地"、"声势浩大地"的意思。*The boss is a real Simon Legree. He works us something fierce.* 老板简直是一个冷酷无情的野兽。他非常凶狠地驱使我们。*My arm hurts something fierce.* 我的胳膊疼得厉害。*It's raining something fierce.* 在下暴雨。*The cats in our neighborhood yowl something fierce every night.* 我家附近的几只猫每天夜里嚎叫得很凶。另外，还用于表示"最佳"的意思。例如：*Nat's not only a good batter, he can pitch something fierce.* 纳特不仅是一个优秀的击球员，在投球方面也是最佳的。◇ terrific(ally) / terrible / terribly / extremely great [hard, sore, well, etc.]

fifty-eleven

fifty- eleven [ˈfɪftiəˈlevən] [话] **许许多多(的)** → FORTY-ELEVEN

fight

throw a fight [ˌθrouə ˈfaɪt] [口] **在拳击的假比赛中败北** → THROW a race [game, etc.]

figure

have a good figure [ˌhævə ˌgud ˈfɪgjər] [口] **丰姿绰约** → be well STACKED

file

the circular file [ðə ˈsə(:)rkjələr ˈfaɪl] [话] **办公室的废纸篓** file 是"文件箱"。公司或其他的单位所用的废纸篓为圆形，故有这一表达法。称废纸篓为 file，而且形容词不用 round，偏用一个具有专业术语性质的 circular，因而使人感到十分轻松，这一点很有趣。这一表达法只用于办公室，一般来说，在家庭中是不使用的。美国那些在家里当主妇的太太们大概听不懂这个习用语。*Put these papers in the circular file, will you please?* 请把这些文件扔到废纸篓里好吗？*I consign all that guy's letters to the circular file.* 我把那个家伙的全部信件都送到废纸篓里去。有时用 *one's* 代替定冠词 the。*My circular file is just about full. May I use yours?* 我的废纸篓就快满了。可以用你的吗？◇ the wastebasket

the rank and file → RANK

fill

fill in for *someone* [fɪˈlɪnfər ～] [话] **临时代替工作** → fill *someone's* SHOES

filling

a filling station → STATION

filthy

filthy rich → RICH

final

a final [ə ˈfaɪnl] [话] **期末考试** a final examination 的简称。学生(中学生以上)

用语。又称 a final exam。*I have a math final [a final in math] tomorrow.* 明天我有数学的期末考试。*Spring finals start next week.* 春季的期末考试下个星期开始。→ a MIDTERM ◇ a final examination

finger

have a finger in the pie [ˌhævə ˈfɪŋgərɪnðə ˈpaɪ] [口] **参与计划、事业、活动** 请读者在头脑里想象一下"把手指头插入馅饼"的状态。"馅饼"是比喻"计划"、"事业"以及"日常生活"等。论姿态,决不是"勉勉强强",因为"馅饼"是好吃的东西,所以在这里含有"积极参加"、"染指"的意思。*Leave me alone! Can't I do anything without your having your finger in the pie?* 别缠着我啦! 我做什么事情,你不插手行不行? *This project sounds like one of Roy's ideas. At least I'm sure he must have a finger in the pie.* 这个计划很象是罗伊的主意。我敢肯定,至少他是起草人之一。*Let me know if you need some capital to start your new company. I'd like to have a finger in the pie, too.* 你开办新公司如果需要资金的话,请对我讲,我也愿意参加这项事业。a finger 可以改换成 *one's* [its] finger(s); the pie 可以改换成 this [that, every, *someone's*] pie。*That company has its fingers in every pie in this region.* 在这个地区里,那个公司要染指每一件有利可图的事情。如果把 have 改为 put, stick, get 等,那就不是指"正在参与"的状态,而是表示"进行参与"的动作了。*He'll be sorry if he tries to stick his finger in our pie.* 如果他硬要参与我们所干的事情,他一定要后悔的。have 也可以改换成 keep,表示"始终参与"的继续状态。*Mrs. Smith got sick because she tried to keep her fingers in too many pies at once.* 史密斯夫人病倒了,因为她同时参加过多的活动。既然有 keep a finger in the pie 的形式,当然也会有 keep ~ out of ~的形式存在。这是"不去参与"的意思。*You keep your fingers out of that pie.* 那件事你不要插手。另外,finger 前可加形容词 greedy 或 fat 作定语,强调"贪得无厌";pie 的前面加上 political (政治的), financial (金融的), private (民间的), rich (富裕的) 以及其他的形容词作定语,则可表示出 pie 的特性。*For some reason, the President thinks it has to have its greedy fingers in every private pie.* 不知为什么,总统认为他对所有的民间事业都非过问不可。*I've never known a man with so many fingers in so many questionable pies.* 我从来没有见过象他那样一个什么斜门歪道都往里钻的人。◇ be involved

fingers

burn *one's* **fingers** [ˌbə(ː)rn~ ˈfɪŋgərz] [口] **吃苦头** 字面意义是"烧伤手指"。原来是一个表示"火中取栗的危险性"的表达法。*I burned my fingers on the stove.* 我在火炉上把手指烫伤了。如此例所示,可以按照字面意义使用。但作为比喻,使用的范围极广。*I burned my fingers trying to help that guy once before. Once is enough.* 从前我为了帮助那个家伙吃过一次苦头。我再也不想干了。*You shouldn't invest your money in gold unless you know something about the market. You may end up burning your fingers.* 除非对于市场有一定的知识,你不能投资去搞黄金生意。要不然你会吃大亏的。*Mrs. Snoopy has burned her fingers so often by sticking her nose into other people's business that you'd think she'd have learned her lesson by now.* 斯努皮太太常常由于爱管他人的闲事而吃苦头,现在她可能已经接受教训啦。除 burn *one's* fingers 外,还有一个句型是 get *one's* fingers burned,意义与用法相同,也经常为人们使用。*Leo has big- gang connections. If you cooperate with him you man get your fingers burned.* 利奥跟一些大的暴力集团有关系。如果你跟他合作,你很可能要吃亏的啊。◇ get hurt [in trouble] / sustain a loss

cross *one's* **fingers** [ˌkrɔ(ː)s ~ˈfɪŋgərz] [话] **把食指与中指交叉祈求减轻说谎的罪过** → keep *one's* FINGERS crossed

have sticky fingers [.hæv .stɪki 'fɪŋgərz] [话] **手不老实** sticky fingers 的字面意义是"发粘的手指"。*Don't touch my book with your sticky fingers!* 不要用你那黏糊糊的手指头摸我的书! 因为"黏糊糊",所以就产生了把什么东西都"粘去"的感觉。*It wouldn't do to let him work in your store. He has sticky fingers.* 叫他在你的铺子里工作可不大好。他手不老实。*I hate to say this about a friend of yours, but I think Mr. Beta has sticky fingers.* 关于你的朋友的事情,我本来不愿意多嘴多舌,不过,贝塔先生手可不老实呀。也使用 sticky-fingered (手不老实的)的形式。*That guy is nothing but a sticky-fingered klepto!* 那个家伙完全是一个手不老实的偷窃狂! ◇ have a tendency to steal things

keep *one's* **fingers crossed** [.ki(:)p ~ 'fɪŋgərz .krɔ:st] [话] **祈求成功[幸运]** 直译为"将两个手指交叉",具体地讲,是把中指弯到食指背后作十字交叉。自古以来就有的一种祈祷形式。当对方有什么困难的或者重大的任务要去完成时,祝愿者就把两指交叉的手背伸向他说 I'll keep my fingers crossed for you. (为你的成功 [幸运]祈祷。)但有时只做手势而不说这句话,或者只说这句话而不做手势。也有自己请求对方祝愿的情况,例如:*I'm going for an interview today. Keep your fingers crossed that I get the job.* 今天我去接受面试。请祈祷我能找到工作吧! 另外,孩子们为了祈求自己的成功[幸运],常对自己以这样的方式进行祈祷,而成年人则如下面的例句所示,一般只用语言来表达。*I don't think anything can go wrong with our plan, but we'd better keep our fingers crossed.* 我认为咱们的计划不会出什么差错,不过咱们最好还是为成功祈祷。*A: Do you think you'll pass the entrance exam? B: I don't know, but I'm keeping all my fingers crossed.* 甲:你认为你能通过入学考试吗? 乙:我不知道,但是我从深心里祷念成功哪。从最后这一例句可以看到,使用 all 能加强语气。动词可用 have 代替 keep, 整个表达法作 have *one's* fingers crossed。这一 have 与上一例句中的 be keeping 大致同义。*Good luck! We'll have our fingers crossed for you.* 祝你运气好! 我们为你祈祷。另有 cross *one's* fingers 的说法,多用分词句。*"Good luck," she said, crossing her fingers.* 她把中指与食指交叉起来说:"祝你成功!"最后讲一下在一般词典中查不到的释义,即孩子们在说谎的时候,也把中指与食指交叉起来。他们认为这样做可以产生"虽然撒谎而祈祷不构成撒谎"的效果,一般是把手转到自己身后再将两指交叉,不叫对方看见。在表示"做虽然撒谎而不算撒谎的祈祷"的意思时,人们很少用 keep *one's* fingers crossed, 普遍使用 have *one's* fingers crossed 或者 cross *one's* fingers。*A: You told me a lie when you said you didn't eat my candy. B: That doesn't count. I had my fingers crossed.* 甲:你告诉我你没有偷吃我的糖果,这是说谎。乙:那不能算是说谎。我已经两指交叉祈祷啦。如果成年人照搬孩子们的这种使用方法,就会产生象下面的笑话:*I'm sorry, Mr. Smith, the judge says you'll be guilty of perjury even if you cross your fingers.* 对不起,史密斯先生,法官说,即便你已经两指交叉进行了祈祷,也要判你伪证罪。◇ pray for (*someone's* [*one's*]) success (in *doing something*) / wish *someone* luck

let *something* [*someone*] **slip through** *one's* **fingers** [.let ~ .slɪp .θru(:) ~ 'fɪŋgərz] [口] **眼睁睁地看着跑掉** 直译"听任……从指缝间溜掉"。在自己认为已经抓住的人或者只要想抓就能抓住的人、以及非常良好的机会等眼看着跑掉的时候使用这一表达法,常伴有"悔之晚矣"的韵味。*How could I be so stupid! I let a golden opportunity to make a lot of money slip through my fingers.* 我怎么会如此愚蠢! 一个发大财的宝贵机会眼睁睁地叫它跑掉了。*Although the police had surrounded the building, they somehow let the culprit slip through their fingers.* 虽然警察包围了那座建筑物,但是不知什么缘故,却让犯人跑掉了。也常常用逃跑的人或失去的机会作主语,而说

slip through *someone's* fingers (从……的指缝间溜掉)。*It was too late. The last opportunity had slipped through Joe's fingers.* 已经太晚啦。乔眼睁睁地错过了最后的机会。*It was the chance of a lifetime for my brother. But to help him take advantage of it meant betraying my best friend. I had no choice but to stand aside and watch it slip through his fingers.* 对于我哥哥来说,那是他一生中难得的好机会。但是,我要是帮助他获得那个机会,就意味着背叛我最好的朋友。因此我没有别的办法,只能站在一旁,默默地看着哥哥的机会溜掉了。◇ let *something* [*someone*] escape

slip through *someone's* **fingers** [ˌslɪp ˌθru(:) ~ ˈfɪŋgərz] [口] **眼睁睁地跑掉** → let *something* [*someone*] slip through *one's* FINGERS

snap *one's* **fingers at** *something* [ˌsnæp ~ ˈfɪŋgərzət ˈ~] [话] **瞧不起** snap *one's* fingers 按字面意义是“捻手指作响”,这是表示轻蔑时常有的动作。例如:*I can beat him just like that.* 我可以这样地揍他。在说最后的 that 的时候,把手指一捻,叭的一声响。意思是说:“要是揍那个家伙,你瞧,就跟捻手指头作响一样,不费吹灰之力。”(→ just LIKE that)。由于人们有这样的习惯,snap *one's* fingers 这一动作以及表达法就用以表示“瞧不起”、“轻视”的意思了。*Men of wealth and power have always been able to snap their fingers at local customs and morals.* 有钱有势的人总是能够不把当地的风俗和道德放在眼里,自己为所欲为。*Just because you don't like the world the way it is doesn't mean you can snap your fingers at reality.* 你不能因为对世界的现状不满而忽视现实。*One of these days he's going to snap his fingers at the law once too often.* 他再三再四地轻视法律,有一天他会受到惩罚的。at *something* 也可以改换为 in the face of *something*,意思相同。*A politician can't afford to snap his fingers in the face of public opinion.* 政治家不能不重视群众的意见。另外有一个 be nothing to snap *one's* fingers at 的形式,意思是“不能瞧不起”,与 be nothing to SNEEZE at 大致同义。*I'd accept their offer if I were you. After all, thirty thousand dollars is nothing to snap your fingers at.* 如果我是你的话,我会接受他们的条件。不管怎么说,三万美元可不是一个小数目啊。◇ scorn *something* / treat *something* lightly

work *one's* **fingers to the bone** [ˌwərk ~ ˈfɪŋgərz təðə ˈboun] [话] **拚死命地劳动** 19 世纪英国和美国的缝纫女工被强制在 sweat shop (血汗工厂)中干很重的劳动,工资极低,一直干到手指不听使唤为止。这一表达法便是由此而来。通常具有“为某某拚命劳动”的意味。如果谈到他人,则用同情的口气;如果谈到自己,则用不满的语调。从印象来说,这一表达法主要用于女性,但对男性使用也未尝不可。*Poor Mrs. Harris works her fingers to the bone to support her children, but they don't appreciate it.* 可怜的哈里斯太太为了养活自己的孩子含辛茹苦,可是她的孩子们没有一个知恩感恩。*I work my fingers to the bone and what thanks do I get?* 我拚死命地劳动,可是又有谁领情呢? ◇ work very hard

finish

Let's finish. [ˌlets ˈfɪnɪʃ] [话] **不干完不收工** → call it a DAY

fire

a ball of fire → BALL

build a fire under *someone* [ˌbɪldə ˈfaɪˌʌndər ~] [口] **催促某人行动起来** 最初的构思是:“为了使对方按照自己的意图行动起来,在他的屁股底下架上柴,点把火”。意思近似汉语的“鼓励”或“鼓舞”,但在英语中使用的范围要广泛得多。*Our son doesn't study nearly as much as he should. I wish there were some way to build a fire under him.* 我们的儿子不大好好用功。但愿有个什么办法促使他努力学习才好。*If our loan application isn't approved soon, we're going* *to be in trouble. I'd better go over to the bank and see if I can't build a fire under them.* 如果我们的贷款申请不能被马上批准,公司就要陷入困境。我还是去银行一趟为好,看看能不能敦促他们快点给办下来。*Some employees were reluctant to go along with the new work rules, so the company built a fire under them by threatening dismissal if they didn't comply.* 有一些工作人员不愿遵守新的工作规程,因此,公司为了叫他们就范,就威胁说:如果他们违犯规程,就将他们解雇。如果主语不是"人",而是"事物"、"情况"、"措施"等等,一般用 put 代替 build。*If he refuses, tell him we won't pay. That'll put a fire under him.* 如果他不答应,你就告诉他我们不付钱。这样将他一军,他就干了。◇ get *someone* to try harder [act, do so]

the fat is in the fire → FAT

fight fire with fire [ˌfaɪtˈfaɪr wɪθˈfaɪr] [口] **以其人之道还治其人之身** 相当于"以火攻火"、"以毒攻毒"的表达法。一般用于以卑鄙手段、恶毒办法、肮脏伎俩互相交锋的场合。有时相当于"以眼还眼",但不含复仇雪恨的韵味。我们可以说这是一个已经考虑过战略的冷静的说法。*If they are going to use dirty tactics, so will we. You have to fight fire with fire.* 如果他们采取卑鄙的手段,我们也要这样干。必须以其人之道还治其人之身啊。*My uncle lost out to his competition because he wasn't willing to fight with fire.* 我的叔父由于不愿采取以毒攻毒的手段,他在竞争中败于对手了。◇ use the same (under-handed) tactics as *one's* opponent

fire away [ˌfaɪrəˈweɪ] [话] **象连珠炮似地提问或发言** 本来是"接连不断打枪"的意思。away 包含有"连续不断地"、"随随便便地"的意味。*As soon as you see the target, fire away.* 看见目标以后,你马上连续射击。转用于表示"象连珠炮似地提问或发言"的意思。*A: I have some questions I would like to ask you. B: Sure. Fire away.* 甲:我有几个问题想请教您。乙:好。请随便讲吧。*A: I think you should hear my side of the story as well. B: Well, fire away.* 甲:我认为您也应该听一下我这方面的话。乙:好,你说吧。如以上两个例句所示,一般使用命令式,但也有普通陈述句的场合。例如:*As soon as the President finished his talk, the reporters began firing away with questions.* 总统刚讲完话,记者们就开始了象连珠炮似的提问。具有同一形式的 ask away 是"连续不断地询问"。*If you have any questions, ask away.* 如果你有什么问题,请随便问好啦。shoot 用命令式也表示"请问[谈]吧"的意思,但是,它与 fire away 或 ask away 的发言或提问必须是复数不同,只是一个问题或一件事也可以。例如:*A: I've got a question. B: Shoot.* 甲:我有一个问题。乙:请问吧。*A: I have something I'd like to talk to you about. B: OK, shoot.* 甲:我有一件事想跟您谈一下。乙:很好,请谈吧。◇ ask [speak] freely

Great balls of fire! [ˈgreɪt ˈbɔːlzə ˈfaɪr] [话] **哎呀!** → Great SCOTT!

have *many* **irons in the fire** → IRONS

jump out of the frying pan into the fire → PAN

like a house on fire [laɪkəˈhauˌsɔ(ː)nˌfaɪr] [话] **热火朝天** → like a HOUSE afire

play with fire [ˌpleɪwɪθ ˈfaɪr] [口] **玩火** 字面意义为"用火游戏"。一般用作比喻。也有照字面意义使用的场合,例如:*Children must be taught not to play with fire.* 应该教育孩子们不要玩火。但在这一场合,一般的表达法为 play with matches (拿火柴玩)。在英语中,"玩火"这一习用语应用范围很广,所表示的意思与汉语成语"玩火自焚"或"惹火烧身"相类似。*I'd advise you not to date a man you know absolutely nothing about. That's playing with fire.* 我劝告你不要跟一个你完全不了解的男人约会,那是在玩火啊。*You're playing with fire to accept favors from the Mafia.* 你接受黑手党的恩惠,那可是玩火呀。*The doctor told my grandfather that anyone who plays tennis at his age is playing with* *fire*. 医生对我的祖父说，任何人到了他那个年纪还打网球都是在玩火。◇ take a great risk

set the world on fire → WORLD

Where there's smoke there's fire. → SMOKE

with fire in *one's* **eye** [wɪθ ˈfaɪrɪn ~ ˌaɪ] [口] **怒气冲冲** 字面意义为"眼睛里有火焰"。是日常使用的一个表达法。*Here comes the boss with fire in his eye. He must have heard about the mistake we made.* 老板怒气冲冲地到这儿来啦。他一定是听说我们的失误了。*I finally arrived home from my date at three o'clock in the morning, and, when I opened the door, there stood my father with fire in his eye.* 与情人幽会后，我到家已经是早晨三点钟了。当我开门的时候，父亲正怒气冲冲地站在那儿。◇, consumed with anger / , obviously very angry

firebug

a firebug [ə ˈfaɪrˌbʌ(:)g] [话] **放火狂** fire 是"火"、"火灾"。bug 一般作"虫子"解，但常作后缀使用，表示"……迷"的意思。因此，fire 加 bug 就成为"放火狂"了。此外，用这一 bug 为后缀的表达法有 the JITTERBUG, a LITTERBUG, a SHUTTERBUG 等。*The police believe that the blaze was the work of a firebug.* 警察认为那场火灾是一个放火狂干的。*The firebug is still at large.* 那个放火狂依然逍遥法外。◇ an arsonist

fireman

a visiting fireman [ə ˌvɪzɪdɪŋ ˈfaɪrmən] [口] **远方来客** 字面意义是"远方来的消防队员"。原指"从地方前来的团体客人"。他们从地方前来参加大会什么的，感到一身轻松，吃喝玩乐，挥金如土。后来，这一表达法不仅指"团体客人"，也指单独的客人，不过"团体客人"的意味依然很浓。 *Hotels and cabarets generally depend for much of their trade on visiting firemen.* 一般来说，旅馆饭店和歌舞餐厅的生意在很大程度上依靠各地前来的团体客人。在现代，已经很少表示这样的意义，越来越多地表示"远方来客"的意义了。一般指重要的商业伙伴(买主或卖主)，有时指高级官员、出来视察的公司老板等，总之，是需要殷勤招待的客人。*I'm behind in my work because our office had three groups of visiting firemen in this week.* 这个星期我们公司有三批远方来的客人，因此我耽误了工作。*I'll be home late tonight. I have to entertain a bunch of visiting firemen.* 今天晚上要晚回家，我必须招待一批远来的客人。 *You don't have to go out of your way to entertain me. I'm not a visiting fireman, you know.* 你用不着特别分神来款待我，因为我并不是一个远道而来的客人。◇ an out-of-town businessman [conventioneer]

firewater

firewater [ˈfaɪrˌwɔ(:)dər] [话] **威士忌** 字面意义是"火的水"，据说为美国印第安语的直译。从 19 世纪上半叶开始在拓荒者间流行，现在除西部影片或戏剧的对白外，专用作诙谐语。*The party's not half over and we're almost out of firewater.* 社交晚会开了不到一半时间，咱们就几乎把威士忌全喝光了。主要指威士忌，但广义指度数高的各种酒，如杜松子酒、朗姆酒等，与啤酒、葡萄酒相对而言。*No beer or wine for me thanks. I'm a firewater man.* 我不要啤酒或者葡萄酒，我是专喝烈性酒的人。◇ whiskey

first

first off [ˈfə(:)rˌstɔ(:)f] [话] **首先** 与 first of all, in the first place 等相同，常用于列举若干理由时的开端。 *A: Why won't you play baseball? B: First off, it's too hot today. Secondly, I have a sore arm. Third,....* 甲：你为什么不打棒球？ 乙：首先，今天天气太热。第二，我的胳臂疼。第三，……。不过，一个句子尽管用 First off 开始，却不一定按照章法非在后边续上 second(ly), third(ly) 不可，有时就用 besides 等词替代。 *A: Why don't you go to Europe with us, Bill? B: Well, first off, I don't have the time. Besides, I'm broke.* 甲：比尔，你跟我们一道去欧洲怎么样？ 乙：好是好，不过，第一

我没有时间，其次我也没有钱。◇ first of all

not get to first base (with *something* [*someone*]) → BASE

not know the first thing about *something* → THING

of the first water → WATER

fish

drink like a fish [ˌdrɪŋk laɪkə ˈfɪ(ː)ʃ] [话] **大喝、贪杯** 字面意义为"象鱼吸水一样喝酒"，当然指饮的量相当大。不过，这一表达法是形容一个人平日喜欢多喝几杯，而不能用于暴饮的场合。*Kirk is a hard worker but he drinks like a fish.* 柯克在工作中很卖力气，但是贪杯。如这一例句所示，根据上下文，有时略含轻蔑的意味，但不限定如此。*Hugh drinks like a fish, but he never seems to get drunk.* 休是大量喝酒的人，但他好象永远也喝不醉。◇ drink a lot

have other fish to fry [hævˌʌðər ˈfɪʃtə ˌfraɪ] [口] **另有要紧的事情** 直译是"有另外的鱼要用油煎"，听起来很奇怪，但从 17 世纪以来，这就是人们常挂在口头上的一个习用语。语源不明。当一个人认为另外的事情比眼前的事情要紧、自己觉得应该去干或者愿意去干的时候，常常使用这一表达法。从工作直到兴趣，使用范围很广。*I haven't got time to be on that committee. I've got other fish to fry right now.* 我没有时间参加那个委员会。我现在有别的事情必须去做。*Joyce isn't going to cooking class today. She says she's got other fish to fry.* 乔伊斯今天不去上烹饪课。她说她另有要紧的事情。*Prof. Higgins had wanted to become dean for many years, but by the time he was offered the job he had other fish to fry.* 希金斯教授多年以来渴望当上学院院长，但是当人家请他担任这个职务的时候，他却另有要紧的事情去做了。◇ have something of greater concern to do

be like a fish out of water [laɪkə ˈfɪʃ audəv ˈwɔːdər] [口] **如鱼离水** 原来的构思是：鱼出了水，不能自由活动，十分可怜。这一表达法常用于表示"不合时宜"、"格格不入"、"局促不安"、"手足无措"等意思。*I can't swim. At the beach, I'm like a fish out of water.* 我不会游泳。到了海岸，我是一筹莫展的。*I'm quitting my job. I'm like a fish out of water here.* 我辞职不干啦。在这个单位，我感到很不适宜。在特别表达本人的心情时，也可以说 feel like a fish out of water。*Mrs. Stone's parties are too high class for me. I feel like a fish out of water with her guests.* 对于我来说，斯通夫人举办的社交晚会太高级啦。跟她的客人在一起，我感到十分局促。有时省略 like。*Finny should go home. He's a fish out of water in China.* 芬尼应该回国。他不服中国的水土。◇ be in an unsuitable environment / feel awkward

be neither fish nor fowl [ˌni(ː)ðər ˈfɪʃnər ˈfaul] [口] **不伦不类** 字面意义为"既不是鱼，又不是鸟"。说是鱼，却有翅膀；说是鸟，却有鳞；乍看起来，谁也不知道是什么东西。这就是本条习用语最初的构思。汉语为"非驴非马"。有些词典译作"莫明其妙"，如果作这一解释，多少要包含着"离奇"的意味。但是，这一习用语本身完全没有此种意味，请读者注意。*Politically speaking, Mr. Horsefeathers appears to be neither fish nor fowl. He claims to be a Democrat but it seems he always votes Republican.* 从政治上说，霍斯费瑟斯先生究竟属于哪一派，谁也弄不清。他自称是民主党，但是永远投共和党候选人的票。*If you ask me, that company is neither fish nor fowl. It's supposed to be an advertising agency, but they seem to spend most of their time doing translation work.* 如果叫我来说，那个公司简直是非驴非马。它应该搞的是广告业务，但是大部分时间从事翻译工作。如以上的例句所示，一般用于在二者之间看不出属于哪一边的场合。但也有不特别指定"二者之间"的使用方法。例如：*That book is neither fish nor fowl. The publisher calls it a dictionary, but there are only five hundred entries and they aren't even in alphabetical order.* 那

部书简直不论不类。出版社称它为词典，但是只有五百个条目，而且不是按字母顺序排列的。另外，这一表达法已经有五百年以上的历史，最初的形式较长，作 be neither fish nor fowl [flesh] nor good red herring (herring 是鲱鱼)。至今还可以极偶然地听见有人用这一原形以及类似的形式，意义相同。◇ have no definite character

a pretty kettle of fish [ə ˈprɪdi ˈkedələv ˈfɪ(ː)ʃ] [口] **真糟糕** 这里的 fish 本来指鲑鱼 (salmon)。古时候，每当鲑鱼的繁盛季节，人们到流经苏格兰与英格兰交界附近的特威德河 (the River Tweed) 的河边去野餐。他们去捕浮游上来的鲑鱼，将活鱼放入釜 (kettle) 中煮食。因此，这种野餐本身就被称为 kettle of fish 了。我们对以上的史实是十分明确的。但是 a pretty kettle of fish 的语源不详，究竟是指野餐时人们喧闹得"一团糟"呢？还是指釜中的鱼煮得"乱糟糟"呢？这就不清楚了。不管语源如何，这里的 pretty 是反语用法，具讽刺的意味，一般在谈到与预期相反的结果时使用。*He's managed to get himself into a pretty kettle of fish.* 他竟把自己搞得个一塌糊涂。*Well, if this isn't a pretty kettle of fish. I ordered sirloin steaks for guests tonight, and look—the store delivered a box of hot dogs.* 唉，这可真糟糕透啦！今天晚上请客，我预订了牛排。可是你瞧，饭馆给送来的却是一箱热狗。*The deal I thought would work so well turned out to be a pretty kettle of fish. One of the participants pulled out at the last moment, and another came up with only half the money he had promised.* 我本来以为事情是一帆风顺的，可是结果一团糟。一位参加者到最后关头甩手不干了，另一个人只出了他所应允的钱数的一半。pretty 有时用 fine 或 nice 代替。*This is a fine kettle of fish. My boss has gone out of his way to land you a good job, and you go and get kicked out of school for cheating just one month before you're supposed to graduate.* 这真糟糕透了。我的老板特意给你找到一份很好的工作，可是你呢，居然在即将毕业的一个月之前，由于考试作弊被学校开除啦。*Lost on a country road with a flat tire— and it's snowing to boot. Talk about a nice kettle of fish!* 由于迷了路，把车开到乡村土路上，轮胎放炮还不算，又下起鹅毛大雪来。甭提多倒霉啦。◇ a terrible situation / quite a mess

fisheye

give *someone* **the fisheye** [gɪv ~ ðəˈfɪ.ʃaɪ] [话] **冷眼凝视** 直译为"给某人一个鱼眼睛"。这里的 eye 应作"目光"解，因此这一表达法的意思是"用好象鱼那样的目光看某人"。仔细分析，它包含着两种意味：一是"冰冷"，二是"怀疑"。在一个句子里，究竟哪一个意味占上风，那要根据上下文来决定。比如说：*The waiter gave the shabbily dressed hobo the fisheye.* 服务员冷冷地盯着衣衫褴褛的流浪汉。这样解释比较自然。但是如果把 The waiter 换成 The policeman，那就应该译成警察以怀疑的目光盯着衣衫褴褛的流浪汉了。*When the boy saw the two toughs giving him the fisheye, he quickly took to his heels.* 少年见到两个恶棍正以冷冰冰的目光凝视着他，他赶快撒腿跑掉了。*The student looked up from his exam paper to see the teacher giving him the fisheye.* 学生从考试答卷上抬头一看，老师正以怀疑的目光盯着他。◇ stare at *someone* coldly [suspiciously]

fist

hand over fist → HAND

an iron fist in a velvet glove [ə ˌnaɪrn ˈfɪstɪnə ˌvelvət ˈglʌːv] [口] **表面笑哈哈，心里毒又辣** → an iron HAND in a velvet glove

rule with an iron fist [ˌru(ː)lwɪðə ˌnaɪrn ˈfɪ(ː)st] [口] **高压统治** → rule with an iron HAND

fit

be dressed up fit to kill → KILL

(as) fit as a fiddle → FIDDLE

be fit to be tied [ˈfɪtːəbi ˈtaɪd] [话] **十分恼**

火 字面意义是“适合于绑上的状态”。原来的构思是:“由于满腔怒火,如果不用绳子捆上,就会爆发出来,不可收拾”。例如使用于这样的场合:本来约好在什么时间见面,可是对方过了一个小时还不来,心里的怒火不断增大,等到对方来临时,已经达到马上就要爆发的程度。*When I finally got to the airport an hour late, the boss was fit to be tied.* 我到达飞机场已经晚了一小时,老板非常恼火。*By the time Roy had mispronounced the name of the guest of honor for the third time, his wife was fit to be tied.* 罗伊第三次叫错贵宾的名字时,他的太太已经怒不可遏了。◇ be extremely angry

have a fit [ˌhævə ˈfɪ(ː)t] [话] **大发脾气** → have a CONNIPTION

laugh fit to kill → KILL

throw a fit [ˌθrouə ˈfɪ(ː)t] [话] **大怒** → have a CONNIPTION

five

a five o'clock shadow → SHADOW

five-and-dime

a five-and-dime (store) [ə ˌfaɪ vənˌdaɪm (ˌsto(ː)r)] [话] **大众百货店** → a FIVE-AND-TEN

five-and-ten

a five-and-ten [ə ˌfaɪ vənˈte(ː)n] [话] **大众百货店** 正式名称为 a five-and-ten-cent store [ˌfaɪ vənˈten-ˈsentˌsto(ː)r]。原意为“出售 5–10 分钱廉价物品的商店”。这种百货店是出售群众日用品的综合商店,在美国,凡是 2–3 千以上人口的城镇大致都有一家。在一万人左右的城镇,一般规模较大,多数为著名的连锁商店,如 Woolworth's, Kresge's 等。这种百货店出售日用品、玩具、文房用具、衣服、家具等等,甚至很多家都设有便餐柜台。现在虽然 5–10 分钱的商品几乎绝迹,但比一般大百货店价钱便宜,商品种类面向群众的居多。*Excuse me, but is there a five-and-ten in this area?* 请问,这一带有大众百货店吗? *I want to stop in at the five-and-ten and buy some Scotch tape.* 我想顺便去大众百货店买点透明胶带。又称 a ten-cent store, a dime store, a five-and-dime (store) 等。◇ a five-and-ten-cent store

five-spot

a five-spot [ə ˈfaɪv ˌspɑt] [话] **五美元钞票** 字面意义是“带有五个点的东西”,相当随便的说法。*I need some ones. Can you break this five-spot for me?* 我需要用一美元的票子。这张五元的你能给破开吗?另外,这一表达法也用于表示“扑克牌的五”、“骰子的五点”、“五号弹子”等意义,但比指金钱的场合要少得多。◇ a five-dollar bill

fix

be in a fix [ɪnə ˈfɪks] [话] **正在困窘** → be in a PICKLE / be in a SPOT

fixed

be fixed for life → LIFE

be well fixed [ˌwel ˈfɪkst] [话] **生活富裕** well 是“充分地”。fixed 的字面意义是“被固定的”。例如说:*The picture was well fixed to the wall.* 图画被牢牢地固定在墙上了。作为比喻,fixed 是“生活安定”的意思。最初的构思是:“因为生活安定,一动不动都可以有饭吃。”另外又加个 well,那就是不但有饭吃,而且有更多的钱,亦即“生活富裕”了。*Why does that guy want to borrow money from you? I thought he was well fixed.* 那个家伙为什么想要向你借钱呢?我本来以为他是非常富裕的啊。在强调的场合,最常使用的是 extremely。*George's family was extremely well fixed.* 乔治的家庭是极其富裕的。◇ have plenty of money

flag

a flag waver → WAVER

nail *one's* flag to the mast [ˌneɪl ~ ˌflæ(ː)gtəðə ˈmæːst] [口] **表明决不屈服的坚决意志** → nail *one's* COLORS to the mast

flak

catch a lot of flak (from *someone*) [ˌkætʃə ˌladəv ˈflæ(ː)k] [话] **受到极大的责难** flak 是在轰炸机周围象黑色花瓣

一样炸裂开的“防空炮火”,在战争影片中经常可以看到。原为德语 *Fl*iegerabwehr*k*anone(高射炮)的缩略,由其中的斜体部分拼写而成。最初是在第二次世界大战期间由英美空军开始使用。因此,在战争的场面中是按照字面意义使用的,如说: *We're catching a lot of flak.* 我们遇到猛烈的高射炮火。转作比喻使用,就是“成为指责的目标”的意思了。*The President is catching a lot of flak from the press for his anti-inflation policies.* 总统由于他所采取的制止通货膨胀政策而受到报刊猛烈的攻击。动词除 catch 外,还使用 get 或 take,意思相同。*I got a lot of flak from my wife for losing five hundred dollars at the races.* 由于在赛马上输掉五百美元,老婆对我百般责难。*Nowadays manufacturers who ignore the problem of pollution must be prepared to take a lot of flak.* 当前,凡是忽视污染问题的工厂都必须认识到它要受社会各方面的谴责。有时用 a bit of 或 some 等形容词(短语)代替 a lot of。*We caught some flak on that.* 关于那件事,我们受到了一些责难。◇ receive a lot of criticism

flake

flake out [ˌfleɪ ˈkaut] [话] **因酒醉或疲劳而酣然入睡** flake 一般是“使成薄片”或“使剥落”的意思。flake out 为什么会是“酣然入睡”的意思呢? 语源不详。有人说这一场合的 flake 乃是 flag (疲乏)、fake (假装)等的形变,但均非定论。*George is not a strong drinker. He usually flakes out after a couple of beers.* 乔治没有什么酒量,他只要喝上两杯啤酒就会酣然入睡的。*I'm tired. I think I'll flake out on the couch for an hour or so.* 我累了。我在长沙发上睡上一个来小时吧。改用被动语态,意思不变。*Dewey isn't up yet. He's still flaked out in his room.* 杜威还没有起床。他还在自己的屋子里睡大觉哪。这个例子中没有表明睡大觉的原因究竟是喝多了酒还是疲惫不堪。下一个例句是由于疲劳而酣睡的场合。*Having worked hard in the garden all morning, the boys were all flaked out on the living room floor.* 男孩子们整个上午一直在花园中辛勤劳动,现在都躺在起居室的地板上酣睡呢。◇ lose consciousness / go to sleep / be asleep ((be flaked out 的场合))

flame

an old flame [ə ˈnoul*d* ˈfleɪm] [话] **老相好** 直译为“昔日的火焰”。flame 单独可作“爱人”解,但极少使用。*I ran into an old flame of yours at the supermarket.* 我在超级市场碰见了你的一个老相好。*I don't know if I should invite Doris to the party or not. She's one of my husband's old flames.* 我不知道是不是应该邀请多丽丝参加社交晚会。她是我丈夫的老相好之一啊。有时模仿 old flame 这一习用语,而说 new flame 或者 latest flame,但都不是定型的表达法。主要用于戏谑。*George has another new flame.* 乔治又有了新相好。*Who's your latest flame?* 你最近跟哪一个女人相好哪? 按照 flame 的意义,用汉语相当的话来翻译,就是:你最近跟谁打得火热呀? ◇ an old girl friend

flames

add fuel to the flames → FUEL

flash

a flash in the pan [ə ˌflæ(ː)ʃənðə ˈpæːn] [口] **昙花一现** flash 是“闪光”,pan 是旧式火枪的“药池”。在使用旧式火枪的时候,虽然搬动枪机,但是只见药池冒出火花,往往发不出子弹。转作比喻,用以表示一时的“走红”或“成功”。*That singer was just another flash in the pan who dropped out of sight after one hit record.* 那个歌手也是昙花一现,只出了一张流行唱片之后,就默默无闻了。另外,也有指对某种事情仅具五分钟热情的场合,例如: *The public's enthusiasm for the plan turned out to be a flash in the pan.* 公众对那项计划的热情转瞬就消失了。◇ a momentary phenomenon

in a flash [ɪnə ˈflæ(ː)ʃ] [话] **象闪电一样** → like a SHOT

flat

fall flat [ˌfɔ(ː)l ˈflæ(ː)t] [话] **以失败而告终** 字面意义是"突然一下子倒下"。例如: *The wall he built so carefully fell flat.* 他那么认真砌起来的墙却突然一下子倒塌了。作为比喻使用,表示"理想完全破灭"的意思。*All the coach's attempts to build a winning tennis team fell flat.* 教练员打算建立一个常胜网球队的尝试完全以失败而告终了。*When the chief withdrew his support from our plan, our hopes of having the board of directors accept it fell flat.* 当科长不再支持我们的计划时,我们对董事会采纳这一计划的一切希望全都化成了泡影。在企图使人发笑而没有成功的时候,也常使用这一表达法。*Dennis likes to tell jokes, but they always fall flat.* 丹尼斯喜欢讲笑话,可是没有一次引得人发笑。为了加强语气,常常使用 completely, 作 fall completely flat。→ fall flat on *one's* FACE ◇ come to nothing / fail (completely)

(as) flat as a pancake → PANCAKE

flatfoot

a flatfoot [ə ˈflætˌfut] [俗] **巡警** flatfoot 本来是"扁平足"的意思。但是,在作"扁平足"解的场合,不能使用 flatfoot 这一词形,必须分成两个词,而且用复数,如说 *I have flat feet.* 我是平足。要不然就采取"名词+-ed"的形式,作为形容词使用,如说 *I'm flatfooted.* 我是平足。与此相反,在作"警察"解时,不分成两个词,而且多半用单数 (亦即指一名警察的时候居多)。偶尔也用此词表示多数的警察,在这种场合,复数形式大多作 flatfeet,但也可以作 flatfoots。另外,人们所以称"警察"为 flatfoot,是由于警察一年到头来回地走,把脚都走成"平足"了。这一意义的 flatfoot 是非常轻松的俚语,主要的使用者是流氓、阿飞或盗匪。一般市民也偶尔使用,表示对警察轻蔑的意思。如果当着警察的面使用,必然引起警察的愤怒。 *Here comes a flatfoot! Let's beat it.* 有巡警来啦! 咱们赶快颠儿吧! ◇ a policeman

flattop

a flattop [ə ˈflæˌtɑːp] [话] **航空母舰** 这一表达法的来源是:航空母舰的上部 (top) 是平的(flat)。为第二次世界大战中流行起来的海军俚语,现在一般人仍广泛使用。航空母舰的正式名称为 aircraft carrier, 而 flattop 一词则使人产生轻快的感觉。*The Brown's son is a sailor on a flattop.* 布朗先生的儿子在航空母舰上当水兵。◇ an aircraft carrier

flea

a flea trap → TRAP

flesh

goose flesh [ˈgu(ː)s ˌfle(ː)ʃ] [口] **鸡皮疙瘩** → goose PIMPLES

press the flesh [ˌpres ðə ˈfle(ː)ʃ] [话] **握手** 字面意义是"压(对方手上的)肉"。20 世纪 40 年代产生的相当轻松的俚语,过去在青年人中间特别广泛使用,例如: *Hey, long time no see. Let's press the flesh.* 嘿,好久没见啦。咱们握握手吧! 现在一般人很少使用,但是报纸和周刊杂志等却把它作为新闻专用语言常常使用。意思是:"政客为了得到群众的拥护,到处游说,与选民们一一握手"。*American politicians have to spend a great deal of time going about the countryside pressing the flesh.* 美国的政治家们必须耗费大量时间去周游全国各地与选民们握手。◇ shake hands

The spirit is willing, but the flesh is weak. → SPIRIT

flick

a flick [ə ˈflɪk] [话] **电影** 在过去无声电影的时代,将动词 flicker (<光>闪烁) 作为名词使用,表示"电影"的意义。这是一个老掉牙了的表达法,现在除了开玩笑的时候外一概不用。但是,把 flicker 去掉 -er 而构成的 flick 却成为青年人特别喜欢使用的俚语了。 *That was a good flick.* 那个电影很不错。在说"去看电影"的时候,flick 的用法与 a movie / the movies 相同,既可以用"a+单数"的形式,如 *Let's go to a flick.* 也可以用"the +复数"的形式,如 *Let's go to the flicks.*

咱们去看电影吧。◇ a movie

flip

the flip side → SIDE

flivver

a flivver [ə ˈflɪvər] [话] **破旧的小汽车** flivver 原为表示"失败"的方言，现在不能用这一解。后来转用作对福特汽车公司 1908–1928 年间生产的"福特 T 型(Model T)"的爱称。例如：*My grandfather bought one of the first flivvers Ford made.* 我爷爷买了一辆福特汽车公司最初制造的 *T* 型小汽车。从那以后又有发展，不仅指福特牌的汽车，而且指一般的廉价、破旧、小型的轿车了，现在使用这一意义的场合最多。*When are we going to get rid of this old flivver and buy a new car, Dad?* 爸爸，咱们什么时候把这个老破车处理掉，买一辆新汽车呢？*Mr. Pennypinch has been driving that same beat-up flivver for I don't know how many years.* 彭尼平奇先生一直驾驶那辆破旧的小汽车，简直都数不清有多少年啦。有时戏指另外的小汽车，特别是闪闪发光的新车。这当然是反语的用法了。*Hi, Steve. Where'd you get the new flivver?* 嗬，史蒂夫，你从哪里弄来一辆新的破车呀？这一表达法又指"个人用的廉价旧飞机"或者"破旧的小轮船"。由于是从汽车转用于其他交通工具，所以仍具有原来的戏谑的语气。*Sam's plane was an old flivver that trailed smoke and oil wherever it went.* 萨姆的飞机是一架破旧的小飞机，不管飞到哪里都留下烟和油的尾迹。另外，上面提到的"福特 T 型"，除 flivver 外，还有一个爱称是 a tin lizzie(其中 tin 是"锡"，lizzie 是 Elizabeth 的爱称)。这一爱称也用于表示"破旧的小汽车"的意思。首先举一个"福特 T 型"的爱称的例句。在这一场合，第一个字母一般要大写。*The Tin Lizzie was a fine car.* 在过去，福特 *T* 型是一种很好的小轿车。其次，再举一个作"破旧的小汽车"解的例子。*Let me go with you. I don't want to ride in that old tin lizzie of George's.* 我跟你一块儿走吧。我可不愿意坐乔治那辆老破车。◇ a (little old broken-down) car [plane, etc.]

floor

floor *someone* [ˈflo(:)r ～] [话] **把(某人)打倒在地** 这里的 floor 是及物动词，意思是"打击某人，使他倒在地板上"，也就是"把某人打倒"。因为用的是 floor (地板或铺砌的地面)，所以这一表达法很少用于"打翻到土地上"的场合。*The champion floored the challenger with a wicked uppercut to the jaw.* 冠军冲着挑战者的下巴狠狠向上一击，把挑战者打倒在地了。*He said he could beat me, did he? It'll take more than a little punk like that to floor me.* 他说他能打败我，是吗？象那样一个小崽子要打倒我，未免太不量力了。在以上的例句中，可以认为 floor *someone* 大致与 DECK *someone* 同义。但是，deck *someone*(把某人击倒)只能按字面意义使用，floor *someone* 则可以作为比喻使用，例如：*I had a bad cold that almost floored me last week.* 上个星期我患重感冒，几乎病倒啦。*I thought I was pretty good at math, but that problem floored me.* 我以为我的数学挺好，但是那道习题却把我难倒啦。也常用 be [get] floored 这样的被动语态。*The champ got floored twice before he finally won the fight.* 冠军在取得最后胜利之前，曾经两次被打倒在地。另外，floor *someone* 还有一个重要的意义，在使用这一意义时，绝大多数采取被动语态。请参阅专条 be FLOORED。◇ knock *someone* down / put *someone* in bed / stymie *someone*

get in on the ground floor [ge.dɪnɔ(:)nðə ˈgraund ˈflo(:)r] [口] **从一开始就参加** 就字面意义来说，the ground floor 与 the first floor 相同，是"楼房的第一层"。这一表达法直译为"从第一层进去"。意思是："不是从中间，而是从最下层入门，沿着楼梯向上爬。"很显然，这是把公司、投资计划等比拟为建筑物的表达法。作为比喻，大多用于表示"自己认为将来有利可图，而比别人早早参加某一事业"的意味。偶尔也用于因为捷足先登而达到升官发财的目标的场合。所参加的机构或投资计划一般是大型的或者将来可能成为大型的。这一表达法似乎来自股票市场用语,现在在日常会话中普遍使用。*Jack's family is rich because his father got in on the ground floor by buying five hundred shares of the Coca-Cola Company when it was first formed.* 杰克的家庭是很有钱的,因为他父亲在可口可乐公司刚刚成立时就参加进去,买了五百股的股票。*Chris has risen to a high position in NASA because he got in on the ground floor. He was one of the first space scientists to join the agency.* 克里斯在航天局的职位很高,这是由于他从该局成立之日起就在那里工作。他是最初参加那个机构的宇航科学家之一。*I came here to invest some money. I believe that this area is going to see a real boom in the near future, and I want to get in on the ground floor.* 我是到这里来投资的。我相信这个地区在最近的将来会迅速繁荣起来,所以我愿意捷足先登,从一开始就参加这里的建设工作。下一个例句讲的是科学的一个分支。在这一场合,也许不是直接意识到金钱的报酬,但仍然具有"早日参加,将来得利"的企图。*In medicine, the study of the effect of the mind on the body is the field of the future. I've decided to specialize in psychosomatic medicine so that I can get in on the ground floor.* 在医学中,研究精神对肉体的影响是大有前途的一个领域。我已经下决心专攻心身医学,以便成为这方面最初的专家之一。另有 a ground-floor opportunity 的表达法,意思是"最早参加能得巨大利益的机会"。*A lot of young college graduates these days are ignoring larger corporations and looking for ground-floor opportunities in small, new companies.* 最近,很多新的大学毕业生都不投奔大型的企业,他们到新成立的小公司去寻求发迹的机会。◇ participate from the very beginning

mop up the floor with *someone* [.mɑ(:).pʌpðəˊ ˈflo(:)rwɪð ~] [话] **把(某人)打得落花流水** 这里的 mop 为动词,意思是"用墩布拖地板"。如果不知道本条的表达法是习用语,而按照字面解释,那就是:"与某人一道用墩布拖地板"。*My wife and I are very close. I discuss business with her, go driving with her, wash the dishes with her—sometimes I even mop up the floor with her.* 我们夫妇真是一唱一随。我和她谈论生意,和她一起驾汽车兜风,一起刷盘子,有时甚至一起用墩布拖地板。然而,mop 所用的工具却是个关键性的问题。如果用的不是"墩布"而是"人"的话,那可就惨极了。按照字面,条头应该译成"用某人当墩布去拖地板",这也就是"把某人打得落花流水"的意思。因此,上边所引用的那位男士的话,实际上不过是一个笑谈,他只是"唯妻命是从"而已。在使用这一表达法时,一般都含有"把对方任意摆布"的意思。*He said that about me, did he? Why that dirty little rat, I'll mop up the floor with him.* 关于我的事情,他是那样讲的吗?这个卑劣的家伙,我非把他砸个稀巴烂不可。有时省略 up。*The champ is expected to mop (up) the floor with his opponent.* 人们预料冠军会把他的对手打得个落花流水。*The Giants mopped (up) the floor with the opposing team.* 巨人队大胜对方的球队。也可以用 wipe (up) 代替 mop (up)。*Bud is an expert chess player. He wipes (up) the floor with everyone who challenges him.* 巴德是国际象棋高手,凡是向他挑战的人都大败而归。◇ thrash [defeat] *someone* soundly

wipe up the floor with *someone* [.waɪ.pʌpðə ˈflo(:)rwɪð ~] [话] **大败某人** → mop up the FLOOR with *someone*

floorboard

floorboard it [ˈflo(:)r.bo(:)rdɪt] [话] **把汽车一下子开足马力** floorboard 原意为"汽车驾驶室的车底板",这里作动词用。it 指"加速器"。两个词合起来,意思是"踩足汽车的油门踏板"。大致与 give her the GUN 同义,但这一表达法只限于汽车。特别是在逃跑的场合使用,语气轻松。*When we heard the police siren behind us, we floorboarded it.* 我们听到后边有警车的鸣笛声以后，立即开足了汽车的马力。*Quick! Into the car! Let's floorboard it out of here.* 快！上车！咱们立即开足马力，离开这里。◇ open the throttle wide / get out of *someplace* fast

floored

be floored ['flo:rd] [话] **事出意外，不禁哑然** 原意为"被打倒在地"。不过在这一场合，"被打倒在地"的不是"身体"，而是"情绪"。因此，这是一个相当强烈的表达法，言外有"简直不知怎么办才好"的意味。*His attitude floored me. I had thought that we were good friends, but he wouldn't even speak to me last night.* 他的态度使我不禁哑然。我本来以为我们是好朋友，可是昨天晚上他连话也不跟我说。如此例所示，有时用主动语态。但一般是用被动语态，例如：*He was floored by the size of the problem.* 问题之大，使他深为震惊，不知所措。这一表达法只是单纯地表示"吃惊"，因此，不论情况比预想的好或坏，全都可以使用。常用 completely 加强语气。*When, on our second date, Simon asked me to marry him, I was completely floored.* 当我们第二次约会的时候，西蒙就向我求婚，把我弄得简直不知所措了。*After treating them so badly, I was floored by their extreme kindness when I was in the hospital.* 我对待他们那么坏，可是当我住医院的时候，他们却对我百般照顾，弄得我实在太难为情了。*I was completely floored when the boss told me that he was promoting me to sales manager.* 老板告诉我他提升我为销售经理的时候，这完全出乎我的意料之外，我简直不知所措了。→ FLOOR *someone* ◇ be dumb-founded

flop

a belly flop [ə 'beli.flɑ(:)p] [话] **腹部先入水的笨拙跳水动作** 跳水动作是头部或脚部先入水，跳水失败时，腹部先拍击水面，发出声响。这种腹部打水的拙笨跳法，英语作 do a belly flop。另外的说法还有 belly flopper, belly whop ['beli.*h*wɑ(:)p], belly whopper, belly buster ['beli.bʌstər]。这些说法的前边加上 do a，与 do a belly flop 的意思相同。*Paul tried to do a back flip but it ended up as a beautiful belly flop.* 保罗本来想做向后空翻，结果却闹了个漂亮的腹部入水。另外，belly flop, belly whop 本身就可以作为动词使用。*Several small children were belly flopping off the side of the pool.* 有几个小孩子从游泳池的边上往下跳，腹部先入水。◇ a dive onto *one's* stomach

flunk

flunk ['flʌŋk] [话] **考试或课程分数不及格** → FLUNK out (of *school*)

flunk out (of *school*) [.flʌŋ'kaut] [话] **因成绩不佳退学** flunk 相当于 fail，是轻松的学生用语。如果只是 flunk 的话，为"某次考试或某种课程分数不及格"，还达不到"退学"的程度。*A: Did you pass the math test? B: No, I flunked.* 甲：你通过数学考试了吗？乙：没有，我不及格。也当作及物动词使用。*I flunked my math test.* 我数学考试没有及格。但是，在这个 flunk 的后边加上 out 构成习用语 flunk out 之后，意思就变成了"由于平均分数达不到规定的标准而给与退学处分"了。也就是说，flunk out 原是 flunk out of *school* 的缩略，按最初的构思，这一表达法的意思是"不合学校的格"。*Eight of my classmates flunked out last semester.* 在上个学期，我班有八个同学因成绩不佳而受到退学处分。*You'd better study harder or you may flunk out of school.* 你最好多用点功，否则会被勒令退学的。*Donwit flunked out of Stanford.* 唐维特因成绩不佳，被斯坦福大学勒令退学了。school 一词包括各种类型的学校。航空学校的学生一般使用 wash out 而不使用 flunk out。*George washed out of flight school because he couldn't master navigation.* 乔治由于未能掌握航空学，从航空学校退学了。另外，虽然用例很少，但 flunk 也可作为名词使用,表示"名落孙山"、"不合格"的意思。*I got a flunk in English lit.* 我的英国文学课程没有及格。◇ be expelled (from *school*) (for not performing satisfactorily)

fly

a fly in the ointment [ə 'flaɪənðɪ 'ɔɪntmənt] [口] **美中不足** 这一表达法源出《圣经·旧约》中《传道书》(Ecclesiastes) 第 10 章 1 节: Dead flies cause the ointment of the apothecary to send forth a stinking savour: so doth a little folly him that is in reputation for wisdom and honor. (死苍蝇使作香的膏油发出臭气。这样一点愚昧也能败坏智慧和尊荣。) 现在, ointment 是"软膏"的意思。在古时,此词指女子化妆以及王公贵族涂发用的、加入高级香料的油。本条习用语直译为"进入高级香料油的一头苍蝇"。*His offer sounds too good to be true. There must be a fly in the ointment somewhere.* 他提出的条件太好了,简直达到令人无法相信的程度。这里面肯定有些蹊跷啊。a fly 可采取 the fly, the only fly, one fly 等种种不同的形式。*Tom is the fly in the ointment of every party we have. He just can't control himself once he starts drinking.* 我们每次开社交晚会,都被汤姆搞糟了。他一旦拿起酒杯,就再也控制不住自己了。*That house is just what we have been looking for. There's only one fly in the ointment—we can't afford it.* 那所房子正合我们的意。只有一点美中不足,那就是我们买不起。在说俏皮话时,常使用这一表达法。*I love living near the seashore. The only fly in the ointment is having to commute so far to work.* 我喜欢住在海滨,唯一的缺点是上班太远。fly 或 ointment 的前边可以加形容词。*I'm a night owl and my husband is an early riser, but once we adjusted to each other's habits, that became only a small fly in our matrimonial ointment.* 我是个夜游神,我的丈夫喜欢早起早睡,但是,在我们相互适应各自的习惯以后,象这样的事情只不过是我们婚姻中一点小小的美中不足罢了。◇ a drawback

straighten up and fly right → STRAIGHTEN

flying

get off to a flying start → START

food

rabbit food ['ræbət ˌfuːd] [话] **生菜** 字面意义是"兔子的食物",可以按照字面意义使用。此外,作为戏谑语或小儿语,又指人吃的"生菜",如白菜、萝卜、黄瓜等。*You should eat lots of rabbit food. It's very good for your health.* 你应该多吃生菜,这对你的健康大有好处。◇ raw vegetables

fool

a fool [ə ˌfu(ː)l] [口] **混蛋** fool 有"笨人"、"笨蛋"、"傻子"、"蠢货"之类的意思,但是,有一点必须认识清楚:在汉语中,这些词可用于轻松的、戏谑的甚至亲昵的场合,说者语调不重,听者并不在意。在英语中,fool 一词却是十分严重的,一般使用的时候,说者心里充满轻蔑对方的感情。因此,不是真正恼火的时候,绝对不要说 You fool. 或者 You're a fool. 即使是亲密的朋友,你说上这样一句话也会引起吵架,千万要注意。*That man once called me a fool. I can never forgive him for that.* 那个人有一次管我叫混蛋。我一辈子也不会饶恕他。另外,在英语中,比 fool 语调轻的表示"笨蛋"、"傻瓜"之类的词简直多的不可胜数,我们在 a DUMBHEAD 条目中列举一些主要的词,请读者查阅。◇ a(n incorrigibly) stupid person

make a fool (out) of *someone* [ˌmeɪkə 'fuːl(aud)əv～] [口] **愚弄某人** → make a MONKEY (out) of *someone*

be nobody's fool [ˌnoubɑdiz 'fuːl] [口] **精明** 直译是"对于任何人都不是傻子",亦即"任何人都不能拿他当傻瓜"。在劝告别人"不要轻视对手"或者提醒别人"那家伙不好对付"的时候,常常使用这一表达法。*You won't trick him that easily. He may be fat and greedy, but he's nobody's fool.* 他可不是容易欺骗的。别看他又肥胖又贪婪,他这个人精得很,谁也斗不了。如此例所示,多在与外观、初步印象作对比时使用。*I'm afraid he's stolen a march on us. I told you he was nobody's fool.* 我看,他大概比咱们先下手啦。我跟你说过,他的心眼儿多。*He insisted on seeing the money before he was willing to talk. It was easy to see that he was nobody's fool.* 他坚持说,他不先见到钱是不愿意谈判的。一眼就可以看出,他是个很精明的人。◇ be very shrewd

fool's

live in a fool's paradise → PARADISE

fools

not suffer fools gladly [nɑt ˌsʌfər ˌfuːlz ˈglædli] [口] **不甘心忍耐愚妄的人[言行]** suffer ~ gladly 是"甘心忍耐……"的意思。在《圣经·新约》中《保罗达哥林多人后书》(Second Corinthians) 第 11 章 19 节有这样一句话: For you suffer fools gladly, seeing you yourselves are wise. (你们既是精明人,就能甘心忍耐愚妄人。) 这话带有一点讽刺的味道。本条的表达法即来源于此。有时用肯定式,表示"忍耐"的意思,如: *A priest must learn to be tolerant and always suffer fools gladly.* 当神父的人必须学会宽容和永远甘心忍耐愚妄的人。但是现在,特别是在会话中,使用否定式或与否定式相等的句法占绝对的多数。在谈到那些对言行轻率者持非常严厉态度的人们时使用。*You'd better be sure that you're right before you give the boss an answer. He doesn't suffer fools gladly.* 在你回答老板的问题的时候,你先考虑好绝对有把握再跟他说。他不甘心忍耐愚妄的言论。*My father is not one to suffer fools gladly.* 我父亲不是一个甘心忍耐愚妄言行的人。*There are few people who are able to suffer fools like Sam Jones gladly.* 很少有人能象萨姆·琼斯那样甘心忍耐愚妄的人。不仅在会话中,在小说里描写人物性格时,也常使用这一表达法。◇ be impatient with people who behave [talk] foolishly [unthinkingly]

foot

cut *one's* **foot** [ˌkʌt ~ ˈfu(ː)t] [话] **一脚踩到粪上** 字面意义是"划破了脚",当然可以按照这一意义使用,如说: *I cut my foot on a piece of glass.* 我的一只脚被玻璃划破了。此外,常常用以表示"由于不小心,一下子踩到(狗、猫等的)粪上了"的意思。这是一个委婉的表达法。在促使人加小心的时候,常说: *Be careful. Don't cut your foot.* 小心点啊! 别踩到粪上。在指明"某种动物的粪"时,用前置词 on ~继续。*I cut my foot on a cow pie.* 我踩到牛粪上啦。◇ step in that [some] (cow, horse, etc.) dung

get off on the right foot (with *someone* [*something*]) [geˌdɔ(ː)fɔnðə raɪt ˈfu(ː)t] [口] **开门红** → get off on the wrong FOOT (with *someone* [*something*])

get off on the wrong foot (with *someone* [*something*]) [geˌdɔ(ː)f ɔnðəˈrɔːŋ ˈfu(ː)t] [口] **出师不利** off 与 on 连用,乍看起来有点奇怪。但这种用法并不罕见,与 get off on the third floor (在三楼下电梯), get off on the wrong side (从相反的一侧下来)的形式相同。不过,本条的 get off 并不是"下来"而是"出发"的意思。on the wrong foot 是"弄错了脚"。军队或军乐队在行进时必须由左脚起步。本条习用语原来的意思是:"弄错了脚,由右脚起步了"。一旦由 wrong foot 出发,就很难改正步调,而且令人看起来十分可笑。用作比喻,则表示"在开始一件新的事情的时候,由于方法错误,给人以不良的印象"的意思。*We got off on the wrong foot when we tried to market this product ourselves instead of using an established distributor.* 由于我们不通过已有的批发公司,而试图自己推销这种产品,结果出师十分不利。这句英语如果使用 ~with *something* 的形式,那就成为 *We got off on the wrong foot with this product by trying to market it ourselves ~.* 可以用 start off 代替 get off, 而说 start off on the wrong foot。*You should wear a coat and tie on your first day at work. You don't want to start off on the wrong foot.* 你头一天上班,应该

穿上衣，结领带。你总不愿意出师不利吧。有时也可以听到表示相反意思的说法 get [start] off on the right foot (with *someone* [*something*])。当然，这里的 right foot 不是"右脚"，而是"正确的脚步"。 *My having read Professor Rodney's new book got me off on the right foot with him.* 由于我读过了罗德尼教授的新著作，我与这位教授的关系很顺利地开始了。◇ make a bad [unpropitious] start / make a bad first impression

have one foot in the grave [hæv ˌwʌnˌfutnðə ˈgreɪv] [话] **一只脚在坟墓里** 即汉语俗语"土埋半截了"。*Me marry an old man like that? You must be joking. He's already got one foot in the grave.* 叫我跟那样一个老头子结婚？你一定是在开玩笑吧。他都已经土埋半截子啦。如这一例句所示，这一表达法是强调年纪大，多少带有轻蔑和嘲笑的意味。不过，在英语中，它的使用范围要比汉语译文"一只脚在坟墓里"或"土埋半截了"更宽广一些。例如：*I knew that Martha had been very ill, but it was a shock to see her looking as if she already had one foot in the grave.* 我知道马莎病情很重，但是看到她那奄奄一息的样子，不免大为震惊。 *Few of the soldiers I fought with seemed to have much fear of death. They lived from day to day as if aware that they already had one foot in the grave.* 跟我一道作战的士兵们，似乎极少有非常怕死的人。他们虽然一天一天地活下去，但好象已经意识到不知什么时候就会牺牲的。这就是说，在英语中不仅指老人而言，也可以应用于面临死亡的病人或青年人，范围比较广。另有一个形式是 with one foot in the grave，意思是"处于不知什么时候会死的状态"。 *The chronic illness I had suffered since childhood made me feel that I was going through life with one foot in the grave.* 我从小的时候得了一种慢性病，使我感到自己在整个一生中始终处于不知几时会死去的状态。◇ be close to death

~ my foot! [~ ˈmaɪ ˈfuːt] [话] **算个屁！** 怎么会产生这样一个表达法，不大了解。有人说源出表示惊讶的成语 My God! 是这一成语的变形。这一说法有道理。当然，与"我的脚"毫无关系。在反驳对方的话时使用，常常把对方的用语放在 my foot 的前边。 *A: They say Dick is a good public speaker. B: Good my foot! He mumbles so badly you can't half understand what he's saying.* 甲：听人家说，迪克是一位很好的演说家。乙：好个屁！他嘴里咕噜咕噜地说些什么，你连一半也听不清。 *A: Jim should be finished with his homework by now. B: Finished my foot! He hasn't even started!* 甲：现在，吉姆一定完成了家庭作业。乙：完成个屁！他还没动手哪。 *A: It'll take five hundred thousand dollars to build a house like that. B: Five hundred thousand dollars my foot! It'll take at least a million.* 甲：盖那样一所房子得五十万美元。乙：五十万美元算个屁！至少得一百万美元。有时说 ~ my eye! ◇ Good [Finished, etc.]? Far from it.

put *one's* **best foot forward** [ˌput ~ ˌbest ˌfut ˈfɔːrwərd] [口] **想尽量给人好印象** 字面意义是："把最好的脚伸到前边"。这是至少从莎士比亚时代就开始流传的古老的表达法。 *Since it was my first date with Sally, I put my best foot forward by wearing my only shirt without a hole in it.* 因为那是我与萨莉的第一次约会，所以我穿上自己唯一一件没有窟窿的衬衣，想尽量给她一个好印象。 *You'd better buy a new suit. You'll want to put your best foot forward at your job interview next week.* 你最好买一套新衣服吧。下个星期就业面谈的时候，你一定想要给人一个最好的印象呀。以这一表达法为模式，有时带几分开玩笑的口吻说 put *one's* worst foot forward(给人最坏的印象)。 *Jack put his worst foot forward by arriving at the dinner party drunk.* 杰克醉醺醺地来到宴会席上，给人留下了极坏的印象。有时作"拚命干"或"赶紧走"解，不过使用频率很低。 *We'll have to put our best foot forward if* *we are to finish this work on time.* 如果我们要按期完成这个工作,我们就必须拚命干。*If we don't put our best foot forward we'll miss the train.* 如果咱们不赶紧走,就赶不上火车啦。另外,在英国不使用“给予好印象”的意义,而使用”竭尽全力”的意义,请读者注意。但与美国口语相同,也使用“拚命干”或“赶紧走”的意义。◇ try hard to make a good impression

put *one's* **foot down** [ˌput ~ ˈfutˌdaun] [口] **采取坚决态度** 最初的构思是:“把脚向下一跺,表示坚强的意志”。“在一定的程度上倾听对方讲话,允许对方自由行动,但超过这一限度就要严格取缔”的场合使用这一表达法。主语仅限于老师、父母等长辈的人。*The boss never complained about our being a little late for work, but when some began showing up at ten o'clock he put his foot down.* 我们上班迟到几分钟,老板从来不说什么,但是,当有人到十点钟才来上班的时候,他采取了坚决的态度。下面的例句是一位父亲的谈话。由于他的儿子学习成绩不大好,他表示了让步:“进不了一流大学也没办法,有个大学就行啦。”可是他的儿子听了父亲的话,更加放任自流。父亲终于忍无可忍,似乎大发脾气了。*When my boy began to talk about not wanting to go to college, I had to put my foot down.* 当我的儿子开始讲他不想上大学的时候,我不得不表示坚决的态度了。◇ adopt a firm attitude

put *one's* **foot in it** [ˌput ~ ˈfu(ː)dɪnɪt][口] **说错话[做错事]** → put *one's* FOOT in *one's* mouth

put *one's* **foot in** *one's* **mouth** [ˌput ~ ˈfutn ~ˌmauθ] [口] **讲话不得体** 直译是“把自己的一只脚放到自己的嘴里”。这一表达法最初的构思就是:“一个人不留神到把脚放到嘴里的程度,他说起话来当然是不加思索,随便云云,很难得体”。用汉语俗语来说,这种人常“说走了嘴”。*You put your foot in your mouth when you told Mr. Crank you didn't trust Yankees. Didn't you know that he was born and raised in New York?* 你对克兰克先生说你不信任北方佬,这话可说走了嘴。你不知道他是在纽约出生和长大的吗? *The defendant might have gone free if he hadn't put his foot in his mouth by mentioning that the murdered man owed him a lot of money.* 被告如果不是走了嘴,说他曾借给被谋杀的人一大笔钱,他可能被无罪释放了。另有一个表达法 put *one's* foot in it 常常与 put *one's* foot in *one's* mouth 发生混淆,因为人们认为后者是用 *one's* mouth 取代了 it (按:it 原指猫、狗、牛等动物的粪,put *one's* foot in it 意为“一只脚踩到粪上”,即踩到不合适的地方)。事实上,不但外国的英语词典,就连美国当前出版的词典,大多都认为这两个习用语完全相同。然而,对这两个习用语必须加以区别,而且美国人在实际使用时也是有所区别的。首先,put *one's* foot in *one's* mouth 只能用于“说错话”的场合,而 put *one's* foot in it 除用于“说错话”的场合外,也可以用于“做错事”的场合,也就是说,“说”和“做”均可使用,范围比较广。我们先举一个“说”的例子:*Every time she opens her mouth she puts her foot in it.* 她一张嘴就说错话。这是美国人常说的一句话,整个句子可以当作定型的表达法,即“她好信口开河”。下面再举两个“做”的例子:*Jack's really put his foot in it this time. He mistakenly mailed a letter to one of his old girl friends in an envelope addressed to his wife.* 杰克这回可真捅大娄子啦。他把给过去的一个女朋友写的信,错装在写有他老婆的名字和地址的信封里邮走了。这位男士可能是在旅行中干下了如此的蠢事。*Foonder has put his foot in it again. He delivered the hush money to the head of the wrong faction.* 封德又干了一件错事。他竟把用于封嘴的贿赂钱送交另一个派系的头头了。关于这两个习用语的不同,还有一点值得注意,这就是二者的意味具有细微的差别。例如说 He put his foot in his mouth. 意思是“他说错了话”,结果可能只是“embarrassing (使人难堪)”一下而已,但也可能“惹起什么麻烦”。至于 He put his foot in it. 就不同了。它的意思是"说错话"或"做错事",其中含有结果必然是要"惹起麻烦"的意味。顺便介绍一个有关的表达法: have [get, suffer from] foot-in-mouth disease。foot-in-mouth disease 是模仿 hoof-and-mouth disease (口蹄疫,牛、羊等有蹄类动物感染的一种病)而构成的一个戏谑的表达法,意思是"总爱信口开河的病症"。中国有人译作"拙语症",容易误解为"嘴笨"。日本有人译为"舌祸病",似乎过于严重。*Something's wrong with me tonight. I seem to be suffering from foot-in-mouth disease.* 今天晚上我不知怎么啦,一说话就走嘴。◇ make a faux pas / say the wrong thing / blunder

put *one's* **worst foot forward** [.put ~ .wə(:)rst .fut 'fɔːrwərd] [话] **给人最坏的印象** → put *one's* best FOOT forward

the shoe is on the other foot → SHOE

wait on *someone* **hand and foot** → HAND

foot-in-mouth

foot-in-mouth disease [.futn'mauθ də .ziːz] [话] **说话惹事病** → put *one's* FOOT in *one's* mouth

footprints

follow *someone's* **footprints** [.fɑ(:)lə ~ 'fut.prɪnts] [口] **沿着某人的足迹(前进)** → follow in *someone's* FOOTSTEPS

footsie

play footsie (with *someone*) [.pleɪ 'futsi] [话] **桌下碰脚调情** footsie 是 foot (脚)的爱称,类似汉语的"脚鸭儿"。例如母亲对幼小的孩子说: *Let's wash your footsies now.* 来,洗洗你的小鸭鸭。play 与 play house (儿童"玩家家"游戏)中的 play 相同。这一表达法直译为"碰脚游戏",颇有儿童玩耍的意味。碰脚的场所是桌子底下或其他有隐蔽的地方,一般是轻轻接触脚尖,相互调情。采取这种行动的往往是一对情人或者新婚夫妇。 *I don't think Mr. and Mrs. Pedwin were sending signals to each other under the card table last night. They were probably just playing footsie.* 我不认为佩德温夫妇昨天夜里是在牌桌底下互相递暗号。他们大概只是小两口碰脚调情。有时是用这一动作轻轻试探异性的心情。*John wasn't brave enough to hold hands with Mary, so he just played footsie with her under the tree.* 约翰没有足够的勇气去握玛丽的手,于是他在大树底下用脚尖碰了一下玛丽的脚尖。也可以用复数形式 footsies。*I think I should warn you, your date was trying to play footsies with me in the theater.* 我觉得应该叫你知道,你那个约会对象在电影院里试图跟我调情哪。作为比喻,用以表示"悄悄来往"或"不即不离"的意思。多用于双方都为了自身利益或搜集情报而试探着保持一定程度的关系的场合。*China is upset over the way many countries continue to play footsie with the Taiwan regime.* 中国对许多国家继续与台湾政权保持接触的作法感到不快。*When you play footsie with the Mafia, you are playing with fire.* 你与黑手党偷偷勾搭,那是在玩火啊。在男女关系方面,也可以用"悄悄来往"这一比喻意义,但在这一场合,仍旧残存着本来的意义,有强烈的"调情"的味道。*Marian Busty often plays footsie with other men when her husband is away on business.* 玛丽安·巴斯蒂在她的丈夫出差的时候,常与其他的男人偷偷地幽会。另外,有时把 footsie 拼写为 footsy。◇ playfully [casually] rub feet / (casually) maintain contacts / (casually) go out

footsteps

follow *someone's* **footsteps** [.fɑ(:)lə ~ 'fut.steps] [口] **顺着某人的脚步声走去** → follow in *someone's* FOOTSTEPS

follow in *someone's* **footsteps** [.fɑ(:)loɪn ~ 'fut.steps] [口] **继承老一辈的衣钵** 字面意义是"自己的脚沿着某人留下的脚印一步一步地走过去"。footsteps 一般指"脚步声"("脚印"是 footprints),但在这里是"足迹"的意思。这一表达法多半用于自己选择与父祖相同的职业的场合,但在学习各行各业的老前辈而决定走他们的道路时也同样可以使用。

Frank decided to follow in his father's footsteps and become a doctor. 弗兰克决定继承父亲的衣钵当医生。*Tom followed in his uncle's footsteps and joined the navy.* 汤姆走他叔父的道路，参加了海军。*Few people can ever hope to follow in Picasso's footsteps.* 很少有人能望毕加索的项背。因为这一表达法基本上具有"走同一人生道路"的意味，所以也可能用以述说反面的情况。*Jake is often in trouble with the police. I'm afraid he is following in his father's footsteps.* 杰克经常给警察局添麻烦。这大概是继承乃父的衣钵吧。顺便提一下，实际上的"踏着某人的足迹"，在英语中的一般说法为 follow *someone's* footprints。*I followed their footprints [tracks] in the snow.* 我踏着他们在雪上的足迹向前走去。同一意义的表达法有 follow *someone's* footsteps, 但这一表达法多用于表示"顺着某人的脚步声走去"。这两个表达法都不加 in。◇ follow the same profession [path] as *someone*

forest

can't see the forest for the trees [ˌkæ(:)nt ˌsi(:)ðəˈfɔ(:)rəst fərðəˈtri:z] [口] **只见树木不见森林** → can't see the WOODS for the trees

forever

forever [fəˈrevər] [口] **老是……** → every TIME *one* turns around

form

a racing form [ə ˈreɪsɪŋ ˌfɔ(:)rm] [口] **赛马新闻** 一般来说，form 是"(申请书等的)格式"的意思。这里指"赛马的成绩"以及刊登成绩单的小报，亦即"赛马新闻"。请读者注意，美国人不用 a racing newspaper 之类的字样。*Almost everyone on the train last Saturday was buried in a racing form.* 在上个星期六，火车上几乎人人都埋头阅读赛马新闻。在美国，另外有一种叫做 a scratch sheet 的东西，它主要刊登当天 scratched horses (退出比赛的马) 的消息，还报导 jockey (骑手)，handicaps (给强马的不利条件)，odds (预计分红率)等的最新消息，可以称为《参赛马快报》。在赛马场及其附近的小摊上出售 (→ SCRATCH *a horse*<from the race>)。又称 a dope sheet。*Have you got today's scratch sheet?* 你有今天的参赛马快报吗？◇ a newspaper dealing with (horse) racing

fort

hold the fort [ˌhouldðə ˈfɔ(:)rt] [话] **坚守岗位** 字面意义是"守住堡垒"。实际上也有按字面意义使用的情况，如：*The American soldiers had difficulty holding the fort against the Indian attack.* 当印第安人进攻的时候，美国兵勉勉强强守住了堡垒。一般使用比喻的意义，例如：*Don't worry about the office while you are on vacation, boss. Harry and I will stay here and hold the fort.* 老板，你去休假，公司的事情不用担心。我和哈里留在这里照料一切。*My wife expects me to stay home and hold the fort while she goes out and plays tennis with her friends every Sunday.* 每星期日，我的妻子与朋友出去打网球，她希望我留在家里照料一切。在以上的两个例句中，都是"坚守岗位"的意思。这一表达法使用此义的情况最多。但也用于表示"坚持立场"的场合，例如：*The power companies are having difficulty holding the fort against the criticisms of anti-nuclear activists.* 在反核动力活动家的指责之下，电力公司勉勉强强坚持住自己的立场。◇ maintain operations / defend *one's* position

fortune

marry a fortune [ˌmæriə ˈfɔ(:)rtʃən] [口] **跟有钱的女人结婚** 古时，fortune 一词除"大量财产"的意义外，还有"有钱的女人(或富翁的女儿)"的意思。现在，只能在本条的表达法中见到这一意义的遗痕。本条习用语的基本意义是"跟有钱的女人结婚"，但根据文章的前后关系，常有"为了财产而结婚"即 marry for MONEY 的意味。比如说 Harry married a fortune. 这句话，一般都解释为 Harry married a rich woman. (哈里娶了一个有钱的女人。) 但是根据文章的前后关系，也可能是这样的意思：Harry married a woman for her money.（哈里贪图女人的财产而同她结了婚。）*I absolutely refuse to marry a fortune.* 我决不与有钱的女人结婚。*Hubert finally succeeded in marrying a fortune.* 休伯特终于达到了与有钱的女人结婚的目的。另外，也有时用于表示"与有钱的人结婚"（不单指女人）的意思，如说：*She married a fortune.* 她嫁给一个财主了。有人说，根据语源，这种用法是错误的。然而，在实际的日常会话中，如此使用的人却屡见不鲜。◇ marry a rich woman

forty

grab forty winks → WINKS

forty-eleven

forty-eleven [ˈfɔ(ː)rdiəˈlevən] [话] **数不过来那么多** 当然，forty-eleven 这样的数字是不存在的。这一表达法的来源是：儿童们在数数儿的时候往往数错，比如应该说 forty-nine, fifty, fifty-one, fifty-two 的时候，他们说成了 forty-nine, forty-ten, forty-eleven, forty-twelve。这一表达法不是指的实际数字，而是强调在心理上感到"怎么那么多"。它意味着从儿童的观点来看"多得数不过来"。原来的构思就是以五十为上限，所以这一表达法仅能用于以十为单位的数字，不能用于以百为单位的数字。这里的"多"，根据上下文，当然会有"许多回"、"许多个"、"许多人"的意思。儿童们经常使用这一表达法。例如：*I've told you forty-eleven times to stop that!* 不要干那个，我已经跟你说过许多回啦！*I can't play today. The teacher gave us forty-eleven problems for homework.* 今天我不能玩啦。老师给我们留了许多回家做的题目。成年人在强调一件事情的时候，也使用这一表达法。*How do you expect me to get this work done with forty-eleven different people trying to give me advice?* 在形形色色的人七嘴八舌地指挥下，你怎么能够期望我完成这项工作呢？有时用 fifty-eleven，意思一样。*Jane must have at least fifty-eleven boy friends.* 简的男朋友多得数不清。也可以说 forty-eleventh 或者 fifty-eleventh，作为序数词使用。*For the forty-eleventh time, stop pestering me!* 我说八百六十次啦，你不要缠着我！◇ I don't know how many / so many

foul

by fair means or foul [ˌbaɪ ˈfeːr ˈmiːnzər ˈfaul] [口] **不择一切手段** → by HOOK or crook

four-bagger

a four-bagger [ə ˈfo(ː)rˈbæːgər] [话] **本垒打** bag 是棒球用语，为 base（垒）的轻松说法。"四垒打"亦即"本垒打"，英语的正式名称是 a home run，也叫做 a homer。*Lewis had a four-bagger his last time up.* 在上次的击球员区，刘易斯打了个本垒打。顺便提一下："三垒打"为 a three-bagger，"二垒打"为 a two-bagger，正式名称分别为 a three-base hit, a two-base hit。但一般常用的是 a triple, a double。*Ned hit a three-bagger to left field.* 内德向左外场击了个三垒打。*That's Alou's second two-bagger in this game.* 在此次比赛中，那是阿鲁的第二次二垒打了。"一垒打"称 a single，也可以叫做 a one-bagger 或者 a one-base hit，不知道为什么，人们不大使用后两个说法。*The batter rapped out a sharp single down the third-base line.* 击球员向三垒线打了一个狠球。◇ a home run

four-eyes

a four-eyes [ə ˈfo(ː)ˌraɪz] [俗] **戴眼镜的人** 戏谑语，通常含有轻蔑的意思。汉语俗称"四眼儿"，与英语的构思巧合。虽然是复数形式，但由于指的是一个人，所以在语法上作单数处理。*We don't need a four-eyes on our team.* 我们队不需要一个四眼儿。常常用于称呼他人。*Hey, here comes old four-eyes.* 喂，那个戴眼镜的又来啦。*Hey, watch who you're running into, four-eyes.* 喂，四眼儿，你别瞎撞呀，看着点儿！◇ a person who wears glasses / a glasses-wearer

four-letter

a four-letter word → WORD

fowl

be neither fish nor fowl → FISH

fox

crazy like a fox [ˌkreɪzi laɪkə ˈfɑːks] **非常狡猾** 直译是"象狐狸一样疯狂"。其实,这是另一个成语 (as) sly as a FOX (象狐狸一样狡猾) 的翻版。只在否定对方的话的时候使用。如果对方说某某人 crazy, 你就接着这个茬回答说 Crazy like a fox. 意思是:"哪里是疯狂,简直象狐狸一样狡猾"。实际对话方式如下: *A: Old Mr. Higgins is crazy—forever changing his mind like that. B: Yeah, crazy like a fox. He figures that if he changes his story often enough, we'll finally give up.* 甲:希金斯老先生发疯啦,一会儿变一个主意。乙:哼,哪里是发疯,他是象狐狸一样狡猾呀。他以为如果多编一些瞎话,咱们最后就会死了这条心。有时作 (as) crazy as a fox。◇ (No,) *someone* is far from (being) crazy.

(as) sly as a fox [əzˈslaɪ əzə ˈfɑ(ː)ks] [口] **象狐狸一样狡猾** 美国人对狐狸的印象与我们中国人相同,他们常把狡猾的、必须提防的人比做狐狸。*Be careful about doing business with Mr. Reddy. He's as sly as a fox.* 跟雷迪先生做生意可要多加小心。他是一个象狐狸一样狡猾的人。主语如果是复数,fox 当然也要改作 foxes。*Their spies are sly as foxes. Every time we think we have one trapped, he slips through our fingers.* 他们的间谍象狐狸一样狡猾。每次我们以为已经抓住一个的时候,他都从我们的指缝间溜掉了。◇ very cunning

ˈfraidy

a ˈfraidy cat → CAT

frail

a frail [ə ˈfreɪl] [俗] **妞儿** frail 一般当作形容词使用,意为"脆弱的"、"身体虚弱的"。在这里变为名词,指"软弱的性"即"女性"。男性用语,指女郎、少妇。一种轻视女性的说法。*Good-looking frails are a dime a dozen in this town.* 在这个城镇里,好看的妞儿拿鞭子赶。*Are you squiring a frail to the party tonight?* 今天的社交晚会,你带个妞儿去吗? ◇ a girl / a (young) woman

freak

an acid freak [ə ˈnæ(ː)səd ˌfri(ː)k] [话] **LSD 的常用者** → an acid HEAD

free

be (as) free as a bird → BIRD

give *someone* a free hand → HAND

have a free hand [ˌhævə ˌfriː ˈhæːnd] [口] **拥有自行决定权** → give *someone* a free HAND

make free with (*someone's*) *something* [ˌmeɪkˈfriː wɪð ～] [话] **擅自使用(他人的东西)** make free 是"随意地"。本条习用语的意思是"把别人的东西当作自己的东西一样随意地处理",也可能是用,也可能是借,也可能是拿走永不归还。不论哪一种情况,对他人来说,总是一种讨厌的、捣乱的行为。如以下的例句所示,这一表达法可以表示多方面的意义。*I'm tired of your brother's coming here and making free with my clothes.* 你弟弟到这儿来随便穿我的衣服,我真讨厌极啦。*You'd better lock your personal effects in your desk before you leave. There are some people around here who are quick to make free with other people's things.* 你在下班以前,最好是把私人物品锁到桌子抽屉里。这里有几个人总爱擅自动用别人的东西。*I'll thank you not to make so free with the use of my secretary.* 你别那样随意使用我的秘书好不好呀? 在"任意吃喝"的场合也可以使用这一表达法。*Our guests certainly made free with the liquor last night, didn't they.* 昨天晚上客人们在我家里喝酒,可真喝个够啊。有时可以采取 make free with (*someone's*) *someone* 的形式,应用于"人"。 *No sooner had I become somewhat friendly with my next-door neighbor, than she began to make free with our maid, asking her to run errands almost every day.* 我跟邻居的太太刚刚有点来往,她就开始擅

自支使我的女仆，几乎每天都叫女仆去替她跑腿。在应用于男女间的关系时，则具有“挑逗”、“调戏”、甚至“奸淫”的意味。*We frequently had fights with the boys from the neighboring village because they often came over and tried to make free with our girls.* 我们经常跟邻村的小伙子们打架，因为他们总来逗弄我们村的姑娘。*Soldiers have traditionally tended to make free with the women of conquered nations.* 自古以来就有一种风气，士兵总是奸淫被征服国家的妇女。◇ use [borrow, take] (*someone's*) *something* freely

freebie

a freebie [ə ˌfri(ː)bi] [话] **免费的东西** 比较新的表达法。过去有 freebee, freeby, freebe 等拼写法，但最近已经逐渐定型，大多采用 freebie。free 意为“免费的”，但 -bie [-bee, -by, -be]的来源不详。恐怕只是为了合辙押韵而加上的，别无它义。*You don't have to pay me for these tickets. They're freebies.* 这几张票你不用给我钱，这是免费赠送的。如此例所示，这一表达法原来专指剧院或体育比赛的免费招待券，现在使用范围扩大了，泛指一切本来收费但是免费赠送的东西。例如：*Don't thank me for the meal. It was a freebie. The restaurant owner is a friend of mine.* 你用不着为这顿饭向我道谢，我没花钱，餐厅的主人是我的朋友。这里讲的是“白吃饭”。*There is a sale on these pens now. If you buy one, the second is a freebie.* 现在甩卖这种自来水笔，买一送一。这里讲的是“白送商品”。也可以采取 a freebie *something* 的形式，即作为修饰名词的定语。*You want to go to the movies tonight? I've got a couple of freebie tickets.* 今天晚上你愿意去看电影吗？我有两张免费招待券。◇ (a) free (*something*)

freeloader

a freeloader [ə ˈfriːˌloudər] [话] **专占便宜的人** 把此词分解开来，则 free 是“不花钱”，load 是“(把饮食物往身体内)装进去”。因此，这一表达法原来专指“白吃白喝的人”，例如：*That guy's a born freeloader. He never offers to pay for a meal.* 那个家伙天生就是讨吃鬼，他吃饭从来不付钱。现在使用范围扩大，除指“白吃白喝的人”以外，泛指一切不出钱白占便宜的人们。*I don't care if he is your brother, he's a freeloader. It's about time he moved out of our house and started taking care of himself.* 我不管他是不是你的弟弟，反正他是一个净白占便宜的人。现在他该从咱们家搬出去，自己照顾自己去啦。这大概是妻子对丈夫讲的话，说的是丈夫的弟弟既不付饭钱，也不付房钱，在哥哥家里当食客，一切都由兄嫂照顾。*Those freeloaders are always wanting to use our house for their parties. Tell them to find someplace else for a change.* 那些专占便宜的人总愿意利用咱们家的房子举办社交晚会。你告诉他们换个地方去搞吧。如这一例句所示，专门利用他人房屋的也叫做 freeloader，因为这是“不花钱使用”。有一个动词 freeload，但与 freeloader 相比，使用频率低得多。*You've freeloaded your last meal off me. From now on you'll bring your own money, or starve.* 你白吃我的饭，这是最后的一顿啦。从今以后，你来吃饭就得掏钱，要不你就饿着。不但有动词，而且有动名词。*I'm sick and tired of his freeloading.* 我对他的白吃白拿简直厌烦透啦。◇ a(n) habitual cadger

freeway

a freeway [ə ˈfriːˌweɪ] [口] **高速公路** → a HIGHWAY

French

Excuse my French. [ɪkˌskjuːz ˌmaɪ ˈfre(ː)ntʃ] [话] **我说句粗鲁的话，对不起。** → Pardon my FRENCH.

Pardon my French. [ˌpɑ(ː)rdnˌmaɪ ˈfre(ː)ntʃ] [话] **请原谅我说句粗鲁的话。** 字面意义是“我的法语说得不好，请原谅”。但是这里的 French 一般指人们忌讳的字眼，即所谓的 a four-letter WORD(→)。本条习用语不是对自己的法语表达能力表示谦逊，而是在说粗俗下流话时进行道歉。*Pardon my French, Mary, but I don't give a damn what your brother thinks.* 请原谅我说句粗鲁话，玛丽，你哥哥怎么想，我只当作一个屁。在这句话里，damn (不顶个屁)就是四字母的粗俗下流词(four-letter word)。*Then he said—pardon my French—"Up you," and walked out.* 然后他说——请原谅我说句粗鲁话——"见鬼去吧，"就走出去了。pardon 也可以换成 excuse。*Where the hell have you been for crissake? —Excuse my French, ladies.* 你究竟到什么鬼地方瞎逛荡去啦？请原谅我说了句粗鲁话，女士们。这句话里的粗俗下流的字眼是 hell 和 crissake (→ for Pete's SAKE)。说话的背景是：同伴来得太迟了，说话者十分恼火，忍不住在女人们面前骂街了。 ◇ Pardon the (bad [vulgar]) language.

fresh

(as) fresh as a daisy → DAISY

Freudian

a Freudian slip → SLIP

Friday

a girl Friday [ə 'gəːrl 'fraɪdi] [口] **得力女助手** 字面意义是"女子星期五"。Friday 是著名小说《鲁宾逊飘流记》(*Robinson Crusoe*) 中出现的忠实的仆人。本条的表达法即来源于此。原来只说 a man Friday (男子星期五)，现在多用 a girl Friday。这种助手不仅协助上级处理公务，而且兼顾私人生活，具有 devoted (献身的)精神。*You can't possibly handle all the details yourself. What you need is a good girl Friday.* 你连一切杂事都亲自处理，这是力所不及的。你需要有一个得力的女助手啊。*This is Sally, my girl Friday. This office couldn't function without her.* 这位是萨莉，我的得力女助手。这个办事处如果没有她，就运转不了啦。下面举个 a man Friday 的例句。 *He started as a mere floor sweeper, but within ten years he had risen to the position of man Friday to the president.* 他最初只不过是一个扫地的勤杂工，但是不到十年的功夫，他已经爬到总经理助手的地位了。但是，如果说话的男性怀有不愿"居人胯下"的思想，这一表达法也含有屈辱的或轻蔑的意思。*My title was Assistant Overseas Sales Manager, but actually I was a sort of man Friday to the president.* 我的头衔是海外销售部长助理，实际不过是总经理的一名杂役而已。◇ a(n indispensable) female assistant

a man Friday [ə 'mæ(ː)n 'fraɪdi] [口] **得力男助手** → a girl FRIDAY

fridge

a fridge [ə 'frɪ(ː)dʒ] [话] **电冰箱** a refrigerator 的缩略。去掉前边的 re-和后边的 -rator，给残余的部分 frige 加个 d，按发音拼写而成。 *I bought a new fridge.* 我买了一台新电冰箱。在实际使用的时候，因为一般来说一家只有一台电冰箱，所以在大多的场合加定冠词。*If you're hungry, there's some pie in the fridge.* 你要是饿了，冰箱里有馅饼。◇ a refrigerator

friend

a fair-weather friend [ə ˌfe(ː)r'weðər ˌfre(ː)nd] [口] **不能共患难的朋友** 直译为"晴天的朋友"。天晴时在你的身边，一下雨就不见影儿了。指"处于逆境时不能依靠的朋友"。*Karl used to have people around him all the time, but most of them turned out to be fair-weather friends who disappeared when he lost all of his money.* 在过去，卡尔总有一群人围着他团团转，但是当他失去了全部财产的时候，那些酒肉朋友大多都不见影儿了。*I was sure that Mary, of all people, would help me. It was a shock to learn that she was only a fair-weather friend.* 我原来认为，在所有的人当中只有玛丽会帮助我。当我了解到她是一位不能共患难的朋友时，简直大吃一惊。也可以象下面的例句这样活用。*You're the only person I can look to now. All of my other friends have turned out to be the fair-weather variety.* 现在，你是我唯一能够依靠的人啦。我的其他一切朋友

都是只能同安乐而不能共患难的人罢了。◇ a friend in good times only

fright

get stage fright [ˌget ˈsteɪdʒ ˌfraɪt] [口] **怯场** stage 是“舞台”, fright 是“恐怖”。一看就会明白,这是“上台胆怯”的意思。*Even great actors sometimes get stage fright.* 即使是著名的演员,也有上台胆怯的时候。转用于舞台以外。*I got stage fright when I was called on to testify at the trial.* 当我被传唤出庭做证的时候,我怯场了。动词也可以用 suffer from 的形式。*I suffer from [get] stage fright whenever I have to make a presentation in front of the class.* 每当叫我在全班同学面前发表什么的时候,我都很胆怯。另外, have stage fright 表示“怯生生的”状态,也可以换用 be suffering from。*Helen is supposed to sing next, but she says she's got a bad case of stage fright and can't go on.* 下一个该海伦上场了,但是她说她太胆怯了,唱不出来。◇ become nervous

Frisco

Frisco [ˈfrɪskou] [俗] **旧金山** 这一表达法是美国加利福尼亚州 San Francisco 市的 Francisco 一词的仿造。为 San Francisco 的俚语名称,美国人广泛使用。但不知为什么,旧金山人 (San Franciscans) 却不喜欢用这个词去称呼他们的故乡。有的旧金山人认为这个词“玷污我们城市的名誉”,十分反感,因此在使用时必须选择对象。*For some reason or other, people from San Francisco hate the word "Frisco."* 不知什么原因,旧金山人非常讨厌“*Frisco*”一词。◇ San Francisco

front

the front desk → DESK

present a united front [prəˌzentə juˌnaɪdəd ˈfrʌ(ː)nt] [口] **结成统一战线** → close RANKS (with *someone*)

frosh

a frosh [ə ˈfrɑ(ː)ʃ] [话] **(特别指)大学一年级生** 大学(或高中)的一年级生称 a freshman [ˈfre(ː)ʃmən], 二年级生称 a sophomore [ˈsɑ(ː)fəˌmo(ː)r], 三年级生称 a junior [ˈdʒu(ː)njər], 四年级生称 a senior [ˈsi(ː)njər]。本条的 frosh 是 freshman 的缩略。有时用此词称呼高中一年级生,但主要为大学用语。*She is still a frosh.* 她还是一个大学一年级生。frosh 词形不变,可代表 freshman 的复数 freshmen。*The frosh are going to have a party tonight.* 一年级的学生们今天举行社交晚会。→ a SOPH ◇ a first-year (college) student

fruit

hen fruit [ˈhe(ː)n ˌfru(ː)t] [话] **蛋** 直译为“母鸡所产的果实”。这是对“蛋”的戏谑的称呼。亦作 hen's fruit。*The truck driver entered the roadside cafe and yelled to the waitress over the counter, "Fix me a plate of ham and hen fruit."* 卡车司机走进路旁的小饭馆,隔着柜台向女服务员喊道:“给我来一盘火腿蛋!” ◇ eggs

fruitcake

be (as) nutty as a fruitcake [əz ˈnʌdiəzə ˈfru(ː)tˌkeɪk] [话] **头脑古怪** nuts 是俚语,意思是“头脑有毛病”,作表语形容词使用。*You're nuts if you think I'd go along with a plan like that.* 如果你认为我会支持那样一个计划,你的头脑未免太古怪啦。nutty 与 nuts 意思相同,也是形容词,但既可作表语也可作定语使用。*I've never seen such a nutty guy.* 我从来没有见过象那样头脑古怪的人。这是用于“人”。也可以用于“事物”或“场所”。*This sounds like one of your boss's nutty ideas.* 这又是你们老板的怪主意吧? *I'm sick and tired of this nutty place. I'm going to find a new job.* 这个鬼地方我实在腻味透啦。我要找个新工作了。本条条头的表达法,按照字面意义是“头脑象水果蛋糕一样发疯”。因为“水果蛋糕”中有许多坚果仁(nut),所以用来加强 nutty 一词的语气。但是请读者注意:这一表达法只能应用于“人”。*If you think I'm going swimming with you in the middle of winter, you're nutty as a fruitcake.*

你如果以为在数九寒天我跟你一道去游泳，那可简直是发疯。*If you think a fruitcake is nutty, you ought to meet my brother.* 如果你想找个狂人，谁也赶不上我的哥哥。下面是讲真正"精神失常者"的例子。*The stranger was a nice-looking man, but when he started speaking I realized that he was as nutty as a fruitcake.* 那个陌生人外表挺帅，但是一说起话来，我发现他疯疯癫癫的。◇ be absolutely crazy

fry

fry [ˈfraɪ] [话] **被电刑处死** 一般来说，fry 是及物动词，意为"油煎"、"油炒"、"油炸"。如果以人为主语，作不及物动词使用，那意思可就非同小可了。这是盗匪、警察使用的俚语，常在电视节目或侦探小说中出现。*You pull that trigger and you'll fry.* 你勾那个枪机试试，你会坐电椅子的。在英语中，"电椅子"是 the electric chair, 因此，把 electric 省略而说 get the chair [ˌgetðə ˈtʃeːr]，意思也一样。*If he's found guilty, he'll get the chair.* 如果他被确定有罪，他就要被电刑处死。◇ die in the electric chair

frying

jump out of the frying pan into the fire → PAN

fuel

add fuel to the flames [ˌæ(ː)d ˌfjuəl təðə ˈfleɪmz] [口] **火上浇油** 字面意义是"往火苗上加燃料"，但没有按照这一意义使用的情况，经常作为比喻使用。*Mark tried to calm the angry crowd, but his words only added fuel to the flames.* 马克企图抚慰愤怒的群众，但是他的话简直是在火上浇油。flames 也可以用单数形式，但极少见。另外，如果要说实际的"增加燃料，使火烧旺"，英语不用 flames，而是用 fire，应该讲 add fuel to the fire。不过，在日常会话中，一般是说出各种燃料的具体名称，而讲 add wood [coal, etc.] to the fire。◇ cause greater excitement [difficulty] (than existed before)

full

be (as) full as a tick → TICK

(a) full bath [(ə)ˈful ˈbæːθ] [口] **带澡盆的卫生间** → the BATHROOM

fun

for fun [fərˈfʌ(ː)n] [话] **闹着玩儿地** → for KEEPS

a fun house → HOUSE

have a barrel of fun [ˌhævə ˈbæ(ː)rələv ˈfʌ(ː)n] [话] **极开心** 直译为"有一桶的乐趣"。a barrel 给人以比 a lot 的量更多的感觉，可以认为这是对习用语 a lot of fun 更加强调的一种表达形式。*Why don't you go to the party with us? We'll have a barrel of fun.* 跟我们一道去参加社交晚会吧，一定有趣极啦。*The children had a barrel of fun at Disneyland.* 孩子们在迪斯尼乐园里玩得极为开心。◇ have a wonderful time

make fun of *someone* [*something*] [ˌmeɪk ˈfʌnəv ~] [口] **取笑** 字面意为"拿……作为乐趣"。同样的表达法有 poke FUN at *someone* [*something*]，取笑的程度比较轻。本条的表达法含有很浓厚的"怀有恶意"或者"真刀真枪"、"冷酷无情"的意味，具有"以……为笑料"的感觉。*You're making fun of me, aren't you.* 你是在耍笑我啊! *We used to make fun of Jimmy for wanting to be President someday.* 吉米说自己将来想当总统，我们经常以此取笑他。取笑的对象不限于"人"，"事"、"物"均可。*When people make fun of my big nose I get angry.* 当人们取笑我的大鼻子的时候，我很恼火。*I had thought that they were my friends until they began to make fun of my accent.* 在他们开始取笑我说话的口音以前，我一直以为他们是我的朋友呢。不是"当面"，在"背后"取笑也可以用这一表达法，例如：*Don't talk like that. You should never make fun of your teacher.* 不能那样说话。绝对不要笑话你的老师啊。*Jim often makes fun of you behind your back.* 吉姆常常在背后笑话你。◇ laugh at *someone* [*something*]

more fun than a barrel of monkeys [.mo(:)r 'fʌ(:)n ðənə .bæ(:)rələv'mʌŋkiz] [话] **最开心的** 美国的桶 (barrel) 特别大,能装许多东西,因此,a barrel of 或者 a barrel full of 有时用以表示"非常多"的意思。也就是说,本条的字面意义为"比很多的猴子还有趣"。如果想象一下群猴嬉戏的场面,会有助于理解这一表达法。多与动词 be 或 have 一起使用。*Why don't you try the roller coaster? It's more fun than a barrel of monkeys.* 你怎么不坐坐快速滑车玩? 简直开心极啦。barrel 的后边有时添加 full, 意思不变。*We had more fun than a barrel full of monkeys last night.* 昨天晚上我们玩得开心极啦。根据上下文或说话口气,偶尔具讽刺性,表示相反的意义。这一点务请读者注意。*Jim is more fun than a barrel of monkeys.* 吉姆是个最有趣的人。(吉姆是个最无聊的人。) ◇ *lots (and lots) of fun*

poke fun at *someone* [*something*] ['pouk 'fʌnət ~] [口] **打趣** poke 是"戳"的意思。本条直译是"对着……戳 fun (乐趣、玩笑)",意思不难理解。也就是说,经常带有嬉戏的韵味。虽然同样是"开玩笑",但这一表达法比 make FUN of *someone* [*something*] 的罪过轻,往往与汉语的"逗弄"、"调笑"等相近。再者,make fun of ~可以是"背后嘲笑",而这一表达法只能是"当面打趣",没有鬼鬼祟祟的阴暗神态。 *When people poke fun at me for my big nose, I just laugh.* 当人们打趣我的大鼻子时,我只是哈哈大笑。*My friends often poke fun at my accent.* 朋友们常常打趣俺的口音。也可以"嘲笑"对方发言的内容。*We used to poke fun at Jimmy for wanting to become President someday.* 吉米说他将来想当总统,我们常为这个拿他打趣。◇ tease *someone* (for *something* [because of *his something*])

funeral

be *someone's* **funeral** [~ 'fju(:)nərəl] [话] **那是某人的事** funeral 是"葬礼",但在这里只是很轻的"不幸[痛苦]"的意味。这一表达法使用的场合主要是:"我是这样想,你[他]偏要那样想也没办法。虽然我感到很遗憾,但是受罪[倒霉]的不是我,而是你[他]啊!" *I don't think you should marry her, but it's your funeral.* 我认为你不该跟她结婚,但是将来后悔的是你,与我无关啊。*If he doesn't want to go with us that's his funeral.* 他不愿意跟我们一起去也没关系,将来后悔的是他,与我们无关。也说 be not my funeral, 与 be your [his, etc.] funeral 意味相同。 *You can quit your job if you want to. It's not my funeral.* 如果你愿意的话,你可以辞掉你的工作。那不关我的事。也偶尔把说法翻转过来,讲 be my funeral 或者 be not your [his, etc.] funeral, 意思是"倒霉的是我,与……无关"。*Why should you care if I lose my job? It's my [not your] funeral.* 我丢掉工作,你怎么会操心呢? 倒霉的是我而不是你呀。◇ be *someone* that will suffer

funny

one's **funny bone** → BONE

tickle *someone's* **funny bone** [.tɪkl ~ 'fʌni .boun] [话] **使人发笑** → *one's* funny BONE

fuse

blow a fuse [.blouə 'fju:z] [话] **勃然大怒** → blow *one's* TOP

have a short fuse [hævə .fɔrt 'fju:z] [话] **容易发怒** 字面意义为"导火线短"。*Be careful. That firecracker has a short fuse.* 当心! 那个爆竹的导火线可短啊。这一表达法应用于人时,则指"容易激动,动辄发怒"。原来的构思是把人的感情比作爆竹,一点火立即爆炸。*My father has a short fuse.* 我父亲性子火暴,动辄发怒。一般用于形容人的性格,但也可以用于说明一时的心情或心理状态。*Be careful. For some reason the boss has a very short fuse today.* 小心点儿。不知什么缘故,老板今天非常不顺气儿。◇ be quick to anger

fussy

fussy ['fʌsi] [口] **爱挑剔的** → PERSNICKETY

fuzz

the fuzz [ðə ˈfʌ(:)z] [俗] **警察** fuzz 本来意为桃一类水果表皮上的“无数细毛”，不知如何变成了“警察”一词的俚语。几乎所有的场合都作为集合词使用，如：*We had a little visit from the fuzz last night, boss. Maybe we better clear out of this place.* 头儿，昨天晚上有警爷光顾了一下。我看还是离开这个地方为妙。也有象下面的说法，但极罕见。*The guy's a fuzz.* 那家伙是个巡警。◇ the police

G

gab

the gift of gab → GIFT

gadget

a gadget [ə ˈgæ(ː)dʒət] [口] **小玩意儿** → a THINGAMABOB

gaga

go gaga [gouˈgɑː,gɑː] [话] **疯疯癫癫** 最初的构思是:人的头脑如果不正常,就会象婴儿般发出 ga——ga——的声音。这是一个轻松的表达法。*Don't mind my grandfather. He's a little gaga.* 我爷爷的话你不要在意,他有点疯疯癫癫的。*That guy's gaga. He wants me to sell him my car for a hundred dollars.* 那个家伙是个半疯儿。他给一百美元,叫我把汽车卖给他。如以上两个例句所示,在表示"疯疯癫癫"的意味时,gaga 可以与动词 be 一起使用,但大多的场合是与 go 结合起来。这一表达法一般含有戏谑的成份。*I'll go gaga if I have to read all these letters.* 如果非叫我看完这么多的信不可,我会发疯的。但也有象下一例句那样,是按照真正"疯"的意思使用的。*She apparently went a little gaga after her husband died.* 自从她丈夫死了以后,她显然有点疯了。◇ become strange in the head

gain

gain on *someone* [*something*] [ˈgei ˌnɔ(ː)n ~] [口] **逼近** → gain GROUND (on *someone* [*something*])

gall

have the gall to *do something* [ˌhævðə ˈgɔːltə ~] [口] **厚脸皮** gall 是"胆汁"。本条的字面意义是"有足够的胆汁去做某事"。根据中世纪欧洲的医学,如果肝脏分泌的胆汁过多,人就脸皮厚,或者傲慢无礼。gall 一词的比喻意义"傲慢"、"无耻"、"厚脸皮"等便是由此而来。have the ~ to 的意思是"有足够的……去干……"的意思。*That man had the gall to call me an antiquated shrew.* 那个男人居然厚着脸皮管我叫老泼妇。*You sit around doing nothing all day every day and still you have the gall to tell me I don't pay you enough salary?!* 你一整天一整天地坐在那里什么也不干,还厚着脸皮说我给你的工资少啊?! *She had the gall to come parading into the reception without being invited.* 我们并没有邀请那个女人,她厚着脸皮自己跑来出席招待会了。◇ be so insolent as to *do something*

play to the gallery [ˌpleɪ təðə ˈgæ(ː)ləri] [口] **哗众取宠** gallery 是剧场中票价最低的顶层楼座。一般来说,在 gallery 里的观众大多欣赏水平低,只要有点特殊的场面或演技,马上就会鼓掌叫好,很不安静。因此,play to the gallery 的字面意义就是"面对 gallery 里的观众表演",也就是"迎合群众的趣味"或"投一般群众的所好"。*He might become a great actor someday if only he would give up his habit of playing to the gallery.* 只要他丢掉迎合顶层楼座观众的习惯,他早晚有一天会成为著名演员的。转用于表示"哗众取宠"的意思,在这种情况下,play 指"发言"的情况最多。*I'm sure that was not Ralph's honest opinion. He was merely playing to the gallery.* 我认为那不是拉尔夫的真实意见,他只不过是哗众取宠而已。*Don't worry about what the president said at the stockholders' meeting about reducing the number of employees. He was only playing to the gallery.* 总经理在股东大会上讲裁减从业人员,你不必为这个自寻烦恼。他只不过是迎合股东们的心理罢了。play 有时指"行动",例如:*The governor doesn't* *really like to visit all those workers' homes. He's just playing to the gallery.* 州长并不是真正喜欢去访问所有那些工人们的家。他只不过为了收买人心而已。有时包括"发言"和"行动"两个方面，例如：*Having to seek re-election after only four years in office often forces Presidents to play to the gallery rather than seek firm solutions to the nation's problems.* 由于仅仅在任四年就得争取再度当选，美国的总统们往往并不努力去切实解决国家的问题，而是不得不用言语和行动去拚命博得群众的欢心。另外，以下的情况可供参考：在 17 世纪以前，这一表达法本是名词词组，指"为 gallery 里的观众而写的剧本"、"迎合低级趣味的戏"。后来逐渐具有动词的作用，直至现在。◇ act [speak] in such a way as to achieve popularity [the approval of the audience, the approval of the people]

gam

a gam [ə ˈgæ(ː)m] [话] **(人的)腿** 关于这个词的来源，说法不一：①原为现在已成废语的英语 gamb; ②原为法国方言 *gambe*; ③原为意大利语 *gamba*(以上三个词均是"腿"的意思)。这是一个相当轻松的表达法。一般用复数，很少指一条腿。 *A boxer has to have strong gams.* 拳击手必须有壮实的腿。不管什么人的腿，也不管什么样的腿，都可以用这一名词表达，但是多用于指女子好看的大腿。*The young actress can't act, but she sure has a beautiful set of gams.* 那个年轻的女演员戏演得不好，但是两条腿的确很好看。◇ a leg

game

the badger game [ðə ˈbædʒər ˌgeɪm] [话] **美人计** 字面意义是"耍獾游戏"。据说这一表达法的来源是：古时候有一种游戏叫 badger-baiting (耍獾)，先引导獾进入大桶或浅洞，然后唆使狗去欺负它。美国常有以女人为诱饵敲诈金钱的现象，在进行恐吓的时候，为了使对方乖乖地掏钱，敲诈者总是指着那个女人说："这是我的老婆！" *George was a victim of the badger game.* 乔治中了美人计。*I'm afraid you've fallen for the old badger game. That woman wasn't his wife. It was just someone he hired for the job.* 我看你是被美人计的老一套手法欺骗了。那个女人并不是他的老婆，是他雇来干这种勾当的。◇ an extortion plot / a method of extorting money by pretending that the woman one has arranged to discover in embarrassing circumstances with another man is one's wife

a con game [ə ˈkɑːnˌgeɪm] [话] **骗局** con 是 confidence (信任)的缩略。先取得他人信任而后进行欺骗，英语叫做 a confidence game。但在日常会话中将其短缩，称 con game。game 是"策略"、"计谋"、"花招"的意思。*Be sure to have the painting appraised before you pay for it. You don't want to find yourself the victim of a con game.* 在付款以前，对那幅画必须鉴定一下。你总不会愿意上当受骗吧？ *How can you be so naïve? You've been taken in by the oldest con game there is.* 你怎么会那么傻气？那是老掉了牙的欺骗手段，你竟然中了圈套。→ a con ARTIST ◇ a swindle

a confidence game [ə ˈkɑnfədənts ˌgeɪm] [话] **骗局** → a con GAME

fair game [ˌfe(ː)r ˈgeɪm] [口] **最适当的攻击对象** 原为狩猎用语，指"准许捕猎的鸟兽"。 fair 是"可以捕猎的"，game 意为"猎物"。本来的用法如：*When deer hunting season opens this year, even does will be fair game.* 当今年的猎鹿季节开始的时候，连雌鹿也准许狩猎啦。从这一意义发展，广泛用于表示"最适当的猎物"、"最适当的目标"。*The terrorists have warned that they consider all government officials to be fair game.* 恐怖分子警告说，他们认为所有的政府高官都是暗杀的对象。*When children are in the mood to tease, they look on their fat classmates as especially fair game.* 当孩子们一心想要去戏弄别人的时候，他们总是把肥胖的同学当作目标。*The moment anyone decides to run for public of-*

fice, he becomes fair game for the political cartoonists. 不论是谁,只要他一竞选去当大官,他就变成政治讽刺漫画家的良好题材了。*As soon as a small firm becomes the least bit successful, it becomes fair game for a take-over bid by a larger company.* 只要一个小公司取得一点点成绩,它马上就成为较大公司吞并的对象。◇ suitable targets / a suitable target

the name of the game → NAME

be onto *someone's* **game** [ˈɔːntə～ˌgeɪm]

[话] **识破阴谋诡计** game 有"策略"、"计谋"、"花招"的意思。be onto *someone* 是定型的说法,意思是"注意到某人要干什么事情"、"识破某人的阴谋诡计"。*I'm onto you.* 我了解你的阴谋诡计。条头的英语是在 be onto (注意到、明了)后边加上 *someone's* game 而构成的表达法。*I may as well tell you that all your efforts to fool us have gone for nought. We've been onto your game for a long time now.* 我可以告诉你说,你要愚弄我们的一切努力都已经化成泡影。我们老早以前就已经识破你的阴谋诡计了。*You needn't try to play up to me. I'm onto your little game.* 你用不着拍我的马屁,我明白你的小心眼儿。◇ be aware of *someone's* scheme

throw a game [ˌθrouə ˈgeɪm] [口] **在骗人的比赛中认输** → THROWa race [game, etc.]

gander

take a gander at *something* [*someone*]

[ˌteɪkə ˈgæ(ː)ndərət ～] [话] **看一看** gander 是"雄鹅"。这一表达法原来的构思是:"鹅总是伸长脖子去看东西"。从意味上讲,与 take a look at *something* 大致相同。*Take a gander at this picture.* 你瞧瞧这张画。如这一例句所示,一般用命令式。因为其中包含着征求对方意见的口吻,所以在回答时多半是说:*Oh, this is beautiful!* 啊!这真好看!或者是说:*I don't care for that.* 我不大喜欢。这是一个轻松的表达法。*A: Take a gander at the bike my dad got for me. B: Wow!* 甲:你瞧瞧我爹给我买的自行车。乙:嘀,真棒! *Take a gander at that girl in the bikini.* 你瞧瞧那个穿三点式游泳服的女郎。有时也可以用记叙体,例如:*I went and took a gander at that house today.* 今天我去瞧了瞧那所房子。即使在这一场合,也包含着命令的意义。比如说,这个人的妻子已经去看过那所房子,又命令他今天去看。他看回来才说了以上的话。"*Take a gander at this little beauty," said the used-car salesman, pointing to a nearby jalopy.* 卖旧汽车的推销员指着身旁的一辆破旧的汽车说:"请瞧瞧这个漂亮的小妞!"◇ (take a) look at *something* [*someone*]

gang

gang up on *someone*[ˌgæ(ː)ŋ ˈʌˌpɔ(ː)n ～]

[话] **结成一伙对付他人** 名词 gang 是 group (群)的轻松的表达法,指歹徒的"一帮",如"四人帮"的"帮"。gang up 是"集在一起"或"成堆儿"的意思,例如说:*Don't gang up. Walk two or three paces behind the person in front of you.* 不要挤在一块儿,要离开你前边的人两三步走。不过,单是 gang up,或者单是 gang up to *do something*(结合一伙做某件事),都没有与人敌对的意味。只有说 gang up on *someone* 才是以对付他人为目的。*The large trading companies ganged up on us to try to force us out of business.* 一些大贸易公司结成一伙对付我们,打算把我们排挤出这一行。这是"结成一伙对付他人"的固有意义,但也常用这一表达法表示在结伙之后实际进行"袭击"、亦即"集体袭击"的意思。如果不注意上下文,是很容易误译的。*The three men ganged up on Jay in an alley and beat him up.* 三个大汉在一条小巷里堵住杰伊,把他狠揍了一顿。在这个例句里,因为有 beat him up,所以意思明确无误。*It wasn't fair to gang up on him like that.* 这句话的意思究竟是"一群人堵住打他,这不光明正大"呢?还是"为了打他而结成一伙,这不光明正大"呢?仅从文字本身是无从理解的,除了细看前后文而外,没有别的办法。另外,在"集体袭击"的场合,"袭击"的内容有上

面例句中那样的"狠揍",也有"七嘴八舌地指责"或者"大家一致进行恫吓"等等,不一而足。◇ band together (unfairly) against *someone*

garden

lead *someone* **up the garden path** → PATH

gas

a gas guzzler → GUZZLER

a gas station [ə ˈgæ(:)s ˌsteɪʃən] [话] **加油站** → a filling STATION

step on the gas [ˌstepɔnðə ˈgæ(:)s] [话] **加快速度** gas 是 gas pedal (油门踏板) 的略语。 step on the gas 的字面意义是"踩油门"。因此,应用于汽车是理所当然的,如说: *Step on the gas or we'll be late for the plane.* 快点儿开! 要不然,我们就赶不上飞机啦。不过,实际上用作比喻的时候比较多。例如: *If we don't step on the gas, we won't finish this work in time.* 如果我们不抓紧,这个活儿到时候就完不成了。*We've got to step on the gas. The boss will be back soon.* 咱们得赶快干,老板就要回来啦。有时用 it 代替 the gas, 而讲 step on it [ˈstepˌɔ(:)nət]。 *Step on it, you guys. Can't you walk any faster?* 喂,大家加点油,你们不能走快一点儿吗? ◇ hurry (up)

gasket

blow a gasket [ˌblouə ˈgæ(:)skət] [话] **勃然大怒** → blow *one's* TOP

bust a gasket [ˌbʌstə ˈgæ(:)skət] [话] **勃然大怒** → blow *one's* TOP

gat

a gat [ə ˈgæ(:)t] [话] **手枪** → a HEATER

gate

crash the gate [party] [ˌkræ(:)ʃðə ˈgeɪt / ˈpɑ(:)rdi] [话] **无票入场** crash 是"砸碎"。本条的字面意义是"破门 (gate) 而入",这个"门"指体育场、剧院、开晚会的大厅等等的门。也就是说"不买票或者没有招待券而混进门去"的意思。*They couldn't get any tickets for the football game, so they tried to crash the gate.* 他们没有弄到一张足球赛的票,因此试图无票入场。*The circus manager found two boys who had crashed the gate.* 马戏团的负责人发现有两个少年无票入场了。crash the party 是"没有招待券而进入社交晚会"的意思,大多指在会堂中举办的大型晚会。但是,高中生或大学生带着没有得到邀请的朋友悄悄走进一般家庭的社交晚会的场合,也可以使用这一表达法。例如: *There seem to be more people here tonight than are on the invitation list. Several people must have crashed the party.* 今天晚上到这里来的人似乎比邀请名单上的多,肯定有几个是不请自来的。根据上下文,当然有时候必须脱离 crash the party 的基本形式,而讲 a party 或者 any party (但 crash the gate 则较少这种情况)。*Sid claims it's easy to crash any party if you're dressed properly and look like you know what you're doing.* 照锡德的说法,只要衣冠楚楚,大模大样,任何社交晚会都可以混进去。也可以用这一表达法开玩笑,例如: *Hello, fellows. I didn't know you were going to eat at this restaurant to-night. May I crash your party?* 哈,哥儿们,我不知道各位今天晚上在这家餐厅吃饭。我没有请帖参加各位的晚宴行不行? "无票入场的人"是 a gate-crasher。*They always put on extra guards for the big games in order to stop gate-crashers.* 在重大比赛的时候,为了防止有人无票入场,他们总是多设一些守卫人员。照理说,可以有 a party-crasher 的说法,但不知什么原因,社交晚会的场合一般使用 gate-crasher。在美国,凡是著名人士举办的大型社交晚会,有一两个 gate-crasher 乃是司空见惯的事,不足为奇,其中也有大家都熟知的职业 gate-crasher。对于这种人也不用 party 一词,而将之称为 a professional gate-crasher。主办晚会者明明知道也装作看不见,甚至认为这很有趣,可为晚会增光。 *Don't you know those two men standing near the hors d'oeuvre table? They're professional gate-crashers.* 你认

识站在小吃桌子旁边的那两个男的吗？他们一向是没有招待券而混入晚会的人。◇ enter without a ticket [invitation]

get the gate[ˌgetðə ˈgeɪt] [话] **被驱逐** → give *someone* the GATE

give *someone* **the gate** [ˌgɪv ~ ðə ˈgeɪt] [话] **驱逐** 逐字翻译是"给予某人门"，意思是"不管三七二十一，把某人撵出门外"。*When it became clear that we didn't have tickets, they gave us the gate.* 他们查出我们没有票，就把我们撵出来了。如此例所示，可用于具体"从某个地方撵走"的场合。除此而外，广泛用作比喻，表示"断绝友情"或者"断绝来往"，也就是"从人际关系中赶走"的意思。*After my girl met Jack, she gave me the gate.* 我的女朋友与杰克相见之后，就把我忘得一干二净了。*Having discovered that his wife was having an affair with another man, he gave her the gate.* 他发现妻子与另一个男人私通之后，就同她一刀两断了。在这个句子里，不一定是"把妻子从家里撵走"，自己从家里出走也可以，主要的意思是"感情告吹，自己主动断绝夫妻关系"。又如：*As soon as Sonny had run through his dead father's money, most of his so-called friends gave him the gate.* 松尼把父亲的大笔遗产花光之后，他的狐朋狗友几乎全都不跟他来往了。另外有 get the gate 的表达法，表示"被驱逐"。*Lyle got the gate for cheating on his expense account.* 莱尔由于虚报交际费，被公司开除了。*I got the gate from my boy friend.* 我被男朋友甩了。◇ throw *someone* out / abandon *someone* / fire *someone*

gate-crasher

a gate-crasher [ə ˈgeɪtˌkræ(ː)ʃər] [话] **无票入场的人或没有招待券而参加社交晚会的人** → crash the GATE [party]

gatepost

between you and me and the gatepost [bətwi(ː)ˌnjuː ənˌmiː ənðə ˈgeɪtˌpoust] [话] **只是咱们私下里说说** 过去曾用过 lamppost (街灯柱)代替过 gatepost (门柱)，而说 between you and me and the lamppost, 现在基本上固定用 gatepost, 有时换用 bedpost (床柱)而作 between you and me and the bedpost。也有时不加 and the gatepost, 如：*Between you and me, I think the man is a fool.* 这只是咱们私下里说说，我认为那个家伙是个混蛋。虽然"不足为外人道也"的意思与条头的表达法相同，但语调却十分严重。and the gatepost 具有和缓或者软化这种语调的功能。也就是说，在不愿意让外人知道而自己又未深刻思索的场合，常用这一表达法作为开场白。*This is just between you and me and the gatepost, but I hear Widow Brown has a new boy friend.* 咱们的话只是随便讲讲，我听说寡妇布朗又交了一个男朋友。其次，如下一例句所示，在轻轻询问对方的意见时，也常把这一表达法放到问话的前边。*Just between you and me and the gatepost, what would you say to moving our office to Atlanta?* 我只是私下问问你，把咱们的办事处移到亚特兰大，你认为如何？◇ confidentially

gay

gay [ˈgeɪ] [话] **同性恋的** → a QUEER

gear

be in high gear [ɪn ˌhaɪ ˈgɪːr] [口] **全力进行** 原为汽车用语，意思是"在最高速档"，亦即"发动机在全速运转"。*The car is in high gear.* 汽车正在全速行驶。作为比喻，表示事物顺利进行或状态极为良好的样子。*After a slow start, the program is now in high gear.* 计划的执行在开始时很缓慢，但是现在上了轨道，顺利得很。下一例句加用其他动词的进行时，与 be in high gear 的意义完全一样。*The work is moving along in high gear and is expected to be completed on schedule.* 工作正沿着轨道顺利进行，预计可以按期完成计划。如果用 go 或 get 等动词代替动词 be, in 要改成 into, 即采取 go [move, get] into high gear 的形式，意思是"上了轨道，开始全速进行"。*Construction on the new hotel went into high gear last month.* 新饭店的建设工程

上个月上了轨道，开始全速进行了。另外还有一个表达法是 get [move] *something* into high gear。*A lack of funds has prevented us from getting our new planning department into high gear.* 由于缺乏资金，我们新成立的计划部没有能够全面展开工作。◇ move forward at top speed

gee

Gee. [ˈdʒiː] [话] **哎呀！** 感叹词。原为 Jesus (耶稣)的委婉语，Gee. 是其第一音节拚音的变形。虽然与 WHEE! 相似，但除表示"高兴"、"感动"而外，Gee. 还具有"出人意外"、"令人惊奇"的意味。*Gee! Look at that tiny airplane!* 哎呀！你瞧那个小飞机！*Gee! Where did you get that neat bike?* 哎呀！你从哪儿弄来那么好的自行车啊？*Gee! You mean I can go with you?* 哎呀！我跟你去也行吗？如以上的例句所示，大多的场合是表示"高兴"或"感动"，但也有时用以表示"失望"。*Aw, gee, Mom. Why can't I go to the movies to-night?* 哎呀！妈妈，为什么今天晚上我不能去看电影？从以上的例句可以看出，一般是中、小学生年龄的孩子们使用这一表达法。但成年人也有使用的场合，一般表示小小的"失望"、"困窘"、"同情"、"钦佩"等，除戏谑时外，通常不把它作为"高兴"、"感动"的表达法。*Oh, gee. I forgot to bring my wallet.* 哎呀！我忘带钱包了。*Gee, that's too bad.* 哎呀！那太遗憾啦。*Gee, that's a beautiful picture, isn't it.* 哎呀！那幅画可真好看呀。下面是成年人开玩笑的用例：*Gee. You mean you'd actually lend me one dollar?* 哎呀！你真舍得借给我一块钱吗？Gee. 加强语气的说法是 Gee whiz. 这也是儿童用语，成年人除戏谑时以外几乎不使用。

gentle

(as) gentle as a lamb → LAMB

gently

break *something* **to** *someone* **gently** → BREAK

George

Let George do it. [ˌletˈdʒɔːrdʒ ˌdu(ː)ət] [口] **把自己的任务推给别人** 本条的来源是：法国国王路易十二世 (1462—1515) 每当有自己不愿过问的事情时，就指着当时的首相、枢机主教昂布瓦斯的乔治(Cardinal Georges d'Amboise) 说："让乔治去办吧！"这成了他的口头禅。但是，在现代美国人的意识中，这个 George 已经不是指一个特定的人物，等于中国人说"张三、李四"一样。请注意：这一表达法不是指把任务分配别人去干或者请求别人去干，而是让别人去干自己职责范围以内的事情。*Our streets are so dirty because no one wants to take responsibility for keeping them clean. Everyone's attitude seems to be "Let George do it."* 我们附近的街道太脏了，因为没有人愿意负责保持它们的清洁。每个人都似乎抱着"让别人去干吧"的态度。如这一例句所示，在讲到不负责任的人或不尽义务的人的时候，常使用这一表达法。*It seems that the more people there are on a committee, the more they are willing to let George do it when it comes to getting anything accomplished.* 委员会的人数越是增多，每当有什么工作要完成的时候，那些委员们就越想叫别人去干本来应该由他们自己去干的事情。*A: I'm glad to see that you, for one, are working very hard. Everyone else I've met today seems happy enough to let George do it. What is your name, by the way? B: George.* 甲：我能见到至少还有你这么一个在拚命工作的人，心里很高兴。今天我碰见的每一个人似乎都充满了"让乔治去干吧"的愉快心情。可是，你叫什么名字呀？乙：我叫乔治。◇ Let someone else do it.

get

Come and get it! → COME

get away with (*doing*) *something* [ˌgedəˈweɪwɪð ~] [口] **逃脱惩罚** 只是 get away，是"逃走"的意思。例如：*The thieves got away.* 几个窃贼逃走了。get away with (*doing*) *something* 中的 (*doing*) *something* 处必须是"坏事"或者

一般人认为不好的事情。这一点务请读者注意。这一表达法指已经干的坏事"没有暴露",或者干坏事的人"没有被捕","虽然就擒但未受处罚"等等,使用范围很广。肯定形式的意思是"干了坏事,巧妙逃走",否定形式的意思是"天网恢恢,疏而不漏"。使用否定形式的场合较多。*You'll never get away with killing us.* 你休想杀了我们而逃脱罪责。*The gang tried to rob a bank but they didn't get away with it.* 一伙强盗抢劫了银行,但是被抓住了。*Jerry got caught because he bragged about getting away with cheating on the test.* 杰里由于吹嘘说他在考试中作弊成功而被捉住了。*He thought he could get away with bribery.* 他以为自己进行贿赂不会被发觉。下面的例句中所讲的不是"坏事",但一般认为不大好。*How do you get away with talking so familiarly with the boss?* 你那么放肆地跟老板讲话,怎么没受到中斥哪?另外,get away with *something* 可以用于表示"巧妙地拿走什么东西"的意思,但是本条条头中的 *something* 一定指的是"坏事"。如果记住这一点,就不致造成混乱。比如说:*The bank robbers got away with the robbery.* 银行抢匪很巧妙地进行了抢劫。这是按照本条条头的用法。但是 *The bank robbers got away with the money.* 这句话就不一样了。虽然从整个句意来看指的是一件"坏事",然而相当于 *something* 的 the money 本身却不是什么"坏事"。因此,这句话翻译时应该按照它的字面意义译为"银行抢匪巧妙地拿着钱逃走了"。◇ escape punishment (for <*doing*> *something*) / not get caught (for <*doing*> *something*) / avoid detection [reprimand] (in <*doing*> *something*)

get away with *something* [ˌgedə ˈweɪwɪð ~] [口] **巧妙地偷走** → GET away with (*doing*) *something*

get back at *someone* (for *something*) [ˌgetˈbæːkət ~] [话] **报复** 指"报一箭之仇"。*Be careful of Martha. She says she's going to get back at you for stealing her boy friend.* 你要留神马莎。她说你抢走了她的男朋友,她一定要报仇。*Don't believe what Hal says. He's just trying to get back at me for refusing to recommend him for promotion.* 不要相信哈尔所说的话。由于我拒绝推荐他提升,他只是要对我进行报复而已。另有一个表达法 get even with *someone* (for *something*),意思和用法均相同。请注意:单单 get even 是"拉平"的意思。*You'll be sorry you did this to me. I'll get even with you for this if it's the last thing I do.* 你对我这样干,你会后悔的。因为不论情况如何,我必进行报复。◇ take revenge on *someone*

get *someone* **down** [ˌget ~ ˈdaun] [话] **使人厌烦** *All this homework every day is starting to get me down.* 每天都是这么一大堆作业,真叫我腻烦死了。如此例句所示,主语大多是使说话者非常厌烦的事情,而且是长期反复去做的事情。*My new roommate's tendency to argue over everything is getting me down.* 我的新室友对每件事情都要议论一番,这种作风真叫我厌烦。*Charles should get married. He says he enjoys the freedom of bachelor life, but that always having to do his own cooking gets him down.* 查理应该结婚。他讴歌独身生活的自由,但是每天得自己做饭吃,这使他厌烦透了。另有一个 let *something* get *one* down 的表达法,意思是"被什么事情弄得郁郁不乐"。这一表达法不是用于多次反复的事情,恰恰相反,大多是用于仅仅发生一次的事情。*I'm afraid Fred has let his mother's death get him down.* 据我看,弗雷德母亲的去世使得他精神十分沮丧。*It's a tough break, but don't let it get you down.* 那是一件痛苦的事情,不过,你不要因此而灰心丧气啊。*He seems to be letting the constant pressure of his studies get him down.* 他似乎被经常不断的学习压力弄得郁郁寡欢了。◇ depress *someone*

get even with *someone* (for *something*) [ˌgeˈdiːvən wɪð ~] [口] **进行报复** → GET back at *someone* (for *something*)

get off scot-free → SCOT-FREE

Get out of here. [ˈge(ː)ˌdaudə ˌhɪːr] [话] **别胡扯啦!** 当然可以按照字面意义使用。例如: *Get out of here! I won't have you kids playing in my yard!* 快给我出去! 你们这些小鬼不要在我的院子里玩。“快出去!”为什么会变成“别胡扯啦!”呢? 大概原来的构思是:“你说的话令人无法相信,快给我滚开吧!”这与中国人常说的“去你的吧!”的用法极相似。说话者具有“受人嘲弄”或“受人欺骗”的心情。本条与 Go on (with you). (怎么会呢!)很相似,但是在说 Go on. 的时候,心里是半信半疑;在使用这一表达法的时候,是完全不相信对方所说的话,语气也强烈得多。 *A: Mr. Brown offered me a thousand dollars for the job. B: Get outa here. Nobody would pay that much money for a simple job like that!* 甲:布朗先生说,如果我干那个工作,他给我一千美元。乙:别胡扯啦! 象那么简单的工作,没有人会出那么大的价钱。在这一场合,不论甲的话是真是假,反正乙完全不相信,所以说“别胡扯啦!” *A: I've never revealed this to anyone before, but actually I'm President Reagan's nephew. B: Get out of here. You don't expect me to believe that, do you?* 甲:这件事我从前没有向任何人透露过,实际上我是里根总统的外甥。乙:别胡扯啦! 你总不会认为我会相信你的瞎话吧? 在这一场合,甲多半是在开玩笑,但也可能是认真说的。也常有象下边的情况,在对明显的诙谐或玩笑进行回答时,用以表示很轻松的“去你的吧!”的意思。 *A: Do you know why Columbus left Spain to go to America? B: No, why? A: Because when he told Queen Isabella that the world was round, she said, "Get outa here!" B: Oh, get outa here!* 甲:你知道哥伦布为什么离开西班牙去美洲吗? 乙:不知道。为什么呢? 甲:因为当他向伊莎贝拉女王讲地球是圆的之后,女王说:“去你的吧!”乙:嘿,别胡扯啦! 在这一例句中,甲所讲的 Get out of here! 包含着“从这里走出去!”和“别胡扯啦!”的双重意味。◇ I don't believe it. / That's ridiculous. / What a lot of nonsense.

get someplace [ˈget ˌsʌmpleɪs] [话] **发迹** → GO PLACES

get *oneself* **up in** *something* [as *something*] [ˌget ～ ˈʌpɪn / ˈʌpəz ～] [口] **打扮** → a GET-UP

get with it → WITH

let *something* **get** *one* **down** [ˌlet ～ ˌget ～ ˈdaun] [话] **被(什么事情)弄得郁郁不乐** → GET *someone* down

not get anyplace [ˌnɑt geˈdeniˌpleɪs] [话] **得不到社会地位** → GO PLACES

tell *someone* **where to get off** → WHERE

Where does *someone* **get off** *doing something*? [ˈhwe(ː)rdəz ～ ˌgeˈdɔːf ～] [话] **到底是要干什么呀?** 直译为“什么地方允许做这种事?”这里的 get off 是“免予治罪或惩罚”的意思。也就是说,本条习用语的字面意义是:“干某种事应该被治的罪,是哪里给免去的?”在说话者向他感到“讨厌”或“生气”的人讲话的时候使用,具有 What right does he have to do that? (他有什么权利那样干?)的意味。 *Where does that guy get off telling us what to do?* 那个家伙指挥我们干这干那,他到底是要干什么呀? *Where do you get off barging into my home and insulting my wife?* 你闯进我的家,侮辱我的妻子,你到底是要干什么呀? *I paid for my ticket on this train. Just where do you get off telling me where to get off?* 我是买了票上这次列车的。你居然指示我在哪儿下车,这到底是什么意思? ◇ *Someone* has no right to *do something*.

get-out

like all get-out [ˌlaɪˈkɔːl ˈgeˌdaut] [话] **极度地** get-out 原意为“脱身之计”。在现代的美国不使用这一意义,只在 like all get-out 这一习用语中还保留它的踪影。据说这一表达法本身从一百年以前就已经开始使用。它令人感到有些乡巴佬的味道,但是城市的人们也常用它作为强调动词内涵的副词短语。 *Lem was duded up like all get-out.* 莱姆又穿又戴,打扮得很厉害。在此句中,Lem 这个名字就具有十足的乡下味儿,而 be duded up (又穿又戴，打扮起来)的说法也同样土里土气，因此就更增强了语感。*We worried like all get-out.* 我们极为担心。在动词表示动作的场合，当然就不是“极度地”，而是“以猛烈的势头”的意思了。*When the old farmer appeared with a gun, we ran like all get-out.* 当老农拿着枪出现的时候，我们撒开鸭子拚命逃走了。*The people in the discotheque were dancing like all get-out.* 进迪斯科舞厅的人们全都在疯狂地跳舞。*I worked like all get-out to finish that report on time, and the boss hasn't even read it.* 我拚命写那个报告，总算按期完成了，可是老板连看都没有看。在修饰形容词的时候，不是用 like all get-out，而是采取 (as) ～ as all get-out 的形式。*That guy is as stupid as all get-out.* 那个家伙愚蠢到了极点。*His sister's beautiful as all get-out.* 他的妹妹美极啦。另外，get-out 有不加连字符而作 get out 的情况。◇ extremely / greatly / very hard [vigorously, etc.]

get-up

a get-up [ə ˈge͵dʌp] [口] **奇装异服** 有 get *oneself* up in *something* [as *something*] 的表达法。意思是“做某种装束[打扮]”，但这种“装束”不是一般的穿戴，而是象在化装舞会中所见到的那种引人注目的“奇装异服”。*He got himself up in a cowboy outfit [as a cowboy].* 他穿起一身牛仔的装束[打扮成一个牛仔]。这个 get *oneself* up 中的 get 与 up 结合起来，变成名词，就是条头出现的 get-up，也可不加连字符，写作 getup。它的意思是“穿戴”、“服装”，但依旧保留作为动词使用时的“奇特”、“与平常不一样”的意味。化装舞会用的“服装”当然不用说了，凡是上下身完全不调和的“服装”，与年龄极端不相称的“服装”，以及三伏穿貂皮大衣的违背时令的“服装”，都算是 get-up。*Did you see the get-up Charlie has on? He looks like an old-time Mississippi gambler.* 你看见查理的怪打扮了吗？他看起来活象早年间的密西西比赌场老板。这里的“密西西比赌场老板”指过去在航行于密西西比河的船只上设赌骗取船客金钱的赌棍。*Did you see old Mrs. Barn's get-up? She must think she's a young girl, with that short skirt and frowsy hairdo.* 你看见巴恩老太太的怪打扮了吗？短短的裙子，流行的飞机头。她准以为自己是个十七八岁的姑娘哪。如上所述，get-up 始终是“穿在身上的服装”，凡是放在衣柜里的、挂在衣钩上的服装，不管多么“奇异”，也不能管它叫做 get-up。因此，象下面这一例句，也是向穿着那种服装的人提出的询问。*Where in the world did you get a get-up like that?* 你从哪儿弄来了那样一套怪打扮？另外，get-up 也有“书籍、杂志的服装”亦即“装帧”的意思。但是，这是出版界的专门术语，一般美国人知者甚少。◇ a (ridiculous) outfit

get-up-and-go

get-up-and-go [͵ge͵dʌpənˈgou] [话] **干劲** 字面意义是“站起来走”，即“要积极去干”的意思。这是含有一半“精力”、一半“意愿”的表达法。*George is one of our hardest-working employees. He has a lot of get-up-and-go.* 乔治是我们公司最努力工作的一个。他的干劲很大。如这一例句所示，大多使用于“工作”。*George will never rise very high in the company. He doesn't have any get-up-and-go.* 乔治在公司里永远不会提升到很高的职位。他没有一点儿干劲。*Ever since Harry was passed over for promotion, he seems to have lost all his get-up-and-go.* 哈里自从没有受到提拔以后，似乎丧失了他全部的工作积极性。有时限定用于“体力”。*I don't know what's wrong with me lately. I don't seem to have any get-up-and-go.* 最近，我的身体不知哪儿出了毛病。我似乎没有一点儿精神啦。也说 get-up-and-get (git-up-and-git)，但这是方言。另外，可省略 -and-go 而单用 get-up。◇ drive

ghost

Great Caesar's ghost! [ˈgreɪt ˈsiːzərz ˈgoust] [话] **哎呀!** → Great SCOTT!

not stand a ghost of a chance [nɑt ͵stændə

'goustəvə 'tʃæ(:)nts] [话] **一点希望都没有** → not have a PRAYER(of *something*)

(as) pale as a ghost [əz 'peɪləzə 'goust] [话] **面无人色** → (as) white as a SHEET

(as) white as a ghost [əz 'hwaɪdəzə 'goust] [话] **吓得面色苍白** → (as) white as a SHEET

gibber

gibber ['dʒɪbər / 'gɪbər] [口] **喋喋不休** → JABBER

gibberish

gibberish ['dʒibərɪʃ / 'gɪbərɪʃ] [口] **喋喋不休** → JABBER

gift

the gift of gab [ðə ˌgɪftəv 'gæːb] [话] **口才** gab 是“瞎扯”或“闲聊”。gift 是“天赐之物”,亦即“才能”。这一表达法直译为“闲聊的才能”,在实际使用时多半都含有“说得挺好听,就是没内容”的意思。但也有用于赞美“口若悬河”、“能说善辩”的场合,也就是不论谈话有没有内容,单指“滔滔不绝地讲话的才能”。 *If you hope to really succeed as a salesman, you have to have the gift of gab.* 要想当一个真正成功的推销员,就必须有一张利嘴。*The gift of gab comes naturally to Ross. Both his father and grandfather are well-known lawyers.* 罗斯的能说会道是天生的。他的父亲和祖父都是著名的律师。其他的形式有 a gift of gab, *one's* gift of gab 等。 *Hitler is often said to have been no more than a small man with a large gift of gab.* 人们常说希特勒不过是个能说会道的渺小人物而已。*Seldom have I met a man with such a gift of gab.* 我几乎没有见过象他这样有口才的人。 *I wish I had a gift of gab like yours.* 我希望有你那样的口才呀。这句话也可以说: *I wish I had your gift of gab.* 另外有个表达法是 the gift of the gab, 但象这样给 gab 加定冠词乃是英国英语。◇ the ability to talk easily and fluently

look a gift horse in the mouth → HORSE

G. I. Joe

a G. I. Joe [ə ˌdʒi(:)ˌaɪ 'dʒou] [话] **一般士兵** → a good JOE

gills

green around the gills [ˌgri(:)nəraundðə 'gi(:)lz] [话] **脸色发青快要呕吐** 字面意义是“两鳃周围呈绿色”。人并没有鳃,但是不知什么缘故,这一表达法单单用以表示人的脸色。脸色发青,有马上就要呕吐的感觉。 *After sailing all day through heavy seas we were all green around the gills.* 在狂风大浪的海上航行一整天,我们大家全都脸色发青,好象马上就要呕吐出来了。 *When he heard how the vultures had eaten the soldiers' bodies, he began to go green around the gills.* 当他听人家讲秃鹫怎样啄食士兵尸体的时候,他脸色发青,快要呕吐了。如以上的例句所示,这一表达法用于因晕车晕船、见到悲惨情景或者闻到难闻气味而“脸色发青,快要呕吐”的场合。*I'm not used to flying, so I'm feeling a little green around the gills.* 我坐不惯飞机,所以有点儿要呕吐的感觉。 *Someone must have told Eric that his blind date was with that ugly fatso Gloria Hogg. He was looking positively green around the gills.* 一定有人告诉埃里克说他的相亲对象就是那个又胖又丑的格洛里娅·霍格了。你瞧他的脸色已经发青啦。另外,在英国英语中,前置词一般不用 around, 而用 about。◇ sick (at the stomach)

be stuffed to the gills [ˌstʌf(:)tðə 'gɪ(:)lz] [话] **吃得饱饱的,几乎动不了地方** be stuffed 是“塞得满满的”。 to the gills 的字面意义是“一直到鳃”。本来人是不会有 gills(鳃)的,但有时用此词作为“腮帮子”的轻松的表达法。正是汉语俗语所说“吃得都堵到嗓子眼儿了”的意思。当别人请吃饭,自己已经吃饱了的时候,常常这样说: *No, thank you. I couldn't eat any more. I'm stuffed to the gills.* 不,谢谢,我不能再多吃了。我已经饱得快动不了地方啦。 *After that giant meal, we were all stuffed to the gills.* 在那么丰盛的一餐之后,我们全都酒足饭饱,几乎连地方都动不了啦。从本来的意义出发，也常用于人以外的事物，表示"塞得满满的"、"挤得满满的"的意思。在这一场合，动词除 stuffed 外，还使用 packed, loaded, crammed 等。后边多用 with ~ 继续，表示"用(什么塞满)"。*The truck was loaded to the gills with furniture.* 大卡车上装了满满一车家具。*The theater was packed to the gills with eager jazz fans.* 剧院里挤满了爵士乐迷。另外，be loaded to the gills 在应用于人的时候，常有"酒灌到 gills"的意味。*He was loaded to the gills.* 他已经酩酊大醉了。◇ be completely full

gimme

gimme [ˈgɪmi] [话] **给我!** → have the GIMMIES

gimmies

have the gimmies [ˌhævðə ˈgɪmiːz] [话] **患伸手病** gimme 是"给我!"，在日常会话中，give me 的发音为 gimme, 所以直接拼写这样一个词。由于孩子们一天到晚地说 Gimme! Gimme! 于是又模仿英语中的病名，创造了个复数形式 gimmies。have 是 have a cold (患感冒) 中的 have。一般在说笑时或半开玩笑时使用。*You've got the gimmies, haven't you. Just be patient and I'll let you have it when I finish.* 你患了伸手病不是? 请你忍耐一下，等我用完了就借给你。如这一例句所示，不仅限于"要"，还有"借"、"看"、"使用"等各种各样的情况。常用 really 加强语气。*That child really has the gimmies. Every time I start using something, he wants to have it.* 那个孩子真的患了伸手病。每次我开始使用什么东西，他总是要。人们在说病症的场合使用 a case of, 可以把这个词组插入本条的表达法，作 have a case of the gimmies, 意思不变。*Maybe we should call a doctor. You seem to have a case of the gimmies.* 咱们应该请大夫来了。你似乎害了伸手病啦。get (a case of) the gimmies 是"得上伸手病"。下面例句中 a bad case of 的 bad 只是加强语气。*Whenever I take Suzy to a department store, she gets a bad case of the gimmies.* 每当我带苏吉去百货商店的时候，她见到什么要什么。with (a case of) the gimmies 是"具有伸手病"。*I've never seen a child with such a bad case of the gimmies as you have.* 我从来没有见过象你这样有严重伸手病的孩子，见什么要什么。◇ want everything / have a case of acquisitiveness

girl

a bachelor girl [ə ˈbæ(ː)tʃələr ˌgə(ː)rl] [口] **年轻的单身女子** a bachelor 是"单身男子"。但是，"单身女子"叫什么呢? 在英语中没有适当的名词。过去曾经叫过 a maid, 然而自从用 maid 表示"女仆"、"侍女"的意思以后，就失去"未婚女性"的意义了。现在只剩下一个 an old maid 的表达法，既然有 old 作定语，当然也不能用于年轻的女性。因此，就出现了 bachelor girl 这样一个新名词。此词并非专指"未婚女性"，而是指那些不依赖父母、靠劳动挣钱、一个人或与其他 bachelor girls 一起住在公寓里过活的女性。主要指二十岁左右的女子，但把三十岁以下的这类女子均称为 bachelor girl 也没有什么问题。*More bachelor girls work in Washington than in any other city in America.* 在华盛顿，参加工作的年轻单身女子比美国其他任何城市都多。◇ an independent, unmarried girl

a girl Friday → FRIDAY

gismo

a gismo [ə ˈgɪ(ː)zˌmou] [话] **叫不出名字的东西** → a THINGAMABOB

git-up-and-git

git-up-and-git [ˌgɪˌdʌpənˈgɪt] [话] **工作积极性** → GET-UP-AND-GO

give

give as good as *one* gets [ˌgɪvəz ˌgudəz ~ ˈge(ː)ts] [话] **不服输** 美国人日常使用的一个表达法。意思是"在打架或辩论中不甘心失败，而要进行相等的反扑或反驳"，亦即"不服输"。这一表达法的前提是"乍看起来很软弱"，在使用时大多伴有表示此种情况的词句。*Tim is small, but when he gets in a fight, he gives as good as he gets.* 蒂姆身材很小，但是在打架的时候，他是决不服输的。常常加助动词 can，但意思不变。*Sarah may seem very demure, but when she gets into an argument, she can give as good as she gets.* 萨拉看起来非常娴静，但是一争吵起来，她是不肯示弱的。*We may be a small company but we've got lots of connections. If you start a price war with us, you'll find that we can give as good as we get.* 我们虽然算是一个小公司，但是业务往来的范围很广。如果你们要搞价格战争，我们决不示弱，要给你们一点颜色看看。◇ compete on even terms

give *oneself* away [ˌgɪv ~ əˈweɪ] [口] **露马脚** → a dead GIVEAWAY

What I wouldn't give for *something*! [ˌhwɑdaɪ ˌwudntˈgɪ(ː)vfər ~] [话] **(如果……)那该多么好啊!** 直译为"为了得到某种事物，我什么不能给呀"，亦即"为了得到某种事物，我什么都豁出去啦"。乍一看好象是表示"一定要把某种东西弄到手"的强烈意志，其实并不是如此。这一表达法是表示一种强烈的愿望，意思是"如果把……弄到手，那该多么好啊"，为了突出这种愿望的强烈程度，所以在语气上便加重了一些。*What I wouldn't give for a car like that!* 我要是能有那样一辆小轿车，那该多么好啊！*What I wouldn't give for a week off this summer!* 今年夏天如果能休息一个星期，那该多么好啊！也可以将 for *something* 的部分换成 to *do something*，采取 What I wouldn't give to *do something*! 的形式。例如，上边两个例句中 for 以下的部分分别可以改作 to have a car like that 和 to have a week off this summer，意思相同。*What I wouldn't give to be able to get into that university!* 我要是能进那所大学，那该多么好啊！另外还可以使用肯定的形式，作 What I would give for *something* [to *do something*]! 上边的所有例句均可改换为肯定式。不过，一般都用条头的否定形式，语气比较强烈。◇ How wonderful it would be to have *something*!

would give anything [wud ˌgɪvˈeniˌθɪŋ] [话] **(如果……)该多么好!** → would give *one's* right ARM

giveaway

a dead giveaway [ˈde(ː)d ˈgɪvəˌweɪ] [口] **无意中暴露的确凿证据** a giveaway 是由 give *oneself* away (露马脚)而来的名词，dead 是强调"彻底"的形容词。本条在谈到只要一看[听、闻、摸、尝]就会了解的事物时使用。*The man let on that he was well-to-do, but his old, scuffed shoes were a dead giveaway.* 那个人装模作样，摆出了有钱人的架势，但是他的那双又旧又破的皮鞋完全揭了他的老底儿。*A: How did you know that someone else had been in the apartment with Charlie? B: The cigarette butts in the ashtray were a dead giveaway. Charlie doesn't smoke.* 甲：你怎么知道在公寓的房间里除了查理还有另外的人呢？乙：烟灰碟里烟头就是确凿的证据，因为查理不吸烟。*He looked like a Chinese and used a Chinese name, but I knew right away that he was an Japanese. His accent was a dead giveaway.* 他的样子象中国人，而且用的是中国姓名，但是我马上就知道他是一个日本人。他的口音完全暴露了他的身份。*Miss Marple knew immediately that the man had been poisoned with potassium cyanide. The faint smell of almonds was a dead giveaway.* 玛普小姐立即明白那个男子是被氰化钾毒死的。轻微的杏仁味就是确凿的证据。◇ (不加动词 be) betray *someone* / betray that fact

giver

an Indian giver [ə ˈnɪndɪən ˌgɪvər] [话] **送东西给人而日后又往回要的人** 这一表达法最初是"给人送礼而指望还礼的人"的意思，不知从什么时候起，已经专指"送东西给人而日后又往回要的人"了。孩子们的习用语。*Toby may have given you these books, but don't start celebrating yet. He's famous for being an Indian giver.* 托比可能送给你这几本书了，

但是不要高兴得太早。他送东西又往回要，是出了名的啊。*Don't be an Indian giver. You gave me this ball, so let me keep it.* 你不要给人东西又往回要啊。这个球你给了我，就算是我的吧。关于这一表达法的语源，有如下的说法：在过去，某些印第安部族中有送礼必须还礼的习俗。因此，有不少印第安人为了得到新奇的东西而向白种人送礼。后来，就把一般给人送礼而指望还礼的人都称为“印第安送礼者”了。另外，“Indian”一词过去有“虚假的”一义，所以本条的表达法也可以解释为“虚假的送礼者”。现在，如果从种族差别的立场出发而对美国印第安人抱有如此侮辱的观念，那是很成问题的。然而，要想把经过一个历史时期在人类社会中已经固定下来的语言一笔勾销，也非易事。另外还有用表示“虚假的”一义的 Indian 作为形容词构成的习用语，而其中丝毫不带轻蔑的意思，甚至如 Indian summer (小阳春) 那样，反倒令人产生愉快的感觉。◇ a person who takes back things *he* has given away

gives

What gives? → WHAT

gizzard

stick in *someone's* **gizzard** [ˌstɪkɪn ~ ˈgɪzərd] [话] **非常讨厌** gizzard 是鸟类的“砂囊”，即把吞下去的固体物质咬碎的器官。stick 在这里是“卡住不动”的意思。因此，本条直译为“在……的砂囊里卡住不动了”。这一表达法最初的构思是：“由于吃了讨厌的东西，食物堵在喉咙里”。汉语成语“如梗在喉”，正是此意。*That guy's attitude sticks in my gizzard.* 那个家伙的态度使我讨厌极了。*The belief of many Americans that the American way is always best has long stuck in my gizzard.* 许多美国人认为他们的生活方式永远是最好的，我始终对这种信念感到非常厌恶。*The way so many politicians make promises only to break them after they're elected sticks in my gizzard.* 许许多多的政治家在当选以后就不信守自己的诺言，我对他们的这种做法万分讨厌。可以使用 craw (鸟的嗉子) 代替 gizzard 而说 stick in *someone's* craw，意思和用法与 stick in *someone's* gizzard 完全相同，任何时候都可以相互替换。◇ be very unpalatable to *someone*

glad

glad rags → RAGS

glass

have a glass jaw → JAW

glove

fit (*someone*) **like a glove** [ˌfɪtlaɪkə ˈglʌːv] [口] **恰到好处** glove 是“手套”。这一表达法来自人们一般的想法：“手套戴到手上必须完全合适”。*My new wetsuit fits like a glove.* 我的新保温潜水服正合身。这是用于服装。*That must be Ned that you're talking about. The description fits him like a glove.* 你所谈的人一定是内德，你的描述恰恰与他吻合。这是用于描述。此外，也可以用于环境、称呼等等。例如：*Reg wasn't sure he would like teaching in a Chinese university, but when he tried it, he found the environment fit him like a glove.* 雷吉原来对于自己是否喜欢在一所中国的大学教书没有信心，但是他试了一段时间之后，发现那个环境对他是非常适宜的。*I don't see why he should object to being called a fool. The appellation fits like a glove.* 我真不明白他为什么反对人家管他叫混蛋。这个名称对他是再合适也没有了。◇ fit [suit] (*someone*) perfectly

an iron hand in a velvet glove → HAND

gloves

handle *someone* [*something*] **with kid gloves** [ˌhændl ~ wɪð ˌkɪd ˈglʌːvz] [口] **小心谨慎地对待** kid (小山羊)的皮柔软光滑，论皮子的质量属于最高级。本条习用语直译为“戴上小山羊皮手套去拿”。不是光着手，而是戴上最高级的、柔软的皮手套去拿，其小心翼翼的神态可谓跃然纸上了。在对待“人”、“物”、“事态”等场合均表示十分慎重的态度，即对“人”注意不惹他恼怒，对“物”注意不使它损坏，对"事态"注意不使它恶化。*You'd better handle the boss with kid gloves today. He got out of bed on the wrong side this morning.* 今天你对老板可要谨慎一些。从早晨起，他就不顺气。*My grandfather is extremely temperamental. You have to handle him with kid gloves.* 我的祖父性情非常暴躁，你对他可要小心谨慎。*This mate very explosive. It has to be handed with kid gloves.* 这种原料极容易爆炸。对它可要万分小心。*The situation between the two countries is extremely delicate. It could explode into war if it is not handled with kid gloves.* 两国之间的情况极端微妙。如果不谨慎从事，就可能爆发战争。◇ handle *someone*[*something*] extremely carefully

glutton

be a glutton for punishment [ə 'glʌtnfər 'pʌniʃmənt] [口] **有受罪的瘾头** glutton 本来是"大肚子汉"的意思，引伸作"贪图者"、"酷爱者"解。*Robert is a glutton for ice cream.* 罗伯特非常爱吃冰淇淋。因此，条头如果直译的话，就是"非常喜欢严厉惩罚(punishment)的人"。*Anyone who would marry a sharp-tongued girl like Hazel must be a glutton for punishment.* 凡是愿意跟黑兹尔那样尖酸刻薄的姑娘结婚的人，肯定是不打不骂不自在的家伙。如这一例句所示，一般含有讽刺的意味，指汉语俗语所说的"天生的贱骨头"。*A: How come you're taking so many courses this term? B: I guess I'm just a glutton for punishment.* 甲：你这一学期怎么选修那么多门课程呀？乙：大概我有点受罪的瘾头吧。常用 real 加强语气。*The challenger is on his last legs, but still he refuses to throw in the towel. He seems to be a real glutton for punishment.* 挑战者眼看支撑不住了，但是他仍然不肯认输。看起来，他真有挨揍的瘾头呢。另外，有的英华词典把 a glutton for punishment 译成"不怕挨打的拳击家"，那并不是这一表达法的真正意义，只不过人们常把它用在拳击等运动员的身上而已。◇ like to suffer

go

from the word go → WORD

go off without a hitch → HITCH

Go on (with you). ['gou.ɔ:n (.wiðju:)] [话] **((半信半疑地))怎么可能呢？** Go on [.gou'ɔ:n]本来是"不要停下，继续往前走！"的意思。*Go on. I'll catch up within a few minutes.* 你先往前走，我两三分钟就会追上你。又用于表示"继续说下去！"。例如：*Go on. Please explain a little further.* 请继续讲下去，解释得更详细一些。以上的 Go on. 的用法极其普遍，人们已经司空见惯了。另外在美国，本条的表达法还常用于表示对对方所说的事情怀抱着半信半疑的态度。在这一场合的 Go on. 发音的语调与作"继续下去！"解的 Go on. 略有差异，即 on 的音要拉长：[ɔ:n—]。*Go on. This picture can't be worth that much.* 怎么可能呢？这张画值不了那么多钱。*Go on. Nobody can read a 500-page novel in 40 minutes.* 怎么可能呢？任何人四十分钟也读不完一部五百页的长篇小说。如果后边加上 with you，语气进一步加强，但 Go on with you. 为女性用语，男子一般不加 with you。*Go on with you. He didn't really say that, did he?* 怎么可能呢？他不会说那样的话吧，是不是？虽然心里愿意相信对方的话，但是又怕对方在开玩笑，为了弄清对方的话是真是假，不免想叫对方进一步说下去。在这种时候，也常使用本条的表达法。*A: You're the prettiest girl in school. B: Oh, go on (with you). There are lots of girls prettier than I am.* 甲：你是咱们学校最漂亮的姑娘啊。乙：怎么会呢？比我好看的女孩子多着呢。顺便讲一下：这里的 Go on (with you). 与 GET out of here. 相似，但前者表示"半信半疑"的语调比较轻。另外，Go on with you. 偶尔表示"赶紧去"的意思，例如：*Go on with you now. Go outside and play.* 喂，走啦走啦！到外边玩去吧！◇ That's impossible [ridiculous].

go out for *something* [.gou'autfər ～]

[口] **参加选拔考试** 这一表达法与 TRY out for *something* 的意义基本上相同，在用法上主要有两点区别：一是专指学校[大学]体育队、乐团、剧团的选拔考试；二是 go out for 下面的 *something* 处不仅可以代入 team 或 club, 而且可以代入 activity (活动)本身，也就是说，不仅可以把组织而且可以把活动放在宾语的地位。具体地讲，我们可以说：*Are you going out for the baseball team?* 你打算参加棒球队的选拔赛吗？也可以说：*Are you going out for baseball?* 你打算参加棒球的选拔赛吗？两句话的意义完全是一码事。*I'm going out for glee club.* 我打算参加合唱团的入团考试。◇ enter the trials to become a member for *something*

go under [ˌgouˈʌndər] [话] **倒闭** 这一表达法是 go under the waves (沉到波浪底下)省略掉 the waves 形成的，原意为"沉没"。*The ship went under.* 船沉没了。转作比喻，用于公司商行等。最初的构思是："公司商行等象船一样沉没"。这一表达法的反义语是 keep *one's* HEAD above water。*If we don't bring in some business from somewhere soon, we're going to go under.* 如果不赶快从什么地方弄点生意做，咱们的公司就得倒闭啦。◇ go bankrupt

(have) got to go [(həv) ˌgɑdəˈgou] [话] **想去解手** 轻松的表达法，一般在朋友之间使用。比 have (got) to go to the toilet 或 have (got) to go to the bathroom 的说法委婉一些。意思是："我憋不住了，必须去厕所啦。"可以按照字面意义("非去不可")使用，例如：*I've got to go. I'll be late as it is.* 我必须走啦。现在出发，已经要晚了。下面是按照条头释义的用例。*I wonder if they have any facilities in this place. I've got to go.* 不知道这个地方有没有厕所之类的设备？我想解个手。*Excuse me just a minute. I gotta go.* 对不起，我出去一下。我想解个手。大厦、加油站等处的厕所一般称 restroom, 高速公路、公园等处单独设立的厕所(即公共厕所)一般称 public toilet。*They should build some public toilets between the airport and city. When people've got to go, they've got to go. They can't just sit around in traffic an hour or more, waiting to get to town.* 在飞机场和城市之间应该修几个公共厕所。当人们想要解手的时候，不去解是不行的。叫他们在车上硬呆一个小时或更多的时间，等到城里再说，那他们可等不了。*My grandfather was quite a card. The last thing he said on his deathbed was, "Don't worry about me. When ya gotta go, ya gotta go."* 我爷爷真是一个有趣的人。他在病床上最后的遗言是："不要为我担心。人到该去的时候非去不可。"这是说的俏皮话，最后一句包含着"人死如去解手，不去不行"的诙谐意味。◇ have to go to the toilet

make a go of *something* [ˌmeɪkəˈgouəv ～] [话] **获得成功** 由 make *something* go (使某事顺利进行) 的表达法而来。本条的意思是"取得成功"、"一帆风顺"。*MMy brother started a company some years ago but was never able to make a go of it.* 我哥哥几年前开设了一家公司，但是生意始终没有能够兴隆。*Do you think he'll make a go of his new restaurant?* 你以为他新开的餐厅生意会好吗？如以上的例句所示，这一表达法多用于商业或工作，但也用于如下的场合：*Jack and Betty never should have married. Though both of them tried to adapt to each other, their personalities were too strong. They just couldn't make a go of it.* 杰克和贝蒂这两个人根本就不应该结婚。虽然他们都曾努力迁就对方，但是两个人的个性都太强。他们的夫妻生活怎么也达不到美满的地步。*something* 处也可以代入动名词。*Jim's got a lot of experience in sales. I'm sure he'll make a go of selling cars as well.* 吉姆在销售方面具有丰富的经验，我敢肯定他推销汽车也一定会成功的。◇ make a success of *something*

be no go [ˈnou ˈgou] [话] **白费劲** 这里的 go 是作为名词使用的。本条最初的构思是："(事情)不进展，不向前走"。在客观情况不容许做某种事情的场合使用。

We tried to get back in time for the meeting, but it was no go. 我们竭力往回赶，准备参加会议，可是误了会期，白费劲了。*If you want to buy one of the houses in that subdivision, I'm afraid it's no go. They've all been sold.* 如果你想要在那个小区买所房子，很遗憾，办不到啦。那里的房屋全都卖出去了。如以下的两个例句所示，在怎样劝说也没有用的场合特别频繁地使用这一表达法。*It's no go. No matter what I say, he refuses to lend us the money.* 瞎子点灯白费蜡。不管我怎么说，他也不肯借给咱们钱。*You can talk until you're blue in the face, but it's no go. You're too young to have a car.* 你就是把嘴唇磨破了也不顶用。你太小了，还不能有辆汽车。◇ be impossible / be no use

be *always* **on the go** [~ ˌɔ(ː)nðə ˈgou] [话] **频繁活动** on the go 与 always going someplace 相同，是"一会儿向东走，一会儿向西走，总是不断地活动"的意思。在使用时经常带有"忙忙碌碌"的意味。 *I get tired just watching Skip. He's always on the go.* 我只是看管斯基普就够累啦。他一刻不停地活动。在这句话里，斯吉普可以是幼小的儿童，也可以是个成年人。若为前者意思是"到处乱跑"；若为后者意思是"转来转去"。除 always 外，还用其他的副词作为时间状语，如 constantly, all the time, all day, all week, all *one's* life, since early this morning 等。 *What with the boss away and two different groups of visiting firemen to entertain, I've been on the go all week.* 老板不在，又得接待两批远方来的贵宾，这一个星期我简直忙得不可开交。 *Hong Kong people seem to be constantly on the go.* 香港人似乎总在忙忙叨叨。◇ be *always* busy

to go [təˈgou] [话] **带走的** 由不定式构成的形容词短语，与 to eat [drink] here (在这里吃[喝]的)相对。在饭馆、汽车餐馆、汉堡包小吃店等处买食品时的用语。*Give me two hamburgers to go.* 给我两个带走的汉堡包。*A: I'll take a chocolate shake. B: To drink here or to go? A: To go, please.* 甲：我要一个巧克力汁。乙：在这里喝的还是带走的？甲：请给我带走。有时用 to take out [tə ˌteɪ ˈkaut]代替 to go。◇ to eat [drink] away from the premises

be touch and go → TOUCH

go-ahead

get the go-ahead (from *someone*) [ˌgetðə ˈgouəˌhe(ː)d] [话] **得到许可** → give (*someone*) the green LIGHT

give (*someone*) **the go-ahead** [ˌgɪv ~ ðə ˈgouəˌhe(ː)d] [话] **批准** → give (*someone*) the green LIGHT

goat

get *someone's* **goat** [ˌget ~ˈgout] [话] **使人恼怒** 字面意义是"取走某人的山羊"。古时，在赛马的头一天夜里，有把马与山羊放在一起的习俗。这样，马可以安心休息，第二天会跑出好成绩。如果在赛马的前夜，把拴在竞争对手的马厩中的山羊取走，就会刺激对方的马的神经，而对自己的马有利。这就是本条习用语的来源。"刺激神经"可能有种种不同的程度，因此在翻译时要根据上下文采取适当的词句，如"使人勃然大怒"、"使人恼火"、"使人生气"、"使人不大高兴"等等。 *That guy gets my goat. He's always inviting me out for a drink and then claiming to have forgotten to bring any money.* 那小子真叫我生气。他总是约我出去喝酒，但是一算帐，他就说忘带钱了。在讲一般情况的场合，常用 the way 导入"使人恼怒"的原因。*It gets me goat the way some people push onto a train before the passengers on board can get off.* 有些人在上火车的时候，不等乘客下车就一拥而入，这种行为真叫我生气。*Politicians get my goat the way they make campaign promises they know they can never keep.* 那些政客们真叫我恼火，他们偏偏在选举中许下他们明知不能信守的诺言。在讲特定情况的场合，一般用 with *something* 或者 by *doing something* 表示"使人恼怒"的原因。 *I'll admit I shouldn't have hit him, but he finally got my goat with his insinuations about* *how I made my money*. 我承认我不应该揍他，但是他含沙射影地讽刺我的钱的来路，使我按不住怒火了。*That chick's a real tiger. She scratched my face when I got her goat by calling her a young heifer*. 那个小娘儿们可真是个母老虎。当我叫她一声小骚货的时候，把她惹恼了，竟抓破了我的脸。◇ irritate [provoke] *someone*

goats

separate the sheep from the goats → SHEEP

gob

a gob [ə ˈgɑːb] [话] **水兵** 原为美国海军俚语。与将校对称，指中士以下的水兵。偶尔也有指将校级而言的时候，但一般用于泛指"下级的水兵"。关于 gob 的语源，有人说它是 gobble (狼吞虎咽) 的缩略。船上的工作是重体力劳动，所以吃得多。此说真伪如何，尚无定论。*When the war started, I joined the air force and my brother became a gob*. 战争开始的时候，我参加了空军，我弟弟当了水兵。*The bar was full of gobs and their girls*. 那个酒吧间挤满了水兵和他们的女朋友。gob 虽然一般指"水兵"，但有时用以表示"普通船员"的意思。例如在下一例句中，gob 可以作"水兵"解，也可以作"驶船的老百姓"解，二者均讲得通。*Henry was a gob for almost thirty years*. 亨利干了 30 来年的水上活儿。a tar 为俗语，意思也是"水手"或"水兵"。此词是自古以来就有的英语，由英伦三岛传入美国。它的来源是：在古时候，水兵戴着用 tarpaulin [ˈtɑrpələn] (柏油帆布) 制作的帽子。虽然是个旧词，至今仍然使用。*Being a tar in the old days was a rough life*. 在过去的时代，当水手是非常辛苦的工作。另有 an old salt 的表达法，令人产生"长年盐渍"的感觉，既指"老资格的水手"，也指"上了年级的水手"。*My uncle's an old salt. He's teaching us how to sail*. 我的叔父是一位老资格的水手，他在教我们怎样驾驶快艇。*There were several old salts sitting around a table talking of the good old days*. 有几个老水手围坐在桌子旁边漫谈过去美好的时代。gob, tar, old salt 都是俗话，一般的称呼为 a sailor 或者 an old sailor。◇ a sailor

God's

for God's sake [fər ˈgɑ(ː)dzˈseɪk] [俗] **无论如何** → for Pete's SAKE

goes

the deal goes through → DEAL

goes-inner

a goes-inner [ə ˌgoˈzɪnər] [话] **凹下的肚脐** → a belly BUTTON

goes-outer

a goes-outer [ə ˌgoˈzaudər] [话] **凸出的肚脐** → a belly BUTTON

go-getter

a go-getter [ə ˈgouˈge(ː)dər] [话] **精力充沛、积极进取的人** 由 go and get (去取来)产生的表达法。指"为了达到目标，精力充沛、到处活动的人"。在使用时，什么年龄或性别都可以。*In the business world, " go-getter" is a term of praise; in the government bureaucracy, it's a criticism*. 在商界，"能钻的人"一词有褒义；在政界，这个名词是指责。一般来说，这是个褒义词，有"活跃"而且"能干"的意思。*Charlie is a go-getter. He'll make an excellent student body president*. 查理是一个精力充沛、积极肯干的人，他会成为一个优秀的学生会主席。在"工作"、"公司"等方面使用的场合最多，例如：*Successful newspaper reporters are all go-getters*. 凡是有成就的新闻记者，都是精力充沛、积极活动的人。*Not being a natural-born go-getter, I was happy to be transferred from sales to the personnel department*. 我天生不是一个好活动的人，因此从销售部调到人事部，我感到很高兴。*Many young go-getters these days are dropping out of big corporations to form their own companies*. 最近有许多精明强干的青年人都脱离大企业而去建立自己的公司。◇ an enterprising person with lots of drive

going

What's going on? → WHAT'S

while the going is good [ˌhwaɪlðə ˌgouənəz ˈguːd] [话] **不失时机** 这里的 going 的本来意义是"道路或路面的状况"。本条的字面意义是:"趁着道路好走的时候"。*The snow is beginning to fall pretty fast. If we hope to get home tonight, we'd better go while the going is good.* 雪开始下大了。如果我们想今天晚上到家,要趁路还好走的时候赶快启程。这是按字面意义的用法,句子的最后部分也可以改换说 *We'd better go before the going gets too bad.* 作为比喻,这个 going 意味着"形势"或"情况"。while the going is good 则是"趁着大好形势"或者"不失时机"的意思。*The police will be here soon. We'd better get out of here while the going is good.* 警察马上就要来啦。我们抓紧时间,赶快溜走吧。*Apparently there's going to be a bad recession soon. I'm going to take my money out of the stock market while the going is good.* 很明显,大萧条时期马上就要到来了,我不能错过时机,要把我的钱从股票市场收回来。如以上的例句所示,这一表达法用于预料情况不妙的场合。good 的前面常添加 still 一词。*In the late 1930's, thousands of Jews were flowing out of Nazi Germany, determined to leave while the going was still good.* 在20世纪30年代后半期,有成千上万的犹太人逃离纳粹德国。他们决心在未受迫害之前赶紧到国外去。也可以不用 going,如说:*We'd better get out of here while the getting is good.* 趁着这功夫,咱们最好赶快离开这儿。这是把前边的动词重复一遍,以代替 going,意思不变。◇ while conditions are (still) favorable / before it's too late

win (*something*) **going away** [ˌwɪn ˌgouənəˈweɪ] [话] **压倒的胜利** 原为赛马用语。going away 是"不断离开",亦即"比其他的马越来越领先"。加上个 win,就成为"大获全胜"的意思了。*Apple Knocker won the Kentucky Derby going away.* 在肯塔基大奖赛中,"乡巴佬"(马名)获得了压倒的胜利。转用于赛马以外的事情。*Muhammad Ali won going away.* 穆罕默德·阿里取得了压倒的胜利。*The Republican candidate won going away.* 共和党候选人取得了压倒的胜利。◇ win (*something*) overwhelmingly

gold

everything *one* **touches turns to gold** [ˌevriθɪŋ ~ ˈtʌtʃəz. tə(:)rnztə ˈgould] [口] **干什么都发财** → have the Midas TOUCH

a gold digger → DIGGER

have a heart of gold → HEART

golden

kill the golden goose [ˌkɪlðə ˌgouldən ˈguːs] [口] **杀鸡取卵** → kill the GOOSE that laid the golden eggs

Golly

Golly. [ˈgɑ(:)li] [话] **天哪!** God. 的委婉语,作感叹词使用。与同义的 GEE. 有别,即大人、小孩均常使用。语气比 Gee. 强一些。*Golly, look at all the people.* 天哪! 你看那里人山人海。*Golly, I didn't know Mr. Friendly was that old.* 天哪! 我不知道弗兰德利先生的年纪有那么大呀。如以上的例句所示,在表示单纯惊异的场合使用频率最高。但与 Gee. 同样用于"同情"、"困窘"、"失望"、"钦佩"的场合,例如:*Golly, that's too bad.* 哎呀! 那太不幸啦! *Golly, did I hurt you? I'm sorry.* 哎呀,伤着你了吗? 太对不起啦。*Golly, Mom. Why do I have to go to bed so early?* 哎呀,妈妈! 我为什么非那么早上床睡觉不可啊? 特别是成年人使用的场合,为了加强语气,前面可以加 My。*My golly, the price of that stock has almost doubled in one month.* 我的天哪! 在一个月的功夫,那种股票的价格竟上涨了一倍左右。另有一个 by golly 的表达法,在出乎意料之外时表示惊讶的场合使用,例如:*By golly, it looks as if he may actually succeed.* 嘿! 看起来,他也许真的会成功呢! 也可以在对方说完话以后,用强烈的口气表明自己的态度时使用,具有"绝对地”的意味。例如：*You made me a promise, and by golly you're going to keep it.* 你向我做了诺言，说话可得绝对算数啊！

gone

be gone on *someone* [ˈgɔː nɔ(ː)n ～] [话] **迷恋(异性)** 直译为“(心)跑到某人身上去了”，也就是已经不能控制自己的感情。*Jack seems to be gone on that new girl in our class.* 杰克似乎迷恋上我们班那个新来的女生啦。如这一例句所示，这一表达法专用于“男女关系”。*Don't be so shy. Ask Sally for a date. She'll be gone on you before you know it.* 你不要那样羞怯嘛，去向萨莉提出约会，她很快就会迷上你的。偶尔有用 over 代替 on 的情况。*I met her on the first of April, and by the end of the month I was completely gone over her.* 4月1日我第一次遇见她，到了4月底，我完全迷上她了。这一表达法始终是相当轻松的。◇ be captivated by *someone*

goner

a goner [ə ˈgɔːnər] [话] **必然垮台的人[物]** 字面意义是“走了的人”。乍看起来是“走向来世，已经无可挽救”的意思，但在实际上并不仅仅用于死的场合，在夸大表现自己处于非常糟糕的状态或绝望的状态时也使用这个词。多半用于条件句“如果……，……就完蛋啦”。*If the enemy discovers our whereabouts, we're goners.* 如果敌人发现我们的所在，我们就完蛋啦。*If my wife finds out, I'm a goner.* 如果我妻子发现了，我就完蛋啦。如上面的例句所示，一般用于虽然前途未卜但是现在还苟安一时的场合。不过，当现在正成为 goner 的时候，也使用这一表达法。在这一场合，实际上专指“处于濒死状态的人”而言。*The man in the wrecked car appeared to be a goner.* 在撞坏的汽车里的那个人，看起来没希望啦。把 goner 应用于物的场合，意思是“肯定垮台的东西”。*One more earthquake and this building is a goner.* 再来一次地震，这座大厦必然倒塌。另外，a dead DUCK 大致与 a goner 同义，但只能用于现在还活泼乱跳的场合，几乎不能用以表示实际上就要死去的人的意思。◇ doomed (to die [to face a difficult time, etc.]) / finished / all but dead

gonna

gonna [gənə] [话] **要(做)** be going to do 中的 going to 的变音，是按照 going to 在日常会话中的发音记写的形式，在漫画、小说等的会话部分经常出现。*I'm gonna study now.* 我现在要学习啦。*Tom's gonna go swimming.* 汤姆要去游泳。*They're gonna come tonight.* 他们今天晚上要来。另外，go 在按本来的意义“去”使用的时候，即使在句子中出现 going to 的形式，也决不发音为 [gənə]，因此也不采取 gonna 这一变音的形式。下面两个例句意味着“吉姆要去纽约”，请比较一下：① Jim is gonna go to [gənə ˈgodə] New York. ② Jim is going to [ˈgoəntə] (正式发音为[ˈgoɪŋ tu]) New York. ◇ going to

goober

a goober [ə ˈguːbər] [话] **落花生** 美国南部方言，现在全国也通用。在南方作家福克纳(William Faulkner, 1897–1962)等人的小说中经常出现。是黑人从非洲带到美洲的安哥拉语 *nguba* 的形变。*I simply love goobers.* 我非常喜欢吃花生。*Want a poke for your goobers?* 要不要一个小口袋把你的花生装起来？有时又称 a goober pea。◇ a peanut

good

be all well and good → WELL

for good [fər ˈgu(ː)d] [口] **永远地** 一般的英华词典都在 good 一词下面收有 for good (and all) 这一成语，但加上表示强调的 and all 者主要是英国英语，在现代的美国英语中只用 for good 的表达法。*Jim is not coming back. He's gone for good.* 吉姆不回来了，他永远地不在了。*You can't talk me into going back to work for that company. I've quit for good.* 不管你怎么说，我也不回那个公司工作了。我已经辞职，再也不干啦。

Though wounded twice, the soldier continued to move forward. Then a third bullet stopped him for good. 虽然两次负伤，那个士兵继续前进。后来，第三颗子弹使他永远停止不动了。虽然与表示"离去"、"辞退"、"停止"等意义的动词一起使用的场合比较多，但并不限定如此，有时也与表示"前来"、"归来"、"恢复"等意义的动词一起使用。*I am never leaving again. I've come home for good.* 我今后哪儿也不去了。我永远留在故乡啦。如以上的例句所示，一般用于"永久"(亦即"无限期")的场合，但有时也用于"有限期"的场合，表示在一定的时间内"一直"如何如何。*I don't think you'll need your umbrella. It looks as if the rain has stopped for good.* 我看你用不着伞了，雨好象已经完全停啦。◇ forever / permanently

give as good as *one* **gets** → GIVE

good and ～ ['gudn '～] [话] **厉害、完全、非常** good and hot 是"非常热"，good and ready 是"完全准备好了"，good and hard 是"狠狠地"。也就是说，good and 的作用是强调它后边的形容词或副词，本身没有固定的意义。因此，在翻译成汉语的时候，必须根据后边的形容词或副词的意义选择适当的词语，不能生搬硬套。由于这一表达法仅仅是加强语气，所以在以下的各例句中，即使完全省略了 good and 也是极为通顺的英语，无损原意。*I like my coffee good and hot.* 我喜欢喝热热的咖啡。*I'm leaving when I'm good and ready, and not a minute before.* 我什么时候想走才走哪。在这之前，我就呆在这儿。*Make sure you hit the ball good and hard.* 你打球一定要卯足了劲儿啊! *Larry won't fight unless he gets good and mad.* 拉里如果不是发疯，他是不会打架的。也可以把 good 换成 nice, 采取 nice and ～ ['naɪsn ' ～]的形式。用法基本上一样，但两者之间略有差别。在加强语气的劲头上，nice 比较弱一些，只表示"适当地"的意味。good 是单纯加强语气，而 nice 则存在着"可爱的"、"愉快的"等意味，因此，它的使用范围比 good 要窄。所有 nice and ～均可用 good and ～代替，但反过来就不尽可能。例如丈夫喝醉了酒回家的时候说 *I was good and drunk.* 这只是我喝得太多了。如果说 *I was nice and drunk.* 则是我喝得很痛快。到第二天早晨，妻子说 *You were nice and drunk last night, weren't you.* 那是怀有好意(或者开玩笑)的话，意思是 你昨天晚上喝得挺痛快吧? 但是，如果换用 good，那就反映出她不高兴的心情，等于说 你昨天晚上猫尿灌多了吧? *I'm nice and tired tonight. I should be able to sleep well.* 今天晚上我很开心，有点累了，一定睡得香啊。*Hit it nice and hard.* 你卯点劲儿，把球打得漂漂亮亮的! ◇ really / very

a good egg → EGG

Good gravy. ['gu(:)d 'greɪvi] [话] **哎呀，天哪!** → Good GRIEF.

Good grief. → GRIEF

a good guy → GUY

a good Joe → JOE

Good night. → NIGHT

be too good to be true [ˌtu(:)ˌgudtəbi 'tru:] [口] **好得令人难以相信** 大多用以表示"说话或情况过于好了"的意思。但是，如果没有上下文，仅仅是这一表达法的话，真正的意思并不十分明确。它究竟是强调"情况好"而讲"好到令人难以相信的程度"呢? 还是表示根本不相信是真的而讲"好得令人产生疑心"呢? 这只有根据讲话或文章的前后关系来确定。例如: *I couldn't believe it. It was too good to be true. But there in black and white was my number. I had won one million dollars in the lottery.* 我真不能相信。天上怎么会往下掉馅饼? 但是白纸黑字，明明写着我的号码。我中了一百万美元的彩了。谁都看得出，这是属于前者，亦即强调"情况好"的场合。与此相反，在下一个例句中，则显然属于后者，表示不信任的态度。*A: My mother says she has decided to live with us after all. B: I knew all her talk about wanting to live alone was too good to be true.* 甲: 结果，我母亲说她已经决定跟咱们住在一起了。乙: 她过去讲想要自己过活，我根本就没相信那套好听的话。其次，这一表达法除了表示"说话好得过火"外，还表示"人或物好得过火"的意思。在这一场合，一般要在 too good 的前边加 almost, just a little 等副词。加上以后，也具有两方面的作用：一是仅仅强调好，一是表示不相信的态度。 *Your mother is a wonderful cook. Her pies are almost too good to be true.* 你的母亲真是烹饪的能手。她烤的馅饼好吃到令人难以相信的程度。 *I don't trust Mr. Goodenough. He's just a little too good to be true.* 我不信任古迪纳夫先生，他这个人好得似乎有点过火。◇ be unbelievably propitious [delicious, favorable, good, etc.] / have to be untrue / (appear to) be so propitious [favorable, good, etc.] that there (just) has to be something wrong

goodness

for goodness sake [fər ˈgudneˈsːeɪk] [话] **哎呀，我的天哪!** → for Pete's SAKE

goods

give *someone* **the straight goods** [ˌgɪv ~ ðə ˌstreɪt ˈgu(ː)dz] [话] **说老实话** straight 是"端正的"、"正直的"；goods 是"货物"、"东西"。本条的字面意义是"把正路来的东西给与某人"。转义为"说正直的话"。原为黑社会用语，现在仍有一点儿流氓无赖的口气。*Would I lie to you, Charlie? I tell you I'm giving you the straight goods.* 查理，我能跟你撒谎吗？我对你说的是大实话。◇ tell *someone* the truth

have the goods on *someone* [ˌhævðə ˈgu(ː)dzɔ(ː)n ~] [话] **掌握某人犯罪的确凿证据** 这里的 goods 原是黑社会和警察的用语，意思是"窃得的物品"。本条换个说法是 have *someone* with the goods on *him*，字面意义为"人赃俱获"。*He was caught with the goods on him.* 他连带所偷的东西被抓获了。但是，本条是一个习用语，它与"窃得的物品"并无关系，直接表示"掌握罪证"的意思。例如：*You may as well confess. We have the goods on you.* 你还是坦白交待为好，我们已经掌握你犯罪的证据了。*You better beat it outa town, Fred. I hear the cops've got the goods on you.* 弗雷德，你最好赶快从城里溜出去，我听到警爷已经掌握你作案的证据啦。这一表达法一般用于"犯罪"，但有时也可以用于并非"法律上的犯罪"的场合。 *My wife is a very suspicious woman. Every time she finds a receipt for dinner for two in my pocket or a long blond hair on my coat, she thinks she has the goods on me.* 我的妻子是一个非常多疑的女人。每当她在我的衣袋里发现一张两份客饭的账单，或者在我的外衣上发现一根金黄色的长头发，她都认为掌握了我干坏事的证据。get the goods on *someone* 是"抓住证据"。 *There's no doubt that Sam did it, but we can't get the goods on him.* 那肯定是萨姆干的，但是我们抓不到证据。◇ have (the) evidence against *someone*

sell *someone* **a bill of goods** → BILL

goof

goof off [ˌgu(ː) ˈfɔːf] [话] **偷懒耍滑** 在工作、学习等方面，自己该干而不着手去干或者虽然着手却偷懒耍滑的场合使用。至于"根本不露面"、"找借口告假"等，那不是 goof off，而要分别说 play HOOKY (from school) (逃学), cut class (逃课), skip work [a meeting] (逃避工作 [会议])。本条主要用进行时。 *Stop goofing off and get to work.* 别偷懒耍滑啦，干活吧！ *That guy is always goofing off—talking to his friends on the telephone or going out for coffee during office hours.* 那个家伙总是偷懒耍滑，在上班时间不是给朋友打电话聊天，就是跑到外边去喝咖啡。经常偷懒耍滑的人称为 a goof- off [ˈgu(ː) ˌfɔːf]。 *Bill has a good mind. He could make good grades if he weren't such a goof-off.* 比尔的头脑很不错，如果他不是那样偷懒耍滑，他会得到很高的分数。◇ waste time

goop

a goop [ə ˈgu(ː)p] [话] **粗鲁的人** 源出美

国幽默作家伯吉斯 (Gelett Burgess)所著小说《粗鲁的人和成为这种人的方法》(*Goops and How to Be Them*, 1900)。在这部小说中破天荒第一次用 goop 一词表示"没有教养的、没有礼貌的、在与人交往时总是出差错的、感觉迟钝的、令人讨厌的人"的意思。该书出版后不久,这个词就流行起来。当时的孩子们如果吵闹得厉害,他们的父母就说: Don't be a goop!(不要学 goop 的样子!)因此,在一个时期,此词曾表示"野孩子"的意思,但是现在,这种意思已经消失,专用于表示"粗鲁的人"的意思了。这一表达法语气很轻松,主要为女性使用。 *I certainly wouldn't date a goop like him.* 要是我的话,绝对不跟他那样粗鲁的人约会啊。 *You're not going? Don't be a goop, Jenny. Everyone else will be there.* 你说不去? 詹妮,别犯傻啦。一会儿大家都到那儿去的。◇ a dull, graceless person

goop [ˈgu(:)p] [话] **黏的东西** 语源为 goo [ˈguː] (黏性物质)+ soup (汤)的 p。有时拚写作 goup。指用不着去摸,一看就感到黏糊糊的,而又不知道它究竟是什么物质的东西。 *What's this goop in this bucket?* 这个水桶里的黏糊糊的东西是什么呀? *You've got some kind of goop on your shirt.* 你的衬衣上粘上什么黏糊糊的东西啦。 *What was that goop they served for dessert?* 他们上的那黏糊糊的甜食是什么呀? ◇ a viscous liquid

goose

cook *someone's* **goose** [.kuk ~ ˈguːs] [话] **使彻底完蛋** 直译为"烧某人的鹅"。这一表达法为什么会有"破坏"的意思,不详。许多词典说是来自如下的传说:在中世纪的时候,瑞典国王率兵出征,来到了某城。于是,该城人民就把象征着"傻瓜"的鹅高悬到一个显眼的地方,质问国王:"你干什么来啦?"国王回答说:"我来烧你们的鹅。"他放火把城烧掉了。故事很有意思,但是可信程度不大。根据 OED (《牛津英语词典》),本条最早的出典是 1851 年。在这一表达法中,goose 除指希望、计划外,还指人的存在本身以及存在价值等等。因此,根据上下文,它的意味会有很大的差异,在翻译时必须灵活运用,不能抱一而终。不过,无论是哪一场合,都离不开"彻底完蛋"这一基本意义。 *My falling down in the ski trials cooked my goose. I can never make the Olympic team now.* 我在滑雪预选赛中摔倒,一切希望都化成泡影。我已经绝对进不了参加奥运会的队了。 *That scandal cooked his goose. Now it's impossible for him to get elected.* 那件丑闻使他彻底完蛋啦。现在,他已经不可能当选了。在应用于人的存在本身以及存在价值时,与 settle *someone's* HASH 大致相同,两者在大多数的场合可以互换。 *The advent of talking pictures cooked the goose of many a silent film star.* 自从有声片出现以后,许多无声片的影星全都完蛋了。goose 前面可以加形容词。 *One more mistake like that will cook my professional goose.* 再犯那样一个错误,我的饭碗就全砸了。在下一例句中,如果没有上下文,就看不出来是指人的存在本身,还是指他的计划或希望。 *Let's tell the teacher what he did. That'll cook his goose.* 咱们把他所干的勾当去汇报给老师。这样,他就会彻底完蛋啦。还有 cook *one's* (own) goose 的说法,意思是"自己搞垮自己"或"自掘坟墓"。 *You've cooked your goose now. Whatever made you criticize the boss in front of those newspaper reporters?* 这一回你算彻底完蛋了。不知你吃了什么药,竟在那些新闻记者面前批评起老板来啦? 请读者注意:主语即使是复数,goose 仍然要用单数。 *It was nobody's fault but our own. We cooked our own goose by trying to bite off more than we could chew.* 这不是任何人的错误,责任完全在我们自己身上。我们不自量力,结果把自己搞得彻底完蛋了。也常使用被动语态,采取 *someone's* [*one's*] goose is cooked 的形式。 *We'd better get out of here while the going is good. Our goose'll be cooked if the cops get here before we leave.* 趁着还来得及走,咱们赶快离开这个鬼地方。如果警爷在咱们溜出去以前到来，咱们就全完蛋啦。◇ ruin *someone's* plans [hopes, career, chances of success, etc.]

goose bumps → BUMPS

a goose egg → EGG

goose flesh [ˈgu(:)s ˌfle(:)ʃ] [口] **鸡皮疙瘩** → goose PIMPLES

goose pimples → PIMPLES

kill the golden goose [ˌkɪlðə ˌgouldən ˈgu:s] [口] **杀鸡取卵** → kill the GOOSE that laid the golden eggs

kill the goose that laid the golden eggs [ˌkɪlðəˈgu:sðətˌleɪdðəˌgouldəˈne:gz] [口] **杀鸡取卵** 直译为"杀产金卵的鹅"。这一表达法源出《伊索寓言》(Aesop's Fables)：有一个农夫得到一只产金卵的鹅，每天下一个。农夫认为鹅的肚子里一定有许多金卵，他发财心切，于是就把鹅杀掉了。有时用现在时 lays 代替 laid，用单数形式的 egg 代替 eggs。*Any company that cuts back on research and development is killing the goose that lays the golden eggs.* 凡是削减研制费用的公司，都等于在杀鸡取卵。*It's too soon to sell those stocks yet. You'll just be killing the goose that lays the golden egg.* 卖掉那些股票为时太早啦。你等于在杀鸡取卵啊。虽然用例不多，但有 kill the golden goose 的说法。*The team's management dropped three of their best-paid players in order to save money. But when their standing fell and attendance also dropped, they realized too late that they had succeeded only in killing the golden goose.* 球队的管理部门为节省经费，裁减了三个薪金最高的队员。当球队的名次降低、观众也减少的时候，他们省悟到自己只不过是杀鸡取卵而已，但是为时已晚了。◇ destroy the source of *one's* income [profits, success]

gosh

by gosh [ˈbaɪ ˈgɑ:ʃ] [话] **不管怎么样** → GOSH.

for gosh sake [fər ˈgɑ(:)ʃˈseɪk] [话] **哎呀，我的天** → for Pete's SAKE

Gosh. [ˈgɑ:ʃ] [话] **哎呀** 原为 God 的委婉语。但一般美国人在说出这个词的时候，没有一个人会意识到它是 God 的委婉说法。意思和用法与 GOLLY 相近，几乎在所有的场合都可以互相代替。Gosh. 是一个感叹词，它表示感叹、焦急、困窘、道歉等多方面的心情。因此，只译作"哎呀"不能适应所有的场合，必须根据上下文改换相宜的字眼儿。如下边的两个例句所示，孩子们常使用这个表达法。*Gosh! That's the biggest truck I've ever seen!* 哎呀！我头一回看见这么大的卡车！ *A: I saw a UFO last night. B: Gosh! Did you really?* 甲：昨天夜里我看见飞碟啦！ 乙：啊呀！真的吗？以下两个例句是表达自己真实的感觉。*Gosh, that's a beautiful picture.* 啊，那是一张美好的图画呀！ *Gosh, it's cold today.* 嗬，今天真冷啊！ 下面两个例子表示着急甚至感到"可不得了"的心情。可以用 my 加强语气。 *Gosh, it's almost ten o'clock! I've got to go.* 哎哟，快十点啦！我得赶紧走啦。*Oh my gosh, it's started raining and the laundry is still on the line.* 哎呀呀，可了不得，下起雨来了，我洗的衣服还在外边晾着呢！下面两个例子是强调抱歉的心情。*Gosh, I'm sorry. Did I hurt you?* 哎呀，真对不起！我伤着你了吗？ *Gosh, I'm sorry, Bill. I just don't have fifty dollars to lend you right now.* 哎，真对不起，比尔。我身上恰恰没带着五十美元，现在无法借给你。by gosh 具有"不管怎么样"或者"绝对地"的意味，一般用于表示决心的场合。*I said I would finish on time, and by gosh I'm going to.* 我说按时完成，所以不管怎么样我也要干下去。

gotta

gotta [ˈgɑ(:)də] [话] **必须** 一种变音形式，即把 (have [has]) got to (非……不可) 中的 got to 按照日常会话的发音拼写而成。一般后边接不定式。在小说、漫画中常常可以见到。在主语为第一人称、第二人称以及第三人称复数的场合，有时加上 have 的省略形式 've，例如：*I've gotta study tonight.* 我今天晚上必须学习。有时也可以不加 've，例如：*They* *gotta go.* 他们必须出发啦。但是，在主语为第三人称单数的场合，不能丢掉 's，例如：*He's gotta go to bed early.* 他必须早睡。如以上各例句所示，一般在后边要接不定式，但也有省略不定式的情况。*Ya gotta help me—ya just gotta!* 你不帮助我不行——无论如何要帮我一下！◇ got to

goup

goup [ˈgu(:)p] [话] **黏糊糊的不知什么东西** → GOOP

grabs

be up for grabs [ˌʌpfər ˈgræ:bz] [话] **有可能争夺到手的** 这里的 grabs 是把动词 grab (抓取)转用作名词。这一表达法的具体形象是："一个球在空中，还没有人拿到手"。有的词典只把它译作"供人竞购"，这很片面。事实上可以在许多的场合使用。例如：*With three undefeated contenders, the boxing championship is still up for grabs.* 有三个拳击选手一直保持不败，他们都有夺得冠军的可能性。也就是说，只要是人们争夺的事情，都可以用这一表达法来表示某些优胜者"有可能争夺到手"的意思。主语当然是"人们争夺的事情"。*When the Prime Minister died in office, the post of president of the majority party was up for grabs.* 首相死在任上，执政党内的一些头头都有可能争夺党总裁的职位了。以上的例句都是表明"争夺"是在竞争对手之间进行的。但是也有并无竞争对手的"争夺"，仿佛空中悬着一个球，谁抢都可以似的。*A: Has anyone bought that house yet? B: No. It's still up for grabs if you want it.* 甲：那所房子还没有人买吗？乙：是的，还没有人买。如果你想买的话，还能够买到手。◇ be undecided / be open to competition / be available (to anyone who wants it)

graceful

(as) graceful as a swan → SWAN

grad

a grad [ə ˈgræ:d] [话] **毕业生** a graduate [ˈgræ(:)dʒuət] 的缩略。*Paul is a Cornell grad, too, isn't he?* 保罗也是康奈尔大学毕业，对吧？与 graduate 同样，也常作为形容词使用。a grad school 是"研究院"，a grad student 是"研究生"，a grad program 是"硕士[博士]课程"。an old grad 是"O.B.(老毕业生)"。与自己同一大学毕业的人称为 a fellow grad。顺便提一下，O.B. 是英国英语，一般美国人不懂。◇ a graduate

a grad student → STUDENT

grade

make the grade [ˌmeɪkðə ˈgreɪd] [口] **达到目标** grade 是"斜坡"的意思。a steep grade 或者 a heavy grade 都意味着"陡坡"。本条的英语本是"向坡上爬"的意思，只要明白这一点，就容易理解它的涵义了。其构思与汉语的"向上爬"有类似之处。当然也可以按照字面意义使用。*The load was so heavy that the truck almost didn't make the grade.* 由于所载的东西太重了，卡车几乎没有爬上坡去。在使用比喻的意义时，有时构成肯定句，例如：*Joan was determined to make the grade in New York's upper society.* 琼下定决心要在纽约的上流社会中大出风头。但是在实际上，构成 can't make the grade 一类的否定句的场合比较多。在这一场合，表示"力量不足，爬不上坡"，亦即在与人竞争中失败，或者达不到自己的目标。*He tried to get into Harvard, but he couldn't make the grade.* 他曾打算上哈佛大学，但是没能考进去。*Will is a nice fellow, but he just wasn't able to make the grade so we had to let him go.* 威尔是一个很好的人，但是他完不成定额，我们只好辞退了他。*I may as well give up. I guess I just don't have the talent to make the grade as a novelist.* 还是断了这个念头为好。我看自己没有能够当一个小说家的天才。◇ succeed / do the work expected of *one*

grain

go against the grain (with *someone*) [ˌgoʊəˌgenstðə ˈgreɪn] [口] **与……性情不合** 这里的 grain 原意"木纹"。本条习用语直译为"逆着木纹走"。*In plan-*

ing wood, it is important not to go against the grain. 在用刨子刨木板的时候，最重要的是不要逆着纹理刨。人与木板一样，也有"纹理"，如果戗着"纹理"，就会受到抗拒。这就是本条习用语最初的构思。作为比喻，grain 意味着人的"性情"、"性格"、"基本想法"、"感情"。整个条头意味着"作为主语的具体事物与 *someone* 的性情不合"。但也可以省略 with *someone*，例如：*It goes against the grain to pay so much money for such poor work.* 对于那样简单的工作不应该付那么多的钱。*His way of doing things goes against the grain with me.* 我看不惯他那一套做法。*Sarah always tries to think well of people. It goes against the grain with her to have to listen to malicious gossip.* 萨拉总是爱想别人好的地方。她不喜欢去听那些怀有恶意的流言蜚语。grain 的前面可以加 intellectual (知识的)、emotional (感情的)、philosophical (理性的)等形容词。再有，*someone* 处如果代人 people 等的复数形式，前置词不用 with，大多用 of。例如：*Reincarnation is an interesting concept, but it goes against the intellectual grain of most people.* "转世"是一个很有意思的概念，但是大多数有知识的人不相信这种说法。另有 go against *someone's* grain 的形式。*It goes against my grain [the grain with me] to make promises I'm not sure I can keep.* 我不愿意言而无信，随便答应人家我做不到的事情。◇ go against *someone's* inclinations [nature]

take *something* **with a grain of salt** → SALT

grandmother

(go) teach *one's* **grandmother (how) to milk ducks**[(ˌgou)ˌtiːtʃ ~ ˈgræ(ː)nˌmʌðər (hau)də ˌmɪlk ˈdʌks] [话] **班门弄斧** → (go) teach *one's* GRANDMOTHER (how) to suck eggs

(go) teach *one's* **grandmother (how) to suck eggs**[(ˌgou)ˌtiːtʃ ~ ˈgræ(ː)nˌmʌðər (hau)də ˌsʌˈkeːgz] [话] **班门弄斧** (how) to suck eggs 是"吮鸡蛋的方法"。本条整体的字面意义是"教奶奶怎样吮鸡蛋"，指"班门弄斧"。这是自古以来就有的表达法。*Someone should take that new eager-beaver employee down a notch or two. He's always trying to teach his grandmother to suck eggs.* 对于新来那个假积极的工作人员，应该有人去挫挫他的傲气。他总爱指手划脚，向老前辈讲一些谁都明白的大道理。如这一例句所示，可以按字面意义"向长辈教导"来使用，但是，这应该算作例外的使用方法。一般的用法是：当别人指手划脚来讲你本来十分熟悉的工作方法时，常用这一表达法回敬一句，意思是"你别班门弄斧啦！"、"多此一举！"、"真是老生常谈！"，含有嘲笑的意思。因此，多用命令式。在同样的场合，也可以只说：Go suck an egg. (见鬼去吧!)在命令句中，这一表达法具有否定的意义，应译成为"不要讲……"。这一点请读者注意。例如：*Go teach your grandmother how to suck eggs. I've been doing this kind of work since I was knee-high to a grasshopper.* 你不要讲这种谁都知道的事情啦。我从很小的时候起就干这一类的工作。如这一例句所示，在命令句中必须用 go。在其他句法中，加 go 的时候居多。how 只是为了加强语气而插入的，不过，一般总是加上它。*When he started putting in his two cents worth, I told him to go teach his grandmother (how) to such eggs.* 当他从旁边插嘴开始那套老生常谈的时候，我告诉他那是谁都知道的事情，不要再说下去了。有时用 tell 代替 teach。*Go tell your grandmother how to suck eggs. I'm tired of your stupid advice.* 别来那些老生常谈啦！我对你那婆婆妈妈的忠告已经腻味透了。*It's not that I don't appreciate your advice, of course, but henceforth I would prefer that you direct your efforts toward telling your grandmother how to suck eggs.* 当然，我对你的忠告是不能不感谢的，不过，如果你竭力不再来那些老生常谈，我就更领你的盛情啦。另有一个句型是：把 suck eggs 换成 milk ducks (挤鸭子的奶)，作

(go) teach [tell] *one's* grandmother (how) to milk ducks。◇ tell someone more expert than *oneself* how to do something / Don't try to tell me how to do it. / not (to) say the obvious

grapes

sour grapes [ˌsauər ˈgreɪps] [口] **由于得不到而说不好** 源出《伊索寓言》(Aesop's Fables) 中的第一节《狐狸与葡萄》。狐狸没有弄到葡萄,就愤恨地说:I'm sure those grapes are sour anyhow. 那葡萄一定是酸的。一般用动词 be, 例如: *Judy says she wouldn't date Fred if he were the last boy in the world, but I know that's only sour grapes.* 朱迪说,即使弗雷德是世界上唯一的小伙子,她也不会跟他约会。但是我知道这只是得不到葡萄而说葡萄酸罢了。*A: I'm glad I wasn't invited to their house tonight. Their parties are always so boring. B: That's a bad case of sour grapes if I've ever heard of one.* 甲:今天晚上他们家没有邀请我,我很高兴,因为他们举办的社交晚会总是很沉闷的。乙:象你这样吃不到葡萄说葡萄酸的人,我还真是少见哪。*Prof. Jones says that the books he writes are very philosophical and so he doesn't really expect them to sell as well as other writers', but I suspect that's just sour grapes on his part.* 琼斯教授说他的著作太深奥,因此他并不期待象别人的著作那样畅销,但是据我看,他是不是自己在吃开心丸呀?◇ feigned indifference

grapevine

hear (*something*) **through the grapevine** [ˌhɪr θruðə ˈgreɪpˌvaɪn] [口] **道听途说** 字面意义是"通过葡萄藤 (grapevine) 听到某事"。如果你考虑一下葡萄藤弯弯曲曲向四面八方伸展的情况,就会了解把它比做道听途说是如何贴切了。*I hear through the grapevine that Joe is getting married.* 我听到小道消息,说乔已经结婚啦。常用 neighborhood 一词与 grapevine 搭配在一起。*I heard the news through the neighborhood grapevine.* 我从邻居的口中听到了这个消息。常用 by 代替 through。*I hear by the grapevine that you're moving to California.* 听别人说,你要搬到加州去啦。hear ~虽然是最常用的习用语,但也可以说 come [spread, etc.] through the grapevine, 或者 learn by [via, etc.] the grapevine。*The news spread quickly through the neighborhood grapevine.* 那个消息很快在左邻右舍传开了。◇ hear (*something*) by way of rumor

grass

The grass is always greener on the other side of the fence. [ðə ˈgræ(ː)səz ˌɔːlweɪz ˈgriːnər ɔnðɪˌʌðər ˌsaɪdəvðə ˈfe(ː)]nts] [谚] **这山望着那山高** 在广阔的牧场的围栏旁边聚集着成群的牛,每头牛都把脖子伸到围栏外边去吃邻居牧场的草。英语中的这个谚语便是由上述景象而来。*A: I wonder why Jeff is always wanting to change jobs. B: You know how it is. The grass is always greener on the other side of the fence.* 甲:我不明白杰夫为什么老要调动工作。乙:这正如俗话所说,这山望着那山高呀。常常省略 of the fence。另一表达法是 The grass always looks greener on the other side (of the fence). 例如:*A: It's strange that many Western men think Oriental women are beautiful, while with Oriental men it's just the opposite. B: Not really. The grass always looks greener on the other side, you know.* 甲:真奇怪,许多西方男子认为东方女性美,而东方男子又恰恰相反,认为西方女性好看。乙:这不足为奇。俗话说,家花不如野花香嘛。有时讲 The grass is always [always looks] greener on the other hill. ◇ Somewhere else [What is not yours] always appears to be better than where you are [your own].

The grass is always greener on the other hill. [ðə ˈgræ(ː)səz ˌɔːlweɪz ˈgriːnər ɔnðɪˌʌðər ˈhɪ(ː)l] [谚] **这山望着那山高** → The GRASS is always greener on the other side of the fence.

not let the grass grow

under *one's* **feet** [nɑt ˌletðə ˈgræːs ˌgrouˌʌndər ~ ˈfiːt] [话] **不错过大好机会** 直译为"不让在自己的脚下生草",也就是"不停留在一个地方"的意思。通常构成否定句。与汉语"莫失良机"的涵义大致相同。 *As soon as Harry hears of a chance to make a sale, he picks up the phone right away. He's not one to let the grass grow under his feet.* 哈里一听到有个推销的机会,马上就打电话。他不是一个坐失良机的懒汉。一般用于表示"不失掉机会"或者"充分利用得到的机会"的场合,例如: *The competition in this business is stiff. You can't afford to let the grass grow under your feet.* 在这一行里,竞争非常厉害。如果一错过机会,就会全盘皆输。grass 的冠词 the 可以用 any 代替。 *I saw Carl out with that new girl in our class last night. He certainly doesn't let any grass grow under his feet, does he?* 昨天晚上我看见卡尔带着我们班新来的那个女生出去啦。他这个家伙有好机会是决不错过的。在下一个例句里,这一表达法不是意味着"不失掉机会",而是形容"转动的速度非常快"。 *Jane didn't let any grass grow under her feet in Europe this summer. She visited eight countries in less than two weeks.* 今天夏天,简在欧洲马不停蹄地到处跑。在不到两个星期的时间,她周游了八个国家。◇ not dilly-dally / not waste time

a snake in the grass → SNAKE

grasshopper

knee-high to a grasshopper [ˌni(ː)ˈhaɪ tuə ˈgræːsˌhɑ(ː)pər] [话] **很小 (儿童时代)** 这是个夸张的表达法。直译为"只有蚱蜢的膝盖那么高"。汉语俗语叫"小不点儿"。有时用于强调人的身材短小,如说: *He's only knee-high to a grasshopper.* 他没有三块豆腐高。一般是在谈到儿时的事情或者遇到幼年的朋友的场合使用。 *I haven't eaten such good watermelon since I was knee-high to a grasshopper.* 自从我长大以后,我没有吃过这么好的西瓜。 *I'm sure you don't remember me, Robert, but I knew you when you were knee-high to a grasshopper.* 罗伯特,你大概不记得我啦,可是在你小不点儿的时候我就认识你。 *I haven't seen Ted since we were knee-high to a grasshopper.* 自从我们撒尿和泥的时代以后,我再没有见过特德。◇ very small

grave

have *one* **foot in the grave** → FOOT

make *someone* **turn over in** *his* **grave** [ˌmeɪk ~ ˌtə(ː)rˌnouvərɪn ~ ˈgreɪv] [话] **做出使死者都感到痛苦的事情** 欧美有一个古老的传说,说"如果孩子行为不好,父母的死尸会在墓中翻身"。这一表达法就是按照古老传说构成的,直译为"使某人在墓中翻身"。 *I swear I don't know what kind of trouble that boy will be into next. He seems determined to see how often he can make his father turn over in his grave.* 我不知道那个男孩子下一步还会惹出什么乱子来。他似乎下定决心要让他老子在九泉之下不得安宁。现在不仅常常用于"父母与子女的关系",此外还用于"亲属关系"、"共同的朋友"、"历史上的著名人物"等等。over 可以省略,但在口语中加上的时候多。 *That orchestra shouldn't try to play such hard selections. Their performance of the Fifth Symphony was enough to make Beethoven turn (over) in his grave.* 那个管弦乐队就不应该选择难度太大的曲子去演奏。他们演奏的第五交响曲足够使贝多芬在九泉之下大哭一场了。另外还有一个 turn (over) in *one's* grave 的表达法,构成主语的当然是"死者"了。 *If my poor dead parents knew how we have redone their house, they would probably turn over in their graves.* 如果我去世的可怜的父母知道我们怎样重新装饰了他们的房子,他们大概会在九泉之下大哭一场的。 *A: What was that noise? B: I'm sure I don't know. But from the way you are wasting your inheritance, it could well have been your father turning over in his grave.* 甲:那是什么声音啊? 乙:我怎样会知道呀。不过,从你挥霍老人遗

产的方式来看，多半是你老子在九泉之下痛哭流涕呢。◇ (do something that would) upset *someone* were *he* still alive

(as) silent as the grave [əz ˈsaɪlentəzðə ˈgreɪv] [口] **象坟墓一样寂静** 有时只是强调"寂静"的状态，如说: *Now that the children have all grown up and gone, our house is as silent as the grave.* 现在孩子们全都长大，而且都离开家了，所以我们家变得非常安静了。一般用法符合字面意义"象坟墓一样寂静"，有点阴森森的意味。*The old house stood silent as the grave.* 那所老房子阴森森的，象坟墓一样寂静。*I called out for help a number of times but there was no answer. The streets were as silent as the grave.* 我多次呼喊求援，但是没有任何回音，街道象坟墓一样的寂静。◇ eerily [extremely] silent

gravy

Good gravy. [ˈgu(:)d ˈgreɪvi] [话] **哎呀，天哪!** → Good GRIEF.

a gravy train → TRAIN

gray

tattletale gray [ˌtæ(:)dl ˌteɪl ˈgreɪ] [口] **白中带灰** a tattletale 是"搬弄是非的小人"。本条逐字翻译为"搬弄是非者的灰色"，这简直令人莫明其妙。原来，这是从 20 世纪 40 年代起美国制造洗衣剂的某大公司在广播电台的商业广告中的用语。广告的大意是:"如果使用我公司的产品，衬衣、内衣都会变得雪一样白；如果一不留神用其他公司的产品去洗，衣服很快就带灰色了。那种灰色等于'搬弄是非的小人'，它会向你的左邻右舍宣传说:'你用不好使的洗衣剂洗衣服啦!'结果，你一定会脸红的。"这里所用的 tattletale gray 不久就成为美国一般人的日常用语了。这一表达法指"white 中略有 gray"，特别指长期使用的东西白中透一点点黑的颜色。off-white [ˈɔ:f ˈhwaɪt] 有时作为同义语使用，但 off-white 也有"白里带一点黄"的意思，所以二者的意义并不完全相同。*The walls of our kitchen used to be white, but now they've become tattletale gray.* 我们家厨房的墙壁原来是雪白的，但是现在有一点儿发黑了。◇ grayish-white

grease

fry in *one's* **own grease** [ˌfraɪən ~ ˌounˈgri:s] [话] **自作自受** → stew in *one's* own JUICE

a grease monkey → MONKEY

use elbow grease [ˌju(:)z ˈe(:)lbou ˌgri:s] [口] **费很大劲** elbow 是"肘部"，grease 是"油脂"。这一表达法最初的构思是:"由于胳膊用力活动的次数多，大量消耗了肘部的油脂。" *My arms are sore from waxing the floors yesterday. I'm not used to using so much elbow grease.* 由于昨天给地板打蜡，我的胳膊很疼。我平常没用过那么大的力气。*Window washers have to use a lot of elbow grease.* 擦窗户的人必须费很大的力气。除用 use 外，有时用 take, put 等动词。*These pans are all very dirty. Cleaning them will take a lot of elbow grease.* 这些平底锅全都太脏啦，要刷干净得费很大的劲儿。*You'll never get the car to shine that way. You have to put more elbow grease into it.* 你那样干，汽车永远也不会闪闪发亮，你必须多费一点力气才行。◇ do so much [a lot of, etc.] (hard) rubbing / use *one's* arm muscles (so much, a lot, etc.)

greased

like greased lightning → LIGHTNING

greased-pig

a greased-pig contest [ə ˌgri:zdpɪg ˈkɑ(:)ntest] [口] **捉涂油猪竞赛** → bring home the BACON

greasy

a greasy spoon → SPOON

great

go great guns → GUNS

Great balls of fire! [ˈgreɪt ˈbɔ:lzə ˈfaɪr] [话] **哎呀，不得了!** → Great SCOTT!

Great Caesar's ghost! [ˈgreɪt ˈsi:zərz ˈgoust] [话] **哎呀，我的天!** → Great SCOTT!

Great day. ['greɪt'deɪ] [话] **哎呀,天哪!** → Good NIGHT.

Great Scott! → SCOTT

the great unwashed → UNWASHED

be no great shakes → SHAKES

Greek

be (all) Greek to *someone* [ˌ(ɔːl) 'griːktə ~] [话] **完全不懂** 源出莎士比亚的名剧《裘力斯·凯撒》(*Julius Caesar*)。在第一幕第二场中有这样的情景:站在凯撒一边的西塞罗向他的朋友讲凯撒要被暗杀的情况时,为了怕别人听见,用的是希腊语。暗杀者的同谋之一吉亚斯卡曾经去偷听。这件事传到其他同谋者的耳朵里以后,他们就问:"那么,西塞罗说了些什么?"吉亚斯卡开玩笑地回答说: For mine own part, it was Greek to me. (对于我来说,那完全是希腊语。)也就是"完全听不懂"的意思。*My grandfather says that half the slang spoken by young people these days is Greek to him.* 我爷爷说,最近青年人所讲的俚语他有一半完全听不懂。为了加强语气,在大多的场合增添 all 一词。 *A: What does this note say? It's written in Chinese. B: I dunno. It's all Greek to me.* 甲:这个便条上说什么?它是用汉语写的。乙:我不知道。我对中文一窍不通。这一表达法应用的对象不限于"语言",也可以是说话者难以理解的事物。例如: *Don't ask me anything about international politics. It's all Greek to me.* 不要问我有关国际政治的任何问题,因为我对这个是一窍不通。 *The old fellow has been teaching Greek for half his life, but still the fact that Greek art has contributed so much to the West's aesthetic values appears to be all Greek to him.* 那个老汉教了半辈子希腊语,可是关于希腊艺术对西方美学价值观念究竟有多大贡献,他是毫无所知的。有时人们戏把 Greek 换成 Hebrew (希伯来语) 或 Arabic (阿拉伯语),意思也通。总而言之,只要是英语圈的人们认为难以理解的语言,不论哪一种都可以,在实际上常常听见人们这样灵活运用。这一切全都是由 Greek 一词派生出来的表达法。◇ be (completely) unintelligible to *someone*

green

get the green light (from *someone*) [getðə 'griːn 'laɪt] [口] **得到批准** → give (*someone*) the green LIGHT

give (*someone*) **the green light** → LIGHT

be green with envy → ENVY

have a green thumb → THUMB

the long green [ðə 'lɔːŋ 'griːn] [话] **现金** → BREAD

greenback

a greenback [ə 'gri(ː)nˌbæk] [话] **美钞** 美国纸币的背面印的是绿色,故俗称"绿背"。用法主要有三种:①指与硬通货相对的美国纸币,②指与他国通货相对的钞票形的美元,③指钞票形式的美元。在表示 ③的意义时,主要用复数形式。① *I had a whole pocketful of coins but not a single greenback left.* 我有大量的硬币,可是连一张钞票都没有了。 ② *I don't want Hong Kong dollars. Haven't you got any greenbacks?* 我不要港币,你没有美元吗?③ *Did you see that? That guy's briefcase is crammed with greenbacks.* 你瞧见了吗?那个家伙的公事包里塞满了美钞。◇ (American [paper]) money

greens

greens ['griːnz] [口] **青菜** 集合名词。greens 意为"青的叶"。具体地说,包括 spinach (菠菜), turnip leaves (芜菁叶), Swiss chard (瑞士甜菜), plantain (大蕉), dandelions (蒲公英)等,指煮、蒸、炒而食之的 herb (草本类)的"叶"。同样是青菜,如经常生吃的 lettuce (生菜),多半生吃的 cabbage (甘蓝) 等,均不包括在内。另外,这些草本类并不都是美国的全国性食物,特别是芜菁叶、大蕉、蒲公英等,把它们当作青菜吃乃是美国南部独特的习惯。 *In the American South, people eat many kinds of greens.* 在美国南部,人们吃许多种绿叶青菜。 *These greens are delicious.* 这些青菜很好吃。各种草本类的名称常被用作 greens 的形容词。*I love dandelion greens.* 我爱吃蒲公英的青叶。*Turnip greens is a typical Southern dish.* 用芜菁叶当菜,是南方特有的风味。◇ (green) leaves

grief

Good grief. [ˈgu(ː)d ˈgriːf] [话] **哎呀,天哪!** 原为 Good God. 的委婉说法。grief 意为"悲伤",但在这里没有特殊意义。与同类的感叹词 Good NIGHT. 相似,但 Good night. 主要表示"震惊",而这一表达法则表示"吓呆了"、"简直令人不能相信"的神情。 *Good grief. There's a hole in the gas tank.* 哎呀,天哪! 汽车油箱竟有一个洞。*Good grief! Where did you get that hat?* 哎呀,天哪! 你从哪里弄来那样一顶帽子? *Good grief! The news says Mount Vesuvius has erupted!* 哎呀,天哪! 据报导,维苏威火山爆发了。*Good grief. Is your mother coming to visit us again?* 哎呀,天哪! 你母亲还要到我们这儿来? *Good grief! Look at the time! If we don't hurry, we'll miss the last train.* 哎呀,天哪! 瞧瞧时间! 如果我们不抓紧,就要误了末班火车。*Good grief, can't you do anything right?* 哎呀,天哪! 你不能干点正经事吗? 在以上各例句中,虽然意思略有不同,但均可用 Good night. 替换。但在下面这样"奇谈怪论,语惊四座"的场合,用 Good night. 就太勉强了。 *Lucy: Of course girls are smarter than boys. That's why men get women to raise their children. Charlie: Good grief.* 露西:当然女孩子的头脑比男孩子的好啦。这就是为什么男人要请女人生孩子的原因。查理:哎呀,妙论妙论! 另外,也可以用 Good gravy. 这一表达法代替 Good grief. ◇ Oh, no!

grin

grin and bear it [ˌgrɪnənˈbe(ː)rɪt] [口] **一声不吭地忍耐** grin 的第一个意义是"露齿而笑"。因此,在英汉词典里常把本条习用语译为"苦笑忍受",甚至误译为"逆来顺受"。但是,除了偶尔在戏谑的场合外,美国人不会从这一习用语中的 grin 直接联想到"笑"。本条具有"把不平不满装在心里,不显露出来"的意思,所以译作"一声不吭地忍耐"或"默默地忍受"好些。 *I'm sorry I can't help you. You'll just have to grin and bear it.* 很抱歉,我帮不了你的忙。你只好自己忍耐一下啦。*I know you don't like the way this organization is run, but if you don't have the courage to quit, you'll just have to grin and bear it with the rest of us.* 我知道你不喜欢这个单位的经营方式,但是,如果你没有勇气辞职的话,你必须跟我们大家一样把不满装在心里,一声不吭地忍耐下去。it 泛指"必须忍耐的事情",但可以把它换成具体的内容。例如:*If you think I'm just going to grin and bear your going bar-hopping with your friends while I sit and wait for you every night, you've got another think coming.* 我每天夜里守在家里等你,你却跟你的狐朋狗友去串酒吧间,如果你认为我会一声不吭地忍耐下去,那你可打错算盘啦。◇ suffer [accept *something*] without complaining

grind

the daily grind [ðə ˈdeɪli ˈgraɪnd] [话] **单调的日常工作[学习]** daily 自然是"每天的"。grind 原意为"碾成粉末",转用于表示"枯燥无味的、非常单调的、既消耗精神又费体力的工作"。 *A: How's school? B: It's a grind.* 甲:学校怎么样啊? 乙:又枯燥,又单调。条头的 the daily grind 是定型的表达法,主要用于"工作"或"学习"。这里的 the 具有"人人都经验过的、照例的"的意味,daily 则令人产生"今后不知道要继续多少年"或"不知道何年何月才能终了"的感觉。*I'm sick and tired of the daily grind. I wish I could take a long vacation.* 每天每日这样枯燥而单调地干活,我已经厌烦透了。我希望得到一个时间长一些的休假。 *A: Are your studies interesting? B: Sometimes. But usually it's just the same old daily grind.* 甲:学习有意思吗? 乙:有时候挺有意思。不过,一般是老和尚念经,天天一个调儿。◇ the everyday dull, arduous routine

grindstone

keep *one's* [*someone's*] **nose to the grindstone** → NOSE

ground

break new ground [ˌbreɪk ˌnju(:) ˈgraund] [口] **开辟新天地** 字面意义是"开垦处女地"。*With our new farm equipment, we'll be able to break new ground and expand our cultivated acreage.* 我们使用新的农业机械可以开垦处女地,扩大耕种面积。转作比喻使用,表示"开发新的领域"、"开辟新天地"的意义。例如:*Companies in the electronics field must be continually breaking new ground or they will fall behind the competition.* 电子企业必须继续不断地开发新的领域,否则就会在竞争中落伍。*Lu Xun broke new ground in Chinese literature by writing his novel The True Story of A Q in conversational style.* 鲁迅用口语体写小说《阿Q正传》,为中国文学开辟了一个新天地。*Alaska has broken new ground by paying its citizens oil royalties instead of collecting state income taxes.* 阿拉斯加不但不征收州民所得税,反而向公民支付石油矿区使用费,在税收制度方面开辟了一个新局面。虽然并非正统的说法,但也有用 fresh 代替 new 的情况。*Medical science has broken vast acres of fresh ground in the field of genetics over the past five years.* 在过去的五年间,医学在遗传学的领域中开辟了非常广阔的新天地。◇ make new developments [a new development]

cut the ground from under *someone* [*something*] [ˌkʌtðə ˈgraund frəˈmʌndər ~] [口] **先发制人挫败某人的计划** → cut the GROUND from under *someone's* feet

cut the ground from under *someone's* **feet** [ˌkʌtðə ˈgraund frə ˌmʌndər ~ ˈfi:t] [口] **使某人的意图[努力]告吹** 直译为"把人脚下的地面砍去"。作为比喻,表示"当别人要开始做什么或者正在准备做什么的时候,抢先破坏别人的计划或者努力的成果"的意思。这种破坏行为有时是故意的,但由于"马虎大意"的场合比较多,也有时是顺水推舟,自然形成那样的结果。*I'm sorry, Jim. I didn't mean to cut the ground from under your feet with my remarks.* 真对不起,吉姆,我虽然发表点不同的意见,可是并非打算拆你的台。*I was just going to tell the teacher that I hadn't been able to study for the test today because I was sick, when Phil cut the ground from under my feet by congratulating me on winning the baseball game yesterday.* 我正准备向老师讲,我由于生病,没有温习功课而不能参加今天的测验,这时菲尔竟来庆贺我昨天在棒球比赛中获得胜利,完全破坏了我的意图。*The opposition party was in the midst of campaigning for the election on a tax-cut platform when the government cut the ground from under its feet by announcing a large tax cut.* 当反对党正在选举运动中提出减税的方案摇旗呐喊的时候,政府推出大幅度的减税政策,先发制人地拆了他们的台。有时去掉 feet, 只说 cut the ground from under *someone*。在以上的各例句中,均可用 *someone* 代换 *someone's* feet。除 *someone's* feet 或 *someone* 外,也可以代入 *something*。*His cutting logic cut the ground from under all my arguments.* 他那锐利的逻辑驳倒了我所有的论点。◇ render *someone's* intentions [efforts] futile

gain ground(against *someone*[*something*]) [ˌgeɪn ˈgraund] [口] **占上风** 包括本条在内,所有的 gain ground ~的表达法都有一个共同的基本意义,就是"获得地盘"。请注意:各个表达法的独特意义是由 ground 后边的前置词 (against, on, toward) 来决定的。against 的表达法用于与敌人战斗争取扩大地盘或势力的场合,即"获得敌方领土 (ground)"的意思。*Day after day, the troops continued to gain ground against the enemy.* 我军连日挺进,继续占领敌方的领土。这是按原意的使用方法。作为足球用语的 gain ground 便是由这一构思而来。*Our football team was unable to gain* *ground against our stronger opponents.* 我们的足球队在强敌之下未能告捷。普遍使用转义,即"压制"、"克服"、"占上风"的意思。例如: *With this new treatment, many patients are rapidly gaining ground in their fight against cancer.* 用这种新的治疗方法,许多癌患者在病痛斗争中迅速取得了战果。*Despite a week of negotiations, neither side has been able to gain any ground (against the other).* 虽然经过一个星期的谈判,双方都未能取得任何的进展(压倒对方)。*In the 1950's, rock and roll began to gain ground against big-band music.* 在20世纪50年代,摇滚乐压倒大乐队音乐而占了上风。另外,在这一场合的 gain ground 的反义语为 lose GROUND (to [against] *someone* [*something*])。◇ advance [win territory, make progress] (against ~)

gain ground (on *someone* [*something*]) [ˌgeɪn ˈgraund] [口] **逼近** gain ground 是"获得地盘",后边加上 on,直译为"得到与前面对手之间的地面",亦即"缩短与前面对手之间的距离"、"追赶上敌人"的意思。on 后边的用语当然就是"前面的对手"。*We'll have to go faster. Our pursuers are gaining ground (on us).* 我们要赶快跑,追赶的人越来越近啦(快追上我们啦)。在这种实际上"缩短距离"的场合,可以省略 ground 或 on *someone* [*something*]。但在会话中,一般只省略 ground,而作 gain on *someone* [*something*]。如: *We'll have to put more money into sales promotion. Our competitors are gaining ground on us.* 为了扩大销售额,我们必须投入更多的资金,我们的竞争对手都追上来啦。*Despite huge outlays for research, Russia has so far been unable to gain any ground on America in the space race.* 苏联虽然投入了大量的研究费用,但是在宇宙开发竞赛中,至今还未能缩短与美国的差距。*In the 1950's, rock and roll began to gain ground on big-band music.* 在20世纪50年代,摇滚乐的流行程度开始赶上大乐队音乐了。另外,这一场合的 gain ground 的反义语为 lose GROUND (to *someone* [*something*])。◇ catch up (with ~) / advance (on ~)

gain ground (toward *something*) [ˌgeɪn ˈgraund] [口] **前进** 字面意义虽然是"获得地盘",但用于以下两个场合:一是表示实际距离的前进;一是作为比喻,表示事情有进展。*After the rainy season was over, the explorers began to gain ground more rapidly toward their destination.* 雨季过了以后,探险家们以更快的速度向着他们的目的地进发了。*Though our throttles were wide open, the swift current prevented our boat from gaining ground.* 虽然我们开足了马力,但是水流过急,我们的小艇未能前进一步。以下是比喻用法。*Not until Uppun Adam became president did we really begin gaining ground toward our goal of doubling productivity.* 我们向着产量翻一翻的目标前进,实际上是从厄彭·亚当就任总经理以后才开始的。ground 常用 any 或 much 作修饰语。*The residents of this area have been fighting hard against the plan to build a new airport here, but so far they have not gained much ground.* 这一地区的居民为反对在当地建造新飞机场的计划而展开了猛烈的斗争,但是至今他们的运动并没有大的进展。有时用表示目的的前置词(短语) for *something* 或者 in *one's* attempt to *do something* 代替 toward。*Educational authorities haven't gained much ground in their attempt to reform the university entrance examination system.* 教育当局企图改革大学入学考试制度,但是没有多大进展。另外,这一场合的 gain ground 的反义语为 lose GROUND (toward <etc.> *something* [*someone*])。◇ advance [move forward, make progress] (toward ~)

something **gains ground** [~ ˌgeɪnz ˈgraund] [口] **越来声势越大** gain ground 是"获得地盘"或"扩大领地"。这一表达法的主语 (*something*) 指思想、主张、运动、样式等等,具体形象是:"它们得到支持者或爱好者,因而扩大自己

的领域”。*As time went by, the idea of universal suffrage gained increasing ground.* 随着时间的推移，普选的思想越来越为人们所接受了。*Darwin's theory of evolution began to gain ground quickly soon after it was introduced.* 达尔文的进化论被介绍过来之后，立即迅速地传播开来了。*The case for energy conservation is gaining ground throughout the country.* 保护能源的主张正在得到全国的响应。*Support for a new international monetary system is gaining ground in Europe.* 新的国际通货制度在欧洲越来越得到广泛的支持。*Rock and roll began to gain ground in the 1950's.* 摇滚乐是在20世纪50年代开始流行起来的。*something* gains ground 的反义语是 *something* loses GROUND。另外，在 gain ground 的后边加上 on, against, toward,可以构成不同的习用语，请参阅各该条目。◇ *something* gains popularity [influence, force]

get in on the ground floor → FLOOR

give ground [ˌgɪv ˈgraund] [口] **让步** ground 的字面意义是“(自己所站的)地面”。give ground 一语来源于战争，意思是“让出自己站在那里打仗的地面”，亦即“节节后退”。*In the face of the fierce attack, the troops had no choice but to give ground.* 在猛烈的进攻之下，部队不得不向后退却。常作为比喻：*Despite the union's strike, management adamantly refused to give ground.* 尽管工会举行罢工，经理部顽固地不肯让步。*The negotiations reached an impasse when neither side would give ground on the question of import tariffs.* 由于在进口税问题上双方都不肯让步，谈判陷入了僵局。在表示“服从他人的意见”的意味时，也常用这一表达法。*Club members opposed to admitting women finally gave ground in the face of Walter's forceful argument.* 反对允许女性参加的俱乐部的人们，在沃尔特的有力的争辩下，终于让步了。在否定句中，可以用 an inch of 加强语气。字面意义是“连一英寸也不后退”。*The mayor refuses to give an inch of ground on that question.* 关于那个问题，市长连一步也不让。另外，在表示“坚持自己的意见，丝毫也不让步”的场合，要说 stand *one's* GROUND。◇ yield

hold *one's* **ground** [ˌhould ~ˈgraund] [口] **坚守阵地** 在各国的英语词典中，包括美国的在内，都把这一表达法与 stand *one's* GROUND (→)等同起来，但两者的意味是有一定的差别的。stand *one's* ground 是带有积极性的表达法，意思是“接受对方的攻击是出于本人的自由意志，即使失败也不让一步”。而 hold *one's* ground 则是表示始终处于被动状态的表达法，只有在被逼无奈的场合使用，意思是“不凭本人的自由意志，不论愿意不愿意，都要去抵挡前来进攻的对手”。按字面意义，ground 是“阵地”。*Though the soldiers were vastly outnumbered, they succeeded in holding their ground.* 虽然在人数方面大大处于劣势，但是士兵们成功地守住了阵地。作为比喻使用的时候，ground 指“现在确保的地步”或“立场”等。*The trial so far seems to be a stand-off, but it is doubtful that the defense will be able to hold its ground if the prosecution succeeds in finding another reliable witness.* 审判到现在为止似乎正处于难见分晓的局面，但是如果检查官能够找到另一个可靠的证人，被告是否能不败诉就成为疑问了。*If the majority party doesn't hold its ground in the coming elections, there will probably be a coalition government.* 如果执政党在即将到来的大选中保持不住自己的席位，就可能成立联合政府了。*Our company is having difficulty holding its ground in the face of today's steep inflation.* 我们公司在当前严重通货膨胀的情况下，是很难维持现状的。不论是比喻也好，按字面意义使用也好，在不能坚守自己的 ground 而“节节败退”的场合，要说 lose GROUND (to [against] *someone* [*something*]); 在已经断定无论怎样坚持也守不住了从而退让的场合，一般用 give GROUND。◇ maintain *one's* position

keep an ear to the ground → EAR

lose ground(to[against] *someone* [*something*]) [ˌluːz ˈgraund] [口] **节节败退** 这是与 gain GROUND (against *someone* [*something*])针锋相对的表达法。字面意义是"在敌人的压力下,不断失去自己的阵地"。lose ground to ～与 lose ground against ～大致相同,但是,如果用 against,主语与 *someone* 以及 *something* 的敌对关系就显得更加突出,"战斗"的意味会溢于言表。*Day after day, the troops continued to lose ground to [against] the enemy.* 在敌人的压力下,部队一天又一天地不断向后撤退。在作比喻使用的场合,ground 是"地步"、"立场"的意思,一般也含有"节节地(败退)"的意思。*Despite its determination to hold the line, over the past decade management has steadily lost ground to the union in wage negotiations.* 虽然说是决心维持现状,但是过去十年间,厂方在工资谈判中总是对工会不断地让步。*New methods of treatment not withstanding, many patients continue to lose ground against cancer.* 由于一些新的治疗方法的疗效还不够稳固,许多癌症患者不断地死去。*In the 1950's, big-band music began to lose ground to rock and roll.* 在 20 世纪 50 年代,大乐队音乐开始逐步让位于摇滚乐了。作为足球用语使用的场合,只意味着"后退"或"失去阵角",不含有"节节"的意思。*Our football team lost a lot of ground on that play.* 在那场比赛中,我们的足球队非常失利。◇ be pushed back (by ～) / lose territory (to ～) / retrogress (against ～) / yield part of its popularity (to ～)

lose ground (to *someone* [*something*]) [ˌluːz ˈgraund] [口] **失去遥遥领先的地位** 这是与 gain GROUND (on *someone* [*something*]) 完全相反的表达法。*The leader is losing ground to the second-place runner.* 处于领先地位的赛跑选手逐渐要被第二名选手赶上了。这是按字面意义的用法。转义,广泛用于一般的竞争。例如: *We'll have to put more money into sales promotion. We are losing ground to our competitors.* 为了增加销售额,我们必须投入更多的资金。竞争的各公司正在逐步逼近我们的领先地位。*If America does not put more money into space research, she may begin losing ground to Russia in the space race.* 如果美国在宇航研究方面不投入更多的资金,它在宇宙开发的竞赛中就可能被苏联追赶上。*In the 1950's, big-band music began to lose ground to rock and roll.* 20 世纪 50 年代,摇滚乐开始压倒大乐队音乐,受到人们的热烈欢迎。◇ lose part of *one's* lead (to ～) / lose in popularity (to ～)

lose ground (toward <etc.> *something* [*someone*]) [ˌluːz ˈgraund] [口] **不得已而向后退** 直译为"对着某物[某人]失去地盘"。可以认为是 gain GROUND (toward *something*) 的反义表达法。意思是:本来正在向着一个目标前进,可是,由于某种原因,与目标之间的距离越来越远了。先举一个实际上"后退"的例子。*Because of the swift current, our boat continued to lose ground.* 由于水流过急,我们的船越来越向后退了。下面举几个比喻用法的例子。事先说明一点:在上边的例句中,表面上没有提到以什么为目标(如河岸),但也可象下边例句那样,直接讲出目标来。在讲出目标的场合,使用条头所举的前置词 toward (etc.),可根据目标的意味和功能进行变换。*The fire in the museum caused the curator to lose ground toward his goal of deciphering the language of the ancient land of Dworp.* 由于博物馆失火,馆长解读古代德沃尔普地方语言的工作不得不搁浅下来了。以"人"为目标时,前置词大多用 with。*I seem to be losing ground with Doris. After two or three dates, she now claims she's too busy to see me.* 我与多丽丝之间的关系似乎越来越疏远了。在两三次约会之后,现在她说她太忙,没有时间见我。有时不是用一个前置词,而是用副词短语导出目标。*I'm afraid we're losing ground in our efforts to raise productivity. It has actually fallen during the last quarter.* 我们努力增产的目标恐怕越来越达不到了。上个季度实际上不是增产,而是减产。◇ retrogress / lose much of *one's* progress (toward ~) / make less than no progress (with ~) / move backward

something **loses ground** [~ ˌluːzəz ˈgraund] [口] **衰退** 这一 ground 是"地步"、"立场"的意思。本条的表达法与 *something* gains GROUND 意义正相反。*As time went by, the belief that the earth was the center of the universe lost ground.* 随着时间的推移,人们越来越不相信地球为宇宙中心的说法了。*The case for prohibition rapidly lost ground throughout the country.* 禁酒法在全国各地越来越得不到支持了。*Big-band music began to lose ground in the 1950's.* 从20世纪50年代开始,大乐队音乐日趋衰落。◇ *something* loses influence [force, popularity]

run *something* **into the ground** [ˌrʌn ~ ɪntəðə ˈgraund] [口] **把同一事情反复到令人讨厌的程度** 字面意义是"使车在一个地方来回转,结果陷入地面",也就是由于反复做一件事而产生不良的效果。如以下的例句所示,多用于讲思想、主意、计划、打算等等,带有"最初很新鲜,可是……"的意味。*George has a lot of good ideas, but he tends to run them into the ground.* 乔治虽然有很多好主意,但是他总反复讲他的想法,令人讨厌。*That is an amusing TV commercial, but they've run it into the ground.* 电视中的那个商业广告很有意思,可是他们来回不断地播放,已经令人厌烦了。*Martha runs some of her interior decorating schemes into the ground. Now she's got pink walls in practically every room.* 马莎滥用她的室内装饰的设计,千篇一律,过于单调。现在她几乎把所有房间的墙都涂成粉红色了。可以用 in 代替 into。*It's okay to borrow my car once in a while, but don't run it in the ground.* 偶尔借我的汽车用一回半回的,那倒没什么,不过,三天两头地老来借,就太令人为难了。→ be in a RUT ◇ use the same idea [method, etc.] too often

run *someone* [*something*] **to ground** [ˌrʌn ~ tə ˈgraund] [口] **查明下落** → run *someone* [*something*] to EARTH

stand *one's* **ground** [ˌstæ(ː)nd ~ ˈgraund] [口] **一步也不后退** 这里的 stand 表示"挺身而立,坚决不让步"的顽强意志。整个条头的意思是:"不管对方如何前来进攻,自己坚守阵地[立场],寸步不让"。人们常把这一表达法与 hold *one's* GROUND (→)等同起来,请读者注意,两者的意味是有若干差别的。本条可按字面意义使用,如说: *Though the soldiers were vastly outnumbered, they stood their ground.* 虽然在数量上处于极端劣势,但是士兵们坚守阵地,寸土不让。作为比喻,专用于"语言"。例如: *The boy stood his ground despite the threats of the bully.* 在小流氓的威胁之下,那小男孩没有让步。在这一场合仅指口头上的"交锋"。如果使用的不是"语言",而是"暴力",那就要用 hold *one's* ground。 *The boy held his ground despite repeated blows from the bully.* 虽然遭受小流氓的再三殴打,那个少年一步也没有后退。如果这句话换用 stand *one's* ground,那便是"虽然挨打,但是坚持自己的主张"的意思了。 *Though the coaches of both teams disagreed with his decision, the umpire stood his ground.* 虽然两个队的教练都不同意他的裁定,但是裁判员坚持自己的意见。*Despite the principal's threat to fire him, the young teacher, believing he was in the right, stood his ground.* 虽然校长威胁说要解雇他,但那个青年教师相信自己是正确的,一步也没有退让。*I tried to talk my wife out of taking a job but she stood her ground, saying that since we didn't have children, there was no reason to stay home every day.* 我劝说妻子不要出去工作,但是她坚持自己的立场,说我们既然没有孩子,就没有每天呆在家里的理由。另外,不论作比喻使用的场合还是按照字面意义使用的场合,如果不 stand 自己的 ground 而进行"让步"的话,要说 give GROUND。◇ refuse to yield / stand firm

suit *someone* **down to the ground** [ˌsu(:)t ~ ˌdauntəðə ˈgraund] [话] **正合某人的意** down to the ground 是"从头顶直到地面"亦即"完全"的意思。它对动词 suit (适合)起强调的作用。*The climate in Arizona suits me down to the ground.* 亚利桑那州的气候太合我的意了。常用 right 进一步加强语气。*Being a forest-fire lookout is lonely work, but it suits me right down to the ground.* 当一个森林防火值班员是很寂寞的,但是正合我的心意。如以上的例句所示,在使用这一表达法时,*someone* 一般为说话人本身(亦即表示"正合说话人本身的意思")。如果在形式上不是说话人本身,也以 appear, seem 等词表示出说话人的主观看法。这是一个特点。*Our plans don't seem to suit Merle exactly down to the ground, but I think she will go along with them.* 我们的计划似乎不完全合默尔的意,但是我认为她是会表示赞成的。→ to a T ◇ be exactly what *one* likes [wants]

worship the ground *someone* **walks on** [ˌwə(:)rʃəpðə ˌgraund ~ ˈwɔ:kˌsɔ:n] [口] **衷心敬爱** 一般来说,只是 worship *someone* 就已经表示出相当强烈的敬爱心情了。本条的表达法直译为"崇拜某人走过的地面",这是表示最高级的热爱和尊敬的语言。*Though Mr. Doe is a very ordinary man, his wife seems to worship the ground he walks on.* 虽然多伊先生是一个极平凡的人,可是他的妻子似乎对他是由衷地敬爱。*Mr. Icon is a very popular teacher. His students worship the ground he walks on.* 艾孔先生是一位很受欢迎的教师,他的学生们从心里敬爱他。常加 very 进一步增强语气。*The old nun has spent her life working in the slums, and the poor people worship the very ground she walks on.* 老修女一生都为贫民窟工作,穷人们从心底里敬爱她。◇ be full of love and respect for *someone*

ground-floor

a ground-floor opportunity [ə ˌgraund ˌflo(:)r ɑpərˈtʃu:nəti] [口] **最初参加者优先获利[升官]的机会** → get in on the ground FLOOR

group

a rap group [ə ˈræ(:)pˌgru:p] [口] **自由坦率的谈话会** → RAP (with *someone*)

grow

grow on *someone* [ˈgrouˌɔ(:)n ~] [口] **越来越让人喜欢** 字面意义是"在某人身上成长",也就是"好感在某人心中发芽,逐渐增大"的意思。主语有时是人,例如: *I had no special feelings for Betty in the beginning, but the more I saw of her the more she grew on me.* 最初我对贝蒂没有特殊的感情,但是我见到她的次数越多,她越让我喜欢。主语也有时是事物,例如: *You don't like classical music? Don't worry. It'll grow on you.* 你不喜爱古典音乐吗? 不用担心。它会使你越来越喜爱的。*Helen didn't care for life in China at first, but she found it grew on her.* 海伦最初不喜欢在中国的生活,但是后来她越来越对它感兴趣了。如以上的例句所示,这一表达法首先令人联想到的"在心中成长的东西"是"好感",但是另外还有"不安"、"习惯"、"欲望"等。在这一场合,是"越来越感觉(不安)"的意思。例如说: *An uneasy feeling grew upon me as I talked to the man.* 当我同那个男人谈话时,我越来越感到不安。*His drinking habit grew on him so quickly that soon he was a complete alcoholic.* 他很快地养成了喝酒的习惯,不久以后就成为一个大酒鬼啦。*As the days went by, the desire grew upon me to be left to myself.* 随着时间的推移,我孤居独处的欲望越来越强了。另外,如这一例句所示,可以用 upon 代替 on。用 upon 时口气比较严肃一些。◇ (*someone*) (gradually) come(s) to like *someone* [*something*]

grub

grub [ˈgrʌ(:)b] [话] **食物** grub 原为动词,意思是"掘土"。同样是"掘",但具体形象不是去寻求黄金或财宝,而是在地面上东刨一下西刨一下,找一些不值钱的东西,一派寒酸相。在"挖蚯蚓"的场合,也常说 grub for worms。后来，就用这一动词表示“为不值钱的东西忙忙碌碌”、“寻求不值钱的东西并想弄到手”的意味了。*I'm tired of having to grub like this for a living.* 象这样为了吃饭而奔波，我已经厌倦了。在这一场合，也包含着如下的心情：“我虽然这样辛辛苦苦拚命劳动，仍然过着毫无价值的、没有幸福的生活。”下面的 grub 是“寻求”、“努力弄到手”。在这一场合，一般加上 up，说 grub up *something*。 *You stay here in hiding. I'll go into town and see if I can grub up some food.* 你在这儿隐藏着，我到镇上去看看能不能弄点吃的。在这一例句中，也同样令人感到“没有什么有价值的食物”。至于 grub 作为名词使用而具“食物”一解，这是因为在过去，当住在城郊的流浪汉和乞丐到城里去找点残羹剩饭的时候，他们常如上一例句那样，说 grub up some food (弄点吃的)。因此，grub 一词仿佛成为乞丐、流浪汉或牛仔等的专用语了。这一 grub (食物)本身也多指“只能充饥的粗糙东西”。女性很少使用这一表达法。 *Got any grub? I'm hungry.* 弄到什么吃的东西了吗？我饿啦。 *You finish fixing the stove. I'll go in the kitchen and see if I can dig up some grub.* 你快把炉子修理好。我到厨房去看看能不能弄点吃的东西。 *How much grub we got left?* 我们还剩有多少吃的东西？有时把 grub 作为 eat 的轻松语使用。 *Jack used to come over and grub with us once in a while.* 杰克有时来跟我们一起吃顿饭。◇ food

grub up *something* [ˌgrʌ(ː)ˈbʌp ～] [话] **搜寻** → GRUB

grunt

a grunt [ə ˈgrʌnt] [话] **大兵** grunt 原为象声词，指猪的呼噜声。*The pig grunted.* 猪发出呼噜声。如此例所示，grunt 可以作为动词使用。转用于表达人在不满意时、用力气时、以及漠不关心地回话时所发出的“哼”的声音，并可用作动词，意思是“发出哼的声音”或“哼了一声”。*He gave a grunt.* 他哼了一声。但是，近年以来，这个 grunt 普遍用于表示“下级士兵”的意思了。原来，在越南战争中，美国海军陆战队的下级士兵背着沉重的背囊，一边走一边要发出用力的“哼”、“哼”的声音，因此他们就用 grunt 一词称呼自己，意思是“哼、哼的人”。不久又传到陆军。现在，不只用这一表达法指海军陆战队的下级士兵，也普遍地指一般的陆军下级士兵。这是一个非常轻松的称呼。另外，从这一表达法的来源也可以了解，使用这一意义的 grunt 一般带有“净干苦差事，永远难抬头”的意味。 *My year as a grunt in Vietnam added ten years onto my life.* 我在越南当了一年大兵，等于老了十岁。 *If I have to go into the army, I want to go to officers' training school. I don't want to end up as a grunt.* 如果我必须参军，我想进入军官训练学校。我可不愿意老当下级士兵。 *Sergeant: OK, you grunts. Get a move on!* 军士：喂，弟兄们！快点！◇ a (foot) soldier / an enlisted man

grunt [ˈgrʌnt] [话] **儿童大便** 由“用力气哼一声”转为“儿童大便”的意思。这是非常温柔的幼儿用语，如果成年人用在自己身上，那就是开玩笑的说法了。*Did you grunt today, Billy?* 比利，你今天拉臭臭了吗？ *Mommy, I have to grunt.* 妈妈，我要拉臭臭。另有 do number two 的说法，也是幼儿用语。这是成年人为儿童创制的一种委婉语，医生也常使用。 *Doctor: Jimmy, do you do number two every day?* 医生：吉米，你每天有大便吗？ *I did a big number two this morning, Mommy.* 妈妈，今儿早上我拉了一大泡臭臭。顺便讲一下：“小便”叫 PEE-PEE，又作 do number one。*Stop the car, Daddy. I have to do number one [pee-pee].* 爸爸，把汽车停一下，我要撒尿。*Child: I have to go to the bathroom. Mother: Number one or number two? Child: I have to pee-pee.* 孩子：我要上卫生间。母亲：大还是小？孩子：我要撒尿。 ◇ have a bowel movement / defecate

guard

catch *someone* **off guard** [ˌkætʃ ～ ˌɔ(ː)f ˈgɑːrd] [话] **乘虚而入** → catch *someone* NAPPING

guess

have another guess coming [hævə ˌnʌðər ˌgesˈkʌmən] [话] **猴儿吃麻花(蛮拧)** → have another THINK coming

Your guess is as good as mine. [ˈjə(:)r ˌgesɪzəz ˌgudəz ˈmaɪn] [话] **我也不了解** 在这里，guess 是"猜测"、"揣度"的意思。直译为"你的猜测跟我的猜测一样好"。这意思就是说："你猜不到，我也猜不到"，亦即"你如果不了解，我也不可能了解"。*A: Do you think Joan will pass the exam? B: Search me. Your guess is as good as mine.* 甲：你认为琼能通过考试吗？乙：我不知道。连你都不知道，我怎么会知道呢？*Don't ask me what the boss's plans are. Your guess is as good as mine.* 别向我打听老板的计划。你不知道，我也是照样不知道啊。◇ I don't know either.

gum

gum *something* **up** [ˌgʌm ～ ˈʌ(:)p] [话] **搞糟** → gum up the WORKS

beat *one's* **gums** [ˌbɪːt ～ˈgʌ(:)mz] [话] **废话连篇** gum 是"牙床"，beat *one's* gums 就是 beat *one's* gums together，按字面解释为"上下牙床互相碰"，即"使嘴一张一合"。这一表达法原来的构思是："一个人净说毫无内容的、非常无聊的话，从听者的角度来看，只不过是他的嘴在一张一合而已"。*I want everyone to listen carefully to what I have to say. I'm not here just to beat my gums, you know.* 我希望在座的每个人都注意听我说的话，因为我不是到这儿来向你们胡诌八扯，说些无聊的话的。*I hate faculty meetings. We have to sit there hours on end listening to the older professors beating their gums.* 我最讨厌开教员会。我们必须在那里白坐几个小时，净听老教授们东拉西扯，废话连篇。根据情况，也可以作 chew the RAG 的同义语使用。在这一场合没有"非常无聊"的意思，只表示"呶呶不休"，北京话叫"闲磕牙儿"。*Several old ladies were sitting around beating their gums.* 有几个老太太一直坐在那里闲磕牙儿。◇ engage in aimless talk / talk (aimlessly)

gun

a BB gun [ə ˈbi(:)ˌbiː ˈgʌ(:)n] [口] **儿童气枪** a BB 是"直径 0.175 英寸(约 4.5 毫米)的圆形子弹"。BB gun 是"BB 型气枪"(多为步枪式)。在美国，小学生以下的儿童常用这种枪做打靶游戏。它的威力可以杀伤小鸟、野鼠之类的小动物。对于人，只要不直接打到脸上，没有大的伤害。尽管如此，小孩子哪怕有一次用气枪去打人，也要受到父母的严厉惩罚。这是家喻户晓的常识。BB gun 只是一种玩具，但在同时也是美国人最初掌握用枪技术的训练工具，因此他们常常把这种气枪作为缅怀少年时代的一种象征物，永远刻在自己的脑海里，一时也不会遗忘。有时称作 an air rifle，但是严格地讲，air rifle 一语包括成年人用的大气枪在内。*Santa Claus brought Jimmy a BB gun for Christmas.* 在圣诞节的时候，圣诞老人送给吉米一支气枪作为礼物。另外，在表示极小物体的大小时，常用 BB 来作对比。*The floor was covered with tiny pellets about the size of BB's [with tiny, BB-sized pellets].* 地板上撒满了象 *BB* 气枪弹那么大的小粒。◇ an air rifle

a big gun [ə ˌbɪg ˈgʌ(:)n] [话] **有影响力的重要人物** a big gun 当然是"一支大枪"的意思。这一表达法原来的构思是："某人为制服对方的巨大武器"。*Mr. Smith is a big gun in the publishing world.* 史密斯先生是出版界的大人物。◇ a powerful person

a burp gun [ə ˈbə(:)rp ˌgʌ(:)n] [话] **自动手枪** → a BURP

give her the gun [ˌgɪvərðə ˈgʌ(:)n] [话] **开足马力** 旧式飞机的节流阀很象枪的扳机，因此就称油门(the throttle)为 the gun。her 指发动机。本条意为"加大油门"。这是一个轻松的说法。常根据会话时的实际发音拼写作 give 'er the gun。除汽车外，也应用于飞机、气艇等，凡是有发动机的交通工具一概都行。有时也用于不是车船类的带有发动机的东西，在这一场合是"增加转数"的意思。不只用在从静止状态到发动的场合，也用在中途加速的场合。*I'll be back in five minutes. As soon as I jump in the car, give 'er the gun and let's get out of here.* 我过五分钟回来。只要我一跳上车，马上开足马力，咱们赶快从这里溜走。*As soon as the pilot sighted the enemy fighter, he gave her the gun and went into a steep climb.* 飞行员发现敌人的战斗机以后，马上开足马力，直线向上冲去。偶尔用 it 代替 her。*As the escapees approached the police blockade, they gave it the gun and tried to crash through.* 当逃跑者接近警察的封锁线的时候，他们立即加大油门，打算猛冲过去。◇ open the throttle wide / (suddenly) accelerate

gun *one's* **engine** → ENGINE

jump the gun [ˌdʒʌmpðə ˈgʌ(ː)n] [口] **过早行动** 这里的 gun 是体育比赛时的"发令枪"。jump the gun 是"赛跑运动员抢跑"的意思。*He was disqualified from the race for jumping the gun.* 他由于赛跑时抢跑而失去了参赛的资格。也转作比喻使用。*Let's not jump the gun. We should plan very carefully before making our first move.* 我们不要过早地行动。在迈出第一步之前，我们必须非常仔细地计划好。如这一例句所示，可以单独使用 jump the gun；但也可以象在下边的例句中那样，采取 jump the gun and *do something* 的形式，即"过早地干什么"的意思。*When speculating in stocks, it's easy to jump the gun and sell before the price has peaked.* 在做股票投机生意的时候，很容易过早行动，不等价钱涨到顶峰就把股票抛出手。*We were supposed to start singing when the teacher gave us the signal, but Lucy jumped the gun and started when the band started playing.* 我们本来应该等到老师打手势才开始唱歌，可是露西急不可待，乐队刚一演奏，她就唱起来了。另有一个形式为 jump the gun by *doing something*，也是"过早地干什么"的意思。*Fred jumped the gun by telling a newspaper reporter about our new product before we were ready to announce it.* 我们还没有准备好公布我们的新商品，弗雷德就过早地把消息透露给新闻记者了。◇ be too hasty / act precipitously

a Tommy gun [ə ˈtɑ(ː)miˌgʌ(ː)n] [话] **汤普森式冲锋枪** Thompson submachine gun [ˌtɑ(ː)mpsn ˌsʌbməˈʃiːn ˌgʌ(ː)n]的爱称。这种枪是以美国军官汤普森 (John T. Thompson) 的姓命名的。在以禁酒令时代(1919～1933) 为背景的影片和描写黑社会的电视中，常常见到匪帮把这种枪放在提琴盒中拿着走的镜头。军队很早以前就改用新型冲锋枪了，但黑社会仍然爱用汤普森式。这一表达法现在泛指手提式机枪，不是汤普森式也可以。*Watch out, Joe! He's got a Tommy gun!* 注点儿意，乔！他拿着冲锋枪哪！如果加连字符写作 Tommy-gun，则变为动词，是"用 Tommy gun 射击"的意思。*A policeman was Tommy-gunned by the bank robbers.* 抢劫银行的匪徒用小型机枪射中了一名警察。也可以用小写字母，写作 tommy gun, tommy-gun。作为黑社会用语，又称 a chopper (→ a CHOPPER①)。◇ a (Thompson) submachine gun

guns

go great guns [ˌgou ˈgreɪt ˈgʌ(ː)nz] [话] **非常顺利** 语源不详。按字面意义，great guns 是"巨大的枪"。但是，人们并不使用这一意义，它与 go 结合到一起，是"有生气地"、"盛大地"、"顺顺当当地"的意味，具副词的功能。我们且不管语源以及语法关系如何，假若把 go great guns 理解成"象大炮(即巨大的枪)一样咚咚咚不断地放"这样的具体形象，可能有助于记忆。下面的几个例句可以证明这一点。*Now that we have a new president, our firm is going great guns.* 自从新的总经理到任以来，我们公司蒸蒸日上。象这样应用于公司或事业的时候，主要指"财源茂盛"。*The stock I bought last year is going great guns.* 去年我买的股票非常顺手。当然，这是指"股票价格不断上涨"。如下面的例句所示，特别应用于老年人的健康状态。*A: How's your* *grandfather these days? B: He's still going great guns.* 甲：最近，你爷爷身体好吗？乙：他仍然非常硬朗。这一表达法在使用时一般采取 be +～ing 的形式，但也有不是如此的情况。*After the war started, industry began to go great guns.* 战争爆发以后，工业开始蓬勃发展起来了。◇ do extremely well

stand by *one's* **guns** [ˌstændbaɪ ～ ˈgʌ(ː)nz] [口] **坚持自己的信念** → stick to *one's* GUNS

stick to *one's* **guns** [ˌstɪktə ～ ˈgʌ(ː)nz] [话] **坚持自己的观点** 字面意义是"贴在自己的大炮上不离开"，亦即"坚守阵地，决不退却"的意思。*Even though completely surrounded by the enemy, the soldiers all stuck to their guns to the very end.* 甚至到被敌人完全包围的时候，士兵们全都守着自己的大炮，一直战斗到最后。转作比喻使用。*Although the President denied the New York Times report, the newspaper stuck to its guns.* 虽然总统否认了《纽约时报》的报导，但是该报始终坚持自己的观点。*Don't give up. Stick to your guns. The company can't fire you as long as you have the union's backing.* 不要屈服。要坚持到底。只要有工会作后盾，公司就解雇不了你。如以上的例句所示，多在上文为"虽然受到攻击"或"虽然情况不利"的场合使用，但并不限定如此。*I knew someone was in the house because I had seen a curtain move. So I stuck to my guns and pounded on the door until it was finally opened.* 我知道房子里有人，因为我看见有一块窗帘动了。于是，我不断敲门，直到门开为止。stand by *one's* guns 的字面意义为"站在大炮旁边"，实际上与 stick to *one's* guns 同义，但后者语气轻松，而前者略嫌呆板。*Though his energy proposals were being denounced on all sides, the governor stood by his guns, refusing to allow them to be diluted.* 州长关于能源的提案受到各方面的谴责，但是他坚持己见，拒绝删除其中的任何部分。另有 stand to *one's* guns 这一表达法，但为英国英语，在美国几乎无人使用。◇ refuse to change *one's* position [approach, opinion, belief, etc.]

gut

bust a gut (*doing* [to *do*] *something*) [ˌbʌstə ˈgʌ(ː)t] [话] **费很大劲** a gut 在口语中指"肚子"。本条直译为"使肚子破裂"，亦即"费了九牛二虎之力"的意思。*I almost busted a gut lifting that log.* 我在抬起那根大圆木头的时候，使的劲儿乎把肚子胀破了。这是按照字面意义的用法，表示实际上用了力气。但是，这是一个大多用作比喻的轻松的表达法。*I almost busted a gut getting into this university. I refuse to take part in any activity that might cause me to be expelled.* 我费了九牛二虎之力才进入这所大学，我可不参加任何会使我被开除学籍的活动。*Jerry busted a gut to get you this job. The least you can do is to show your appreciation.* 杰里为了给你找这个工作，费了很大的劲儿。你至少应该表示一下谢意啊。*Why bust a gut—that's my motto. I never do any more than is expected of me in this job.* 不出力气不费劲——这就是我的格言。在这项工作中，叫我干多少我就干多少，决不多做一点儿。◇ have an extremely difficult time (*doing something*) / exert yourself

guts

hate *someone's* **guts** [ˌheɪt ～ ˈgʌ(ː)ts] [话] **恨之入骨** guts 是"内脏"。这一表达法主要是强调 hate 一词，直译为"连某人的内脏都恨"。可以在脑子里把 hate 当作为 love 的反义词，有时意为"讨厌"，有时意为"仇恨"。但是，guts 一词不大文雅，特别是与 hate 结合起来就更加粗俗，所以有些人避免使用。*I'm sure Jed would never lift a finger to help me. He hates my guts.* 杰德肯定不会帮我一把，他对我是恨之入骨。*Don't put those two in the same work group. They hate each other's guts.* 不要把他们俩放在一个组里干活，他们是水火不相容的。◇ despise *someone*

guy

a bad guy[①] [ə ˈbæːdˈgaɪ] [话] **不好的人** 原为专用于否定句的表达法，如说：*He's not such a bad guy*. 他不是个那么坏的家伙。最近，特别是在青年人中间，一般在肯定句中也使用起来了，如说：*He's a bad guy*. 他是一个坏家伙。在肯定句中使用的场合，不是按字面意义专指“坏人”，而是泛指“不可心的人”、“不相宜的对手”，具有“敬而远之”的主观的心情。这是一个把自己的这种主观心情稍微夸大的表达法，只应用于男性。 *John Smith is a bad guy*. 我对约翰·史密斯这个人敬而远之。另外，以轻松的口吻半开玩笑地使用的场合居多，这时含有“不随和”、“冷冰冰”、“太严厉”等意思。*Professor Green is a bad guy. He only gave me a 55 on my history test*. 格林教授真不开面儿，历史测验他只给我55分。◇ a bad person

a bad guy[②] [ə ˈbæ(ː)dˌgaɪ] [话] **坏蛋** 在西部影片中或者电视的儿童节目中，指企图干掉“正义的一方”的“大坏蛋”。请注意重音与 a bad GUY①(不好的人)不同。与 bad guy①的另一个不同点是复数的场合必须加 the。与 a good GUY②的场合相同，这是个男性名词，不能用于女性。 *The bad guys always lose in the end*. 坏蛋最终必败无疑。*A bad guy shot the sheriff*. 一个坏蛋开枪打死了县保安官。◇ an enemy of justice

a good guy[①] [ə ˈgu(ː)dˈgaɪ] [话] **善良的人** 在以亲切的口吻夸奖他人的性格或品质的时候使用，只应用于男性。与 a good EGG 大致同义，但 good guy①没有上级对下级、长辈对晚辈的意味。 *Biff is a good guy. I really like him*. 比弗是一个很不错的小伙子，我真心喜欢他。*You're really a good guy, Joe. It's just that I don't love you enough to marry you*. 乔，你的确是一个好人。只不过我对你的爱还没有达到要与你结婚的程度。◇ a nice person

a good guy[②] [ə ˈgudˌgaɪ] [话] **好人** 在西部影片中或电视的儿童节目中，指“正义的一方”。请注意重音与 a good GUY①(善良的人)不同。另一个与 good guy①的不同点是在复数的场合必须加 the。只应用于男性。*The good guys always win*. 正义者总是会胜利的。*A good guy bit the dust*. 一个好人被枪打死了。*In the old cowboy movies, you could tell the good guys because they always wore white hats and rode white horses*. 在过去的牛仔影片中，你马上会看出谁是好人，因为他们总是戴白帽子，骑白马。◇ a defender of justice

a wise guy [ə ˈwaɪz ˌgaɪ] [话] **狂妄自大的家伙** wise 本来是“聪明”的意思，a wise man 是“智者”。但在这里却是一种讽刺，不是指真聪明，而是指“自作聪明”。guy 是“家伙”，常为男性。这一表达法用于形容“自以为什么都知道[懂得]，信口开河或任意行动的人”。 *Alec's all right, I guess, but sometimes he's such a wise guy*. 据我看，亚历克这个人还不坏，不过有时候太狂妄自大了。*I don't know where Jim got the reputation for being such a wise guy. I thought he was very nice*. 我真不知道吉姆怎么弄来个狂妄自大的名声？我认为他这个人很好嘛。*Why did you have to make all those smart remarks at the meeting? It's wise guys like you that always gum up the works*. 为什么你非在会议中发表一套谬论不可呢？把事情搞糟的永远是象你这样狂妄自大的家伙。 *Oh, a wise guy, huh? How would you like to step outside with me for a moment?* 嗬，又不知天高地厚，自吹自擂啦？咱们到外边去比试比试如何？有时是朋友之间带半开玩笑的口吻使用。*OK, wise guy. If you know all the answers, tell me how I'm supposed to write a letter when we don't have any paper*. 好啦好啦，你算个聪明人。如果你什么都知道的话，请你告诉我：当我们没有一张纸的时候，我应该怎样去写一封信。大概那位“聪明人”说的是“没有电话，可以写封信嘛！”因此有以上的讽刺性的回答。在上面的一些例句中，主要讲的是“好说大话的人”。但是，在“狂妄自大的人”当中，也包括“哗众取宠的人”，这种人主观地以为自己很聪明会把大家逗乐。*Who's the wise guy that took my lunch box?* 哪位机灵的大爷把我的饭盒拿走啦？另有 a smart aleck 与 wise guy 大致同义，但使用的人不同：wise guy 主要是中学以上的学生相互间使用，而 a smart aleck 一般是大人对孩子或者儿童们相互间使用。另外，a wiseacre 也是与 wise guy 意味大致相同的表达法，但接近书面语，在会话中很少使用。◇ an impudent, self-assured fellow / ((讽刺)) a genius

guzzler

a gas guzzler [ə ˈgæ(ː)s ˌgʌzlər] [口] **大量耗油的汽车** 这是一个很早就有的表达法，但是自从资源问题或能源问题被不断地提出后，使用频率更为提高了。guzzle 为象声词，意思是“咕嘟咕嘟地大口喝”。例如：*The old men sat around guzzling beer and swapping tall tales.* 几个老头围坐在一起咕嘟咕嘟地喝啤酒，你一言我一语，正在高谈阔论。*You'd better not guzzle your milk. That's all there is.* 你不要咕嘟咕嘟地大口喝牛奶。就那么一杯，再没有啦。这是本来的用法。因此，gas guzzler 就是“咕嘟咕嘟大口喝 gas(汽油)的东西”的意思了。大多指大量消耗汽油的大型车辆。*In these days of high oil prices, Americans are deserting their big gas guzzlers for more fuel-efficient cars.* 最近汽油价格上涨，美国人正在放弃他们那些消耗汽油的大型汽车，而改用节省燃料的小轿车了。这一表达法不仅指大型汽车，也可以指赛车、运转不灵的车、破旧的老爷车。*This sports car may be small, but it's a real gas guzzler.* 这辆赛车大概算是小型的，但是它可真能消耗汽油啊。*I've got to get rid of this old gas guzzler or I'll go broke.* 我必须处理掉这辆消耗汽油的老车，不然我就得破产啦。◇ a car that consumes great quantities of gas / a gas consumer

gym

gym [ˈdʒɪ(ː)m] [话] **体育(课)** gymnastics [dʒɪmˈnæ(ː)stɪks] (体育、体操)的缩略，学生用语。从中学生到大学生普遍使用，但大学生有喜欢使用另一表达法 PHYS ED (→) 的倾向。请读者注意：如果说“体育课”，不使用 gymnastics 一词，一定要用 gym 这个形式。*Gym is my favorite class.* 体育是我最喜欢的课程。也可以说 (a) gym class，意味相同。*I have (a) gym class at three.* 我三点钟有体育课。gym 的前边加 a 便形成名词，为作“体育馆”解的 gymnasium [dʒɪmˈneɪʒəm] 的缩略，一般人也使用。*I hear there are plans to build a new municipal gym.* 我听说正在计划修建一座新的市体育馆。另外，在这一场合，不只用 gym，也常常使用 gymnasium。◇ physical education

H

habit

kick the habit [.kɪkðə 'hæ(:)bət] [话] **戒除恶习** habit 本来是"习惯",在这一习用语中常加定冠词,为"恶习"的意思。kick 是"踢","踢掉恶习"就是"完全戒除"。*I'd like to quit smoking, but I just can't kick the habit.* 我想不再吸烟,可是怎么也没能完全戒除恶习。有时把表示具体"恶习"的词放在 habit 的前边,如 kick the drug habit 中的 drug。*Once Carl kicked the drug habit, he became a model citizen.* 卡尔自从戒绝吸毒的恶习以后,他变成一个模范公民了。如以上所讲,这一表达法一般用于"对身体健康有害的恶习",但有时也用于其他的"恶习"。在这种场合,与 quit (*something*) cold TURKEY 不同,并没有特殊的戏谑味道。*I think my brother has finally kicked the gambling habit.* 看起来,我的哥哥总算完全戒除赌博的恶习啦。这一表达法在用于本来不知道是不是"恶习"的一些事情的场合,可以感到有戏谑的成份。例如:*I really can't afford to date so many girls, but it's tough to kick the habit.* 老实说,我没有充裕的金钱去跟那么多的姑娘们约会,不过恶习难改啊。◇ rid *oneself* of the habit (completely)

had

have been had [hæv.bɪn 'hæ:d] [话] **受骗** 有些英汉词典在 have 条目下列有"欺骗"一解,实际上不能单独把 have 按这一意义使用。一般采取本条条头的形式:完成时的被动语态。*You've been had. This receipt hasn't been signed.* 你受骗啦。这个收条上没有签字啊。*When the man we had given our money to hadn't returned after thirty minutes, we realized that we'd been had.* 我们把钱交给了一个人,当他过了半个钟头还没回来的时候,我们明白受他欺骗了。本条习用语不只表达"对方进行欺骗",而是强调"自己上当"这一后果。因此,也可以用于表示与对方的意图无关。仅仅自认"倒霉"的意思。在打扑克时,如果分到极坏的牌,人们常说:*I've been had. These are the worst cards I've ever seen.* 真倒霉,我从来没有见过这么糟糕的牌。在这一场合,丝毫没有发牌的人搞斜门歪道的意思,只表示"自己倒霉"这一结果。在本条开头的两个例句中,可以将 been had 改换成 been tricked,意思基本上一样,只是语气严厉得多,带有很明显的"对方进行欺骗"的意思。如果在打扑克时说 been tricked,可能会吵起架来。◇ have been tricked [taken advantage of]

hafta

hafta ['hæ(:)ftə] [话] 将 have to 按普通的日常会话中的发音拼写而成。主语为第三人称单数时的 has to 作 hasta ['hæ(:)stə]。这两个形式在小说和漫画中常常可以见到。*I hafta get to work.* 我得干活啦。*She hasta fix dinner.* 她得准备饭啦。如以上的例句所示,一般后接不定式,但也有省略的情况。*A: Eat your spinach, Jimmy. B: Gee whiz. Do I hafta?* 甲:吉米,你把菠菜吃啦。乙:哎哟!我非吃不可呀?◇ have to

hair

curl *someone's* **hair** [.kə(:)rl ~ 'he:r] [话] **令人毛骨悚然** 字面意义是"卷头发"。*The beautician curled my hair.* 美容师给我卷了头发。作为比喻,使用方法如下:*Haven't you read what the newspaper said about you this morning? It'll curl your hair.* 你看到今天早上的报纸上关于你的报导了吗?哎哟,简直吓死人。*That's a comfortable hotel but the breakfasts they serve will really curl your hair.* 那是一家很舒适的旅馆,不过那里的早

餐却实在吓人。这一表达法不仅在表示心中不快的感觉时使用，也用于由于恐怖而毛骨悚然的场合。*I went to see a gory movie about zombies. It really curled my hair.* 我去看了一部以幽灵为题材的恐怖影片。那可真是令人毛骨悚然。还有一个相似的表达法是 make *someone's* HAIR stand on end (吓得浑身发抖)。直译是"使头发从根上竖起来"，对于中国人说，这意思也很容易理解。但原因只能是恐怖，不能用于表示"怒发冲冠"。另外，curl *someone's* hair 这一表达法也可以采取 make *someone's* hair curl 的形式，但这是英国式的说法，在美国极少使用。◇ make *someone* shudder

get in *someone's* **hair** [ˌgedən ~ ˈheːr] [话] **使人讨厌** 直译为"进入某人的头发中"。最初的构思可能是："象虱子一样呆在头发里，总也不离去"。现在已经没有虱子的意味，而用于"在身边转悠，哓哓不休，令人又急又恼，但又毫无办法"的场合。*I wish there were some way to avoid that guy. He's always getting in my hair.* 我希望有个什么方法躲开那个家伙。他老是缠在我身边，讨厌极啦。*Our work would go much more smoothly if it weren't for that guy. He seems to enjoy getting into everyone's hair.* 如果没有那个家伙，我们的工作一定会进行得顺利得多。他好象拿打扰每一个人当作一件乐事。be in *someone's* hair 是"打扰某人"甚至"成为累赘"的意思。*I never should have agreed to help that fellow. Now he's in my hair from morning till night.* 我真不应该同意去帮助那个家伙。现在，他从早到晚无时无刻不扰乱我。也常使用 with *someone* in *one's* hair 这一表达法，意思是"被某人扰乱"。*It's not that I don't like my roommate. He's a nice fellow. But I just can't study with him in my hair all the time.* 我不是不喜欢我同屋的伙伴。他是一个很好的人。但是他无时无刻不打扰我，使我一点儿也不能温习功课。*Let's not invite my brother. I can't stand having him in our hair all weekend.* 咱们别约请我弟弟啦。整个周末都叫他打扰，我可受不了。→ stay out of *someone's* HAIR ◇ get in *someone's* way / bother *someone*

let *one's* **hair down** [ˌlet ~ ˈhe(ː)r ˌdaun] [话] **无拘无束** 字面意义是"把头发散开放下"。*She always lets her hair down before going to bed at night.* 每天晚上上床以前，她总是把头发散开放下来。最近，女人们有了各式各样的发型，但在过去的时代，除了家族和亲人之外，不能叫外人见到梳头或散开头发的姿影，这是一般的常识。因此，let *one's* hair down 就有了"不拘礼节"、"随随便便"的比喻意义了。*You're always so stiff. You should let your hair down and enjoy yourself once in a while.* 你老是板着个脸，有时候应该无拘无束地快乐一下子。*Heads of state seldom have a chance to let their hair down in public.* 一成为国家首脑，就很少有机会在群众面前说说笑笑了。下面是"不拘谨"、"推心置腹"的例子：*After acting aloof for so many months, Jay finally let his hair down and told us of his financial difficulties.* 杰伊采取超然离群的态度已经很多个月了，最近他终于推心置腹地对我们讲述了他的经济困难状态。◇ relax *one's* reserve

make *someone's* **hair stand on end** [ˌmeɪk ~ ˈhe(ː)r ˌstændə(ː) ˌnend] [话] **使人毛骨悚然** 字面意义是"使某人的头发从根上站起来"。*The static electricity in the room made our hair stand on end.* 由于室内的静电作用，我们的头发立起来了。转作比喻使用，表示在恐怖时头皮发凉、"头发立起"的感觉。顺便讲一下：在美国的漫画中常常可以看到为表示内心恐怖而绘出的头发竖立的形象。*The sudden noise from the upstairs of the supposedly deserted old house made my hair stand on end.* 当从一所本以为是无人居住的老房子的楼上突然传来了声响时，我不禁毛骨悚然。*The ghost stories my uncle told us when we were children always made our hair stand on end.* 我们还是孩子的时候，伯父向我们讲的鬼怪故

事，都使我们毛骨悚然。*When Bess opened the door, the scene that met her eyes made her hair stand on end.* 当贝丝打开门的时候，映入她的眼帘的情景使得她毛骨悚然。◇ fill *someone* with fear

stay out of *someone's* **hair** [ˌsteɪ ˌaudəv ~ ˈheːr] [话] **不打扰他人** get in *someone's* HAIR (→)的反义语。直译为"不进入某人的头发"，即"不做妨碍他人的讨厌事情"的意思。*I'm willing to take him with us as long as he stays out of my hair.* 只要不妨碍我，可以叫他跟咱们一起去。*I'm sorry to bother you again, but I have one more question. After this, I promise to stay out of your hair.* 对不起，还要麻烦你一下，我再提一个问题。这以后，我保证不打扰你了。*I won't fire him because he's your brother, but you tell him from now on to stay out of my hair.* 因为他是您的弟弟，所以我不免他的职。不过请你告诉他，今后不要给我找麻烦。也可以用 keep 代替 stay。*You can stay if you want, but keep out of my hair.* 如果你愿意的话，你可以在这儿呆着，不过千万不要打搅我。还有一个形式为 keep *someone* out of *one's* [*someone's*] hair，意思是"不要叫某人去打搅另一个人"。*The boss wants you to keep your brother out of his hair.* 老板希望你叫你的弟弟不要去打扰他。*Keep that guy out of my hair.* 不要叫那个家伙来打搅我。◇ stay out of *someone's* way / not bother *someone*

without turning a hair [wɪˌðautːˌərnɪŋə ˈheːr] [口] **保持冷静态度** 勉强直译为"头发一丝不乱"。有人说这一表达法是形容马的镇定，但语源不详。这一表达法虽然是强调"镇静"、"沉着"，但从它本身看不出内心是否平静。总之，从外观上看是采取了毅然的态度，即"面不改色"的意思。*My father picked up a stick and faced the bear without turning a hair.* 我的父亲抄起一根棒子，毫不惊惶地面对着熊。这一表达法的应用面极广，从面对"恐怖"、"震动"起，一直到"羞耻"、"疲劳"等等。*The woman listened to the news of her husband's death without turning a hair.* 那个女人在听到丈夫死去的消息时毫不动容。*Though the woman had lost her bathing suit in the strong tide, she thanked us for saving her, and, without turning a hair, turned and walked up the beach.* 那个女人被激流冲走了游泳衣，我们救了她，她向我们道了谢，然后就转过身去，光着身子毫不羞惭地向海岸走去了。*That old man can jog ten kilometers a day without turning a hair.* 那个老头儿每天能跑十公里，毫无倦容。这一表达法虽然用 without 的场合占绝大多数，但也可以不用 without，而讲 not turn a hair。*A: Did he take the news calmly? B: Didn't turn a single hair.* 甲：他听到那条新闻后很冷静吗？乙：简直毫不动容啊。如这一例句所示，常用 single 加强语气。*Even when the doctor told him he would soon be completely bald, he never turned a hair.* 尽管医生告诉他不久就要完全变秃了，而他却是毫不在乎的样子。◇ without any sign of fear [distress, embarrassment, fatigue, etc.]

hairs

split hairs(over *something*) [ˌsplɪt ˈhe(ː)rz] [口] **作不必要的过细分析** 直译是"把头发一根一根分开"，指过细的、毫无意义的行为。这一表达法常在"罗罗嗦嗦列举一些说不说都行的事例"的场合使用。特别指叫听众感到毫无意味的发言。*John always slows up the progress of our departmental meetings by splitting hairs over such things as a few cents' difference in monthly manufacturing costs.* 约翰在我们部门的会议上，总是罗列每月生产成本有几分钱差异之类的数字来拖延会议的进程。*I don't want to split hairs, but I think that if a student gets a grade of 59.9 rather than 60.0, he should be failed.* 我不愿说鸡毛蒜皮的事情，不过我认为如果一个学生得了 59.9 分而不是 60.0 分，就必须叫他留级。*Let's not split hairs over a few minutes' difference in arrival time.* 我们不要为了到达

时间相差三两分钟这点鸡毛蒜皮的小事而争辩吧。◇ make unnecessarily fine distinctions

hairsplitter

a hairsplitter ['he(:)r͵splɪtər] [口] **做不必要过细分析的人** 即 split HAIRS 的人。一般指没有必要过细分析而他偏要仔细区分的人,即"好抠字眼儿的人"或"好讲歪理的人"。 *Ralph is a real hairsplitter. If you say the train got in on the dot, he'll claim it was at least thirty seconds late.* 拉尔夫实在是个好抠字眼儿的人。如果你说列车是准时到达的,他硬要说至少误点有三十秒。◇ a person who makes unnecessarily fine distinctions (real <hairsplitter> → really <unnecessarily>)

hairsplitting

hairsplitting ['he(:)r͵splɪtɪŋ] [口] **过细分析** split HAIRS 的名词形式。常用于"讲话"。 *We have to reach a quick decision. This is no time for hairsplitting.* 我们必须赶快做出决议来,没有时间去抠鸡毛蒜皮的小事啦。另外,这一名词可以原封不动当作形容词使用,意思是"拘泥于细枝末节的"。用汉语俗语来说,就是"鸡蛋里挑骨头(的)"。 *I'm tired of your hairsplitting arguments.* 你那些议论纯粹是鸡蛋里挑骨头,我听腻了。◇ making unnecessarily fine distinctions / overly fastidious

half

one's **better half** [~ ͵bedər 'hæ:f] [话] **妻子** 一种轻松的说法。直译为"一对夫妇较好的那一半"。这一表达法是以基督教的男女结婚合成一体的教义为基础的。 *I promised to take my better half shopping this afternoon.* 我答应妻子今天下午带她去买东西。另外,妻子用此习用语指"丈夫"而言的例子不是没有,但极罕见。◇ *one's* wife

Half a loaf is better than none. → LOAF

(a) half bath [(ə) 'hæ(:)f 'bæ:θ] [口] **无洗澡设备的卫生间** → the BATHROOM

be half the battle → BATTLE

half-cocked

go off half-cocked [gou͵ɔ(:)f ͵hæ(:)f 'kɑ:kt] [话] **仓促行事** cock 是"扳起枪的击铁"。cock 分为两个阶段,第一阶段是 half cock (半击发状态),第二阶段是 full cock (全击发状态),到了这一阶段,一扣枪机,子弹应声而出。如果停留在第一阶段,即使扣枪机也不能发射子弹。因此,添加上具有"发射"意味的 go off 而讲 go off at half cock,那就意味着"射击的准备只做了一半,子弹就飞出去了"。转作比喻,就变成"没有准备好就贸然行动"即"仓促行事"的意思。但 go off at half cock 已经有些陈腐,人们在日常会话中不喜欢用这一表达法。现在几乎全都使用 go off half-cocked 的形式。 *Phil has a lot of good ideas, but they usually come to naught because he's always going off half-cocked.* 菲尔有一肚子好主意,但是由于他总是仓促行事,把好主意都化成了泡影。人在一怒之下,常常不加思考,草率行动。下面就是在这一场合的普通对话。 *I know you're angry about the way the boss has treated you, but don't go off half-cocked. If you quit your job now, it won't be so easy to find another.* 我知道老板对待你的方法使你很恼火,但是可不要贸然行事。如果你辞去目前的工作,再找一个可不那么容易啊。一说 go off half-cocked,必定含有"移诸行动"的意味,但有时这种行动只是"说话"而已。 *Don't go off half-cocked. Hear me to the end.* 你别认为自己已经全懂了,听我把话讲完。◇ act without sufficient thought [preparation] / be too [so] hasty

half-crocked

half-crocked ['hæ(:)f'krɑ(:)kt] [话] **半醉的** → half CROCKED

half-wit

a half-wit [ə 'hæ(:)f͵wɪt] [口] **弱智者** 意思是"只有一般人智慧 (wit) 的一半 (half)的人"。 *That half-wit locked the keys in the car.* 那个傻瓜把钥匙锁到汽车里了。也可以以 half-witted ['hæ(:)f 'wɪdɪd]的形式作为形容词使

用。 *That half-witted brother of mine forgot the tickets.* 我那个缺心眼儿的弟弟忘记把票带来了。*It's pathetic, but their second son is half-witted [a half-wit].* 真可怜,他们的二儿子大脑发育迟缓[是个低能儿]。有时如这一例句所示,按照字面意义使用。务请读者注意上下文的关系。 → a DUMBHEAD ◇ a stupid person

hall

a chow hall [ə ˈtʃau ˌhɔːl] [话] **(军队、大学、工厂等的)食堂** CHOW (→) 是"食物"、"食品"、"一顿饭"的轻松说法;hall 是"大厅"。因此,本条整体的意义是"吃饭的大厅"亦即"食堂"。主要为军队的俚语,但除军队外,学生与工厂职工的专用食堂也称为 chow hall。*Are you going to the chow hall now?* 你现在去食堂吗? *Is the chow hall in this building?* 食堂在这座楼里吗? *That building is the university chow hall.* 那座建筑物是大学的食堂。◇ a mess [dining] hall

hammer

go at *something* **hammer and tongs** [ˌgouət ~ ˈhæmərən ˈtɔːŋz] [话] **拼命地** 打铁工人用钳子 (tongs) 夹着烧红了的铁,抡着大锤(hammer) 拼命去打。本条的表达法正是从这一火热劳动的具体形象产生的。常用于学习、工作以及吵架等。*Jim has finals next week. He's upstairs now going at his homework hammer and tongs.* 吉姆下个星期有期末考试。他现在正在楼上拼命温习功课呢。*Mr. and Mrs. Jones seldom quarrel, but when I called on them yesterday, they were going at it hammer and tongs.* 琼斯夫妇很少吵嘴,但是昨天我去拜访他们的时候,两个人正吵得脸红脖子粗呢。如果 *something* 的部分长,可以把 at *something* 放在 tongs 的后边,例如: *Bill is going hammer and tongs at his new job.* 比尔竭尽全力从事他的新工作。◇ work vigorously at *something* / quarrel vigorously

put *something* **under the hammer** [ˌput ~ ˌʌndərðə ˈhæːmər] [口] **拍卖** 这里的 hammer 为"拍卖者使用的木槌"。本条直译是"把某物放在木槌底下",即"公开拍卖"的意思。 *I hate to put this painting under the hammer, but otherwise I won't be able to pay my taxes.* 我极不愿意拍卖这幅画,可是不拍卖它,我就付不了税金呀。动词 put 最有代表性,但有时使用 send, bring, 意思相同。另外,"被拍卖"在英语中说 come [go] under the hammer。*I've decided to send my classic car collection under the hammer.* 我决定把自己收藏的古典式轿车送去拍卖了。 *When the Hadrocks went bankrupt, all their belongings went under the hammer.* 哈德罗克斯家破产的时候,他们所有的东西都被拍卖了。*When I arrived at the auction, the table I wanted to bid on was just coming under the hammer.* 当我到达拍卖市场的时候,我想出个价钱的那张桌子正好在开始拍卖。◇ auction *something*

Hancock

put *one's* **John Hancock on** *something* → JOHN HANCOCK

hand

bite the hand that feeds *one* [ˌbaɪtðə ˌhæ(ː)ndðət ˈfiːdz ~] [口] **恩将仇报** 直译为"动物咬饲养者的手"。经常作比喻使用。在按字面意义使用的场合,必须补加 of the person, 例如: *That dog always tries to bite the hand of the person that feeds him.* 那只狗总是要咬饲养者的手。有时用于实际养育者,在这一场合也含有"恩"的意义在内,在中国叫"父母之恩"。例如: *I can't go against my father's wishes. That would be biting the hand that feeds me.* 我不能违背父亲的意愿,否则就等于忘恩负义了。一般场合如: *If you refuse to support the boss's proposal, you'll be biting the hand that feeds you.* 如果你不支持头头的建议,就等于恩将仇报呀。◇ repay kindness with injury

be eating out of *someone's* **hand** [ˌiːdɪŋ audəv ~ˈhæːnd] [口] **言听计从** → have *someone* eating out of *one's* HAND

force *someone's* **hand** [ˌfors ~ ˈhæːnd] [口] **迫使某人行动** 这里的 hand 原为纸牌游戏中的"一手牌"。在纸牌游戏中, force *someone's* hand 是"迫使对手把他准备在紧要关头使用的牌提前亮出来"。有时是利用巧妙的战术达到这一目的,有时则是自然形成如此的结果。*I didn't want to play my ace of spades so soon, but Sam forced my hand.* 我不想那么早就亮出黑桃 *A*,可是萨姆逼得我非出不可了。作为比喻使用的场合,一般是这一表达法的主语"有意识地"这样做:*The President hadn't planned to announce his tax-reform bill so soon, but the opposition forced his hand.* 总统并没有打算那么早就公布税制改革法案,但是在野党迫使他提前发表了。有时是"结果不得不如此"或者"在某种情况下只好这样做"的意思。*The police hadn't planned to make any arrests, but the rioters forced their hand.* 警察并没有打算逮捕什么人,但是暴徒的行动迫使他们这样做了。*I had hoped to hold on to this property a while longer before selling, but the economic situation has forced my hand.* 我本来希望过一个时候再卖掉这份产业,但是经济情况不容许我往后拖。◇ prompt *someone* to take action [reveal *his* intentions] sooner than *he* desires

gain the upper hand [ˌgeɪnðɪ ˌʌpər ˈhæːnd] [口] **占上风** upper hand 古时曾表示"有权威的地位"的意味,现在只在这一表达法中残存着此解的踪影。*The fighting was even at first, but because our soldiers were better equipped, we slowly began to gain the upper hand.* 在最初的时候,双方的战斗未分胜负。但是由于我们士兵的装备较好,我方逐渐开始占了上风。*Our lack of adequate sales promotion has let our rivals gain the upper hand.* 由于我们缺乏提高销售量的相应措施,使得一些竞争对手占了上风。动词除 gain 外还常用 get,意思相同。*The important thing in wrestling is never to let your opponent get the upper hand.* 摔跤中的秘诀是永远不让对手占有优势。也可以说 have the upper hand,表示处于优势的状态。*We have no choice but to accept their conditions. They have the upper hand.* 我们没有别的办法,只好接受他们的条件,因为他们占上风嘛。gain [get] the upper hand 的反义语是 lose the upper hand (失去优势)或者 give *someone* the upper hand (让别人占了上风)。*As their lawyer refuted my arguments one by one, I realized that without new evidence I would quickly lose the upper hand.* 对方的律师把我的论点一一驳倒之后,我已经看出如果没有新的证据,我很快就要处于不利状态了。*I'm afraid our mistakes have given them the upper hand.* 看起来,咱们由于失误而使对方占了上风。另外,几乎所有的英汉词典都加个 of,把这一表达法写作 gain the upper hand of ~ (占上风,占优势),但是在实际上使用这一表达法时,大多不加前置词,只采取 gain [get, have] the upper hand 的形式。即使在加前置词的场合,不论是英国英语还是美国英语,那个前置词也不是 of,一般用的是 over。*I'm afraid I've let George get the upper hand over me for the position of section chief.* 看起来,争夺科长这个位子,乔治比我占有优势了。◇ gain the advantage [the stronger position]

get a big hand [ˌgedə ˌbɪ(ː)g ˈhæːnd] [口] **受到鼓掌欢呼** → give *someone* a HAND (for *something*)

get out of hand [geˌdaudəv ˈhæːnd] [口] **失去控制能力** hand 在这里指"握着缰绳的手"。最初的构思是"有如脱缰之马",用于表示"自己已经控制不了、处理不了"的意味。*The fire soon got out of hand.* 火势凶猛,很快就无法控制了。*If you are not firm with the children, they will get out of hand.* 如果对孩子不严厉,他们就会如脱缰之马,不服管教了。自己控制不住自己的感情,这在英语中也有个定型的表示法,即 let *one's* temper get out of hand (发脾气)。*My husband sometimes lets his temper get out of hand.* 我丈夫有时候发脾气。这一表达法大多使用 get,但也常用动词 be。*If* *the government doesn't act soon, the economic situation will soon be out of hand.* 如果政府不立即采取行动，经济情况很快就会失控。→ out of HAND ◇ reach a point where *something* [*someone*] can no longer be controlled

give *someone* **a free hand** (to *do something*) [ˌgɪv ～əˌfriː ˈhæːnd] **给某人自由处理权** 直译为"给与某人自由的手"。这里的 free hand 是"随意处置"或"行动自由"的意思，其原义大概是"可以自由活动的手"或"按自己的心意活动手的自由"。这一表达法多用于工作。*Our workers tend to grow lazy if they are given a free hand.* 如果任凭我们的工作人员自由行动，他们就会懒惰起来了。*The boss has given us a free hand to handle this project the way we see fit.* 老板给予我们充分的自由，这项计划可以按照我们认为合适的方式进行。*Gardeners will often do a better job if you give them a free hand.* 如果对园丁们放开手，他们的工作往往更出色一些。如果为 have a free hand, 那是"对某事有自由处置权"的意思。*I don't care if Mr. Graves did put up most of the money. As the director of the play, I insist on having a completely free hand to hire the actors I want.* 格雷夫斯先生是不是把大部分经费都支出去了，这我不管。作为这出戏的导演，我要聘用哪个演员必须有绝对的自由权。*I have to show up at the office every day. Otherwise I have a free hand.* 我每天必须到办公室露个面，除此而外，一切都随我的便了。另有一个 get (*one*) a free hand 的形式，意思是"(为某人)取得自由处置权"。*I'll talk to the boss and see if I can't get (us) more of a free hand.* 我去跟老板谈一下，看看是不是能给我们更多一些的处置权。◇ allow *someone* the freedom to do things as *he* wishes [to *do something*]

give *someone* **a hand** (for *something*) [ˌgɪv ～ə ˈhæːnd] [话] **为某人鼓掌** hand 除"手"以外，有"鼓掌"(applause)"的意思。加上 give ～就是"给予某人鼓掌"了。*Let's give Jake a hand for the fine job he did in preparing for the meeting.* 杰克为会议的准备做了极出色的工作，让我们大家为他鼓掌。hand 前边加一个表示强调的 big，那就是"热烈鼓掌(great applause)"的意思。*When the singer came onto the stage, everyone gave her a big hand.* 歌唱家刚一走上舞台，每个听众都向她热烈地鼓了掌。但是，give *someone* a hand 又有"帮助某人"的意思，如果不注意上下文，就会造成意外的误会。不过，在这一场合，后面不是接 for ～，而是接 with *something*。*Give me a hand (with this), will you? I can't lift it by myself.* 你帮我一下好吗？这东西我自己提不起来。以 *someone* 为主语，有 be given a (big) hand 或 get [receive] a (big) hand 的表达法。其中最常使用的是 get a big hand。例如：*Harry got a big hand when he stood up.* 哈里站起来的时候，得到人们热烈的掌声。◇ applaud *someone*

give *someone* **a hand** (with *something*) [ˌgɪv ～ə ˈhæːnd] [话] **给予某人帮助** → give *someone* a HAND (for *something*)

hand it to *someone* (for *something*) [ˈhæ(ː)ndɪt(ː)ə ～] [话] **称赞(某人的能力、努力、功劳等)** 这里的 it 是所谓的"虚指情况的 it"，并无特定意义，如果牵强一些，可以说指"称赞"或"称赞的话"。本条直译为"给予某人称赞[称赞的话]"。*I'll hand it to you, George. You certainly have a way with women.* 我算佩服你，乔治。你跟女人打交道真有一套办法。如这一例句所示，可以单独使用 hand it to *someone*，但有 90%左右是象下边所举的例句那样，在前面加 have to 而使用 have (got) to hand it to *someone* 的形式。因此，有时译作"心服口服"、"心悦诚服"甚至"佩服得五体投地"则十分贴切。在单独使用的场合，现在时要改成将来时，但在添加 have to 时，并不限定这样。*I'll have to hand it to you, George. You certainly did a fine job.* 乔治，我对你算是佩服得五体投地。你干的工作的确非常出色。*I've gotta hand it to you, Jane. I never thought you could beat me in the speech contest.* 简，我对你

是甘拜下风呀。我从来没有想到在讲演比赛中我会被你击败。在具体陈述称赞对方的内容时，用 for ~的形式接在后面。*You may not like Bill, but you have to hand it to him for the way he has brought new business into our company.* 你也许不喜欢比尔这个人，但是你不能不称赞他那种卖力气给我们公司兜揽新生意的精神。*The former President may have been a liar, but you've got to hand it to him for his foreign policy successes.* 前任总统可能是个说谎大王，但你不能不承认他的外交政策取得了成功。*He's not very capable, but you have to hand it to him for trying so hard.* 他不是一个能力很强的人，但你对他的刻苦努力是不能不竖起大拇指的。◇ give *someone* credit

hand over fist [ˌhæ(ː)nˌdovər ˈfɪ(ː)st] [话] **迅速大量地** 这一表达法最初的构思是：在收获粮食的时候，两只手交替着去抓，抓到的一只手形成拳头 (fist) 往回收，另一只手(hand)则往前伸去，反反复复，迅速而紧张。这是强调抓取的动作迅速以及数量之多。几乎所有的场合本条都用于谈论金钱的会话，特别在形容"财源滚滚而来"的样子时常常使用。因此，大多与 make money (赚钱) 或 rake in the money (拼命赚钱) (→ RAKE it in)等动词词组结合在一起。*Since Ed started investing in the stock market, he claims he's been making money hand over fist.* 自从埃德开始在股票市场上做投机生意以来，他说自己的手里有大批的钞票源源而来。*John had a streak of luck at last night's bridge game. He was raking in the money hand over fist.* 约翰昨天晚上打桥牌运气一直不错，他赢了很多钱。*That new chain restaurant appears to be making money hand over fist ever since the supermarket opened nearby.* 自从附近开设了超级市场以来，那家新的联号餐厅似乎大赚钞票哪。与此相反，虽然这种情况极少，但是也有用以表示"减利"、"亏本"意味的场合。*My father's grocery store has been losing money hand over fist ever since that new supermarket opened nearby.* 自从附近开设超级市场以来，我父亲的食品杂货店日益萧条，收益不断下降。另外，有时可以形容具体的动作，但这完全是例外的用法。*The fishermen were pulling in the fish hand over fist.* 渔民们一网又一网地迅速捕鱼。hand over hand 是"两手交替着拉绳子"，专用于实际的动作。*In gym class we have to climb a rope hand over hand all the way to the roof.* 在上体育课的时候，我们必须两手交互使用，沿着绳子一直爬到屋顶。◇ in large amounts

hand over hand [ˌhæ(ː)nˌdovər ˈhæːnd] [口] **(爬绳等时)两手交互使用** → HAND over fist

have a free hand [ˌhævə ˌfriː ˈhæːnd] [口] **可以自由处置** → give *someone* a free HAND

have a hand in *something* [ˌhævə ˈhæ(ː)ndɪn ~] [口] **参与某事** 字面意义是"伸进一只手"。一般用于犯罪以及干其他的坏事。*They've arrested the section chief for the embezzlement, but I'll bet that boss of his had a hand in it as well.* 科长由于盗用公款而被捕了，但是我敢打赌，他上边的头头肯定也参与了这一非法活动。*Larry pretended to be sorry when I was fired, but dollars to doughnuts he had a hand in it.* 当我被解雇的时候，拉里假装一副同情的面孔，但是，十有八九他也参与了开除我这件事。*I can't believe that she had a hand in such a terrible crime.* 我不能相信她参与了那样骇人听闻的犯罪活动。有时也应用于好的事情，例如：*Don't thank just me for the success of the party. Everyone had a hand in making the preparations.* 不要为了社交晚会的成功而仅仅感谢我一个人，大家都参加了准备工作。也常用 see *someone's* hand in *something* 的形式。see *someone's* having a hand in *something* 是"某人肯定参与了某事"的意思。*I see Willie's hand in this. It would be just like him to start such a rumor.* 威利肯定参与了这件事。造这类谣言是他的拿手好戏。这个表达法也可

以用于实际上不坏的行为，例如：*A present for me? Joan, I see your hand in this.* 给我一份礼物？琼，这里面一定有你搞鬼。◇ be involved in *something*

have *someone* **eating out of** *one's* **hand** [ˌhæv ～ ˌiːdɪŋ audəv ～ ˈhæːnd] [口] **使人完全服从** 如果用于动物和鸟类，要按照字面意义"用手喂食吃"解释，这表示非常驯服的状态。*Jake is an excellent horse trainer. In only a few weeks, he has even the wildest horse eating out of his hand.* 杰克是一位优秀的驯马员。只用三两个星期，他连最剽悍的野马都能驯服，叫它吃自己手里拿着的草料。在作为比喻应用于"人"的时候，"驯服"的韵味依然很强。*Marilyn is a charming woman. She has all the men eating out of her hand.* 玛里琳是一位迷人的女性，所有男人都拜倒在她的石榴裙下。*The Godfather has all the gang bosses eating out of his hand.* 所有各匪帮的头目对黑手党大头目是唯命是从，服服贴贴。*That guy's as greedy as they come. Just wave a little lettuce in front of his nose, and you'll have him eating out of your hand.* 那个家伙见钱就眼开，只要你拿两张钞票在他的鼻子前边一摇，你叫他干什么他就干什么。有时使用 be eating out of *someone's* hand 这一表达法，意思是"唯命是从"。*Mr. Oatcruncher is a fool. Just mention that you know someone important, and, before you know it, he's eating out of your hand.* 欧特克兰切尔先生是个混蛋。只要你说你认识某个要人，他对你马上就俯首贴耳，唯命是听。◇ have *someone* doing anything *one* wants *him* to / have *someone* completely under *one's* control

have *something* **on hand** [ˈhæv ～ɔnˈhæ(ː)nd] [口] **在手头上** → have *something* on *one's* HANDS

an iron hand in a velvet glove [ə ˌnaɪrn ˈhæ(ː)ndɪnə ˌvelvət ˈglʌːv] **外柔内刚** 字面意义为"丝绒手套中的铁手"，转而表示"内心很残酷，但是由于态度温和，从表面上看不出来"的意思。*The king rules his country with an iron hand in a velvet glove.* 国王治国，外柔内刚。如这一例句所示，本条的表达法广泛用于"国王"、"政治家"、"父亲"等处于统治地位的人。16 世纪以来就有的古老说法，原来象条头所写那样只用不定冠词，现在多换用具有"那个……"意味的 the。*He was ruthless in his pursuit of money, but he treated his employees with the proverbial iron hand in the velvet glove.* 他在追求金钱方面是残酷无情的，但是他在对待职工方面却如常言所说：外柔内刚。也可以加上几个连字符，构成 iron-hand-in-the-velvet-glove，作为形容词使用。*My father always says he believes in the iron-hand-in-the-velvet-glove approach, but when he is angry it's sometimes hard to feel the velvet.* 我父亲总是说，处事必须外柔内刚，但是当他恼怒的时候，有时就很难见到外柔的踪影了。下面是套用这一习用语的两个例子。*I'll admit my will is iron, but if you marry me I promise you that you'll never feel anything but the velvet glove.* 我承认自己是"内刚"，但是如果你跟我结婚，我保证你永远只会感觉到我的"外柔"啊。*I suddenly realized that I had gone too far in giving the boss my frank opinion. The look in his eye told me that the velvet glove was off.* 我突然醒悟过来，我向头头坦率陈述自己的意见说得太多了。从他的眼神看得出来，他那温和的面纱已经揭掉了。另外，有时用 fist 代替 hand，意思不变。◇ a gentleness that conceals *one's* severity [strictness, ruthlessness, etc.] (不加 the proverbial)

keep *one's* **hand in** [ˌki(ː)p ～ˈhæ(ː)ndɪ(ː)n] [口] **经常练习以免生疏** 字面意义是"对于过去大搞特搞的东西，现在还插一只手"。为什么要如此呢？一般来说，是由于"为了不使技艺生疏，不使感觉迟钝"。*I don't have much time for tennis anymore, but I try to play enough to keep my hand in.* 我再也没有很多时间去打网球了，但是我仍然尽可能地练习，不让球艺有所荒废。*My husband doesn't have much chance to use his English these days, but he subscribes to an English* *newspaper just to keep his hand in.* 我的丈夫最近没有多少使用英语的机会,但是他订了一份英文报纸,使他对英语不会荒疏下去。除技艺、感觉外,有时用于表示"不让知识荒废,不使兴趣降低"的意思。*My father has retired from his law practice, but he goes to the office once a week just to keep his hand in.* 我的父亲是律师,现在业已退休,但是为了不荒废业务知识,他每星期去法律事务所一次。◇ keep in practice / stay involved

know *someplace* **like the back of** *one's* **hand** → BACK

live from hand to mouth [.lɪvfrəm 'hæn(:)tə 'mauθ] [口] **勉强糊口** 这一表达法的意思是:食物入"手"(hand)之后,没有存下的份儿,必须马上送给"嘴"(mouth),就这样"过生活"(live)。*When I was first married I didn't have a job, and we had to live from hand to mouth.* 我结婚初期,自己没有工作,因此,我们两个人只得过吃一顿算一顿的生活。另外有个表达法是 lead a hand-to-mouth existence [.li(:)də 'hæ(:)ntə.mauθ 'ɪgzɪstəntś],意思相同。*If I don't find a job soon, we'll be leading a hand-to-mouth existence.* 如果我不马上找到工作,我们就得过吃上顿接不上下顿的悲惨生活了。◇ lead an impoverished existence

lose the upper hand [.lu(:)zðɪ .ʌpər 'hæ:nd] [口] **处于不利地位** → gain the upper HAND

be an old hand at *doing something* [ə .nould'hæ:nd] [口] **老手** 这里的 old 是"老练"、"熟练"的意思。hand 是"人"。这一表达法具有"在某方面是老资格"或"对某种工作很熟练"的意味,广泛应用于各种不同的领域。*Why don't you ask Abe to help you? He's an old hand at fixing cars.* 你为什么不请阿贝帮你一下?他是个修理汽车的老手呀。*You should never have played poker with that fellow. He's an old hand at cheating.* 你根本就不应该跟那个家伙一起玩扑克,他是作弊的老手。*The Foreign Minister is an old hand at negotiating with the Arabs.* 外交部长是个同阿拉伯人谈判的老手。也可以应用于不要什么特殊专门技艺的事情,例如:*Sue is an old hand at getting her way with men.* 苏是个任意摆布男人的老手啊。*I don't mind cleaning up after dinner. I'm an old hand at washing dishes.* 吃完饭的善后工作我可不在乎,因为我是个刷盘子的老手啊。也可以省略 at *something* 而仅讲 old hand,但这可以说是例外的说法。*If there is anything you don't understand, there are several old hands here who would be happy to help you.* 如果你有什么不明白的地方,这里有几位老手,他们都乐于帮助你。◇ be a veteran when it comes to *doing something*

out of hand [.audəv 'hæ:nd] [口] **不假思索地** 直译为"从手中出去"。最初的构思是:"对于各种事物,丝毫也不通过大脑,刚一来到手里马上就进行处理"。这一表达法的意义为"一点儿也不认真考虑,立即……",根据上下文,有时突出"轻率"的意味,有时把"立即"的韵味表面化。*This is a serious problem. We must not act out of hand.* 这是一个严肃的问题,咱们不能草率地行动。*After Mr. Greely understood my intentions, he apologized for condemning me out of hand.* 格里利先生明白了我的意图以后,他因为轻率地谴责我而向我赔礼道歉。*The union rejected our proposals out of hand.* 工会当即拒绝了我们的建议。另外,从"脱手"这一构思出发,这一表达法又具有"告终"、"完了"的意味,虽然并不普遍,但有人这样使用。但是,请读者注意:不能用它来代替表现"(把问题、事情)移交他人之手"的意义的 be out of *someone's* HANDS 使用。*Those were tough negotiations. I'm glad they're finally out of hand.* 那些谈判可真够费劲的。现在总算结束了,我真高兴。→ get out of HAND ◇ hastily / right away / without (even) thinking

overplay *one's* **hand** [.ovər'pleɪ ~ 'hæ:nd] [口] **做得过火** 这一表达法源出扑克游戏,意思是:"对于自己手中的牌

过分自信,因而胃口增大,猛冲猛打,结果失利”。 *Charlotte lost the game by overplaying her hand.* 夏洛特自信手中的牌有把握,打得过火,结果输了一局。作为比喻,常在如下的情况中使用:“由于过分自信而胃口增大,或是去干超越自己能力的事情,或是为了使对方理解而说话过火,结果产生相反的效果”。 *When I saw his reaction to my remark, I realized I had overplayed my hand.* 当我见到他对我所说的话的反应时,我明白自己做得过火了。 *Be sure not to overplay your hand. Mr. Vixen is a shrewd man. If you try to bluff him, he'll be sure to sense it.* 你千万不要做得太过火。维克森先生是个很精明的人。如果你想虚张声势去吓唬他,那肯定会被他识破的。如这一例句所示,有显然是在“言语”方面“做得过火”的场合;如下面的例句所示,有在“行为”方面“做得过火”的场合;还有包含两方面的场合。 *I'm afraid we may have overplayed our hand. If we don't get some more new orders quickly, we won't be able to pay off our bank loan.* 据我看,咱们可能做得过火啦。如果咱们不赶快多弄到几批新的订货,就还不上银行贷款啦。 *I know you want to impress her, but don't overplay your hand. If she comes to think you have a lot of money, she'll expect you to take her to expensive places every time you go out.* 我知道你想要使她对你产生好印象,但是你可不要做得太过火。如果她认为你是个大财主,你每次带她出去玩的时候,她都要去最花钱的地方了。主语不仅仅是人,有时是国家、组织等等。 *Japan overplayed its hand in attacking Pearl Harbor.* 日本袭击珍珠港是过火的行动。◇ go too far / overextend *oneself*

play a lone hand [ˌpleɪə ˈloun ˈhæːnd] [口] **依靠自己的想法[力量]去干** 这一表达法来自打桥牌等分为两家的扑克牌游戏,手起好牌的人可以不需同家牌手的援助便能与对家相对抗。直译为“用自己的一手牌 (lone hand) 玩下去”。下面是按字面意义使用的例子: *My partner had so many good cards in that last game that he was able to play a lone hand.* 在那最后一局中,我的同家牌手来了许多好牌,他用自己的一手牌就能够打赢了。作为比喻,多用于工作,凡是能够 play a lone hand 的人一般都具有“强人”的形象。 *You're welcome to invest some money in my new company if you wish, but I'll have to ask you to be a silent partner. I intend to play a lone hand.* 如果你愿意向我开办的新公司投资的话,我很欢迎,但是我希望你做一个只出钱不出声的伙伴。我打算按照自己的想法经营下去。 *At first, everyone thought he was acting under orders from his superiors, but we later found that he was playing a lone hand.* 最初,大家认为他是上级叫干什么才干什么,但是后来我们发现他是一个依靠独立思考进行工作的人。 *He was always playing a lone hand in investment circles.* 在搞投资的人们当中,他总是单枪匹马地去干。也可以用 a lone hand 表示“一直依靠自己的想法[力量]去干的人”。 *I'm not surprised that Craig turned your offer down. He's always been a lone hand.* 克雷格不接受你的好意帮助,这我一点儿也不感到惊奇。他一向是喜欢单枪匹马地去干的人。◇ act [operate] independently [alone, on *one's* own]

reveal *one's* **hand** [rəˌvi(ː)l ～ˈhæːnd] [口] **摊牌** → show *one's* HAND

rule with an iron hand [ˌru(ː)lwɪðə ˌnaɪrn ˈhæːnd] [口] **铁腕统治** rule 是“统治”, an iron hand 是“铁的手”,亦即“戴有铁甲的手”。二者合起来,意思大致已经清楚了,与“实行铁的纪律”之类的说法相似。用法如下:主语即使是复数, iron hand 仍然用单数的形式。例如: *The tsars ruled Russia with an iron hand.* 沙皇以铁腕统治了俄国。在这里, tsars 是复数形。另外,也可以用 an iron fist 代替 an iron hand。fist 是“拳头”。 *The rebellion occurred because the people were no longer willing to be ruled with an iron fist.* 所以发生叛乱,是由于人民再也不愿忍受高压统治了。“采取高压手

段”的当然是“为政者”了,但作为比喻,这一表达法可以应用于为政者以外的人。*Mr. Cooley rules his family with an iron hand.* 库利先生治家极为严厉。*Until his death last year, George Hendry ruled his far-flung financial empire with an iron hand.* 乔治·亨德里直到去年亡故为止,一直用铁腕统治着他那庞大的金融帝国。此外,这一表达法可以以形容词的方式构成 an iron-handed rule, an iron-fisted rule 使用。*The American colonists rebelled against the iron-handed rule of England.* 美洲殖民地开拓者起来反抗英国的铁腕统治。◇ govern *someplace* [*someone*, *something*] very [so] severely

see *someone's* **hand in** *something* [ˌsi(ː) ˈ～ ˌhæ(ː)ndɪn ～] [口] **某人显然参与其事** → have a HAND in *something*

show *one's* **hand** [ˌʃou ～ ˈhæːnd] [口] **摊牌** 原为打扑克等纸牌游戏用语,后为人们普遍应用。字面意义是“给人看自己手中的牌”。例如说: *Bill's no fun to play cards with. He's always showing people his hand.* 跟比尔打扑克太没有意思了,他总给人看自己手中的牌。作为比喻,是“告诉对方自己要做什么”。但这一表达法与 tip *one's* HAND 不同,并没有“疏忽大意”的因素存在。如果上下文毫无“疏忽大意”的意思,它永远是“故意”的。*Don't show your hand unless you are forced to.* 不到万不得已,你不要表明自己的真实意图。*When the police became suspicious of my actions, I had no choice but to show my hand.* 当警察认为我的行动可疑的时候,我没有别的办法,只好老实交代了。有时采取 show *someone one's* hand 的形式。*Being convinced of Mr. Straight's sincerity, I decided to show him my hand.* 我确信斯特雷特先生怀有诚意之后,就决心向他交底了。有时也说 reveal *one's* hand。◇ reveal *one's* plans [intentions] (to someone)

strengthen *someone's* **hand** [ˌstreŋkθən ～ ˈhæːnd] [口] **帮助某人** 源出《圣经·旧约》中《撒母耳记·上卷》(First Samuel) 第 23 章 16 节: And Jonathan Saul's son arose, and went to David in the wood, and strengthened his hand in God. (扫罗的儿子约拿单起身前往那树林里去见大卫,使他倚靠神得以坚固。)但在现代的一般美国人中间,hand 指“手中的牌”,因此,strengthen *someone's* hand 通常表示“使手中的牌更好”的意味,在日常会话中也按照这一意义使用。*I was able to win because that ace you passed to me strengthened my hand.* 我所以能够赢,是因为你转给我的 A 加强了我手中的牌。除象这样在实际上应用于扑克游戏外,也广泛转用于其他方面。*I think we will win the case anyway, but this additional evidence should strengthen my hand.* 据我看,不论如何,这个官司我们是会打赢的。再加上这个证据,我们的胜利就更有把握啦。hand 有时用复数形式。*Whatever you do, don't lose your temper. That will only serve to strengthen their hands.* 不管有什么事情,你也不要大发脾气。那只会对他们有利啊。另外,*someone's* hand 也常常采取 the hand of *someone* 的形式。*Growing inflation was strengthening the hand of the opposition party.* 通货膨胀越来越严重,使在野党的地位日益增强了。如果用 weaken 代替 strengthen 而说 weaken *someone's* hand,意思当然就相反了。*The boss's vacillating attitude is weakening our hand against the union.* 老板犹豫不决的态度动摇了我们对工会的立场。◇ strengthen *someone's* position

throw in *one's* **hand** [ˌθrouɪn ～ ˈhæːnd] [话] **舍去老本不干了** 字面意义是“抛弃自己手中的牌”。也就是“中途退出赌局”,常伴有“舍弃以前下的赌注”的意味。*When my opponent was dealt two aces in a row, I threw in my hand.* 当对方连续甩出两张 A 的时候,我抛弃手中的牌不再打下去了。转作比喻使用。*As a partner in the venture I had struggled to keep the company going, but when the oil shock came I threw in my hand.* 作为合资经营的伙伴,我曾经为公司的生存而斗争,但是在石油危机来临的时候,我舍

去老本不干了。◇ (give up *one's* investment thus far and) quit

tip *one's* **hand** [ˌtɪp ～ ˈhæːnd] [口] **无意中亮底** tip 是"倾斜", hand 是"自己手中的一把牌"。本条的字面意义是"由于歪着拿牌,所以被对方看了去"。例如说: *Jack inadvertently tipped his hand when he reached for his cigarettes.* 杰克伸手取纸烟的时候,不留神歪着拿牌,结果都叫人家看去了。作为比喻,则表示"把今后的工作计划顺嘴说出,叫对方听去了"的意思。*Be sure not to tip your hand before you are ready to act.* 没有做好行动的准备之前,千万不要信口亮自己的底。*Although they absolutely refused to tell us where they were planning to buy their oil, fortunately Mr. Low tipped their hand by mentioning that he was going to Saudi Arabia next week.* 虽然他们绝对不肯告诉我们究竟计划到哪里去买石油,幸运的是,洛先生顺口说出他下个星期去沙特阿拉伯,这就完全露了底儿。如这一例句所示,一般使用时都具有"无意中"的意味,但有时也用于"故意去干"的场合,例如: *He purposely tipped his hand to us.* 他特意地向我们亮了底。不过,在这一场合,一般具有"假装着无意识地(实际上故意地)亮底"的意味。由于特别添加 to *someone* 的情况较多,所以在下一例句中,如果没有前后关系,就弄不清实际上是有意还是无意。*Let's not tell Lew about our plan until we absolutely have to. He's always tipping our hand to someone.* 不到非讲给他听不可的时候,先别把咱们的计划告诉卢。他总是对别人亮我们的底。另外,在显然是故意那么做的场合,一般用 show *one's* HAND。◇ (inadvertently) reveal *one's* plans [intentions]

try *one's* **hand at** (*doing*) *something* [ˌtraɪ ～ ˈhæ(ː)ndət ～] [口] **试试身手** 这里的 hand 是"才能"、"能力"的意味。*I think I'll try my hand at tennis today.* 今天我想打打网球。这与 have a TRY (at <*doing*> *something*) 之类的表达法用法相同,只是表示"玩玩看"这样一种轻松愉快的心情。但一般用于如下的场合:对过去没有搞过的事情进行挑战,试验一下自己究竟有没有掌握它的本事或才能。挑战对象是需要经过很长时间的艰苦奋斗才能取得成功的工作、体育运动、技艺等等。*Upon mastering golf, Phil decided to try his hand at tennis.* 菲尔在掌握了高尔夫球的技巧之后,又决定试试打网球了。*After working for several years in a large trading company, Mr. Cook tried his hand at the restaurant business.* 库克先生在一家大贸易公司干了几年之后,自己试着去开餐厅了。*I'd like to try my hand at translating.* 我很想在翻译方面试试身手。另外,在 *something* 处可代入 it, 如说: *I'm thinking of trying my hand at it next year.* 我准备明年干干那个看。请读者注意:在这时候, it 的发音不是[ət], 而变为[æt]。◇ try (*one's* capabilities at) (*doing*) *something*

wait on *someone* **hand and foot** [ˌweɪdɔ(ː)n ～ ˈhæ(ː)ndənˈfu(ː)t] [口] **侍奉得无微不至** wait on 在这里大致与 attend (伺候)同义,指"照顾各种身边琐事",具有"不惜力气,总是忙着给你干这干那"的意味。hand and foot 是强调的词组,意为"从手到脚",亦即"又给你戴手套,又给你穿鞋,从上到下全部服侍,无微不至"。这一表达法令人感到"忠心耿耿"的味道。但是现在的用法不同了,大多是从照料者的立场出发,表示"这可受不了"或者"你不能连那样一点事也叫别人伺候"的意思。*When my mother was sick, I had to wait on her hand and foot.* 当我母亲有病的时候,一切都由我伺候,真够呛啊。*Go get your own tea. You can't expect me to wait on you hand and foot.* 你自己倒碗茶喝吧! 你不能样样事都等我来伺候呀。*My husband never does anything for himself around the house. He seems to think I should wait on him hand and foot.* 我丈夫回到家里什么也不干。他似乎认为一切事情都得由我去伺候他。这一表达法也可以应用于工作。*Lee has a faithful secretary. She waits on him hand and foot.* 李有一位忠心耿耿的秘书。她无微不至地为他服务。也常用被动语态 be waited on hand and foot。*Having grown up in a wealthy family with lots of servants, he is used to be being waited on hand and foot.* 他生长在一个雇用许多仆人的富裕家庭里，因此养成了事事要人侍奉的习惯。◇ take care of *someone* completely / seeto *someone's* every need

weaken *someone's* **hand** [ˌwi(ː)kən ~ ˈhæːnd] [口] **拆台** → strengthen *someone's* HAND

handle

fly off the handle [ˌflaɪ ˌɔ(ː)fðə ˈhæ(ː)ndl] [话] **大发雷霆** 这里的 handle 是"(斧子的)柄"。这一表达法是把"自我控制"比做"斧头"。本条的意思是:"象斧头突然脱离斧柄飞了出去一样，人自我失控而大发脾气"。过去也常用于"恼怒"以外的"自我失控"，现在极少表示这种意义。这一表达法与 lose *one's* TEMPER (with *someone* over *something*) (动肝火)相似，但多用于如下的场合：由于不调查不研究，自己贸然断定是怎么回事，或者由于自己对一件事情任意作片面的解释，因而勃然大怒。*There's no need to fly off the handle. I'm sure he has an explanation.* 没有必要那么大发雷霆嘛。我敢肯定，他会说明理由的。*The boss flies off the handle at someone almost every day.* 老板几乎每天都要对某个职工大发脾气。◇ (suddenly) get extremely angry

one's **handle** [~ ˈhæ(ː)ndl] [话] **人的名字** 如果水壶、煎锅等没有 handle (柄)，如果汽车或冰箱的门没有 handle (把手)，这些东西使用起来就非常不便。同样，人们在相互接触时如果没有名字，也是很不便利的。这一表达法原来的构思就是如此。也就是说，名字乃是人们相互交往所不可缺少的 handle。handle 可以指 full name，但一般指教名、爱称、通称、假名乃至头衔。总之，当有人问 What's your handle? 的时候，你可以回答 It's John Jacob Jinglehammer Smith, Junior. 但一般的回答是 It's John. 或者 It's Smith. 假如平常使用 "Jingles" "Smitty"这样的 nickname，那就回答说 It's Jingles.或者 It's Smitty. 这是一个相当轻松的表达法。◇ *one's* name

hand-me-down

a hand-me-down [ə ˈhæn*d*miˌdaun] [口] **传下来的东西** hand down 具有"传给下边的人"的意味。这一表达法最初的构思是 hand down to me (传给我)。一般是指大孩子的东西传给小的孩子，但是，不管父母、亲戚、朋友，谁用旧的东西都算数。*Being the youngest child, I always had to wear hand-me-downs.* 我是家里最小的孩子，所以儿时老是要穿大孩子们传下来的旧衣服。*This coat is a hand-me-down, but it's practically like new.* 这件上衣是传下来的东西，但是几乎跟新的一样。*I don't want to wear my sister's old hand-me-downs. Why can't I have a new evening dress?* 我不愿意穿姐姐的旧衣服。为什么不能给我买一套夜礼服呀? 也可以用于衣服以外的用过的东西。*Most of our children's toys are hand-me-downs from older cousins.* 我家孩子们的玩具大部分是他们的表哥表姐玩过的旧东西。由于这一表达法包含着"人家已经用得破旧不堪"的意思，所以在用作比喻的时候，可以表示某一思想、小说情节、笑谈等是"老一套"、"二手货"的意思。*This book is well written, but the plot is an old hand-me-down.* 这本书写得挺不错，但故事情节是老一套。也可以当作形容词使用。*This is a hand-me-down sweater that my sister outgrew.* 这件圆领毛衣是姐姐已经穿不下去的旧货，传给我了。*That guy is full of hand-me-down ideas. I don't think he's ever had an original thought in his life.* 那个家伙一脑子都是趸来的思想。据我看，他有生以来还没有过任何独立的思考。过去还有"现成的廉价衣服"一义，现在不使用这一解释。顺便讲一下：英国英语另有一个说法是 a reach-me-down，但在美国不通用。◇ *one's* older brother's [sister's, cousin's, etc.] old clothes [coat, dress, toy, etc.] / (a) second-hand clothes [article, dress, toy, plot, story, idea, etc.]

hands

change hands [ˌtʃeɪndʒ ˈhæːndz] [口] **易手** 字面意义是"换手"。*The suitcase was so heavy I had to stop and change hands every few minutes.* 那手提箱太重了,我每隔几分钟就得停下来换换手。如此例所示,可以用于表示"换手拿东西"的意思。但一般美国人听到 change hands 一语,首先想到的是"改换所有人"。从 change hands 的字面上就可以判断,这一表达法的含义是"人从这个手移到那个手"、"在不同的人们中间转移"或者"把东西移交给别人"。总之,它的构思与意义与汉语的"易手"完全一致。*That house changed hands just last month.* 那所房子上个月刚换了主人。如这一例句所示,可以用于"一次换所有人"的场合。但是,大多是用于表示"多次易主"或者"不断地传下去"。例如:*That house has changed hands numerous times over the years.* 这些年来,那所房子已经换了许多主人。*Expensive works of art like this don't change hands very often.* 象这样高价的艺术品不会频繁地易手。*This car looks pretty beat up. I wonder how many times it has changed hands.* 这辆汽车看起来是十足的老爷车啦,不知道已经转过多少个主儿了。◇ change ownership

have *one's* **hands full** (*doing something*) [ˌhæv ~ ˈhæːndz ˌfu(ː)l] [口] **忙得不可开交** have *one's* hands full 是"手里拿满了东西"的意思,指"再也不能多拿了"的状态。*Put those boxes there, please. I've got my hands full right now.* 请把那些盒子放在那儿吧,现在我的手头已经是满满的了。*I had my hands full of apples.* 我的两只手全都拿着苹果。这是按照字面意义使用的例子。这一表达法经常作为比喻使用,表示忙碌的状态。*With a full-time job and a family to care for, Mrs. Rusharound has her hands full.* 拉夏朗德夫人既要全天上班,又要照顾家庭,简直忙得不可开交。这是表示经常忙。但不仅用于这一场合,大多是表示一时的忙。例如说:*Don't bother me with that now. I've got my hands full trying to get this report finished.* 现在不要用那件事来烦我。我为了完成这个报告书正忙得不可开交。*I won't be able to help you next week. I'm going to have my hands full entertaining a group of visiting businessmen from Europe.* 下个星期我帮不了你的忙。有一批商人从欧洲来,我必须用全部时间去招待他们。◇ be very busy / have all *one* can do

have *something* **on** *one's* **hands** [ˌhæv ˈ~ ɔn ~ ˌhæ(ː)ndz] [口] **有待处理** 字面意义是"手上粘着油、油漆之类的液体",例如说:*I have paint on my hands.* 我手上粘着油漆。在作为比喻使用的场合,*something* 处代入"问题"、"责任"、"麻烦"等等。这一表达法给人的感觉是:"手里的东西很沉重,不容易处理"。*Don't bring me any more problems. I've got enough trouble on my handsalready.* 不要再给我添麻烦了。我手里的麻烦事已经够多的啦。*Car dealers are complaining because they still have some of last year's models on their hands.* 汽车代销店正在叫苦,因为他们手里还有一些去年的型号难以脱手哪。*I can't go to parties like you do. I've got three children on my hands.* 我不能象你那样自由自在地去参加社交晚会。我手里有三个孩子哪。with *something* on *one's* hands 是"拥有……"。*When Jill's father died, she was left with a large debt on her hands.* 吉尔的父亲死去的时候,给她留下了一大笔债。be on *someone's* hands 是"手头正有……"。*Is this the only case on our hands now?* 咱们手头就这一个案子吗? have time on *one's* hands 是个定型的表达法,意为"手里有难以处理的时间",亦即"空闲的时间多"。*When young people get into trouble, it is often because they have too much time on their hands.* 年轻人出去闹事,往往是由于他们的空闲时间太多。读者千万注意:不要把本条的表达法与 have *something* on hand 混淆起来,后者完全没有"难以处理"的意味。它的基本意义是"手头有某物,可以应急"。*I'd better buy some more wine. We have only a* *small bottle on hand.* 最好还是再买点儿葡萄酒吧。家里只剩下一小瓶啦。◇ be burdened with *something*

be in good hands [ɪn.gu(ː)d'hæːndz] [口] **可以放心** 在一般词典中见不到这一表达法,但是比较常用。good hands 的意思是"可以令人安心使用的手"。因此,本条习用语的意思是"交到可靠的手中"。*Don't worry about your operation. You'll be in good hands with that doctor.* 你不必担心做手术。由那位大夫主刀,你尽可以放心。*If Mr. Toplex is your lawyer, you're in good hands.* 如果托普列克斯先生给你当律师,那你就放心好啦。如以上两个例句所示,good hands 一般指"能使自己的事情顺利进行的人"。下面的例句虽然表面讲的是"学校",但具体地指"学校的老师"。*That's a fine school. Your children's education will be in good hands if you send them there.* 那是一所很好的学校。如果你把孩子们送进那所学校,你就可以放心他们的教育啦。*After I had talked to the investment broker my brother had recommended, I knew my money would be in good hands.* 与我哥哥所介绍的投资经纪人谈过话以后,我觉得把钱交给他是可以放心的。还有一个形式是 leave *someone* [*something*] in good hands, 意思为"把……交给可靠的人"。*I need a baby-sitter I can trust completely. I have to be away from home a lot, and I naturally want to leave my children in good hands.* 我要找一个我能完全信赖的保姆。我经常需要外出,当然希望把孩子交给可靠的人看管。*We left our house in good hands. My brother is living there while we are abroad.* 我把家委托给可靠的人照看了。在我们全家出国期间,我弟弟住在我家。◇ be well cared for / be being well cared for

leave *someone* [*something*] **in good hands** [.li(ː)v ~ɪn.gu(ː)d'hæːndz] [口] **把某人[某物]交给可靠的人** → be in good HANDS

be no longer in *someone's* **hands** [nou.lɔ(ː)ŋgərɪn ~'hæːndz] [口] **不再负责** → be out of *someone's* HANDS

be out of *someone's* **hands** [.audəv ~'hæːndz] [口] **不再负责** 直译是"从某人手中出去"。用于本人不再负责而把问题、事情等移交他人的场合。*According to a police announcement, the FBI had taken over the case so the matter was out of their hands.* 据警察宣布说,那个案子已经移交联邦调查局了,不再由他们负责。如果说 be no longer in *someone's* hands (已经不在某人手中),意思也是一样。*You'll have to talk to the department head about the problem. It's no longer in my hands.* 关于那个问题,你应该跟部长去谈,因为它不再归我管了。如果正在负责解决某一问题的时候被撤消了该项权力或责任,则使用 take *something* out of *someone's* hands 的被动语态 be taken out of *someone's* hands [.teɪkə .naudəv ~'hæːnd] (从某人手中被取走)。*When I had failed to find a solution after three weeks, the problem was taken out of my hands.* 我三个星期未能解决那个问题,因此就不再叫我负责去解决了。→ take *something* [*someone*] off *someone's* HANDS ◇ be no longer *someone's* responsibility

play into *someone's* **hands** [.pleɪ ɪntə ~'hæːndz] [话] **正中某人下怀** 这里的 hand 原是打扑克时分配的"一手牌"。本条的字面意义是"所出的牌于对手有利",即"正中对手的下怀"。*She kept playing into my hand.* 她总打出对我有利的牌。象这样的说法是常见的。在作为比喻使用的场合,很少用 hand, 大多是用复数 hands。*They have a top team of lawyers. We'll have to be careful not to play into their hands.* 他们有几个一流的律师。我们必须小心谨慎,别叫他们钻我们的空子。如这一例句所示,这一表达法多用于"陷入对方玩弄的圈套"的场合。但是,也可以用于"不论对方策划与否,自己去干有利于对方的蠢事,使对方有机可乘"的场合。*Jack's a good tennis player, but his overconfidence caused him to lose by playing into the hands of* *his opponent.* 杰克是一位优秀的网球选手,但是由于狂妄自大,使对方有机可乘,并战胜了他。如果要加强语气,可添上 right, 而作 play right into ～。*They're trying to make you angry. If you don't control your temper you'll be playing right into their hands.* 他们正在设法使你发怒。如果你扰不住火儿,那就正中他们的下怀了。◇ play [act. say something] to *someone's* advantage

take *one's* **life in** *one's* **(own) hands** → LIFE

take *something* [*someone*] **off** *someone's* **hands**[ˌteɪk ～ˌɔ(ː)f ～ˈhæːndz] [口] **解除负担** 直译为"从某人手中取掉 *something* [*someone*]", *something* [*someone*] 处代入相当于责任、负担、包袱等的"事物"或"人"。*My mother took the children off my hands for the afternoon so that I could go shopping.* 下午,我母亲帮助我看孩子,这样我就能去买东西了。另有一个近似的形式是 take *something* out of *someone's* hands (→ be out of *someone's* HANDS)。不同点在于前置词,一个是用 off,另一个是用 out of。但是,请读者注意:仅仅前置词不同,意思就完全不一样了。下面两个例句请比较和研究。*When Jim's work load proved too heavy, the boss took part of it off his hands.* 当吉姆的工作量过多的时候,老板给他减轻了一部分负担。*When Jim proved incompetent to do the work properly, the boss took it out of his hands.* 当了解到吉姆完全不能胜任那个工作时,老板就不让他再干下去了。这两个例句的字面意义全是"从……取掉……",但前者是"为了减轻对方的负担而取掉",后者则是"即使违反对方的利益也要取掉",也就是前者是"照顾",后者是"免职"。*If you don't want that old refrigerator anymore, I'll be happy to take it off your hands.* 如果你不再用那个旧电冰箱,我愿意替你保存。*I wish someone would take these old books off my hands.* 我希望有人能给我保存一下这些旧书啊。在这两个例句中,也是把"旧冰箱"和"旧书"当作一种包袱,而"给人保存"则是"解除负担"的意思。下面是使用被动语态的例句: *Fortunately, the case was taken off my hands so that I could take my vacation.* 幸好把我从那个事件中解脱出来,我可以去休假了。另有一个 be off *someone's* hands 的形式,意思是"(从责任、负担、包袱等中)被解放了",以相当于那种责任、负担、包袱的词或词组为主语。*Thank goodness that problem is off my hands now.* 谢天谢地,我现在算是从那个问题中解放出来啦。◇ relieve *someone* of (the responsibility [burden, etc.] of) *something* [*someone*]

take the law into *one's* **own hands** → LAW

be taken out of *someone's* **hands** [ˌteɪkəˌnaudəv ～ˈhæːndz] [口] **被解除权力或职务** → be out of *someone's* HANDS

tie *someone's* **hands** [ˌtaɪ ～ˈhæːndz] [口] **捆住手脚** 字面意义是"捆上两只手",如说: *The kidnapper tied his hands.* 绑架者捆上了他的两只手。用作比喻,表示"使人不能活动"的意思。它与 TIE *someone* down (→)不同,一般有不能活动的理由,用于因不能活动而达不到目的的场合。*Fred was willing to help me change jobs, but his promise to my wife not to do so tied his hands.* 弗雷德很想帮助我调换个工作,但是他曾向我的妻子保证不这样做,所以一筹莫展。使用被动语态的场合比较多。*I'd like to help you, but my hands are tied.* 我很想帮助你,可是我的手脚被捆住了,无能为力。*The FBI was anxious to take part in the investigation, but its hands were tied by the refusal of the local police to issue a call for aid.* 联邦调查局急欲参加调查,但是地方警察不请求援助,使它无可奈何。◇ prevent *someone* from taking action

time hangs heavy on *someone's* **hands** → TIME

wash *one's* **hands of** *something* [*someone*] [ˌwɑ(ː)ʃ ～ ˈhæ(ː)ndzəv ～] [口] **洗手不干** 源出《圣经·新约》中《马太福音》(Matthew) 第 27 章 24 节。So when Pilate saw that he was gaining nothing, but rather that a riot was beginning, he took water and washed his hands before the crowd, saying, "I am innocent of this man's blood; see to it yourselves." (彼拉多见说也无济于事,反要生乱,就拿水在众人面前洗手,说:"流这义人的血,罪不在我,你们承当吧!")彼拉多洗手这一动作表示他对处理耶稣没有任何责任。按《新约》原文,并没有后续的 of ~。但是,如果只是 wash *one's* hands,则仅具字面意义("洗手"),毫无"不干"的意思,这一点务请注意。至于为什么"洗手不干",可能有各种原因。*Maybe you can do something with that guy. I wash my hands of him.* 你可以照料照料那个家伙嘛,我不管他的闲事啦。*When his colleagues refused to take his advice, he washed his hands of the entire affair.* 当同事们不接受他的忠告的时候,他对所有的事情都不过问了。这是由于"嫌麻烦"、"感到厌倦"。*They tried to wash their hands of the affair just before the scandal broke, but it was too late. They were already too deeply involved.* 在丑闻暴露之前,他们打算摆脱那个事件,可是为时已晚了。他们已经陷得太深啦。这是由于"要逃避责任"。*Disgusted with the constant factional infighting, the senator decided to resign his seat in the Senate and wash his hands of politics.* 由于厌恶经常不断的派系斗争,那位参议员决心放弃他在参议院的席位,退出政治舞台了。可以用 completely 加强语气。*From now on it's your problem. I completely wash my hands of it.* 从现在起就是你的问题了。我完全不管啦。另外,偶尔用 wipe 代替 wash。◇ cut all ties with *something* [*someone*] / refuse to take further responsibility for *something* [*someone*]

win (*something*) **hands down** [ˌwɪn ˈhæ(ː)ndz ˈdaun] [话] **毫不费力地取得胜利** 直译是"垂着手就得胜了",换句话说就是"一点儿没费劲就取得了胜利"。汉语叫"唾手可得"、"不费吹灰之力"。*George won the speech contest hands down.* 乔治在讲演比赛中很轻易地获得优胜了。*The English soccer team is expected to win hands down.* 人们预料英国足球队会轻易取胜。这一表达法与 win (*something*) GOING away 不同,可以认为仅能应用于人或者以人为主体的体育比赛、竞赛等。也有人用以表示"参加比赛的马轻易获胜",但在这一场合不免有些滑稽之感。◇ win easily

wipe *one's* **hands of** *something* [*someone*] [ˌwaɪp ~ ˈhæ(ː)ndzəv ~] [口] **对(某事或某人)不再负责** → wash *one's* HANDS of *something* [*someone*]

hand-to-mouth

lead a hand-to-mouth existence [ˌli(ː)də ˈhæ(ː)ntəˌmauθ ˈɪgzɪstən*t*s] [口] **勉强维持生活** → live from HAND to mouth

handwriting

the handwriting on the wall [ðə ˈhæ(ː)n*d*ˌraɪtɪŋ ɔnðə ˈwɔːl] [口] **厄运临头的预兆** 直译是"墙上的字迹"。这一表达法源出《圣经·旧约》。据《但以理书》(Daniel) 第 5 章:在巴比伦王国尼布甲尼撒一世的儿子伯沙萨国王所设的酒宴当中,突然出现一只人的手,用手指在王宫的墙壁上写下了谁也不认识的字。国王将以色列的先知但以理召来,经他解释,那些字的意思是:"由于一直忽视神的存在,巴比伦要灭亡,伯沙萨将被杀。"后来一一应验。因此,"墙上的字迹"就成为习用语而表示"厄运临头的预兆"的意味。这一表达法常与 see 或 read 搭配使用。 *When his boss stopped asking him to attend important company meetings, Jack saw the handwriting on the wall and began looking for another job.* 当老板不再叫杰克参加公司的重要会议的时候,杰克感到这是不吉的预兆,就开始另找工作了。*Even though the world's oil reserves were rapidly being depleted, the advanced nations continued to ignore the handwriting on the wall.* 尽管全世界的石油资源迅速枯竭,但一些发达国家依然无视这不吉的前兆。*After my boy friend had canceled two dates in succession, I could read the handwriting on the wall.* 在我的男朋友连续两次取消约会以后,我明白我们两个人的关系快告吹了。有时省略 hand 而作 the writing on the wall。◇ the portent of disaster

hang

get the hang of *something* [ˌgetðə ˈhæ(ː)ŋəv ～] [话] **掌握窍门** 这里的 hang 是"决窍"、"正确的做法"。条头整个的意思是"掌握工作等的窍门"。*I'll get the hang of it pretty soon.* 我很快就能够掌握它的窍门。*I haven't gotten the complete hang of it yet.* 我还没有完全掌握它的窍门。如以上的例句所示，大多使用 get the hang of it 这一表达法。但也使用具体的名词 the thing, the work, the machine 等代替 it。*It usually takes about a week to get the hang of this machine.* 掌握这种机器的使用方法通常大约要一个星期的时间。◇ learn how to do [run, etc.] *something*

hang around [ˌhæ(ː)ŋə ˈraund] [话] **闲呆着** → STICK around

hang in there [ˌhæ(ː)ŋ ˈɪ(ː)nˌðə(ː)r] [话] **坚持下去** 具有牢牢抓住什么不放手的含义。在不论如何艰难困苦也毫不后退的场合使用。这一表达法表示一种积极的姿态。语气相当轻松，书面一般不用。*If we don't hang in there, we're going to lose this game.* 如果不坚持下去，这场比赛咱们就要输掉啦。这是用于"比赛"、"竞赛"。也可以用于"议论"或"工作"等，例如：*Once Nevers gets hold of an idea, he doesn't believe in giving it up, does he. He hung in there against the arguments of almost everyone at the meeting.* 内维尔斯一旦有了个想法，他是舍不得放弃的。在会议中，几乎每个人都反对他的想法，而他却毫不退让，硬要坚持下去。*I don't think we can finish on time, but we're still hanging in there.* 我不认为我们能够按时完成，但是我们仍然坚持下去。*Hang in there, Bill. Don't let her talk you out of it.* 比尔，你要坚持到底！不要叫她一说，你就不干了。*We hung in there hour after hour, hoping to sight some sign of civilization before our food and water ran out.* 我们坚持了一小时又一小时，希望在我们的吃食和水用尽之前能够见到有人烟的地方。在新的表达法中也可以省略 there，意义和用法均不变。例如：*We're hanging in, but I don't know how much longer we can last.* 我们在坚持，不过我不知道我们还能够坚持多久。*I'll continue to hang in as long as there is the slightest chance of success.* 只要有一线成功的希望，我就要继续坚持下去。*Despite accusations of malfeasance from all sides, the governor hung in, refusing to resign.* 州长虽然受到各方面的责难，说他有渎职行为，但是他始终坚持，不肯丢掉乌纱帽。◇ try harder / persist (tenaciously) / not give up

hang loose → LOOSE

hanger

a paper hanger [ə ˈpeɪpər ˌhæ(ː)ŋər] [话] **常开空头支票的人** paper hanger 的 paper 一般指 wallpaper (壁纸)。hanger 是"糊墙的人"。因此，paper hanger 通常是"糊壁纸的工人"的意思。但在黑社会中，paper 一词指"假支票"，因而 paper hanger 直译应为"向各商店去贴假支票的工人"。这一表达法的意义便是由此而来。通过小说和电影的传播，现在不仅黑社会和警务人员使用，一般也广泛使用起来了。这是一个相当轻松的表达法。*The man was arrested on suspicion of being a paper hanger.* 那个男子由于有使用空头支票的嫌疑而被捕了。*I never cash checks for people unless I know them. This city is full of paper hangers.* 不是认识的人，我决不给他的支票兑付现金。这个城市到处都是开空头支票的人。paper hanger 所进行的活动叫做 hang paper (到处乱开空头支票)，原来也是黑社会用语，现在已成为日常口语了。 pass bad checks (here and there) 为同义的表达法。 *Louie hung paper all over town before the police finally caught him.* 路易在整个镇内到处乱开空头支票，直到他被警察逮住为止。 → bounce a CHECK ◇ a bad-check passer

happy

(as) happy as a lark → LARK

hard

go hard with *someone* [ˌgouˈhɑːrdwɪð ~] [口] **吃苦头** 直译是“对(with)某人变得(go)困苦(hard)”，也就是“使某人难受或痛苦”。*He's trying to fool the police, but it [things] will go hard with him if he's found out.* 他打算愚弄警察，但是如果被抓住了，他会大吃苦头的。如这一例句所示，主语一般用 it 或 things。但两者之间有细微的差别。也就是说，如果以 it 为主语，意思主要是“要吃某人(在上个例句中是警察)的苦头”，而以 things 为主语时，这种意味则很淡薄，突出的是“情况[事情]很严重”，以“情况[事情]”为重点。*We're just about out of money. If this venture fails, things'll go pretty hard with us.* 我们的钱快用光了。如果这项事业失败的话，我们的情况可就严重啦。在这一例句中，如果用 it 代替 things，那就要译为“在大股东面前，我们得吃不了兜着走啦”。*After my company went bankrupt, things went pretty hard with us for a while.* 我开的公司破产以后，我们的情况一度惨极了。*It'll go hard with you if I catch you smoking again.* 如果再叫我看见你吸烟，你可要吃不了兜着走。◇ be difficult [painful] for *someone*

be hard up [ˌhɑ(ː)rˈdʌ(ː)p] [话] **缺钱** 这是 be HARD up for *something* 省略了 for *something* 的表达法，只用于“金钱”。*When I was a kid, we were always hard up.* 在我小的时候，我家总是缺钱花。*Can you lend me some money? I'm a little hard up this week.* 你可以借给我点儿钱吗？这个星期我手头紧一些。如以上两个例句所示，“长时间”可以用，“短时期”也可以用。*I don't know if Jenny will be able to go to college or not. Her family is pretty hard up.* 我不晓得詹妮是不是能够上大学，她家里很穷。◇ be poor / be short of cash / be in financial straits (pretty→ fairly narrow)

be hard up for *something* [ˌhɑ(ː)rˈdʌpfər ~] [话] **由于缺什么而感到困难** 这是把“缺乏”和“困难”两种意思合而为一的表达法。*Will you help me write this paper? I'm hard up for some good ideas.* 你帮助我写这篇论文好不好？我缺乏新的思路，写不下去啦。*My wife wants me to go to a concert tonight, and I'm hard up for an excuse to get out of it.* 我的妻子要我今天晚上陪她去听音乐会，我找不到逃避的口实，实在难办。当然，在缺少具体的“物”的场合也可以使用。*Business is fairly good these days, but we're a bit hard up for ready cash.* 最近生意倒是挺不错，但是我们缺现金，所以有一点困难。*The nation's farmers are pretty hard up for rain this year.* 今年缺雨，全国农民十分困难。◇ be having difficulty finding *something* / be suffering from a lack of *something* ((pretty→ pretty much))

someone **is hard on** *someone* [*something*] [~ɪzˈhɑːrˌdɔ(ː)n ~] [口] **对人严厉或对物粗暴** 这里的 hard 与 take *something* HARD 中的 hard 相同，是“令人难受”的意思。be hard on ~就是一个习用语，但在 on 后边接 *someone*，还是接 *something*，意思有一点儿区别。我们首先研究一下 *someone* is hard on *someone*。*The boss is a very fair man, but I feel he's a bit too hard on employees who make mistakes.* 老板是一个很公正的人，但是我觉得他对犯错误的职工有点过于严厉了。*The police here are quick to stop traffic violators, but they tend not to be very hard on first offenders.* 这里的警察能够很迅速地阻止违反交通规则的行为，但是他们对于初犯的人却有些手软。不限于“严厉对待过错”。*Mr. Legree was not a kind man. He was always hard on the men who worked under him.* 列格里先生不是一个和善的人。他对部下始终是非常严厉的。以上所讲 *someone* is hard on *someone* 的特征是：主语经常“有意识地对人 hard (严厉)”。而 *someone* is hard on *something* 则相反，主语一方并没有那样的意识，只不过产生“hard 对待”的结果而已。因此，be hard on 的译文也要相应地改变，作“对

……粗暴”亦即“不爱护某种东西”。*My son is very hard on the car.* 我的儿子总是胡乱开车。*Jack is very hard on his clothes. It seems I'm forever having to mend them.* 杰克穿衣服实在太费啦，我仿佛一年到头都得补衣服似的。此外，如以上的各例句所示，这一表达法无论是 on *someone* 的场合还是 on *something* 的场合，在 hard 前面通常要加副词。◇ *someone* is severe [harsh] with *someone* / *someone* treats *something* roughly

something **is hard on** *something* [*someone*] [~ɪzˈhɑːrˌdɔ(ː)n ~] [口] **对某物[某人]产生不良影响** 这里的 hard 本身与 *someone* is HARD on *someone* [*something*]中的 hard 在意义上基本相同。但主语为 *something*(即非生物)，因此，主语一方当然不会有“hard 对待”的自我意识。另外，只就主语并无意识这一点来说，这一表达法与 *someone* is hard on *something* 是相同的。但主语为 *someone* 和主语为 *something* 时，译文不能一样。在以 *something* 为主语的场合，正如本条的条头所示，又分为 be hard on *something* 和 be hard on *someone* 两种形式。与以 *someone* 为主语时的情况不同，be hard on *something* 这一形式的使用范围比较广。*You shouldn't drive so fast over rough roads. It's hard on the car.* 你不要在崎岖不平的道路上把车子开得那么快，这对车大有损害。*Drinking too much is hard on your health.* 喝酒太多有害于你的身体健康。*Washing dishes with strong soap is hard on your hands.* 用强烈的洗涤剂洗盘子对你的手有害。下面讲 *something* is hard on *someone* 的形式。这里既然是 *someone*，那就会有意识或感觉。在翻译 be hard on 一语的时候，也要根据具体情况有所变化。*His wife's death was quite hard on him.* 他妻子的去世使他万分悲痛。*Having to work until late at night is hard on an old man like me.* 对于我这样一个老头子来说，干活要干到深夜实在苦极了。◇ *something* is bad for *something* / *something* is difficult [not good for] *someone*

play hard to get (with *someone*) → PLAY

take *something* **hard** [ˌteɪk ~ ˈhɑːrd] [口] **心情沉重** 直译是“对……感到难以接受”。在因不幸、灾难、厄运而精神受到严重打击时使用。hard 的前边常加 very, pretty, a bit 一类的副词。*Alf took his sister's death very hard.* 阿尔夫的姐姐死了，他心里十分难过。*Tim's wife told him she wanted a divorce, and he's taking it pretty hard.* 蒂姆的妻子说她想离婚，他听了万分难过。根据上下文，有时更具体地表示“失意”、“烦恼”等等的意味。*Don't take it so hard. It's tough losing your job, but I'm sure you'll find something else soon.* 不要那么垂头丧气嘛。丢掉了饭碗肯定不好受，但是我相信你很快就会找到别的事情去干。*A: Arnold shouldn't blame himself for the accident. It wasn't his fault. B: I know. But still he's taking it pretty hard.* 甲：阿诺德不应该为了那起事故责怪自己，那不是他的过错。乙：我晓得。但是，他的心里仍然感到十分痛苦。如以上的例句所示，这一表达法几乎完全用于因精神上受打击而悲观失望、灰心丧气的场合。但也有时候表示由于精神上受打击而引起的愤怒或憎恨，例如：*The Iranians took America's past support for the Shah very hard.* 伊朗人民由于美国过去支持巴列维国王而对它恨之入骨。◇ be depressed [distressed] (by *something*) / be bitter (about *something*)

harness

die in harness [ˌdaɪən ˈhɑ(ː)rnəs] [口] **在工作岗位死去** 美国人听到 harness 一词，首先浮现在头脑中的是“马拉车时套上的挽具”。对本条英语一般的理解是：“马在拉车中(＝执行任务中)死去”。但正本求源，harness 的古义为“铠甲”，本条英语的意思是“穿着铠甲死去”，过去曾与 die with *one's* BOOTS on (阵亡)(→)按大致相同的意义使用。现在是“死于任内”或“死在工作岗位上”的意思。其中暗含着“虽然上了年纪但不退休”的意思，因此一般对坚持工作的老年人使用。另外，有的词典译作“工作时死去”，但请读者注意，不一定非上着班一命呜呼不可。*Mr. Horsey died in harness at the age of sixty-three.* 霍西先生死于任内，卒年 63 岁。*I like my work, but I'm not going to die in harness. I'm going to retire while I'm still young enough to enjoy it.* 我热爱我的工作，但是我不打算干到死那一天为止。我要留下足够的余年享点儿清福哪。如下面例句那样，如果 harness 带有定语，则要加冠词，作 the harness。*Jimmy Durante fought his way to the top of the entertainment world and never retired. He died in the harness of a professional entertainer.* 吉米·杜兰特努力奋斗，在文艺界达到了最高的地位。他一直没有退出舞台，是作为职业演员而去世的。◇ die while still working [actively engaged in *one's* profession (of ~)]

Harry

every Tom, Dick and Harry → TOM

has-been

a has-been [ə ˈhæːz.bı(ː)n] [口] **过时的人[东西]** 这一表达法原为习用语 a person who has been (but is no longer) great 的一部分。 *The singer used to be extremely popular, but now he's just a has been.* 那个歌手曾经红极一时，现在已是明日黄花了。*Many people believe that England, once the most powerful country on earth, is rapidly becoming a has-been.* 英国一度是世界上最强盛的国家，许多人都认为它在迅速衰退，已经日落西山了。为了明确 has-been 的性质，可在它的前面加形容词，例如：*Everyone thought that George Andwell was a literary has-been until his latest book became a best-seller.* 乔治·安德韦尔在他的最新作品成为畅销书之前，谁都认为他已经是一位过时的作家了。has-been 本身也常作为形容词使用，如说 a has- been author (过去的作家)。 *A has- been politician like that can never hope to become President.* 那样一个落伍的政治家是永远没有希望当总统的。◇ a person (etc.) of the past

hash

a hash house → HOUSE

settle *someone's* **hash** [ˌsedl ～ ˈhæːʃ] [话] **制服某人** settle 是“处置”的意思。hash 是把肉和蔬菜煮得稀烂的糊状物，可以单独吃，也可以抹到土豆或面包片上吃。对这种“肉菜泥” (hash) 加以“处置” (settle) 怎么就具有“制服”的意义了呢？不清楚。但这是一个习用语。这一表达法的表面意义是“给与某人以决定性的损害”，而“给予损害”的对象常常是“怀有敌意[反感]的人”乃至”处于敌对关系的人”，因此在实际使用时含有“这下子对方可完蛋啦！真痛快！”的意思。*America thought that it could settle Vietnam's hash by sending in a few troops, but it soon learned that their hash was not so easily settled.* 美国原来以为派上几个兵就可以制服越南，但是它不久就明白了事情并不那么一厢情愿。在这句话里含有“彻底消灭越南，好不痛快”的意思。因此，在预先示明“给与决定性损害”的方法时，后面接续的 settle *someone's* hash 如果译成“告终啦”、“完蛋啦”、“垮台啦”等等，就能更忠实地表达原文的精神。*Why don't we tell the tax office he's been cheating on his taxes? That would settle his hash.* 他偷税漏税，咱们为什么不向税务局告发？一告发，他就彻底完蛋啦。*Let's tell the teacher what he did. That'll settle his hash.* 咱们把他干的事情去汇报给老师。这样，他就完蛋啦。◇ inflict decisive damage on *someone*

sling hash [ˌslıŋ ˈhæːʃ] [话] **在小饭馆当服务员** hash 为“肉菜泥”，是一种典型的廉价饭食(→ a hash HOUSE)。sling 是“投掷”。本条的表达法直译为“把肉菜泥往餐桌上扔去”。*Her boy friend slings hash at some cheap restaurant.* 她的男朋友在一家廉价小饭铺里当服务员。在不设服务员的自助食堂 (a cafeteria) 中，则用这一表达法表示“往盘子里盛食物”的意思。*Joy slings hash in the school cafeteria.* 乔伊在学校的自助食堂中干杂活。a hash-slinger 是"端出食品的人"。这是一个戏谑的表达法,含有"在小饭馆或学校食堂干活"的意味,但也常指一般餐厅的男女服务员。*Pierre is a hash-slinger at Maxim's.* 皮埃尔在马克西姆饭店当服务员。但 hash-slinger 不仅为"服务员",有时指"(廉价饭馆的)厨师"。因此,在下面的例句中,要通过上下文来了解究竟指的是服务员还是厨师。*George used to be a hash-slinger at The Greasy Spoon.* 乔治曾在低级小饭馆当过服务员[厨师]。◇ work as a waiter [waitress]

hash-slinger

a hash-slinger [ə ˈhæʃ:ˌlɪŋər] [话] **低级小饭馆的服务员或厨师** → sling HASH

hasta

hasta [ˈhæ(:)stə] [话] **必须** → HAFTA

hat

at the drop of a hat → DROP

I'll eat my hat. [ˌaɪ ˈli:tˌmaɪ ˈhæ(:)t] [话] **我把脑袋给你** 字面意义是"我会吃掉我的帽子"。最初的构思为:"我敢打保票,肯定没有错,如果我的话有错,我可以吃掉我的帽子给你瞧"。这是强调自己的话完全正确时使用的表达法。典型的说法有两种,一是 If~, I'll eat my hat. (如果……,我把脑袋给你);二是 ~ or I'll eat my hat. (要不是……,我把脑袋给你)。两者比较,前者的使用率高。*If that horse doesn't come in first, I'll eat my hat.* 如果那匹马不跑第一,我把脑袋给你。*If he succeeds, I'll eat my hat.* 如果他能成功,我把脑袋给你。*It'll rain tomorrow or I'll eat my hat.* 明天要不下雨,我把脑袋给你。如以上的例句所示,大多应用于未来的事情,但有时也应用于过去的事情,目的是表示自己确实相信。例如:*It was Jim that did it for sure. If not, I'll eat my hat.* 那肯定是吉姆干的。如果不是,我把脑袋给你。◇ I'll be extremely surprised.

keep *something* **under** *one's* **hat** [ˌki(:)p ~ ˌʌndər ~ ˈhæ(:)t] [口] **保密** 直译为"把某种东西放在自己的帽子底下",也就是"只放在自己的头脑里,不向外泄漏"的意思。*Keep it under your hat.* 不要对别人讲啊。*I had no choice but to tell Tom, but he promised to keep it under his hat.* 我只好对汤姆讲了,但是他保证决不外传。*one's* 处如果是复数,hat 也要复数。*For the time being, we'll have to keep this plan under our hats.* 在目前,这个计划无论如何也不能外传。◇ keep *something* secret

be old hat [ˌouldˈhæ(:)t] [口] **现在不算什么了** 对于这一表达法,英语词典(包括美国出版的在内)都解释为"过时的"(behind the times)、"老式的 (old-fashioned),这不算错,但是按现在的使用方法,解释得不够充分。当然可以这样使用:*You should buy some new shoes. Those are too old hat.* 你得买双新鞋啦,你穿的那双样子太老了。*Nobody listens to the Rolling Stones any more, Dad. They're old hat.* 爸爸,没人再听"滚石"音乐了。那早过时啦。但是,现在的用法不一样了,例如:*When I first became famous, all the attention was a real ego trip. Now it's old hat.* 当我刚刚出名的时候,受到人们注目实在使我飘飘然。现在这已经不算什么了。也就是说,人们用这一表达法表示"过时"、"老式"的意思的场合已经减少,大多是用以表示"现在已经不算什么"的意义了。至于这一表达法的来源,可能是由于帽子是耐久之物,因而容易过时的缘故。由此一转,就变成"经历多次,已经没有新鲜味道,现在不算什么了"的意味。请读者注意:hat 虽然是物质名词,但在这一表达法中不能加冠词。*Nowadays putting satellites into orbit is old hat to space scientists.* 现在,对于航天科学家来说,发射人造卫星进入轨道已经不算一回事了。*I don't care to go to see a magician pull rabbits out of a hat. That's old hat.* 我不想去看魔术师从帽子里变出小兔来。现在那已经不算一回事啦。◇ be nothing new / be very [too] commonplace

a ten-gallon hat [ə ˌtenˌgælənˈhæ(:)t] [口] **高牛仔帽** a gallon 是液量单位(加仑),约等于 3.8 升。a ten-gallon hat 的字面

意义是“能装十加仑的帽子”,实际上当然不会有这种帽子。这是一种夸张说法,形容帽子很高。*The man was wearing a black ten-gallon hat.* 那个人戴着一顶很高的牛仔帽子。◇ a (tall) cowboy hat

throw *one's* **hat in(to) the ring** [ˌθrou ~ ˈhæ(ː)tn(tə)ðə ˌrɪ(ː)ŋ] [口] **参加竞选** 古时,在竞技或庙会中,有普通人向职业拳师挑战的节目。在这种时候,就“把自己的帽子扔进拳击场”,表示挑战,也就是报名的意思。由此一转,人们就用这一表达法表示“宣告参加竞选”的意味了。*By the time the presidential campaign had opened, five Republicans had thrown their hats into the ring.* 当竞选总统活动开始的时候,有五位共和党人宣布参加竞选。*The club could use a president like you, Bill. Why don't you throw your hat in the ring?* 比尔,俱乐部需要有你这样一个人当主席。你为什么不参加竞选哪? 如果用 toss 代替 throw, 则含有“轻松愉快”的意思,但在实际会话中并没有那样严格的区别。toss 是“轻投”的意思。*The post of mayor of this town is a low-paying, thankless job. So far no one has tossed his hat into the ring.* 这个镇的镇长职位是一个工资低而又不讨好的工作。直到现在还没有一个人愿意出来竞选。如以上的例句所示,这一表达法一般是“出来参加竞选”的意思,但有时也用于选举以外的事情。*As soon as the government opened bidding on the giant development project, all of the big construction companies threw their hats in the ring.* 自从政府对大规模开发工程项目进行招标以来,所有的大建筑公司都争先恐后地投了标。*At first only two countries were arguing over possession of the island. Now two more have tossed their hats into the ring.* 最初只有两个国家对该岛的所有权争议不休。现在又有两个国家提出主权要求了。◇ stand as a candidate / enter the competition

toss *one's* **hat in(to) the ring** [ˌtɔːs ~ ˈhæ(ː)tn(tə)ðə ˌrɪ(ː)ŋ] [口] **参加竞选** → throw *one's* HAT in(to) the ring

hatch

a booby hatch [ə ˈbu(ː)bi ˌhæ(ː)tʃ] [话] **精神病院** booby hatch 原为海上用语,指“帆船船尾的舱口”。booby 是一种鸟,学名“鲣鸟”。hatch 是“舱口(盖)”。在热带的海洋,鲣鸟常停在舱口盖上,故名。但是,booby 一词另有“笨蛋”、“傻瓜”的意味,因此,booby hatch 又有了“精神病院”的新解。也就是说,“鲣鸟常停的地方”变成了“收容疯子的场所”。在使用这一意义的时候,一般语调轻松,带戏谑成分。*That's a booby hatch.* 那是一所精神病院啊。如这一例句所示,有时用不定冠词。然而,所谓 booby hatch,一般来讲,每个地方只能有一个,所以习惯上大多使用定冠词。*This was really a hectic week. A little more and I'd have been ready for the booby hatch.* 这个星期我实在忙得不可开交,再差一点儿我就得进精神病院啦。另外,这一表达法过去还有“监狱”的意味,现在不用此解。 → a BOOB ◇ an insane asylum

hatchet

bury the hatchet [ˈbe(ː)riðə ˈhæ(ː)tʃət] [口] **言归于好** 字面意义为“把斧子埋掉”。这里的 hatchet (手斧)指美洲印第安人的武器 tomahawk (将石片捆在木棒头上的战斧)。这一表达法来源于印第安人的习惯,他们在讲和时要把 tomahawk 埋入土中。不过,虽然说是“埋斧”,却不一定非用于实际动武的场合不可,在双方仅仅抱有敌意的场合也可以使用。另外,这一表达法原来只是“息争”的意思,后来又演绎为“相互和好”、“言归于好”了。*It's foolish for us to continue quarreling. What say we bury the hatchet?* 咱们继续争吵下去实在太蠢了。相互和好好不好? *After the war of 1812, America and England buried the hatchet.* 1812 年战争以后,美英两国敦睦邦交了。再有,bury the hatchet 的反义语为 take up the hatchet (挑起争端)。不过,后者还算不上习用语,使用频率也很低。*We are surrounded by people who would like to see us fail. Let's not take up the hatchet against each oth-*

er. 周围有许多人幸灾乐祸地看着我们，希望看见我们失败，我们不要相互争斗啦。这意思是说相互打架，两败俱伤，只能使看热闹的人们高兴而已。◇ give up our [their] animosities (toward each other) / become friends again

have

have it coming (to *one*) [ˌhævɪt ˈkʌmɪŋ] [话] **活该** 字面意义是"它来到某人的地方"，言外之意是"与该人的言行相符合"。在实际使用时，绝大多数是表达"恶有恶报"、"天网恢恢，疏而不漏"的意思。因此，it 虽然并无特指的名词，但也含有"惩罚"之类的意义。*I don't like to see anyone get beat up like that, but he had it coming to him for the way he always bullies the younger kids.* 我不愿意看见任何人挨那样的狠揍，但是他平常总是欺负比他小的孩子，所以挨揍也是活该的啊。*Sue got extremely angry with me, but I guess I had it coming. I should have been more sensitive to her feelings.* 苏对我非常恼火，但是我想这也是理所当然的。我应该更加体谅她的感情啊。也有象下边的例句那样，偶尔用于表示"善有善报"的意思。在这一场合，it 当然指"善果"之类的事情了。*Peter got an extraordinarily large raise, but considering how hard he works, everyone felt he had it coming to him.* 彼得的工资一下子提高了很多，但是考虑到他工作的勤奋，每个人都感到这是理所当然的。◇ deserve it

have it in for *someone*[ˌhævɪˈtɪ(ː)nfər ～] [话] **对某人有恶感** 另有一个相似的说法为 have a grudge against *someone* (对某人怀恨在心)。虽然从一般词典中的译文看，两者的意思完全一样，但是两者之间是有细微差别的。也就是说，条头的表达法含有"一旦有机会就要报复"的意味，而相似的说法则是只停留在感情上而已。例如：*I don't understand George's attitude recently. He seems to have it in for me for some reason.* 我不理解乔治最近的态度。不知为什么，他对我怀有恶感。从这句话可以体会出：乔治对"我"说了不三不四的话，或者干了蛮横无礼的事。*Professor Green has had it in for Charlotte ever since he heard her say that his class wasn't very interesting.* 格林教授自从耳闻夏洛特说他讲课没有什么意思以后，就对她怀有恶感。人们听了这句话，不禁要问："他对夏洛特给什么小鞋穿了？" *I'd stay clear of Russ if I were you. He's got it in for you for stealing his girl.* 如果我要是你的话，我可要远远地躲着拉斯。你把他的女朋友偷偷抢走了，他对你的恶感可大啦。在用这一表达法的时候，常加 long, 例如说：*The Arabs and the Israelis have long had it in for each other.* 阿拉伯人与以色列人相互之间长期仇视。◇ have an active grudge against *someone*

have it out (with *someone* over *something*) [ˌhævɪˈdaut] [话] **通过讨论解决问题或通过斗争解决争端** it 指"对于对方的一肚子不满"。本条直译为"把不满倾泻出去"，也就是"把一肚子不满发泄出去，求得解决问题"。有时是舌剑唇枪，有时则文武带打。但是，不论有多少不满 have it out, 往往是仅以吵几句嘴而告终。*You two have been at swords' points for too long now. Don't you think it's about time you had it out?* 你们两个人水火不相容，到现在时间已经太长了。你们不认为该解开疙瘩了吗？ *I'm tired of that guy's always trying to block my proposals. I'm going to go have it out with him right now.* 那个家伙总是妨碍我的提案得到通过，我已经不能再忍耐下去了，现在马上就找他算帐去。下面的例子是用决斗的方式解决争端。*Get your gun and meet us at the O.K. Corral, Doc. We're gonna have it out with those guys once and for all.* 多克，拿着你的枪，咱们到 *OK* 牧场会齐。这回，咱们要跟那帮家伙决一死战。在下面的两个例句中，"口角"的意味强。*Better stay out of the kitchen. Jack and his wife are in there having it out over something or other.* 最好不要到厨房去。杰克和他的老婆不知为什么事情正在里边吵嘴哪。*We had it out for over an hour last night, but we* *didn't reach an agreement.* 昨天晚上我们争论了一个多小时，但是没有达成协议。◇ (try to) settle *one's* quarrel

have *someone* **there** [ˈhæ(ː)v ～ ˈðeːr] [话] **把某人问住了** 如果勉强直译，就是"在那一点上 (there) 把某人抓住"。这里的 have 原意为"使对方陷入窘境"、"战胜"，类似在下国际象棋时的用法: *When he moved his knight in front of his king, I knew I had him.* 当他把他的马移到自己的国王前边的时候，我知道我已经战胜他了。在对应该能够回答的问题瞠目结舌的时候，或者在议论中刺中对方的痒处和抓住对方不合逻辑的地方的时候，使用这一表达法。但是，语气极为轻松，在一般的会话中不一定用于有意识地难倒对方的场合。例如，You have me there. 这句话常与 I don't know.同样表示"我不知道"的意思。 *A: What time are they coming tonight? B: You have me there. I forgot to ask them.* 甲：今天晚上，他们几点钟来？ 乙：不晓得。我忘问他们啦。在这一场合，把 You have me there. 换上 I don't know. 也可以，不过在说 You have me there.的时候，多少含有"自己应该打听而没有打听，叫人一问实在难为情"的意思。 *A: Since the Japanese spend so many years studying English, why aren't there more fluent English speakers in Japan? B: You've got me there.* 甲：既然日本人费那么多年的功夫学习英语，为什么在日本能够很流畅地讲英语的人并不多呢？ 乙：这个问题你可把我问住啦。在这一场合也令人感到"无法作答，只好认输"的意味。也可以用于第三者身上，例如: *A: If, as you say, the Democrats are always so powerful, how come we have a Republican President now? B: .... C: Looks like he's got you there.* 甲：如果照你所说，民主党人的力量总是很强大的，那么，为什么我们的现任总统是共和党人呢？ 乙：…… 丙：看起来，这下子把你问倒啦。在这一场合，意思是"甲给你出了个难题"。另外，虽然同是 have *someone* there, 而在下面的句子里使用时意思就大不一样: *We go to our summer cottage every August and often have them there.* 我们每年八月前往避暑山庄，常常在那里招待他们。◇ have *someone* stymied / I don't know.

have what it takes (to *do something*) → WHAT

hay

hit the hay [ˌhɪtðə ˈheɪ] [话] **上床睡觉** 字面意义是"(用身体)打干草"。hay 本来是喂牲口用的"干草"。但是古时曾用 hay 填塞到垫子里，因此，hit the hay 中的 hay 就意味着"垫子"。这是个轻松的表达法，平时经常使用。一般来说，多用于"要上床去睡觉"的场合，如说: *Let's hit the hay. It's getting late.* 咱们上床睡觉吧，时间不早啦。 *I think I'll hit the hay.* 我要上床睡觉啦。但有时也用于指过去的行为或现在的习惯。 *What time did you hit the hay last night?* 你昨天晚上几点钟睡的觉？ *I hit the hay early every night.* 我每天晚上睡得早。另有 hit the SACK, 同义 ◇ go to bed

make hay while the sun shines [ˌmeɪkˈheɪ ˌhwaɪlðə ˈsʌnˌʃaɪnz] [口] **晒草要趁太阳好** 字面意义是"在太阳照耀的时候制作好干草"。如果用命令式作 Make ～，则为民间谚语。但现在几乎完全不用命令式了。农民们可能这样说: *You can't make hay in all this rain. You have to make hay while the sun shines.* 老这样下雨，根本制不了干草。必须在有太阳的时候制干草。但一般是作为比喻使用。 *My wife is worried about my health, but business conditions are good now. I told her I have to make hay while the sun shines.* 我的妻子总担心我的身体健康，但是现在正是做生意的好时候。我告诉她说，晒草要趁太阳好，良机可不能错过呀。 *You're young and strong now. If you want to succeed, you'll have to make hay while the sun shines. Soon you'll be too old for this kind of work.* 你现在年轻力壮，如果想有所成就的话，俗语说"晒草要趁太阳好"啊。等到年老力衰，这种工作就干不了啦。另外，请注意这一表达法与 strike while the IRON is hot (趁

热打铁)的不同。所谓 while the iron is hot (在铁正热的时候),是指热铁很容易冷,所以良好的机会只在一瞬之间。因此,“趁热打铁”这一表达法含有很强烈的“紧急行动”、“分秒必争”的意味,通常用于“不放过一瞬间的好机会”的场合。与此相反,晒干草是需要很长时间的,因此,while the sun shines 不可能指一天半天。“晒草要趁太阳好”虽然也是“勿失良机”的意思,但只能用于比较长时期的良好机会的场合。◇ utilize an advantageous condition while it lasts

That ain't hay. [ˈðæ(ː)ˌdeɪntˈheɪ] [话] **那可不是一笔小数目** ain't 在俗语中为 is not 的缩略,但在这一表达法中不能用 is not, 习惯上用 ain't。 hay 是“不值钱的东西”、“一点点钱”的意思,但只在 That ain't hay.这一表达法中作此解释。本条全部直译为“那不是很少量的金钱”。这是一个轻松的表达法,实际上指钱的数量大。 *Why not apply for a job where I work? They pay twelve dollars an hour there. That ain't hay.* 到我干活那个地方找个工作怎么样?他们一小时给 12 美元啊。那可不是几个小钱啊。*The publisher gave him a million-dollar advance on his new book, and that ain't hay.* 他要新写一本书,出版社预付给他一百万美元。那可不是一个小的数目啊。也可以用金额作主语以代替 That。*I'd accept his offer if I were you. I know you hope to get more, but a hundred thousand dollars for a five-room house ain't hay, you know.* 如果我是你,我就接受他所提出的条件了。我知道你想再多捞点儿,不过,一所五室的住宅能卖十万美元可不算少啊。◇ That's a lot of money.

haymaker

a haymaker [ə ˈheɪˌmeɪkər] [话] **挥拳猛烈的一击** hay 是“干草”。因此,haymaker 原意“制干草的人或机械”。但在现代,特别是在会话中,极少使用这一意义。一般用法如下: *The champ floored his opponent with a haymaker in the first round.* 冠军在第一回合就猛烈一击把对手打倒在地上了。但不一定非击中对方要害不可。例如: *I ducked the man's wild haymaker and grabbed him from behind.* 我躲过那人猛烈的一击,从他身后抓住了他。也就是说,本条条头的 haymaker 中的 hay,与 hit the HAY 中的 hay 相同,意思是“床”或“垫子”。在这里,haymaker 的字面意义是“使人睡到 hay 上之物”,亦即“使人昏倒到 hay 上那么猛烈的一拳”。虽然说“使人昏到”,但并不是仅指一拳把人打得失去知觉(拳击术语叫 knockout,十秒钟内不能站起比赛),只要是把人打趴下的一拳就叫 haymaker。“挥拳猛击”在英语中也有固定的说法,叫 throw a haymaker。例如: *Chuck threw a haymaker that caught the punk right on the chin.* 查克挥拳猛击一下,正打中小流氓的下巴。另外,haymaker 除“挥拳猛烈的一击”外,还作比喻使用,表示“具有决定性力量的东西”、“撒手锏”的意思。 *A: So far, the committee doesn't seem impressed with any of your ideas. B: Don't worry. I'm saving my haymaker for the end.* 甲:到目前,委员会似乎对你的想法无动于衷。乙:甭担心。我准备的撒手锏留在最后才用哪。*The comedian's last joke was a real haymaker.* 喜剧演员最后的插科打诨真正赢得了观众的哄堂大笑。◇ a knockout [powerful] punch / most impressive idea / (a) hilarious (joke) ((real→really))

hayseed

a hayseed [ə ˈheɪˌsiːd] [话] **乡巴佬** → a country HICK / a country BUMPKIN

haystack

be like looking for a needle in a haystack→ NEEDLE

haywire

go haywire [ˌgou ˈheɪwaɪr] [话] **乱了套** haywire 是“捆干草用的铁丝”。现在,这种铁丝一般叫做 baling wire。本条习用语的来源是:捆干草的铁丝很容易纠缠到一起，一旦纠缠到一起就令人束手无策了。首先联想到的是“机械”、“计划”等出了毛病的场合。*The plan worked smoothly at first, but then things began to go haywire.* 计划最初进行得很顺利，但是后来开始乱了套。*My new FM radio seems to have gone haywire. I can't get half the stations.* 我新买的调频收音机似乎出毛病啦。我连一半的台都收不到。*There must be something wrong with the computer system. Our production schedule has gone haywire.* 电脑系统一定有什么地方出故障了。我们的生产计划已经乱了套。*Something's gone haywire. I can't get this machine to work.* 什么地方出毛病啦。这个机器开不起来了。除“机械”、“计划”外，也可以应用于“人”。*He appeared to be all right when he first got out of the mental hospital, but then he started going haywire again.* 当他刚从精神病院出来的时候，一切都似乎很正常，但是后来他又开始发狂了。可以省去 go，把 haywire 当作形容词使用。*Something's haywire. They should have been here long ago.* 一定出了什么岔子。他们老早以前就应该到这儿啦。*That guy's haywire, if you ask me.* 要叫我说的话，那个家伙发疯啦。◇ get mixed up [out of order] / go crazy

head

an acid head [ə ˈnæ(ː)səd.he(ː)d] [话] **LSD 的常用者** 原为嬉皮士用语，后来普遍化了。acid 本来是化学中的“酸”，但在嬉皮士用语中，特指“LSD”。LSD 为致幻药物 lysergic acid diethylamide [lɪˈsərdʒɪk ˈæsɪd ˈdaɪˈeθələ.maɪd] (麦角酸酰二乙胺)的缩略，也是“酸”的一种。又，在嬉皮士用语中，head (头)指“麻药的常用者”。*He became an acid head and dropped out of school.* 他变成 LSD 的常用者，从学校退了学。acid 又与 freak [ˈfriːk] (原意“怪物”，但在嬉皮士用语中为“特别喜好某种东西的人”)结合起来，作 an acid freak，也是“LSD 的常用者”的意思。head 又与其他的词结合起来使用，例如与 pot (本来的意思是“壶”，在俚语中为“大麻”)结合成一个词，作 a pothead [ˈpɑ(ː)t.he(ː)d]，意为“大麻的常用者”；在它的后边加 shop (商店)，作 a head shop [ˈhedˈʃɑ(ː)p]，意为“出售麻药常用者必需品(注射器、小镊子等)的专门商店”。*The supreme court ruled that local authorities could ban head shops.* 根据最高法院的裁定，地方当局有权查封出售麻药常用者必需品的专门商店。◇ an habitual LSD user

beat *one's* **head against a brick wall** [.bi(ː)t ～ ˈhe(ː)də .genstə .brɪkˈwɔːl] **白费力气** 直译为“把自己的脑袋往砖墙上撞”。意思很明白，就是“去干不可能成功的事情”，有时可译为“枉费心机”、“螳臂挡车”、“以头碰壁”等。*There's no use trying to make them see that they're wrong. You'd just be beating your head against a brick wall.* 你想叫他们明白自己做错了，那毫无用处，简直等于用你的脑袋去撞墙。*I gave up trying to solve that problem. I realized I was just beating my head against a brick wall.* 我放弃解决那个问题的尝试了。我已经明白那是白费力气，不会取得成功的。如以上的例句所示，常用 just 加强语气。有时用 stone wall (石壁)代替 brick wall。*Don't ask me to try to convince him. I'm not about to beat my head against a stone wall.* 不要叫我去说服他吧。我不打算白费唇舌。有时既不加 brick 也不加 stone，只说 the wall。*I give up. I've beat my head against the wall long enough.* 我不干了，再也不想白费力气啦。另外，动词除 beat 外，可以用 bang, butt, run，按使用频率，bang 仅次于 beat，而 butt 和 run 则很少使用。bang 与 beat 相同，是“往上碰”，butt 与 run 则是“(拿脑袋)往上撞”。*Challenging the tax office is like banging your head against a brick wall.* 硬要违抗税务局，那岂不是螳臂挡车？◇ attempt the impossible

bite *someone's* **head off** [.baɪt ～ ˈhe(ː).dɔːf] [话] **气势汹汹** bite 是“咬”，bite off 是“咬掉”。本条直译为“咬掉某

人的脑袋”。如果一个人正在气头上，而你并不知情，有时你向他说一句话，打个招呼，他都气势汹汹地向你发火。世间常有这类的事情。这就是 bite *someone's* head off 的涵义。汉语俗话叫“拿别人撒气”。*What's eating Frank today? I only said good morning and he almost bit my head off.* 今儿个弗兰克吃了什么耗子药啦？我只向他问个早安，他几乎就暴跳如雷，对我发起火来了。*A: May I have the day off tomorrow, chief? B: No! Certainly not! What do you think this is, a nursery school? A: You don't have to bite my head off. I was only asking.* 甲：主任，我明天告一天假行吗？乙：不行！绝对不行！你把这里当成什么地方了？幼儿园？甲：你用不着这样气势汹汹呀！我只是来请示一下啊。*Don't take what the boss said so hard. He's biting everyone's head off today.* 老板说的那些话，你不要往心里去。今天他拿着每个人撒气哪。有时说 take *someone's* head off。◇ answer *someone* very angrily

bring *something* **to a head** [ˌbrɪŋ ～ tuə ˈhe(ː)d] [口] **使事情达到决定性的地步** → come to a HEAD

bury *one's* **head in the sand** [ˌberi ～ ˈhe(ː)dɪnðə ˈsæːnd] [口] **逃避现实** 据说驼鸟一感到有危险的时候，就只把头部插到砂堆中，它认为这样就算完全隐蔽起来，不会被发现了。本条习用语即是由此说法而来。意思是：“尽管从客观上看，事态非常严重，但是却不去正视”，亦即所谓的“采取驼鸟政策”。有时是“假装看不见”，有时则是“熟视无睹”，对现实估计不足。*The situation is getting desperate. We can't just bury our heads in the sand and hope the problem will go away.* 形势越来越糟糕啦。我们不能象驼鸟似地把头埋到砂子里，希望问题自己烟消云散。*World War II might not have occurred if so many nations hadn't buried their heads in the sand during Hitler's rise to power.* 如果在希特勒上台的时候，许多国家不采取驼鸟政策，第二次世界大战也可能不会发生。又说 hide *one's* head in the sand (把头藏到砂子里)。*That doesn't sound like Tim. He's not the type to hide his head in the sand when problems arise.* 那可不象是蒂姆的表现。他不是那种一发生问题就躲躲闪闪的人。have *one's* head buried in the sand 的意思是“不想了解现实情况”。*We can't depend on him to help us. He's got his head buried in the sand.* 我们不能指望他来帮助我们。他是闭上眼睛不看现实的。另有一个说法为 keep *one's* head buried in the sand。*You can keep your head buried in the sand if you want to. I'm going to try to do something about it.* 如果你愿意把脑袋埋在砂子里，那随你的便。我对那件事却打算搞一下试试看。play ostrich (象驼鸟一样行动)与 bury *one's* head in the sand 同义，但不象后者那样普遍使用。*Everyone seems to be playing ostrich while the world is threatened with nuclear disaster.* 明明世界受到核灾难的威胁，可是大家似乎熟视无睹。另有一个模仿本条的表达法是 take *one's* head out of the sand，意思是“从砂子里伸出头来”，亦即“睁开眼睛正视现实”。*Stop playing ostrich and take your head out of the sand. You've got to face the facts.* 不要象驼鸟那样，把脑袋从砂子里伸出来吧。你应该面对现实。◇ ignore [shut *one's* eyes to] reality

can't make head or tail of *something* [ˌkænt meɪk ˌhedər ˈteɪləv ～] [口] **完全弄不明白** 直译为“看不出哪里是头哪里是尾”。在“完全不了解是什么东西”的场合使用这一表达法。主要应用于“字迹”、“文章”、“说话”等。*His writing is so bad I can't make head or tail of it.* 他的字太潦草了，我完全认不清。复数形式为 can't make heads or tails of ～ [ˌhedzər ˈteɪlzəv～]。*I can't make heads or tails of this sentence. Can you help me translate it?* 这个句子我弄不清楚是什么意思，你能给我翻译一下吗？另外，有时不用 or，而说 can't make head nor tail of ～ [ˌhednər ˈteɪləv ～]。*Sally called me, but she was so excited I couldn't* *make head nor tail of what she was saying.* 萨莉给我打电话来了，但是她过于兴奋，我简直听不懂她在说什么。◇ can't understand *something* at all

come to a head [ˌkʌmtuə ˈhe(ː)d] [口] **事情达到决定性阶段** 这里的 head 是"白色的脓包头"。这一表达法的字面意义为"化脓"。*The painful boil on my leg finally came to a head.* 我大腿上很痛的疖子终于化脓了。转作比喻使用，表示"事情或问题经过迂回曲折，达到最后阶段"的意思。一般用于如下的场合：与脓疱一样，如果处置错误，就会进一步恶化；如果适当地处理，问题可以解决。*After many long days of negotiation, things were finally coming to a head. If all went well, the union would soon be back at work.* 经过许多日子的谈判，事情总算达到了决定性的阶段。如果一切顺利，工会不久即可复工啦。*The world economic crisis is fast coming to a head.* 世界经济危机迅速达到严重关头。*Relations between Japan and America came to a head when President Roosevelt ordered exports of oil and steel to Japan cut off.* 当罗斯福总统下令禁止向日本输出石油和钢的时候，日美之间的关系就达到了决定性的阶段。但也可以用于仅仅表示"达到顶点"(reach a peak) 的意思。*The anti-Vietnam War movement came to a head that year.* 反对越南战争运动在那一年达到了高潮。另有一个 bring *something* to a head 的形式，意思是"使某事达到决定性的阶段"。*There had been bad blood between them for many years, but their rivalry over the same woman brought things to a head.* 他们之间的恶感已经持续很多年了，但是由于争夺一个女性，相互的敌对达到了顶点。*I think most of the people have swung their support to our side. It's time to bring matters to a head.* 我认为绝大多数的人都支持我们这一边。现在是该最后解决问题的时候了。◇ reach the [a] critical point

fall head over heels [ˌfɔːl ˌhedovər ˈhiːlz] [话] **倒栽葱** → fall HEAD over heels in love (with *someone*)

fall head over heels for *someone* [ˌfɔːl ˌhedovər ˈhi(ː)lz fər ~] [话] **(为异性) 神魂颠倒** → fall HEAD over heels in love (with *someone*)

fall head over heels in love (with *someone*) [ˌfɔːl ˌhedovər ˈhi(ː)lz ɪnˈlʌ(ː)v] [话] **(为异性) 神魂颠倒** fall 是"落下"。head over heels (头朝上，脚跟在下)本来是 heels over head (脚跟在上，头朝下)，意思是"倒栽葱"，不知从什么时候起，意思不变，而 heels 与 head 换了位置。因此，fall head over heels 的字面意义(头朝上落下)与实际意义(头朝下落下)显然是矛盾的。*I fell head over heels into a ditch.* 我头朝下掉到沟里去了。后边加上 in love，那就是"头朝下掉到爱河中去"了。可以认为这是 fall in love (坠入情网)的强调说法。*The moment John saw Mary, he fell head over heels in love with her.* 约翰对玛丽是一见倾心，为她弄得神魂颠倒了。*There are many young couples who fall head over heels in love only to find later that they aren't suited to each other.* 有许多情侣先是沉溺于爱河，后来却发现两个人性情合不来。如以上的例句所示，这一表达法决不是"爱情一点点萌生"的意味，而是"一下子燃烧起来"。fall head over heels 的后边有时不接 in love with *someone*，而接 for *someone*，成为 fall head over heels for *someone* 的形式。两者意思大致相同，但使用 in love with *someone* 这一形式者比较多。使用 in love with *someone* 的形式与使用 for *someone* 的形式对比起来，从意义上说，前者更"严肃"一些，因此如下一例句所示，将后者用于小孩子们的场合，就具有几分夸大的感觉了。*When I was in the second grade, I fell head over heels for the little girl who sat behind me.* 我上小学二年级的时候，为坐在我身后的那个小女孩神魂颠倒了。另外，这个 fall head over heels for *someone* 可以认为是 FALL for *someone* 的强调说法。另有一个说法是不用 fall，而用动词 be，作 be head over heels in love (with *someone*)。例如：*Louis is* *head over heels in love with my sister.* 路易斯为我的妹妹神魂颠倒了。再者,当使用动词 be 的场合,可以不用 in love,而用 in debt,作 be head over heels in debt(债台高筑)。例如说: *I'm head over heels in debt.* 我欠债太多,被压得喘不过气来了。◇ fall deeply in love

get it into *one's* **head that** ~ [ˌgedɪdɪntə ~ ˈhe(ː)d ðət ~] [口] **错误地认为……** 字面意义是"将 that 以后的事情装进脑袋里"。这是一个非常习用的表达法,在把不合情理的事情认为"正确"的时候使用。 *Meg seems to have gotten it into her head that I don't like her.* 梅格似乎认为我不喜欢她。这一表达法的要点是经常在言外含有"与事实相反"的意思。 *Our little boy has somehow gotten it into his head that all foreigners are Americans.* 不知怎么搞的,我家的小男孩竟然认为所有的外国人都是美国佬。有时不用 it,而承前启后地说 get that [such an] idea [notion, etc.] into *one's* head 或者 get an idea [a notion, etc.] like that into *one's* head。例如: *You thought I would refuse to help you? How did you get that idea into your head?* 你认为我会拒绝帮助你?你怎么会产生这样的想法呢?◇ (mistakenly) come to believe that ~

get it through *one's* **head** (that ~) [ˌgedɪtˌθru(ː) ~ ˈhe(ː)d] [口] **深切体会** 字面意义是"使某物完全通过脑子"。在对一件事情不仅理解而且深有体会的场合使用。 *You've got to get it through your head. If you don't study harder, you won't be able to graduate.* 你必须认识清楚:如果不加把劲儿学习,你就不能毕业了。 *When will nations get it through their heads that true peace does not mean simply the absence of war?* 各国什么时候才能真正体会到真正的和平并不仅仅意味着没有战争呢?常用 just 加强语气。 *Susan just can't seem to get it through her head that her affair with Frank is over and that she is never going to see him again.* 苏珊似乎还没有深切地感觉到:她与弗兰克之间的恋爱已经告吹,她再也不会见到他了。另有 get it through *someone's* head 的说法,意思是"使某人深切体会到……"。 *I think I've finally gotten it through Stu's head that I'm not going to lend him any more money.* 我认为我已经使司徒切实地了解到,我不会再借给他一分钱了。 *How can I get it through your head? The answer is No! No! No! No matter what you say, I'm not going to marry you.* 我怎样才能使你切实明白哪?我的回答是:不!不!不!不管你说什么,我决不跟你结婚。在这一场合,也常用 just 加强语气。 *You've just got to get it through John's head that it's too dangerous for him to go spelunking by himself.* 你应该使约翰切切实实地明白,他单枪匹马地去洞窟探险,那太危险啦。◇ (fully) realize

get it through *someone's* **head** (that ~) [ˌgedɪtˌθru(ː) ~ ˈhe(ː)d] [口] **使某人深切体会到……** → get it through *one's* HEAD (that ~)

give *someone his* **head** [ˌgɪv ~ ˈhe(ː)d] [口]**给与某人行动自由** 原来的形式是 give a horse its head。这是骑马用语,意思是"让马自由驰骋"。 *This is a good horse. If you get lost, just give her her head and she'll bring you right back home.* 这是一匹好马。如果你迷了路,你就让它随便走,它一定会把你送回家的。作为比喻,在把某件事情交给一个人自由处理的场合使用。 *My son wanted to become an actor so badly that I finally decided to give him his head.* 我的儿子无论如何也想去当演员,我最后决定随他的便好啦。有时用 some, a little more 等代替 his, her, their。 *As children grow older, it is wise to give them a little more head.* 孩子们越来越大,就逐渐多给他们一些行动自由,这样做才是明智的。也可以说 let *someone* have *his* head。 *Once an employee shows that he knows his job, the chief lets him have his head.* 一个职工一旦表明他已经熟悉了自己的工作,领导就给予他行动的自由。◇ let *someone* do as *he* wishes / give *someone* freedom of action

go to *someone's* **head** [ˌgoudə ~ ˈhe(:)d] [口] **冲昏头脑** 直译为"走向某人的脑袋",而"走"的主体本来是"酒"。因此,原意是"酒上某人的头"。例如说:*Because he hadn't eaten anything, the wine quickly went to his head.* 因为他没吃什么东西,葡萄酒很快就使他醉了。*There is an old popular song which goes, "You go to my head, like a glass of bubbling champagne."* 有这样一句古老的民歌:"你象一杯起泡的香槟使我迷醉。"后来又进一步发展,用以表示"兴奋"、"权力"等"冲昏人的头脑"的意思。*Their sudden freedom following the riot went to the evildoers' heads, and they ran through the streets breaking windows and looting the stores.* 骚乱发生之后,歹徒们突然感到自由,他们如醉如狂,在大街上奔跑,又砸玻璃,又抢商店。*I'm sorry I hit you. I guess all the excitement went to my head.* 实在抱歉我打了你。周围的一切如此令人激动,使我的头脑都发昏了。*Unlimited power went to his head, and he began issuing orders which were impossible to fulfill.* 无限制的权力冲昏了他的头脑,他开始发布一些根本不可能执行的命令。如以下的两个例句所示,也可以用以表示"使人骄傲自满"的意思。*The adulation of his fans went to the young singer's head.* 他的狂热听众的过分称赞使那位青年歌手骄傲自满起来了。*I'm afraid she has let her good looks go to her head.* 很遗憾,她由于貌美而骄傲自满起来啦。◇ intoxicate *someone* / make *someone* conceited

hang *one's* **head in shame** [ˌhæŋ ~ ˌhedɪn ˈʃeɪm] [口] **羞愧地垂下头** hang *one's* head 是"垂下头",再加上 in shame (羞愧地),这一表达法就具有"羞愧得抬不起头来"的意味了。*When the boy was caught cheating on the test, he hung his head in shame.* 那个男生在考试中作弊被抓住了,他羞愧地耷拉着脑袋。这是用于实际上"垂下头"的场合。但更多的是用作比喻,不带有"低头"动作。在这一场合,可以认为是强调 be ashamed (害臊) 的说法。*What a terrible thing for you to do! You should hang your head in shame.* 你怎么会干这样极坏的事情!你应该知道羞耻啊。*When I learned that the man I had thought to deceive was trying to help me, I could have hung my head in shame.* 当我了解到我想欺骗的人正是要帮助我的那个人的时候,我羞愧得无地自容了。◇ be extremely ashamed

have a head like a sieve [ˌhævə ˌhed laɪkə ˈsɪ(:)v] [话] **记性太坏** → have a memory like a SIEVE

have a head on *one's* **shoulders** [ˌhævə ˈhe(:)dɔn ~ ˌʃouldərz] [话] **扎扎实实** 直译为"肩膀上有个脑袋"。这一表达法的含义是:"不是有一个什么也不懂的糊涂脑袋,而是有一个端端正正的好脑袋"。指的是具有"理解力强"、"有条不紊"、"绝对不干不合理的事情"、"辨别是非,不犯错误"等各种优点的人。这种人的头脑精于实际生活,不一定是学识丰富、聪明绝顶、有发明创造的天才。*Why don't you ask Carl to help you? He lacks experience, but he has a head on his shoulders.* 找卡尔帮你一下怎么样?他虽然缺乏经验,但是非常扎实。*June will make a good wife. She's not all that smart, but she has a head on her shoulders.* 琼会成为一位好妻子。她的头脑虽然说不上聪明,但是非常扎实。在这一场合,是"扎扎实实,会过日子"的意思。在加强语气时,说 good head 或 real head, 或者把二者加在一起,说 real good head。*I realize your brother has a good head on his shoulders, but we'd prefer to hire someone with more education.* 我了解你的弟弟非常扎实,但是我们想雇用一个多受过一些教育的人。*I've always admired Mr. Ray. He's got a real head on his shoulders.* 我一向钦佩雷先生。他非常稳重,不出差错。另有一个 with a head ~ 的形式。*This job requires someone with a head on his shoulders.* 这项工作非有一位扎扎实实的人去干不可。◇ have (a lot of) practical ability and common sense

have *one's* **head in the clouds** [ˌhæv ～ ˌhedɪnðə ˈklaudz] [口] **脱离现实，满脑子幻想** 最初的构思是"脱离实际，好象把脑袋伸到云彩里似的"。*Jack would never make a good lawyer. He always has his head in the clouds.* 杰克永远也成不了一个好律师。他总是脱离现实，满脑子的幻想。*That guy has had his head in the clouds so long he's forgotten what the real world looks like.* 那个家伙脱离现实，在幻想中过日子太久了，已经忘记真正的世界是个什么样子啦。这一表达法也用于表示"组织、机构等充满幻想"的情况，例如：*Some say that the Socialist Party has had its head in the clouds for too many years ever to hope to come to power.* 有人说，社会党多年以来一直脱离现实、总在做梦，根本没有希望取得政权。也常采取 with *one's* head in the clouds 的形式。*How do you ever expect to get into college if you spend your high school days with your head in the clouds like this?* 如果你在高中时期如此脱离现实，满脑子都是幻想，怎么能够指望考上大学呢？如以上的例句所示，这一表达法一般用于表示"头脑里是在想什么，但总是脱离实际，想入非非"的意思。不过，有时也用于表示"头脑里什么也不想，只是发呆"的意思。*What are you doing sitting there with your head in the clouds?* 你干吗坐在那儿发呆呀？ ◇ be lost in unrealistic thoughts / be day-dreaming

have rocks in *one's* **head** → ROCKS

be head over heels in debt [ˌhedovər ˈhiːlzɪn ˈde(ː)t] [话] **债台高筑** → fall HEAD over heels in love (with *someone*)

a head shop [ə ˈhe(ː)dˌʃɑ(ː)p] [话] **吸毒用具商店** → an acid HEAD

hit the nail on the head → NAIL

keep a civil tongue in *one's* **head** → TONGUE

keep *one's* **head** [ˌki(ː)p ～ ˈhe(ː)d] [口] **保持冷静** 这里的 head 指"冷静思考的能力"。本条的意思是：在混乱时期或者非常时期能够毫不放松地 keep (保持) 这种能力。*George always keeps his head in emergencies.* 乔治在紧急时刻始终保持冷静的头脑。*After the accident, Phil kept his head and led the survivors to safety.* 事故发生以后，菲尔保持镇静，把幸存者引导到安全的地方。*In case of fire, keep your head. Walk, don't run, to the nearest exit.* 万一发生火灾，务请镇静。要走向最近的太平门，不要跑。这一表达法比青年人爱用的 keep *one's* COOL 正规一些。反义语为 lose *one's* HEAD。◇ remain calm

keep *one's* **head above water** [ˌkɪ(ː)p ～ ˈhedəbʌvˌwɑ(ː)dər] [口] **经济上过得去** 直译为"保持头在水面以上的状态"。按字面意义使用的场合，一般采取 ～ above *the* water 的形式，例如：*I can't really swim, but I can keep my head above the water.* 我实际上不会游泳，但是我能够使脑袋保持在水面上。作为比喻使用的场合，仍然残留着这种在水里努力挣扎的形象。有些英汉词典译为"不负债"，在原版的英语词典中也释义为 keep out of debt, 但在实质上，这一表达法与借钱不借钱并没有什么关系，它的本来意义是"不破产"。严密地说，就是"保持支付必要费用的状态"。为了保持这种"勉强度日"的状态，也可能在某个时期借一点钱，但是只要能够支付利息和到期还本，仍然算是 keep *one's* head above water。反之，即使不负债，而囊空如洗，在经济上过不去，那就不能说 keep *one's* head above water。总起来讲，这是一个表示财政困难的习用语，可应用于个人，也可应用于机关团体。*Our office managed to keep its head above water by securing a bank loan.* 我们公司弄到一笔银行贷款，日常开支能够过得去了。*They aren't rich but they seem to be keeping their heads above water.* 他们虽然不是有钱的人，但是日子似乎过得去。为了加强语气，常添加 just。*During periods of recession, many families have a hard time just keeping their heads above water.* 每当经济衰退的时期，许多家庭维持生计都非常困难。◇ remain financially solvent

let *someone* **have** *his* **head** [ˌlet ～ ˌhæv ～ ˈhe(ː)d] [口] **让某人随意处理** → give *someone his* HEAD

lose *one's* **head** [ˌluːz ～ ˈhe(ː)d] [口] **失去自制** 字面意义是"失掉脑袋"。*The king's army was defeated, and the king lost his head.* 国王的军队打败了,国王也被斩首了。可以这样地使用。但在现在的日常会话中,人们很少遇到使用这一意义的机会。一般是在发怒、惊恐、以及因男女关系而头脑发胀的场合使用。*I'm sorry I hit you. I guess I lost my head.* 我揍了你,太对不起了。我似乎失去自制能力啦。*As soon as he saw the three men coming at him, he lost his head and began shooting.* 他一看见有三个人向他走来,他就慌了神,开始射击。*How could you lose your head over a girl like that?* 你怎么会为那样一个姑娘神魂颠倒哪? 这一表达法比青年人爱用的 lose *one's* COOL 正规。反义语为 keep *one's* HEAD。◇ become excited

run around like a chicken with its head cut off → CHICKEN

take a head count [ˌteɪkə ˈhedˌkaunt] [话] **数头数** → count NOSES

take *someone's* **head off** [ˌteɪk ～ ˈhe(ː)ˌdɔːf] [话] **对某人粗暴无礼** → bite *someone's* HEAD off

take *one's* **head out of the sand** [ˌteɪk ～ ˈhe(ː)daudəvðə ˈsæːnd] [口] **正视现实** → bury *one's* HEAD in the sand

take it into *one's* **head to** *do something* [ˈteɪkəˌdɪntə ～ˈhe(ː)dtə ～] [口] **突然决定** 直译为"把做什么事情放到脑袋里",具有"不管周围人的反对或批评"的意味。汉语俗语叫"心血来潮"。一般是以第三者为主语。基本精神是:说话的人对作为主语的第三者的言行持批判的态度,表示"自己决不那样做"的心情。偶尔以 I 为主语,在这一场合当然是反省的言词了。*For some reason the boss of our little company has taken it into his head to open a branch office in New York.* 不知为什么,我们这家小公司的老板突然决定要在纽约开设一个分号。*Once my husband has taken it into his head to do something, there is no way in the world to stop him from carrying it out.* 我的丈夫一旦决定去干什么事情,世界上就没有任何办法能够阻止他去做。*My son has taken it into his head to emigrate to South America.* 我的儿子突然决定移居南美洲了。*I shouldn't have taken it into my head to attempt it by myself.* 我不该决定自己一个人去干。◇ decide (unadvisedly)

talk *someone's* **head off** [ˌtɔ(ː)k ～ ˈhe(ː)ˌdɔːf] [话] **唠叨得使人厌烦** → talk *someone's* EAR off

talk off the top of *one's* **head** → TOP

talk to hear *one's* **head roar** [ˈtɔːktə ˌhɪr ～ ˈhe(ː)ˌdro(ː)r] [话] **为说话而说话** 直译为"为了听自己的声音在脑袋里响而喋喋不休"。这一表达法原来的构思是:"不论有没有内容,只是由于喜欢听自己的声音而说个不停",也就是"为说话而说话"。*I'd take anything she says with a grain of salt. She's always talking to hear her head roar.* 对于她讲的话,我总是半信半疑。因为她一向是为说话而说话,喜欢闲扯淡。*Pay attention! I'm not just talking to hear my head roar, you know.* 大家注意听! 我不是闲着没事在这里磨嘴皮子。*I'm not going to any more protest rallies. I'm tired of standing around for hours listening to a bunch of malcontents talking to hear their heads roar.* 今后我不再去参加任何的群众抗议大会啦。一连几个小时站在那里听一群不满分子胡说八道,我已经腻烦透了。◇ talk (just) because *one* likes to (hear *oneself* talk)

turn *someone's* **head** [ˈtə(ː)rn ～ˈhe(ː)d] [口] **使某人骄傲自满** 逐字直译是"把某人的脑袋转到旁边去",这究竟为什么会成为"使某人骄傲自满"的意思呢? 不详。这一表达法另外还有一个意义是"使某人神魂颠倒"。不论是哪一个意义,都含有"令人不能从正面去看一切事物"的意义。既然"把某人的脑袋转到旁边去",他当然不能从正面去看东西,于是就"骄傲自满"或"神魂颠倒"了。这也许是最初的构思,至少说,通过这一联想，可能有助于对本条习用语的记忆。*It looks as if all the attention Jay is getting has turned his head. He hardly speaks to his old friends anymore.* 杰伊那样引人注目，似乎使他骄傲自满起来了。他对老朋友们连句话都不说了。*I'm afraid Maria's success as an artist has turned her head completely.* 玛丽在绘画方面成名成家，似乎使她完全不知道天多高地多厚啦。另外，上面已经讲过，这一表达法还有"使某人神魂颠倒"的意味。在使用这一意义的时候，总是伴随着"丧失理性"或者"精神失常"的意味。*Stu is hopeless. Every pretty girl he sees turns his head.* 司徒已经不可救药啦。他一见到个漂亮的姑娘就心猿意马，魂不守舍。*He is tall, dark and handsome— and rich to boot. It's no wonder he turned your head.* 他身材高大，皮肤浅黑，又帅又有钱，无怪乎使你神魂颠倒啦。如以上两个例句所示，大多应用于男女关系。但并不限定如此，例如说：*He used to be a very modest man, but I'm afraid his sudden wealth has turned his head.* 他原是一个非常谦虚的人，但我看他被暴富冲昏了头脑。◇ make *someone* conceited [think too highly of *himself*] / excite *someone*

headstrong

(as) headstrong as a bull [əz ˌhed.strɔ(ː)ŋəzə ˈbu(ː)l] [口] **死顽固** → (as) stubborn as a MULE

health

give *someone* **a clean bill of health** → BILL

be not in *something* **for** *one's* **health** [nɑ.dın ~ fər ~ ˈhe(ː)lθ] [话] **不是无偿地干工作** 字面意义是"不是为了健康而从事 *something*"。如果只是 for *one's* health，可以按照字面意义使用，例如：*A: Did you take up tennis for your health? B: No, I play because I enjoy it.* 甲：你是为了锻炼身体而开始打网球吗？乙：不，我是因为有这种兴趣。如果在前面加上 be not in *something*，就一定用比喻的意义。*something* 处代入"生意"、"工作"或者其他相当的语词。*I can't give you a lower price than that. I'm not in this business for my health, you know.* 我不能够再让价了。你要知道，我做这种生意可不是为了喝西北风啊。*You say you want me to use my influence for you, but you haven't said what you are offering in return. After all, I'm not in politics for my health.* 你说你希望我大力支持你，但是你没有讲你给我什么报酬啊。我搞政治这玩意儿，毕竟不是为了白干呀。另外，有时可以变形如下：*I don't work like this for my health, you know. I've got a wife and four children to feed.* 你要知道，我这样辛辛苦苦地工作可不是因为有这个瘾头。我得养活老婆和四个孩子啊。◇ be not engaged in *something* just because *one* enjoys it

hearing

hearing range [ˈhı(ː)rıŋ ˌreındʒ] [口] **听力所及距离** → within EARSHOT

heart

Absence makes the heart grow fonder. → ABSENCE

break *someone's* **heart** [ˌbreık ~ ˈhɑ(ː)rt] [口] **使某人心碎** 字面意义是"弄坏某人的心"。表达极度悲伤的习用语。与汉语的"心如刀割"、"悲痛欲绝"等说法近似。*Don't tell Jane that you saw her boy friend out with another girl. It'll break her heart.* 不要告诉简你看见她的男朋友跟另一个姑娘一起出去，那会使她非常伤心的。*The bank's having to foreclose on the old farmer's mortgage would surely break the old man's heart.* 如果银行一定要取消老农民赎回抵押品的权利，那位老翁肯定会悲痛欲绝的。有时只表示"太可怜啦"的意味，用者女性特别多。*Look at this picture of starving children in Africa. Doesn't it just break your heart?* 你看看这幅非洲饥饿儿童的照片。真是太可怜啦！这一表达法本来是应该在严肃的场面使用的，但是也有象下面的例句那样用于戏谑的场合。用者男性居多。*A: That makes two hundred dollars you've won off me in this* *poker game. B: That breaks my heart.* 甲：在这此扑克游戏中，你一共从我手里赢去二百美元啦。乙：这使我连心都碎啦。从 break *someone's* heart 又产生了形容词 heartbroken (或作 brokenhearted)。 *Alice was heartbroken when her fiancè broke off their engagement.* 艾丽斯在未婚夫撕毁婚约的时候，心都碎了。象这样用作表语的情况较多，但有时也用作定语。*He lost all his family in the war and died a heartbroken man.* 他在战争中失去了所有的亲人，自己也在悲痛欲绝中死去。另有一个表达法是 a heartbreaker。从它的来源 break *someone's* heart 推论，意思应该是"使人极度悲伤的事物"，但在实际上专指男女关系中或体育运动中令人大失所望的人或者"比赛"。 *Don't get too intimate with Joe. He's known as a heartbreaker.* 不要跟乔太亲密了。他玩弄女人感情已经出名了。 *The game was a real heartbreaker. We lost in the last minute of play.* 那次比赛实在令人惋惜，我们在最后一分钟输掉了。◇ cause *someone* great grief / be a sorrowful blow to *someone* / make *someone* feel like crying / make *someone* extremely sad

can't find it in *one's* **heart to** *do something* [ˌkænt ˈfaɪndɪdɪn ～ˈhɑ(ː)rtːə ～] [口] **怎么也不忍心去做某事** 这里的 it 是形式宾语，表示"做 to 以下的事情所必要的东西"，亦即"做……的勇气"。这一表达法的整个意思是"在自己的心里找不到做某件事的勇气"。与 not have the HEART (to *do something*) 的意义大致相同，但语气强一些。一般用于"由于不忍心"、"由于觉得可怜"的场合。过去曾用于肯定句，现在几乎见不到这种情况。*My son has had his heart set on going to Europe for so long that I couldn't find it in my heart to refuse.* 我的儿子从很早以前就一心想去欧洲，我怎么也不忍心拒绝他的要求。*Although the little dog was suffering, we couldn't find it in our hearts to kill it.* 虽然那只小狗病得很痛苦，我们怎么也不忍心杀掉它。以上的两个例子是用于否定句。也可以用于疑问句，例如：*Can't you find it in your heart to forgive me?* 你怎么也不愿意原谅我吗？ *How could you ever find it in your heart to do such a terrible thing?* 你怎么竟会做这样可怕的事情呀？ ◇ can't bring *oneself* to *do something*

can't find the heart to *do something* [ˌkænt ˌfaɪndðə ˈhɑ(ː)rtːə ～] [口] **不忍心去做某事** → not have the HEART (to *do something*)

cross *one's* **heart (and hope to die)** [ˈkrɔ(ː)s ～ˈhɑ(ː)rtn ˌhouptəˈ daɪ] [话] **在胸口划十字发誓** cross *one's* heart 直译虽然是"用手指在胸前划十字"，但一般划的是 X 字。儿童用语。小学生以及年龄相仿的孩子们使用，如果成年人使用则具有戏谑的成份。用法如下：有时一边说一边划十字，但大多只是口头上讲，实际上并不划十字。 *It's the truth. Cross my heart it is.* 这是真的。我可以发誓。在强调 cross *one's* heart 的时候，加上 and hope to die (直译为"并且希望去死")。*I didn't tell the teacher on you—cross my heart and hope to die.* 关于你的事情，我没有向老师讲。如果我对你说谎，天打五雷轰。 *A: Promise you'll come tomorrow? B: Sure. A: Cross your heart? B: Yes. Cross my heart and hope to die.* 甲：你答应明天来？ 乙：准来。甲：真的能来吗？ 乙：真的哟！如果我说谎，天打五雷轰。◇ I [you, etc.] swear I didn't [you will, etc.]

cry *one's* **heart out** [ˌkraɪ ～ˈhɑ(ː)rˌtaut] [口] **痛哭** 直译是"把心都哭出来了"。汉语叫"肝肠寸断"。一讲到 cry 这个动词，因为它有"叫喊"一义，所以人们很容易认为是"哭出声来"，其实并不一定如此。cry 可以是"放声大哭"，也可以是"暗自流泪"或者"默默抽泣"。在讲动词的用法时，人们常拿 weep 与 cry 作比较。也有 weep *one's* heart out 这一表达法，意思与本条相同，但文学的味道强，在会话中几乎不使用。 *When Jennie's dog died, she cried her heart out for a whole week.* 珍妮的狗死去以后，她痛哭了整整一个星期。*Jane is up in her room crying her heart out. Her fiancé just broke off their engagement.* 简在二楼自己的房间里痛哭哪。她的未婚夫刚刚解除了他们的婚约。类似的表达法有 cry *one's* EYES out,但请注意两者之间的细微的差别。cry *one's* eyes out 这一表达法是强调 cry (哭)的状态,而 cry *one's* heart out 则是以悲痛的心情为重点,并不计较哭的方式如何。因此,如果上面的第一个例句使用 cry *one's* eyes out,意思则为"接连不断地哭了一个星期",这在实际上是不大可能的。第二个例句可以使用 cry *one's* eyes out,意思是"一直在哭",这是有可能的。但是,从文章的美感来讲,"一直在哭"是强调"哭"这一行为本身,而"痛哭"则是突出内心的情感,原例句更生动而深刻。◇ cry as if *one's* heart would break

do *someone's* **heart good** [.du(:) ~ 'hɑ(:)rt'gu(:)d] [口] **使某人高兴** 直译为"对某人的心起好作用"。如果把词的顺序改变一下,说 do good to *someone's* heart 就更容易明白了,但一般不这样说。在美国,经常可以听到当母亲的人这样说:*It does a mother's heart good to see her children so healthy and happy.* 见到孩子们这样健康和幸福,真使妈妈高兴啊! *It did my heart good to hear how successful you have become.* 我听说你获得巨大的成就,十分高兴。另外,常常使用 really 来强调"高兴"。*So my rival finally went bankrupt, did he? Well, that really does this old heart (of mine) good.* 你是说,我做买卖的对手终于破产了,是吧? 哈哈,这真使我万分高兴啊。◇ make *someone* happy

eat *one's* **heart out** [.iːt ~'hɑːr.taut] [话] **悲痛欲绝** 字面意义为"吃掉自己的心"。原来的构思是"由于过分悲哀而狠狠折磨自己的心"。一般应用于因自己的责任而引起的事故。*No one can get Candy to cheer up. She's been eating her heart out because she blames herself for her brother's death.* 谁也没办法使坎迪高兴起来。她把弟弟的死归咎于自己,一直悲痛欲绝。这一表达法的后边常接续 over ~ 的形式。*Joe is eating his heart out over not having gotten into Stanford University.* 乔正在为了未能考取斯坦福大学而极度伤心。*So you dropped a hundred thou at the races. So what? That's nothing to eat your heart out over.* 这么说,你在赛马场损失十万美元啦。那又算得了什么呀? 就这么一点儿小事,也犯不上伤心啊。也有不论本人心情如何,从客观上看并没什么了不起的场合。*Little Jimmy ate his heart out when his best friend was angry and wouldn't come to his birthday party.* 小吉米的最要好的朋友生气了,没有参加他的生日晚会,这使他伤心得不得了。这一表达法常常用于表示"由于不能如愿以偿而闷闷不乐"的意思。*The front lines were filled with fresh teenage recruits eating their hearts out because they couldn't get home for Christmas.* 前线到处是不满二十岁的新兵,他们由于不能回家过圣诞节而闷闷不乐。◇ grieve / be greatly distressed

have a change of heart → CHANGE

Have a heart. ['hæ(:)vә 'hɑːrt] [话] **发发慈悲吧!** 这里的 heart 有"同情心"的意思。本条习用语的意思是"请你以慈悲为怀",在诉诸对方的同情心而有所恳求的时候使用。几乎所有的场合都用祈使式,放在句子的开头。*Have a heart, Pete. Give us back our ball.* 你行行好吧,皮特。把我们的球还给我们吧。*Please, Mom. Have a heart and let me go to the movies tonight. I promise I'll study tomorrow.* 妈妈,请你发发慈悲,让我今天晚上去看电影吧。我保证明天用功。如以上的例句所示,孩子们常常使用这一表达法。成年人也有使用的时候,例如:*Have a heart, Boss. Don't fire Jim just because he has a habit of being late for work.* 老板,你发发慈悲吧。请不要只因为吉姆常常迟到而开除他。◇ Be reasonable [kind]. / Please.

have a heart of gold [.hævә .hɑ(:)rtәv 'gould] [口] **有一颗美好的心** heart of gold (黄金的心)指温存、体贴、

善良、纯真等各种美德兼备的"象黄金一样美好的心灵"。在各种美德中,这一表达法所包含的"温存"的意味特别强,因此多应用于女性和老年人。这是一个最高度的褒义语。 *Lillian isn't all that pretty, but she has a heart of gold.* 莉莲长得不算很美,但是她有颗美好的心。在强调时,可以说 heart of pure gold (纯金的心)。*Mary never believes bad about anyone. She has a heart of pure gold.* 玛丽对任何人都不往坏处想。她有一颗真正美好的心。有时是把重点完全放在"温存"上边。例如: *Sue will make someone a wonderful wife. She has a heart of gold, and she loves children.* 苏会成一位极为出色的妻子。她非常温柔,而且喜欢孩子。with a heart of gold 的意思是"具有一颗美好心灵的"。*If you want to criticize her you could say she is naïve, but I prefer to think of her as a woman with a heart of gold.* 如果你想挑她的毛病,你可以说她不通世故人情,但是我恰恰认为她是一位具有美好心灵的女性。有时也应用于男性。*If there ever was a man with a heart of gold, it's Ralph. He is forever going out of his way to help other people.* 如果说世界上有一位具有美好心灵的男子,那就是拉尔夫。他永远不辞劳苦地去帮助他人。◇ be very [extremely] kind and unselfish ((pure→extremely))

have *one's* **heart in** *one's* **mouth** [hæv ~ ˈhɑ(ː)rtn ~ ˈmauθ] [口] **吓得要命** → *one's* HEART is in *one's* mouth

have *one's* **heart in the right place** [ˌhæv ~ ˈhɑ(ː)rtnðə ˌraɪtˈpleɪs] [话] **心怀善意** 字面意义为"心在正当的地方"。*I'm sorry what I did hurt you. I had my heart in the right place.* 真对不起,我干的事情伤害了你。我本来是一片好心啊。如这一例句所示,在本来出于好意或者无意识地干某种事情、而结果却损害了对方的时候,或在为某人进行辩护的时候,常常用这一习用语表白自己的态度。因此,在它的前边往往加上 but。*I'll admit that Mary shouldn't have spoken to your father about the incident, but she had her heart in the right place. She thought she was helping you.* 我承认玛丽不应该把那件事情告诉你父亲,不过,她是出于好意啊。她觉得这样做会对你有帮助。在"无意识"的场合,当然谈不到"心怀善意"与否,可以译成"没有恶意"或"并无歹心"。*Dave often says or does the wrong thing, but he always has his heart in the right place.* 戴夫常常说错话,做错事,但是他绝对没有坏心眼儿啊。这一表达法也可以用 *one's* heart is in the right place 的形式。论使用频率,两者差不多。*Tom's words are often harsh, but his heart is in the right place.* 汤姆说话常常很难听,但是他并没有什么坏心眼儿。*Once a well- intentioned President's actions lead to war, it does no good to say that his heart was in the right place.* 总统的一切行动即使动机是好的,但是一旦导致战争,那就很难说他心怀善意了。◇ *one's* intentions are good

have *one's* **heart set on** (*doing*) *something* [ˌhæv ~ ˈhɑ(ː)rt ˌsedɔ(ː)n ~] [口] **一心想要** 直译为"把心放在(干)某件事上",也就是"下定决心"的意思。这表示强烈的愿望。*My wife had her heart set on a red car, but only blue and yellow were available.* 我的妻子一心想要红颜色的汽车,可是只能买到蓝的和黄的。*Once she's got her heart set on something, she won't take no for an answer.* 她一旦想要什么东西或者想要做什么事情,决不容人说个"不"字。on 的后面可以用动名词。*Bob has his heart set on becoming [being] a doctor.* 鲍勃一心想要当个医生。*We had our hearts set on going to Hawaii this summer, but our daughter got sick and we couldn't go.* 我们本来打算今年夏天无论如何也要去夏威夷,但是女儿病了,未能去成。另外,除 have *one's* heart set on ~外,还有一个 set *one's* heart on ~的形式,在以上的例句中,都可以换用这一表达法。但在实际上,前者的使用率高一些。◇ very much want (to *do*) *something*

one's **heart is in** *one's* **boots** [~ ˈhɑːrtɪz ɪn ~ˈbuːts] [口] **沮丧** → *one's* HEART sinks

one's **heart is in** *one's* **mouth** [~ 'hɑ(:)rtɪzɪn ~ 'mauθ] [口] **吓得要命** 字面意义为"心跑到嘴里来"。这一表达法是形容正被吓得缩成一团的状态。*Was I scared? My heart was in my mouth.* 你问我害怕没有?哎呀,简直把我吓死啦。*Jimmy's heart was in his mouth as he opened the door to the haunted house.* 吉米打开闹鬼的房屋的门的时候,简直害怕得掉了魂儿。这一表达法可以使用以下各种形式。首先是 have *one's* heart in *one's* mouth,这是条头的表达法的变形,两者几乎在所有的场合都可以互换。但是,条头的表达法使用率高一些。*I had my heart in my mouth as I turned to face the intruder I sensed behind me.* 我觉察背后有歹人前来袭击,回过身去一看,简直快被吓死了。with *one's* heart in *one's* mouth 是"战战兢兢"、"提心吊胆"的意思。*Bob moved toward the strange sounds with his heart in his mouth.* 鲍勃提心吊胆地向着奇怪的声响走去。bring *someone's* heart into *his* mouth 是"把某人吓得魂飞魄散",可以用于"突然"的场合,也可以用于"徐徐"的场合。*The sound of baying police dogs, which suddenly came from behind him, brought the fugitive's heart into his mouth.* 突然身后传来警犬的叫声,简直把逃犯吓得魂飞天外了。*one's* heart leaps into *one's* mouth 也是"吓得要命",但它的本意为"心跳到口中",所以只用于"突然"的场合。*June's heart leapt into her mouth when she saw the truck swerve toward her.* 当琼看到一辆卡车突然改变方向向她冲过来的时候,她吓得魂儿都没了。◇ *one* is filled with fear

one's **heart sinks** [~ 'hɑ(:)rt 'sɪ(:)ŋks] [口] **大失所望** 直译为"心往下沉",即汉语俗语所说的"情绪低落"。多用于表示大失所望的情况。根据前后文,可以译作"沮丧"、"伤心"、"失意"、"垂头丧气"、"心灰意懒"、甚至"蔫了"、"打不起精神"等等。*My heart sank when I saw the exam results.* 我看到考试的成绩时,完全灰心了。*Fred had hoped that by driving fast he would get to the airport on time, but his heart sank when he heard the police siren behind him.* 弗雷德为了及时赶到机场,加快了车速,但听到后边有警笛以后,他感到非常沮丧。如果是下面这样严重的情况,那就不只是"失望",而是"绝望"了。*The boy's parents' hearts sank when they saw the face of the doctor as he emerged from the operating room.* 当外科大夫从手术室里走出来的时候,少年的父母看到他的面部表情就感到绝望了。在强调失望的状态时,可以说 *one's* heart sinks into *one's* boots,直译为"心落到自己的靴子(boots)里"。*I had been fairly confident that the boss hadn't discovered my mistake, but when I heard his angry voice calling my name, my heart sank into my boots.* 我一直认为老板没有发现我的错误,但当我听到他喊我的名字的恼怒声音时,简直被吓得三魂掉了两魄。另一个变形是 *one's* heart is in *one's* boots,直译为"心在自己的靴子里"。*I began my new job full of confidence, but after one week and I still hadn't make a single sale, my heart was in my boots.* 我开始干新的工作的时候充满了信心,但是过了一个星期,我还没搞成一笔交易,就大失所望了。也使用 with sinking heart (带着沮丧的心情)的形式。*With sinking heart Joan read in her husband's letter that his return home would be delayed for another month.* 琼怀着沮丧的心情阅读丈夫的来信,信上说他又得推迟一个月才能回家。◇ *one's* hopes sink / *one* loses hope

lose heart [ˌluːz 'hɑ(:)rt] [口] **丧失信心** 这一表达法除了"灰心丧气"而外,还包含着很大的"绝望"成份。一般来说,先是对于某一件事抱有 heart (热情和希望),后来发现并不能如愿以偿,于是逐渐失望,丧失了热情。这个总的过程叫做 lose heart。过程的最初阶段叫做 begin to lose heart,中间阶段叫做 be losing heart,最后阶段叫做 (have) lost heart。有时又说 suddenly lose heart,意思不是指一瞬间的现象,而是指过程极为迅速。如果把这一过程倒过来，就用 take HEART 这一表达法。*I know it's difficult to find a job now, but don't lose heart. Keep looking. I'm sure something will turn up.* 我知道现在找个工作是困难的，但是不要丧失信心，继续去寻找，我相信一定会找到的。*After twenty-four hours had passed and still there was no news of the missing plane my father was on, we began to lose heart.* 24 个小时过去了，依然不知道我父亲所乘飞机的下落，我们开始丧失信心了。*The other team may be winning, but it's too early to lose heart. We can still overtake them in the second half.* 对方的球队虽然占上风，但是丧失信心可为时太早啦。在下半场比赛中，我们还可以转败为胜啊。同义语有 become disheartened，不过在日常会话中很少使用。◇ become discouraged

not have the heart (to *do something*) [ˌnɑtˌhævðə ˈhɑ(ː)rt] [口] **不忍心(去做某事)** 这里的 heart 原来是"勇气"的意思，肯定形式作 have the heart to ～，意为"有勇气(或决心)去做某事"。但这是古老的表达法，现在 heart 已经带有"残酷"、"无情"的意味。这里的 the 有"充分的"、"足够的"的意思。本条条头整个直译为"没有足够的残忍去做某事"。*The boy was so downcast at having broken the window that his teacher didn't have the heart to punish him.* 那个男孩儿打破了窗户玻璃以后，连头也不敢抬，老师觉得他很可怜，没有处罚他。*How could you have ever had the heart to do such a cruel thing?* 你怎么会忍心去干那样残酷的事情呢？如以上两个例句所示，一般用于否定句或疑问句。*My aunt says she wouldn't have the heart to kill a deer, but she certainly loves to eat venison.* 我的婶娘说她不忍心去杀鹿，但是她肯定是爱吃鹿肉的。*How did you ever have the heart to make her study on New Year's Day?* 你怎么忍心叫她在元旦这一天还啃书本哪？下面的例句是与旧的用法相近的表达法。*Go ahead—shoot me. I don't believe you have the heart.* 你动手吧，向我开枪。我不相信你有那么大胆子。也可以用 can't find the heart to do *something* 的说法，意思一样。*Although the little bird was obviously suffering, I couldn't find the heart to kill it.* 那只小鸟虽然很痛苦，但是我没忍心杀了它。◇ can't bring *oneself* to *do something*

search *one's* **heart** [ˌsə(ː)rtʃ ～ˈhɑ(ː)rt] [口] **扪心自问** 字面意义为"探索自己的心"，也就是"从自己的内心深处去寻求答案"。经常伴有"要有充分时间"和"本着良心和诚意"的意味。因此，通常用于本人感到严重的事情。*Susan was a recalcitrant employee but her boss was a kind-hearted man. He searched his heart for many days before he finally decided to fire her.* 苏珊是一个桀骜不驯的职工，但是她的领导却是一个面慈心软的人。他左思右想了好多天，最后才把她解雇了。*Should I forgive him? I searched my heart for many sleepless nights, but I couldn't find the answer.* 我应该宽恕他吗？我在许多个无眠之夜扪心自问，可是未能找到答案。*If you will search your heart, I'm sure you will discover that you are as much to blame as he.* 如果你能够扪心自问的话，你肯定会发现你与他负有同样的责任。另外有一个定型的表达法是 SOUL-SEARCHING，这可以说是 search *one's* heart 的名词形式或形容词形式。但是，不知什么原因，却极少见 search *one's* soul 或者 heart-searching 的说法。◇ examine *one's* conscience [deepest motivations]

set *one's* **heart on** (*doing*) *something* [ˌset ～ˈhɑ(ː)rtɔ(ː)n ～] [口] **一心想要得到某物(做某事)** → have *one's* HEART set on (*doing*) *something*

be sick at heart [ˌsɪkət ˈhɑ(ː)rt] [口] **心里非常难受** 源出莎翁名剧《哈姆雷特》(*Hamlet*) 第一幕第一场。原文如下：For this relief much thanks; 'tis bitter cold, and I am sick at heart. (在这里换班，我万分感谢；天气这么冷，我又打不起精神。) 至于条头译文所写的"心里非常难受"，可以分为两大原因。第一，是由于"自己责备自己"。*I was sick at* *heart when I learned that my hasty words had caused my friend to quit his job.* 由于我轻率地说几句话,我的朋友就辞去了工作。我听到这件事心里非常难过。*Laura was sick at heart for having run over her little sister's cat.* 劳拉因为开车压死了小妹妹的猫,心里非常难受。如以上的例句所示,大多是由于"疏忽大意犯了过错"而"自责"。第二个大原因是"未能如愿以偿"。例如:*Alice was sick at heart when, despite all the time and effort she had taken to make herself beautiful, Tom scarcely noticed her at the party.* 艾丽斯虽然花费了很多时间,竭尽一切力量去把自己打扮得花枝招展,但在社交晚会中,汤姆却几乎连看都不看她一眼,使得她心里万分难受。*After working so hard to prepare for the picnic, we were sick at heart when it had to be canceled because of the rain.* 我们费了很大劲准备野餐,在由于下雨而停止举行的时候,心里非常难受。如以上的例句所示,在"未能如愿以偿"的背后大多具有"可惜费了那么多力气"的悔恨心情。还有一个 make *someone* sick at heart 的表达法。*It made me sick at heart to realize what a wonderful opportunity I had wasted.* 我知道自己白白丢掉一个大好的机会,心里难过极了。*It makes me sick at heart to think that we won't be able to finish the work on time.* 一想到我们不能按期把活儿干完,我的心里难受极了。◇ be filled with anguish / be grief-stricken / be extremely disappointed

take heart [ˌteɪk ˈhɑ(ː)rt] [口] **鼓起勇气** 这里的 take 是"拿回来"的意思。heart 是"热情和希望"。本条习用语直译为"把热情和希望拿回来",也就是"树立信心,鼓起勇气,重新振作精神"的意思。多用于因受到鼓励而振作精神的场合。反义语为 lose HEART (→)。*I had been worried about failing English, but I took heart at my teacher's words of encouragement.* 我原来很担心英语不及格,但是听了老师鼓励的话,我又树立了信心。*Mom began to take heart when my father showed signs of recovery.* 母亲见到我父亲有康复的兆头,精神又振作起来了。常用作命令。*Take heart. Being jilted is tough, but Mary isn't the only girl in the world.* 要把精神振作起来!被女人甩掉固然很痛苦,但是玛丽并不是世界上唯一的姑娘呀。同义语有 become heartened, 但在日常会话中极少使用。◇ become encouraged

take *something* **to heart**① [ˌteɪk ~ tə ˈhɑ(ː)rt] [口] **认真接受忠告或教训** 字面意义是"把某事记在心里"。不仅仅是 take seriously (认真考虑),而且含有 be affected by (受到感化) 的意味。例如:*Jim took his father's advice to heart.* 吉姆认真地接受了他父亲的忠告。在这句话里,可以想象到吉姆的内心有一定的变化。*Mary took her mother's advice to heart and decided to get married.* 玛丽听从了母亲的劝告,决定结婚了。advice 多用作宾语,但并不限定如此。*At first I was repelled by Mr. Blanton's harsh manner, but when I realized he was trying to help me, I began to take his words to heart.* 最初我很讨厌布兰顿先生的冷峻态度,但是当我了解到他是要帮助我的时候,我就认真听他所说的话了。*I gave him my thoughts on his plans. If he doesn't want to take them to heart, that's his business.* 关于他的计划,我向他陈述了自己的想法。如果他不认真考虑,那就与我无干了。可以用 lay 代替 take, 而作 lay *something* to heart, 但这一表达法很生硬,会话中很少使用。◇ give *something* serious consideration / take *something* seriously / accept *something*

take *something* **to heart**② [ˌteɪk ~ tə ˈhɑ(ː)rt] [口] **往心里去** 意思是"听了别人的话,遇到不顺心的事,在肚子里憋得难受"。这一表达法用以表示"为了芝麻大的小事而过分烦恼"的不良意味。这是一个比较轻松的说法,在有关人的生死之类的严重问题上一般不使用。*I'm afraid Fred took my criticism to heart. He hasn't spoken to me since that day.* 弗雷德大概对我提的意见有些想不通。自从那天以后,他没有跟我说过话。*Don't* *take it to heart. I'm sure she didn't mean what she said.* 不要往心里去嘛。我认为她的话并不是她自己的本意。*Joan tends to take criticism too much to heart.* 琼一听到别人的批评,总爱往心里去,老是想不开。*Our son has taken the death of his dog very much to heart.* 我儿子的狗死了,他为此伤心不已。另外,这一表达法与 take *something* to HEART[①] 的区别只能靠文章或讲话的前后关系来判断,不过在一般的场合是很容易看或听得出来的。例如说:*I hope Fred took my criticism to heart.* 我希望弗雷德能听进去我的批评。在这句话里,"往心里去"反倒具有良好的意味了。◇ take *something* too [so] seriously / be upset by *something*

wear *one's* **heart on** *one's* **sleeve** [ˌwe(:)r ~ ˈhɑ(:)rtən ~ ˈsliːv] [口] **立即表现内心的感情** 逐字翻译是"把心挂到袖子上"。这一表达法的来源是:古时英国有一种风俗,男人常把恋人赠送的缎带或手帕等缝到袖子上。这是一个古老的习用语,莎士比亚曾经使用过。*A woman has to learn to play hard to get. Men won't be interested in you if you are always wearing your heart on your sleeve.* 女人必须学会使男人焦急不安的本领。如果你总是有什么说什么,对男人就没有吸引力了。如这一例句所示,首先联想到的是男女关系。一般是指人的个性,如果控制不住自己的感情,结果往往失利或受到损害。*She seemed uninterested in him, but then she was not the type to wear her heart on her sleeve.* 从表面上看,她对他很冷淡,然而她并不是外向类型的人。这一表达法在用于男女关系以外的事情时,总含有"单纯"、"幼稚"等否定的意味。*Our little boy often has his feelings hurt by other children because he wears his heart on his sleeve.* 我家的小男孩由于心直口快,常常被别的孩子伤害了感情。*It's not clear yet whether they'll do business with us or not. Japanese businessmen are not noted for wearing their hearts on their sleeves.* 他们是不是跟我们做生意,现在还不清楚,因为日本商人总是不露声色。可以用前置词 with 代替动词 wear,例如:*You can't go around with your heart on your sleeve like a little puppy dog and not expect people to take advantage of you sometimes.* 如果你象一条小狗那样心里有什么脸上就表现什么,而又希望不为人们所利用,那是办不到的事情。◇ (constantly) allow others to know *one's* (true) feelings

with sinking heart [wɪθ ˈsɪŋkɪŋ ˈhɑ(:)rt] [口] **灰心丧气** → *one's* HEART sinks

heartbreaker

a heartbreaker [ə ˈhɑ(:)rtˌbreɪkər] [话] **令人大失所望的人[比赛]** → break *someone's* HEART

heartbroken

heartbroken [ˈhɑ(:)rtˌbroukən] [口] **使人心碎的** → break *someone's* HEART

heartened

become heartened [bəˌkʌm ˈhɑ(:)rtənd] [口] **精神振作起来** → take HEART

heart's

to *one's* **heart's content** → CONTENT

heat

a dead heat [ə ˈde(:)d ˈhiːt] [口] **同时到达终点(的比赛)** 原为赛马用语。dead 是"不分胜负"的意味。heat 是 a trial heat (预赛)、a final heat (决赛)等用法中的 heat, 即 race (比赛)的一个赛次。a dead heat 指在比赛中同时到达,不分胜负。这一表达法不表示竞争的过程,只表示最后的结果。*The two leading runners finished in a dead heat.* 在赛跑中,领先的两名选手同时到达了终点。*The race appeared to be a dead heat between the three top runners, but a study of photographs showed that the French contestant's breast touched the tape first.* 在赛跑中,领先的三名选手似乎同时到达了终点,但是,检查照片的结果表明法国选手的胸部是第一个触拉绳的。如以上的例句所示,这一表达法一般用于"竞赛"、"赛跑"。人们也常把选举比做"竞赛"。

The election finished in a dead heat, with both candidates receiving exactly the same number of votes. 两个候选人所得的选票张数几乎相同，这次选举以未分胜负而告终。另外，最近美国人常常误用这一表达法表示“短兵相接”的意味，如说：*The horses came down the home stretch in a dead heat.* 参加比赛的马猛烈竞争，冲向终点线。◇ a tie

heater

a heater [əˈhiːdər] [话] **手枪** 字面意义为“加热的东西”。谁都知道这是“加热装置”的意思。 *It's too hot. Let's turn off the heater.* 太热啦。把电炉关了吧。但是，就是这个 heater 又被用作暗语，表示“手枪”的意思。原为黑社会用语，后在小说或电视描写黑社会的场面中，匪徒和警官们常常使用。现已成为家喻户晓的一个表达法。 *Have you got a heater on you?* 你带着手枪吗？ *I've got to get some shells for my heater.* 我得给我的手枪弄几颗子弹啦。pack a heater 为定型的说法，意为“持有手枪”。pack 本来是“包装”的意思，在这里与 carry 同义。也说 carry a heater。不论用 pack 还是用 carry，都不是“手里拿着”，而是“携带在衣袋里(或者身上的其他地方)”。*Be careful. He may be packing a heater.* 当心！他身上可能有手枪。pack heat 与 pack a heater 一样，也是黑社会用语，意思相同。 heat 原意为“热”，是不可数的名词，因而不用冠词。但 heat 与 heater 不同，在作“手枪”解时，不用于 pack heat 以外的形式。另外，在黑社会用语中，“手枪”一词还有 a gat [ˈgæ(ː)t], a rod [ˈrɑːd] 等说法，其中 a gat 已略嫌陈旧，最近没有象 heater 或 rod 那样普遍应用。再有，gat 和 rod 在搭配动词时，一般用 carry 而不用 pack。◇ a gun

heaven

be in seventh heaven [ɪnˈsevənθ ˈhevən] [口] **高兴极了** 根据伊斯兰教和犹太教，天国 (heaven) 有七个，第七个 (seventh) 是“极乐之地”，为上帝的住所。英美口语中以 seventh heaven 作“最高的幸福”解即由此而来。*John has been in seventh heaven ever since he learned he'd passed the entrance exam.* 约翰知道他已经考上大学以后，简直高兴极了。有时不用 in，只使用 seventh heaven。 *Wetting my feet in puddles of water was seventh heaven for me when I was a kid.* 在我小的时候，使我最高兴的事情是把脚浸到水坑里。另外，在一般的英汉词典里，常常可以见到加定冠词，作 in the seventh heaven，但是，这是英国英语特有的说法，而在美国英语中，只要不是采取 ~ of delight 之类的形式，一概不加定冠词。 → be on CLOUD nine ◇ be extremely happy

move heaven and earth (to *do something*) [ˌmu(ː)v ˈhevənəˈnəːrθ] [口] **想尽一切办法** 直译为“搬动天 (heaven) 和地 (earth) 去做某事”。大多用于因不能顺利进行而达不到目的的场合，但也有时用于经过努力可以达到目的的场合。例如：*You know I would move heaven and earth to help you, but my hands are completely tied.* 你知道，为了帮助你，我可以赴汤蹈火，万死不辞，但是我的手脚完全被捆住了，连窝儿都动不了。*Joe moved heaven and earth to try to get transferred back to the home office.* 乔千方百计地要调回总公司。有时，这一表达法相当于汉语的“排除万难”。*I promised to move heaven and earth to be there on time.* 我已经保证，要排除万难准时到达那里了。◇ do everything possible

heaven's

for heaven's sake [fər ˈhevənzˈseɪk] [话] **无论如何** → for Pete's SAKE

heavy

a heavy date → DATE

heck

Heck. [ˈhe(ː)k] [话] **真糟糕！**感叹词之一。 heck 是 hell (地狱)的委婉语。 hell 也与 God 一样，不能信口乱说。 *Aw, heck, Why can't I go, too, Mom?* 哎呀，真糟糕！妈妈，为什么我也不能去？ *Oh, heck. Now I'll have to start all over again.* 唉，真糟糕！现在我必须从头开

始,整个重来一遍。如以上的例句所示,多用于表示沮丧、失望等情绪。但也有时表示轻蔑的心情。*Heck. That's not so great. Anybody can do that.* 哼,那没什么了不起!谁都能干得了。在下一例句中是用这一表达法表示轻蔑自己,结果就等于表示谦逊了。*A: Thank you so much. B: Heck. It was nothing.* 甲:太感谢你啦!乙:嘿,那没什么。另外,大家还应该知道,heck 除作感叹词使用外,又与 hell 同样,可以用以加强语气。*What the heck are you doing here?* 你到底在这儿干什么呀? *What the heck do you care?* 你操这份心干什么? *I had a heck of a time finding it.* 我费了多大的劲才找到它。*I have a heck of a lot of work to do.* 我要干的事情堆积如山。虽然 heck 与 hell 几乎在所有的场合都可以互相替换,但 hell 的语气强,显得粗暴,特别是孩子们对父母说话时使用,一般是要受到申斥的。

heebie-jeebies

give *someone* **the heebie- jeebies** [.gɪv ~ ðə .hi(:)bi ˈjiː.bɪ(:)z] [话] **使某人坐立不安** 美国漫画家德贝克 (W. De Beck, 1890～1942) 曾经发表著名的连环漫画《巴尼·古戈尔》(Barney Google)。古戈尔是一个老农民,他常使用 heebie-jeebies 一词。这就是本条习用语的来源。1925 年左右开始流行,现在依然使用。heebie-jeebies 指"不安定的心理状态",意思是"只要风吹草动,便要战战兢兢"。*I don't know who that guy is, but I wish he'd stop hanging around the neighborhood. He gives me the heebie-jeebies.* 我不知道那个人是谁,但是我希望他不要在这附近来回转悠。他使我有点毛骨悚然。*The sounds that came intermittently from the darkened old house gave everyone the heebie-jeebies.* 从那黑黝黝的老屋断断续续地传出来的声音,使得每个人都毛骨悚然。有这样"令人毛骨悚然"的场合,也有象下面例句那样"令人提心吊胆"的场合。*Stop waving that gun around. You're giving me the heebie-jeebies.* 你不要挥舞那枪啦。叫我有点心惊肉跳。*The way Jake keeps looking backwards while driving gives me the heebie-jeebies.* 杰克在开车的时候老是回头往后瞧,真叫我提心吊胆。偶尔用这一表达法形容酒精中毒的症状。*Too much drink will give you the heebie-jeebies.* 喝酒过多会中毒,使你浑身发抖。get the heebie-jeebies 是"神经紧张",have the heebie-jeebies 是"焦燥不安"的意思。*I get the heebie- jeebies whenever I see someone walking on a high tightrope.* 我一见到在高处走钢丝绳的人,就感到神经紧张。*We all had the heebie-jeebies waiting to learn what our exam results were.* 我们大家都在焦燥不安地等待着考试成绩的公布。另外,有时把 heebie 拼写为 heeby,但极罕见。◇ make *someone* nervous

heeled

be well heeled [.we(:)l ˈhiːld] [话] **很有钱** 在资本主义社会,饭馆、酒楼等服务行业往往根据客人的鞋判断他的腰包里是否有钱。也就是说,鞋跟完好(即没有磨破)乃是"不缺钱"的证据。本条习用语的构思与此相同。与 be rich 或 wealthy 同义,但富有会话的韵味。不能按字面意义("鞋跟完好")使用。*Corey Gashy may be well heeled, but he's certainly no gentleman.* 科里·加西可能很有钱,但他肯定不是一位绅士。*The customers in this restaurant seem to be fairly well heeled.* 这家餐厅的客人似乎都相当有钱。如以上的例句所示,这一表达法主要以人为对象,但也有用于组织、企业等的场合。*That union is well heeled.* 那个工会很有钱。又可以加连字符,作 well-heeled,大多放在名词前边。*That's a well- heeled union.* 那是个有钱的工会。◇ be wealthy

heels

cool *one's* **heels** [.kuːl ~ ˈhiːlz] [话] **久等** 直译为"使脚后跟冷下来"。乍看起来,这与"久等"有什么关系呢?令人莫名其妙。原来,这一表达法的语源是:古时用马作交通工具,走的路程太长了,马的蹄子就发热。骑马的人必须让马休息，等待马的蹄子凉了以后再走。也就是说，从骑马的人立场来讲，他是为马而久等。后来形成固定的表达法，表示由于对方的原因而要等候很长的时间。本来应该是“使马蹄凉下来”，不知为什么变成了“使人的脚后跟凉下来”。一般不用于虽然等候但是受到礼遇的场合。*Newspaper reporters must learn to accept cooling their heels as part of their job.* 新闻记者必须牢记：久等也是工作的一部分。往往与 be left 一起使用，如说：*I was left cooling [to cool] my heels outside the manager's office for almost an hour.* 我在经理办公室的外边足足等了一个来钟头。有时候不是由于对方无礼或摆架子而等候，而是等候的人产生了这样的感觉。在此种场合，也可以使用这一表达法强调自己的不满或埋怨。*Where in the world have you been? I've been cooling my heels on this corner since six o'clock.* 你究竟到哪儿去啦？从六点钟以后，我一直在这个角落等你。◇ wait

down at the heels [ˌdaunətðə ˈhiːlz] [口] **破旧的** 字面意义为“鞋跟磨破”。*You should have your shoes fixed. They're getting pretty down at the heels.* 你的鞋应该送去修理了，鞋跟大部分都磨破了。有时从“连修鞋的钱都没有”这一构思出发，表示“穷得不象样子”的意思。*At the end of the war, everyone looked down at the heels.* 在战争末期，每个人都衣衫褴褛，穷得不象样子。有时与有没有钱毫无关系，只是“本人不注意穿戴，非常邋遢”而已。*Mary dresses nicely, but her brother is always down at the heels.* 玛丽打扮得非常整洁，而她的弟弟永远是那么邋遢。不仅应用于人，在谈到房屋、街道等风景时也可以使用。*We should have the house painted. It's beginning to look down at the heels.* 我们得把房屋油漆一下，它已经开始显得破旧不堪了。再者，可以用连字符全都连接起来，用于名词之前。*Somehow the town had a down-at-the-heels look about it.* 这个城镇的外观看起来太破旧啦。有把 heels 改成单数而说 down at the heel 的时候，但极罕见。◇ shabby

fall head over heels in love (with *someone*) → HEAD

take to *one's* **heels** [ˌteɪktə ～ ˈhiːlz] [口] **逃走** 这里的 take to 是“开始使用”的意思。heels 是“脚后跟”。二者合起来为“开始使用脚后跟”，与北京话的“撒鸭子”意思相同。*Jack suddenly took to his heels.* 杰克突然逃走了。*When the boys who broke the window saw the owner coming, they took to their heels.* 当男孩子们打破了人家的玻璃窗户，见到房主前来的时候，他们一溜烟儿逃走了。◇ run away

hell

catch hell (from *someone* for *something*) [ˌkætʃ ˈhe(ː)l] [俗] **大受申斥** 直译为“捕捉地狱”。意思与 CATCH it (from *someone* for *something*) 一样，但语气比较强烈，是富有男子气概的表达法。但是，也有人认为 hell 的这一用法非常庸俗，因此在使用时，千万要注意分寸。如果你心里犯嘀咕，可以使用 catch it (受责备)，保管平安无事。*Jack caught hell from the president for losing the company's biggest customer.* 杰克由于丢掉公司最大的主顾，被总经理狠狠地申斥了一番。*Was he mad?! Man, I caught hell.* 难道他生气啦?! 哎呀，叫我挨了顿臭骂。可以换个说法，作 give *someone* hell (for *something*) (为某事而对某人大加申斥)。*The boss gave him hell (for losing a big customer).* 由于他丢掉一位大主顾。老板狠狠地申斥了他一番。◇ be severely reprimanded (by *someone* for *something*)

come hell or high water [ˌkʌm ˈhelər ˈhaɪ ˈwɔːdər] [话] **不管发生什么情况** 换个普通说法是 even should hell or high water come (不管 hell [地狱] 来也好，high water [洪水] 来(也好)。表示“哪怕有千难万险”的坚强意志。*I'm going to see my son in that school come hell or high water.* 不管有多大困难，我也要让我的儿子进那所学校。*My grandfather is a* *spry old coot. He says he's going to live to be a hundred come hell or high water.* 我祖父是一位精力旺盛的老人。他说,他无论如何也要活到一百岁。*I'm determined to finish this job come hell or high water.* 不管发生什么情况,我也决心完成这项工作。→ go through HELL and high water ◇ no matter what *one* has to do (to do it) / no matter what the hardship [what happens]

give *someone* **hell** (for *something*) [ˌgɪv ～ˈhe(ː)l] [俗] **大加申斥** → catch HELL (from *someone* for *something*)

go through hell and high water [ˌgou, θru(ː) ˈhe(ː)lən ˈhaɪ ˈwɔːdər] [话] **经受重重困难** 字面意义为"通过地狱和洪水往前走"。这是一种夸张表达法。在强调为了达到目的而经受重重困难的时候常常使用。因此,绝大多数是用过去时。*I went through hell and high water to win this contract. We're going to deliver on time or heads will roll.* 我费了千辛万苦,才签订这个合同。我们必须按期交货,要不就全完蛋啦。*I went through hell and high water to get tickets for tonight's concert and now Jane says she can't go.* 我费了九牛二虎之力才弄到今天晚上音乐会的票,可是现在,简居然说她去不了啦。下面的例句是用将来时,但在这一场合也可以与 come HELL or high water 互相替换。*I'm going to see my son in that school (even) if I have to go through hell and high water to do it. (= I'm going to see my son in that school come hell or high water.)* 不管怎样,我也要让我的儿子进入那所学校。但请读者注意: go through ～的场合固定要用 and,而 come ～的场合固定要用 or。◇ ((to *do something* → in *doing something*)) have an extremely difficult time / experience untold difficulties

until hell freezes over [ənˌtɪl ˈhelˌfri(ː)zəˌzovər] [俗] **直到地老天荒** 直译为"一直到地狱冰封为止",这肯定需要极长极长的时间。因此,这一表达法就具有"永远"、"永恒"的意味了。它相当于 forever,而语气强烈。使用范围比 forever 窄,主要用于坚决反对对方的主张或断然拒绝死乞白赖的请求的场合,表示"不管你怎样坚持也白搭"的意味。造句大多采取如下的形式:"指对方的主语+can+动词原形+ until hell ～"。*You can beg until hell freezes over, but my answer will still be "no."* 不论你恳求到什么时候,我的回答也是一个"不"字。*He can wait until hell freezes over. I absolutely refuse to see him.* 不论他等到什么时候,我也绝对不见他。可以用 till 代替 until。*It's hopeless. You can talk to her till hell freezes over; she'll never change her mind.* 没有用处。不论怎样跟她谈,她也坚决不改变自己的主意。◇ forever

help

so help me [ˌsou ˈhelpˌmɪ] [话] **上天作证** 在信奉基督教的国家,当在法庭上宣誓时,把左手放到《圣经》上,举起右手说: *I swear to tell the truth, the whole truth, and nothing but the truth, so help me God.* 我发誓讲真话,字字是真,句句是真,上天作证。这是他们的风俗习惯。本条的 so help me 则是从上述誓词的最后一句去掉 God 一词,作为轻松的誓言被人们广泛使用。意义和用法与 I swear 相同,在以下各例句中均可互换使用。*I didn't mean to do it. So help me, it was an accident.* 我不曾有意识地那样做。上天作证,那的确是一次事故。*It's the truth. So help me it is.* 那是真的。上天作证,的确如此。*If you say that once more, so help me I'll hit you.* 如果你敢再说一遍这种话,我可真地要狠狠揍你一顿。有时又恢复 God 一词,而讲 so help me God [ˈsou ˈhelp ˈmiː ˈgɑːd]。在这一场合也不是特别具有"上帝"的意味,只是加强语气而已。*If you so much as lay a finger on my brother, so help me God I'll kill you.* 如果你敢碰我的弟弟一指头,我说话算数,一定杀了你。*I didn't know the man I insulted was your father. So help me God I didn't.* 我不知道我侮辱的那个人是你的父亲。上天作证,我做梦也没有想到啊。◇ I swear (to God)

hen

hen fruit → FRUIT

a hen party → PARTY

(as) mad as a wet hen [əz ˈmæ(ː)dəzə ˌwetˈhe(ː)n] [话] **非常生气** wet hen 意思是"湿的母鸡"。给鸡的身上浇水,鸡就兴奋得发狂。这便是本条习用语的来源。*Mom was as mad as a wet hen when she found we had eaten the pie.* 妈妈发现我们把馅饼全都吃光了以后,非常恼火。动词如果用 get, 意思是"大为恼火起来"。*My wife gets as mad as a wet hen whenever anyone drops ashes on the rug.* 谁要是把烟灰掉落到地毯上,我的妻子就会大为恼火起来。可能由于用的是 hen (母鸡),这一表达法大多用于女性。但也有用于男性的场合,例如: *Better not try to talk to the boss now. He's mad as a wet hen because you didn't meet your deadline.* 现在最好不要向老板讲。因为你没有遵守限期,他正在非常生气哪。另有 (as) mad as a hornet (象大黄蜂一样生气)的说法,与 (as) mad as a wet hen 大致同义。两个说法同样,在 mad 之前可加 as, 也可以不加。◇ extremely angry

an old hen [ə ˌnouldˈhe(ː)n] [俗] **老婆子** 男性用语。除显然开玩笑的场合外,女性肯定是不会欢迎这一称呼的。old hen 的字面意义是"老母鸡"。这一表达法的来源是:从男人们的眼光来看,母鸡来回乱跑,凑在一起咕咕叫,或者互相掐架,简直象人类世界中的"婆娘"。专用于中年以上的女性。大多不是指一个人,而是用复数。*Three old hens from the neighborhood were standing on the corner gossiping.* 有三个邻居的老婆子站在街角上说长道短哪。◇ a(n old) woman

hen-pecked

hen-pecked [ˈhenˌpe(ː)kt] [口] **怕老婆的** 直译为"被母鸡啄的"。意思是:"就象软弱的公鸡经常被强壮的母鸡啄头部一样,男子慑于女性的淫威,总是服服贴贴"。这是一个相当古老的表达法,在 1690 年发表的德莱顿 (John Dryden, 1631～1700) 的喜剧《安菲特律翁》(*Amphitryon*) 中和 1712 年发行的杂志《旁观者》(*The Spectator*) 中都出现过。*Giles is a hen-pecked husband if there ever was one. His wife almost never lets him out of her sight.* 象贯尔斯那样怕老婆的丈夫,可以说世界上是绝无仅有的。他的老婆几乎永远不准他离开她的眼皮底下。*The trouble with you is you're too hen-pecked. At my house I'm the lord and master.* 你最糟糕的是太怕老婆了。我在家里是一品大老爷啊。《旁观者》杂志的总编辑和撰稿人艾迪生 (Joseph Addison, 1672～1719) 曾使用 the henpecked 这一形式。*Addison referred to men who let their wives dominate them as "the fraternity of the henpecked."* 艾迪生把那些让妻子骑在自己头上的男人们称为"怕老婆分子联谊会"。动词 henpeck 是由 hen-pecked 转化而来,意思是"对丈夫唠唠叨叨责骂不休"。*Mrs. Batttleaxe is a real ogre. She henpecks her husband all the time.* 巴图阿克斯夫人真是一个母夜叉。她一天到晚对丈夫唠唠叨叨责骂不休。这一表达法不仅用于妻子,也可以用于姐妹、女儿、甚至家族以外的人际关系。*Poor Mr. Milquetoast is henpecked not only by his wife but by his sisters and daughters as well.* 米尔克托斯特先生真可怜,不但受太太的气,而且受姐妹和女儿们的气。*Old Miss Biddy, who has been in the office for over thirty years, tries to henpeck all the younger employees.* 比迪小姐在我们公司已经有三十年以上的工龄了,这位老处女企图对所有年轻的工作人员颐指气使,施展她的雌威。◇ wife-dominated / dominated by *one's* wife

Henry

put *one's* John Henry on *something* [put ～ ˌdʒɑ(ː)n ˈhenriə(ː)n ～] [话] **亲笔签名** → put *one's* JOHN HANCOCK on *something*

hen's

be like pulling hen's teeth → TEETH

(as) scarce as hen's teeth → TEETH

herd

ride herd on *someone* [*something*] [ˌraɪd ˈhəːrdɔn ~] [口] **管束** herd 是大动物的"群"。本条的字面意义是"牛仔骑着马监督牛群"。*It's Luke and Randy's turn to ride herd today.* 今天该卢克和兰迪去牧牛了。作为比喻,主要用于对人进行监督,使其严守纪律的场合。*I enjoy my work as an elementary school teacher, but I'm always very tired in the evenings after riding herd on a roomful of rowdy pupils all day.* 我很喜欢小学教师这个工作,但是由于整天管束一屋子的淘气学生,到了晚上总是疲惫不堪。*I wish I could go to America, but I have to ride herd on a group of teachers going to Europe this summer.* 我虽然很想去美国,但是今年夏天我必须率领一群教师去欧洲旅行。不仅用于监督人,也用于对计划、工作、法案等实行监督的场合。*It's my job to ride herd on all the work in progress in the survey department.* 我的任务是在测量部监督正在进行的全部工作。*There is a special legislative assistant who rides herd on the bills in Congress that the President wants passed.* 国会里设有一个特别立法助理,专门监督总统提出并希望通过的法案。◇ supervise [oversee] *someone* [*something*]

here

Get out of here. → GET

Here goes! [ˌhɪ(:)r ˈgouz] [话] **我开始啦!** → Here goes NOTHING.

Here goes nothing. → NOTHING

look here and there (for *something* [*someone*]) [ˌluk ˈhɪrən'ðe(:)r] [口] **到处寻找** → look HIGH and low (for *something* [*someone*])

be neither here nor there [ni(:)ðər ˌhɪ(:)rnər ˈðe(:)r] [口] **无关紧要** 自古以来就有的表达法,在莎翁名剧《奥瑟罗》(*Othello*) 中就可以见到。字面意义为"这里那里全都没有",当然可以按照这一意义使用,例如:*If my book is neither here nor there, then where could it possibly be?* 如果我的书这儿没有,那儿也没有,那么它可能在什么地方呢?在实际上,象这种用法极为罕见。一般作为比喻使用。它的发展途径是:"这里没有,那里也没有"→"不是这个,也不是那个"→"当前,这个不成问题,那个也不成问题",也就是"在目前来说,某事对于某人无关紧要(怎么都可以)"的意思。言外之意是"重要的事情在别的方面"。*The amount of money is neither here nor there. The important thing is that you give something.* 钱数多少现在无关紧要。重要的是你得掏掏腰包。*He doesn't trust us, it seems. Well, that's neither here nor there. What I want to talk to you about is something quite different.* 他似乎不信赖我们。不过,那没什么要紧的。我要跟你讲的完全是另外的事情。*It seems they've offered to reduce the price if we permit delivery of the merchandise a week late, but that's neither here nor there. We must have delivery on time.* 如果我们同意晚一个星期交货,他们似乎可以降低价格,但现在这是无关紧要的。我们到期不进货是不行的啊。*A: Don't be angry. I'm sorry I can't keep our date, but I have an important meeting tonight. B: That's neither here nor there. You told me you wouldn't break this date no matter what!* 甲:请你别生气。我不能遵守约会,实在过意不去。不过,我今天晚上得参加一个重要的会议。乙:这不成为理由。你跟我讲过,不论有什么事情你都不会破坏这次约会呀! 如以上各例句中的"现在无关紧要"的说法那样,多用于表示"现在"的场合。但有时不是如此,仅在一般的评论中使用。例如:*Whether a mountain cabin has modern conveniences is neither here nor there to the real hiker.* 对于真正的远足者来说,山上小屋是否有现代化的设备,那是无关紧要的问题。◇ be immaterial

hick

a country hick [ə ˈkʌntri ˈhɪ(:)k] [口] **乡巴佬** 现在很少使用。Hick 是 Richard 的

昵称。在过去，乡村里姓 Richard 的人特别多，如中国的“张王李赵遍地刘”一样，所以 Hick 就成为“土包子”的代名词了。这是城市人对乡下人的称呼，含有相当侮蔑的意味。*I don't understand why my daughter wants to marry a country hick like Lem Clodhopper.* 我不理解，我的女儿为什么要跟莱姆·克劳德霍珀那样一个乡巴佬结婚。如这一例句所示，一般指男性。*Ever since the price of farm land went up, the city has been swarming with country hicks rubbernecking all over the place.* 自从田地价格上涨以来，城市拥满了乡巴佬，他们伸着脖子到处东张西望。省略掉 country 意思也不变。*Ask that hick over there how to get to the next town.* 你去问问那个乡巴佬，往下一个城镇怎么走。表示“乡巴佬”的名词另外还有很多，如 a bumpkin, a clodhopper, a hayseed, a yokel 等等。其中，按使用频率来说，本条的 country hick 与 bumpkin 并列第一，如果硬要区别二者意味的不同，则可以说前者是“土气”，后者是“粗鲁”。◇ an uncultured, country-bred fellow [person]

hick [ˈhɪ(ː)k] [口] **乡巴佬(似)的** 在过去，Hick 是 Richard 的昵称。乡下人姓 Richard 特别多。可能由于这个原因，就称“乡巴佬”为 a country HICK 了。意思是：“土里土气的理查德”。hick 可为名词，与 a country hick 同义，但主要作为形容词使用，意思是“乡巴佬(似)的”，“乡下的”，或者“土里土气的”。在使用时通常含有若干侮蔑的意味。*I wonder if there's a decent hotel in this hick town.* 我很怀疑，在这个土里土气的小镇里是否能有一家象样的旅馆。*Mr. Greenshade is the editor of some hick newspaper in Georgia.* 格林西德先生是佐治亚州某家土报纸的编辑。下一例句中的 hick ideas 是“象 a country hick 所想出来的土主意”。*I'm tired of that guy's hick ideas.* 我对那个家伙的土主意已经腻烦透啦。◇ countrified

hide

tan *someone's* **hide** [ˌtæ(ː)n ~ ˈhaɪd] [话] **痛打一顿** 这里的 hide 是“生皮”(raw hide)。本条习用语直译为“鞣生皮”。这是强调严重体罚的表达法。一般用于打孩子的场合，大多是用树枝或尺子打屁股或腿。不论怎样打法，反正这一表达法是指体罚。常用 really 加强语气。*My father really tanned my hide for disobeying him.* 因为我不听话，我爸爸把我狠狠地揍了一顿。有时不一定是真打，常作为恫吓的话使用，表示“我可不饶恕你”的意味。*Mr. Grumpy told us that if he found us playing ball in his yard again he would tan our hides.* 格兰皮先生对我们说，如果他发现我们再在他的院子里玩球，他要狠揍我们一顿。在应用于成年人的时候，也是作为恫吓的话，专对晚辈、下级的人使用，表示“给你点厉害颜色看看”的意思。*If he's late to work once more, I'll tan his hide.* 如果他上班再迟到一次，我要给他点厉害看看。另有 tan the hide off *someone* 的句型，直译为“鞣到剥掉皮的程度”，即“狠揍”的意思。*If you do that again, I'll tan the hide off you.* 如果你再做那种事情，我剥掉你的皮。此外还有 give *someone* a tanning 的说法，语调比 tan *someone's* hide 更软一些。在使用这一形式的时候，除 really 外，常用 good 加强语气。*The principal gave me a tanning for playing hooky.* 我因为逃学，受到校长的体罚。*Boys who behave like that should be given a good tanning.* 凡是有那种行为的男孩子，应该受到体罚。“受到体罚”这句话，除 be given a tanning (by *someone*) 外，还可以说 get a tanning (from *someone*)。*I really got a tanning from my dad.* 我被爸爸狠揍了一顿。◇ spank *someone* / make *someone* sorry

tan the hide off *someone* [ˌtæ(ː)nð ˈhaɪˌdɔ(ː)f ~] [话] 狠揍 → tan *someone's* HIDE

high

high [ˈhaɪ] [话] 喝醉了的 → be (as) high as a KITE

be (as) high as a kite → KITE

hit the high spots → SPOTS

be in high gear → GEAR

It's high time *someone did something.* → TIME

leave *someone* **high and dry** [ˌli(ː)v ~ ˈhaɪənˈdraɪ] [口] 把某人丢下不管 high and dry 直译为"高而干燥的地方",亦即"没有水的地方"。leave 是"丢下"。本条习用语本来的意思是:"大浪或潮水退后,把冲到海岸上的小船丢在那里搁浅了"。*The receding tide left the ship high and dry on the beach.* 落潮把船搁浅到海岸上了。把船搁浅到岸上,当然是使船处于极为困难的状态了。因此,这一表达法在应用于人的场合,常常具有"使处于困难状态"甚至"使处于进退维谷的状态"的含义。*The boys promised to help Betty work in the garden, but when the baseball game started on TV, they left her high and dry.* 男孩子们答应帮助贝蒂在花园里干活,但是当电视里开始播放棒球比赛的时候,他们就把她丢下不管了。*My date got angry at me and left me high and dry on the side of the street.* 我的约会对象生我的气,把我丢在街道上,甩头走了。*The woman's husband disappeared over a year ago, leaving her high and dry with three children to care for.* 那个女人的丈夫在一年多以前不辞而别,丢下她和三个小孩子不管了。*The students were left high and dry in a foreign country because the travel company that had promised to pay their return fare had gone bankrupt.* 那些学生被丢在国外了,因为答应付给他们回国旅费的旅行社已经破产。不仅人的行为,周围的情况也可以成为"被丢下"的原因。*The tremendous popularity of action novels has left the writer of more serious literature high and dry.* 由于情节小说的大肆泛滥,比较严肃的文学作家都被打入了冷宫。也有应用于人以外的事情的场合。*The new craze for tennis left the previously popular sport of bowling high and dry.* 最近网球风靡一时,使得过去十分流行的保龄球无人问津了。偶有不用 leave 一词的情况。*There I was, high and dry in a strange city with only five dollars in my pocket.* 我被抛弃在一个陌生的城市里,口袋里只剩下五美元。◇ desert *someone* / leave *someone* in a difficult position

look high and low (for *something* [*someone*]) [ˌluk ˈhaɪənˈlou] [口] 到处寻找 字面意义为"高处也寻找,低处也寻找"。与 look [search] all over (for *something* [*someone*])同义。虽然和 look [search] here and there (这里那里寻找)相似,但寻找的热心程度强烈得多。这是一个强调"拚命"的心情的表达法。大多用于要找的东西"找不到"的场合。*I've looked high and low for my watch, but I can't find it anywhere.* 我到处寻找我的表,但是怎么也找不到。*Where have you been? I've been looking high and low for you.* 你到哪儿去啦?我到处找你呢。动词有时用 search 代替 look,但在这一场合,与用 look 的时候不同,可在 search 的后边加"寻找"的场所,句型如下:search (*someplace*) high and low (for *something* [*someone*])。*The police searched (the house) high and low but were unable to find a single piece of evidence.* 警察把房屋的所有部分都搜遍了,但是未能找到一件证据。◇ look everywhere [very thoroughly]

hightail

hightail it [ˈhaɪ ˌteɪlɪt] [话] 急奔 这一表达法的来源是:兔子、鹿等在飞奔的时候,高高 (high) 竖起它们的尾巴(tail)。形象很生动,全速飞奔的动物的尾巴(内侧白色)仿佛就浮现在我们的眼前。it 没有特殊意义。*As soon as we heard the news, we hightailed it into town.* 我们一听到消息,马上跑进城镇去了。*Here's a dollar. Hightail it over to the store and* *get some flashlight batteries.* 这是一美元,赶快到商店去买几节手电筒用的电池。特别是逃跑的时候常常使用,在这一场合,多伴有 out of *someplace*。 *A red sports car was hightailing it down the highway with a police car on its tail.* 一辆红色的赛车在公路上急驰,警车在它后边紧追。 *When we heard a gun go off, we hightailed it out of there.* 当听到一声枪响的时候,我们急忙从那里逃走了。◇ run / hurry / go at high speed

a highway [ə 'haɪ.weɪ] [口] **交通干线** highway 一般译为"公路"。在美国,highway 一词指直接连结城镇的交通干线。"高速公路"叫 freeway ['fri:.weɪ]。"首都高速公路"专有一个名称,叫 expressway [əks'pres.weɪ]。交通干线大致有两种,一种是一般公路,即 highway; 另一种是高速公路,即 freeway; 而在英语中, freeway 的正式名称为 limited access highway, 某些地方又称"收税高速公路"为 turnpike ['tə(:)rn.paɪk]。 *How many highways are there between Beijing and Shanghai?* 北京与上海之间有几条交通干线? *I turned into the highway from a side road.* 我从一条支路驶入了干线。 *We went by highway number one.* 我们走的是一号公路。 *We were on the same highway all day.* 我们一整天都在同一的公路上行驶。 *I pulled off the highway.* 我把车停在公路旁边了。◇ a main road

hill

The grass is always greener on the other hill. [ðə 'græ(:)səz .ɔ:lweɪz 'gri:nər ɔnðɪ.ʌðər 'hɪ(:)l] [谚] **这山望着那山高** → The GRASS is always greener on the other side of the fence.

not amount to a hill of beans → BEANS

be not worth a hill of beans [nɑt .wə(:)rθə .hɪlə'bi:nz] [话] **毫无价值** → not amount to a hill of BEANS

hills

(as) old as the hills [ə 'zouldəzðə 'hɪ(:)lz] [话] **非常古老** 字面意义为"象 hills (山) 一样老"。人们认为 hills 自远古以来就一直保持同样的形态,因而用来作为古老的象征。 *That building is as old as the hills.* 那座建筑物太古老啦。 *I don't know how old Mr. Fisher is, but he must be as old as the hills.* 我不晓得费希尔先生多大岁数,但是他一定很老啦。如以上的例句所示,这一表达法用于强调建筑物、场所的"旧"或人的"老"。此外,多用于故事、趣谈、笑话等。在这一场合,不仅仅强调"旧",一般带有若干轻蔑的意味,即"陈腐"、"老掉了牙似的"。 *Everybody knows that story. It's as old as the hills.* 谁都知道那个故事,它已经老掉牙啦。 *Lem knows lots of jokes but most of them are old as the hills.* 莱姆知道很多的笑话,但是大多数都已经陈腐不堪了。另外,除戏谑的场合外,这一表达法不大用于汽车之类寿命不长的消费品。◇ extremely old

hip

shoot from the hip [.ʃu(:)t frəmðə 'hɪ(:)p] [话] **信口开河** 原意为"手枪在腰上挎着就射击"。这意思就是"没有很好地瞄准"。由此转用到人的说话上,便具有"不考虑说话方法和对方的立场"的意味了。 *Sorry I said that. I shouldn't have shot from the hip.* 我说了那种话,实在对不起。我不应该信口开河。如果仅说 Don't shoot from the hip. 则是"不要轻率发言"或"不要叫人抓住话把儿"的意思。在下边的例句中,除"信口开河"的意思外,还加上"说不上喷出什么话来"的含义。 *Watch out for that guy. He has a habit of shooting from the hip.* 当心那个家伙,他有随口往外乱喷的习惯。◇ speak without thinking / speak impulsively

hit

hit *someone* ['hɪt ~] [口] **(某人) 突然想起** → like a ton of BRICKS

a hit man → MAN

a scratch hit [ə 'skræ(:)tʃ 'hɪ(:)t] [口] **偶然安打** 棒球用语。这里的 scratch 本来是台球用语,即"球偶然进入袋中"。本条习用语指的不是由于打得准确,也不是由于守方失误，而是瞎猫碰见死耗子似的幸运的安打。 *Rose got to first base on a scratch hit.* 罗斯由于偶然安打而到达了一垒。◇ a lucky hit

hitch

go off without a hitch [ˌgou'ɔ(:)f wɪˌðaudə 'hɪ(:)tʃ] [话] **非常顺利地进行** go off 本身就是一个习用语，意思是"(事情)进行"。*Things went off beautifully.* 事情进行得很好。如这一例句所示，一般用于"直到最后都很顺利"或"完满成功"的场合。hitch 是"钩住"、"挂住"、"套住"。例如传送带正在顺利运转，忽然被什么东西挂住了，这就叫 hitch。因此，without a hitch 是"没有什么东西挂住"，亦即"毫无阻碍，极为顺利"的意思。 *Our plans went off without a hitch.* 我们的计划进行得非常顺利。 *Their trip went off without a hitch until they ran into a snowstorm in the mountains.* 在山中遇到暴风雪之前，他们的旅行是一帆风顺的。根据上下文，go off 有时可以省略。 *A: How did everything go off? B: Without a hitch.* 甲：事情进行得怎么样？乙：一切顺利极啦。有时可以用 go off 以外的动词。 *We completed the job without a hitch.* 我们非常顺利地干完了那个工作。 *It came off without a hitch.* 那件事是一帆风顺。 *The gang brought off the train robbery without a hitch.* 那帮匪徒十分顺手地抢劫了火车。◇ go very smoothly

hitched

get hitched [ˌget 'hɪtʃt] [话] **结婚** hitch 是"用绳子拴住"。加上 get，就成"被拴住"了。原为地方方言，后来作为戏谑语，在标准话中也常常使用。 *Let's get hitched.* 咱们结婚吧。 *Jack and Betty got hitched last week.* 杰克和贝蒂上个星期结婚了。◇ get married

hog

eat high off [on] the hog [ˌi(:)t ˌhaɪɔ(:)fðə / ˌhaɪɔ(:)nðə 'hɔ:g] [话] **生活富裕** hog 是"猪"。猪身上最好的肉，如 loin (腰肉)，roast (适于烤肉的嫩肉)等，均在脊背的高处。这就是本条习用语的来源，直译为"吃猪身上高处的肉"。off 和 on 均常使用，而且可以自由替换。 *The Joneses have been eating high off [on] the hog ever since Mr. Jones' book became a best seller.* 自从琼斯先生的著作成为一部畅销书以后，琼斯一家就过着富裕的生活。eat 可以换成 live。 *Most Washington politicians live pretty high off [on] the hog.* 华盛顿的大多数政客都过着非常富裕的生活。也可以把 high 换成 low，而说 eat [live] low off [on] the hog，直译为"吃猪下身的肉"，带有开玩笑的成份。意思是"勒紧腰带，过着拮据的日子"。 *With the inflation rate so high, we're going to have to start eating lower on the hog.* 由于通货膨胀率太高，我们不得不勒紧腰带，过俭朴的生活。◇ live well / enjoy an affluent life

eat like a hog [ˌi(:)t laɪkə 'hɔ:g] [话] **狼吞虎咽** hog 是"猪"，但与 pig 相比，有大而肥的形象。例如"小猪"，只能说 a little pig，而不能说 a little hog。两者是同一种类的东西，但在语言形象上是有差别的。也有 eat like a pig 的说法，这是 eat sloppily 的意思，指完全不晓得吃饭的规矩，象猪吃食一样，瞎拱一阵。 *Don't eat like a pig.* 不要象猪吃食那样没规矩。eat like a hog 可以说是把 eat like a pig 与 eat like a HORSE (吃得非常多)合在一起的表达法，也就是不但"没有规矩"，而且"吃得非常多"。 *I don't mind your eating like a horse, son, but you mustn't eat like a hog.* 小家伙，你吃多少我都不在乎，但是不要象猪拱食一样没个规矩。 *It's easy to see why Mr. Smith looks like a hog. He eats like a hog.* 很容易看出来史密斯先生为什么象一只大肥猪，他吃饭的时候狼吞虎咽，没个规矩，就象只肥猪。◇ eat huge amounts in a sloppy manner

go (the) whole hog [ˌgou(ðə) 'houl 'hɔ:g] [话] **干到底** 在 17 世纪的英国，hog (猪)作为俚语，有"先令"的意思。也就是说，go the whole hog 的原意为"把整个一个先令都用光吧"。后来转作比喻使用，表示"一直要追求到最后阶段"

的意思。定冠词可有可无,在会话中以不加为好。*After discussing for many days where to go on our vacation, we decided to go the whole hog and take a trip around the world.* 关于放假期间到什么地方去的问题,我们讨论了许多天,最后终于决定一不做二不休,来个周游世界的大旅行。*Whenever Chet takes up a new hobby, he goes whole hog.* 切特只要迷上什么新的玩意儿,他就一心扑在那上面。*At first I was only going to write a short story about it, but, after consideration, I decided to go the whole hog and write a book instead.* 关于那个题材,最初我只打算写一个短篇小说,可是经过仔细考虑以后,我决定一不做二不休,干脆写成一本书了。有象下面这样轻松的用法。*I know it's good chicken, but you don't have to go whole hog. Leave some for the rest of us, will you?* 我知道那鸡肉的味道很香。但是你不应该一扫光啊。给我们几个人留点儿好不好? ◇ throw off all restraints / do a complete and thorough job of it / eat everything

hog the road → ROAD

live high off [on] the hog [.lɪ(:)v .haɪɔ(:)fðə / .haɪɔ(:)nðə 'hɔ:g] [话] **过阔绰的日子** → eat high off [on] the HOG

make a hog of *oneself* [.meɪkə 'hɔ:gəv ~] [话] **贪得无厌** → make a PIG of *oneself*

a road hog [ə 'roud .hɔ:g] [口] **在马路上乱开车、妨碍后边车辆行驶的司机** → hog the ROAD

hold

hold out [.hou*l*'daut] [口] **维持** → STICK 'it out

hold *one's* **own** → OWN

hold *someone* [*someplace*] **up** [.hould ~ 'ʌp] [口] **持枪抢劫** → STICK 'em up.

holdup

a holdup [ə 'hou*l*'dʌ(:)p] [口] **持枪抢劫** → STICK 'em up.

hole

an ace in the hole → ACE

in the hole [ɪnðə 'houl] [话] **亏空** 最初的构思是:在"地面"为零,地上算作加,地下(洞)算作减,亦即负号。经济用语,特别应用于"金钱"。动词一般用 be 或 go [get],说 be in the hold (正在亏空)或 go [get] in the hole (形成亏空)。有时用 put ~ in the hole 的形式,例如: *That project put our company in the hole.* 那项计划使我们公司亏空了。很多场合象以下两个例句那样,具体示明金钱的数额。*I went almost a million yuan in the hole on that deal.* 在那笔交易中,我损失了将近一百万元。*I was twenty dollars in the hole until that hand.* 在来那把牌之前,我输了二十美元。可用 deep 或者 way 加强语气。*I can't afford to borrow any more money. I'm already deep in the hole.* 我不能再借一点钱了。我已经亏空太多了。有时不直接用于"金钱"而用于游戏、比赛的分数,在这一场合指的是输了多少分。*Tom has the worst score. He's thirty-five points in the hole.* 汤姆的得分记录最糟糕。他是负 35 分。另外,这一表达法又作为棒球用语使用,表示"分数被追赶上"的意思。*The count is three and oh, and the pitcher suddenly finds himself in the hole.* 投手三次不得分,他的分数马上要被追上啦。这是球类比赛讲解员的台词。*The batter is in the hole at oh and two.* 击球员两次不得分,他的分数要被追上啦。◇ in a minus position financially / in the red / minus ((在数字之前)) minus / behind

be (like) a round peg in a square hole [(laɪk)ə .raun*d*'pe(:)g ɪnə .skwe(:)r 'houl] [口] **对工作、环境等不适合** ◇ be (like) a square PEG in a round hole

be (like) a square peg in a round hole → PEG

hollow

have a hollow leg → LEG

Holy

Holy cats [mackerel, Moses, smoke]! ['houli 'kæ(:)ts / 'mæ(:)krəl / 'mouzəs / 'smouk] [话] **哎呀,天哪!** → Holy cow!

Holy cow! → COW

home

bring home the bacon → BACON

bring home to *someone something* [ˌbrɪŋ ˈhoumtə ~] [口] **使人深切体会** 字面意义为"给在家 (home) 的 *someone* 带来 *something*"。home 一般来说是人最宝贵的场所。这一表达法最初的构思是:"使 *someone* 深切体会到 *something* 对于最宝贵的家是很有影响的事物"。因此,这一表达法不仅意味着"使人在头脑中很好地理解",而且意味着"使人深切地感受到"或者"使人切身地体会到"。*The lawyer's attitude brought home to me the seriousness of the charge against me.* 律师的态度使我深深地感到对我的控告的严重性。*The loss of nearly all our funds brought home to us the need for greater caution when investing in the commodities market.* 我们几乎损失了所有的资金,这使我们深切地体会到:在向商品市场投资的时候,我们必须格外多加小心。另外,这一表达法是一习用语,通常采取 bring home to *someone something* 的形式,但是,如果代入 *something* 的语句很短,也可以采取 bring *something* home to *someone* 的形式。例如:*I tried to bring the magnitude of Jimmy's stupidity home to him.* 我试图使吉米深切体会到他糊涂到了什么程度。◇ make *someone* realize (keenly) *something*

eat *someone* **out of house and home** → HOUSE

hit home [ˌhɪt ˈhoum] [口] **击中要害** → strike HOME

be nothing to write home about [ˌnʌθəntə ˌraɪtˈhou məˌbaut] [话] **没什么了不起** 直译为"不值得写在住宅上"。但是使用这一表达法时,与写字并没有特殊关系。*The food at that restaurant is not bad, but it's nothing to write home about.* 那家餐厅的饭菜不坏,但是也没有什么了不起。*It was an interesting play, but certainly nothing to write home about.* 那出戏很有意思,但是并没有什么了不起的地方。*I certainly don't know why she wants to marry him. He's as ugly as sin, and his brains are nothing to write home about.* 我简直不明白她为什么想跟那个男人结婚。论相貌,其丑无比;论头脑,也是稀松平常。如以上的例句所示,几乎全用于否定句。但有时用 something 代换 nothing,意思变成"实在应该大书特书",亦即"真是好极啦"。*Our visit to New York was really something to write home about.* 我们到纽约去游览,实在是美不胜收。*Did you meet Jack's girl? She's something to write home about.* 你见过杰克的女朋友了吗? 她简直好极啦。◇ be nothing remarkable

be something to write home about [ˌsʌ-mtə ˌraɪtˈhou məˌbaut] [话] **好到了极点** → be nothing to write HOME about

strike home [ˌstraɪk ˈhoum] [口] **击中要害** 按字面意义,home 是"目标"、"要害";本条习用语为"枪弹打中目标"。*The first shot missed, but the second struck home and the man toppled from his horse.* 第一枪没有打中,第二枪打中了目标,那个男子从马上掉下来了。作为比喻,意思是:**"我说的话恰恰击中对方的要害,从而得到所期望的反应"**。*When I saw the look of consternation on her face, I knew my words had struck home.* 当我见到她脸上的狼狈表情时,我知道我的话已经击中了要害。*The President struck home with his warning that our children may have to study in cold classrooms next winter if we do not conserve oil now.* 总统警告说,如果我们不节约石油,明年冬天我们的孩子们在教室里就得挨冻,这话打动了我们。有时说 hit home。◇ have the intended effect / evoke a strong psychological response

home ec [ˌhoˈme(ː)k / ˈhouˈmeːk] [话] **家政学** home economics [ˌhou. mekəˈnɑ(ː)mɪks] 的缩略。高中和大学生用语。*She's majoring in home ec.* 她的专业是家政学。*I wonder why boys don't have to take home ec.* 不知道为什么男生可以免修家政学。◇ home economics

honcho

a honcho [ə ˈhɑ(:)nˌtʃou] [话] **头儿** 语源是日语"班长"。日语的"班长"本应拼写为 hancho,但美国人对 hancho 的发音为 [ˈhæ(:)n.tʃou],离日语的原音过远,反倒不如 honcho 与原音相近。这是驻日美军官兵带回本国的一个广泛使用的表达法,使用者为比较小的机关团体的成员,含有亲密的意味。一般指特定的人,因此大多加定冠词 the。*I don't know. Ask Dick. He's the honcho.* 我不知道。你问问迪克,他是头儿。*Okay, I'll do it. I don't like the idea, but you're the honcho.* 好啦,我去干。我不喜欢这个主意,但是你是头儿呀。也常使用 *one's* honcho 的形式。*Who's your honcho?* 你们头儿是谁? 在呼喊的时候,当然不加冠词。*Hey, honcho! Where do you want us to put this stuff?* 喂,头儿! 这东西放在哪儿好啊? 一般指头儿的场合,说 a honcho。例如在下一例句中,a good honcho 的意味是:"作为所谓的头儿,他是个好的"。*I don't mind taking orders from Graham. He's a good honcho.* 我不担心接受格雷厄姆的命令,他是一个好头儿。有时在说笑中称大公司的董事长或总统为 honcho,具有非常轻松的意味。例如: *He's the new honcho of General Motors.* 他是通用汽车公司的新董事长。*Both of J.F. Kennedy's brothers dreamed of becoming the big American honcho.* 约翰·富·肯尼迪的两个弟弟都曾梦想当美国的总统。◇ a boss

honest

(as) honest as the day is long → DAY

make an honest woman of *someone* → WOMAN

hoof

hoof it [ˈhufit] [话] **一步一步地走** hoof 本来是有蹄动物的"蹄子",后用于指人的"脚",这是一个轻松的说法。又以 hoof it 这样一个固定的词组作为动词使用。这一表达法表示"不愿意走而又必须走"的无可奈何的心理状态,大多用于"本来有交通工具前往一个远地方,但由于某种原因不得不徒步走去"的场合。*When our car broke down, we had no choice but to hoof it to the next town.* 当我们的汽车发生故障的时候,我们没有别的办法,只好一步一步地向下一个城镇走去了。*The last bus has already left. I guess we'll just have to hoof it.* 末班公共汽车已经开走了。我看,咱们只好一步一步地走啦。不仅用于实际距离远的场合,也可以用于在心理上感觉远的场合。例如,距离车站不远,徒步只需 5~10 分钟,一般来说,走着去并不算啥,但是由于下瓢泼大雨,走着去就显得太远了。这种场合就想叫一辆出租汽车。*You can wait for a taxi if you want to. I'm going to hoof it.* 你想等出租汽车,那你就等吧。我决定步行啦。这意思很明显:虽然讨厌走,但是久等更不耐烦。另外,hoof it 又用于表示"跳舞"(dance)的意思。*Cal's cousin hoofed it for over ten years in that theater.* 卡尔的表妹在那个剧院当舞蹈演员已经有十多年了。如这一例句所示,一般用于职业舞蹈演员,但有时也用于非职业的跳舞者。不过,由于职业舞蹈演员一般是在狭窄的舞台上跳舞,因此在用于非职业的跳舞者时,也具有舞池不大的意味。例如: *There were two or three couples hoofing it around the dance floor.* 有两三对舞伴在舞池里旋转。总而言之,这一表达法绝对没有大型舞会那样你拥我挤的印象。顺便提一下: a hoofer 是"职业舞蹈演员"的意思。*She is a hoofer in the opera house.* 她是一位歌剧院的舞蹈演员。◇ walk

hoofer

a hoofer [ə ˈhufər] [话] **职业舞蹈演员** → HOOF it

hook

by hook or crook [ˌbaɪ ˈhukər ˈkru(:)k] [口] **千方百计地** hook 是"钩子",crook 为 shepherd's crook,即"牧羊人的曲柄杖"。本条直译为"hook 也用,crook 也用",听起来令人莫明其妙。原来,在英国的封建时代有这样的风习:佃农在打柴的时候不准砍树,但允许在 hook 或 crook 所能达到的高度取树上的枯枝。

这一表达法根据上下文也有表示"用不正当手段"的场合,但原来并没有那种意思。大概是后来 crook 又带有 crooked ['krukɪd] (不正当的)的意味,于是,本条习用语也象现在这样具有"不择手段"的意味了。 by hook or crook 与另一习用语 by fair means or foul (用正当手段也好,不正当手段也好)大致同义,但后者直接表示用不正当的手段,而前者则含有"如果用合法手段能行就用合法手段,实在不行再采取非法手段"的意思。这一表达法更具有会话的气氛,常用于表示"不达到目的决不罢休"的坚强意志。 *I'll get into that school by hook or crook.* 我要想尽一切办法考入那个学校。*Their team was determined to win the game by hook or crook.* 他们那个队下了决心,千方百计地要在比赛中取胜。为了加强语气,crook 的前面也增添个 by。*By hook or by crook, we've got to get that information.* 我们不管用什么手段,必须把那个情报搞到手。◇ by whatever means necessary

get *someone* **off the hook** [ˌget ~ ˌɔ(:)fðə 'hu(:)k] [话] **使某人脱离困境** 这一表达法原来的构思是:"不把钓上来的鱼放到鱼笼里,而摘下钩(hook) 将它放跑"。hook 作为比喻,是"陷入必须去干自己不愿意干的事情的困境"的意思。 *We were about to lose our house because we couldn't meet the payments, but a friend got us off the hook by lending us some money.* 由于我们无法偿还贷款,房子险些就要失掉了,幸好有一位朋友借给我们钱,使我们摆脱了困境。*I was supposed to make a speech tonight, but my boss got me off the hook by calling up and telling them I had to work.* 我今天晚上必须去做一次演讲,幸亏我的上司给对方打电话,说我有工作要完成,才算使我摆脱了困境。*My wife expects me to take her to the opera tonight. I wish there were some way I could get off the hook.* 我的妻子期待着我今天晚上领她去看歌剧,有个什么妙计打退堂鼓才好啊。还有一个 let *someone* off the hook 的说法,意思是"免除某人去干他不愿意干的事情"。*If you'll let me off the hook this time, I'll do a favor for you someday.* 如果你这一次饶恕了我,我总有一天会报答你的。◇ get [help] *someone* out of trouble [a difficult situation]

hook, line and sinker ['huk 'laɪnən 'sɪŋkər] [话] **完全地** hook 是"鱼钩",line 是"鱼线", sinker 是"鱼线的坠子"。本条直译为"连鱼钩带鱼线和坠子",这是"鱼吃食饵已经上钩"的夸张的表达法。*The big trout swallowed [took] the bait hook, line and sinker.* 大鳟鱼已经完全上钩了。但象这样按字面意义使用的情况极少,作为比喻使用的场合占绝大多数。例如: *The poor fool swallowed the story hook, line and sinker.* 可怜的傻瓜完全相信了那套瞎话。一般用动词 swallow (轻信,囫囵吞枣)搭配,但也有时与其他动词结合使用(→ swallow *someone's* LINE)。*A: Did he fall for our trick? B: Yep. Hook, line and sinker.* 甲:他上了我们的圈套了吗? 乙:是的。完全上套啦。FALL for *something* 是"上当"的意思。*The facts seem to indicate that he's on the up and up, but I'm not about to accept them hook, line and sinker.* 从事实上看,他似乎非常正直,但是我根本不相信那些事实。accept 是"承认"的意思。*It was a fantastic story, but he went for it hook, line and sinker.* 那本来是一个荒诞的故事,而他却完全信以为真了。go for 也表示"鱼向鱼饵扑上去"的具体形象。 ◇ completely / unquestioningly

on *one's* **own hook** [ən ~ ˌoun 'hu(:)k] [话] **依靠自己的力量[思考]** 字面意义为"用自己的鱼钩"。实际上表示三种意思:"独立地去干"、"按照自己的想法去干"和"自己负责去干"。*If you won't help me, I'll do it on my own hook.* 如果你不帮我的忙,我就依靠自己的力量去干。*A: Did his father set him up in business? B: No, he did it all on his own hook.* 甲:他的父亲在事业方面给他打下基础了吗? 乙:没有,他完全是靠自己的力量干起来的。以上两个例子都是"独立地去干"的意思。下面举两个表示"想法"

和"责任"的例子。*Someone must have asked him to come. He would never have come here on his own hook.* 一定是有人叫他来。如果按照他自己的意思,他是决不会到这儿来的啊。*A: Who gave you permission to do this? B: No one. I did it on my own hook.* 甲:谁许可你做这件事啦? 乙:没有人许可,我做这件事是由自己负责。如果不用 hook 而仅采取 on *one's* own 的形式,也具有"依靠自己的力量或思考"的意味,但用 hook 的表达法语气比较强烈。◇ on *one's* own resources [initiative]

hooky

play hooky (from school) [ˌpleɪ ˈhu(ː)ki (frəm ˈskuːl)] [口] **逃学** 这里的 hooky 的原形大概是 hook。hook 古时作为动词使用,可能有"开小差"的意味,至今在俚语中仍然残留着 hook it (逃走)的说法。 *When we saw the teacher coming, we hooked it out of there.* 当我们看见老师走来的时候,我们就一溜烟似地从那儿逃走了。这一表达法一般用于整天逃学到其他地方去玩的场合,而不能用于假托有病呆在家里的场合。典型的情况是:早晨假装上学走出家门,然后去游戏乐园之类的地方消磨时间,晚上又大模大样地回到家里来。*The truant officer caught the boys playing hooky.* 训导主任抓住了逃学的男生。*If I catch you playing hooky from school once more, you're going to be severely punished.* 如果我再一次发现你逃学,可要严厉处罚你。作为戏谑语,可以用于逃学以外的偷懒行为。*Don't count on Bill's being here. He often plays hooky from Saturday meetings.* 不要指望比尔会到这儿来,星期六的会议他是经常不出席的。另外,也可以拼写为 hookey。◇ not attend school

hoosegow

the hoosegow [ðə ˈhusˌgau / ˈhuːzˌgau] [话] **拘留所** 在美国开拓西部的时代,牛仔们模仿西班牙语 *juzgado* (法庭)创造的英语。现在不仅西部使用,整个美国都通行,但除西部戏剧或影片外,在使用时大多含有戏谑的成分。*Terry spent a week in the hoosegow for getting mad and punching a policeman in some hick town up north.* 在北方的某一个农村集镇上,特里由于一时发火,殴打警察,被拘留了一个星期。 *Brent is in the hoosegow because he lost his wallet and didn't have the money to pay for a speeding ticket.* 布伦特因为丢了钱包,未能付汽车超速的罚金,被关进了拘留所。the calaboose [ˈkæ(ː)ləˌbuːs]与本条条头一样,也是"拘留所"的意思,源出西班牙语 *calabozo* (土牢),同为戏谑语。 *Let's get out of this town. If the sheriff catches us, it's the calaboose for sure.* 咱们溜出这个城镇吧。如果叫保安官抓了去,肯定进拘留所。hoosegow, calaboose 二者一般均指"警察局的拘留所",但也有用于表示"监狱"的场合,例如: *He's a criminal who's spent almost half his life in the hoosegow [calaboose].* 他是一个罪犯,几乎在监狱[牢房]中度过了半生。另外,hoosegow 有时去掉 e 而拚写为 hoosgow。◇ jail

horn

blow *one's* **own horn** [ˌblou ~ ˌoun ˈhɔ(ː)rn] [话] **自吹自擂** → blow *one's* OWN TRUMPET

toot *one's* **own horn** [ˌtu(ː)t ~ ˌoun ˈhɔ(ː)rn] [话] **老王卖瓜,自卖自夸** → blow *one's* OWN TRUMPET

hornet

(as) mad as a hornet [əz ˈmæ(ː)dəzə ˈhɔ(ː)rnət] [话] **勃然大怒** → (as) mad as a wet HEN

horns

on the horns of a dilemma [ˌɔ(ː)nðə ˈhɔ(ː)rnzəvə dəˈlemə] [口] **进退两难** dilemma 的 *di-* 为希腊语,意思是"双重的",*lemma* 是"假定"、"前提"。本条的字面意义为"在双重假定的角上"。这里的 horns 系指拉丁文 *argumentum cornutum*(有角的争论)的"角"。*argumentum cornutum* 是由对方提出两个假定,你不论选择哪一个假定,在争论中都要输。这两个假定是两只"角",你硬要往上碰,必被刺穿无疑。因此,本条习用语只能用于不论你选择哪一条路也躲不开坏的结局的场合。也可以单讲 be in a dilemma,而本条条头则是更进一步强调的表达法。*I'm in a dilemma. Should I leave now and get wet, or wait for Sam to bring my umbrella and be late?* 我现在是进退两难啊。是现在就走挨雨淋好呢?还是等萨姆拿来雨伞而迟到好呢?这是 be in a dilemma 本来的使用方法,即内心为"选择"而烦恼。后来又进一步发展,与"选择"根本无关,只用以表示"困惑"的意义,例如:*I'm in a dilemma about the dinner. I don't have the money to buy enough to feed everyone.* 我正为晚饭发愁哪。我手里的钱不够给所有的人买吃的东西啊。on the horns of a dilemma 与此不同,只能用于为"选择"而烦恼的场合。*I was on the horns of a dilemma. If I left Jim alone he might die, yet if I didn't go and try to find help, we both might die.* 我当时是左右为难了。如果我把吉姆丢下,他也许会死,可是,如果我不前去求救,我们两个人大概都得一命呜呼。*Fred found himself on the horns of a dilemma. To say "yes" meant humiliation, to say "no" meant financial ruin.* 弗雷德陷入进退两难的境地了。如果说"是",就意味着屈服;如果说"不",就意味着破产。dilemma 的前边可以加形容词。*The knowledge that her beloved husband was a murderer put Jane on the horns of a horrible dilemma.* 简知道她所热爱的丈夫是一个杀人犯之后,陷入了极可怕的窘境。同样的表达法还有 between the DEVIL and the deep blue sea,意思、用法均相似,也常互相代换使用,但在意味上仍有一点不同。on the horns ~是"有充分的时间去进行思考",而 between ~则是"迫不及待,非赶快想个主意不可"。◇ in a position of having to choose between two undesirable options / in a serious predicament

take the bull by the horns → BULL

hornswoggle

hornswoggle *someone* [ˈhɔrnsˌwɑ(ː)gl ~] [话] **欺骗** → I'll be HORNSWOGGLED

hornswoggled

I'll be hornswoggled. [ˈaɪlbi ˈhɔ(ː)rnsˈwɑ(ː)gld] [话] **吓,真惊人!** 19 世纪上半叶在美国产生的表达法,语源不详。多少有点方言的味道。hornswoggle 意为"欺骗"、"哄骗",如说:*I was hornswoggled.* 我受骗啦。但这一意义很少使用,大多使用本条条头的形式。*I'll be hornswoggled! There are three legs on that chicken!* 吓,真惊人!那只鸡有三条腿!也可以采取如下的形式:I'll be hornswoggled if *someone* [*something*] + 过去时否定式。这是对否定式后面叙述的事实表示自己的惊异的反语表达法。*I'll be hornswoggled if he didn't give me a hundred dollars!* 太惊人啦!他居然给了我一百美元!*When I entered the room, I'll be hornswoggled if they hadn't taken all the furniture.* 我进屋之后大吃一惊,全部家具都被弄走了。I'll be darned (if ~), I'll be damned (if ~), I'll be doggoned (if ~), I'll be a monkey's uncle (if ~), 均按同样的意味使用。但有些人对 damned 一词感到讨厌,所以常根据具体情况改用该词的委婉说法 darned 或 doggoned。◇ I'm dumbfounded. / I was dumbfounded. He gave ~ [They had taken ~].

horse

back the wrong horse [ˌbækðə ˌrɔ(ː)ŋ ˈhɔ(ː)rs] [话] **下错赌注** 字面意义为"支持(back)并非胜利的马"。原为赛马用语。自己下了赌注的马一跑起来却完全不行,这就是本条习用语的来源。当然可以按照字面意义使用,如说:*Phil is an expert at losing at the races. He's forever backing the wrong horse.* 菲尔是赛马场上有名的输钱人物,他总是下错赌注。从结果来讲,他是"把赌注下在失败的马身上"了,所以人们常把这一表达法理解为"有意识地支持失败的一方"。其实不是这样,因为在下赌注时,他本来认为那匹马是会获胜的。本条习用语的正确意义应为"下赌注时选错了马"。在作为比喻使用时也是同样,务请读者注意这一点:在表示支持的当时,并未判明胜利或失败。一般英语词典往往释义为“支持失败的一方”或“支持软弱的一方”,严格来说,这是错误的。*Mike had expected Mr. Green to make him the next department head, but when Mr. Green failed to become president, he realized too late that he had backed the wrong horse.* 迈克本来指望格林先生上台后,能派他接任部长,但是,当格林先生未能当上董事长的时候,他才明白自己捧错了人,可为时已晚了。*The supporters of the enemies of Cao Cao soon discovered that they had backed the wrong horse.* 支持曹操的敌对者的人们,很快就发现他们选错了拥护的对象。支持的“对象”不一定总是“人”,“政策”、“计划”等均可。*When the Republicans were defeated because of their tax-reduction policy, they realized they had backed the wrong horse.* 共和党人由于提出减税政策而在竞选中失败之后,他们明白自己宣布的政治纲领是错误的了。有时可以说 bet on the wrong horse。◇ (mistakenly) support the wrong person [side, policy, plan, etc.]

bet on the wrong horse [ˌbedɔ(:)nðə ˌrɔ(:)ŋ ˈhɔ(:)rs] [话] **支持错了对象** → back the wrong HORSE

a charley horse [ə ˈtʃɑ(:)rli ˌhɔ(:)rs] [话] **抽筋** 据说 Charley 是一匹瘸腿的参赛马的名字,本条习用语即由此而来。此说正确与否不明。在体育运动中,常常由于碰撞处于紧张状态的肌肉而发生这种现象。但不限于跌打碰撞,在过度使用肌肉的场合也会出现抽筋。*The quarterback's injury was fortunately only a charley horse, so he was able to re-enter the game after only a few plays.* 四分卫幸好只是碰抽了筋,没过几个球,他就又能上场参加比赛了。*Take it easy on my arm. I've got a bad charley horse.* 别碰我的胳臂,它现在抽筋很厉害。get a charley horse 是“抽筋了”的意思。*I got a charley horse on my leg from falling on the ball.* 我由于跌倒到球上,大腿抽筋了。还有一个 give *someone* a charley horse 的说法。在孩子们一起游戏的时候,常常故意淘气,猛击别人处于紧张状态的胳臂或大腿上的肌肉,使其产生 charley horse。*Ow! You gave me a charley horse.* 哎呀,好痛!你把我弄抽筋啦! ◇ a muscle cramp (in ~)

eat like a horse [ˌi(:)tlaɪkə ˈhɔ(:)rs] [话] **吃的非常多** 如果一惯吃得多,这一表达法即相当于汉语的“肚子大”或“饭量大”。但 eat like a horse 也用于一时吃得多的场合。一惯吃得多的人,亦即“大肚子汉”,在英语中叫做 a big eater。如果讲经常多吃,可以认为 eat like a horse 与 be a very big eater 大致相同。*Ralph is not a big man, but he eats like a horse.* 拉尔夫身材不大,但是吃得非常多。*Since Tom joined the football team, he's been eating like a horse.* 汤姆自从参加足球队以后,他的饭量大得很。在这两个例句中,原文可以分别换成 ~ he's a very big eater. ~ he's become a very big eater. 意思相同。但是在下一例句中,如果代换就不合适了: *He's been eating like a horse all week.* 整个一星期,他吃得特别多。另外,这一表达法没有 eat like a PIG 那样的讽刺意味,可以安心使用。顺便提一下:与 eat like a horse 正相反的说法是 eat like a BIRD。◇ eat a huge amount

a horse biscuit → BISCUIT

(that's) a horse of another color [(ˈðæ(:)ts)ə ˌhɔrsəvə ˌnʌðər ˈkʌlər] [话] **那完全是另一码事** 直译为“那是一匹颜色不同的马”。相当古老的表达法。莎士比亚在《第十二夜》(*Twelfth Night*,1601) 中曾用 a horse of the same color (同样颜色的马) 一语表示“完全是一码事”的意思。本条的表达法似乎由此而来,但正确的语源不详。在会话中讲“那完全是另一码事”的场合使用。*I'm happy to send you on a trip abroad after you graduate from college, son. But if you want to stay and work there, that's a horse of another color.* 孩子,你从大学毕业以后,我很高兴让你到外国去游历一番。但是,如果你想留在外国长住和工作,那就完全是另一码事啦。*So you* want to be a doctor instead of an artist. Well, that's a horse of another color. 是吗？你不是想当艺术家而是想当医生啦。果然如此，那就完全是两码事了。常用 entirely 加强语气。*Of course, I said I could lend you a thousand dollars. However, if you need ten thousand, that's a horse of entirely another color.* 不错，我说过，我可以借给你一千美元。不过，如果你需要一万美元的话，那可就完全是两码事啦。也可以说 a horse of a different color，在这一场合，加强语气时除用 entirely 外，还常用 completely。*I told Tim we couldn't use him on the project, but if he's willing to work for nothing, then that's a horse of a completely different color.* 我对蒂姆说，我们不能聘用他参加这项事业，但是他如果自愿工作，不要报酬，那就完全是两码事啦。◇ (that's) a different situation

a horse opera → OPERA

look a gift horse in the mouth [ˌlukə ˈgɪftˌhɔrs ɪnðə ˈmauθ] [话] **对礼物吹毛求疵** 要了解马的年龄，先打开马的嘴看牙。当别人赠送一匹马的时候，立即打开嘴去观察，这是怀疑赠马者的好意的非常没礼貌的行为。人们常把这一表达法译为"对人家给的东西挑毛病"。当然，这样译也未尝不可，但是，在这一表达法中并没有"挑毛病"那样故意的性质，只是从第三者的眼光来看，"受赠者没有表示足够的谢意"；从受赠者本人来看，"若是给点别的东西就更好了"。一般使用时都含有这种得陇望蜀的意思。*A: This is a nice scarf Jim gave me, but I wish it were a darker color. B: Don't look a gift horse in the mouth. I'd be happy if a boy gave me any scarf.* 甲：吉姆送给我的这条头巾非常好，不过，颜色再深一点就好啦。乙：对礼物不要吹毛求疵吧。如果有男朋友送给我头巾，什么样的我都喜欢。在否定句中使用的情况占绝大多数。*Perhaps the present your father gave you for your birthday wasn't exactly what you wanted, but you shouldn't look a gift horse in the mouth.* 也许你父亲送给你的生日礼品不完全如你的意，但是对人家赠给的东西可不要吹毛求疵呀。不仅用于赠送的东西，也可以用于借用的东西。*The sweater they lent me was a little tattered, but it was a terribly cold day I wasn't about to look a gift horse in the mouth.* 他们借给我的毛衣有点开线了，可是那一天冷得厉害，我也顾不得吹毛求疵啦。除"具体的东西"外，也用于"无形之物"亦即"人家给做的事情"。*The ride the man offered me was only for halfway to my destination, but being cold and almost broke, I was hardly one to look a gift horse in the mouth.* 我搭那个人的车前往目的地，而他只送了我一半路程。可是天气很冷，我又几乎身无分文，也就没有吹毛求疵的资格了。◇ complain about something *one* receives (free) from someone

put the cart before the horse → CART

work like a horse [ˌwɔ(ː)rklaɪkə ˈhɔ(ː)rs] [话] **辛辛苦苦地干活** 具体形象是："象马拉车一样用力地劳动"。比较起来，这一表达法多用于男性，令人产生"满头大汗，拚命劳动"的感觉。*The part-time job I had with that construction company paid good money, but I had to work like a horse.* 我在那家建筑公司打零工挣的钱倒不少，但是必须卖命地去劳动。*Real estate prices are just too high. I work like a horse six days a week, and still I can't provide my family with a decent place to live.* 不动产的价格太高啦。我每个星期拚死命干六天的活，还不能为我的家庭弄到一处象样的住所。*Jim will go far in this company. He works like a horse on every project the boss gives him to do.* 在这家公司里，吉姆会步步高升的。不管领导交给他什么任务，他都拚命地去完成。如这一例句所示，也可以用于称赞他人的场合。不过，这一表达法总含有"做牛做马"的意味，如果用它来当面去称赞人就有点儿不礼貌了。另外，也有主要用于女性的表达法，即 work *one's* FINGERS to the bone。◇ work very hard

You can lead a horse to water, but you can't make him drink. [ˌjukənˌliːdə

ˌhɔrstəˈwɔːdər bətʃə ˌkæ(ː)ntˌmeɪkɪm ˈdrɪ(ː)ŋk] [谚] **带马溪边易,强马饮水难** 字面意义为"你能够把马引到有水的地方,但是你却没有办法逼它饮水"。也可以用 bring 或 take 代替 lead,但一般使用 lead。water 的前面有时加 the。这是一个古谚,在 1546 年约翰·海伍德 (John Heywood)所编的《格言集》(*Proverbs*)中就收有如下的谚语: *A man may bring a horse to the water, but he cannot make him drink without he will.*(without he will 在现代英语中应该说 if he doesn't want to)。现在,这一表达法仍在日常生活中广泛流行。 *I've learned that you can lead a horse to water, but you can't make him drink. Take my son, for example. We've provided all the best educational opportunities for him, and still he refuses to study.* 我可是体会到"带马溪边易,强马饮水难"的意思了。拿我的儿子来说吧。我们向他提供了所有最好的受教育的机会,可是他依然不肯努力学习啊。 *I'll talk to him, but he may not agree to do it. You know as well as I that you can lead a horse to water, but you can't make him drink.* 我要跟他谈一下,但是他很可能不答应去干那件事。你我都很清楚:带马溪边易,强马饮水难啊。 *You won't have to force him. Just lead him to the water. With an offer as good as this, he'll drink.* 你不要去逼他干。先把他往河边一领,给他这样的甜头,他会去饮的。◇ You can provide an easy opportunity for a person to do something, but you can't make him do it.

horselaugh

give *someone* **the horselaugh** [ˌgɪv ~ ðə ˈhɔ(ː)rsˌlæːf] [口] **哈哈大笑** horselaugh 直译为"马的笑",也就是"象马嘶一样狂笑"。大多针对那些胡说八道的人们使用。有用于实际大笑的场合,也用于有比喻的场合。 *When the candidate said that there wasn't a single dishonest politician in his party, the audience gave him the horselaugh.* 当候选人说他的党内没一个不诚实的政治家时,听众报以哄堂大笑。 *Whenever Archie Leach said that he planned to be a famous movie star someday, his friends would all give him the horselaugh.* 每当阿奇·利奇说他准备将来成为电影明星的时候,他的朋友们总是报之以哈哈大笑。(按: Archie Leach 为美国著名电影演员卡里·格兰特 <Cary Grant>的原名。)下面是作为比喻使用的例子。也就是说,尽管不是面对面哈哈大笑,在心里也是狂笑不已的。 *There's no chance of borrowing the money from a bank when you don't even have a job. They'd just give you the horselaugh.* 一个人没有工作,还要向银行贷款,那连门儿也没有啊,只会遭到他们的嘲弄罢了。◇ laugh mockingly (at someone)

horsepower

not spare the horsepower [nɑt ˌspe(ː)rðə ˈhɔ(ː)rsˌpauər] [话] **开足马力** → not spare the HORSES

horses

change horses in the middle of the stream [ˌtʃeɪndʒ ˈhɔ(ː)rsəz ɪnðə ˌmɪdləvðə ˈstriːm] [口] **在关键时刻换人或改变计划** 直译为"在河的中流换马"。如果换马,应该在渡河之前,到河的中间去换马,这是十分愚蠢的做法。在这里,horse 意味着"人"或"计划"等,middle of the stream 则指"一个事情正在热火朝天进行的时候"。 *That guy's always wanting to change horses in the middle of the stream.* 那个家伙老爱中途变卦。如这一例句所示,有时使用肯定句。但使用否定句或类似否定句的句型的场合占绝大多数,表示"事情正在进行,现在不能改变,很难改变,或者以不变为好"的意思。 *I realize now that we should have followed our original plans, but it's too late now. We can't change horses in the middle of the stream.* 现在看起来,我们按照原来的计划去干就好了。但是,后悔已经太晚了,我们不能中途再折腾啊。 *I know the team needs a new coach, but it's difficult to change horses in the* *middle of the stream.* 我知道球队需要一个新教练，但是现在很难换人啊。有时说 in midstream。*Though most of the board members saw that the president was ill equipped to handle the company's recession-related difficulties, they felt it best not to change horses in midstream.* 虽然大多数的董事们认识到现在的董事长没有能力克服公司由于不景气而带来的种种困难，但是他们觉得最好不要中途换人。◇ change plans [personnel, etc.] after work [the season, the recession, etc.] is in progress

get it straight from the horse's mouth (that ～) → MOUTH

hold *one's* **horses** [.hould ～ 'hɔ(:)rsəz] [话] **耐心等待** 原意为"用手抓住要往前跑的马的缰绳"。*A: Hurry up! Let's go! B: Hold your horses. I'll be ready in a minute.* 甲：别磨蹭啦！走吧！乙：你耐心等一下，我马上就来。*"Just hold your horses," the inspector said to the jostling reporters. "I'll answer your questions one by one."* "请诸位耐心等一下，"督察员对纷纷提问的新闻记者们说："我现在一一回答你们的问题。"如以上的两个例句所示，绝大多数用祈使语气。同时，象第二个例句那样，常加 just 一词。下面是一个非祈使语气的例子。*Jimmy is always too impatient. He's got to learn to hold his horses once in a while.* 吉米总是一副心急如焚的样子，他应该知道有时候要耐心等一会儿。一般来说，hold *one's* horses 是用以表示"耐心等待"的意味，但有时则用以表示"不要凭着一时冲动急着去干"的意味。*Now, just hold your horses. There is no need to lose your temper.* 喂，你等一下好啦，用不着急躁嘛。这意思就是说，你沉着地考虑一下，等考虑好了，该发脾气再发脾气。◇ be patient

not spare the horses [nɑt .spe(:)rðə 'hɔ(:)rsəz] [话] **(汽车)开足马力** 由 spare the [*one's*] horse 的说法而来。spare 是"爱惜使用"、"节省"的意思。因此，这一表达法直译应为"小心乘用，不要使马累着"。*The cowboy rode slowly in order to spare his horse.* 那个牛仔骑着马慢慢地走，怕累坏他的马。not spare the horses 则是把交通工具的引擎比拟为马，意思为"不用管引擎损坏与否，开足了马力往前飞奔"。请读者注意：在使用这一意义时，一定要用 horses（复数形式）。一般用于汽车。*Quick, driver, to the airport! And don't spare the horses.* 司机，赶快！去机场！开足马力！*Don't spare the horses. We have to get there by ten o'clock.* 开足马力！我们十点钟以前必须赶到那儿。也可以采取否定的形式，例如：*This is no time to spare the horses. We're already late for the meeting.* 这不是慢慢吞吞的时候。我们参加会议，时间已经晚啦。下面是与 be 动词结合的例子：*I don't know how fast he was going, but he certainly wasn't sparing the horses.* 我不知道车速究竟是多少，但是他肯定是开足马力了。偶尔有用于汽车以外的交通工具的情况，当然，这种交通工具必须有引擎。*This is a powerful boat. If you don't spare the horses, it'll do about thirty knots.* 这是一艘马力很大的快艇。如果开足了劲儿，每小时可行驶三十海里左右。horses 也可以改用 horsepower（马力），意思相同。*Don't spare the horsepower. Our plane leaves in less than an hour.* 开足马力！我们乘坐的班机离起飞不到一小时啦。◇ go as fast as possible / not dawdle / go full speed

play the horses [.pleɪðə 'hɔ(:)rsəz] [话] **沉溺于赛马赌博** 这里的 play 是由"游戏"一义发展而来，意思是"在游戏中进行赌博"。the horses 是"赛马(马)"。这一表达法经常用于赌博性的赛马活动。请不要与 play with the horses（骑马玩）混同。*He likes to play the horses.* 他喜欢赛马赌博。horseracing 也是"赛马"的意思，但是如果说 He likes horseracing. 并不一定含有"赌博"的意味。因为在这一场合，赌钱不赌钱完全是另一码事，它只意味着"我喜好赛马这一体育活动"，也就是"我喜欢看赛马和参加赛马"。为了避免混淆，在表示"赛马赌博"的时候，就使用 play the horses 这一表达法了。

His hobby is playing the horses. 他爱好赛马赌博。*Mr. Jones lost all this money playing the horses.* 琼斯先生在赛马场上输掉了所有的财产。→ play the MARKET ◇ bet on the (horse) races

Wild horses couldn't drag it from me. [.waɪld ˈhɔ(:)rsəz kudnt ˌdræ(:)gɪt frəm:i] [话] **我向天发誓,绝对保守秘密** 字面意义为"就是野马,也不能把它从我这里拉走"。"它"指"秘密"。当有人向你公开一个秘密并且叮嘱不要告诉别人的时候,你用坚定的口气说这一句话,意思是:"我对天地神明发誓,绝对不向其他任何人讲这件事。"相当庄重的用语。因为用"野马"一词,很象是男子的口气,其实女性也常常使用。*A: Promise me you won't tell anyone. B: Oh, no. Wild horses couldn't drag it from me.* 甲:你答应我,你决不告诉任何人。乙:哦,我不会说的。我对天发誓,决不泄密。◇ I'll never reveal it to anyone.

hot

blow hot and cold [.blou ˈhɑ(:)tn ˈkould] [口] **出尔反尔** 出典《伊索寓言》(*Aesop's Fables*)。故事大意是:半人半兽的森林之神 (satyr [ˈsæ(:)tər]) 遇见一个由于寒冷而向手上呵气的旅行人,就把他请到山洞里,招待他喝热菜汤。可是,那个旅行人对着热菜汤也是呵气。森林之神见到这一情况,就说"用同一张嘴又呵热气又呵冷气的家伙给我滚出去",把那个旅行人赶走了。多以"人"或"团体"为主语。*Gene blew hot and cold over whether to accept the job or not.* 对于是否去干那个工作,吉恩出尔反尔,没个准主意。*The government blows hot and cold on the question of increasing the defense budget.* 政府在增加国防预算的问题上犹豫不决。根据上下文,也常有以 enthusiasm, ardor, feelings 等表示"心情"的名词为主语的情况。*A: Do you think Doris will go to Europe with us this summer? B: I don't know. Her enthusiasm blows hot and cold.* 甲:你认为今年夏天多丽丝会跟咱们去欧洲吗?乙:我不晓得。她的热情是随时有变的。*I don't know if Tom loves me or not. His feelings seem to blow hot one day and cold the next.* 我不知道汤姆是不是爱我。他的感情天天变化,忽冷忽热。另外,与本人的感情或爱好毫无关系,这一表达法也适用于人际关系之类可能有"忽冷忽热"现象的事情。*Our relationship with the Smiths blows hot and cold. For a period we'll get together often, then, for some reason, a year or more will go by without our seeing each other again.* 我们跟史密斯夫妇的关系忽冷忽热。有一个时期,我们常常见面,然后,不知因为什么,又一年多互不来往。◇ change *one's* mind back and forth / vary (from day to day)

be full of hot air [.fuləv.hɑ(:)ˈde:r] [话] **夸夸其谈** → be full of BEANS②

get hot under the collar → COLLAR

Hot diggity (dog)! [ˈhɑt:.dɪ-gɪdi / ˈhɑt: ˈdɪ-gɪdi ˈdɔ:g] [话] **棒极啦!** → Hot DOG!

Hot dog! → DOG

a hot potato [ə ˌhɑtpəˈteɪdə] [话] **棘手的问题** → drop *something* [*someone*] like a hot POTATO

be in hot water → WATER

it gets [things get] hot for *someone* [.ɪt gets ˈhɑ(:)tfər~ / ˌθɪŋzget ˈhɑ(:)tfər ~] [话] **日子不好过** → make it [things] HOT for *someone*

make it [things] hot for *someone* [.meɪk ɪt / ˌθɪŋz ˈhɑ(:)tfər ~] [话] **使某人日子不好过** it 或 things 是"情况"的意思。这一表达法最初的构思是:"把热度升高,使某人呆不下去"。"把热度升高"(加热)可以认为是"刁难"的委婉语。至于"刁难"的方法,则有各种各样,如使用暴力、找碴儿、令人难受等等。*Stay out of our territory or we'll make it hot for you.* 不要向我们的圈子里插手,否则我们会叫你的日子不好过。*Our section chief has been making things hot for me ever since I disagreed with him at last month's meeting.* 自从在上个月的会议中我不同意科长的意见以后,他一直给我小鞋穿。*I'm going to make it hot for the next guy that puts a frog in my bed!* 下一回哪

个小子敢往我的床上放青蛙,我一定不让他舒服了! hot 前面也可以加修饰语。 *The cops have been making things pretty hot for us recently.* 最近,警察大找我们的麻烦。可以用 it 或 things 作主语,构成 it gets [things get] hot for *someone* 这一表达法,意思是"日子不好过"。 *It got too hot for us to stay in Europe once the Nazis got wind of our activities.* 自从纳粹分子听到有关我们活动情况的风声后,我们便很难在欧洲呆下去了。 *Things are going to get hot for you around here if you try to interfere again.* 如果你再要捣乱的话,你在这里就不会有好日子过了。◇ make the situation [make things] uncomfortable [difficult, dangerous] for *someone*

not so hot [ˈnɑ(ː)tˌsou ˈhɑːt] [话] **不大好**

hot 是口语,意思为"极好"、"极棒"。 *The pitcher is hot tonight.* 在今天晚上的棒球比赛中,投手棒极了。not so hot 与 not so good [well]同义,在以下的例句中均可互相代换,但 hot 的说法比较轻松一些。 *A: How did you do on the test? B: Not so hot. I didn't understand some of the questions.* 甲:你考试考得怎么样? 乙:不大好,有几个问题我不明白。如这一例句所示,这一表达法多在青年人的会话中出现。 *As a basketball player, he's not so hot. I could probably do better myself.* 他当篮球选手不怎么样,可能我打的都比他强。 *A: How do you feel? B: Not so hot. I think I have a fever.* 甲:你感觉如何? 乙:不大好,我觉得可能发烧啦。◇ not so well [good]

sell like hot cakes → CAKES

hotfoot

hotfoot it [ˈhɑtˌfudət] [话] **匆匆地走**

hotfoot 的字面意义是"热脚",原来主要是儿童搞的恶作剧。他们见到有人打盹儿,就偷偷地往他的鞋底与鞋帮之间的隙缝里插火柴,先插进有硫磺的头部,把尾部留在外边点火。当火烧到火柴头部的时候,打盹儿的那个人当然就醒了,他一边喊"好烫呀!",一边慌慌张张地用力跺脚,企图把火踩灭。大家见到这一情景,就笑得前仰后合。这种游戏的性质不太高尚。 *Slim is always sleeping at his desk. Let's give him a hotfoot. That'll wake him up in a hurry.* 斯利姆总是趴在书桌上睡觉。咱们给他来个"热脚"吧,那他就会一下子醒过来啦。从拚命往地面上跺脚的样子加以联想,后来就把 hotfoot 一词作为动词使用,表示"快跑"乃至"急走"的意思了。it 虚指情况,没有特定的意义。 *As soon as I heard of the accident, I hotfooted it to the hospital.* 我一听到发生了事故,就急忙奔向医院了。 *I can't get through on the phone. You'd better hotfoot it over there and see what's wrong.* 我打电话打不通。你最好赶快跑到那儿去,看看发生了什么事情。 *Hotfoot it over to the store and buy me some cigarettes, will you?* 你赶紧去商店给我买几盒烟好吗? 偶尔也有不用 it 的时候。 *As a special maintenance engineer working for an airline, my husband is always having to hotfoot around the country.* 我的丈夫是航空公司的专门维修工程师,总是急匆匆地在全国各地飞行。◇ hurry / run

hots

have the hots for *someone* [ˌhævðə ˈhɑ(ː)tsfər ～] [话] **(对异性)神魂颠倒**

the hots 为俚语,即 love 的意思。本条直译为"为某人而发热",是一种轻快的表达法。 *I've had the hots for Sally ever since last year, but she just won't give me a tumble.* 自从去年开始,我就为萨莉神魂颠倒,但是落花有意,流水却无情啊。 *A: I've got the hots for you, baby. B: Yes, I know. And for Mary and Sue and Sally and how many other girls?* 甲:宝贝儿,我非常爱你啊! 乙:是的,我明白。你不但爱我,还热爱玛丽、苏、萨莉以及其他许许多多的姑娘哪,是吧? *Watch out, Gil. I hear Sue has the hots for you.* 吉尔,注意点儿。我听说苏迷上你啦。可以用 get,说 get the hots for *someone* (迷上异性)。 *Talk about fickle! Estelle gets the hots for a different boy every few weeks.* 甭提多么水性杨花啦! 埃斯特尔每过两三个星期,就勾搭

上另外一个男朋友。the hots 又有 sexual desire 的意思，偶尔可以见到如下的用法：*That guy gets the hots for every girl he sees in a bikini.* 那个家伙一见到穿三点式游泳服的姑娘就心猿意马。◇ have strong feelings for *someone* / love *someone*

hound

an autograph hound [ə ˈnɔːdə,græ(ː)f ˌhaund] [话] **爱请人签名题字的人** autograph 是"亲笔签名"，hound 是"有瘾的人"(→a ~ HOUND)。二者合在一起，意思是"有瘾头去搜集著名演员、作家、音乐家、运动员等的亲笔签名的人"。*George is a dyed-in-the-wool autograph hound. He's collected the autographs of every pitcher in the Pacific League.* 乔治是一个地地道道的亲笔签名搜集家。太平洋联队的每个棒球投手的亲笔签名，他都搜集到了。有时并不特指搜集家，仅指请求名人签字的一般人。如说：*After the concert the rock star was surrounded by autograph hounds.* 音乐会结束后，摇滚乐歌星被请求签字的人们围住了。◇ an autograph collector [seeker]

a booze hound [ə ˈbuːz ˌhaund] [话] **酒鬼** BOOZE 是"酒"。hound 一般指"狗"，在这里是"有瘾的人"或"……迷"的意思。本条习用语的意思是"非常喜欢喝酒，一有机会就要狂饮的人"。*Stu is really a booze hound. He goes barhopping almost every night.* 司徒真是一个酒鬼。他几乎每天晚间逛酒馆。另有 a booze fighter 的说法，但比 booze hound 陈腐，不大使用。◇ (a person who) really likes to drink

a chow hound [ə ˈtʃau ˌhaund] [话] **贪吃的人** CHOW(→) 是"饭"，a hound 是"猎犬"。本条习用语指"大肚子汉，象狗一样一闻到食物的香味就馋的人"(→ a ~ HOUND)。戏谑语。*Chet is a real chow hound.* 切特简直是一个贪吃的家伙。*OK, you chow hounds, let's chow down.* 喂，馋鬼们！咱们来吃吧。有时写成 chowhound 一个词。◇ a glutton

a ~ hound [ə ˈ~ ˌhaund] [话] **……迷** hound 是"狗"，特指"猎犬"。因为猎犬热烈地追赶猎物，所以把它加在种种不同的词的后边，表示"热心追求……的人"、"有……瘾的"、"特别喜好……的人"、"……迷"的意思，如 an autograph HOUND, a booze HOUND, a chow HOUND, a news HOUND, a rock HOUND 等等。◇ a(n) ~ enthusiast

a news hound [ə ˈnjuːz ˌhaund] [话] **热心的新闻记者** 这里的 hound 是"热心追求……的人"(→ a ~ HOUND)。本条习用语多用于报纸的记者，但也可以用于广播、电视、杂志等的一切采访人员。*If there's any kind of a story there, Roy will find it. That guy's a real news hound.* 只要那里有新闻素材，罗伊总会采访到的。他真是一位热心的记者呀。如这一例句所示，常含有"热心"的意味。但也有时只是"记者"一词的轻松说法而已。*My brother is a TV news hound.* 我哥哥在电视台当采访记者。有时拚写为一个词，作 newshound。另外，由于 hawk (鹰)具有捕获猎物的锐利目光，所以又称 a news hawk，但这一表达法略有陈腐之感。◇ a(n avid) news reporter

a rock hound [ə ˈrɑ(ː)k ˌhaund] [话] **地质学家** rock 是"岩石"，hound 是"热心追求……的人"或"非常喜好……的人"的意思 (→ a ~ HOUND)。*My boy is a rock hound. He's collected almost every type of rock in this area.* 我的儿子热心搜集岩石。这个地区的各种类型的岩石，他几乎全都采集来了。如这一例句所示，这一表达法可以用于表示"作为趣味，热心搜集岩石的人"的意思。但是，在大多的场合为"地质学家"的戏谑语。*My father is a rock hound.* 我父亲是地质学专家。也可以用于以地质学为专业的学生。*We rock hounds are going on a field trip tomorrow.* 我们地质系学生明天出去进行实地考察。◇ a geologist

hour

every hour on the hour [ˌevri ˈaur ɔnðɪ ˈaur] [口] **每小时整点** every hour 是"每一小时"，on the hour 是"分针正指十二点的时候"。在英语的广播新闻、电视节

目、以及公共汽车和飞机等的时间预告中，每天会多次听到象条头这样的用语。*The express leaves every hour on the hour.* 快车每小时整点发车。*That station broadcasts the news every hour on the hour.* 那家电台每小时整点广播新闻。*The chimes in the tower ring every hour on the hour.* 那个塔楼上的钟每小时整点响一次。也常说 every hour on the half-hour (每半小时整点)。*The boat arrives every hour on the half-hour.* 船每半小时整点到达。也可以用 quarter (四分之一) 一词，而说 every hour on the quarter-hour (每 15 分钟整点)，但用者不多。◇ each time the minute hand points to twelve

house

the big house [ðə ˈbɪg ˌhaus] [话] **(美国各州或联邦) 监狱** 字面意义是"那所大房子"。必须用定冠词 the。原为黑社会用语，通过电影、小说等，现已家喻户晓。*Louie spent fifteen years in the big house.* 路易蹲了 15 年监狱。◇ the penitentiary

bring down the house [ˌbrɪŋ ˌdaunðə ˈhaus] [口] **博得满堂喝彩** house 为 play house，即"剧场"；bring down 是"使倒塌"的意思。本条直译为"由于人们热烈欢迎，鼓掌喝彩达到使剧场倒塌的程度了"。*That new comedian is very funny. He brings down the house wherever he appears.* 那位新的喜剧演员非常有趣。不管他在哪里演出，总博得满堂的喝彩。*The soprano's soaring aria brought down the house.* 那位女高音的响彻云霄的咏叹调博得了满堂的喝彩。另外，相当于 the house 的场所，也不一定非是"剧场"不可，大会堂也可以，社交晚会的会场也可以。*Jimmy's antics at the party last night brought down the house.* 昨天晚上，吉米在社交晚会上的滑稽表演博得了满堂的喝彩。但是，即使为社交晚会，如果受约请向全体到会人员表演的人没有"博得满堂喝彩"，那也不能用这一表达法。也就是说，在社交晚会上，如果只是与少数人一边闲聊一边做什么有趣的即兴表演，即便大受欢迎，一般也不能使用 bring down the house 来表达。另外还有 bring the house down 的说法。*Falstaff's last line in that scene never fails to bring the house down.* 在那一场中，福斯塔夫的最后几句台词永远博得满堂的喝彩。◇ make the audience clap and cheer (wildly)

a crazy house [ə ˈkreɪzi ˌhaus] [话] **精神病院** 字面意义为"疯子之家"，由此可以想象得出，这是一个戏谑的说法，主要是儿童们喜欢使用。与 the hospital 的场合一样，大多加定冠词。*If you don't stop picking on me, I'm going to call my daddy and have him put in you in the crazy house.* 如果你还要继续欺负我，我去叫我爸爸，让他把你送进精神病院。有时，孩子们用 a fun HOUSE(→) 表示同一意义。◇ an insane asylum

eat *someone* **out of house and home** [ˌi(:)t ~ˌaudəv ˈhausənˈhoum] [口] **吃光某人的家当** 直译为"由于吃得太多，使某人连房屋带家私都变卖了"。实际上，不管怎样"吃得太多"，也没有因此而"变卖"房屋和家私的情况。这一表达法只不过是强调"吃得太多"的一种夸张说法而已。多作戏谑语使用。出典是莎士比亚名剧《亨利四世》(*Henry IV*)下部第二幕第一场，奎克利夫人(Mistress Quickly)在讲述大胖子骑士福斯塔夫 (Falstaff) 时，有这样一段话：He hath eaten me out of house and home, he hath put all my substance into that fat belly of his. (他吃光了我的家当，把我的全部财产塞进了他的肥大的肚皮。) 在这一场合，当然也是夸张的表达法了。一般来说，house 指"房屋"，home 指"家庭"，但在这里，问题并不在于意义上的区别，只是为了追求 alliteration (头韵法) 的效果，将 house 的 h 与 home 的 h 并列，用以增强这句话的韵味。因此，这两个词合在一起，可作"房屋财产"解。*Our son is growing so fast he'll soon be eating us out of house and home.* 我家的儿子长得太快了，这样下去，他很快就会吃光我们的家当啦。这正如汉语俗话所说："半大小子，吃死老子"。*A mob of visiting rela-*

tives almost ate us out of house and home. 一大群亲戚前来串门儿，几乎把我们的家当全吃光了。*Our daughter may look small and delicate, but I pity the man she marries. She'll eat him out of house and home.* 我家的女儿看起来小巧玲珑，但是我可怜娶她当老婆的男人。她会吃光他的全部家当啊。如以上的例句所示，这一表达法只用于"吃得太多"的场合，不能用于"由于吃喝玩乐而荡尽家产"的场合。◇ eat so much as to make a pauper of *someone*

a fun house [ə 'fʌn,haus] [口] **游乐宫** fun 是"娱乐"，fun house 是"充满乐趣的房子"的意思。在游乐园中常常可以见到这样的建筑物，里边有倾斜房间、活动地板、哈哈镜等设备，令人惊吓而富有趣味。*Does that amusement park have a fun house?* 在那个游乐园里，有惊险的游乐宫吗？*We've still got a little more time. Why don't we visit the fun house?* 我们还有一点儿时间。为什么不去游乐宫里看看呢？◇ a special house with many amusingly tricky devices

a hash house [ə 'hæ(:)ʃ ,haus] [话] **经济餐馆** hash 原为动词，是"(把肉等)剁碎"的意思。后来进一步发展，用作名词，意思是"肉末菜泥"。由于 hash (肉末菜泥)是廉价小饭馆经常备有的、具有代表性的便宜菜，所以就产生了 hash house 的表达法。*I worked part time at a hash house when I was a college student.* 当我上大学的时候，我在一家经济餐馆打工。◇ a cheap restaurant

a house dick [ə 'haus,dɪ(:)k] [俗] **便衣侦探** → a DICK

a house of cards [ə ,hausəv 'kɑ:rdz] [口] **象用纸牌搭成的房子一样不坚固的东西** 儿童们常常用纸牌一张一张地搭房子玩，但是不论怎样加小心，稍微一碰就会房倒屋塌。由于原意为"认真搭起来的东西倒塌"，所以这一表达法总是以由许多因素组成的东西(如计划、组织、建筑物等)为对象。如下面的例句所示，大多使用 be a house of cards 或者 like a house of cards 的形式。*The plan proved to be a house of cards. It all came to naught once the bank withdrew its support.* 那个计划象用纸牌搭成的房子一样，只要银行停止贷款，便会全部垮台。*The company was held together by the president. When he died, it collapsed like a house of cards.* 那家公司是由董事长来维持的。他一死，公司就象用纸牌搭成的房子一样马上崩溃了。◇ a fragile affair

a johnny house [ə 'dʒɑ(:)ni ,haus] [话] **自家专用的室外厕所** 在没有抽水马桶的时代，每家是在住宅外边专修一个小的房子当厕所。这种厕所叫作 johnny house。现在，在美国的某些乡村中，还有很多使用 johnny house 的家庭。原是由 a JOHN (→)发展而来的表达法。*When my father was a boy, almost every home had a johnny house.* 当我父亲还小的时候，几乎每家都有室外厕所。*Our weekend place doesn't have running water, so we built a johnny in the backyard.* 我们的别墅没有自来水，因此我们在后院修了一个室外厕所。也可以说 an OUTHOUSE。◇ an outdoor toilet

like a house afire [,laɪkə 'hausə,faɪr] [话] **猛烈地** 直译为"象房子失火一样"。这一表达法是用火烧房子时的激烈和迅速来形容势头的凶猛。afire 是"正在燃烧"，与 on fire 相同。如以下的例句所示，本条习用语可以用于各种不同的场合。*With the deadline only two hours away, everyone was working like a house afire.* 到最后限期只剩两个小时了，每个人都拚命地在干活。*Enemy troops moved over that country like a house afire, and in only three months their government surrendered.* 敌军以排山倒海之势侵入那个国家，仅仅三个月，他们的政府就投降了。*The Republican Party is capturing votes like a house afire.* 共和党获得的票数猛增。afire 可以用 on fire 代换。*The last time I saw him he was running down the street like a house on fire.* 我最后一次见到他的时候，他正在大街上飞奔。◇ very vigorously [quickly, fast]

how

And how! ['æ:nd 'hau] [话] **可不是吗!** 首先请读者注意:And 和 how 的发音均为重音。 *A: I hear you're in trouble with the boss. B: And how! I forgot to tell him that he had an appointment at the White House yesterday.* 甲:我听说你跟老板发生矛盾啦。乙:可不是吗! 我昨天忘记告诉他白宫的约会啦。如这一例句所示,本条习用语是在强调对方所说的话时使用。And how! 直译为"并且(And)达到如何严重的程度啊 (how!)",拿上边的例句来说,如果在 how 的后边补充上 great a trouble I am in! 意思就容易明白了。在汉语中,相当于这一表达法的有"那当然啦!","那还用说!"等等。 *A: How's business? Pretty good? B: And how! We're making money hand over fist.* 甲:生意如何? 很好吗? 乙:那还用说! 我们发大财啦! *Am I broke? And how! I haven't even got thirty cents for a cup of coffee.* 我钱花光啦? 可不是吗! 连喝杯咖啡的三十美分都没有啦。◇ Very much so.

How come? [ˌhau 'kʌ(:)m] [话] **为什么?** 意思与 Why? 相同,为日常会话中经常使用的表达法。它与以 why 开始的疑问句不同,后边接续的文句不必改变词序,这一点很方便。例如: *Why isn't he coming?* 他为什么不来? 如果用本条的表达法,就说: How come he isn't coming? 也就是说,只要把 How come 放在肯定句的前边就行了。 *How come she wants to go mountain climbing in December?* 她为什么要在十二月去爬山哪? 另外,与 Why? (怎么?为什么?) 同样,人们也常常单独使用 How come? 另外,How come? 虽然令人产生比较轻松的感觉,但在实际上并不是新的表达法,而是旧语的残余。在过去的疑问句中,一般是把主语放在动词的后边。例如现代英语说 What did you go to see? (你去看什么来着?) 在古代英语中,这句话的说法是 What went you to see? 同样,现代英语说 How do you come to be here? (你怎么会在这儿?) 而在过去,一般的说法是:How come you to be here? 不知什么原因,在过去的造句法中,只有 How come 现在仍为活生生的英语,被人们频繁地使用。How come you are here? 是由上面的表达法演变出来的,但从规范语法的立场来讲,必须象 How come you to be here? 那样,How come 要求带 to 的不定式。有的语法学家认为 How come you are here? 的说法"不标准"。然而在实际会话中,一般人却不大使用前者,而把后者当作标准的表达法。◇ Why?

how-de-do

a fine how-de-do [ə 'faɪn ˌhaudi'du:] [话] **太糟糕啦! 太不象话啦!** → a fine HOW-DO-YOU-DO

a fine how-do-you-do [ə 'faɪn ˌhaudəjə'du:] [话] **太糟糕啦! 太不象话啦!** 直译为"良好的问候"。这是一句反语。在这里,fine 是"非常的"、"极糟的"的意思。本条习用语强调一种吃惊的心情,含有"天下竟有如此糟糕的问候"的意味。多用于对自己不利的事情,但基本上总是从客观的立场上来看的"糟糕"。常常使用 That [This, It] is a fine how-do-you-do. 的形式。 *This is a fine how-do-you-do. I apply for three day's vacation and your folks aren't coming to visit us after all.* 这真太糟糕啦。我告了三天假,结果你的父母并没有前来作客啊。 *That's a fine how-do-you-do. After all the taxes we pay, they're going to stop mail deliveries on Saturday.* 简直太不象话啦! 我们交了那么多的税,星期六居然停止送信。正中间的 do-you 可以按俗语的发音拼写,作 a fine how-de-do ['faɪn ˌhaudi'du:] (书写时亦可作 d'ye)。 *It's a fine how-de-do, if you ask me, when even college graduates can't get jobs.* 如果叫我说的话,连大学毕业生都找不到工作,那可糟糕透啦。◇an irritating turn of events

How's

How's about (*doing*) *something*? ['hauzə 'baut ~] [话] **你觉得怎么样?** 这是一个非常有趣的表达法。乍看起来,How's 很象是缩写,其实不是。大概由于说起来好听，才在 How about ～? 这一表达法中加一个不必要的 -'s。在日常会话中经常使用，与 How about ～? 的意思完全相同。 *How's about my speaking to the prof about it?* 关于那件事情，我向老师谈一下怎么样呢？ *How's about some Chinese food tonight?* 今天晚上吃中国饭怎么样？ *How's about minding your own business?* 你别管闲事好不好？ *How's about my calling Betty tomorrow?* 明天我给贝蒂打个电话好不好？ *How's about you and I getting hitched?* 咱们俩结婚好不好？ ◇ How about (*doing*) *something*? / What do you think of the idea of (*one's*) (*doing*) *something*?

hubby

one's **hubby** [～ 'hʌbi] [话] **丈夫** husband (丈夫) 的缩略变体。主要是女人们相互间使用。 *My hubby is simply crazy about football.* 我丈夫真是一个疯狂的足球迷啊。 *Her hubby is an insurance salesman.* 她的丈夫是保险公司的推销员。◇ *one's* husband

huh-uh

huh-uh ['hʌ.ʌ] [话] **不** 相当于 no 的轻松说法。用鼻子发出 [ʌ]，即在发音时好象在一瞬之间将声堵在喉内。 *A: Are you going? B: Huh-uh. (I'm not going.)* 甲：你去吗？ 乙：不去。又作 uh-uh ['ʌ.ʌ]。与这一表达法相对的是 UH-HUH，意思为 yes，在美国人的日常会话中同样经常出现。 ◇ no

human

a human dynamo [ə .hjumən 'daɪnə .mou] [口] **猛烈活动的人** → a BALL of fire

humble

eat humble pie → PIE

hump

get over the hump [ge.dou*v*ər*ð*ə 'hʌ(:)mp] [口] **飞过高山** → be over the HUMP

be over the hump [.ou*v*ər*ð*ə 'hʌ(:)mp] [口] **已经渡过难关** hump 有"山脉"、"驼峰"等各种不同的意义。作为航空用语，指"必须飞越的最高山脉"，如说：*It will be a fairly dangerous flight, but after you're over the hump the rest will be easy.* 这一段飞行相当危险，但是过了那个山脉，其余就没什么啦。转作比喻使用，hump 一般具"危机"、"难关"等意味。 *The negotiations have been extremely difficult, but we're finally over the hump. The rest is a matter of tying up the loose ends.* 谈判极端困难，但是我们终于渡过了难关。其余只是收尾工作了。 *The Prime Minister announced that though the recession had been long and difficult, the nation was at last over the hump.* 总理宣布说，经济萧条虽然时间很长，也很严重，但是国家终于渡过了难关。 *The patient is over the hump. If his fever stays down, he should recover completely in a couple of weeks.* 病人已经脱离了危险期。如果他不再发烧，有两个星期就可以完全康复了。 get over the hump 是"飞过高山"。 *If we can just get over the hump, the rest should be easy.* 只要我们能够飞过这座高山，其余的路程就轻松啦。 ◇ be over the most difficult part / be past the crisis

hunch

have a hunch (that ～) [.hævə 'hʌntʃ] [口] **预感到** hunch 是"直觉"、"第六感觉"，与 intuitive feeling 同义。 *A: What makes you think that? B: I dunno. Just a hunch, I guess.* 甲：你为什么会那么想呢？ 乙：不晓得。我想，这是第六感觉。 *My hunch was right.* 我的直觉应验啦。 *The hunch I had was off. The market went down instead of up.* 我的第六感觉错了。行情不是涨而是落啦。 *A: Why do you think she may have gone to New York? B: Oh. I just have a hunch, that's all.* 甲：你为什么以为她可能去纽约呢？ 乙：哦，我只不过是有这样一种直觉罢了。本条条头 have a hunch (that ～) 也是个定型的说法，人们常常使用。 *I have a hunch (that) it may rain tomorrow.* 我感觉到明天可能有雨。常用 strong 加强语气。 *I have a strong hunch* *that Mr. Shady may not show up tonight.* 我总觉得谢迪先生今天晚上可能不会露面。◇ have a feeling (that ~)

play a hunch [ˌpleɪə ˈhʌntʃ] [口] **靠着直觉去试试看** 这里的 hunch 是"预感"、"直觉"的意思。同样的表达法有 act on a hunch, 在只表示"靠着直觉去干"的场合,用这一表达法比较合适。本条条头中的 play 有"打赌"或者"试试看"的意味。play a hunch 不是用于"如果有了直感,干一下试试看"的场合,而是用于"靠着已经有的直觉,干一下试试看"的场合。I've always played my hunches. 的意思不是"我一向是靠着自己的直觉去行动",而是"在有直觉的时候,我总是靠着它去行动"。因此,务请读者注意这一表达法的确切用法,在讲"如果不知道,就靠直觉去干"(If you don't know, follow your feelings [intuition].) 的场合不能使用。*I'm not sure, but I'm going to play a hunch.* 我没有什么把握,但是我要靠着直觉去干一下试试看。*I played a hunch and won three thousand dollars on a long shot.* 我靠着直觉下了一次大赌注,结果赢了三千美元啊。特别是在作一般论的场合,如说"搞赌博这玩艺儿,必须学会靠着直觉去碰运气"(A gambler has to learn to play his hunches.) 大多用 play *one's* hunches 的形式。*If you want to be a successful detective, you should always play your hunches.* 如果你想当一个了不起的侦探,就必须永远在有了直觉的时候马上去试试看。另有 play *someone's* hunch 的形式,意思是"靠着某人的直觉去试试看"。*I think we ought to play Lew's hunch. He's got more experience in this field than we have.* 我认为我们应当靠着卢的直觉去干一下试试看,因为他在这方面的经验比我们丰富。◇ act on *one's* feelings [intuition]

hunky-dory

be hunky-dory [ˌhʌŋkiˈdo(ː)ri] [话] **挺不错** hunky-dory 表示"很满意"或"没说的"的心情,是一个非常轻松的表达法,为专与 be 动词搭配使用的形容词。*A: How do you like your new job? B: So far everything's hunky-dory.* 甲:你的新工作怎么样? 乙:到目前为止,一切都挺不错。关于 hunky-dory 的语源,有好几种说法:①原为美国南北战争时期 Christy Minstrels (化装黑人乐队)所唱的歌的歌词。②过去,美国海军的舰艇在日本横滨的港口停泊时,士兵们常到横滨最主要的大街"本町通 (Honcho-dori)去游逛。只要一到那条大街,吃喝玩乐,一切都"挺不错"。而这 Honcho-dori 到了美国人嘴里,就变成 hunky-dory 了。此外还有一些语源说。其中,②的说法似乎是可信的。在实际会话中,常用 just 加强语气。*A: If you don't like your room, I'm sure the hotel will change it for you. B: No, this is just hunky-dory. Much better than I expected.* 甲:如果你不喜欢这个房间,旅馆肯定会给你换一个房间的。乙:不,这一间就挺不错的,比我所预料的强多啦。*Waitress: Can I get you something else, sir? Customer: No, thanks. Everything's just hunky-dory.* 女服务员:先生,还要我给你拿什么吗? 顾客:不用了,谢谢。一切都挺不错啦。在"不满意"的时候,也有时用这一表达法表示讽刺的意味。*A: Your date just called to say she won't be able to make it tonight. B: Well, isn't that just hunky-dory. And after all the trouble I went to to get tickets for tonight.* 甲:跟你约会的那个女的刚才来电话说,她今天晚上不能赴约啦。乙:哈,这倒挺不错呀。我为了今天晚上相会,费了九牛二虎之力才弄到两张票。◇ fine / great

hurry up [ˌhə(ː)riˈʌp] [口] **快点!** → make it SNAPPY

I

ice

break the ice [ˌbreɪkðɪ ˈaɪs] [口] **缓和紧张空气** 字面意义为“破冰船(ice-breaker)冲碎坚冰”。原来的构思是:“破冰之后,可以使其他船只通行”。因此,就产生了如下的意义:①最先去做,成为先驱者。*Ever since Henry Ford broke the ice by applying mass-production techniques to the manufacture of automobiles, mass production has been indispensable to the industrial world.* 自从亨利·福特破天荒第一次把成批生产技术应用于汽车制造业以来,成批生产方式便成为工业领域不可缺少的东西了。*Each of us club members is going to make a five-minute speech now. Bill, why don't you break the ice?* 从现在开始,我们俱乐部的每个成员都必须做五分钟的演说。比尔,由你开头怎么样?②打破冷冰冰的局面,使他人能够感到轻松,亦即“首先去把紧张的气氛缓和下来”。现在,特别是在会话中,最多使用的是这 ②的意义。至于“缓和气氛”的方法,既可以是讲些有趣味的话,也可以是首先采取热情的待人接物的行动。*The atmosphere of the party was at first very stiff, but the host broke the ice with an amusing story.* 社交晚会最初的气氛非常沉闷,但是主人讲了一个有趣味的故事,使得场面活跃了起来。如这一例句所示,本条的表达法大多用于表示缓和全场的人的气氛,但也有时缓和气氛的对象只是一个人。*I was tense and nervous when the president called me to his office, but he broke the ice by offering me a drink and asking about my children.* 当总经理把我叫到他的办公室的时候,我精神紧张,忐忑不安,但是,他让我喝饮料,又打听我孩子的情况,使我的心情平静下来了。还有一个表达法 an ice-breaker,意思是“消除紧张气氛的手段”。*We decided to use a guessing game as an ice-breaker at the beginning of the party.* 我们决定用猜谜游戏作为打破社交晚会刚一开始时的沉闷空气的手段。顺便提一下,break the ice 还有一个从 ①派生出来的意义,即“首先得分”。但一般人们很少使用这一意义,主要使用者是报纸或广播电台的体育新闻。*UCLA broke the ice with a touch-down early in the first half.* 在橄榄球比赛的上半时开始不久,加州大学洛杉矶分校队即触地得分,首开记录。◇ relax the tense [formal] atmosphere

something **cuts no ice with** *someone* [~ ˌkʌts nouˈaɪs wɪð ˈ~] [口] **不起作用** 在滑冰运动中,冰刀要锋利,滑行时划破冰面。在滑冰用语中,冰刀的刀刃锐利叫做 cut the ice, 如果刀刃太钝,就是 cut no ice (在冰上留不下痕迹)了。cut no ice 是滑冰的专门术语,如果用一般的英语来说,就是 make no impression on the ice。但是,这个 make no impression 可以构成 make no impression on *someone* 的句型,作为比喻,又表示“在人的心里不留痕迹”→“打不动人的心灵”→“对人不发生影响”的意思。在这一句型的影响之下,本为滑冰专门术语的 cut no ice 也构成本条条头的 cut no ice with *someone* 的句型,作为比喻使用起来。*His money cuts no ice with me. I still refuse to marry him.* 他的金钱打动不了我,我仍然拒绝同他结婚。*He may be a big man in the community, but that cuts no ice with me. I'm not going to be pushed around.* 他在这个地方可能是个了不起的人物,但是那对我不起任何作用。我这个人是不听人家摆布的。*Once my father makes up his mind, nothing anyone says ever cuts any ice with him.* 我的父亲一旦下了决心,不管谁说什么,都改变不了他的主意。如以上的例句所

示，大多的使用方法是讲“对 *someone* 不起作用”，在这一场合，原则上要带 with *someone*。有时表示“客观上不起作用”，在这一场合，当然不能带 with *someone*，例如：*That argument cuts no ice.* 那个论据一点也没有说服力。◇ makes no difference (to *someone*) / be unimportant (to *someone*) / makes no impression (on *someone*)

skate on thin ice [ˌskeɪ dɔ(ː)n ˈθɪ ˈnaɪs] [口] **如履薄冰、冒风险** 这是一个广泛使用的表达法，可以用于因为去干与自己的身份不相称的事情而招来祸害的场合，因为有不正当言行而被周围的人们愤怒谴责的场合，以及因为受警察的怀疑而置身危险境地的场合，等等。按照字面意义，与汉语成语“如履薄冰”非常相似。但是，在英语方面，大多是在客观地观察事物的时候使用。可以用以表达本人的主观的心情，如说 *I broached the subject with the feeling that I was skating on thin ice.* 我怀着如履薄冰的心情提出了那个问题。除此而外不宜使用。在使用时大多采取进行时。*The president will be skating on thin ice if he puts his new expansion plans into effect without the approval of the major stockholders.* 总经理如果不得到大股东们的许可而执行他的新的扩展计划，那就如履薄冰，是要承担风险的。*Scientists who claim that there is no life on other planets are skating on thin ice.* 一些科学家声称其他行星上没有生物，那是有若干臆断的危险的。*You're skating on thin ice when you talk to the boss that way.* 你用那种口气对老板说话，可是很危险啊。有时用 be 动词代替 skate。特别是在这一场合，常用 pretty, very, extremely 等修饰 thin ice。*I can't say it's exactly against the law, but you're certainly on pretty thin ice.* 我不能说那就是违法，但你肯定是有很大的危险。另外还有 walk [tread] on thin ice 的说法，但是使用频率很低。◇ venture onto dangerous [questionable] ground

iceberg

the tip of the iceberg → TIP

ice-breaker

an ice-breaker [ə ˈnaɪsˌbreɪkər] [口] **消除紧张气氛的手段** → break the ICE

idea

The idea (of *doing something*)! [ˌðɪ ˈaɪˈdɪːə] [话] **太不象话啦!** 母亲在申斥孩子的时候，一个人在气愤的时候，常使用这一表达法。意思是：“太荒唐啦，怎么会干出这种事来!”发音不是 [aɪˈdɪːə]，而是 [ˈaːɪˈdɪːə]，即两个音节都是重音，[aɪ] 要提高嗓门，拉长声音。女性专用的语言。只用于实际上看见或听见的场合，不能用于未来的事情。*The idea of going to school without a shirt on! I'm ashamed of you.* 太不象话啦，你居然要不穿衬衫上学。你不觉得害臊吗? *The idea!— That woman all but telling me I have poor taste in clothes!* 太不象话啦！那个女人差不多是在教训我对衣服的趣味太低了。常用 very 加强语气。*The very idea! Playing in the snow in your bare feet! You'll catch your death of cold!* 简直太不象话啦！你居然光着脚在雪里玩！你会伤风的，简直找死！◇ I can hardly believe it! (*Doing something*!)

toy with the idea of *doing something* [ˈtɔɪ wɪðːˌaɪˈdɪə(ː)v ～] [口] **心里盘算** toy with ～是“耍戏”、“玩弄”的意思。*Stop toying with your food and eat your dinner.* 不要摆弄食物，赶快吃饭。这是父母叱责孩子的话。本条直译为“玩弄要干某件事的想法”。这一表达法表示“在头脑中漠然考虑”的状态。大多用于有“试一下看”的心情的场合。*I'm toying with the idea of trying for Harvard University.* 我心里盘算着去考哈佛大学。*Sam appears to be toying with the idea of quitting his job.* 萨姆的心里似乎在盘算着辞职哪。*We toyed with the idea of taking a trip to Europe this summer but then decided it would be too expensive.* 我们本来盘算着今年夏天去欧洲旅行，但是由于可能花钱太多，后来决定不去了。◇ think (off and on) about *doing something*

The very idea! [ðə 've(:)ri 'aɪ'dɪːə] [话] **简直太不象话啦!** → The IDEA (of *doing something*)!

idiot

an idiot [ə 'nɪdiət] [口] **傻子** 原为心理学专门术语,指"精神发育年龄两岁以下的白痴"。后来转用于日常会话,表示"傻子"、"笨蛋"、"糊涂虫"等意思。多带有"缺乏判断能力"的含义。 *There will always be a chance of war as long as the world is peopled by so many idiots.* 只要世界上有这么多的白痴,就永远有发生战争的可能性。可以放在名词前面作为形容词使用。如果在词尾加上 -ic, 就构成正式的形容词 idiotic [ˌɪdi'ɑ(:)dɪk],既可作定语,亦可作谓语使用。 *Where is that idiot [idiotic] brother of mine?* 我的那个傻兄弟在哪儿呢? *Wars are idiotic.* 战争是极为愚蠢的。另外,由心理学名词转为日常口语、并与 idiot 同义的有 an IMBECILE, a MORON。请参见 a DUMBHEAD 条。◇ a stupid person

an idiot box → BOX

ifs

No ifs, ands or buts. [ˌnou 'ɪf 'sæ(:)ndzər 'bʌ(:)ts] [话] **不要找任何的借口** 当对方进行辩解的时候,用这一表达法堵住他的嘴,意思是"用不着花言巧语"。 *A: But I could make good grades, too, if only .... B: No ifs, ands or buts. I expect you to improve your grades by the end of the term.* 甲:但是,我是可以取得好分数的,只要是…… 乙:不要找任何的借口啦。我希望到本学期末,你的分数能有所提高。 *A: But, Mom .... B: No ifs, ands or buts. You will do as I say.* 甲:但是,妈妈…… 乙:不要找任何的借口。你照我说的去做。◇ You will make no excuses [complaints].

ignoramus

an ignoramus [ə ˌnɪgnə'reɪməs] [口] **无知之辈** *ignoramus* 原为拉丁文,意思等于英语的 We ignore.(我们不理。)有一个早年的故事说:英国的大陪审团 (Grand Jury) 在确定没有审判必要的案件之后就写上 ignoramus (驳回)的批语贴到外面。人们怀着讽刺的心情,把这一批语解释为"我们无知"(We are ignorant.)。1916 年,在这个故事的启发下,拉格尔 (G. Ruggle) 写成剧本《无知之辈》(*Ignoramus*),登场人物是一个无知的律师,名字即叫 Ignoramus。此后,这一表达法被人们广泛使用,指"无知的人"。 *Of course I don't believe that. What kind of ignoramus do you take me for?* 我当然不会相信那种话。你难道认为我是那样浑噩无知吗? *If you don't start studying harder, your teachers are going to give up on you as an incorrigible ignoramus.* 如果你不更加努力地用功学习,你的老师们就会把你当作无可挽救的低能儿而丢开不管啦。 *My grandfather says there is little hope for the world. Half the population is made up of fools and the other half of ignoramuses.* 我的祖父说这个世界是没有多大希望的。人口的一半是由傻瓜组成的,而另一半则是无知之辈。◇ an ignorant person / an imbecile

ignorance

parade *one's* **ignorance** [pə'reɪd ~ 'ɪgnərənts] [口] **暴露出自己的愚昧无知** → parade *one's* KNOWLEDGE (of *something*)

imagination

stagger the imagination [ˌstæ(:)gərðɪ əˌmædʒə'neɪʃən] [口] **令人难以想象** → boggle the MIND

imbecile

an imbecile [ə 'nɪmbəsəl] [口] **笨蛋** 原为心理学专门术语,指"精神发育年龄 3~7 岁的低能儿(即在 an IDIOT (→) 与 a MORON (→) 之间)"。转用于日常会话,意思是"傻瓜"、"糊涂虫"、"笨蛋",多带有"无知无识"、"非常迂阔"的含义。 *If that imbecile makes one more mistake, he's fired.* 如果那个笨蛋再搞错一次,就把他开除。imbecile 虽然有形容词 imbecilic [ˌɪmbə'sɪlɪk],但在会话中很少使用。→ a DUMBHEAD ◇ a stupid person

in

have it in for *someone* → HAVE

inch

Give *someone* **an inch and** *he*'**ll take a mile.** [ˌgɪv ～ əˈnɪ(:)ntʃ ən ～ l ˌteɪkə ˈmaɪl] [口] **得寸进尺** 直译为“给他一英寸,他拿一英里”。原来不用 a mile, 而用 an ell, 不知从什么时候起变成了现在的表达法。ell (厄尔)为英国旧时量布的长度单位,等于 45 英寸(约 114 厘米),最初的意思是 forearm (前臂),亦即“从肘到中指尖”。 *You have to be careful about showing kindness to George. Give him an inch and he'll take a mile.* 你对乔治不要太和颜悦色,因为他这个人是得寸进尺的。*Give my brother-in-law an inch and he'll take a mile. I told him he could stay with us two or three days until he found an apartment of his own, and he's been living with us for over a month now.* 我的内弟真是得寸进尺。我跟他说,在他找到公寓之前可以在我家住两三天,但是现在已经一个多月了,他还赖在我家不走。除了用 Give *someone* ～ 这样的命令式开头之外,还可以用连词开始,如 If you give ～或者 Every time you give ～等形式。*Don't offer the other party any more concessions. Every time you give them an inch, they take a mile.* 不要向对方做更多的让步,他们总是得寸进尺。◇ Yield to *someone* a little bit and *he*'ll want [(try to) take] much more.

Indian

an Indian giver → GIVER

(an) Indian summer [(ən)ˌɪndɪən ˈsʌmər] [口] **小阳春** → an Indian GIVER

info

info [ˈɪn(:)ˌfou] [话] **情报** information 的缩略,意思与 information 完全一样。是很轻松的口语,书写的场合很少使用。使用方法如: *I'll bring you all the info tomorrow.* 我明天把所有的情报都给你送来。*I can't make a decision without a little more info.* 没有更多一些情报,我做不了决定。◇ information

inside

gain the inside track (for *something*) [ˌgeɪnðɪ ˈɪnˌsaɪdˈtræ(:)k] [话] **占有利地位** → have the inside TRACK (for *something*)

have the inside track (for *something*) → TRACK

put *someone* **on the inside track** (for *something*) [ˌput ～ ɔnðɪ ˈɪnˌsaɪdˈtræ(:)k] [话] **给与某人有利地位** → have the inside TRACK (for *something*)

inspiration

an inspiration [ə ˌnɪnspəˈreɪʃən] [口] **灵感** → a BRAIN-STORM

interview

a man-in-the-street interview [ə ˌmænɪnðə ˌstri(:)t ˈɪntərˌvju:] [口] **街头访问(记)** → the MAN in the street

into

be into *something* [ˌɪntə ˈ～] [话] **卷入** 直译为“连身体都投入某事物当中”,换个说法就是 be involved in *something*。这一表达法本身只是“卷入”的意思,并不含有“热衷”、“入迷”之类的强烈的意味。但是根据上下文,也有带此类意味的情况,例如: *I was into the peace movement a little when I was younger, but my interest didn't last.* 在青年时代,我曾经参加过和平运动,但是不久就失去了兴趣。这句话仅仅是“有点关系”。*I love philosophy. I'm really into Kierkegaard now.* 我非常喜爱哲学,现在还对克尔恺郭尔的著作百读不厌哪。这个例子有两个句子。后一个句子承接前一个句子的意思,因而有“入迷”、“专心致志”之类的含义。*Charles likes to cook exotic dishes. Right now he's into snails.* 查尔斯喜欢烧一些稀奇古怪的菜,现在他正烧蜗牛哪。*Tom is too much into cars to be interested in girls.* 汤姆对汽车过于迷恋了,没有功夫去注意姑娘们。另有 get into *something* 的说法,同义。但是,这一表达法一般用于否定句。*French literature is interesting, but* *somehow I just can't seem to get into it.* 法国文学是很有意思的，但是不知为什么，我却钻不进去。◇ be involved [interested] in *something*

iron

an iron hand in a velvet glove → HAND
rule with an iron hand → HAND

a shooting iron [ə ˈʃu(ː)tn ˌaɪrn] [话] **枪** 字面意义为"射击用的铁器"。有时也指"步枪"，但一般指"手枪"，特别是指美国西部的牛仔们使用的"六响左轮"(<six-chambered> revolver)。在西部开发时代，是作为正规的日常用语使用的，如说：*Did you bring a shooting iron?* 你带来枪了吗？但是现在，在使用这一表达法时大多带有戏谑的口吻。*Shooting irons aren't exactly my favorite playthings.* 我对于玩枪没有多大兴趣。而且，在使用这一表达法的时候，即使不是西部人，也往往模仿西部方言的口音，作 [ˈʃu(ː)tn ˈɑ(ː)rn]。*The Injuns is acomin'. Lemme git mah shootin' arn. (= The Indians are coming. Let me get my shooting iron.)* 印第安人上来了，我去拿枪。那些喜欢看以西部生活为题材的戏剧、电影的人们，对这一类的对白是会很熟悉的。◇ a gun

strike while the iron is hot [ˈstraɪk ˌhwaɪlðɪ ˌaɪrnəz ˈhɑːt] [口] **不失机会，立即行动** 字面意义与汉语成语"趁热打铁"完全一样。strike 是"一击"。原来作命令句 Strike ~. 为英国的谚语。在现代，很少使用命令式。这一表达法虽然可以译作"趁热打铁"或"趁火补漏锅"，但两者之间是有一定距离的。先看例句。*When it comes to the stock market, you can't spend hours and hours thinking about a transaction. You have to strike while the iron is hot.* 就股票市场而言，你不可能用几小时的时间去反复研究一笔交易的问题。你必须看好机会，马上采取行动。*If you really want to quit your job, you should strike while the iron is hot. Later you may not be able to get another job so easily.* 如果你真打算辞职，就要立即采取行动。时间迟了，你就未必能够很容易地找到另外的工作了。*We must strike while the iron is hot. If we wait another single day, the opportunity may be gone forever.* 我们必须立即采取行动。如果耽搁一天，就可能永远失掉这次机会。在第一个例句中，股票市场是投机活动，有赔有赚，也就是说铁"热"或"不热"，并不能预先知道。第二个例句是讲的"辞职"，无法说"趁热辞职"。第三个例句勉强与"趁热打铁"相近。这一表达法所指的"机会"大多是商业上或工作上的机会，这种机会总是一瞬间的或者极短时期的。另外，也可以见到省略 strike 的使用方法，例如：*You should accept his offer now, while the iron is hot. By tomorrow he may have changed his mind.* 你应该接受他现在的开价，不要放掉好机会。到明天他也许会变卦的。→ make HAY while the sun shines ◇ act at the most favorable moment / act without delay

irons

have *many* **irons in the fire** [ˌhæv ~ˈaɪrnz ɪnðəˌfaɪr] [口] **同时从事许多事业或活动** 这一表达法最初的构思是："正如铁匠炉的火中插着许多铁棒一样，有许多事情同时去做"。*Lyle has many irons in the fire. I'm sure that even if one of his enterprises went bankrupt, he could survive on the rest.* 莱尔同时干着许多生意。我敢肯定，即使他的公司有一个破了产，他也能够依靠其余的公司经营下去。*It's no wonder Mrs. Fidgit got sick. She has so many irons in the fire that she doesn't have time to take proper rest.* 费吉特夫人病了，这不足为奇。她要去干各种各样的事情，没有时间适当地休息。除了 *many* 外，还可以用各种各样的形容词。*A: Have you gotten a job yet? B: No, but I have a number of irons in the fire. I'm sure one of them will develop into something.* 甲：你已经找到工作了吗？乙：没有。不过，我已经有了许多目标。在不久的将来，肯定会搞成其中的一个。*Thanks for the invitation to spend the night, Jim, but I've got to be getting back to the city. I've got a few* *other irons in the fire this weekend.* 吉姆,非常感谢你留我在这里过夜。不过,我还是得回到城里去,因为在这个周末,我有一些其他的事情非办不可。*Dick is always busy. He's not satisfied unless he has five or six irons in the fire at one time.* 迪克永远很忙,他在同一时间干五、六种事情才觉得过瘾。*I don't understand the kids nowadays always wanting to go steady. When I was young I always had several irons in the fire.* 我真不明白,现在的年轻人为什么总爱跟固定的一个女朋友经常来往。当我年轻的时候,我同时交上好几个女朋友。◇ be involved in *many* things / be testing *many* opportunities

itching

have an itching palm [ˌhævə ˌnɪtʃɪŋ ˈpɑːm] [口] 贪婪 → have an itchy PALM

be itching for a chance to *do something* → CHANCE

be itching to *do something* [ˈɪ(ː)tʃɪŋtə ~] [话] 渴望 → be itching for a CHANCE to *do something*

itchy

have an itchy palm → PALM

ivories

tickle the ivories [ˌtɪklðɪ ˈaɪvri(ː)z] [话] 弹钢琴 ivories 为 ivory (象牙)的复数,这里指"钢琴的键"。tickle 是"使发痒"。本条习用语是一个轻松的、幽默的表达法,直译为"咯吱琴键"。*Sue likes to tickle the ivories.* 苏喜欢弹钢琴。*Ted can really tickle the ivories.* 特德弹钢琴弹得很好。◇ play the piano

J

jabber

jabber ['dʒæ(:)bər] [口] **叽叽喳喳地闲聊** 象声词。乍看起来与 BLABBER 相似,但 blabber 只是"信口胡扯",并不一定要"叽叽喳喳"。jabber 是"叽叽喳喳地闲聊",重点在于"喋喋不休"。*How can I study with you guys jabbering like that!* 你们这些家伙叽叽喳喳说个没完,我怎么能够温习功课呀? 如果后边加上 away,就具有"一个劲儿地(说下去)"的意思。例如: *Whenever those two fellows get together they always begin jabbering away about nuclear physics.* 只要那两个人碰到一起,他们就开始谈核物理学,叽叽喳喳一直没个完。也可以作及物动词使用。*I said "Ni hao?" and he began jabbering Chinese at me [jabbering at me in Chinese].* 我说了句"你好?",他就喋喋不休地向我说起汉语来了。另外,gibber ['dʒɪbər / 'gɪbər] 也与 jabber 同义,但不象 jabber 使用得广泛。*They were gibbering away in French.* 他们用法语闲聊了起来。jabber 除作动词使用外,还可以作名词使用,只不过使用频率极低。gibber 的名词形式为 gibberish ['dʒɪbərɪʃ / 'gɪbərɪʃ],与动词的场合相反,使用频率很高。gibber 本身可以作名词使用,但使用者极少。*When I asked him when he was going to pay me back, he gave me a lot of gibberish about the high cost of living.* 当我问他打算什么时候还给我钱的时候,他对我喋喋不休地谈起生活费高的问题来了。"叽叽喳喳地闲聊的人",一般称 jabberer。也有 gibberer 的说法,但几乎无人使用。*You're a real jabberer, aren't you.* 你真是一个喋喋不休的人啊。另外,有些英汉词典把 jabber 一词释义为"(猿猴、鸟类)吱吱喳喳地叫"或其叫声,但除文学作品以外,极少以 jabber 作为这些动物的象声词,相应的英语是 CHATTER (→)。◇ talk (on and on) / talk (on and on) unfathomably ((at *someone*→ to *someone*))

jack

every man jack ['evri 'mæ(:)n 'dʒæk] [口] **每一个人** → every last MAN

jack ['dʒæ(:)k] [话] **金钱** 这一表达法来源于扑克牌游戏。在某一个人取胜之前,所有参加游戏的人都不断地往桌面上下赌注,这些赌注的总额称为 the pot。在扑克牌游戏中,赌注很大的往往会是 draw poker (暗扑克)。在打暗扑克时,赢钱的最起码条件是必须有两张以上的 J(杰克)。因此,人们把 draw poker 的 pot (赌金) 称为 the jackpot。后来,就把"金钱"本身叫做 jack 了。这是一个相当轻松的表达法。*How much jack ya got?* 你带了多少钱? *Got any jack you can lend me?* 你能借给我点儿钱吗? *Those folks've got a real pile of jack.* 那些家伙有很多很多的钱啊。◇ money

jackpot

hit the jackpot [ˌhɪtðə 'dʒæ(:)kˌpɑ(:)t] [话] **获得很大的成功** 在扑克牌游戏中,起决定性作用的牌(两张以上的 J)出来以前,每个玩牌的人都要往桌面正中间的地方放赌注(钱),那些赌注的总和称为 jackpot(累积赌注)。hit the jackpot 的意思是"手持强牌,把赌注一扫而光"。*We played poker for almost an hour before I finally hit the jackpot.* 我们玩扑克将近一个小时,我终于把全部赌注一扫而光了。这是按照本来意义的用法。但是现在,人们从 jackpot 一词联想到的并不是扑克牌,而是吃角子老虎机(slot machine)。只要具备规定的图样,机器就吐出全部硬币,来个所谓的"满堂红"。*My brother hit the jackpot on the* *nickel slot machine.* 我弟弟去玩五分镍币老虎机,得了个"满堂红"。作为比喻,广泛用于表示"获得很大的成功"的意味。*That company hit the jackpot with its new line of electronic games.* 那家公司搞电子游戏的新制品,获得了很大的成功。*Duffy hit the jackpot on a quiz show and won a set of furniture and a trip to Europe.* 达菲在智力测验节目中中了头奖,得到一套家具并去欧洲旅游一次。在加强语气时,常在 hit 前面添加 really 一词。*I really hit the jackpot on my last blind date—a beautiful blond!* 我最近一次相看对象,真是大走红运,居然是一位金发美人! 可以省略 hit,单独使用 jackpot,例如: *Jackpot! Look at my report card! I got all A's.* 好极啦! 请看我的成绩单! 全部是"*A*"。*You now have won five hundred dollars. Would you like to try for the jackpot?* 你现在已经赢了五百美元。你愿意试试看,争取个"满堂红"吗? ◇ have great success [luck]

jag

go on a ~ing jag [ˌgouɔ(ː)nə ˈ~ ˌdʒæːg] [话] **大搞一阵** jag 原意为 a light load。load 是"负荷",因此,如果说 a light load,那意思就是"人或马所能运送的轻装载量"。然而,load 又有"酒的致醉量"的意味。比如"他喝多了"这句话,过去在英语中说 He has a load on. 现在一般是说 He is loaded. (→ LOADED) 这样一来, jag (= a light load) 也就有了 an early stage of intoxication (微醉)的意味。后来又进一步发展,先作 a drinking party (酒会)解,又转为 a drinking splurge (狂饮),同时产生了 go on a jag (如疯似狂地不断喝酒)的表达法。因此, go on a jag 本来是表达喝酒状态的用语。到了现代,在 jag 的前边加上各种各样的形容词,采取 go on a ~ing jag 的形式,除了饮酒而外,广泛地作为比喻使用。*Sue went on an eating jag last month and gained fifteen pounds.* 苏上个月猛吃了一阵儿,结果长了 *15* 磅肉。*My girl went on a crying jag just because I couldn't take her to the dance.* 由于我未能带她去跳舞,我的女朋友痛哭了好一阵儿。常用 real 加强语气。*What's wrong with Ralph? He's gone on a real studying jag.* 拉尔夫是怎么的了? 他如疯似狂地用起功来啦。如以上的例句所示,自从 go on a jag 的比喻用法大大推广以来,就必须在 jag 的前面加相应的形容词。现在,即便使用这一表达法的本来意义(即饮酒),也必须说 go on a drinking jag, 否则就弄不清是什么 jag 了。但是,在从上下文可以判明是什么意义时,省略 drinking 也行。例如: *We went out on a (drinking) jag last night and all have hangovers.* 我们昨天晚上狂饮了一阵儿,今天大家全处于宿醉状态。除 go on a ~ing jag 外,还有 get on a ~ing jag 的表达法。将 go 换成 get 以后,具有"一旦开始干某事之后,如疯似狂,决不罢休"的含义。*Every once in a while I get on a reading jag.* 我有时候读起书来爱不释手。还有一个句型为 be on a ~ing jag, 意思是"处于如疯似狂地……的状态"。*There is no reasoning with her when she's on a crying jag.* 当她痛哭时,她是没有理智的。此外,作为 go [get, be] on a ~ing jag 的变形,还有一个常为人们使用的表达法,就是 go [get, be] on one of *one's* ~ing jags, 意思为"经常如疯似狂地…… (*one's* ~ing jags),这是其中的一回(one of)",亦即"又照例如疯似狂地……来了"。◇ embark on an extended period of ~ing

go on a jag [ˌgouɔ(ː)nə ˈdʒæːg] [话] **狂饮一大阵** → go on a ~ing JAG

jailbait

jailbait [ˈdʒeɪlˌbeɪt] [话] **祸水妞儿** jail 是"监狱", bait 是"饵"。合起来的意思是"人一去吃就会进监狱的饵"。是不可数名词,不能加不定冠词,也没有复数形式。一般指 11~15 岁有姿色的少女。*She's a beautiful girl—but beware, she's jailbait.* 她是个很好看的姑娘,但是要当心,是个祸水妞儿啊。*There're a lot of available girls in this town, but most of them are jailbait.* 这个镇里有许多可以弄到手的姑娘,不过,她们大多数是与之发生性关系即构成犯罪的未成年少女。有时仅指未成年,没有姿色也可以。*Stu doesn't seem to care about what the girls he dates look like, so long as they're not jailbait.* 司徒似乎不在乎他所约会的姑娘的姿色,只要不是未成年的祸水妞儿就行。◇ (an) underage (girl)

jam

be in a jam [ɪnə ˈdʒæːm] [话] **陷入困境** jam 本来是动词,意思是"把……塞满"。转用作名词,意思是被危险、困难等塞满而使人动不了地方的"窘境"。*You've got to help me. I'm in a jam. The police have discovered I was the hit-and-run driver.* 你得设法救救我,我正陷入困境,警察已经发现我是肇事后逃跑的司机啦。下面是说俏皮话的例子:*If you hadn't been so fresh, we wouldn't be in the jam.* 如果你不是那么冒冒失失,咱们不会吃这样的苦头。如以上的例句所示,有单独使用 be in a jam 的情况,但与 with *someone* 结合起来表示"在与他人的关系上陷入困境"的场合非常多。例如:*George is in a jam with the tax office because he cheated on his taxes.* 乔治由于偷税漏税而受到税务局的追查,正在陷入困境。*He's been in several jams with the police.* 他有好几次与警察发生纠纷,陷入困境。如果用 get 代替 be 动词而作 get in(to) a jam (with *someone*),意思是"发生困难"。*Whenever he gets in a jam, his brother always helps him out.* 当他有困难的时候,他的哥哥总是去帮助他。另有一个表达法是 get *someone* in(to) a jam (with *someone*)。例如说 *A gets B in(to) a jam with C.* 由于甲的关系,乙和丙不睦。*The rumors got me into a jam with my superiors.* 由于那些流言,我和上级之间的关系很糟糕。如果说 get out of a jam (with *someone*),则是"摆脱困境"的意思。*Can you help me get out of a jam?* 你能帮助我摆脱困境吗? get *someone* out of a jam (with *someone*) 是"帮助某人摆脱困境"。*His lawyer got him out of a jam with the police.* 在律师的帮助下,他摆脱了与警察的纠葛。◇ be in trouble [a predicament]

Jane

a plain Jane [ə ˈpleɪnˈdʒeɪn] [话] **不起眼的女人** 这里的 plain 是"不惹人注目"、"朴素"的意思。Janc 是一般女人名,中译为"简"。plain [ˈpleɪn] 与 Jane [ˈdʒeɪn] 这两个词合辙押韵。*I wonder why a handsome man like Jeff married such a plain Jane.* 我真奇怪,象杰夫那样一个英俊的男子怎么会与一个很不起眼的姑娘结婚。*She calls herself a plain Jane, but when she dresses up she's actually quite attractive.* 她自称是一个不起眼的女人,但是当她打扮起来的时候,的确十分迷人哪。*Beautiful women are too fickle. Give me a plain Jane any day.* 美貌的女子总是水性杨花,但愿我有一天得到个朴素的姑娘。◇ an ordinary-looking girl

java

java [ˈdʒɑ(ː)və] [话] **咖啡** 在第二次世界大战以前,爪哇 (Java) 是世界闻名的大量出产高级咖啡的地方,因此就用这一地名作为咖啡的代名词了。本条习用语不是所谓的"爪哇咖啡"的意思,而是一种轻松的表达法,泛指各种咖啡。*Let's stop in somewhere and get a cup of hot java.* 咱们在什么地方停下车,喝杯热咖啡吧。有时第一个字母大写,作 Java。有些地方发音 [ˈdʒæ(ː)və]。◇ coffee

jaw

have a glass jaw [ˌhævə ˌglæ(ː)s ˈjɔː] [话] **不堪一击的下巴** 直译为"有一个玻璃的下巴"。拳击用语。*That fighter has a very strong punch, but unfortunately he also has a glass jaw.* 那个拳击运动员的出拳很有力量,遗憾的是下巴不堪一击。*I can beat that guy any day. He may be stronger than I am, but he has a glass jaw. One good right to the chin will finish him.* 任何时候我都能够打败那个家伙。他也许比我力量强,但是他的下巴不堪一击。只要用右勾拳猛击他的下巴,他就会完蛋啦。◇ be easily knocked out

jawbreaker

a jawbreaker [ə ˈdʒɔːˌbreɪkər] [话] **难发音的词** 直译为"破碎下巴的东西"。原为 20 世纪 30 年代推出的一种内含泡泡糖的大块硬糖的商品名称。*Jawbreakers were my favorite kind of candy when I was little.* 在我小的时候,"破碎下巴"是我喜爱的一种糖果。转用于指很长的、发音困难的词。这一表达法与 a tongue TWISTER(绕口令)不同,一般为一两个单词。*The names of those Polish towns are real jawbreakers.* 那些波兰城镇的名字实在很难发音。*I wonder why the poet Emil Frida chose a jawbreaker like Jaroslav Vrchlicky for a pen name.* 我真不明白为什么诗人埃米尔·弗里达会选择雅罗茨拉夫·弗尔赤利斯基这样一个难以发音的笔名。*A: What's the full name of the chemical tetryl? B: It's quite a jawbreaker: trinitrophenyl methylnitramine* [ˌtraɪˈnaɪtrouˈfenəl ˌmeθəlˈnaɪtrəˌmiːn]. 甲:化学品特屈儿的正式名称是什么? 乙:这个名称非常绕嘴:三硝基苯(替)甲硝胺。◇ (a) difficult-to-pronounce (word [name, phrase, etc.])

jaywalk

jaywalk [ˈdʒeɪˌwɔːk] [口] **乱穿马路** 这一表达法指步行的人们不从人行横道过马路、或者虽然走人行横道但不顾交通信号的行为。jay 一词现代很少单独使用,过去则用以表示"头脑迟钝、没有经验的乡巴佬"。因此,本条习用语的字面意义是:"象刚进城的土包子那样走路"。不过,现在几乎没有人知道 jay 这个词,所以在使用本条习用语时不含有轻蔑的意味在内。*Don't jaywalk!* 不要乱穿马路! 乱穿马路的行为英语作 jaywalking。*In most American cities you can be fined for jaywalking.* 在美国大多数的城市里,如果乱穿马路是要被罚款的。"jaywalking 的人"是 a jaywalker。*Jaywalkers are a problem in New York.* 在纽约,乱穿马路的人太多,形成一个大问题。◇ cross the street without regard to traffic rules

jerkwater

jerkwater [ˈdʒə(ː)rkˈwɔ(ː)dər] [话] **乡下的** 含有轻蔑意味。这里的 jerk 原来是"把满桶的水猛地提起来"的意思。在早年间,当蒸气机车补充水的时候,如果是在没有水塔的小镇,就必须用水桶去提水,然后往机车上面吊,倒入水箱。因此,人们就把这样偏僻的农村集镇称为 a jerkwater town (火车头要用水桶上水的小镇)。*Sometimes I just don't understand my husband. He wants us to spend our vacation in some little jerkwater town way up in the mountains.* 有时候我对自己的丈夫实在无法理解。他居然要叫我们到深山里的一个土里土气的小集镇去度假。现在,人们听到 jerkwater 一词之后,首先联想到的依然是 town,不过后边有各种各样的名词接续。*He graduated from some jerkwater college by the name of Podunk University.* 他从一个叫做波敦克大学的乡下学院毕了业。*Sam used to work for a jerkwater airline in Alaska.* 萨姆过去在阿拉斯加州的一个地方航空公司工作。有时省略 water,只说 jerk。*Let's get out of this jerk town. I'm bored stiff.* 咱们离开这个乡下集镇吧,我在这里快憋死啦。◇ country / out-of-the-way / insignificant (rural)

jet

jet lag → LAG

jiff

in a jiff [ɪnə ˈdʒɪ(ː)f] [话] **不大一会儿** → in a JIFFY

jiffy

in a jiffy [ɪnə ˈdʒɪfi] [话] **不大一会儿** 意思与 right away, in a second, in a very few minutes 等相同,但这一表达法轻松得多。语源不明。可能为拟态语。*Can you wait a minute? I'll be ready to go in a jiffy.* 你等一下好吗? 我马上做好出门的准备。也可以说 in just a jiffy,这里的 just 只是调整语调,别无意义。*Customer: Is there anything seriously wrong with my car? Mechanic: No, I can have it* *fixed in just a jiffy.* 顾客：我的车有严重的毛病吗？修理工：没有，我一会儿功夫就会修好。可以讲 jiff，这个词要比 jiffy 更使人产生轻松的感觉。 *Wash your hands, everyone. Dinner'll be ready in just a jiff.* 大家都洗洗手，晚饭马上就好啦。可以省略 in，只用 jiffy，jiff。*I can't answer that question. Just a jiff. I'll call Jim and find out.* 我回答不出那个问题。请等一下。我给吉姆打个电话，问问他看。在这一例句中，Just a jiff. 省略了 wait 一词。*My office is just around the corner. It'll only take me a jiffy to get the papers you want.* 我的办事处就在那个街角上。你要的文件我马上就可以取来。(in) half a jiffy [jiff] 按字面来说是"不大一会儿"的一半时间，实际上只是与条头的说法不同，意思还是一样。*Let me go mail these letters. I'll be back in half a jiffy.* 我去寄这几封信，不一会儿就回来。◇ very soon / right away

jig

The jig is up. [ðə ˌdʒɪ(:)gɪ'zʌ(:)p] [话] **一切都完啦** 这里的 jig 是"吉格舞"或"吉格舞曲"，据说始于 16 世纪。现在仍然使用这一意义。古时，在大戏的幕与幕之间表演滑稽的吉格舞，因此 jig 一词又具有"玩笑"、"捣鬼"、"计策"等意义。但在作此解时，jig 不能单独使用。人们所使用的只有条头的一种形式。 up 是 over (终了)的意思。 *Come out with your hands over your heads. The jig is up.* 赶快举起手，从里边走出来。你们已经全完蛋啦。*The jig is up. The cops have found the getaway car with your billfold in it.* 一切都完蛋啦。警察已经发现逃跑用的汽车，车里有你的钱夹。如以上两个例句所示，这一表达法用于表示坏事、犯罪、作恶等"已经到了尽头"的意思。按照字面意义是"吉格舞表演完毕"，也就是一直在表演的舞蹈节目收了场。同样，在使用这一表达法时，必须反映接连不断地干某种不正当的事情，而现在把戏已经拆穿，无法进行了。 *As soon as we saw the principal coming toward us with an angry look on his face, we knew the jig was up.* 当我们见到校长一脸怒气向我们走来时，我们知道一切都完蛋啦。 *The jig's up, Stu. No more afternoons at the baseball game. The boss saw you coming out of the stadium yesterday.* 司徒，一些都完蛋啦。再也不能下午去看棒球比赛了。昨天老板看见你从球场出来啦。◇ *Someone* is finished. / It's all over.

jillion

a jillion [ə 'dʒɪljən] [话] **多得数不过来** 这是一个夸张的表达法，极力强调数目之大。有点童稚气味。成年人只在戏谑时使用。形式虽为名词，但一般作形容词处理，例如：*It was a great party. There must have been a jillion people there.* 那是一次规模很大的社交晚会，参加的人数一定多得不得了哇。 *I don't know what's wrong with Dave. I've written him a jillion letters and he hasn't answered a single one.* 我不晓得戴夫发生了什么事。我给他写了好多好多的信，可是他连一封回信也没有啊。 *There are umpteen jillion people in this world, and I had to end up with a creep like that for a roommate.* 天下的人何止千千万万，而我却非得跟那样一个讨厌鬼住一个房间不可。另有 zillion 一词，意思和用法与 jillion 完全一样，但使用频率低一些。*I can't go with you. I've got a zillion things to do today.* 我不能跟你一起去，今天我有好多好多的事情非干不可呀。◇ millions / billions / I don't know how many

jitterbug

the jitterbug [ðə 'dʒɪdər.bʌ(:)g] [口] **吉特巴舞** 一种活泼欢快的社交舞。由于这种性质，可能有人马上就把这一表达法解释为"不安定的 (jitter) 虫子 (bug)"。其实，这里的 jitter 指"上上下下的细碎动作"，而 bug 则是后缀，具有"对某事极有兴趣的人"的意味 (→ a FIREBUG)。但是现在不用于指"人"，只用于指舞蹈本身。这一表达法的特征是：前面不能加 a，经常与定冠词一起使用。 *The jitterbug became popular in America in* *the 1940's*. 20 世纪 40 年代,吉特巴舞在美国流行起来了。也可以把 the 去掉,作为动词使用。*Can you jitterbug?* 你会跳吉特巴舞吗?另外还有 do the jitterbug (跳吉特巴舞) 的说法,如: *Can you do the jitterbug?* 你能跳吉特巴舞吗?

jitters

have (a case of) the jitters [ˌhæv(ə ˌkeɪsəv)ðə ˈdʒɪdə(ː)rz] [话] **忐忑不安** 这里的 case 是"病症",jitters 是表示"心里紧张、惴惴不安"的一种拟态语。*Most of the actors in our school play had the jitters just before the curtain.* 我们学校演剧的时候,演员们在即将开幕时都象怀里揣个小兔子似的,忐忑不安。*Smith was a veteran pilot, but even he had a case of the jitters while waiting to take off on the bombing raid over enemy territory.* 史密斯是一位老资格的飞机驾驶员,即使是他,在等待起飞前往轰炸敌人领土的一瞬间,心里也是忐忑不安的。上面的第一个例句中可以加上 a case of;相反,第二个例句则可以省略。case 前面可以加形容词。*I don't know if I can play my solo well or not. I've got a bad case of the jitters.* 我不晓得我的独奏能不能演得成功,我心里非常紧张。也可以用 be suffering from 代替 have (got)。*After being in the secret room for over an hour waiting for the police to finish searching the house, we were all suffering from a bad case of the jitters.* 为了等待警察搜查完住宅,我们在秘密房间里藏了一个多小时,大家都象怀里揣个小兔子似的,极为紧张不安。可以把 have 换成 get,构成 get (a case of) the jitters 的表达法。*Every time Ben thought about asking Janice to the dance party, he began to get the jitters.* 每当本心里想请贾尼丝参加舞会的时候,他就开始忐忑不安起来。另外, give *someone* the jitters 也是定型的说法,意思是"使人忐忑不安"。在这一场合,一般不加 a case of。*All the talk about the possibility of war was giving everyone the jitters.* 关于可能发生战争的一切言论,使得每个人都忐忑不安起来。除此而外,虽然并不构成句型,但有如下的用法: *Don't worry about me. It's just the jitters* (= *I've just got the jitters.*). *I'll be all right once the action starts.* 不要为我担心,我只是有点紧张而已。一旦开始行动,就会完全没问题啦。◇ be nervous ((a bad case of → very))

job

do a bang-up job [ˌdu(ː)ə ˌbæ(ː)ŋˌʌp ˈdʒɑ(ː)b] [话] **做得十分出色** bang-up 一词的意思是"极出色的"、"第一流的"、"最好的"。do a ~ job 是广义的"做",并不限定"干工作"的场合使用。*Let's ask Lew to be the speaker at the lecture meeting. He always does a bang-up job.* 咱们请卢做报告吧,他做的报告总是非常出色的。在表示 job 的内容时,大多是在后面接 of + 动名词(短语)。例如: *The coach has done a bang-up job of training the new players.* 教练对新选手的训练干得十分出色。*We're glad we had the Pushmelon Agency advertise our new product. They did a bang-up job.* 我们委托普什梅隆广告社去为我们的新产品做广告,真是太好啦。他们干得很出色。有时只把 bang-up 与其他的动词短语或名词结合在一起使用。*The drama club put on a bang-up performance of The Taming of the Shrew.* 剧社非常出色地上演了《驯悍记》。*It was a bang-up performance.* 完成得太出色啦。◇ perform outstandingly (in *doing something*)

do a snow job (on *someone*) [ˌdu(ː)ə ˈsnou ˌdʒɑːb] [话] **用花言巧语进行欺骗** 这一表达法是把花言巧语或者阿谀奉承比喻为暴风雪。最初的构思是:"在对方的眼前刮起语言的暴风雪,使他看不见现实的世界(即不了解真实的情况)"。意思是用各式各样的美好言词或者拍马屁的话使听的人上当受骗。这一表达法可以用于诈骗金钱的案件,但一般没有那么恶劣的性质,如商人为了卖某种物品而吹嘘几句,下级为了讨好上司而恭维一番,大多是这类无足轻重的事情。*Some salesman did a snow job on my* *wife and she ended up buying a whole new set of living room furniture.* 有一个推销员对我的妻子花言巧语了一番,结果她为起居室买了一整套新家具。*I don't trust politicians. If you ask me, the successful candidates are simply the ones who can do the biggest snow jobs (on the public).* 我不信任政客们。如果叫我说的话,那些当选的人物只不过是最善于用花言巧语欺骗群众的政客而已。这一表达法也常用于为了讨好女性而甜言蜜语的场合。*Slim did a real snow job on that girl. He actually had her believing that he was the President's nephew.* 斯利姆对那个姑娘来了一大套花言巧语,居然使她相信他是总统的外甥啦。另外有 give *someone* a snow job 的形式,其意思与 do a snow job on *someone* 相同。例如:*That was quite a snow job you gave the boss.* 你对老板拍马的手段真高明啊。这句话里的 you gave the boss 可以改换为 you did on the boss。*The guy gave me a real snow job. It wasn't until later that I learned that most of what he told me was pure fabrication.* 那个家伙的花言巧语简直把我骗住了,后来我才了解,他对我讲的事情绝大部分是凭空捏造的。*Don't try to give me another of your snow jobs. Just tell me exactly what happened.* 不要对我再来你那套花言巧语了吧,你只讲发生了什么事情就行啦。由此又产生了 snow *someone* 的说法,意思与 do a snow job on *someone*, give *someone* a snow job 相同。*Be firm with Ralph this time. Don't let him snow you like he did before.* 这次对拉尔夫要持坚决的态度,别象上次那样被他的花言巧语哄骗啦。snow job 也可以单独使用,例如:*Cut out the smooth talk. I want a rational explanation, not a snow job.* 不要净说好听的了吧。我想听的是合乎逻辑的说明,而不是花言巧语。◇ overwhelm [fool] *someone* with a lot of plausible words ((the biggest → the most people / a real → really))

fall down on the job (of *doing something*) [ˌfɔ(ː)lˈdau nɔnðə ˌdʒɑ(ː)b] [话] **敷衍了事** 直译为"在工作时跌倒了"。在如下的场合使用:本来干得了,但是不愿意干,因而没有干出预期的效果。一说 job,首先会联想到"工作",但是,job 比 work 范围广,包含"应该做的事情"的意思。本条习用语也是一样,可以认为包括工作、学习、体育运动等一切"应该做的事情"。*The chief reprimanded Jerry for falling down on the job.* 杰里由于马马虎虎,被头儿申斥了一顿。*If you fall down on the job of studying once more, you won't pass this course.* 如果你再不认真学习,这门课程就要不及格啦。这一表达法也用于表示过分马马虎虎、几乎"完全不干"的意味。*Jack is falling down on the job. This makes three days he hasn't come to practice now.* 杰克偷懒啦,他已经三天没有练习了。另外有一个类似的表达法,即 lie down on the JOB。◇ fail to work as hard as one should (at *doing something*)

give *someone* **a snow job** [ˌgiv ～ ə ˈsnou ˌdʒɑːb] [话] **用花言巧语哄骗某人** → do a snow JOB (on *someone*)

lie down on the job [ˌlai ˈdau nɔnðə ˌdʒɑ(ː)b] [口] **偷懒** 直译为"在工作中躺下"。这里的 job 不仅指"工作",泛指"应该做的事情"。本条习用语大多用于因为不愿意干而把应该做的事情丢下不管的场合,但也用于磨洋工或者消极混泡的场合。*Kyle's been lying down on the job lately. He hasn't even started that work I gave him last week.* 凯尔最近躺下不干啦。我上个星期交给他的工作,他至今还没有动手哪。*When are you going to stop lying down on the job and start studying properly?* 你到什么时候才能不再偷懒,开始认真学习呢? *You were supposed to be watching him. You would have seen him leave if you hadn't been lying down on the job.* 你的任务是看守他。如果你没有偷懒,是应该见到他走出去的啊。*Father to son: From the size of the weeds in the yard, it's obvious that you've been lying down on the job (of keeping them pulled).* 父亲对儿子说:从院子里杂草丛生的情况看,非常明

显，你偷懒啦（没有拔草）。顺便讲一下：在会话中，有些人用 lay（置放）代替 lie，而讲 lay down on the job。由于 lie (lay, lain) 与表示"置放"意味的 lay (laid, laid) 容易混淆，即使是美国人，也常常张冠李戴。尽管是误用，但由于耳朵听的多了，也并不觉得怎么别扭。*You've got to keep after Bumsley. He'll lay down on the job if you don't watch him very closely.* 对于巴姆斯利这个人，你非经常督促不可。如果你不严加看管，他马上就要偷懒的。◇ shirk *one's* responsibility / dawdle (over *one's* work [studies, etc.])

the patience of Job [ðə ˈpeɪʃəntsəvˈdʒoub] [口] **极大的忍耐性** 源出《圣经》。Job 是《圣经·旧约》中《约伯记》(Job) 的主人公，希伯来人的族长之一。他非常虔诚，正直无私，经受住了上帝种种的考验。关于这位 Job，在《圣经·新约》中的《雅各书》(James) 第 5 章 11 节曾经提到：(You have heard of) the patience of Job ....（你们听见过约伯的忍耐……）。the patience of Job 的字面意义就是"约伯的忍耐"。由于人们认为世界上没有一个比约伯更有 patience（耐性）的人，所以这一表达法便意味着"具有超人的忍耐力"或"极有耐性"了。*Mrs. Button is wonderful with rowdy children. She has the patience of Job.* 巴顿太太善于对付那些淘气的孩子们，她的耐性超人一等。*Joe is the ideal person to be in charge of customer complaints. He has the patience of Job.* 乔是负责应付顾客提意见的最适当的人选，他有超人的忍耐力。如以上的例句所示，这一表达法常与 have 结合使用。但也有使用其他动词的情况。*This job requires the patience of Job.* 这个工作需要有极大的耐性。◇ a tremendous amount of patience

jockey

a desk jockey [ə ˈdesːˌdʒɑ(ː)ki] [话] **坐办公室的人** 与主要干外勤工作的人相对，专指坐办公室从事事务性工作的人。大多指公司的职员，但也可以指一般干部、军人等，也就是说，任何机关、团体的成员都行。这是一个模仿 a disc JOCKEY 而来的幽默的表达法。*I wish I could be transferred to the sales department. I'm sick of being simply a desk jockey.* 我多么希望能够调到推销部去啊，老坐办公室实在腻味透顶啦。◇ a desk worker

a disc jockey [ə ˈdɪsːˌdʒɑ(ː)ki] [口] **流行音乐唱片节目播音员** 这一表达法的来源如下：田径赛中有一个项目是"掷铁饼"，在英语中，"铁饼"叫做 a discus [ˈdɪskəs]。discus 这个词源出古拉丁语，现在将词尾 -us 去掉，作 disc，泛指一切平而圆的东西（只有掷铁饼的"铁饼"仍用 discus）。到了 20 世纪，自从唱片工业兴盛以后，人们就将"唱片"也很轻松地称为 disc 了。jockey 的意思是"职业赛马骑师"，按英语的感觉来说，是"操纵马的人"。因此，disc jockey 就是"操纵唱片的人"的意味。这就是本条习用语最初的构思。由于 disc 的拼写不符合英语的传统缀字法，一般均写成 disk。但不知什么原因，在作"唱片"解的场合，人们总喜欢按古典的方式拼写。当然，也有不少人写作 disk jockey。另外，请读者注意 jockey 的发音。*That disc jockey used to be a news announcer.* 那个流行音乐唱片节目播音员过去是报告新闻的。*Late-night disc jockey programs are very popular these days.* 最近一个时期，深夜播放流行音乐唱片颇受人们欢迎。又称 a DEEJAY。◇ an announcer who plays records on the radio

jockey for position → POSITION

Joe

a G. I. Joe [ə ˌdʒi(ː)ˌaɪ ˈdʒou] [话] **美国兵** → a good JOE

a good Joe [ə ˌgudˈdʒou] [话] **大好人** a Joe 与 a fellow 或者 a guy 相同，是"小子"、"家伙"的意思。*I was walking down the street when some Joe comes up to me and asks me to lend him a dollar.* 当我在大街上漫步的时候，有一个小子向我走来，要我借给他一美元。a G. I. Joe 是"普通一兵"，一般指美国兵。*I'm just a G. I. Joe. I only do what my Uncle Sam tells me to.* 我只是个普通美国兵，山姆大叔（即美国）叫我干啥我就干啥。a good Joe 也是习用语，意思是 a nice everyday type of fellow (善良的老百姓)。主要是男性用语。*He hasn't got all that much on the ball, but he's a good Joe.* 他没有多大能耐，但是一个大好人。Joe 的第一个字母一般大写，但也可以小写。*You'll like Alfonso. He's a good joe.* 你会喜欢阿方索的，他是一个大好人。另外，偶尔也有女性使用的情况。*Frank's a good Joe, but he's not the type I would ever want to marry.* 弗兰克是个大好人，但是他不是我想与之结婚的那一类人。◇ a nice fellow

John

a Dear John letter → LETTER

a john [ə ˈdʒɑ(ː)n] [俗] **厕所** 由男子名 John 而来。John 是一个非常普遍的名字，正如厕所一样，不论什么地方都有。可能由于这个原因，人们就把 John 作为厕所的代名词了。这是美国制造的一个表达法，已有相当长的历史，至迟是 18 世纪的产物。这一表达法虽然并没有特别坏的意味，但为男性专用的一种轻松的俚语，因此在使用时，必须考虑时间、地点和场合。*Is there a john around here?* 这附近有没有厕所呀？*He lives in a big house with two baths and three johns.* 他住在一所大房子里，有两个浴室，三个厕所。*I gotta go to the john.* 我憋不住啦，得上厕所。◇ a toilet

John Hancock

put *one's* **John Hancock on** *something* [put ～ ˌdʒɑ(ː)n ˈhæ(ː)nˌkɑkɔ(ː)n ～] [话] **签字** 这里的 put 是"写"的意思。John Hancock (1737—1793) 因担当通过美国独立宣言的大陆会议 (the Continental Congress) 的主席而闻名。他首先用又粗又大的字体在宣言上签名，因此，John Hancock 这一人名本身就具有"署名"的意味了。*After some deliberation, Bill put his John Hancock on the contract.* 稍微考虑一下之后，比尔在合同上签了字。*There's nothing to it. Just put your John Hancock on the dotted line.* 这很简单，你只要在虚线上边签个字就行啦。如以上的例句所示，这一表达法大多用于合同之类文件通过签字产生法律效力的场合，但并不限定如此。*The baseball player put his John Hancock on the little boy's ball.* 那个棒球运动员在小男孩的球上签了名。另外，说不清由于什么原因，从 19 世纪下半叶起，美国西部开始流行一个意思相同的表达法：put *one's* John Henry on *something*。现在，这一表达法与 put *one's* John Hancock on *something* 并驾齐驱，全国通用。◇ sign *something*

John Henry

put *one's* **John Henry on** *something* [put ～ ˌdʒɑ(ː)n ˈhenriɔ(ː)n ～] [话] **签名** → put *one's* JOHN HANCOCK on *something*

johnny

a johnny house → HOUSE

Johnny-come-lately

a Johnny-come-lately [ə ˈdʒɑ(ː)ni ˌkʌmˈleɪtli] [口] **新来的人** Johnny 是 John [ˈdʒɑ(ː)n] 的爱称。John 是美国极为普遍的人名，常用作统称某一类人的代名词(→ a JOHNNY-ON-THE-SPOT)。*Everyone was surprised when a Johnny-come-lately with no experience in national politics won the Democratic Party's presidential nomination.* 当一个对于国家政治毫无经验的新手赢得民主党总统候选人提名的时候，所有的人都大吃一惊。在下面的例句中是"新参加者"的意思，根据上下文，常含有轻蔑的意味。*Our club has grown too fast. There are too many Johnny-come-latelies who want to change the rules.* 我们的俱乐部发展得过快了，想要改变俱乐部规章的新参加者实在太多啦。◇ a (green) newcomer

Johnny-on-the-spot

a Johnny-on-the-spot [ə ˈdʒɑ(ː)ni ɔnðə ˈspɑ(ː)t] [话] **机灵的人** 这里的 on the spot 是"在现场"的意思。本条字面可译作"永远在场的约翰"。这个 Johnny 当然不是指某个特定的人，而是"好助手"的代名词。这种人用不着吩咐，恰恰在你需要的时候前来给你做你想叫他做的事情。Johnny 虽然为男子名,但对男女均可使用。另外,Johnny-on-the-spot 虽然是可数名词,大概由于其中包含有人名,在使用时多不加冠词。*I was just about to ring for something for my callers to drink when my secretary, always Johnny-on-the-spot, appeared at the doorway carrying a tray of coffee.* 我正想按铃,为客人们要点饮料,我那位一向非常机灵的秘书在门口出现了,端的盘子里放着咖啡。当事人是不是天性如此,一向是个"机灵鬼",这没有关系,本条也用于偶然在做什么时"机灵"一次的场合。*Just as we had begun to fear that the power failure would prevent our holding the meeting as scheduled, Jud was Johnny-on-the-spot with a portable generator.* 我们正在开始担心停电会妨碍我们举行预定的会议,贾德这个机灵鬼拿来了一架手提式发电机。大多使用 real 加强语气。*My daughter is a real Johnny-on-the-spot. She's always there when I need her to help me in the kitchen.* 我的女儿真是个机灵鬼。当我在厨房里需要有人帮忙时,她总是出现在我的身旁。◇ (someone who is) helpful in answer to the need of the moment

John Q. Public

John Q. Public [.dʒɑ(:)n .kjuː ˈpʌblɪk] [口] **一般市民** → the MAN in the street

johns

long johns [ˈlɔ(:)ŋ .dʒɑːnz] [话] **男子的长内衣** 冬季用的内衣,连手腕和脚腕都能遮住,即所谓的 combinations。这一表达法来源于又瘦又高的男子的浑名 Long John (细高挑儿约翰)。正式的名称为 a union suit,比较轻松的说法是 LONGIES,有点戏谑的说法是 long-handle(d) underwear。自从使用集中供暖以来,城市人与这种旧式内衣早已无缘;可是,在农民、工人、猎户、钓翁、山林劳动者和户外工作者之中,依然有很多人爱用它。*Where are my long johns?* 我的长内衣在哪儿? *I always wear long johns when I go deer hunting.* 我去猎鹿的时候,总是穿长内衣。现在,如果是长内衣,即使是衬裤分为两件,也称为 long johns。◇ long underwear

joint

case the joint [ˈkeɪsðə .dʒɔɪnt] [话] **探路** 原为黑社会用语。这里的 case 是"为了犯罪的目的仔细侦察"的意思。joint 指住宅、银行、商店以及其他各种成为犯罪对象的建筑物或场所。*We'd better case the joint to make sure there are no cops hanging around.* 咱们最好先探探路,看看有没有警察在巡逻。*Lou is casing the joint now. He's going to give us a call when the coast is clear.* 卢现在正在探路哪。如果无人妨碍,他就给咱们打电话。象以上这样的台词,在小说、电视、电影里是经常出现的。一般人有时也模仿坏人的口气,把这一表达法作为戏谑语使用。*There's a likely restaurant over there. Let me go over and case the joint first. There's no use in all of us getting out of the car if there are no tables available.* 对面有一家看起来还可以的餐厅。我先去打探一番。那儿如果没有空着的座位,我们用不着全都下车啊。*I'm supposed to go there for a job interview tomorrow, so I think I'll go over today just to case the joint.* 明天是我就业面试的日子,因此,我想今天前去探探路。◇ look the place over

a clip joint [ə ˈklɪp .dʒɔɪnt] [话] **索价特别高昂的商店** clip 一词有 cheat (欺骗)或 overcharge (乱要价)的意思。例如: *That guy clipped me for fifty dollars.* 那个家伙从我手里骗走了五十美元。joint 大致与 place 同义,是一个非常轻松的说法。一般指商店、住宅等建筑物乃至房间。*Let's get out of this joint.* 咱们离开这家商店[这个地方]吧。因此,clip joint 是"索价特别高昂的商店"的意思,与 a rip-off joint 相同 (→ RIP *someone* off)。*You should never go to a bar in New York that you haven't been introduced to by an acquaintance. There are too many clip joints around.* 如果没有熟人介绍,你千万不要走进纽约的酒吧间。漫天要价的酒吧间太多了。*Stay* *away from that cabaret. It's a real clip joint.* 你可要离那个卡巴莱远着点。那可真是一个大敲竹杠的地方啊。当你一听到 clip joint 这个名词的时候,你首先会想到酒吧间、卡巴莱、大餐馆之类漫天要价的地方,但有时也可以用于普通的商店。*That guy runs a chain of clothing stores, but they're all clip joints.* 那个家伙经营衣着用品系列商店,索价全都特别高。◇ a place that charges outrageous [fraudulent] prices ((不加 real))

a rip-off joint [ə ˈrɪ.pɔːf .dʒɔɪnt] [话] **大敲竹杠的商店** → RIP *someone* off

joke

crack a joke [.krækə ˈdʒouk] [话] **开玩笑** 这里的 crack 与 crack a whip (甩响鞭)中的 crack 在构思上完全相同。这一表达法不能用于"讲个有趣的故事"(tell a funny story) 的场合,一般仅指说一句半句的俏皮话。*This is a serious meeting. Crack another joke like that and out you go.* 这是一个严肃的会议。你如果再开玩笑,就叫你出去啦。如这一例句所示,joke 可以用单数,但使用复数的时候居多。*Phil is forever cracking jokes.* 菲尔总爱开玩笑。*The men were sitting around the stove cracking jokes.* 那几个人坐在火炉边上说笑哪。◇ make a joking remark / tell a joke

Joneses

keep up with the Joneses [ki(ː)p.ʌp wɪðə ˈdʒounzəz] [口] **与左邻右舍斗富** the Joneses (琼斯一家)是社会地位、经济情况与自己相等的人们的代名词,不限于邻近的人,但"左邻右舍"的意味很强烈。keep up with 是"紧跟上去,不要落后"的意思。这一表达法所表现的行动"哲学"是:别人买一辆新汽车,我不买不行;别人去海外游览,我不去不成;一切的一切,都要向社会潮流看齐。*The urge to keep up with the Joneses is a phenomenon that can be found in almost every society.* 几乎在任何社会里都可以见到极力与左邻右舍斗富的现象。*We're never able to save money because my wife thinks we always have to keep up with the Joneses.* 由于我的妻子认为我们家无论如何不能落后于左邻右舍,所以我们家永远也存不下钱。*Mrs. Jones is concerned only with keeping up with the Joneses.* 琼斯太太只关心一件事,那就是与左邻右舍斗富。◇ compete with others in demonstrating *one's* social level

josh

josh (*someone* about *something*) [ˈdʒɑ(ː)ʃ] [口] **逗趣** 有开玩笑的意味。比 KID (*someone* about *something*) 的使用范围窄得多,在认真的场合(如恼怒时)不能使用。与 tease 有相似的一面,但 tease 有时表示"恶意的嘲笑",josh 则是"说点俏皮话",毫无恶意在内。*Jacques often joshes me about my American accent.* 雅克常常拿我的美国口音逗趣。Jacques 是个法国人。*We were joshing Jack about his new girl, when suddenly he got angry.* 杰克新交了一个女朋友,我们拿这件事打趣他,而他却突然恼火啦。*They're the best of friends, always joshing each other back and forth.* 他们是极要好的朋友,经常互相逗趣。也可以用作不及物动词。*Don't take it so seriously. They were only joshing.* 你不要那么认真吧,他们只是逗个趣罢了。另外,josh 也有名词用法,但极少使用。joshing 和 josher 为派生词,其中 joshing 常常使用,而 josher 则很少使用。*We gave Harriet a good joshing over her mistake.* 哈丽特搞错了,我们大大地逗弄了她一番。◇ tease *someone* (lightly) / banter *someone*

joy

a joy stick → STICK

judge

(as) sober as a judge [əz ˈsoubərəzə ˈdʒʌ(ː)dʒ] [口] **头脑清醒** sober 一词有"清醒"和"严肃"两方面的意思。as a judge (象法官那样)只是用以加强语气,基本意思不变。唯一的变化是,在加上 as a judge 之后,用于表示"清醒"意思的时候多,而用于表示"严肃"意味的场合少。另外，在表示“清醒”的场合，这一表达法为 (as) drunk as a LORD 的反义习用语。*I haven't had much to drink. I'm still sober as a judge.* 我并没有喝多少呀，我的头脑还完全清醒着哪。*Stu can hardly stand up, but he claims he's as sober as a judge.* 司徒几乎站不起来了，可是他还硬说自己一点儿也没有喝醉哪。在用于表示“严肃”的意味时，总是指“表情”而言，亦即“板着一副面孔”。*The little boy didn't laugh when I fell down. He just stood there watching me, as sober as a judge.* 在我摔倒的时候，那个小男孩并没有笑。他只是站在那里绷着脸望着我。◇ completely sober

juice

cow juice [ˈkau ˌdʒuːs] [话] **牛乳** 这一表达法已经有一百多年的历史。虽然富有儿童用语的稚气，但成年人也很喜欢使用。*How about some cow juice?* 喝点牛奶好吗? ◇ milk

sky juice [ˈskaɪ ˌdʒuːs] [话] **水** 有点儿童气味的戏谑语。*Better take an umbrella. Looks like we may get a little sky juice.* 最好带把伞走，天似乎要下雨啦。如这一例句所示，本条习用语原是“雨”的意思。后来转用于泛指“水”。*Gimme a glass of sky juice.* 给我一杯水吧! ◇ water

stew in *one's* **own juice** [ˌstuːən ~ ˌounˈdʒuːs] [话] **自作自受** 这一表达法是具有同一意义的习用语 fry in *one's* own grease (用自己的脂肪去油炸自己) 的翻板。历史相当悠久，在 13 世纪所写的关于英王查理一世 (Richard I) 的传说中即已经出现。原来似乎应用于处火刑的囚犯。 stew 为动词，意思是“用文火炖”。juice 是“汁”，在这里指“体液”。整个表达法的字面意义为“用自己的体液煮自己”。但 stew 另有“忧虑”、“着急”一义，所以这一表达法就有了在悔恨或者恼怒的时候内心焦躁不安的意味，也就是自己给自己找苦恼，结果便是“自作自受”了。*I warned him that if he didn't follow my advice he would fail. Of course I intend to bail him out, but not yet. Let him stew in his own juice for a while.* 我对他说过，如果他不听从我的忠告，他必然失败。我当然打算使他脱离困境，但是为时尚早。叫他先自己尝尝苦头再说吧。*I left Nelson to stew in his own juice for about a week after I got his telephone call.* 纳尔逊给我打电话来之后，大约有一个星期左右我没有理他，叫他自己去尝尝苦头吧。如以上的例句所示，这一表达法大多用于说话者心怀“活该!”、“你瞧瞧!”等有思想准备看人笑话的场合。*You enjoy stewing in your own juice, don't you. You'd rather do that than risk hurting your foolish pride by letting your friends help you.* 你很喜欢自作自受吧。你不如丢掉愚不可及的自尊心，让你的朋友们帮助你为好。*Taxes are so high now because the people of this country were stupid enough to vote in a so-called Democratic government. Well, they can stew in their own juice for all I care. I'm going abroad to live.* 现在赋税这样多，都是由于本国人民太愚蠢了，投票选举所谓的“民主”政府。好啦，叫他们自作自受吧，这与我无干，我要到外国去住了。◇ suffer (from the consequences of *one's* own actions)

jump

get the jump on *someone* (by *doing something*) [ˌgetðə ˈdʒʌ(ː)mpɔ(ː)n ~] [话] **抢在前边** 本来的意思是“在赛跑中比人先起一步”。可以按字面意义使用，如说: *Ted got the jump on the other runners at the start of the race and led all the way to the finish.* 特德在赛跑的起点比别的选手抢先起跑，直到终点一直领先。转义不限于赛跑，广泛应用于一切”有胜负”、“争成绩”的事情。*I don't know if we'll be able to get the contract with ABC Corporation or not. One of our rivals got the jump on us by contacting them first.* 我不晓得咱们公司能不能跟 ABC 公司签订合同。咱们的一家竞争对手已经抢先一步跟该公司洽谈了。*Nixon got the jump on the other would-be Republican candidates for Pres-*

ident by securing the backing of party bigwigs before the campaign started. 尼克松在选举运动开始之前,就已经比其他争取共和党总统候选人提名的一些人抢先一步得到了党内有势力人物的支持。get the DROP on *someone* (by *doing something*)的意味和用法几乎与本条的表达法完全一样,但严密地讲,二者之间仍有细微的差别。例如: *Roy got the jump on his classmates by starting to study for the test a week early.* 罗伊抢先一步,比同班同学早一个星期开始复习功课准备考试。在这一例句中,可以将 jump 换成 drop,但前一表达法强调"首先采取行动",而后一表达法的重点在于"占有优势"。也有用 have 表示状态的场合,作 have the jump on *someone*(一步占先)。 *Several other teams have the jump on us for the conference championship, but we can still win it if we work hard.* 在联合锦标赛中,有几个其他的队比我们占先一步,但是只要我们努力拚搏,我们仍然有优胜的希望啊。◇ gain an early start on [over] *someone*

just

just like that → LIKE

K

kayo

kayo *someone* [ˈkeɪ.ou ～] [话] **击倒** 按 knock out 的缩略语 KO [ˈkeɪ.ou] 的发音拼写而成。拳击以外也使用,但只限于用拳头把人击倒或击昏的场合。这是一个比 knock out 更轻松的说法,变化如下:kayos(第三人称单数),kayoed(过去时,过去分词)。*I'll kayo him in the first round.* 我在第一轮就要把他击倒。*The champ has never been kayoed.* 冠军迄今没有被击倒过。*He kayoed the burglar with a hard right to the jaw.* 他用右勾拳狠狠给强盗的下巴一下,把强盗击倒了。也可以使用大写字母,拚写为 KO, KO's, KO'ed [K.O., K.O.'s, K.O.'ed]。*He called me that, did he? Where is he? I'll KO the bum.* 他管我叫那个,是吗?他在哪里?我把这个讨吃鬼一拳打翻在地。◇ knock *someone* out [unconscious]

keel

on an even keel [.ɔnə ˈniːvənˈkiːl] [口] **平平稳稳** keel 是"船的龙骨",即船底的脊棱。整个习用语直译为"龙骨处于水平状态"。这一表达法原指船不向前后左右倾斜,十分平稳的样子。*We'd better shift this cargo. The boat isn't on an even keel.* 我们最好把这个货物移动一下,现在船不平稳。作为比喻,广泛应用于经济状况、政局情况以及心理状态等。*We'll have to work to keep the company on an even keel during the coming recession.* 在即将到来的经济萧条时期,为了保持公司的稳定,我们必须苦干一番啊。 *Even ten years after the revolution, the country was not yet back on an even keel.* 革命以后已经十年了,国家还没有稳定下来。*Women like her seldom stay on an even keel. Even the smallest things upset them.* 象她那样的女人很少有情绪稳定的时候,一点小事也会使她们心烦意乱。◇ in a stable condition / calm

keeps

for keeps [fərˈkiːps] [话] **一本正经地** for keeps 来自儿童游戏。特别是在玩玻璃球的时候,常常可以听到这句话。意思是"输了不许往回拿",用儿童的话来说就是"玩真格的"。反义语是 for fun(闹着玩儿)。 *Shall we play for fun or for keeps?* 咱们是随便玩儿,还是来真格的?另有一个定型的说法是 play for keeps(玩真的)。*Jimmy is the best marble shooter, so he always wants to play for keeps.* 吉米最善于弹玻璃球,所以他总愿意玩真的。作为比喻,这个 for keeps 有各式各样的用法,但是万变不离其宗,它始终具有上边所讲的"真格的"的精神,这个精神的实质是:"一旦得出结论,这个结论永远不能变更"。因此,在一般的英汉词典中有"当真地"、"永远地"的释义。在作为比喻使用的场合,也与玩玻璃球的场合一样,play for keeps 是个固定的句型。 *I wouldn't mess around with Sally unless you're serious. She's the type who plays for keeps.* 如果你不持严肃的态度,最好不要跟萨莉交往。她是那种非常认真的类型的人。这意思就是说:"一旦跟她交朋友,就永远不能变心"。下一例句是讲和生意上的敌人"干到底",即"要将对方打翻在地,使其永远站不起来"的意思。*Our competitors would be happy to drive us out of business if they could. They believe in playing for keeps.* 我们的竞争对手只要有可能的话,是很高兴把我们赶出做买卖这一行的。他们认为搞生意就必须斗争到底。在情节小说中常常可以见到如下的叙述: *When I heard the bullet whistle by my head, I realized they were playing for keeps.* 当我听到子弹从我的脑袋旁边呼啸而过的时候，我明白他们是动真刀真枪啦。在这一场合，“动真刀真枪”的意思并不是恫吓一番或者生俘，而是要“杀头”的。其次，for keeps 也可以与 play 以外的动词搭配。当然，即使搭配其他动词，for keeps 的含意并不改变。例如向借钱的人要帐，而对方却嘻皮笑脸，这时说：*Don't laugh. It's no joking matter. This is for keeps.* 你不要笑，这可不是开玩笑，这是正经事。在这一场合中，for keeps 一语也令人感到说话者的强烈意志，表示“如果你不还钱，我要采取一定措施”、“我要叫你吃不了兜着走”，甚至在某种情况下意味着“我要杀了你”。*When I saw my bride coming down the aisle toward me, it struck me as never before that this was for keeps.* 当我见到我的新娘从教堂坐椅的通道向我走来的时候，我从来没有象这样强烈地感觉到：一切都已成定局了。这就是说：“要想反悔，为时已晚”。同时，在这一例句中，也很明显地表达出 for keeps 所含有的 for GOOD (永久地)的意味。在下一个例句中，这个意味就更明显地与词典中的译文“永久地”完全吻合。*I'm going to settle that guy's hash for keeps.* 我要使那小子一败涂地，永世不得翻身。◇ in terms of permanent results / very serious / forever

keg

be sitting on a powder keg [ˌsɪtɪŋɔ(ː)nə ˈpaudər ˌke(ː)g] [口] **一触即发之势** 字面意义是“坐在火药桶(powder keg)上”。在作为比喻的时候，powder keg 是“不知什么时候会爆发的危险局势”。但只能在周围情况对本人危险的场合使用，不能用于当事者之间关系恶化、一触即发的场合。本人有时了解这种情况，也有时对此一无所知。*With the demonstrations increasing in violence day by day, the capitalists were well aware that they were sitting on a powder keg.* 由于示威运动日益猛烈，资本家们心里十分清楚，他们周围的情况万分危险，大有一触即发之势。*Little did the Americans in Iran realize that they were sitting on a powder keg.*。在伊朗的美国人并没有注意到他们正在一触即发的危难当中。*The town had suddenly become quiet, but I could not escape the feeling that we were sitting on a powder keg.* 城镇突然一片寂静，但是我未能摆脱这样的感觉：我们正在面临一场一触即发的危机。也可以单独使用 a powder keg。*With more and more countries developing atomic weapons, the world is fast becoming a huge powder keg.* 由于越来越多的国家发展原子武器，世界正在迅速地变成一个巨大的火药库。◇ be in a potentially explosive situation

kettle

(a case of) the pot calling the kettle black → POT

a pretty kettle of fish → FISH

key

a church key [ə ˈtʃərtʃ ˌkiː] [俗] **瓶起子、开罐器** 字面意义是“教堂的钥匙”。这是一个戏谑的说法，一是因为它们形状极其相似，二是因为教会各宗派大多禁止酒类。本条原指“开饮料(特别是啤酒)瓶盖的前端呈圆形的起子”，现在也指开罐头的工具。另外，这虽然是一个轻松的表达法，为广大群众所使用，但是所谓的正统派基督教徒则很讨厌它，所以在使用时，最好看准对象。*We brought lots of beer but forgot to bring a church key.* 我们拿来了许多啤酒，但是忘带瓶起子啦。◇ a bottle [can] opener

kick

get a kick out of (*doing*) *something* [ˌgedə ˈkɪkaudəv ～] [话] **有干某种事情的乐趣** kick 原意为因喝酒、吸毒等而产生的“飘飘然的感觉”，后又转义为“刺激性”(thrill)。在本条内，指在干自己所喜好的事情时产生的飘飘然的心情和极轻松的快感。整条直译为“从干某一事情中得到极大的乐趣”。*I get a kick out of cowboy movies [skin diving].* 我很爱看西部影片［潜泳］。*Our son gets a kick out of collecting insects.* 我的儿子很喜欢采集昆虫。在加强语气时用 a big kick。*My wife seems to get a big kick* *out of just window shopping*. 我的妻子似乎对到处观看商店的橱窗有莫大的乐趣。◇ enjoy (*doing*) *something* very much

kick *something* **around** [ˌkɪk ~ əˈraund] [话] **多方面研究** 直译为"东踢一脚,西踢一脚"。最初的构思是:把空罐头盒或者石块往这里踢一下,然后又往那里踢一下,从各种不同的角度仔细端详。虽然有"从各种不同的角度观察"的意味,但这一表达法并不用于严肃对待和深刻考虑紧急情况的场合。*We kicked the plan around for a week or so, and then decided it wouldn't work after all*. 我们对那个计划研究了一个来星期,结果认为它根本没有实行的可能性。*That sounds like a fairly good approach. Let's kick it around at the next meeting*. 那似乎是一个很好的建议,咱们在下次的会议中研究一下吧。*We kicked around the idea of buying a new house, but then decided that it would be wiser to stay here*. 我们从各方面研究了一下买新房子的想法,后来得出结论说,还是住在这里为上策。一般来说,二人以上相互谈论的场合比较多,但不是限定如此。有时也用于一个人在头脑中左思右想的场合。*Here's an idea I've been kicking around in my mind for the past few weeks. Tell me what you think of it*. 我有一个想法,在过去的几个星期中,我已经反复考虑多次了。现在我想听听你的意见。◇ consider *something*

kick *someone* **downstairs** [ˌkɪk ~ ˌdaunˈstɛːrs] [话] **降低某人的级别** → kick *someone* UPSTAIRS

kick *someone* **out** [ˌkɪt ~ ˈaut] [话] **撵走** 本来的意思是"把某人踢出去"。有时是"一时地把某人从某个场所撵走",也有时是"从公司、团体、机关等永远地开除"。这一表达法的使用范围相当广。*The boys were making so much noise during the movie that the manager finally kicked them out*. 演电影的时候,一些男孩吵得太凶了,影院经理终于把他们撵出去了。*You can't kick me out. I'm a member of this club*. 你不能把我撵出去,我是这个俱乐部的会员。*We kicked him out of the club for not paying his dues*. 由于他不交会费,我们把他从俱乐部开除了。可以用 get [be] kicked out 这样的被动语态,在这一场合,一般具"永远地"的意味。*I got kicked out of school because of low grades*. 由于学习成绩太差,我被学校勒令退学了。*The D. A. was kicked out of office for taking bribes*. 由于受贿,地方检查官被开除了公职。可以将 kick 换成 boot, 有 boot *someone* out, get [be] booted out 等表达法。意思和用法完全相同;但用 kick 的时候比较多。kick [boot] *someone* off the *something* 也与 kick *someone* out 同义,但用法略有差异。out 变成 off 以后,意思是"取消作为团体成员的资格"。也就是在讲构成某个俱乐部、球队的人员时,使用 off。*The coach kicked Jim off the basketball team for smoking*. 吉姆由于抽烟,教练把他赶出了篮球队。*Several policemen were kicked off the squad for drinking on duty*. 有几个警察由于在值勤中饮酒,被队里开除了。◇ remove *someone* / take away *someone's* membership

kick the habit → HABIT

kick *someone* **upstairs** → UPSTAIRS

a top kick [ə ˈtɑ(ː)p ˌkɪk] [话] **上司** 原为陆军俚语,指的是 first sergeant(军士),但空军和海军也使用。*Who's your top kick?* 你班的军士是谁?现在转义,用于表示"在机关、团体、组织、工厂、工地、车间等等拥有最高决定权、统治权的人"的意味,如董事长、部长、科长、主任、工头、工长、现场指挥之类,在翻译时,可根据上下文确定适当的名称。一般语调轻松,在朋友、同事之间使用。*I can't answer that. I'll have to ask the top kick*. 那个问题我回答不了。我必须去请示部长。*Our top kick is a real taskmaster*. 我们的工长实在严厉得很啊。如以上的例句所示,大多不用不定冠词 a, 而用定冠词或代词所有格。◇ a boss

kicking

be alive and kicking → ALIVE

kid

handle *someone* [*something*] **with kid gloves** → GLOVES

kid (*someone* about *something*) ['kɪ(:)d] [话] **取笑** 大多语调轻松，"取笑"的程度一般不达到使对方恼怒的地步。"取笑"一词的内涵包括"逗弄"、"开玩笑"、"哄骗"等等，多种多样。*He likes to kid people.* 他喜欢拿别人开心。*Don't get mad. I'm only kidding you.* 不要恼火，我只不过跟你开个玩笑罢了。*The boss's daughter wants a date with me?—Wait a minute. You wouldn't be trying to kid me, would you?* 你说老板的女儿想跟我约会？哎呀，且慢。你不是在哄骗我吧？*Tom's always kidding me about my scraggly beard.* 汤姆总爱拿我的稀稀拉拉的胡子开心。以上所讲都是 kid 的本来用法。此外，有很多使用 kid 的定型的表达法。第一个就是 I'm not kidding. 直译为"我不是在开玩笑"。大多在恼怒的时候使用，意思是"我说的是实在话"。*I'm not kidding. If you're late once more, you're fired.* 我不是跟你说笑话。如果你再迟到一次，我就开除你。最近，在应该说 I'm not kidding. 的场合，有些人仿照莎士比亚时代的英语，把 not 移到后边，作 I kid you not. 大多用于戏谑。第二个表达法是 kid *oneself*，直译为"哄骗自己"，意思是"把事情想得太天真了"、"把现实看得太简单了"。*Don't kid yourself. Nobody's going to pay that much for you old car.* 你想得太天真啦。对你那辆旧汽车，谁也不会出那么大的价钱。另外还有 No kidding. Are you kidding? 以及 You've got to be kidding. 等，这些都是日常的习用语。在听完对方的话时，用这几种说法表示"是吗？"，"真的吗？"、"不能吧！"或者"哪儿的话！"的意思。如果勉强直译的话，这三个表达法分别是"别开玩笑啦！"、"你是开玩笑吧？"和"你一定是在开玩笑呀！"。使用时语调大多十分轻松，但也有时碰到严重情况，包含着一腔怒火。语气增强的顺序如下：No kidding. → Are you kidding? → You've got to be kidding. 其中，No kidding.的使用范围特别广，从"真的吗？"一直到"不可能吧"。*A: Ben called me last night. B: No kidding? What did he say?* 甲：昨天晚上，本给我打电话来啦。乙：是吗？他说什么来着？ *A: I'm getting married next month. B: No kidding! Are you really?* 甲：我下个月结婚。乙：不可能吧！你是说真的吗？ *No kidding. It's really true.* 不是开玩笑。是真而又真的。*Are you kidding? I wouldn't date Hester Hoghock if she were the last girl in the world!* 这是哪儿的话呢！即使世界上只剩下赫斯特·霍格霍克这样一个姑娘，我也决不会跟她约会的。*Me? Get up at four in the morning? You've got to be kidding!* 我？早晨四点起床？这简直是开玩笑！还有名词 a kidder (爱拿别人开心的人)，a kidding (戏弄) 等。*Phil's a great kidder.* 菲尔是一位爱拿别人开心的人。*What's the matter? Can't you take a little kidding?* 怎么回事？开个小玩笑你就受不了啦？ ◇ tease / fool / be not serious

kid *oneself* ['kɪ(:)d ~] [话] **自己哄骗自己** → KID (*someone* about *something*)

kidder

a kidder [ə'kɪdər] [话] **爱拿别人开心的人** → KID (*someone* about *something*)

kill

be dressed up fit to kill [ˌdrestˌʌp ˌfɪtə 'kɪ(:)l] [话] **盛装打扮** 如果只是 be dressed up，意思为"打扮"。后面加上 fit to kill，意思为"达到最高的程度"。fit to kill 的字面意义是"适合于被人杀死"。这一表达法直译为"打扮得宁愿当场被人杀死"，极度夸张，当然在使用时不能考虑这一意义。*Everyone at the Prime Minister's reception was dressed up fit to kill.* 在首相的招待会上，每个人都盛装打扮了起来。如这一例句所示，一般用于表示"盛装"的意味，但也有时指"打扮得太过分"，例如：*Mr. and Mrs. Jones arrived at the picnic dressed up fit to kill.* 琼斯夫妇出席野餐会的时候，打扮得未免太花哨啦。这一表达法在使用时常作被动语态 be dressed up ～，但不限定如此。*She dresses up fit to kill even to go* *out shopping*. 她甚至在去买东西的时候,也打扮得花枝招展。另外,也可以去掉 up,而说 be dressed fit to kill 或者 dress fit to kill。在被动语态的场合,也可以省去 fit,只说 be dressed to kill。顺便提一下:fit to kill 脱离这一表达法,可以独立使用,为强调其他动词的短语,意思是"极度地"。→ laugh fit to KILL ◇ be very smartly dressed

kill *someone* **with kindness** → KINDNESS

laugh fit to kill [ˌlæ(ː)ˈfɪːtə ˈkɪ(ː)l] [话] **哈哈大笑** fit to kill 的字面意义为"虽然被杀,也无遗憾",表示极度的强调。*When Jim appeared on the stage in an evening gown, everyone laughed fit to kill*. 当吉姆穿着晚礼服在舞台上出现的时候,全体观众都哈哈大笑起来了。一般仅用以表示"哈哈大笑"的意思,但也常有含讽刺意味的场合,表示"耻笑"对方的失误等,如说:*I laughed fit to kill when that guy's company went bankrupt*. 当那个家伙的公司倒闭的时候,我简直笑掉了大牙。在包含 fit to kill 的习用语中,最常用的除 laugh fit to kill 外,还有 be dressed up fit to KILL。有时作为强调的短语,fit to kill 也与其他动词结合使用。◇ laugh very hard

killing

be killing *one* [ˈkɪlən ~] [话] **疼得厉害** 字面意义为"在杀某个人"。这是一个夸张的表达法,与汉语的"疼死我也"完全一致。*After the hike my feet were killing me*. 远足之后,我的脚简直疼极啦。*The hand I had caught in the car door was killing me*. 我的一只手被夹在汽车门上,简直把我疼死啦。*I don't think I can play golf today. My back is killing me*. 今天我不能打高尔夫球啦,我的背部疼得要命。◇ be extremely sore [painful]

make a killing [ˌmeɪkə ˈkɪlən] [话] **发大财** killing 为什么作"发大财"解,语源不详。在股票市场上大发利市的时候常常使用。*Ned's father made a killing on the stock market*. 内德的父亲在股票市场上大发利市啦。*He tried to make a killing by cornering the silver market, but ended up losing millions of dollars instead*. 他企图在银市场上发个大财,但是结果却赔了几百万美元。当然,也可以用于与市场无关的发大财。*Mr. Fisher has made a killing by opening his land to hunters at fifty dollars a head*. 费舍先生由于向猎人开放自己的土地,每人收五十美元,因而发了大财。如果把 a 改成 *one's*,作 make *one's* killing,这是由于发大财已经成了富翁的意思。 *He made his killing on the summer people*. 他之所以成为富翁,是在夏季游人的身上发了大财。◇ make a tremendous amount of money

killjoy

a killjoy [ə ˈkɪ(ː)lˌdʒɔɪ] [话] **令人扫兴的人** 字面意义为"杀死快乐"。这一表达法与 a wet BLANKET 相似。但是,a wet blanket 为"由于自己心情不好而在言语行动上消极地使大家扫兴的人"的意思,与此相反,a killjoy 则正如字面所示,一般用于表示"积极地或有意识地妨碍他人快乐的人"的意味。*I don't understand Sally. Sometimes I think she enjoys being a killjoy*. 我不理解萨莉这个人,有时我觉得她以扫别人的兴致为乐趣。*Don't be a killjoy, Dad. Let us use the car tonight*. 爸爸,你不要扫大家的兴吧,今天晚上让我们用一下汽车。使人扫兴的一般手段是以规章、道德为盾牌,或者以权力、立场为依靠。 *The guy's a real killjoy. Every time we come up with an idea for having a good time, he thinks of some reason why we shouldn't do it*. 那个家伙是个专门泼冷水的人。每当我们想起什么有意思的事情,他必然要找出若干我们为什么不应该干的理由。如这一例句所示,常用 real 加强语气。 *That prof is a real killjoy. He always gives us a lot of homework to do during spring vacation*. 那位教授的确是一个令人扫兴的老师。每当春假的时候,他总是给我们留下一大批作业。有时不仅用以表示"人",也可以用以表示"物"。*Rain on a picnic is always a killjoy*. 对于野餐会来说,雨总是非常令人扫兴的。◇ a person who spoils other people's enjoyment

kimono

a wooden kimono [ə ˌwudnkəˈmounə] [话] 棺材 → a wooden OVERCOAT

kindly

take kindly to *something* [*someone*] [ˌteɪk ˈkaɪndlitə ～] [口] **乐意接受** kind 原来是"天然的"(natural)的意思，经过漫长的历史时期，才变成现在的意味"亲切的"。原来意味的 kind 如今已成废语，仅在 take kindly to ～这一表达法中还残存着它的遗韵。因此，这里的 kindly 不是"亲切的"，而是"天然地"(naturally)。 *Roses take kindly to this type of soil.* 直译为"蔷薇天然地接受这类土壤"，也就是"蔷薇适应于这种土壤"。take to 在这里是"接受"的意思，作为比喻则经常有"爱好"、"喜欢"的意思，可以认为与下一例句中的 take to 相近。 *He doesn't take to cold places.* 他不喜欢寒冷的地方。总起来讲，这一表达法的整体就是"由于喜欢，自然而然地、很痛快地接受"，一般在否定句、疑问句、条件句中使用。 *Mr. Hobbs didn't take kindly to my suggestion that he should think about retiring.* 我劝霍布斯先生考虑退休的问题，他不乐意接受我的建议。 *Do you really think the boss will take kindly to your quitting your job?* 你真认为老板会乐意叫你辞职吗？ *If anything would make Japan take kindly to Russia's overtures, it would be the return of the northern islands.* 如果问日本在哪一个问题上乐意接受苏联的建议，那就是归还北方四岛。下面的例句是把这一表达法作为反语使用，表示讽刺的意味。 *For some reason, the Indians never took too kindly to the white man's efforts to civilize them by killing them off and stealing their land.* 不知什么原因，印第安人对于那些用枪杀他们和夺取他们土地的方式使他们文明化的白种人的种种努力，从来也没有乐于承受的意思。接受的对象也可以是"人"。 *It would be healthier for you to leave town in a hurry, mister. People around here don't take kindly to nosy strangers.* 先生，赶快离开这个城镇对你的健康会有益处的。这里的老百姓不乐意接待好管闲事的外地来客。 *I don't know why, but apparently Bob's never taken kindly to me.* 我不知道为什么，但是很显然，鲍勃对我从来没有好感。◇ accept *something* [*someone*] in good spirit / appreciate [like, care for] *something* [*someone*]

kindness

kill *someone* **with kindness** [ˈkɪl ～ ˌwɪð ˈkaɪnːəs] [话] **以过分的好意使人不自在** 字面意义为"用亲切的态度杀人"。出典是莎士比亚的《驯悍记》(*The Taming of the Shrew*) 第四幕第一场、主人公培特尔吉奥的台词中的一部分：This is the way to kill a wife with kindness. And thus I curb her mad and headstrong humour. (这是用亲切的态度驯服老婆的方法。就这样，我治好了她那疯狂的和顽固的性情。) 在过去，这一表达法包含有"口蜜腹剑"的意味，现在完全没有这种意思了。对人亲切，希望对方报答，这种情况是可能有的，但是至少说，这一表达法不用于有意使对方为难的场合。 *I advise you to avoid accepting any favors from Mrs. Gushaton. Once you let her do something for you, she'll kill you with kindness.* 我劝告你千万不要接受古夏顿太太的任何好意。一旦你让她为你做点什么事情，她的亲切简直叫你受不了。 *When we visited Fred's relatives, they all but killed us with kindness. We had absolutely no time to ourselves.* 当我们去拜访弗雷德的亲属的时候，他们招待得无微不至，简直叫人受不了。我们连一丁点儿自己的时间都没有。如以上的例句所示，这一表达法一般用于"对方一片好意，本人却不自在"的场合。但也有如下一例句那样，仅用于强调"亲切"的场合。 *We had a wonderful time in China. The Chinese almost killed us with kindness.* 我们在中国度过一段极好的时光，中国人对我们是非常亲切的。◇ be so kind it becomes a burden (to *someone*)

kiss

a butterfly kiss [ə ˈbʌdər.flaɪ .kɪs] [口] **蝴蝶吻** 接吻有很多变种。自己眨巴着眼睛，让睫毛象蝴蝶 (butterfly) 扇动翅膀一样去接触对方的面颊，这就叫 butterfly kiss。幼儿常有这样的动作。成年男女以此为戏。*My little granddaughter likes to give butterfly kisses.* 我的小孙女喜欢蝴蝶吻。*Sally kissed me three times last night— but unfortunately they were only butterfly kisses.* 萨莉昨天晚间吻了我三次，遗憾的是，三次都是蝴蝶吻而已。*Butterfly kisses are for the birds.* 蝴蝶吻太没有意思啦。接吻的另一个变种是 an Eskimo KISS。◇ a flutter of *one's*eyelashes against *someone's* cheek

an Eskimo kiss [ə ˈneskə.mou.kɪs] [口] **碰鼻礼** 模仿爱斯基摩人见面时鼻子碰鼻子的礼节，幼儿常这样做，情人们也戏而为之。*Here is a picture of our children giving each other an Eskimo kiss.* 这是我家孩子互相碰鼻子的照片。*No matter how many times I date Mary, she refuses to let me have any more than an Eskimo kiss.* 不管我跟玛丽约会了多少次，她也只容许我对她行碰鼻礼。*I suppose I could get to like Eskimo kisses better if I were an Eskimo.* 如果我是个爱斯基摩人，那我一定更喜欢接爱斯基摩吻啦。◇ (a) rubbing (of) noses

the kiss of death [ðə .kɪsəv ˈde(ː)θ] [口] **致命的东西** 字面意义为"死的接吻"。这一表达法源出《圣经·新约》中的《马可福音》(Mark) 第 14 章 44～45 节：Now the betrayer had given them a sign, saying, "The one I shall kiss is the man; seize him and lead him away safely." And when he came, he went up to him at once, and said, "Master!" And he kissed him.（卖耶稣的人曾给他们一个暗号，说："我与谁亲嘴，谁就是他；你们把他拿住，牢牢靠靠的带去。"犹大来了，随即到耶稣跟前说"拉比！"，便与他亲嘴。）大家一读就会了解，就是犹大向官府出卖耶稣的有名的场面。也就是说，对于耶稣来说，犹大的一吻乃是 the kiss of death。转义"致命的东西"，在会话中广泛使用。*It was foolish of him to go jogging so soon after his operation. That was the kiss of death.* 他太愚蠢了，刚做完手术就去练跑步，结果把命也搭上啦。这是按照字面意义使用的情况。但大多用于比喻。*Support by the radical faction proved to be the kiss of death to the candidate.* 激进派的支持使得那个候选人一败涂地。*He's a powerful man in this organization. A bad report from him is the kiss of death.* 在这个单位里，他是一个实权人物。只要他打一个对你不利的报告，你就完蛋啦。*I had thought that getting that big loan would save our company, but when the recession came and we couldn't pay it back, it turned out to be the kiss of death.* 我本来以为得到那么大一笔贷款，咱们的公司就有救了，但是，当经济萧条来临的时候，咱们还不上钱，结果倒要了咱们的命。有时为了说个俏皮话而使用这一表达法，如：*Age fifty-five in most American companies is the kiss of death.* 在大多数的美国公司中，人到了 55 岁就完蛋啦。当然这指的是"退休"。如以上的例句所示，"致命"的原因大多是"事"或"物"，但有时也会是"人"。*If you ever hope to rise in this company, stay away from that guy. He's the kiss of death.* 如果你希望在这个公司爬上去，千万别跟那个家伙接近。一跟他来往，你就永无出头之日了。◇ ruinous

kisser

a kisser [ə ˈkɪsər] [话] **脸或嘴** 最初的构思是"接吻时使用的东西"。这一表达法是 19 世纪中叶流行起来的，当时指"嘴"或"嘴唇"。后来，意义的范围不断扩大，现在泛指"口"、"唇"、"颚"以至"整个脸"。*No wonder Mary's so fat. She's forever stuffing her kisser with something sweet.* 无怪乎玛丽那么肥胖。她那嘴里总离不开甜食。除了象这一例句，从上下文可以断定是用"嘴"的场合外，一般解释为"脸"，大致不会出错。这是一个极为轻松的说法。另外，kisser 尚有"接吻者"一义，但实际上几乎完全不用这一意思。*A: What happened to you? B: I* *got hit in the kisser with a baseball.* 甲:你怎么啦? 乙:一个棒球打到我的脸上啦。这一表达法也可以用不定冠词,如说:*What an ugly kisser!* 多么丑陋的一张脸! 但是,如前面的例句所示,大多的场合用 the 和所有格。◇ a face [mouth]

kitchen

everything but the kitchen sink → SINK

kitchy-koo

kitchy-koo [ˈkɪtʃi ˈku:] [话] **你瞧你瞧** 对婴儿的寒暄语。不管谁见到可爱的婴儿,都想摸他一下。在这种时候,美国人是用食指轻轻地胳肢一下婴儿的下颚或脸蛋,嘴里说 kitchy-koo。这是象声词。*What a cute little baby! Kitchy-koo.* 多么可爱的宝贝呀! 你瞧你瞧! 另作 kitchy-kitchy-koo。还有一个表达法是 kitchy-kitchy, 不仅用于婴儿,对稍微大一点的儿童也可以使用。小孩子们游戏的时候,相互间常说 kitchy-kitchy。◇ tickle-tickle

kite

Go fly a kite. [ˌgouˌflaɪə ˈkaɪt] [话] **滚开!** → Go jump in the LAKE.

be (as) high as a kite [əz ˈhaɪəzə ˈkaɪt] [话] **酒醉飘飘然欲仙** 在讲 He is high.的时候,high 的意思是"情绪高涨"。它表示"心里飘飘然"的样子,也就是"喝醉了"。be (as) high as a kite 直译为"象风筝一样飞舞到天空",这表示"由于喝醉而晕晕忽忽"的状态。喝醉酒的人当然感觉很痛快,但与 dead DRUNK (烂醉如泥)不同,他有时又蹦又跳,有时要高歌一曲,精神饱满,非常活跃。*By the time we got to the party, everyone there was as high as a kite.* 在我们来到社交晚会的时候,已经在场的每一个人都喝得有些飘然欲仙了。*You can't drive home tonight. You're high as a kite.* 你今天晚上不能开车回家啦。你已经喝得晕晕忽忽的了。有时用 get 代替 be 动词。*I can't drink very much. I get as high as a kite off of one beer.* 我酒量不大,只喝上一瓶啤酒,就会晕晕忽忽的了。◇ be very drunk

kitten

(as) weak as a kitten [ə ˈzwi(:)kəzə ˈkɪtn] [口] **软弱无力** 字面意义为"象小猫(kitten)一样软弱"。指由于运动少或者有病而身体软弱、以及由于运动而大量消耗体力的状态。*My temperature has gone down, but I'm still weak as a kitten.* 我的热度降低了,但是我仍然没有一点力气。如这一例句所示,这一表达法大多用于说明自己身体情况的场合。*After swimming over three kilometers to the shore, I felt as weak as a kitten.* 游了三公里到达岸上以后,我身上连一点劲儿也没有啦。*The medicine made me as weak as a kitten.* 由于药的作用,我的身体软弱无力。有时也说 (as) weak as a baby。◇ extremely weak

kittens

have kittens [ˌhæv ˈkɪtnz] [话] **暴怒** 直译为"生小猫"。主语为"人"。乍看起来,令人莫明其妙,怎么会"人生小猫"呢? 原来,最初的构思是:母猫在产小猫的前后,脾气特别暴躁。这一表达法是把作为主语的"人"比做"母猫"。*My father had kittens when he found I'd quit school.* 我的父亲知道我不上学以后,暴跳如雷。*Better get with it, you guys. The boss'll have kittens if he comes back and we're not finished.* 你们这些家伙卖点力气呀。老板回来的时候,如果我们还没有干完,他会大发脾气的。下一例句中的 a (whole) litter of 是强调的用语,这个 litter 是"狗、猫、猪等一窝的仔畜"的意思。因为一窝要生许多只仔畜,所以此词起强调的作用。*Mom's going to have a (whole) litter of kittens when she sees this report card.* 妈妈若是看见这张成绩通知单,一定会大发雷霆的。这一表达法以内心的状态为重点,用于表示"恼怒"的场合最多,但也有用于表示"兴奋"、"忧虑"、"恐怖"等的时候。又,动词 have 一般不用进行时,但在表示"生产仔畜"的意义时不在此例。下一例句里的 be about to 常与本条习用语搭配使用,意思与 be having 相同。*We'd better open the Christmas presents soon. The kids are about to have kittens.* 我们马上把圣诞节的礼物打开吧。孩子们已经急不可待啦。*It's about time you got home. Don't you realize it's two o'clock in the morning? Your mother has been having kittens.* 你该回家啦。你不知道现在已经是早晨两点钟了吗? 你母亲会非常焦急的啊。*Doris is deathly afraid of lightning. She has kittens every time there's a thunderstorm.* 多丽丝对于闪电害怕得要命。每当雷雨的时候,她都感到非常恐怖。◇ be extremely angry [excited, worried, afraid, etc.]

klepto

a klepto [ə ˈklepˌtou] [话] **有盗窃癖的人** a kleptomaniac [ˌkleptəˈmeɪ niˌæ(ː)k] (盗窃病患者)的缩略,轻松的表达法。*The guy's a klepto. He's been caught shoplifting in department stores three times this year.* 那个家伙有盗窃癖。他在百货店行窃,今年被人抓住三次了。也用作戏谑语。*My roommate's a real klepto. He's forever using my socks and ties without asking.* 我同屋的朋友真是一个盗窃病患者。他总是不打招呼就穿我的袜子,用我的领带。◇ a person with a constant urge to steal

knock

knock *something* [*someone*] [ˈnɑ(ː)k ~] [话] **说坏话** knock 一般是"敲"、"打"的意思。*She knocked on the door.* 她敲门。*The batter knocked the ball out of the park.* 击球员把球打出场外去了。*I knocked him down with one blow.* 我一拳把他打倒在地了。此外,人们常用 knock 表示 criticize (批评、批判) 的意思,这是个轻松的说法。但是比 criticize 的使用范围窄,只用于"说坏话"的场合。*He's been knocking my pitching.* 他对我的投球褒贬起来了。*How do you know it's no good? Don't knock it until you've tried it.* 你怎么知道它不好呢? 在你自己试试看之前,先不要挑剔嘛。*Ok, if you're so good at knocking other people's ideas, why don't you come up with a solution?* 好啦,你既然这样善于贬低别人的想法,为什么你自己不提出一个解决办法呢? 如以上的例句所示,宾语大多是 *something*,但也有时为 *someone*。*Don't knock him. He's doing the best he can.* 不要找他的岔子。他在做最大的努力了。◇ criticize *something* [*someone*]

knock back *a drink* [ˌnɑ(ː)kˈbæk ~] [话] **一口气喝下** 请读者注意:这一表达法与 knock *something* back 不同。knock *something* back 的意思是"敲打某种东西回到原来的位置"。*I knocked the loose nails back into place.* 钉子松了,我又把它敲进去了。*I knocked the ball back over the fence.* 我把球打回篱笆那边去了。乍看起来,条头的 knock back *a drink* 与这一表达法十分相似,但是原来的构思完全不同。条头的习用语无法直译,其语源可能是这样:"仰起头来 (throw *one's* head back),把液体往喉咙的深处 (the back of *one's* throat) 一下子灌进去"。*a drink* 的地方,除戏谑的场合外,一定要代入 an alcoholic drink (某种酒精饮料)的名称。*Stu knocked back three straight whiskies in a row.* 司徒一连喝了三杯纯威士忌酒。*He knocked back his drink and calmly set the glass on the table.* 他咕嘟一下喝完自己的酒,很平静地把杯子放到桌子上了。另有一个类似的表达法是 toss off *a drink* (把酒一气喝干)。两者的区别是: knock back 的重点在于表示"猛然一下子"的动作,而 toss off 则有"从从容容喝下去,毫不在乎"的意味。*He can toss off five or six martinis without showing any effect.* 他能够一连串喝上五、六杯马丁尼酒,毫无醉意。◇ (quickly) drink

knock off (work, study, practice, etc.) [ˌnɑˈkɔːf] [话] **停止(工作、学习、练习等)** 主语一般是几个人,如 we, they 等。有时用 our office (我们公司) 为主语,在语法上是单数,但仍然是指多数的人。在习惯上不用 I knock off 这样的说法。*We knocked off work about ten o'clock last night.* 昨天夜里,我们在十点钟左右停止了工作。*They knock off at noon on Saturdays.* 他们每星期六在中午下班。*Everyone was tired. so we knocked off* *soccer practice early today.* 大家都很疲乏,所以我们今天提前停止了足球练习。有时用于表示“停止一下”、“中断片刻”亦即“休息”的意思。*Well, let's knock off for lunch, shall we? We'll start again at one-thirty.* 好啦,咱们停下来去吃午饭。一点半再开始干。*We studied for about three hours and then knocked off for a twenty-minute coffee break.* 我们学习了三个小时左右,然后停下来喝点咖啡,休息了二十分钟。这一表达法的来源是:古时,在由奴隶、囚犯划桨的大木船(galley)上,为了划桨的步调一致,其中有一个人用木槌敲木块打拍子,并且有一种特别的敲打 (knock) 方式,作为“划桨休息”的信号。由于用这一方式使划桨的动作停下来 (off),所以就产生了 knock off 这一表达法。另外,这一 off 与 sign off (广播完毕) 或 switch off (关上电门) 中的 off 同义。◇ quit

knock off *something* [ˌnɑ(:)ˈkɔ:f ~] [话] **抢劫** → KNOCK over *something*

knock *someone* **off** [ˌnɑ(:)k ~ ˈɔ:f] [话] **杀死** knock off 本来是“把人击倒”或“把物击落”的意思。*He knocked the vase off the table.* 他把桌子上的花瓶推到地下去了。转义为“杀人”,是一种轻松的说法。原为黑社会用语,现在已经一般化了。*The gang decided to knock the FBI agent off.* 匪帮决定干掉联邦调查局的侦探。*The terrorists have so far knocked ten army officers off.* 到现在为止,恐怖主义分子已经暗杀了十名军官。另有使用 bump (撞)的表达法,作 bump *someone* off, 与本条同义。但与 knock *someone* off 相比,黑社会用语的色彩依然十分浓厚,几乎完全不用于象以 terrorists 为主语的最后一个例句那样与黑社会无关的会话。◇ kill *someone*

knock *oneself* **out** [ˌnɑ(:)k ~ ˈaut] [话] **拚命干** knock out 在拳击中是“击倒对手”的意思。knock *oneself* out 是“自己把自己击倒”,亦即“使自己意识不清,站不起来了”。虽然这样讲,并不是真的自己殴打自己。这一表达法专门作为比喻使用,表示“为了某种目的拚出死命去干,达到身子晃晃悠悠几乎要倒下的程度”的意味。在实际上,当然不一定非“达到身子晃晃悠悠的程度”不可。这一表达法只是一种夸张的说法,人们常用它来强调“拚命干”的状态。*She knocks herself out trying to make a happy home for that guy, then what does he do? He up and leaves her for another woman.* 她为了那个家伙拚出命来建立一个幸福的家庭,可是你猜他如何呢? 他突然把她丢开,找另一个女人去了。*I'm not going to knock myself out for that guy. What has he ever done for me?* 我没有必要为那个男人去粉身碎骨。他究竟为我干了些什么呢? 如以上的例句所示,这一表达法大多用于“虽然百般努力却得不到报答”的场合。但并不限定如此。*We all knocked ourselves out getting the gym ready for the school dance.* 我们全都在体育馆内为准备学校舞会而卖尽所有的力气。也有象下面这样用于讽刺的情况。*A: Sure, I'll be glad to help you ... maybe next week ... if I find the time. B: Thanks a lot. Don't knock yourself out.* 甲:可以可以,我很愿意去帮助你……嗯,下个星期……如果我有时间的话。乙:多谢多谢。您多保重贵体,可不要累坏啦。◇ make a great effort

knock over *something* [ˌnɑ(:)ˈkovər ~] [话] **抢劫** knock over 按字面意义是“打翻”、“击倒”、“撞倒”。*The dog knocked over the stove.* 狗把火炉子撞倒了。转用于表示 rob *someplace* (rob 发音为 [ˈrɑ(:)b]) 亦即“进屋抢东西”的意思。这是一个轻松的说法。在这一场合,knock over *something* 中的 *something* 处当然要代入与房屋同类的名词,如 a bank, a store, a home 等等。*The gang knocked over five banks in one month.* 那个匪帮在一个月内抢劫了五家银行。另外,有时用 off 代替 over, 而说 knock off *something*。◇ rob *someplace*

knock *someone* **up** [ˌnɑ(:)k ~ ˈʌ(:)p] [俗] **使女人怀孕** knock up 的字面意义为“把……向上击”。*He knocked me up in the air.* 他把我打得脚跟都离地了。如果用非常轻松的口吻,这一表达法意味

着"使女人怀孕",在美国,一般认为是下流话,难登大雅之堂。但在英国,这一表达法却是"敲门叫人起床"的意思,为极其普通的日常用语。由于一般的英美人互不了解双方用法的差异,就产生了意外的麻烦。例如,一位英国女士对美国人说 *He knocked me up.* 她本来的意思是讲"他敲门把我叫起来了",可是在美国人听来却会误解为"他使我怀孕了",真是南辕北辙。在这种场合,美国人说 He got me up. 或者 He woke me up. ◇ make *someone* pregnant

Knocked

You could have knocked me over with a feather. → FEATHER

knocks

the school of hard knocks → SCHOOL

knowledge

parade *one's* knowledge (of *something*) [pəˈreɪd ~ ˈnɑ(ː)lɪdʒ] [口] **卖弄学问** 这一表达法从字面意义"夸耀自己的知识"就可以理解它的内涵。 *That guy's always parading his knowledge in front of other people.* 那个家伙总在别人面前卖弄他的学问。*George likes to parade his knowledge of airplanes.* 乔治喜欢卖弄他对于飞机的知识。 *Charles is a smart guy, but he's not one to parade his knowledge.* 查理是一个很聪明的人,但是他并不卖弄自己的学问。顺便提一下:"暴露某人的无知"在英语中说 parade *one's* ignorance, 特别用于"明明不知道而硬要蒙混过关"的场合。 *Whenever you don't know the answer, keep your mouth shut. There's no need to parade your ignorance before everyone at the meeting.* 如果你回答不出,就闭上嘴别出声。在会议中没有必要当着大家暴露自己的无知啊。◇ (ostentatiously) display *one's* knowledge

knuckle

knuckle down (to *something*) [ˌnʌkl ˈdaun] [口] **开始认真工作** → BUCKLE down (to *something*)

knuckles

give *someone* a rap on the knuckles → RAP

rap *someone* on the knuckles [ˌræ(ː)p ~ ɔ(ː)nðə ˈnʌ(ː)klz] [口] **申斥** → give *someone* a RAP on the knuckles

KO

KO *someone* [ˈkeɪˌou ~] [话] **击倒** → KAYO *someone*

L

L. A.

L. A. [eˈleɪ] [话] **洛杉矶市** 美国加利福尼亚州(California)城市 Los Angeles 的略称。 *Dick's little sister lives in L. A.* 迪克的妹妹住的洛杉矶。 Los Angeles 原为西班牙语“天使”的意思,因此,这一城市的别名叫做 The City of the Angels (天使城)。 *L. A. is sometimes called “The City of the Angels.”* 洛杉矶市有时被人们称为“天使城”。◇ Los Angeles

lab

a lab [ə ˈlæ(:)b] [话] **实验室** lab 为 laboratory [ˈlæ(:)brə.to:ri] 的缩略,指“以 theory (理论)为基础进行实验或研究的场所”。原为学生用语,现在已普遍使用。 *Dr. Heckel has a lab in his home.* 赫克尔博士的家里有个实验室。这是讲个人的 lab。也有附属于各种单位的 lab,例如: *I work in a hospital lab.* 我在医院的实验室里工作。 *Most large universities now have language labs.* 现在大多数规模较大的大学,都有语言实验室。 *The lieutenant sent the fingerprints to the lab for identification.* 警尉把指纹送化验室去核对了。 *The students gathered in the physics lab.* 学生们集合到物理实验室。此外,lab 一词还常用于表示“大学的实验课程”的意味。特别是学生们在使用这一解释时,一般都用 lab,而很少用 laboratory。在这一场合,大多不加冠词。 *I have three labs this semester.* 我这学期有三个实验。在美国的大学中,一般标准是:每种课程由三次讲课与一次“实验”循环组成,这位学生说有“三个实验”,就是每周有三次实验的意思。 *I've got (a) chem lab this afternoon.* 今天下午我有化学实验。有时可作形容词使用。 *This is a lab course with no lectures.* 这是一门实验课程,不讲课。◇ a laboratory

lady

one's **old lady** [~ .ouˈl:eɪdi] [俗] **老娘** an old lady 是“老太太”,但在 *one's* 这样的所有格后边却是“(某人的)母亲”的意思。与 *one's* old MAN 的情况一样,年纪并不一定要“老”。 *Her old lady is very young.* 她的老娘非常年轻。这样的说法也是很自然的。这是一个很轻松的俚语,主要是男子相互间使用。也有人很讨厌这个词,因此,在使用时要注意时间、情况和地点。 *Her old lady used to be a teacher.* 她的老娘过去是学校的老师。如果谈到自己的母亲,有时可以加定冠词,作 the old lady。 *The old lady's already gone to bed.* 俺娘已经睡下了。另外,偶尔也有人用本条称自己的妻子。◇ *one's* mother

lag

jet lag [ˈdʒet.læ:g] [口] **喷气飞行时差综合症** jet plane (喷气式飞机)的 jet 与 time lag (时差)的 lag 的合成语。虽然是新近出现,但是已经定型了。 *It is said that jet lag is often the cause of pilot error.* 据说喷气飞行时差综合症往往成为飞行员失误的原因。 suffer from jet lag (患喷气飞行时差综合症)是一个定型的表达法。 *International travelers often suffer from jet lag.* 国际旅游者常患喷气飞行时差综合症。同样,recover from jet lag (解除喷气飞行时差综合症) 也是一个定型的表达法。 *It usually takes me several days to recover from jet lag.* 我通常要用好几天的功夫才能从喷气飞行时差综合症中恢复。另有一个与 jet lag 意思相同的表达法为 jet syndrome [ˈdʒet .sɪndrəm],因为是专门术语,一般不通用。◇ fatigue due to rapid travel through different time zones

laid

be laid up (with *something*) [ˌleɪ ˈdʌ(ː)p] [话] **在家休息** 指由于有病或受伤，完全不能工作、外出或游玩，处于无法自由行动的状态。不一定非卧床不可。*I was laid up with a broken leg for over a month last year.* 去年我由于腿部骨折，在家休养了一个多月。*Charles hasn't been to work this week. He's laid up with the flu.* 查尔斯这个星期没上班。他患流感，在家里休息哪。*I've been laid up often recently.* 最近我常在家里休养。有时用 *something* lays *someone* up 这样形式的主动语态。*An accident laid Mr. Kern up for two weeks.* 由于发生事故，克恩先生在家里休息了两个星期。◇ be confined (to bed [at home])

lake

Go jump in the lake. [ˈgouˌdʒʌmpənðə ˈleɪk] [话] **滚开！** 直译是"去往湖里跳"也就是"这里没你的事"。成年人也使用，但用这一表达法的大多为儿童。语气相当严厉。一般只能用于朋友或亲近的人之间。*Go jump in the lake. If I want your opinion, I'll ask for it.* 滚开！如果我想听你的意见，我会去问你的。*Go jump in the lake, will you? Can't you see I'm trying to study?* 你给我滚开好不好？你看不见我正要学习吗？如以上的例句所示，本条是在讨厌别人多嘴或者前来纠缠的时候使用的，意思等于"真烦死人！"，"别闹啦！"此外，还用于表示"别胡扯啦！"，"岂有此理！"，"难以令人相信"的意味。其中，用于表示"难以令人相信"的意味的情况比较少。通常用命令句，也有例外的场合。*Paul wants me to pay five hundred dollars for his old jalopy? Tell him he can go jump in the lake.* 保罗那么一辆又旧又破的汽车，要我付给他五百美元？你告诉他，滚他的蛋吧！ *Go jump in the lake. Nobody can drive from New York to San Francisco in only two days.* 别胡说八道啦！只用两天时间从纽约开车到旧金山，任何人也办不到啊。在非命令句的场合，可以省略 go。 *If you don't like the way I do things, you can just (go) jump in the lake for all I care.* 如果你不喜欢我的做法，你爱怎么办就怎么办吧。另有一个同样的表达法是 Go fly a kite. 直译为"去放风筝好啦！"意义和用法与本条完全一样，只是极少用于表示"难以令人相信"的意味。*Go fly a kite, will you? Your stupid ideas are only making us more confused.* 你一边呆着去吧！你那些愚蠢的意见只能给我们添乱。*Go fly a kite. I'm not about to give you five dollars for a rusty old knife like that.* 你别胡扯啦！我不会为那么又旧又锈了的小刀，给你五美元的。◇ Keep quiet. / Stop bothering [pestering] me. / that's ridiculous / suffer

lam

be on the lam [ˌɔ(ː)nðə ˈlæːm] [话] **在潜逃中** → take it on the LAM

take it on the lam [ˌteɪkɪˌdɔ(ː)nðə ˈlæːm] [话] **急忙逃走** 过去专指"犯罪分子躲避警察逃走"，现在也用于与警察毫无关系的场合。本条有"一溜烟似地逃跑"的意思，与汉语的"撒鸭子"相等。it 没有什么意义。lam 原为表示"急急逃逸"的动词，现在还常这样使用。 *As soon as we heard the ball go through the window, we lammed it out of there.* 我们一听到球打破窗户玻璃的声音，赶紧从那儿逃走了。后来 lam 被用作名词，出现了 take it on the lam 的表达法，而且与动词 lam 的语气一样轻松。 *As soon as we heard the police siren, we took it on the lam.* 我们一听到警报器的声音，马上就撒鸭子跑了。 *When Nick heard that he was suspected of the robbery, he decided he'd better take it on the lam.* 当尼克听说他被列为抢劫嫌疑犯的时候，心里就决定以从速逃走为上策了。*When we saw the principal coming out of his office, we took it on the lam.* 当看到校长走出他的办公室的时候，我们撒鸭子逃走了。另有 be on the lam 的表达法，只能用于表示"(从警察那里)在潜逃中"的意思。*Lennie is on the lam for that supermarket robbery.* 伦尼因为那次抢劫超级市场的案件，正在潜逃中。◇ run (away) / leave in a hurry / leave town

lamb

(as) gentle as a lamb [əz ˈdʒentl əzə ˈlæːm] [口] **象羊羔一样老实** 主要用于平常不大 gentle (温顺)的动物,偶尔也用于人。 *Our dog barks viciously at strangers, but it's as gentle as a lamb with the children.* 我家的那条狗见到陌生人就狂吠,但是跟孩子们在一起的时候却象羊羔一样老实。*The lions seem gentle as lambs when the trainer is in their cage, but he knows better than to turn his back on them.* 当训兽员在狮子笼里的时候,狮子象羊羔一样老实,但是他知道自己决不能转过身去背对着它们。◇ extremely gentle

lamb's

in two shakes of a lamb's tail → SHAKES

lame-brain

a lame-brain [ə ˈleɪm.breɪn] [口] **呆子** 直译为"残废的头脑",指"头脑一点也不灵活的人"。 *You want me to hire that lame-brain? You must be kidding!* 你希望我雇用那个呆子吗?你简直是在开玩笑。本条条头的原形加上 -ed,就构成 lame-brained [ˈleɪmˈbreɪnd]这样一个形容词。 *What a lame-brained thing to do!* 你做了多么糊涂的事情! → a DUMBHEAD ◇ a stupid person

lamppost

between you and me and the lamppost [bətwi(ː).njuː ən.miː ənðə ˈlæm.poust] [话] **咱们只是私下说说** → between you and me and the GATEPOST

land

how the land lies [.hauðə ˈlæ(ː)nd.laɪz] [口] **情况** → the LAY of the land

the lay of the land → LAY

landing

make a belly landing [.meɪkə ˈbeli .lændɪŋ] [话] **以机腹着陆** → make a pancake LANDING

make a pancake landing [.meɪkə .pæ(ː)n.keɪk ˈlæ(ː)ndɪŋ] [话] **以机体着陆** 直译为"进行烙饼着陆"。在烙饼的时候,把饼翻上翻下,平放在锅中。本条以此为比喻。*The pilot couldn't lower the wheels so he had to make a pancake landing.* 飞机的轮子放不下去了,飞行员不得不以机体着陆了。可以用 come [go] in for 代替 make。*The plane came in for a pancake landing.* 飞机以机体着陆了。又,pancake 词形不变可以作动词使用。例如: *The plane pancaked on the water.* 飞机以机体降落到水面上了。另外,也可以用 belly (腹)代替 pancake 而说 make [come in for, go in for] a belly landing。◇ make a wheels-up landing

land-office

do a land-office business (in *something*) → BUSINESS

language

speak the same language [.spi(ː)kðə .seɪm ˈlæ(ː)ŋgwɪdʒ] [口] **有共同语言** 直译为"说同样的语言"。最初的构思可能是:"既然说同样的话,想法也会是同样的"。这一表达法使用于想法、意见一致,而且情感交汇的场合。*The boys in my club are a great bunch of guys. We all speak the same language.* 我那个俱乐部的青年们都是极好的人,大家有共同的语言。*In a small office like ours, it's very important to have a partner who speaks the same language.* 在我们这样一个小公司里,能有一个志同道合的伙伴是非常重要的事情。*He and I don't speak the same language.* 我跟他没有共同语言。即使与外国人一道,两种语言不同,也可以使用这一表达法,因为通过翻译,两个人说得来,也与用同一种语言讲话一样。在下一例句中,埃默森和"我"可以是操不同语言的两个国家的人。*I feel very much at ease with Mr. Emerson. We both speak the same language.* 我与埃默森先生交往感到心情非常舒畅。我们两个人非常谈得来。◇ think the same way

lap

live in the lap of luxury [.lɪvɪnðə

ˌlæ(:)pəvˈlʌkʃəri] [口] **过豪华的生活** 最初的构思是把 luxury (奢侈)神化，所以说"坐在奢侈(女神)的膝头 (lap) 上过日子"。这一表达法的意味是："极尽奢侈之能事，过着优裕舒适的日子"。*Not all rich people live in luxury.* 不是所有的富人都过着豪华的生活。本条习用语是强调这一例句中的 live in luxury, 具有骄奢淫逸达到顶点的含义。*All her life she has lived in the lap of luxury.* 她的一生都过着极为豪华的生活。*Even though he was very rich, he was not satisfied just to live in the lap of luxury.* 尽管他已经是一个非常有钱的人，但是并不满足于过骄奢淫逸的生活。◇ live an extremely rich and comfortable life

lard

a tub of lard [ə ˌtʌbəˈlɑ(:)rd] [话] **大胖子** tub 是"大桶"，lard 是"猪油"。本条的意思是"象一大桶猪油那样肥胖"，汉语俗话也说"肥得象一篓油"，构思相同。本条与 a tub of BLUBBER 同义，但使用频率高。*Sue is such a nice girl. I wouldn't mind marrying her if she just weren't such a tub of lard.* 苏是一个非常好的姑娘。如果她不是肥得象一篓油，我是可以跟她结婚的。◇ an obese person / obese ((such a → so))

large

be at large [ət ˈlɑ:rdʒ] [口] **逍遥法外** 这里的 large 与 freedom 或者 liberty 一样，是"自由"的意思。*Three escaped cons are at large in this area.* 在这一地区，有三个逃犯正在逍遥法外。可以这样原封不动地使用，但一般要在 be 与 at large 之间加一个 still(仍然)。*The murderer is still at large.* 杀人犯还没有被捉拿归案。往往用 remain (依然) 代替 be still。*The police have recaptured most of the escaped convicts, but three remain at large.* 警察把大部分越狱的囚犯都抓回来了，可是还有三个人逍遥法外。如以上的例句所示，这一表达法绝大多数场合是用于"囚犯"、"嫌疑犯"、"越狱的犯人"等，但也有时用于表示"(被告)尚未被逮捕"的意思。*The defendant remained at large pending the outcome of his appeal to a higher court.* 被告向上级法院申诉，在没做出结论之前，他尚未被逮捕。此外，也可以用于表示"家畜未被控制"的意味，但在这一场合，大多不用动词 be 或 remain。*The cattle roamed at large over the open range.* 牛群在一望无际的大牧场上自由自在地游荡着。◇ be being sought / be roaming free / be free

lark

(as) happy as a lark [əz ˈhæpiəzə ˈlɑ(:)rk] [口] **高高兴兴** 一般的鸟总是停在树上啼叫，而云雀一边飞一边鸣，叫人听起来感到它们是非常高兴的样子。这一表达法便是由此而来。主要指孩子们的高高兴兴的情态，具有天真无邪的意味。当然，也可以指一般的现象。*The child was as happy as a lark with his new toy.* 那个孩子有了件新玩具，简直高兴极了。*The little girl, happy as a lark, set off for her friend's birthday party.* 那个小女孩高高兴兴地前去参加她的朋友的生日晚会了。*The old woman became as happy as a lark when she heard that her grandchildren were coming for a visit.* 老奶奶听说她的孙子孙女们要来家里玩，简直高兴极了。◇ extremely happy

last

breathe *one's* **last** [ˌbri:ð ～ ˈlæ:st] [话] **咽气** 直译是"做最后的呼吸"。*After a long illness, Mr. Smith breathed his last at two o'clock this morning.* 史密斯先生长期患病，今天早晨两点钟逝世了。正如这一例句所示，过去本条是广泛应用的 die (死)的委婉语。在现代，人们有时也使用这一个极普通的委婉的表达法，但更主要的是男人们用它来恫吓别人或者开玩笑，这种情况日益增多。*Try moving into my territory again and you'll breathe your last.* 你如果再敢侵入我的地盘，我就叫你去见阎王。特别是儿童们相互间常用作戏谑语。*Whoever ate my piece of cake is about to breathe his last.* 谁吃了我的蛋糕，我马上要他的命啦。◇ die

every last man → MAN
(I'm telling you) for the last time → TIME
if it's the last thing *one* **does** → THING
last rites → RITES

late

Better late than never. [ˌbedərˈleɪt ðəˈnɪːvər] [谚] **迟做总比不做强** 这是对罗马时代历史学家李维(Livy,公元前 59 ~公元 17) 的名言 *Potius sero quam num quam.*的直译。虽然是个谚语,但没有死板的感觉,语调非常轻快。美国人在使用时简直都不汴意到它是一个谚语。 *A: Sorry I'm late. B: That's OK. Better late than never.* 甲:对不起,我来晚啦。乙:没什么。迟到总比不到强啊。如这一例句所示,使用最多的是"迟到"的场合。但在其他的情况下也可以使用,例如: *I realized it's a bit late in the day for an old man like me to be learning to drive, but better late than never, I always say.* 我明白,象我这么大年纪学习驾驶汽车的确有点晚了,但是,不管什么事情,迟做总比不做强啊。 *A: Isn't January a little late to be writing Christmas cards? B: Yes, but better late than never, don't you think?* 甲:到了一月才写圣诞节贺卡,有点儿晚了吧? 乙:是的。不过,迟写总比不写强,对不对? *Oh, I forgot to introduce you two, didn't I. Well, better late than never. Sally, this is Jim Jones. Jim, Sally Smith.* 哎呀,我忘记给你们二位介绍啦。不过,晚介绍总比不介绍好。萨莉,这位是吉姆·琼斯。吉姆,这位是萨莉·史密斯。◇ It is better to be late in doing something than never to do it at all.

a late bloomer → BLOOMER
be late in the day for *something* → DAY

Latin

pig Latin [ˈpɪ(:)gˌlæ(:)tn] [口] **(儿童游戏的)假拉丁语** 直译为"猪的拉丁语"。在这里,pig 是"伪的"、"假的"的意思。拉丁语的单词多以 a (按英语读作[eɪ]) 为词尾,因此就产生一种语言游戏,即把英语的单词改变一部分拼法,再在末尾加上 ay [eɪ],冒充拉丁语。方法极为简单,只要把英语单词最初的辅音(群)移至最后,再加上 ay 就行了。例如: Can you speak pig Latin? 这句话的假拉丁语为 Ancay ouyay eakspay igpay Atinlay? [ˈænˌkeɪ ˈuːˌjeɪ ˈiːkˌspeɪ ˈɪ(:)gˌpeɪ ˈæ(:)tnˌleɪ]。如果是以元音开始的单词,一般的方法是将该元音及与其相连的辅音(群)一起后移;但另有一种方法是:字母的次序完全不变,仅在最末尾加 ay。例如说: How long have you been studying English? 这句话的假拉丁语为 Owhay onglay avehay ouyay eenbay udyingstay Lishengay [Englishay]? 发音作 [ˈauˌheɪ ˈɔːŋˌleɪˈæ(:)v ˌheɪˈuːjeɪ ˈenˌbeɪ ˈʌdiɪŋˌsteɪ ˈlɪʃənˌgeɪ / ˈeŋlɪˌʃeɪ]。现在,请解读下面一句假拉丁语: Et'slay ayplay ennistay terafay [afteray] oolschay odaytay. [ˈetˌsleɪ ˈeɪˌpleɪ ˈenɪˌsteɪ ˈterəˌfeɪ / ˈæ(:)ftəˌreɪ ˈuːlˌskeɪ uˈdeɪˌteɪ]。答: Let's play tennis after school today. 在这一例句中,是将 play 和 school 两词的最初的辅音群(即 pl 和 sch) 一起后移。另外有一种方法是只将最初一个字母后移,剩下的 l 和 ch 仍留在原处: Et'slay laypay ennistay terafay choolsay odaytay. 美国人使用这一方法相当困难。另外,一个字母的单词(如 I) 以及以元音开始的极短的单词(如 in, own),只要后边加上 ay 就可以了。 Iay on'tday owknay. [ˈaɪˌeɪ ˈontˌdeɪ ˈouˌneɪ] 就是 I don't know. pig Latin 是儿童们之间使用的一种隐语,一般只是口头说,几乎不写。只要熟悉了之后,就可以顺口说出来。所以出现这种游戏,是因为过去的学校把拉丁语列为必修课程。

laugh

laugh in *one's* **sleeve**(at *someone* [*something*]) [ˌlæ(:)fɪn ~ˈsliːv] [口] **在肚子里笑** → laugh up *one's* SLEEVE (at *someone* [*something*])

laurels

rest on *one's* **laurels** [ˌrestɔn~ˈlɔːrəlz] [口] **固步自封** a laurel (tree) 是"月桂(树)"。用这种树的小枝编成的"月桂冠",在英语中叫做 a laurel wreath, 或者简称 a laurel。古希腊的运动会以此物

作为对优胜者的奖品。转义为“突出的成绩、巨大的成功,以及由此而来的良好的评价、名声、荣誉等”。因此,所谓“在月桂冠上休息”,就是“躺在功劳簿上睡大觉”的意思。laurels 为复数,表示功劳簿上不只是一笔帐。*An ambitious man is never satisfied to rest on his laurels.* 一个有雄心壮志的人决不满足于过去取得的成就。*We've succeeded in repulsing the enemy attack, but that doesn't mean we can rest on our laurels. They'll no doubt soon be back with reinforcements.* 我们是击退了敌军的进攻,但这并不意味着我们可以躺下睡大觉。他们会马上带着增援部队卷土重来的。*When an old man has achieved the success and fame in life that he has, he deserves to rest on his laurels.* 一个老年人象他那样在一生中获得巨大的成功和崇高的声誉,满足于过去的一切也是理所当然的。不仅限于本人的 laurels, 有时用于躺在自己家族或祖先的成功与名誉上面睡大觉的场合。*George may be the scion of a famous family, but he is not one to rest on the family laurels.* 乔治也许是个名门之子,但是他不是一个靠着家庭的声誉混日子的人。另外,不仅以人为主语,常常以企业、团体等为主语。例如:*With the rapid advance of world's computer technology, IBM can't afford to rest on its laurels.* 由于全世界电脑技术的飞速进步,美国的国际商用机器公司也难以靠吃老本过日子了。*That used to be an outstanding school, but I'm afraid it's just resting on its past laurels.* 那个学校过去是一个非常出色的学校,可是很遗憾,它只是躺在过去的声誉上睡大觉了。如这一例句所示,有时用 past 等词修饰 laurels。◇ be satisfied with past achievements [successes, fame, honors, etc.]

law

lay down the law (to *someone* for *something*) [ˌleɪ ˌdaunðə ˈlɔː] [口] **严厉斥责** 直译为“(独裁者等片面地)立下(lay down)法律(law)”。 *The ruler laid down the law that common people could not own swords.* 统治者立下一条法律:老百姓不得有剑。作为比喻,具有“(权威性地)庄严宣告”的意味,用于严厉责备或批评错误言行和过火做法的场合。由于在责备时大多怒气冲冲,所以常用于表示“申斥”的意思。有的词典释义为“以自大的态度命令”或“发号施令”,但这一表达法的本意为“严厉责备[批评]”,至于当时的态度是否“妄自尊大”或“发号施令”,那是次要的问题。例如: *The foreman laid down the law to the workmen.* 这句话的意思并不是“工头以妄自尊大的态度向工人们下命令”,而是他“严厉批评工人们所干的活或干活的方式”。*The section chief laid down the law to his men for being late almost every morning.* 由于部下几乎每天早晨迟到,科长对他们进行了严厉的批评。*I laid down the law to my wife for running up so many shopping bills.* 我的妻子老是随意买东西,所以我对她进行了严厉的批评。有时用于“从最初起庄严宣告”的场合,例如: *On the first day of work, the department head laid down the law as to what would be expected of us.* 上班的头一天,部长就很严肃地向我们讲了他对我们的要求。在加强语气时插入一个 really。*My steady really laid down the law to me for two-timing her with Sally.* 由于我偷偷与萨莉乱搞,我的女朋友兴师问罪,狠狠责难了我一大顿。*When our teacher caught some of the students cheating, he really laid down the law.* 当我们的老师发现有几个学生考试作弊的时候,他进行了狠狠的批评。另外,在英国英语中,这一表达法也可用于表示“武断地讲”或“用武断的说法”,但在美国英语中完全没有“独断独行”的意思。◇ reprimand *someone* severely

take the law into *one's* own hands [ˌteɪkðəˈlɔː ɪntə ~ ˌoun ˈhæ(ː)ndz] [口] **不通过法律擅自处理** 直译为“把法律拿在自己手中”。*Give me that gun, Jim. You're not going to take the law into your own hands.* 吉姆,把枪给我。你不通过法律擅自处理,那是不行的。*When* *the man suspected of murdering his wife was found not guilty, the distraught husband vowed to take the law into his own hands.* 当杀害他妻子的嫌疑犯被宣告无罪时，悲痛欲狂的丈夫发誓要不通过法律而自行用武力报复。如上边的例句所示，“擅自处理”的方法绝大部分是“干掉”，但也偶尔有不是如此的时候。*If they don't give back the money I'm going to run them out of town. Sometimes you have to take the law into your own hands.* 如果他们不还钱，我就把他们赶出这个城镇去。有时候必须不通过法律自己进行处理。另外，前置词一般用 into，但在会话中有脱落 -to 而只剩下 in 的时候。*"I'm responsible for this man until he stands trial," said the sheriff to the crowd in front of the jail. "I'll shoot anyone who tries to take the law in his own hands."* “在送法院审判之前，这个人由我负责看管。”县保安官向聚集在拘留所前边的群众说：“谁要不顾法律擅自处理，我就开枪打他。”◇ administer justice without recourse to legal procedures

lay

lay it on (thick) [ˌleɪədɔːn / ˌleɪədɔ(ː)n ˈθɪ(ː)k] [话] **言过其实** → SPREAD it on thick

lay it on with a trowel [ˌleɪdɔ(ː)n wɪðə ˈtrauəl] [话] **过分吹捧** → SPREAD it on thick

the lay of the land [ðə ˌleɪəvðə ˈlæ(ː)nd] [口] **情势** 古时，当船接近未知的岛屿或陆地的时候，首先观看“陆地(在海上)的走向”(the lay of the land)，亦即“地理形势”。可以按字面意义使用，例如：*The fog in the offing prevented the ship's crew from ascertaining the lay of the land.* 海面有大雾，船员们未能判明陆地的走向。*I think I'll walk up to the top of that hill to see the lay of the land.* 我到那山顶上去观察一下地理形势吧。转义“状况”、“情势”、“事态”，为人们广泛使用。*I have a feeling that her father is against our marriage. After my appointment with him next week I should know the lay of the land.* 我总感觉到她的父亲不同意我们的婚事。我已经约定下个星期与他会面，情况究竟如何，会面之后便知分晓了。*As soon as I entered the room, from the angry looks on their faces I knew the lay of the land.* 我一走进屋内，见到他们的满面怒容，便知道情况如何了。除 the lay of the land，还有一个表达法是 how the land lies，意思相同。*Read this report. It'll show you how the land lies.* 你读读这篇报导，自然就会明白情况啦。如果象 get [see] the lay of the land 或者 see how the land lies 这样，在前边加上 get, see 等动词的时候，大多表示“事先调查情况”的意味。*I think I'll visit their office tomorrow to try to get the lay of the land before I make a decision.* 我想明天先到他们的办事处去一趟，事先了解一下情况，然后我再做决定。*We may enter into a joint venture with a Chinese company. Our sales manager is going to Shenzhen next week to see how the land lies.* 我们可能跟一家中国公司搞合资企业。我们的销售经理预定下个星期前往深圳，事先调查一下情况。在英国英语中，有时用 the lie of the land 代替 the lay of the land。◇ the situation ((get / see → ascertain))

lay *someone* **out** [ˌleɪ ～ˈaut] [话] **打倒** 在这里，out 是“伸得长长地”的意思。*The champ laid out the challenger with one punch in the first round.* 在第一回合，冠军猛击一拳就把挑战者打倒了。如这一例句所示，一般是用手殴击，但也有如下的用法。*The pitcher laid the batter out with a bean ball.* 投手向击球手头部投了一个犯规球，把击球手给打倒了。常用 really 加强语气。*A board fell from a building under construction and really laid me out.* 从正在施工的大楼上掉下来一块木板，简直把我砸扁啦。lay *someone* out 还用于表示“在埋葬之前，给死者化妆，放入棺材里”的意味。*We were pretty hard up when my granddaddy died, so they just laid him out in an old wooden box.* 我爷爷死的时候，我们家非常穷，因此，只把他装到一个旧的木盒子

里了。如果是“把活的人横放在地面上”,一般要用 on,而讲 lay *someone* on the floor。还有 lay *something* out 的说法,意思是“把东西摊开”。*His wife always lays his clothes out for him.* 他的妻子总是给他摊开衣服。◇ knock *someone* out ((really → completely))

lay *something* **out** [ˌleɪ~ ˈaut] [口] **摊开** → LAY *someone* out

pick 'em up and lay 'em down → PICK

lays

something **lays** *someone* **up** [~ ˌleɪz ~ ˈʌ(:)p] [话] **(由于有病或受伤)在家休养** → be LAID up (with *something*)

lead

get the lead out of *one's* **pants** [ˌgetðə ˈle(:)daudə ~ ˌpæ(:)nts] [话] **赶快干[走]** 这里的 lead 是“铅”。本条直译为“把铅从裤子里取出来”。最初的构思是“只要把屁股上的铅块从裤子里取出来,身子轻快,速度就会加快了”。主要用于“赶快干什么事或到什么地方去”的场合。*Get the lead out of your pants!* 你们赶快干! 如此例所示,经常用命令式。但也可以这样说: *He's got to get the lead out of his pants or else he won't finish on time.* 他必须赶快干,否则到时候完不了活儿。有时省略 of *one's* pants, 例如: *If we don't get the lead out we're going to miss the train.* 如果我们不赶快走,就会误了火车。◇ hurry (up)

go over like a lead balloon → BALLOON

throw lead (at *someone*) [ˌθrou ˈle:d] [话] **打枪** lead 是“铅”,但在这里指“子弹”。因此,本条直译为“扔子弹”。一种轻松的表达法。 *A guy behind that tree over there suddenly started throwing lead at us.* 藏在那边树后的一个家伙突然向我们开枪了。*One of the gangsters ran out throwing lead.* 一个歹徒一边打枪一边跑。◇ shoot

leading

a leading question → QUESTION

leaf

shake like a leaf [ˌʃeɪklaɪkə ˈli:f] [口] **打哆嗦** 直译为“(由于寒冷或恐怖而)象树叶一样颤抖”。 *When Jimmy got home from school, he was shaking like a leaf from the cold.* 当吉米从学校回到家里的时候,他冻得直打哆嗦。*The weird sounds coming from the darkened house left me shaking like a leaf.* 我听到那所昏暗的房子里发出来的令人毛骨悚然的声音,身上直打哆嗦。也可以说 tremble like a leaf, 但只限于“恐怖”的场合。*Ten minutes after the danger had passed, I was still trembling like a leaf.* 危险已经过去十分钟了,可是我依然直打哆嗦。◇ quiver

tremble like a leaf [ˌtrembəlːaɪkə ˈli:f] [口] **吓得直打哆嗦** → shake like a LEAF

turn over a new leaf [ˌtər ˌnovərə ˌnju: ˈli:f] [口] **洗心革面** 这里的 leaf 不是“树叶”,而是“书籍的一页”。因此,本条直译为“掀开新的一页”。用作比喻,表示“改正缺点,重新起步”。应用范围很广,从“改正恶习”、“改正不良行为”,一直到“犯罪分子洗手不干,重做新人”。*Jimmy is late for school almost every morning. If he doesn't turn over a new leaf he'll have to be punished.* 吉米几乎每天早晨上学迟到。如果他不改正这一缺点,必然要受到处罚的。*This year I've decided to turn over a new leaf. I'm not going to criticize people just because they disagree with me.* 今年我下决心改正自己的不良作风了。我不再仅仅由于人家不同意我的意见而对他们进行批评。*This is a model prison. By the time most inmates are released, they are determined to turn over a new leaf and go straight.* 这是一座模范监狱。在被释放的时候,大多数犯人都决心改恶从善,重新做人。◇ change *one's* ways / make a new beginning

leak

take a leak [ˌteɪkə ˈli:k] [俗] **撒尿** 直译为“使漏出”。男性用语。*Stop at the next filling station. I've got to take a leak.* 到下一个加油站停车。我得撒泡尿。◇ urinate

lean

lean on *someone* (to *do something*) ['li:.nɔ(:)n ~] [话] **施加压力** 按照字面意义,这是一个表示亲密无间的习用语,例如说: *The old man leaned on his son as he walked.* 老汉依靠着他的儿子向前走路。但在作为比喻使用的时候,立场就完全相反了。有时是表示强者以势欺人,施加压力;有时是表示抓住对方的弱点,以此为本钱,向对方指手划脚。*The finance company is leaning on us to pay back the loan.* 金融公司正在向我们施加压力,叫我们偿还贷款。*The President found that bureaucrats are not quick to comply unless he leans on them a bit.* 总统已经看到,如果不对那些官僚们施加一点压力,他们是不会唯命是从的。友人之间也可以轻松地使用,在这一场合,并不一定有谁强谁弱的立场问题。*Stop leaning on me, will you? I told you I would help you when I get the time.* 不要逼我好不好?我已经告诉你了,只要我有功夫,我就去帮助你。◇ pressure *someone* (to *do something*)

leap

Look before you leap. → LOOK

learn

I'll learn *someone* **to** *do something*. ['aɪl .lə:rn ~tə ~] [话] **我要叫你好瞧** → I'll TEACH *someone* to do *something*.

learning

book learning ['buk .lə(:)rnən] [话] **书本知识** 如字面所示,指从 book (书) 得来的学问。不一定与学校教育有关系。*In this job, experience and common sense are more important than book learning.* 在这种工作中,经验和常识比书本知识更为重要。book learning 这一名词本身有点土气,因此,除了戏谑的场合外,在有教养人的会话中是见不到的。换个说法就是 education。*I came up through the school of hard knocks, so I ain't got much book learning.* 我是从艰难困苦之中磨练出来的,因此肚子里没有多少墨水儿。*The trouble with this outfit is that it's run by scholars with lots of book learning but no practical experience.* 这个单位的毛病是由一些学者经营,他们有很多书本知识,但是缺乏实际经验。◇ formal education

leash

keep *someone* **on a short leash** [.ki(:)p ~ ɔnə .ʃɔrt'li:ʃ] [口] **严格控制** leash 是"系狗的绳子"。本条直译为"把狗拴在一条短绳子上"。*My dog has a habit of biting people, so I always keep it on a short leash when I take it out.* 我的狗有咬人的习惯,因此,当我带它出去的时候,我总是把拉着它的皮带弄得很短。"拴在短绳子上"的目的就是"限制其任意行动",因此,本条常作为比喻使用。例如: *Mrs. Jones keeps her children on a short leash. She doesn't even allow them to go to the movies.* 琼斯太太对她的孩子们管得很严。她甚至不准他们去看电影。*The board of directors keeps the president on such a short leash that he has very little authority.* 由于董事会对总经理控制得极严,他的权限很小。*Mr. Milquetoast doesn't go out at night much. His wife keeps him on a short leash.* 米尔克托斯特先生夜里很少外出,因为他是"妻管严"。另外,可以用 tight 代替 short,而说 keep *someone* on a tight leash。◇ sharply control *someone's* freedom of action

keep *someone* **on a tight leash** [.ki(:)p ~ ɔnə .taɪt'li:ʃ] [口] **管得很严** → keep *someone* on a short LEASH

leatherneck

a leatherneck [ə 'le(:)ðər.nek] [话] **美国海军陆战队士兵** 直译为"皮脖子"。因旧时美国海军陆战队制服上有皮领,故名。*Craig has been a leatherneck for fifteen years now.* 克雷格参加海军陆战队已经 15 年了。海军陆战队全体士兵为 the leathernecks。*Leave it to the leathernecks.* 把那个任务交给海军陆战队吧。顺便讲一下:美国的海军陆战队专门负责登陆作战,正式名称是 the Marine Corps [.ko(:)r]。在行政上由海军部长管辖，但既不属于海军也不属于陆军，是一支独立的军队。如果用英语说明，就是：The Marine Corps is an independent armed service. ◇ a marine

leave

leave well enough alone [li(:)v ˌweləˌnʌfə ˈloun] [口] **原封不动** 直译为“让它非常良好地独自呆着”，亦即“原封不动”，意思是“本来已经令人十分满意的事物，如果硬要画蛇添足，反倒弄巧成拙，不如维持现状为妙”。 *I changed many of the answers on my test paper, but most of them turned out to be right the first time. I should've left well enough alone.* 我在考试的答卷上改动了许多答案，但是，几乎所有最初的答案反而是正确的。我原封不动就好啦。let well enough alone 同义。 *The steaks were a little rare, but I should have let well enough alone. When I tried to cook them some more, I ended up burning them.* 牛排煎得有点嫩，可是我不动它就好了。我又去回锅，结果却炸焦啦。真是“悔之晚矣”。如果表示“今后再也不乱动手了”，就说 *Next time I'll leave [let] well enough alone.* 便可以了。◇ not attempt to improve the result

take it or leave it → TAKE

left

left and right [ˌleftənˈraɪt] [口] **依照次序** → RIGHT and left

leftist

a leftist [ə ˈleftɪst] [口] **左派人物** → a LEFTY

lefty

a lefty [ə ˈle(:)fti] [话] **左撇子** a left-handed person 的轻松说法。美国人中有很多左撇子。*I hadn't realized he was a lefty until I saw him sign his name.* 在我看到他签名之前，我没注意到他是个左撇子。*I write with my right hand, but in most other things I'm a lefty.* 我写字用右手，但是干其他的大多数事情时是个左撇子。本条也表示“棒球左手投球员”(a southpaw) 的意思。 *Two of the pitchers on that team are lefties.* 那个队里有两个左手投球员。如下一例句所示，也可以作为形容词使用。*Against a lefty pitcher, it'd be better to send in a right-handed batter.* 为了对付左手投球员，最好是派出一个右手击球员。在英国英语中，lefty 可作“左翼人士”解。在美国英语中，“左翼人士”为 leftist, 如果用 lefty 则含有一些轻蔑的意味。*I'm not sure whether he's a communist or not, but I know he's a lefty.* 我不敢肯定他是不是共产主义者，但是我知道他是个左派人物。*This town is full of lefty politicians.* 这个城镇里充满了左派政治家。◇ (a) left-handed (person)

leg

have a bone in *one's* **leg** → BONE

have a hollow leg [ˌhævə ˌhɑlə ˈleːg] [话] **海量** 直译为“有一只中空的腿”。意思是说：不管喝多少酒，都流进了“中空的腿”，因此怎么也不醉。汉语叫“海量”，不管有多少条江河注入，海都能容纳。*You'll never drink Stu under the table. That guy's got a hollow leg.* 你永远也灌不醉司徒，那个家伙是海量的酒仙。*No more for me thanks. I'm afraid I don't have your hollow leg.* 谢谢，请不要给我倒酒啦。很遗憾，我没有你那样的海量。*The chief usually has only one or two drinks, but tonight he somehow seems to have developed a hollow leg.* 咱们的头头平常只喝一两杯，今天晚上怎么啦，他好象变成了一位海量的酒仙。◇ have a great capacity (for alcohol)

not have a leg to stand on [nɑt ˌhævə ˌle(:)gtə ˈstæːnˌdɔːn] [话] **完全没有根据** 直译为“没有一只能够站立的腿”。在想要贯彻自己的主张或者通过法律解决而又“缺乏确实的根据”时，常使用本条。*Let them sue us if they want to. They don't have a leg to stand on.* 他们愿意告咱们，就叫他们上法院起诉好了。他们没有任何的根据。当然也可以说 have not (got) a leg to stand on。例如：*Their case hasn't got a leg to stand on.* 他们的诉讼没有一点儿依据。常用 single 加强

语气。*After Ben refuted my first argument, I didn't have a single leg to stand on.* 本驳倒了我的第一个论点之后，我就完全站不住脚了。另有一个说法为 be left without a leg to stand on, 意思是“失去立足的根据”。*When the section chief refused to support my proposal, I was left without a leg to stand on.* 当科长拒绝支持我的建议的时候，我就失去一切立足的根据了。◇ lack a valid basis (for *one's* position, argument, proposition, etc.)

pull *someone's* **leg** [ˌpul ～ ˈleːg] [话] **开玩笑** pull 是“拉”，leg 是“腿”。如果把本条译为“拉某人的后腿”，那就大错特错了。本条的意思是：“毫无恶意地说个谎，向某人开个小玩笑”。*Don't let Luke fool you. He's forever pulling someone's leg with a tall story.* 你不要上卢克的当。他总是编一套谎话拿别人开心。*When I first met Mr. Tanaka, he told me he was Chinese. Only later did I find out that he had been pulling my leg.* 当我第一次与田中先生见面的时候，他对我讲他是中国人。直到后来，我才发现他是开我的玩笑。*A: Go on! You're pulling my leg. B: No. It's true, I tell you.* 甲：得啦！你净拿我开心。乙：不，这是真的。一点儿不假！“拿别人开心者”是 a leg-puller。常用 great 加强语气。*My grandfather is a great leg-puller.* 我的祖父最喜欢开别人的玩笑。◇ deceive *someone* jokingly / tease *someone*

shake a leg [ˌʃeɪkə ˈleːg] [话] **赶快** 直译为“摇动脚”。不限定“用脚急走”的场合，一般在步行时，在乘交通工具时，或者正在做出行动的准备时使用。很少用于表示“赶快干活”的意思，在这一点上，比 get a MOVE on 或者 get a WIGGLE on 的使用范围窄多了。*We'd better shake a leg or we'll miss the bus.* 我们得赶快走，不然就赶不上公共汽车了。*Hurry and get dressed. If we don't shake a leg, we'll be late for the party.* 赶快换衣服。如果我们不抓紧时间，参加社交晚会就要迟到了。◇ hurry (up)

legit

legit [ləˈdʒɪ(ː)t] [话] **合法的** 原为 legitimate (合法的)一词的缩略，可以认为是 legitimate 的轻松的表达法。一般用于表示“法律上有效的”、“法律认可的”，以及“严肃的”、“认真的”等意义。另外，作为艺术用语，还有相对于杂耍、电视、电影等的“正统的舞台剧”的意味。总而言之，legit 的使用范围非常宽广。*This contract isn't legit if you ask me. You'd better get it rewritten.* 如果叫我来讲，这个合同在法律上不完备。最好是叫他们重写一下。这里的 legit 是指“在法律上有效”。在下一例句中，则是“合法”的意思。*I'd like to do it that way, but we'd better check with a lawyer first. It may not be legit.* 我喜欢那样办，但是我们还是先请教一下律师为好，万一不合法呢。go legit 与 go STRAIGHT 同义，是“犯法者改邪归正”乃至“严格遵守法律办事”。*You can't make me believe that shyster lawyer has gone legit.* 你无法让我相信那个卑鄙无耻的律师已经改邪归正了。下面的例子与法律没有直接关系，仅用于表示“严肃”、“认真”的意味。*Is his offer legit? I don't want to waste time considering it unless he is really serious.* 他的开价是真的吗？除非他是真心实意，我不愿意花费时间去考虑它。下面的例句是表示“正统的舞台剧”的意味。*He is a former comedian who succeeded on the legit stage.* 他原是一下喜剧演员，曾在正统的舞台剧中取得成功。*She has given up movie acting and gone back to legit.* 她放弃了演电影，又回来搞正统的舞台剧了。◇ legitimate / legal / (become) honest / serious

leg-puller

a leg-puller [ə ˈle(ː)gˌpulər] [话] **拿别人开心者** → pull *someone's* LEG

Legree

a Simon Legree → SIMON LEGREE

legs

be on *one's* **last legs** [ˌɔn ～ ˈlæːstˈleːgz] [口] **就要倒下了** 直译为“在某人最后的

腿上”。语源不详。但 last 指“腿已经不能再动”,亦即“腿的机能达到了最后的限度”。*When we got home from the hike, we were all on our last legs.* 当我们从远足回到家里的时候,大家都精疲力竭,快要倒下了。*I was on my last legs by the end of the race.* 在赛跑到终点的时候,我精疲力竭,都快要倒下了。以上的例句是表示“精疲力竭,一时地快要倒下”的意思。也有表示“寿命将尽,快要永远躺下”的场合。*I haven't much longer to live. I'm on my last legs.* 我活不多久了。我快要倒下啦。如果在讲到“人”的场合,使用“一时快要倒下”的意味占绝大多数;但在讲到人以外的“动物”的场合,情况恰恰相反,一般使用“快要永远倒下”的意味。*This has been a fine horse, but it's on its last legs.* 这是一匹好马,但是寿命已经不长啦。在讲到“动物”的时候,也有表示“精疲力竭”的用法。*Dogged doggedly by a dog, the rabbit appeared to be on its last legs.* 在狗的穷追猛赶之下,小兔子似乎已经精疲力竭,快要倒下了。如果讲的不是人或动物,而是“事物”,当然只能考虑是“就要永远垮台”的意思。*My old car is on its last legs.* 我的那辆破旧的汽车就要报废啦。*The old capitalist regime is on its last legs.* 旧的资本主义制度行将灭亡。有一点请读者注意:在“事物”的场合以及“动物”的大多场合,条头中的 *one's* 要改为 its。◇ be very tired [old, worn out, weak, etc.] / won't last much longer

with *one's* **tail between** *one's* **legs** → TAIL

lemme

lemme ['lemi] [话] **让我……** let me 的音变。按照日常会话的发音拼写而成。在漫画、小说的对话中常可见到。*Lemme try it, too.* 让我也试试看。*Lemme go!* 放开我! *Lemme have that.* 把那个给我。*Lemme see it!* 让我看一下! *He wouldn't lemme do it.* 他不让我干那个。◇ let me

length

keep *someone* **at arm's length** [ˌki(ː)p ~ ˈədɑːrmz ˈleːŋkθ] [口] **保持一定距离** 直译为“使某人离开有一臂的距离”。用于“人际关系”,不是“完全不来往”,而是“达不到亲密的程度”。汉语成语叫“不即不离”。*After Jane heard about his background, she decided that she'd better keep him at arm's length.* 简了解到他的出身情况以后,决定对他采取不即不离的态度。*A man as rich and handsome as Ron is has difficulty keeping the girls at arm's length.* 象罗恩那样一位既有钱又英俊的男子,要想与姑娘们保持一定的距离是很困难的。条头中的 *someone* 的部分有时要改成 *something*(物),在这一场合,本条可以译作“躲避”、“逃避”。*Jim is the type who likes sports but prefers to keep intellectual pursuits at arm's length.* 吉姆是这样一种类型的人:喜好体育运动,逃避文化学习。*Any kind of physical labor was repugnant to him, and he did his best to keep it at arm's length.* 他讨厌任何种类的体力劳动,竭尽一切力量去躲避它。可以将 keep 换成 hold,采取 hold *someone* [*something*] at arm's length 的形式。在这一场合,有时用法与 keep 相同。例如: *He wasn't a popular person. Everyone held him at arm's length.* 他没有人缘儿。每个人对他都敬而远之。但是,大多是按照字面意义使用,表示“把什么东西放在伸胳臂能达到的地方”的意思。例如: *He held his wife at arm's length, admiring her new dress.* 他伸出两只手,轻轻拉住妻子,欣赏她的新装。如果把这句话译成“他一边欣赏妻子的新装,一边躲开了她”,那就大错特错了。在按照字面意义使用的场合,不能把 hold 换成 keep。*She held the book at arm's length, trying to read without her glasses.* 她手拿着书,将两臂伸平,试着不戴眼镜阅读。◇ prevent *someone* from becoming too friendly

less

much less [ˌmʌtʃ ˈle(ː)s] [口] **更不用说** → LET alone

let

let alone [ˌledəˈloun] [口] **更不要提……** 意义和用法与 much less 相同,在以下各

例句中完全可以互换。但是，let alone 的语气比较强烈。*My son would never tell a lie, let alone steal.* 我的儿子绝对不说一句谎话，更不要提偷东西了。*That guy can't even do his own work, let alone run a company.* 那个家伙连他自己的工作都干不了，更不消说经营一个公司了。如以上的例句所示，alone 的后边可以用动词。但是为了避免同一动词的重复，有时直接连续名词，例如：*He is too busy even to talk to his wife, let alone (to) Miss Jones.* 他太忙了，连跟妻子谈话的功夫都没有，更何况跟琼斯小姐了。在这一场合，省略的顺序是：to talk to Miss Jones → talk to Miss Jones → to Miss Jones → Miss Jones，而且使用其中的任何一个都可以。不过，避免使用动词 talk 的方式乃是最好的表达法。*When I was young, we hardly had enough money to feed ourselves, let alone our relatives.* 在我年轻的时候，连养活自己家人的钱都不够，更不要说照顾亲戚了。◇ much less

let *someone* **down** [ˌlet ~ ˈdaun] [口] **使某人失望** 同义语为 disappoint。Don't let me down. 与 Don't disappoint me.的意思大致相同。在以下各例句中，均可用 disappoint 代换。本条的重点在于"使沮丧"、"使失望"的"心情"。*Jack promised to come and help us, but it looks as though he's let us down.* 杰克答应来帮助我们，可是现在看起来，他使我们失望啦。如这一例句所示，常用于负约的场合。*That guy has let me down for the last time. I'm never going to ask him to do anything for me again.* 这是那个家伙最后一次使我失望啦。今后我决不再求他给我干任何的事情。*I'm counting on your getting good grades on your exams this time. Please don't let me down.* 我想你在这次考试中会取得良好的成绩。请不要使我失望。*Tom won't let us down. As soon as he realizes we may be lost, I'm sure he'll come looking for us.* 汤姆是不会叫我们失望的。他一想到我们可能迷路，肯定会前来寻找我们。◇ disappoint *someone*

let *someone* **down easily [easy]** [ˌlet ~ ˌdau ˈniːzəli / ˈniːzi] [口] **委婉地讲，不使人伤心** → LET *someone* down gently

let *someone* **down gently** [ˌlet ~ ˌdaunˈdʒentli] [口] **婉转地说，不伤他人的心** → LET *someone* down (→) 的字面意义为"使某人的情绪下降"，是 disappoint (使失望)的同义语。加上 gently，就是"温和地使之失望"了。这个 gently 表达对他人的关怀，也就是说，在向别人传达不幸的消息时，结果必然会使对方沮丧，然而努力婉转去讲，可能缓和剧烈的悲痛。*When I decided not to marry Alan, I tried to let him down gently.* 当我决定不同阿伦结婚的时候，我极力用委婉的话对他讲，不使他太伤心。*I know you have no choice but to refuse my mother's request. I only ask that you let her down gently.* 我知道你不能不拒绝我母亲的要求。我只是请求你委婉地对她讲，不伤她的心。有时不用 gently，而用 easily 或者 easy。这两个词的意义与 gently 相同，但 easy 比 easily 更具有会话的味道。*What can I say to her? When telling a mother that her son is dead, there's no way of letting her down easily.* 我怎么对她说才好呢？当向一位母亲讲她的儿子已经死了的时候，没有任何方法使她听了不悲痛欲绝啊。*There's no need to beat around the bush. I know I'm fired. But thanks for trying to let me down easy.* 没有转弯抹角的必要了。我知道我已经被解雇了。不过，你们努力委婉地对我讲，怕我伤心，这一点我很感谢。◇ give *someone* the news in a way that doesn't hurt (*him*)

let *someone* **in on** *something* [ˌlet ~ ˈɪn.ɔ(ː)n ~] [口] **告知** 意思是"让 *someone* 参加 *something*"。*What are you whispering about? Let me in on the secret.* 你们在说什么悄悄话哪？把秘密也告知我吧。*If you hear any good tips on the stock market, let me in on them, will you?* 你如果听到股票市场上有什么好消息，也告知我一下好吗？有时不仅仅指"告知"秘密或消息，而且指"参加"随后的行动"。*My big brothers won't let* *me in on the camping trip. They say I'm too little to go.* 我的几个哥哥不让我参加他们的野营旅行。他们说我太小了，不能去。*The thieves decided to let Tenderfingers in on the next robbery because he was a good safe-cracker.* 窃贼们决定让"巧手指"参加下一次的抢劫活动，因为他是一个破坏保险柜的能手。◇ tell *someone* (a secret, etc.) / include *someone* in *something*

let on [.le(:)'dɔ:n] [口] **假装** 详细解释就是："用动作、态度、语言等显示出若有其事的样子"。换句话说，就是"假装"。但是，否定式的 not let on 却不是"不假装"的意思，而是"不由动作、态度、语言等泄露出来"，相当于汉语成语的"不动声色"。肯定式大多采取 let on that ～的句型。*Jane let on that she didn't care about falling the exam, but I knew she was deeply disappointed.* 简没有通过考试而假装满不在乎的样子，但是我了解她是大失所望的。有时用 like [as though, as if] 代替 that。*Grandpa's not all that deaf. He just lets on like he doesn't hear.* 爷爷的耳朵并不太聋。他只是假装听不见的样子。let on about ～大多指在言语上"假装"，而不是在动作和态度上"假装"。*She's always letting on about how happy she is.* 她总是从口头上显露出她是多么的幸福。that [like] 或 about 以下的部分如果不言而喻，可以省略。*Mary is not really sick. She's just letting on.* 玛丽不是真有病。她完全是装的。*He's not so dumb. He knows more than he lets on.* 他并不那么傻。别看样子傻，他知道的东西可多着呢。也有如下的说法。*She's not as happy as she lets on to be.* 她并不象外表装的那样幸福。在否定的场合，用法如下。*When we meet Mr. Plotter, don't let on that we know about his plan.* 当我们见到普洛特先生的时候，不要暴露出我们了解他的计划。not let on to *someone* (不让某人了解)这一句型使用较多。*I saw Margaret at the party, but I didn't let on to other people that I knew her.* 我在社交晚会中见到了玛格丽特，但是我没叫别人知道我认识她。*I didn't let on to my wife that I had lost my job.* 我不动声色，没有叫妻子了解我已经失业。◇ pretend / make a false show / let *someone* know

let well enough alone [let .welə.nʌfə 'loun] [口] **别去管它** → LEAVE well enough alone

not let on to *someone* [nɑt.le'dɔ:ntə ～] [口] **不要让某人了解** → LET on

letter

a bread-and-butter letter [ə .bredn'bʌdər .ledər] [口] **感谢款待的信** 直译为"对用面包和黄油招待表示感谢的信"。在别人家里的宴席上吃饭，或是在别人家里过夜又吃饭，事后写信表示感谢。*After returning from my trip around the country visiting friends, I had to write a lot of bread-and-butter letters.* 在我走遍全国访友归来之后，我不得不写了许多封感谢款待的信。*You should send your grandmother a bread-and-butter letter thanking her for the week you spent at her house.* 你在外婆家里呆了一个星期，应该给她去一封感谢招待的信。可以用 note 代替 letter。*There was no particular news in Anne's letter. It was just a bread-and-butter note thanking us for inviting her to the party.* 安妮的信里没有什么特殊的事情。那只是一封感谢信，感谢我们请她参加了社交晚会。◇ a thank-you letter [note]

a Dear John letter [ə .dɪ(:)r'dʒɑ:n .ledər] [话] **绝情信** 朝鲜战争时期，美国流行一首名为"Dear John"的西部歌曲。这是一首男女别离歌，第一句为"Dear John, oh how I hate to write....."。本条来源于此。原来为士兵用语，而且指的是妻子的来信。例如：*Corporal Higgins' morale is pretty low right now. He got a Dear John letter from his wife.* 希金斯下士现在的情绪非常低落。他的老婆给他寄来一封绝情信。现在，一般指年轻人收到的恋人的绝情信。*A: Why the long face? B: I just got a Dear John letter form my girl.* 甲：你干吗愁眉苦脸呀？

乙:我刚收到女朋友的绝情书。有时可以省去 letter 一词。 *Jack got a Dear John from his fiancée just one week before they were to be married.* 杰克在就要结婚的前一个星期接到了未婚妻的绝情信。◇ a farewell letter

lettuce

lettuce ['ledəs] [话] **钞票** → BREAD

level

level with *someone* ['le(:)vəl wɪð ~] [话] **坦率地说话** 动词 level 是"把凸凹不平的地方弄平,将弯曲的地方裁直"的意思。加上 with *someone* 作为比喻使用,则意味着"不使说话的内容弯曲,笔直地→坦率地讲"。在向对方和盘托出过去没有讲过的事情或者过去没有交待清楚的思想感情的时候使用。 *I'll level with you. I don't like the way you're running this company. You're trying to expand too fast.* 我坦率地对你讲,我不喜欢你经营这个公司的方式方法。你扩大规模搞得过于快啦。 *My husband finally leveled with me on the true state of our finances.* 我的丈夫终于向我坦率说出我家经济的实际状况。根据上下文,not level with 有"隐瞒"的意味。 *I don't like the way Ben sometimes disappears for days on end. I have a feeling he's not leveling with us.* 本有时候一连几天不见影儿,这种做法我不喜欢。我总觉得他有什么事在隐瞒我们。有时候表示从一开头就"坦率地讲",但在这一场合总含有"平常的时候多少有点隐私也没什么"的意味。 *Mr. Ernest was very frank. He leveled with me right from the beginning.* 欧内斯特先生是非常直爽的。他从一开始就坦率地对我讲了。◇ be frank with *someone* / tell *someone* frankly (about *something*) / be(come) open and sincere with *someone*

be on the level [ˌɔ(:)nðə 'le(:)vəl] [话] **真诚的** on the level 本来是"不斜不弯,正在水平上"的意思。 *The plane flew on the level for a while, but then it began banking and turning.* 飞机水平飞行了一会儿,然后开始倾斜并转弯。转用于比喻。 *That's a lot of money. Do you think his offer is on the level?* 那是很大一笔钱啊。你认为他真开那么大的价吗? *I'd advise you to avoid any and all transactions with that company. They're suspected of not being on the level.* 我劝你还是尽量避免跟那家公司做生意为好。他们有弄虚作假的嫌疑。有时候,在句子里明显地表示出"不说谎,不弄虚作假"的意思。 *You can trust Jack. He's always on the level.* 你可以信赖杰克。他这个人一言一行都没有虚假。 *I don't trust that guy. How do you know the information he gave you is on the level?* 我不信任那个家伙。你怎么知道他给你的情报是真的呢? on the level 除了象以上那样与 be 动词一起使用外,还可以用作副词短语。 *I spoke to him as I would (to) a child, half teasingly, half on the level.* 我跟他讲话是半真半假,象逗弄一个孩子似的。◇ be genuine / be honest

lick

give *something* **a lick and a promise** [ˌgɪv ~əˌlɪkənə 'prɑ:məs] [话] **草率从事** lick 是"舔"的意思,在这里是"马马虎虎地赶快干什么事"。promise 意味着"自己心里打算以后再仔细收拾"。本条来源于英国的古代童话,据说:猫没有时间好好地洗脸,它只是舔一舔,并且对自己保证以后再认真地去洗。在打扫卫生时或擦或洗,要弄干净的场合使用本条。 *There wasn't time to clean the house well, so I just gave it a lick and a promise.* 我没有时间去好好地打扫屋子,因此只是大概齐地搞了一遍。 *I told the maid to polish the furniture carefully, but she only gave it a lick and a promise.* 我告诉女仆把家具仔仔细细地擦一遍,可是她只是马马虎虎地划拉了一下。 *Go back and wash your hands again. And this time give them more than a lick and promise.* 你回去再把手洗一遍。这回可不能猫洗脸,一划拉啊。◇ give *something* a very perfunctory cleaning [polishing, washing, etc.]

lie

lie in *one's* **teeth** → TEETH

a white lie [ə ˌhwaɪt ˈlaɪ] [口] **没有恶意的谎言** 直译为"白色的谎言"。这是一个非常巧妙的表达法。在英语中，white(白色)是"纯洁"、"善良"的意思，所以"白色的谎言"指无害的、有时为善意的谎言，十分贴切。*No one likes a real liar, but sometimes one has to tell white lies in order to spare others' feelings.* 谁也不喜欢一个真正爱说谎话的人，但是有时为了不伤别人的感情又非撒点小谎不可。*When I told you I had to leave the country right away on business, it was actually only a white lie to get you to promise to see me tonight.* 当我告诉你我必须立即出国办事的时候，实际上是撒了个谎，为的是要你答应今天晚上来看我。◇ an innocent falsehood

life

can't for the life of *one* [ˈkæ(ː)ntfərðə ˈlaɪfəv ~] [口] **怎么……也不行** for the life of *one* 直译为"拿生命交换也……"、"豁出命也……"，强调"怎么也不行"的意思。本条比 at all (全然) 的语气更强烈得多。*Would you explain this math problem to Bill? He says he can't understand it for the life of him.* 你给比尔讲一讲这个数学问题好吗？他说他怎么也弄不明白。*I had long waited to meet Sally, but when I was finally introduced to her, I couldn't for the life of me think of anything to say.* 我很久以来一直想与萨莉见面。但是，当我被介绍给她的时候，我怎么也想不出该说点什么。*I can never for the life of me remember Carl's telephone number.* 我怎么也想不起来卡尔的电话号码。如以上的例句所示，本条与"不明白"、"想不出"、"记不得"等表达法一起使用的场合非常多，但并不限定如此。*I couldn't for the life of me convince Judy to come.* 我怎么也没能把朱迪劝来。*For the life of me I don't seem to be able to stop smoking.* 我似乎怎么也戒不了烟。如最后这一例句所示，can't 可以采取 not be able to 的形式。另外，可以象 for the very life of *one* 这样，用 very 加强语气。本条大多放在句子的最前端。*For the very life of me I can't recall his name.* 我无论如何也想不起他的名字了。◇ no matter how hard *one* tries

be fixed for life [ˈfikst fər ˈlaɪf] [话] **一辈子生活富裕** be fixed 是"被固定住"，在这里把它解释为"不动弹"就容易明白了。be fixed for life 的意思是"一辈子不用费力气过富裕的生活"。*If this venture succeeds we'll be fixed for life.* 如果这项投机生意成功，我们一辈子就不愁吃不愁穿啦。常用 become 代替 be 动词。但是不知为什么，在本条中不用表示同样意义的 get。*Mr. Jones became fixed for life when oil was discovered on his farm.* 在琼斯先生的农场上发现石油以后，他就成为一辈子不必劳动的富家翁了。◇ have enough money to spend *one's* life without working

for dear life [fər ˈdɪːr ˈlaɪf] [口] **拼命地** 这里的 dear 有"宝贵的"、"可爱的"的意味。本条直译为"为了宝贵的、可爱的生命"。*Upon seeing the man pull a knife, Sally ran for dear life.* 看见那个男人拔出刀子，萨莉拼命地逃跑了。如这一例句所示，这个"拼命"是在遇到危险时"拼命逃跑"的"拼命"，如果没有特殊的情况，在讲"拼命用功"、"拼命吃饭"的场合不能使用本条。*As the waves grew higher, I found a bucket in the bottom of the boat and began bailing for dear life.* 风浪越来越大，我见到船的底部有一个水桶，就开始拼命地往外舀水。*I've never seen such a confirmed bachelor as Jake. A girl has only to look at him twice and he runs for dear life.* 我从来没有见过象杰克这样一个坚定的独身主义者。只要有一个姑娘看他两眼，他就拼命地逃走了。◇ in desperation

have the time of *one's* **life** → TIME

lead a charmed life [ˌli(ː)də ˈtʃɑːrmdˈlaɪf] [口] **命好** 源出莎翁名剧《麦克佩斯》(*Macbeth*)。charmed life 是"受魔法保护的生命"的意思。charmed 由及物动词 charm (对……施魔法) 而来，是"好象有魔法保护似的"的意思。动词原来不

是用 lead,而是用的 bear。但是在美国英语中,bear 一词有文绉绉的感觉,所以会话时不使用。*As a soldier, Charles bore a charmed life. Though he was wounded many times, he always completely recovered.* 查尔斯当兵好象有魔法保护似的,他虽然多次负伤,但总能彻底全愈。这是按照原意的用法。现在,lead a charmed life 不仅表示"不死",而且还更广泛地表示"逢凶化吉","命好"。但是,不论按本来的意义还是比喻的意义,只要涉及"生命"的事情,全都是表示"不死"。*That guy must lead a charmed life. He's come out of two bad automobile accidents without a scratch.* 那个家伙的命真叫大。他遇到两次严重的车祸,连一点皮都没擦破。这句话的前半部可以译成"他的生命一定有魔法保护",也可以理解为"运气好,没有被撞死"。但是,在下一例句中就不能译成"不死"。*Talk about leading a charmed life. Every time Stu loses a job, two or three weeks later he ends up getting an even better one.* 甭提命有多好啦。司徒每当失业的时候,过不上两三个星期,他就会找到另一个更好的工作。lead 可以用 enjoy, have 等动词代替。*Oliver may be rich, but, far from having enjoyed a charmed life, he seems to have suffered more misfortune than most.* 奥利弗可能很有钱,但是他的命运很不好,好象比一般的人有更多的不幸。◇ have continuous good fortune

lead a dog's life [ˌli(ː)də ˈdɔːgz ˌlaɪf] [话] **过着悲惨的生活** 直译为"过着狗的生活"。最初的构思是:狗的生活"没有自由"。而人"没有自由"的原因有多种多样,或者"由于监视很严",或者"由于没有金钱",或者"由于受人奴役",等等。*I led a dog's life in Europe.* 我在欧洲过了一段悲惨的生活。*Sam married a rich woman, but she keeps him on such a short leash that he leads a dog's life.* 萨姆取了一个有钱的老婆,但是"妻管"极严,弄得他的日子很惨。*Hank led a dog's life until his uncle died and left him some money.* 汉克的伯父死了,给他留下一些钱,在此以前,他的生活悲惨得很啊。◇ have a miserable existence

live the life of Riley [ˌlɪvðə ˌlaɪfəvˈraɪli] [口] **享清福** 过去,在歌舞杂耍表演(vaudeville)中曾经流行一首名为 Are you *the* O'Reilly? [ˌoˈraɪli] 的歌,内容为一个叫做 O'Reilly 的人在发财时的空想。本条来自这首歌的歌词,用于表示在物质上、精神上都没有不自由的生活状态,重点在于"享清福"。*Since Pat married a rich widow, he's been living the life of Riley.* 帕特自从娶了一个有钱的寡妇,就过上了自由自在的安乐日子。*You told me that if we moved to the South Seas we would be living the life of Riley, and here we are slaving away selling hot dogs to tourists.* 你告诉我说,如果我们移居南太平洋,我们就会过上安乐的日子。你瞧,我们在这里靠向旅游者卖热狗为生,整天象牛马一样劳动。可用 really 加强语气。*Have you seen the way Jack's wife waits on him hand and foot? He really lives the life of Riley.* 你看见杰克的老婆对他服侍得无微不至的样子了吗?他的确是享清福啦。另外,常用 lead 代替 live,而讲 lead the life of Riley,特别是在家庭生活以外的场合,使用 lead 比较自然。*You shouldn't envy my position. Just because I have a big office and a secretary doesn't mean I'm leading the life of Riley.* 你用不着羡慕我的地位。尽管我有一个大的办事处,而且有个秘书,但这不意味着我在过舒服的日子啊。有时,Riley 拼写为 Reilly。◇ lead a life of comfort and ease

Not on your life. [ˈnɑ(ː)dɔnjər ˈlaɪf] [话] **绝对不!** 表示极端的厌恶和强烈的拒绝,有"无论如何也不会答应"的意味。使用方法如下:*A: Will you lend my brother five hundred dollars? B: Not on your life. He hasn't paid me back the last money I lent him.* 甲:你能借给我弟弟五百美元吗?乙:绝对不行。上次他借我的钱还没有还清哪。*A: Would you take a ride on a UFO if you had the chance? B: Not on your life. I wouldn't get on one* *of those things for a million dollars.* 甲：如果你有机会的话，愿意乘一下飞碟吗？乙：绝对不干。即使给我一百万美元，我也不乘那类东西呀。*Not on your life would I ride in on airplane. I get acrophobia just climbing the stairs to my bedroom.* 我绝对不乘飞机。我连上楼梯去卧室，都会犯恐高症。◇ Certainly not. / Not for any reason.

the staff of life → STAFF

take *one's* **life in** *one's* **(own) hands** [ˌteɪk ~ ˈlaɪfɪn ~(ˌoun) ˈhæ(ː)ndz] [口] **冒生命危险** 直译为"自己的生命拿在自己的手中"，也就是"冒着极大的危险，稍一不慎就有生命之虞"的意思。用法如下：*Firemen take lives in their own hands every day in the line of duty.* 消防队员为了完成自己的任务，每天都冒着生命危险。*The blizzard is terrible. Anyone who goes out on a night like this is taking his life in his own hands.* 暴风雪可怕极了。谁要在这样的夜晚外出，简直是冒生命的危险。在会话中一般用 own，但有时可把 own 省去。另外，in 也可以改用 into，但在会话中还是应该用 in。*Mountain climbers are willing to take their lives into their hands in order to conquer lofty peaks.* 登山家们为了征服陡峭的山峰，自愿去冒生命的危险。实际上虽然没有生命危险，但为了夸张，也有用本条的时候。*You'll be taking your life in your own hands if you try to talk to the boss while he's in such a foul mood.* 在老板的情绪那么坏的时候，你却要找他谈话，那不是往老虎嘴里送食找死嘛！古时，本条不是用 take，而是用的 put。《圣经·旧约》中的《士师记》(Judges) 第 12 章 3 节有这样一段话：And when I saw that ye delivered me not, I put my life in my hands and passed over against the children of Ammon, and the Lord delivered them into my hands. (我看你们不来，就冒生命的危险越过边界去打亚扪人。上主使我打了胜仗。) ◇ risk death

lifer

a lifer [ə ˈlaɪfər] [俗] **无期徒刑犯人** 意思是"终身在监狱中度过的人"。这是一个极轻松的说法。*Many lifers try to do away with themselves.* 许多无期徒刑的犯人企图自杀。◇ a person in prison for life

lift

get a lift (to *someplace* from *someone*) [ˌgedə ˈlɪ(ː)ft] [话] **搭车** → give *someone* a LIFT (to *someplace*)

get a lift from *something* [ˌgedə ˈlɪft frəm ~] [话] **精神振奋** → give *someone* a LIFT

give *someone* **a lift** [ˌgɪv ~ əˈlɪ(ː)ft] [话] **使精神振奋** lift 是"提起"，但与 give *someone* a LIFT(to *someplace*) 中的 lift 不同，系指"提起人的精神"。本条与 The good news gave my spirits a lift. (大好消息令我精神振奋。) 一句话里的 give *someone's* spirits a lift 同义，用以表示"给垂头丧气或闷闷不乐的人打气"的意思。*Thank you for your letter last week. I was feeling blue when it arrived, but your words of encouragement gave me [my spirits] a lift.* 谢谢你上星期的来信。收到信的时候我的情绪处于低落，但是你的鼓励的词句使我的精神振奋起来了。*My husband somehow hasn't been feeling himself recently, but your visit yesterday seemed to give him somewhat of a lift.* 不知为什么，我的丈夫最近精神萎靡不振，但是你昨天的来访使他的情绪似乎有些好转啦。*Have a drink. It'll give your a lift.* 来喝一杯。它会使你的精神振作起来。如果讲 get a lift from *something*，则是以人为主语，表示"精神振奋"的意思。*I got a lift from your words of encouragement.* 在你的鼓励之下，我精神振奋起来了。◇ revive *someone's* spirits

give *someone* **a lift** (to *someplace*) [ˌgɪv ~ əˈlɪ(ː)ft] [话] **让某人搭车** lift 是"提起"。本条直译为"用车将某人提起运至某处"。*Mrs. Jones gave Trudy a lift to school.* 琼斯太太让特鲁迪搭她的车去学校了。*Fred gave two hitchhikers a lift to the next town.* 弗雷德把两个免费搭车的

人带到了下一个城镇。*Can you give me a lift part way?* 你能允许我搭车走一段路程吗? get a lift (to *someplace* from *someone*) 意思恰好相反,是"搭别人的车"。*I'll get a lift from Don.* 我要搭唐的车子走。◇ give *someone* a ride

lift *something* ['lɪft ~] [话] **偷东西** lift 一般是"提起"的意思。本条最初的构思是"把别人的东西提起来,使之成为自己的东西"。因此,lift 一词在口语中表示"偷"。*The burglar lifted three hundred dollars from the supermarket.* 窃贼从超级市场偷了三百美元。如这一例句所示,有以现金为宾语的场合。但是在大多数场合,是用以表示"偷东西(包括钱包)"或"在商店行窃"。*Jake was caught trying to lift a watch at the jewelry store.* 杰克在珠宝商店偷一块手表,叫人家抓住了。*Hey! That guy just now lifted my wallet.* 喂!那个家伙刚才偷了我的钱包。*Somebody broke into my place and lifted my TV set.* 有人闯进我家,把我的彩电偷走了。转义"剽窃他人的文章"。*The professor was accused of lifting his dissertation from an already published work.* 那位教授受到控告,他的论文被指责是剽窃一部已经出版的著作。◇ steal *something*

light

get the green light (from *someone*) [ˌgetðə ˈgriːn ˈlaɪt] [口] **获准** → give (*someone*) the green LIGHT

give (*someone*) **the green light** [ˌgɪv ~ðə ˈgriːn ˈlaɪt] [口] **批准** green light 是"交通的绿灯"。加上 give,就是"给绿灯",亦即"可以通行"。本条是由此产生的用作比喻的表达法。从下面的例句可以看出,"批准"的主体大多是各种机关团体的头头。*The president of the university can't begin the expansion program until the board of trustees gives him the green light.* 不得到理事会的批准之前,大学校长是无法开始实行扩充计划的。*The railroad wants to raise fares, but so far the government hasn't given the green light.* 铁路想要提高运费,可是至今政府还没有批准。顺便讲一下:另外还有个表达法是 get the green light (from *someone*),这当然是"获准"的意思。*The plans for the new project are completed, but we can't proceed until we get the green light from the board of directors.* 新工程的计划已经完成,但是在得到董事会批准之前,我们是不能开始实行的。另外,可以用 the go-ahead (许可) 代替 the green light,而讲 give (*someone*) the go-ahead 或者 get the go-ahead (from *someone*),意思完全一样。◇ give (*someone*) permission

hide *one's* **light under a bushel** [ˌhaɪd ~ ˈlaɪˌdʌndərə ˈbuʃəl] [口] **不露锋芒** 直译为"在蒲式耳斗下面隐藏光"。bushel 一词汉语音译为"蒲式耳",是英美的谷物、水果等的容量单位,在英国约等于 36 升,在美国约等于 35 升。在古时,除作容量单位外,还有计量使用的容器"蒲式耳斗"的意味(现在用 a bushel basket 表示"蒲式耳斗")。那末,"在蒲式耳斗下面隐藏光"怎么会成为"隐藏才能"的意思呢?《圣经·新约》中的《马太福音》(Matthew)第 5 章 14~16 节有下面这样一段特别有名的话。耶稣对弟子说: You are the light of the world. A city set on a hill cannot be hid. Nor do men light a lamp and put it under a bushel, but on a stand, and it gives light to all in the house. Let your light so shine before men, that they may see your good works and give glory to your Father who is in heaven. (你们是世上的光;城造在山上,是不能隐藏的。人点灯,不放在斗底下,是放在灯台上,就照亮一家的人。你们的光也当这样照在人前,叫他们看见你们的好行为,便将荣耀归给你们在天上的父。)也就是说,hide *one's* light under a bushel 来源于《圣经》,在《圣经》中是用以表示"隐藏好行为"的意思。在现代,与宗教有关系的一部分人仍用本条表示"隐藏好行为[信仰]",但在日常会话中,它只表示"隐藏才能"的意味。至于隐藏的原因,有时是因为"内向"。*You have a wonderful singing voice, Jimmy. Why don't you stop* *hiding your light under a bushel and join the glee club?* 吉米,你的歌喉棒极啦。你别隐藏自己的才能,参加合唱团好不好?也有时是因为"谦虚"。*I wouldn't go so far as to call George a braggart, but one has to admit that he's not exactly one to hide his light under a bushel.* 我不能言过其实,称乔治为牛皮大王,但是,你必须承认,他无论如何不是一个不露锋芒的人啊。在下一个例句中,认为是"内向"或"谦虚"都可以。*You are a talented boy, but if you hope to get anywhere in this world you've got to learn not to hide your light under a bushel.* 你是个很有才能的少年。但是,如果你希望在这个世界上得一席之地,就必须学会展示自己的才华。◇ hide [be modest about] *one's* ability [talent]

not stand the light of day [nɑt ˌstændðə ˌlaɪdəv'deɪ] [口] **立即露出马脚** 直译为"耐不住白昼的光线"。最初的构思是:在黑暗的地方还可以敷衍,但在光天化日之下,缺点便暴露无遗。*You'd better think of a better alibi. That one will never stand the light of day.* 你还是找一个更好点儿的口实吧。你那个口实是站不住脚的。*The company's carefully thought-out explanations concerning its smuggling operations didn't stand the light of day.* 关于走私活动,公司认真准备了一套很周密的解释。但是一说出来,立即露了马脚。*You'd better be careful about accepting Dave's excuses. Most of the things he says won't stand the light of day.* 你在听戴夫的辩解的时候,务必多加小心。他所说的话大部分是纸糊的窗户,一戳就破。◇ not stand up under examination

be out like a light [ˌautlaɪkə 'laɪt] [话] **一下子完全失去知觉** 直译为"象电灯一样,一下子就灭了"。在20世纪20年代,本条有"酩酊大醉,人事不省"的意思,现在几乎完全不用于醉酒的场合。因为原意为"象电灯一样,一关就灭,然后是一片漆黑",所以转用于表示"突然一下子失去知觉,完全不省人事"的意味,重点一是"完全地",二是"一下子"。*I only hit him once and he was out like a light.* 我只用拳头击了他一下,他马上就完全失去知觉了。如这一例句所示,应用最多的是"向脑袋上打一拳"的场合。*Don't worry about the guard. Just stick this under his nose. One whiff and he'll be out like a light.* 你不必担心那个警卫,只要把这东西往他的鼻子底下一杵就行啦。他吸一下,马上就会完全失去知觉了。*That's powerful medicine. One swallow and I was out like a light.* 那药的劲儿真大啊。我喝上一口,马上就完全失去知觉啦。也可以表示"一下子就睡着了"的意思,例如:*She was exhausted. As soon as her head touched the pillow, she was out like a light.* 她实在精疲力竭了。脑袋刚一挨着枕头,马上就睡着了。有时候不含有"一下子"的意思,只用以表示"完全失去知觉"或者"酣睡"的意味。不论如何,处于完全没有意识的状态这一点是与条头相通的。*He was struck so hard that he was out like a light for several hours.* 他挨了狠狠的一拳,一连几个小时完全人事不省。*I didn't hear any noise, I was out like a light all night.* 我没有听见任何的动静。我整整酣睡了一夜。有时使用 go out like a light 或者是 put *someone* out like a light 的形式。*I barely touched him and he went out like a light.* 我只是碰了他一下,他就马上完全失去知觉了。*The blow put him out like a light.* 他被那一拳打得一下子人事不省了。◇ be completely unconscious / lose consciousness instantly / be instantly asleep / be in a deep sleep

see the light at the end of the tunnel [ˌsi(ː)ðə 'laɪdətðɪ ˌendəðə 'tʌnl] [话] **终于有了一线曙光** 人们把"长时间的劳动"、"痛苦的经验"、"经济萧条"、"大病"等比做"黑洞洞的隧道",而在好容易达到尽头时,常说"隧道快完了,见到光亮了"。正是苦尽甘来,曙光在望的情景。*After four years' work on the project, we're beginning to see the light at the end of the tunnel.* 这个规划我们搞了四年,总算有点眉目啦。*It's been a long recession, but* *we're finally seeing the light at the end of the tunnel.* 经济萧条的时期很长，但是我们终于看见恢复繁荣的迹象了。*My wife has been very sick, but the doctor says he now sees the light at the end of the tunnel.* 我妻子的病很重，不过大夫说，她现在有康复的希望了。◇ approach the end / see the beginning of (complete) recovery

trip the light fantastic → FANTASTIC

lightning

like greased lightning [ˌlaɪkˈgriːzd ˈlaɪtnɪŋ] [话] **闪电似地** like lightning (象闪电一般)是自古以来就有的表达法，用"闪电"比喻"迅速"。*As soon as I said that, like lightning her attitude changed.* 我刚一谈到那件事，她的态度立即就改变了。本条又加上了 greased (抹上了油)一词，是强调"迅速"的意思。只有喜好夸大其词的美国人，才会有"抹了油的闪电"的奇怪想法。*The car zipped around the track like greased lightning.* 那辆小汽车象闪电一般从卡车的旁边飞驶过去了。*I had struggled with English for many years without completely mastering it, but when we went to live in America our children picked it up like greased lightning.* 我拼命学了好多年英语，也没有完全掌握它，可是在我们移居美国之后，孩子们一转眼的功夫就学会了。*Charles is very good at math. He always whips through his homework like greased lightning.* 查尔斯很善于学数学。他的家庭作业总是在一转眼的功夫就做完了。faster than greased lightning 是对这一夸张的表达法的进一步夸大。*The brakes on my bicycle broke and I went down the hill faster than greased lightning.* 我的自行车上的刹车坏了，在下山的时候车速简直比闪电还要快。*Once George makes up his mind to do something, he moves faster than greased lightning.* 一旦乔治下定决心干什么事情，他行动起来比闪电还要快。◇ very quickly

white lightning [ˈhwaɪtˈlaɪtnən] [话] **家庭自制威士忌** 这种酒酒劲儿非常大，喝上一口，全身有受雷击 (lightning) 的感觉，故名。这里的 white 是"无色透明"的意思。本条主要指玉米制造的威士忌。另有 white MULE, MOONSHINE 等说法，意思大体相同。*Tim's grandpa makes his own white lightning.* 蒂姆的爷爷用玉米自制威士忌。◇ homemade (corn) whiskey

like

I like that! [ˈaɪ ˈlaɪk ˈðæ(ː)t] [话] **亏你说得出口！** I like that. (我喜欢那个。)这句话，由于重音所在位置的不同，会有种种不同的意味。例如，一般来说，如果强调"喜欢"，就把重音放在 like 上；如果强调"那个"，把重音放在 that 上就行了。这条规律是不言而喻的。然而，如果把 I, like, that 这三个词全加上重音，而且一个单词一个单词分别很清楚地来发音，那就与"我喜欢那个"的意思恰恰相反，表示与 I don't like that. (我不喜欢那个。)相同的韵味了，亦即成为 I like that.的反义语。在使用本条时，经常带有愤慨的口气，意思是说："为你费了这么大劲，而你却……，亏你说得出口！""对你如此期待，而你却……，亏你说得出口！"使用者大多为女性，而且是在听到或见到令人愤慨的言语和事情之后立即脱口而出。为了加强语气，通常在本条前边加 Well。*Well, I like that! After all the trouble I went to get him the job, he says he isn't going to take it.* 哼，亏他说得出口！我费了九牛二虎之力给他去找工作，而他却说他不打算去就职！*You're not going to eat the meal I fixed for you? Well, I like that!* 我特意给你做了饭，而你却不打算吃？哼，亏你说得出口！*He says he's not going to take us with him? Well, I like that!* 他是说他不打算带咱们一起去吗？哼，亏他说得出口！◇ That makes me angry!

just like that [ˌdʒʌst ˌlaɪk ˈðæt] [话] **极其简单地** *We thought it would be very difficult, but we were able to do it just like ... that.* 我们原来认为这件事非常难，但是我们轻而易举地把它干完了。美国人在说这句话的时候，常常在讲到最后的

that 处弹一下手指，意思是“就象弹手指那么容易”。这就是本条的来源。在遇到困难的、要紧的、严重的事情而敢说敢做的时候使用。具有“简单、干脆到了惊人的程度”的韵味。当然可以按照字面意义“就是那样地”使用。但是，本条的准确意思只能通过上下文来判断，别无其他办法。例如说 *We did it just like that.* 这句话，既可以理解为“我们就是那样做的”，也可以理解为“我们轻而易举地做了那件事”，两种解释全说得通。*When I told him I didn't have that part for his car, he told me to make one, just like that.* 当我告诉他我这里没有他的汽车所需要的那种部件的时候，他站着说话不嫌腰疼，叫我给他制作一个。*After fifteen years of married life, he tells me he wants a divorce, just like that. Can you imagine?* 我们结婚都 15 年啦，他告诉我他想要离婚，说得多轻巧啊？你能想象得到吗？这是很简单地顺嘴一说的例子。下面是简单地顺手去做的例子。*When he saw that my car was stuck in the ditch, he picked it up and set it on the road, just like that.* 当他看见我的车陷在沟里的时候，他轻而易举地把它端起来，放到公路上了。*He must be loaded. I said I was a little short of cash, so just like that he pulls out a roll of hundred-dollar bills and asks me how much I want.* 他一定是非常有钱。我说我缺一点儿现金，他很随便地掏出一卷百元的钞票，问我想要多少。*I come late for work and just like that he fires me.* 我上班迟到了，他不容分说就开除我。◇ just as if it were nothing.

like anything → ANYTHING

liking

take a liking to *someone* [*something*] [ˌteɪkə ˈlaɪkɪntə ～] [口] **对……产生好感** → take a SHINE to *someone*

limb

go out on a limb (for *someone*) [ˌgou-ˈaudɔnə ˈlɪ(:)m] [口] **(自愿)赴汤蹈火**

limb 是“树枝”。本条最初的构思是：离开树干，而 out on a limb（走到树枝上）。go 是表示“自愿”的意味。树干是安全的地方，树枝容易折断或者容易被人锯断，因而是危险的场所。*You know I'm going out on a limb (for you) by giving you this much information. If my boss should find out about it, I could be fired.* 你要知道，我是冒着很大危险（为你赴汤蹈火）向你透露这么多消息的。如果我的老板发现，他会把我解雇的啊。*I don't think you should guarantee a loan that large. That's going too far out on a limb, even for a friend.* 我认为你不应该为那么大一笔贷款担保。即使是为朋友两肋插刀，象这样的风险也未免过大了。如以上的例句所示，out on a limb 与 go 结合在一起使用的场合是最多的。但可以用 put *oneself* 代替 go，意思相同。*It was clear that Davis believed me to be innocent, but still he wasn't willing to put himself out on a limb (for me) by saying so publicly.* 很明显，戴维斯相信我是无罪的，但是，他并不愿意冒着危险（为我赴汤蹈火），把事情向大家说清楚。out on a limb 还可以与 put *someone*, be, find *oneself*, leave *someone* 等结合起来使用。在这一场合，由于这些动词(+宾语)在性质上与 go 或 put *oneself* 不同，当然就失去了“自愿”的意味。另外，out on a limb 除了“处于危险的境地”的意义外，还有“处于尴尬的境地”的意思。先讲 put *someone* out on a limb (使某人陷入危险的[尴尬的]境地)。*Jimmy's statement to the boss that I had talked privately with one of the union leaders put me out on a limb.* 吉米把我与一位工会领导私自谈话的事情汇报给老板了，使我陷入了危险的[尴尬的]境地。其次讲 be out on a limb (处于危险的[尴尬的]境地)。*Me and my big mouth! Now I was out on a limb and all my enemies were just itching for a chance to cut it off!* 怨我自己说走了嘴啊！现在我陷入危险的[尴尬的]境地了，我的所有的敌人正抓耳挠腮地等待着把我弄倒的机会呢。再其次是 find *oneself* out on a limb (感到自己处于危险的[尴尬的]境地)。*When George and Pat refused to confirm my story, I found myself out on a limb.* 由于乔治和帕特不肯证明我所讲的话是真实的，我感到自己处于危险的[尴尬的]境地了。最后看一看 leave *someone* out on a limb (把某人抛在危险的[尴尬的]境地)的用法。*America's sudden recognition of the Chinese government left Japan out on a limb.* 美国突然承认中国政府，把日本抛在尴尬的境地了。◇ put *oneself* in a risky position

leave *someone* **out on a limb** [ˌliːv ~ ˌaudɔnə ˈlɪ(ː)m] [口] **把某人抛在危险的[尴尬的]境地** → go out on a LIMB (for *someone*)

put *oneself* **out on a limb** (for *someone*) [ˌput ~ ˌaudɔnə ˈlɪ(ː)m] [口] **自愿冒着危险** → go out on a LIMB (for *someone*)

put *someone* **out on a limb** [ˌput ~ ˌaudɔnə ˈlɪ(ː)m] [口] **使某人陷入危险的[尴尬的]境地** → go out on a LIMB (for *someone*)

limit

the sky's the limit → SKY'S

line

a chow line [ə ˈtʃau ˌlaɪn] [话] **在食堂等候开饭的队伍** 一种通俗的说法。直译为"饭的队"(→ CHOW)。主要指在 a chow HALL(公共食堂) 排队吃饭的人，但是，在自助餐馆(cafeteria) 或是团体野餐等凡是要排队等待吃饭的场所，也称为 chow line。*Because of the long chow line in the school cafeteria, we decided to eat at a nearby restaurant.* 由于在学校食堂排的队太长，我们决定到附近的一家饭馆吃饭去了。◇ a food service line

draw the line (at *something*) [ˌdrɔːðə ˈlaɪn] [口] **划界线** line 指"不能超越的限度"。因此，本条的构思与汉语完全一致。它可以表示"绝对不干某种事情"的坚强意志，例如：*I believe your cause is just, but I draw the line at terrorism.* 我相信你的奋斗目标是正确的，但是我绝对不搞恐怖活动。*You should refuse to work on Sundays. I know that pleasing your boss is important to your career, but you have to draw the line somewhere.* 你应该拒绝在星期日上班。我知道，对于你的前程来说，讨好老板是一件重要的事情，但是，要有个限度。*I am willing to do business with Mr. Blackheart, but I prefer to draw the line at inviting him into my home.* 在工作中我愿意跟布莱克哈特先生打交道，但是我绝对不请他到我家来做客。有时候相当于"知道限度"或"掌握分寸"。例如：*A bit of familiarity from your subordinates once in a while is fine, but you've got to know where to draw the line.* 对待部下有时可以随便一点儿，但是必须掌握住分寸。*She may be a good artist, but she doesn't know where to draw the line.* 她也许是一位优秀的画家，但是她不懂得掌握分寸。常常使用 that 承接上边所讲的"不能容忍的事情"，而说 That's where I draw the line。意思是"那是我不能允许的"或者"我绝对不干那样的事情"。这句话的语气十分强烈。*I don't mind his using my clothes, but when he starts borrowing my car without permission, that's where I draw the line.* 他穿我的衣服，我倒不在乎；可是他开始不经我同意就使用我的汽车，那是我绝对不能允许的。*I know it's important for me to pass my exams, but cheating? That's where I draw the line.* 我知道，对于我来说，考试及格是很重要的事情，但是，作弊吗？我绝对不干那样的事情。◇ (absolutely) object (to *something*) / set limits (*someplace*) / refuse (to *do something*)

drop *someone* **a line** [ˌdrɑp ~ əˈlaɪn] [话] **写信** 这里的 a line 是"一行"，因此特别指短信，但并不限定如此。一般指没有急切的事情，在闲暇的时候书写的信件。drop 是"投入(邮箱)"的意思，因此，本条不能用于写了信又改变主意而并不寄出的场合。*Having nothing to do, I decided to drop Mary a line.* 我闲着没事，决定给玛丽写封信寄去。*I'll drop you a line when I get to San Francisco.* 我一到旧金山就给你写信。*Drop me a line sometime.* 有功夫给我来封信。◇ write to *someone*

fall for *someone's* **line** [ˌfɔ(ː)lfər ~ ˈlaɪn] [话] **上当受骗** → swallow *someone's* LINE

feed *someone* **a line** (about *something*) [ˌfiːd ~əˈlaɪn] [话] **甜言蜜语** → hand *someone* a LINE (about *something*)

give *someone* **a line** (about *something*) [ˌgɪv ~əˈlaɪn] [话] **说讨好的话** → hand *someone* a LINE (about *something*)

hand *someone* **a line (about** *something*) [ˌhæ(ː)nd ~əˈlaɪn] [话] **说好听的话** 这里的 line 本来有两种意思,一是"钓鱼竿上的线",一是"台词"。如果是前者,本条的意思是"垂下钓丝";如果是后者,便是"讲漂亮的台词"。两者有共同之处,即都是"有所企图"的行为。*The real estate agent handed me a line about how cheap the property was.* 房地产经纪人对我一派花言巧语,说那片产业价钱如何便宜。*Be careful of Paul. He always hands the girls a line.* 要对保罗多加小心。他对姑娘们一向是花言巧语。a line 的冠词 a 可以用 *one'* usual 或 some 等代替。*A: Did you see Mr. Fisher? B: Yeah. He handed me his usual line.* 甲:你见到费布尔先生了吗? 乙:见到啦。他照例是那套冠冕堂皇的话。从这一意义发展,又用于表示"推托"。*When I asked him why he wouldn't help us, he handed me some line about being busy.* 当我问他为什么不能帮助我们的时候,他推托说他很忙。*A: What did he say when you asked to borrow some money? B: He handed me a line about losing a pile at the race track.* 甲:你向他借钱的时候,他说什么来着? 乙:他推辞说,在赛马场输掉一大笔钱。动词 hand 可以用 feed 或者 give 代换。*The beggar fed me a line about how he had a sick wife and five children.* 乞丐对我说,他的老婆有病,又有五个孩子,求我发发慈悲。*Don't give me that line. I wasn't born yesterday, you know.* 不要对我推三挡四吧。你要知道,我不是刚吃奶的孩子。◇ give *someone* a deceptively smooth [an unlikely] story

hook, line and sinker → HOOK

lay it on the line (for [to] *someone*) [ˌleɪədɔ(ː)nðə ˈlaɪn] [话] **坦率地说** 最初的构思是"把事情的真象都摆到眼前的线上",即汉语的"摆到桌面上"。意思为"把对方还没有弄清楚的事情合盘托出"。*I'll lay it on the line for you. We don't have enough money to go on the trip we planned.* 我要对你讲清楚。我们没有足够的钱按照预定计划去旅游啦。*Since you won't take a hint, I'll lay it on the line (for you). I want to break our engagement.* 由于你不明白我的暗示,我只好向你直言不讳了。我想解除我们之间的婚约。也常使用于在过去压抑着一腔怒火、而现在已经忍不住了的场合。在这一场合,后边接续 to *someone*。例如:*The principal really laid it on the line to the students. He said that, from now on, anyone who cut classes would be severely punished.* 校长对学生们斩钉截铁地下了命令。他说:从现在起,谁要是逃课,一定受到严厉的惩处。偶尔讲 put it on the line (to *someone*)。*I'm going to put it on the line (to you). I'm tired of your goofing off. Either get to work or get out.* 我要对你说清楚。我对你的闲荡已经腻味透啦。要不你好好工作,要不你离开这里。另外有一个意义完全不同的表达法是 lay *something* on the LINE,这一表达法有时根据上下文而采取 lay it on the line 的形式。请读者注意不要把二者弄混。◇ put it plainly and bluntly

lay *something* **on the line** [ˌleɪ ~ ɔ(ː)nðəˈlaɪn] [口] **冒风险** 最初的构思是:赌博台上划有一条线,示明下赌注的地方。与下赌注的情况一样,把 *something* 放到 line (指风险) 上,也就是以 *something* 打赌决胜负的意思。*I'm laying my reputation on the line to help you. Don't let me down.* 我冒着名誉受损害的风险助你一臂之力。不要辜负我的一片好心啊。动词大多使用 lay,但也有时讲 put *something* on the line 或者 place *something* on the line,意义和用法与用 lay 的场合相同。*The family has put [laid, placed] a hundred thousand dollars* *on the line in hopes of having the boy returned by the kidnappers.* 男孩子被绑架了。他家指望把他赎回来，出了十万美元。在这句话里，"出了十万美元"也和下赌注一样，是冒着风险的。*The boss has placed [laid, put] his entire fortune on the line in this venture. It's up to us to see that it succeeds.* 老板把他的全部财产都投入这个企业了。成败如何全靠咱们大家的努力了。另有 be on the line 的说法，意思是"由……决定"。*The Prime Minister's political future will be on the line at tomorrow's lower-house session.* 首相的政治生命将由明天的下院会议来决定。还有一个表达法是 have *something* on the line，意思为"下赌注"。*I've got one million dollars on the line in this venture.* 我对这一事业投入了一百万美元的资金。此外，lay [put] *something* on the line 只用于金钱，例句极少。这一表达法没有"下赌注，冒风险"的意思，仅仅是"拿出钱来"。例如：*Whenever I needed cash, he laid [put] it on the line for me.* 在我需要现金的时候，他总是拿出钱来给我。→ lay it on the LINE(for [to] *someone*) ◇ gamble [risk] *something*

the punch line [ðə ˈpʌntʃ ˌlaɪn] [口] **画龙点睛的妙语** 这里的 punch 与 knockout punch (把人击昏在地的一拳)中的 punch 相同。line 是"一行"。二者合起来，意思是"令人昏倒的最后一行台词"，亦即"画龙点睛的妙语"。*Fred loves to tell jokes, but he's always forgetting the punch lines.* 弗雷德爱讲笑话，但是他总忘记最后画龙点睛。如这一例句所示，joke 必然要有 punch line。另外，漫画、小故事、广告节目等的重要词句也都是 punch line。例如酒店的 an advertising sign (广告牌子)上写着 Rigor Mortis Saloon—Feel free to come in and get stiff. (尸僵高级酒店——飘然座上客，请君一醉休。) Feel free 以下可以叫做 punch line。由于 get stiff 有"僵直"和"喝醉"两方面的意义，因此与酒店名称的 rigor mortis (尸僵)联系起来，就语意双关，妙不可言了。◇ the point (of a joke, etc.)

a stag line [ə ˈstæ(ː)g ˌlaɪn] [口] **不带舞伴的男子们** 本条的来源是：在社交舞会中，常有一些 stag (不带舞伴的男子)排列在舞池周围评头论足，看哪个正在跳舞的女子可以与自己同舞。*A stag line had formed near the door.* 在门的附近，不带舞伴的男子已经站成一排。实际上不在一起排队也可以，本条算是单身参加舞会的男子的总称。当 stag 的人数众多的时候，可以讲 a lot of stags。但是，人们常用的说法是"stag 的队列很长"，如 *There's a long stag line at the party tonight.* 在今晚的舞会中，不带女伴的男子们排了很长的一列。◇ (a line [group] of) men [boys] without dates

step out of line [ˌstep.audəv ˈlaɪn] [口] **任意而为** line 是"队列"，因此，step out of line 就是"脱离队列"。先按照字面意义举两个例子。line 有加 the 的场合和不加 the 的场合，请注意两者的不同。*I stepped out of the line to get a drink of water and when I came back my place was gone.* 我走出队列去喝一杯水，当我回来的时候，我站的地方已经没有了。*The drummer stepped out of line to pick up his drumstick.* 鼓手离开队列去拾他的鼓槌。在前一句里，line 意味着"按次序排队等候着干什么的一长列人"，指具体的事物，因此经常加 the。与此相反，在后一句里，line 不是意味着具体的"一长列人"，而是表示"笔直的一条线"这一抽象的概念，所以不加 the。当 step out of line 作为比喻使用的时候，line 的前边自然是不能加 the 的。在这一场合，line 是抽象名词，意味着"规章"、"命令"、"统一控制"等等。*That guy may be a spy for another gang. If he steps out of line, take care of him.* 那个家伙可能是给另一个帮派当探子的，如果他有轨外行动，就把他干掉。*The sergeant was demoted to corporal for stepping out of line.* 中士由于违犯纪律，被降成下士了。从以上的例句可以看到，step out of line 一般用于表示"任意的行动"。但是，有时可以表示"任意的发言"，或者兼指"行动"和"发言"两方面。*As long as you work for this company, you must speak and act as expected of you. If you* *step out of line you will be reprimanded.* 只要你在这个公司里工作，一切言行都必须合乎要求。如果随意胡来，就会受到严厉的惩处。使用 step out of line 的时候最多，偶尔有用 get 代替 step 的情况。但是，step out of line 一般是"有意识的言语行动"，而 get out of line 则可以是"有意识的"，也可以是"无意识的"。换句话说，后者可以用于"因为漫不经心而有出轨的言行"的场合。与前者相比，后者使用于"随意乱说"的频率高。*Tom has been getting out of line recently. Better talk to him and make sure he understands what is expected of him.* 最近，汤姆乱说乱动起来啦。你最好跟他谈谈，一定要让他了解自己的职责。另外有使用 be 动词的形式，即 be out of line。这个表达法同样用于"行动"和"言语"两方面，是"过火"、"冒昧"的意思。*You're out of line, Smith. Don't offer advice unless you're asked for it.* 史密斯，你做得太过分啦。我不请教你，你不要提出什么忠告。◇ ignore regulations [the rules, accepted procedures]

swallow *someone's* **line** [ˌswɑ(ː)lə ～ ˈlaɪn] [话] **轻易相信花言巧语** 这里的 line 与 hand *someone* a LINE (about *something*) 中的 line 相同，原来的意思是"钓丝"或"台词"。在这里解释为"钓丝"是顺理成章的，因为在头脑里会浮现出"把鱼饵和钓丝一下子吞进去"的具体形象。swallow 原意"连嚼都不嚼，一下子吞咽"，在这里指"对别人的话完全信以为真"。*Don't tell me you swallowed that guy's line.* 你不至于轻易相信那个家伙的花言巧语吧。*someone's* line 亦可作 that (old) line 或者 a line like that 的形式。*You certainly don't expect me to swallow that line, do you?* 你一定不希望我轻信那种花言巧语吧？*How could you have swallowed a line like that?* 你怎么能够轻信那样的瞎话呢？fall for *someone's* line 是"上当受骗"的意思。fall for 是"听了对方的花言巧语而为之倾倒"的韵味。例如：*Somehow the girls always fall for his line.* 不知什么原因，姑娘们听了他的话全都心醉神迷。在使用本条时，可以先从作"垂下钓丝"一解的 hand *someone* a LINE (about *something*) 开始。*He handed me a line about being from some bank, and I was stupid enough to swallow it.* 他花言巧语说自己是某家银行派来的人，我糊涂极了，竟完全相信了他的话。在加强语气时，常增添 HOOK, line and sinker。当然，这是从钓鱼的情景而来，"连钩子、钓丝和坠子全都吞下去"为"完完全全地"的意思。*A: Did you hand him the usual line? B: Yeah, and he swallowed it hook, line and sinker.* 甲：你对他讲了那套惯常的瞎话了吗？乙：讲啦，他完完全全信以为真了。◇ believe *someone's*(unlikely) story

toe the line [ˌtouðə ˈlaɪn] [口] **认真执行** 直译为"赛跑运动员把足尖抵在起跑线上"。*The runners toed the line, waiting for the starting signal.* 赛跑运动员把足尖抵在起跑线上，等待起跑的信号。在这一场合，只要足尖稍微跨出线外，就是犯规。也就是说，虽然事情非常细微，却成为很严重的问题。因此，本条作为比喻使用时，语气也十分强烈，不仅指"遵守规章制度"，而且表示"认真执行上级的命令或指示，不得有误"。*The boss is fair, but he makes us all toe the line.* 老板为人彬彬有礼，但是他严格要求我们完成自己的任务，不得有误。*If you want to get ahead in this company, you have to toe the line.* 如果你想在这个公司有很好的前途，就必须做好一切应该去做的事情。*Our homeroom teacher is very strict. If we don't toe the line, he keeps us after school.* 我们的班主任非常严格。如果我们不认真完成一切应该做的事情，他在放学以后就不许我们走。另外，有时用 mark 代替 line，而讲 toe the mark。在以上的所有例句中都可以互换。不过，一般是用 line。◇ do exactly as is expected of *one*

linen

air *one's* **linen in public** [ˌe(ː)r ～ ˌlɪnənɪn ˈpʌblɪk] [口] **家丑外扬** → wash *one's* dirty LINEN in public

wash *one's* **dirty linen in public** [ˌwɑʃ ~ dərdi ˌlɪnənɪn ˈpʌblɪk] [口] **家丑外扬** 字面意义为"在群众面前洗肮脏的内衣裤"。linen 除作"内衣裤"解外，泛指家庭日用的亚麻 (linen)织品，如枕套、餐巾、手巾等。把这些东西的肮脏样子暴露在他人的眼前，也是不体面的事情。*It's embarrassing to listen to Mrs. Lawndress talk. She seems to enjoy washing her dirty linen in public.* 听朗德列斯夫人的谈话实在叫人难为情。她似乎把外扬家丑当作一种乐趣。这一表达法不仅用于家庭的丑事，而且广泛用于同伙的、公司的、以及其他各种团体的"内部丑闻"。*When the Secretary of State described his policy misgivings at a press conference, he was later reprimanded by the President for washing the Administration's dirty linen in public.* 在记者招待会上，国务卿讲述了他对于一些政策的忧虑，事后，他以暴露政府的"家丑"而受到总统的严厉批评。动词也可以用 air (使通风)来代替 wash。但是，在这一场合一般不加 dirty，只讲 air *one's* linen in public。◇ talk in public about private problems [problems within *one's* own circle]

lines

blow *one's* **lines** [ˌblou~ ˈlaɪnz] [话] **说错台词** → BLOW *something*

lining

Every cloud has a silver lining. → CLOUD

lion's

the lion's share → SHARE

lip

button *one's* **lip** [ˈbʌtn ~ˈlɪ(ː)p] [话] **闭上嘴** 直译为"把嘴唇的纽扣扣上"。多用命令式。特别是在"真烦死人，别多说啦"的场合以及"这种见不得人的事儿，不要对别人说"的场合，更常常使用命令的口吻。*Button your lip or I'll button it for you.* 闭上你的嘴！不然的话，我要使你把嘴闭上啦！*The man kept interrupting until the policeman lost his temper and told him to button his lip.* 那个男子说话没完没了，警察终于忍不住发火，叫他闭上嘴。*Button your lip. Do you want to reveal all our secrets?* 闭上你的嘴！你打算把咱们的全部秘密都泄露出去吗？经常使用 keep *one's* lip buttoned (缄口不言)的形式。*Keep your lip buttoned about this. We'll catch it if the chief finds out about it.* 关于这件事情，你要保持缄默。如果叫头头知道了，咱们就要吃家伙啦。◇ keep quiet

keep a stiff upper lip [ˌki(ː)pə ˌstɪfʌpər ˈlɪ(ː)p] [口] **意志坚定，不怕困难** 美国有很多人认为本条是英国英语最有代表性的习用语之一，实际上它是19世纪上半叶在美国产生出来的。直译为"保持紧绷绷的上嘴唇"。最初的构思是：在遭到苦难而想要哭泣的时候，下唇虽然颤抖，只要顽强地勒紧上唇，脸上的表情就不会从刚毅转为怯懦，一垮到底。本条也有用于内心感情的时候，但是一般来说，不管心里如何，只用于表示"在对手或世人面前保持坚定不移的态度"的意味。*Throughout her many years of difficulty, Mrs. Pennypacker has kept a stiff upper lip.* 彭尼帕克夫人是以坚强不屈的态度度过多年的苦难岁月的。*Surrounded though he was by a howling crowd of demonstrators, the ambassador kept a stiff upper lip.* 虽然被一群狂呼乱喊的示威者包围，大使表现出坚强不屈的态度。*You mustn't let their criticism bother you. You've got to keep a stiff upper lip.* 用不着为他们的批评而烦恼。你必须坚强起来。◇ remain (outwardly) strong in the face of adversity

pay lip service to *something* [*someone*] → SERVICE

liquor

(can) hold *one's* **liquor** [(kən) ˌhould ~ ˈlɪkər] [话] **保持不醉** "无论喝多少酒，既不胡闹，也不睡觉，更没有心里难受的感觉"。这就是 hold *one's* liquor 的含义。*Don't worry about Tom's getting drunk. He can hold his liquor.* 你不用害怕汤姆喝醉。他能够保持自己不醉。*If you want to succeed in business in this* *country, you'll have to learn to hold your liquor.* 在这个国家里，如果你想做生意发财，就必须学会喝多少酒都不醉。*It's no fun to go drinking with Bic Sieve. He can't hold his liquor.* 跟比克·西夫一道去喝酒没有意思，他喝上几杯就醉了。◇ drink without getting drunk

lit

lit [ˈlɪ(ː)t] [话] **文学(课程)** literature 的缩略。高中生和大学生用语。*He teaches lit.* 他讲授文学课。如这一例句所示，本条可以单独使用，不过这种情况较少。一般用法是：可以作为形容词，如：*I'm taking two lit courses this term.* 这一学期我选修两门文学课程。也可以把表示文学种类的形容词放在前边，如：*Phil is majoring in American lit.* 菲尔专攻美国文学。*I hate classical lit.* 我非常讨厌古典文学。◇ literature

be lit up [ˌlɪdʌ(ː)p] [话] **喝醉** → be lit up like a Christmas TREE

litterbag

a litterbag [ə ˈlɪdərˌbæ(ː)g] [口] **废物袋** 在美国，买汽油时常常免费赠送。多为塑料制品。一般挂在开车窗的拉手上，口朝上。有一些州规定，如果从车窗往外扔垃圾，要处以 25～150 美元的罚金，因此，这种 litterbag 最近大为流行。*Car litterbags are especially convenient for long trips.* 在长途旅行时，汽车上的废物袋是特别方便的。但是，本条不仅指汽车用的废物袋，也指在野餐、远足的时候为了处理饮食残物而携带的小口袋。*We always take a litterbags on picnics.* 我们去野餐的时候，总是带着废物袋。请读者注意：不要把 a litterbag 与 a LITTERBUG[ˈlɪdərˌbʌ(ː)g] 的发音弄混了。*Litterbugs should use litterbags.* 乱扔废物的人必须使用废物袋。◇ a (handy sized) trash bag

litterbug

a litterbug [ə ˈlɪdərˌbʌ(ː)g] [口] **乱扔废物的人** 动词 litter 是"乱扔废弃物"的意思。用法如下：*The tourists littered the beach with empty cans and bottles.* 旅游的人们把空罐头盒和空瓶子乱扔到海滩上。*The yard was littered with the children's toys.* 院子里乱扔着儿童们的玩具。litterbug 的 bug 与 a FIREBUG, a SHUTTERBUG 等的 bug 相同，是"有某种癖好的人"的意思。*In Singapore litterbugs are made to pay heavy fines.* 在新加坡，乱扔废物的人要被处以大量的罚款。*Don't be a litterbug.* 不要乱扔废物。litterbug 一般指在公共场所乱扔废物的人，但有时也指在院子或房屋内乱扔废物或乱放自己物品的人。*Jimmy is a real litterbug. He leaves his things all over the house.* 吉米真是一个喜欢乱扔东西的人。在整个屋子里，到处都有他的东西。◇ a person who scatters trash (in public places)

little

a little brother → BROTHER

a little sister [ə ˌlɪdl ˈsɪstər] [口] **妹妹** → a big SISTER

the little woman → WOMAN

live

live it up [ˌlɪvədˈʌ(ː)p] [话] **狂欢** → BOOZE it up

live music → MUSIC

lizzie

a tin lizzie [ə ˌtɪnˈlɪzi] [话] **旧的廉价小汽车** → a FLIVVER

load

get a load of *something* [ˌgedə ˌloudəv ˈ～] [话] **看或听不寻常的事物** get a load of 原来是"得一堆(货物)"的意思。*Take the bucket and go get a load of coal.* 拿着提桶去取一下煤来。转义"把一堆东西装入眼睛或耳朵"，也就是"看"或"听"的意思。但是用法有限制，一般是在促使对方注意特别令人惊奇或感动的事物的时候使用，而且采取祈使句或疑问句的形式。主要是男性用语。*Did you get a load of that guy's coat? It was purple with orange stripes.* 你瞧见那个家伙的外套了吗？紫底带橙色的条纹。"看"或"听"的对象有时是人。*Hey! Get a load of that pretty girl over there.* 喂，你看看那个姑娘多漂亮啊。这句话里包含的意思是:“那可是举世无双的美人儿呀!”“那可是天下少有的美人儿呀!” *Hey, get a load of George. He says he wants me to lend him a thousand dollars.* 喂,你听听乔治的话! 他说,他想向我借一千美元。在这句话里包含着“简直太出人意料”的意味。当人们在报纸上看到意外的消息而向他人讲述时,开头常常使用本条。例如: *Hey, get a load of this. It says here that the price of beef is going to be reduced by fifty percent.* 喂,请听大好消息! 报纸上说,牛肉价格降低50%啦。◇ look at [listen to] *something*

take a load off *one's* **feet** [ˌteɪkə ˈloudə(ː)f ~ˌfi(ː)t] [话] **坐下** 直译为“从脚上卸下重荷(指身体上部)”,也就是为了使腿休息而“坐下”的意味。常与 sit down 一起使用,例如: *Sit down. Take a load off your feet.* 你坐下,歇歇脚。从这一例句可以看出,本条的最初构思与汉语的“歇歇脚”如出一辙,同是表示“休息一会儿”的意思。大多使用命令式。在这一场合,是朋友、伙伴之间的一种极其轻松的说法。但在叙述句中使用时,就没有什么轻快的味道了,例如: *When you work standing up all day, it really feels good to come home and take a load off your feet.* 当你站着劳动了一整天的时候,回到家里坐下休息一会儿,实在是舒服极了。◇ sit down

loaded

loaded [ˈloudɪd] [话] ①**钱很多的**; ②**喝醉了的** loaded 原来的意思是“装满或超过负荷”。 *The ship is loaded.* 船已经满载了。转用于表示“金满仓,银满仓”,亦即“有很多钱”的意思。 *Look at that mansion. The people who live there must be loaded.* 你看那个大公馆。住在里边的人一定很有钱啊。 *You have to be loaded to be able to afford a yacht like that.* 如果没有很多钱,置备不了那样一艘游艇啊。也可以用于“一时有钱”的场合,例如说: *I'm loaded tonight. I just got a big bonus.* 我今天晚上是财主。我刚刚领了一大笔奖金。其次,loaded 也可以形容“体内装满酒精”亦即“喝醉了”的状态。 *I feel like going out and getting loaded tonight.* 今天晚上我想出去,来个一醉方休。 *By the time we left our third bar, we were all loaded.* 当我们走出第三家酒吧间的时候,大家全都喝醉啦。 *We weren't exactly loaded in those days, so we usually got loaded on cheap wine.* 在那个时期,我们没有多少钱,因此我们总是用廉价的葡萄酒灌醉自己。◇ ① (have) a lot of money ② (be very) drunk

a loaded question → QUESTION

play with loaded dice → DICE

loaf

Half a loaf is better than none. [ˈhæ(ː)fə ˌloufəz ˌbedərðən ˈnʌ(ː)n] [谚] **有一点总比没有好** 本条的原形大概是约翰·海伍德(John Heywood) 所编 *Proverbs* (《格言集》,1546年)中收录的谚语 Better is half a loaf than no bread. (半个面包胜于没面包。) 另外,过去美国人也讲 Half a loaf is better than no bread. 但现在只是英国英语还有这一说法。loaf 是一般面包房出售的“面包的一块”,也有按照字面意义使用的场合 (例如野餐会)。 *If you don't have a whole loaf of bread, bring what you've got. After all, half a loaf is better than none.* 如果你没有整块的长方形大面包,有多少带多少来吧。总而言之,半个也比没有强啊。但是,一般是作为比喻使用。在这一场合,不要拘泥于 half 这个数量,也不要考虑“面包”代表一种具体东西,因为大多用于指抽象的时间或条件。 *I had hoped to get three week's vacation this year. I only got one week, but I guess half a loaf is better than none.* 我本来指望今年有三个星期的休假,结果却只有一个星期。不过,俗话说,有一点总比没有好呀。 *We didn't exactly get all the conditions we wanted in the contract, but at least we did get the contract, and half a loaf is better than none.* 我们没有能够把我们所提出的条件全都写在合同里,但是至少我们订立了合同,这就是俗话所说有一点总比没有好啊。◇ Getting even a part of what you want is better than getting nothing at all.

lock

lock, stock and barrel ['lɑ(:)k 'stɑ(:)kən 'bæ(:)rəl] [口] **所有的一切** lock, stock, barrel 全是枪上的东西,分别指"枪机"、"枪托"和"枪管"。本条的原意是"枪上的一切东西",在美国独立战争时期开始使用。当时,枪是非常宝贵的东西,所以说"枪上的一切"就等于"一切的一切"了。 *When my father retired, he sold his store lock, stock and barrel.* 我的父亲退休的时候,把他的铺子整个卖掉了。*We bought his farm from him lock, stock and barrel—including the chickens and cows.* 我们从他手里买了整个的农场,包括鸡和牛在内。如以上的例句所示,在买卖物品时经常使用本条。但也有象在下一个句子中使用的情况。*America's economic policy makers took over the ideas and philosophy of Keynes lock, stock and barrel.* 美国经济政策的制定者们完全照搬凯因斯的理论和哲学。◇ completely as is

log

(as) easy as falling off a log [ə 'zi(:)ziəz ˌfɔ(:)lənɔfə 'lɔ:g] [话] **极容易** 逐字直译为"象从圆木上掉下去一样简单"。剥了皮的圆木很难爬上去,但是极容易掉下来。本条是由这一情况产生的。为了加强语气,也说 easier than falling off a log (比从圆木上掉下来还容易)。不过,从容易的程度来说,两种说法并没有什么差异,因此可以同样地使用。 *A: Did you succeed? B: Sure. It was as easy as falling off a log.* 甲:你成功了吗? 乙:一点不假。实在太容易啦。*Making an apple pie is easier than falling off a log.* 苹果馅饼太容易做啦。有时用 rolling off (滚落)代替 falling off, 而说 (as) easy as rolling off a log。二者可以自由替换。还有一个说法是 (as) easy as (apple) pie (象做苹果馅饼一样容易),也表示"极容易"的意思。 *A: Can you do it? B: Sure. Easy as (apple) pie.* 甲:你干得了吗? 乙:当然啦。不费吹灰之力。◇ very easy

sleep like a log [ˌsli(:)plaɪkə 'lɔ:g] [口] **酣睡** 直译为"象横在地上的圆木(log)一样,一动不动地熟睡"。另有一个同义语是 sleep like a TOP,具"睡得很香"的意思。*I slept like a log last night.* 昨天夜里,我睡得很熟。本条特别用于因体力劳动筋疲力尽而熟睡的场合。*My husband always sleeps like a log after a day of working in the garden.* 我的丈夫只要在花园里干一整天活,夜里就睡得很熟。◇ sleep very soundly

loggerheads

be at loggerheads (with *someone* over *something*) [ət 'lɔ:gərˌhe(:)dz] [口] **顶牛儿** 本条来源于中世纪。loggerhead 是一种熔解柏油的用具。当时熔解柏油的方法是:把一个好象大水桶那样的金属盆吊到圆木 (log) 的前端 (head),然后点上火堆烤。后来用作武器,在海战中,敌对的两只船相互用 loggerheads 泼柏油。这种作战方法被称为 at loggerheads(泼柏油法)。到了 16 世纪,这一表达法更用于比喻,表示人们的相互争执。在莎士比亚的剧本里也曾常常出现。现在,很少用于人们互相吵架,大多是用于在重要问题的争论中意见对立而互不让步的场合,特点是并不包含憎恨的感情在内。*The President is at loggerheads with the Congress over next year's budget.* 关于下一年度的国家预算,总统与国会意见对立。*Those two are always at loggerheads over something.* 那两个人经常为某件事顶牛儿。*Mike is at loggerheads with his father over which college he should apply to.* 关于应该考哪所大学的问题,迈克与他父亲的意见是对立的。◇ be in a head-on dispute

lollipop

a lollipop [ə 'lɑ(:)liˌpɑp] [口] **棒糖** → a SUCKER②

lone

play a lone hand → HAND

long

be (about) as broad as it is long → BROAD

by a long shot → SHOT

the long green [ðə ˈlɔːŋ ˈgriːn] [话] **现金** → BREAD

long johns → JOHNS

a long shot → SHOT

long-handle

long- handle underwear [ˈlɔ(ː)ŋ ˌhændl ˈʌndərˌwer] [话] **(男性用上下连接的)长内衣** → long / JOHNS

longies

longies [ˈlɔ(ː)ŋiz] [话] **(男性用上下连接的)长内衣** 构成方式: 将 long underwear (长内衣) 中的 long 加指小词 -y, 又改成复数形式 -ies, 即为本条。 *It's cold today. I wish I'd worn my longies.* 今天很冷。穿上我的长内衣就好啦。longies 还有一个意义是"(少年用的)长裤"。现在几乎不使用这一意义。在第二次世界大战结束之前, 12 岁以下的男孩子规定不穿长裤 (long pants), 只穿短裤 (short pants), 因而常用 longies 一词与 short pants 相对照。 *Jimmy was bursting with pride upon receiving his first pairs of longies.* 吉米第一次得到长裤, 简直神气极啦。→ long JOHNS ◇ long underwear / long pants

long-sighted

long-sighted① [ˈlɔ(ː)ŋˌsaɪdəd] [口] **远视的** → FAR-SIGHTED①

long-sighted② [ˈlɔ(ː)ŋˈsaɪdəd] [口] **有先见之明的** → FAR-SIGHTED②

looey

a looey [ə ˈluːi] [话] **少[中]尉** lieutenant [ˌlu(ː)ˈtenənt] (少[中]尉)的 lieu-按发音拼写为 loo, 然后加指小词 -ey 而成。在第一次世界大战中, 此词在陆军内大为流行, 是"少尉"的轻松说法, 不久即普及于空军、海军陆战队以及一般老百姓之间。在现代, 不仅指"少尉"(正式名称 second lieutenant), 而且指"中尉"(first lieutenant)。为了防止混同, 大多不单独使用, 而采取 first looey, second looey 的形式。 *My brother is a second looey in the army.* 我的哥哥是陆军少尉。 *He's recently been promoted to first looey.* 他最近已经晋升中尉啦。looey 与 lieutenant 有一点不同, 即不能作为呼语。另外, 也可以拼写为 looie(改变词尾)。◇ a lieutenant

look

Look before you leap. [ˈluk bəˌforjə ˈliːp] [谚] **三思而后行** 直译为"在跳之前, 先要看看"。 *If you had looked before you leaped, you wouldn't have broken your leg.* 如果你在跳之前看一下, 就不至于摔断了腿啊。可以认为有这样说的情况, 但一般用作比喻。是一种训诫的语言: "不经过仔细考虑, 不可轻举妄动。" *You want to marry Carol? I'll admit she's a beautiful girl, but I know her better than you do. I'd advise you to look before you leap.* 你想跟卡罗尔结婚? 她的确是一个美丽的姑娘, 但是我比你更了解她啊。我劝你三思而后行为好。 *He says he'll pay you twenty percent interest if you'll lend him ten thousand dollars? It sounds like a nice offer, but you'd better look before you leap.* 他是说你借给他一万美元, 他付 20%的利息吗? 这个条件听起来倒不错, 不过, 你可要三思而后行啊。有时不用命令式或者直接训诫的方式。 *Mr. Stumble is always getting into trouble because he never looks before he leaps.* 斯坦布先生由于不三思而后行, 总是惹起麻烦。◇ Think carefully before you act.

look down *one's* **nose at** *someone* [*something*] → NOSE

look down on *someone* [*something*] [ˌluk ˈdaunɔ(ː)n ~] [口] **看不起** 有按照字面意义使用的场合, 如说: *From my window I looked down on the people.* 我从窗户向下看那些人。不过, 在这一场合, 一般采取 look down at *someone* [*something*] 的形式, 作 ~ I looked down at the people. 除了实际的从上往下看而外, 本条又常常用于表示一种心理状态: 把自己作为"上", 而把"对方(人)"或"对象(事物)"当作"下"去看待。 *Children should be taught never to look down on anyone simply because he is poor.* 应该教育孩子

们不要因为某个人穷就看不起他。如这一例句所示，一般来说，大多用于看不起"人"的场合，但并不限定是"人"。*Harriet pretends to look down on football as being too rough a sport, but I've never heard of her turning down a date with a football player.* 哈丽雅特硬说踢足球太野蛮，摆出一付看不起足球的架势，但是我从来没有听说她拒绝过与足球运动员的约会。◇ regard *someone* [*something*] with condescension

not look forward to *doing something* [nɑt ˌluk ˈfɔ(ː)rwərdtə ~] [口] **不感兴趣** → not relish the PROSPECT of (*doing*) *something*

things look up [ˌθɪŋz ˌlukˈʌ(ː)p] [话] **情况好转** things 是"情况"、"局势"。look up 是"抬头望"，在这里为"向好的方面活动"的意思。*He hasn't asked me for a date yet, but at least he has become a lot more friendly, so things are looking up.* 他还没有跟我约会，不过，至少说，他比从前可友好多啦。因此，情况正在好转啊。*The first year for our new company has been difficult, but now things are looking up.* 我们新开办的公司头一年非常困难，可是现在情况一天比一天好啦。如以上的例句所示，大多用进行时，但是也有例外。*The depression isn't over by any means, but things have begun to look up.* 不管怎么说，经济萧条还没有结束。但是，情况已经开始好转啦。◇ the situation gets better

Someone **would just as soon** *do something* **as look at you.** [~ (wu)d ˌdʒʌstəzˌsu(ː)n ˈ~ əzˈlu(ː)kətʃu] [话] **根本不当作一回事** *I would just as soon read a book as go to the movies.* 在我来说，去看电影跟读一本书是相同的。如这一例句所示，would (just) as soon *do something* as *do something* 表示"做某种事情与做另一事情相同"的意思。也就是从兴趣来说没有什么两样，如果勉强区分，则是比较喜欢去做前者。这是一个定型的说法。本条是把这一说法中的第二个 *do something* 处代入了 look at you。just 在这里不是表示强调，而是说话的一种口气，有时省去。look at you 当然是"看你"的意思，在这里指"最简单的行为"。本条直译为"干某种事情跟看人相同"、"与拿眼睛看人一样简单地干某种事情"，这等于说"毫不在乎地干某种事情"或者"根本不当作一回事"。*I don't trust that guy. He would just as soon cheat you as look at you.* 我不信任那个家伙。他把骗人当作家常便饭。*Mr. Godfeather's bodyguard looked to be an ugly customer who would just as soon shoot you as look at you.* 戈德菲泽先生的保镖看起来是一个暴躁的家伙，他会毫不在乎地开枪把你打死。*Prof. Shoeleather is a tough teacher. He'd just as soon flunk you as look at you.* 休立泽教授是一位严厉的老师。他毫不在乎地给学生打不及格的分数。◇ *Someone* would *do something* without hesitation. / *Someone* would not hesitate to *do something*.

look-see

have a look-see (at *something*) [ˌhævə ˈlukˌsiː] [话] **瞧一瞧** 在一般的英华词典中，有的不收 look-see 一词，有的则只收 look-see 而无 have a look-see。本条与经常使用的 have a look (at *something*) (查看)大致相同。但是，在用 look-see 的时候，语调显得很轻松，更加强了"瞧一下"的意味。*Customer: The engine of my car seems to be making a strange noise. Mechanic: Bring it around tomorrow and I'll have a look-see.* 主顾：我的汽车的发动机的声音有点不对头。修理工：明天开来吧，我给瞧一瞧。*I won't be gone long. I just want to have a look-see at the store's new fall collection of dresses.* 我一会儿就回来。商店里有新的秋季服装展览，我想去瞧一瞧。有时使用 for a look-see 的表达法，意思是"为了瞧一瞧"。*I heard you were thinking of selling your house, so I just thought I'd drop by for a look-see.* 我听说你有意出售你的住宅，所以我顺便前来，想要看一看。◇ take a (quick) look

loony

a loony bin → BIN

loose

be at loose ends → ENDS

hang loose [.hæ(:)ŋ 'lú:s] [话] **不着急** 本条本来的意思是"筋疲力尽,浑身松软",但是并不用于表示身体的状态,而专用于表示人的心情或精神状态,指"消除紧张,轻松愉快"。*Hang loose? How can I hang loose when my company is on the verge of going bankrupt?* 不着急?我的公司都快要破产了,我怎么能够不着急啊? *That guy really hangs loose, doesn't he. When the boss told him he was fired because his work was unsatisfactory, he just grinned and said, "Fine. I find this company unsatisfactory, too."* 那个家伙真够得上是个乐天派。当老板告诉他由于他的工作不能令人满意而他被解雇的时候,他只是咧着嘴笑着说:"好极啦。我对这个公司也很不满意哪。"有时用 just 加强语气。 *Your girl threw you over? Don't worry. Just hang loose. She'll be back.* 你的女朋友把你甩了吗?不必烦恼。你把心放宽好啦。她会回来的。 *When you go to take an exam, just hang loose. You can't do a good job if you're all uptight about it.* 当你参加考试的时候,心里千万别紧张。如果你紧张得不得了,决不会考出好成绩来。也有象下面这样轻快的用法: *Hang loose here a minute. I'll be right back.* 你在这里呆一会儿。我马上就回来。这里的"呆一会儿"具有"不要着急"亦即"要轻松愉快"的意思。同样,在告别的时候也用本条表示"那么,告辞了"这样轻松的意味。 *Hang loose. I'll see you next week.* 那么,告辞了。下星期再见。在这一场合,可以认为与 Take it easy. 相同 (→ take it [things] EASY)。本条是一个比较新的而且轻松的表达法,特别是在青年人中间经常使用。◇ relax / be nonchalant

play fast and loose with *something* [*someone*] → FAST

tie up the loose ends → ENDS

lord

(as) drunk as a lord [əz 'drʌŋkəzə 'lɔ(:)rd] [话] **烂醉如泥** 直译为"醉得象贵族似的"。英国乔治三世统治时期(1760~1820),自从失去美洲殖民地之后,在国王和 lord (贵族) 之间普遍流行一种奇妙的想法: Drunkenness is the mark of a gentleman. (酒醉是绅士的标志。) 有许多 lord 一天喝光两三瓶威士忌,从早到晚处于泥醉状态,发挥了"风流"gentleman 的本色。现在时代变了,人们不把 drunkenness 当作高尚的行为了,只剩下一个用 lord 表现"酩酊大醉"状态的习用语还未消失。 *We'd better take the chief home. He's drunk as a lord.* 我们最好是把头头送回家去。他已经喝得烂醉如泥啦。 *Stu arrived at the dinner party as drunk as a lord.* 司徒出席宴会的时候,已经是烂醉如泥了。◇ extremely drunk

lord it over *someone* [.lɔrdə'douvər ~] [口] **摆架子** 直译为"象君主一样支配他人",即对他人妄自尊大的意思。对成年人或孩子们皆可使用。 *Our section chief doesn't have much ability, but he enjoys lording it over everyone under his control.* 我们的科长没有多大本领,但是喜欢向每一个部下逞威风。 *Mary tries to lord it over us just because she's got more money than we have.* 玛丽只是因为比我们多有几个臭钱,就对我们摆架子。 *Jimmy Jones lords it over all the other kids in the neighborhood.* 吉米·琼斯是附近所有儿童的孩子王。◇ adopt a domineering attitude toward *someone*

loser

a born loser [ə 'bo(:)rn 'lu:zər] [话] **废物点心** 指无论主观上还是客观上都被认为干什么也不成的人。好象"天生就是失败者"似的。 *You'd better not go into business with Willie. He's a born loser.* 你最好不要跟威利一起做生意。他是个废物点心。 *I guess I'm just a born loser.* 看起来,我天生就是个废物。◇ a person who never succeeds at anything

a sore loser [ə .so(:)r 'lu:zər] [话] **一输就恼火的人** → a SOREHEAD

a sorehead loser [ə ˌso(:)rˌhe(:)d ˈlu:zər] [话] **一输就翻脸的人** → a SOREHEAD

a three-time loser [ə ˈθri: ˌtaɪm ˈlu:zər] [话] **坐过三次牢的人** → a two-time LOSER

a two-time loser [ə ˈtu(:) ˌtaɪm ˈlu:zər] [话] **坐过两次牢的人** two-time 是"两次", loser 是"(在法律面前的)失败者"。美国有些州的法律规定:一个人如果因重罪坐过两次牢,第三次犯重罪而又被判刑时,要无条件地被判无期徒刑。two-time loser 处于一种十分微妙的地位,它意味着"再也没有回旋的余地了"。 *You'll never take me alive, copper! I'm already a two-time loser.* 巡警,我决不会叫你把我活着抓去。我已经坐过两次牢啦! *If Joe is caught, he's sure to get life. He's a two-time loser.* 如果乔被捕,肯定是无期徒刑。他已经坐过两次牢啦。后来,本条又应用于在结婚、事业等方面两次失败的人,也是"再失败一次就完蛋了"、"再也没有回旋的余地了"的意味。 *I'm a two-time loser. I'm not anxious to get married again.* 我已经失败两次了,再也不急着结婚啦。 *I'd like to start another company, but banks are wary of lending to a two-time loser.* 我想再开办一个公司,但是各银行都很慎重,不肯向两次失败的人贷款。由于重罪而三次坐牢的人,亦即 a three-time loser, 当然是"无期徒刑的犯人"了。 *Why don't you go straight, Snyder? You don't want to end up a three-time loser like your old man.* 斯奈德,为什么你不改邪归正?你不愿意象你老子那样终身坐牢吧。loser 在作"坐过牢的人"解释时,原为警察、法院、流氓无赖等的用语。因此,在一般会话中,只是在谈到结婚或事业两次失败的人的时候,以开玩笑的口吻讲 a two-time loser 而已。也有 a one-time loser, four-time loser, five-time loser 等说法,但在日常会话中是绝对听不见的。◇ a man who (already) has two crimes [mistakes, failures] on his record

loss

be at a loss [ədə ˈlɔ:s] [口] **茫然不知所措** 本条用于"不知道怎么想才好"、"不知道怎么做才好"、"不知道怎么说才好"的场合。 *I'm at a loss. I've looked everywhere and still can't find it.* 简直不知道怎么办才好。我到处都找遍了,还是找不到。请读者注意:这句话不是"我找不到所以很为难"(I'm in trouble.) 的意思。为什么呢?因为本条虽然表示"由于不知道怎么办而困惑"的状态,但重点不在于"困惑",而在于"不知道怎么办"。 *He was at a loss as to what he should do next.* 他完全不知道下一步该怎么做。常用 complete(ly) 或 utter(ly) 加强语气。 *I'm completely at a loss to understand why he did it.* 我完全无法理解他为什么干那种事情。 *The stranger suddenly whispered to me, "Why didn't you call me yesterday?" "There must be some mistake," I protested, utterly at a loss.* 一个陌生人突然小声对我说:"你昨天为什么没给我打电话?"我完全没明白是怎么回事,就回答说:"你弄错了吧。" *Joe appeared to be at a complete loss for an explanation.* 乔似乎完全不知道怎样理解才好啦。be at a loss for words 是一个定型的说法,意思是"不知说什么好"。 *Wise guys like Harvey are never at a loss for words.* 象哈维那样狂妄自大的家伙永远不会无言以对的。leave *someone* at a loss 是"使某人处于茫然不知所措的状态"。 *Her unexpected question left me at a loss for an answer.* 她的突如其来的问题,使我简直茫然不知如何回答才好。 *The strange murder seems to have left the police at a complete loss.* 那件奇异的凶杀案似乎使警察完全不知道怎样解决才好啦。◇ be baffled (as to what to ~ [how to ~, why ~, etc.]) ((complete → completely))

be at a loss for words [ədə ˌlɔ:s fərˈwə:rdz] [口] **不知说什么好** → be at a LOSS

lost

Get lost. [ˈge(:)t ˈlɔ:st] [话] **走开!** 原来是"迷了路"的意思,如说: *They got lost in the mountains.* 他们在山里迷了路。

把这句话改成命令式，就是“你迷路去吧！”意思为“你走开，别在我的眼皮底下！”本条是对同辈或晚辈使用，语气相当强烈。*Get lost. We don't want you trailing after us.* 走开！不要跟着我们。*Get lost! Can't you see I'm trying to study?* 走开！你看不见我要温习功课吗？也可以采取间接表达法，说 tell *someone* to get lost。*Tell that guy to get lost. I don't have time to waste on him today.* 你去告诉那个家伙走开。我今天没有跟他磨牙的时间。*I couldn't believe it. When I asked him for the money I had lent him, he told me to get lost.* 简直令人难以相信啊。当我向他要账的时候，他竟叫我滚开。◇ Go away. / Stop bothering me [*someone*].

be a lost cause → CAUSE

louse

louse *someone* **up** [ˌlaus ～ ˈʌ(:)p] [话] **把某人搞得一团糟** → LOUSE up *something*

louse up *something* [ˌlauˈsʌ(:)p ～] [话] **把某事搞得一团糟** louse 作为名词，是“虱子”的意思。本条直译为“使某事物满是虱子”。原来肯定有这样的意味，但是现在完全没有虱子的形象在内了。本条的意义和用法大致与 ruin *something* 相同。*Harold loused up the whole deal by mistakenly stating our final offer first.* 哈罗德弄错了，他开门见山地提出我们最后的条件，结果把整个交易搞糟啦。*The rain loused up our picnic.* 雨水把我们的野餐搞得一团糟。*He loused up his marriage by getting involved with another woman.* 他由于跟另外一个女人勾搭，把自己的婚姻搞得一团糟。*Don't push that button. You'll louse up the recording.* 不要按那个键。你会把磁带搞坏的。如果代入 *something* 的词极短，一般采取 louse *something* up 的形式。*The deal is almost set. Don't say any more or you may louse it up.* 买卖大致谈妥了。你不要再多说一句话啦，否则也许会砸锅的。有时应用于人，说 louse *someone* up，意思是“把别人的想法或所要干的事情搞得一团糟”。*Don't listen to that guy's advice. He'll only louse you up.* 你不要听那个家伙的建议。他只会把你的事情搞得一团糟。还有一个表达法是 louse *someone* up with *someone*，意思为“把某人与某人的关系搞得一团糟”。*The rumors she spread have loused me up with the boss.* 她散布的流言蜚语把我与老板之间的关系搞得一团糟。再者，louse up 也可以作为不及物动词使用。在这一场合，是“失败”的意思。*Dooley has loused up again. It seems he just can't do anything right.* 杜利又弄错了。他好象没有能够做对的事情。*You have your orders. Don't louse up.* 你要听从命令，不得有误。◇ ruin *something*

louse *someone* **up with** *someone* [ˌlaus ～ ˈʌp wɪð ～] [话] **把某人与某人的关系搞得一团糟** → LOUSE up *something*

lousy

be lousy with *something* [*people*] [ˈlauzi wɪð ～] [话] **有很多的东西或人** lousy 是 louse [ˈlaus] (虱子)的形容词。be lousy 直译为“爬满大量的虱子”，但是实际上已经失去“虱子”的形象，只剩下“大量”的部分了。作为比喻，以 be lousy with *something* [*people*]的句型广泛为人们所使用。从语感来讲，lousy 并不仅形容东西或人“多”，而且近似拟态语，指“爬得满满地”或者“成群地蠕动”。这是一个非常轻松的表达法。从本条的性质(形容“多”)来讲，with 后边的名词当然经常要用复数形式。*This dog is lousy with fleas.* 这条狗浑身都是跳蚤。*Let Fred pay. He's lousy with dough.* 叫弗雷德付款。他有的是钱。*The garden is lousy with weeds.* 花园里长满了杂草。由于失去了“虱子”的形象，所以在应用于人的时候，也不会产生丝毫肮脏的感觉。*Why can't you get a date? This town is lousy with nice girls.* 你怎么没找到约会的对象？这个城镇漂亮姑娘多极啦。*I wonder what's going on. The streets are lousy with cops.* 不知出了什么事情，满街都是警察。类似的表达法有 be SWARMING with *people* [*something*]。be swarming 强调"成群蠕动"的咕咕容容的状态,因而不能用于静止的东西。本条则不管动与不动,只是"很多很多"的意思。尽管可以按照字面意义"爬满虱子"来用,例如说 *This dog is lousy*. 但是,可能由于人们使用 be LOUSY 的其他意义的时候比较多,就产生了竭力避免使用字面意义的倾向,因而在讲 This dog is lousy. 这句话的场合,一般采取 This dog is covered with lice. 的说法。◇ have innumerable [a surfeit of] *something* / be full of [overflowing with] *something* [*people*]

love

All's fair in love and war. [.ɔ(ː)lz 'feːrɪn .lʌ(ː)vən 'wɔːr] [谚] **恋爱与战争不择手段** 实际上不限于"恋爱与战争",作为比喻广泛地使用。特别是在发生竞争的情况时,人们常用这一谚语为自己采取的手段辩护。*What do you mean I shouldn't fire Jones because my fiancée has jilted me for him? All's fair in love and war, isn't it?* 你说我不应该因为琼斯挖走我的未婚妻就把他解雇,这是为什么?谚语说得好:恋爱与战争不择手段,是吧? *Don't you tell me it's unethical to use our competitor's new invention without their permission. All's fair in love and war, you know.* 你不要对我讲不经我们的竞争对手许可而利用他的发明是什么不道德的事情。要知道,恋爱与战争是不择手段的啊。◇ In love and war [In fierce competition] any tactic is permissible.

fall head over heels in love (with *someone*) → HEAD

be no love lost between *them* [.nou 'lʌːv .lɔ(ː)s*t* bət.wi(ː)n ~] [口] **相互之间没有一点感情** 直译为"相互之间没有失落的爱情",亦即"相互之间都不是值得去爱的对象"。有趣的是,过去曾经按照完全相反的意义使用:*No love between them was lost. Each was kind to the other.* 他们相亲相爱,每个人都体贴对方。在以上的两种不同的用法中,lost 都是 wasted (浪费掉的)的意思。也就是假定"爱情"有一定的数量,不能白白地浪费。在过去,人们把本条解释为"热烈相爱",可是不知从什么时候起却向相反的方向转化,由"不向对方白白浪费爱情"而达到"根本不爱对方",所表示的意思来了个一百八十度大转弯。*I wouldn't say that those two hate each other, but there is certainly no love lost between them.* 我不能说那两个人互相仇恨,但是他们之间肯定没有感情。从这一例句可以了解,本条不是用于剑拔弩张的互相仇恨,而是用于冷淡的关系。*Don't expect them to cooperate. They may be brothers, but there is no love lost between them.* 不用指望他们会通力合作。他们俩可能是弟兄,但是相互之间没有什么感情。*Though they were formally polite to each other at offices, there was never any love lost between them.* 他们虽然在办公室里相互客客气气,但是彼此丝毫没有一点交情。可以用 no love is lost ~ 的形式替代 be no love lost ~。另外,在应用于动物时,本条具有诙谐的味道。例如:*No love is lost between our cat and the one next door. The fur flies whenever they meet.* 我家的猫与邻居的猫没有什么感情。它们一见面就掐架。◇ have no love for each other

not *do something* **for love or money** [nɑt ~fər'lʌ(ː)vər .mʌni] [话] **无论怎样也不** 直译为"给多少爱情 (love) 或者金钱 (money) 都不情愿[都不干]"。这是一个表示非常强烈的否定意味的习用语。所以把 love 一词放在前边,是为了加强语气,因为人们认为"爱情"是最宝贵的东西。*I wouldn't spend the night in that old house for love or money.* 不管怎样我也不愿意在那所老房子里过夜。这是直接表示自己的心情。*You talk to her. I can't get her to change her mind for love or money.* 你跟她谈一谈。不管怎样我也改变不了她的想法。也有象这样讲"他人的想法"的场合。*Phyllis says you'll never get her to live in New York for love or money.* 菲利斯说,不管你怎样费尽苦心,她也决不移居纽约。*I* *don't know what's wrong with that boy. He just won't study for love or money.* 我不知道那个男孩子出了什么毛病，他无论如何也不肯学习。对象不限于"人"，一般来说，也用于"非常困难的事情。" *During the war, unless you had connections you couldn't get a hotel room in Washington for love or money.* 战争时期，除非走后门，在华盛顿无论怎样也弄不到一个旅馆的房间。◇ not *do something* for any reason whatsoever / not *do something* no matter what *someone* says [does]

The City of Brotherly Love [ðə ˈsɪdiəv ˈbrʌðərli ˈlʌ(:)v] [口] **费城** → PHILLY

low

look high and low → HIGH

luck

crowd ***one's*** **luck** [ˌkraud ~ ˈlʌ(:)k] [话] **贪心不足，想再交好运** → push *one's* LUCK

be down on ***one's*** **luck** [ˌdaunən ~ ˈlʌ(:)k] [口] **不走运** 直译为"运气(luck)一蹶不振"。在玩扑克牌的时候，常这样说：*I seem to be down on my luck tonight. I haven't had a good hand all evening.* 我今天晚上似乎没交好运，一晚上没起过一把好牌。除赌博以外，多用于表示"一生倒霉"或"一时落魄"的意味。 *Try not to be discouraged. The world is full of people like you who are sick, out of a job, or otherwise down on their luck.* 不要灰心丧气嘛。社会上有许许多多的人象你一样，或是疾病缠身，或是没有工作，或是在其他方面没交好运。 *Harry's a generous guy. He's always ready to lend money to friends or former colleagues who are temporarily down on their luck.* 哈里是个很有义气的人。每当朋友或过去的同事一时不走运，他总是马上借钱给他们。*The Salvation Army has a long tradition of serving hot meals to people of the city who are down on their luck.* 救世军有一个悠久的传统，就是向落魄的城市居民提供热的饭食。*I hate to see an old friend so down on his luck.* 我见到老朋友那种落魄的样子，心里很难受。◇ be suffering a period of bad luck [misfortune]

have the devil's own luck [ˌhævðə ˈdevəl.zoun ˈlʌ(:)k] [话] **大走红运** 直译为"有恶魔本身的运气"。本条来自西方人的传统思想，他们认为恶魔本身创造命运，他们干什么都会成功。*Mr. Smith always seems to have the devil's own luck. He bought lottery tickets twice last year and won ten thousand dollars both times.* 史密斯先生似乎永远在大走红运。去年他买了两次彩票，两次都得了一万美元。如这一例句所示，意思只是"世界上没有比这再好的运气了"。*Barny may be a tremendous pilot, but he's going to have to have the devil's own luck to make it through this storm.* 巴尼可能是一位最优秀的飞机驾驶员，但是要通过这么凶猛的暴风雨，他没有最好的运气是不行的啊。*We're completely surrounded by the enemy. We're going to need the devil's own luck to get out of this one.* 我们完全被敌人包围了。要想脱出重围，我们没有最好的运气是不行的。*That guy has the devil's own luck. He applied the wrong formula to the toughest problem on the math exam, but he got the answer right because he made a mistake in his calculations.* 那小子真是大走红运啊。在考试数学的时候，他对最难的一道题用错了公式，可是由于计算失误，他却歪打正着答对了。a stroke of luck (意外的幸运)也是一个习用语。下一个例句是这一习用语与本条的结合。由于 a stroke 是"一击"之意，所以这一结合不能用于幸运持续不断的场合，务请读者注意。 *By a stroke of the devil's* *own luck, the clouds parted for just a moment and we saw the airport directly ahead of us.* 实在太幸运了，云层分开了片刻，我们看到机场就在眼前。另有一个 have the luck of the devil 的形式，意思相同。*In order to be successful in the commodities market, you have to have nerves of steel and the luck of the devil.* 如果想在商品市场上取得成功，一是要有钢铁般的意志，二是要有最好的运气。◇ be very lucky

have the luck of the devil [ˌhævðə ˈlʌkəvðə ˈde(ː)vəl] [话] **大走红运** → have the devil's own LUCK

press *one's* **luck** [ˌpres ~ ˈlʌ(ː)k] [话] **得寸进尺** → push *one's* LUCK

push *one's* **luck** [ˌpuʃ ~ˈlʌ(ː)k] [话] **乘着运气前进** 本条的具体形象是："有了 *one's* luck (幸运)，把它 push (往前推)"。也就是"相信好运气会继续下去，再碰一碰看"的意思。*Fortunately, our climb up the mountain had been faster than we had expected, so we decided to push our luck and see if we couldn't reach the top before nightfall.* 幸运的是，我们登山的速度比预计的快，因此，我们决定乘着运气前进，看看是否能在日落之前到达顶峰。本条常用于反省或警告的场合，例如：*I was tempted to go for broke on the three queens I held, but then I decided I'd better not push my luck.* 我本来打算用我手里的三张 *Q* 孤注一掷，但是后来我心想还是不要乘着运气前进为妙。*So far the boss has turned a blind eye to your being late to work so often, but I wouldn't push my luck too far.* 到现在为止，老板对你上班经常迟到总是睁一个眼闭一个眼，但是可不要得意忘形做得太过分啊。有一点应该注意：即使在这样的场合应用 push *one's* luck，其本身的意思仍然是"乘着运气前进"，并没有"得寸进尺"、"得意忘形"之类的成语所包含的批评的意思。除了 push *one's* luck 而外，还有 crowd *one's* luck，press *one's* luck 等说法，意思相同。但是，push *one's* luck 的使用率很高，而且具有会话的性质。*It's true that we've done very well so far by depending almost exclusively on one product for most of our business, but I have a feeling that we're beginning to crowd our luck.* 不错，到现在为止，咱们的生意几乎仅仅依靠一种产品而取得很好的成绩，但是我总觉得咱们好象在开始盲目地撞大运了。*If you want to be a successful race driver, sometimes you have to press your luck.* 如果想要作为一名赛马选手取得成功，有时必须豁出去撞大运。◇ take a chance [chances, the chance] / depend too much on luck

a stroke of luck [ə ˌstroukəv ˈlʌ(ː)k] [口] **意外的幸运** → have the devil's own LUCK

lucky

thank *one's* **lucky stars** → STARS

lulu

a lulu [ə ˈlu(ː)ˌluː] [话] **出众的人(或事物)**

Lulu 是 Louise 的昵称。它为什么成为具有"冒尖儿"意义的俚语，不详。本条指"突出的人或事物"，不论是好的方面还是坏的方面。例如：*Talk about a beautiful woman, our new secretary is a lulu.* 要讲美人儿嘛。我们那里新来的秘书可算冒尖儿啦。这是对花容月貌的惊叹之辞。下面的例句说法相似，而意思却恰恰相反。*Our new secretary is a lulu. Not only can she not type, she can't even spell.* 我们那里新来的秘书可是个出类拔萃的人物。她不但不会打字，连字母都拼不出来。这就是说，本条的意味要根据上下文来确定。*Jim seldom makes a mistake, but when he does it's a lulu.* 吉姆很少出错，但是，他一出错就是个大错。*That belly flop of yours was a real lulu.* 你那胸腹先着水的动作可真笨拙到家啦。*Nick's drive off the tee was really a lulu. The ball landed right on the green.* 在打高尔夫的时候，尼克的发球实在棒极啦。球正好落到球穴区里。*The math final was a lulu.* 数学的期末考试实在难极啦。如这一例句所示，a lulu 常用于表示"困难的事情"。*Most of Cal's serves are hard to return, but that last one in particular was a lulu.* 卡尔发的球大半很难接，而刚才这个球可算是刁到极点啦。在以上的各例句中，本条都是"达到极点"的意思。但是，也有表示"值得一看"的场合，例如：*Did you see Jack's black eye? It's a lulu.* 你看见杰克被人打得眼青鼻肿了吗？真好玩儿。◇ unbelievably beautiful [bad, big, atrocious, good, difficult, etc.]

lummox

a lummox [ə 'lʌməks] [话] **傻大个** 来源不明。可能是 a dumb ox (笨牛) 与 a lump (傻瓜) 的结合体。意思是"身材不小，头脑迟钝"。应用于男性。在会话中，多含有亲密的意味。*That lummox has lost our tickets.* 那个傻大个把咱们的票全丢了。另外，dumb ox 几乎与本条同义，在任何文句中都可以互换。→ a DUMBHEAD◇ a (big) stupid man [boy]

lump

feel a lump in *one's* **throat** [ˌfi(:)lə 'lʌmpɪn ～ ˌθrout] [口] **心里感到难受** lump 是"块"。直译为"感到喉咙里有个硬块"。似乎可以译作汉语成语"如鲠在喉"，其实意思不一样。美国人在受感动的时候，在产生感激或者强烈的同情心的时候，说"好象有个什么东西堵在嗓子眼儿里"。*I felt a lump in my throat on seeing the pictures of the starving children.* 我看到那些饥饿儿童的照片，心里感到很难受。*No one who heard the little girl's story could help feeling a lump in his throat.* 凡是听到那个少女的故事的人，没有一个不感到一阵辛酸。本条有各种各样的变形。首先是 get a lump in *one's* throat 的形式，意思相同。*I get a lump in my throat whenever I see a tragic movie.* 我一看悲剧的影片，心里就不好受。其次是 have a lump in *one's* throat 的形式。*After hearing her story I had such a lump in my throat that I couldn't speak.* 我听到她的情况之后，心里一阵辛酸，简直连话都说不出来了。第三个形式是 *something* leaves a lump in *someone's* throat, 直译为"把一个硬块留在某人的喉咙里"。*Rachmaninoff's piano concertos always leave a lump in my throat.* 拉赫玛尼诺夫的钢琴协奏曲永远震动我的心灵。第四个形式是 *something* brings a lump to *someone's* throat, 直译为"给某人的喉咙送来一个硬块"。*The recollection brought a lump to my throat.* 我一想起那件事来，心里便堵得慌。此外还有一个说法是 a lump comes to *someone's* throat, 意思也一样。*A lump came to my throat when I saw the little blind girl smile.* 当我见到那个盲少女微笑的时候，我的喉咙哽住了。◇ be greatly moved

If *someone* **doesn't like it,** *he* **can lump it.** [ˌɪf ～ ˌdʌzn'laɪkət～ kən'lʌmpət] [话] **即使不愿意，也只好忍受** 这里的 lump 是"勉强忍受"的意思。这里的 can 不是"能够"，而是 may (可以)的意思。本条直译为"如果不满意，就忍受好啦"。反过来说，就是"没有选择的余地"。有翻脸不认人的感觉。除朋友、伙伴之间使用外，一般来说，这是一个打架吵嘴的用语。*This is all I'm going to give you. If you don't like it, you can lump it.* 我就给你这些。你如果不满意，就忍耐点好啦。在 lump 之前常加 just 增强语气。*He's not going to quit now. We're all in* *this together. If he doesn't like it, he can just lump it.* 现在不能叫他辞职。咱们大家是风雨同舟啊。如果他不愿意,就叫他忍耐点好啦。也可以用 have to 代替 can。 *If they don't like the way I do things, they'll have to lump it. I'm not about to change my methods for them.* 如果他们不喜欢我的做法,就叫他们忍耐点好啦。我不打算为了他们而改变自己的方法。一般来说,can lump it 不能单独使用,必须与 if 以下的部分成龙配套。但在承接前边的话的场合,if 以下的部分可以省略。 *A: I don't like the idea of leaving at two o'clock in the morning. B: Then you'll just have to lump it. We can't change our plans.* 甲:我不喜欢早晨两点出发的主意。乙:那你也只好克服啦。我们不能改变我们的计划。 ◇ If *someone* doesn't like it, that's (just) too bad.

lunch

be out to lunch [ˌautːə ˈlʌ(ː)ntʃ] [话] **心不在焉** 本条本来的意思当然是"出去吃午饭"了。*I'm sorry, but Mr. Smith is out to lunch right now.* 对不起,史密斯先生出去吃午饭了。*Most of the kids in my class are out to lunch. They can't even answer the simplest questions.* 我们班的同学们大部分都魂不守舍。就连最简单的问题,他们也回答不出来。如这一例句所示,特别是年轻人爱用本条,戏谑地表示"心不在焉"的意味。按字面解释就是:这个心不在身体内部,而是"吃午饭去了",也就是"头脑不在家"。常用 really 加强语气。 *That guy's really out to lunch. I asked him if he wanted to go by himself and he said, no, he'd rather go alone.* 那个家伙简直是心不在焉。我问他是不是愿意自己去,他说:"不是。我想一个人去。" *The boss is really out to lunch if he thinks union members are going to work overtime for nothing.* 如果老板以为工会会员加班不要报酬,他的头脑真的不在家了。◇ stupid

lungs

shout at the top of *one's* **lungs** → TOP

lurch

leave *someone* **in the lurch** [ˌli(ː)v ～ ɪnðə ˈlə(ː)rtʃ] [口] **弃之不顾** lurch 是 16 世纪法国流行的一种棋戏。在玩这种棋的时候,如果说 leave *someone* in the lurch, 那就是"连连得胜,使对手陷入不管怎样奋战也没有赢的希望的困难境地"的意思。lurch (法语 *lourche*) 这种棋戏早已不再流行,只有本条作为它的遗迹残存下来,现在广泛用于表示"对于陷入极为困窘的状态的对手弃之不顾,扬长而去"的意思。大多的场合具有"不顾自己应尽的责任"的含义。 *As the enemy approached, many of the soldiers threw down their guns and ran, leaving their comrades in the lurch.* 当敌人逼近的时候,许多士兵把枪扔掉,对战友弃之不顾,逃之夭夭了。 *My secretary left me in the lurch by taking an unauthorized vacation at the busiest time of the year.* 在一年最忙的时候,我的秘书对我弃之不顾,私自休假去了。 *Here comes the boss with fire in his eye. Don't leave me in the lurch.* 老板来了,两眼冒火。你别扔下我不管呀。 *For three hours the bride waited at the church before she finally realized she had been left in the lurch.* 新娘在教堂里等待三小时,她才明白自己是被丢在那儿没人管了。◇ desert *someone* / leave *someone* in a difficult position

luxury

live in luxury [ˌlɪvɪn ˈlʌkʃəri] [口] **过豪华的生活** → live in the LAP of luxury

lying

take *something* **lying down** [ˌteɪk ～ ˌlaɪɪŋ

'daun] [话] **甘心忍受** 指对别人的辱骂、欺侮、慢待等逆来顺受,不做正面斗争。一般用于否定句,有时用于含有否定意味的疑问句或者反语表达法。例如:*I refuse to take her insults lying down.* 我决不甘心受她的侮辱。*That's a terrible way for him to treat you. I wouldn't take it lying down if I were you.* 他对待你的方式太不象话啦。如果我是你的话,决不甘心忍受这种侮辱。*We've succeeded in stealing a few of their customers, but we can't expect them to take it lying down. They'll find some way of retaliating.* 我们是把对方的几个客户拉拢过来了,但是不能指望对方会善罢干休。他们一定会想方设法进行报复的。*He called you a fool. Are you going to take that lying down?* 他管你叫混蛋。你甘心受这种侮辱吗? ◇ accept *something* docilely [without resisting]

lynching

a lynching party [ə 'lɪntʃɪŋ ˌpɑ(:)rdi] [话] **暴乱分子私处的绞刑** → a necktie PARTY

M

machine

a slot machine [ə 'slɑ(:)t mə.ʃi:n] [口] **吃角子老虎** → a one-armed BANDIT

mackerel

Holy mackerel! ['houli 'mæ(:)krəl] [话] **哎呀,天哪!** → Holy cow!

mad

like mad [.laɪk'mæ:d] [话] **猛烈地** 直译为"象疯了似的"。这是一个被非常广泛应用的表达法,形容势头的凶猛。*It's raining like mad.* 正在下瓢泼大雨。*The dogs are barking like mad.* 狗在狂吠。*Inflation is increasing like mad.* 通货膨胀急速加剧。在翻译成中文时,要根据上下文寻求适当的字眼。*I had hoped to go to bed early, but it was already past twelve and I was still working like mad to finish my homework.* 我本来想早上床睡觉,但是已经过十二点了,我仍然在拼命去完成家庭作业。*Cockroaches multiply like mad during the summer.* 蟑螂在夏季繁殖特别快。*We ran like mad to catch the bus.* 我们拼命奔跑去赶公共汽车。*The weeds in our yard are growing like mad.* 我家院子里的杂草在猛长。◇ very hard [wildly, loudly, rapidly, etc.]

(as) mad as a hornet [əz 'mæ(:)dəzə 'hɔ(:)rnət] [话] **大发雷霆** → (as) mad as a wet HEN

(as) mad as a wet hen → HEN

mad money → MONEY

made

have it made [.hævɪt'meɪd] [话] **以后就万事大吉了** 直译为"那个已经做成"。it 虚指情况,不是代替某一特定名词,意思大致为"以后的事情"。"以后的事情已经做成"意味着"以后就万事大吉了"、"以后就没有问题了"。*If this deal goes through, we'll have it made.* 如果这笔生意顺利进行的话,咱们以后就好办啦。如这一例句所示,在使用本条时,总是承接"某一事情顺利进行"的前提,而表示"因此,以后就好办了"的意味。*Once we get past the guard, we'll have it made.* 我们只要过了岗哨,以后就没有问题啦。*With two best sellers under his belt, that author has it made.* 那位作家已经出了两部畅销书,他以后就是锦绣前程啦。◇ be sure of success

magpie

chatter like a magpie [.tʃæ(:)dər laɪkə 'mæ:gpaɪ] [口] **喋喋不休** → CHATTER

main

the main drag → DRAG

make

make away with *something* [*someone*] [.meɪkə 'weɪ wɪð ~] [口] **偷东西或拐走人** → MAKE off with *something* [*someone*]

make do with *something* [*someone*] [.meɪk'du: wɪð ~] [口] **凑合** 这里的 make 与 You must make him go. (你必须叫他走。)中的 make 的用法一样,是"强制叫人干什么"的意思。do 如同在问 Which pen do you want? (你要哪一只钢笔?)而回答说 Either will do. (哪一只都行。)的时候所用的 do 一样,是"将就"、"凑合"的意思。二者合起来,就是"勉强用什么来凑合"。*You really need a larger wrench for this job, but if you don't have one, you'll just have to make do with what you have.* 干这个活儿,的确需要一个大一点儿的扳子。如果没有大一点儿的,那就只好拿现有的扳子凑合啦。*We can't afford a new car this year. We'll have to make do with the old one for a while.* 我们今年买不起新汽车啦。我们必须用旧车凑合一段时间。

Since I didn't have time to go shopping, I made do with leftovers. 因为我没有时间去买东西，就用残羹剩菜凑合了一顿。*We ought to hire another man. It's difficult to make do with only three employees.* 我们应该再雇一个人。只雇用三个人实在应付不了。◇ manage [get along] with *something* [*someone*]

make do without *something* [*someone*] [ˌmeɪk'duː wɪ'ðaut ～] [口] **没有也凑合** make do 是"勉强凑合"的意思(→ MAKE do with *something* [*someone*])。加上 without ～，就意味着"没有……，也勉强凑合"或者"如果没有……，就用现有的……凑合"。*It's possible to make do without money, but not without food.* 没有钱也可以凑合，没有吃的就凑合不了啦。如果 without 的后边接 something，而 something 处又用的是代词，这个代词可以省略。*I forgot to take any bread on the picnic, so we had to make do without (it).* 在野餐的时候，我忘了带面包，大家只好不吃面包而凑合一顿了。*A: What did you do when you discovered you'd forgotten to take a map? B: We made do without (one).* 甲：你们发现忘带地图了的时候，怎么办啦？乙：我们没有(地图)也勉强凑合啦。但是，如果在 without 的后边接 someone，哪怕用的是代词，也不能省略。*Joe is the only one who knows the road, but since he couldn't come on this trip, we'll have to make do without him.* 乔是唯一知道路的人，但是，由于他不能参加这次旅行，我们就只好勉为其难，摸索前进了。◇ manage [get along] without *something* [*someone*]

make it big [ˌmeɪkɪt 'bɪːg] [话] **大获成功** make it 是一个习用语，意思是"成功"。加上 big，则表示"在社会上取得巨大的成功"。*Shirley has made it big in the entertainment world.* 雪莉在娱乐界获得很大的成功。可以用 really 或 so 加强语气。*Though many of today's young would- be authors may achieve some degree of success, only a few will make it really big.* 虽然现在有许多想当作家的青年会获得一定程度的成功，但是只是极少数人能够真正取得伟大的成就。*When Jimmy first went into business, we never dreamed that he would make it so big.* 当吉米开始步入商业界的时候，我们连做梦也没有想到他会取得那么巨大的成功。◇ become truly successful

make off with *something* [*someone*] [ˌmeɪ'kɔːf wɪð ～] [话] **攫取** 直译为"拿走"。可以用于表示"偷窃"，例如：*Someone made off with my billfold while I was in the bath.* 在我洗澡的时候，有人把我的钱夹偷走了。也可以用于表示"夺得"，例如：*Frank made off with the top prize in the speech contest.* 弗兰克在讲演比赛中夺得一等奖。*Thieves broke into our home while we were away and made off with most of our furniture.* 当我们不在家的时候，小偷破门而入，偷走了我们的大部分家具。*Hey, Joe. Don't make off with my umbrella. I've got to use it myself today.* 喂，乔！你别把我的伞拿走。今天我自己要用哪。不仅限于"物"，也可以应用于"人"。*Ringo made off with my date while I was dancing with someone else.* 当我跟另一个姑娘跳舞的时候，林戈把我的女朋友给弄走了。*If we don't start paying higher wages, other companies are going to start making off with our best employees.* 如果我们不付出更高的工资，别的公司就要把我们公司最优秀的工作人员挖走了。可以用 away 代替 off，而讲 make away with *something* [*someone*]，但实际上，这一表达法一般仅作"偷窃"解。*A burglar made away with my wife's jewelry.* 一个窃贼偷走了我老婆的珠宝。*The kidnappers made away with the bank president's daughter.* 绑架的匪徒把银行总经理的女儿诱拐走了。◇ take [steal] *something* [*someone*]

make-up

a make-up [ə 'meɪ.kʌ(ː)p] [话] **补考** 由于有病或其他原因未能参加考试的学生"进行补考"，在英语中叫做 make up an exam [a test]。这里的 make up 是"补"的意思。 *I have to make up an econ exam next week.* 下个星期我必须补考经济学。由这一 make up an exam [a test] 进一步发展,又产生了 a make-up exam [test] (补考)的表达法。这里的 make-up 是形容词,意思为"找补的"。上边的例句可以使用这一表达法改换为 *I have to take a make-up exam in econ next week.* 本条条头的名词 a make-up 就是由这一 a make-up exam [test] 脱落 exam [test] 而成,为 a make-up exam [test] 的缩略,主要是学生们使用。*I can't go out tonight. I've got a make-up in American lit tomorrow.* 今天晚上我不能外出啦。我明天得补考美国文学。另有 do a make-up 的说法。 *Susan got sick during finals and had to do four make-ups.* 苏珊在期末考试时生病了,她必须补考四门课。如以上的例句所示,a make-up 一般用于表示"对未参加考试的学生进行的补考"的意思,但是,也可以用于表示"对不及格的学生进行的补考"的意思。不过,根据美国当前的教育情况,为不及格学生进行补考的老师有如凤毛麟角,自然这方面的用例也就罕见了。 *Prof. Acerb is very strict. He never gives make-ups for people who fail.* 阿塞布教授是非常严厉的人。他绝对不给不及格的学生进行补考。◇ a special exam [test] (to cover one that *one* missed)

a make-up exam [test] [ə 'meɪkʌp ɪg,zæ:m / ,test] [口] **补考** → a MAKE-UP

malarkey

malarkey [mə'lɑ(:)rki] [话] **胡说八道** → BALONEY

mama's

a mama's boy → BOY

man

a big butter-and-egg man [ə ,bɪg ,bʌdərə'ne(:)g,mæ(:)n] [话] **地方阔佬** 古时,有一个男子走进卡巴莱(有歌舞等助兴的餐馆),毫不吝惜地宴请在座的客人,对舞女和艺人挥金如土。卡巴莱的女老板表示深深感谢,为了向大家介绍而请教他尊姓大名。那个男子不肯透露姓名,只说他是一个酪农场主。因此,女老板向大家做介绍的时候说: He's a big butter-and-egg man. (他是由黄油和鸡蛋起家的大财主。)从这一传说进一步发展,a big butter-and-egg man 便成了一个定型的表达法,意指"在地方上有钱有势的大人物",特别是实业家或者商人。*Many downtown cabarets are frequented by big butter-and-egg men from the provinces.* 在闹市区的卡巴莱中,许多家是地方阔佬经常光顾的。 *Lem Knott may be nothing to you big city businessmen, but around here he's a big butter-and-egg man.* 莱姆·诺特与你们大城市的实业家相比可能算不了一回事,但是在这一带他可是一个大阔佬啊。 *I have to entertain a big butter-and-egg man from Texas tonight.* 今天晚上我必须接待一位从得克萨斯州来的地方阔佬。◇ an important (business) man

a confidence man [ə 'kɑnfədənts ,mæ(:)n] [话] **骗子手** → a con ARTIST

be a disgrace to man and beast → DISGRACE

every last man ['evri 'læst'mæn] [口] **所有的人** 直译为"每一个最后的人",叫人摸不清是什么意思。其实,这里的 last 只是加强 every man (每一个人)的语气,并无"最后"的意义。 *Every last man has to be here by eight o'clock in the morning.* 早晨八点,所有的人都必须到这儿来。又说 every man jack。◇ every man without exception

every last man and his wife [,evri 'læ:st'mæ(:)nənhɪz 'waɪf] [口] **不管张三李四,有一个算一个** → every TOM, Dick and Harry

a hit man [ə 'hɪt,mæ(:)n] [话] **职业杀手** hit 是"击",hit man 使用的武器一般是手枪,但也可能是匕首之类。*The gang boss was double-crossed by his own hit man.* 匪帮的头子被他自己的杀手出卖了。 *There are those who don't believe that Kennedy was killed by a lone assassin. They claim that Oswald was only the* *hit man for an international conspiracy.* 有些人不相信肯尼迪是被一个单独的暗杀者刺死的。他们认为奥斯瓦德只是国际阴谋集团的一个职业杀手。在下一个例句中,不是字面意义的"职业杀手",而是作为比喻使用。*I refuse to be the boss's hit man. If he wants to fire Joe, he should do it himself.* 我不愿意给老板当枪使,如果他想解雇乔,他自己去做好啦。◇ a hired [professional] killer

(the) low man on the totem pole [(ðə) 'lou 'mæ(:)nonðə 'toudəm.poul] [话] **身份最低的人** 原意是"图腾柱最下边的雕像"。这些最下边的雕像,看起来好象要被图腾上方排列的雕像压偏似的。因此,美国的著名喜剧演员弗烈德·艾伦(Fred Allen)在几十年前就开始使用本条习用语。直至今日,凡是有自卑感的人,还常用半开玩笑的口吻使用它。不过,在严肃的会话中使用的情况比较多。不论是严肃还是诙谐,语调是十分轻松的。本条指某一社会、阶级、组织、集团中身份最低的人(有时指处于最下层的民族)。拿公司来说,指"最低级的职员";拿整个社会来说,指"最下层的老百姓"。本条强调完全没有权力或者发言权的意味。*I've only been working here for less than a year, so I'm still the low man on the totem pole.* 我在这儿工作不到一年,所以还是最低级的人员。*You were born into a rich and influential family. You've never known, like I have, how it feels to be low man on the totem pole in this society.* 你出生于一个有钱有势的家庭。你绝对不会象我一样理解这个社会最底层的人们的心情。也可以用于家族关系,例如:*Being the youngest son in our family, I was always low man on the totem pole.* 在我们家里,我是最小的儿子,所以总是小菜一碟,没人当回事。另有 the bottom of the totem pole 这样一个活用的形式。*Blacks in America have too long been on the bottom of the political totem pole.* 美国的黑人有很长一个时期没有一点政治地位。◇ the lowest man in the hierarchy / a member of the lowest layer (of this society) / (the one who is) treated the most lightly / the bottom of the political structure

a man Friday [ə 'mæ(:)n 'fraɪdi] [口] **男助手** → a girl FRIDAY

the man in the street [ðə .mænɪnðə 'stri(:)t] [口] **一般市民、群众** 形式是单数,意思是复数。与当政者、阔佬、名人、伟人等相对,指平凡的一般老百姓。特别是在谈论政治问题或者进行民意调查时,本条常常出现。前置词 in 有时用 on 代替。*The man in the street has no choice but to trust the elected politicians to look after his interests.* 老百姓没有别的办法,只能相信那些当选的政客们会为他们谋福利。*The man in the street may not seem very important, but it is he who decides who will rule the country.* 一般群众看起来可能不很重要,但是正是他们决定由谁管理国家。man-in-the-street 为形容词,但是除了 a man-in-the-street interview (街头访问记)这一习用语外,几乎无人使用。*The local TV station conducted a series of man-in-the-street interviews.* 地方电视台摄制了一系列的街头访问记。John Q. Public [.dʒɑ(:)n .kju: 'pʌblɪk] 是仿照人名构成的习用语,与本条同义。John 是美国最普遍的男子名,Q. 没有特别意义,Public 当然是"公众"。*John Q. Public is not satisfied with the present economic situation.* 一般市民对于当前的经济情况是不满意的。the man in the street 又与某一领域的专家、权威、内行相对,常用于表示"一般人"或"外行"的意思。但是 John Q. Public 不表示这一意思。*The function of the commodities market is not well understood by the man in the street.* 一般人不大理解商品市场的作用。◇ the ordinary citizen

a man of the world [ə 'mæ(:)nəvðə 'wə:rld] [口] **通达世故的人** 这里的 the world 指"人间"或"社会",但也包含着实际的 world (即世界)的意思。*George is only twenty-five years old and three years out of college, but because he has been to Europe, he considers himself a* *man of the world.* 乔治虽然只有 25 岁，大学毕业刚刚三年，但是由于去过欧洲，他就认为自己对世界上的事都懂了。*Ben was quite a man of the world in view of the fact that he had spent most of his life in a small country town.* 本大半生是在一个乡村小镇度过的，根据这一事实来评价，他就算是十分通达世故的人了。由"通达世故的人"这一意义进一步发展，又用于表示"潇洒不俗的人"的意思。*In contrast to what you would expect of an ambassador to a major country, there was little of the man of the world about him.* 他虽然是驻某大国的大使，却没有一点精通世故、优雅大方的风度。本条一般应用于男子，但对女性也有 a woman of the world 的说法。*Sara was enough of a woman of the world to know that men enjoyed flattery.* 萨拉已经通达一些世故人情，懂得了男人们喜欢奉承。◇ a knowledgeable man of sophisticated views

one's **old man** [~ ˌouldˈmæn] [俗] **爸爸** 如果只是 an old man，为"老翁"、"老人"的意思。加所有格 *one's*，则为"(某人的)父亲"的意思。中国人在某些场合，同样称自己或他人的父亲为"老头儿"。虽然有个 old，却不一定非"老"不可。例如象下面这样说也是极其自然的：*His old man is thirty.* 他的老头儿[爸爸]三十岁。这是一个相当轻松的俚语，主要是男子使用。*My old man says I can use his car tomorrow.* 我爸爸说，明天我可以使用他的汽车。在讲"家父"时，有时加定冠词，作 the old man。*I'll hafta ask the old man.* 我得问问我爸爸。另外，也有个别女人称自己的丈夫为 old man，等于中国女人称"我家老头子"或"孩子他爸爸"。→ *one's* old LADY ◇ *one's* father

be *one's* **own man** [~ ˌoun ˈmæːn] [口] **不受他人支配，按照自己想法行事** 直译为"是自己所有的人"。最初的构思是："如果受雇于人，则身子归雇主，不归自己"。因此，本条的含义是"自己不是别人的东西，而归自己所有"，换句话说，就是"在思想行动上完全独立的人"。在讲某个人的基本态度或想法时使用。*I can never tell my husband what to do. He's very much his own man.* 我绝对不能向我的丈夫讲做这个或做那个。他总是按照自己的意图行事。*You can't rise in the army if you insist on being your own man.* 如果你总坚持自己的那一套，在军队里是晋升不了的。*Tom is anxious to quit his job and go into business for himself. He's not happy unless he can be his own man.* 汤姆急欲辞去工作，专搞自己的事业。除非他能按照自己的想法去干，否则他的心情是不会舒畅的。请读者注意：如果加上 again，而成为 be *one's* own man again，译法就不同了。但是，"独立的人"这一基本意义不变，因为原来的构思是："从疾病、疲劳、郁闷的状态中解放出来，又能够按自己的意志行事了"。例如：*After sleeping almost twelve hours, I was finally my own man again.* 我睡了将近 12 个小时之后，终于恢复了精力。这是"象原来一样精神饱满"的意思。在用于表示这一意义的场合，不仅用动词 be，也可以用 feel。另外，也可以改变 again 的位置，把它提到前边，例如：*Soon after his operation, he was again feeling his own man.* 他做完手术以后，马上就恢复健康了。再有一点需要注意：即使加上 again，根据上下文，也有表示条头的意义的场合。例如：*After twelve years of working for someone else, I was finally my own man again.* 在为他人工作 12 年之后，我终于能够独立自主地干事情了。◇ be a free agent

be *one's* **own man again** [~ ˌoun ˈmæːnə ˌge(ː)n] [口] **恢复原来的精力** → be *one's* OWN MAN

to a man [ˌtu(ː)ə ˈmæːn] [口] **所有的人** 这是被妇女解放运动者们斥为大男子主义用语的表达法之一。直译是"一直到每一个人"。因为用的是男人 (man) 一词，在完全是女人群体中不便使用。本条的使用范围很广。*We were against the idea to a man.* 我们所有的人都反对那个主意。*Those present supported the motion to a man.* 所有出席的人都支持那项动议。*They appear weak and effeminate* *almost to a man.* 他们几乎全都弱不禁风,没有一点男子气概。*They are, to a man, all willing to die for their country.* 他们所有的人都愿意为国捐躯。*To a man, they were seeking only to benefit themselves.* 他们那些人没有一个不是在追求自己的利益。◇ unanimously / without exception

man-about-town

a man-about-town [ə ˌmæ(:)nə bauˈt:aun] [口] **浪荡公子** 直译为"(喜欢在)城里各处游逛的男人"。所谓"城里各处",系指高级夜总会、剧场、一流的酒吧间、大餐厅、舞厅等。这些人当然以有大量金钱为先决条件,他们的打扮极为阔绰,虽无妻室,却永远有美女陪伴。*I'm not exactly what you could call a man-about-town, but I prefer not to sit home every night.* 我实际上够不上所谓的浪荡公子,但是每天晚上在家里呆不住。*As soon as she was divorced, all the young men-about-town looked on her as fair game.* 她刚一离婚,所有的纨绔少年都把她当作自由猎取的对象了。常用 quite 加强语气。*Since his rich uncle died, Paul has become quite a man-about-town.* 自从富有的伯父去世后,保罗完全变成一个浪荡公子了。本条也有在前面加形容词的时候,例如:*I don't care if he is rich and handsome. I don't care to date some fickle man-about-town.* 我不在乎他是不是有钱,长得帅不帅。我不愿意跟一个朝三暮四的浪荡公子约会。也可以不加连字符,写作 man about town。◇ a (socially knowledgeable) frequenter of fashionable places

manger

a dog in the manger → DOG

man-in-the-street

a man-in-the-street interview [ə ˈmænɪnðə ˌstri(:)t ˈɪntərˌvju:] [口] **街头访问记** → the MAN in the street

many

have one too many → ONE

marbles

have all *one's* **marbles** [hæˌvɔ(:)l ~ ˈmɑ(:) rblz] [话] **头脑正常** → have all *one's* BUTTONS

lose *one's* **marbles** [ˌlu(:)z ~ ˈmɑ(:)rblz] [话] **头脑不正常** 直译为"失掉了(儿童游戏用的)弹子",亦即"失去正常的判断能力或思考能力"。一般用完成时。*You want to quit school and join the army? Have you lost your marbles?* 你想要退学去参军?难道你的头脑有毛病了吗?常用 all 加强语气。*If you think I'd ask Mary Lapigg for a date, you've lost all your marbles.* 如果你认为我会请求玛丽·拉皮格与我约会,你的想法未免太可笑啦。*When I explained our plan to the chief, he looked at me as if I had lost all my marbles.* 当我向科长说明我们的计划时,他眼睛盯着我,好象我发疯了似的。→ have all *one's* BUTTONS ◇ become strange in the head

be missing a few marbles [ˌmɪsən əfju(:) ˈmɑ(:)rblz] [话] **头脑有一点儿不正常** → have a few BUTTONS missing

march

steal a march on *someone* [ˌsti(:)lə ˈmɑ(:)rtʃən ~] [口] **偷偷地抢先** 本条的语源是:古时,在打仗时似乎也有一种骑士风格。双方相互默契,遵守一定的规约。其中之一是从清晨战斗到黄昏,夜里各自休息。如果一方采取卑鄙手段,在夜里偷偷地行军,抢在对方的前面,那就叫"偷(steal)一次行军(march)"了。从使用 steal 一词也可以了解,在当时来说,这是一种不能容许的卑鄙行为。然而到了今天,即使按照字面的意义使用,也不会含有这种意味。*The army stole a march on the enemy by quietly moving into an advantageous position by night.* 部队在夜间悄悄开入一个有利的地点,比敌人占据了优势。现在,绝大多数的场合是作为比喻使用。*We stole a march on our competitors by not publicly announcing our new product until we had secured orders from several large distributors.* 在我们得到几家大批发商订货之前，我们没有公开宣布我们的新产品，这样偷偷地抢先我们的竞争对手一步。*That guy knew I wanted to buy that house, so he stole a march on me by contacting the owner first.* 那个家伙知道我想买那所房子，所以他偷偷地比我抢先一步去和房主联系。◇ outmaneuver *someone*

Maria

a Black Maria [ə ˌblæk məˈraɪə] [话] **囚车** → a paddy WAGON

marine

a dead marine [ə ˈde(ː)d məˈriːn] [话] **空酒瓶子** 美国人一般称空酒瓶子为 a dead SOLDIER，但有时也叫做 a dead marine (死了的海军陆战队员)。这两个表达法都是把倒着的空酒瓶比做士兵的死尸。有些词典把 a dead marine 解释为“葡萄酒的空瓶”，其实并没有这种限制，它与 a dead soldier 完全一样，只要是装酒精饮料的瓶子，什么样的都可以。*This bottle's empty, too. That makes five dead marines so far.* 这一瓶也喝光啦。到现在，一共有五个空瓶了。◇ an empty whiskey [beer, wine, sake, etc.] bottle

marines

Tell it to the marines. [ˌtelɪtːəðə məˈriːnz] [话] **胡说八道** 直译为“这种话你跟海军陆战队员们说去”。英国海军最初使用本条习用语。皇家海军陆战队 (the Royal Marines) 是英国陆军的一个部门，专门负责登陆作战，自创始以来，就是海军舰艇把他们送到目的地。从海军舰艇上的官兵的眼光来看，他们无论对于大海或是对于船只都毫无所知，不管胡说些什么，他们马上就相信，简直是“一群大傻瓜”。因此，自然而然地产生了本条的说法，它的含义是：“象这种话你跟海军陆战队说去吧，他们听了也许会相信的，我可不是那样容易被欺骗的人啊！” *A: There's a lawyer on the phone. He says you've inherited a million dollars. B: Tell it to the marines. I've never even met anybody with a million dollars.* 甲：一位律师打电话来了。他说你继承了一百万美元的遗产。乙：简直胡说八道。我从来还没有遇到过有一百万美元的人哪。*A: I'm innocent, I tell ya. B: Tell it to the marines. We know it was you that killed him.* 甲：我跟你说，我是无罪的呀。乙：简直胡说八道。我们知道你是杀死他的凶手。根据上下文，it 可用 that 等代替。*A: Dick says he's been invited to dinner at the White House. B: He can tell that to the marines. If he means "a white house" I'll believe it.* 甲：狄克说他受邀请去参加白宫的宴会啦。乙：别听他胡说八道啦。如果他指的是“白房子”，那我还可以相信。另有一个说法是 Tell it to the horse marines. [~ ˈhors məˌriːnz]。horse 一词是为了说话有力而后来加上的，它本身在这里没有任何意义。这一表达法很少使用。◇ I don't believe it.

mark

toe the mark [ˌtouðə ˈmɑ(ː)rk] [口] **规规矩矩办事** → toe the LINE

market

a drug on the market → DRUG

be in the market for *something* [ɪnðə ˈmɑ(ː)rkətfər ~] [口] **正在寻求** 直译为“为了寻找某物而在市场上”。*I'm in the market for a good used car.* 我正在寻求一辆好一点的半新汽车。*Our company is in the market for an experienced sales manager.* 我们的公司正在寻求一位富有经验的销售经理。本条虽然有“在市场上”的字样，但是并不限定用于“出钱去买”的场合。*Stop trying to have me meet so many bachelors. I'm not particularly in the market for a husband.* 别给我介绍那么多的单身汉了吧。我并不急着要找丈夫呀。◇ be looking for *something*

play the market [ˌpleɪðə ˈmɑ(ː)rkət] [话] **做股票投机生意** 这里的 play 与 play the HORSES 的场合相同，是“玩耍”的意思。market 指“股票市场”(stock market)。*Mrs. Gottrocks enjoys playing the market.* 戈特罗克斯太太以玩股票投机为乐趣。也可以添加 stock。*Phil thought he'd try making a little money by* *playing the stock market, but he ended up losing a bundle.* 菲尔原来打算搞股票投机赚几个钱,结果却赔了老本儿。也可以使用 commodities (商品)一词,构成 play the commodities market (搞商品投机)。 *I used to play the commodities market a lot.* 我过去常搞商品投机。◇ speculate on the stock market

marriage

a shotgun marriage [ə ˈʃɑ(:)t.gʌ(:)n ˈmæ(:)rɪdʒ] [口] **由于使未婚女子怀孕而迫不得已的结婚** → a shotgun WEDDING

marry

marry a fortune → FORTUNE

marry for money → MONEY

mast

nail *one's* colors to the mast → COLORS

mat

put out the welcome mat (for *someone*) [pu.dautðə ˈwelkəm .mæ(:)t] [口] **热烈欢迎** welcome mat 是"门前擦鞋垫",因经常在垫上写有 Welcome (欢迎)字样,故名。put out 是"拿出"、"展开"的意思。 *Let us know when you're coming, and we'll put out the welcome mat.* 请告诉我们你什么时候来,我们好热烈欢迎啊。 *The Japanese government put out the welcome mat for the visiting Chinese premier.* 日本政府对于前去访问的中国总理表示了热烈的欢迎。常用 really 加强语气。 *Jack and Betty really put out the welcome mat for us.* 杰克和贝蒂的确对我们表示了热烈的欢迎。也可以用 the welcome mat is out (for *someone*) 表示"热烈欢迎"的意思。 *The welcome mat is out for you whenever you can come.* 你什么时候能够光临,我们都热烈欢迎。◇ give *someone* a warm welcome

match

throw a match [.θrouə ˈmæ(:)tʃ] [口] **在骗人的假比赛中输掉** → THROW a race [game, etc.]

math

math [ˈmæ(:)θ] [口] **中学以上的数学** mathematics [.mæθə ˈmæ(:)dɪks]的略语。原为轻松的学生用语,现在一般人也比使用 mathematics 更广泛地使用本条。 *I wasn't very good at math when I was in school.* 我上中学的时候,数学不太好。 *Mr. Henry is a math teacher.* 亨利先生是数学老师。小学的数学为算数,那不是 math,一般称 arithmetic [əˈrɪθ mə.tɪk]。中学也有时称 arithmetic,但听起来比 math 或者 mathematics 显得幼稚。高中以上的数学绝对不称 arithmetic。◇ mathematics

matter

no matter what [no.mædər ˈhwɑ(:)t] [话] **不管怎样** 本条是省略了某些语句中 what 后边的部分,如: no matter what happens (不管发生什么事情), no matter what the conditions (不管条件如何), no matter what anybody says (不管谁说什么), no matter what I have to do (不管要我做什么),等等。因此,可以分别使用于上面所列举的各种场合。重音放在 what 上。 *We have to carry out our plan no matter what.* 不管怎样,我们也必须实行我们的计划。 *I plan to succeed no matter what.* 不管怎样,我也是打算取得成功的。 *He says he doesn't care about other people's opinion, he's going to do it no matter what.* 他说他不管别人有什么意见,不管怎样他一定要干那件事情。◇ regardless of circumstances

maybe

maybe [ˈmeɪbi / məbi] [口] **也许** 有些英华词典把 maybe 一词译为"大概"、"多半",从英语使用的意思来考虑,这种译法不恰当。例如说: *It's clouding up. Maybe it'll rain this afternoon.* 如果译成"天阴上来了,今天下午多半要下雨。"就不如译成"今天下午也许有雨。"更接近英语的意思。maybe 是从 It may be that ~发展而来,用于可能性占 50%的场合。意义与助动词 may 几乎相同,表示“也许”、“或许”、“说不定”。与“多半”相当的英语为 PROBABLY(→),它比 maybe 的准确率高。因此,对于 *Do you think she'll really come?* (你认为她真的会来吗?)这一问题,可以回答说: *Maybe. But probably not.* (也许。不过,多半不会来。) *maybe* 还有一点与 *probably* 不同,一般放在句子的开头部分,例如: *Maybe it's better to go.* 也许去了好。 *A: Maybe the boss will give us a whole month's vacation. B: Hah! Fat chance!* 甲:老板也许会给我们整整一个月的休假哪。乙:哈! 天上真能掉馅饼吗! *A: Do you think you'll get the job? B: Maybe. Maybe not. Who knows?* 甲:你认为可以得到那份工作吗? 乙:也许行,也许不行。谁知道呢? perhaps 与 maybe 的意思完全相同,但有点儿一本正经的意味,中学生以下的孩子们几乎不使用。在成年人的日常会话中,maybe 的使用频率绝对高。◇ perhaps

McCoy

the real McCoy [ðə ˌri(:)l məˈkɔɪ] [话] **真货** 本条在强调并非假货(仿制品、代用品、玩具)时使用。 McCoy 原来是人名,这一点可以肯定;但是本条的语源至今尚无定论。大多使用 It's the real McCoy. 的形式。 *Careful how you handle that gun. It's the real McCoy.* 你摆弄那支枪可要当心。那是真枪啊。 *Hey, this isn't fool's gold! It's the real McCoy!* 喂,这不是黄铜! 这是真金啊! *Look at this ring I found in the street. It's the real McCoy.* 你瞧瞧我在街上捡的这个戒指。这可是真东西啊。 *Mom, your cooking is the real McCoy.* 妈妈,你在烹调上的确是真本领。也可以象 This is the McCoy. 这样省略 real,但此种情况极少见。 ◇ the real thing

meal

a square meal [ə ˌskwe(:)r ˈmi:l] [话] **一顿正经饭** square 一般是“正方形的”的意思,在这一场合是“充实的、令人满意的”。本条大多用于说“由于没有钱或者由于忙而吃不上一顿正经饭”的场合。 *I've been so busy I haven't had a square meal in three days.* 我由于太忙,已经三天没有吃上一顿正经饭了。另外,在讲“一天吃三回正经饭”的时候,可以省略 meal,只说 three squares a day。 *All I need is a place to sleep and three squares a day.* 我只要有个睡觉的地方和一天三顿饱饭就心满意足啦。 ◇ a proper [complete] meal

mealy-mouthed

mealy-mouthed [ˈmi:liˈmauθt / ~ˈmauðd] [口] **说话暧昧的** mealy 是 meal 的形容词。但是,这里的 meal 不是“饭”,而是“未筛过的粗粉”。本条的最初构思是:“嘴里塞满了粗粉,连话都说不清楚了”。在实际上,mealy-mouthed 不是指由于发音不清或者口吃而令人难以听懂,乃是指在有话难于出口而又不愿撒谎的场合,或者拐弯抹角,或者油嘴滑舌地说几句。也就是“遣词造句十分暧昧”。 *Horace may have a lot of ability, but the mealy-mouthed way he talks gives me the creeps.* 赫列斯也许非常有能力。但是,我很讨厌他那种言语暧昧的方式。 *What this country needs is some real statesmen instead of all these mealy-mouthed politicians.* 这个国家所需要的是一些真正的政治家,而不是所有那些口是心非的政客们。如前所述,mealy-mouthed 并没有“撒谎”的意思,甚至是因为不愿意撒谎才“含糊其词”(mealy-mouthed)。尽管如此,从旁观者来看,有时还是与“撒谎”无异。 *How can you say that Mr. Soapstone is sincere? He's a mealy-mouthed liar if you ask me.* 你怎么老说索普斯通先生为人诚实呢? 如果叫我说的话,他言语暧昧,是个说谎大王。也可以用做表语,但这种情况很少。如说: *He's too mealy-mouthed* [ˈmi:liˌmauθt / ~ˌmauðd]. 他说的话太暧昧啦。 ◇ round-about / insincere-talking / purposely ambiguous

mean

mean business → BUSINESS

mean well [ˈmi:n ˌwe(:)l] [口] **出于好心** 虽然想把什么事情做好,但是事与愿违,结果弄得很糟；虽然出于好心，要替别人做些什么，或是提出建议，结果却伤害了别人的感情，不欢而散。本条使用于这样的场合。*Harvey means well, but he is forever making stupid mistakes.* 哈维的动机是好的，但是他总犯愚蠢的错误。*I'm sure you mean well by your advice, Mother, but this is a question I have to decide by myself.* 妈妈，我知道你的忠告是出于一片好意，但是这是一个必须由我自己决定的问题。*You mustn't be offended. I'm sure Sue meant well by her remarks.* 你不要生气嘛。苏所说的话肯定是出于好意啊。◇ (*someone*) has good intentions (with <*his*> *something*) / (<*someone's*> *something*) is well intended

means

by fair means or foul [ˌbaɪ ˈfeːr ˈmiːnzər ˈfaul] [口] **不择手段地** → by HOOK or crook

meat

be *someone's* **meat and drink** [~ ˈmi(ː)tnˈdri(ː)ŋk] [口] **精神寄托** 古时，在本条出现的时候，meat 不仅有"肉"的意思，而且指一般的食物。与 drink (饮料)合在一起，构成 meat and drink，意思是"营养"，亦即"维持肉体不可或缺的东西"。后来进一步发展，到现在已具有"维持精神不可或缺的东西"或者"精神食粮"的意义了。在一般的词典里，常常释义为"无上的乐趣"或"最大的乐趣"，是有这种意思，但是，从下边的例句中也可以看得很清楚，虽然同是"乐趣"，这种"乐趣"却完全是"令人感到生活有意义的东西"、"可以作为精神支柱的东西"。这一点请读者注意。在使用时，语气大多很轻松。 *Travel is more than an enjoyment for Mrs. Gadabout. It's her meat and drink.* 对于加达保特夫人来说，旅行不仅仅是一种享乐，而且是她的精神寄托。*Joan loves all kinds of books. Reading is her meat and drink.* 琼喜爱各种各样的书。读书是她的精神寄托。*Being a playwright, praise from the critics is naturally my meat and drink.* 作为一个剧作家，批评家们的赞扬当然是我的精神支柱。*For Ronald, politics is not just a job, it's his meat and drink.* 对于罗纳德来说，政治不仅仅是一种工作，而且是他的精神上的寄托。◇ be *someone's* spiritual sustenance

One man's meat is another man's poison. [ˌwʌn ˌmæ(ː)nz ˈmiːdɪzə ˌnʌðər ˌmæ(ː)nz ˈpɔɪzn] [谚] **各有所好** 直译为"一个人的肉为另一个人的毒物"，简直有点儿令人莫名其妙。其实，在出现这一谚语的时候，meat 的意思不是"肉"，而是"食物"。 *A: I wonder why he likes English so much. I really hate it. B: Well, you know the old saying, one man's meat is another man's poison.* 甲：不知道他为什么那么喜欢英语。我实在讨厌。乙：古语说的好，各有所好嘛。*My brother loves the army and has made a successful career of it, but I just couldn't stand army life. It just shows that one man's meat is another man's poison.* 我的哥哥喜爱陆军，他在陆军中有锦绣的前程，但是我却非常讨厌军队生活。真是"各有所好"，这话一点儿也不错。◇ What one person likes, another may hate.

medical

a medical checkup [ə ˈmedəkl ˈtʃeˌkʌ(ː)p] [口] **身体检查** → a PHYSICAL

a medical exam [ə ˈmedəkl ɪgˌzæːm] [话] **身体检查；医学实验** → a PHYSICAL

medicine

give *someone* **a dose of** *his* **own medicine** [ˌgɪv ~ əˈdousəv ~ˌoun ˈmedəsn] [口] **以其人之道还治其人之身** → give *someone* a taste of *his* own MEDICINE

give *someone* **a taste of** *his* **own medicine** [ˌgɪv ~ əˌteɪstəv ~ oun ˈmedəsn] [口] **以其人之道还治其人之身** 这里的 medicine (药) 指"对方使你尝到的苦头"。你感到"他居然给我这样的苦头来尝"，因而怀恨在心，"一定叫他尝尝同样的苦头"——这便是本条的含义。*Harry is always making fun of me. I'd like to give him a taste of his own medicine.* 哈利总是取笑我。我想以其人

之道还治其人之身。a taste 可以用 a dose ['dous](一剂药)或者 some, a little 等代替。*Jill never shows up on time for an appointment. Today I gave her a dose of her own medicine by making her wait for twenty minutes.* 吉尔没有一次遵守过约会的时间。今天我以其人之道还治其人之身,叫她等了二十分钟。如果把立场倒过来,当然可以使用 be given a ~这样的被动语态,但是在这一场合,大多使用 get [have] a taste [a dose, some, etc.] of *one's* own medicine 的表达法,意思是"自己也尝到同样的苦头"。*You run and tell the teacher every time someone does something wrong. How would you like to have a taste of your own medicine?* 谁要是做错了什么事情,你总是马上去报告老师。你也想尝尝同样的滋味吗? *Brian finally got some of his own medicine.* 布雷恩终于尝到了同样的苦头。◇ make *someone* undergo the (unpleasant) experience (*he* makes *one* [other people] undergo)

take *one's* **medicine** [ˌteɪk ~ˈmedəsn] [口] **甘愿受罚** medicine 是"药",在日常会话中一般指"液体的药"。在现代,medicine 往往是甜的,很容易喝;但在本条习用语出现的时候,medicine 大多非常苦,必须咬着牙往下喝。*You have to take your medicine or you won't get well.* 你必须把药喝下去,否则病好不了啊。作为比喻,"自己的苦药"就变成了"由于自己的失败或罪恶而应该接受的苦果或惩罚"。这里的 take 是"忍受"、"忍耐"的意思。*It was your fault that it happened. Now you'll have to take your medicine.* 所以发生那种事,都是你的过失。现在,你当然必须甘心受到惩罚啦。*I admit it was wrong of me to cheat on the exam. I'm ready to take my medicine.* 我承认自己在考试中作弊是错误的,我甘心受处罚。在男性的场合,常加上短语 like a man (象男子汉大丈夫一样)。*He freely admitted his mistake and took his medicine like a man.* 他坦率地承认自己的错误,以大丈夫的气概接受了惩罚。◇ (readily) accept *one's* punishment

memory

have a memory like a sieve → SIEVE

have a memory like an elephant → ELEPHANT

play (*something*) **from memory** [ˌpleɪ frəˈmɪːemri] [口] **凭着记忆演奏听来的音乐** → play (*something*) by EAR

men

separate the men from the boys [ˌsepəˌreɪtðə ˈmen frəmðə ˈbɔɪz] [话] **真假男儿见高低** 意思是"区分出是强壮的男子还是软弱的男子",不是指有无"才能"或"技术",而是指有无"体力"、"气力"、"活力"、"勇气"等等。*Football is a game that separates the men from the boys.* 足球是真假男儿见高低的一种体育活动。*Deep-sea diving is dangerous work. It separates the men from the boys.* 深海潜水是很危险的作业。它能使真假男儿见高低。*Our training methods separate the men from the boys.* 我们的训练方法可以使真假男儿见高低。◇ separate the strong and courageous (men) from the weak

mend

mend *one's* **ways** → WAYS

be on the mend [ɔ(ː)nðə ˈmend] [口] **病情日渐好转** mend 一词首先令人想到的是表示"修补"意义的动词,但是这里的 mend 当然是个名词。be on the mend 这个句型几乎完全在谈到疾病或受重伤的场合使用,有"在恢复的道路上迈进"的意思。*My father has been sick for the past two weeks, but now he's on the mend.* 我父亲已经病了两个星期,但是现在他的病情日渐好转了。*Mr. Jones appeared to be on the mend until just before he died.* 琼斯先生在临死之前,病情好象有所好转似的。有时用于表示"事态有所好转"的意思。*Relations between Japan and China have recently been on the mend.* 最近,中日关系在向好的方面发展。◇ be getting better

meow

the cat's meow [ðə ˌkæ(:)ts ˈmiau] [话] **最了不起** 1920～1930 年间流行的俚语。直译为"猫的咪咪叫"。本条的语源不详。在小说或电影中经常出现。但现在有些陈腐的味道,青年人很少使用。*Debbie's new coat is the cat's meow.* 戴比的新外衣简直棒极啦。*That guy thinks he's the cat's meow.* 那个家伙认为自己最了不起啦。如以上的例句所示,可以用于物,也可以用于人。*Can Amy cook?! Her pies are the cat's meow!* 你问艾米会不会做饭?! 她做的馅饼好极了! *When I was a kid, Benny Goodman's orchestra was the cat's meow.* 在我小的时候,本尼·古德曼的管弦乐队是首屈一指的乐队。meow 也可以用 pajamas, whiskers 等词代替。*Rod's sports car is the cat's pajamas [whiskers].* 罗德的赛车棒极了。另外,在英国英语中,把 meow 拼写为 miaow 或 miaou, 把 pajamas 拼写为 pyjamas, 但美国人看不惯这种拼法。◇ the height of fashion [manhood, etc.] / absolutely delicious [beautiful, marvelous, etc.]

mercies

leave *someone* **to the tender mercies of** *someone* [*something*] [ˌli(:)v ～ təðə ˌtendər ˈmə(:)rsizəv ～] [口] **丢下某人任凭……摆布** tender mercies 直译为"温柔的仁慈",但在这里为反语,是"粗暴对待"、"野蛮蹂躏"的意思。本条经常含有"任意地"或"片面地"的意义。语源为《圣经·旧约》中的《箴言》(Proverbs) 第 12 章 10 节: A righteous man regardeth the life of his beast: but the tender mercies of the wicked are cruel. (义人顾惜他牲畜的命,恶人的怜悯也是残忍。)用例: *The British army had no choice but to retreat and leave the French people to the tender mercies of the advancing Nazis.* 英军没有别的办法,他们只好撤退,把法国人民丢给向前推进的纳粹,任凭纳粹野蛮地蹂躏。*After attacking the two hunters on the mountain, the thief tied them up and left them to the tender mercies of the wolves.* 强盗在山中袭击两个猎人之后,把他们捆了起来,任凭野狼去摆布了。本条也常用于戏谑的场合。*My wife went on a week-long trip with her friends, leaving me to the tender mercies of my mother-in-law.* 我老婆跟她的朋友们一道出去旅行一个星期,把我丢给岳母任她摆布了。可以用 entrust (委托)代替 leave,特别是在被动语态的场合。*The slaves were entrusted to the tender mercies of their cruel master.* 奴隶们任凭他们的残酷主子随意宰割。◇ expose *someone* to the harsh treatment of *someone* [*something*]

mercy

be at the mercy of *someone* [*something*] [ətðə ˈmə(:)rsiəv ～] [口] **完全受某人的支配** mercy 是"仁慈"。本条直译为"任凭某人的仁慈"。但请读者注意: 本条一般用于做句子主语的人不能期待 *someone* 的仁慈的场合,它强调做句子主语的人站在多么没有力量的立场。*We were at the mercy of our captors.* 我们完全受俘获者们的支配了。当然也有 be at *someone's* mercy 的说法。*You are at my mercy.* 你完全由我支配。如果进一步强调,则用 entirely 或者 complete(ly)。*After we lost our sail in the storm, our boat was entirely at the mercy of the waves.* 在暴风雨中失去帆以后,我们的船就完全随着波浪移动了。*The poor people in this area are at the complete mercy of their circumstances.* 这一地区的穷人完全受环境的支配。另有一个 find *oneself* at ～的形式代替 be at ～这一表达法。*When the storm struck, we found ourselves at the mercy of the raging elements.* 当暴风雨袭来的时候,我们完全任凭大自然的威力支配了。反义语有 have *someone* at *one's* / MERCY /。◇ be under *someone's* complete control / be controlled entirely by *something* / have no defense against *someone* [*something*]

have *someone* **at** *one's* **mercy** [ˌhæv ～ət ～ˈmə(:)rsi] [口] **对某人随心所欲地摆布** mercy 是"慈悲"、"怜悯"。本条中的

one's mercy 可以解释为"使对方不能抵抗,只好任凭我来摆布的状态"。*Our landlord has us at his mercy. If we don't agree to his raising the rent, he can force us to move out.* 我们的房东对我们是任意摆布。如果我们不答应提高房租,他就会撵我们搬家。*Just when we had that guy at our mercy, you had to let him get away!* 我们刚刚把那个家伙掌握在手心里,而你却叫他跑掉啦! *If we don't do something soon, Mr. Hardheart will have us at his mercy.* 如果我们不赶快下手,就得任凭哈德哈特先生随意摆布了。反义语有 be at the MERCY of *someone* [*something*]。◇ have *someone* in a defenseless position

throw *oneself* **on** *someone's* **mercy** [ˌθrou ~ɔn ~ˈmə(:)rsi] [口] **完全依靠他人的宽宏大量** 本条具有一种无可奈何的意味:现在已经没有其他的办法,只能指望人家宽大为怀了。*After being abandoned by her lover, Mrs. Hotpoo returned home and threw herself on her husband's mercy.* 霍特普太太被情夫甩掉以后,返回家中,完全指望丈夫宽大为怀原谅她了。*The defendant decided to tell the whole truth and throw himself on the mercy of the court.* 被告下决心坦白交代,听任法院宽大处理了。有时用 upon 代替 on,但具书面语言的感觉。*I know I can't expect you to forgive me, so I am throwing myself upon your mercy.* 我知道你不会原谅我,因此就希望你以慈悲为怀了。◇ (ask for forgiveness for *one's* misdeed and) leave *one's* fate to *someone's* magnanimity

mercy's

for mercy's sake [fər ˈmɜːrsizˈseɪk] [话] 哎呀呀! → for Pete's SAKE

merrier

The more the merrier. [ðəˈmo(:)r ðəˈmeriər] [口] **非常欢迎** 英国有个古代谚语说:The more the merrier, the fewer the better fare. (人越多越快乐,人越少吃得越香。)本条即由此而来。但是,在一般的美国人中,很少有人知道谚语的后半部分。在实际使用的场合,如果有人问 May I join you? (我可以参加吗?),就可以很轻松地回答说:The more the merrier. (非常欢迎。)在这一场合,几乎完全没有"人越多越快乐"的本来意义,只不过是表示欢迎的一种随意应答的寒喧之词而已。*A: May I bring a friend with me to your party tonight? B: Sure. The more the merrier.* 甲:我可以带个朋友参加你今天的社交晚会吗?乙:当然当然,非常欢迎。本条一般用于参加有三、四个人以上活动的场合,如果一个人与一个人合在一起,则不能使用。*A: Got room for me to ride in your car? B: Of course. Climb aboard. The more the merrier.* 甲:你的汽车还有空位子让我坐吗?乙:当然啦。上来吧,非常欢迎。不过,本条也有使用原意的情况,例如:*What say we invite the whole class? The more the merrier, I say.* 我们邀请全班同学好不好?依我说,人越多越热闹啊。*Japanese and English alike have always been borrowing languages. Both have always warmly welcomed foreign words and phrases with the spirit of the more the merrier.* 日语与英语自古以来就吸收其他民族的语言,双方都以丰富本国语言的精神,始终不断地热心引入他国的单词和成语。◇ Happy to have you [him, them, etc.]. / The more there are, the more fun there is [the better it is].

merry

lead *someone* **a merry chase** → CHASE

Midas

have the Midas touch → TOUCH

middle

knock *someone* **into the middle of next week** [ˌnɑk ~ ˌɪntəðə ˌmɪdləv ˌnekst ˈwiːk] [话] **猛烈一击打翻在地** 直译为"痛打某人,直到下星期的正中间"。最初的构思是:"一拳打得非常凶猛,直到下个星期正中间才能恢复意识"。原为拳击用语,意思是"把某人打倒在地,完全昏了过去"。*A powerful uppercut* *from the champ knocked the challenger into the middle of next week.* 冠军猛烈地向上一击,把挑战者打翻在地了。这一表达法本来是对打击的猛烈程度的夸张,因此在实际上并没有打得昏迷不省人事的场合也常常使用。意思是:"一拳打得极猛,即使打昏过去也不足为奇。" *He said that about me, did he? Wait'll I catch him. I'll knock him into the middle of next week.* 他是那样讲我的坏话吗?你等我抓住他再说,我会狠狠揍他一顿的。大多指饱以猛拳,但也可以指用拳头以外的东西(如棍棒)打击,或者指非人为的一击。 *I took a blow from behind that almost knocked me into the middle of next week.* 有人从后边给我猛烈一击,使我几乎昏了过去。 *As Hans was walking by a construction site, a board fell off a scaffold and just about knocked him into the middle of next week.* 当汉斯从一个建筑工地的旁边走过的时候,脚手架上掉下一块木板,正砸中他,他几乎昏了过去。偶尔用于表示"大吃一惊"的意思。 *The bill for my wife's new fur coat just about knocked me into the middle of next week.* 我的妻子买的一件新毛皮外套的帐单简直吓得我快昏过去了。 ◇ knock *someone* (completely) unconscious

middling

fair to middling [ˈfeːrdə ˈmɪdələn] [话] **马马虎虎** → SO-SO

midnight

burn the midnight oil → OIL

midsemester

a midsemester [ə ˌmɪdsəˈme(ː)stər] [话] **期中考试** → a MIDTERM

midterm

a midterm [ə ˈmɪd.tə(ː)rm] [话] **期中考试** a midterm examination 的简略说法,学生(中学生以上)用语。又作 a midterm exam。mid-是"中间(的)", term 与 semester 同义,是"学期"。 *The English midterm [midterm in English] was tough.* 英语的期中考试题目很难。 *How were your midterms?* 你期中考试成绩如何?有时也可以说 a midsemester [ˌmɪdsəˈme(ː)stər]。 *I have two midsemesters tomorrow.* 明天我有两门功课期中考试。可以加连字符写作 mid-term, mid-semester。→ a FINAL ◇ a midterm examination

mile

Give *someone* **an inch and** *he***'ll take a mile.** → INCH

go the extra mile [ˌgouðɪ ˈekstrə ˈmaɪl] [口] **干额外的事** 这一表达法是把《圣经》中的文句改成了习用语(→ an EYE for an eye and a tooth for a tooth)。在罗马帝国统治下的以色列人,只要罗马士兵下命令,就有义务给罗马士兵扛着东西,随着走一英里路。耶稣根据这一情况,教诲说:"有人强逼你走一里路,你就同他走二里(go the extra mile)"。也就是除了尽义务之外,主动地干额外的事情。 *In order to win your customers' complete confidence, it is not enough simply to do your duty. You must go the extra mile.* 为了赢得顾客们的完全信任,仅仅完成你的义务是不够的,你必须做进一步的工作。 *If you want me to help you, you are going to have to give me more of your cooperation. I'm tired of always having to go the extra mile.* 如果你想要我帮助你,你就必须跟我进一步合作。你老叫我白尽义务,我实在腻味透啦。 *The American President was willing to go the extra mile in order to secure a peace treaty between Egypt and Israel.* 美国总统为了埃及与以色列签订和平条约,不辞辛苦,干了一些额外的工作。 ◇ do more than what is required of *one*

miss (*something*) **by a mile** [ˌmɪs baɪə ˈmaɪl] [话] **相差十万八千里** 直译为"偏离目标一英里"。经常用于表示"虽然确定目标,结果相差太远"的意思。如说 miss the ball by a mile (球一点也不着边),这是表示"实际上离目标太远",用于体育比赛等场合。也可以用做比喻,表示"距离标准太远",如说 miss the answer by a mile (回答是驴唇不对马嘴), miss becoming a hit song by a mile (离一炮打响的歌相差十万八千里)。用例如下: *Jud missed the target by a mile.* 贾德远远没有打中目标。*A: Did you get the right answer to the problem? B: No, I missed (it) by a mile.* 甲:那道题你答对了吗? 乙:没有,相差十万八千里。*Everyone thought the book would become a bestseller, but it missed (becoming a best seller) by a mile.* 每一个人都认为那部书会成为畅销书,可是它差的太远了。◇ miss (*something*) by a wide margin

A miss is as good as a mile. → MISS

milk

cry over spilt milk [ˌkraɪ ovər ˌspɪltˈmɪlk] [口] **后悔也晚了** 英语中有一句大家所熟知的谚语是 There's [It's] no use crying over spilt [spilled] milk. 直译为"牛奶洒了,哭也没有用处",相当于汉语成语"覆水难收"。常常按照谚语原来的形式使用,例如: *It's too bad that we failed, but there's no use crying over spilt milk. We'll just have to make up our minds to do better next time.* 我们失败了,这非常遗憾,但是牛奶洒了,哭也没有用处啊。我们只能下定决心,下次做得更好一些。不过,cry over spilt milk 部分单独使用的情况非常多。而在这一场合,前面又大半加否定词。*Mr. Hairyheart is not one to cry over spilt milk.* 海里哈特不是那种专吃后悔药的人。*A busy man has no time to waste crying over spilt milk.* 一个忙人没有吃后悔药的时间。本条大多用于表示"对自己所造成的错误后悔"的意思,但也有时用于表示"对客观情况所造成的恶果痛心"的意思。◇ lament a result that cannot be changed

mill

a diploma mill [ə dəˈploumə ˌmɪl] [话] **文凭工厂** 直译为"大学毕业证书制造厂"。有人把这一表达法应用于高中,但极罕见。主要指以营利为目的而滥发文凭的大学。*You can't expect to get a good job when you graduate from a diploma mill like that.* 从那样一所文凭工厂毕业,你就休想找到好工作。◇ an inferior (large-scale) university

run of the mill [ˌrʌnəðəˈmɪ(:)l] [口] **平平常常** 字面意义为"刚从工厂制造出来的",但从来不按这一意义使用,专门用做比喻。这一表达法最初的构思是:"象工厂里一般生产过程中制造出来的大路货那样平平常常"。广泛作为表语使用。*As a woman, she's pretty much run of the mill.* 作为女人,她的姿色平平常常。*Bill's grades are only run of the mill.* 比尔的学习成绩平平常常。可以以 run-of-the-mill 的形式作为定语使用。*You paid too much money for such a run-of-the-mill car.* 你买那样一辆平平常常的汽车,花的钱过多了。◇ average / mediocre

million

feel like a million [ˌfi(:)laɪkə ˈmɪljən] [话] **身体感觉极佳** → feel like a million DOLLARS

feel like a million dollars → DOLLARS

millstone

a millstone around *someone's* **neck** [əˈmɪlˌstounə ˌraund ~ ˈnek] [口] **沉重的包袱** 本条源出《圣经·新约》中《马太福音》(Matthew)第 18 章 5–6 节: Whoever receives one such child in my name receives me; but whoever causes one of these little ones who believes in me to sin, it would be better for him to have a great millstone fastened round his neck and to be drowned in the depth of the sea. (凡为我的名,接待一个象这小孩子的,就是接待我。凡使这信我的一个小子跌倒的,倒不如把大磨石拴在这人的颈项上,沉在深海里。) a millstone 是"大磨石",把它"挂到脖子上" (around *someone's* neck),当然是沉重的负担了。*Calvin's drunken brother was a millstone around his neck that prevented him from attaining the success in life he so intensely desired.* 酗酒的哥哥是卡尔文的一个沉重包袱,他热切地希望在人生的大道上获得成功的心愿因此没有实

现。*I'm not going to get married. A wife and family would only be a millstone around my neck.* 我不打算结婚。妻子儿女只能成为我沉重的包袱。本条一般指具体的束缚,很少指精神的负担。例如: *The debts left by his father remained a millstone around Kevin's neck for many years.* 从结果来讲,凯文会有种种的苦恼,但是这句话的真正意义决不是"债务成为精神的负担",而是"凯文为了偿还父亲留下的债务,辛辛苦苦劳累了许多年"。*someone's* 当然也可以采取 of *someone* 的形式,例如: *Inflation and unemployment became millstones around the neck of the Republican government, finally dragging it down to defeat.* 通货膨胀和失业成为共和党政府的沉重包袱,终于把它拉垮了台。顺便讲一下:在英国英语中,一般喜欢用 round 而不用 around,因此,本条通常也作 ~ round *someone's* neck。相反,美国英语一般使用 around,有竭力避免 round 的倾向。◇ a liability [handicap, burden] ((of→to))

mince

not mince (*one's*) **words** (with *someone*) → WORDS

mincemeat

make mincemeat (out) of *someone* [*something*] [ˌmeɪk ˈmɪnts.mi(ː)d(aud)əv ~] [话] **打得落花流水** 许多人记得 mincemeat 是"肉末"的意思,现在美国出版的英语词典也是这样释义的,但是,在这个意义上,此词可以说是废语。也就是说,人们用 mincemeat 作"肉末"解乃是过去的皇历,现在只表示"百果馅饼的馅"。因此,本条在出现的当时(17 世纪)原是"把某人剁成肉末"的意思,而到了现代,大多数美国人则理解为"把某人剁成碎块,就象百果馅饼的馅一样"。所谓"百果馅饼的馅",一般不包括肉类,是把切碎的苹果、葡萄干、剁碎的果仁等调上香料搅拌而成。这样一讲,大家对于本条会有个大致的印象。当然,本条只能作为比喻使用。以下示明主要的使用方法。*The champ made mincemeat of the challenger.* 冠军把挑战者打得个落花流水。*The advancing Nazi army made mincemeat of the Polish forces.* 入侵的纳粹军队把波兰的武装力量打得一败涂地。*The opposing team made mincemeat out of us.* 我们队惨败于对方。也可以用于"击败某种思想或论断"的场合,例如: *Modern science has made mincemeat of many earlier beliefs.* 现代科学粉碎了许多古老的信条。*His cutting logic made mincemeat of my argument.* 他那尖锐的逻辑完全驳倒了我的论点。在以上的例句中,有的加 out,有的不加,而加 out 更具有会话的味道。另外,在现代,"肉末"一般叫做 (finely) chopped meat, 有时称 minced meat 则为烹调术语。◇ defeat *someone* thoroughly / completely destroy *something*

mind

blow *someone's* **mind** [ˌblou ~ˈmaɪnd] [话] **晕晕忽忽** 主要是年轻一代使用的轻松的表达法。这里的 mind 是"头脑"、"精神"。blow 是与 blow a fuse (烧断保险丝)同一的 blow。本条最初的构思是:"由于过分激动,大大超过负荷,头脑用保险丝烧断了"。原为 LSD 用语,意思为"以 LSD 致幻,迷醉不醒",亦即"头脑因 LSD 致幻而反常"。*He had to quit school after he blew his mind on LSD.* 他由于 LSD 致幻头脑反常后,不得不退学了。*Stay away from LSD. It'll blow your mind.* 别用 LSD 致幻,它会使你的头脑反常的。后来广泛用于表示"由于惊异、喜欢而大为激动"的意思。这是一种非常夸大的表达法,经常含有"晕晕忽忽"、"神志不清"的意味。本来,本条与事情的善恶毫无关系,但是在实际上大多用于表示比较好的意义,例如因非常有趣或精美绝伦而"激动",而"欣喜若狂"等等。首先举两个表示"非常有趣,令人意想不到"的例子。*That's a terrific book. The ending'll blow your mind.* 那是一本非常有趣的书,结局令人激动极了。*Some of Prof. Scattershot's ideas are so fantastic they almost blow your mind.* 斯卡特肖特教授的一些思想奇妙极了，简直令你心醉神迷。下面再举两个表示"精美绝伦"的例子。*It blows my mind just to think of being able to date a girl like that.* 我一想到能跟那么美的姑娘约会，心里就感到飘飘然。*When I was a student it practically blew my mind to think of having a job that took me overseas several times a year. Now that I have one, I'm sick and tired of having to travel all the time.* 在我当学生的时候，我非常醉心于得到一个每年能去几次国外的工作。现在我已经有了这种工作，却对于一年到头东奔西跑感到厌烦极了。下一个例句是怀着非常惊奇的心情讲的。*Just think! The US government spends more than one billion dollars a day! Doesn't it just blow your mind?* 你想一想啊！美国政府每天要花费十亿多美元！这多么让人吃惊啊？如果用否定形式，意思是"不太感兴趣"或"不喜欢"。*A: What do you think of the idea of taking in a movie tonight? B: It doesn't exactly blow my mind.* 甲：今天晚上去看电影，你认为怎样？乙：我没有多大兴趣。本条可以用做反语。也就是说，在本来想说"没有多大意思"或者"不值得大惊小怪"的时候，却用讽刺的口吻说"真是奇妙极啦"。*A: It says here that cockroaches can live three months without water. Isn't that something? B: Yeah. It blows my mind.* 甲：这本书上说，蟑螂没有水可以活三个月。这真了不起啊，是吧？乙：是啊，真够惊人的呀！◇ overwhelm *someone*

boggle the mind [.bɑ(:)glðə 'maɪnd] [口] **令人头晕眼花** 这里的 mind 是"头脑"、"想象力"；boggle 是"使困惑"、"使为难"。本条直译为"使想象力为难"，也就是"想象不到"、"连做梦也没有想到"。*His stupidity boggles the mind.* 你简直想象不出他是多么愚笨[他简直糊涂极啦]。*The vast number of stars in the universe boggles the mind.* 宇宙间星辰之多，简直令人头晕眼花。*The amount of money it takes to run the government for one year boggles the mind.* 政府每年开支总额之大，实在令人咋舌。另有 the mind boggles (at *something*)的形式，意思是"大吃一惊"。*The mind boggles at the thought that there may be millions of human civilizations in the universe.* 宇宙间可能有上百万的人类文明，这使人感到万分惊奇。也可以以 mind-boggling (令人惊奇的)的形式作为形容词使用。*That's a mind-boggling idea.* 那是一个令人惊奇的想法。另外有一个定型的表达法是 stagger the imagination, 意思与 boggle the mind 大致相同。◇ The very thought of *something* overwhelms one.

change *one's* **mind** [.tʃeɪndʒ ~ 'maɪnd] [口] **改变想法** → have a CHANGE of heart

give *someone* **a piece of** *one's* **mind** (for *something*) [.gɪv ~ ə.pi(:)səv ~ 'maɪnd] [话] **严厉责备** 直译为"把自己的一部分心给与某人"。这里的 mind 指"心中考虑的批评意见"。give *someone* 是把这种意见"当面向某人说出来"。本条的基本意思是"严厉责备"，但是根据对方处于平等的或者下属的地位，意思多少有一些差别。例如，在父母对子女讲的场合，"申斥"的因素强；如果对方处于平等的地位，则"直言不讳"的因素强。*I gave Jimmy a piece of my mind for being so bad as to be kept after school every day.* 我严厉申斥吉米说：你怎么表现那么差，每天放学后都被留下呢？ *I'm going to go and give Jimmy's teacher a piece of my mind. No matter how bad he is, that's certainly no reason for keeping him after school day after day.* 我打算去找吉米的老师提点意见。不论吉米这孩子多么淘气，也不能每天放学不让回家呀。对于上级或长辈，一般不使用本条。但是，在自己认为绝对正确而表示不满的时候，也可以用于表示"毫不客气地进行质问"的意思。*The boss's secretary gave him a piece of her mind for having peremptorily canceled the Christmas party he had promised that the company would give for the orphanage.* 老板原来答应公司为孤儿院举办圣诞晚会，而他又武断地取消了，他的秘书

为这件事坦率地对他提出了意见。◇ bluntly rebuke *someone*

go out of *one's* **mind** [ˌgou ˌaudəv ~ ˈmaɪnd] [口] **疯狂** → lose *one's* MIND

have a good mind to *do something* [ˌhævə ˈgu(ː)d ˈmaɪndtə ~] [话] **很想去干某事** 一般不是用于表示"非常想去干某事",而是用于表示"有干某事的意图"。*She says she has a good mind to buy two new coats since they're on sale.* 她说现在外套大减价,她有意买上两件新外衣。可以这样使用。但是,绝大多数是用于心怀不满或者愤怒的场合。*I've got a good mind to call that guy up and tell him to mind his own business.* 我很想给那个家伙打个电话,告诉他少管闲事。*I've got a good mind to write to him myself.* 我很想亲笔给他写封信。言外包含着"对他不满"的情绪。本条表示强烈的意志,实行与否则是另外一回事了。*If that's the way you're going to talk, I've got a good mind not to go with you.* 如果你这样讲话,我不打算跟你一道走。*I have a good mind to tell her the truth, no matter how much it hurts.* 不管怎样刺伤她的心,我都想对她吐露真实情况。尽管这种情况极少,但可以用 great 代替 good。*I've got a great mind to poke you in the nose.* 我真想冲你鼻子打上一拳。◇ be halfway determined to [halfway convinced *one* should] *do something*

have a mind like a sieve [ˌhævə ˌmaɪnd laɪkə ˈsɪ(ː)v] [话] **记性太坏** → have a memory like a SIEVE

have a mind like a sponge → SPONGE

have a mind like a steel trap → TRAP

have a one-track mind [hævə ˌwʌnˌtræ(ː)k ˈmaɪnd] [口] **只有一个心眼** one-track 是"(铁路)单轨的"。本条直译为"有一个单轨的头脑"。一般用于表示不好的意思,有时指只考虑一件事情的天性,也有时指在某一段时间脑子里只装着一件东西。*Chet has a one-track mind. All he ever thinks about is food.* 切特是个单线脑筋,他考虑的只是吃。*I've often tried to get Franz to donate some of his time to teaching English to poor students, but unfortunately he has a one-track mind. All he's interested in is making money.* 我常常请弗兰茨腾出一些时间教贫苦学生学英语,但是很遗憾,他只有一个心眼,就是向钱看。*Can't you talk about anything else besides some stupid TV program? I've never seen anyone with such a one-track mind.* 除了一些无聊的电视节目外,你不能谈其他的任何事情吗?我从来没见过象你这样一根筋的人。*All Gracie ever talks about is boys, boys, boys. Talk about (having) a one-track mind!* 格雷西的嘴里没有别的,一讲就是男朋友、男朋友、男朋友。真没见过这样一个心眼的人! ◇ be obsessed by one idea [with one subject]

have half a mind to *do something* [ˌhæv ˈhæ(ː)fə ˈmaɪndtə ~] [话] **有心要去干某事** 直译为"有一半心情去干某件事情"。在使用时语调极为轻松,表示"心里有那么一点儿意思"。实际上是否真去实行,那是另外的问题。*It's such a nice day. I've half a mind to stay home from work and practice my golf game.* 天气真好啊。我很想不去上班,呆在家里练一练高尔夫球。*I know Wilma only invited me to her party to be polite, but I have half a mind to go anyway.* 我知道威尔玛邀请我参加她的社交晚会只是出于礼貌,但是不管怎样,我是有心前去的啊。*I'm fed up with studying. I've got half a mind to quit school and become a truck driver.* 我对于学习已经厌倦啦。我有心退学去当卡车司机。有时用于表示因为"恼怒"或者"不满"而"很想怎样干"的意思。*I was so angry with Roy that I had half a mind to get out of the car and walk home.* 我对罗伊极为恼怒,很想下车,走回家去。不过,在这一场合如果使用 have a good MINDto *do something*, 那就更贴切了。◇ be tempted to *do something*

lose *one's* **mind** [ˌlu(ː)z ~ ˈmaɪnd] [口] **精神失常** 虽然同样是"疯狂"的意思,但本条一般不用于乱吵乱闹的情况,而用于神态稳静但头脑异常的场合。*By the time he was found after he had wandered* *four days in the desert without water, he had lost his mind.* 他没有一点水，在沙漠里乱走了四天，等被人发现的时候，他已经精神失常了。*He lost his mind soon after his entire family had been killed in an automobile accident.* 在全家人由于交通事故而丧生之后，他马上就精神失常了。*I often hear strange noises in the house at night. Sometimes I think I must be losing my mind.* 在夜里，我常听到房子里有奇怪的声响。有时我想自己是不是精神失常啦。have lost *one's* mind 是"精神已经失常"，与 be out of *one's* mind 同义。*Have you lost your mind? [Are you out of your mind?] We can't afford a vacation in Europe!* 你是不是精神失常啦？[你是不是头脑有点那个？]咱们没有到欧洲去休假的功夫啊！如果是 go out of *one's* mind，根据上下文，既可以用于"神态稳静"的场合，也可以用于"乱吵乱闹"的场合，因此比 lose *one's* mind 的使用范围广，以上的例子均可用它来替换。相反，下一例句如果使用 lose *one's* mind 就不适宜了。*The man suddenly seemed to go out of his mind. It took three men to hold him.* 那个人似乎突然发疯了。三个人才把他抓住。也常添加上 with ～，而讲 go [be] out of *one's* mind with *something*。在这一场合，一般是强调 with 后续词所表示的状态。*We've got to find some water soon. I'm going out of my mind with thirst.* 我们必须马上找到点儿水啊，我渴得要发疯啦。*Where have you been all this time? I was almost out of my mind with worry.* 你这些时候都在哪儿来着？我着急得快要发疯啦。◇ go insane [crazy]

mind *one's* **own affairs** [ˈmaɪnd ～ ˌou nəˈfe:rz] [口] **少管闲事好啦** → mind *one's* OWN BUSINESS

mind *one's* **own business** → BUSINESS

be of one mind (on *something*) [əvˈwʌn ˈmaɪnd] [口] **同心合意** 源出《圣经・新约》中《哥林多后书》(Second Corinthians) 第 13 章 11 节：Be perfect, be of good comfort, be of one mind, live in peace; and the God of love and peace shall be with you. (要作完人，要受安慰；要同心合意；要彼此和睦；如此仁爱和平的上帝必常与你们同在。) 这里的 mind 是"意见"或"想法"的意思。本条是强调 think the same way (about *something*) 的表达法。*I never saw my mother and father disagree. They seemed to be of one mind on everything.* 我从来没有见到过我的母亲与父亲意见不和。他们似乎对于任何一件事都是同心合意的。*My partner and I are usually of one mind on most things, but this time we just can't seem to agree.* 我的合伙人与我几乎在所有的事情上都是同心合意的，但这一次我们似乎不能持一致的看法。在强调的场合常用 entirely 或 completely。*We should discuss our ideas on the project. We must be entirely of one mind before we attend the meeting.* 我们应该讨论一下大家对这个计划的想法。在参加会议之前，我们必须完全统一思想。也可以改变 one 的部分，而讲 be of a mind 或者 be of the same mind。不过，前者是略为生硬的说法。*The Allies were not all of a mind as to how to conduct the war in Europe.* 各同盟国关于怎样在欧洲进行战争，意见并不一致。the same 与 one 没有意义上的不同，但在谈到各种问题时，人们有使用 same 的倾向。*Joe and I are of the same mind on this subject.* 关于这个问题，乔和我的看法是一致的。◇ agree completely / be in complete agreement

be out of *one's* **mind** [ˌaudəv ～ ˈmaɪnd] [口] **发狂** → lose *one's* MIND

Out of sight, out of mind. → SIGHT

slip *one's* **mind** [ˌslɪp ～ ˈmaɪnd] [口] **不留神忘掉了** 直译为"从某人的头脑里滑落了"。*It slipped my mind.* 我不留神把它忘掉了。以"不留神忘掉了"的对象为主语。slip 是"刺溜一下子滑出去"的意思，为了表达这一意思，不能把本条只译作"忘记"，而要译成"不留神忘掉了"才比较传神。*I'd better make a note of* *that. It may slip my mind if I don't.* 我最好还是把这件事写到笔记本上。如果不写下来，一不留神就会忘掉啦。*A: Did you mail the letter I handed you this morning? B: No. It slipped my mind.* 甲：今天早晨我交给你的那封信，已经寄出去了吗？乙：没有。我一不留神把它给忘掉啦。slip *one's* mind 的后边加上 for the moment (暂时)，大致是"一时想不起来"的意思。*I know his name almost as well as my own. It's just slipped my mind for the moment.* 我对他的名字几乎跟对自己的名字一样熟悉。只是一时记不起来啦。*A: Don't tell me you've forgotten our date tonight! B: No, I haven't forgotten. It just slipped my mind for the moment.* 甲：你总不会是忘记我们今天晚上的约会吧！乙：当然没有忘记啦。只不过一时想不起来了。◇ forget ((it →I))

weigh on *someone's* **mind** [ˌweɪɔ(ː)n ~ ˈmaɪnd] [口] **心事重重** 按照字面意义，可以说：*The pack weighed heavily on my back.* 行李很沉重地压在我的背上。本条即来源于此。作为比喻，既可以用于心事重重的场合，也可以用于比较轻一些的场合。*Dad has been very quiet recently. He seems to have something weighing on his mind.* 爸爸最近很少说话。他似乎有什么心事。可以用 upon 代替 on，但有点儿生硬。*The question has been weighing upon my mind for some time now. I will have to do something about it soon.* 那个问题最近始终压在我的心头。我非赶快设法解决不可。与按字面意义使用的场合相同，以 heavily 加强语气。*The matter of his daughter's impending marriage to a near- stranger weighed heavily on Mr. Minnick's mind.* 女儿即将与一个近似陌路人一样的男子结婚，这件事很沉重地压在明尼克先生的心头。◇ worry *someone* (considerably) ((heavily → deeply))

mind-boggling [ˈmaɪndˌbɑ(ː)gəlɪŋ] [口] **令人头晕眼花的** → boggle the MIND

minds

be of two minds [əvˈtuː ˈmaɪndz] [口] **下不了决心** of two minds 直译为"好象有两个心似的"。意思是："在两个心之间来来往往，确定不下来"。*I'm of two minds. I can't decide whether to go without permission or ask first and risk being refused permission.* 我心里正在游移。究竟是不经许可去呢？还是冒着不被批准的危险先去请示呢？一时确定不下来。of two minds 的后边大多接 as to+名词短语、about+名词[代名词]等。*I'm of two minds as to what should be done.* 究竟应该采取两种办法中的哪一种，我下不了决心。*I don't think Brent is capable of making a decision. He always seems to be of two minds about everything.* 我认为布伦特是不可能做出决定的。不管什么事情，他似乎总是游移不定。about 的后边，除 everything 外，还常用 it, that 等代名词。前置词除 about 外，有时用 on。在这一场合，后续的名词多为 point, question 等。*A: Are you going with us? B: I don't know. I'm still of two minds on the subject.* 甲：你跟我们一起去吗？乙：我不晓得。关于这个问题，我还没有确定下来。另外，在一些词典中只收录了英国英语 be in two minds。美国英语中不说 in two minds，不过意思一样。◇ be torn between two different thoughts / be undecided

mines

go back to the salt mines [ˌgou ˌbæktəðə ˈsɔ(ː)ltˌmaɪnz] [话] **回到那令人苦痛的工作岗位** salt mines 是"岩盐坑"。本条直译是"回到岩盐坑去"。俄国把囚犯送到西伯利亚的岩盐坑去干苦活，本条即来源于此。在工作岗位或大学里经常使用，为戏谑语，一般含有开玩笑的意味。*Well, let's go back to the salt mines.* 好啦，咱们回车间干苦活去吧。*After such an enjoyable trip through Europe with my wife and family, I didn't look forward to having to go back to the salt mines of New York.* 在带着老婆孩子到欧洲痛快地玩了一圈之后，我并不想回到纽约的工作岗位去干苦活。动词常用 get 代替

go, 或者使用 be 动词采取 it's back to ～的形式。*Please stay and finish your lunch. It's time for me to get back to the salt mines.* 请你们留下,把午饭吃完吧。到上班的时候了,我得受罪去啦。*Today is the last day of my vacation. Tomorrow it's back to the salt mines.* 今天是我的休假的最后一天,明天又得上班受罪去啦。如上面的例句所示,休息终了、返回工作岗位或学校是最常使用的场合。*I have to finish this history report this week. Monday it's back to the salt mines.* 这个星期,我必须写完这篇历史学报告。星期一又要回到那难受的教室去了。◇ go [get, be] back to work [the office, etc.]

ministry

enter the ministry [ˌentərðə ˈmɪnɪstri] [口] **就圣职** → take the TONSURE

miss

miss (*something*) **by a mile** → MILE

A miss is as good as a mile. [əˈmɪs ɪzəzˌgudəzə ˈmaɪl] [谚] **失败终归是失败** 如果把这句话的英语补足,作 A miss (by even a bit) is as good as (a miss by) a mile. 那就容易明白了。意思是:"哪怕偏离一丁点儿,也与偏离一英里相等"。用英语换句话来说,就是: Whether one misses by one centimeter or one kilometer, the result is the same. (偏离一公分与偏离一公里,结果是相同的。) 这一谚语使用 as good as 的说法。所以用 good (好) 一语,是因为原来系指"对方的 miss (失误)"而言,在我方看来,对方的失误当然是 good 了。实际上,即使在今天,当使用这一谚语时也偏重于表达同样的意义。*Their last batter missed hitting a homerun by only one foot, but fortunately for us a miss is as good as a mile.* 他们最后的击球员所打的球离本垒打只差一英尺,但是毕竟没有打中,对我们来说是很幸运的。*The Republican candidate missed being elected by only ten votes, but a miss is as good as a mile.* 共和党候选人只以十票之差没有当选,但是失败终归是失败啊。有时也用于"自己失误"亦即"不好"的场合。*I missed the target by only a fraction. Unfortunately, a miss is as good as a mile.* 我只差一点点,没有击中目标。遗憾的是,失败终归是失败啊。◇ To miss by a little is the same as missing by a lot.

missus

the missus [ðə ˈmɪsəs / ˈmɪsəz] [话] **老婆** 带有一点戏谑的说法,具有乡巴佬的味道。在会话中主要指 my wife (我的妻子)。*I'm fine, but the missus has been a little under the weather recently.* 我身体很好,但是我老婆最近有点儿不舒服。*I'm a bachelor tonight. The missus couldn't come.* 今天晚上我是孤零零一个人。老婆来不了。虽然一般指自己的妻子,但也有指对方或第三者的妻子的场合。*Hello, Jim. How's the missus these days?* 哈罗,吉姆。你太太最近好吗? missus 与 Mrs. 相同,原为 mistress 的土音。在过去的上等家庭中,仆人对女主人表示敬意,称呼 the mistress 或者 the missus (太太)。现在,有些地方还用 missus 表示"太太"的意思,在这一场合当然没有戏谑的味道。*I'm a salesman. Is the missus in?* 我是推销员。太太在家吗? 也可以拼写为 missis。◇ *one's* wife / the lady of the house

mistake

a bonehead mistake [ə ˈbounˈhe(:)d məˈsteɪk] [话] **愚蠢的错误** → pull a BONER

mitt

a mitt [ə ˈmɪ(:)t] [话] **手** mitt 是 mitten (仅拇指分开的"两指手套",主要为妇女儿童防寒用)的缩略。mitt 虽然也是"两指手套",但是使用的目的在于防止受伤,一般指棒球接球员的手套或者车间里拿热东西时用的手套等,后在俚语中转作"手"的意思。*The man gripped a shovel in his work-hardened mitt.* 那个人用他在劳动中锻炼出来的手紧紧握着一把铁锹。*Just wait'll I get my mitts on that guy.* 我要是抓住那个家伙,决不白饶他。◇ a hand

moderator

a moderator [ə ˈmɑ(:)də͵reɪdər] [口] **主席** → an EMCEE

modesty

throw modesty to the winds [͵θrouˈmɑ(:)dəsti təðə ˈwɪ(:)ndz] [口] **丢掉一切顾虑** → throw CAUTION to the winds

molehill

make a mountain out of a molehill → MOUNTAIN

Molotov

a Molotov cocktail → COCKTAIL

money

for *one's* **money** [fərˈ ~ ͵mʌni] [话] **在……看来** 原为赌博时说的话，意思是"如果把自己的钱押上"。"既然是赌钱，那就要按照自己的意思去赌"——从这一构思出发，本条就产生了"依照我的意见"、"按我的想法"、"叫我来说"之类的意思了。 *Whisky is fine, but for my money nothing is better than a nice, cold beer on a hot day.* 威士忌当然很好，不过在我看来，在烈日炎炎的日子里，什么也不如冰镇的好啤酒啊。 *Greased Lightning is the fastest horse for my money.* 据我来看，"油光闪电"是最快的马。 *For my money, there's nothing to be gained by being nice to them. They'll give in only if we force them to.* 依我说，对他们客客气气是没有用处的。我们只有硬逼着他们，他们才会屈服。 *Rex says that for his money Mr. Good is the best man for chairman.* 雷克斯说，按照他的意思，古德先生是当主席的最好人选。 *If you're looking for someone you can completely trust, Mr. Upright is the man for my money.* 如果你找完全能够信赖的人，依我看，阿普赖特先生是最合适不过了。 ◇ if you ask me [*someone*]

give *someone* **a (good) run for** *his* **money** → RUN

have money to burn [͵hæv ˈmʌni təˈbə:rn] [话] **钱多得用不完** burn 是"烧"。直译为"有烧的钱"，亦即"钱多得很，烧也不可惜"。 *Let's ask Jay to put up some cash. He's got money to burn.* 咱们去请杰伊掏点钱吧。他钱多得用不完。 *How could I ever buy a big house like that? I haven't exactly got money to burn, you know.* 我怎么能买那么大的一所房子呢？要知道，我可没有花不完用不尽的钱啊。have money to burn 虽然是一个定型的表达法，但有时也可以用于 money 以外的东西，而讲 have *something* to burn (某种东西多得用不完)。 *I wish I were as popular as Jake. I know hardly anyone in this city, while he has friends to burn.* 我希望自己能象杰克那样有人缘儿。在这个城市里，我几乎连一个熟人都没有，而他的朋友却多得不得了。常用 with 代替 have，构成 with money [*something*] to burn 这样的形容词短语。 *I don't understand why you don't want to marry a man like him —young, handsome, and with money to burn.* 我不明白你为什么不想嫁给他那样一个年轻、英俊而且有用不尽的金钱的男人。 ◇ have plenty of money / have more money than *one* needs

be in the money [ɪnðə ˈmʌni] [话] **钱多得很** → be in the CHIPS

mad money [ˈmæ(:)d ͵mʌni] [话] **女人手头准备的一点零钱(万一与约会的对象吵嘴，用做单独回家的车费)** mad 是 angry (恼怒、生气)的意思，也就是"为了万一吵架而发怒时准备使用的"的意思。在汽车万能的美国，男子与女子约会时，一般是用汽车接送。但是，也有可能发生意外的情况，两个人吵起来不欢而散。在这种场合，如果女方连回家的车费都没有，那就只能听男方摆布了。因此，mad money 等于有力的护身符。 *I would have gone home alone, but I didn't have enough mad money with me.* 我当时很想一个人回家，可是我身上没有足够的车费啊。 *A smart girl never goes on a date without a little mad money.* 一个聪明的姑娘身上不带点回家用的车费，决不出去与男人约会。另外，mad money 除指"与男朋友吵嘴后分手时所用的车费”外，还泛指“女性为不时之需备用的金钱”，也可以认为是一种“私房钱”。在美国人的感觉中，这一场合的 mad 不是 angry，而接近 crazy。因为这种钱本来是为不时之需储存的，但女人们大多是发疯 (crazy)似地把它用掉。从这一点也可以看出美国人特有的一种性格。 *That's such a beautiful dress, I'm tempted to use some of my mad money and buy it.* 那件衣服太漂亮啦。我真想用自己的一些私房钱买下它。◇ (emergency) money

marry for money [ˌmærifər'mʌni] [口] **为财产而结婚** 字面意义为“为金钱而结婚”。这是个一般的表达法，例如：*He married for money.* 他为得到财产而结婚了。如果谈到特定的结婚对象，就必须在 money 前面加上人称代词的所有格，而说 marry *someone* for his [her] money。例如：*He married Mary for her money.* 他为了玛丽的财产而同她结了婚。就是在不举出具体人名的场合，虽然罗嗦，也必须把代词重复一遍。例如：*He married her for her money.* 他为了她的财产而同她结了婚。 *It's foolish to marry for money.* 为财产而结婚是愚蠢的。 *She foolishly married him for his money.* 她很愚蠢，为了他的财产嫁给他了。◇ marry in order to become rich

not *do something* **for love or money** → LOVE

put *one's* **money where** *one's* **mouth is** [ˌput ~ 'mʌni *h*wer ~ 'mauˌθɪz] [话] **拿出钱来打赌** 本条的意思是：“光是口说不行，要打赌就实际掏钱”。当对方说“绝对如此，我敢打赌”的时候，人们常回答说：“你如果真认为那样，拿出钱来真的打赌好啦！”本条就是在这样的场合使用。因此，大多用命令式。 *A: I'll bet you 50 dollars the Yankees will win the pennant. B: You think so? Okay, put your money where your mouth is.* 甲：扬基棒球队肯定会夺得锦标，我和你赌五十美元。乙：你真这样想吗？好啦，空口无凭，把钱先拿出来。即使对方口头上没有明说打赌，而说话的内容包含有打赌的意思，当然也可以使用本条。 *A: We can beat your team any day. B: Oh, Yeah? Put your money where your mouth is.* 甲：我们随便哪一天都能击败你们球队。乙：哦，真的吗？光说不算，你拿出钱来打赌吧！象这样面对面使用命令式的情况很多，但也偶尔有如下的用法： *He says he's not afraid to finance our venture, but he won't put his money where his mouth is.* 他说他并不害怕向我们的企业提供资金，但是这只是口头一说，他并不真地掏钱。在这一场合，是把 venture (企业)看作一种赌博了。也可以用过去时。 *I made him put his money where his mouth was.* 他由于净说大话，我逼着他把钱拿出来了。◇ I accept the bet. Show me your money. / follow *one's* words with an actual outlay of money

be strapped for money [ˌstræp*t*fər'mʌni] [口] **缺钱** 名词 strap 是“电车、公共汽车上乘客用的拉手吊带”。作为动词，则是“用吊带捆上”。本条直译是：“在金钱方面被束缚住手脚”。 *I'm a little strapped for money tonight. Can you lend me a ten-spot?* 今天晚上我缺一点儿钱。能借给我一张十美元的票子吗？ *We're strapped for money to pay our debts.* 我们缺钱，还不上债。有时将 for money 省略。 *I'd like to help you, Frank, but I'm strapped, too.* 我很愿意帮助你，弗兰克，不过我也缺钱啊。如果是象第一个例句那样“缺乏现金”的场合，可以用 cash ['kæ(:)ʃ]代替 money，而说 be strapped for cash。更文雅一点的说法有 be financially strapped。例如：*Our company is financially strapped at the moment.* 目前，我们公司经济很困难。◇ not have any [enough] money

throw good money after bad [ˌθrou 'gud ˌmʌni æftər 'bæ:d] [口] **再多花钱也是白费** bad 是 bad money 的略语。本条直译为“往坏的钱的去处投入好的钱”。在这里，“好的钱 (good money)”指“能用的钱”；“坏的钱 (bad money)”指“白白浪费掉的、自己已经不能用的钱、等于扔到臭水沟里的钱”。也就是说，本条的中心意思是：“为了达到某种目的而花了钱，可是没有成功的迹象。尽管如此,仍然为达到这个目的而投资”。 *I wouldn't go into debt any further to try to save your company. You'd just be throwing good money after bad.* 我不想再为拯救你的公司去欠债啦。因为再多花钱也是白费。*Our son simply refuses to study. I'm not going to throw good money after bad by hiring another tutor for him.* 我们的儿子根本不肯念书。我不想再给他请家庭教师,因为多花钱也是白费。*We'll just have to buy a new car. I'm tired of throwing good money after bad by trying to get our old rattletrap fixed.* 我们只好买一辆新汽车了。我不愿意再白白花钱去修理我们那辆老破车啦。◇ spend more money in order to save a hopeless investment

moneybags

a moneybags [ə 'mʌni.bæ:gz] [话] **财主** a moneybag 直译是“钱袋”、“钱包”,当然可以按照这一意义使用。但在日常会话中,常在后边加 -s 做 moneybags,表示“有很多钱的人”的意思。最初的构思是“持有很多 moneybag 的人”。本条是复数形式,但可以当做单数、复数使用。*I'd like to be a moneybags like Bea Richman.* 我想成为象比·里克曼那样的一个财主。*The people who live in those big houses must be real moneybags.* 住在那些大房子里的人一定都是腰缠万贯的财主。◇ (a) rich (person)

monkey

a grease monkey [ə 'gri(:)s .mʌŋki] [话] **修理工** 原意为“给马达或发动机注油的人”。现在指“修理马达或发动机的人”,特别指在加油站或汽车修理厂从事这种工作的人。直译为“油猴子”,从这一称呼就可以明白,本条为戏谑语,但并没有侮蔑的意思。 *My brother is a grease monkey in a downtown garage.* 我哥哥在闹市区的一个汽车修理厂当修理工。*I'm not going to be a grease monkey all my life. Someday I plan to have my own filling station.* 我不打算一辈子总当修理工。我计划将来自己有一个加油站。*Jack was a grease monkey in the air force during the war.* 战争时期,杰克曾在空军当修理工。◇ a mechanic

have a monkey on *one's* **back** [.hævə 'mʌŋkiən ~ .bæ(:)k] [话] **成瘾** 最初的构思是:“把一个不能控制自己欲望的猴子背在身上”。本条原来只用于麻药中毒,如说:*He started taking drugs just for the fun of it, but now he has a monkey on his back.* 他最初用麻醉药只是为了好玩,但是如今已经中毒成瘾了。现在不限于麻醉药品,也常以开玩笑的口吻应用于“食品”、“烟草”或者“趣味”等等。*A: You eat a lot of chocolate. B: Yeah, I've got a monkey on my back.* 甲:你吃很多巧克力哪。乙:是啊,我已经中毒成瘾啦。 *Carl never talks about anything but baseball. He has a real monkey on his back.* 卡尔一张口就谈棒球。他真是中毒成瘾啦。如这一例句所示,常用 real 加强语气。◇ an [a drug, etc.] addict

make a monkey (out) of *someone* [.meɪkə 'mʌŋki(aud)əv ·~] [话] **嘲弄他人** 按照本条的词序翻译,为“用某人制作猴子”,也就是“使某人叫人看起来象个猴子”的意思。与 make a fool (out) of *someone* (愚弄他人) 大致同义,在以下的例句中也可以互相替换。不过,本条比较轻松一些。有一点请读者注意:它不仅仅是“开玩笑”的意思。 *Lulu made a monkey of me by telling me that the party was a masquerade.* 璐璐嘲弄我,告诉我社交晚会是一次化装舞会。如这一例句所示,省略 out 也未为不可。然而,在日常会话中,一般采取 out of ~ 的形式。 *I'll be waiting here tomorrow at noon for you to bring the money you owe me. And you'd better show up. You know what happens to people who try to make a monkey out of me.* 我明天正午在这儿等候,你要把欠我的钱送来。你还是按时前来为好。你大概知道凡是敢嘲弄我的人会是怎样的下场。 *My boy friend made a monkey out of me in front of all my friends by dancing with Sally all night.* 我的男朋友嘲弄我,整个晚上当着我所有朋友的面与萨

莉跳舞。make a monkey (out) of *oneself* 是"成为笑柄"。*I'm not about to make a monkey (out) of myself before hundreds of people. Get someone else to make the speech.* 我不想在几百人的面前使自己成为笑柄。你找个别的人讲话吧。◇ make *someone* [*oneself*] look foolish / humiliate *someone* [*oneself*]

monkey's

I'll be a monkey's uncle. [ˈaɪlbiə ˈmʌŋki ˈʌŋkl] [话] **真令人意想不到** → I'll be HORNSWOGGLED.

monkeys

more fun than a barrel of monkeys → FUN

month

a month of Sundays → SUNDAYS

moola

moola [ˈmuːˌlɑː] [话] **金钱** 在一般词典中,此词的发音均写作 [ˈmuːlə],但日常会话时发音为 [ˈmuːˌlɑː],最后的 [ɑ] 拉长。这是一个轻松的说法,在使用时与 money 完全相同。*I'm out of moola.* 我没钱了。*Wow! A hundred thousand dollars is a lot of moola!* 哎呀!十万美元可是一大笔钱啊! 也可以拼作 moolah。◇ money

moon

once in a blue moon [ˌwʌnts ɪnə ˈbluː ˈmuːn] [话] **千载难逢** 直译为"在蓝色月亮出来的时候有一次",亦即"只是在蓝色月亮出来的时候才能遇到的事情"。与汉语俗语"太阳打西边出来"的构思完全相同。在 16 世纪左右,这一表达法与 never 同义,不知什么原因,到了现代变成"极为罕见"的意思了。有人说由于气象的关系,月亮会"偶尔"看起来为蓝颜色,故云。此说不确。不管来源如何,可以认为这是强调 seldom 词义的一个表达法。常用 only 加强语气。*Earthquakes occur in this area only once in a blue moon.* 这个地区只是偶尔地发生一次地震。*He only comes here once in a blue moon.* 他只是偶尔地到这儿来一回。*I see her but once in a blue moon.* 我只是偶尔地碰见她一次。如上面的例句所示,本条主要用于表示"很少有"这样一种否定的意思,但有时也用于表示"虽然少有,但是有"这样一种肯定的意思。*Once in a blue moon I get the urge to go hiking all by myself.* 我偶尔产生一种自己去徒步旅行的愿望。顺便提一下:在歌曲或电影的题名中常常出现的 blue moon 并不是本条的"罕见的蓝色月亮",而意味着"悲伤的月亮"。◇ very seldom / (only) once in a long while

moonlight

moonlight [ˈmuːnˌlaɪt] [口] **兼差** 直译为"月光"。本条来源于如下的构思:"白天干完工作之后,在月亮出来的时候,又去干另外一种工作"。名词为 moonlighting。"moonlight 的人"叫做 a moonlighter。moonlighting 与所谓的"业余劳动"不同,大多是正式的工作。也就是说, moonlighter 指有两个 full-time job 的人,即一身兼二职。*Mr. Williams is a policeman, but he also moonlights as a night watchman at a factory.* 威廉斯先生是一位警察,夜里又在一家工厂里当看守。*Moonlighting is against the rules at our company.* 我们公司不准工作人员在别处兼差。*Many of our drivers are moonlighters.* 我们公司的许多司机在别处兼职。另外,请不要与 MOONSHINE(私酿威士忌酒)混同。◇ work at a second (nighttime) job

moonshine

moonshine [ˈmuːnˌʃaɪn] [口] **私酿威士忌** 特指美国南方农村的"私酿玉米威士忌"。人们对一般的威士忌也戏称为 moonshine。直译为"月光"。为了不被保安官或税务员看到,南方农民常在夜里,于月光照耀的山窝中私自酿造威士忌。本条即来源于此。*Many mountaineers in the South still make moonshine.* 南方的许多山地居民现在仍然私酿威士忌。moonshine 的私酿者、运输者、私卖者,一概称为 a moonshiner。*The Kamen family is proud of their tradition as moonshiners over many generations.* 卡门一家以祖祖辈辈私酿威士忌的传统而自豪。moonshine 也可以作为形容词使用,而说 moonshine whiskey (私酿的威士忌)。 *Some moonshine whiskey is very good.* 有些私酿威士忌味道很不错。◇ homemade (corn) whiskey

moron

a moron [ə ˈmoːˌrɑ(ː)n] [口] **傻瓜** 原为心理学专门名词,指"智力发育停留在 8~12 岁儿童水平的鲁钝者"。转用于日常会话,表示"傻瓜"、"笨蛋"、"呆子"等意思。多带有"判断能力不足"的意味。*Oh, why was I such a moron!* 唉,我当时怎么那样傻! 形容词为 moronic [moˈrɑ(ː)nɪk]。 *That guy is full of moronic ideas.* 那小子一肚子笨主意。另外,从心理学名词转用于口语而与 moron 当做同义词使用的有 an IDIOT, an IMBECILE,请参见 A DUMBHEAD ◇ a stupid person

Moses

Holy Moses! [ˈhouli ˈmouzəs] [话] **哎呀,天哪!** → Holy cow!

most

make the most of *something* [ˌmeɪkðə ˈmoustəv ～] [口] **最大限度地利用** 请读者注意这一表达法与 make the BESTof *something* 不同。 make the best of *something* 是"在失败、背运等不利条件下,尽到最大的努力",而 make the most of *something* 则是"最大限度地利用良好的机会、幸运等有利的条件"。 *You must learn to make the most of your opportunities.* 你必须学会最大限度地利用自己的机会。 *They are not really bad boys. It's just that when the teacher leaves the room they tend to make the most of it.* 那几个男孩子并不是真正的淘气包。他们只是在老师离开教室的时候,想要最大限度地利用一下当前的机会而已。 *This contact represents a big chance for our company, and the boss intends to make the most of it.* 这种接触对我们公司来说是一个大好机会,老板打算最大限度地去利用它。 *It's okay to stay out late tonight, isn't it, Mom? It's the biggest school dance of the year and I want to make the most of it.* 妈妈,今天晚上晚回来可以吧? 这是一年一度的最大的学校舞会,我想尽兴玩个痛快。◇ take as much advantage as possible of *something*

motion

make a motion [ˌmeɪkə ˈmouʃən] [口] **提出动议** → make a PASS at *someone*

mountain

make a mountain out of a molehill [ˌmeɪkə ˈmauntˌnaudəvə ˈmoulˌhɪ(ː)l] [口] **夸大其词,小题大作** 直译为"拿田鼠丘当做山"。16 世纪就存在的古谚。*The situation is not as serious as the newspapers make it out to be. They're just trying to make a mountain out of a molehill.* 情况并不象报纸上所说的那么严重。他们只是在竭力渲染而已。*I said I was sorry I forgot your birthday, didn't I? Stop making a mountain out of a molehill.* 我不是为忘掉你的生日而向你道歉了吗? 是吧? 不要小题大作啦。也可以用复数形式,作 mountains, molehills。*Don't let yourself be affected by what that ninny said. That guy goes through life making mountains out of molehills.* 你不要把那个傻瓜所说的话放在心上。那个家伙一向好夸大其词啊。*I was very worried at first, but as I turned the problem over in my mind, I realized I was only making a mountain out of a molehill.* 我最初曾经非常焦急,但是经过反复思索,已经明白原来我是把针尖大的问题看得比骆驼还大了。◇ (try to) make something insignificant into something big / make much ado about nothing

mountain dew → DEW

mouse

(as) poor as a church mouse [əz ˈpurəzə ˈtʃə(ː)rtʃ ˌmaus] [口] **非常穷** church mouse 是"教堂里的老鼠"。古时,教堂很穷,伙食很差。因此,教堂里的老鼠也必然经常挨饿。本条会令人想到如此贫寒的情景。 *Mr. Jones is as poor as a church mouse, but he is as honest as the* *day is long.* 琼斯先生虽然一贫如洗，但是为人非常正直。*Most of the people in this area are poor as church mice.* 这一地区的大部分人都非常穷。◇ extremely poor

(as) quiet as a mouse [əz ˈkwaɪədəzə ˈmaus] [口] **非常老实** 与 rat 恰恰相反，mouse (小老鼠)给人以老实可爱的印象。因此，as a mouse (象小老鼠一样)是在强调 quiet 一词。形容的对象只限于生物，特别多用于儿童。*Do you think Jimmy is sick? He's been quiet as a mouse all day today.* 你看吉米是不是病了？他今天一整天都安安静静。在应用于儿童的场合，言外一般含有"老实得实在值得表扬"的意味。*The children are quiet as mice now. They must be up to something.* 孩子们现在非常安静。他们一定是在淘什么气哪。在会话中可以这样说，但是一般说来，人们不用本条表示对儿童的老实"不值得表扬"的意思。另外，如这一例句所示，当主语是复数的场合，相应地要说 as mice，务请读者注意。一般用例如下：*I had expected Seth to make some suggestions at the meeting, but he sat there the whole time as quiet as a mouse.* 我本来期望塞斯在会议中会提出一些意见，但是他始终坐在那里一言未发。*People are basically selfish. They yell bloody murder when their own rights are ignored, but if it's someone else's rights that are being trampled, they remain as quiet as mice.* 人基本上是自私的。当他们自己的权利受到忽视的时候，他们大嚷大叫；如果是别人的权利受到践踏，他们就默不作声。也可以用 quietly 代替 quiet。*Amy has been in her room playing as quietly as a mouse all afternoon.* 整个下午，爱米一直安安静静地在她自己的屋子里玩。◇ very quiet / very quietly

mouth

Someone **and** *his* **big mouth.** [ˈ~ ən ˈ~ ˈbi(:)g ˈmauθ] [话] **多嘴多舌** big mouth 是"喋喋不休的大嘴"。*his* 是 *someone* 的所有格。本条逐字翻译是"某人与他那张喋喋不休的大嘴"。在由于说错话或多说话而造成严重事态的场合使用。*You and your big mouth. Why did you have to tell my wife I didn't have to work tonight?* 就是你多嘴多舌！你为什么要对我老婆讲我今天晚上不加班也可以呢？如这一例句所示，本条一般放在句子的开头部分。它不仅用于指责别人的场合，也可以用于自己多说了话的场合。在这时候不是用 I，常采取 Me and my ~.的形式。*Me and my big mouth. If I hadn't told the chief I could read German, I wouldn't have to be doing all this translation work.* 怨我自己多嘴多舌。如果我不告诉头头我能读德文，他也不会叫我干全部的翻译工作啦。*Someone* 处也可以用专有名词代替。*Jane and her big mouth. We would still be on that airplane if she hadn't complained to the stewardess that someone had stolen our passports.* 简总爱多嘴多舌。如果她不向女服务员叨唠有人偷了我们的护照，我们现在还会在那架飞机上呢。◇ *Someone* talks too much.

be born with a silver spoon in *one's* **mouth** → SPOON

be down in the mouth [ˌdaunɪnðə ˈmauθ] [话] **垂头丧气** 直译为"两个嘴角向下耷拉着"。从具体形象来看，这是一副沮丧的嘴脸。但是，从本条的意义来说，它所指的不是面部表情，而是内心的状态，至于是否有沮丧的嘴脸，则是次要的问题。可能由于自己看不见自己的 mouth，本条很少用于说话人本身，在谈到本身的场合，一般使用 be down in the DUMPS。按垂头丧气的程度来说，be down in the mouth 比 be down in the DUMPS 轻一些。*Harry is down in the mouth because he was passed over for promotion.* 哈利由于没有被晋级而垂头丧气的。除 be 动词外，常用 feel, look, seem 等。*George is feeling down in the mouth because he didn't get the job he wanted.* 乔治由于未能干上他所想望的工作而垂头丧气了。*What's the matter? You look down in the mouth today.* 怎么回事？今天你愁眉苦脸的。◇ be sad

get it straight from the horse's mouth (that ~) [ˌgedɪt ˈstreɪt frəmðə ˌhorsəz ˈmauθ] [话] **直接从本人那里打听** 原来 it 指 the horse's age(马的年龄)。本条是"马的年龄可以从马嘴里直接得知"的意思。要想知道马的年龄,只要看它的牙就没有错。这便是本条习用语的来源。转义使用时,horse 表示"本人", it 指"一般信息"。这里的 get 具有"见而得知"和"听而得知"两方面的意味。*The information about the president's retirement can't be wrong. I got it straight from the horse's mouth.* 关于总经理退休的情报不会有错。我是亲自听他本人讲的。*I got the information [news, figures, etc.] straight from the horse's mouth.* 我是直接从他(她)本人那里听到的信息[新闻、数字等]。如这一例句所示,可以用名词(短语)代替 it。另外,在某些场合,horse 也可能是"可靠方面"(如侧近人士、有关人士、详细了解情况的人士等)的意思。例如前边例句中的 president 如果不是"总经理"而是"总统"的话,一般来说,就不可能被认为是"直接从本人口中听到"。*We've got it straight from the horse's mouth that the United States is going to lower its import taxes.* 我们从可靠方面得悉,美国将要降低进口税。在这一例句中,horse 一词究竟指什么并不明确。动词一般使用 get,此外也可以用 hear, learn, find out 等。*She says she learned it straight from the horse's mouth.* 她说她是直接从当事人那里听到的。但是,在使用 get 以外的动词而后边接续 that ~的场合,不要 it。*I found out straight from the horse's mouth that they're about to go bankrupt.* 我直接听内部的人说,那个公司马上要破产啦。还有一些简单的说法,如: *This is straight from the horse's mouth.* 这是直接听当事人说的。*It came straight from the horse's mouth.* 这是他(她)本人亲自对我说的。◇ hear [get] it directly from the person(s) concerned

have *one's* **heart in** *one's* **mouth** [ˌhæv ~ ˈhɑ(:)rtn ~ ˈmauθ] [口] **吓得要命** → *one's* HEART is in *one's* mouth

one's **heart is in** *one's* **mouth** → HEART

leave a bad taste in *someone's* **mouth** → TASTE

live from hand to mouth → HAND

look a gift horse in the mouth → HORSE

put *one's* **foot in** *one's* **mouth** → FOOT

put *one's* **money where** *one's* **mouth is** → MONEY

put words into *someone's* **mouth** → WORDS

take the words out of *someone's* **mouth** → WORDS

wash *someone's* **mouth out with soap** [ˌwɑ(:)ʃ ~ ˈmauˌθaut wɪθˌsoup] [口] **用肥皂洗嘴,作为说脏话的惩罚** 最初的构思是:"说脏话会脏了嘴,要用肥皂把它洗干净"。一般的洗的方法是:用水浸湿毛巾,打上大量肥皂,然后去擦嘴的内部。*The little boy's mother washed his mouth out with soap for using a dirty word.* 那个小男孩因为用一个脏字眼儿,他母亲用肥皂洗他的嘴。有这样实际去洗刷的场合,但有时只是吓唬孩子说:"我要给你用肥皂洗嘴啦。"另有 have *one's* mouth washed out with soap 的说法,意思是"被人用肥皂洗嘴"。*Watch your language, young man. You should have your mouth washed out with soap!* 小伙子,你说话可留点神。该用肥皂给你洗洗嘴啦! ◇ *one* should be ashamed of the way *one* talks

mouthpiece

a mouthpiece [ə ˈmauθˌpi(:)s] [话] **(刑事)律师** 本来是"乐器的吹口"、"电话的送话器口"的意思。人们认为通过律师讲话就等于通过送话器打电话一样,于是就产生了本条。一般指办理刑事案件的律师。为黑社会的俚语,如果一般市民使用,就有诙谐的意味了。*Any half-decent mouthpiece should be able to beat that rap for you.* 任何二流的律师都能够使你免受刑事处分。*Mafia bosses seldom get sent up because they can afford to hire the best mouthpieces.* 黑手党的头子们很少有进监狱的,因为他们雇得起最好的律师。本条进一步发展，又用于表示“发言人”(spokesman) 的意思。*The press secretary is the President's official mouthpiece.* 新闻秘书是总统的官方发言人。因此，如果说 *He refuses to talk to me except through his mouthpiece.* 他只通过律师[发言人]同我对话。就不能明确的指出是律师还是发言人，只好根据上下文来判断。◇ a lawyer

move

get a move on [.gedə 'mu: .vɔ:n] [话] **赶快** 直译为“行动起来”。*We'd better get a move on or we'll be late.* 最好快一点，不然我们就会迟到了。*Come on, you guys, get a move on. At this rate we'll never get the work finished.* 喂，伙计们，抓紧点！照现在这样，咱们的活永远干不完呀。get a WIGGLE on 大致同义。◇ hurry (up)

movie

a blue movie [ə 'blu: 'mu:vi] [口] **色情影片** blue 除“悲伤的”一义外，还有“淫秽的”的意思。本条来源不明。大概是由于过去表演脱衣舞时常打蓝色的灯光。从黄色内容来说，可以作为在一般电影院放映的 pornographic movie 的同义语使用，但 blue movie 主要指在男人俱乐部或集会中上演的短片。*Our club shows a blue movie every Thursday night.* 每星期四晚间，我们俱乐部放映一部色情影片。*That studio specializes in blue movies.* 那个制片厂专门拍色情影片。◇ a pornographic movie

much

much less [.mʌtʃ 'le(:)s] [口] **何况** → LET alone

mud

(as) clear as mud [əz'klı(:)rəz 'mʌ(:)d] [话] **一点也不明白** 直译为“象污泥一样透亮”，这显然是个反语。不仅用于讲的话，也可以用于写的字、数学问题等等。as ~ as 中的前一个 as 常因前后的语调关系省去。*Maybe you understand it, but it's clear as mud to me.* 你也许懂，可是我一点也不明白呀。*How do I know what he's going to do? His intentions are always as clear as mud.* 我怎么会知道他想要干什么呢？他的意图永远令人摸不清楚。下一个例句是开玩笑或者是冷嘲热讽。*Thanks for your wonderful explanation. Now everything's as clear as mud.* 谢谢你的精采的说明。现在，我完全进入五里雾中了。◇ very unclear

Here's mud in your eye. [.hırz 'mʌ(:)dnjər .aı] [话] **干杯** → BOTTOMS up.

mug

a mug [ə 'mʌ(:)g] [话] **嘴脸** 本条的来源是：18 世纪时期，人们制作的陶瓷大杯(喝啤酒等用)称 (drinking) mug，上面常有人的脸部的图形。此词常含有“不大值得夸耀的面相”的意味，因此在大多的场合添加形容词 ugly (丑陋)。这是一个相当轻松的用语。*I ain't got such a bad mug, have I?* 我长得不太丑吧，是不是？*Look at the ugly mug on that guy.* 你瞧瞧那个家伙的脸，简直丑极啦。*Get your ugly mug out of the way, will ya? I can't see.* 把你那副丑陋的嘴脸缩回去好不好？我看不见了。如以上的例句所示，男人们之间常用这一表达法逗弄取笑。→ a mug SHOT ◇ a face

a mug shot → SHOT

mule

(as) stubborn as a mule [əz 'stʌbərnəzə 'mju:l] [口] **非常固执** stubborn 是“顽固”。(as) ~ as a mule 是强调“顽固”的程度的用语。mule (骡子)是一种极端顽固的动物，它一旦不想动，你怎么叫它动它也不动。*You're just wasting your breath trying to persuade Don Key. He's as stubborn as a mule.* 你劝说笨驴先生，那是徒费唇舌。他是个非常固执的家伙。*What do you mean I'm as stubborn as a mule? When it comes to being stubborn, you take the cake!* 你怎么老说我顽固透顶呢？要论顽固，老兄可是冠军啊！另外，“顽固”与“顽强”不同，(as) stubborn as a mule 的具体形象是“不论如何也不动地方”，而 (as) headstrong as a bull (象公牛一样顽强)则完全相反，它

的具体形象是"不论说什么也要前进"。◇ extremely stubborn

white mule ['hwaɪt'mjuːl] [话] **私酿玉米威士忌** 直译为"白色的骡子"。英美人在形容强烈的威士忌时,常说 It has quite a kick. (这酒真有劲儿。) 原文的 kick 本是"踢"的意思,所以这句话的字面意义为"这一脚踢得够厉害的"。人们从这个"踢"字马上想到爱踢人的骡子(mule),因而产生了本条。这里的 white 是"无色"的意思。刚酿出来的没有进行勾兑的玉米威士忌一般是无色透明的。也就是说"白色的骡子"是"无色的烈性威士忌",主要指用玉米酿造出来的。*Jeb's pappy makes the best white mule in the world.* 杰布的爸爸酿造的玉米威士忌世界第一。◇ homemade (corn) whiskey

mum

keep mum (about *something*) [ˌki(ː)p 'mʌ(ː)m] [口] **保持沉默** mum 是形容词,与 silent 同义。为双唇紧闭发音时的象声词。在作为名词使用时,有 mum's the WORD 这样一个习用语,意思是"不要声张!"本条用例如下: *We'll have to keep mum about our plans for the time being.* 关于我们的计划,目前必须严守秘密。*I'm sure they know what's going to happen. They're just keeping mum.* 他们肯定知道今后要发生什么事情。他们只是保持沉默而已。*The company has kept mum about its alleged payoffs to high government officials.* 据传那个公司贿赂政府高级官员,而那个公司则对此保持沉默。◇ remain silent (about *something*)

mum's

mum's the word ['mʌ(ː)mzðə 'wəːrd] [话] **不要声张** mum 是中古英语时代开始使用的象声词,意思是"别说话"、"别出声"。这里的 the word 是"暗号"的意思。本条直译为"沉默是暗号",使用方法与 Don't tell anyone. (不要对任何人讲) 相同。*I'm planning to change jobs, but mum's the word until after I tell the boss.* 我打算调换工作,在我向老板谈过之前,你不要声张啊。"*Mum's the word,*" *said Flo, after telling Sally of her plan to hold a surprise birthday party for her mother.* 在弗洛告诉萨莉她打算为她妈妈开一个她意想不到的庆贺生日的晚会后,又对萨莉讲:"千万别说出去啊!"使用 mum 一词的习用语还有 keep MUM。◇ don't tell anyone

murder

get away with murder [ˌgedə 'weɪwɪð 'məːrdər] [话] **做什么坏事也不受处罚** get away with 在这里是"做坏事得逞"的意思。murder 是"杀人",当然是最严重的犯罪行为。因此,作为比喻,本条具有"不论干多大的坏事也不受惩罚"的意味。这是一个夸张的表达法。*Don't kill me. You'll never get away with murder.* 你不要杀我。你杀了人,是绝对逃不出法网的。这是按本来的意义使用的例句。除此而外,一般使用肯定句。*Our office is very lax. As long as you come to work on time and always kowtow to the boss, you can get away with murder.* 我们单位是非常随便的。只要你按时上班,对头头总是卑躬屈膝,你犯天大的错误也不会受到处罚。let *someone* get away with murder (不论某人犯多大错误,对他也不处罚)这一表达法也常使用。*That teacher lets his students get away with murder.* 不论学生们干什么坏事,那位老师也不闻不问。*It's not fair. Whenever I do something wrong I always get punished, but my parents let my big brother get away with murder.* 太不公平啦。只要我做错了什么事情,总是受到惩罚,可是我大哥不管干什么坏事,爹妈却一概不问。◇ do anything *one* pleases without being reprimanded [punished]

yell bloody murder [ˌje(ː)l 'blʌdi 'məːrdər] [话] **大吵大闹** yell 是"大声喊叫"。bloody murder 是"杀人流血事件"。本条的意思是:好象见到杀人流血事件以后大喊"杀人啦"那样地叫嚷。语气非常强烈,实际是否大声喊叫并没有直接关系。*My husband will yell bloody* murder when he learns how much I've paid for this dress. 如果我的丈夫知道我这套衣服花了多少钱，他一定要大吵大闹的。Dad never says anything when Mom dents a fender, but just let me put one little scratch on the car and he yells bloody murder. 妈妈把汽车的挡板撞出凹坑，爸爸没有抱怨过一句，而我只要把汽车擦破一点皮，他就大叫大嚷起来。The union yells bloody murder every time the capitalists try to change the work rules. 资本家们一要改变劳动规章，工会便起来声嘶力竭地表示抗议。也可以应用于人或组织以外的事物。下一例句是戏谑的说法。How come dinner is so late? My stomach is yelling bloody murder. 晚饭怎么开得这么晚？我的肚子在大吵大闹哪。一般是表示愤怒，但也偶尔有由于恐怖而"吵闹起来"的场合。When the child saw the strangely dressed man approach, he started yelling bloody murder. 当那个小孩见到一个穿着奇怪衣服的男子走近的时候，吓得大嚷大叫起来了。有时用 scream [cry] bloody murder 这一表达法。Whenever a member of the government mentions revising the Constitution, the opposition starts screaming [crying] bloody murder. 每当一位政府人士提出修改宪法，反对党便大嚷大叫起来。另外，英国英语认为 bloody 一词刺激性太强，改用 blue，而讲 scream blue murder，但美国英语不使用这一表达法。◇ raise a big fuss

music

canned music [ˈkænd̩ˈmjuːzɪk] [话] **唱片音乐** 直译为"罐装的音乐"。与现场演奏的音乐相对，指用唱片或磁带录音的音乐。流行音乐唱片节目播音员的习用语。*We have some especially cool canned music coming your way to-night, folks.* 各位听众，今天晚上特别向大家播出唱片冷音乐。*They couldn't hire a dance band so we'll have to make do with canned music tonight.* 由于没有能够雇到乐队，今天晚上咱们就得用唱片音乐凑合了。→ live MUSIC ◇ recorded music

chin music [ˈtʃɪ(ː)n ˌmjuːzɪk] [话] **聊天** 直译为"下巴的音乐"。*I'm tired of you guys' chin music.* 你们这些家伙山南海北地胡侃，我已经腻味透啦。动词使用 make。*My wife loves to make chin music.* 我的老婆最喜欢聊天。◇ idle talk

face the music [ˌfeɪs ðə ˈmjuːzɪk] [话] **承担后果** 这是由美军处罚士兵的方法而来的表达法。直至不久以前为止，如果一个士兵已经被定罪，必须从营里被开除，就要全营列队，宣读此人的各种罪状。每宣读一种罪状，就敲一阵鼓。因此，face the music 就是"面对敲响的音乐"的意思。这个 music 指"自己失误或胡作非为的后果"，根据情况的不同，包括处罚、批评、责难、申斥、对方的恼怒等等。*If you continue doing something wrong long enough, sooner or later you're going to have to face the music.* 如果你继续不断地作恶，时间长了，早晚有一天会受到应有的惩罚。*Almost all Americans were angry because the President refused to face the music.* 由于总统拒绝接受批评，几乎所有的美国人都被激怒了。*The boss is waiting in his office for us to come and explain why we failed to finish this work on time. The sooner we go and face the music the better.* 老板在他的办公室里等着咱们前去说明未能按期完成这个工作的理由。咱们还是早点去接受批评为好。*I got a very bad report card this time. Now I've got to go home and face the music.* 我这回得到的成绩通知书实在太坏了。现在得回家挨一顿训斥啦。◇ accept the consequences (of *one's* actions)

live music [ˈlaɪvˈmjuːzɪk] [口] **现场演奏的音乐** 直译为"活的音乐"，与用唱片或磁带录音的音乐相对。*Mary's stereo is great. It's just like listening to live music.* 玛丽的立体音响棒极啦。简直跟听现场演出一样。→ canned MUSIC ◇ music played in person

be music to *someone's* **ears** [ˈmjuːzɪktə ~ ˈɪːrz] [口] **声音悦耳** 直译为"对于某人

的耳朵是音乐”，这是“象音乐一样好听”的意思。究竟什么声音“好听”，这是极端主观的事情。因此，在使用本条时，“好听”的对象会因人而异，决不能千篇一律。例如，对于穿越大沙漠而来到海边的人来说，*The sound of the waves was music to his ears.* 他感到波涛的声音非常悦耳。幼儿哭叫，他人听起来完全是噪音，但由他的父母看来，*The sound of our baby's crying is music to our ears.* 我家小宝宝的哭声简直跟音乐一样。另外，“悦耳”的东西不限于声音，言语也可以。*When the management agreed to raise our salaries ten percent, it was music to our ears.* 当听到公司领导同意将我们的工资提高10%的时候，我们感到非常高兴。◇ be a most welcome sound / be delightful to listen to / be wonderful news

muster

pass muster [ˌpæ(:)s ˈmʌstər] [口] 及格

pass 是“通过检查”的意思。muster 是“召集士兵”的意思，在这里当然是名词。在军队里，每次集合以后，照例由军士或军官检查衣服、鞋帽等。本条的原义就是“集合时检查合格”。*The soldier didn't pass muster because his shoes were not shined. (= The soldier's shoes were not shiny enough to pass muster.)* 那个兵由于皮鞋擦得不亮而没有通过检查。但是，在军队平日的集合时，检查并不十分严格。因此，当本条用于比喻的时候，也有“凑合过得去”的意味。*Though a rather dull student in college, he was able to pass muster as a scholar in the country village where he went to teach upon graduating.* 他在大学读书时并不出众，但是毕业后去农村任教，在那里够得上一个学者了。*I don't have the money to buy any new clothes for my job interview. Do you think this old, frayed suit will pass muster?* 我根本没有钱去为就业面试买一套新衣服，你认为这身磨破的旧衣服能凑合过去吗？也有为了期待对方的夸奖而使用本条的场合，例如：*I bought a new dress and had my hair done for our date tonight. Do I pass muster?* 为了今天晚上约会，我买了一套新衣服，又做了头发。你看我够漂亮了吗？◇ be accepted / be [look] good enough

mutt

a mutt [ə ˈmʌ(:)t] [话] 狗 → a POOCH

N

nah

nah [ˈnɑː] [俗]不 → NAW

nail

a coffin nail [ə ˈkɔ(ː)fən ˌneɪl] [话] **一支烟** 直译"棺材钉"。这是对"纸烟"的一种黑色幽默的称呼,意思是:"吸一支烟就等于往自己的棺材上钉一颗钉子"。*Buy me a pack of coffin nails, will you?* 去给我买合烟,好吗? *Can I bum a coffin nail from you?* 你能赏给我一支烟吗? 此外,亦称 a cancer STICK 。◇ a cigarette

fight (*someone* [*something*]) **tooth and nail** → TOOTH

hit the nail on the head [ˌhɪtðəˈneɪl ɔnðəˈhe(ː)d] [口] **抓住要点** 直译为"打钉子的帽儿"。可以按这一意义使用,例如:*Be sure to hit the nail on the head or you'll mar the wall.* 你钉钉子一定要打到帽儿上,否则会弄坏墙的。作为比喻是"抓住要点"、"十分中肯"的意思。*Mr. Smith is good at discussing generalities, but when it comes to specifics he never quite hits the nail on the head.* 史密斯先生在讨论一般性的问题时说得头头是道,但是在研究每个细节的时候,他一向抓不住要点。常用 right 加强语气。*The President's remarks hit the nail right on the head.* 总统的几句话恰恰说到点子上了。*Jack hit the nail right on the head when he said that our biggest weakness is in product development.* 杰克讲我们最大的弱点是在产品研制方面,他的话十分中肯。本条几乎完全用于"说话"的场合,但也偶尔有如下的说法:*We hit the nail on the head with our new product.* 我们的新产品一炮打响。◇ express things accurately and concisely

nailed

everything that isn't nailed down [ˌevriθɪŋ ðəˌdɪdnːeɪldˈdaun] [口] **一切的一切** → everything but the kitchen SINK

name

the name of the game [ðə ˈneɪməðə ˈgeɪm] [话] **最要紧的事** 直译为"游戏的名称"。最初的构思大概是这样:"一种游戏如果没有名称,这种游戏就不能成立",也就是说"对于一种游戏来说,最重要的是它的名称"。*Schools seems to have gotten off the track somewhere. Nowadays, instead of a well-rounded education, the name of the game seems to have become high test scores.* 学校似乎在什么地方迷失了正确的方向。现在,不是推行全面的教育,而是把在考试中取得好的分数当作最要紧的事情。*Alcohol-free beer will never become popular. After all, for people who like to drink, getting high is the name of the game.* 没有酒精的啤酒绝对不会受到欢迎。对于喜欢喝酒的人来说,兴奋陶醉毕竟是最重要的事情。根据最初的构思"一种游戏没有名称就不能成立",这一表达法又用于表示"规则"、"规定"、"规律"的意味。*I can't give you a raise apart from the other people in your section. I'm sorry, but that's the name of the game.* 我不能不顾你们科里其他的人而单独给你提高工资。非常遗憾,但这是规章制度呀。*In the capitalist world, dog-eat-dog is the name of the game today.* 在资本主义社会,弱肉强食是当前司空见惯的现象。◇ the most important thing / the way things are

name-dropper

a name-dropper [ə ˈneɪmˌdrɑ(ː)pər] [口] **常以仿佛很熟悉的口吻谈到著名人物的人** 这里的 drop 是"从嘴里掉出来",即"若无其事地说"的意思。本条用于那些由于虚荣心作怪而到处乱提许多著名人士的名字的人。所谓“著名人士”并不限定全国知名的人物，也包括本地区的“名人”，如富豪、公司总经理、市镇首长等。另外，还用于把只有一面之交的人当作自己的亲密朋友来讲的场合，例如采取“As I was telling Mrs. Kaneari the other day ....”(前几天我告诉卡奈阿莉太太说……)之类的方式提名道姓信口雌黄的场合。*Mrs. Mureeda is a name-dropper if there ever was one. To hear her talk, you'd think that the mayor and half the company presidents in town come to dinner almost every week at her house.* 象穆利达夫人那样爱讲著名人士的名字的人简直举世无双。你一听她的谈话，就会以为市长和一半公司的总经理几乎每个星期都到她家里去吃晚饭。*Most social climbers are name-droppers.* 那些削尖脑袋往上流社会钻营的人，大多喜欢提著名人士的名字。如果不是出于虚荣心，而是真正熟悉著名人士，当然就不算是 name- dropper 了。*He's not a name- dropper. He actually knows all those people he mentions.* 他不是一个从虚荣心出发爱讲著名人士的名字的人，凡是他提到的人物，他的确都相识。还有 name-dropping 的形式，意思是“爱讲著名人士的名字的狂热病”。*I'm sick and tired of that guy's name- dropping. You'd think he doesn't know anyone who isn't listed in Who's Who.* 对于那个家伙爱讲著名人士的名字的狂热病，我简直头痛死啦。你会以为凡是《名人录》上查不到的人他一个也不认识呢。◇ a person who intimates that *he* knows (many) well-known people

names

call *someone* **names** [ˌkɔːl ～ˈneɪmz] [口] **骂人** 由于 names 是复数形式，所以挨骂者一般也是一个以上。*When the soldiers set fire to the woman's house, she screamed at them, calling them names.* 当士兵们纵火烧毁那女人的房子的时候，她拚命叫喊，对他们破口大骂。如下一例句所示，挨骂者是一个也可以。*A: Lem's a dirty coward. B: Let's not have any of that talk. I don't hold with calling a man names behind his back.* 甲：列姆是一个卑鄙的胆小鬼。乙：咱们不谈这类的话吧，我不赞成在背地骂人。常用被动语态，例如：*I've been called all kinds of names in my life, but never an omphaloskeptic!* 我这一辈子挨过各种各样的骂，但是还从来没有人叫我“梦想猪”！omphaloskeptic [ˌɑmfəloˈskeptɪk] 是“望着自己的肚脐苦思冥想的人”，因为这个词非常新奇，所以在戏谑的场合把它当作骂人的用语了。*A: I don't care for fools and liars. B: You wouldn't be calling me names now, would you?* 甲：我不喜欢混蛋和说谎的人。乙：你这不是在骂我吧？请读者注意：这一表达法不是指打情骂俏之类的骂，而是指使用肮脏字眼的大骂或臭骂。◇ give *someone* uncomplimentary labels

nap

a cat nap → a CATNAP

napping

catch *someone* **napping** [ˌkætʃ ～ ˈnæːpɪŋ] [口] **乘虚而入** 直译为“发现某人在打瞌睡”。*The boss caught me napping at my desk today.* 今天老板发现我在办公时间打瞌睡了。转用于表示“乘其不备”、“乘虚而入”的意思。这里的 catch 与 catch *someone* by surprise (出其不意)或 catch *someone* off guard (攻其不备)中的 catch 相同。又，nap 本义“打盹儿”、“假寐”，转义为“放松警惕”、“松懈”、“发懒”。*The sudden attack by carrier- based planes caught the whole country napping.* 正当整个国家放松警惕的时候，从航空母舰上起飞的飞机进行了突然的袭击。*As a spy, your first duty is to remain alert. You must never be caught napping.* 作为谍报人员，你的第一个职责是保持警惕，绝对不能麻痹大意。以上两个例句中的 catch *someone* napping 可以用前边谈到的 catch *someone* off guard 代换，意思几乎相同。但是在下一例句中，如果使用后者就有些不自然了。*The chief seemed de-*

termined to find some excuse to fire me, but try as he might, he was never able to catch me napping. 科长似乎有意寻找某种口实把我开除，但是不论他怎样费尽心机，却始终抓不住我工作中的缺点。catch *someone* off guard 原为击剑用语，本来的意思是"在比赛中，对于防守严密的对手，要乘其一点点的疏忽进行攻击"。在使用这一表达法时，总是设想有一个能攻能守的对手，而表示"抓住对手的空挡"的意思。因此，前面的两个例句可能使用这一表达法。但是，最后一个例句中的 catch *someone* napping 是"工作上的疏忽或偷懒"，并没有设想科长直接前来进行攻击的情况，所以换上表示"抓住空挡"的 catch *someone* off guard 就有些不自然了。◇ take *someone* by surprise / come upon *someone* in an inalert condition

narrow

have a narrow squeak [ˌhævə ˌnærə ˈskwiːk] [话] **幸免于难** → have a close SHAVE

native

go native [ˌgou ˈneɪdɪv] [口] **入乡随俗**

这里的 native (本地的或本地人的)为形容词，是系动词 go (成为某种状态)的表语。本条意为"按照当地人的方式去进行"。在过去英国拥有许多殖民地的时代，go native 的意思是"模仿未开发地区的风俗习惯"，在现代，不是指"模仿土著"，大多用于表示"模仿他国的或相异的风俗习惯"的意味。也就是说，美国人到法国去，可以 go native；汉族人前往少数民族地区，学习当地的风俗习惯，同样能够叫 go native。*George has really gone native since he has been living in Bavaria. He wears short pants, drinks nothing but beer, and has even learned to yodel.* 乔治自从居住在巴伐利亚以后，已经完全入乡随俗了。他穿短裤，只喝啤酒，甚至学会了唱约德尔调。*Going native is becoming meaningless in Japan for Westerners nowadays since so many Japanese sleep in beds, eat with knives and forks, and wear Western clothes.* 现在，西方人到日本入乡随俗越来越没有意义了，因为许许多多的日本人睡在床上，用刀叉吃饭，身穿西服。*Mrs. Jones was looking forward to going native until she found that the natives didn't wear any clothes.* 琼斯太太一直想要学习土著的风俗习惯，等到她发现土著居民一丝不挂之后，满腔热情才凉了下去。◇ follow the dress and customs of the natives

naught

come to naught [ˌkʌmtə ˈnɔːt] **化为泡影**

naught 又拼写作 nought，两者发音相同，意思是"无"，作为数字使用时则表示"零"。come to naught 直译为"结果达到无"。汉语成语叫"化为乌有"，俗话说"结果等于零"，构思相同。本条有点生硬，常用 all 加强语气。*Though they fought long and hard against the rising flood waters, when the dam broke all their efforts came to naught.* 虽然他们面对不断上涨的洪水苦战很长时间，但当水坝决堤的时候，他们所有的努力都化成了泡影。*Unless we can borrow the money by Friday, our efforts to save the company will come to naught.* 除非我们能够在星期五之前借到钱，我们拯救公司的一切努力都将化为泡影。*I raised my son as best I could, but I'm afraid all my efforts have come to naught.* 我曾千方百计把我的儿子培育成人，但是很遗憾，我的一切努力似乎都白搭了。*If you don't cooperate, all our plans will come to naught.* 如果你不合作的话，咱们的整个计划就会化为泡影了。如以上的例句所示，一般使用 come to naught，但也说 come to nothing。◇ end in failure / become meaningless

naw

naw [ˈnɔː] [俗] **不** no 的轻松表达法。使用率低于 yes 的轻松说法 YEAH。特别是有文化的人，除了同伴之间，很少讲这个词。*A: Goin' to the movies tonight? B: Naw, I gotta stay home and study.* 甲：今天晚上去看电影吗？乙：不，我得在家里温习功课。有时也说 nah [ˈnɑː]。◇ no

NCO

an NCO [ə ˌnenˌsi(ː)ˈou] [话] **军士** → a NONCOM

near-sighted

near-sighted [ˈnɪ(ː)rˌsaɪdəd] [口] **近视的** 人们常这样说: a near-sighted person (近视的人), I'm near-sighted. (我的眼睛近视。)有时 SHORT-SIGHTED [ˈʃort-ˌsaɪdəd] 也用于表示同一意义,但此词如果第二音节的重音与第一音节相同,作 [ˈʃortˈsaɪdəd],则一般表示"鼠目寸光"的意味。反义词"远视的"为 far-sighted (→ FAR-SIGHTED①)。*I'm a bit near-sighted.* 我的眼睛有一点儿近视。*Our daughter has been near-sighted since birth.* 我们的女儿生下来就是近视眼。最近,near-sighted 常被去掉连字符,而拼写为 nearsighted。◇ able to see only nearby objects clearly

neck

break *one's* **neck** (*doing*[*to do*] *something*) [ˌbreɪk ~ ˈne(ː)k] [话] **千辛万苦** 可以按照字面意义使用,如说: *Mr. Smith fell down and broke his neck.* 史密斯先生摔倒了,折断了颈骨。一般来说,颈骨一断就活不成了。因此,在作为比喻使用的时候,只用否定式,或者加上 almost 等修饰性副词,实际上表示"颈骨没有折断就行了"的意思。这一表达法在拼命干什么事情而被弄得筋疲力尽的场合使用。*We almost broke our necks getting Mr. Smith to the hospital on time.* 我们把史密斯先生及时抬到医院,简直累得快断了气。*I all but broke my neck trying to finish my homework on time.* 我为了按期完成家庭作业,简直快把命都搭上了。常在说讽刺话的时候使用。*A: Yeah. I'll be glad to help you if I ever find time. B: Thanks. Don't break your neck.* 甲:是的,只要我有时间,愿意为您效劳。乙:太感谢了。可不要有伤贵体呀。*The government doesn't seem to be breaking its neck to help the unemployed.* 政府好象并没有费尽力气去救济失业者。◇ take great trouble and effort (in *doing* [to *do*] *something*) ((不加 almost 等))

a millstone around *someone's* **neck** → MILLSTONE

neck (*with someone*) [ˈne(ː)k] [话] **搂脖子** 男女互相拥抱,爱抚肩膀以上的部分。*When I walked into the living room, my son was necking with his fiancée on the sofa.* 当我走进起居室的时候,我的儿子正在沙发上同他的未婚妻搂着脖子亲热呢。*There were several couples necking on benches in the park.* 在公园的长凳上,有几对情侣在搂着脖子亲热。◇ kiss and caress (*someone* [each other])

be neck and neck [ˌnekəˈnːe(ː)k] [口] **势均力敌** 由赛马用语发展而来。原指两匹或更多的马把脖子 (neck) 并成一排向前奔跑。汉语成语叫"并驾齐驱"。*The two horses were neck and neck as they entered the homestretch.* 那两匹马一进入终点直道就并驾齐驱了。作为比喻,在汽车比赛、选举、猜谜比赛、以及其他各种竞赛中广泛使用。*When the votes were half counted, the two candidates were still neck and neck.* 当选票已经计算一半的时候,两个候选人依然势均力敌,不相上下。在一定的情况下,也可以使用 be 动词以外的动词,例如: *The three leading teams are fighting neck and neck for the pennant.* 最佳的三个队势均力敌,正在为夺得锦标而奋斗。另外,也可以以 neck-and-neck 的形式作为专门修饰名词的形容词使用。*The two debating teams are in a neck-and-neck battle for first place.* 两个辩论小组正在为夺魁展开势均力敌的斗争。◇ be battling evenly

a neck of the woods [ə ˌnekəðə ˈwu(ː)dz] [话] **地带** 原是"森林地带的村落"的意思,后来仅指"地带"而言,主要是在谈到不大熟悉的场所时使用,所指范围一般也都很模糊,如"这一带"、"那一带"等。如果与城市名称一起使用,不仅意味着那个城市,也包括那个城市的周围地区在内。为了统一起见,本条条头用的是 a neck of the woods,但在实际上,用不定冠词的情况很少,大多使用 this, that, your 等,并把第一重音放在这些词的上边。*You're from the South, are you? I've never been in your neck of the woods.* 你是南方人吧?我从来没有到过你们那一带。*We visited Alaska last fall. It really gets cold in that neck of the woods.* 去年秋天,我们到阿拉斯加去了。那个地区可真够冷的啊。*Maine, you say? That's a neck of the woods I'd like to visit someday.* 你是说缅因州吗?我很想在什么时候去那一带走一走。◇ an area

a pain in the neck → PAIN

save *one's* **own neck** [ˌseɪv～ ˌouˈnːe(ː)k] [话] **只顾自己逃命** → save *one's* own SKIN

stick *one's* **neck out** [ˌstɪk ～ˈne(ː)ˌkaut] [话] **挺身而出** 本条用于自己冒着危险出来说话或行动的场合。最初的构思是:鸡在被宰的时候,很愚蠢地把脖子伸出去,仿佛在说:"你割头好啦!"大多指一种有意识的坚决行动。*If we don't stick our necks out once in a while and take some risks, this company will never grow any larger.* 如果我们不偶尔出动去冒一些风险,这个公司就永远扩大不了。*Mr. Green's proposal offers us a wonderful opportunity. I think we should stick our necks out and accept it.* 格林先生的提议向我们提供了一个极好的机会。我认为我们应该敢于冒风险,接受它。*When I got into trouble with the boss, Walt stuck his neck out and interceded for me.* 当我与老板发生纠纷的时候,沃尔特挺身而出为我斡旋。也常使用 stick out *one's* neck 的形式。*I wouldn't stick out my neck for that guy. He never appreciates a favor.* 我不愿意为那个家伙去冒风险。他从来不感激别人的好意。◇ act boldly (despite the risk) / risk (the) danger

be up to *one's* **neck**(in *something*) [ˌʌptə ～ˈne(ː)k] [话] **转动不开** 直译为"连脖子都泡到里边"。*The river was deeper than we had anticipated, and we were soon up to our necks in the current.* 那条河比我们想象的深,我们下去不一会儿,水就没脖子了。作为比喻,用法如下: *I won't have time to see you this week. I'm up to my neck in work.* 这个星期我没有时间与你相会了。我工作排得满满的,动不了窝。*We can't afford a new car. We're up to our necks in debt already.* 我们没有余钱去买一辆新汽车。我们已经满身是债,周转不开啦。除了工作繁忙或债务缠身外,在由于发生纠纷而不得脱身的场合,或者由于刑事犯罪眼看要东窗事发的场合,也使用这一表达法。*If the police discover that those gloves are mine, I'm going to be up to my neck in trouble.* 如果警察发现那付手套是我的,我可就没有脱身的余地了。*Sam wanted to back out but couldn't. He found that he was already up to his neck.* 萨姆想要中途撒手,但是已欲罢不能了,他发现自己陷入得太深了。in *something* 可以移到前边,例如: *I'm in this thing up to my neck, thanks to you.* 托你的福,我在这件事情上已经动不了窝儿啦。有时也可以用 be up to *one's* ears [eyebrows, eyeteeth, eyeballs] (in *something*),意思是"一直泡到耳朵、眼眉、犬齿、眼珠"。*I'm up to my ears in homework.* 家庭作业太多,我简直动不了地方。偶尔用 the 代替 *one's*,而说 be up to the neck。◇ be buried / be completely involved

necktie

a necktie party → PARTY

need

do away with the need for *something* [ˌduəˈweɪ wɪðːə ˈniːdfər ～] [口] **使失去某种必要性** → DO away with *something* [*someone*]

needle

be like looking for a needle in a haystack [laɪk ˌlukənfərə ˈni(ː)dl ɪnə ˈheɪˌstæ(ː)k] [口] **如海底捞针一样** 这一表达法非常古老,在莎士比亚以前已经定型。直译为"象在干草垛 (haystack) 上寻一根针 (needle) 似的",任何人都很容易理解。经常用于在极大的范围内搜寻一个相对来说极小的对象的场合。*We gave up trying to find my father at the football* *game. With thousands of people in the stadium, it was like looking for a needle in a haystack.* 在足球比赛的时候，我们放弃了去找我父亲的念头。体育场中人山人海，那简直象大海捞针一样。也可以说 be like trying to find a needle in a haystack。*I lost a contact lens somewhere in the park, but I didn't even look for it. It would have been like trying to find a needle in a haystack.* 我在公园的什么地方丢失了隐形眼镜片，我连找都没有找。那象大海捞针一样，找也没有用处。◇ be all but impossible to find (*something* [*someone*])

needles

be on pins and needles → PINS

nerve

get up the nerve (to *do something*) [ge,dʌpðə 'nə:rv] [口] **鼓起勇气** nerve 一词自古以来被认为具有"精力、胆量、勇气的源泉"的意味，现在人们用它表示精力、胆量或勇气。在本条中，nerve 是"勇气"，get up 是"鼓起"。the 有"充分的"的意思。整体直译为"鼓起足够的勇气"。*She finally got up the nerve to jump from the burning building.* 她终于鼓足勇气，从失火的建筑物上跳了下去。人们常这样说，但比较起来，与表示"能力"的 can 或 be able to 一起使用的情况更多一些。*I wish I could get up the nerve to ask the boss for a raise.* 我真希望自己能够有足够的勇气去请求老板给我提高工资啊。*The sheriff wasn't able to get up the nerve to challenge the gunfighter.* 保安官没能鼓起勇气向那个持枪的歹徒挑战。常用 enough (足够的)取代 the，意思不变。*Jack wants to ask Betty for a date, but apparently he can't get up enough nerve.* 杰克很想与贝蒂约会，但是他显然未能鼓起足够的勇气。另外还有生硬一点儿的说法，即用 call forth (唤起)或 gather (聚集)代替 get up，而讲 call forth [gather] the [enough] nerve。也可以用 sufficient 和 courage 分别代替同义词 enough 和 nerve，而讲 get up [call forth, gather] sufficient courage。在写正式文章的时候，如果全部代换，作 call forth [gather] sufficient courage (to do *something*)，这要比部分代换高雅得多。◇ gather sufficient courage

have the nerve to *do something* [,hævðə 'neə:rvtə ～] [话] ①**有……的勇气**；②**厚着脸皮……** 直译为"有足够的神经去干某事"。在这里，nerve 是"粗大的神经"，从好的方面说，指"勇气"、"胆量"；从坏的方面说，指"厚颜无耻"、"死皮赖脸"。在使用解 ①的时候，否定句和虚拟语气占绝大多数。*I wish I had the nerve to go up in an airplane.* 但愿我有乘飞机的勇气啊。*He didn't have the nerve to pull the trigger.* 他没有射击的胆量。在使用解 ②的时候，几乎没有否定句。*He had the nerve to get up and walk out in the middle of my speech.* 我正在讲演的时候，他居然厚着脸皮站起来走了。另外，有一种情况是：在本人看起来是"勇气"，而在他人看来却是"厚颜无耻"或"死皮赖脸"。因此，同样一件事会产生两种说法：① *I wish I had the nerve to tell him how sloppy his work is.* 但愿我有足够的勇气告诉他他的工作是多么草率。② *You mean you have the nerve to tell me how to do my job?* 你这是厚颜无耻地来教导我怎样干我的工作啦？在 ② 的场合，have the nerve to *do something* 的 *something* 当然必须是讲话者感到不适宜、不愉快的内容。不过，这一表达法在一个句子中究竟应该是 ①的意义还是 ②的意义，并没有决定性的准则，最后只能根据上下文来判断。与 ②的意义、用法完全相同的表达法有 have the GALL to *do something*。◇ ① have enough courage to *do something* ② be so insolent as to *do something*

nerves

get on *someone's* **nerves** [,gedɔ(:)n ～ 'nə:rvz] [口] **使人心烦** 这里的 get on 是"刺激"、"扰乱"的意思。本条直译为"刺激(或扰乱)某人的神经"。*Talkative women [Taciturn men] get on my nerves.* 多嘴多舌的女人[一杠子压不出屁来的男人]最使我心烦。*That guy gets on my* *nerves. He's always bragging about how he's going to be somebody someday.* 那个家伙烦死我啦。他一天到晚吹牛,说他将来一定会成为伟大人物。*The constant noise and bright lights of the big city get on some people's nerves.* 有些人对大城市的不断的噪音和耀眼的灯光感到厌烦。*Small children soon get on my husband's nerves.* 一有幼小的孩子,我的丈夫马上就感到心烦。通过以上的例句可以看出,get on *someone's* nerves 是一个多次反复刺激神经的过程,因此,这一表达法只能用于"不断地对神经产生恶劣影响"的场合。如果只是一次半次或者在一瞬之间觉得心里不痛快,在汉语里同样可以说"使人心烦",但在英语中不能使用本条。这一点务请读者注意。◇ irritate *someone*

set *someone's* **nerves on edge** [ˌset ~ ˈnəːrvzɔ(ː) ˌneːdʒ] [口] **使某人心烦意乱** 直译为"使人感到自己的神经好象用砂轮研磨一般"(关于 set ~ on edge 的说明,请参阅 set *someone's* TEETH on edge 条)。类似的表达法有 get on *someone's* NERVES,但没有本条语气强烈。例如说 *The noise gets on my nerves.* 这种闹声使我心烦。表示这种 noise (闹声)还可以勉强忍耐;如果说 *The noise sets my nerves on edge.* 这种闹声使我心烦意乱。这就超过忍耐的限度了。*The constant bickering that goes on in the office every day sets my nerves on edge.* 每天每日办公室里经常不断有人吵嘴,实在弄得我心烦意乱。*I'm sorry I barked at you. This long wait for news of my son's whereabouts has set my nerves on edge.* 我对你发了脾气,对不起。由于久等关于我儿子的下落的消息,我心烦意乱。*one's* nerves are on edge 表示状态,是"正在心烦意乱"的意思。*I don't know what's wrong with me today. For some reason my nerves are on edge.* 今天我似乎出了什么毛病,不知为什么总是心烦意乱。◇ drive *someone* to distraction / make *someone* extremely irritable.

nest

feather *one's* **nest** [ˌfeðər ~ ˈne(ː)st] [口] **自饱私囊** 直译为"往自己的巢里铺羽毛",这指的是小鸟;如果是人类的话,往自己的家里弄的就是"金钱"了。大多用于"以不正当的方法"捞钱的场合,但不限定如此。不论哪种情况,都没有什么好的意味。*It was discovered that the chairman of the board was feathering his nest with company funds.* 董事长把公司的资金饱了私囊,这事已经被人发现。特别是在会话中,为了加强语气,常在 nest 之前加上 own。*The mayor was accused of using the taxpayers' money to feather his own nest.* 市长被指责为用纳税人的钱饱自己的私囊。*I wouldn't do business with that man. He's only interested in feathering his own nest.* 我可不跟那个人做生意。他一心一意往自己的腰包里弄钱。◇ enrich *oneself*

new

spanking new [ˈspæŋkəˈnːjuː] [口] **崭新的** spanking 是强调 new 的词。本条与 brand-new 类似,但 brand-new 用于形容抽象的概念,如说 a brand-new idea (崭新的想法),而本条则专用于具体的东西,如引人注目的新产品等。*This boat is spanking new.* 这只小船是崭新的。主要用于"物",但也可以用于"人",例如:*The Browns have a spanking new baby.* 布朗家有一个新出生的婴儿。◇ absolutely new / brand-new

What's new? → WHAT'S

news

bad news [ˈbæːdˈnjuːz] [话] **添麻烦的人** 本条最主要的意义当然是"坏消息",但也可以指人而言,意思是"添麻烦的人"、"危险人物"、"讨厌鬼"。最初的构思是:"那个家伙到哪里,哪里就必定出麻烦,因此,只要那个家伙一露面,本身就是个坏消息"。单数和复数主语皆可使用。*That guy's bad news. He's always telling tales out of school.* 那个家伙是个添麻烦的人,他总是泄漏别人的秘密。*Loan sharks are bad news.* 放高利贷的是一些非常讨厌的家伙。◇ (a person) best avoided

a news hound → HOUND

nibs

his nibs [ˌhɪz ˈnɪ(ː)bz] [话] **那位老爷** 关于 nibs 的语源,最有说服力的主张是:此词原为 nobility (贵族),后简称 nob,又按发音转成 nab,最终变为 nibs 了。经常采取 his nibs 的形式,这是模仿对国王或皇帝的敬称 His Majesty (陛下)而来的一种讽刺语,一般用作对自己所讨厌的上级或长辈的轻蔑的称呼。因此,不能对人当面使用这一表达法。*What's eating his nibs today? He almost took my head off.* 那位老爷今天吃什么耗子药啦?他老是对我气势汹汹地叫嚷。*His nibs, the section chief, wants to see you.* 科长老爷叫你去。有时模仿 His Majesty,将 h 和 n 大写。*A: What did the boss call you for? B: His Nibs desired to inform me that my work was not up to scratch.* 甲:老板找你有什么事情?乙:经理大人想要告诉我说我的工作不够水准。另外,因为是 his nibs,所以一般指男性而言,但在某种情况下,用 her nibs 也未为不可。◇ the boss [chief, etc.] / his majesty

nice

nice and ~ [ˈnaɪsn ˈ~] [话] **非常** → GOOD and ~

nick

in the nick of time [ˌɪnðə ˈnɪkəv ˈtaɪm] [口] **在恰好的时候** 3 世纪以前就有的表达法。nick 的字面意义为用刀子在木头上刻出的 V 字形凹槽。古时候,为了记载时间、竞技的分数、金额等,常采取在木头上刻槽的方法。例如,在踢足球的时候,刚要结束又踢进一球,这次得分就叫做 the nick in time,也就是"在恰好的时候又刻一个槽"。有人说本条来源于此,但无确切证据。不管来源如何,这里的 the nick 解释为"很小的一段时间"比较妥当。本条的整个意思是"正在节骨眼的时候赶上了"。*The burglar was just about to get away, but the police arrived in the nick of time.* 窃贼正要逃走的时候,警察恰好赶到了。*A: Did I make it? B: In the nick of time. They were just about to leave without you.* 甲:我赶上了吗?乙:刚刚赶上。再差一点儿,他们就扔下你启程啦。*The ball arrived at the plate in the nick of time to get the runner out.* 球在最关键的时刻回到本垒,使跑垒的人出局了。在强调的场合,一般是采取 just in the nick of time 或者 in the very ~的形式。例如:*When the company announced it was bankrupt only two days after I had sold my stock, I realized that, unknowingly, I had acted just in the nick of time.* 我卖出股票刚刚两天,那家公司就宣布破产了,这时我感到,冥冥之中我正在节骨眼上搞对了。*In the very nick of time I raised my head to see the car bearing down upon me.* 我正巧抬头看到汽车向我冲了过来。◇ just in time

night

Good night. [ˈguːdˈnaɪt] [话] **哎呀,天哪!** 同样意义的 Good God. 的委婉说法。因为人们认为在这种场合使用 God (神)一词是大不敬,所以用 night 代替 God, night 没有特殊意义。与 GEE. 或 GOLLY. 相似,但按 Gee. < Golly. < Good night. 的顺序,语气一个比一个强烈。因此, Good night. 与 Gee 或者 Golly.不同,一般用于真动感情,特别震惊的场合。*Good night! Look at all those termites!* 哎呀,天哪! 怎么这么多白蚁呀! *Good night! Do you mean to tell me they're all dead?* 哎呀,天哪! 你是告诉我说他们全都死了吗?根据上下文,有时不是表示大吃一惊,而是强烈地表示失望的心情。*Good night. This is the worst hand I've ever been dealt.* 哎呀,天哪!我一辈子也没有起过这么坏的一手牌。也可以说 Great day. 意思和用法与 Good night.完全相同。*Great day! Look at this mess the children have made.* 哎呀,天哪! 你看孩子们把屋里搞得乱七八糟的样子。Great day! 是 Great God! 的委婉表达法,如果加上 in the morning,语气就更进一步增强了。*Great day in the morning! The bridge has been washed away!* 哎呀,我的老天爷!桥被大水冲跑啦! Good GRIEF . 是一

个与 Good night. 或 Great day.大致意义相同的表达法,但 Good grief! 不仅表示吃惊和失望,而且充满令人目瞪口呆或令人难以相信的意味。◇ Oh, no!

make a night of it [ˌmeɪkə ˈnaɪdəvɪt] [口] **通宵饮酒作乐** 直译为“制作一夜”。it 虚指情况,并不特代某一名词,只能算是成语的一个部件。例如: *On the evening of our graduation, we all went out and made a night of it.* 在我们举行毕业典礼那天晚上,我们全体出动,通宵饮酒作乐。在这句话里,也可以认为 it 是指 graduation。但在下一例句中,从上下文就看不出指的是什么了。*I'm feeling a bit under the weather today. I'm afraid that I made too much of a night of it last night.* 我觉得今天还有几分醉意。昨天夜里饮酒作乐,我大概喝得太多啦。所谓“制作一夜”,当然是“通宵达旦”的意味,但是在实际上,如果是“直到深夜”或“直到半夜”,也可以使用 make a night of it。也就是说,这是一个夸张的表达法,“通宵达旦”的字眼只是形容酒宴比平日盛大而已。因此,仅从 make a night of it 这一表达法本身,有时就断定不了是不是真正喝到了天明。不过,象下一个例句就绝对没有误解的可能了。*We've already missed the last train. Why don't we just make a night of it?* 咱们已经误了末班车,何不来个通宵饮酒作乐呢? 以上所讲,都是指的喝酒度过一夜,但是 make a night of it 却并不以喝酒为前提。打一夜麻将牌,疯狂地跳一夜舞,只要是“整夜作乐”,全都可以说 make a night of it。同样,在这种场合,也不限定一直玩到天亮为止。*My husband got a promotion today. I'm to meet him after work and the two of us are going to go out and make a night of it.* 今天我丈夫得到了提升。下班时我去找他,我们俩打算在外边痛痛快快玩它一晚上。◇ spend the (whole) night [evening] enjoying *oneself* [carousing]

a night owl → OWL

a night person → PERSON

a night spot → SPOT

nightie

a nightie [ə ˈnaɪti] [话] **化妆衣** a nightgown (女睡衣)的 night 加上爱称指小词 -ie 构成的新词。*I bought my wife a new nightie for her birthday.* 在妻子过生日的时候,我给她买了一件新化妆衣。除“化妆衣”一义外,还指“婴儿或幼儿的小睡衣”。在这一场合,不仅指上下连身的睡衣,也包括上下身分开的睡衣。如果是上下身分开的,一般用复数形式 nighties。*Quick, now, put on your nighties. It's time for bed.* 喂,快穿上你的睡衣,该上床睡觉啦。有时拼写为 nighty。◇ a nightgown / pajamas

nightie-night

nightie-night [ˈnaɪtiˌnaɪt] [话] **晚安** 小儿语。如果成年人相互使用,就有戏谑的味道了。*Nightie-night, Jimmy. Don't forget to say your prayers.* 晚安,吉米。你不要忘了祈祷呀。又可以拼写为 nighty-night。另有一个表达法 night-night, 同义。◇ good night

night-night

night-night [ˈnaɪtˌnaɪt] [话] **晚安** → NIGHTIE-NIGHT

nighty

a nighty [ə ˈnaɪti] [话] **化妆衣** → a NIGHTIE

nighty-night

nighty-night [ˈnaɪtiˌnaɪt] [话] **晚安** → NIGHTIE-NIGHT

nincompoop

a nincompoop [ə ˈnɪŋkəmˌpu(ː)p] [口] **傻瓜** 语源不明。有人说可能是英美法律用语中沿袭拉丁语固定词组 non compos mentis [ˈnɑn ˈkɑmpəs ˈmentɪs] (心神丧失的)的转讹。*The great political leaders of the past are gone. Today's voters are forced to vote for dummies and nincompoops.* 过去的伟大政治领袖已经一去不复返了。现在的选民不得不去投笨蛋和傻瓜的票。→ a DUMBHEAD ◇ a stupid person

nine

be on cloud nine → CLOUD

ninny

a ninny [ə ˈnɪni] [口] **呆子** “呆子”、“傻瓜”、“笨蛋”在英语里有很多词汇,“呆”、“傻”、“笨”的程度也有种种的不同。ninny 一词含有由于是新手、由于没有经验而发呆的强烈意味。从语源来看也是如此,它似乎是 an innocent (不谙世故的人)一词的转讹,即脱落其中的 a-和 -ocent,再加上爱称指小词 -y,成为 (a)n inn(ocent)+y。*Don't just stand there like a ninny—say something.* 别光站在那儿发呆,说几句话。→ a DUMBHEAD ◇ a stupid person

nitwit

a nitwit [ə ˈnɪ(:)t.wɪ(:)t] [话] **糊涂虫** 关于这里的 nit, 有人说是来自德国的方言,意思是“没有”。但一般美国人听到 nit 以后,首先想到的是“虱子的幼虫”。也就是说,按一般的想法,nitwit 是“只有虱子幼虫那样程度的智慧 (wit)”的意思。特别指“没有分辨能力的人”,亦即俗话所说的“糊涂虫”。语调十分轻松,多用作戏谑语。*Has that nitwit lost his coat again?* 那个糊涂虫又把他的外衣丢了吗?形容词为 nit-witted [ˈnɪt.wɪ(:)dɪd]。*Have you seen that nit-witted Charlie?* 你见到那个糊里糊涂的查理了吗? → a DUMBHEAD ◇ a stupid person

no

No way. → WAY

nobody

a nobody [ə ˈnou.bɑdi] [口] **无名之辈** 作为不定代词, nobody 是“没有人”的意思;作为名词,是“名声、地位全都没有的人”的意思。在作为名词的场合,一般加冠词,作 a nobody, 不加冠词的情况极少。常用 just 加强语气。根据上下文,有时具轻蔑的意味。*I'm sure the governor will refuse to see me. I'm just a nobody.* 州长肯定不会接见我,因为我只是个无名之辈啊。*I may be a nobody, but he can't treat me like that just because he's a big company president.* 哪怕我是个无名之辈,他也不能因为自己是一位大公司经理就那样对待我呀。*That guy gets on my nerves. He's just a nobody pretending to be a somebody.* 那个家伙实在令人讨厌。他明明是个无名之辈,却装成大人物的模样。有时用复数。*I'm not going to put myself out for them. They're just a bunch of nobodies.* 我不打算帮他们的忙。他们只是一群毫不足取的人。◇ an unimportant person ((just →very))

nodding

have a nodding acquaintance (with *someone*) → ACQUAINTANCE

noggin

a noggin [ə ˈnɑ(:)gən] [话] **人的脑袋** 原意为“小啤酒杯”。在一般词典中,对于作“脑袋”解的 noggin, 都写着“语源不明”。但是,古时人们常在酒杯上画出人脸的图形,这一表达法大概由此而来 (→ a MUG)。*The ball hit me on the noggin.* 球打在我的脑袋上了。*Use your noggin.* 你要动动脑筋呀! ◇ a head

no-host

a no-host party → PARTY

noncom

a noncom [ə ˈnɑ(:)n.kɑːm] [话] **军士** noncommissioned officer [ˌnɑnkə.mɪʃənd ˈɔːfəsər] 的缩略语。轻松的军队用语。与“有委任状的军官” (commissioned officer) 相对,在陆军和空军中指准尉 (warrant officer), 中士 (sergeant), 以及下士 (corporal) 等。又叫做 an NCO [ə ˌnensi(:)ˈou]。*Capt. Parks was a noncom for many years.* 帕克斯上尉当过很多年军士。*This billet is for noncoms.* 这是军士们的住宿地。◇ a noncommissioned officer

no-no

a no-no [ə ˈnou.nou] [话] **不行的事情** 母亲常对孩子说 No, no! (不行,不行!) 成年人原封不动地借用这句话,改为名词的形式。特别应用于违反习惯、规章制度或常识的行动。在使用的时候,大多是半开玩笑的口气。*Beards are a no-no in our company.* 在我们公司不许留胡子。*Keeping bananas in the refrigerator is a no-no.* 香蕉不能放在冰箱里保存。*Hey, don't drink my beer. That's a no-no.* 喂,别喝我的啤酒,那可不行啊。◇ (something) not permitted / something you shouldn't do

nonsense

talk nonsense [ˌtɔːk ˈnɑːnˌse(ː)nts] [口] **胡说八道** → talk SENSE

nope

nope [ˈnoup] [话] **不不** 强调 no 的表达法。发音是把 no 的尾音上挑,略微用力,再加上 [p] 就行了。[p] 是闭合音,发音终了时不吐气,将两唇紧闭。此词给人以冷漠无情的感觉,所以在使用时必须注意对手和场合。这一表达法比 no 直截了当,在朋友或同事之间特别经常使用。Won't you go with us, Bill? (比尔,你愿意跟我们一块儿去吗?) 对于这一问话,如果比尔回答的是 No. 那还有商量的余地,他最后可能说: Well, maybe I'll go too, then. (好,那么我也去吧。) 如果比尔一开始就明确地说 Nope. 那就表明"怎么说我也不去",毫无商量的余地了。假定有人死气白赖地跟你借钱,而你并不想借,也许一开始就说 Nope. 为上策。反义词是 YEP。◇ no

nose

cut off *one's* **nose to spite** *one's* **face** [kʌˌdɔ(ː)f ~ ˈnouz təˌspaɪt ~ ˈfeɪs] [话] **与人呕气伤害自己** 这里的 spite 是"为了解恨而刁难对方"、"使坏"的意思。因此本条直译为"为了刁难自己的脸而把鼻子割去"。当然,这一表达法只作为比喻使用。例如儿童使坏反倒伤了自己,妻子吵架扔掉丈夫特意给买的貂皮外衣,等等。不论具体情况如何,总是由于"想要刁难别人"或者"想要使别人揪心"而使自己吃了亏。多用 only 或 just 加强语气。*Jimmy only cut off his nose to spite his face when he refused to eat his steak because he was mad at his mother.* 吉米因为与母亲呕气而不吃他那一份牛排,结果只是自己吃了亏。*If you quit the company just because you're mad at your boss, you'll just be cutting off your nose to spite your face.* 如果仅仅由于跟老板呕气而辞去在公司的职务,吃亏的只是你自己而已。*Russia cut off its nose to spite its face by boycotting the UN Security Council in order to demonstrate its dissatisfaction with American moves.* 苏联为了表示对美国的行动不满,拒绝参加联合国安全理事会,结果使自己受到了损失。◇ hurt *oneself* [harm *one's* own interests] in attempting to hurt [spite, annoy, etc.] someone else ((by boycotting→when it boycotted))

follow *one's* **nose** [ˌfɑlə ~ ˈnouz] [话] **凭第六感觉** 直译为"跟着自己的鼻子走",鼻子在脸的中央,当然是一直前进了。因此,这一表达法是"笔直地走"的意思。例如说: *The store is on the next street. Turn right at the next corner and just follow your nose. You can't miss it.* 那家商店在下一条街上。再遇见街角向右拐,笔直地走就行了。很容易找,错不了。不过,这一表达法按照"凭第六感觉"一义使用的场合最多。狗的嗅觉灵,就凭着鼻子走;人的嗅觉不灵,就凭着直觉走。凭着直觉辨别的主要是方向。*I hadn't been to Mary's house for over ten years, but I was able to find my way there again just by following my nose.* 我有十几年没去过玛丽的家了,但是凭着第六感觉走,我又找到了地方。然而,不仅限于"方向",也常用于"凭第六感觉采取行动"的场合。*In office politics, it's often difficult to know how to react. You just have to follow your nose.* 对于公司的经营方针,往往很难知道下一步应该如何应付,只有凭第六感觉采取行动。如以上的几个例句所示,多用 just 加强语气。◇ be guided by instinct

have a(good) nose for *something* [ˌhævə (ˌgud) ˈnouzfər ~] [口] **嗅觉灵敏** 本条来自谈论猎犬鼻子的好坏。*This dog has a good nose for deer.* 这只狗的鼻子对于鹿的气味很敏感。这是按原义的用法。在按原义使用的场合,一般均加

good。在作为比喻的场合,如下边的例句所示,常常省略此词。省略的原因多半是语调的关系,但有时是由于说话的人对于他人的灵敏嗅觉感到不快。例如:*That reporter has a nose for the unusual news story.* 那位记者对于一些奇闻怪事嗅觉很灵敏。*Mrs. Looselips has a nose for juicy gossip.* 卢思里普斯太太对于流言蜚语的嗅觉很灵敏。*Paul has a good nose for profitable business deals.* 保罗对于赚大钱的买卖嗅觉很灵敏。nose 的前边可以加 excellent, outstanding, uncanny 等形容词。*Flora is one of the best editors we have. She has an uncanny nose for potential best sellers.* 弗洛拉是我们出版社最好的编辑之一。她有不可思议的嗅觉,能够发现未来的畅销书。◇ be good at searching out [recognizing] *something* ((excellent 等 → very / extremely))

keep *one's* **nose clean** [.ki(:)p ~ 'nouz .kli:n] [话] **规规矩矩** 本条最初的构思是:"如果把鼻子往肮脏的地方伸,鼻子就会污染。如果不伸进去,就会保持清洁"。*I've kept my nose clean for three years now. I'm not about to risk getting into trouble with the law again.* 到现在为止,我已经老实三年了。我再也不冒着被惩罚的危险去触犯法律了。*The cop warned us to keep our noses clean or he'd run us in.* 警察警告我们不要去干坏事,否则他就把我们抓进去。*I've kept my nose clean all my life.* 我这一辈子没干过坏事。如以上的例句所示,本条一般用于表示"不干违法的事"或"不犯罪"的意思。但有时也很轻松地用于犯罪以外的事情。*Since I lectured him about cheating on tests, he seems to be keeping his nose clean.* 自从我严厉批评他在考试时作弊以后,他似乎谨言慎行了。另有 *One's* nose is clean. 的表达法,但用者比较少。*My nose is clean. I didn't steal the car.* 我是无辜的,我没有偷汽车啊。◇ avoid getting into trouble / obey the law [the rules] / behave *oneself*

keep *one's* **nose out of** *something* [.ki(:)p ~'nouzaudəv ~] [话] **不介入他人的事情** → poke *one's* NOSE into *something*

keep *one's* [*someone's*] **nose to the grindstone** [.ki(:)p ~ .nouztəðə 'graɪnd.stoun] [口] **(自己或使他人)一直去干** 直译为"把鼻子总是贴到磨石 (grindstone) 上"。因为在转动磨石时,脸要离磨石很近,于是产生了这一表达法。至少说,本条并不用于本人喜欢去干的场合,但是也不含有"拼出死命"的意味。可以认为它的重点在于"一刻不停"。*If I don't keep my nose to the grindstone, I won't be ready for my college entrance exams.* 我如果不日以继夜地努力,就完不成考大学的准备工作了。*I have to keep my nose to the grindstone in order to meet my work schedule each month.* 我每个月为了完成任务都必须孜孜不倦地工作。如果把 *one's* 变成 *someone's*, 那就是"使人一直去干"了。*Our English teacher keeps our noses to the grindstone.* 我们的英语老师督促我们一刻不停地学习。*I don't have much time for relaxation. The boss keeps our noses pretty close to the grindstone.* 我没有多少休息的时间,老板对我们的工作抓得紧极啦。◇ (make *someone*) work [study] constantly

lead *someone* **around by the nose** [.li:d ~ ə.raund.baɪðə 'nouz] [口] **牵着某人的鼻子走** 原来的意思是"给牛的鼻子穿上铁环,随意拉着它走"。虽然按字面意义来说是"牵着鼻子走",但在英语中并没有不管三七二十一地生拉硬拽的意思。大多用于以花言巧语等哄骗手段使他人听从摆布的场合,其中一定含有坏的意味。*The world is full of fast-talking politicians who are good at leading people around by the nose.* 世界上到处都是满嘴花言巧语的政客,他们善于蛊惑群众跟着他们走。常使用 let *someone* lead *one* around by the nose 的形式。*Phil should take a stronger stand with his wife. He's always letting her lead him around by the nose.* 菲尔对他的老婆应该采取更强硬的态度。他老是让她牵着鼻子走。*Whatever you do, son, always exercise your own judgment. Don't let* *other people lead you around by the nose.* 孩子,不论你做什么事情,都要按照你自己的判断去干。不要让别人牵着你的鼻子走。◇ manipulate *someone*

look down *one's* **nose at** *someone* [*something*] [ˌluk ˌdaun ~ ˈnouzət ~] [话] **轻视** 把鼻子向上翘,沿着鼻子的边缘,将视线投向对方,这是非常看不起对方(以及事物)的表情。本条是比 LOOK down on *someone* [*something*] 更强烈的表达法,语言本身就带有若干令人讨厌的意思。*That guy looks down his nose at people that aren't as smart as he is.* 那个家伙看不起不如他精明的人。*I could sense the other people at the reception looking down their noses at my old, out-of-fashion suit.* 在招待会上,我感到其他的人以轻蔑的眼光看着我的一身陈旧的、老式的服装。实际上不仅用于"拿眼睛看"的场合,也用于"采取瞧不起人的态度"的场合。*If you want to succeed in office politics, never look down your nose at a secretary.* 如果你想在公司里向上爬,可不要对秘书表示瞧不起的态度。◇ regard *someone* [*something*] with contempt

be no skin off *someone's* **nose** [nouˌskɪˌnɔ(ː)f ˈ~ ˌnouz] [话] **与某人没有瓜葛** → be no SKIN off *someone's* back

One's **nose is clean.**[~ ˌnouzəz ˈkliːn] [话] **无辜** → keep *one's* NOSE clean

nose out *someone* [ˌnou ˈzaut ~] [话] **险胜** → win by a NOSE

the parson's nose [ðə ˈpɑ(ː)rsənz ˈnouz] [话] **(烹调的)鸡屁股** → the Pope's NOSE

pay through the nose [ˌpeɪ ˌθru(ː)ðə ˈnouz] [话] **付出过多的钱** 直译为"通过鼻子付钱"。语源尚未确定。根据最有力的说法,本条可能来自 bleed (非法榨取钱财)与 nosebleed (鼻子出血)之间的密切关系。虽然指"巨款"的场合多,但并不限定金额绝对的大。也用于"比一般的或应有的价格高得多"的场合。*Beef is very expensive in Japan. You pay through the nose even for low-grade hamburger.* 在日本,牛肉是非常昂贵的东西。哪怕买劣等牛肉糜,也要付极多的钱。*Real estate is so expensive nowadays that no matter what you buy, you end up paying through the nose.* 房地产现在非常昂贵,不论你买怎样不起眼的地方,也得付出令人吃惊的巨款。*Jack has a beautiful sports car, but he had to pay through the nose to get it.* 杰克有一辆很漂亮的赛车,但是他在购买的时候可花了好大好大一笔钱啊。◇ pay a very high [an eye-popping] price

be (as) plain as the nose on *someone's* **face** [əz ˈpleɪ nəzðə ˌnouzən ~ ˈfeɪs] [话] **明明白白**脸上有没有鼻子,一看就知道——事情就是这样"明明白白"。*Whaddya mean you don't understand? It's as plain as the nose on your face.* 你说什么? 不明白? 这不是明明白白的吗? ◇ be very clear

poke *one's* **nose into** *something* [ˌpouk ~ ˈnouzɪntə ~] [话] **插手别人的事情** 直译为"把鼻子插进某事",意思是"为了干涉或者刨根问底而去过问与自己无关的事情"。*something* 的部分经常代入与本人无关的事情。*I can't stand that woman. She's always poking her nose into other people's business.* 我忍受不了那个女人。她总是插手别人的事情。常用同义的 stick 代替 poke。此外还有 put [shove, thrust] *one's* nose into *something* 等说法,但极少使用。*How many times have I told you not to stick your nose into things that don't concern you?* 你不要去管与你无关的事情,我已经跟你说了多少次啦? keep *one's* nose out of *something* 是"不插手别人的事情"。*I'll thank you to keep your nose out of my affairs.* 你别插手我的事情好不好? ◇ interfere in *something* / pry into *something*

the Pope's nose [ðə ˈpoups ˈnouz] [俗] **(烹调的)鸡屁股** 直译为"罗马教皇的鼻子"。戏谑语。本条的来源是:鸡、鸭、火鸡等的"屁股(肉)"的尖尖的形状很象"罗马教皇的鼻子"(罗马教皇的鼻子代表人类的鼻子)。有些天主教徒讨厌这个习用语,因此在使用时必须慎重。也可以说 the parson's nose (牧师的鼻子),意思相同,在天主教徒面前使用不会惹起麻烦。基督教徒对这两个习用语都不在乎。*She says her favorite parts of the chicken are the gizzard and the Pope's nose.* 她说她最喜欢吃鸡肫和鸡屁股这两个部分。◇ the tail

see beyond *one's* **nose** [ˌsiː biˌɑ(ː)nd ~ ˈnouz] [话] **有远见** → see beyond the end of *one's* NOSE

see beyond the end of *one's* **nose** [ˌsiː biˌɑndðɪ ˌendəv ~ˈnouz] [话] **考虑未来** 直译为"看自己鼻子尖的那一边"。当然是作为比喻使用,意思是"把眼光放远,视野广阔,考虑未来"。与"有先见之明"(预见未来事情的能力)的意思不一样。用法:前边一般用助动词 can, be able to, 或同类的词引导。有时用肯定式,例如:*I save my money because, unlike you, I'm able to see beyond the end of my nose.* 我把钱存起来,因为不象你,我能够考虑未来。但大多构成否定句。在这一场合,不是"不考虑未来",而是"只考虑目前的事情"的意思。*I don't care if he is the department head. I'm tired of taking orders from a man who can't see beyond the end of his nose.* 我不管他是不是部长。听一个鼠目寸光的人指挥,我已经腻味透啦。*The grasshopper, unable to see beyond the end of his nose, played all summer while the ants worked.* 蚱蜢只顾眼前,当蚂蚁辛勤劳动的时候,它玩了整整一个夏天。*The difference between a statesman and politician is that the latter has difficulty seeing beyond the end of his nose.* 政治家与政客的不同之处在于后者目光短浅。这里的 have difficulty ~ing 也是 can [be able to]+否定的一种变形。即使不构成否定句,也如下面的例句所示,大多采取疑问句或条件句的形式。在这一场合,同样具有否定句中的意味。*When are you going to learn to see beyond the end of your nose? If you spend so much on one project, we'll soon be bankrupt.* 你为什么总是只考虑眼前呢?如果你在一个计划上花那么多的钱,我们公司很快就会破产啦。在这句话里,learn to 具有 can 的意味。*If you could see beyond the end of your nose, you'd understand the importance of getting a good education.* 如果你不只顾眼前,你会理解受良好教育的重要性。可以用 farther than 或 past 等代替 beyond, 也可以把 beyond the end of ~ 中的 the end of 省略。但在使用 farther than 或 past 的场合,省略 the end of 就不自然了。◇ (have the sense to) think in terms of [plan for] the future / view things in the long term

stick *one's* **nose into** *something* [ˌstɪk ~ ˈnouzɪntə ~] [话] **插手他人的事情** → poke *one's* NOSE into *something*

thumb *one's* **nose at** *someone* [ˌθʌm ~ ˈnouzət ~] [口] **作鬼脸** → thumb *one's* NOSE at *something*

thumb *one's* **nose at** *something* [ˌθʌm ~ ˈnouzət ~] [口] **瞧不起** thumb (拇指)作动词使用。thumb *one's* nose 是"把拇指按在鼻子头上,张开其他的手指左右活动"的意思。这是孩子们侮辱或嘲弄对方的一种把戏。与中国的儿童们做鬼脸的情况相似。可以按照字面意义使用,例如:*When I told the boy to come to where I was, he just thumbed his nose at me and ran away.* 当我叫那个男孩到我跟前来的时候,他只对我做个鬼脸就跑掉了。这是用的 at *someone*。*The student stood respectfully as the teacher reprimanded her, but as soon as the teacher turned away, the girl thumbed her nose at him.* 当老师批评她的时候,那个学生毕恭毕敬地站在那里,但是,老师刚一转过身去,她就冲着他做了个鬼脸。如果变成 at *something*,就是比喻用法了,表示"瞧不起"、"忽视"的意思。*There would be fewer traffic deaths if people would stop thumbing their noses at the speed laws.* 如果每个人都不忽视关于车速的规定,因交通事故死亡的人数就会减少啦。*The chief called Stu on the carpet for thumbing his nose at company regulations.* 司徒由于忽视公司的规章制度,被总经理狠狠批评了一大顿。*You can't go through life thumbing your nose at social conventions if you* *want people to accept you.* 如果你想要人们容纳你，在生活中不遵从社会习惯是不成的。◇ ignore *something* / treat *something* lightly

turn up *one's* **nose at** *something* [*someone*] [ˌtə(ː)rˌnʌp ~ ˈnouzət ~] [口] **根本不理睬** 直译为"对某事或某人把鼻子往上翘"。人们常"哼"上一声，把鼻子翘起来，表示轻蔑。这一动作便是本条的来源。意思是"不加理睬"、"断然拒绝"，有"象我这样的大人物能与他为伍吗?"的意思。*Jobs are hard to find these days. You shouldn't turn up your nose at Mr. Smith's offer just because it's not exactly what you want.* 现在，工作是很难找的。对于史密斯先生提供的机会，你不要因为不很如意就一口回绝呀。*When I had plenty of money she was very friendly. Now she turns up her nose at me.* 当我腰缠万贯的时候，她对我亲热极了。现在，她根本不理我啦。也有时用"动物"作主语。*Our dog has been eating food from our table so long that he turns up his nose at canned dog food.* 我们的狗一直同家人一起吃饭，他对罐头的狗食连闻都不闻。◇ scorn *something* [*someone*]

under *someone's* **very nose** [ˌʌndər ~ ˈveri ˈnouz] [话] **就在眼皮底下** 直译为"就在某人的鼻子下边"。汉语一般是"在眼皮底下"，也可以说"在鼻子尖儿底下"。very 是强调，相当于"就"字。当然这是一种比喻说法，实际上也可以指眼睛看不见的地方。即使是眼睛看得见的地方，也经常含有"当事人没有注意到"的意味。*The murder took place under the policeman's very nose.* 谋杀案件就是在那个警察的眼皮底下发生的。也就是说，谋杀事件距离那个警察很近，而他没有觉察。看看下一个例子，对这一点就会更清楚了。*If the kidnappers came to the city last month, that means they have been under our very noses all the time.* 如果那些诱拐犯上个月就已经来到这个城市，那就是说，他们一直就在咱们的眼皮底下啦。常用 right 代替 very 加强语气，有时为了进一步强调而一齐使用。*Jim said he couldn't find his watch, when there it was, right under his nose all the time.* 吉姆说找不到他的手表了，而手表却一直就在他的眼皮底下。*The students were cheating right under the teacher's very nose.* 学生们考试时，就在老师的鼻子尖儿底下作弊。也可以在 under 之前加 from，而说 (right) from under *someone's* very nose。*The thief took the jewelry right from under the guards' very noses.* 小偷就从警卫们的眼皮底下把珠宝盗走了。→ before *someone's* very EYES ◇ very nearby / (right) within (*someone's*) immediate reach / (right) in *someone's* very presence / with *someone* very nearby

win by a nose [ˌwinbaɪə ˈnouz] [话] **险胜** 直译为"以一鼻子之差获胜"。本条来源于赛马，也常按照字面意义使用。*The favorite won by a nose.* 最有希望的那匹马以一鼻子之差获胜了。用作比喻时，是"以微小的差别获得胜利"的意思。*The Republican candidate won by a nose.* 共和党候选人以微弱的优势当选了。同样的表达法还有 win by a slight margin (以一线之差获胜)、barely win (勉强获胜)等，在以上的例句中均可互换。另有 nose out *someone* 的说法，原来的构思与 win by a nose 相同，例如：*The Republican candidate nosed out his Democratic rival.* 共和党候选人以微弱的优势击败了他的民主党对手。◇ win by a very small margin

noses

count noses [ˌkauntˈnouzəz] [话] **数人数** 原来是为了知道有多少匹马而"数鼻子"。现在几乎所有的场合是用于表示"数人数"的意思。*We'd better count noses to see how many drinks we'll have to serve after the meeting.* 我们最好是数一下人数，看看在开会之后要准备多少份饮料。*To make sure no members of the tour get lost, we count noses every time they get back on the bus.* 为了保证旅行团团员没有走失，每当他们回到大汽车上来的时候，我们都清点人数。另有 take a head count 的说法，字面意义

就是“数脑袋”。以上各例句皆可换用。两者的区别是 take a head count 的使用范围比较广，例如在数赞成和反对的票数时，一般不用 count noses，而用 take a head count。*We took a head count to decide the issue.* 我们进行表决，数了一下赞成和反对的票数。count noses 的同义语有 tell noses，但这是英国英语，美国不用。◇ count the number of people

no-show

a no-show [ə ˈnou.ʃou] [话] **买了机票而不乘飞机的人** 航空公司和传播媒介的习用语。如果乘客买了机票不乘该次飞机，航空公司原则上对这些人要按整个票价退款，或者允许他们用该票转乘另一班飞机。因此，航空公司对此极为头痛。*No-shows are a problem for the airlines.* 买了机票不来乘机是航空公司的一大问题。写宣传标语为对付这种人的方法之一：*Don't be a no-show.* 买了机票，务请登机。◇ a person who fails to board a flight for which he has a reservation

nosy

nosy [ˈnouzi] [口] **爱管闲事的** 指对别人的事情都想知道、爱“把鼻子插进”与自己无关的事情的人而言。但是，并没有去帮助人的积极性。又拼写为 nosey。*She's a nosy woman.* 她是一个爱管闲事的女人。*Don't be so nosy!* 不要那么刨根问底！ ◇ (a person who is) overly interested in other people's affairs

notch

be a notch above *someone* [ə.nɑ(:)tʃə-ˈbʌ(:)v ～] [口] **略胜一筹** notch 是“刻痕”或“切口”的意思。古时在游戏或比赛时，把一根木棍插在地上，从下往上将得分刻在木棍上面。这种记分方法就是本条的来源，直译为“高出一个刻痕”，也就是“比对方多得一分”。转作比喻使用，表示“略微强一点”的意思。*When it comes to chess, he's a notch above me.* 要论国际象棋，他比我略胜一筹。*someone* 处常常代入 other people、most people，以及具有“周围的人”之意的 the others 或 those around *one*。*I'm sure Hank will be the next department head. He's a notch above the others when it comes to handling people.* 我看下一次准是汉克当部长。他在处理人际关系上比别人强一点。a notch 如果换成 a few notches 或者 several notches，那就是“强几分”或“强一些”的意思。*As a public speaker, Bill is several notches above most people.* 作为演说家，比尔比普通人强一些。◇ be clearly better than *someone*

take *someone* **down a notch** [.teɪk ～ ˈdaunə .nɑ(:)tʃ] [话] **挫其傲气** → take *someone* down a PEG

note

a bread-and-butter note [ə .bredn'bʌder .nout] [口] **对别人在家中款待表示感谢的信** → a bread-and-butter LETTER

nothing

come to nothing [.kʌmtə ˈnʌ(:)θɪŋ] [口] **终成泡影** → come to NAUGHT

something **does nothing to** *do something* [～ .dʌ(:)z ˈnʌθɪŋtə ～] [口] **雪上加霜** 意思是“由于某种事情，更加使人不想去做……”。这是一个语气很强的表达法。*The recent spate of airplane accidents has done nothing to whet my appetite for flying.* 最近大量的空中事故使得我更不想去坐飞机了。在这句话的背后，有“过去就不爱坐飞机”的意味。有时用 little 代替 nothing，意思不变。又，常用 certainly 或 absolutely 等加强语气。*I'll admit I'm in a bad mood today, but your attitude has certainly done little to improve it.* 的确，我今天的情绪很不好。不过，你的态度对于我来说更是雪上加霜了。如以上的例句所示，这一表达法大多使用完成时，但并不限定如此。*This meal does nothing to make me think better of this restaurant.* 本来我对这个餐厅的印象就不好，这顿饭更增加了我的恶感。*Another bribery scandal will do nothing to enhance the image of politicians.* 如果再发生受贿的丑闻，政客们就会更加名誉扫地啦。◇ *something* blunts [worsens, lowers my [*someone's*] estimation of, diminish, etc.] *something* (even further)

Here goes nothing. [ˌhɪr ˌgouz ˈnʌθən] [话] **试一试看吧** 本条是由 Here goes. (我开始啦!)加 nothing 构成的。Here goes. 是在去干困难的事情或者危险的事情的紧要关头,为了给自己打气或者为了引人注目而喊叫的话,与 Here I go.的意义和用法大致相同。例如: "*Here goes!*" *shouted the boy as he started running toward the end of the high-diving board.* 那个少年在高高的跳水台上开始向跳水板前端跑的时候,大声喊道:"我跳啦!" "*Well, here goes,*" *whispered the sergeant before moving out of the thicket.* "*The rest of you stay here until I've taken out the guard at the front gate.*" 在离开灌木丛之前,中士小声说:"喂,我去啦! 在我消灭大门前的那个卫兵之前,你们呆在这儿不要动。"Here goes nothing. 与 Here goes.的不同点在于:同样是困难的事情或危险的事情,但前者只在成功的可能性极少的场合使用。它表达这样一种心情:"虽不大可能成功,不过既然非干不可,那也只好去试一下。"或者是:"不干一下不甘心。"本条不是象 Here goes. 那样为自己打气的、精神抖擞的呼喊,只是自言自语、顺口溜出的喃喃的话。"*Here goes nothing.*" *That was all the agent said before stepping through the door of the airplane and disappearing into the darkness over enemy territory.* "试一试看吧。"那个特工只说了这样一句话,就从飞机的舱门跳出去,消失在敌境上空的黑暗中了。在 Here goes nothing. 的场合,有时说出声来,也有时是在自己的心中暗暗嘀咕。*When the bell sounded for the start of the entrance exam, Jimmy gave a wry smile.* "*Well, here goes nothing,*" *he thought as he reached for his pencil.* 当入学考试开始的铃声响起来的时候,吉米苦笑了一下。"好吧,试一试看吧!"他这样想着,伸手去取铅笔。在下一例句中,实际上是否说出声来,不清楚。"*Well, here goes nothing,*" *said Bill to himself as he threw back his shoulders and started toward the boss's office to ask for a raise.* "好,试一试看吧!"比尔自言自语,他挺起胸膛,为了要求提高工资向老板的办公室走去。◇ (Chances of success may be slim, but) there's no choice but to give it a try.

Nothing doing. [ˌnʌθən ˈdu:ən] [话] **绝对不行** 对于"请求"表示拒绝或对于"提议"表示否定的时候使用。可以认为与加强语气的 no 相同。*A: Let's go to the movies. B: Nothing doing. I've gotta study today.* 甲:咱们去看电影吧。乙:绝对不行。我今天得学习啊。*A: How about lending me your car to-night? B: Nothing doing. I'm squiring Helen to a dance tonight.* 甲:今天晚上把你的汽车借给我怎么样? 乙:不成不成。今天晚上我要陪海伦出席舞会哪。在这一例句中,是用与对方无关的事情为理由表示拒绝,因而和一般的 no 没有什么两样。但在大多数的场合,包含有"已经吃过苦头,再也不干了"的心情。例如: *A: How about lending me your car to-night? B: Nothing doing. The last time I lent it to you, you brought it back with a dent in the fender.* 甲:今天晚上借用一下你的汽车好吗? 乙:绝对不成。上次我借给你的时候,挡泥板都给撞出坑来了。*A: Let's ask the Dalla-Shenigh Company to do the work. B: Nothing doing. They never finish on time.* 甲:我们把这个活包给达拉西奈公司吧。乙:不成不成。他们从来没有按期完成过任务。◇ Absolutely not.

Nothing to it. [ˌnʌθənˈtu(:)ət] [话] **容易极啦!** 一般是当对方问"你干得了吗?"的时候回答使用,it 指对方所问的事情,直译是"做那件事不费吹灰之力"。本条为 There is [was, will be, etc.] nothing to it. 的缩略形式。*A: How can I lose weight? B: There's nothing to it. Just stop eating.* 甲:我怎样才能减肥呀? 乙:那容易极啦! 只要不吃饭就行了。如这一例句所示,可以带 There is,但在会话中通常省略,因此就与动词的时间变化无关,使用起来十分方便。例如: *A: Can you finish this work by three o'clock? B: Nothing to* *it. I have only a few pages to go.* 甲：你到三点钟能完成这个作业吗？乙：那没有什么。我只剩两三页啦。*A: How did you ever get here so soon? B: Nothing to it. I just borrowed my son's motorbike.* 甲：你来得怎么这么快？乙：那没有什么，我不过借我儿子的摩托车用了一下。另外，如果带 There + be 动词，而作 There is [was, will be, etc.] nothing to it. 还有"那种话毫无根据"的意思，如说：*I heard that story, too. There's nothing to it.* 我也听到那种说法了，那完全是无稽之谈。这一点请读者注意。◇ It is [was, will be, etc.] very easy.

There is nothing to it. [ðərəz ˌnʌθɪŋ ˈtu(:)ət] [口] **毫无根据** → NOTHING to it.

notice

sit up and take notice (of *something* [*someone*]) [sɪ.dʌpən ˌteɪk ˈnoudəs] [口] **刮目相看** 本条最初的构思是："一些人原来认为没有什么了不起的事情，逍遥自在地坐在那里，现在他们直起身来 (sit up and) 注意去瞧 (take notice)"。在实际上，并不是都要有"直起身来"的动作，只是用于表示"原先并没有注意，现在突然注意了"的意思。*He has long been considered a second-class writer, but his most recent novel has at last made the critics sit up and take notice.* 他长期以来被认为是个二流作家，但是他最近发表的长篇小说终于使批评家们刮目相看了。*Though the fortune-teller had been widely ridiculed, when his first predictions came true the people began to sit up and take notice.* 虽然那个算命先生曾经被大家嘲弄，而当他的最初的预言应验的时候，人们开始刮目相看了。如果要讲"对……注目"，在本条后边接 of *someone* [*something*] 的句型。*If Sally won't give you a tumble, go out and date some other girls. That ought to make her sit up and take notice of you.* 如果萨莉不给你满意的答复，你就去另外找几个姑娘约会好啦。这样一来，她就会对你刮目相看了。◇ (suddenly) pay attention (to *something* [*someone*]) / (suddenly) take an interest (in *something* [*someone*])

nought

come to nought [ˌkʌmtə ˈnɔːt] [口] **化为泡影** → come to NAUGHT

nowhere

be getting nowhere fast [ˌgetn ˈnouˈhwe(:)r ˈfæːst] [话] **没有进展余地；不能解决问题** 直译为"向任何地方都快去不了"。这里的 fast (快)是反语，强调毫无进展的情况。*We're getting nowhere fast in this heavy traffic. We'd better find another road.* 这里的交通太拥挤了，往前一步也走不了。咱们最好另找一条路吧。这是按照字面意义的用法。作为比喻，用以表示"事情没有进展"、"问题不能解决"的意思。*We seem to be getting nowhere fast in this discussion. Perhaps we'd better go back to the beginning and start over.* 咱们这样讨论下去，似乎永远解决不了什么问题。我看不如从头开始，再仔细研究一下为好。*We've been trying to save some money, but with inflation being higher than bank interest, we're getting nowhere fast.* 我们本来打算存几个钱，但是通货膨胀高过银行利息，一切都是白搭了啊。*We're getting nowhere fast trying to push the car out of the mud this way. We'd better call a wrecker.* 咱们象这样从泥塘里往外推汽车，怎么也推不出去，我看不如叫个救险车为好。*A: How are you doing with Betty? Has she given you a tumble yet? B: Not yet. I seem to be getting nowhere fast.* 甲：你跟贝蒂的关系怎么样啦？她还没有肯定的答复吗？乙：还没有。我简直毫无办法啊。如以上的例句所示，绝大多数使用进行时，但也有例外。*I can tell you now you'll get nowhere fast trying to borrow money from that skinflint.* 现在我告诉你说，你别想从那个吝啬鬼那里借到钱。◇ make absolutely no progress

number

do number one [ˌdu(:)ˌnʌmbər ˈwʌn] [话]

小便 → GRUNT

do number two [ˌdu(ː)ˌnʌmbər ˈtuː] [话] **大便** → GRUNT

something **has** *someone's* **number on it** [~ ˌhæz ~ ˈnʌmbərɔnɪt] [话] **中弹或中箭而死** 与 *someone's* NUMBER is up 同样,基本上来源于一种宿命论的说法:"人在出生时,死亡的顺序就已经确定了"。本条直译为"子弹或箭上写有自己死亡顺序的号码",换句话说就是"那颗子弹或那支箭使你死亡,是命中注定的事情"。因此,本条的构思是:"不管你在什么地方,那颗子弹或那支箭总有一天会向你飞来,这是命中注定,躲避不了的"。一般用于表示"中弹或中箭而死"的意思,但不一定指"当场死去",有时只指"中弹"或"中箭"。但在这一场合也包含有"致命"的意味。当然,使用于战争或战斗的情况比较多。*Watch out! That bullet almost had your number on it!* 当心!刚才那颗子弹差一点儿打中你! *War is always a risky business. Who knows when the next bullet will have his number on it?* 战争时刻存在着危险,谁也不晓得下一颗子弹是否会轮到自己身上。*As soon as the Indian raised his bow, I knew the next arrow had my number on it.* 那个印第安人刚一抬起他的弓,我就感到自己会中他的箭。*A shell exploded nearby. But luckily it didn't have my number on it.* 炮弹在附近爆炸了,但是我幸免于难。也可以转用于子弹或箭以外的东西。*You'd better be more careful crossing the street. That taxi almost had your number on it.* 你在过马路的时候可要多加小心,那辆出租汽车差一点撞到你的身上啦。也可以应用本条采取如下的说法:*I may not return from the war. I have a feeling there's a bullet somewhere with my number on it.* 我可能从战场上回不来啦。我总感觉到在什么地方有颗子弹在等着我。在这句话里,there's a bullet 以下的意思是"不知在什么地方有一颗子弹上有我的号码"。顺便讲一下:过去英国海军有一句俚语是 lose the number of *one's* mess (失去自己吃饭的号码牌子),美国陆军则把这句话改为 lose *one's* mess number,全都是"死"的意思。构思很简单:每个士兵在开饭时都有带号码的牌子 (mess number),只有死了的人,才会没有这种牌子。这一俚语与条头颇有相似之处,但从语源上讲,二者没有什么关联。◇ (be destined to) hit [kill] *someone*

have *someone's* **number** [ˌhæv ~ ˈnʌmbər] [话] **知道某人的底细** 这里的 number 究竟是什么意思,不明确。如果勉强解释,这个"数目"指的是"出生年月日"。也就是说,本条直译为"根据出生年月日了解某人的性格",即对"某人的底细一清二楚"。*I've got your number.* 我了解你的底细。根据上下文,这句话中的"底细"可能指对方的"人品"、"企图"或者"手段",也可能指所有这几方面的综合。*You may as well come clean. We've got your number.* 你最好是坦白交代,我们已经掌握了你的材料。如这一例句所示,本条言外总含有"抓住对方的小辫儿"的意思,一般不用于好的事情。*That ploy won't work on me again. I've got your number now.* 你那种花招对我再也不会起作用了,我现在已经知道你的底细啦。*I couldn't understand for a long time why that guy was being so friendly. Now I think I've finally got his number.* 我有很长一个时期不理解那个家伙为什么表现得如此友好,现在我总算知道他的企图啦。get *someone's* number 是"了解"、"看出"。*That guy's not so smart. I got his number the first time I met him.* 那个家伙不大聪明。我第一次会见他就看穿了他的企图。◇ realize what *someone* is / be aware of *someone's* modus operandi / understand *someone's* tactics [motives, aims, etc.] / have *someone* figured out

look out for number one → ONE

someone's **number is up** [~ ˌnʌmbərəˈzʌ(ː)p] [话] **死期已至** 直译为"某人的号码出来了"。本条来源于人死由天的思想,仿佛一个人临终时,眼前有一个写着死亡号码的牌子。*I can't go any farther without water. You go on ahead without me. My number is up.* 没有水,我连一步

也走不动啦。你们把我丢下,往前进吧。我的死期到了。*When I saw that big truck bearing down on me, I thought my number was up.* 当我见到那辆大卡车向我直冲过来的时候,我想自己的命算完蛋了。*Another big wave like that against this little boat and our number will be up.* 这条小船如果再遇见那样一个大浪,我们就全完蛋啦。西部影片或者描绘盗匪的电影常有这一类的对白。*Drop your gun and say your prayers. Your number is up.* 扔下你的枪,向上帝祷告吧。你的死期到啦。也可以说 *someone's* number comes up (寿命已尽)。*Don't mourn for me when I'm gone. Everyone's number has to come up some time.* 当我离开人世的时候,不要为我悲伤。任何人的寿命都有终了的一天啊。◇ *someone* is fated to die

an unlisted number [ən ˌʌnˈlɪsted ˈnʌmbər] [口] **保密电话号码** unlisted 是"不列入的"。本条的意思是"不载入电话簿的电话号码"。一些有名人物为了保密,往往要求电话局不要把他们的电话号码刊登到电话簿上,而只告诉亲戚朋友或其他有关人士,另外的人不论以怎样的理由向电话局询问,交换台都绝对不能告知。即便是亲戚朋友,一旦把那个电话号码丢了,也只能用书信或电报向本人再问询一次。绝对保密电话的处理是电话公司的营业项目之一。*I wanted to call John Stonefeller, but unfortunately he had an unlisted number and the operator refused to tell me what it was.* 我想给约翰·斯通斐勒打个电话,偏巧他的电话保密,交换台不肯告诉我号码。◇ a secret telephone number

numbskull

a numbskull [ə ˈnʌm:skʌ(:)l] [口] **笨蛋** 直译为"麻木的(numb)头盖骨(skull)",也就是"脑子笨的人"的意思。也可以按照发音拼写为 numskull。*You're not a numbskull. If you'd only study you could make good grades.* 你的头脑并不笨。只要好好用功,就会取得良好的成绩。→ a DUMBHEAD ◇ a stupid person

nut

be a tough nut to crack [ə ˈtʌf ˈnʌt:ə ˈkræ(:)k] [话] **不好对付的人或事物** 直译为"很难砸开的坚果"。*The Brazil nut is a tough nut to crack.* 巴西核桃是一种很难砸开的坚果。转作比喻使用。这里的 crack 不是"砸开",而有"开一条缝"的意味。"很难开一条缝"就是"很难找到头绪"的意思。*This physics problem is a tough nut to crack.* 这道物理问题很难找到解答的头绪。*It was difficult enough to deal with our rivals when they were fighting among themselves. The reconciliation among them will be a tough nut to crack.* 我们的竞争对手们在相互斗争的时候,就已经使我们难以应付了。如果他们和解,那就使我们更感到棘手了。下面是个别的人难以对付的例子。*I don't know whether I'll be able to make a sale to Mr. Bighand or not. He's a tough nut to crack.* 我不知道能不能向比格汉德先生推销出去一批货。他这个人是不好对付的。*A: Have you succeeded in getting a date with Ellen yet? B: No, she's a tough nut to crack.* 甲:你已经跟埃伦约会了吗? 乙:没有,她不容易弄到手啊。有用 hard 代替 tough 而说 be a hard nut to crack 的表达法,但一般使用 tough。◇ be a difficult problem [situation, person, etc.] to (know how to) deal with [approach]

nuts

nuts [ˈnʌ(:)ts] [话] **精神不正常** → be (as) nutty as a FRUITCAKE

nutty

nutty [ˈnʌdi] [话] **疯疯癫癫** → be (as) nutty as a FRUITCAKE

be (as) nutty as a fruitcake → FRUITCAKE

oats

feel *one's* **oats** [ˌfi(ː)l ～ ˈouts] [话] **精神饱满** oat 是"燕麦"。一般使用复数。本条的来源是:据说,马吃了燕麦,立刻就有精神。按字面解释,本条的意思为"象吃过燕麦以后那样的感觉"。从旁观者的立场来看,就是意气风发、精神抖擞的形象。经常含有"与平日相比"或"从来没有这样"的意味。大多指人或马而言,但也有时应用于驯养的动物。不论是人还是动物,本条只能用于平日非常熟悉的对象。*The horses were really feeling their oats that day. I was able to finish plowing the field in record time.* 那一天,几匹马真是精神十足。我能够在从未有的短时间内耕完了地。*My husband must have been feeling his oats today. He usually doesn't play ball so long with the children.* 我的丈夫今天一定是精神极啦。他跟孩子们玩棒球,从来没有玩过这么长的时间。本条除"精神饱满"的意味外,还进一步发展,表示"得意洋洋"甚至"骄傲自满"的意思。*Ralph must be feeling his oats today. I've never heard him disagree with the boss like that before.* 拉尔夫今天一定是得意洋洋起来了。在过去,我从来没有听见他象那样对老板表示不同的意见。*I'd like to take that guy down a notch or two. He's been feeling his oats a bit too often lately.* 我很想挫一挫那个家伙的傲气,他最近常常显示出自高自大的神情。另外,也可以用以表示把"精神饱满"与"骄傲自满"加在一起的意味。*By the end of the nineteenth century, America was like a strong but as yet ill-formed youth just beginning to feel his oats.* 在19世纪末,美国好象一个虽然意志坚强但是还没有发育成熟的小伙子,刚刚开始具有自己能够干点什么的信心。◇ feel energetic / feel extremely [overly] confident

sow (*one's*) **wild oats** [ˌsou ˌwaɪl ˈdouts] [口] **青年男子结婚前的放荡不羁** 16世纪左右开始使用的古老的表达法。直译为"播种野生的燕麦"。wild oats 只是一种被称为"假大麦"的杂草,无论怎样播种,也不会产生出大麦来,因此,其中包含有"白费劲"的意味。这里的 wild 从"野生"的意思转成了"野性",亦即"放荡不羁"。*By the time I was twenty-five, I was through sowing my wild oats. I had begun to look upon life as something more serious than a flagon of beer at one hand and a pretty girl at the other.* 到了25岁,我总算结束了自己的放荡生活。我开始认为人生比一手啤酒杯、一手美小妞有更重要的意义了。如这一例句所示,这一表达法特别用于青年男子结婚前过花天酒地生活的场合。*More than a few young men look upon college as an opportunity to sow wild oats.* 许多男青年认为进大学是个玩乐的好机会。*After three years of sowing wild oats in Europe, Francis returned home ready to settle down and raise a family.* 弗朗西斯在欧洲过了三年放荡生活之后,回国准备安定下来、成家立业了。如果只是讲与女性的关系,也可以这样说:*George only meant to be sowing some wild oats. He didn't mean to become a father.* 乔治的意思只是玩玩女人,他并不想结婚生孩子。如这一例句所示,*one's* 可用 some 或 a few 等形容词代替。*Don't worry about your son, Martha. Every healthy boy feels he has to sow a few wild oats before he settles down.* 玛莎,不要为你的儿子烦恼。每一个健康的男孩子都认为自己在成家立业之前应该放荡一番。◇ live a prodigal life / have a little wild fun

off

an off day → DAY

offense

give offense (to *someone*) [ˌgɪvə'fe(ː)nts] [口] **得罪某人** → take OFFENSE (at *something*)

be quick to take offense (at *something*) [ˌkwɪktə ˌteɪkə'fe(ː)nts] [口] **爱生气** 直译为“不高兴 (take offense) 来得快(be quick)”。主要用于表示人的性格,意思与 (be) THIN-SKINNED (神经过敏)相近。*Be careful of what you say to Mr. Thinpelt. He's very quick to take offense.* 你对辛培尔特先生说话要多加小心,他这个人很爱生气。*You shouldn't be so quick to take offense at what people say about you. At this rate, you soon won't have any friends left.* 不管别人怎样谈论你,你也不要马上就火冒三丈啊。照这样下去,用不了多久,你会连一个朋友都没有了。*Mr. Reinough is fairly thick-skinned about most things, but he's quick to take offense at the least criticism of his company.* 雷诺先生对于大多的事情都感觉十分迟钝,但是如果有人稍微批评一下他的公司,他马上就来气了。→ take OFFENSE (at *something*) ◇ be easily angered [upset]

be slow to take offense (at *something*) [ˌsloudə ˌteɪkə'fe(ː)nts] [口] **不爱生气** 直译为“不高兴(take offense) 来得慢(be slow)”,为 be quick to take OFFENSE (at *something*) 的反义语。主要用于表示人的性格,意思与 (be) THICK-SKINNED (神经迟钝)相近。*I'm sure Jack was not bothered by what you did. He's very slow to take offense.* 我敢肯定,杰克对你所做的事情是不会放在心上的。他这个人最不爱生气啦。*You shouldn't be so slow to take offense at what people say about you. They'll think you have no backbone.* 你对于别人谈论你的话不应该一点儿也不来火,他们会认为你太没骨气啦。*Mr. Rarebird is an unusual fellow. Though generally thin-skinned, he is apparently slow to take offense at criticism of his family.* 列尔波德先生是一个与众不同的人。他平常对别人的话很敏感,但是如果有人批评他的家族,他似乎并不大生气。→ take OFFENSE (at *something*) ◇ be not easily angered [upset]

take offense (at *something*) [ˌteɪkə'fe(ː)nts] [口] **恼火** 从“不高兴”、“不痛快”一直到强烈的“恼怒”、“愤慨”,本条的意味范畴相当宽广。take umbrage ['ʌmbrɪdʒ] (at *something*) 大致同义,但可能由于高级一些,显得生硬,在日常会话中不如 take offense 一般化。*Please don't take offense at what I have to say, but I feel I must speak frankly.* 我觉得应该向你直言不讳,请听了我讲的话之后不要恼火。*Gary is too thin-skinned. He's always taking offense at what other people do or say.* 盖利这个人太神经过敏。别人不管做什么或说什么,他总爱生气。*I know what Mr. Brown said is right, but I couldn't help take offense at the way he said it.* 我知道布朗先生所说的话是对的,但是我禁不住对他的说话方式恼火。“令人生气”英语作 give [cause] offense (to *someone*)。*Please try to overlook what Mr. Fink said. He didn't mean to give offense.* 请你宽容芬克先生所说的话吧。他并不是想惹你不高兴。→ be quick to take OFFENSE (at *something*) / be slow to take OFFENSE (at *something*) ◇ get angry [upset]

office

office politics → POLITICS

play post office [ˌpleɪ 'pouˌstɔːfəs] [口] **邮信游戏** 美国人在举办家庭晚会的时候,小学生那么大的孩子们常常聚在一起,搞一种“邮信游戏”。游戏方法虽然多种多样,但最普遍的是:孩子们每个人拿着一张写有号码的纸。号码男女有别,一是奇数,一是偶数。每个号码都保密,只有他本人知道。首先公推一个邮政局长,他到邻室去。然后,一个和局长性别不同的孩子在纸上写出与自己的号码不一样的号码(经常是异性的号码),称为“信”,把它送到邻室(即邮局),在局长颊上吻一下,算是邮资。于是这个孩子充当局长,留在那里。原来的局长拿着那封已经邮寄的信回到孩子群里,宣读那封信上的号码。持有那个号码的人(与新局长异性的孩子),又写一个另外的号码,送到邮局去。局长与发信人就是这样一个一个轮流替换。*Larry's parents are very strict. They wouldn't let us play post office at his birthday party.* 拉里的父母是非常严厉的人。在拉里的生日晚会上,他们不允许我们搞邮信游戏。*Carol is stuck up. When we played post office, she only gave me a butterfly kiss.* 卡罗尔自高自大。当我们玩邮信游戏的时候,她只给我一个蝴蝶吻。有时成年人也借用本条戏指男女之间的卿卿我我的行为。*I saw Mr. Sweetlips playing post office the other day with his secretary.* 我看见斯威特利普斯先生前几天跟他的女秘书玩邮信游戏呢。◇ play a kissing game

offing

in the offing [ˌɪnðɪ ˈɔːfiŋ] [口] **不久的将来** 直译为"船在海面上"。*From my position on the shore, I could see two or three ships in the offing.* 从我在岸边采的地方,可以看见海面上有两三只船。作为比喻,offing 与 be 动词结合在一起,表示"不久的将来[马上、一会儿]就会有[发生]……"的意思。原来的构思是:"已经看见船在海面上了,因此,用不多大工夫,它就会驶入港口啦"。大多用于不确实的预测、预想或预感。*When the boss called me into his office, I had a feeling that something unpleasant was in the offing.* 当老板叫我到他的办公室去的时候,我感到马上就要发生什么不愉快的事情了。*From the looks of those two, I'd say there may be a wedding in the offing.* 从那两个人的神情看,可能在不久的将来他们就要举行婚礼啦。*The news was getting worse day by day, and everyone was sure that war was in the offing.* 消息一天比一天坏,大家都认为战争已经为期不远啦。也有与 be 动词以外的动词结合使用的时候。*Every time I step out the back door with something in my hand, my dog, sensing a meal in the offing, makes a beeline for his dish.* 每当我手里拿着东西从房屋后门走出的时候,我的狗就意识到马上要吃饭了,向它的食盘一直跑去。◇ about to happen [take place] / in the near future / impending

off-the-cuff

off-the-cuff [ˌɔ(ː)fðəˈkʌ(ː)f] [口] **即席的(讲话等)** → speak off the CUFF

often

once too often → ONCE

oil

burn the midnight oil [ˌbə(ː)rnðə ˌmɪdˌnaɪ ˈdɔɪl] [话] **用功或工作到深夜** 直译为"燃烧午夜的油"。这是爱迪生出世以前就有的表达法,现在人们仍然常常使用。*He's been burning the midnight oil for a week straight now, getting ready for finals.* 他为了准备期终考试,已经有一个星期天天复习到深夜了。如这一例句所示,主要用于"学习",但有时也用于"工作"。不过,请读者注意,在用于"工作"的场合,不是指肉体劳动,而是指案头工作,即所谓的 desk work。*We're really going to have to burn the midnight oil tonight if we're going to complete this spec sheet by tomorrow.* 如果我们要在明天以前完成这份产品说明书,今天晚上非干到深夜不可。*I burnt the midnight oil last night filling out my income tax forms.* 我昨天晚上填写所得税报表,一直干到深夜。◇ study [work] until late at night

pour oil on troubled waters [ˌpoˈrɔɪlɔn ˌtrʌbld ˈwɔːdərz] [口] **平息风波** 本条的来源是:船在航行时遇到风暴,就把油倾入波涛汹涌的大海 (troubled waters),使大浪减少冲力,保住船体。troubled waters 是极富有诗意的语言,在口语中决不按照字面意义使用,一般作为比喻,如说 fish in troubled WATERS (混水摸鱼)。因此,本条也只能作为比喻使用。如果要表达"把油倾入波涛汹涌的大海"这一固有的意义,则说 pour oil on the rough waves [the rough sea, etc.]。"风波"的内容包括"纷争"、"吵架"、"动乱"

等。*When two of my best friends began to quarrel, I knew it was up to me to pour oil on troubled waters.* 当我的两个最要好的朋友开始吵嘴的时候，我知道该由我来平息这场风波了。如果是特定的 troubled waters，要加定冠词 the。*England and America tried to pour oil on the troubled waters of Africa.* 英国和美国试图解决非洲的纷争。*How dare you accuse me of seeking my own interests! I'm here to try to pour oil on troubled waters, not to fish in them.* 你怎么竟敢指责我追求自己的利益！我在这里是要平息风波，不是要混水摸鱼。◇ (take action to) calm the situation (in *someplace*)

ointment

a fly in the ointment → FLY

okey-doke

okey-doke [ˈouki.douk] [话] **行，好** O.K.(亦作 OK, okay,okey, 发音均为 [.ouˈkeɪ]) 的变形。O.K. 是 19 世纪上半叶开始出现的。okey-doke 比 O. K.的说法轻松得多，是 20 世纪的产物。请读者注意：okey-doke 中的 okey 与 O.K.的发音不一样。doke 是为语调好听而添加的，没有实际意义。*A: Will you do some shopping for me? B: Okey-doke. What do you want me to buy?* 甲：你可以去给我买点东西吗？乙：行。你想要买什么呢？为了合辙押韵，有时把 okey-doke 说成 okey-dokey [ˈoki.doki]，并将前者拼写为 okie-doke，后者拼写为 okie-dokie。◇ all right

old

(as) old as the hills → HILLS

be an old hand at *doing something* → HAND

be old hat → HAT

an old hen → HEN

***one's* old lady** → LADY

***one's* old man** → MAN

an old salt [ə .nould ˈsɔ(:)lt] [话] **经验丰富的水手** → a GOB

an old wives' tale → TALE

once

for once [fər ˈwʌnts] [口] **就这一次** 意思是"与从来的情况不一样，破题儿第一遭"。根据上下文，常有"仅仅这一回"的意味。*This time try not to be late for once.* 这一回可别迟到啦。如果用过去时，则表示"这回终于……"。*For once our son got a good grade on his English test.* 这回我们的儿子在英语考试中终于取得了好成绩。为了表示"哪怕是一回"的强烈愿望，可添 just 加强语气。*Just for once I'd like to see that guy fall flat on his face.* 哪怕是一次，我也愿意看见那个家伙一败涂地。◇ as opposed to *someone's* usual habit [performance, etc.] / just (this) one time

(for) once and for all [(fər)ˈwʌntsən fəˈrɔ:l] [口] **一劳永逸** once 是"只这一回了"。for all 是 for all time，即"此后永久地"。本条的含义是："就是这一回了，以后永久保持这一回出现的状态"。古时讲 once for all，为了加强语气，中间插入一个 and。但现在 and 已失去强调的作用，于是在前边又加上个表示强调的 for。*Let's go and talk to him. I want to get this matter settled once and for all.* 咱们去跟他谈一下。我愿意把这个问题彻底解决，一劳永逸。*This'll cook his goose for once and for all.* 这回可以使他彻底完蛋啦。根据上下文，有时可以译作"以此为限"、"只此一遭"、""干干脆脆"等，但有一个共同点，就是都具有"这是最后一次"的意味。*For once and for all, stop calling me Tommy. My name is Thomas.* 这是最后一回，别再叫我汤米啦。我的名字叫托马斯。*If we can get a new part for this machine, we can solve the problem once and for all.* 如果我们能给这台机器弄到一个新部件，问题便可以永远解决啦。*I'm telling you for once and for all, if you don't stop pestering me you'll be sorry.* 我这是最后一次警告你。如果你不停止纠缠我，你将来会后悔的。◇ finally and conclusively / for the last time

once too often [.wʌnts .tu(:)ˈɔ:fən] [口] **屡次三番，引来恶果** 直译为"又来一次，太

过分了”。严格地说，本条不是指“程度”，而是指“次数”。在如下的场合使用：一个人的言语、行为或危险的做法，过去已经多次引起对方的反感或愤怒，现在又来一次，这就超过最后的界限，“太过分了”，终于造成一定的灾祸。请读者注意：不仅仅是“常常”或“终于”的意思。例如说：*He was caught calling his boss names once too often and lost his job.* 这句话的意思不是“他常说老板的坏话，终于被抓住了，因而失掉了自己的工作”，正确的意思是：“他虽然屡次三番被发现说老板的坏话，可是都得到了原谅，这回却是最后的一次，他被革职了”。本条没有与它相当的汉语成语或习语，只能根据上下文的意思翻译，无法生搬硬套。*One of these days you're going to make me angry once too often.* 你老惹我生气，早晚有一天我要给你点儿颜色看看。*Pete has finally thumbed his nose at the law once too often. He was arrested last night.* 皮特老是犯法，终于难逃法网，昨天晚上被捕了。*I'm a patient man, but some day that fellow's going to take advantage of my good nature once too often.* 我是一个能忍耐的人，不过，那个家伙老是利用我的善良的天性，总有一天会有他好瞧的。*Carl often passes other cars on blind curves. One of these days he's going to do it once too often.* 卡尔常常在看不清前方的拐弯处超车。早晚有一天他会惹祸的。有时用 just 加强语气，而讲 just once too often。*This is the last straw. You've ignored my orders just once too often.* 这一回再也不能忍受啦。你多次不听我的命令，现在可不能再放过你了。◇ once more than is wise

once-over

give *something* **a once- over** [.gɪv ~ ə'wʌn.tsouvər] [话] **简单搞一下**

once-over 是“粗略地做一回”的意思。*I didn't have time for the hairdresser to do my hair properly, so I just had him give it a once-over.* 我没有时间做头发，只叫美发师简单地搞了一下。*I'll be with you in a minute. Just let me give my mail a once-over.* 我马上跟你一起走，让我把信件整理一下。可以用 quick 加强语气，作 a quick once-over (极简单地搞一下)。*You needn't clean the living room carefully today. Just give it a quick once-over.* 今天你不必仔细打扫起居室，只稍微弄一下就行啦。*I didn't read the contract carefully. I just gave it a quick once-over.* 我没有仔细看那份合同，只是过了过目。a good once-over 虽然也是“草草了事”的意思，但有“大概搞了一遍”的意味。*I give the newspaper a good once-over on the train every morning.* 我每天早晨在列车上把报纸浏览一番。*The car wasn't very dirty, so I just gave it a good once-over with a rag.* 汽车并不太脏，所以我只用湿抹布把它简单擦了一遍。→ give *someone* [*something*] the ONCE-OVER ◇ give *something* a brief treatment [examination]

give *someone* [*something*] **the once- over** [.gɪv~ ðə'wʌn.tsouvər] [话] **瞧一眼**

once-over 加不定冠词 (a once-over) 后，意义有变化，因而容易混淆(→ give *something* a ONCE-OVER)。the onceover 和 a once-over 不同，专用于表示“对人、物、地点瞧一眼”的意思。*All the men in the office gave the new secretary the once-over.* 办公室里的所有男子，都向新来的女秘书瞧了一眼。*When I entered the room I felt everyone giving me the once-over.* 当我走进房间的时候，我感到每个人的视线都集中到我身上了。*There's a guy outside who claims he's on the lam from the cops. You'd better go out and give him the once-over.* 外面来了个小伙子，说是从警察手里逃出来的。你最好出去瞧一瞧。以下是“对物瞧一眼”的场合。*As I drove into the parking lot, a suspicious-looking man gave my car the once-over.* 当我把汽车开入停车场的时候，一个神情可疑的男子向我的车瞧了一眼。下边是“地点”的场合。*I don't know what the man wanted. He just came in, gave the place the once-over, and went out again.* 我不晓得那个男子要干什

么。他走进屋里,向周围打量一番,又走出去了。◇ give *someone* [*something*] a rapid examination / run *one's* eyes over *someone* [*something*]

one

do number one [ˌdu(:) ˌnʌmbər ˈwʌn] [话] **撒尿** → GRUNT

have one too many [ˌhæv ˌwʌn.tuː ˈme(:)ni] [话] **饮酒过多** one too many 是"多余一个"。用法如下: *I'd like to return this handkerchief. You sent me one too many.* 这个手帕还给你,因为你多送给我一个。*I never want to have another experience like that. I've had one too many.* 我永远不想再有一次那样的经历了,那一次已经够多的啦。如果没有上下文,只说 have one too many, 这是"饮酒过多"的意思。也就是说,这是一个成语。这里的 one 与 one drink 相同,是"一杯酒"的意思。按字面意义, have one too many 应该是"多喝了一杯",但这是习用语,并不限定"一杯"。*I had one too many last night.* 我昨天晚上酒喝多了。可以象这样用过去时,但一般是用完成时。例如: *No more, thanks. I've already had one too many.* 谢谢,别给我斟酒啦。我已经喝多了。*From the way the man walked, I could tell he had had one too many.* 从那个人走路的样子,我敢肯定他喝多了。*When my stomach started turning over, I realized I had had one too many.* 我一开始恶心,就知道自己已经喝得太多啦。另有一个说法是 have a few too many, 可以认为意思完全相同。*Jack had had a few too many. As soon as he got into the car, he fell asleep.* 杰克已经喝得太多了。他刚一上汽车就睡着了。◇ drink too much

look out for number one [ˌlu.kautfə ˌnʌmbər ˈwʌ(:)n] [话] **把自己的利害放在第一位** 这里的 number one 是"自己"的意思。据说,本条的来源是由于数字的"1"与英语的"I"(我)很相似。有"最重要的东西 (number one) 是自己(I)"的意思。在狄更斯 (Charles Dickens, 1812-1870) 的小说中多次出现,历史相当悠久。look out for 在这里与 look after 或者 take care 相同,有"爱护"、"珍惜"的意思。根据上下文,有时含有"自私自利"的贬意,但一般用以表达"不是完全不顾他人,而是首先考虑自己的利害"的意思。*This is a tough world, Jimmy. You've got to learn to look out for number one.* 吉米,这是一个冷酷无情的世界。你必须学会维护自己的利益。*Bill ran away when we were attacked by those bullies yesterday. As usual, he thought only of looking out for number one.* 昨天那些小霸王袭击我们的时候,比尔赶紧逃走了。和平常一样,他只顾保全自己。如这一例句所示,常用 only 或 just 调整语调,加强语气。*I'm not being selfish. I'm just looking out for number one.* 我不是出于自私,我只是爱护自己而已。*It's not that I don't trust you when I ask payment at the time of delivery. All sorts of things can happen, and I'm just looking out for number one.* 我要求你在交货时付款,这并不是我不信任你。现在什么事情都可能发生,我只不过考虑自己的利益而已。也可以采取如下的形式。*In the world of business, it's only natural to look out first of all for number one.* 在做生意这一行,首先维护自己的利益是理所当然的事情。look out for 可以用 look after、take care of、think of [about] 等代换。*Don't think me greedy. You have to admit that it's only natural that I look after number one.* 你不要认为我贪多无厌。你应该承认,我维护自己的利益是理所当然的事情。也有如下的应用形式。*Chuck'll never risk his life on my behalf. All he ever thinks about is old number one.* 查克绝对不会为我去冒生命的危险。他心里所想的照旧是他自己。◇ look after *oneself* [*one's* own interests]

ten to one [ˈte(:)ntə ˈwʌ(:)n] [话] **十拿九稳** → DOLLARS to doughnuts

tie one on [ˌtaɪ ˌwʌ(:) ˈnɔːn] [话] **痛饮** 本条从何而来,语源未定。*I feel at loose ends. Let's go out and tie one on tonight.*

我闲着太闷得慌。今天晚上咱们出去痛痛快快喝一顿吧。如这一例句所示,一般指到外边去与朋友一起喝,但"在家里与朋友一道喝"、"在外边一个人喝"或者"在家里一个人喝",也都可以使用本条。*No wonder you have a headache today. You really tied one on last night.* 难怪你今天头痛,昨天晚上你实在喝太多啦。这句话是表示"数量大",但也可以用于与喝酒数量无直接关系的"吵吵嚷嚷"的场合。*The whole staff tied one on at the office party.* 在公司的晚会上,全体职工饮酒作乐,热闹极了。*Charlie usually doesn't drink much, but once in a while he really ties one on.* 查理平日不大喝酒,有时却痛饮一番。如这一例句所示,本条习用语常用 really 加强语气。◇ get (gloriously) drunk / have a wildly good time (drinking)

one-armed

a one-armed bandit → BANDIT

one-horse

a one-horse town → TOWN

one-track

have a one-track mind → MIND

onions

know *one's* **onions** [ˌnou ～ˈʌnjənz] [话] **精通业务** 为什么说"知道自己的葱头",不详。在这里,onions 意味着"内容和方法"。本条是指对自己所干的工作具有丰富的知识,非常熟悉工作的方法。相当轻松的说法。*We don't have many employees in our office, but they all know their onions.* 我们公司没有很多职工,但是他们全都精通自己的业务。*Not many English teachers are fluent in speaking, but when it comes to grammar, most of them know their onions.* 英语教师中能流利讲英语的人并不多,但一谈到语法,他们几乎个个精通。常用 really 加强语气。*If you want to know about pottery-making, you should ask Kay. She really knows her onions.* 如果你想了解有关制作陶瓷的事情,去问凯好啦。她真是精通此道啊。另有 know *one's* stuff 的说法,也很轻松。*When it comes to automobile engines, that guy really knows his stuff.* 要讲汽车的引擎,那家伙真是精通啊。◇ have a thorough knowledge of what *one* is doing / know everything about *something*

on-the-spot

on-the-spot [ˈɔnðəˈspɑ(ː)t] [口] **当场(的)** → on the SPOT ①

onto

be onto *someone* [ˈɔːntə ～] [话] **识破某人的阴谋** → be onto *someone's* GAME

oodles

oodles [ˈuːdlz] [话] **非常多** 与 lots [ˈlɑ(ː)ts] (许多)的用法相同,但使人感到比 lots 还多得多。自古就有的说法,原为方言,1890 年左右变成普通话,1900～1920 年间最为流行。现在仍然可以常常听到。不过,近年以来,由于此词带有脂粉气或童稚气,一般男性几乎无人使用了。这是一个轻松的表达法。*I've got oodles of homework.* 我有非常多的家庭作业。*Why don't we have something to eat? There's oodles of time before the movie starts.* 咱们吃点东西去吧。离电影开演还有好长时间哪。顺便提一下:贝尼·古德曼 (Benny Goodman, 1909～)的古典爵士乐名曲中有一支曲子叫做"Oodles of Noodles",这没有什么意义,只是一个合辙押韵的顺口溜式的题名。◇ a lot of

open

an open secret → SECRET

an open sesame (to *something*) → SESAME

opera

a horse opera [ə ˈho(ː)rˌsɑ(ː)prə] [口] **西部剧** 直译为"马的歌剧",亦即"有马上台的歌剧",即"西部剧"。广播、电视、电影均可,特别指用十天左右时间、花很少本钱拍出来的老一套的"牛仔影片"。*There's a horse opera on at the Orion.* 奥利昂影院在上演一部西部剧。在这句话里，“西部剧”只不过是 cowboy movie (牛仔影片)的代名词而已。但在一般的场合，都含有轻蔑的意义。*I want to see a good Western, not just any old horse opera.* 我想看的是真正的西部剧，而不是任何老一套的瞎凑合的东西。一些根本瞧不起西部剧的人也会这样说：*All Westerns are horse operas to me.* 在我看来，所有的西部剧都是耍弄牛仔的无聊的东西。◇ a cowboy movie

a soap opera [ə ˈsou ˌpɑ(:)prə] [口] **肥皂剧** 这一名称的来源是：从前，美国广播电台在白天主要播放由肥皂公司赞助的情节剧。现在专指电视中的情节剧。一般带有若干轻蔑的意味。*Japanese and American women are much alike in that both are fond of soap operas.* 日本妇女与美国妇女有一点很相似，她们都喜欢看肥皂剧。*Some American daytime soap operas have been running for years and still the heroine hasn't gotten married.* 美国有几部白天播放的肥皂剧已经连续播了好几年，至今女主角还没有结婚哪。*The Joneses have two television sets because she likes soap operas and he likes horse operas.* 琼斯家有两台电视机，因为太太喜欢看肥皂剧，丈夫喜欢看西部剧。◇ a (daytime) melodrama

operation

a shoestring operation [ə ˈʃu(:)strɪŋ ˌɑpeˈreɪʃən] [口] **用很少的资金仔细经营的事业** → operate on a SHOESTRING

opportunity

a ground-floor opportunity [ə ˌgraund.flo(:)r ɑpərˈtʃu:nəti] [口] **由于最初参加而享有的优先获利或提升的机会** → get in on the ground FLOOR

oral

an oral [ə ˈnɔ(:)rəl] [话] **口头答辩** 请注意 an oral exam(ination) 与 an oral 的区别：前者指一般的所谓“口试”。如果省略 exam(ination)而只说 an oral，通常仅指博士等的“口头答辩”或“论文答辩”。许多教授面对一名学生，根据他所写的论文提出种种问题，有时需要好几个小时。*I have an oral in philosophy tomorrow.* 明天我要进行哲学的口头答辩。一般集中在一天或两天进行，所以多用复数形式。*When do you have orals?* 你什么时候进行口头答辩？也可以采取 *one's* orals 的形式。*I can't take a vacation this summer. I have to prepare for my Ph. D. orals.* 今年夏天我不能休假了。我得准备取得哲学博士学位的口头答辩。*His orals are scheduled for next spring.* 他的口头答辩预定在明年春季进行。◇ an oral examination

order

in apple-pie order [ɪ ˈnæ(:)pəlˈpaɪ ˈɔ(:)rdər] [话] **整整齐齐** 直译为“象苹果馅饼一样有秩序”。但本条的意思与“苹果馅饼”毫无关系。语源不详，据一般的说法是：这一 apple pie 的祖先是法语的 *nappes pliées* [ˈnap pliˈje]。*nappes pliées* 则与英语的 folded linen 相同，是“衬衣、枕套、餐巾、桌布等折叠得干干净净、整整齐齐的亚麻布类”的意思。这一法语传入英语之后，讹误为在意义上与之毫无关系但发音相似的既存的英语 apple pie，以 in apple-pie order 的形式为人们所使用。*The guest room was in apple-pie order.* 客室非常整洁。*Except for a pair of dirty shoes in the foyer, the whole house appeared to be in apple-pie order.* 除了门廊有一双脏的鞋而外，整个家似乎非常整洁。如这一例句所示，与 be 动词一起使用的场合最多，当然并不限定如此。*Amy always keeps her desk in apple-pie order.* 艾米总是把她的书桌收拾得很整齐。◇ very tidy

a tall order [ə ˈtɔ:l ˈɔ(:)rdər] [口] **难完成的任务** 这里的 tall 与 a tall STORY 的 tall 相同，作“规模大”讲。tall story 的意思是“说的话太玄，令人难以相信”；tall order 的意思是“要求得过高，很难完成任务”。使用范围很广，不仅按照字面意义用于向裁缝铺定做衣服，而且用于朋友间、父母子女间相互委托的事情，以及上级的命令等。*You want us to make two suits for you by next Monday? That's a tall order, but I think we can do it.* 你定做两套衣服，要下星期一交活吗？这很难办哪。不过，我们可以努力完成。常用 mighty 加强语气。*A: Would you pay my way to study abroad for two years, Dad? B: That's a mighty tall order, son. I'll have to think about it.* 甲：爸爸，我想到外国留学二年，你能供给我学费吗？乙：孩子，你这给我出了个好大的难题。我得考虑考虑才行。*A: I want you to finish this work by the end of the week. B: That's a mighty tall order, boss. Can't I have until Monday?* 甲：我希望你本周末完成这个工作。乙：老板，这个要求太难达到了。到星期一行不行？◇ a (very) difficult request [order]

ostrich

play ostrich [ˌpleɪ ˈɑːstrɪtʃ] [口] **掩耳盗铃** → bury *one's* HEAD in the sand

ounce

An ounce of prevention is worth a pound of cure. [ə ˈnaunʦəv prəˈve(ː)nʧənəz ˌwə(ː)rθə ˈpaundəv ˈkju(ː)ər] [谚] **一分预防等于十分治疗** 直译为"一盎司的预防与一磅的治疗价值相等"。这一谚语说明预防的重要性，意思是："预防并不费什么劲，一旦有了病，那就要大吃苦头了"。可以按照字面意义使用，也可以作为比喻使用。*I know that smallpox shots are no longer necessary for overseas travel, but we had the children vaccinated anyway. After all, an ounce of prevention is worth a pound of cure.* 我知道去海外旅行已经没有必要注射天花疫苗了，但是我叫孩子们都种了痘。不论如何，一分预防等于十分治疗啊。*It's true that a lot of tax money goes into the national defense budget, but an ounce of prevention is worth a pound of cure.* 不错，国防预算是占用了大量的税收，但是一分预防等于十分治疗啊。有不少成语是以这一谚语为基础，仅代换名词，句子的构造完全不变。例如，有一个表达法是：An ounce of practice is worth a pound of theory. (一分实践等于百分理论。) 不过，这一表达法不如本条的使用率高。*All they do in those meetings is talk, talk, talk. If you ask me, an ounce of practice is worth a pound of theory.* 他们在那些会议中所干的事情，就是不住嘴地说，说，说。如果叫我讲，一分实践等于百分理论啊。另外有 An ounce of hard work is worth a pound of good intentions. (一分艰苦的工作等于百分良好的意图。) An ounce of solid fact is worth a ton of mere gossip. (一分确切的事实等于百分的捕风捉影。) 如果利用 An ounce of ~ is worth a pound of ~. 这一句型，改换名词，随时随地都可以自己制成谚语。◇ A small measure of precaution is as effective as large amounts of remedial action.

out

be down and out → DOWN

be down but not out [ˈdaun bətˌnɑ(ː)ˈdaut] [话] **虽然占下风，但并非投降** → be DOWN and out

feel down and out [ˌfi(ː)l ˌdau nəˈnaut] [话] **一点也打不起精神** → be DOWN and out

have it out (with *someone* over *something*) → HAVE

be out like a light → LIGHT

Out with it! [ˈautˌwɪðət] [话] **坦白交待！** out 是"(从嘴里)向外吐出"的意思。it 指打算叫对方说出来的事情。经常使用命令式。*Out with it! You were the one who stole that candy, weren't you?* 你说实话！是不是你偷了那糖果？如这一例句所示，可以对小孩子这样说。但在成年人之间也可以使用。*Where were you when you were supposed to be attending the sales meeting? Come on, out with it!* 你本来应该出席推销会议，可是你跑哪儿去啦？喂，坦白交代吧！◇ Tell me!

outa

outa [ˈaudə] [话] **从(什么地方)** out of 的音变。在轻松的日常会话中，out of 的 of 大多不发 f 音。因此，特别是在表示"从(什么地方)"的场合，在漫画或小说的对话部分，往往拼写作 outa。*It won't come outa the bottle.* 从瓶子里出不来呀。*Come outa there!* 从那里走出来！*Get outa here!* 从这里滚出去！◇ out of

outhouse

an outhouse [ə ˈnaut.haus] [口] **一家专用的室外厕所** 直译为“与住宅离开的屋子”。在美国，多年以来，这是“室外厕所”的委婉语。一提到 outhouse, 美国人的头脑里首先浮现出来的是在旧式农民住宅或山村房屋后边孤零零地立在那儿的古老的小厕所。因此，当你打算说“我的父母住在另外一所房子里”而用英语讲 My parents live in an outhouse. 的时候，是会使对方大吃一惊的。在这一场合，美国人一般回避 outhouse 这一表达法，而讲 a detached house [ə də.tæ(:)tʃt ˈhaus] 或者 an outbuilding [ə ˈnaut.bɪl-dɪŋ]。 *We still use an outhouse at our summer place.* 在我们的夏季别墅里，我们还使用室外厕所哪。又称 a johnny HOUSE。◇ an outdoor toilet

outs

be on the outs (with *someone*) [.ɔ(:)nðɪˈauts] [话] **失和** 美国英语的独特表达法。语源不明。本条不失 out 的本义，有“相互脱离”的意味。*For some reason, Lyle has been on the outs with his brother ever since their father died.* 不知什么原因，莱尔在父亲去世以后与他的哥哥感情不和。如这一例句所示，本条是以往日有过相互来往为前提的。*You and I have been on the outs for a long time. Why don't we bury the hatchet?* 你我二人已经有很长时间失和了。咱们言归于好如何？ *He and his wife seem to be on the outs these days.* 他和他的妻子最近似乎感情很不好。偶尔也有人用 be at outs (with *someone*), 意思和用法相同。*Those two have been at outs with each other since last summer when they had an argument over who should pay for the new fence between their property.* 自从去年夏天，那两个人为了他们的地产之间新修一道栅栏应该由谁付钱的问题发生争论之后，他们便失和了。◇ be on bad terms

outside

an outside chance → CHANCE

an outside possibility [əˈnəut.said .pɑsəˈbɪləti] [口] **只有一线希望** → an outside CHANCE

over

look all over (for *something* [*someone*]) [.lukɔː ˈlovər] [话] **到处搜索** → look HIGH and low (for *something* [*someone*])

overboard

go overboard [.go ˈouvər.bo(:)rd] [话] **过火** 直译为“从船上掉进[跳入]海中”。*When the big wave hit our boat, all of our gear went overboard.* 当大浪袭击我们的船的时候，所有的帆具都掉进海里去了。转用于形容“过度”、“过火”的样子，使用范围很广。例如：*I think it's a good idea, too. But let's not go overboard.* 我也认为这是一个好主意。不过，咱们不要做得太过火了。在这一场合，可能对方由于自己想出一个主意而兴高采烈，为了实现他的计划，什么也不考虑，一心要把人力物力全都投进去。说话的人则告诫他说：如果草率从事，以失败而告终，则鸡飞蛋打，不但得不到利，连本钱也要赔上，因此要“慎重”，也就是“不要过火”。下面我们看看各种“过度”或“过火”的状态，当然，在翻译成汉语时，应该根据具体情况仔细斟酌。*I'm sorry my dog tore your pants. He's so friendly that he often goes overboard.* 真对不起，我的狗撕破了你的裤子。它见人自来熟，往往亲昵得太过分了。*Roger went completely overboard over Nancy.* 罗杰对南希迷恋得如疯似狂了。如这一例句所示，常用 completely 加强语气。另外，go overboard 后边的 over 如果用 for 代替，就是“过度支持……”的意思。*For a while, every one went completely overboard for rock and roll.* 一时之间，人人都迷醉于摇摆舞了。以下也是同样，请注意前置词的变化。*His music is interesting, but it's nothing to go overboard about.* 他的音乐挺有意思，但是并不值得大吹大擂。*John has gone overboard on health foods.* 约翰过于注重保健食品了。如这一例句所示，如果前置词用 on, 则永远表示“做得过分”的意思。在这一场合是"吃保健食品过多",因而有"对身体并没有好处"的意思。此外,go overboard 的后边除接前置词+名词外,还可以接前置词+动名词,例如:*He's gone overboard in trying to create a new art style.* 他过分热衷于创造一种新的艺术风格,结果失败了。按照以上所讲,go overboard 的后边接前置词也好,不接前置词也好,或者是不论所接的前置词有什么变化,"过度"、"过火"的意思是始终不变的。也就是说,其中包含着若干批评的或者反省的味道。然而,从"过度"(即"去做不干也行的事情")一义进一步发展,本条习用语也可以表示强调,具有"拼命去干"的意味。*You should be more appreciative, Frank. Everyone's going overboard to help you.* 弗兰克,你应该表示更多的感谢才对。所有的人都在拼命地帮助你啊。从这一例句也可以看出,go overboard 在表示这种意味时,后边大多接 to+不定式。◇ become overly [very] excited (about *something* [*someone*]) / fall completely in love (with *someone*) / go too far (on *something*) / do *one's* best (to *do something*)

overcoat

a wooden overcoat [ə ˌwud'nouvər͵kout] [话] **棺材** 直译为"用木头制作的大衣"。黑社会用语。*Come with us. We've brought a wooden overcoat we want you to try for size.* 跟我们来。我们带来一个棺材,想叫你试一下尺寸合适不合适。又称 a wooden kimono [ˌwudnkə'mounə]。◇ a coffin

Ow

Ow! ['au / 'æ(ː)ou] [话] **好疼呀!** 用法如下:*Ow! I stubbed my toe!* 好疼呀! 我戳了一下我的脚趾! *Ow! Cut it out! I've got a sunburn.* 好疼呀! 快停止吧。我快晒焦了。本条是借用 Ouch! (好疼!)一词的前两个字母,按照发音拼写而成,与 Ouch! 完全同义,所有的 Ouch! 均可用它代换。尽管只能用于表示疼,但不仅表示肉体的疼,也可以表示心理上的"疼痛"。*A: Why should I care if I hurt your feelings? You didn't seem to care about mine last night! B: Ow! I guess I deserved that.* 甲:我为什么要注意是否伤了你的感情呢? 昨天夜里你似乎并没有注意我的感情呀! 乙:喔唷! 这就算我自作自受吧! 这一句话的构思是:"你这样说,真叫我痛心"。为了强调 Ow!,另有个表达法是 Ow-witch! ['auwɪtʃ / 'æːouwɪtʃ]。*Ow-witch! I banged my finger with the hammer.* 哎呀好疼! 榔头砸伤了我的手指。Ow-witch! 是把 Ouch! 的发音分成两节拼写而成。Ow! 和 Ow-witch! 都是极为轻松的说法。◇ Ouch!

owl

a night owl [ə 'naɪ͵daul] [口] **夜游神** 直译为"夜里活动的猫头鹰"。专作比喻使用。汉语俗语又称"夜猫子"。*I've always been a night owl. I never go to bed before twelve o'clock.* 我一向是个夜游神。我从来没有在十二点以前上床睡觉的时候。*Why don't you night owls go to bed? It's past three o'clock in the morning.* 你们这些夜猫子,怎么还不上床睡觉呀? 已经早晨三点多钟啦。→ night PEOPLE ◇ a person who habitually stays up late / a late stayer-upper

own

hold *one's* **own** [ˌhould ～'oun] [口] **坚持奋斗** own 的意思是 that which belongs to oneself (属于自己的东西),亦即指 position (立场), condition (状态)等。hold 是"保持"。本条习用语使用最多的场合是:"尽管对手强"、"尽管情况不利"或者"尽管自己处于劣势",而要 hold *one's* own (坚持到底,寸步不让)。有时则表示"虽然痛苦,但能坚持"的意味。*Jake may be small, but he can hold his own in any fight.* 别看杰克个子小,不管跟什么人打架,他都毫不让步。*Though our team lost in the end, it succeeded in holding its own against a much stronger opponent for most of the game.* 我们队虽然最后是输了,但是在大部分比赛时间内,一直不畏强敌,努力拼搏。*Our son is weak in English, but he has no difficulty holding his own in any mathematics class.* 我们的儿子英语差一些,但是在数

学方面不次于班上的任何人。以上是“坚持奋斗，一步不让”的例子。以下的例句则具有“极力维持”或“努力挣扎”的意味。*America appears to be having difficulty holding its own in international markets these days.* 最近，美国在国际市场上拼命挣扎保持它自己的地位。*Though extremely weak, the patient is holding his own.* 患者虽然非常虚弱，还勉强支撑着自己。*Despite constant pounding by heavy waves, our little boat was holding its own.* 我们的小船虽然不断受到大浪的冲打，却依旧向前航行。◇ compete evenly / maintain *one's* position / not regress [falter]

be *one's* **own man** → MAN

own up (to *something*) [ˌou ˈnʌ(ː)p] [口] **坦率承认** 一般说来，比 confess 或 admit 积极，本条充满“好汉做事好汉当”的意味。*When his father accused him of having broken the window, Jimmy immediately owned up.* 当父亲责问吉米打破窗户玻璃的时候，吉米立即承认了。*The suspect admits that he stole the money, but he refuses to own up to the murder.* 嫌疑犯承认他偷了钱，但拒不坦白杀了人。*Own up! You cheated on the exam, didn't you!* 坦率承认！你在考试的时候作弊了，是吧！◇ confess

Ow-witch

Ow-witch! [ˈauˈwɪtʃ / ˈæːouˈwɪtʃ] [话] **哎呀真疼！** → Ow！

OX

a dumb ox [ə ˈdʌ(ː)ˈmɑːks] [话] **笨牛** 指身材高大的笨蛋。→ a LUMMOX

(as) strong as an ox [əz ˈstrɔ(ː)ŋ əzə ˈnɑ(ː)ks] [口] **力气特别大** ox 是“去势的役牛”，一般认为这种牛力气非常大，体质特别壮。*That guy is as strong as an ox. He pulled the car out of the mud single-handed.* 那个家伙力大如牛，他一个人就把小汽车从泥塘中拉上来了。*You can never hope to beat him. He's strong as an ox.* 你永远也甭指望打败他。他的力气非常大。ox 除如以上所述，有“力气非常大”的意味外，还有“愚笨”的形象。这与中国人的观念完全一致，既可以说“力大如牛”，也可以说“其笨如牛”。*Tim is as strong as an ox, and just as stupid, too.* 蒂姆力大如牛，其笨也如牛。as strong as an ox 一般是在谈到“力气”的时候使用，有时从“强壮的体格”这一具体形象出发，在谈到“健康”的场合也用它来形容，表示“顽健”、“非常结实”的意思。*I'm strong as an ox. I never get sick.* 我象牛一样强壮，从来也不生病。◇ extremely strong [healthy]

P

packing

send *someone* **packing** [ˌsend ~ ˈpæ(ː)kɪŋ] [话] **马上撵出去** pack 是"打包"。因此, send *someone* packing 原来是"叫某人去打包",亦即"叫某人收拾行李走出去"的意思。专作比喻使用,例如: *If your brother shows up at my office again, I'll send him packing.* 如果你的弟弟再到我的办公室来,我要马上把他撵出去。但在下一例句中,仍残留着几分原来的意味。*Any student discovered cheating on an exam will be sent packing.* 凡是在考试中作弊的学生,一经发现,将被勒令退学。这与汉语俗语"卷铺盖走人"的说法不谋而合。另外,本条习用语本身并没有"解雇"的意思,但在某种情况下,也可能表示这一意义。*When the boss found Ron loafing on the job, he sent him packing.* 当老板发现罗恩在磨洋工,他马上把他辞掉了。◇ order *someone* to leave / immediately dismiss *someone*

pad

hit the pad [ˌhɪtðə ˈpæːd] [话] **上床睡觉** → a PAD

a pad [ə ˈpæ(ː)d] [话] **公寓** 直译为"填料"、"垫子"。原为黑社会歹徒们的用语,指"床"。后来爵士音乐家们用它指"有床的地方",又进一步发展为"公寓"的意思并固定了下来。虽然说是"公寓",但一般不包括全家居住的套房,仅指单身汉租用的房间。这一表达法本来带有"狭窄"或"简陋"的意思,但现在并不一定指这一类房间,也可以指豪华的房间。*I've rented a pad in Long Island.* 我在长岛租了一间公寓。*Al and I have a three-room pad near the office.* 阿尔和我在公司附近租了一套三室的公寓。也可以使用 *one's* pad 的形式。*Come on to my pad. It's not far from here.* 到我的公寓去坐坐吧。离这儿不远。*Let's go to Jim's pad and listen to records.* 咱们到吉姆的公寓去听唱片吧。现在,有时仍用以表示"床"或"寝室"的意思。*If you're sleepy, you can use my pad. It's in the next room.* 如果你困啦,可以到我的床上去睡。就在隔壁房间。*The three of us rent an apartment together, but it has three bedrooms so we each have our own pad.* 我们三个人共同租了一套公寓,不过它有三个卧室,因此我们各有自己的房间。hit the pad 是"上床睡觉"的意思 (→ hit the HAY)。◇ a place / an apartment

pad *something* [ˈpæ(ː)d ~] [口] **虚报** → pad the BILL (with *something*) / pad *someone's* ACCOUNT (with *something*) / pad *one's* expense ACCOUNT / pad the ROLLS (with *something*)

paddy

a paddy wagon → WAGON

pain

a pain in the neck [əˌpeɪ nɪnðə ˈne(ː)k] [话] **讨厌的人或事物** 如果是 a pain in *one's* neck, 这是"脖子痛",例如: *I've got a pain in my neck.* 我脖子痛。如果是 the neck, 一般用比喻的意义,经常含有"非常麻烦"、"令人焦躁"的意味。与各种不同的动词一起使用,但结合 be 动词的时候最多。*That guy is a pain in the neck. Every time I see him he either wants to tell me his troubles or borrow some money.* 那是一个讨厌的家伙。每次我见到他,他不是向我诉苦,就是要借几个钱。*Apple polishers are a pain in the neck to conscientious teachers.* 对于有良心的教师,送礼拍马的学生实在讨厌极了。常使用 real 加强语气。*Being chairman of that committee is a real pain in the neck. I realize it's an honor, but it takes too much of my time.* 当那个委员

会的委员长简直令人头痛死啦。我知道这是一种荣誉，但是它使我花费的时间太多了。*This car is a real pain in the neck. It's always breaking down on me.* 这部汽车实在让人头痛死啦。它三天两头总出毛病。也常使用 give *someone* a pain in the neck 的形式，但在这一场合，以人作主语的时候居多。*That guy gives me a pain in the neck. He's forever complaining about something or other.* 那个家伙让我讨厌极了。他不是对这件事不平，就是对那件事不满。*I didn't mind this job at first, but recently it has become a pain in the neck.* 我最初没有把这个工作当作一回事，但是近来它使我感到讨厌极了。◇ be extremely bothersome

paint

paint the town [ˌpeɪntðə ˈtaun] [话] **在闹市出入酒吧狂饮作乐** → paint the TOWN red

pajamas

the cat's pajamas [ðə ˌkæ(ː)ts pəˈdʒɑːməz] [话] **了不起的人或物** → the cat's MEOW

pale

(as) pale as a ghost [əz ˈpeɪləzə ˈgoust] [话] **面无人色** → (as) white as a SHEET

palm

grease *someone's* palm [ˌgriːz ～ ˈpɑːm] [口] **向某人手里塞钱** 在 18 世纪以前，似乎不是用 palm，而是用 hand。现在的形式是中世纪法语 *oindre la paume à quelqu'un* 的直译，逐字翻译是"向某人的手心涂油"。语源没有定论。由于这是为了有利于自己而使用金钱的行为，所以使用范围很广，从给服务员小费一直到犯罪性质的贿赂，都可以说"向手心涂油"。*The restaurant was so crowded that we had to grease the waiter's palm in order to get a table.* 餐厅里挤满了人，为了找个座位，我们不得不往服务员手里塞点钱。*The old man will help you for nothing, but it's best to grease his palm a bit if you don't want to listen to his grumbling all day.* 那个老头可以白尽义务去帮助你，但是，如果你不想听他整天发牢骚，最好还是塞给他一点钱。塞钱的对象如果是"复数"(不止一个人)，则用 palms。*The building contractor was indicted for greasing a few official palms.* 那个建筑业承包商被指控向一些官员行贿。条头中的 *someone's* 可以换成定冠词 the，构成 grease the palm of *someone* 的形式。*That's a terrible country. Though we had reservations, we couldn't get on the plane until we had greased the palm of the man at the check-in counter.* 那是一个可怕的国家。虽然我们预订了座位，但是直到我们向验票人员的手里塞钱，我们才获准登机。◇ give *someone* some money

have an itchy palm [ˌhævə ˌnɪtʃi ˈpɑːm] [话] **贪脏** 前一条所讲的 grease *someone's* PALM 是"行贿"的意思，这一条 have an itchy palm 则是"受贿"的意思。正式说法是 have an itching palm，但在轻松的日常会话中，大多不用 itching 而用 itchy。直译为"手心发痒"，亦即"想捞点钞票"的意思。*It's a sad state of affairs when even the Prime Minister turns out to have an itchy palm.* 连首相都一心要捞外快，这种情况实在可悲。可以用于比"贿赂"轻的场合，例如：*Do you have any loose change? The reservation clerk seems to have an itchy palm.* 你带着零钱吗？预约处的人似乎想要点好处费。*You can't do anything in that country without slipping people money. Practically everyone you meet has an itching palm.* 在那个国家里，你不偷偷地塞给人家钱，任何事情也办不成。实际上，你遇见的每个人都想捞点外快。因为原意为"手心发痒"，所以只要搔一下就行了。可以使用 scratch (搔)一词构成如下的独特说法：*He won't tell you, you say? Here. Here's a ten-dollar bill. Try scratching his palm with this.* 你是说，他不愿意告诉你吗？喏，这是一张十美元的钞票，你往他手里塞一下看。◇ want to be given (some) money

scratch *someone's* **palm** [ˌskræ(:)tʃ ～ ˈpɑːm] [话] **行贿** → have an itchy PALM

pan

a flash in the pan → FLASH

jump out of the frying pan into the fire [ˌdʒʌmˌpaudəðə ˈfraɪɪŋˌpæ(:)n ˌɪntəðəˈfaɪr] [话] **跳出油锅,又落火坑** 汉语中这类俗话很多,如:"正离狼窝,又逢虎口","从屎窝挪到尿窝",反正是躲过了这一灾,又遇到更大的祸。*I realize you're in a difficult position, but borrowing from high-interest loan sharks to pay off your debts is just jumping out of the frying pan into the fire.* 我知道你的处境很困难。但是,如果为了还债而向放高利贷的人借钱,那可真是跳出油锅又落火坑啊。有时用 from 代替 out of。*When I ran into the hallway to escape the heat and smoke in my room, the flames leaping up on all sides told me that I had simply jumped from the frying pan into the fire.* 当我为了逃避自己室内的热浪和浓烟而奔到走廊里的时候,周围全是熊熊的火焰。这使我明白:自己刚离狼窝,又进了虎口啊。动词 jump 可以用 fall 或 leap 代换。*I think we should wait a while before we act. We don't want to risk falling out of the frying pan into the fire.* 我认为咱们在行动之前应该等待一下,我们总不愿意去冒跳出油锅又落火坑的危险吧。以本条条头的英语为基础,可以有各种各样的说法。把习用语稍加改变,逗人发笑,这是英语报章杂志常用的手法之一。*Cinderella says that as much as she dislikes her stepmother, she is not ready to exchange the frying pan of her terrible home life for the uncertain fires of marriage.* 灰姑娘说,虽然她不喜欢她的继母,但是她还不准备跳出她那油锅般可怕的家庭生活,而跳入难以预料的结婚的火坑。◇ go from a bad situation into a worse (one)

pan out [ˌpæ(:)ˈnaut] [话] **一帆风顺** 名词 pan 是"淘金的大锅"。作为动词使用,则是"选矿 (淘沙金等)"。out 是副词,表示"顺利淘出沙金等"的意味。如果按照字面意义使用 pan,一般不加 out。例如:*We panned two ounces of gold yesterday.* 昨天我们淘出了两盎司黄金。也就是说,如果象条头那样采取 pan out 的形式,则专用于表示比喻的意义。又,pan out 多在疑问句或否定句中使用。例如:*What do you think of Paul's plan? Do you think it will pan out?* 你认为保罗的计划如何?你觉得会一帆风顺地执行吗? *Don't fret about a little failure like this. You can't expect things to pan out every time.* 不要为这样小小的挫折而烦恼。你不能期望事情总是一帆风顺的啊。请读者注意以下两个否定式的差异。*Our trip to Europe didn't pan out. My office canceled my vacation at the last minute.* 我们去欧洲旅行的计划告吹了。在临出发之前一分钟,公司取消了我的假期。*Our trip to Europe didn't pan out very well. We were stuck in our Paris hotel most of the time because of a transportation strike.* 我们的欧洲旅行并非一帆风顺。由于交通系统的罢工,我们大部分时间被困在巴黎的旅舍里了。第一句是"完全告吹",没有去成。第二句由于后边加上 (very) well, 便是"虽然有曲折,但是达到了目的"的意思了。◇ be successful / work out (well)

pancake

(as) flat as a pancake [əz ˈflædəzə ˈpæ(:)nˌkeɪk] [话] **压扁** 直译为"象薄饼一样平"。*The land stretching to the far horizon was as flat as a pancake.* 大地一马平川,直伸到天边。可以象这样使用,强调陆地的"平坦"。但是,这一表达法一般用于形容有一定厚度的东西和有一定形状的东西被压瘪的样子。*Mr. Bigbum sat on my hat and mashed it flat as a pancake.* 比格巴姆先生一屁股坐到我的帽子上,把它压瘪啦。*I accidentally ran over the girl's doll and mashed it flat as a pancake.* 我一不留神开车压了小女孩的洋娃娃,把它完全弄瘪了。有时与外来的压力无关,而用本条形容"不够厚度"或"发育不足",如说:*Her chest is as flat as a pancake.* 她的胸部扁平。◇

perfectly flat

make a pancake landing → LANDING

pancake (on *something*) [ˈpæ(ː)nˌkeɪk] [话] **机身着陆** → make a pancake LANDING

panic

hit the panic button [ˌhɪtðə ˈpæ(ː)nɪk ˌbʌtn] [话] **惊慌失措** → push the panic BUTTON

push the panic button → BUTTON

pansy

a pansy [ə ˈpæ(ː)nzi] [俗] **男子同性恋者** → a QUEER

pants

by the seat of *one's* **pants** → SEAT

catch *someone* **with** *his* **pants down** [ˌkætʃ ~wɪð ~ ˈpæ(ː)nts ˌdaun] [话] **使人措手不及陷入窘境** → be caught with *one's* PANTS down

be caught with *one's* **pants down** [ˌkɔ(ː)t wɪð ~ˈpæ(ː)nts ˌdaun] [话] **措手不及陷入窘境** 这里的 be caught 不是"被抓住",而是"使人陷入窘境"或"使人现出窘状"。with *one's* pants down 的意思是:"裤子还未提起,正在脚面的时候"。本条习用语的整个意思是:"刚要穿裤子,在还没有把它提起来的时候,想不到有人走进屋里来了。"碰到这种情况,任何人也要感到狼狈不堪的。*Sally shouldn't have entered the bedroom without knocking. I was caught with my pants down.* 萨莉不敲门就走进卧室,实在太不应该了。我正要提裤子的姿态叫她碰上了。可以象这样按照字面意义使用。但一般使用其比喻的意义。作为比喻,意思是"在没有准备的情况下 (with *one's* pants down) 被人捉住了 (be caught)",经常含有"处于狼狈状态"的意思。*We hadn't expected a test before finals so we were caught with our pants down when the professor gave us a pop quiz today.* 我们没有预料在期终考试之前还会有测验,因此,今天老师搞突然袭击的测验时,我们都被弄得措手不及,陷入了窘境。*We were caught with our pants down when the bank unexpectedly gave notice that they were going to foreclose the mortgage on our home.* 银行突如其来地通知要取消我们住宅的抵押权,使我们陷入非常困窘的境地。这一表达法虽然大多使用被动语态,但也有 catch *someone* with *his* pants down 这样的主动语态。*The president's unexpected visit caught our branch office with its pants down.* 总经理突然前来,使得我们分公司狼狈极了。另外,从这一表达法所使用的文字来考虑,很象是男性的语言,但是,由于 native speaker 对于习用语并不死抠字面的意义,所以女性使用也没有什么奇怪之处。另外,这一表达法完全没有其他的恶意,在任何地方都可以安心使用。◇ be completely unprepared [off guard]

get the lead out of *one's* **pants** → LEAD

have ants in *one's* **pants** → ANTS

wear the pants in the family [ˌwerðə ˈpæ(ː)nts ɪnðə ˌfæ(ː)məli] [话] **当家** 直译为"在家庭中穿裤子"。过去,在夫妇之间掌握大权的是男性,而男性经常穿着长裤,因而产生了本条的比喻意义。*Most men make it very clear to their wives who wears the pants in the family.* 大多数的男人都使他们的妻子明确究竟由谁当家。如果自己认为已经说得很清楚,而妻子却不听从,男人就要大喊大叫了:*I told you I wear the pants in this family! Don't forget it!* 我已经跟你讲过了,这个家由我当! 你不要忘记这一点! 不过到了最近,丈夫的威风扫地,象下面这种情况已经不足为奇:*Mrs. Whozis seems to wear the pants in her family.* 胡吉斯家似乎由太太当家。顺便提一下:在一般的英文词典里大多译作"妇女当家"、"老婆掌权",但是,从上面的例句可以看出,这一表达法本身并没有如此的区别,对男女双方同样可以使用。另外,in the family 除可改用 in this [*one's*] family 外,还可以变换为 in this house, around here 等。又,在英国英语中,一般不用 wear the pants ~,而讲 wear the trousers ~,但在美国一定要说 wear the pants ~。◇ wield the power in the household

paper

be not worth the paper it's written on [nɑt ˌwərθðə ˌpeɪpərɪts ˈrɪtˌnɔːn] [口] **如同废纸** 直译为"纸上所写的东西还没有那张纸有价值"。可以认为这是强调 worthless (没有价值)的一种表达法。多用于"约定某种事情的文件",如 a contract (合同)、an agreement (契约)、a promissory note (期票)、an IOU (借据)等。*You've been swindled. This contract is not worth the paper it's written on.* 你被人欺骗啦。这张合同如同废纸一样。有时也用于契约类文件以外的东西。*That's the dullest book I've ever read. As a novel, it's not worth the paper it's written on.* 我头一次读这么索然寡味的书。象这样的长篇小说,简直跟擦屁股纸一样。◇ be absolutely worthless

a paper hanger → HANGER

ruled paper [ˈruːld ˈpeɪpər] [口] **带格的纸** 这是美国人极常用的表达法,但是一般英汉词典却不收录,因此本书列为专条。ruled 为形容词,意思是"用 ruler (尺)划了线的"。英语是横写的,ruled paper 当然是"横格纸",例如横格笔记本可以叫做 a ruled notebook。不过,在有必要区分"横格"或"竖格"的场合,前者可称 horizontally [ˌhɑrəˈzɑntəli] ruled paper,后者可称 vertically [ˈvərdəkli] ruled paper。再有,无格的纸英语叫做 unruled [unlined] paper,称 plain white paper (素白纸) 也可以。*Term reports must be written in ink on ruled paper.* 学期成绩报告单必须用钢笔在格纸上书写。顺便提一下:"方格纸"称 graph paper [ˈgræ(ː)f ˌpeɪpər]。◇ paper with horizontal lines

papers

get *one's* **walking papers** [ˌget ～ ˈwɔːkɪŋˌpeɪpərz] [话] **被开除** → give *someone his* walking PAPERS

give *someone his* **walking papers** [ˌgɪv ～ ～ ˈwɔːkɪŋˌpeɪpərz] [话] **开除** walking papers 直译为"使人走出工作单位的文件",也就是"解雇通知" (notice of dismissal) 的意思。*He was given his walking papers.* 他接到了解雇通知。如这一例句所示,本条习用语的意思是"用书面通知某人被解雇",但实际上并不问方法如何,一般只用于表示"开除"的意味。*The boss gave George his walking papers yesterday.* 昨天老板把乔治开除了。get *one's* walking papers 是"被开除"。*If you aren't careful, you're going to get your walking papers.* 如果你不小心谨慎,你就要被开除啦。有时使用其他的动词。*I picked up my walking papers last week.* 上个星期我被解雇了。◇ fire *someone*

Go peddle your papers. [ˌgou ˈpedl jərˈpeɪpərz] [话] **走开!** go peddle 的形式是在 go 与 peddle 之间省略了 and,这是美国英语的特征。也可以加上 and,而说 Go and peddle your papers. 不过欠缺一些劲头。peddle *one's* papers 原是"沿街卖报"的意思,不是在街角的报摊坐着卖,而是把报纸装在袋子里,向等信号灯的人或者步行的人们兜售。*He used to peddle papers when he was young.* 他年轻的时候曾经沿街卖报。在卖报的时候,或者呼喊当天新闻的大标题,或者死乞白赖地推销,都很令人讨厌。由于人们对报童讨厌,后来进一步发展,就对一切令人讨厌的对手以比喻的方式说 Go peddle your papers. (讨厌死啦,你赶紧卖报去吧!) 按语源来讲,这是对报童十分不敬的一个表达法。*Go peddle your papers. I'm certainly not going to pay you for an accident that wasn't my fault.* 你走开吧!事故不是由于我的过错造成的,我一分钱也不付给你。这是对方"令人讨厌地"找上门来的例子。一个人正在工作的时候,旁边的同事"令人讨厌地"向他讲话,他急得直发脾气,也使用本条。*Go peddle your papers, will you? Can't you see I'm busy?* 你走开好不好?你看不见我正在忙着吗?但是,周围的人们不论如何"令人讨厌",只要对方不直接前来说话,就不能使用本条。如以上的各例句所示,典型的用法是采取命令的形式,但也可以用 tell *someone* to go peddle *his* papers 的形式,这是本条的变形。又,在祈使句的场合必须有 Go，但在采取 tell *someone* ～的时候，可以省略 go。*When he came around wanting to borrow more money, I told him to go peddle his papers.* 当他前来说还要借些钱的时候，我对他讲："赶快给我走开吧！"这句话没有省略 go，而下一个例句是省略了的。*If that salesman shows up again, tell him to peddle his papers elsewhere.* 如果那个推销员再露面，你告诉他赶快到别处去吧。正如这一例句所示，在省略 go 的场合，大多要加个 elsewhere (到别处)。也就是说，加上 elsewhere (或者 somewhere else, to someone else), go 就有省略的可能性。不过，如果加上 elsewhere 或 somewhere else, 并不是非省略 go 不可，常有两者并存的情况。在实质上，这些副词无论加与不加，意思是相同的。总而言之，只不过是根据说话的语气，有时加有时不加而已。◇ Stop pestering me [*someone*]. / Go away.

par

be par for the course [ˈpɑ(:)r fəðə ˈko(:)rs] [话] **一般标准** par 是高尔夫球用语，即"标准打数"。be par for the course 直译为"合乎那个高尔夫球场的打数标准"。*Sam shot a seventy. That's par for the course.* 萨姆打了七十分，正够这个球场的标准。转用于高尔夫球以外的事情，也是"根据某项标准，恰恰合格"，亦即 be just about average 或 be nothing unusual 的意思。*I got only a 70 on the test but the teacher told me not to worry, that that was par for the course.* 我在考试中只得了个七十分，但是老师告诉我不必担心，那个分数正是合格的标准。*Don't worry about making only three sales this month. That's about par for the course for a new employee.* 不要为本月只卖掉三个而烦恼。对于新职工来说，这就合乎标准了。常用戏谑的语气使用这一表达法。*You say my wife smashed the fender on our car? Well, that's par for the course. She ruins four or five fenders every year.* 你是说我老婆把我家汽车的挡板撞坏了吗？是呀，那是合乎标准的。她每年都要撞坏四、五个挡板。*George is late again? Well, that's par for the course.* 乔治又迟到啦？是呀，这是老规矩。◇ be average [typical]

parade

parade *one's* ignorance [pəˈreɪd ～ ˈɪgnərən*t*s] [口] **暴露出愚昧无知** → parade *one's* KNOWLEDGE (of *something*)

parade *one's* knowledge (of *something*) → KNOWLEDGE

paradise

live in a fool's paradise [ˌlɪ(:)vɪnə ˈfu:lz ˈpæ(:)rəˌdaɪs] [口] **陶醉在虚无缥缈的乐境之中** 这一表达法因在莎翁《罗密欧与朱丽叶》(*Romeo and Juliet*) 第二幕第四场的对白中出现而有名。但实际上，在此以前本条就存在。直译为"在愚人的乐园中生活"。根据上下文，有时直译就可以理解它的含义。*After my fortune was gone and my seeming friends had turned their backs on me, I realized I had been living in a fool's paradise.* 在财产用光了、所谓的朋友视我如陌路人之后，我才明白自己过去是陶醉在虚无缥缈的乐境之中了。*Anyone who believes there is no danger of a nuclear war is living in a fool's paradise.* 凡是认为没有核战争危险的人，都是陶醉在虚无缥缈的乐境之中。a fool's paradise 大多与 live in 配套使用，但也有如下的用法。*Some claim that the welfare state is a fool's paradise which protects the lazy from having to face the realities of life as their country slides to its destruction.* 有些人认为福利国家是一种虚幻的幸福，当祖国日趋崩溃的时候，它使那些懒人不去面对人生严竣的现实。◇ be foolishly naïve

park

put *someone* in the ball park [ˌput ～ ɪnðə ˈbɔ:l ˌpɑ(:)rk] [话] **使人了解大致情况** 直译为"把某人放在棒球场内"。最初的构思是："如果有一定的情况，即便不让某人坐在棒球场的特定席位上，也应该让他进入球场之中"。作为比喻，是"使人了解某种情报的主要内容”的意思。*This formula won't give you the exact figure for the cost of the project, but it should put you in the ball park.* 这个计算式不能使你知道工程费用的精确数字，但是它会使你了解大致的情况。*A: How many planes does the enemy have? B: We don't know. But if we can learn the size of their pilot-training program, that should at least put us in the ball park.* 甲：敌人有多少架飞机？乙：我们不知道。但是，如果我们能够得知他们训练飞行员计划的大小，至少可以了解大致的情况。有时用 get 代替 put，意思不变。*These figures are awfully vague. I'm not sure they'll even get us in the ball park.* 这些数字太含糊啦。据我看，咱们通过这些数字连大致的情况也了解不到。也可以用 be 动词，作 be in the ball park，意思是“大致差不多”。*Our thinking as to how the market would go was way off. We weren't even in the ball park.* 我们关于市场动态的预测完全失败了，连一点边儿也没有沾啊。还有 ball-park 这样一个形容词，意思是“八九不离十的”。用法：只能做名词前的定语。*This is only a ball-park estimate. I'll give you the exact amount later.* 这只是一个大致的估计。准确数字容后奉告。以上的几种表达法都比较新，特别是商人和职员之间常常使用。◇ give *someone* a rough idea

parson's

the parson's nose [ðə ˈpɑ(ː)rsənz ˈnouz] [话] **(烹调的)鸡屁股** → the Pope's NOSE

particular

particular [pərˈtɪkjələr] [口] **爱挑剔的** → PERSNICKETY

parting

a parting shot → SHOT

party

a bachelor party [ə ˈbæ(ː)tʃələr ˌpɑ(ː)rdi] [口] **告别独身晚会** 男性友人为即将成为新郎的人举行的晚会，主要是在结婚典礼的前一夜聚集在一起，通宵狂欢作乐。有时也举行正式的晚宴，这种晚宴又称 a bachelor dinner [ˈbæ(ː)tʃələr ˈdɪnər]。无论是晚会或晚宴，都是主人公独身 (bachelor) 时代终结的纪念会。*The groom was late for the wedding because he drank too much at the bachelor party his friends gave for him.* 新郎由于在朋友们为他举办的告别独身晚会中喝得太多，迟误了结婚典礼的时间。另外，本条偶尔用于表示“单身汉晚会”的意思。◇ a party celebrating *someone's* last day(s) as a bachelor

crash the party [ˌkræ(ː)ʃðə ˈpɑ(ː)rdi] [话] **没有请柬闯入晚会** → crash the GATE [party]

a hen party [ə ˈhen ˌpɑ(ː)rdi] [话] **女人的聚会** hen 本来是“母鸡”，在这里为俚语指“女性” (→ an old HEN)。party 是“聚会”的意思。本条主要是男性使用，但与 old hen 不同，没有那种坏的意味，所以女性也有使用的。典型的女人聚会是摆上咖啡和糕点，大家闲聊，但并不以此为限，凡是只有女人参加的社交性的聚会，一概叫做 hen party。*My wife had a hen party at our house yesterday, so I escaped to the movies.* 我的妻子昨天在家里举行女人的聚会，所以我逃出来去看电影了。◇ a party for women only

a lynching party [ə ˈlɪntʃɪŋ ˌpɑ(ː)rdi] [话] **由群众处的绞刑** → a necktie PARTY

a necktie party [əˈnekˌtaɪ ˌpɑ(ː)rdi] [话] **由群众处的绞刑** 这里的 necktie (领带) 是“绞索”的意思。这种私刑是由某一群人执行，所以称为 party (聚会)。这是一个讽刺性的表达法，意思是“绞人的社交集会”。由于在西部电影的对话中经常出现，所以美国人家喻户晓。*When we catch that guy, we're going to have a necktie party.* 我们抓住那个家伙的时候，大家要对他处以绞刑。也称 a lynching [ˈlɪntʃɪŋ] party。◇ a hanging

a no-host party [ə ˌnouˌhoust ˈpɑ(ː)rdi] [口] **费用分担的社交集会** no-host 是“没有东道主”。这种社交集会由参加的人各自分担费用，形式上有主办者，但没有担负全部费用的东道主(host)。特别是美国西部常用本条。场所与一般的社交晚会相同,在家里可以,在店铺里也可以。大家不分摊现金而由各人带食品和饮料也行。*No-host parties have become very popular recently.* 最近非常流行费用分担的社交集会。*Our class is going to have a no-host party next week.* 我们班下个星期举行费用由各人分担的社交集会。本条又衍生出另外一些说法,如 no-host dinner (费用分摊的晚宴), no-host affair (费用分担的社交活动)等。*Our neighborhood has a no-host dinner at someone's house two or three times a year.* 我们的街坊每年有两三次在某一家举行费用分摊的晚宴。这一例句所讲的 no-host dinner,或是由大家凑钱买现成的菜(或自己烹调的原料),或是自带已经做好的饭菜。*Since our club's finances are pretty low, we've decided to make the Christmas party a no-host affair.* 由于我们俱乐部的财政状况很糟,所以我们决定在圣诞节时举行费用分担的社交晚会。◇ a party where everybody pays [brings food and drink]

a stag party [ə 'stæ(:)g ˌpɑ(:)rdi] [口] **男人的聚会** 特别指放映黄色影片或谈女人不堪入耳的话的社交集会。但是,只要没有女人参加,任何男人的聚会都可以使用这一表达法。参加的男性是单身汉也可以,不是单身汉也可以。*We're going to have a stag party this Saturday night.* 这个星期六晚间,我们准备来一个男人的聚会。在举行 a bachelor PARTY 时,也可以使用本条。◇ a party for men only

party-pooper

a party-pooper [ə 'pɑ(:)rdi.pu(:)pər] [话] **在社交活动中使大家扫兴的人** → a wet BLANKET

pass

make a pass at *someone* [ˌmeɪkə ˈpæ(:)sət ~] [话] **向女人调情** 这里的 pass 是击剑用语,意思是"刺"。*The fencer in black made three passes, but all of them were parried skillfully by his opponent.* 穿黑衣服的剑客刺了三次,但是都被对方巧妙地闪开了。这是按字面意义的用法。本条习用语就是由"刺"的意思转来的。可以用于飞眼吊膀子的场合,但一般指用花言巧语去挑逗女人。*A stranger began making passes at me, so I got up and left.* 一个陌生的男子开始向我调情,所以我站起来走开了。如这一例句所示,对于大部分女性来说,这是一种令人不愉快的行为。*Better be careful, Joe. That guy's making passes at your girl.* 乔,你最好多加小心。那个家伙在向你的女朋友调情哪。*When Stu gets drunk, he makes passes at anything with a skirt and two legs.* 当司徒喝醉了的时候,只要是穿裙子、有两条大腿的,他一概去挑逗。调情者肯定是男性,但也偶尔有如下的例子: *When the woman sitting next to me at the bar started making passes at me, I realized she was probably a prostitute.* 在酒吧间,当邻座的女人开始向我调情的时候,我看出她可能是个妓女。另外,motion 一词虽然有"动作"、"眼色"等意义,但在把"调情"二字译成英语时,不能说 make a motion。make a motion 是在开会时"提出动议"的意思,如说: *Mr. Smith made a motion that the meeting be recessed for an hour.* 史密斯先生提出了休会一小时的动议。◇ make a romantic overture

pass away [ˌpæ(:)sə'weɪ] [口] **去世** 直译为"走过去了",汉语也说"过世"、"过去了",意思相同。这是 die (死) 一词的最常用的委婉表达法,而且不论是文章和会话,一概可以使用。*Mrs. Jones' husband passed away last autumn.* 琼斯夫人的丈夫去年秋天故去了。◇ die

pass out ['pæ: 'saut] [口] **昏迷过去** pass out 除"昏迷"的意思外,还有种种不同的意味。例如说 pass out of *someplace* 是"从某个地方出去"。*She walked quickly by me and passed out of the building.* 她脚步很快地走过我的身边,从大楼里出去了。pass *something* out 以及 pass out *something* 则是"分配某种东西"的意思。*The union members are passing out leaflets to passersby.* 工会会员们向路上的行人散发传单。作"昏迷"解时,用法

如下：*Where am I? I must have passed out.* 我这是在什么地方呀？我一定是昏迷过去啦。*Two soldiers passed out from the heat.* 两名士兵由于天气太热而晕倒了。可以用 cold 加强语气。*The nervous young man stood up to speak, and promptly passed out cold.* 那个神经质的青年站起来要讲话，但是马上昏迷不醒了。也用于因过分高兴而晕过去的场合。*Sue passed out when she heard she had won a million dollars in the lottery.* 苏听说她买的彩票中奖一百万美元，乐得晕过去了。pass out 的应用范围很广，除以上所述外，在因麻醉而失去知觉或者因狂饮而不省人事的时候也可以使用。*The patient passed out within seconds of the doctor's administering the anesthetic.* 医生给他打上麻药之后，仅过几秒钟，病人就失去知觉了。*The noisy drunk at the next table finally passed out.* 邻桌的那个大嚷大叫的酒鬼终于醉倒过去了。◇ faint / lose consciousness ((cold → completely))

pass out *something* [ˌpæ(ː) ˈsaut ~] [口] **分配东西** → PASS out

pass out of *someplace* [ˌpæ(ː) ˈsaudəv ~] [口] **从某个地方出去** → PASS out

passel

a passel [ə ˈpæ(ː)səl] [话] **许多** 原为 parcel [ˈpɑrsəl] (小包)一词的方言表达法。现在是轻松的普通话，表示"许多"的意思。*I've got a passel of work to do.* 我有许多非做不可的工作。常用 whole 加强语气。*There is a whole passel of reporters waiting in the hall.* 有大批的新闻记者在大厅里等待着。◇ a lot

past

one **wouldn't put it past** *someone* (to *do something*) → PUT

paste

paste *someone* **one** [ˈpeɪst ~ ˌwʌn] [话] **用拳头狠狠地一击** 这里的 one 是"一击"的意思。本条条头直译为"把一击给某人贴上"。一般指用拳头猛击脸面，例如：*I pasted him one on the jaw.* 我一拳打在他的下巴上。*He pasted me one in the mouth.* 他一拳打在我的嘴上了。但也有使用球棒等作武器的场合。*She pasted him one over the head with a baseball bat.* 她用棒球的球棒狠狠地往他的脑袋上一击。请读者注意：前置词根据狠击的部位而有所不同。一般来说，face, stomach, mouth, eye 的场合用 in，其他部位的场合用 on，只是 head 有用 over 的时候。这条规则不限于 paste *someone* one，凡是具有"打"的意思的动词，如 strike, hit, bang 等，均适用。另外，paste *someone* one 的 one 可以省略，但是这就弄不清打几回了。◇ hit *someone* (hard)

pat

get *something* **down pat** [ˌget ~ ˌdaun ˈpæ(ː)t] [话] **完全记住** 这里的 get 是"理解"的意思，pat 是具有"完全地"、"正确地"的意味的副词。down 是用以调整语调，没有特定意义。整个条头的意思是："完全理解，而且记牢"。*Don't bother me now. I've got to get the answers to these problems down pat for my test tomorrow.* 现在别打扰我。明天考试，对于这些问题的答案，我必须完全记住才行啊。*I practiced my speech for over a week before I finally got it down pat.* 我把讲演稿足足练习了一个多星期，终于完全记住了。*The steps involved in running this machine are rather complicated. It usually takes a new employee quite a while to get them down pat.* 这台机器的操作程序相当复杂。一般来说，一个新职工要花很长的时间才能完全记熟。如果把 get 换成 have，就是"已经完全记住"的意思。*A: Have you studied the plans carefully? B: Yes, I think I've got them down pat now.* 甲：你仔细看过那个计划吗？乙：是的，我觉得我现在已经记得滚瓜烂熟了。有时省略 down。*Now I've told you everything you have to do. Do you think you have it pat?* 凡是你应该做的事情，我已经全对你讲啦。你觉得都记住了吗？◇ learn [remember] *something* perfectly

have *something* **down pat** [ˌhæv ~ ˌdaun

ˈpæ(:)t] [话] 已经完全记住 → get *something* down PAT

stand pat (on *something*) [ˌstæ(:)nd-ˈpæ(:)t] [话] **保持现状** 这里的 pat 是副词，表示"这样正合适，不做变动"的意思。*No more cards for me. I'll stand pat.* 我不再要牌啦，就用这把牌打。如这一例句所示，本条常在扑克游戏中使用，表示"用发到手的牌决一胜负"的意味。但在此以外也广泛使用。*The government has decided to stand pat on the question of import quotas.* 关于进口限额问题，政府已经决定保持现状。*There is nothing we can do now. We'll just have to stand pat until we see what move our competitors make.* 我们现在没有任何能做的事情。在我们了解竞争对手所采取的行动之前，只能保持现状。*His offer is still a good bit below your asking price. I suggest you stand pat and see if he won't offer you more.* 他给的价钱依然比你的要价低得多。我建议你稳住不动，看他是否会开更大的价钱。◇ not make a move / maintain *one's* present position

pate

a pate [ə ˈpeɪt] [话] **人的脑袋** 因为类似俚语，使人会以为是最近出现的表达法。其实它来源于中世纪英语，一直保持原状为人们所使用。*He's had a bald pate since he was thirty.* 他从三十岁起就秃顶了。*Harvey's pate is as empty as a drunkard's wine bottle.* 哈维的脑瓜象醉鬼的酒瓶子一样空。也可以与 bald, empty, shallow 等结合在一起作为形容词使用。*You seldom meet such a shallow-pated fellow.* 象那样头脑浅薄的家伙实在罕见。◇ a head

path

lead *someone* **up the garden path** [ˌliːd ~ ʌpðə ˌgɑ(:)rdn ˈpæːθ] [话] **欺骗某人误入歧途** 在过去，英国有许多大的宅邸，庭院里栽满了树木。当有不速之客来临、走进大门之后，仆人并不领他往居室走，而是一边客客气气地应酬，一边领他走向通庭院的道路 (garden path)，等到客人明白过来的时候，已经到达出口了。这一表达法直译即为"领某人走庭院的小径"，后来发展作为比喻使用，表示"欺骗某人，使人误入歧途"的意思。*Phil led me up the garden path by pretending that he loved me.* 菲尔假装爱我的样子，使我信以为真了。*The murderer led the police up the garden path by telling them that he had heard the murdered man threaten to commit suicide.* 杀人犯欺骗警察说，他曾听见那个被杀的人说要自杀，警察竟信以为真了。*I wouldn't believe what that guy tells you. He's only trying to lead you up the garden path.* 我决不相信那个家伙对你所说的话。他只是打算欺骗你，使你误入歧途而已。◇ deceive *someone*

patience

the patience of Job → JOB

patrol

a patrol wagon [ə pəˈtroul ˌwæ(:)gən] [口] **囚车** → a paddy WAGON

Paul

rob Peter to pay Paul → PETER

pay

hit pay dirt → DIRT

pay *someone* **back** [ˌpeɪ ~ ˈbæ(:)k] [口] **报复** → pay *someone* back in *his* own COIN

strike pay dirt [ˌstraɪk ˈpeɪˌdə(:)rt] [话] **出门恰遇金凤凰** → hit pay DIRT

peace

hold *one's* **peace** [ˌhould~ ˈpiːs] [口] **保持沉默** 这里的 peace 是 silence (沉默) 的意思。If anyone present knows of any reason why these two should not be joined together as man and wife, let him speak now or forever hold his peace. (凡是在座的人，如果对这两个人结为夫妇持有异议，必须立即提出来，否则要永久保持沉默。) 这是在教堂举行结婚典礼时，牧师必定要说的一句台词。当然，在日常生活中，也可以用于各种各样的场面。*Hold your peace a moment until I have finished explaining.* 在我做完解释

之前，你们暂时不要出声。*I knew he was lying, but I had no choice but to hold my peace.* 我明明知道他在撒谎，但是我除了保持沉默之外没有别的办法。另外，如条头所写的那样，使用动词 hold 的场合占绝大多数，但有时可以采取 keep *one's* peace 的形式。*How do you expect me to keep my peace when I'm being cheated so openly?* 我这样公然地受到欺骗，怎么能够一声不吭呀？顺便讲一下：另有一个表达法是在 peace 之前加定冠词，作 keep the peace。这一表达法的意义与上面所讲的 keep *one's* peace 完全不同，请读者注意不要把两者弄混。keep the peace 的 peace 是"治安"，而 keep 是"维持"的意思。*It's the sheriff's job to keep the peace.* 维持治安是保安官的工作。◇ remain silent

keep *one's* **peace** [ˌki(ː)p ～ ˈpiːs] [口] **保持沉默** → hold *one's* PEACE

keep the peace [ˌki(ː)pðə ˈpiːs] [口] **维持治安** → hold *one's* PEACE

peanuts

peanuts [ˈpiːˌnʌ(ː)ts] [话] **微不足道的一点钱** 最初的构思是"象花生米那样小而不值钱的东西"。意义和用法与 chicken FEED 完全相同。英语中的 peanuts 没有"不正当的、肮脏的钱"的意味，只是表示"钱的数目极小"。*Only a thousand dollars for keeping my mouth shut? That's peanuts.* 仅仅拿一千美元堵我的嘴吗？这个数目可太小啦。常加 only 调整语调。*I've been slaving for that company for over ten years, and I still get only peanuts.* 我在那个公司辛辛苦苦干了十几年，论报酬依然是一点点。◇ a very small amount (of money)

pearls

cast pearls before swine [ˌkæ(ː)st ˈpə(ː)rlz bəfor ˈswaɪn] [口] **把珍珠丢在猪前** 大致相当于汉语成语"明珠暗投"，有时可以解作"对牛弹琴"。源出《圣经·新约》中的《马太福音》(Matthew) 第 7 章 6 节。耶稣说：Give not that which is holy unto the dogs, neither cast ye your pearls before swine, lest they trample them under their feet, and turn again and rend you. (不要把圣物给狗，也不要把你们的珍珠丢在猪前，恐怕它们践踏了珍珠，转过来咬你们。) 这段话的意思是："对于满脑子都是庸俗念头的人，不能讲解宗教的奥秘。他们不但理解不了其中的妙处，甚至会加害于讲解的人。"如果把 cast pearls before swine 翻译成现代英语的会话体，就是 throw pearls in front of pigs。但是，人们并不使用这种现代化的表达法，至今仍然照搬古语，丝毫不爽。*No use trying to explain Shakespeare to those guys. It's just casting pearls before swine.* 向那帮家伙讲解莎士比亚是白费劲，简直象对牛弹琴一样。如这一例句所示，一般用于"试图向没有理解能力的人说明"以及"试图向分不清好坏的人赠送什么东西"的场合。常采取 like + 动名词的形式。*Playing Bach for my husband is like casting pearls before swine.* 给我丈夫弹巴赫的曲子，那可真是对牛弹琴啊。*Giving jewelry to such small children is like casting pearls before swine.* 把珠宝给与那么幼小的孩子，真好象将珍珠丢到猪的面前一样。◇ do something for [give something to] someone who can't appreciate it ((不加 like))

pecker

keep *one's* **pecker up** [ˌki(ː)p ～ ˈpekərˌʌp] [俗] **振作精神** 几乎所有的词典都把本条当作英国英语的俗语，其实在美国英语中也照样使用。*When Mr. Jones' wife died, all his friends spoke kind words to him, encouraging him to keep his pecker up.* 当琼斯先生的妻子死去的时候，他所有的朋友都极力安慰他，劝他振作精神。这是一句纯粹的英国英语。如果美国的女人听到这句话，一定会把脸羞得通红或者大笑起来的。因为 pecker 原意为"啄的工具"，即"鸟的嘴"，后在英国英语中又转用于表示"人的鼻子"。keep *one's* pecker up 原意"把鼻子往上翘"，用作比喻，就是"打起精神"的意味了。但是在美国英语中，pecker 指"男性生殖器”，因此，虽然 keep *one's* pecker up 这一习用语本身的意思与英国英语相同，但一般人把它当作“粗俗语”，特别是在女性面前忌讳使用。在男性之间，除亲密朋友外，一般也避免说这句话。在美国英语中实际使用的场合，一般采取祈使句的表达形式。例如：*Keep your pecker up. I'm sure you'll find a job soon.* 你要打起精神来。我相信你很快就会找到工作的。*It's tough getting jilted, but keep your pecker up. After all, Jane is not the only fish in the sea.* 被人甩了当然会很痛苦，但是你要振作起精神来。世界上两条腿的女人毕竟不只是简一个啊。在这一场合，只表示“振作精神”的固有意味，并不使人产生粗俗的感觉或联想。另外，在使用 tell＋(人)＋to ～的形式时，因为具有间接的祈使句的性质，也表示本来的意味，而无粗俗感。例如：*I hear Jimmy failed his entrance exams. If you see him, tell him to keep his pecker up.* 我听说吉米没有考上大学。如果你见到他，请告诉他振作起精神来。◇ not become disheartened

peddle

Go peddle your papers. → PAPERS

peddler

a pill peddler [ə 'pɪ(ː)l ˌpedələr] [俗] **医生** → a pill PUSHER

pee

pee ['piː] [俗] **撒尿** 这是粗俗的字眼 piss (主要是男性使用) 的委婉表达法，只取第一个字母按发音拼写而成。即使已经是委婉的表达法，一般来说，在女性面前不能使用。*Tom and Dick peed on the side of the road.* 汤姆和迪克在马路旁边撒尿了。*I have to take a pee.* 我得撒尿啦。在这一例句中是把 pee 当作名词使用。take a pee 与本条条头意思相同。◇ urinate

take a pee [ˌteɪkə 'piː] [俗] **撒尿** → PEE

pee-pee

pee-pee ['pi(ː)ˌpiː] [话] **尿尿** 把 PEE(→)重复一次，儿童用语。*Mommy, I have to pee-pee.* 妈妈，我要撒尿。也可以作为名词使用。*Be careful. That's dog's pee-pee.* 当心。那是狗尿。有时说 wee-wee ['wi(ː)ˌwiː]。◇ urinate

peepers

peepers ['piːpərz] [话] **眼睛** 直译为“窥视之物”。这是一个轻松的表达法。*There's nothing wrong with my peepers. I tell you, I saw a UFO.* 我的眼睛绝对没有毛病。我告诉你，我看见了一个飞碟。*She has lovely peepers.* 她的眼睛很好看。另外，最近在青年人中间，常用 peepers 表示“太阳镜”(sunglasses) 的意味。*That guy wears peepers even indoors.* 那个家伙在屋内还戴太阳镜哪。◇ eyes

peeve

one's **pet peeve** [～ˌpet 'piːv] [口] **平日特别不喜欢的事情** 这里的 pet 为形容词，是“最喜爱的”的意思。peeve 来自形容词 peevish (性情乖僻的、爱发怒的)，先构成动词 (使恼怒、使焦急)，后又转为名词 (惹人气恼的事情、讨厌的事物)。从词义来讲，把 peeve 与 pet 结合在一起似乎是自相矛盾。但是，这是一种反语的表达法，而且已经成为习用语，在日常会话中经常使用。它表示“平日最不喜欢的事情”，亦即“平日心里特别讨厌的事情”的意思。*My pet peeve is people who borrow things and then forget to return them.* 我平日最讨厌的是有些人借了东西然后就忘记还。*I don't think Mr. Grump has any pet peeves. He always seems to be equally peeved about everything.* 我不认为格兰普先生有什么特别不喜欢的事情。他似乎永远对每件事情都同样感到恼火。同一类的表达法有 *one's* pet theory, *one's* pet aversion，都是习用语，前者是“某人一贯的理论”，后者是“最厌恶的事情或东西”的意思。*My husband's pet theory is that all women are stupid, especially the one he married.* 我丈夫的一贯理论是：所有的女人都是愚蠢的，尤其是同他结婚的女人。*That the government is the source of all inflation is Mr. Friedman's pet theory.* 弗里德曼先生的一贯的理论是：

政府为一切通货膨胀的根源。*Stu's pet aversion seems to be work.* 司徒最讨厌的事情似乎是工作。*Snakes are her pet aversion.* 她最厌恶的东西是蛇。◇ *one's* favorite [most- voiced] complaint [dislike]

peg

be (like) a round peg in a square hole [(laɪk)ə ˌraund'pe(:)g ɪnə ˌskwe(:)r 'houl] [口] **工作、环境等不适合** → be (like) a square PEG in a round hole

be (like) a square peg in a round hole [(laɪk)ə ˌskwe(:)r'pe(:)g ɪnə ˌraund 'houl] [口]**工作、环境等不适合** 直译为"象一个方木钉进入圆的洞",用以表示"不适应"、"不合适"、"不配合"的意思。主语是"人",在大多的场合包含"他不适合于承担某种责任或解决某一问题"的意味。这一表达法常用于工作和环境。*Nothing seems to go well in my new job. I guess I'm a square peg in a round hole.* 我在新的工作中干得一点也不顺手。看起来,我不适合这个工作。*I've been a square peg in so many round holes that I've almost forgotten how it feels to belong.* 我跑了很多地方,全都觉得不合适,因此,我几乎完全忘记与环境溶为一体的心情了。*At school, Einstein was (like) a square peg in a round hole. He made poor grades and often got into trouble with the other children.* 爱因斯坦在小学时很不适应那里的环境。他的成绩很不好,而且常跟其他孩子发生纠纷。*Manuel is good at making things with his hands, but when it comes to paper work he's (like) a square peg in a round hole.* 曼纽尔在制作东西的时候,他的手很巧,但是搞文书工作,他就很不合适了。常用 feel like 代替 be 动词,意思是"感到不合适"。*My new job doesn't suit me. I feel like a square peg in a round hole.* 我的新工作不适合于我。我总感到与之格格不入。*Libby's parties are too wild for me. I always feel like a square peg in a round hole.* 利比举行的社交晚会实在太闹得慌,我总感到跟他们合不来。square 与 round 可以互换位置。*I'm afraid we'll have to let Frank go. He's like a round peg in a square hole in this office.* 据我看,我们只好把弗兰克辞退了。他和这个公司的气氛格格不入。◇ be a misfit

take *someone* down a peg [ˌteɪk ~ 'daunə ˌpe(:)g] [话] **灭某人的威风** peg 是"木钉"。过去,在英国的军舰上有一种习惯:每当有人前来访问的时候,要根据他的社会地位改变桅杆上升旗的高度,以表示相应的敬意。为了调整旗子的高度而钉一列木钉。本条习用语直译为"把某人降低一个木钉",就是"比过去所表示的敬意下降一度"的意思。受到这种待遇的人肯定会觉得"有失尊严"了。现在,这一表达法一般对那些令人感到过于趾高气扬或骄傲自满的人使用。*That guy is far too big for his britches. Someday I'd like to take him down a peg.* 那个家伙实在太骄傲自大啦。等哪一天我来杀杀他的威风。a peg 也可以改用 a peg or two, a few pegs 等,意思相同。*Herb is always trying to order us around. He needs to be taken down a peg or two.* 赫布总想对我们指手划脚。需要灭一灭他的威风啦。由于本人的失误或过错而灭自己的威风时,要用 bring 来代替 take。*I'd like to see Fritz make a big mistake for once. That would bring him down a few pegs.* 我非常想看见弗里茨犯大错误,哪怕是一次也好。这样会使他灭一灭自己的威风。另外还有 take [bring] *someone* down a notch (or two) [a few notches, etc.] 的说法,意思和用法一样。这里的 notch 的来源与 be a NOTCH above *someone* (→) 的来源相同。◇ make *someone* less proud

pencil

a pencil pusher → PUSHER

pennies

pinch pennies ['pɪntʃ 'peni(:)z] [口] **节俭** 这里的 pinch 是"紧紧捏住,不让它跑掉"的意思。penny [-ies] 是"便士"(英国硬币)。本条习用语的具体形象是:"把硬币紧紧挟在指缝间,尽可能不放松"。

意思是"对于每一分钱都认真考虑,仔细使用",亦即"极力节约"。多用于表示勤俭节约的良好意味。*Though we live fairly comfortably now, we often had to pinch pennies when we were first married.* 现在我们的日子过得很舒服啦,可是我们刚结婚的时候,经常连几个小钱都得算计着花。*Many parents have to pinch pennies in order to put their children through school.* 许许多多的父母为了孩子上学都必须省吃俭用。*I decided to go out and get a job because I was tired of pinching pennies on my husband's small salary.* 我对于靠丈夫微薄的工资过节俭日子已经腻味透了,所以我下决心走出家门,找个工作干。如果用否定式,则是"毫不吝惜"的意思。*They certainly look as if they didn't pinch any pennies when they built the governor's mansion. It looks like a palace.* 在给州长建造官邸的时候,他们简直是不惜工本啊。这所官邸看起来好象一座宫殿一样。至于 a penny PINCHER (→) 可不是"节俭的人",而是"吝啬鬼"的意思,一般有贬义。◇ scrimp

penny

A penny for your thoughts. [ə 'peni fəjə 'θɔ:ts] [话] **你呆呆地想什么呢?** 非常古老的习用语,在约翰·海伍德(John Heywood)所编的《格言集》(*Proverbs*, 1546 年)中就曾出现过。古时英国的 penny 与现在的"便士"不同,是相当大的银币,币值也高。因此就产生了 A penny for your thoughts. 的说法,作为 What are you thinking about? (你在想什么?)的委婉语,直译为"把你的想法告诉我,我给你一个 penny"。但是,请读者注意:在实际使用时,仅限于相当亲密的伙伴之间。"*A penny for your thoughts,*" *said Ellen as she watched her husband staring at the ceiling.* 埃伦看到她的丈夫凝视着天花板,就说:"你呆呆地想什么呢?" *A: A penny for your thoughts. B: Huh? Oh, I was just wondering how the children are getting along.* 甲:你呆呆地想什么呢? 乙:嗯? 哦,我只是在想不知孩子们现在情况如何。*A: A penny for your thoughts. B: I'm afraid they're not really worth that much.* 甲:你呆呆地在想什么呢? 乙:没有什么了不起的事情。◇ What are you thinking about?

a penny pincher → PINCHER

a pretty penny [ə ˌprɪdi 'peni] [话] **相当多的钱** 在美国人的感觉中,这一表达法的具体形象是"闪闪发光的 (pretty) 一个便士的硬币 (penny)"。但在实际使用时,则指"相当数额的金钱"。也就是说, penny 象征着"金钱"。*He's put a pretty penny into that coin collection.* 他在收集货币上投入了很多钱。*He'll probably sell you that house, but it'll cost you a pretty penny.* 他大概想把那所房子卖给你,可是你得出相当多的钱啊。*I hear Caleb paid a pretty penny for that dog.* 我听说凯莱布买那条狗花了很多钱。◇ a lot of money

people

night people ['naɪt ˌpi(:)pl] [话] **夜猫子** → a night PERSON

perhaps

perhaps [pər'hæ(:)ps] [口] **也许** → MAYBE

pernickety

pernickety [ˌpər'nɪkəti] [话] **吹毛求疵的** →PERSNICKETY

persnickety

persnickety [ˌpərs'nɪkəti] [话] **爱挑剔的** 原来的形式是 pernickety [ˌpər'nɪkəti]。在英国英语中只用这一形式。但在美国英语中,这一形式与条头的美国造 persnickety 同时并存。以前 persnickety 是方言,不加 s 的 pernickety 是标准的说法。现在 persnickety 变成标准语,而使用 pernickety 的人却越来越少了。*Byrd is very persnickety about his food. There are many things he won't eat.* 伯德对于食物太挑剔了。有很多东西他绝对不吃。*When it comes to clothes, she is the most persnickety woman I know.* 一讲到穿衣服,据我所

知，她是一个最爱挑剔的女人。也可以用于表示“对人的挑剔”。*Frieda is very persnickety about the kind of company she keeps.* 弗丽达在交朋友方面挑剔得很厉害。下面是“吹毛求疵”的例子。*So I made a few mistakes typing your paper for you. Don't be so persnickety.* 我给你的论文打字的时候，有几处打错了，不过用不着那么吹毛求疵。如果总爱挑剔别人，周围的人们必然会认为他 stuck-up (自高自大)。因此，persnickety 也作为 stuck- up 的同义语使用。*That persnickety Jill Jones won't even speak to me when we meet.* 那个吉尔·琼斯实在自高自大，我们碰见时，她连一句话都不跟我说。另外，persnickety 还有“非常微妙，需要小心处理”的意思，可以用于“人”以外的 machine, problem 等。*This is a very persnickety machine. I have to tune it every week.* 这是一架非常精密的机器，需要细心对待。我每个星期必须调试一次。这一用法是把“机器”比做“性情乖僻的人”，“如果不小心谨慎地对待，就会出麻烦”。*We are faced with a very persnickety problem in human relations.* 我们在人际关系方面面临着一个非常微妙的、难以处理的问题。这句话的意思也是“情况非常微妙，走错一着棋就会酿成大问题”。从以上各例句可以了解，条头与副词 very, most, so 等结合使用的情况非常多。另外，从意义和用法来讲，本条习用语与 particular 或 fussy 十分相似，在最初的四个例句中均可用这两个形容词代换。如果勉强区分的话，可以说 persnickety 是主要在会话中使用的表达法，而其他两个形容词则常常用于文章之中。再者，有时拼写为 persnickity。◇ particular / fussy

person

a night person [ə ˈnaɪt ˌpərsn] [话] **夜里活动的人** 指白天睡觉、夜里工作或行动的人，特别指喜好此种生活方式的人。20 世纪 50 年代，纽约广播电台的唱片音乐节目主持人开始使用 night people [ˈnaɪt ˌpi(:)pl] 一词，于是便流行起来。现在也多用复数形式。*Larry sleeps until noon every day. He's a night person.* 拉里每天一直睡到中午。他是个夜猫子。*There are a lot of night people among disc jockeys and writers.* 在唱片音乐节目主持人和作家中间，有许多夜猫子型的人。◇ a person who likes to work [live, etc.] at night

persuader

a persuader [ə ˌpərsˈweɪdər] [话] **手枪** 直译为“威慑物”，亦即“不容对方分说的东西”。主要为黑社会用语。本条已经有一百年以上的历史，通过电影和小说的传播，现在一般人都很熟悉。*If he refuses to come with you, use your persuader.* 如果他拒绝跟你来，你使用手枪好啦。另外，persuader 不仅指手枪，也可以指“大枪”、“匕首”、“皮鞭子”等，但一般不这样使用。◇ a pistol

pet

one's **pet aversion** [～ˌpedə ˈvəːrʒən] [口] **最讨厌的事情或东西** → *one's* pet PEEVE

one's **pet peeve** → PEEVE

one's **pet theory** [～ˌpetˈθɪ(:)ri] [口] **一贯的理论** → *one's* pet PEEVE

Peter

rob Peter to pay Paul [ˌrɑːb ˈpiːdər təˌpeɪˈpɔːl] [口] **拆了东墙补西墙** 直译为“抢彼得的钱去还保罗的钱”。语源未定。有一种说法是：12 世纪有一句拉丁语，译成英语为 crucify Peter to redeem Paul (为了拯救保罗而把彼得钉在十字架上)，把其中的两个动词分别换上 rob 和 pay，就构成了本条习用语。在基督教中，保罗 (Paul) 和彼得 (Peter) 是同样重要的人物，为了拯救一方而损害另一方，这当然是毫无意义的事情了。*What's the sense in borrowing from one bank just to repay a debt at another? That's just robbing Peter to pay Paul.* 为了向一家银行还债而去向另一家银行贷款，这有什么意义呢？那只是拆了东墙补西墙而已。如这一例句所示，在“勉强去做没有意义的事情”、“勉强去做毫无进展的事情”、“勉强去做解决不了的事情”等场合使用本条。*When a govern-*

ment taxes the food out of the mouths of one group of poor people in order to put it into the mouths of another, it is merely robbing Peter to pay Paul. 如果一个政府为了使一部分穷人吃上饭，而从另一部分穷人身上征税、使他们吃不上饭，这只不过拆了东墙去补西墙而已。这种勉强周转的作法不仅是"毫无意义"，有时还会造成整体的"损失"。*We can't continue to rob Peter to pay Paul by using money from retirement funds in order to pay current salaries.* 我们不能继续拆东墙补西墙地挪用退休基金去发工资啊。如以上的例句所示，本条一般用于金钱问题，但并不限定如此。*I know you're behind in your English studies, but you're only robbing Peter to pay Paul when you do your English homework in math class.* 我知道你在学习英语方面落后了，但是你在上数学课时做英语的家庭作业，那只是拆了东墙补西墙呀。◇ fill in one minus by creating another (minus)

Pete's

for Pete's sake → SAKE

Phew

Phew! ['fju:] [话] **呸!** → WHEW !

Philly

Philly ['fɪli] [话] **费城** Philadelphia (在宾夕法尼亚州东部)的爱称。1776 年 7 月 4 日美国《独立宣言》曾在此发表。*Ralph has to go to Philly on business next week.* 拉尔夫下个星期必须出差去费城。这个城市还有 The City of Brotherly Love (兄弟爱城)、The Quaker City (贵格会教徒城)等别名。前者是由于 Philadelphia 一名源出希腊语 *phil* (爱) + *adelphos* (兄弟)，后者是由于创立这一城市的是以 brotherly love 为信条的基督教贵格会的教徒 (The Quakers) 而得名。◇ Philadelphia

Phooey

Phooey. ['fu:i] [话] **见鬼** 感叹词。象声词 Phew! (→ WHEW!) 变化成 Phoo! (此词也使用)，随后进一步变化成 Phooey. 有时又拼写为 Fooey. *Phooey. I just can't get this lighter to work.* 见鬼！这个打火机怎么也打不出火来啦。*Aw, phooey. Do I have to go, Mom?* 唉，真见鬼！妈，我非去不可吗？如以上的例句所示，这一表达法与 HECK. 非常相似，它们的区别是: Heck. 表示轻蔑的心情，而 Phooey. 则表示不信任的念头。*Phooey. I don't believe it.* 见它的鬼去吧！我就不相信。以上是单独使用，这是普遍的情况。但有时采取 Phooey on someone [*something*]. 的形式。*Phooey on that guy. If he won't help me I'll do it myself.* 叫那个家伙见鬼去吧！他不愿帮我，我自己干。

phys ed

phys ed [.fɪ(:)'ze:d] [话] **体育** physical education (身体的教育)的缩略。学生用语。*Bill Bodey is majoring in phys ed.* 比尔·博迪专修体育。*I have a phys ed class at three.* 我三点钟有体育课。*Last year I had phys ed on Tuesdays and Thursdays.* 去年我每星期二和星期四都有体育课。◇ physical education

physical

a physical [ə 'fɪzəkl] [话] **身体检查** 正式名称是 a physical examination，也使用它的缩略形式 physical exam。同义的说法有 physical checkup 和 medical checkup，而 checkup 是"查点"的意思。另外还有 medical exam(ination) 的说法，不过，这一说法可能由于又有"医学实验"的意思，人们不大使用。*I'm to go in for a physical next week.* 下星期我要去做身体检查。◇ a physical examination

a physical checkup [ə .fɪzəkl 'tʃekʌp] [口] **身体检查** → a PHYSICAL

a physical exam [ə .fɪzəkl ˈɪgzæ:m] [话] **身体检查** → a PHYSICAL

pick

pick 'em up and lay 'em down [.pɪkə.mʌpən .letəm'daun] [话] **撒开腿跑** 'em 为 them 的音变，在这里指"两只脚"。这一表达法的字面意义为"把它们(脚)拾起来，再把它们放下"。*When Joe* *saw the bear, he really started pickin' 'em up and layin' 'em down.* 乔一看见熊，撒开鸭子就跑起来了。美国的体育老师和教练常说这句话。*OK, you guys. Pick 'em up and lay 'em down! Faster!* 喂，你们快跑！再快一点！◇ run fast

pickings

be slim pickings ['slɪ(:)m'pɪkənz] [话] **几乎没有可用的东西** 这里的 slim 不是"纤细"、"苗条"，而是"没有把握"、"缺乏"、"少"的意思。pickings 是"摘取物"，亦即"从中选出的东西"。整个表达法直译为"选取的东西很少"，意思是："即使挑选，也几乎没有有价值的东西或正合我意的东西"。这一表达法的使用范围极为广泛，包括商店里的商品、工作单位、住宅用的土地、结婚对象等各个方面。造句一般采取 there + be 动词的形式。*There are slim pickings in the job market this year.* 今年在就业市场找不到什么好的工作。常用 mighty 加强语气。*I was thinking of taking you to an interesting movie tonight, but there're mighty slim pickings.* 我本想今天晚上带你去看一场有意思的电影，可是连一个好片都没有啊。在日常会话中，pickings 大多脱落 g 而发音作 ['pɪkənz]，因而有时拼写为 pickin's。*I went to that bargain sale yesterday, but by the time I got there, there were mighty slim pickin's.* 昨天我到那家拍卖商店去了，但是当我到那里的时候，简直没有一样可买的东西了。有时用 the pickings are slim 的表达法，例如：*There used to be a lot of residential land for sale in this area, but now the pickings are rather slim.* 在这个地区，过去有许多出售的住宅土地，可是现在呢，好的土地实在太少啦。*That store has a few coats for sale, but the pickings are slim.* 那家商店倒是有几件上衣出售，但是没有一件象样的。the pickings become [get] slim 是"好的东西几乎没有了"的意思。*There never were very many eligible bachelors around here, and the pickings got even slimmer after the war started.* 这一带本来就没有几个可以作为结婚对象的单身男子，自从战争爆发以后，连这寥寥可数的几个人也几乎不见影了。◇ be few choices / be little to select from

pickle

be in a pickle [ɪnə 'pɪkl] [话] **为难** 几百年前移入英语的荷兰语。按字面意义，pickle 一般作"咸菜"解，在这里指"腌咸菜的盐水"。in a pickle 是荷兰习用语 *in de pekel zitten* (坐在盐水上)的直译。在处于必须做某种事情而不知怎样做才好的状态或立场时，常用轻快的语调使用本条。*I'm in a pickle. I'm supposed to take Betty to the movies, but I don't have enough money.* 我真为难啊。我必须带贝蒂去看电影，而手里的钱却不够。在请求对方帮助的时候，常用这一表达法作为"开场白"，然后接着说：Can you lend me a little? (你能够借给我一点儿吗？) 另外，在同时必须去干两种事情因而为难的场合，也常用这一表达法。*I'm in a pickle. We're having guests for dinner and the boss wants me to work late tonight.* 真为难死啦。我家请了一些客人来吃晚饭，而老板叫我今天晚上加夜班。另有 get in(to) a pickle 的说法，意思是"陷入困境"，但不大使用。be in a fix 也大致同义。◇ be in a predicament

pickled

pickled ['pɪkld] [话] **酩酊大醉** 本条是 pickle 的过去分词，直译为"被咸菜水泡了"。也就是说，喝得酩酊大醉的人是"被酒泡了"。主要用 get pickled (喝醉了) 和 be pickled (灌醉了) 的形式。*I got pickled last night.* 我昨天晚上喝醉了。*George was so pickled that he couldn't walk straight.* 乔治烂醉如泥，走起路来东倒西歪。一般用 completely 加强语气。*He got completely pickled on one highball.* 他喝完一高杯酒，已经酩酊大醉了。◇ drunk

pick-me-up

a pick-me-up [ə 'pɪkmi.ʌp] [口] **解乏酒(或其他饮料、食品)** 直译是"把我的疲劳的身体 pick up (拾起来)"，也就是消除疲劳，振作精神。一般的英汉词典把这一表达法译作“兴奋剂”或“强壮剂”，但 pick-me-up 并不是一种药。在下班回家的路上，如果说 Let's have a pick-me-up. 那是“咱们去喝一杯”的意思，并不是要去打一针强壮剂。*Fred often stops by a local bar for a pick-me-up on the way home from work.* 在下班回家的路上，弗雷德常常在当地的酒吧门口停车，去喝一杯解乏酒。如这一例句所示，大多用于酒精类，但并不限定如此，也可以指能够恢复精神的其他饮料，有时甚至可以指食品。又，pick-me-up 中的 me，不论主语是第几人称，永远用 me。*A hot cup of tea serves as a good pick-me-up around the middle of the afternoon.* 在下午三点来钟，喝上一杯热茶的确可以提神。*My favorite pick-me-up on a hot day is a cold green salad.* 在夏天的炎热日子里，蔬菜沙拉是我的消暑妙品。◇ a (bracing) drink / a tonic

pickpocket

a pickpocket [ə ˈpɪkˌpɑkət] [口] **扒手** → a DIP

picnic

be no picnic [ˌnou ˈpɪknɪk] [话] **不是轻松的事情** picnic (野餐)是令人感到一身轻松的娱乐之一。用 no 加以否定，作为比喻，就是“不轻松”、“苦头多”的意思了。*It's nice to be able to travel, but being a tourist guide is no picnic.* 能够出去旅游是一件美事，但是当导游可不轻松。*Moving was no picnic. It rained all day and we had no one to help us lift the heavy furniture.* 这次搬家苦极了。下了一整天雨，而且没有一个人帮我们抬沉重的家具。*I think we can do it, but it won't exactly be a picnic.* 我以为我们干得了那件事，可是决不是轻而易举啊。◇ be no easy task

picture

get the picture [ˌgetðə ˈpɪktʃər] [话] **掌握大概情况** 这里的 picture 是“大概的情况”。get 是“了解”、“掌握”的意思。本条习用语的具体形象是：“picture (图画)的细部姑且不谈，先了解一下这是一张什么画”。例如，当就某件事情进行说明之后，而向对方询问“大致明白了吧？”的时候，在英语中常这样说：Get the picture? 对方回答：I've got the picture. (大致明白了。) 或者：I've just about got the picture. (大体上明白啦。) 如果对整个的轮廓还不清楚，就回答说：No, I haven't got the complete picture yet. (不，我还没有完全了解。) 如果站在相反的立场，即“使人了解大概情况”或“讲解大概情况”，英语为 give *someone* the picture。例如：*A: Have you heard anything about the new project? B: Yes, the chief is going to give us the picture at this afternoon's departmental meeting.* 甲：关于新的计划，你听到什么消息了吗？乙：是的，今天下午我部开会的时候，部长要给我们做概括的说明。另有 put *someone* in the picture 的表达法，同义。*I'll put you in the picture.* 我来向你介绍一下大概情况。再有，get the picture 不仅用于听别人讲述或说明而理解的场合，也用于通过自己观察而掌握大概情况的场合。*After seeing my girl sitting in the park with Andy for two days in a row, I began to get the picture.* 我一连两天见到我的女朋友与安迪一起坐在公园里之后，开始明白大概是怎么回事了。请读者注意：不管是用哪一个表达法，picture 的前边全是加 the。如果说 get a picture，那仅仅是“照相”或者“去取一张画”的意思。◇ grasp the (overall) situation

give *someone* the picture [ˌgɪv ~ ðə ˈpɪktʃər] [话] **使人了解大概情况** → get the PICTURE

put *someone* in the picture [ˌput ~ ɪnðəˈpɪktʃər] [话] **使人明白大概情况** → get the PICTURE

pie

a cow pie [ə ˈkau ˌpaɪ] [话] **牛粪** 直译为“牛制作的馅饼”。这一表达法是由其形状联想产生的。既是一种轻松的说法，也是一种委婉语。*Jerry cut his foot on a cow pie.* 杰里的一只脚踩到牛粪上了。*Cow pies make good fertilizer.* 牛粪可以成为很好的肥料。◇ (a piece of) cow dung

(as) easy as (apple) pie [ə ˈzi(ː)ziəz (ˌæpl) ˈpaɪ] [话] **容易极了** → (as) easy as falling off a LOG

eat humble pie [ˌi(ː)t ˌhʌmbl ˈpaɪ] [口] **低头谢罪；忍辱含垢** 直译为“吃卑躬屈膝的馅饼”。古时，英国贵族在猎鹿之后，把鹿的内脏(umbles) 给与从者和仆人吃。有人说，本条习用语即来源于此。自古以来，在英国的所谓下层阶级的群众之间，humble 一词脱落 h，一般发音[ˈʌmbl]。也就是说，humble 与 umble 在发音上没有区别。既然鹿内脏制的馅饼是给身份低的人吃的饭食，当然 umble pie 也就变成了 humble pie。如果作为讲故事，这一说法倒很有趣。不过，从历史上来考证，尚存在一些疑问。我们涉猎了若干文献，原来不仅身份低下的人们吃用鹿内脏制成的馅饼，对于上层阶级的人来说，这也是大受欢迎的美味佳肴。据可靠的记载，著名的日记作家、英国海军大臣佩皮斯 (Samuel Pepys, 1633-1703) 和苏格兰的诗人、作家司各脱 (Sir Walter Scott, 1771-1832) 等也都爱吃这种馅饼。再往前追溯，15 世纪有一本叫做 *Babees Book* 的菜谱，把鹿内脏馅饼列入“供贵族用的佳肴”的项目内。因此，从语源来说，这样考虑是比较妥当的，即：把 umble pie 改成 humble pie 只不过是一种语言游戏而已。基本意思是“心里感到屈辱”。根据上下文，也可能有“点头哈腰”、“低三下四”等的意思。这一表达法当然用于实际上去完成“屈辱的行为”(例如“低头谢罪”) 的场合，但在仅仅有“屈辱的心情”的场合也可以使用。按情况来讲，“过去自己有不好的言行，结果必须承认错误，低头谢罪”的场合比较多，但是并不限定这样的因果关系。相似的表达法有 eat CROW，但使用的范围比较窄，主要用于不得不在口头上承认自己言行的错误的场合。*I refuse to eat humble pie for him just because he's rich and I'm not.* 我绝对不因为他是富人而我是穷人就向他低三下四。这是一个没有因果关系的句子，如果换上 eat crow 就显得很不自然了。*I'll admit my error, but I refuse to eat humble pie.* 我承认自己的错误，但是我决不卑躬屈膝。在这一例句中，“承认自己的错误”本身就是 eat crow，所以在这一场合进行代换也是不自然的。在以下的两个例句中，二者是可以替换的。*You'd better be careful about what you say if you don't want to end up eating humble pie.* 如果你不愿意得到忍辱含垢的后果，最好是在说话时多加小心。*You'd think that George would learn not to brag so much. He almost always ends up having to eat humble pie.* 乔治似乎应该懂得不要吹牛吹得太大啦。每当他吹牛的时候，几乎都是以被迫收回自己的话而告终。◇ adopt a humble attitude / be humiliated (by having to admit *one* was wrong [to apologize])

have a finger in the pie → FINGER

piece

a conversation piece [əˌkɑ(ː)nvərˈseɪʃən ˌpiːs] [口] **可当作话题的东西** 本来是艺术用语，意思是“一家团圆图”。但在一般会话中决不使用这一意义，而指的是“家具”、“绘画”、“古玩”、“摆设”等珍贵物品。这里的 conversation 是“成为话题的”的意思。*That ashtray is very inconvenient to use, but its unusual shape makes it an interesting conversation piece.* 那个烟灰缸使用起来很不方便，可是它的形状特殊，遂成为一个有趣的话题。*The Joneses have furnished their home with so many interesting things. Practically everything they have is a conversation piece.* 琼斯夫妇的家装饰着许许多多有趣的东西。他们所有的每一件东西实际上都是珍品。◇ something that arouses interested comment

give *someone* **a piece of** *one's* **mind (for** *something***)** → MIND

be a piece of cake → CAKE

say *one's* **piece** [ˌseɪ ~ ˈpiːs] [话] **讲心里话** → speak *one's* PIECE

speak *one's* **piece** [ˌspi(ː)k ~ ˈpiːs] [话] **讲自己想说的话** 这里的 piece 是“在整个的话中，自己的那一小部分”，亦即“自己要说的话”的意味。大多用于对一个以上的对手发言的场合。常采取 let *someone* ~的形式。*Quiet everybody! Let him speak his piece!* 大家安静一下!让他说说自己的意见。*Let me speak my piece and then I'll shut up.* 让我说说自己的意见,然后我就不再开口啦。象以上这种说法,实际上往往是倾诉不平不满的前奏,因此本条常用于表示"发泄一腔不满"的意思。例如 *He got into trouble when he spoke his piece to the boss's face.* 这句话,根据上下文的意思,很有可能解释为:他当着老板的面发泄积存已久的一腔不满,因而给自己带来了麻烦。有时讲 say *one's* piece [.seɪ ~ 'piːs]。另外,speak *one's* piece 偶尔用于表示"求婚"的意思,务请读者注意。*George can't seem to get up enough nerve to speak his piece to Debbie.* 乔治似乎拿不出向戴比求婚的勇气。◇ say (frankly) what *one* wants to say / propose (marriage)

pig

buy a pig in a poke [.baɪə 'pɪ(:)gɪnə 'pouk] [话] **隔山买老牛** poke (袋子) 主要为美国南部方言,但 buy a pig in a poke 则全国通行。直译为"买一只在口袋里的猪",也就是"不看货色如何就买"的意思,与汉语俗语"隔山买老牛"相当。*Of course I want to see it first. I'm not about to buy a pig in a poke.* 当然啦,我想先看一看货色。我不打算隔山买老牛啊。*Buying a used car without road testing it is like buying a pig in a poke.* 不在路上开一下试试就买旧的小汽车,那等于隔山买老牛。◇ buy *something* without first inspecting it

eat like a pig [.i(:)t laɪkə 'pɪ(:)g] [话] **吃饭象猪拱食一样没有规矩** → eat like a HOG

make a pig of *oneself* [.meɪkə 'pɪ(:)gəv~] [话] **贪得无厌** 直译为"使自己成为猪",也就是"简直跟猪一样"。本条来自"猪贪得无厌、大吃特吃"的形象。*Mother: Don't make a pig of yourself. You should leave some for other people.* 母亲:你不要贪食无厌。你应该给别人留下一些。*Jimmy has been invited to eat at a friend's house tonight. I do hope he doesn't make a pig of himself.* 今天晚上,吉米应邀去一位朋友家吃饭。但愿他规矩一些,不那么狼吞虎咽。在应邀前去别人家吃饭的时候,常用这一表达法作客套话。*This meal is so good that I'm afraid I'm making a pig of myself.* 这顿饭太香了,很抱歉,我狼吞虎咽起来啦。如以上的例句所示,这种"贪得无厌"一般是指吃或连吃带喝(只是喝的场合很少使用)。不过,并不仅限于大吃二喝。*I know my father left his estate entirely to me, but I'd be making a pig of myself if I didn't share some of it with my brother.* 我知道父亲是把他的财产全部遗留给我的,但是不分给我的弟弟一些,我就成为一个贪得无厌的人了。另外用 hog 代替 pig,而有 make a hog of *oneself* 的说法。不过,一般通用本条条头的表达法。◇ be greedy / eat [have] more than *one's* (proper) share

pig Latin → LATIN

pigeon

a dead pigeon [ə .de(:)d 'pɪdʒən] [话] **注定要完蛋的人或事物** → a dead DUCK

pigeon-toed

pigeon-toed ['pɪdʒən.toud] [口] **内八字脚的** 本条的来源是:pigeon (鸽子) 在走路时,toe (足指) 内向。*A pigeon-toed boy came up to me in the park.* 在公园中,一个内八字脚的少年向我走来了。"以内八字脚走路"的英语是 walk pigeon-toed。*Suzy walks a little pigeon-toed.* 苏吉走路有点小内八字儿。反义词"外八字脚的"是 slue-foot ['sluː.fut],或者是 slue-footed ['sluː.fudəd]。slue 是"向侧面弯曲"的意思。*It's disgusting to see a pretty young girl walking slue-foot.* 看见一个漂亮姑娘走路外八字,实在令人作呕。slue 也拼写作 slew。*You should concentrate on pointing your toes straight ahead when you walk. You have a tendency to be slew-footed.* 当你走路的时候,你要注意把脚尖向正前方伸。你已经有外八字脚的苗头啦。◇ with *one's* toes pointing inward((a little 放在句末))

piggy

a piggy [ə ˈpɪgi] [话] **脚趾** 本来为幼儿用语，意思是“小猪”。“小猪”的正式英语叫做 piglet。这是由儿歌集《鹅妈妈》(1781年出版)而来的表达法。This little pig went to market. / This little pig stayed home. / This little pig had roast beef. / This little pig had none. / This little pig cried, "Wee, wee, wee," all the way home. 这只小猪去了市场。/这只小猪呆在家里。/这只小猪吃了烤牛肉。/这只小猪什么也没吃。/这只小猪在回家的路上一直“呜，呜，呜”地哭。母亲一边念这首诗，一边把膝头上的孩子的脚指，从大指开始，一个一个地捏。到了最后，她捏着孩子的小脚指，一边摇晃，一边说 Wee, wee, wee。于是，孩子嘎嘎地乐了。由此，piggy 一词就有了 toe (脚指)的意义。这是学龄前儿童的用语。*Come on, Tommy. Let's wash your piggies.* 来，汤米。洗洗你的脚指。*Mommy, I hurt my piggy.* 妈妈，我的脚指受伤啦。◇ a toe

pigskin

a pigskin [ə ˈpɪg.skɪ(:)n] [话] **美式足球** 因为 Footballs are made of pigskin. (足球是用猪皮制作的。) 所以人们常说以下这类的话: *Throw me the pigskin.* 把足球扔给我。◇ a football

pill

be a bitter pill (for *someone*) **to swallow** [ə ˌbɪdər ˌpɪltə ˈswɑ(:)lə] [口] **难以接受的事物** bitter pill 是“苦的丸药”。后边加上 to swallow，就成为“苦到难以下咽程度的丸药”了。但这一表达法专作比喻使用。虽然表示“难以接受”或“难以忍耐”，可是含有“不得不接受”或“不得不忍耐”的意味。*Losing his job just before retirement was a bitter pill for him to swallow.* 他在刚要退休时丢掉了工作，这对他来说，真是一个难以下咽的苦果。*Learning that his insurance had lapsed just two days before his house burned down was a bitter pill to swallow.* 他了解到在住宅失火的前两天，保险已经到期，心里难过极了。也可以在 swallow 之前加 have to，构成 a bitter pill (for *someone*) to have to swallow，意思不变。*John's failure to get into college was a bitter pill for his mother to have to swallow.* 约翰没有考上大学，对他的母亲来说，这是一个难以下咽的苦果。相反，有时把 for 以下的部分完全省略，只说 a bitter pill。*I know it's a bitter pill, but you'd best admit your mistake and apologize.* 我知道这是一件难以接受的事情，但是你最好是承认错误并道歉。◇ be an unpleasant fact [act] to have to accept [perform]

a pill peddler [ə ˈpɪ(:)l ˌpedələr] [俗] **医生** → a pill PUSHER

a pill pusher → PUSHER

a pill roller [ə ˈpɪ(:)l ˌroulər] [俗] **医师** → a pill PUSHER

sugar the pill [ˌʃugər ðə ˈpɪ(:)l] [口] **给点甜头安慰一下** sugar 当然是动词，意思为“加糖”。pill 是“丸药”。最初的构思是“给药丸涂上糖”。当叫人去干他不愿意干的事情的时候，给他一点甜头，使他高兴，安慰安慰。这等于吃药加糖，减小一下苦的味道。*I didn't want to be transferred from the home office, but the boss gave me an extra bonus to sugar the pill.* 我不愿意从总公司调出去，可是老板发给我一笔额外的奖金，作为安慰。*I told my son I wouldn't be able to take him skiing this week as I had promised, and sugared the pill by giving him the money to take his friends out to a movie or somewhere.* 我告诉我的儿子说，虽然我答应过他，但是我不能在这个星期带他去滑雪了，为了安慰他，我给他一些钱，叫他跟朋友们去看电影或到别的什么地方去玩。有时用 sweeten (弄甜)代替 sugar，而说 sweeten the pill。另有 gild the pill (gild 为“镀金”)的说法，但不是美国英语。◇ make it less disagreeable

sweeten the pill [ˌswi(:)tən ðə ˈpɪ(:)l] [口] **给点甜头作为安慰** → sugar the PILL

pimples

goose pimples [ˈgu(:)s ˌpɪmplz] [口] **鸡皮疙瘩** goose 是"鹅", pimples 是"疙瘩"。也就是说,汉语的"鸡皮疙瘩"在英语中为"鹅皮疙瘩"。*Air conditioning always gives me goose pimples.* 一开空调,我的身上就起鸡皮疙瘩。*Whenever I hear a scary story, I get goose pimples.* 我一听人讲可怕的故事,身上就起鸡皮疙瘩。如以上的例句所示,这一表达法常用作 give 或 get 的宾语。另有 goose BUMPS 和 goose flesh,也是"鸡皮疙瘩"的意思。bump 是"隆起物",flesh 一般作"肉"解,在这里是"皮肤"的意思。下面讲一下这三者的关系。直到最近为止,最普遍的是条头的 goose pimples,无论是在会话中还是在文字中,一向为人们广泛使用。但是近来,这一表达法日益衰微,至少作为口头语言,goose bumps 已经后来居上。goose bumps 当前主要是在会话中使用,特别是青年人喜欢使用这一表达法。goose flesh 是在 goose pimples 出现以前最流行的表达法,在会话与书写两方面都广泛使用,但现在除了老年人之外几乎没有人使用它,特别是在会话中已经快成为废语了。另外,有些英汉词典把 goose skin 解释为"鸡皮疙瘩",但这是英国英语,在美国英语中只有字面的"鹅皮"的意思,这一点请读者注意。

pinch

in a pinch [ɪnə ˈpɪ(:)ntʃ] [话] **一旦有事的时候** pinch 一词当然有"紧迫"、"危机"的意思,但在这一表达法中并不指那么严重的状态。因此, in a pinch 只是"在一旦有事的时候"、"在没有别的指望的时候"、"在没有选择余地的时候"的意思,一般使用时语调非常轻松。例如在借钢笔的时候,人家只有铅笔,借的人可以这样说: *This will do in a pinch.* 没有钢笔,这个也凑合啦。*I don't have much money myself, but in a pinch I could lend you about a hundred dollars.* 我自己并没有多少钱,不过,你一旦需要,我可以借给你一百美元左右。这句话并不是明确指出对方有什么"急用",而且很轻松地、含含糊糊地表示一下自己的心情。*Steve is not the best public speaker, but he'll do in a pinch. Let's ask him.* 史蒂夫不是最好的演说家,但是一旦有需要的时候,还可以凑合一阵子。我们就去请他吧。*We don't have a weapon, but this hammer will do in a pinch.* 我们连一件武器都没有,一旦有事,这把榔头也顶点用啊。*I don't like to work on Sundays, but I'm willing to do it in a pinch.* 我不喜欢在星期日工作,但是一旦需要,我可以加班。如果用 at 代替 in,而说 at a pinch,那是英国英语,美国英语一定要用 in。另外也有用 on 或 upon 的例子,但都是古老的词句,现在,在英美两国都见不到。◇ if there is no better choice [no alternative] / in an emergency (situation)

pincher

a penny pincher [ə ˈpeni ˌpɪntʃər] [口] **吝啬鬼** pinch PENNIES 是"节约开支"的意思,在通常的观念中是属于美德的行为。因此,人们很容易由此类推,认为 penny pincher 是"节约家"的意思。我们即使不能断言这是绝大的错误,但是,把"pinch pennies 的人"在意义上与 penny pincher 等同起来的例子是极为罕见的。当然,在"连一分钱也不想出"这一点上,两者是一致的,然而, pinch pennies 是人的一种良好的行为,而 penny pincher 则完全相反,通常令人怀有恶劣的印象,用轻蔑的口气去使用它。例如说: *Don't waste your time trying to borrow money from that penny pincher.* 你不要白白浪费时间去跟那个守财奴借钱。*My husband is a wealthy man, but unfortunately I didn't realize until I married him what a penny pincher he is.* 我的丈夫是一个富翁,但不幸的是,直到结婚以后,我才明白他是一个多么吝啬的人。另外,一般英汉词典所收录的动词 penny-pinch 是 penny pincher 的逆成语,但实际上很少使用。◇ a miser / a stingy person

pinch-hit

pinch- hit for *someone* [ˌpɪntʃ ˈhɪtfər～] [话] **代替** 这一表达法是棒球用语,原来的意思是"代打"。*Smith pinch-hit for* *the pitcher in the bottom of the ninth.* 在第九局的后半局,史密斯出场代替投手。转用于比喻。pinch-hit 中的 pinch,在棒球比赛中多指"良好的机会",但在比喻用法,仅意味着 emergency (非常时刻,紧急情况)。*My lawyer is sick so his assistant is pinch-hitting for him in court today.* 我的律师病了,因此,他的助手今天代他出庭。*The principal pinch-hit for our math teacher while she was recuperating from her accident.* 我的数学老师发生事故,在她养伤期间由校长代课。◇ substitute for *someone*

pineapple

a pineapple [ə ˈpaɪ ˌnæpl] [话] **手榴弹** pineapple 的第一个意义当然是"菠萝"。在中世纪英语中,称"松球"为 pinapple (松树的苹果,中间无 e)。后来,在夏威夷等地出产的象大松球形状的水果也称为 pinapple (即菠萝)了。至于"松球",在现代英语中不是 pineapple,而是 pine cone。由于形状相似,在美军的俚语中,把"手榴弹"称为 pineapple。*Sergeant Lauck lobbed a pineapple toward the enemy position.* 劳克中士向敌人阵地投了一颗手榴弹。◇ a hand grenade

pink

be tickled pink [ˌtɪkəld ˈpɪŋk] [话] **非常高兴** tickle 的主要意义是"使发痒"。因此,本条习用语乍看起来是"被胳肢得发粉红色"的意思。但在日常会话中,常用 tickle 表示"使喜欢"、"使高兴"的意思。*I'm tickled.* 我很高兴。pink 是强调"最高"、"非常"等意味的名词。本条有一点女性的味道,但在表示单纯的高兴时,男性也使用它。*I'm tickled pink that you came.* 你来了,我非常高兴。*Everyone was tickled pink to hear that you were promoted.* 听说你被提升,大家都非常高兴。◇ be very happy

pinkie

a pinkie [ə ˈpɪŋki] [话] **小手指** 源出荷兰语 *pinkje* 的表达法。*pink* 是"小指",*-je* 是指小词,相当于英语的 -ie。原为幼儿用语,但成年人也常常使用。*Mommy, I caught my pinkie in the door.* 妈妈,我的小手指被门夹住了。*He ran his pinkie over his eyebrow.* 他用小手指抚摸眼眉。有时用于表示"全部手指或脚趾"的意思。*My pinkies are frozen.* 我的指头全冻僵了。又拼写作 a pinky。◇ a little finger

pins

be on pins and needles [ɔ(:)n ˌpɪnzən ˈniːdlz] [口] **坐立不安** pin 是"别针",needle 是"针"。本条习用语直译为"坐在别针和针上"。汉语这类成语很多,如"如坐针毯"、"坐卧不宁"等。意指恨不得一下子逃出去的心情,应用的范围极广。*We were on pins and needles, waiting to hear whether Dad had finally gotten a job or not.* 我们坐立不安,等待听到爸爸是否找到工作的消息。如这一例句所示,这一表达法一般用于怀着"不安"或者"期待"的心情等待某种"结果"的场合。*I was on pins and needles lest Paul should blurt out the truth and get us both in trouble.* 我坐立不安,生怕保罗走嘴说出真相,使我们俩都陷入困境。*While the stranger talked on and on, we were all on pins and needles for fear that the police would arrive before we were able to leave.* 当那个陌生人滔滔不绝地讲下去的时候,我们如坐针毯,生怕警察会在我们逃走之前赶来。have *someone* on pins and needles 是"使某人坐卧不安"的意思。*You've got me on pins and needles. Never mind the details, just tell me how it all ended.* 你真急死人。不要管细节,光谈结果如何。*The close game had us on pins and needles till the very end.* 由于比赛双方势均力敌,我们一直坐立不安,到结束时才平静下来。keep *someoneon* pins and needles 是"使某人处于坐卧不安的状态"。*Don't keep us on pins and needles! What happened?* 不要使我们着急嘛! 究竟发生了什么事情? ◇ be in a state of excitement [anxiety]

pipe

Pipe down. [ˈpaɪp ˈdaun] [俗] **安静一点!** 原为海军用语。过去在海军中曾经使用 stand down 一语作为表示“作业完了!”或“工作停止!”之意的号令。每到这种时候,要鸣笛 (pipe) 通知,因此就产生了本条条头的表达法,也就是把 stand down 中的 stand 改成了 pipe。后来,在海军俚语中表示“安静!”的意思,1930 年左右开始,为一般人广泛使用。这一表达法与 shut up 相似,但是 shut up 的意思是“闭嘴!”,只限于表示“停止说话!”,而 pipe down 除“闭嘴!”外,还用以表示“不要发出大的声音”的意思。这是个男性的、粗暴的表达法。*Pipe down, will ya? Can't you see I'm trying to study?* 安静点,好吗? 你看不见我在学习吗? 大多象这一例句似地使用命令式,但也有如下的用法。*We'd better pipe down. The teacher will be back in a minute.* 咱们最好是安静下来。老师马上就要回来啦。◇ Be (more) quiet.

put that in *one's* **pipe and smoke it** [ˌputˈðæ(ː)tn ～ ˌpaɪpən ˌsmoukɪt] [话] **你仔细考虑考虑吧!** 原来的意思是:“象装到烟斗里去吸那样地仔细琢磨”。在表示这一意义时,put 的宾语一般用 it 而不是 that。*I really don't agree with you but if that's your advice, I guess I'd better put it in my pipe and smoke it for a while.* 我实际上不同意你的意见,但是,如果这是你提出的忠告,我还是仔细考虑一下好。但是,到了现代,已经极少使用本条习用语表示这样的意义。大多是采取 Put that ～. 这样的命令句形式,只表示说话者单方面的意思,仿佛说:“你呆着去吧,不要多管闲事。”另外,Put that ～. 这一命令句,虽然我们根据它本来的意思译作“你仔细考虑考虑吧!”,但是在实际上,说话的人并不期待对方替他去考虑。也就是说,“仔细考虑考虑吧!”的意思已经退到背后,这一表达法一般包含着怒气,表示近似“不要再罗嗦啦!”的意思。*Father: I won't have you dating that girl again! Son: I'm twenty years old now and I'll date whoever I like, so put that in your pipe and smoke it!* 父亲:不许你再跟那个姑娘约会! 儿子:我现在已经二十岁了,我喜欢谁就跟谁约会。请你头脑清醒一点儿吧! 除了命令句而外,还常见 you can put that ～ 或者 you can just put that ～的说法,实际上这也是命令式的一种。*A: You'd better go now. It's getting pretty late. B: I'll go when I'm good and ready, so (you can) put that in your pipe and smoke it.* 甲:你现在该走啦。时间已经很晚了。乙:我什么时候想走,我就什么时候走。所以,你的头脑要清醒一点。如上边的例句所示,一般是直接向对方讲,但也有时向不在场的第三者表示这种意思。*I don't care what the boss says, my vacation is scheduled for July and I'm going to take it in July. He can just put that in his pipe and smoke it.* 我不管老板说什么,我的休假规定在七月,我就在七月去休假。让他头脑清醒一点吧。◇ *one* may as well resign *oneself* to it / ((不加 so)) (I don't care) whether *someone* likes it or not

piper

He who pays the piper calls the tune. [ˈhi(ː)*h*u ˌpeɪzðə ˈpaɪpər ˌkɔːlzðə ˈtjuːn] [谚] **谁出钱,谁有发言权** → pay the PIPER / call the TUNE

pay the piper [ˌpeɪðə ˈpaɪpər] [口] **自食其果** 这里的 piper 是“吹笛子的人”。古时,在英国的酒吧间里,可以付钱叫人吹笛子。因此,这一表达法的本来意义是“向吹笛子的人付钱”。英国有一句谚语是 He who pays the piper calls the tune. (由付钱的人指定吹笛者吹什么曲子。) 谚语后一半的 call the TUNE (→) 可单独使用,表示“拥有决定权”的意思。后来,这句谚语的字面意义除戏谑的场合外已经无人使用,一般来说,它只表示“付钱的人有发号施令的权利”的意思了。例如: *Why do they complain when I tell them what to do? They should have realized when they asked me for financial support that he who pays the piper calls the tune.* 我告诉他们要做什么的时候,他们为什么要发牢骚呢? 他们在请求我给与经济援助的时候就应该明白“谁出钱，谁有发言权”啊。本条条头 pay the piper 是独立使用谚语的前半部分，本来为“担负费用”的意思。例如：*I agree that holding a big party would be great, but who's going to pay the piper?* 我也认为开个大型社交晚会很有气派，但是由谁出钱呢？*I'm paying the piper, so I'm going to call the tune.* 钱由我出，所以得我说了算。由本来的意义进一步发展，就有了“自食其果”的意思。乍看起来，这两种意思风马牛不相及。这一表达法是由如下的构思产生的：指定吹什么歌曲(call the tune)的人不仅是“担负费用”，而且是“不管认可与否，非拿钱不可”，因此可以说这是他自己给自己找出来的麻烦。*Someday he's going to have to pay the piper for treating his friends this way.* 他这样对待自己的朋友们，总有一天会自食其果的。*Go ahead and ruin your health with fast living if you want. You're the one who's going to be paying the piper.* 如果你愿意的话，你就去过花天酒地的生活，毁坏自己的身体。因为将来自食其果的是你自己。*Lem has lost his job, family and friends. He's paying the piper for years of self-serving behavior.* 列姆失掉了工作、家庭和朋友。他多年以来自私自利，现在自食其果了。下面的例句是这一表达法的变形。*Even such a powerful man as Napoleon found that in the end the piper was waiting to be paid.* 就连拿破仑那样一个有权威的人物，最后也发现必须自食苦果了。◇ pay (the bill [bills]) / suffer

pitchers

Little pitchers have big ears. [ˌlɪdl ˈpɪtʃərz hæv ˌbɪˈgɪːrz] [口] **小孩子耳朵尖** 这是把“小孩子”比做 pitcher (水罐)的一个谚语式的表达法。pitcher 的“把儿”一般叫做 handle，但自古以来又称为 ear。本条的来源是：英国的小水罐上往往装有一个比例不协调的大把儿。这一表达法只能用于“在小孩子面前说话必须谨慎”的场合。*Be careful of what you say in front of the children. Little pitchers have big ears.* 你当着孩子们的面说话可要小心。小孩子耳朵尖。*I was surprised that our little boy was worried because I might lose my job. I guess little pitchers have big ears.* 我家的小男孩竟为我可能失业而担心，真叫我大吃一惊。小孩子耳朵真尖啊！另外，旧日还有 Little pitchers have long ears. 的说法，但在现代的美国口语中，不说 long ears。◇ Children hear more than one imagines they do.

pitchforks

rain pitchforks [ˌreɪn ˈpɪtʃˌfɔ(ː)rks] [话] **倾盆大雨** 直译为“天上落下干草叉”。夸张的表达法。同义的表达法有 rain cats and dogs，可以随便替换使用。*We'd just arrived at the picnic ground when it started raining pitchforks [cats and dogs].* 我们刚一到野餐的场地，就下起倾盆大雨[瓢泼大雨]来了。◇ rain very hard

pity's

for pity's sake [fər ˈpɪdizˈseɪk] [话] **无论如何……** → for Pete's SAKE

p.j.'s

p.j.'s [ˈpiːˌdʒeɪz] [话] **上下身分开的睡衣** pajamas [pəˈdʒɑːməz] 的缩略，只摘取其中 p, j, s 三个字母。它与 pajamas 一样，总用复数。*How do you like my new p.j.'s?* 你看我的新睡衣如何？*These p.j.'s aren't mine.* 这套睡衣不是我的。顺便提一下，pajamas 或 p.j.'s 所以用复数形式，是由于上下身两件为一套(上下身连在一起，习惯上也作复数考虑)。因此，如果只是“上身”，则使用单数，叫做 pajama top [pəˈdʒɑːmə ˌtɑːp]。但是“下身”仍然用复数，叫做 pajama bottoms [pəˈdʒɑːmə ˌbɑ(ː)dəmz]，因为它是裤子型，与 pants 或 trousers 同样，每件睡裤有两条腿。*This pajama top is mine, but those aren't my pajama bottoms.* 这件睡衣是我的，但是，那条不是我的睡裤。◇ pajamas

place

put *someone* **in** *his* **place** [ˌput ~ ɪn ~

'pleɪs] [口] **使张牙舞爪的人老实下来** 最初的构思是："使忘记自己应该呆的地方(place)而跑出来乱动的人回到原来的场所 (put in)"。这里的 *his* place 指"他本来的立场、身份、地位、职责等"。本条习用语直译为"叫某人了解其原来的立场,退缩回去",特别常常应用于那些忘乎所以说一些没有礼貌的话的人或者嬉皮笑脸采取一种狎昵态度的人。*The boss is very quick to put overly familiar employees in their place.* 老板很快使那些过于放肆的职工老实下来了。*Mr. Stonebrow is a very strict teacher. He can put an unruly student in his place with just a stern glance.* 斯通布劳先生是一位非常严格的老师。他能用严厉的一瞥使不守规矩的学生老实下来。*Ralph talks as if he runs the whole company. I wish someone would put him in his place.* 拉尔夫的口气很大,仿佛整个公司是由他经营的。但愿有人能教训他一番,叫他老实下来。这一表达法也可以用于男女关系。*If Bob starts getting fresh with you again, just remind him that his father works as a janitor in your father's store. That should put him in his place.* 如果鲍勃再要对你放肆无礼,你就提醒他,说他父亲在你父亲的商店里看门。这样就会使他老实下来了。keep *someone* in *his* place 是"使某人老老实实守本分"的意思。*My grandfather is very much against women's lib. He thinks what modern women need is to be kept in their place.* 我的祖父非常反对妇女解放运动。他认为必须使现代妇女恪守妇道,规规矩矩。◇ make *someone* behave as befits *his* position [as *he* should]

a wide place in the road [ə ˌwaɪdˌpleɪs ɪnðə'roud] [口] **乡村小镇** 按照字面意义,当然可以解释为"道路加宽的地方"。但是,一般来说,这是一个强调镇的规模太小的表达法。例如说: *When we got there we were surprised. It was only a wide place in the road.* 当我们到达那里的时候,我们大吃一惊,原来那只是一个乡村小镇。有时连镇都谈不到,仅指有一家商店和两三所住房的地方。◇ a small country village

places

go places ['gou ˌpleɪsəz] [话] **发迹;成功;发展** 直译为"到许多地方去[旅行]"。例如说: *He likes to go places and meet people.* 他喜欢到各地去会见各行各业的人。作为比喻,是"大大发迹"、"非常成功"、"达到极好的地步"的意思。相似的表达法有 get someplace [somewhere],但是本条的 go places 是更强烈的说法,令人产生"蒸蒸日上"的感觉。*He has a good mind. If he'd only get off his rear end and get to work, he'd go places.* 他的头脑很灵。只要他把沉重的屁股抬起来,认真地干活,他很快就会有所成就的。也常用 really 加强语气。*I understand Shirley is really going places in Hollywood.* 我听说秀兰在好莱坞大红特红起来了。也可以用于公司,意思是"迅速发展"。*This company would go places if only we could get rid of the deadwood at the top.* 这个公司只要去掉那些无用的头头,就会迅速发展起来。否定式作 not get [go] anyplace [anywhere],直译为"哪里也去不了",根据上下文,有"不发迹"、"抬不起头"或者"不成功"的意味。*He'll never get anywhere as long as he stays in this little town.* 只要他呆在这个小镇里,他永远也发迹不了。*This business is not going anyplace unless we can borrow some money.* 这个公司如果借不到钱,怎么也发展不起来。◇ succeed in a big way

plague

avoid *something* [*someone*] **like the plague** [ə'vɔɪd ~ ˌlaɪkðə 'pleɪg] [口] **极力躲避** a plague 是"猛烈的传染病"。如果把 a 换成 the,则为最可怕的传染病之一 the bubonic plague (腺鼠疫) 的略语。本条习用语的意思是:"象躲避腺鼠疫一样躲避某事或某人"。但是在实际使用时,往往脱离本来的意思,语调比较轻松,成为一种夸张的表达法,大多用于"因为不喜欢"、"因为觉得麻烦"或者"因为不方便"的场合。*My husband avoids yard work like the plague.* 我丈夫极力躲避收拾庭院的活儿。*Ever since Dick ate some bad fish last year, he's avoided seafood like the plague.* 迪克自从去年吃了一些变质的鱼以后，他极力避免吃海产品。*Mrs. Smith is quite a chatterbox. Everyone in the neighborhood avoids her like the plague.* 史密斯太太是一个大话匣子。左邻右舍每一个人都对她敬而远之。◇ absolutely shun *something* [*someone*]

plain

be (as) plain as the nose on *someone's* **face** → NOSE

a plain Jane → JANE

plainclothesman

a plainclothesman [ə ˈpleɪnˈklouzmən] [口] **便衣警察** → a DICK

plane

a shuttle plane [ə ˈʃʌtl ˌpleɪn] [口] **短程航班飞机** → an air SHUTTLE

plans

one's **plans fall through** [~ ˈplæ(:)nz ˌfɔ:lˈθru:] [口] **计划落空** 这是一个习用语，在计划实行之前、亦即在正在计划的阶段内失败的时候使用。fall through 与 collapse 同义，是“事业、计划等在中途突然失败”。也可以说 the plans 或者 this [that] plan，但一般用 *one's* plans。哪怕只是一个计划，习惯也用复数形式 plans。*Our plans fell through at the last minute because my husband had to work.* 由于我丈夫必须去工作，我们的计划在即将实现时落空了。大多采取 plans for *something* 或者 plans to *do* [for *doing*] *something* 的形式。*Doris's plans for the winter vacation fell through when she fell through the ice while skating and caught pneumonia.* 多丽丝在滑冰的时候，由于冰面破裂而掉进水里，得了肺炎，因此，她的冬季休假的计划落空了。*Phil's plans to go to Europe fell through at the last minute.* 菲尔前往欧洲的计划在最后的一分钟落空了。◇ *one's* plans collapse [are ruined]

plastered

plastered [ˈplæ(:)stərd] [话] **喝醉了** 直译为“用石膏涂上了”。既然用石膏涂上，当然要 stiff (僵硬)了。而 STIFF 一词自古以来就用以表示“喝醉”的意思。在相当于 drunk 的许多俚语中，本条条头是最广泛使用的一个。可以作表语使用，例如：*That man is plastered.* 那个人喝醉了。常用 really 加强语气。*We were really plastered last night.* 昨天晚上我们喝得酩酊大醉。“一醉方休”的英语是 get plastered。*Let's get plastered.* 咱们痛痛快快地喝一顿吧。这句话大有“不醉不止”的含义。◇ drunk

plate

the plate [ðə ˈpleɪt] [口] **本垒板** 在棒球用语中，人们常用 the plate 代替 home plate。在这一场合，home plate 前边不用 the。但是，请读者注意，the plate 必须有 the。plate 一词首先令人想到的是“浅而圆的皿”，它原来是“用坚硬物质制成的薄而平的东西”的意思，(home) plate 一语源出于此。*The batter reshouldered his bat and stepped up to the plate.* 击球员又把他的球棒搭在肩上，向本垒板走去了。◇ home plate

platter

a platter [ə ˈplæ(:)dər] [话] **唱片** 在日常会话中，这个名词一般指“大皿”。因为形状相似，又转用于表示“唱片”的意思。由于是俚语，多用于爵士乐或摇滚乐的唱片，很少用于古典音乐唱片。这是青年人或广播电台音乐唱片节目主持人的用语。*Play the flip side of that platter.* 把那个唱片翻过来放唱。◇ a (phonograph) record

the platter [ðə ˈplæ(:)dər] [话] **本垒板** 本垒板 (home plate) 常简称 the PLATE (→)，而 plate 一词首先令人想到的是“浅而圆的皿”。后来进一步发展，具有“长圆形浅的大盘子”意味的 platter，在俚语中也当作 home plate 的一种表达法了。*Put it right across the platter.* 投个好球啊！如这一例句所示，platter 前边必须加 the。◇ home plate

play

a bonehead play [ə ˈbounˈhe(:)d ˈpleɪ] [话]

运动或比赛中愚蠢的失误 → pull a BONER

child's play [ˈtʃaɪldz ˌpleɪ] [口] **不费吹灰之力** 直译为"儿童的游戏",但是,这一意义几乎完全无人使用。这一表达法的意思是:"象儿童游戏一样极其简单的事情"。*That job is child's play.* 那个工作容易极啦。为了加强语气,常把 mere 放在前边。*Defeating Ugly Knuckles will be mere child's play for the champ.* 对于冠军来说,打败丑八怪纳库尔斯简直不费吹灰之力。◇ (a) very easy (task)

make a play for *something* [*someone*] [ˌmeɪkə ˈpleɪfər ~] [话] **千方百计去求得……** 在体育运动中,常说 make a play for three points。比如说在篮球比赛快要终了的时候,这句话的意思是"要特别卖劲夺得三分,才能取胜"。这是本条习用语原来的用法,基本意义是"为了求得 *something* 而 play"。*Both candidates are making a play for the labor vote.* 两个候选人在千方百计争取工人们的选票。*When the president retires, there are several men set to make a play for the top job.* 当总经理退休的时候,有好几个人出来争夺这个领导工作。*The political situation is very unsettled in that country. If things get any worse, the army may make a play for power.* 那个国家的政局非常不稳定。如果情况恶化,军队可能出来夺权。*something* 处有时是 *someone*。在一般的词典中,大多释义为"勾引异性"或"向异性求爱"。*someone* 处大多代入异性。但不限定如此,也有象上边的最后一个例句那样的场合。也就是说,"勾引"或"求爱"是由"为了求得……而 play"发展而来,这只是这一表达法的意义的一部分。*Watch out for Rick. He seems to be making a play for your wife.* 你要注意里克啊。他似乎在勾搭你的老婆哪。*That company is very aggressive in its hiring tactics. It has already made a play for three of our top engineers.* 那个公司采取了非常积极的用人策略。它已经来对我们公司的三位高级工程师进行活动了。◇ try to get *something* / make advances toward *someone*

play for time → TIME

play hard to get (with *someone*) [ˌpleɪ ˌhɑrdtə ˈge(ː)t] [话] **拿架子** 直译为"做出使人难以到手的姿态"。主要用于男女关系。这是女性为了吸引对方常用的手段之一。*I'm sure it's not that Sue doesn't want to date you. She's only playing hard to get.* 我认为,苏并不是不愿意跟你约会。她只是故意拿架子而已。*Don't play hard to get with me. You aren't the only fish in the sea, you know.* 你不要跟我故意拿架子吧。你要知道,两条腿的女人不只你一个。在男性应用的场合,一般不是讲男女关系,而是别人来找他干什么工作时,他以此作为讲价钱的一种手段。*Lou is one of America's top baseball players. He can afford to play hard to get with club owners.* 卢是美国最佳棒球运动员之一。在与俱乐部的老板办交涉时,他有讨价的本钱。◇ feign disinterest (in *someone's* overtures)

play it cool (with *someone*) → COOL

play it safe → SAFE

play safe [ˌpleɪ ˈseɪf] [口] **谨慎从事** → play it SAFE

play up to *someone* [ˌpleɪˈʌptə ~] [话] **拍马屁** 原为演剧用语,意思是"当配角","给主角锦上添花"。例如:*The new actor played up perfectly to Humphrey Bogart's performance.* 那个新演员给汉弗莱·博加特当配角,真是锦上添花啊。但是,一般很少使用这一意义,特别是在会话中很少听到有人这么说。作为比喻是"为了取悦对方而献殷勤、说好话"的意思,主要用于口头。*Look at that guy, will ya? He thinks he can get a good grade by playing up to the prof.* 喂,你看看那个家伙!他以为拍教授的马屁就能得到好分数哪。*I refuse to play up to the section chief or anyone else just to get a promotion.* 不管是科长也好,或是其他的什么人也好,我决不为了自己向上爬而去拍他的马屁。*It's disgraceful the way that woman plays up to Mr. Stokes just because he's a rich man.* 那个

女人只是由于斯托克斯先生是个富翁就向他谄媚,这种行为实在可耻。◇ make *oneself* overly agreeable to *someone*

Turnabout is fair play. → TURNABOUT

pledge

take the pledge [ˌteɪkðə ˈpleːdʒ] [话] **发誓戒酒** 可以认为是 take a pledge to stop drinking (宣誓停止喝酒)省略了 to 以下的部分。take a pledge 只是"宣誓"的意思。*Pink elephants I don't mind, but when I began to wake up and see giant spiders in my bed every morning, I decided it was time to take the pledge.* 幻觉我不在意,但是每天早晨一睡醒就看见床上有大蜘蛛的时候,我觉得该发誓戒酒了。在这一例句中,pink elephant 据云是酒精中毒的人在幻觉中必然会看到的"粉红色的大象",所以作"幻觉"解。*Charlie's drinking got so bad that his wife threatened to divorce him if he didn't take the pledge.* 查理喝酒喝得太不象话了,以至他老婆威胁他说,如果他不发誓戒酒,就跟他离婚。*Alcoholics Anonymous is an organization designed to help alcoholics who have taken the pledge.* 嗜酒者互诫协会是一个以帮助已经发誓戒酒的酒精中毒者为宗旨的组织。与戒烟的宣誓一样,戒酒的宣誓也往往是一而再,再而三。*Stu takes the pledge every time he wakes up with a hangover, but it never lasts until the next day.* 每当宿醉醒来之时司徒必发誓戒酒,但是他的誓言绝对持续不到第二天。◇ renounce alcohol

plumb

plumb [ˈplʌ(ː)m] [话] **完全的(地)** 作为名词,plumb 是"测锤"的意思,转义"垂直"。在日常会话中作为形容词"完全的"或副词"完全地"使用。也就是说,在作为形容词、副词时,与 complete(ly) 或 absolute(ly) 同义。这一表达法原来富有方言色彩,人们往往怀着这种心情,为了故意显示乡土味或者滑稽味而使用它。在这种场合,为了加强效果,一般是极力模仿方言,大大拉长声音,作 [ˈplʌːm] 或者 [ˈplʌːːm]。另外,这一表达法不只用于打算突出乡土味或滑稽味的场合,一般说来,用于形容令人很不满意的事情的时候比较多。当然也有例外,如说:*Yore plumb beeyootiful.* [ˌjɔːr ˌplʌːm ˈbiːˌjuːdifəl] (= *You're plumb beautiful.*) 你简直漂亮极啦。以下,用例句示明 plumb 的典型使用方法。这些例句,根据说话人、说话方式以及发音的不同,有时显示出乡土味或滑稽味,也有时显示不出来。但仅根据文字,什么味也体会不到。*That's plumb nonsense.* 那完全是胡扯! *That guy's a plumb fool.* 那个家伙是个大混蛋。*You're plumb crazy.* 你简直发疯啦。*It's certainly a wonderful boat. When I stepped into it, the water came plumb up to my belly button.* 那的确是一只奇妙的小船。在我上船以后,水就立即往上涌,一直没到我的肚脐。◇ absolute(ly) / complete(ly)

plunge

take the plunge [ˌteɪkðə ˈplʌ(ː)ndʒ] [口] **下定决心去干** 这一表达法用于表示有实行的勇气和胆量。按字面意义,plunge 是"向水里猛然一跳"。*I stood on the edge of the pool for some minutes gazing at the cold water, trying to get up enough nerve to take the plunge.* 我凝视着冰冷的水面,在池边站了几分钟,试图鼓起足够的勇气往下跳。作为比喻,表示"下决心去干"或者"大胆尝试"的意思。plunge 前边经常加定冠词 the,这是因为此种 plunge 是"经过仔细思考,而且烦恼过、犹豫过的特定行动"。也就是说,这一表达法不论是按字面意义或按比喻意义使用,都是表示在"实行"之前有过犹豫和左思右想的阶段。*Graham had been debating for a long time whether to quit his job and go into business for himself. Finally, in September, he took the plunge.* 格雷厄姆对于是否辞去现有的工作而自己独立经商的问题,反复考虑了很长一个时期。最后,在九月,他下决心采取行动了。也常用于狠一下心把存款花光的场合。例如说:*We've been wanting to take a trip to America for many years, but, with prices* *so high there, it's difficult to get up enough nerve to take the plunge.* 我们多年以来就想去美国旅游,但是那里的物价太高,总没有足够的勇气付诸实现。求婚,对于害怕遭到拒绝的腼腆的人来说,也是需要拿出勇气的事情之一。*Lew has been on the verge of asking Fay to marry him many times, but he's too shy to take the plunge.* 卢已经多次想要请求费伊同他结婚了,但是由于过于腼腆,话到舌尖却没有出口。下一个例句是半开玩笑的用法,把结婚看作"可怕的事情"。*A: Hear you're getting married. B: Yep. Finally decided to take the plunge.* 甲:听说你已经结婚啦。乙:是啊,终于一狠心跳进水里去啦。◇ take the decisive step

points

be at swords' points (with *someone* over *something*) [ət'so(:)rdz 'pɔɪnts] [口] **剑拔弩张,大有一触即发之势** 直译为"双方的刀尖正碰在一起",表示激烈的对立状态。从表面上看,与 be at LOGGER-HEADS (with *someone* over *something*) 很相似,但是 be at logger-heads 一般没有憎恶的感情,而这一表达法则大多具有明显的憎恶的感情和紧张的心情。*Henry used to date Betty, but last year he started going with Doris. The two girls have been at swords' points ever since.* 亨利过去曾与贝蒂约会,但是去年却与多丽丝开始交往了。从那以后两位小姐互相敌对,大有一触即发之势。*India and Pakistan are at swords' points over the position of the border between the two countries.* 印度和巴基斯坦由于两国之间的国境线问题而剑拔弩张,大有一触即发之势。有时使用 be 动词以外的动词。*You should make up with Dick. It's silly to stay at swords' points with him over such a trivial thing.* 你跟迪克言归于好吧。为了芝麻大的一点小事而相互仇视,实在太愚蠢啦。◇ be (extremely) antagonistic (to *someone* over *something*)

poison

One man's meat is another man's poison. → MEAT

poke

buy a pig in a poke → PIG

pole

a bean pole [ə 'biːn ˌpoul] [口] **细高挑儿** → a string BEAN

(the) low man on the totem pole → MAN

poli

poli sci [ˌpɑ(:)li 'saɪ] [话] **政治学(课程)** political science 的缩略。学生用语。直译为"政治科学"。在美国英语中,如果说 politics,一般指"政治活动"。*Poli sci is a tough course.* 政治学是一门很难的课程。*I've decided to major in poli sci.* 我决定专修政治学了。也可以作为形容词使用。例如说: *Bergen is a poli sci prof.* 伯根是一位政治学教授。◇ political science

polisher

an apple polisher [ə 'næ(:)pl ˌpɑ(:)lɪʃər] [口] **拍马屁的人** → polish the APPLE

politics

office politics [ˌɔ(:)fəs 'pɑlətɪks] [口] **企业政治** 直译为"公司的政治活动"。似乎哪个国家的公司内部,都有勾心斗角和党派存在。*Promotions often seem to depend more on office politics than ability.* 提升似乎多半是靠企业政治,而不是靠能力。*We thought Edgar Beaver would be the next department head, but he became a victim of office politics.* 我们原来以为埃德加·比弗会是下一任的部长,但是他却变成了企业政治的牺牲品。◇ transactions in office power and influence

pond

the big pond [ðə ˌbɪg 'pɑ(:)nd] [话] **大西洋** 直译为"那个大水池子"。戏谑的表达法。*I'd like to cross the big pond by sailboat.* 我想乘帆船横渡大西洋。也可以大写作 the Big Pond。偶尔指太平洋而言。◇ the Atlantic Ocean

pooch

a pooch [ə 'pu(:)tʃ] [话] **犬** 语源不明。相当于 dog (犬)的最广泛使用的俚语之一。*That's a cute pooch.* 那是一条很可爱的狗。这一用法仅仅是代替 dog 一词而已。当一个爱狗的人招呼陌生的狗时,特别常用这一表达法。*Here, pooch. Ah, that's a good boy.* 来来,小狗! 啊,这小家伙真不错。至于那些讨厌狗的人,则对任何狗都轻蔑地称呼为 mutt ['mʌ(:)t],意思是"杂种狗"。*It may be a thoroughbred, but a mutt is a mutt if you ask me.* 它也许是一条纯种狗,但是叫我来说,所有的狗都是杂种,没一个好东西。◇ a dog

poop

poop *someone* **out** [.pup ~ 'aut] [话] **使人筋疲力尽** → POOPED

pooped

pooped ['pu(:)pt] [话]**筋疲力尽** 这是 poop (使人筋疲力尽)的过去分词。关于 poop 的语源,有人说是中世纪英语中的象声词 poupen (噗的一声),不确。这一表达法大多用于构成简单句子,例如在激烈的运动之后,把大腿往外一伸说:*I'm [I feel] pooped.* 我筋疲力尽啦。常用 all 或 completely 加强语气。*I'm [I feel] all [completely] pooped.* 我简直累死啦。又常加副词 out 表示"完全、彻底"的意思,如说:*I'm pooped out.* 我累垮了。*You look all pooped out.* 你似乎累得完蛋啦。另外,还有发音强调法,即将声音拉长,把 ['pupt]发音为 ['pu:pt]或 ['pu::pt]。如以上所述,poop 的过去分词形式一般作为表语使用 (不能作定语使用),也有时采取 poop *someone* 这样的动词+宾语的形式。在这一场合,大多伴有副词 out。例如说"刚才的比赛使得我筋疲力尽",译成美国口语并不是 That game pooped me. 一般要讲 That game pooped me out. 当然这句话也可以使用过去分词,而说 That game left me pooped out. 这里的 leave *someone* pooped out 也是惯用句型之一。◇ exhausted

poor

(as) poor as a church mouse → MOUSE

pop

a pop quiz → QUIZ

a pop test [ə 'pɑp 'te(:)st] [话] **突然袭击式的测验** → a pop QUIZ

Pope's

the Pope's nose → NOSE

popsicle

a popsicle [ə 'pɑ(:)psɪkl] [口] **冰棍** pop (咯噔一声响)与 icicle (冰柱)的合成语,原为商品名称。指的是"冰棍",不包括"冰淇淋"。*There's nothing better than an ice-cold popsicle on a hot day.* 在炎热的日子里,再没有比凉凉的冰棍更好的东西了。*I loved popsicles when I was a child, and they're just as popular with my children.* 我小的时候喜欢吃冰棍,我的孩子们对于冰棍也是非常欢迎。p 字可以大写。*My favorite flavor of Popsicle is orange.* 我最爱吃的是橘子冰棍。"雪糕"叫做 (an) ice cream on a stick。*I like ice cream on a stick.* 我喜欢吃雪糕。*Do you want an ice-cream-on-a-stick?* 你吃雪糕吗? 如这一例句所示,可以用连字符全连起来。◇ flavored ice [sherbet] on a stick

position

jockey for position [.dʒɑ(:)kifər pə'zɪʃən] [口] **争先恐后谋地位** 这一表达法源出赛马用语。jockey 在这里是"骑马竞赛", position 是"有利的位置"。本条的意思是:"争抢占好的位置"。在讲赛马或赛汽车的时候,用法如下: *The three leading drivers were still jockeying for position as they entered the last lap of the race.* 三个领先的驾驶员在进入赛程的最后一圈时,依然在抢占好的位置。作为比喻使用,表示"争先恐后"的意味。本条的主语一般用复数。*As soon as the incumbent announced that he would not run for re- election, the gubernatorial hopefuls began jockeying for position.* 现任州长刚一宣布他不参加下届竞选,那些希望当选州长的人们就开始争夺这一

官职了。*Laura is a very popular girl. As soon as she arrives at a dance party, all the young stags begin jockeying for position.* 劳拉是一个很有人缘的姑娘。她刚一来到舞会,所有没带舞伴的小伙子都争先恐后地来约请她跳舞。这一表达法也可以用于公司团体。*Many companies are jockeying for position in hopes of winning government contracts.* 许多公司都在谋取能够获得与政府订合同的有利地位。◇ vie (with one another) to gain an advantageous position

possibility

an outside possibility [ə ˌnautˌsaɪd ˌpɑsəˈbɪləti] [口] **一线希望** → an outside CHANCE

possum

play possum [ˌpleɪ ˈpɑ(:)səm] [口] **装死,装睡,装不知道** possum (飞袋貂)据说在遇到危险时装死,本条习用语即由此而来。possum 的正式名称为 opossum,但一般人称呼为 possum,而且不能说 play opossum。在谈到动物时,只使用“遇到危险时装死”这一个意义。*There is a kind of snake in America that plays possum when caught.* 美国有一种蛇,一被抓住就装死。在谈到人时,一般用于表示“装死”乃至“装睡”的意味。*The fallen soldier escaped notice by playing possum until the enemy troops had passed by.* 那个倒下的士兵在敌军开过去之前始终装死,没有被敌军发觉。常用 just, only,以及 merely 加强语气。*He looks like he's still asleep, but maybe he's only playing possum.* 看起来他好象还在睡觉,但是,他也许只是装睡哪。也有用于表示“装不知道”或“装病”的时候,但用例极罕见。*Our rivals appear to be unaware of what we are planning to do, but they may be merely playing possum.* 我们的竞争对手表面上好象没注意我们在计划干什么,但是,他们也许只是装不知道而已。*I don't think he's really sick. He's probably just playing possum.* 我不认为他真的有病。他可能只是装病而已。◇ pretend to be dead [asleep] / feign ignorance

post

play post office → OFFICE

posted

keep *someone* **posted** (on *something*) [ˌki(:)p ~ ˈpoustəd] [口] **详细通知** 本来的意思是“不断写信报告情况”。在实际使用时,不管用什么方式“传送消息”都可以。*Don't worry about how Jack and the other boys are getting along. They'll keep us posted.* 不用惦记杰克和其他几个孩子的情况如何,他们会详细通知我们的。这是指用电话或者书信的方式。*The President asked his advisers to keep him posted on events in the Middle East.* 总统要求他的顾问们向他详细汇报中东发生的各种情况。这大概是用口头吧。总而言之,这一表达法的意思是:“不问手段,详细地、不断地报告情况或消息”。*Please write to us and keep us posted. We'll be looking forward to hearing whether Bill got the job he wanted.* 请给我们写一封详细的信,我们很想知道比尔是否找到了他想得到的工作。on *something* 的 on 可以改用 about 或者 as to。*He promised to keep us posted as to his father's health.* 他答应向我们详细报告他父亲的健康状况。此外,在商业书信的末尾常用本条,如 *We'll keep you posted.* 容后奉告。*Please keep us posted.* 务请告知。这都是定型的客套话。◇ keep *someone* informed

pot

go to pot [ˌgoudə ˈpɑ:t] [话] **没落** 如果说 go to the pot,则是“到厕所去”的意思,这是一个非常轻松的表达法,等于中国人说“上茅房”。请读者注意:本条条头没有冠词 the。pot 一般作“锅”、“壶”等解。关于“到锅或壶去”为什么会表示“没落”的意思,有两个说法:①因为吃剩下的肉不扔,而放在“锅”里煮。煮的时候切得很碎,原来的形状没有了。②因为死人用火葬,剩下的骨灰有放在“壶”里埋了的习俗。在以上两个说法中,可能与后一说有关联,某些词典把 go to pot

译为"死亡"。古时且作别论,反正在现代决不使用这样的意义。*The company has gone to pot since the president died.* 自从总经理去世之后,那个公司就衰败了。*I've been so busy lately I'm afraid I've let the garden go to pot.* 最近我太忙,把花园全都荒废了。不仅用于"物",也有用于表示"人垮台了"的场合。*Lynn has let himself go to pot since he lost his wife last year.* 林恩自从妻子去年去世之后,就颓废下来了。他多半是经常喝酒,连胡子也不刮就去公司上班。pot 另外还有"大肚子"的意思,因此有如下的戏谑的说法。*I'm afraid everything I eat goes to pot.* 我看,我所吃的每样东西全都往大肚皮里走啊。◇ go to ruin

(a case of) the pot calling the kettle black [(ə ˌkeɪsəv) ðə ˈpɑ(ː)t ˌkɔ(ː)lənðə ˌkedl ˈblæ(ː)k] [口] **乌鸦笑猪黑** 也可以用前置词 like (好象)代替 a case of (如同),而说 like the pot calling the kettle black。pot 是"锅",kettle 是"烧水的壶"。本条习用语直译为"(如同)锅说水壶黑"。也就是说,由于经常烧,锅底也是黑的,实际上与水壶的情况一样。汉语有很多这类的俗语,如"乌鸦笑猪黑","乌鸦落在猪身上,只看见别人黑,看不见自己黑"。作为比喻,意思是:"把自己的问题搁在一边,专指责他人的缺点"。*The Democrats accusing the Republicans of political opportunism is a case of the pot calling the kettle black.* 民主党人指责共和党人在政治上搞机会主义,这只是五十步笑百步罢了。*You accuse me of stealing other people's boy friends? Talk about the pot calling the kettle black!* 你指责我夺走了别人的男朋友?简直是乌鸦落在猪身上,只看见别人黑,看不见自己黑呀! 如以上的例句所示,本条大多相当于汉语的"五十步笑百步",但根据具体情况,有时不能死译。*The chief is forever complaining that we spend too much on entertainment, but don't worry about it. That's a case of the pot calling the kettle black.* 科长总是抱怨咱们花的招待费太多,但是不必为这件事烦恼。他花的决不比咱们少。另外,本条在塞万提斯 (Cervantes) 著《堂·吉诃德》(*Don Quixote*) 的第一个英译本(1701年)中首先见于文字,原作 The pot calls the kettle black. 一些英汉词典也把它作为谚语收录。其实,根本无人使用 The pot calls ~. 这样主语+动词的句型。一般如本条所示,用动名词的形式表达。◇ (<an instance of> one person [group, etc.]) accusing another of faults identical with *his* [*its*] own

potato

drop *something* [*someone*] **like a hot potato** [ˈdrɑ(ː)p ~laɪkə ˈhɑtpəˈteɪdə] [话] **赶紧抛弃** 只要想象一下手里拿不住热土豆慌忙丢掉的场面,对这一表达法就很容易理解了。*When Mr. Skinflint learned that his latest idea would cost such a pile of money, he dropped it like a hot potato.* 当斯金弗林特先生了解到他最近的一个方案需要很大一笔经费的时候,赶紧把它放弃了。*As soon as the Prime Minister realized the depth of opposition to his new proposal, he dropped it like a hot potato.* 首相了解到人们如何强烈地反对他的新提案之后,马上就把它撤消了。除了"方案"、"提案"等之外,又用于"舍弃人"的场合。例如: *The boss has political ambitions. If he ever discovers that you have underworld connections, he'll drop you like a hot potato.* 老板有政治野心。他只要发现你与黑社会有关系,马上就会辞退你。*Lois was a gold digger. When she found that I wasn't really rich, she dropped me like a hot potato.* 洛伊丝是一个以色相骗取男人钱财的女子。她一发现我其实并不富有之后,马上就把我甩掉了。也有独立使用 a hot potato 的场合,意思是"棘手问题"。*Soon after the President agreed to allow the Shah of Iran into the country; he realized that he had been handed a political hot potato.* 美国总统刚一批准伊朗国王入境,他就注意到自己引起了麻烦的政治问题。◇ abandon *something* [*someone*] very quickly

a hot potato [ə ˈhɑtpəˈteɪdə] [话] **棘手问题** → drop *something* [*someone*] like a hot POTATO

potatoes

be small potatoes [ˌsmɔːl pəˈteɪdəz] [话] 微不足道 → be small BEER

potbelly

a potbelly [ə ˈpɑtˌbeli] [口] **大腹便便** → a bay WINDOW

pothead

a pothead [ə ˈpɑ(ː)tˌhe(ː)d] [话] **吸毒者** → an acid HEAD

potluck

a potluck dinner → DINNER

take potluck [ˌteɪk ˈpɑ(ː)tˌlʌk] [话] **吃便饭** take 与说 take *someone's* offer (应某人约)时的 take 相同。potluck 的 pot 是"锅",luck 是"运气",二者合在一起是"锅的运气"。原来的构思是:"因为是用手头现有的材料做成的,所以不晓得会出现什么样的饭菜",亦即"吃的人碰运气的饭菜"。*Shall we go out for dinner tonight? Or would you rather stay home and take potluck?* 今天晚上咱们到外边去吃饭吗?要不然,在家里凑合点便饭吃好吗? *I didn't have time to go shopping today, so you'll just have to take potluck.* 我今天没有时间出去买东西,所以你只好凑合着吃顿便饭了。如以上的例句所示,这一表达法本来是对家里人使用的,但是在来客人的时候,如果没有功夫去特别准备,就怀着抱歉的心情使用它。*We'd be happy to have you stay to dinner if you're willing to take potluck.* 如果你愿意凑合吃点便饭,我们很欢迎你留在这儿一起用晚餐。take potluck 虽然是定型的表达法,有时也单独使用 potluck。*A: What's for dinner tonight, Mom? B: Just potluck.* 甲:妈妈,今天晚上吃什么菜?乙:全是现有的东西。take potluck 作为比喻,也可以用于饭菜以外的东西。例如:*When we arrived at the resort, most of the inns were full, so we didn't have a choice of accommodations. We were forced to take potluck.* 我们到达游乐胜地的时候,大多数旅馆都已经住满了人。因此,我们没有选择住处的余地,只要有个睡觉地方就凑合了。但是,potluck 几乎完全不能按照比喻的意义单独使用。→ a potluck DINNER ◇ have [take] whatever happens to be available

pours

It never rains but it pours. → RAINS

powder

be sitting on a powder keg → KEG

take a powder [ˌteɪkə ˈpaudər] [话] **溜走** 直译为"吃药粉"。上一代的黑社会用语有一个说法是 take a run-out powder (直译为"吃跑掉的药粉")。本条习用语是省略了其中的 run-out。现在,这一习用语已经与黑社会没有什么连带关系了。主要是男性用语,在有什么不相宜的事情时走开的场合使用。*Let's take a powder.* 咱们走开吧。这句话与 Let's get out of here. 意思一样。*When we heard the teacher coming back, we took a powder.* 当我们听到老师回来的声音时,我们赶紧溜走了。◇ leave in a hurry

power

more power to *someone* [ˌmo(ː)r ˌpauər ˈtu ~] [话] **祝你成功** 原形为英国英语的 more power to your elbow。过去英国人认为只要肘部有力,就能多喝酒。因此,这句话在干杯时使用,意思是"但愿你的肘部有更多的力量"。原形似乎是戏谑语,美国人绝大部分不知道这个古老的说法。在美国英语中,条头的表达法是鼓励对方的用语,有"加油干"的意味,经常在严肃的场合使用。例如:*I don't think you'll succeed, but if you're determined to try, more power to you.* 我不认为你能够成功,不过,如果你决心要试一下的话,祝你一帆风顺。*I'm not willing to give my time and energy to the women's lib movement, but for those that are, more power to them.* 我不想花费时间和精力去搞妇女解放运动,但是,我祝愿那些积极参加这一运动的人们取得成功。在 more power to *someone* 的后边,常有接续 I say [ˈaɪ ˌseɪ] 的情况。这一短语有“不管别人如何,要叫我说的话……”的意思。*There's no need to get upset because your son has decided not to go to college. If he thinks he can succeed in life without a college education, more power to him, I say.* 你的儿子已经决定不上大学,你无需为了这件事烦恼。要叫我说的话,如果他认为不受大学教育而能在人生大道上取得成功,那就应该祝他一帆风顺啊。*You shouldn't laugh at him for challenging the club's tennis pro to a match. More power to him, I say.* 你不应该笑他向俱乐部职业网球选手挑战,我倒祝愿他取得成功啊。◇ *someone* should be wished the best of luck / *someone* is to be commended for *his* spirit

praise

damn (*something* [*someone*]) **with faint praise** [ˌdæːm wɪð ˈfeɪntˈpreɪz] [口] **看起来是夸奖,实际上是毁谤** 18 世纪英国著名诗人蒲柏(Alexander Pope)的诗篇《给阿巴斯诺特博士的信》(“Epistle to Dr. Arbuthnot”) 中有这样一节: Damn with faint praise, assent with civil leer, / And, without sneering, teach the rest to sneer. (欲贬形似褒,横眉示赞同。此公不冷笑,偏传冷笑风。) 这就是本条的出处。这里的 damn (咒骂) 是动词, faint 是“微弱的”。本条直译为“用少量的表扬话去咒骂某人”。不论东方或西方,这都是批评家常用的手段。*The critic damned the novel with faint praise by saying that the first half was rather interesting.* 批评家说那部长篇小说的前半部还有点意思,看起来似乎是表扬,实际上是竭力贬低它的价值。也有以人为对象的时候,例如: *Newspapers damned the President with faint praise by saying he had surely done his best.* 各报都说总统确实尽到了最大的努力,这话看起来好象是表扬,实际上是批评他无能。这一表达法一般来说是指故意用夸奖的方式贬低人或物,但也有说者并无此意而听者却如此感觉的场合。*A: How did the professor like your paper? B: He said it was better than average. That's what's known as damning with faint praise.* 甲:教授对你的论文如何评价? 乙:他说比一般水平强点。这正是俗话所讲:看起来是夸奖,实际上是毁谤啊。◇ criticize *something* [*someone*] in an oblique [a roundabout] manner

praise *someone* [*something*] **to the skies** (for *something*) → SKIES

praises

be full of praises for *someone* [*something*] [ˌfuləv ˈpreɪzəz fər ～] [口] **极力称赞** → sing *someone's* PRAISES (for *something*)

sing *one's* **own praises** [ˌsɪŋ ～ ˌoun ˈpreɪzəz] [口] **老王卖瓜,自卖自夸** → sing *someone's* PRAISES (for *something*) / blow *one's* own TRUMPET

sing *someone's* **praises** (for *something*) [ˌsɪŋ ～ ˈpreɪzəz] [口] **颂扬** 由 sing the Lord's praises (歌颂上帝)一语而来。*The chief is singing Jack's praises for capturing a big contract.* 杰克捞到一笔大合同,经理见人就夸奖他。如这一例句所示,一般不是对本人说夸奖的话,而是向大家称颂那个人的事迹。*I don't know why you're always singing that guy's praises. I don't think he's so great.* 我不知道你为什么老是赞扬那个家伙。我认为他没有什么了不起。*Don't sing my praises. It was mainly due to Roy's efforts that we succeeded.* 请不要表扬我。我们主要是靠罗伊的努力取得成功的啊。sing *one's* own praises 是“老王卖瓜,自卖自夸”。*That guy gives me a pain in the neck. He's always singing his own praises.* 我觉得那个家伙太讨厌啦。他永远是老王卖瓜,自卖自夸。有时候不是用于称赞人,而是以 sing the praises of *something* 的句型用于被赞美物。*Everyone in the office is singing the praises of our new computer.* 公司里的每一个职工都称赞我们新置的计算机。同义语有 be full of praise(s) for *someone* [*something*], be full of *one's* own praises。◇ give *someone* a lot of [so much] praise / praise *someone* (so) highly

sing the praises of *something* [ˌsɪŋðə ˈpreɪzəzəv～] [口] **称赞某种东西** → sing *someone's* PRAISES (for *something*)

prayer

not have a prayer (of *something*) [nɑt ˌhævə ˈpre(ː)r] [话] **完全没有希望** prayer 是"祈祷",在这里是"成功的可能性"。本条的原来构思是"一个祈祷也没有",亦即"怎样祈祷也没有用处"。这是一个习用语,常用否定式。*He doesn't have a prayer of getting into that university.* 他完全没有进那个大学的可能性。*The ship sank so quickly that no one had a prayer (of being saved).* 那只船沉没得太快了,连一个人也没有生还的(得救的)希望。如上面的例句所示,of 后边多接动名词,但也有象下面这种场合。*She doesn't have a prayer of success.* 她完全没有成功的希望。另有一个表达法是:not stand a chance, 意思大致相同,但语气比较弱。如果讲 not stand a ghost of a chance, 亦即加上 a ghost of, 其分量与 not have a prayer 大体相等。这里的 stand 是"持有"的意思,ghost 是"幽灵",所以这一表达法直译应为"连成功的影子都没有"。不论有无 a ghost,这一表达法均可与 not have a prayer 自由代换。◇ have absolutely no hope [chance] (of *something*)

praying

be past praying for [ˌpæ(ː)st ˈpreɪɪŋ ˌfɔ(ː)r] [口] **无可救药** 直译为"为之祈祷的阶段过去了",例如说:*No one is so bad that he is past praying for.* 天下没有比他再坏的人,为他祈祷完全没有用处了。作为比喻,表示"不管采取什么手段都没有恢复或改善的希望"。广泛应用于人、动物、东西、事态等等。在讲生物的场合,一般是"快死啦!"的意味,但根据上下文,有时表示"已经死了"。*One glance at the injured man lying beside the road told me that he was past praying for.* 我瞧了一眼躺在路边的那个受伤的男子,就知道他已经无可挽救了。*The soldier was already past praying for. Rigor mortis had begun to set in.* 那个士兵已经完全没救啦。尸首都开始僵直了。*I'm afraid this old car is past praying for.* 据我看,这辆旧汽车已经完全不行啦。*I'd say that the government's anti- inflation program is past praying for.* 据我看,政府的反通货膨胀计划已经完全不灵了。◇ be in such bad condition that recovery [repair] is impossible / be dead

preemie

a preemie [ə ˈpriːmi] [话] **早产儿** premature [ˌpriməˈtʃu(ː)r] (发生过早,时期尚早)的缩略。最初曾仿效 premature, 第一音节只用一个 e, 写作 premie。但在英语中,premie 发音为 [ˈpremi],而不发音为 [ˈpriːmi]。可能由于要保持原来的发音 [ˈpriːmi],最近多加一个 e 而拼写作 preemie 的占绝大多数。有时也可以看到 preemy 的拼法。*Our next- door neighbor gave birth to a preemie last week.* 上个星期,我们的邻居生了个不够月的孩子。◇ a premature baby

pretenses

act under false pretenses [ˌæktʌndər ˌfɔ(ː)ls ˈpri(ː)ˌtentsəz] [口] **采取欺骗手段** 原为法律专门用语,汉语译作"虚伪陈述"或"诈欺取财"。后来在口语中使用。*The swindler was indicted for acting under false pretenses.* 诈骗犯以虚伪陈述罪被起诉了。这是作为法律术语使用的例子。在一般会话中使用时,语调十分轻快。例如:*I finally realized that Hugh was acting under false pretenses. He only wanted to marry me for my money.* 我终于明白了休对我耍的完全是一套假招数。他只是图我的钱才想跟我结婚的。有时候,虽然同样是欺骗对方,但从结果来看,这种行动却是正确的。例如:*Although Frank appeared to befriend the swindler, he was only acting under false pretenses. His real aim was to gather enough evidence to have him arrested.* 虽然看起来弗兰克跟诈骗犯很亲近,但那只是一种伪装而已。他的真实目的是搜

集足够的证据，使诈骗犯落入法网。◇ have ulterior motives / pretend

pretty

a pretty penny → PENNY

be sitting pretty [ˌsɪtn ˈprɪdi] [话] **处于安乐的状态** 具体形象是"以优美的姿态坐着"，当然是"处于安乐的状态"了。至于"安乐"的内容，有时是经济上很富裕，有时是工作轻松、计划顺利实现等等，也有时具备这两方面的"安乐"条件。*Frank is sitting pretty now since his grandfather left him a lot of money.* 弗兰克现在享福啦，因为他爷爷留给他一大笔钱。*If we can win that contract, we'll be sitting pretty.* 如果我们能把那份合同争取到手，我们的日子就好过了。*Doug is sitting pretty now that he has gained the support of most of the board members in his bid to become the next president.* 道格企图当下一任的总经理，他已经得到绝大多数董事的支持，现在是稳坐钓鱼台了。常用 really sitting 或者 very pretty 的形式加强语气。*I was really sitting pretty [sitting very pretty] until that guy came along and started messing up my plans.* 在那个家伙前来并且开始打乱我的计划之前，我一直是进行得非常顺利的。◇ be in a very comfortable position [situation]

prevention

An ounce of prevention is worth a pound of cure. → OUNCE

price

a fancy price [ə ˌfæntsi ˈpraɪs] [话] **过高的价钱** 直译为"精致的、需要高度技巧的价钱"，本来是带有讽刺意味的表达法。现在已经没有那种新鲜的味道了，只用于表示 (very) high price 的意味。这里的 fancy 在美国出版的词典中常释义为 exorbitant(不在法律范围之内的)，但在一般的文句里并没有那么强烈的意味，这一点请读者注意：*That's a fancy price to pay for a book.* 对于一本书来说，那个价钱太高了。*I like that store, but their prices are too fancy for my pocketbook.* 我喜欢那家商店，但是那里的价钱过高，与我的钱包不相配。不仅是 price, rent (房租)、bid (投标)、bill (帐单)、price tag (价格标签)等词的前边也可以加 fancy 表示数字过高的意味。*I'll bet they're paying a fancy rent for this place.* 这个地方的房租肯定很高。*We can't compete with such fancy bids.* 投标的底价那么高，我们无法竞争。*Wow! Talk about a fancy price tag!* 哎呀！标签上的价钱竟有这么高！◇ a (very) high price

pride

pocket *one's* **pride** (and *do something*) [pɑkət ～ˈpraɪd] [口] **抑制自尊心** 直译为"把自尊心放到口袋里"，亦即"自尊心即便受到伤害，也竭力压抑自己的感情，不表现出来"的意思。常用 pocket *one's* pride and *do something* (抑制自尊心去干某事) 的形式。*Although I felt that Jim was in the wrong, for the sake of harmony in our group I pocketed my pride and shook hands with him.* 虽然我觉得吉姆有错误，但是为了集体的和睦，我抑制住自尊心，同他握了手。*Because of the recession, I was forced to pocket my pride and join my younger brother's company.* 由于经济衰退，我不得不放下架子，参加我弟弟的公司。*Mary left home after a big fight with her husband. But after living for a month with her unsympathetic mother, she pocketed her pride and returned home.* 玛丽与她的丈夫大吵大闹之后离开了家。但是到娘家住了一个月，母亲对她丝毫不表示同情，她只得抑制着自尊心回家了。同义的表达法有 swallow *one's* pride (swallow 是"吞"，这一表达法可以译作"忍气吞声")，但大多使用 swallow *one's* pride and *do something* 的形式。◇ sacrifice *one's* pride

swallow *one's* **pride** (and *do something*) [ˌswɑlə ～ ˈpraɪd] [口] **忍气吞声** → pocket *one's* PRIDE (and *do something*)

private

a private dick [ə ˌpraɪvətˈdɪ(:)k] [俗] **私人**

侦探 → a DICK

a private eye → EYE

privates

the privates [ðə ˈpraɪvəts] [口] **阴部** "生殖器"的委婉语，同义的 the private parts (不宜显露的部分) 的缩略，在日常会话中使用。*Your bathing suit is too loose. I can see your privates.* 你的游泳衣太宽松啦。我能看见你的阴部了。如这一例句所示，有时用 *one's* privates 的形式。但一般要象条头所写那样加定冠词 the。*He kicked his attacker in the privates.* 当对方向他袭击的时候，他踢了那个人的阴部。◇ the genitalia [ˌdʒenəˈteɪlɪə]

prize

a booby prize [ə ˈbu(:)bi ˌpraɪz] [口] **末名奖** prize 是"奖"。a booby (→ a BOOB) 是"笨蛋"。两者的意思合起来，是"最不行的人领到的奖"，这很容易理解。*I'm no good at this game. I always get the booby prize.* 我不擅长这种运动，总是得末名奖。如这一例句所示，一般按照字面意义"末名奖"，在社交集会或比赛中使用。但也有时用于表示"显然不行"、"最差劲"等意味。*When it comes to manners, that guy takes the booby prize.* 如果谈到礼貌，那个家伙最差劲。由于在一项比赛中只能有一个末名奖，因此，如上边的两个例句所示，使用定冠词的场合占绝大多数。◇ a prize for last place

probably

probably [ˈprɑːbəbli / ˈprɑ(:)bli] [口] **大概** 中国学英语的人，甚至一些英汉词典，往往把 probably 一词与 MAYBE [perhaps] 混同起来。但是，无论在意义上或用法上，两者都有显著的差别。首先，probably 是在概率或可能性大于50%的场合使用的语言，表示"大概"、"多半"、"基本上"、"很可能"、"差不多"的意思。与此相对，maybe 和 perhaps 则用于概率或可能性将近 50%的场合，表示"也许"、"也有可能"的意思。另外，maybe [perhaps]大多是放在句子的前端，而 probably 可以说完全没有放在句子前端的情况。*He probably left yesterday.* 他多半昨天出发了。基本上如这一例句所示，放在主语与动词之间。如果句子里有助动词，有时可以把它放在助动词的前边，但标准句型是把它夹在助动词与动词之间。*He will probably leave tomorrow.* 他多半是明天出发。*He has probably left already.* 他大概已经出发了。如果动词是 be，则放在 be 动词的后边。*It is probably better to go.* 大概现在去为好。否定式的时候，同此。*He will probably not leave tomorrow.* 他明天大概不会出发。*There is probably not enough money.* 钱大概不够了。但是，当 not 与助动词或 be 动词成 won't, isn't 等的时候，则放在这一类结合词的前边。例如：He probably won't leave tomorrow. 或者 There probably isn't enough money. 关于 probably 在句子中的位置问题，以上所述只是一些原则。由于在会话中可以把它放在打算强调的词的前边，因而会出现各种例外。例如说 *He will leave ... probably tomorrow.* 他要出发喽……多半是明天。这句话强调 tomorrow，打破了正常的顺序。◇ most likely

prof

a prof [ə ˈprɑːf] [话] **教授** professor 的缩略，学生用语。前边一般加修饰语，单独使用的情况很少。*Dr. Hunt is an anatomy prof.* 亨特博士是一位解剖学教授。*My English prof is Mr. Allsberry.* 我的英语教授是奥尔斯贝里先生。*Who's the new prof?* 那位新来的教授是谁？◇ a professor

prom

a prom [ə ˈprɑːm] [口] **大学或高中举行的正式舞会** 特指学期末或学年末高年级学生举行的大规模舞会。原为 promenade (一般正式舞会) 的缩略。现在，promenade 已经不作此解，代替此解的说法是 a formal dance。"学校的正式舞会"只能用 prom 的形式。*Who are you taking to the spring prom this year?* 今年春季的舞会你带谁去啊？三年级和四年级学生常举行只有本年级学生参加的舞会,三年级学生的舞会称 junior prom,四年级学生的舞会称 senior prom。*Next week is the junior prom.* 下星期是三年级学生的舞会。◇ a formal school dance

promise

give *something* **a lick and a promise** → LICK

proof

The proof of the pudding is in the eating. [ðə ˌpruːfəvðə ˈpudɪŋəz ənðɪ ˈiːdɪŋ] [谚] **布丁香不香,要靠嘴来尝** 这与汉语的"实践出真知"、"实践是检验真理的唯一标准"是一个意思。汉语俗语中也有很多类似的表达法,如"不吃高粱,不知粗细"、"不吃黄连,不知味苦"等等。*I'll admit that the plan appears sound, but the proof of the pudding is in the eating.* 我承认那个计划看起来很不错,但是,布丁香不香要靠嘴来尝啊。*It's a beautiful car all right, but I'd like to drive it a day or two before I agree to buy it. After all, the proof of the pudding is in the eating.* 那的确是一辆很漂亮的汽车,但是在我同意购买之前,我想试开一两天。俗话说:布丁香不香要靠嘴来尝啊。为了加强语气,可在 proof 的前边加 only。*Marriage is a high-risk proposition. A man or a woman may appear to be good mate material, but the only proof of the pudding is in the eating. And once you have taken a bite, it's too late to change your mind.* 结婚是一桩高度冒险的事情。一个男人或一个女人,乍看起来可能是般配的一对,但是布丁香不香,唯一的试验方法是用嘴来尝。而等你已经咬上一口的时候,要想改变主意就太迟了。◇ Whether *something* works well [*someone* is the proper person] or not can be known only by trying it [*him*].

prospect

not relish the prospect of (*doing*) *something* [nɑt ˌreləʃðə ˈprɑ(ː)ˌspektəv ~] [口] **不感兴趣** relish 是"喜好"或"有兴趣",prospect 是"预料"或"估计"的意思。这一表达法与 not look forward to (*doing*) *something* 同义,但比较文雅。*I really don't relish the prospect of (spending) August in New York.* 在纽约过八月,我实在不感兴趣。*I myself certainly wouldn't relish the prospect of marrying a man like that.* 如果是我的话,我绝对没有跟那样一个男人结婚的兴趣。◇ not (really) want to *do something*

prospector

a (gold) prospector [ə (ˈgould) ˌprɑ(ː)s-pektər] [口] **探金矿的人** → a gold DIGGER

prudence

throw prudence to the winds [ˌθrouˈpru(ː)-dəns təðə ˈwɪ(ː)ndz] [口] **鲁莽行事** → throw CAUTION to the winds

prunes

be full of prunes [ˌfuləv ˈpruːnz] [话] **说的话非常无聊** → be full of BEANS ②

p's

mind *one's* **p's and q's** [ˌmaɪnd ~ ˈpiːzənˈkjuːz] [口] **注意言行** 这里的 mind ~与 be careful about ~相同,是"对……注意"的意思。英美儿童在写 p 的时候常写成 q,在写 q 的时候又常写成 p,p 和 q 是两个容易弄混的字母。在进行纠正的时候,过去的老师们常说 Mind your p's and q's. (你们要注意 p 和 q 啊!)后来,由"请注意字母的写法"进一步发展,广泛用于表示"请注意言语和行动"的意思,也就是"要规规矩矩,很有礼貌"。主要是对孩子们使用的表达法,但现在对成年人也常常使用。无论是对什么人使用,都有"谨小慎微"的含义。它与具有"言行谨慎"意味的 be on *one's* best behavior 可以互相代换。*Be sure to mind your p's and q's when the new department head is around. He doesn't care for loose talk or behavior.* 当新来的部长在场的时候,你千万要注意自己的言行。他不喜欢自由散漫的言语和行为。*The children were told to mind their p's and q's when the preacher comes* *to visit.* 家长告诉孩子们说，当牧师前来造访的时候，他们必须规规矩矩，很有礼貌才行。有时讲 watch *one's* p's and q's。◇ be careful of *one's* deportment

public

in the public eye → EYE

John Q. Public [ˌdʒɑ(:)n ˌkju: ˈpʌblɪk] [口] **一般市民** → the MAN in the street

pudding

The proof of the pudding is in the eating. →PROOF

Pudgy

Pudgy [ˈpʌ(:)dʒi] [俗] **大胖子** → FATSO

puff

a cream puff [ə ˈkri:m.pʌ(:)f] [话] **软弱无能的人** 具体形象是："象奶油点心一样软绵绵的家伙"。指"弱不禁风"而且"不要强"的男性，但这一表达法主要强调"没有力气"。*So you beat up Jimmy Tate? So what? Anybody can lick that cream puff.* 你把吉米·塔特狠揍了一顿吗？那有什么了不起？任何人都能够打败那个大窝囊废。*"The champ's a cream puff," said the challenger. "I'll finish him off in one round."* "冠军是个大软蛋，"挑战者说，"一个回合我就会把他打倒。"如以上两个例句所示，这一表达法大多用于"打架"或"体育运动"。*That guy's a cream puff. He talks big at first, but he always backs down when he's threatened.* 那个家伙是个窝囊废。在开始的时候大夸海口，人家一吓唬就把脖子缩了回去。cream puff 还有一个与以上完全不同的用法，意思是"保养良好的旧汽车"。在向顾客出售的时候，营业员特别爱用这一表达法。*"This car is a cream puff," purred the used-car salesman. "It was owned by a nice old lady that never drove it over forty miles an hour."* "这辆汽车保养得极好，"旧汽车推销员花言巧语地说，"它原来的主人是一位上流社会的老夫人，她开车的时速从来没有超过四十英里"。◇ a weakling

puke

puke [ˈpju(:)k] [俗] **呕吐** 从前，当莎士比亚使用这个词时，本来非常古雅。曾几何时，它的格调日趋低落，至今在表示"呕吐"的各种说法中，已经成为最不堪入耳的下流话了。*He puked on the platform.* 他在站台上吐起来了。 → lose *one's* DINNER ◇ vomit

pull

pull [ˈpu(:)l] [话] **政治或经济影响** → CLOUT

pull a fast one (on *someone*) [ˌpulə ˈfæ(:)stwən] [话] **行骗** → PUT one over on *someone*

pull down (*money*) [ˌpulˈdaun ~] [话] **挣钱** 直译为"把钱拉下来"。意义与 earn 或 make 相同，但 pull down 指挣大量的钱，因此不能说 I pull down only a hundred dollars a month. (我一个月只挣一百美元。) *A: I wonder how much he's pulling down. B: I dunno, but he must pull down at least half million dollars a year.* 甲：不知道他有多少收入啊？乙：不晓得。不过，他每年至少会挣五十万美元。◇ make

pull *oneself* **together** [ˌpul ~ təˈgeðər] [口] **恢复平静** 本条的具体形象是："把各处分散的精神(*oneself*)再聚拢到一起(pull together)"。也就是重新振作精神的意思。具体地讲，就是"在悲哀、恼怒、失望、恐怖、不安以及其他的精神震动之后，又恢复原来的状态"。*Helen had been on the verge of tears, but she soon pulled herself together.* 海伦的眼泪都快掉出来了，但是她很快地使自己平静下来。在这一场合，海伦在一时之间肯定是有所悲伤、悔恨或者羞愧。*Sid had been in an uncontrollable rage the night before. I was relieved to see that this morning he had pulled himself together and was behaving normally.* 锡德昨天晚上忍不住他的一腔怒火。今天早晨见到他恢复平静、一切照常之后，我心里的石头总算落了地。*Pull yourself together. If we're to escape from here, we've all got to remain calm.* 你要镇静下来。如果咱们要从这里逃出去，所有的人都必须保持冷静的头脑才行。在这一场合，在一

群人当中，一定是有谁由于过分恐惧而失去常态了。*I looked at my shaking hands and realized I had to pull myself together before the police arrived to question me.* 我望着自己两只颤动的手，心里想：在警察前来盘问我之前，我必须使自己平静下来。◇ regain *one's* composure

punch

beat *someone* **to the punch** [ˌbi(:)t ~ təðə ˈpʌntʃ] [话] **先发制人** → beat *someone* to the DRAW

the punch line → LINE

punches

pull *one's* **punches** [ˌpul ~ ˈpʌntʃəz] [话] **悠着劲儿** 这一表达法来源于拳击用语。意思是"在拳击时，不是 follow through (卯足劲)去打，而是适当地控制自己的力量"。按字面说，有"把拳头往回拉 (pull)"的意味。*Many people suspected the fight had been fixed because the challenger appeared to be pulling his punches.* 因为挑战者好象故意不用力打，所以有许多人怀疑这是一场预先定了胜负的假比赛。作为比喻，大多用于用口头批评或叱责的场合。*The boss's reprimands weren't as harsh as they often are. I think he was pulling his punches in order to avoid discouraging the new employees.* 老板的叱责没有平时那么严厉。我想，他是为了不使新来的职工灰心丧气才故意缓和口气的。使用否定句比使用肯定句的场合多。*When Mr. Harsh decides to lay it on the line, he's not one to pull his punches.* 哈什先生一旦决定把话摊开的时候，他不是那种话到舌尖留半句的人。在否定句的场合，可以如这一例句使用 *one's* punches, 但一般是把 *one's* 改为 any。*I'm sorry I have to speak to you this way, Frank, but I'm not going to pull any punches for you or anyone else.* 很遗憾，弗兰克，我必须用这种方式对你讲话，但是不只是对你，对其他的任何人，我也没有话到舌尖留半句的意思。*Once they set out to take over our company, they didn't pull any punches.* 他们从一开始接管我们的公司，手下就没有留情。◇ soften *one's* words [actions]

punishment

be a glutton for punishment → GLUTTON

purple

be born to the purple [ˌbo(:)rn təðə ˈpəːrpl] [口] **生在有钱有势的人家** 紫色(purple)自古以来就是王侯穿用的服装的颜色，成为王室的象征。在没有贵族制度的美国，一谈到 the purple, 则指兼具门第、金钱、巩固的社会地位这三者的"望族"。洛克菲勒一家和肯尼迪一家便是所谓的美国的 the purple。请读者注意：purple 前面必须加 the。*Having been born to the purple, John Stonechap was thought from an early age to be destined for high office.* 约翰·斯通查普生在有钱有势的人家，从幼年起，人们就认为他将来必当大官。◇ be born into a wealthy and prestigious family

purse

make a silk purse out of a sow's ear [ˌmeɪkə ˈsɪlk ˈpəːrs ˌaudəvə ˈsauˌzɪ(:)r] [口] **用朽木做雕刻** 直译为"用母猪耳朵制作丝钱包"。这是一个来源于谚语的表达法。原形是 You can't make a silk purse out of a sow's ear. 但在实际上，You can't 的部分有各种各样的变形。又，原形在许多场合与汉语俗语"乌鸦生不出凤凰"相似，但也常见以下各例句中的用法。基本的意思是："用不好的材料制作不出好的东西来"。*Mrs. Blindly has hired many tutors in hopes of seeing her son become a scholar someday, but what she doesn't realize is that you can't make a silk purse out of a sow's ear.* 布林德里夫人指望她的儿子将来成为学者，因此雇了许多家庭教师。但是，她有一点没弄明白：她的儿子并不是那样一块材料。以下是 You can't 的变形。*I was asked to polish up this translation into a publishable work, but it's impossible to make a silk purse out of a sow's ear.* 我受委托润饰这篇翻译稿件，要求达到出版

水平，但是原译太差，怎么加工也不行。*You want me to make Hal into a competent salesman? That's asking me to make a silk purse out of a sow's ear.* 你想叫我把哈尔培养成一个合格的推销员吗？那等于叫我把一块朽木雕成工艺品一样啊。不仅是 You can't 部分变形，还有象下面这样极端的变形：*We have a good training program, but if they want us to turn out silk purses, they're going to have to send us something besides sow's ears.* 我们有一个很好的训练计划。但是，如果他们想叫我们培训出来优秀的人材，他们必须送一些不是废物的好材料。◇ make something of quality out of shoddy materials

pusher

a pencil pusher [ə ˈpentsəl ˌpuʃər] [话] **办公室职员** 直译为“铅笔 (pencil) 的推者 (pusher)”，即“在纸上写字的人”。一般与体力劳动者 (a blue-collar worker) 相对，指坐办公室的领取工资的人员。*My father wanted me to go to college and become a pencil pusher, but I'm glad I didn't. I'm happier working on a factory assembly line.* 我父亲曾经指望我上大学，然后变成一个坐办公室的人。我真高兴我没有那样做。我在工厂的装配线上工作，快乐得多。坐办公室的人很容易发生运动不足的毛病，在美国也是如此。*Give me the outdoor life. Secretaries and pencil pushers never get enough exercise.* 让我过户外生活吧。秘书和办公室职员总是发生运动不足的毛病。本条常用于表示“没大能力”、“没有资质”等轻蔑的意思。*Those pencil pushers in the head office are always screwing things up.* 总公司的那些坐办公室的人总是把事情搞得一塌糊涂。也可以如下一例句那样，用于记者、作家、会计师等以 desk work 为主的专业知识分子，在这一场合当然不含有轻蔑的意味了。*My family are almost all pencil pushers. My uncle is a novelist, my father is a CPA, and both my brother and sister are reporters.* 我家的人几乎全是耍笔杆子的。我叔叔是一个小说家，我父亲是一个职业会计师，我哥哥和姐姐都是记者。另外，虽然这种情况极少，但有不说 pencil pusher 而说 pen pusher 的场合。◇ a white-collar [desk] worker / a person whose work involves writing

a pill pusher [ə ˈpɪ(:)l ˌpuʃər] [俗] **医生** 直译为“丸药 (pill) 的推销者 (pusher)”。同义的表达法有 pill peddler (卖丸药的小贩)和 pill roller (滚丸药的人)，但在三者之中，pill pusher 的使用频率最高。这是一个戏谑语，使用时一般含有轻蔑的意味。*Pop wants me to become a pill pusher.* 我爹叫我将来当医生。*That pill pusher charged me twenty-five dollars just to look down my throat.* 那个大夫只检查了一下我的喉咙，就要我 25 美元。有时根据上下文是“药剂师”(pharmacist) 的意思。*Bill wants to become a drugstore pill pusher [pill peddler, pill roller].* 比尔说将来要当一名药剂师。◇ a doctor

pushover

a pushover [ə ˈpuˌʃouvər] [话] **容易对付的人** 将 push over (推倒) 合成一词，并转为名词的表达法。直译为“稍微一推就倒下的人”，但不使用这一意义，专门用作比喻。在应用于人的场合，是“容易打倒的拳击对手”、“容易欺骗的对手”的意味，总之，是“容易对付的人”。*The champ claimed that the challenger would be a pushover.* 冠军声称，他很容易把挑战者击倒。*He's no pushover. You'll need real proof to convince him.* 他不是一个好对付的人。你要说服他，必须有真凭实据。*A: Did he give you the money? B: Yeah. He was a real pushover.* 甲：他给你钱了吗？乙：给啦。他这个人太容易对付了。在应用于人的场合，a pushover 可以用 a sucker (容易上当的人)代换。但使用 sucker 时含有“愚蠢”、“无知”等不良的意味，而 pushover 只表示某人是个“老好人”、“实心眼”，并没有坏的感觉 (→ a SUCKER ①)。be a pushover for *something* 本来的意思是“一碰见某种事物马上就倒下去”，作为比喻是表示“禁不起”、“禁不住”。*Just* *polish the apple a bit. She's a pushover for flattery.* 你拍一拍马屁好啦。她这个人禁不起人家奉承。*Dick's a real pushover for blonds.* 迪克一见到金发美人就魂不守舍了。在应用于人以外的场合,是"太容易啦"、"不费吹灰之力"的意思。大多用于"事情",也常用于"比赛"或"比赛对手"。*Selling ice cream on a hot day is a pushover. Why don't you try it?* 在热天卖冰淇淋,这工作太容易啦。你为什么不试试看? *Translating this into English should be a pushover for Lee. He's been to school in America.* 李把这个译成英语,一定不费吹灰之力。他是在美国上过学嘛。*Why should I pay him that much for the job? He said himself that it was a real pushover.* 他干那个工作,我为什么要付给他那么多钱呀?他本人讲过,那个工作不费吹灰之力啊。*We may be the stronger team, but don't expect tomorrow's game to be a pushover.* 我们可能是比较强的队,但是不要认为明天的比赛会很容易拿下来啊。*There are no guards at that bank. It'll be a pushover.* 那家银行没有警卫。搞它非常容易。◇ easy competition / an easy person to persuade [win over] / (a person) easily won over by flattery [blonds, etc.] / (a) very easy (thing to do) / an easy victory [job, etc.]

be a pushover for *something* [ə ˈpuˌʃouvər fər ~] [话] **禁不起** → a PUSHOVER

pussyfoot

pussyfoot around [ˌpusiˌfudəˈraund] [话] **由于过分小心谨慎而采取暧昧的态度**

美国第 26 任总统西奥多·罗斯福(Theodore Roosevelt)首创的一个表达法。印第安准州(Indian Territory)负责人约翰逊 (W. B. Johnson)在追查迫害或欺诈印第安人的白人犯罪分子时,总是采取小心翼翼的态度,不敢下手,因此,罗斯福称他为 Pussyfoot Johnson。这就是本条习用语的来源。罗斯福的原意是指约翰逊办事象 pussy (猫)的 foot (足)走路一样,不出声音,总是悄悄地干。随后,pussyfoot 一词被用作名词,意思是"象猫一样小心谨慎,不轻举妄动的人"。后来又作为动词,加上 around 使用,基本意思是"对环境和对手过分注意,采取暧昧的态度",但不限于态度,也可指言语、行动、思考等,范围极广。有"令人非常着急"的感觉,一般含有非难的意味。可以按照字面意义"象猫一样走路不出声音"使用,如说: *Miss Steno pussyfoots around the office so quietly that half the time you don't even realize she's there.* 斯泰诺小姐在办公室里走路跟猫一样悄然无声,在大部分时间你甚至都理会不到她在上班。一般用例如下: *After pussyfooting around for several months, he finally got up enough nerve to ask the boss for a raise.* 在几个月的犹犹豫豫之后,他终于鼓足勇气去向老板要求提高工资了。*The Nazis took over most of Europe while the rest of the world pussyfooted around.* 在世界各国采取观望态度的时候,纳粹夺取了大半个欧洲。*The chief doesn't pussyfoot around. Once he makes up his mind, he does it.* 头头不是一个裹足不前的人。他一旦下了决心,马上就干。*Why are we pussyfooting around? We know the mayor is guilty. Let's arrest him.* 我们犹豫什么呀?我们知道市长有罪。咱们逮捕他吧。*We don't have time to pussyfoot around on this question. We have to give an answer by tomorrow.* 我们没有时间来来回回地研究这个问题了。我们必须不迟于明天做出答复。本条在应用于语言的时候,意味与 beat around the BUSH 相近。*Cal is not one to pussyfoot around. He always says exactly what's on his mind.* 卡尔不是一个说话爱兜圈子的人。他一向是心里有什么就说什么。a pussyfooter 是"优柔寡断的人"。*York is hardly the man for a job like that. He's too much of a pussyfooter.* 约克这个人不适合于那样一个工作。他过于优柔寡断啦。◇ (timidly) adopt an indecisive attitude / hesitate [dawdle] (timidly) / (timidly) speak in a roundabout manner

pussyfooter

a pussyfooter [ə ˈpusi.fudər] [话] **优柔寡断的人** → PUSSYFOOT around

put

feel put upon [.fi(:)l ˈpudə.pʌ(:)n] [口] **感到很委屈** 可以认为，这是 feel that *one* is put upon 的缩略表达法。这里的 put upon 源出 put responsibility (etc.) on *someone* (使负责任等) 一语，但专用被动语态。在用 be 动词构成 be put upon 时，具体形象是："把本来可以不拿的沉重东西硬放在那个人的身上"。在由于别人豪不客气的委托而感到苦恼和麻烦的场合使用。*He has been greatly put upon by his relatives for many years.* 他为自己的亲属吃了许多年的苦头。feel put upon 大多含有"自己非常冤枉"的意味。除 greatly 外，常用 much 加强语气。*My husband feels put upon because his boss often asks him to work late for no pay.* 我的丈夫感到自己受到虐待，因为他的老板常常叫他加班而不给任何报酬。*I shall naturally feel much put upon if they insist on my taking responsibility without having been involved in the decision-making process.* 我并没有参加决策的过程，如果他们硬要我去负责任的话，我当然会觉得非常不合理啦。*George is feeling greatly put upon because we told him to do a little work for a change.* 我们告诉乔治以后也干点活儿，他感到深受委屈。◇ feel unjustly treated

put *someone* **on** [.put ~ ˈɔ:n] [话] **哄骗** 这一表达法中的前置词 on 必须放在 *someone* 的后边。不论 *someone* 是名词还是代词，都采取 put *someone* on 的形式。例如：*Of course it's true. Would I put you on?* 当然是真的啦。我还能哄骗你吗？这一例句的后半部分也可以用 Would I pull your leg? 代换。也就是说，put *someone* on 与 pull *someone's* LEG 是意义与用法完全相同的表达法，在下边的两个例句中可以互换。如果说这两个习用语有什么不同，那就是 put *someone* on 这一说法新，使用频率高。*Ralph doesn't make that much money. He was just putting you on.* 拉尔夫挣不了那么多钱。他只不过是哄骗你罢了。*Come on. You're putting me on. You're not really the governor's cousin, are you?* 得了吧，你是在哄骗我。你并不真是州长的表弟吧？把 put *someone*on 名词化，就构成 a put-on，意思是"弥天大谎"或者"恶作剧"。*Even after I learned the truth it was difficult to believe that everything Tom had told me was nothing but a put-on.* 甚至在了解真相之后，我还很难相信汤姆向我所讲的事情全部都是谎言。*The story in the newspaper turned out to be a monstrous put-on.* 报纸上的消息原来是个弥天大谎。◇ (try to) fool *someone*

put one over on *someone* [.put .wʌnˈouvərən ~] [话] **欺骗** 在使用时，大多是很轻快的意味，例如在比赛的时候，一个人说：*Ho, ho! You put one over on me that time.* 嗬！上次我吃了你一家伙啊。但有时用于比较严肃的场面。例如在谈生意时：*A: Do you think Fred is trying to put one over ˈon us? B: I wouldn't put it past him.* 甲：你认为弗雷德是打算欺骗咱们吗？乙：那家伙很可能干得出来。这句话的语调就郑重得多了。pull a fast one (on *someone*) 也是"欺骗他人"，但经常用于表示深刻的意味。因此，在上边的两个例句中，第二个例句有时可以变换说 *Do you think Fred is trying to pull a fast one (on us)?* 但是，如果在第一个例句那样轻快的场合，变换使用就不相宜了。又，put one over on *someone* 的 one 有时用 something 代替，构成 put something over on *someone* [.put .sʌ-ˈmouvərən ~]，意思不变。◇ trick *someone*

put *oneself* **out** [.put ~ ˈaut] [口] **关照** 直译为"把自己放在外边"。通常在后边接续表示"为了……"之意的 ~ for *someone*, ~ to help *someone*, ~ on *someone's* account 等。*Frances is always putting herself out to help you. Don't you think you should show a little more appreciation?* 弗朗西丝总是对你关怀备至的。你不认为应该更多地表示一

点感激之情吗？*I'm not going to put myself out for that guy again.* 我再也不去关照那个家伙啦。*Please don't put yourself out on my account. I'm sure I'll be able to manage by myself.* 请不要为我操心啦。我觉得自己能行。◇ inconvenience *oneself*

put something over on *someone* [ˌput ˌsʌ- mouvərɔn ～] [话] **欺骗** → PUT one over on *someone*

put up or shut up [ˌpu.dʌp ər'ʃʌ(ː).dʌp] [话] **要么出钱，要么闭嘴** put up 等于 put up the money (for *something*)，至于对什么事情"出钱"，当然根据具体情况而有所不同。*My big brother has long insisted that I give up painting and go back to medical school, so I finally decided to do as he said if he'd pay my way. However, when I told him to put up or shut up, he shut up.* 很久以来，我的哥哥就主张我放弃绘画而返回医学院，最后我也下了决心，如果他出学费，我就照他的话办。但是，当我向他讲"要么出钱，要么闭嘴"的时候，他一声不吭了。*I'm tired of your rattling on every day about how the Giants are going to win the pennant. O. K. Here's a hundred dollars that says they won't. Now put up or shut up.* 你每天喋喋不休地讲巨人队将会怎样夺得锦标，我已经听腻了。好啦，我拿一百美元打赌，押在他们败北的一边。现在，你要么出钱，要么闭嘴。◇ put forth *one's* money or be quiet

put *someone* **up to** *something* [ˌput ～ 'ʌptə ～] [口] **唆使** 直译为"从身后推某人去干某种事情"。在通过各种各样的 suggestion (例如说"去干吧，管保没问题"、"干了大有好处"或者"这样干准保成功") 而唆使他人去干坏事的场合使用。多用于恶作剧和犯罪活动。*I'm sure Carl wouldn't have gone there on his own. Someone must have put him up to it.* 我认为，卡尔决不会自动到那种地方去的。一定有人唆使他去。*Sam and Jim were the ones who painted the mustache on the principal's picture, but it seems it was some of the older boys who put them up to it.* 在校长的照片上画胡子的人是萨姆和吉姆，但是，好象有几个高年级学生唆使他们去干这件事。*Why should I take all the blame? You're the one who put me up to it.* 为什么要叫我承担全部责任呢？是你唆使我去干的呀。本条也常用于表示"给人出主意"的意思。*Who put you up to this? I eertainly can't believe you're smart enough to have thought of it by yourself.* 你这样做是谁给出的主意啊？我当然不能相信你自己的头脑会有想到这一点的聪明智慧。◇ get *someone* to do *something*

put up with *something* [ˌpu'dʌpwɪð ～] [口] **忍耐** 从 13 世纪左右开始，put up *something* 有"把某种东西装到衣袋、口袋、瓶子里"的意味。后来用作比喻，表示"把不满、愤怒等放到心怀里"亦即"忍耐"的意思。到了 18 世纪，增添一个 with，构成 put up with *something*，至于 put up *something* 在比喻意义上已成废语。现在本条不仅用于对不满或侮辱的"忍耐"，而且广泛地用于对不方便或不相宜的事情的"克服"。*We enjoyed our trip to Timbuktu, though we had to put up with a good deal of inconvenience.* 虽然我们必须忍受种种的不方便，去廷巴克图旅游一番还是很快乐的。如这一例句所示，本条习用语一般用于"本来可以躲避、但是甘愿忍受"的场合。*I wonder how much longer the American people will put up with their government's inflationary policies.* 美国人民对于他们政府的通货膨胀政策不知还会忍耐到几时。*I'm not going to put up with the noise from that factory any longer. If the city office refuses to act, I'm going to sue.* 我再也忍受不了那家工厂的噪音啦。如果市政府不肯采取措施，我就要提起控诉了。如这一例句所示，在使用这一表达法时，常在后边说明处理方法。*I've put up with your insolence long enough. Open your mouth once more and you're fired.* 我对你的傲慢态度已经忍耐好长时间了。如果你再开一次口，我就开除你。*I refuse to put up with your philandering any longer. Either you stop it or I want a* *divorce*. 你到处勾搭女人,我再也不能忍受下去了。如果你不停止这种行为,我就跟你离婚。◇ endure *something* / tolerate *something*

one **wouldn't put it past** *someone* (to *do something*) [ˌwudnt ˌpudətˈpæ(ː)st ～] [话] **如果是他,是干得出来的** 这里的 past 是与 beyond 同义的前置词,意思是"超过 *someone* 能够干的界限"。*one* wouldn't put it past *someone* 的意思是"*one* 不把这种事放在 *someone* 能够干的界限之外"。换句话说,就是"*one* 认为,如果是 *someone*,是会干这种事的",或者"如果叫 *one* 来讲,*someone* 最有干这种事的可能性"。本条一般用于表示"有可能干坏事或不相宜的事情"的意思。*A: Do you think Jake stole the money? B: I wouldn't put it past him*. 甲:你认为那钱是杰克偷去了吗?乙:他是干得出来的。*Jane says she wouldn't put it past her brother to sell her mother's jewelry*. 简说,她的弟弟很有可能卖了她母亲的珠宝。如以上的例句所示,原文一般用否定式,但也偶尔有如下的变形:*Would you really put it past him?* 你真以为他不会干那种事情吗?◇ *one* believes *someone* might well *do* [have *done*] *something*

put-on

a put-on [ə ˈpuˌdɔːn] [话] **欺骗人的事情** →PUT *someone* on

Q

q's

mind *one's* **p's and q's** → p's

q.t.

on the q.t. [ɔnðə 'kjuː 'tiː] [话] **秘密地** q. t. 为 quiet 的缩略，在这里是名词。一般英汉词典作 on the quiet，这种说法极少。有时用大写字母，作 on the Q. T. 但一般是如条头那样用小写字母表示。这是一个非常口语化的表达法，除报纸、期刊杂志之类外，正式文章不使用它。在翻译成中文时，可以根据具体情况，适当地译为"偷偷地"、"私下地"、"悄悄地"等，总之，只要是"秘密地"的意思就行。*He told me on the q. t. that the company he works for is on the verge of bankruptcy.* 他偷偷地告诉我说，他上班的那个公司正处于破产的边缘。*I found my girl has been meeting him on the q.t.* 我发现自己的女朋友与他偷偷地幽会了。*Don't tell anyone what I've said. It's strictly on the q. t.* 不要把我所讲的事告诉任何人。这是绝对秘密啊。*It's no wonder that Rube's suddenly become such a good dancer. He's been taking dancing lessons on the q.t.* 鲁布突然成为那么优秀的舞蹈家，也没有什么奇怪的。他曾经悄悄地上舞蹈班学习过。◇ private(ly) / secret(ly)

Quaker

The Quaker City [ðə 'kweɪkər 'sɪdi] [口] **费城** → PHILLY

queer

a queer [ə 'kwɪːr] [俗] **同性恋者(主要指男性)** 直译为"奇妙的(人)"。这是 queer 作为名词使用的唯一的一般用例，含有轻蔑的意味。*Joan has been dating that fellow for more than three months now. I wonder if she knows he's a queer.* 琼跟那个家伙约会已经有三个多月了。不晓得她知不知道他是一个同性恋者。用轻蔑口吻讲搞同性恋的男子的表达法，另外还有 a fag ['fæːg], a pansy ['pæ(ː)nzi], a fairy ['fe(ː)ri]。其中，pansy (三色紫罗兰)和 fairy (妖精)专指在男性同性恋中扮演女性角色的人。直至最近，queer 是最一般通用的表达法。20 世纪 60 年代开始流行 gay 一词，现在人们广泛使用。在英语中，gay 不分男女，而且与 queer 等不同，不含有轻蔑的意味。常有同性恋者自称为 gay 的情况。以上所讲的几个同义词均可换入本条开头的那个例句。在使用 gay 时应该注意的是：它很少作为名词使用，当表语使用的场合占绝大多数。也就是说，尽管可以讲 He's a gay. (他是一个同性恋者。)但是一般要讲 He's gay. (他是搞同性恋的。) queer 却恰恰相反，一般讲 He's a queer. 很少讲 He's queer. 顺便提一下：fag 虽然可以用作形容词，但与 queer 或 gay 不同，它只能放在名词(词组)的前边，例如：*He went to a fag party.* 他去参加了一个同性恋者晚会。pansy 与 fairy 永远是名词。◇ a homosexual

question

a leading question [ə 'liːdɪŋ 'kwestʃən] [口] **诱导性问题** leading 是"从对方口中巧妙地诱导出自己所期待的答话"的意思。question 当然是"质问"。本条本来是法律用语，如律师在法庭上说：*I object. That's a leading question.* 我有异议。那是诱供。后来扩大范围，警察也使用起来。用法：前边大多用动词 be 或 ask 引导。*The police tried to trap the suspect by asking him a series of leading questions.* 警察向嫌疑犯提出一系列诱导性问题，企图使他自陷罗网。从法庭、警察方面又进一步发展，在日常生活中也用这一表达法表示比较轻松的意味了。*My girl friend is always asking me lead-*

ing questions like, "You don't think Jane is prettier than I am, do you?" 我的女朋友常常向我提出诱导性问题,例如:"你不认为简长得比我好看吗?" ◇ a question designed to elicit a specific response

a loaded question [ə 'loudəd 'kwestʃən] [口] **哄骗性问题** 一般的诱导性问题,英语为 a leading QUESTION, 这也是法庭用语。a loaded question 包括在前者之内,是极为普遍的表达法。loaded 是"装上子弹"的意思,由此也可以看出这种"问题"该有多么危险了。*A: Was the woman you were seen talking to in that restaurant last night pretty, dear? B: That's a loaded question if there ever was one.* 甲:昨天晚上在那家餐厅里,人家看见你与一位女士谈话,亲爱的,那位女士漂亮吗? 乙:我还没听到过这么厉害的哄骗性问题哪。在这个例句中,对于甲的质问不论回答 Yes 还是 No, 乙都同样是承认与另外的女人在一起这一事实。下一个例句也是一样,嫌疑者如果从正面回答,就等于承认自己是杀人犯。*"Why didn't you use a knife to kill him with?" said the policeman, hoping to trap the suspect with a loaded question.* 警察问嫌疑犯:"你杀死他的时候为什么不用刀子呢?"他企图用哄骗性问题诱供了。◇ a question meant to entrap *someone* / a tricky question

pop (*someone*) **the question** [ˌpɑp ðə 'kwestʃən] [话] **向女方求婚** pop 是"突然提出"。the question 是"询问"或"问题"。典型的问题是:*Will you marry me?* 你能跟我结婚吗? 美国人所以说 pop the question (突然提出询问),是由他们的求婚方式而来的。这种求婚方式是:男方鼓足勇气,向女方提出是否愿意结婚的询问。但是不管是不是采取这种询问方式,人们经常用本条习用语表示"求婚"的意思。又,这一表达法用的是 the question (那个问题),即 question 要加定冠词,这是因为所讲的是"那个重要问题",如果说 pop a question, 那就仅仅是"突然提出一个问题"的意思了。*You've been going with Nancy for over three years now. Why don't you pop her the question?* 你与南希交往已经有三年多了。怎么还不向她求婚呀? *I want to marry Betty, but I can't seem to get up the nerve to pop the question.* 我很想与贝蒂结婚,但是,我怎么也鼓不起勇气去求婚啊。◇ propose (to *someone*)

quick

make quick work of *something* [*someone*] [ˌmeɪk 'kwɪk 'wərkəv ~] [话] **简单处理** → make short WORK of *something* [*someone*]

a quick one [ə 'kwɪkwən] [话] **喝一杯(酒)** 这里的 quick 不是"急速的",而是"简单地"的意思,有"来一下"的意味。one 是 one drink 的 one, 即"一杯酒",等于中国人说"咱们喝上一杯"中的"一杯",不是指数量上整整的一杯。*How's about it? Got time for a quick one?* 怎么样? 有时间喝上一杯吗? *There's still a little time before the plane leaves. What say we stop off here for a quick one?* 飞机起飞前还有一点时间。我们到这里喝上一杯如何? *Nothing for me, thanks. I just had a quick one while I was waiting.* 我什么也不要,谢谢。我在等待的时候,刚刚喝了一杯啦。◇ a (short) drink

quiet

on the quiet [ɔnðə 'kwaɪət] [话] **秘密地** → on the Q. T.

(as) quiet as a mouse → MOUSE

quits

call it quits [ˌkɔ(:)lət 'kwɪ(:)ts] [口] **作罢** 这里的 quits 原是"不分胜负的"、"成为平局的"的意思,并不是在 quit (停止)后边加 -s 构成的。古时,在还清借款的时候,要在借据上盖一个印。图章上的字是中世纪拉丁语 *quittus*, 意思是"还讫"。后来英语采取此词,以 quits 的形式,用于表示"不分胜负的"、"成为平局的"的意味。原来的构思是:"债权者和债务人由于欠帐已还而处于平等地位。"因此,如果根据原来的意味直译的话,则 call it quits 为"称之为平局"。现在人们依然使用 quits 一词表示"不分胜负的"的意思,但其背后经常含有"因此,到这里就停止吧"的意思。例如，孩子们在吵架时，有的孩子向先动手打人或出口骂人的对方进行报复之后，常说 Now we are quits. 意思与 Now we are even. (现在咱们谁也不欠谁啦。) 相同。call it quits 有时象下一例句这样使用: *It's foolish for us to remain enemies like this. Why don't we call it quits?* 咱们象这样敌对下去，双方都没有好处。就此罢休如何? 现在一般来说，call it quits 与"不分胜负"无关，仅表示"作罢"的意思，根据情况，专用于"在未达到目标之前作罢"的场合。也就是说，一般含有"再努力也没有用"、"舍不得也不行"之类的"心灰意冷"的情绪。call it quits 的意义所以象这样由"称之为平局"变成"作罢"，大概是受相似的词 quit 的影响。在实际上，一般的美国人意识不到这个 quits 与 quit 是两码事，他们顶多是对于为什么要加 -s 有点纳闷而已。*After struggling for many years to make their marriage work, Mr. and Mrs. Quarles decided to call it quits (and get a divorce).* 夸尔斯夫妇为了美满的婚姻生活奋斗了好多年，他们终于心灰意冷，决定离婚。*If we haven't reached the top of the mountain by nightfall, we'll have to call it quits and make camp.* 如果我们在天黑以前到达不了山顶，就只好停下来宿营了。*Let's call it quits. We're not going to find your purse in all this snow.* 算了吧。在这样的大雪里，我们不给你去找钱包啦。*We had to call it quits for this year because we used up our budget, but we plan to continue our research next year.* 我们的预算已经花光了，今年只好停下来。但是，我们计划明年继续我们的研究工作。有时与"心灰意冷"的感情无关，只是很轻松地表示"结束当天的工作"的意味。在这一场合，一般加 for the day, 但不限定如此。*I'm tired. Let's call it quits (for the day).* 我疲倦了。今天的工作就到此结束吧。→ call it a DAY ◇ give up / stop [quit] (for the present)

be quits [ˈkwɪ(:)ts] [话] **不分胜负** → call it QUITS

quiz

a pop quiz [ə ˈpɑp ˈkwɪ(:)z] [话] **突然袭击式的测验** pop 为形容词，意思是"突然的"、"出其不意的"。quiz 是"小测验"。a pop test 也是一种"突然袭击式的测验"，但性质略有不同。*The prof is famous for giving pop quizzes.* 那位教授是以搞突然袭击测验而闻名的。→ a QUIZ ◇ an unannounced quiz [short test]

a quiz [ə ˈkwɪ(:)z] [口] **小测验** 电视、广播节目中的所谓"猜谜"，当然叫做 quiz。在各级学校中，quiz 是"测验"的意思。"测验"还有 a test, an EXAM 等说法，但 quiz 是其中时间最短的，大多为十分钟，少则 2～3 分钟，至多二十分钟左右。exam 指大的"考试"，特别是大学里，有长达三小时以上者。一般仅用于 a midterm exam (期中考试), a final exam (期末考试) 和 an entrance exam (入学考试)。test 本来是"考试"和"测验"的总称，包括 quiz 和 exam 在内，但在学校用语中，一般指比 quiz 时间长、比 exam 时间短的"考试"或"测验"，大多使用一次授课时间进行。*Our chemistry prof gives a quiz at the beginning of every class.* 我们班的化学老师每次上课先进行短时间的测验。*A: Are we going to have a test tomorrow, Mr. Butler? B: No, not a real test. Just a quiz.* 甲：巴特勒先生，明天我们有考试吗? 乙：不，没有正式的考试，只是小测验。◇ a short test

R

rabbit

rabbit food → FOOD

race

a drag race [ə ˈdræ(ː)g ˌreɪs] [口] **减重短程高速汽车赛** 两辆以上汽车的加速度竞赛，从 0 开始出发，加速度最快者胜。有躲开警察的眼睛在一般公路上进行的，也有举行正式比赛在规定的赛车道上进行的。后者一般使用 0.25 英里(约 400 米)的赛车道，称为 a drag strip [ˈdræ(ː)g ˌstrɪp]。参加比赛的汽车一般叫作 a drag racer [ˈdræ(ː)g ˌreɪsər]，或者简称 a dragster [ˈdræ(ː)gstər]，这是为 drag race 而加以改造过的汽车。*The dragsters were lined up on the drag strip waiting for the start of the drag race.* 减重高速汽车在赛车道上排成一线，等待短程比赛的开始。*Let's have a drag race.* 咱们进行减重短程高速汽车赛吧。有时把 drag 作为动词使用，代替 have a drag race。例如：*Let's drag.* 咱们进行减重短程高速汽车赛吧！ *Ya wanna drag?* 你愿意进行减重短程高速汽车赛吗？ ◇ a contest to compare accelerating power

throw a race [game, etc.] → THROW

racing

a racing form → FORM

rag

chew the rag [ˌtʃu(ː)ðə ˈræːg] [话] **聊天儿** chew 的主要意义是"嚼"，但在古时曾用以表示"反复讲同一的事情"的意思。rag，在这一场合，美国人也会联想到"破布条子"，但有人说这是动词 rag (意思是"欺负"、"斥责")的名词化。实际上，在英国英语中，确实是用 chew the rag 表示"唠唠叨叨"、"发牢骚"的意味。在美国英语中，过去 rag 一词也似乎有过那样的意义，不过现在连半点影子都没有了。本条的意思是"随便聊天儿"、"心情舒畅地漫谈"。*The bar was full of the same old men every night, chewing the rag until closing time.* 每天晚间，那家酒吧间都拥满了经常前去的老人，他们一直闲聊到关门的时间为止。如这一例句所示，本条指长时间的、没有一定目标的谈话，言外有"悠闲舒畅"的意味。*I don't have time to sit around chewing the rag with you. I've got to go to work.* 我没有坐下来跟你闲聊的时间，我得去上班啊。 *You can learn a lot about local customs by taking a little time to chew the rag with some of the old-timers around town.* 如果你费一点时间去跟镇内的一些老人聊天儿，就会熟悉当地的许多风俗习惯。 *At first I thought Tim was an interesting talker, but, after going with him a while, I realized that he's always chewing the same old rag.* 最初，我认为蒂姆是一个讲话很有意思的人，但是跟他交往不久，就了解到他是陈谷子烂芝麻，老是那一套。也可以用 fat (肥肉)代替 rag，意思完全一样。*When I arrived, everyone was just chewing the fat, waiting for the meeting to start.* 当我到达的时候，大家都正在聊天儿，等待会议的开始。◇ engage in idle conversation

rage

fly into a rage [ˌflaɪəntuə ˈreɪdʒ] [口] **怒火冲天** 直译为"飞进激怒的状态"，亦即由于某种原因，在一瞬之间大发雷霆。*The colonel flew into a rage when he learned that his order had been disobeyed.* 上校了解到下级没有听从他的命令，立即火冒三丈了。◇ (suddenly) become intensely angry

be in a towering rage [ɪnə ˈtauərɪŋ ˈreɪdʒ] [口] **大发雷霆** rage 是"狂怒"。towering 是"高耸的"，在这里的意思为"压倒对方

的"。本条的具体形象是:"愤然挺起身来,怒吼一声,把对方吓得缩成一团"。*When I got home at two o'clock in the morning, my father was in a towering rage.* 当我凌晨两点钟回到家里的时候,我父亲大发雷霆了。*The boss is in a towering rage because you didn't show up for the meeting.* 由于你没出席会议,老板在大发雷霆哪。有时不带 be 动词。*I wonder what happened. One of our big clients just stormed into the office in a towering rage.* 不知发生了什么事情。刚才,咱们的一位大主顾怒火冲天地闯进公司里来了。◇ be furious

rags

glad rags ['glæ(:),dræ:gz] [话] **出门的服装** 直译为"令人高兴的破布条子"。这是 best [fanciest] clothes (最考究、最漂亮的服装) 一语的非常有趣、非常轻松的表达法。虽然说是"服装",当然不仅指上衣、裤子或裙子,也包括衬衣、服饰、首饰等在内。如果"出门的服装"有很多,这一表达法可以指其中的一套,也可以指全部。*Put on your glad rags, and let's go out and celebrate my promotion.* 穿上你出门的服装,咱们出去庆祝一下我的提升吧。*I've got to buy some new glad rags. These are getting out of style.* 我非买几件新的出门服装不可啦。这几件的式样已经过时了。如以上的例句所示,本条一般用于表示"出门的服装"的意思,但有时也用于表示 formal evening wear (夜礼服)的意味。*I've been invited to a formal party. Can I borrow your glad rags?* 我受邀请参加一个正式的社交晚会。你能把夜礼服借给我吗? ◇ best [good] clothes

rain

give *someone* **a rain check** [,gɪv ~ ə'reɪn,tʃe(:)k] [话] **请下次赏光** → take a rain CHECK

take a rain check → CHECK

rains

It never rains but it pours. [ɪtnevə'rɪeɪnz bədət'po(:)rz] [谚] **祸不单行** 直译为"只要一下雨,必定如瓢泼"。*A: Raining pitchforks, isn't it? B: Yes, recently it seems it never rains but it pours.* 甲:雨下得够大的,是吧? 乙:是的,最近似乎只要一下雨就必然有如瓢泼。有象这样按照字面意义使用的情况。但一般用作比喻,表示"不幸或灾难一齐到来"的意思,与汉语俗语"福无双降,祸不单行"相当。*First I lost my job. Then my wife caught pneumonia, and as I was going to visit her in the hospital, I fell down and broke my leg. Now I know what they mean when they say it never rains but it pours.* 首先,我失了业。然后,我的妻子得了肺炎,而当我去医院看望她的时候,我摔倒了,折断了腿。现在我算明白俗话所说"祸不单行"是什么意思啦。本条与汉语俗语的不同处,是在极例外的场合,可以解释为"福能双降"。*Soon after our son was born I got a promotion and a raise. It never rains but it pours.* 新添个儿子不久,我又提级长工资。真是双喜临门啊。◇ Bad things always come at one time.

rainy

save (*something*) **for a rainy day** → DAY

rake

rake it in [,reɪkɪ'dɪ(:)n] [话] **发大财** rake 作为名词,是"耙子";作为动词,rake in 是"用耙子搂"的意思。这里的 it 暗指"金钱"、"利益"。也就是说,这一表达法原来的构思是:"金钱滚滚而来,达到非用耙子往怀里搂不可的程度"。*Because of the strength of the dollar, American oil companies are raking it in this year.* 由于美元升值,今年美国各石油公司都发大财了。常用 really 加强语气。*Popular fashion designers really rake it in.* 有名气的服装设计师挣钱多极啦。也可以不用 it 而代入表示 it 的具体内容的词,如 the money (钱), the cash (钱), the profits (利益)等。但在这一场合,这类词不能直接代入 it 的位置,而要放在 rake in 的后边。*Loan sharks are really raking in the profits recently.* 放高利贷的人最近获得大量的利润啦。◇ make great profits [a lot of money]

range

hearing range [ˈhɪ(ː)rɪŋ ˌreɪndʒ] [口] **听力所及的范围** → within EARSHOT

rank

break rank (with *someone*) [ˌbreɪk ˈræ(ː)ŋk] [口] **分袂** → break RANKS (with *someone*)

pull rank (on *someone*) [ˌpul ˈræ(ː)ŋk] [话] **仗势** 原为军队用语,意思是"以自己的等级 (rank)压人一头"。后来一般人也广泛使用。本条用于如下的场合:预料下级或晚辈不能违抗,便不顾对方的思想或情况而发命令,使事情按照自己的意图去进行。*At the school cafeteria the upperclassmen often pull rank by cutting in at the front of the line.* 在学校的食堂里,高年级学生常常仗势,往队列的前边加塞儿。*A: I thought you were flying home tonight. B: I was, but Captain Freebie pulled rank on me and took my seat.* 甲:我以为你今天晚上坐飞机回家啦。乙:我是那样打算的,但是弗里比上尉对我滥用职权,占了我的座位啦。*I don't care for the new section chief. He'll treat you like a buddy while you're out with him at night, but the next day he'll pull rank on you the first chance he gets.* 我不喜欢新来的科长。在晚上跟他一起出去玩的时候,他会与你称兄道弟,但是第二天一上班,只要有个机会,他便对你滥用职权;强行发令。有时用于开玩笑。*I hope you won't mind if I pull rank on you and ask your wife for the first dance.* 我利用特权,请求你的夫人首先伴舞,希望你不要介意。另外有 pull *one's* rank (on *someone*)的说法,但极少使用。◇ take (unfair) advantage of *one's* rank (with *someone*)

the rank and file [ðə ˌræŋkənˈfaɪl] [口] **一般群众** 直译为"横列与纵列"。集合名词。原为军队用语,指"一般士兵"。现在广泛使用,指"一般人民、市民"、"一般职工"、"工会的一般会员"等各种各样的"群众"。*Jimmy rose from the rank and file to become state governor in only ten years.* 吉米仅仅在十年之间,从一般市民一跃而成为州长了。*Union leaders' strength depends on the support of the rank and file.* 工会领导的力量依靠一般会员群众的支持。这一表达法既可以作为单数使用,也可以作为复数使用,例如:*The rank and file is [are] up in arms over the low bonus.* 职工们由于奖金太少而十分愤慨。另有 rank and filers (单数形式为 a rank and filer) 的说法,但极少使用。例如我们可以听到这样的话:*We can't give this job to just any rank and filer.* 这个工作并不是随便哪一个人来都可以的。在这一场合,一般的说法是: ~ to just anyone from the rank and file. ◇ the ordinary members [membership] of society [the organization, etc.]

ranks

break ranks (with *someone*) [ˌbreɪk ˈræ(ː)ŋks] [口] **分道扬镳** rank 原为"军队的横列"的意思,与之相对的"纵列"叫作 file。因此,按字面意义来讲,break ranks 是"打乱队形"。*When a solitary plane appeared high overhead, the unseasoned soldiers broke ranks and ran for cover.* 在高高的天空中出现一架单独的飞机,新入伍的士兵便乱了套,到处奔跑寻求躲避的场所。转用于表示"与已往合作的对手分开、向另外的方向走"即汉语成语"分道扬镳"的意思。*China broke ranks with Russia, bringing about a split in the international communist movement.* 中国与苏联分道扬镳,国际共产主义运动出现了分歧。有时不用复数形式 ranks 而用单数形式,作 break rank,意思不变。*Sutherland and Norman, feeling the pure naturalism of their fellow writers was too confining, broke rank and founded a new literary movement.* 萨瑟兰和诺曼感到他们同辈的作家们的纯自然主义过于单调,遂独树一帜,发起了新的文学运动。◇ separate *oneself* (from *someone*)

close ranks (with *someone*) [ˌklouz ˈræ(ː)ŋks] [口] **团结一致共同对敌** 来源于军队用语。rank 是士兵排队的"横

列"; close 是"收缩队形"。按照字面意义,用法如下: *The troops had to close ranks in order to march through the narrow street.* 部队为了穿过狭窄的街道,不得不收缩队形向前行进。作为比喻,这一表达法用于过去分散的个人或组织团结起来互相合作的场合,大体上与 present a united front (结成统一战线)同义。典型的句型是: X closed ranks with Y against Z. (甲与乙团结一致对付丙。) *The constantly warring tribes stopped fighting and closed ranks (with one another) against the invading army.* 那些经常打内战的部族停止了纷争,团结起来,共同对抗侵略军。*We are going to have to close ranks with our domestic rivals in the face of foreign competition.* 在国外的竞争者面前,我们必须团结国内的竞争对手一致对外。*The American unions closed ranks and won concessions from their government.* 美国各工会团结一致,迫使他们的政府让步了。◇ unite

come up through the ranks [kʌ.mʌp θru(:)ðə ˈræ(:)ŋks] [口] **依靠实力而发迹** → rise through the RANKS

rise through the ranks [.raɪz θru(:)ðə ˈræ(:)ŋks] [口] **依靠实力而出人头地** ranks 原为军队用语,意思是"士兵排队的横列"。因此,the ranks 则指"全体士兵"。一般的校官和将官必须受过特殊教育,最初任少尉,然后逐步上升。但也有个别人是根据实际能力由普通一兵开始而上升到校官或将官的。这种情况就叫作 rise through the ranks。现在,一般的公司、机关、团体也应用本条。*General Hardnose rose through the ranks to become one of the nation's top military leaders.* 哈德诺斯将军行伍出身,由士兵变成了全国最高军事统帅之一。这是本来的用法。*Starting as a copy boy, he rose through the ranks to become editor of the paper.* 他从递送稿件的内勤开始,一直上升到报纸的编辑。这是应用到公司。不论哪一个场合,所依靠的都不是自己的门第或人际关系,而是"实际能力"或者"努力"。*In a large company it's very difficult to rise through the ranks to a top managerial position.* 在大公司里,很难依靠实际能力上升到经营部门的领导地位。*Japan quickly rose through the ranks of the have-not nations, and by the 1960's had become a leading industrial nation.* 日本迅速摆脱穷国的地位,在 20 世纪 60 年代已经成为主要的工业国。另有一个说法是 rise from [out of] the ranks, 意思相同。但是条头 through 的重点是"一步一步上升",而这一说法的重点是"青云直上"。*Very few men rise from the ranks as fast as Mr. Gogetter did.* 很少有人象戈盖特先生那样青云直上,一步登天。又,动词可用 come up 代替 rise。*Tom is the boss's son, but he didn't start at the top. He came up through the ranks just like the rest of us did.* 汤姆是老板的儿子,但是他不是一开始就担任领导职务。他跟我们其余的人完全一样,是依靠自己的实力一步一步上升的。◇ rise from the lower echelons

rap

beat a rap [.bi(:)də ˈræ(:)p] **逃脱罪责** 黑社会用语。这里的 beat 是"战胜"。条头是"通过斗争,免除刑事处分"的意思。因此,这一表达法不能用于"被捕之前逃走"的场合,而用于"被捕之后设法逃脱罪责"的场合。言外有"不择手段"的韵味,即可以采取各种不同的方法,如"正当地辩明自己无罪"、"行贿"、"说谎"等等。根据上下文,冠词 a 可用 the、this、that、one 代换。*The cops are after me for that burglary job. You've got to help me beat the rap.* 为了那桩抢劫案件,警察正在追查我。你设法帮助我逃脱罪责吧。*A good mouthpiece can beat that rap for you.* 一个能言善辩的律师,可以使你被无罪释放。下面两个例子是条头的变形。*We've got the goods on Pruneface this time. This is one rap he's not going to beat.* 这回我们掌握了普伦菲斯作案的证据,他再也抵赖不了啦。*He's under a perjury rap that he knows he can't possibly beat.* 他犯了伪证罪,他知道自己没有逃脱罪责的可能性了。◇

defeat a charge

a bum rap [ə ˌbʌ(:)m ˈræ(:)p] [话] **不实之罪** a RAP 原为黑社会用语,是“嫌疑”、“犯罪”、“处刑”的意思。这里的 bum 是“错误的”、“不负责任的”、“靠不住的”的意思。例如:*You gave me a bum steer.* 你告诉我的话靠不住。这里的 a bum STEER 是 unreliable information [advice] (靠不住的信息[忠告])的轻松的说法。a bum rap 的说法也非常轻松,多用于不管事情真假、说话人在主观上相信“不实”的场合。*My son was sent to prison on a bum rap.* 我的儿子以不实之罪被投入监狱了。*A: It'll go hard with you if you don't confess, Lannie. You've already been in prison once. B: That don't count. That was a bum rap.* 甲:兰尼,如果你不坦白交待,就要对你从严惩处呀。你已经蹲过一次监狱啦。乙:那没什么关系。因为那是无实之罪。*Al says that when he gets out of the big house he's going to get you for having him sent up on a bum rap.* 阿尔说,你以无实之罪把他送进监狱,等他出狱的时候一定要报仇。◇ a false charge

give *someone* **a rap on the knuckles** [ˌgɪv ～ə ˌræ(:)pɔ(:)nðə ˈnʌ(:)klz] [口] **责备** a rap on the knuckles 本来是“用尺子之类敲打手指的关节”的意思,这是在教室中,老师对学生的一种轻的体罚。*The teacher gave the naughty pupil a rap on the knuckles with a ruler.* 老师用一把尺子打那个淘气学生的指节。转作比喻使用,表示“申斥”的意味,但申斥的方式很轻,顶多是“责备”的程度。*The Prime Minister gave the Justice Minister a rap on the knuckles for injecting his own personal opinion into the press conference.* 首相责备司法大臣在记者招待会的发言中夹杂着个人的意见。rap 前面加上 good、sharp、hard、severe 等形容词,则是“严厉指责”的意思。*The judge gave the defense lawyer a good rap on the knuckles for arriving late at court.* 法官对出庭迟到的被告辩护律师给予了严厉的批评。也可以把 rap 作为动词使用而说 rap *someone* on the knuckles, 意思不变。例如:*The general rapped the captain on the knuckles for speaking out of turn.* 上尉说话太过火了,将军给予了批评。同样把 rap 当作动词使用,而有省略 on the knuckles 的表达法。*The President rapped the CIA for giving him mistaken information.* 总统由于中央情报局送给他错误的情报而对其进行了批评。如果说 get [receive] a rap on the knuckles,就是“受责难”了。*You were lucky to get only a rap on the knuckles. The boss could have fired you if he had wanted to, you know.* 你只受到一顿批评,真算是幸运。你要知道,老板如果想开除你,是可能把你赶走的。有时可以单独使用 a rap on the knuckles。*Because the student was usually well-behaved, the dean let him go with only a rap on the knuckles.* 那个学生由于平时品行端正,院长只批评他一下,就不深究了。◇ give *someone* a reprimand / reprimand *someone*

have a rap (with *someone*) [ˌhævə ˈræ(:)p] [话] **敞开思想谈话** → RAP (with *someone*)

a rap [ə ˈræ(:):p] [话] **嫌疑;犯罪;处刑** 原来的意思是:“警察局把嫌疑犯排成一列 <a police line-up>,让目击者从中认出犯人”。后来发展成为警察和黑社会的用语,表示“嫌疑”、“犯罪”或者“处刑”的意思。以下的例句均不超出这三种意义的范围。*A: You're under arrest. B: Oh yeah? What's the rap?* 甲:现在你被逮捕啦。乙:哦,是吗?什么罪名呀? *He was arrested on a hot-car rap.* 他因有盗窃汽车的嫌疑被逮捕了。*What kind of rap was he found guilty of?* 他因为什么而被治罪? *Joe was sent up the river on a murder rap.* 乔由于犯杀人罪而进了监狱。*Slick got a three-year rap for income-tax evasion.* 斯利克因偷漏所得税而被判处三年徒刑。在电影和电视的影响之下,孩子们在日常会话中轻松地使用这一表达法。例如:*You're the one who broke the window. I'm not going to take the rap.* 打破窗户玻璃的就是你。我不叫你承担罪责。a rap sheet 为警察用语，指“过去的犯罪记录”。*Sgt. Friday wants to know if we have a rap sheet on Frank Knuckles.* 弗里代巡官想要了解一下我们有没有弗兰克·纳克勒斯过去的犯罪记录。◇ charge / crime / sentence / blame

rap (with *someone*) [ˈræ(ː)p] [话] **自由而坦率地交谈** 这一表达法来源于已在英语中落户的法语单词 rapport [rəˈpoːr]。rapport 是精神医学用语，指“意思的沟通性”。在日常口语中，是“融洽的关系或气氛”的意思。rap 是在 20 世纪 60 年代定型的一个相当新的习用语，青年人特别喜欢使用。意思是“谈话”，在以下的所有例句中均可用 talk 代换。它与 talk 的不同点在于含有“自由地”、“坦率地”、“轻松地”的韵味。*Prof. Franklin is a good teacher. He often stays after class to rap with his students.* 富兰克林教授是一位好老师。他在下课之后往往不走，跟学生们聊天儿。*I've never been able to rap with my father. He's never understood me.* 我从来没有能够跟我父亲坦率地交谈。他始终不理解我。*There's nothing uptight about Sam. He's easy to rap with.* 萨姆这个人一点儿架子都没有。跟他是容易说心里话的。但在最近几乎与 talk 同样使用，并不含有“轻松地”的韵味了。例如：*I got to rapping with this dude on the train yesterday about coin collecting.* 昨天我在火车上跟这个人曾经谈论搜集钱币的事情。也可以把它名词化，采取 have a rap with *someone* 的形式。*I don't think the boss understands how you feel about the matter. Why don't you go in and have a rap with him?* 据我看，老板不了解你对那件事的感想。你为什么不去找他坦率地谈一下呢？a rap group 是人们恢复本来的面貌、相互坦率地谈话的团体，定期在一起集会。创始于加州。*I belong to a rap group that meets every Wednesday night.* 我参加了一个谈心会，每星期三晚上开会。rap group 召开的会叫做 a rap session。但是现在具有更广泛的意义，凡是敞开思想随便谈论的会都可以叫做 rap session。*Every once in a while the boss invites all the department heads into his office for a rap session.* 总经理时常把所有的部长请到自己的办公室，举行座谈会。rap session 也可以仅仅表示“凑在一起闲聊”的意思。例如：*Every time I want to study, you guys are having another rap session in my room.* 每当我想要功的时候，你们这几个小子准到我的房间里来闲聊大天儿。◇ talk (openly and frankly)

a rap group [ə ˈræ(ː)pgruːp] [口] **谈心团体** → RAP (with *someone*)

a rap session [ə ˈræ(ː)p ˌseʃən] [话] **谈心会；座谈会** → RAP (with *someone*)

rat

a rat [ə ˈræ(ː)t] [话] **告密者** → RAT on *someone*

rat on *someone* [ˈræːˌdɔ(ː)n ~] [话] **告密** 名词 rat 是黑社会用语，意思为“告密者”(an informer)。后来，作这一解的 rat 动词化了，例如说：*Somebody must've ratted to the cops about our plans.* 一定有人把我们的计划密告警察了。在匪盗影片的影响下，一般人也广泛使用这一表达法。15 岁以上的男性用语，大多用于把难以见人的丑事向老师、上级、父母等告密的场合。在表示告密的具体内容时，可以象上面的例句那样使用 about ~的形式，但在后面接动名词的时候，一般使用 for ~。*Dick ratted on Jim for breaking the window.* 迪克把吉姆打破窗户玻璃的事情汇报了。又，如果加上“向谁”告密，则后边接 to *someone*。*Joel ratted on me to the boss (for padding my expense account).* 乔尔把我虚报开销的事情向老板汇报了。有时省略 on *someone* 的部分。*Somebody must've ratted.* 一定有人告密了。黑社会用语 SQUEAL on *someone* 与本条同义。儿童用语有 tell [snitch, tattle] on *someone* (→ TELL on *someone*)。◇ inform on *someone*

smell a rat [ˌsmelə ˈræ(ː)t] [话] **觉得可疑** 直译为“有老鼠的气味”。本条来源于：猫注意到有老鼠的气味之后，就向周围张望，出现神经紧张的样子。作为比喻，用于表示在注意到某人企图干什么的时候，觉得“奇怪”、“可疑”的意思。*The man insisted that if I invested with him he could double my money, but the cheapness of his clothes made me smell a rat.* 那个人坚持说，如果我向他投资，他可以使我的钱增加一倍，但是，他穿的那套廉价衣服使我感到他的话靠不住。*I smell a rat. Both those guys claim they're loyal to me, but they're never around when I need them.* 我真有点儿怀疑。他们两个人都说忠实于我，但是当我需要他们帮忙的时候，他们没有一次来到我的身旁。*Every time I returned to the office, the papers on my desk had been rearranged. I was beginning to smell a rat.* 每次我回到公司的时候，办公桌上的文件都有人整理过。我开始觉得可疑了。◇ be suspicious

Rats

Rats. ['ræ(:)ts] [话] **活见鬼** 在英语的骂人话中，有 Shit.（狗屁！）Crap.（瞎说！）等，但这些词都是禁忌语，在使用时有一定的限制。Rats. 则是比较委婉的表达法，连妇女和儿童们都使用。*Rats! I forgot to bring my cigarettes.* 见鬼！我忘带烟啦。*Oh, rats! I just can't get this calculus problem.* 真见鬼！我怎么也解不开这个微积分问题。如以上两个例句所示，这一表达法专用 Rats. 或 Oh, rats. 这样独立的形式。*Rats. This screw is too small.* 见鬼！这个螺钉太小啦。除了“活见鬼”的意思外，本条偶尔用于表示“胡说”、“胡扯”的意味。*Rats. I don't believe it.* 简直胡扯！我才不相信呢。

rattletrap

a rattletrap [ə 'ræ(:)dl.træ(:)p] [口] **破旧的汽车** rattle 是象声词，表示“嘎嗒嘎嗒的响声”。trap 是“捕兽的陷阱”。直译为“捕住嘎嗒嘎嗒的响声不放的东西”，亦即“发出嘎嗒嘎嗒的讨厌响声的东西”的意思。*I hope this old rattletrap will get us to New York.* 我希望这辆老破车能把咱们送到纽约。*The whole neighborhood knows when Chet gets home. You can hear his rattletrap coming a mile away.* 当切特回家的时候，所有的邻居都会知道。你离一英里远就能听到他那辆破汽车的声音。如以上的例句所示，这一表达法指小汽车的场合占绝大多数，但偶尔也可以指船、飞机等。*If you want a boat, don't buy that rattletrap. I know a better one you can get even cheaper.* 如果你想要一条小船，别买那只破旧货。我知道有一只更好的船，而且价钱比它还便宜。有时也用于破旧的各种机器，但在这一场合，大多采取 rattletrap of a *something* 的形式。*Let's get rid of this rattletrap of a washing machine and buy a new one.* 咱们处理掉这台破旧的洗衣机，买个新的吧。◇ a(n old rattly) car [boat, etc.]

raw

in the raw [.ınðə 'rɔ:] [话] **裸体** in the raw 是“生的状态”的意思。但这一表达法不使用字面意义，例如说“生肉”时，只能讲：*The meat is raw.* 肉是生的。人生 (life)、自然 (nature)等如果说 raw，那就是“未经加工的实际情况”的意思。*That novelist depicts life in the raw.* 那位小说家如实地描写生活。*The early settlers were forced to experience nature in the raw.* 初期的开拓者不得不领略原始自然界的滋味。后来转用于日常会话，表示“人体的天然情况”，也就是“裸体”的意思。*When I was a kid, I often went swimming in the raw.* 我小的时候常光着屁股游泳。一般用 completely 加强语气。*When I opened the door, she was standing there completely in the raw.* 当我打开门的时候，她正一丝不挂地站在那儿。然而，在下一个例句的场合，用两种意义解释全都说得通，因此只能根据前后关系进行判断。*I like to enjoy nature in the raw.* 我喜欢欣赏未经加工的自然风光／我喜欢赤身投入大自然的怀抱。◇ in the nude

reach

a boardinghouse reach [ə .bo(:)rdıŋ.haus 'ri:tʃ] [话] **在饭桌上伸手去取远处的东西** 我们常听到西方人吃饭时讲这样的

规矩:在自己眼前的东西,由自己去取;东西在远处,自己的手够不到,如果想要的话,就必须请别人递给你,例如说:*Please pass me the salt.* 请把盐递给我。假如不守这个规矩,自己胡乱伸手去够在远处放着的东西,那就叫 a boardinghouse reach。boardinghouse 是"供膳食的寄宿舍", reach 是"伸手"。也就是说,在寄宿舍里大家同桌吃饭,没有注意什么吃饭规矩的必要,而且菜量有限,常有你抢我夺的情况。在这种场合,伸手向远处取东西的现象当然是司空见惯的了。这就是本条的来源。*With a boardinghouse reach like Tom's, I'm sure he'll never go hungry.* 象汤姆那样一个吃饭不懂规矩、向远处伸手够东西的人,我敢肯定,他永远饿不着。*Since Lily has started living in the college dorm, she's developed a boardinghouse reach.* 莉莉自从在大学住宿舍以后,她就养成了在饭桌上伸手向远处够东西的坏习惯。如果东西在不太远的距离,在不知道伸手去够是否有失体统的场合,往往是在伸手去够的时候,嘴里这样说: *Excuse my boardinghouse reach.* 请原谅我没规矩。这是一种诙谐的说法,说话的人所考虑的是:即使是真的破坏了规矩,如此一讲也就混过去了。◇ a long [impolite] reach

Reach. ['ri(:)tʃ] [话] **举起手来!** → Reach for the SKY.

rear

bring up the rear [.brɪŋ.ʌpðə 'rɪ:r] [口] **走在后头** 原来为军队用语,意思是"殿后"或"压后阵"。这里的 the rear 是"最后列"。*The cavalry moved out first, and the infantry brought up the rear.* 骑兵先行,步兵殿后。一般指在多数人中的"最后",但也有指两个人中在后面的一个或两个集体中在后边的一个的场合。*You all go first. We'll bring up the rear in Lyndon's car.* 你们全都先走。我们乘林顿的汽车后走。*Three clowns, throwing flowers to the spectators, brought up the rear of the parade.* 三个丑角走在行列的末尾,向观众们扔着鲜花。*The men went first with the fishing gear, and the women, carrying the picnic baskets, brought up the rear.* 拿着钓鱼工具的男人们走在前边,提着野餐篮子的妇女们跟在后头。在体育运动或学习中,可以用本条表示"倒数第一"的意思。*When the league standings were published, our team as usual was bringing up the rear.* 当公布各队名次的时候,我们队照旧是倒数第一名。*Why do you always insist on bringing up the rear? If you'd only study harder, you could be in the top half on your class.* 为什么你老是停留在最后一名哪?你只要用点功,在班里就会列入中上等名次呀。◇ come [follow, be] last [at the end]

red

see red [.si: 're:d] [话] **怒上心头** 直译为"看见红的"。来源是:西班牙人喜好斗牛,在斗牛时,斗牛士拿一块大红布在公牛的眼前不住闪动。公牛一看见红的东西,就如疯似狂地活动起来。本条主要用于因某种原因或情况而使人"火冒三丈"的场合。*I see red whenever I hear that man's name.* 我一听到那个人的名字,心里便火冒三丈。◇ become (quietly) angry

red-eye

red-eye ['redaɪ] [话] **廉价威士忌酒** 本条的来源是:喝上少量的这种酒,眼睛就会发红。特指 bootleg WHISKY (私酿威士忌),但不限定如此。凡是价廉、质劣的威士忌,美国人一概称之为"红眼"。*We drank a lot of red-eye when I was in college.* 在大学念书的时候,我们喝了许多廉价威士忌酒。又,有时用本条戏指一般的威士忌酒。*How about a shot of this red-eye? It's smooth stuff.* 喝一杯这种威士忌怎么样?味道是很不错的。◇ cheap whiskey

red-handed

catch *someone* **red-handed** [.kætʃ ~ .re(:)d'hæ:ndəd] [口] **在犯罪现场被捕** 直译为"趁着手还红的时候抓住"。这一表达法最初的构思是:"一个用刀杀人的凶犯,在手上染满鲜血的时刻被人抓住”。用法:不限于用刀或匕首之类,如说:*The murderer was caught red-handed, the gun still in his hand.* 杀人犯当场被捕了,枪还在他的手里。被捕的人也不限于杀人犯,如说:*The police caught the thief red-handed.* 警察当场捉住了扒手。另外,不仅用于实际的犯罪活动,往往很轻松地用于日常生活。*Jimmy's mother caught him red-handed at the cookie jar.* 吉姆正把手伸进饼干罐子的时候,被母亲逮住了。另有不用 catch 而讲 have *someone* red-handed 的表达法,一般来说,具有“等于在现场抓住对方一样”的韵味。*When I heard footsteps outside the door, I knew they had me red-handed.* 当我听到门外的脚步声的时候,我明白他们已当场抓住了我。◇ catch *someone* in the (very) act (of *doing something*)

have *someone* **red-handed** [ˌhæv ~ ˌre(:)dˈhæ:ndəd] [话] **已经等于当场逮捕** → catch *someone* RED-HANDED

red-letter

a red-letter day → DAY

regs

regs [ˈre(:)gz] [话] **规章制度** regulations [ˌregjəˈleɪʃənz] 的缩略。为可数名词,可以用单数,但极罕见。*I didn't know there was a reg about that.* 我不知道有一条关于那件事的规定。大多是用复数形式,而且加定冠词,表示“整个规章制度”的意思。主要为士兵和学生用语。*We can't do that. You know the regs. If we get caught, we'll be thrown out of school.* 我们不能干那种事。你是知道规章制度的。如果我们被逮住,就会被学校开除啦。◇ regulations

rein

give rein to *something* [*someone*] [ˌgɪv ˈreɪntə ~] [口] **放任** give rein to 直译为“把缰绳交给马”(即“让马自由走”),与 keep a tight REIN on *someone* [*something*] 的意义相反。*As long as we stay within our budget, I usually give rein to my employees to use whatever methods they think best.* 只要不超出我们的预算,我一贯允许职工们自由运用他们认为最好的方法。如这一例句所示,give rein to 的后边可以接 *someone*,但比较起来,接 *something* 的场合多。而且,*something* 处所代入的通常是表示“思想”或“感情”的语言,如 imagination、emotions、passions、feelings 之类。*When trying to solve a difficult problem, I first relax and give rein to my imagination.* 每当要去解决一个困难问题的时候,我首先使身体放松,给与想象以充分的自由。在这一场合,常加 free 调整语调。*The young lovers gave free rein to their passions.* 年轻的恋人们任凭他们的热情汹涌奔腾。也常使用 give *something* [*someone*] (free) rein 的形式。*You're always too serious. Everyone has to give their feelings free rein sometimes.* 你这个人老是过于古板。每个人都必须有自由表现自己的真实感情的时候。*As children grow older they should be given more free rein.* 孩子越长大,就应该越多给他们行动的自由。◇ allow *one's something* to lead *one* / give *someone* freedom of action

keep a firm rein on *someone* [*something*] [ˌki(:)pə ˌfə:rmˈreɪ nɔ(:)n ~] [口] **严格控制** → keep a tight REIN on *someone* [*something*]

keep a tight rein on *someone* [*something*] [ˌki(:)pə ˌtaɪtˈreɪ nɔ(:)n ~] [口] **严加控制** 直译为“把缰绳牢牢抓紧,使马不能乱蹦乱跳或者突然向前奔跑”。*Because of the thunder, he kept a tight rein on his horse as he rode through the forest.* 由于打雷,当他骑着马穿过森林的时候,他牢牢地握着缰绳。转用于比喻。不论用字面意义的场合还是比喻的场合,都包含着这样一种意味,即:虽然牢牢抓住马的缰绳,或者是对人进行严格的监督,但在已经确定的范围内是允许自由行动的。*It is my duty as a teacher to keep a tight rein on my pupils.* 对学生严加管教,这是我作为一个教师应负的责任。*We don't have much freedom to innovate. The boss keeps a rather tight rein on our activities.* 我们没有多少革新的自由。老板对我们

的活动控制得相当严。*The Prime Minister intends to keep a tight rein on government spending.* 首相打算严格控制政府的开支。本条不仅用于对行动的控制，也用于对精神方面的控制。特别是在控制精神的场合，常用 firm 来代替 tight。*A policeman must learn to keep a firm [tight] rein on his emotions.* 当警察就必须学会严格控制自己的感情。有时用 maintain 代替 keep。反义的表达法是 give REIN to *something* [*someone*] ◇ maintain firm control over *something* [*someone*]

relish

not relish the prospect of (*doing*) *something* → PROSPECT

reprimand

reprimand *someone* (for *something*) ['reprəˌmæ(ː)nd ~] [口] **斥责** → SCOLD *someone* (for *something*)

required

a required course [ə rəˈkwaɪrd ˈko(ː)rs] [口] **必修课** → an ELECTIVE

restroom

the restroom [ðə ˈrestˌruːm] [口] **卫生间** → the BATHROOM

retreat

beat a hasty retreat [ˌbi(ː)də ˌheɪsti rəˈtriːt] [口] **急忙逃走** 原来，beat a retreat 是"鸣金收兵"的意思。除历史影片、历史小说外，在现代专作比喻使用。*The students who were trying to sneak out of school beat a retreat when they saw the principal coming down the hall.* 那些打算偷偷溜出学校的学生们，一看到校长从走廊另一端走来，便急忙撒腿跑开了。如这一例句所示，可以使用 beat a retreat 的形式。但是加 hasty (匆忙的)的用例占绝大多数。*When two of my friends suddenly appeared, the bully beat a hasty retreat.* 当我的两个朋友突然出现的时候，那个恶霸匆忙逃走了。*Upon seeing the boss entertaining a lady friend, I closed the door softly and beat a hasty retreat.* 我见到老板正与他的一个女朋友调情，就轻轻关上门，赶紧走开了。*Just as the thieves were about to smash the window a policeman rounded the corner, so they had no choice but to beat a hasty retreat.* 正当窃贼们要打破窗户玻璃的时候，有一个警察从街角转了过来，因此，他们不得不一溜烟跑掉了。偶尔有用 hasty 以外的形容词的情况。*When the crowds started giving him the Bronx cheer, the candidate beat a dignified retreat.* 当群众向候选人开始发出嘘声的时候，他不失尊严地走开了。◇ make a hurried retreat run (away)

rib

rib *someone* (about *something*) [ˈrɪb ~] [话] **开玩笑** 语源不明。最有力的说法是：本条是由 poke *someone* in the ribs (戳某人的肋骨→逗人发笑)而来。用于口头开玩笑的场合，语调很轻松。*Don't mind what Beau says. He likes to rib people.* 对于博说的话，你不要介意。他爱跟别人开玩笑。*He likes to rib me about my fondness for loud ties.* 我喜欢用颜色花哨的领带，他总爱以此开我的玩笑。*Jim is always ribbing his wife about her cooking.* 吉姆总爱拿他老婆的烧菜手艺开心。◇ give *someone* a RIBBING (about *something*) ◇ tease *someone*

ribbing

give *someone* **a ribbing** (about *something*) [ˌgɪv ~ əˈrɪbɪŋ] [话] **开个玩笑** 与 RIB *someone* 同义，但用法不一样。一般来说，不能象 rib *someone* 那样用进行时。这是因为：如果说 giving ~ a ribbing，连续来两个 ~ing，语调很难听。因此，表示"老是"、"总是"的意思的副词几乎不能与 give *someone* a ribbing 一起使用。例如，人们常说 She's always ribbing me.(她总开我的玩笑。)可是极少讲 She's always giving me a ribbing. 在普通会话中的说法是这样：*He gave me a ribbing yesterday.* 他昨天开了我个玩笑。*I'll give her a ribbing when I see her.*

等我见到她，我要开她个玩笑。在加强语气时，常用 good。再进一步加强时，用 terrific。例如：*I'll give Jane a good ribbing about that when I see her next week.* 关于那件事情，等下星期我见到简的时候，要好好地开她个玩笑。*The guys gave me a terrific ribbing about taking Sue to the movies.* 由于我带苏去看电影，哥儿们狠狠地拿我开了一顿心。如果是被动语态，一般不用 about，而用 for。*I was given a good ribbing for arriving an hour early.* 我早到了一个小时，成为人们的一个大笑柄。be given a ribbing (by *someone* for *something*) 这一被动语态的表达法如果用主动语态来讲，就是 get 或 take a ribbing (from *someone* for *something*)，意思为"受到取笑"。*I got [took] a terrific ribbing from my father for rushing out to go to school on Sunday morning.* 星期天早晨我慌忙从家里跑出去上学，被我父亲大大取笑了一阵。◇ give *someone* a teasing

take a ribbing (from *someone* about *something*) [ˌteɪkə ˈrɪbɪŋ] [话] **受到取笑** → give *someone* a RIBBING (for *something*)

ribs

stick to *someone's* **ribs** [ˌstɪktə ～ ˈrɪːbz] [话] **耐饿** rib 是"肋骨"。本条条头直译为"粘到肋骨上"，也就是"吃下去的东西象粘到肋骨上一样，不容易掉出来"，即"耐饿"的意思。*Toast and eggs don't stick to my ribs, so I always get hungry again before lunch when I eat a Western-style breakfast.* 对于我来说，面包片和煎鸡蛋不顶事，所以我要是吃了西式早点，不到午饭时间肚子就又饿啦。*Have some more roast beef. It'll stick to your ribs.* 再吃点烤牛肉吧，这东西耐饿。也可以不用 *someone's* ribs 而说 the ribs，这一表达法比较生硬，多用于一般论述的文句。*People who work outdoors have to have food that will stick to the ribs.* 在户外干活的人必须吃耐饿的食物。另外，有些英华词典把这一表达法译成"有营养的"，实际上不用此种意义。例如，象下面这样的说法是可能的：*Rice isn't all that nutritious, but it sticks to the ribs.* 大米没有太多的营养，但是吃了耐饿。◇ stay in *someone's* stomach

rich

filthy rich [ˈfɪlθi ˈrɪ(ː)tʃ] [话] **非常有钱的** filthy 是"肮脏的"，加上 rich，就是"一身铜臭，怎么洗也洗不掉的"的意思。这里的 filthy 仅仅是加强语气，丝毫没有这钱很"肮脏"或"来路不明"的意思。*George's uncle is filthy rich.* 乔治的伯父非常有钱。也可以说 stinking RICH。两者均如上面的例句所示，作为表语使用。◇ extremely wealthy

stinking rich [ˈstɪŋkən ˈrɪ(ː)tʃ] [话] **极富有的** 这里的 stinking 是副词，意思为"极端地"、"非常地"。因为 stink 一词的主要意义为"恶臭"，所以这一表达法有"钱太多了，简直铜臭扑鼻"的意味。主要用作表语，放在 be 动词的后边。*They say the new couple down the street are stinking rich.* 听说新搬到咱们邻近的两口子非常有钱。又说 filthy RICH。◇ extremely wealthy

riddance

good riddance (to bad rubbish) [ˈgu(ː)d ˈrɪdənts (tə ˈbæ(ː)d ˈrʌbɪʃ)] [话] **有了它[他]是累赘，没有它[他]倒松快** 这里的 riddance 是动词 rid (除掉)的名词形式。rubbish 是"废物"、"垃圾"。bad rubbish (臭垃圾)指"谁也不想要的讨厌东西"或者"累赘"。本条换一个通俗易懂的说法就是：It's good to be rid of such bad rubbish. 有时应用于"人"，但不限定如此。*A: Have you heard that Roy Stinks has been expelled from school? B: Good riddance, I say. He always was a troublemaker.* 甲：你听说罗伊·斯廷克斯被学校开除了吗？乙：我说开除他倒松心。他一向是个捣乱分子。如这一例句所示，本条习用语用于表示"他走了好"这样一种如释重负的心情。在孩子们的会话中，常加 to bad rubbish，例如：*Jimmy: You don't play fair. I'm going home and I'm not coming back! Jenny: Good riddance to bad rub-*

bish. 吉米:你耍赖。我要回家去,不再来啦! 珍妮:没有讨厌鬼,玩得倒松心。有时在成年人的会话中也出现同样的说法:*I lent Charles my husband's old sweater and if he never returns it, good riddance to bad rubbish.* 我把丈夫的旧毛衣借给查尔斯了,如果他永远不还,我去掉一件废物倒松心啦。*Though everyone in the family outwardly sympathized with Tim when someone stole his drum set, in reality their only thought was "Good riddance!"* 当有人偷走了蒂姆的那套鼓的时候,虽然全家没有一个人不在表面上同情他,实际上他们心里所想的是:"去掉麻烦物,这倒很松心!"另外,请读者注意:在美国英语中,这一表达法前边不加 a,不能说 a good riddance。◇ I'm glad *someone* [*something*] is gone [going].

ride

let *something* **ride** [.let ~ 'raɪd] [话] **听其自然** let 当然是"使……",ride 是"乘……前去"。至于使什么东西乘什么前去的问题,请先看一下以下的两个例句。*We don't have to make a final decision yet. Let's just let things [it] ride for a while.* 我们不必要做最后的决定。暂时听其自然好了。*They haven't agreed to our proposal, but I'm sure they will if the business climate gets any worse. For the time being, we'd best let things ride.* 他们不同意我们提出的方案,但是我敢肯定,如果商情进一步恶化,他们是会同意的。目前,我们最好是听其自然啦。这就是说,发生了某种事情。对于这种事情,有必要做出结论或者采取措施。但是,事情还在演变,没有定局。在这样的时候,不是马上就下结论或者讲求对策,而是"任凭"(let)"事情"(things, it)"乘着势头发展下去"(ride)。当然不是永远"听之任之",因此一般要加上表示时间的词句,如 for a while、for the time being 之类。*The police seem to have decided to let things ride until they hear from the kidnappers.* 警察似乎采取这样的方针:在绑架者提出什么要求之前,他们静观事情的演变,不采取行动。◇ withhold action

take *someone* **for a ride** [.teɪk ~ fərə'raɪd] [话] **欺骗** 直译为"带某人出去坐汽车兜风"。但作为黑社会和匪盗团伙的用语,含有可怕的意味。例如:*It's obvious Louie's been squealing on us. Find him and take him for a ride.* 很明显,路易是去警察那里把咱们出卖了。咱们找到他,用汽车把他引诱出去,干掉他。这意思就是:"用好话欺骗那个人,说有事跟他商量,然后带他坐上汽车,到适当的地方把他杀掉。"根据上下文关系,go for a ride 也表示同样的意义,但这一表达法没有 take *someone* for a ride 语意明确,比较含糊。*A: Whaddya want? I ain't done nothing to you guys. B: Don't get excited, Joe. We're only going for a nice friendly little ride.* 甲:你们想干什么?我没做什么对不起哥儿们的事情呀。乙:乔,你不必激动。我们只是要带你友好地、高高兴兴地兜一会儿风而已。在讲这种话的场合,从表面上看,只不过是"一起乘汽车兜风"的意思,但是骨子里一般含有"如果谈崩了,我们就干掉你"的意思。如上所述,take *someone* for a ride 一般表示"欺骗"的意思,但是,当用轻松的语调来讲的时候,也常表示"使人以假当真"的意思。大多用于长时间令人发生错觉的场合。常加 only 或 just 增强语气。*I thought she was in love with me, but I found she was only taking me for a ride.* 我原来以为她爱我,但是我发现她只是虚情假意而已。*Maybe they're not really serious about doing business with us. Maybe they're just taking us for a ride.* 他们也许没有认真跟我们做生意的意思。但也许故意这样哄骗我们。*Don's a wise guy who thinks he knows all the answers. It really does my heart good to see him taken for a ride.* 唐是一个自高自大的家伙,他认为自己无所不知,无所不晓。见到他被人蒙住,我真开心极啦。在这一场合,Don 一定是把别人胡说八道的事情一直信以为真了。下一个例句的语气更加轻松,大致与 pull *someone* LEG 相同,只表示汉语俗语"糊弄"的意思。*Joan's father isn't really the mayor. She was only taking you for a ride.* 琼的父亲实际上不是市长。她只是糊弄你罢了。◇ deceive *someone*

rifle

an air rifle [ə 'ne(:),raɪfl] [口] **气枪** → a BB GUN

right

right and left [,raɪtn'le(:)ft] [口] **一个接一个** 直译为"右和左",当然可以按这个意思使用。*Drivers should always look right and left before coming out of a side street.* 汽车司机在从小路把车开上大马路的时候,总得向左右观看。作为比喻,这一表达法用于表示"一个接一个"、"源源不断地"的意味。*The advanced nations have been squandering the world's natural resources right and left.* 先进的国家在把世界的天然资源——地浪费掉了。*We've got to do something to make our club more interesting. People have been quitting right and life recently.* 我们必须采取一些措施使我们的俱乐部更能引起大家的兴趣。最近,会员们一个接一个退出去了。*Everyone likes Jane. She makes friends right and left wherever she goes.* 每个人都喜欢简。她走到哪里都能交上许多朋友。另外,有时颠倒地说 left and right,但意思与 right and left 完全相同。◇ in great amounts [numbers] / one after another

serve *someone* **right** → SERVE

rights

have *someone* **dead to rights** [,hæv ~ ,de(:)dtə 'raɪts] [话] **铁证如山** dead to rights 的语源不详。原来的构思是这样:"主张无罪的权利死掉了",也就是完全没有那种权利了。have *someone* 是"使某人处于那种状态"的意思。这一表达法原为黑社会以及警察们的用语,是"当场捕获"的意思,现在不限于犯罪,广泛用于表示"抓住干坏事的确凿证据"的意思。大多是在这样的场合使用:一个人说谎或不老实被对方揭穿,陷入理屈词穷的状态。*The woman claimed she had never been to that store, but the police had her dead to rights when they found the stolen bracelet in her handbag.* 那个女人声称她从来没有进过那家商店,可是警察在她的手提包里搜出了被窃的手镯,抓住了确凿的证据。*Tim says he always listens very carefully in class, but when he dropped his comic book on the floor the teacher had him dead to rights.* 蒂姆说他一向非常注意听课,但是,当他把一本连环漫画书掉在地板上的时候,老师抓住了他撒谎的确凿证据。*Don't tell your wife that you went to the movies. She'll have you dead to rights if you can't describe the story.* 你不要跟你太太说你去看电影了。如果她叫你讲影片的情节,你讲不出来,那她就抓住你的把柄啦。顺便提一下:在英国英语中,可以用 bang to rights 代替 dead to rights, 但在美国不通行。◇ have proof that *someone* is guilty [lying]

Riley

live the life of Riley → LIFE

rims

run on the rims [,rʌnɔnðə 'rɪ(:)mz] [话] **经济上紧巴巴的** rim 是"轮圈"。因此, run on the rims 是"汽车没有轮胎,单靠轮圈行驶"的意思。*The tires on this car are so worn out that we're practically running on the rims.* 这辆汽车的轮胎已经磨损得太厉害了,我们实际上是靠轮圈行驶的。这是按字面意义的用法。人们广泛把这一表达法作为比喻使用,表示"没有多余的钱"的紧巴巴的样子。*We can't afford to lose any more customers. This company is already running on the rims.* 我们再也不能失去任何的主顾了。公司在经济上已经非常拮据了。*My husband has decided to spend his vacation at home this year. We don't have enough money to stay at the good hotels, and he says vacationing isn't any fun if you've got to run on the rims.* 我丈夫已经决定今年在家里度过假期。我们没有足够的钱住上等旅馆。他说,如果手头

很拮据,到哪里去玩都没什么意思。虽然最普遍使用 run on the rims 的形式,但有时采取 run 以外的动词。*This company is on the rims.* 这个公司在经济上非常拮据。*I've got to get a better-paying job. I'm tired of living on the rims.* 我得找一个挣钱多的工作了。我已经过够这种紧巴巴的生活啦。◇ operate [live] on a precarious budget

ring

give *someone* **a ring** [ˌgɪv ~ ə ˈrɪŋ] [话] **给某人打电话** 这里的 ring 是"玎玲玲"的声音。本条条头直译为"给某人一个玎玲玲"。但 ring 另有"戒指"的意义,所以有注意上下文的必要。例如:Joe gave me a ring last night. 仅凭这句话,就弄不清究竟是"乔昨天晚上跟我订婚了。"还是"乔昨天晚上给我打电话了。"如果后边接着说 I've never been so happy in my life.(我从来没有如此地幸福。)那是前一种意思;如果下文为 He said he's caught a cold.(他说患感冒啦。)那肯定是电话了。*I'm tied up right now. Can you give me a ring later?* 我现在忙极了,脱不开身。你过一会儿给我打电话好吗? 又说 give *someone* a BUZZ [call]。◇ call *someone* (on the telephone)

throw *one's* **hat in(to) the ring** → HAT

toss *one's* **hat in(to) the ring** [ˌtɔːs ~ ˈhæ(ː)tn(tə)ðə ˌrɪ(ː)ŋ] [口] **宣布参加竞选** → throw *one's* HAT in(to) the ring

ringer

be a dead ringer (for *someone* [*something*]) [ə ˈdeːdˈrɪŋər] [话] **一模一样** ringer 原为赛马用语,是"顶替应该上场的马去竞赛的好马"的意思。后来进一步发展,人们用这个名词表示"非常相似的人或物"。由于这两种意思很容易弄混,在表示"一模一样"的场合,一般添加强调的词 dead。这种强调的表达法与汉语"高兴死了"、"讨厌死啦"的表达法几乎完全一样。*That man is a dead ringer for my big brother.* 那个人长得跟我哥哥一模一样。*That car isn't mine, but it's sure a dead ringer.* 那辆汽车不是我的,但是的确跟我那一辆很相似。顺便讲一下:这一表达法在用本来的意义作"替身"解时,不仅限于赛马,现在可以用于各种竞赛、比赛以及考试的场合。◇ look exactly like (*someone* [*something*])

rings

run rings around *someone* [ˌrʌnˈrɪŋz əraund ~] [话] **绝对出众** 最初的构思是:"在马拉松比赛的时候,哪怕是在那些拼命往前奔跑的人们的周围兜圈子跑,也会稳拿第一。"意思是"绝对冠军"。例如"I'll run rings around that tortoise," said the hare. 这句话的意思为:"兔子说:'我慢慢跑,也能胜过那只龟呀!'"如果按这一表达法原来的构思忠实地翻译,则应该是:"我就是在那只龟的周围绕着圈儿跑,也会取胜的啊!"这一表达法不仅用于田径赛,几乎也可以用于一切的竞争。作为比喻,用法如下:*When it comes to speaking French, Jim runs rings around all his classmates.* 如果讲到说法语,吉姆比他同班的任何人都强。*In space exploration, the Russians and Americans are running rings around the rest of the world.* 在太空探索方面,苏联人和美国人比世界其他各国都绝对领先。*You were foolish to challenge Buck to a fight. He'll run rings around you.* 你向巴克挑战,真太愚蠢啦。他比你占绝对的优势啊。◇ be incomparably better than *someone*

riot

read (*someone*) **the riot act** → ACT

rip

rip *someone* **off** [ˌrɪp ~ ˈɔːf] [话] **敲竹杠** 按字面意义,rip off 是"剥去"。如果说 rip the door off the hinges, 那是"使门脱开铰链"的意思。把这个词组应用于人,就构成 rip *someone* off。这是在 20 世纪 60 年代初产生的一个比较新的表达法。原来的构思是:"从某人身上剥去某种东西"。最初表示"抢劫"、"偷盗"的意思,后来进一步发展,又具有"敲竹杠"、"索高价"的意义了。"抢劫"的英语是 rob,"偷盗"的英语是 steal,而 rip off 则用于表示两方面的意义。*Burglars ripped off the bank.* 强盗们抢劫了银行。*A thief ripped me off for three hundred dollars.* 一个窃贼偷了我三百美元。按照"敲竹杠"、"索高价"亦即 overcharge (算钱过多)的意义使用的场合,经常含有"欺诈"、"诈骗"的意味。*Stay away from that store. They'll rip you off every time.* 离那家商店远着点吧。你每次去它都会敲你的竹杠。*That cabaret ripped us off by charging 50 dollars per drink.* 那家酒馆敲我们的竹杠,一杯酒就要五十美元。本条也可以用于如下的情况,意思不是"敲竹杠",而是接近"欺骗"。*That house painter ripped me off. The first rain washed away half the paint.* 那个油漆房屋的工匠坑害了我。刚下一场雨,油漆就被冲掉了一半。名词形式 a rip-off 除"抢劫案"、"骗局"外,还有"仿制品"、"冒牌货"等意味,可在多种情况下使用,例如: *There was a big rip-off at that bank last week.* 上个星期,那家银行发生一起大抢劫案。*Horse racing is a big rip-off if you ask me. It's fixed so that the big money goes to the people who run it.* 如果叫我说的话,赛马是一个大骗局。谁举办赛马比赛,大批的钱进入谁的腰包,这是预先安排好了的。*In a capitalist country, most political promises are a rip-off. The people who make them never intend to keep them.* 在一个资本主义国家里,大多数的政治诺言都是骗人的把戏。许诺的人根本就不打算遵守那些诺言。*These prices are a real rip-off.* 这里的定价简直高得没边儿。*Star Wars has been the only good sci-fi movie. All the others are just rip-offs.*《星球大战》是唯一一部优秀的科幻影片。其他的全都是仿制品。rip-off 还可以修饰名词。*My grandmother lost her savings to a rip-off artist.* 我的祖母上了一个骗子手的当,失掉了全部的体己钱。这里的 rip-off artist 与 a con ARTIST 大致相同。*That bar is a rip-off joint.* 那个酒吧间是个敲竹杠的铺子。这里的 joint 与 place 同义,指"人们聚集的场所"。◇ cheat *someone*

rip-off

a rip-off [ə ˈrɪˌpɔːf] [话] **抢劫案;骗局;仿制品;冒牌货** → RIP *someone* off

a rip-off joint [ə ˈrɪˌpɔːf ˌdʒɔɪnt] [话] **敲竹杠的铺子** → RIP *someone* off

rise

get a rise out of *someone* [ˌgedə ˈraɪˌzaudəv ～] [话] **刺激某人得到预期的反应** rise 为 rise to the BAIT 中的 rise 的名词用法,原是"鱼见到食饵后从水下浮上来"的意思。从钓鱼人的立场来说,这是预期的反应。也就是说,get a rise out of *someone* 最初的构思是:"象使鱼浮上来吃食饵一样,求得所期待的对方的反应"。这里的"所期待的反应"是对方认真对待、为之着急或生气的意思。本条习用语一般用于"半开玩笑地故意刺激他人"的场合。*If you want to get a rise out of Bela, just mention his big feet.* 如果你想刺激一下贝拉,只要讲他的脚大就行啦。*There's no need to get angry. I was just trying to get a rise out of you.* 你用不着生气呀。我刚才只是想刺激你一下而已。*Joe is from Texas. You can always get a rise out of him by teasing him about Texas's being only the second largest state now that Alaska has joined the union.* 乔是得克萨斯州人。如果你逗弄他说现在阿拉斯加已经并入合众国,得克萨斯只不过是第二大州了,那家伙总是会当真生气的。这一表达法在绝大多数的场合表示"刺激他人得到预期的反应",有时用于表示"使对方上当"的意味。但是,这仍然属于"使对方当真对待"的范围。*Let's tell Jim that the boss's daughter wants a date with him. That should get a rise out of him.* 咱们告诉吉姆,就说老板的女儿想跟他约会。那家伙一定会上咱们的当。另外,也可以用 take 或 have 代替 get,但那是英国英语,在美国不这样说。◇ get a reaction from *someone* / provoke *someone*

rites

last rites [ˌlæːstˈraɪts] [口] **葬礼** 直译为"最后的仪式"。在文章中或者郑重其事的谈话中,常用这一表达法代替 funeral ['fjunərəl]。*Last rites for Prof. Black [Prof. Black's funeral] will be held at the university chapel at three o'clock.* 布莱克教授的葬礼将于三点钟在大学的礼拜堂中举行。◇ a funeral

river

sell *someone* **down the river** [ˌsel ～ ˌdaunðə ˈrɪvər] [话] **出卖同伴或朋友** 直译为"在河的下游卖某人"。这里的 river 从语源上讲系指密西西比河。在过去的时代,美国的农场主把奴隶们卖到密西西比河下游的农场去。他们不仅出卖一直为他们辛勤劳动的奴隶,而且毫不讲人道地拆散奴隶的家庭,把丈夫与妻子、父母与孩子分别卖到不同的地方去。这就是本条习用语的来源。*When the police showed up at their hideout soon after their leader had left, the gang realized they had been sold down the river.* 匪帮的头头刚一离开他们的巢穴,警察就到来了。这些家伙省悟过来,原来他们被出卖了。*That guy achieved his present success by selling his friends, one after another, down the river.* 那个家伙靠着一个又一个地出卖自己的朋友而取得今日的成功。如这一例句所示,本条习用语主要用于表示"见利忘义,出卖朋友"的意思,偶尔用于表示"把用不着的部下调走"的意思,但在这一场合,仍然含有"违背本人的心愿"亦即"出卖同伴"的意思。*Just before I reached retirement age, I was sold down the river to a subsidiary company.* 在我快到退休年龄的时候,我竟然被调到下属公司去了。◇ betray *someone* / transfer *someone* (unfairly)

send *someone* **up the river** [ˌsend ～ ˌʌpðə ˈrɪvər] [话] **送入监狱** 直译为"把某人送到河的上游"。这个河指 Hudson River (哈得孙河)。哈得孙河流经纽约市,在此段上游有著名的 Sing Sing (兴兴监狱)。这就是本条习用语的来源。原为黑社会用语,相当通俗。*Jake's an outstanding cop. He's sent more criminals up the river than anyone else on the squad.* 杰克是一位优秀的警察。他比小队中的任何人往监狱里送的罪犯都多。*Looey was sent up the river for bank robbery.* 路易由于抢劫银行而被投入监狱了。讲话的内容由于前后关系而十分明确的时候,可以省略 the river。*He was sent up for three years for tax evasion.* 他由于逃税而被送进监狱服刑三年。本条条头虽然是一个定型的表达法,但也可以用 send 以外的动词,例如说:*How long has he been up the river?* 他坐牢有多长时间啦? *This is Al. He's just got back from up the river.* 这是阿尔。他刚从监狱出来。*Stoolie should be getting out soon. He's been up almost five years now.* 斯图利快该出来了。他坐牢已经将近五年啦。◇ put *someone* in prison

road

burn up the road [ˌbə(ː)rˌʌpðə ˈroud] [话] **快速飞奔** 直译为"烧毁道路"。这意思就是说:在快速开车时,不仅轮胎发热,连道路也热起来。*We burned up the road on the way to the hospital.* 我们快速开车,向医院飞奔去了。*The lead car burned up the road, pulling a full lap ahead of the rest of the field.* 最前边的那辆赛车快速飞奔,遥遥领先,把其余的车落下足有一圈。如以上两个例句所示,这一表达法一般用于汽车,但不限定如此。*The motorcycle cop and the car he was chasing were both burning up the road.* 警察的摩托车和他所追捕的汽车都在快速飞奔。有时还可以应用于人。*We really burned up the road in Europe, visiting seven countries in only ten days.* 我们在欧洲简直是风驰电掣,仅仅十天的时间里就访问了七个国家。◇ drive [travel] extremely fast

hit the road [ˌhɪtðə ˈroud] [话] **出行** 直译为"打路"。原来是"为了搭别人的车而到马路上去等"的意思,现在一般指"长途旅行的启程或出发",也就是"出行"的意思。这种"旅行"的概念,从 the road 一词中显示得很清楚,不管路途多么远,主要是指徒步或者乘汽车的"旅行",至于以飞机、轮船、火车为载体的"旅行",则不能说 hit the road。*As soon as my* *last exam is over, I'm hitting the road for home.* 最后的一次考试终了以后，我就打道回府。拿这个例句来说，根据现代美国的具体情况，认为说话人坐汽车走是最合理的。另外，所谓的"出行"并不仅指在整个行程中的第一次出发，凡是中途停留或者休息之后的再度启程，也同样是 hit the road. *There is no chance of finding a job in this town. Let's hit the road again.* 在这个城镇里，没有找到工作的可能了。咱们再上路吧。*We stayed at small inns at night, hitting the road early every morning.* 我们夜里住小店，每日大清早继续赶路。毫无目标地出去流浪，也是 hit the road。大概由于这个原因，有的词典就把本条译作"流浪"。*When I lost my job I hit the road for several years, traveling wherever my fancy took me.* 当我失业的时候，我出去转了好几年。我随心所欲，想往哪里走就往哪里走。当对其他人讲"你走开"的时候，也使用本条，意思是"你快到远远的地方旅行去吧！"例如：*Hit the road, buddy. We don't want your type around here.* 老兄，你到别的地方去吧，我们不希望你这种人到此地来。◇ set out / leave

hog the road [ˌhɔːgðə ˈroud] [口] **驾驶汽车在路上横行** hog 的第一个意义是"大的猪"。在这里是动词，意思为"贪得无厌"。本条条头直译是"对道路贪得无厌"。*We got behind a truck that purposely hogged the road so that we couldn't pass.* 我们的车跟在一辆大卡车的后面，那辆卡车故意在马路上横行，不让我们的车开过去。如这一例句所示，本条可以用于"有意识地"开车挡住其他车辆的场合，但一般用于形容初学驾驶汽车者或者不把其他驾驶者放在眼里的老太太之流的开车作风。*Most inexperienced drivers have a tendency to hog the road.* 绝大部分没有经验的汽车驾驶者有独占路面的倾向。*I've been trying to pass the car in front of me for the past fifteen minutes, but the driver keeps hogging the road.* 我打算超越前边那辆汽车已经有 15 分钟了，可是那辆车的司机始终横行驾驶，占着路面。这样肆无忌惮的汽车驾驶者叫做 a road hog。*Why is it that whenever I'm in a hurry, I always seem to get behind a road hog?* 不知为什么每当我有急事要办的时候，总是遇见一个横行霸道的开车者堵在前面？◇ drive in the middle [all over] the road

one for the road [ˈwʌ(ː)nfərðə ˈroud] [话] **回家之前的一杯酒** 这里的 the road 是"回家的道路"。有本来已经喝醉、为了路上保持醉态而更饮一杯的场合，也有本来并未喝酒、在归去之前来上一杯的场合。有时是"临别干上一杯"或"最后喝上一杯"的意思，但这只是在临走的时候的一种极其普通的寒暄，决不表示永别之类深沉的感伤情绪。*It's cold outside to-night. How about one for the road before you go?* 今天夜里外边很冷。你走之前喝上一杯如何？*That old man used to come to my bar every night at nine and order two drinks. At exactly ten he'd always say, "I guess I'll have one more for the road."* 那个老头每天晚上九点钟到我的酒吧间来，要两杯酒。到了十点整，他总是说："我在回家之前还得来上一杯啊。"如以上所述，这一表达法一般是指"一杯酒"，但也可以有如下的用法：*All right. I'll have one more for the road if you insist. But make it coffee, will you?* 好啦，你一定叫我走之前再喝一杯，那我就领受了。不过，来杯咖啡怎么样？◇ one last drink

a road hog [ə ˈroud ˌhɔːg] [口] **不顾后面车辆而在马路上横行的司机** → hog the ROAD

a wide place in the road → PLACE

Robin Hood's

go around Robin Hood's barn → BARN

rock

a rock hound → HOUND

swim like a rock [ˌswɪm laɪkə ˈrɑːk] [话] **一点儿也不会游泳** 直译为"象石头一样游泳"。意思是"一点儿也不会游泳，就跟石头掉在水里一样"。*My big brother is an excellent swimmer, but I swim like a rock.* 我的哥哥游泳非常好，而我却一点

儿也不会。◇ can't swim at all

rocker

go off *one's* **rocker** [gou.ɔ(:)f ～ 'rɑːkər] [话] **发疯** → be off *one's* ROCKER

be off *one's* **rocker** [.ɔ(:)f ～ 'rɑːkər] [话] **发疯** 这里的 rocker 是"摇动木马底部的弧形架"。本条原意为"木马脱离了底架"。结果,木马就不能正常摇动了。由此引伸,就成为"人的头脑不能正常活动"亦即"发疯"的意思。*The old man's a bit off his rocker, but not enough to be put in an institution.* 那个老头的头脑有点不正常,但还不到被送进疯人院的程度。这是指真正的"疯"。*You're off your rocker. I wouldn't date that girl if you paid me to.* 你简直是发疯。要是我的话,即使你付给我钱,我也不跟那个姑娘约会。这不是真"疯",而是极轻松的用法。这一表达法的使用范围极广。常加 a bit 或者 a little 表示头脑有点儿不正常。*When I read the newspapers, sometimes I feel the whole country's a little off its rocker.* 我看报的时候,有时感觉到整个国家都有一点儿发疯。在强调"确实发疯"的场合,使用 really。*That guy must really be off his rocker. He wants me to jump out of an airplane with a parachute.* 那个家伙肯定是疯啦。他叫我带着降落伞从飞机上往下跳。另外,又有 go off *one's* rocker 和 send *someone* off *his* rocker 的说法,前者是"发起疯来"、后者是"使人发疯"的意思。*When Jeb saw you holding hands with his girl friend, he went off his rocker. That's how you got in this hospital.* 杰布看见你握着他的女朋友的手,他发起疯来了。这就是你进入这家医院的原因。*Losing all his money on the stock market apparently sent him off his rocker.* 在股票市场上失去了所有的财产,这显然使他发疯了。◇ be crazy

send *someone* **off** *his* **rocker** [.send ～ ɔ(:)f ～ 'rɑːkər] [话] **使人发疯** → be off *one's* ROCKER

rocks

have rocks in *one's* **head** [.hæv 'rɑːksən ～ .he(:)d] [话] **头脑出了毛病** 本条的意思是:"脑袋里没有脑子,而是一些大石头"。在中国学习英语的人往往有这样的印象:rock 是"岩石",stone 为一般的"石头"。但在美国口语中,rock 和 stone 一样,全指一般的"石头"或"石头子儿"。只有一点不同,即讲"岩石"的时候,要说 a big rock,不能说 a big stone。当别人提出十分愚蠢的建议或约请的时候,自己往往用这一表达法回答。意思是:"自己无论如何也不会有那样奇怪的想法啊!"*Me? Lend that guy a hundred dollars? You've got rocks in your head!* 你叫我借给那个家伙一百美元?你的头脑出毛病啦!*If you think I'm going to spend the night with you in an old house where three people have already disappeared, you've got rocks in your head!* 你居然想叫我陪你在那所已经有三个人失踪的老房子里过夜,你的头脑简直出了毛病啦!在不是直接听到建议或约请的场合也可以使用本条,但仍含有"自己决不会有那种奇怪想法"的意味。*Anyone who goes hiking in the desert just for the fun of it has got to have rocks in his head.* 凡是为了玩乐而到沙漠里徒步旅行的人,他的头脑准是出了毛病啦。*one's* head 有时可作 the head。*You've got rocks in the head if you think I'd go out with that creep.* 如果你认为我会跟那个讨厌鬼一起出去参加社交,你的头脑简直出了毛病啦。◇ be crazy

be on the rocks [.ɔ(:)nðə 'rɑːks] [话] **陷入困境** 本来的意思是"触礁",如说 *The ship is on the rocks.* 船触礁了。后来转作比喻使用。有时不离原意,仍具有"触礁"的意味,例如:*Their marriage is on the rocks.* 他们的婚姻撞到暗礁上了。*Unless some compromises are made, the negotiations will soon be on the rocks.* 除非做出一定的妥协,谈判马上就要触礁了。*Relations between the two countries appear to be on the rocks.* 两国之间的关系似乎触到暗礁上了。也有形容阮囊羞涩、一筹莫展的状态的场合,表示"在经济上触礁了"的意味。*I could see from my old friend's clothes that he was on the* rocks. 从老朋友的一身穿戴,我看出他陷入贫困的境地了。在钱的问题上,这一表达法用于公司、团体的场合比较多。*I'm going to have to find another job. The company is just about on the rocks.* 我必须另找一个工作了。我们的公司马上就要倒闭啦。*I didn't have many toys when I was little. My family was always on the rocks.* 我小的时候没有多少玩具,因为我家的生活一向很困难。go on the rocks 是"破裂"的意思。*May's marriage went on the rocks last year.* 梅的婚姻去年破裂了。*Another oil shock and our company will go on the rocks.* 再来一次石油危机,我们公司就要破产啦。leave *someone* [*something*] on the rocks 是"造成破裂状态"的意思。*Their latest quarrel has left their marriage on the rocks.* 最近的一次吵架使他们的婚姻处于破裂的状态。*The Great Depression left us on the rocks.* 大萧条使我家处于破产的状态。◇ have broken down / be financially insolvent

rod

a rod [ə ˈrɑ(:)d] [话] **手枪** → a HEATER

roller

a pill roller [ə ˈpɪ(:)l ˌroulər] [俗] **医生** → a pill PUSHER

a roller coaster → COASTER

rolls

pad the rolls (with *something*) [ˌpæ(:)d ðə ˈroulz] [口] **虚报人数** 这里的 pad 与 pad the BILL (with *something*) (→) 中的 pad 相同。the rolls 是"名册"。这一表达法用于为了多领经费而虚报名额的场合。*In order to get a budget increase, the Welfare Bureau padded the rolls with over five hundred nonexistent people.* 为了增加预算金额,福利局虚报了五百多名不存在的人员。*It looks as if they've padded their rolls.* 看起来,他们虚报人数了。如这一例句所示,可以使用所有格 their, its 等代替 pad the rolls 的 the。◇ illegally increase the number of names listed (on the [*one's*] rolls)

Rome

fiddle while Rome burns [ˈfɪdl ˌhwaɪl ˈroumˈbəːrnz] [口] **大事不管,只计较小事** 直译为"罗马失火拉提琴"。本条来源于如下的传说:当公元 64 年罗马城着大火的时候,臭名昭著的暴君尼禄(Nero)一边望着正在燃烧的罗马,一边弹竖琴唱歌作乐。实际上,这一传说丝毫没有历史根据。据同时代的历史家塔西佗(Tacitus)所述,尼禄曾经千方百计地设法扑灭大火。另外,当时还没有提琴这一种乐器。本条习用语所以不用"竖琴"而用意味着"拉提琴"的 fiddle,是因为 fiddle 一词还有"干无聊的、没有意义的事情来消磨时间"、"什么也不干、一味瞎胡混"的意义。因此,fiddle while Rome burns 用于如下的场合:"尽管发生了重大事情,必须赶快采取措施,而在实际上却注意一些琐碎的或者毫无意义的末节。既忽视重大问题的前兆,又安于现状,不去想办法解决。" *Rampant inflation is destroying the nation's economy and what is the British government doing? Discussing tobacco prices, arguing over whether cats should be licensed, and otherwise fiddling while Rome burns.* 猛烈的通货膨胀在破坏国家的经济,可是英国政府在干什么呢?他们在讨论烟草的价格,争辩养猫是否应该办许可证,另外还有一些诸如此类鸡毛蒜皮的问题。本条常用于表示"不问大事,袖手旁观"的意味。*While the Nazis were dragging Europe ever closer to war, most of the world seemed content to fiddle while Rome burned.* 当纳粹日益把欧洲拖入战争的时候,世界上大多数国家都好象在贪图安乐,把严重的局势搁在一边儿。*You guys can sit around and fiddle while Rome burns if you want to, but I'm going to try to do something to prevent this company from going bankrupt.* 你们这些家伙可以任意袖手坐在那里不顾大局,但是为了防止这个公司破产,我一定要做点什么事情。◇ fritter away the time with unimportant matters (while doing nothing to solve the problem) / sit by and do nothing (to resolve the crisis)

roof

hit the roof [ˌhɪtðə ˈruːf] [话] **勃然大怒** → hit the CEILING

room

have no room to talk [hæv ˌnouˌru(ː)mtə ˈtɔːk] [口] **没有资格笑话别人** 直译为"没有谈论别人的事情的余地"。有些人自己有同样的不足或缺点,却把它束之高阁,反而向别人提意见或者说三道四,正是"乌鸦落在猪身上,看见猪黑,看不见自己黑"。本条习用语专用于这种人,表示反驳的情绪:"你不是也一样吗?"或者"你不是更糟糕吗?" *A: You should lose a little weight. B: You have no room to talk. You're heavier than I am.* 甲:你应该减少一点儿体重。乙:你没有资格说这种话。你比我还重哪。*A: She says your nose is too long. B: She has no room to talk. Her nose is as long as mine.* 甲:她说你的鼻子太长。乙:她没资格说我。她的鼻子跟我的一样长呀。根据上下文,也可以表示"不应该说这种话"的意味。*A: Mary has it in for you for stealing her boy friend. B: She's got no room to talk. She's been stealing people's boy friends for years.* 甲:玛丽因为你拐走了她的男朋友在埋怨你哪。乙:她不应埋怨我呀。这些年来,她一直在偷别人的男朋友啊。也可以使用 little room 代替 no room。*When it comes to wasting money, they have little room to talk.* 如果谈到浪费金钱的话,他们没有笑话别人的资格。*someone* has a lot of room to talk 以及 a lot of room *someone* has to talk 也都是定型的表达法。直译为"有很多说这种话的余地"。乍看起来,与本条条头的意思似乎相反,但是,这是一种反语的说法,实际上是强调 have no room to talk 的意味。*A: Brent is always complaining about reckless drivers. B: A lot of room he has to talk! Look at the way he's always racing around in that sports car of his!* 甲:布伦特总是发牢骚,说一些司机胡乱开车。乙:他还有脸说别人哪! 你瞧瞧他驾驶那辆赛车总是东撞西撞的样子吧。◇ be in no position to criticize

not room (in *someplace*) **to swing a cat** [nɑt ˌru(ː)m təˌswɪŋə ˈkæ(ː)t] [话] **几乎没有容身的地方** 这一表达法的字面意义好象是"没有挥舞猫的地方"。实际上,这里的 cat 并不是"猫",而是旧时人们使用的 cat-o'nine-tails (九尾鞭)的缩略。因为现在已经没人使用这种鞭子,所以当今的美国人也不会想到本条条头固有的意义为"没有挥动鞭子的余地"。他们只用这一表达法表示"非常狭窄"的意味。常用否定式。大多构成 isn't even, don't have enough 的形式。*We can't have the party in my apartment. I don't have enough room to swing a cat.* 我们不能在我住的公寓房间里举行社交晚会。那太狭窄啦,连个容身的地方都没有。*I wish I had a bigger office. There isn't room in here to swing a cat.* 我希望有一个比较大的办公室。这里太狭窄了,连个转身的地方都没有。◇ (It [This room, etc.] is) too small and cramped.

roost

rule the roost [ˌru(ː)lðə ˈruːst] [口] **掌权** roost 是"鸡架",也指"有架的鸡舍"。在这里用的是后一个意义。本条直译为"统治鸡舍",一个鸡舍是由雄鸡掌握实权的,它是首领。*The government in that country is so fragmented that it's difficult to know who actually rules the roost.* 那个国家的政府四分五裂,很难了解实权掌握在谁手里。*It appears to be the vice-president, rather than the president, who rules the roost in that company.* 在那家公司里,掌握实权的似乎是副总经理,而不是总经理。如以上的例句所示,本条可以应用于政府机关、公司等,但用于表示"掌握家庭内的实权"的场合比较多。*Mr. Brown is a very mild man, but at home he clearly rules the roost.* 布朗先生是一个非常温和的人,但是在家庭里,他显然是掌握实权的。*Every time your mother comes to visit, she tries to rule the roost.* 你母亲每次前来探亲的时

候，她都要在这里当家做主。*A clever wife rules the roost without her husband's ever being aware of it.* 一个聪明的妻子是在丈夫不知不觉之间掌握家中的实权的。顺便讲一下：由于在请客的时候，主人要负责用刀切开肉分给大家，所以旧时曾经使用 roast (烤肉)代替 roost，现在一般没人这样做。◇ be in charge [control] (of *something*) / give the orders

rope

the end of ***one's*** **rope** [ðɪ ˌendəv ~ ˈroup] [口] **山穷水尽** → be at the END of *one's* tether

ropes

know the ropes [ˌnouðə ˈroups] [话] **精通业务** the ropes 指帆船上控制帆的“索具”。古时，帆船是否能够顺利行驶，完全要依靠控制帆的索具。因此，在航海时要由“懂得索具”的老手担任这个工作。后来进一步发展，这一表达法遂具有“了解整个机构”、“懂得操作窍门”的意义了。常应用于公司、机关等。*I know nothing about investing in the commodities market. Why don't you ask Hal to help you? He knows the ropes.* 我对商品市场上投资的问题一无所知。你为什么不请哈尔协助你？他是精通此道的啊。*You'd best keep a low profile until you know the ropes.* 你在精通业务之前，最好是保持低姿态。可以用 all 加强语气，而讲 know all the ropes。*I was very fortunate when I started working. I was befriended by an old veteran who knew all the ropes.* 我在开始工作的时候是非常幸运的。我得到一位精通业务的老手的热心帮助。show *someone* the ropes 是“指点窍门”。*This is a new member of our organization. Show him the ropes, will you?* 这是我们单位新来的人。你向他指点一下工作好吗？learn the ropes 是“学会窍门”。*Don't worry. It isn't hard once you learn the ropes.* 不必烦恼。你一旦学会窍门，事情就不难办了。◇ know how things work

learn the ropes [ˌlə(ː)rnðə ˈroups] [话] **学会窍门** → know the ROPES

on the ropes [ɔ(ː)nðə ˈroups] [话] **即将完蛋** 原为拳击用语，指软弱的一方被追赶到围栏索上的状态。*The challenger is on the ropes.* 挑战者被逼到围栏索上，马上就要倒下了。作为比喻，用于“已经走投无路，即将万事休矣”的场合。*Our company is on the ropes. If we don't get a big order soon, we'll go bankrupt.* 我们的公司快完蛋啦。如果我们不马上搞来大笔的订货，公司就要倒闭了。常常使用 have *someone* on the ropes 这一表达法，意思是“逼人到达快要完蛋的地步”。*The champion has the challenger on the ropes.* 冠军把挑战者逼到围栏索上，使他快要倒下去了。*The recession has our company on the ropes.* 由于经济萧条，我们公司快倒闭啦。*Though I am usually very strong and healthy, my vigorous schedule of work and study had me on the ropes.* 虽然我平日非常强壮和健康，但是由于工作和学习安排得过于紧张，我快要累垮了。◇ in a very weakened condition

show ***someone*** **the ropes** [ˌʃou ~ ðə ˈroups] [话] **指点窍门** → know the ROPES

roses

be no bed of roses → BED

rotten

be rotten through and through [ˈrɑ(ː)tn ˈθru(ː)ənˈθruː] [口] **腐烂透顶** → be rotten to the CORE

Something is rotten in the state of Denmark. → DENMARK

row

a hard row to hoe [ə ˈhɑːr ˈdroudə ˈhou] [口] **艰难困苦** hard 本义为“硬”，转义为“难”。row 是“畦”，亦即“为了栽培作物而不断堆砌的垄”。hoe 是“用锄头锄”。本条条头直译为“很难去锄的畦”，但不使用这一意义。这一表达法专用作比喻，表示“工作困难”、“人生辛苦”、“处境险恶”等等的意味。另外，从 row 一词的具体形象可以想象得到，这种“艰难困苦”总是有相当长的时间性，也就是“从什么时候起到什么时候止，是非常艰难困苦的”的意思。*Anyone who hopes to become an Olympic-class athlete has a hard row to hoe.* 不论是谁，凡是希望成为奥运会级运动员的人，都必须经过艰苦卓绝的训练。这句话的意思是：“从下决心当运动员起，到取得参加奥运会的资格，是经过长时间的艰难困苦的”。*Medical school is a hard row to hoe, but if that's what you want, more power to you.* 医学院很难念。但是，如果你有这个志向的话，那就要多加油啦。这就是：“从入学到毕业，要经过长期的艰难困苦”。*The atmosphere was stiff and the conversation lagged. It would have been a difficult row to hoe if it hadn't been for Jane's lively chatter.* 气氛紧张了，谈话冷场了。如果没有简谈笑风生，闲聊了一大阵，情形一定非常尴尬。这种“艰难困苦”是短时间的，但也有长达一辈子的情况，例如：*Life for Jed, who was born on the wrong side of the tracks to drunken parents with nine other children, has been a hard row to hoe.* 杰德生于贫民窟，父母都是醉鬼，还有九个兄弟姊妹，生活对于他来说实在苦极了。◇ (a) very difficult (job)

rub

rub it in [ˌrʌbəˈdɪːn] [话] **哪壶不开提哪壶** rub in 是“擦进去”的意思。it 指“对方的失败、弱点、缺陷等”。本条条头的基本意思是“触及对方的痛处”。说话人并无恶意，只是拿对方开开心。本条在使用时表示很轻快的意味。*Please don't tell Jimmy about my mistake, will you? He'd rub it in every chance he got.* 请你不要把我的失误告诉吉米，好吗？他这个人一得到机会就拿别人开心。*OK, OK, I know the German isn't my best subject. You don't have to rub it in.* 得啦，得啦，我知道我的德语不行。你不必哪壶不开提哪壶呀。如果失败、弱点等的情况很明确了，一般使用 rub it in; 如果不明确，要用示明内容的名词或相当的词语代替 it，亦即采取 rub in *something* [ˌrʌ(ː)ˈbɪn ～] 的形式。*My husband delights in rubbing in the fact that I was over an hour late to our wedding.* 我在结婚的时候迟到了一个多小时，我的丈夫喜欢拿这件事作为话柄。◇ keep reminding *someone* of it [*something*]

rub *someone* **out** [ˌrʌb ～ ˈaut] [话] **消灭某人** → ERASE *someone*

rub *someone* **the wrong way** → WAY

rubber

a rubber check → CHECK

rubberneck

a rubberneck [ə ˈrʌbərˌne(ː)k] [话] **游览的人** → RUBBERNECK at *something*

rubberneck at *something* [ˈrʌbərˌnekət ～] [话] **伸长脖子好奇地观看** 意思是：“把脖子 (neck) 象橡皮 (rubber) 一样拉长，东张西望”。注意：不是“盯着瞧一个固定点(比如人的脸)”，而是“转动脖子去巡视”。*What are you rubbernecking at?* 你在张望什么呢？可以这样使用。但是，一提到这一表达法，首先令人联想到的是“旅游者”。*Our path was blocked by a group of country bumpkins, rubbernecking at the tall buildings.* 我们的路被一群乡下佬挡住了，他们正在伸着脖子好奇地观看高楼大厦。偶尔有省略 neck 的情况。*After my first week in China, my neck was sore from rubbering at all the unusual sights.* 我来中国一个星期之后，由于观览各种不平常的美景，把脖子都累疼了。rubbernecking 作为形容词使用，意思是“爱看热闹的”。*The country seems to have been taken over by rubbernecking tourists.* 这个国家好象被好奇的旅游者们占领了似的。rubberneck 作为名词使用，是“游览的人”；rubberneck bus [wagon] 是“游览车”，二者都带有诙谐的意味。*I take my vacation in August. That's when all the rubbernecks come to town.* 我在八月份休假。到那时候，所有游山逛景的人都回城里了。*Our progress was slowed when we got behind a rubberneck wagon.* 因为前边是一辆游览车，所以我们的车开不快了。◇ gawk at *something*

a rubberneck bus [wagon] [ə ˈrʌbərˌnek

'bʌ(ː)s / ˌwæ(ː)gən] [话] 游览车 → RUBBERNECK at *something*

rude

a rude awakening → AWAKENING

rug

cut a rug [ˌkʌdə 'rʌːg] [话] **跳快步舞** 直译为"切割地毯"。最初的构思是:"这种跳舞方式的特点为脚的动作非常快,有如用鞋在切割地毯一样"。这一表达法已经有些过时,中年以上的人还常常使用,特别是在"跳吉特巴舞"的场合。*Come on, Mary, let's cut a rug.* 来,玛丽,咱们跳快步舞吧! ◇ dance (a fast dance)

pull the rug out from under *someone* [ˌpulðə 'rʌ(ː)ˌgaut frə ˌmʌndər ~] [口] **拆台** 最初的构思是:"拉某人脚下的地毯,使那个人摔倒"。一般指"故意拆台",但也有时指"造成拆台的后果"。另外,这一表达法大多伴有 by *doing something* 的句型,说明拆台时所采取的手段。*We had hoped to form a joint venture with that company, but a rival firm pulled the rug out from under us by buying up most of their stock.* 我们曾希望与那家公司搞一个合资企业,但是有一家敌对的公司收购那家公司的大部分股票,拆了我们的台。rug 后边的 out 也可以省略。*The leading candidate failed to be elected because labor pulled the rug from under him by suddenly withdrawing its support.* 最有希望的候选人没有当选,因为工会突然撤消对他的支持而拆了他的台。可以用 *someone's* feet 代替 *someone*。*I had thought I was going to win this hand, but you pulled the rug (out) from under my feet when you played that ace of spades.* 我原来以为这手牌一定会赢的,可是你出了张黑桃 *A*,拆了我的台。rug 前可以加形容词。*America pulled the diplomatic rug out from under Japan by approaching China without conferring with Japanese leaders first.* 美国事前没有跟日本的领导人商量就与中国接触,在外交上扯了日本的后腿。*The advanced nations' decision to restrict imports pulled the economic rug from under many developing countries.* 先进国家关于限制商品进口的决定,在经济上扯了许多发展中国家的后腿。◇ undercut *someone's* position

ruled

ruled paper → PAPER

ruminate

ruminate ['ruːməˌneɪt] [口] **左思右想** → chew the CUD

run

cut and run → CUT

give *someone* **a (good) run for** *his* **money** [ˌgɪv ~ə ('gud) 'rʌnfər ~ 'mʌni] [口] **虽然未能取胜,但是奋战到底,使对方苦于应付** 直译是"他出多少钱,给他跑多远"。这一表达法来自赛马的俚语,意思为"他下赌注的那匹马虽然不能取胜,但是给他一个劲儿地跑"。good 只是调整语调,没有特殊意义。按照字面意义,用法如下:*I don't mind losing at the races as long as the horse I bet on gives me a good run for my money.* 在赛马场里,只要我下赌注的那匹马一个劲儿地给我跑,我输了钱也不在乎。在按照字面意义使用的场合,马与在这匹马身上下赌注的人的利害关系是一致的;但在作为比喻使用的场合,两者的利害关系有时是一致的,也有时是相反的。在一致的时候,意思是"投桃报李",谁也不欠谁的情;在相反的时候,意思是"拼命斗争",我赢不了你,也不叫你好过。一般使用后一个意义。在这一场合,本条习用语的重点不在于"对方如何难于应付",而在于"我方如何顽强善战",含有"虽然略逊一筹,但是极力拼搏"的意思。*Our giant rival finally won the contract, but we gave them a good run for their money.* 与我们敌对的大公司终于把那份合同夺走了,但是我们拼命斗争,也没叫他们的日子好过。这句话的意思是:"也叫他们费了九牛二虎之力才弄到手"或者"我们并不是那么轻易地认输的"。run 的前边有时用其他的形容词。*The out-of-town team gave us an* *unexpected run for our money*. 想不到外埠来的球队非常善战，使我们只有招架之功，并无还手之力。*I realized there was little chance of reaching the border before the secret police found me, but I was determined at least to give them a good run for their money*. 我明明知道在不被秘密警察发现之前很难到达国境线，但是我下决心出走，至少要好好找一下他们的麻烦。这句话的含义是："我不会叫他们毫不费劲地抓到我的"。在使用"投桃报李"的意思时，一般加 good。"*I've known many failures and disappointments, but I'm not complaining*," *said the old man*. "*Life has given me a good run for my money*." "我有过许多的失败和失望，但是我不怨天尤人。"那位老人说："人生给了我足够的回报啊。"另有 get [have] a run for *one's* money 的形式。一般是"难于应付"、"不好对付"、"非常棘手"的意思。如果与对方的利害关系一致，则是"得到相应的报答"的意思。*The challenger put up an extremely good fight. I'm sure the champ wasn't expecting to get such a run for his money*. 挑战者进行了极为猛烈的搏斗。我敢肯定，冠军决没有料到他会如此难以应付啊。*The army, not expecting the guerrillas to be such tenacious fighters, is having a run for its money*. 军队没有料到游击战士是如此顽强，他们简直束手无策了。在"得到相应的报答"的场合，一般也加 good。*I was sorry to have to sell that farm. I raised a family and in many other ways got a good run for my money there*. 我必须卖掉那个农场时，心里很不好受。我在那里养育大了儿女，并且在其他方面得到了许许多多的好处。*This is a good business and I've had a good run for my money, but it's about time for me to retire*. 这是一个很好的职务，我辛勤的汗水也没有白流，不过，我该要退休啦。◇ make *someone* work hard for *his* victory ((unexpected → unexpectedly)) / prove to be a worthy opponent ((unexpected → unexpectedly)) / give *someone* a lot of satisfaction

runaround

get the runaround (from *someone*) [ˌgetðə ˈrʌnəˌraund] [话] **被人敷衍搪塞** → give *someone* the RUNAROUND

give *someone* **the runaround** [ˌgɪv ~ ðəˈrʌnəˌraund] [话] **敷衍搪塞** runaround 一词来源于 run around(兜圈子跑)，意思是"托辞"、"借口"。本条条头直译为"瞎说一阵，使对方到处乱转"。如果你在头脑中勾画出下面例句所讲述的情景，对于这一表达法的固有意义就容易理解了。*When I asked to see Mr. slippery, they sent me from one office to another until I realized they were just giving me the runaround*. 当我求见斯利泼里先生的时候，他们叫我到这个办公室，然后又叫我到那个办公室，后来我才醒悟过来，原来他们是搪塞我，故意让我到处转。一般用法是：不管是不是在实际上使人到处乱转，仅表示"托辞"、"借口"的意思。*I've been trying to get a date with Doris for over a month now, but she always gives me the runaround*. 我想跟多丽丝约会已经有一个多月了，可是每当我向她提出的时候，她总是敷衍搪塞。*There's no use trying to borrow from that penny pincher. He'll just give you the old runaround*. 你想跟那个吝啬鬼借钱是白费唾沫。他还会用老一套话来搪塞你。*Don't try to give me the runaround. I know you've got the money. Where is it?* 甭打算搪塞我。我知道你已经把钱弄到手了。钱在哪儿？get the runaround (from *someone*) 是"被人敷衍搪塞"。*I've approached the boss for a raise any number of times, but I get nothing but the runaround*. 关于提高工资的问题，我已经向老板讲过无数次了，可是，我所得到的只是敷衍搪塞而已。*Why don't you ask Dick to help you? You'd just get the runaround from Harry*. 你为什么不找迪克帮助你？你找哈里，他只会敷衍搪塞你。◇ give *someone* evasive answers [excuses]

running

running water → WATER

run-of-the-mill

run-of-the-mill [ˈrʌnəðəˈmɪ(ː)l] [口] **平凡的** → run of the MILL

rut

get into a rut [geˌdɪntu əˈrʌ(ː)t] [口] **落入俗套** → be in a RUT

get out of the rut [geˌdaudəðə ˈrʌ(ː)t] [口] **打破常规** → be in a RUT

be in a rut [ɪnə ˈrʌ(ː)t] [口] **千篇一律** rut是车在泥路上走时留下的印,即"车辙"。本条条头的字面意义与汉语成语"如出一辙"相当。但英语的意思指生活、思想、工作方式程式化,总是老一套,没有任何变化。*Our life is in a rut. Maybe we ought to take a vacation.* 我们的生活是老一套。也许应该出去度假啦。也可以用人作主语。*That author is in a rut. He's always writing the same old stories.* 那位作家千篇一律,老是写同样的旧故事。"落入俗套"的英语为 get into a rut,"打破常规"的英语为 get out of the rut,请读者注意:前者用 a rut,后者用 the rut。*Our talks this time have gotten into a rut. Let's take a couple hours' break.* 我们的谈话已经变成来回扯皮,没什么新鲜的了。休息两个钟头吧。*If we don't get out of the rut and come up with some new ideas, we'll lose out to our competitors.* 如果我们不打破常规,搞一些新道道儿,那就会败给竞争对手了。◇ be fixed in a monotonous routine

S

sack

hit the sack [ˌhɪtðə ˈsæ(ː)k] [话] **就寝** 直译为"用身体碰撞口袋"。这里的 sack(口袋)指"床垫"。同义语有 hit the HAY,意思和用法一样。但 hit the hay 为一般人广泛使用,而 hit the sack 主要在学生、士兵等青年人中间使用。*I think I'll hit the sack early tonight.* 今天晚上我想早点儿睡觉啦。◇ go to bed

sack in [ˌsæ(ː)ˈkɪ(ː)n] [话] **上床睡觉** sack 是"口袋",俚语又作"床"解。本条是把它作为动词使用,后边加个 in,意思是"钻进被窝儿",等于说 go to bed。*It's getting late. I think I'll sack in.* 时间不早了,我该睡觉啦。→ SACK out ◇ go to bed

sack out [ˌsæ(ː)ˈkaut] [话] **和衣而卧** sack 是"口袋",俚语指"床"。本条习用语是把它作为动词使用,后边加个 out。如果不细分析,也可以作为 SACK in 的同义语使用。但是,一般来说,人们用 sack in 表示"上床睡觉",用 sack out 表示"不钻被窝儿,和衣而卧",有时甚至表示"在床以外的地方睡觉"的意味。虽然这两个习用语不分昼夜,但在实际使用时,当然夜里睡觉的场合多用 sack in,昼寝的场合则多用 sack out。更严密地讲,如果没有床铺、被褥、睡袋,就不能讲 sack in,而 sack out 则不限于床铺被褥等,地板也好,地面也好,桌子上也好,只要是能够躺下的地方,不管哪里都行。*I was up late last night. I think I'll sack out for an hour or so.* 我昨天熬很长时间的夜。我想眯上一个来小时啦。*After having been playing football all afternoon, Al came home and sacked out on the floor.* 阿尔玩了一下午足球,回到家里躺到地板上就睡了。◇ take a nap

sacred

a sacred cow → COW

safe

crack a safe [ˌkrækə ˈseɪf] [话] **撬保险箱** 这里的 crack 与 crack a BOOK (→)的用法相同。本条条头直译为"砸开保险箱",但与 crack a book 一样,并没有"砸开"二字的直接的意味。虽然一般用于爆破或撬开保险箱的场合,但不限定如此。有时是悄悄地拧标度盘打开。*A thief broke in and cracked a safe in our company last week.* 上个星期,一个窃贼光顾我们公司,撬开一个保险箱。→ a SAFE-CRACKER ◇ rob a safe

on the safe side [ɔ(ː)nðə ˈseɪf ˌsaɪd] [口] **谨慎地** → play it SAFE

play it safe [ˌpleɪət ˈseɪf] [口] **小心谨慎** 原为体育运动用语。it 泛指"现在正在干的或正要干的事情"。本条整体的意思是:"稳扎稳打,不要大意失荆州"。一般用于如下的场合:在打算干什么事情的时候,为了准确无误地达到目的,预先估计万一发生的情况,做好准备,小心谨慎地去进行。大多表示"以防万一"、"以备不虞"的意味。*I think ten thousand dollars will be enough, but we'd better play it safe and borrow twelve.* 我想有一万美元就足够了,不过,为了万无一失,还是借一万二千美元为好。*Jim hoped to enter Harvard University, but he decided to play it safe by applying to two other universities as well.* 吉姆想入哈佛大学,但是他还报考了另外两所大学,以防万一。有时省掉 it。*I think the train leaves at ten, but just to play safe we'd better get to the station by nine-thirty.* 我想火车是十点钟开,不过,为了保险起见,咱们九点半左右到车站为好。另有同义表达法 (just to) be [stay, remain] on the safe side,几乎在所有的场合都能与 play (it) safe 换用。◇ maintain a margin of safety

play safe [ˌpleɪ ˈseɪf] [口] **谨慎从事** → play it SAFE

safe and sound [ˈseɪfən ˈsaund] [口] **平安无事** safe 是"安全的", sound 是"健全的"。在瞬息万变的语言世界里,这一习用语却是个罕见的现象:自从 13 世纪以来,它形式不变,意义不变,一直使用至今。*The missing mountain climbers were found safe and sound.* 失踪的登山运动员们已经被找到了,他们全都平安无事。*When they found the boy, he was safe and sound.* 当人们找到那个少年的时候,他平安无事。如上面的例句所示,这一表达法常与动词 find 搭配使用。另外,在书信中,常与表示"归来"之意的动词一起使用。*We finally arrived at our destination safe and sound.* 我们终于平安抵达目的地。*I got home safe and sound.* 我平安到家了。原来只用于表示"人平安无事"的意思,现在也用于"物平安无事"的场合。*The money was safe and sound all along.* 那笔钱一直安然无恙。◇ unharmed and in good condition

safe-cracker

a safe-cracker [ə ˈseɪf ˌkrækər] [口] **撬保险箱的匪徒** 直译为"砸开保险箱的人"。"砸开保险箱"这一行动本身,在英语为 safe-cracking。*There is no safe that is absolutely safe from safe-crackers.* 没有撬保险箱的匪徒绝对打不开的保险箱。也可以去掉连字符,拼写为 safecracker。→ crack a SAFE ◇ a criminal who specializes in opening safes

said

Easier said than done. → EASIER

sails

take the wind out of *someone's* **sails** → WIND

sake

for Christ's [God's] sake [fər ˈkraɪˈsːeɪk / ˈgɑ(ː)dzˈseɪk] [俗] **哎呀天哪!** → for Pete's SAKE

for goodness [gosh,heaven's,mercy's,pity's] sake [fərˈgudneˈsːeɪk / ˈgɑ(ː)ʃˈseɪk / ˈhevənzˈseɪk / ˈməːrsizˈseɪk / ˈpɪdizˈseɪk] [话] **啊呀,天哪!** → for Pete's SAKE

for Pete's sake [fər ˈpiːtsˈseɪk] [话] **哎呀,天哪!** 感叹词。用以强烈表示自己的心境或感情。有些词典译作"看在上帝面上"、"千万"、"务必"等,在某些场合有这种意思,但不全面,也不适宜。这可能是因为忽视了这一表达法的特点:它虽然由三个词组成,其实是一个词,这个词不是"千万"、"务必"之类的副词,而是感叹词。从下边的例句也可以看出,在某些场合硬译为"千万"、"务必"就难免驴唇不对马嘴了。本条条头原为 for Christ's sake [fər ˈkraɪˈsːeɪk] (根据发音,也可以拼写作 Chrissake [chrissake] 或 Crissake [crissake]) 的委婉表达法。Christ 一词与 God 同样,如果不按照该词的正解使用,就会被人认为亵渎神明。条头中的 Pete 是耶稣大弟子 St. Peter (圣彼得) 的昵称。另外还有 for God's [gosh, goodness, heaven's, pity's, mercy's] sake 等说法,其中 gosh 和 goodness 是 God's 的委婉语。goodness 可加撇号作 goodness', 但一般不加。*For Pete's sake, stop making so much noise.* 哎呀,天哪! 别弄出那么讨厌的声音啦。*For Pete's sake, don't let him leave before I get there.* 无论如何,在我到达那里之前,不要放他走。*Cut it out, for Pete's sake!* 哎呀,快停下来! *For God's sake, don't shoot! It's me.* 哎呀,不要开枪! 是我呀。*For goodness sake, stop crying!* 哎呀,你不要哭啦! 如以上的例句所示,这一表达法常在恳求他人时使用。此外,还应用于种种不同的场合。*I said I was sorry. What else do you want me to do, for Pete's sake?!* 我已经说对不起了。请问,你还想叫我怎样哪?! *For gosh sake, can't you do anything right?* 哎呀,你不能做点儿象样儿的事情吗? *Well, for heaven's sake, if it isn't Charles!* 哎呀呀,这不是查尔斯吗! *For pity's sake! Why did you have to go and get your clothes so dirty?* 哎呀,天哪! 你为什么非去把你的衣服滚得这么脏不可呀? *For mercy's sake, aren't they* *cute*. 哎呀，这些孩子多么逗人喜爱啊！以上所使用的几种与条头同义的表达法，严格地讲，也多少有一些不同的地方。首先，如前所述，for Christ's sake 与 for God's sake 有亵渎神明之嫌，一般避免使用。但在发生性命交关的严重事件的场合，如本条第四个例句所示，是可以使用 for God's sake 的，不受限制。正因为是在严重事件的场合使用，所以 for God's sake 的语气最强，次强的是 for Pete's sake, 其余的可以认为大致相同。另外，在使用时男女有别。for Pete's sake 和 for gosh sake 多为男性使用。for goodness sake, for heaven's sake 和 for pity's sake 的使用者以女性居多，但男性在表示特别强烈的感情时也可以使用。又，for mercy's sake 几乎只有女性使用。为了调整语调，sake 可加 -s, 而讲 for Pete's [God's, gosh, goodness, etc.] sakes, 意义、用法不变。

salt

go back to the salt mines → MINES

an old salt [ə ˌnoul*d*ˈsɔ(ː)lt] [话] **富有经验的水手** → a GOB

salt *something* **away** [ˌsɔ(ː)lt ～əˈweɪ] [话] **储蓄** salt *something* down 是"把肉类腌起来"，如说：*We salted down a lot of meat for the winter*. 我们腌了许多肉准备过冬。salt *something* away 是 salt *something* down and put it away 的简略，字面意义为"(把肉类)腌起来，加以贮存"。salt *something* down 几乎不作为比喻使用，而 salt *something* away 则用以表示"储蓄金钱等，以备不时之需"的意思，如说 *I always salt away part of my husband's salary in the bank*. 我总是把丈夫工资的一部分存入银行。*A prudent spender, George had salted away fifty thousand dollars by the time he was thirty*. 乔治是一个精打细算的人，到三十岁的时候他已经存下五万美元了。*I'm salting away a little every month for an eventual trip to Europe*. 我将来必去欧洲旅行，因此每个月都存上一点儿钱。除了"钱"而外，这一表达法也可以应用于"信息"以及"可以换成钱的东西"。*I salted away the information for future reference*. 我存储了这些信息，以备将来参考。*There was a pile of stocks salted away in the closet*. 在壁橱里存有一大沓子股票。另有 have *something* salted away 的形式。*When the old man died, they found he had almost a hundred thousand dollars in cash and bonds salted away in his mattress*. 老人死的时候，人们发现他在床垫里藏有将近十万美元的现金和债券。◇ save [store] *something*

salt *something* **down** [ˌsɔ(ː)lt ～ˈdaun] [口] **把肉之类腌起来** → SALT *something* away

the salt of the earth [ðə ˈsɔːltəvðə ˈəːrθ] [口] **值得学习的好榜样** 出典《圣经·新约》中的《马太福音》(Matthew)第 5 章 13 节：You are the salt of the earth; but if salt has lost its taste, how shall its saltness be restored? It is no longer good for anything except to be thrown out and trodden under foot by men. (你们是世上的盐；盐若失了味，怎能叫它再咸呢？以后无用，不过丢在外面，被人践踏了。) 最初的构思是："世上有盐，可以防腐"。但这一表达法并不是指象慈善家之类有特殊贡献的人物，或者什么"社会中坚分子"，一般指的是朴素的、不引人注目的、极其平凡的老百姓，但是心地非常温厚而善良。*Mr. Wrightman doesn't have much education, but he's a very good man—the salt of the earth*. 赖特曼先生没受过多少教育，但他是一位非常善良的人——值得学习的好榜样。*Everyone in town admired your mother. She was the salt of the earth*. 全镇的人没有一个不钦佩你母亲。她为人忠厚善良，是大家学习的好榜样。*I can't keep up with the boss's changes of mood. One day you're a lazy incompetent, but if the next day you do something he happens to like, suddenly you're the salt of the earth*. 我可捉摸不透老板瞬息万变的心情。头一天他说你是懒鬼，不顶用，等到第二天，如果你做了一件顺他心的事情，他又说你是好样的，可做学习的榜样了。salt

是不可数名词,因此,这一表达法为单、复数同形。*You can't find any finer people than the Camerons. They're the salt of the earth.* 没有比卡梅伦一家再好的人啦。他们实在是非常善良。◇ a solid, exemplary person

take *something* **with a grain of salt** [ˌteɪk ~ wɪðə ˌgreɪnəv ˈsɔːlt] [口] **听话打折扣** 直译为"吃的时候加一粒盐"。原来,with a grain of salt 是罗马帝国时代所通行的古拉丁文成语 *cum grano salis* 的直译。这一表达法是把"不能相信的话"比喻为"没有咸味的食物",最初的构思为"那种食物不加一粒盐就不能吃",亦即"那种话不加分析就不能相信"。经常用以表示"对他人所说或所写的东西抱着怀疑态度去听或读"的意思。*You'd best take his words with a grain of salt.* 对他的话最好要打折扣。*That's not a very reliable newspaper. I always take its reporting with a grain of salt.* 那种报纸不太可靠。我读它的报道时总是注意不要上当。◇ not accept *something* without reservations

be worth *one's* **salt** [ˌwə(ː)rθ ~ ˈsɔːlt] [口] **所干的活对得起工资** 直译为"值自己的盐"。在罗马帝国时代,salt 是珍贵的物品,不容易弄到手,因此,罗马军队发盐作为兵饷的一部分。后来,盐成为市场上出售的一般物资,支付买盐所用的钱就叫做 *salarium*(盐补贴)。salary (工资、薪金)一词即来源于此。如果把本条条头的 salt 改换成 salary, 意思就非常明确了。*Fred showed that he was worth his salt as a car salesman by selling ten cars during his first month on the job.* 弗雷德上班头一个月就卖掉十辆汽车,作为汽车推销员来说,他是堪当此任的。*The labor market is not very tight now. Every engineer who is worth his salt already has a job.* 现在的劳动力市场不太紧张。每一个有本事的工程师都已经就业了。*Even though it was Sunday, everyone worth his salt was hard at work to meet the contract deadline.* 虽然是个星期天,为了按合同日期完成任务,每一个对得起自己工资的人都拼命地干活。常加 not, hardly 等构成否定句。*That worker is not worth his salt.* 那个工人干不出与工资相应的活儿来。*Many of our employees are hardly worth their salt.* 我们的很多雇员的劳动对不起他们的工资。有时与金钱或工资无关,只用以表示"顶用"的意味。在这一场合,主语不是人也可以。*I'm going to have to get a new hunting dog. This one isn't worth its salt.* 我非弄一条新猎犬不可了。这一条不顶用。◇ be worthy of *one's* pay

sand

bury *one's* **head in the sand** → HEAD

take *one's* **head out of the sand** [ˌteɪk ~ ˈhe(ː)daudəvðə ˈsæːnd] [口] **面对现实** → bury *one's* HEAD in the sand

sandwich

a Dagwood sandwich [ə ˈdæːgwu(ː)d-ˌsændwɪtʃ] [话] **多层特厚三明治** 来源于著名的连环漫画《布隆迪》(*Blondie*),这一漫画的登场人物 Dagwood Bumstead 喜欢吃几十公分厚的夹肉面包(三明治)。不过,几十公分厚的三明治是漫画中的描写,在实际生活中,这种面包最多只有十公分左右的厚度。单片面包的长、宽、厚与一般的食用面包片无异,只不过中间夹的东西层数多而已,材料有肉、莴苣、干酪、西红柿、花生酱、调料以及其他,什么都可以。也有只用两三种东西夹心而加厚的。*I made a Dagwood sandwich from a little of everything I found in the fridge.* 我把在冰箱里找到的东西一样弄一点儿,制成了一个多层特厚三明治。*Neil claimed he wasn't hungry, but did you see that Dagwood sandwich he put away?* 尼尔嘴里硬说他不饿,但是你看见他吃掉的那个多层特厚三明治了吧?也可以省略 sandwich,只说 a Dagwood。*Look at that sandwich! That's a real Dagwood.* 你瞧那个三明治!那可真是一个多层特厚三明治呀。◇ a big, thick sandwich

sap

a sap [ə ˈsæ(ː)p] [话] **傻瓜** 意思是"智力

不足的人”，特指“容易同情他人、很快钻他人圈套的所谓老好人”。与口语 a SIMPLETON 的意义大致相同。 *That sap thinks she loves him more than his money.* 那个傻瓜以为她爱他这个人而不是爱他的钱。后面加上 -py，就成为形容词 sappy ['sæ(:)pi]了。 *What a sappy idea.* 多么傻的主意啊！ → a DUMBHEAD ◇ a stupid person

Saturday

a Saturday night special → SPECIAL

sauce

hit the sauce [ˌhɪtðə 'sɔːs] [话] **酗酒** → hit the BOTTLE

sawbones

a sawbones [ə 'sɔːˌbounz] [俗] **医生** 意思是 a bonesawer (锯开骨头的人，实际上英语中不用这个词)。原来仅指“外科大夫”，现在可指任何科的医生。对医生有点嘲弄味道的一种轻松的说法。亲友之间或是以轻蔑的口吻，或是带有客气的成份，在说笑时使用。 *I'm certainly not going to entrust my body to that sawbones.* 我决不把自己的身体交给那个医生。 *Dad seems to be a pretty good sawbones.* 我爸爸似乎是一位比较不错的医生。◇ a doctor

sawbuck

a sawbuck [ə 'sɔːˌbʌk] [话] **十美元的钞票** 原意为“两端为 X 字形的锯木架”。此系荷兰语 *zaabok* 的直译。saw 是“锯”，buck 是“雄鹿”。因锯木架两端为 X 字形，很象雄鹿的角，故产生这一表达法。 *Every large farm in America has a sawbuck.* 美国的每个大农场都有锯木架。由于锯木架两端的 X 字形使人联想到罗马数字的 X (即十)，这个 sawbuck 就转为“十美元的钞票”的轻松说法了。 *Can you lend me a sawbuck till Friday?* 你能借给我十美元吗？星期五归还。又因为锯木架的两端均为 X 字形，这一表达法有时指“二十美元的钞票”。 *A sawbuck, you say? You mean a ten or a twenty?* 你说“一个锯木架”？你是指十美元还是二十美元呀？另外，最近的“锯木架”已经没有 X 字交点以上的部分(即角的部分)，因此，在表示“锯木架”的意义时，一般不用 sawbuck，而用 sawhorse。◇ a ten-dollar bill

sawhorse

a sawhorse [ə 'sɔːˌhɔ(:)rs] [口] **锯木架** → a SAWBUCK

sax

a sax [ə 'sæ(:)ks] [话] **萨克斯管** a saxophone 的缩略。 *Do you have a sax?* 你有萨克斯管吗？不论任何乐器，在讲“演奏”的场合，一般要在乐器名前加定冠词，如 play the sax (吹萨克斯管)，play the piano (弹钢琴)。 *George can play the sax.* 乔治会吹萨克斯管。但是，如果是在管乐队或管弦乐队中演奏，即担负整体中的一部分任务时，一般不加 the，而作 play sax, play piano。 *He used to play sax in the high school band.* 他过去在高中的管乐队中吹萨克斯管。◇ a saxophone

say

What do you say I [we] *do something?* [ˌhwʌdəjə'seɪ ˌaɪ / ˌwi(:) ～] [话] **我[我们]做……如何？** → WHAT say I [we] *do something?*

What say I [we] *do something?* → WHAT

You don't say! [jə'dountˈseɪ] [话] **真的啊！** 在惊异的时候，特别是感到津津有味的时候使用。这一表达法不包含怀疑或否定对方所说的话的意思，也就是说，不能直译为“你不要说”或解释为“你说的不是真话吧”。如果把它当做 Oh, really? 的强调说法，就容易明白了。 *A: Jill's husband graduated from college when he was only sixteen. B: You don't say! That's quite remarkable, isn't it.* 甲：吉尔的丈夫 16 岁就从大学毕业了。乙：真的啊！那可真有点儿不同寻常，是吧？ *A: Jim Jones is a good friend of mine. B: You don't say! We lived next door to each other when we were kids.* 甲：吉姆·琼斯是我的好朋友。乙：真的啊！我们小的时候是邻居。有时含有奚落或讽刺的意味。 *A: I saw a beautiful* *mink coat in the store today, dear. It was on sale for only two thousand yuan. B: You don't say! Then why don't you buy two or three?* 甲：亲爱的，我今天在商店里看到一种漂亮的貂皮外衣，大减价，只要两千元。乙：真的啊！那你怎么不买两三件来？在一般的词典里往往收录 You don't say so. 的说法，意思与本条相同，但这一说法很生硬，实际上无人使用。再有 Don't TELL me (that) ~.(→)，它与 You don't say! 语调不同，用法完全不一样，千万不要弄混。◇ Is that right?

'scairdy

a 'scairdy cat → CAT

scales

tip the scales (in *someone's* favor [against *someone*]) [ˌtɪpðə ˈskeɪlz] [口] **扭转局势** the scales 是"天平"。tip 是"使倾斜(少许)"。本条条头直译为"使天平稍微向一方倾斜"。大多在如下的情况使用：当局势正处于相持不下、难解难分的微妙阶段，在某一方面稍微加上一点儿力量。由于局势非常微妙，只要有少许的外力就会使之失去平衡。*I thought for a while that I would lose the election, but the mayor's backing tipped the scales in my favor.* 我曾经认为自己在这次选举中会失败的，但是市长的支持于我有利，扭转了局势。*On a dry field the two sides are evenly matched, but the wet weather tipped the scales against the lighter team.* 在干的比赛场上，双方势均力敌，但是由于下雨，局势变得不利于轻捷的一队了。有时候，局势的扭转是"向有利方面"还是"向不利方面"，只能根据上下文来确定。*The committee finally accepted our plan, but it was touch and go for a while. I'm sure it was your telephone call to the chairman that tipped the scales.* 虽然曾经一度处于成败未卜的危险状态，但是委员会终于采纳了我们的计划，我敢肯定，是你给委员会主席的电话扭转了局势。有时用单数形式，作 tip the scale。*Russia's entering the war tipped the scale in favor of the allied nations.* 苏联的参战使形势向有利于同盟国的方向发展了。另有 turn the scales 和 tip the balance 的说法，但在会话中皆不常使用。tip the scales 还有"体重大"的意思，这是一种轻松的表达法。*The champion tips the scales at one hundred eighty pounds.* 冠军的体重达 *180* 磅。◇ weight the odds / provide the decisive factor / determine the outcome

scalp

be after *someone's* **scalp** [ˌæftər ~ ˈskæ(ː)lp] [口] **对某人发怒** → be out for *someone's* SCALP

be out for *someone's* **scalp** [ˌautfər ~ ˈskæ(ː)lp] [口] **对某人非常恼火** 原意是"印第安人出去寻找仇人，要剥那个人的头皮(scalp)"。这一表达法来源于印第安人旧时的风俗习惯。由于此种风习令人感到复仇的烈火在胸膛里熊熊燃烧，所以产生了本条条头表示"恼火"的比喻意义。它的意思不仅仅是"恼怒"，而且包含着"抓住仇人以后要狠狠整他一顿"的意味。be on the WARPATH 也是白人与印第安人接触后产生的表达法，意思是"大发雷霆"。不过，由于 be out for *someone's* scalp 的意思是找到仇人之后要剥他的 scalp，所以在作为比喻使用的场合，语气也比较强烈，从对方看来，不知要遭多大的殃。*Be careful. The boss is out for your scalp because you didn't attend the meeting yesterday.* 你要多加小心。由于你昨天没有参加会议，老板对你非常恼火。*Our neighbor, Mr. Grumpy, is out for our scalps because we hit a baseball through his living room window.* 我们的邻居格拉皮先生非常恼火，因为我们的棒球打碎了他的起居室的窗户玻璃。*Mary is out for my scalp for standing her up last night.* 昨天晚上由于我失约，玛丽对我非常恼火。有时讲 be after *someone's* scalp。◇ be very angry with *someone*

scarce

make *oneself* **scarce** [ˌmeɪk ~ ˈskeːrs] [话] **溜之大吉** scarce 是"不足以满足需要"

的意思。本条条头直译为"使自己变得稀少",也就是"使别人不容易找到"。*Oh, oh. Here comes Jack, and I haven't got the money I promised I'd pay him back today. Excuse me. I think I'll make myself scarce.* 哎呀,杰克来啦。我答应今天还他钱,可是我还没弄到。对不起。我还是溜走为好。如这一例句所示,这一表达法总是含有"在这里不相宜"的意味。*Whenever I have friends in for tea, my husband makes himself scarce.* 每当我约几个朋友前来喝茶的时候,我的丈夫就悄悄溜走。*Here comes the boss. He's still mad at me from yesterday. I'd better make myself scarce.* 老板来啦。他从昨天就对我恼火,现在还没有消气哪。我还是溜走为好。*Louie seems to be making himself scarce around here since he got into trouble with the police last year.* 路易自从去年跟警察发生纠纷以后,似乎就不在这一带露面了。有时用以表示"从最初就不露面"亦即"不出席"的意思。*I think I'll make myself scarce at tonight's meeting.* 我不打算参加今天晚上的会议。*I try to make myself scarce at my wife's tea parties.* 我尽可能不参加我妻子举行的茶会。◇ disappear / absent *oneself*

(as) scarce as hen's teeth → TEETH

scaredy

a scaredy cat [ə ˈske(ː)rdi ˌkæ(ː)t] [话] **胆子小的人** → a ˈscairdy CAT

scene

be a bad scene [ə ˈbæːd ˈsiːn] [话] **最糟糕**

新的表达法,年轻人喜欢使用。bad scene 直译为"坏的场面",有"尽可能不看见为妙的悲惨情景"的意思。一般指"不愉快的事物"。这是从青年人的独特的感觉产生的所谓 feeling language (直觉的语言)。当他们谈到不愉快的事情或讨厌的人的时候,常带有夸张的语调使用这一表达法,相当于汉语俗语中的"最糟糕啦"、"太惨啦"、"太不怎么样啦"、"太没意思啦"、"太无聊啦"等等,使用范围很广。下面举几个情况各自不同的例子,请读者自己体会这一表达法所包含的意味。*That test was a bad scene. I missed every question but one.* 那次考试太惨啦。我只做对一道题,其余的全都错了。在这里是讲"情景太凄惨了"。*Marriage is a bad scene. I'm going to stay a bachelor.* 结婚最糟糕啦。我要保持独身。这是说结婚"只增加累赘,没有幸福可言"。*That country is a bad scene for tourists. Poor transportation, and everything's very expensive.* 对于旅游者来说,那个国家最糟糕啦。交通不便,什么东西都非常贵。以下是应用于人的例子。*Beautiful girls are a bad scene for my money. Give me a nice, steady plain Jane any day.* 在我看来,漂亮的姑娘没有什么意思。我宁愿要一个极普通的、极平凡的女子。这是说跟漂亮姑娘交往"令人感到不快,十分讨厌"。*Better stay away from that guy. He's a bad scene.* 离那个家伙远一点儿好。他这个人太差劲啦。这是说"跟他交往会令人感到不快"。◇ terrible / is to be avoided (by *someone*)

create a scene [ˌkrɪeɪdə ˈsiːn] [口] **大吵大闹** → make a SCENE

make a scene [ˌmeɪkə ˈsiːn] [口] **乱吵乱闹**

直译为"制造场面 (scene)",因此不能用于"在人看不见的地方",只用于"当着他人的面或哭或喊,乱吵乱闹"的场合。请注意:不是"由于高兴而叫嚷"。例如:*Every time he gets drunk he makes a scene.* 这句话的意思不是"他每次喝醉了酒就兴奋得或者高歌,或者呼喊",而是"毫不体面地吵架或骂街",总之,是制造是非。*The children started crying and made a scene in the doctor's office.* 在医院的候诊室里,孩子们又哭又闹。*My wife is the jealous type. If I so much as look at another woman, she starts making a scene.* 我老婆妒忌成性。我只要瞧一下别的女人,她就歇斯底里发作了。*I know you're unhappy, but stop crying. You're making a scene.* 我知道你心里不好受,不过,别哭啦。当着别人的面,太有失体统了。scene 的前边可以加 big, great, tremendous 之类的形容词。*My girl got angry at me and made a big scene in the restaurant last night.* 我的女朋友对我火了，昨天晚上在餐厅里就大嚷大叫起来。动词用 make 时最多，但 create a scene 也是习用语。 *Don't create such a scene. If you want to quarrel, let's go home and do it.* 不要当着别人的面那么乱吵乱闹吧。如果你想吵架的话，咱们回家去吵。也可以只用 scene 这一个词表示"大吵大闹"的意思。 *There was a tremendous scene at the restaurant when the manager asked two drunks to leave and they refused.* 当餐厅经理请两位喝醉的客人离去而他们拒绝走开的时候，这里便出现了喧嚣鼓噪的场面。◇ make a (public) display of emotion [anger] / make people look at *one*

make the scene [ˌmeɪkðə ˈsiːn] [话] **前去、参加** 20 世纪 60 年代初期开始流行的一个比较新的、青年人特别喜欢用的轻松的表达法。这里的 make 与讲 Can you make the party tonight? (今天晚上你能参加社交晚会吗？) 这句话时的 make 相同，是 go to ～ (前去某处) 的意思。the scene 是"场所"或"文娱活动"，往往含有"可能很有兴趣"的意味。但在实际翻译的时候，make 和 the scene 放在一起，在大多的场合，只译作"前去"或"参加"就行了。例如：*Trudy's having a party tonight. You gonna make the scene?* 特鲁迪今天举行社交晚会。你去吗？ *Thousands of kids made the scene at the rock concert.* 有好几千青年人出席了摇滚乐演奏会。scene 前可加修饰语。 *Gonna make the disco scene to-night?* 今天晚上去跳迪斯科吗？make the scene 除"前去"的意思外，还可以用以表示"做"的意思。下一个例句中的 make the scene 应该认为是"去"和"做"二者之间的意思。 *My girl friend wants me to take her to Maxim's, but I don't have the money to make the scene.* 我的女朋友希望我带她到马克西姆餐厅去，但是我没有钱去那里[那样做]。以下是"做"的例子。但在这一场合，一般要把 make the scene 中的 the 改换成指示形容词，作 make that scene，或者是在 scene 的前边加修饰语。 *Smoke marihuana? Not me, friend. I can't make that scene.* 吸大麻？不是我，朋友。我不会干那种事情。 *If only I had some musical talent, I'd try to make the jazz scene.* 如果我有点音乐才能的话，我很想去搞爵士乐。◇ go (to *something* [*someplace*])

scent

throw *someone* **off the scent** (by *doing something*) [ˌθrou ～ ˌɔ(ː)fðə ˈse(ː)nt] [口] **转移视线** throw ～ off 是"使人误解"、"使人迷路"的意思。scent 是动物或人的"遗臭"。 *The deer plunged into the river, throwing the dogs off the scent.* 鹿跳进河里，使狗无法闻着它的遗臭跟踪了。本条条头可以象这样按照字面意义使用。 *The murderer threw the police off the scent by leaving another man's lighter at the scene of the crime.* 杀人犯把别人的打火机扔在犯罪现场，转移了警察追踪的目标。 *The trading company hoped to throw the tax office off the scent by listing the bribes as political contributions.* 那家贸易公司在帐面上把贿赂用的钱款写成政治捐献，企图逃避税务署的追查。 *I told my steady that the girl I went to the movies with last night was my cousin, but she didn't believe me. She thought I was just trying to throw her off the scent.* 我告诉我的未婚妻说，昨天晚上跟我一起去看电影的姑娘是我的表妹，可是她不相信我的话。她以为我只是糊弄她罢了。主语也有不是"人"的场合。 *His plausible lies threw us off the scent.* 他那说得真而又真的谎言转移了我们的视线。有时讲 put *someone* off the scent，也有时用 track (人或动物的足迹) 代替 scent，而说 throw [put] *someone* off the track。不论哪一个说法，均可代入上边的各例句。不过，用 scent 也好，用 track 也好，在日常会话中，搭配的动词以 throw 占大多数。◇ mislead *someone*

school

the school of hard knocks [ðə ˌsku(ː)ləv ˈhaːrd ˈnaːks] [口] **严峻的现**

实社会 hard knocks 直译为"沉重的敲击",在这里是"种种痛苦的经验"的意思。本条条头的整个意思为"积累痛苦经验的学校"。这是把严峻的现实社会比喻为一所大学校,很多人是通过这所学校受到锻炼和教育。一般指没有进过学校的人或者只受过义务教育的人而言。*I ain't got a fancy school education. I was educated in the school of hard knocks.* 我没有受过什么正式学校教育。我是在充满艰难困苦的社会中锻炼出来的。*On this job, an education from the school of hard knocks is often more valuable than a college degree.* 干这个工作,社会锻炼往往要比大学学位更有实用价值。*In my grandfather's time, few people went past the third or fourth grade. All other learning came from the school of hard knocks.* 在我祖父的时代,很少人念到小学三、四年级。其他的一切知识都是从社会这所大学校中学来的。有时省略 the school of, 只用 hard knocks 表示"痛苦的经验"。 *Jed has taken many hard knocks during his life.* 杰德在人生的道路上备尝艰苦与辛酸。◇ the hard experiences of life ((in→by))

tell tales out of school → TALES

sci

poli sci → POLI SCI

scold

scold *someone* (for *something*) [ˈskould ~] [口] **叱责** scold 是"申斥"、"叱责"、"责备"的意思,但使用范围比这些汉语词语狭窄,只用于"大人对孩子以严厉管教的口气申斥"的场合。主要是在父母或老师教训孩子的时候使用,但在主从关系十分明确的场合 (如饲养者对猫、狗等,或者主人对仆人) 也有使用的情况。如果是机关、公司等单位内的上下级关系,决不使用这个词。假如都是成年人,在叱责对方的场合,一般用 reprimand [ˈreprəˌmæ(ː)nd] *someone*, 如说: *The boss reprimanded me for being late.* 由于迟到,老板批评了我一顿。常用的轻松说法有 CHEW *someone* out 和 bawl *someone* out。 *The mother scolded her son for playing in the mud.* 母亲叱责她的儿子在泥里玩耍。*The students were scolded by the teacher.* 学生们受到了教师的叱责。 *Jimmy scolded his dog for wetting the floor.* 吉米呵斥他的狗,因为它在地板上撒尿了。另外,也有这样的说法: *My secretary is always scolding me for not eating lunch.* 我的秘书常常责备我没吃午饭。在这一场合,是把秘书比做自己的母亲,表示"亲密"的意思。也有时用 scold 一词表示"(主要是女性) 哓哓不休"的意思。在这一场合,常用 about *something* 代替 for *something*。例如: *Dona Litsketash is forever scolding her husband about something or other.* 利茨凯塔什太太老是哓哓不休地叱责她的丈夫,不是这样不行,就是那样不对。◇ reprimand *a child, etc.*

score

have a score to pay off [ˌhævə ˈsko(ː)rdə peɪˌɔːf] [话] **有非报不可之仇** → have a SCORE to settle (with *someone*)

have a score to settle (with *someone*) [ˌhævə ˈsko(ː)rdə ˌsedl] [话] **有非报不可之仇** score 原是"分数"的意思,后转义为"帐目"→"欠款"→"宿怨"。同样,settle 也由"付钱"→"还债"的意义转用于比喻,而有"报仇"的意思了。 *I have a score to settle with that guy before I leave.* 在我启程之前,我对那个家伙非报仇不可。 *You've got to stop him! He muttered something about having an old score to settle and rushed out with a gun.* 你快把他拦住!他嘴里叨咕着什么旧仇必报,拿着枪冲出去了。不说 have a score to settle, 而用 settle a score 的形式,也可以表示同样的意思。例如,第一个例句不说 I have a score to settle ~. 而换用 I'm going to settle a score ~,第二个例句 about 以后简化为 settling an old score ~,结果意思一样。但是,按照英语的习惯,一般不说 settle a score, 而说 have a score to settle。另外,score 不是总用单数形式,也可以加上 a few, several, some 等形容词而采取复数形

式。*Where is he? I've got a few scores to settle with him.* 他在哪儿？我跟他有点儿仇，非报不可。有时可以见到下面这样的变形：*Old scores in the West were often settled with guns.* 在美国西部，往往是用枪报仇雪恨的。在以上的例句中，动词全是用的 settle，但有时也用 pay off，而说 have a score to pay off 或者 pay off a score。在这一场合，英语的习惯也是同样：多用前者，而少用后者。但有一点与 settle 不同，即 pay off 的后边不能接 with *someone*。◇ have a wrong [an injury] to avenge

know the score [.nouðə 'sko(:)r] [话] **熟悉情况** 直译为"知道球赛的得分"。换句话说，就是"对比赛的情况或谁胜谁负都清楚了解"。作为比喻使用，则表示"对于情况了如指掌"。the score 的意义要根据上下文来决定，可能为"实际知识"、"事情的前因后果"、"事情的真相"、"一般社会情况"或"内幕"等等，不一而足，在翻译时切勿胶柱鼓瑟，生搬硬套。首先，在下列两个例句中，the score 指的是"实际知识"。*I know Fred's a competent stockbroker, but are you sure he knows the score on commodities as well?* 我知道弗雷德是一个很有能力的股票经纪人，可是你能肯定他同样熟悉商品的情况吗？*Let's get Jed to help us. When it comes to patent rights, he really knows the score.* 让杰德来帮助咱们吧。关于专利权的问题，他实在是精通。在下一例句中，指的是"事情的真相"乃至"前因后果"。*From the bewildered look on Jim's face when he found us together, it was obvious that he didn't know the score.* 当吉姆见到我们两个人在一起的时候，他脸上显出困惑的神情，很显然，他不曾知道事情的真相。在下边的两个例句中，the score 指的是"社会情况或内幕"。*He told me that anyone who thinks he can get rich and stay completely honest just doesn't know the score.* 他对我说，如果有人认为他既有办法发财而又是个十足的君子，那么这人真是对社会情况一窍不通。*You don't have to talk down to me like that. I've been in this world long enough to know the score.* 你不应该以轻蔑的态度对我讲话。我活这么大岁数了，对人情世故是非常熟悉的啊。也常使用 know what the score is 的形式，意思是"对情况非常熟悉"。*You look like a fellow who knows what the score is. How'd you like to make a quick buck?* 看起来，你是一个熟悉社会情况的人。麻麻利利地去搞一笔钱怎么样？◇ have a thorough knowledge (of *something*) / know the situation / know what is going on / know how things work [the world works]

pay off a score [.peɪɔ(:)fə 'sko(:)r] [话] **报仇** → have a SCORE to settle (with *someone*)

settle a score [.sedələ 'sko(:)r] [话] **报仇** → have a SCORE to settle (with *someone*)

Scotch

Scotch tape → TAPE

scot-free

get off scot-free [.gedɔ(:)f 'skɑ(:)tfri:] [口] **无罪释放** 英国在 17 世纪以前征收 scot (市民税)。scot-free 的意思是"不纳市民税也没受到处罚"。在废除 scot 这种税金之后，scot-free 一词仍然保留下来，但与税金脱离关系，只表示"一点儿也没有受到惩罚"的意思。这里的 get off 是"逃脱惩罚"，如果把 scot 换成 punishment，意思就很清楚了。大致可以认为本条习用语是 get off without punishment 的强调说法。*Because of a lack of evidence, the murderer got off scot-free.* 因为证据不足，杀人犯被无罪释放了。*He shouldn't be punished too harshly for his carelessness, but at the same time he shouldn't get off scot-free, either.* 他是由于疏忽而犯错误，对他不应该严厉惩罚，但在同时，也不应该无罪释放。也可以讲 go scot-free。*How come you punish me when my big brother goes scot-free?* 为什么单单处罚我，而让我哥哥逍遥自在哪？let *someone* off [go] scot-free 是"完全赦免，不加惩处"的意思。*Teenagers who break the law shouldn't be let off* *scot-free simply because they are minors.* 十几岁的孩子犯了法,不应该仅以未成年为理由而完全赦免,不加惩处。◇ go completely free / escape punishment completely

go scot-free [ˌgou ˈskɑ(:)tˈfriː] [口] **无罪释放** → get off SCOT-FREE

let *someone* **off scot-free** [ˌlet ～ ˌɔ(:)f ˈskɑ(:)tˈfriː] [口] **完全赦免,不加惩处** → get off SCOT-FREE

Scott

Great Scott! [ˈgreɪt ˈskɑːt] [话] **天哪!** Great God! 的委婉表达法。与用 Holy cow! (→) 代替 Holy Christ! (哎呀,天哪!),用 Good NIGHT.代替 Good God. (天哪,哎呀!)的办法相同。当然,某人在某时某地也可能直接讲 Great God! 或者 Holy Christ!,但是,无论如何,这种表达法过于强烈,难免疏忽大意,在完全不相宜的时间地点冒冒失失说出上帝的名字。 *Great Scott! The house is on fire!* 天哪! 房子失火啦! *Great Scott! You're not wearing that to the dance, are you?* 天哪! 你不会穿那件衣服去跳舞吧,是不是? 有时在吃惊之外,又表示强烈的否定。 *Me? In love with your sister? Great Scott! Where did you ever get that idea?* 你说我爱上了你妹妹? 我的天老爷! 你怎么会产生了这样的想法啊? 也有人用同义语 Great Caesar's ghost! (直译为"伟大凯撒的亡灵"),但有陈腐的感觉。 *Great Caesar's ghost! She's dead!* 天哪! 她死啦! 另外还有 Great balls of fire! (直译为"伟大的火球")的说法。这一表达法有些农村气息,带泥土的味道。 *Great balls of fire! Grandpa's run off with Widow Brown?* 我的老天爷! 爷爷跟布朗寡妇私奔啦! ◇ Oh, no! / You must be joking!

scour

scour the countryside → COUNTRYSIDE

scram

scram [ˈskræːm] [话] **赶紧走开** 原为匪帮、马戏团艺人的隐语。从 20 世纪 20 年代后期开始,由于广播剧的盛行,这一表达法亦为一般群众使用。关于语源,最有力的说法是:这一表达法为 scramble (向前猛冲) 的缩略。意思与 beat it 相同,在以下的例句中均可用 beat it 代换。这是个相当随便的表达法,语气很强。孩子们之间、伙伴之间以及长者对晚辈使用。*I don't know what happened next. As soon as that big dog started barking at us, we scrammed.* 我不知道以后发生了什么事情。当那条大狗开始向我们狂吠的时候,我们便赶紧撒腿跑掉了。如这一例句所示,这一表达法可以在肯定句中使用。但一般用于命令句,例如: *Scram, kid. You're not old enough to be in this bar.* 赶紧走开吧,小家伙。象你那么小的年纪还不能进这个酒吧。 *Scram. I can't play with you now. I've got homework to do.* 快给我走开。我现在不能跟你一起玩,我必须写家庭作业。 *Didn't I tell you to scram? Now go on, beat it.* 我不是叫你走开吗? 现在就走,赶快! 孩子们特别喜欢用 pig LATIN 的方式将 scram 说成 amscray [ˈæ(:)mˌskreɪ]。不过,在这一场合,用命令式居多。 *Amscray! We're too busy to play with a little kid like you.* 赶紧走开! 我们很忙,不能跟你这样的小孩子玩。◇ go away / leave [get out of *someplace*] (in a hurry)

scrape

bow and scrape → BOW

scratch

(start) from scratch [(ˌstɑ(:)rt) frəm ˈskræ(:)tʃ] [口] **从零开始** 这里的 scratch 原为体育比赛用语,意思是"起跑线"、"出发点"。本条条头直译为"从起跑线开始",亦即不是从途中开始。转用作比喻,应用很广,表示"从零开始"的意思。例如,有的人一不靠父母的余荫,二没有资本,白手起家,经过艰苦奋斗当上了公司的总经理。这时就可以象如下的例句一样来讲: *Starting from scratch, Mr. Jones became president of the nation's largest mining company.* 琼斯先生白手起家,成为了全国最大的矿业公司的总经理。*I've never baked a cake* *(starting) from scratch.* 我从来没有自己准备材料制作烤饼。在这一场合，bake a cake (starting) from scratch 的意思为"不用配制好的现成材料，从头到尾都是由自己完成烤饼工作"。*Mr. Smith built this boat (starting) from scratch in only three months.* 史密斯先生只用了三个月的时间就从零开始制造了这只游艇。如以上的例句所示，这一表达法除了在句子前端的场合，一般来讲，start 可有可无。在日常会话中，省略的时候居多。◇ (start) with nothing [from the very beginning]

not up to scratch [nɑˌdʌptə ˈskræ(ː)tʃ] [话] **达不到要求** 这里的 scratch 泛指达到某一水平的"线"，即汉语"够格"的"格"。be not up to 是"达不到"。因此，本条习用语是"不够格"或"不理想"的意思。主要用于否定句或准否定句。*My tennis game isn't up to scratch these days.* 最近几天，我的网球打得很不理想。*The orchestra's performance wasn't quite up to scratch last night.* 昨天晚上管弦乐队的演奏太不理想了。如以上的例句所示，本条大多用于表示"达不到日常的水平"的意思。此外，也有以表示"达不到所期望的水平"或者"达不到别人那样的水平"等意思为重点的场合。*The boss asked me to speak to you. He's worried because your work hasn't been up to scratch recently.* 老板叫我告诉你说，你最近的工作达不到要求，这使他非常着急。动词不仅用 be，有时用 come 或 bring。*I'm afraid we're going to have to give Job's job to someone else. His work just doesn't come up to scratch.* 咱们大概非把乔布的工作交给别人去干不可啦。他干的工作太不合要求了。*If you don't do something to bring your batting up to scratch you may not make the team this year.* 如果你不努力使你的击球技术符合要求，今年也许不能参加球队了。◇ not match *one's* usual [the expected] standard

only a scratch [ˌounliə ˈskræ(ː)tʃ] [口] **只是一点擦伤** 当然可以按照字面意义"擦伤"使用。但是，负有重伤的人为了显示刚强或者为了使对方安心，也常用这一表达法。*The wound looked pretty bad, but he insisted that it was only a scratch.* 伤口看起来相当深，但是他硬说只擦破一点儿皮。又作 just a scratch。◇ not (a) serious (wound)

scratch [ˈskræ(ː)tʃ] [话] **钱** → BREAD

scratch *a horse* **(from the race)** [ˌskrætʃ ～(frəmðə ˈreɪs)] [口] **在赛马中，取消某匹马参赛资格** scratch 本来是"用爪搔"或者"被尖头的东西刺伤"的意思。从这一意义引申，又表示"用笔勾掉名册上的名字"的意味。例如：*The coach scratched three names off the players' roster.* 教练从选手名单上勾掉了三个名字。在赛马的场合，指从参赛马的名单中取消某匹或某几匹马。*The racing commission scratched two horses from the third race.* 赛马委员会从第三场比赛名单中勾消了两匹马的名字。*The famous Citation has been scratched.* 名马"嘉奖"被从参赛名单中勾掉了名字。如这一例句所示，大多用被动语态。◇ remove a horse (from the race)

scratch around for *something* [ˌskrætʃə ˈraund fər ～] [口] **到处搜索** scratch 是"乱翻"。around 是"在……各处"。for 是"寻求……"。这一表达法令人联想到鸡在地面上到处寻食的样子。*He scratched around in his drawer for a pen.* 他为找一支钢笔在桌子抽屉里乱翻。*The police are still scratching around for evidence.* 警察仍然在到处搜寻证据。*I've been scratching around for a job for over a month.* 我到处找工作，已经有一个多月了。◇ look here and there for *something*

a scratch hit → HIT

a scratch sheet [ə ˈskræ(ː)tʃ ˌʃi(ː)t] [口] **赛马快报** → a racing FORM

screw

have a screw loose [ˌhævə ˈskruː ˌluːs] [话] **精神不正常** 直译为"有一个螺钉松了"。但是，如果按照字面意义讲机器上的螺钉松了的时候，一般的词序是 have a loose screw [ˌluːs ˈskruː]。*This heater* *has a loose screw someplace.* 这个加热器上有个地方的螺钉松了。至于 have a screw loose 则主要用作比喻。也就是说,这是把“头脑的机能”比做“机械的结构”的表达法。*You must have a screw loose if you think I'm going to stay up all night to help you study.* 如果你认为我会整夜不睡来帮助你学习,你的精神一定失常啦。*Everyone thought da Vinci had a screw loose when he claimed that man could fly.* 当达·芬奇说人类能够在空中飞翔的时候,大家全都以为他精神失常了。如以上例句中的 if ～或 when ～那样,这一表达法在使用时大多伴有示明某种条件或状况的从句。◇ be mentally unbalanced

screws

put the screws on *someone* [ˌputðə ˈskruːzɔ(ː)n ～] [话] **施加压力** 这里的 screws 来源于旧时的刑具 thumb screws。这种刑具称为“拇指夹”,是把拇指夹在两条木板中间,然后用螺丝(screw)徐徐拧紧。也就是说, put the screws on *someone* 原来是“用拇指夹进行逼供”的意思。在英国,又作 apply the screws to *someone*。在作“施加压力”解释时,从“强求”到“非法威胁”,其内容的幅度很大。*America and Europe decided to put the screws on Japan to get her to "voluntarily" reduce automobile exports.* 美国和欧洲决定施加压力,要日本“自动”减少汽车的出口。*I know he's lying. Someone must be putting the screws on him.* 我知道他是在说谎。肯定有人对他施加压力了。*The cops are putting the screws on me to tell who did it.* 警察在对我施加压力,叫我招供是谁干的那件事。*Loan sharks often use gangsters to put the screws on people who do not meet their payment deadlines.* 高利贷者常利用流氓对不按期还钱的人们进行威胁。◇ put pressure on *someone*

tighten the screws (on *someone* [*something*]) [ˌtaɪtnðə ˈskruːz] [话] **加强控制** 直译为“拧紧螺丝”。这是由 put the SCREWS on *someone* (→) 发展而来的表达法。*If he won't cooperate, we'll just have to tighten the screws a bit.* 如果他不合作,咱们必须加强一些控制。*The new road-traffic law is designed to tighten the screws on drunken driving.* 新公路交通法的宗旨是对酒后开车加强控制。*Management tried to tighten the screws on the union by refusing to let it hold meetings on company property.* 资方不许工会利用公司的设施开会,以加强对工会的控制。*The government has begun tightening the screws on doctors who overcharge patients insured under the national health plan.* 政府开始对那些为参加国民健康保险的病人多开医药费的医师加强控制。screws 的前边可以加形容词。*Many people are for tightening the commercial screws on South Africa because of its apartheid policy.* 许多人都拥护对实行种族隔离政策的南非当局实行经济制裁。另外有 give another turn of the screw 或者 give the screw another turn 的说法,但这都是从 tighten the screws 演变而来,意思相同,使用频率较低。◇ increase the pressure / put increased pressure on *someone* / tighten restrictions on *something* [*someone*]

sea

be (all) at sea [(ˌɔ(ː)l) ətˈsiː] [口] **如堕五里雾中** at sea 是“在海里”或“航行中”的意思,如说: *The ship is at sea.* 船在海上航行。由于想到“大海茫茫无际,没有任何路标”,所以在作为比喻使用的时候,就具有“不知往哪边走,不知如何是好”的意味,用成语来说,就是“如堕五里雾中”。不过,at sea 极少单独使用,一般用 all 或 completely (完全), plainly 或 obviously (显然), hopelessly (无望) 等副词修饰,其中具有代表性的是 all。*I was all at sea as to how to run the sales campaign for our new product.* 关于怎样展开推销我厂新产品的活动,我好象堕入五里雾中,摸不到一点门路。*He has expert technique in the scientific laboratory, but when it comes to even the simplest cooking he is hopelessly at sea.* 他在

科学实验室里有专门技术，但是一进厨房，哪怕是最简单的菜，他也茫茫然不知所措。也常使用比较级。*After hearing such a strange explanation, I was more at sea than ever.* 听了那么古里古怪的说明，我更如堕五里雾中了。◇ be (completely) lost [mystified]

between the devil and the deep blue sea → DEVIL

seams

come apart at the seams [ˌkʌməˌpɑrdətðə ˈsiːmz] [话] **崩溃** come apart 是"破碎"，at the seams 是"在各接合处"的意思。本来是对衣服之类使用的表达法，意思是"到处都开了线，已经破烂不堪"，带有"完全无法修补"或"不可救药"的意味。*This old coat is coming apart at the seams.* 这件旧外衣到处开线，已经穿不得了。转作比喻使用。*When the president died, the company began to come apart at the seams.* 总经理一死，那个公司就开始垮台了。*If inflation and unemployment get much higher, the whole country will begin to come apart at the seams.* 如果通货膨胀率和失业率继续增长，整个国家就要开始崩溃了。这一表达法也可以应用于人。*After his wife died, he just seemed to come apart at the seams. He quit his job and started drinking heavily. He finally ended up in a mental hospital.* 自从他的妻子死了以后，他就好象失魂落魄了似的。工作不干了，开始酗酒，最后进了精神病院。除了 come apart at the seams 外，还有 fall apart at the seams 的说法。fall apart 有"哗拉哗拉直往下掉"的意味。两个表达法意思都是"崩溃"，但是速度不一样。前者是"徐徐地"、"一点一点地"，而后者是"一下子垮下去"、"眼看着塌了"。*After playing well for the first four innings, our team just fell apart at the seams.* 我们球队在前四个回合打得很漂亮，但是后来完全垮下去了。◇ break down / unravel

Search

Search me. [ˈsə(ː)rtʃ ˈmiː] [话] **我不明白** 直译为"找我！"这种说法有点令人莫明其妙。最初的构思是："你不理解，可以来找我；但是，即便找我，我也回答不出来。"也就是汉语里常说的"你问我，我问谁去？"的意思。在日常会话中，当人家问 WHAT'S up? WHAT gives? WHAT'S cooking? 等的时候，往往很简单地回答一句 Search me. *A: Look at that crowd over there. I wonder what's up. B: Search me. Maybe it's an accident.* 甲：你看那边围了一大帮人，不知出什么事啦。乙：不晓得，可能发生事故了。*A: Why is Mary so mad? B: Search me.* 甲：为什么玛丽那么生气？乙：我不知道。Don't ask me. [ˈdouˌnæ(ː)skˈmiː] 与本条习用语大致相同。*A: What gives? B: Don't ask me. I just got here.* 甲：怎么回事？乙：不晓得。我刚来到这里。◇ I don't know.

seat

by the seat of *one's* pants [baɪðə ˌsiːdəv ～ˈpæːnts] [话] **凭着经验(办事)** 直译为"根据某人裤子的屁股部分"。原来的形式是 fly by the seat of *one's* pants，意思为：当飞机在驾驶中表盘失效的时候，根据自己的"臀部的稳定感觉来驾驶"，也就是"凭着经验驾驶"。现在也有按字面意义使用的场合，例如：*In the old days, a pilot had to fly by the seat of his pants.* 在老早以前，飞行员必须凭着自己的经验进行驾驶。此外，广泛用于"凭着经验办事或行动"的场合。*Without market data, a sales manager has to operate by the seat of his pants.* 在没有市场数据的情况下，销售经理只能凭着自己的经验进行交易。*A national leader needs many sources of information. He can't run a country just by the seat of his pants.* 一个国家的领导人需要很多的信息来源。他不能只凭自己的经验管理国家。◇ by (depending on *one's*) intuition

take a back seat (to *someone*) [ˌteɪkə ˈbæ(ː)k ˈsiːt] [口] **居于人下** 最初的构思是："把好的席位让给别人，自己坐到后边的位子"。本条的意思为"居于人下"或"让人一步"，既有本人主动谦让的场合，也有被迫退后的场合。只能用于比喻。如果照字面意义“坐到他人后边的席位”来讲，英语要用 take a seat behind *someone* [*something*]，例如：*I took a seat behind Mrs. Smith.* 我坐到史密斯夫人后边的座位上了。以下为本条习用语的例子。*Recently there has been an increase in the number of women who are no longer satisfied to take a back seat to their husbands.* 最近，不甘居于丈夫之下的妇女的人数增多了。*If I enter the office, it must be as a full partner. I will not take a back seat to anyone.* 如果叫我参加这个公司，必须是作为有充分权利的合伙人。我可不能居于任何人的下边。如以上的例句所示，在谈到地位、身份或者长期的职务时，大多用否定句。在一时之间对下级或同事“让一步”的场合，则大多用肯定句。*You take the initiative in these negotiations. I'll take a back seat this time.* 在这次谈判中，你采取主动吧。这回我退下一步。*Why do I always have to take a back seat to that guy?* 为什么我老是要让那个家伙一步呢？在讲才能或能力的差距时，也使用这一表达法。*As a salesman he doesn't have to take a back seat to anyone.* 作为一个推销员，他不比任何人逊色。◇ accept a lower position (than *someone*)

sec

a sec [ə ˈse(:)k] [俗] **一会儿** sec 为 second (一秒)的缩略，但比 second 的使用范围窄，不能当作表示时间单位的“一秒”使用。这一表达法只能作为副词使用，常在叫别人等待的场合说 Wait a sec. (等一会儿。) 通常用单数形式，以 just (有时为 only) 调整语调。*I'll be with you in just a sec.* 等一小会儿我就跟你走。*A: Ready yet? B: Just a sec.* 甲：还没准备好吗？乙：只一小会儿就行啦。在以上各例句中，所有的 sec 均可用 second 代换。◇ a moment

second

get *one's* **second wind** → WIND

give *someone* **second thoughts** (about *something*) [ˌgɪv ~ ˌsekənd ˈθɔːts] [口] **使某人重新考虑** → have second THOUGHTS (about *something*)

have second thoughts (about *something*) → THOUGHTS

on second thought [ɔ(:)n ˈsekənd ˌθɔ(:)t] [口] **(经重新考虑后)仍然** → have second THOUGHTS (about *something*)

play second fiddle to *someone* [*something*] → FIDDLE

secret

an open secret [ə ˈnoupən ˈsiːkrət] [口] **公开的秘密** 这里的 open 原是“没有房顶、墙壁等遮挡的东西，暴露于大自然的”之意，转义为“暴露于社会的”亦即“公开的”。*It's an open secret that the two are planning to get married.* 他们俩计划结婚的事儿已经是公开的秘密了。◇ a well-known “secret”

see

Long time no see. → TIME

sees

if *one* **never sees** *someone* **again it'll be too soon** [ɪf ~ ˌnevər ˈsiːz ~ əˈgen ˌɪdl ˌbi(:) ˈtuː ˈsuːn] [话] **永远不想再见到他** 直译为“如果永远再见不到他，也觉得相见太快了”，这是强调 *one* never wants to see *someone* again 的意思的表达法。*You tell that guy that if I never see him again it'll be too soon.* 你告诉那小子，我再也不想见到他了。*Alfonso's accounting was so loose that he almost caused the company to go bankrupt. The president says that if he never sees him again it'll be too soon.* 阿方索的核算太马虎，几乎使公司破产。总经理说再也不想见到他啦。有时用 meet(s) 代替 see(s)。◇ *one* doesn't want to see *someone* ever again

sell

sell *someone* **down the river** → RIVER

send

send *someone* **up** [ˌsend ~ ˈʌ(:)p] [话] **投入监狱** → send *someone* up the RIVER

sense

talk sense [ˌtɔ(ː)k ˈse(ː)n*ts*] [口] **说话合情合理** 这里的 sense 为名词，意思是“合情合理的事情”。 *He isn't talking sense. He must be under the influence of a drug or something.* 他说话杂乱无章。他一定是吸毒或者吃了什么药啦。在这句话里，“杂乱无章”指的不是“说话没有次序”，而是“说话的内容不合情理”。*Talk sense! You're so excited I can't understand what you're saying.* 有条有理地讲！你过于兴奋，我听不懂你说的是什么事情。*A: If you won't sell it to me for a hundred dollars, how about two hundred? B: Now you're starting to talk sense.* 甲：如果你一百美元不卖，我给你二百美元怎么样？乙：现在你给的价才表明你有点打算卖的意思啦。反义语为 talk nonsense (说没有意义的话)，与汉语俗语的“胡扯”、“瞎说八道”、“讲废话”等大致相同。*You're talking nonsense. You can't buy a house today for five thousand yuan.* 你竟讲废话。现在拿五千块钱就买不了一所房子。◇ talk rationally [reasonably]

talk sense into *someone* [ˌtɔ(ː)k ˈsen*ts*ˌɪntə ~] [口] **开导** sense 的意思是“道理”、“合情合理的事情”。本条条头直译为“把道理给某人灌输进去”。*Send him to me. I'll talk sense into him.* 叫他到我这里来。我开导开导他。常常加 some (一些) 或 a little (一点儿) 调整语调，但对意义没什么影响。*I've tried to talk some sense into my son, but he still insists on quitting his job.* 我对儿子进行了说服教育，可是他仍然坚持辞掉工作。*Jack just won't listen to reason. See if you can talk a little sense into him.* 我跟杰克讲道理，他根本就不听。你开导他一下试试。◇ persuade *someone* to act rationally [reasonably]

serve

serve *someone* **right** [ˌsə(ː)rv ~ ˈraɪt] [口] **自作自受** serve 是“报应”，right 是“正当地”。这一表达法在某人发生不好的事情的时候使用，表示“理所当然”、“自作自受”的意思。根据上下文，也可能有“活该！”的意思。*It's too bad you caught cold, but it serves you right for going out without a coat on.* 你伤风了，真太不幸啦。不过，你出去的时候不穿外衣，这也是自作自受啊。*I'm out ten dollars, but it serves me right. I should have known better than to lend money to a stranger.* 我损失了十美元。不过，这是自作自受。我应该知道不能把钱借给一个陌生人。*That was a terrible thing for her to do to Jim. It'll serve her right if he never speaks to her again.* 她对吉姆干出那种事，实在太糟糕了。如果吉姆永远不再跟她讲话，这也是理所当然的。*A: Ow! You stepped on my foot! B: Serves you right. You're always pushing people.* 甲：喔唷，好疼！你踩着我的脚啦！乙：那才活该哪！你经常推人嘛。◇ be proper retribution

service

pay lip service to *something* [*someone*] [ˌpeɪ ˈlɪp ˌsəːrvəstə ~] [口] **口头表示敬意** pay service to *someone* 古时是“为某人服务”的意思，现在是“怀着尊敬、感激的心情认可”的意思。lip 是“口头的”。lip 的这一用法来自《圣经》。在《圣经·新约》中的《马太福音》(Matthew)第 15 章 8 节有这样一句话：This people honors me with their lips, but their heart is far from me. (这百姓用嘴唇尊敬我，心却远离我。)本条条头可以单独使用，例如：*That teacher pays lip service to the idea of Spartan education, but in reality he is very lenient with his students.* 那位老师口头上信奉斯巴达式的教育思想，但是在实际上，他对自己的学生非常温和。在大多的场合，把 only, little more than 等加到 lip service 的前边调整语调。*The president suspects that some members of the board are paying him only lip service while actually plotting to take over the company.* 董事长感觉到有几名董事只是口头上对他表示敬意，实际上正阴谋夺取公司的权力。有时用动词 give 代替 pay。*Many so-called statesmen appear to pay [give] little more than lip service to the ideals of de-*

mocracy. 许多所谓的政治家只不过是在口头上尊崇民主主义的理想而已。◇ support *something* [*someone*] (only) verbally / give *something* [*someone*] (only) superficial support [backing]

a service station [ə ˈsəːrvəs ˌsteɪʃən] [口] **加油站** → a filling STATION

sesame

an open sesame (to *something*) [ə ˌnoupən ˈsesəmi] [口] **法宝** sesame 是"芝麻"。Open sesame! 是《天方夜谈》中所写的开门咒的咒文。这一表达法具有"实现梦想的法宝"的意味。*His experience plus his skill in foreign languages proved to be an open sesame to almost any job he desired*. 他的丰富经验,再加上精通几种外国语,这些变成了一件法宝,使他想干什么工作几乎就能得到什么工作。*Jack's friendship with the President was an open sesame which gained him many important contacts in the world of big business*. 杰克与总统的友谊是一件法宝,使他能与各大财团发生千丝万缕的联系。*A college education is no longer an open sesame to a successful career*. 大学教育已经不是飞黄腾达的法宝了。an 有时改用 the。*My connections were not the open sesame I thought they would be*. 原来以为我走的后门很硬,结果并不是件法宝。◇ a key (which opens the door to *something*)

session

a brainstorming session [ə ˈbreɪnˌstɔrmɪŋ ˌseʃən] [口] **集体自由讨论** session 是 meeting (会议)的意思。为了解决困难问题或者提出新的方案而召开的会,当场各抒已见,不加评论,汇总到一起,会后再仔细研究。 brainstorming 一词可以单独使用,例如说:*I took a class in college that taught brainstorming*. 我在大学里选修了一门讲授集体自由讨论的课程。但一般与 session 搭配使用。*Our department had a brainstorming session yesterday to try to come up with some new marketing ideas*. 我们部门昨天开献策会,探讨了一些市场销售的新方法。*We have solved many of our problems through regular brainstorming sessions*. 我们通过定期的集体自由讨论,已经解决了许多问题。◇ a free-for-all idea session

a rap session [ə ˈræ(ː)p ˌseʃən] [口] **谈心会** → RAP (with *someone*)

set

a set of threads → THREADS

set *someone* **straight** (on *something*) → STRAIGHT

seven

be on cloud seven [ɔ(ː)ŋˈklaudˈsevən] [口] **极为幸福** → be on CLOUD nine

seventh

be in seventh heaven → HEAVEN

sex

the fair sex [ðə ˈfeːr ˈseks] [口] **女性** 集合名词。这里的 fair 不是"公平的"而是"美丽的"的意思。*Where would the world be without the fair sex?* 如果没有女性,这个世界不知会成为什么样子啦? → the weaker SEX ◇ women

the weaker sex [ðə ˈwi(ː)kər ˌseks] [口] **女性** 集合名词。直译为"比较软弱的性"。在妇女解放运动 (women's lib)风起云涌的今天,这是一个不得人心的表达法。*We men must learn to respect the rights of the weaker sex*. 我们男子应该懂得尊重女性的权利。在英语中,即使讲这类的话,由于 weaker 一词的存在,也不会收到良好的效果。为了保险起见,还是使用 the fair SEX (→) 一语为妙。◇ women

Shaddap

Shaddap! [ˌʃæˈdæ(ː)p] [俗] **住嘴!** 将 Shut up. [ˈʃʌˈdʌ(ː)p]一语按照美国北部人的发音直接拼写而成的表达法。常见于漫画和通俗小说。*Shaddap! I'm sick and tired of your complaining*. 住嘴吧! 我对你的满腹牢骚已经腻味透啦。◇ Be quiet!

shadow

a five o'clock shadow [ə ˌfaɪvəˌklɑk

ˈʃæ(ː)də] [话] **早上刮过到傍晚又长出来的短须** 直译为"下午五点钟的阴影",意思是早上刮得很仔细的胡子,到了下午五点钟 (five o′clock) 又象一片阴影 (shadow) 似地冒了出来。这一表达法最初见于销售刮脸肥皂的广告:"请君使用此种肥皂,保证不出 five o′clock shadow"。由于广告渗透各个阶层,这一表达法也成为一般用语了。*I'll have to shave my five o'clock shadow before I go out tonight.* 早晨刮的脸,现在胡子又冒头了。我今天晚上出去之前必须再刮一遍。虽然这一表达法用的是 five o′clock,但并不拘泥于"五点钟",主要是讲胡须的浓度看起来已经象一片阴影了。因此,胡须特浓的人在当天下午二时左右、胡须很稀的人在第二天早晨,全部都可以说 I have a five o′clock shadow。◇ a thin stubble of whiskers

shadow *someone* [ˈʃæ(ː)do ～] [口] **盯梢** 意思是"象影子 (shadow) 一样紧跟在别人屁股后面走"。*The investigator shadowed the suspect continuously for three days.* 侦探一连三天跟踪那个嫌疑犯。have *someone* shadowed 是"使人被盯梢"。*Mrs. Smith had her husband shadowed by a private eye.* 史密斯太太雇一名私人侦探盯她丈夫的梢。另外,也可以把作"尾巴"解的 tail 当动词用,而讲 tail *someone*, have *someone* tailed, 这与汉语的"尾随"、"派人尾随"的构思完全一致。◇ (secretly) follow *someone*

shake

give *someone* **the shake** [ˌgɪv ～ðəˈʃeɪk] [话] **乘机逃走** → give *someone* the SLIP

in a shake [ɪnə ˈʃeɪk] [话] **立刻** → in two SHAKES of a lamb′s tail

in half a shake [ɪnˈhæ(ː)fə ˈʃeɪk] [话] **马上** →in two SHAKES of a lamb′s tail

shake *someone* [ˈʃeɪk ～] [话] **甩掉(某人)** → give *someone* the SLIP

shakes

in two shakes [ˌɪnˈtuː ˈʃeɪks] [话] **立即** → in two SHAKES of a lamb′s tail

in two shakes of a lamb's tail [ˌɪnˈtuː ˈʃeɪksəvə ˈlæːmz ˌteɪl] [话] **马上** 观察一下羔羊尾巴摇动的方式,可以看出:不知什么原因,它决不摇摆一次,必定连着摇摆两次。而且,在摇动的时候速度非常快,连一秒钟都不到。因此,自古以来就用"在羔羊尾巴两次摇动之内"这句话表示"立即"、"马上"的意思。本条习用语大多是在有人等待自己的时候,特别是在由于自己手头工作放不下而要请对方稍等片刻的时候使用。几乎只能放在将来时的句子中。*Just a sec. I'll be with you in two shakes of a lamb's tail.* 稍等一会儿,我马上跟你一块走。*Can you wait just a minute? I'll be finished here in two shakes of a lamb's tail.* 你能稍等一下吗?我的活儿马上就完啦。有时省掉 of a lamb′s tail, 只说 in two shakes。例如:*He said he'd be down in two shakes.* 他说他马上就下楼来。如果更加夸大,也可以说 in a shake (在尾巴一摆的瞬间)或者 in half a shake (在尾巴半摆的刹那),基本意味与本条条头一样。◇ (very) soon

be no great shakes [ˌnou ˈgreɪt ˈʃeɪks] [话] **并不出色** shake 是"摇"。有人认为这一表达法原来的意思是"你摇骰子,也不出好点儿",这一说法正确与否不详。主要在评论能力、工作、作品等的质量、程度、内容的时候使用,也有时为谦逊之词。*A: How do you like your new job? B: It's no great shakes, but the pay is pretty good.* 甲:你的新工作怎么样?乙:工作不怎么样,不过工资比较高。*The President is no great shakes as a speaker, but he is completely honest.* 总统的演说口才并不出色,不过他是非常坦率的。*Jim's a fairly good piano player, but he's no great shakes.* 吉姆钢琴弹得很不错,但是并没有太大的了不起。*I'm afraid I'm no great shakes as a poet.* 我作为诗人,恐怕没有什么惊人之处。◇ be not all that outstanding

shame

hang *one's* **head in shame** → HEAD

share

the lion′s share [ðə ˈlaɪənz ˈʃeːr] [口] **最大的一份** 出典《伊索寓言》(*Aesop's*

Fables)。狮子、狐狸、驴共同弄死了一个动物,把它分成了四份。这时狮子说:"我出的主意,所以分四分之一;我是最勇敢的,所以又分四分之一;我是最有力量的,所以再分四分之一。剩下四分之一,你们俩分吧。不过,你们不要忘了,我虽然吃四分之三,肚子还不饱呀!"根据语源来考虑,这"最大的一份"可以说是"不正当的",但是根据上下文,这一表达法本身并没有"不正当"的意味。*Sam did most of the work. We should let him have the lion's share of the profits.* 萨姆干了工作的大部分。我们分所赚的钱,应该给他最大的一份啊。*My big brother is extremely fat. He always eats the lion's share of every meal at our house.* 我哥哥非常胖。在我们家里,每顿饭他都吃得最多。对于实际上并不能分割的抽象概念,如"名誉"、"爱情"等,也考虑全体与部分的对比,而使用这一表达法。*Mary is a beautiful girl. She always gets the lion's share of the attention at every dance.* 玛丽是一位美丽的姑娘。在每一次的跳舞会上,她总是最受人们的恭维奉承。◇ the greatest part

sharp

(as) sharp as a tack → TACK

shave

have a close shave [.hævə .klo'ʃ:eɪv] [话] **幸免于难** close 的意思是"险些",这里指"剃刀的刀刃险些划破皮肤"。shave 是"刮脸"。*This razor is too dull. It doesn't give me a close [clean] shave.* 这把剃刀太钝了,刮脸刮不干净。转作比喻使用,表示"险些遭难"的意思。有时可以译作"死里逃生"、"九死一生"等等。*As a soldier, I had many close shaves during the war.* 我当兵的时候,在战争期间有许多次是死里逃生。*I had a close shave on the plane yesterday. The man sitting next to me came down with food poisoning just before I started to eat.* 昨天我在飞机里幸免于难。当我刚要开始就餐的时候,邻座的男子食物中毒了。如以上的例句所示,close shave 作为动词 have 的宾语使用的场合最多。但也有如下的用法:*That was a close shave. You almost hit that car.* 真是太危险啦。你几乎撞到那辆汽车上。*Talk about a close shave! I almost ran into the boss as I was coming out of the ball park this afternoon.* 甭提多么危险啦!今天下午我正从棒球场出来的时候,差一点没跟老板撞个满怀。*Close shaves are a part of a professional spy's job.* 冒生死危险是职业间谍的工作的一部分内容。*Race drivers have to take close shaves in stride.* 赛车选手必须去冒险。另外,也有时用 call 代替 shave,而讲 have [be] a close call。call 是"体育比赛中裁判员进行判决"的意思。又有用 narrow 代替 close 的表达法 have a narrow shave,这是英国英语,在美国几乎完全不用。不过,美国倒可以讲 have [be] a narrow squeak ['skwi:k],这一表达法相当轻松,一般不用于人命关天的重大事情,而用于事情不很严重的场合。*I had a narrow squeak last night. My steady almost saw me out with another girl.* 昨天晚上真好险啊。我跟另外一个姑娘出去玩,差一点儿没叫我的未婚妻碰上。又,squeak 为象声词,如老鼠叫的吱吱声,东西相挤的轧轹声等,在上一个例句中,也使人感到把一种东西从极狭窄的地方拔出时的磨擦声。◇ have a narrow escape

shaver

a little shaver [ə .lɪdl 'ʃeɪvər] [话] **男孩子** 指 3–10 岁左右的小男孩。a shaver 是"刮胡子的人",古时作"骗子"解,因为这种人"刮掉 (shave off) 别人的钱"。后来此词失去坏的意味,只表示"家伙"、"男子"之类的意思。现在,在某些地方的方言中还残存着这样的用法,但是一般来讲,little shaver (有时作 young shaver) 则仅表示"小宝宝"、"小小子"、"小男孩"的意思了。*There were lots of cute little shavers playing on the school ground.* 有许多可爱的小男孩正在校园里玩耍。*Hello, little shaver. How're you?* 喂,小宝宝,你好啊?如这一例句所示,这一表达法常在对不知叫什么名字的小男孩讲话

时使用。◇ a little boy

sheep

the black sheep of the family [ðə ˈblæ(:)k ˈʃi:pəðə ˌfæməli] [口] **有辱门楣的人** 这一表达法来源于谚语 There is a black sheep in every flock. (群群羊里有黑羊。) 现在,人们很少使用这一谚语的原形,一般是把 flock 换成 family,而讲 There is a black sheep in every family. (家家都有抹黑人。) black sheep (黑绵羊)为什么成为"有辱门楣的人"呢? 原因是这样:第一,黑绵羊的毛不值钱;第二,它的黑颜色使其他的羊害怕。因此,自古以来,人们就认为黑绵羊是给羊群添麻烦的东西。这一表达法在使用时,多半含有不好的意味。*Jimmy is the black sheep of the family. He never studies and often plays hooky.* 吉米是一个给全家抹黑的人。他根本不学习,而且常常逃学。the family 除指一个家庭,也有指"一族"、"一姓"以及俱乐部之类的团体的场合。of the family 有种种不同的形式,如 of *someone's* family, of that family, of the ~ family 等。*Uncle Ned was always considered the black sheep of our family. He refused to go to college or to enter Grandfather's company. He finally ran off to Australia and become a sheep rancher.* 内德伯伯总被认为是给我们家丢脸的人。他不肯上大学,也不进祖父的公司任职。结果,他跑到澳大利亚放羊去了。*Many people still consider Edward VIII, the only English king to ever abdicate voluntarily, to have been the black sheep of the House of Windsor.* 许多人至今仍然认为英国唯一自动逊位的国王爱德华八世是有辱温莎王室门楣的人。本条有时省略 of the family,但在这一场合,一般要把 the black sheep 改为 a black sheep。*Louis was a black sheep, always getting into trouble in the neighborhood.* 路易斯很不叫家里省心,总在附近惹事生非。*I guess every club has at least one black sheep. Kelvin's ours. He often does things that disrupt the group's activities.* 我看,每个俱乐部至少有一个丢人现眼的家伙。我们俱乐部里有凯尔文,他经常破坏集体的活动。◇ the disgrace [undesirable member] of the family

separate the sheep from the goats [ˈsepəˌreɪt ðə ˈʃi(:)p frəmðə ˈgouts] [口] **区分有能之士与无能之辈** 这一表达法的出典是《圣经·新约》中的《马太福音》(Matthew)第 25 章 32 节: Before him will be gathered all the nations, and he will separate them one from another as a shepherd separates the sheep from the goats, and he will place the sheep at his right hand, but the goats at the left. (万民都要聚集在他面前;他要把他们分别出来,好象牧羊的分别绵羊山羊一般;把绵羊安置在右边,山羊在左边。)《圣经》的意思是"区别善人与恶人",现在也常这样用,例如: *I know all politicians are not dishonest, but it's difficult to separate the sheep from the goats.* 我知道不是所有的政治家都不正直,但是善恶难分啊。但是,一般的倾向是:大多用于表示"区别有能者与无能者"的意味。经常以"人"为对象。在把"思考"、"方法"等当作对象的场合,使用 separate the WHEAT from the chaff。*The purpose of our company's trial employment period is to separate the sheep from the goats.* 我们公司规定的试用阶段,目的在于区分能够胜任工作和不能胜任工作的人。*So many young people are graduating from college these days that it's difficult to separate the sheep from the goats.* 最近从大学毕业的青年人太多了,很难区分哪一些人真有用处。◇ separate the good [qualified] (people) from the bad [unqualified]

sheep's

a wolf in sheep's clothing → WOLF

sheepskin

get *one's* sheepskin [ˌget ~ˈʃi(:)pˌskɪn] [话] **大学毕业** 直译为"得到羊皮"。由于大学毕业证书(diploma)常用羊皮纸制成,所以 sheepskin 便成为 diploma 的同义词。这是一个轻松的表达法,如说:

Show me your sheepskin. 给我看看你的毕业证书。不过，大多是用 get *one's* sheepskin 的形式，表示"毕业"的意思。*That guy's smart. It took him only three years to get his sheepskin.* 那家伙头脑聪明，只念三年就从大学毕业了。◇ graduate (from college)

sheet

a dope sheet [ə 'doup.ʃi(:)t] [话] **赛马快报** → a racing FORM

a scratch sheet [ə 'skræ(:)tʃ .ʃi(:)t] [口] **赛马快报** → a racing FORM

a spec sheet [ə 'spek .ʃi:t] [话] **产品说明书** a specification sheet [.spesəfə'keɪʃən .ʃi:t] 的缩略。sheet 是"一张纸"。在这一场合，即使是用了几张纸，一般也用单数，因为是一种产品的说明书。*Have you got a spec sheet for the new machine?* 你有新机器的说明书吗？◇ a specification sheet

(as) white as a sheet [əz 'hwaɪdəzə 'ʃi:t] [话] **脸色象白纸一样** 指由于震惊、疾病、恐怖等而面色苍白的状态。古时，sheet (被单) 必然是白的，所以有这种表达法，一直流传到今天。*What happened? You're white as a sheet.* 怎么啦？你的脸色象白纸一样啊。*Ned hasn't been looking well recently. He's as white as a sheet.* 内德最近的样子不好看，他的脸色象白纸一样。*When Aunt Martha heard the terrible news, she suddenly turned as white as a sheet.* 当马莎姨妈听到这个坏消息的时候，她的脸色突然变得象纸一样白了。美国人认为幽灵的头上常蒙着白单子，所以有时说(as) pale as a ghost。也有时讲 (as) white as a ghost，但一般只限于恐怖的场合，因此，它只能用于上边的第一个例句，如果用于第二和第三个例句就不自然了。另外，一般讲"非常白"的时候，英语用 (as) white as SNOW (雪白)。◇ extremely pale

sheets

three sheets to the wind [.θri: .ʃi:ts təðə 'wɪ(:)nd] [口] **(由于喝酒过多而)晃晃悠悠** 原为海上用语。sheet 是"帆脚索"，即把帆系到船上的绳子。如果这条绳子脱落了，随风飘动(to the wind)，船就会失去安定性，左摇右摆，象醉鬼一样，在海面上直晃悠。假如三条索(three sheets)全都脱落，那就晃悠得更加厉害了。虽然可以按照字面意义使用，但是，除了帆船的水手一般人是决不会讲这种话的。*By the time I left the third bar, I was three sheets to the wind.* 当我走出第三个酒吧间的时候，我的身子已经直晃悠了。*A sailor, three sheets to the wind, was trying to talk to a girl at the next table.* 一个喝得醉醺醺的水手要跟邻桌的女郎搭话。有时可听到 three sheets in the wind 的说法。◇ unsteady on *one's* feet (from too much drink) / drunk

shekels

shekels ['ʃekəlz] [话] **钱** shekel 原为古犹太王国使用的银币名。美国曾用此词作为 silver dollar (一美元银币) 的俗称。但现在已不使用一美元的银币，所以这一俗称便如同废语一样。这一表达法只作为 money 的同义语使用，比 money 轻松一些。请读者注意：它经常用复数形式。*Hey, Rube. Got any shekels on you?* 喂，鲁布，你带着钱吗？*The Browns seem to have a lot of shekels, don't they.* 布朗一家似乎非常有钱，是吧？◇ money

shift

shift for *oneself* [.ʃɪftfər '~] [口] **独立生活** 这是一个定型的说法，意思是"自己照料自己"。同义的表达法有 do *something* for *oneself*，这是指靠自己的力量干一件事情。本条习用语则与此相反，一般指靠自己的力量干各种各样的事情，所指比较广泛。例如说：*Kyle was an orphan who learned to shift for himself at a very early age.* 凯尔原是孤儿，他从很小的时候就能独立生活。*Dick studied Chinese for three years before he was able to shift for himself in Chinese society.* 迪克能够在中国社会中独立生活之前，曾经学习了三年汉语。*I'm not going to take my son into my company as* *soon as he finishes his schooling. I want him to learn to shift for himself first.* 我的儿子从学校出来之后，我不打算马上叫他进我的公司。我希望他先学会独立生活的本领。*We're happy that you like to live with us, son, but don't you think it's about time you got out and learned to shift for yourself?* 儿子，你喜欢跟我们住在一起，我们感到很高兴，但是，你不认为你已经到了出去独立生活的年龄吗？也有象下一例句中极轻松的用法：*I won't be home in time to fix dinner, dear, so you'll have to shift for yourself tonight.* 亲爱的，今天晚上我不能按时回家做晚饭了，你必须自己动手啦。◇ fend for *oneself*

shine

take a shine to *someone* [ˌteɪkə ˈʃaɪntə ~] [话] **一见就中意** 这里的 shine 是"喜好"或"中意"的意味。本条条头是非常轻松的表达法。意思相近的表达法有 take a liking to (喜欢上……)，take a fancy to (忽然迷上……)等，但在英语中，这两种说法的语调比 take a shine to 深重，后者则含有"随时有变"的意味。它们最大的不同点在于：本条习用语用于"一看见马上就喜欢"或者"一见钟情"的场合。可以应用于"人"和"动物"，但极少应用于"物"。 *Looks like Helen has taken a shine to the new boy in our class.* 看起来，海伦对我们班新转来的男生一见钟情啦。*The little girl took a shine to the old man from the first day they met in the park.* 从在公园里相遇的第一天，小女孩就喜欢上那位老人了。 *Don't worry about what kind of blind date you get for George. He seems to take a shine to every girl he meets.* 你不用考虑给乔治安排一个什么样的姑娘与他初次见面为好。他似乎不管什么样的姑娘，一见面就会喜欢上。"动物"与"人"，"动物"与"动物"，在句子里怎样结合全可以。又，shine 也可以加形容词。*The little dog we found took an immediate shine to our son.* 我们弄来的小狗立即喜欢上我们的儿子了。*The problem developed when the neighbor's mongrel took a shine to our pedigreed poodle.* 当邻居的杂种狗跟我家的纯种长卷毛狗一见钟情的时候，麻烦就来了。◇ take a (spontaneous) liking to *someone*

shiner

a shiner [əˈʃaɪnər] [话] **受伤后青肿的黑眼圈** 这是一个轻松的表达法，与 a black eye 同义。 *Boy, you've got a beautiful shiner. Did you have a fight with your wife or something?* 好家伙，你弄了个漂亮的黑眼圈。莫不是跟你太太打起来啦？◇ a black eye

ship

run a taut ship [ˌrʌnə ˈtɔːtˈʃɪ(ː)p] [口] **对部下严格要求** → run a tight SHIP

run a tight ship [ˌrʌnə ˈtaɪtˈʃɪ(ː)p] [口] **对部下要求严格** run 与 operate 相同，是"经营"、"管理"的意思。 tight 指帆船上的帆脚索"绷得很紧"。如果帆脚索松弛了，那就表明船员工作松懈了。因此，run a tight ship 的意思是："船长指挥整条船，使船员们始终保持紧张状态"。这一表达法原为海军用语，现在不但在其他领域，而且在日常生活中，都被人们广泛地作为比喻使用。例如说：*Captain Nemo is a strict commander who runs a tight ship.* 舰长[陆军上尉]尼莫是一个严厉的指挥官，对部下要求严格。这句话可以说是讲的海军，也可以说是讲的陆军，因为 captain 一词有几个释义，没有上下文就不会知道怎样解释是正确的。另外，run a tight ship 的意思虽然是"对部下要求严格"，但并不是经常不断地对部下怒吼，而是在心平气和之中不容许工作松弛或者违反纪律。也就是说，本条具有"不许部下散散漫漫"、"要求部下规规矩矩"的意味。 *There was no wastefulness or goofing off at the White House when Eisenhower was President. As might be expected from an ex-army general, he always ran a tight ship.* 在艾森豪威尔任总统期间，白宫里没有浪费或者怠惰的现象。从他原来是陆军将军这一点可以想象得到，他对部下一向是要求严格的。*You're treated* *fairly in our company, but you're expected to work hard and always be on time. The boss runs a tight ship.* 我们公司给你们的待遇很不错，但是希望你们勤勤恳恳，总能按时上班。老板对部下是严格要求的。有时用 taut (拉紧) 代替 tight，而讲 run a taut ship，但是在一般会话中均用 tight。 *It's the managers who don't run a taut ship that have the most difficulty in meeting deadlines.* 对按期完成任务最感到困难的人，是那些不严格要求部下的经理们。◇ be an exacting leader

shirt

give *someone* **the shirt off** *one's* **back** [ˌgɪv ～ ðə ˈʃə(ː)rˌdɔ(ː)f ～ ˈbæːk] [话] **毫不吝惜地接济别人** off *one's* back 是"从自己的背上"。本条直译为"把身上穿着的衬衫脱下来送给某人"。这是形容"慷慨大方"，但如下面第二个例句那样，常含有"喜欢对方"的积极意味。*Hal is so generous he'd give you the shirt off his back.* 哈尔非常慷慨大方，他能毫不吝惜地接济别人。*You know I'm willing to give you the shirt off my back, but I just don't have any money to spare.* 你知道，我有什么就愿意给你什么，不过，我手头没有一点余钱啊。◇ give *someone* anything *one* has

keep *one's* **shirt on** [ˌki(ː)p ～ ˈʃəːrˌdɔːn] [话] **别着急** 直译为"一直穿着衬衣"。最初的构思是："不论要干什么，也不慌忙地脱衬衣"。从意义上讲，相当于 be patient (忍耐)。但是，这一表达法轻松得多。特别是常用命令的口气，采取 Keep your shirt on. 的形式。大多应用于如下的情况：当对方催促说"快一点儿!"的时候，被催促者不耐烦地讲："着什么急? 稍微等一下嘛!" *A: Aren't you ready to go yet? B: Keep your shirt on. I'm coming.* 甲：还没做好走的准备吗? 乙：甭着急嘛。我就来。常用 just 调整语调。 *A: Haven't you finished your homework yet? I want to go out and play. B: Just keep your shirt on. I'll be through in a minute.* 甲：你还没做完家庭作业吗? 我想出去玩啦。乙：你别那么着急嘛。我马上就做完了。*A: I wonder why my girl hasn't written recently. B: Just keep your shirt on. I'm sure you'll hear from her soon.* 甲：不知为什么我的女朋友最近没有来信。乙：千万不要着急。我敢肯定，她马上就会给你写信的。除命令式外，有如下的用法：*Let's not give up yet. I'm sure he'll be along eventually if we just keep our shirts on.* 咱们还是不要失去希望。我认为，只要咱们耐心地等待，他准会来的。顺便讲一下：在英国英语中，除 keep *one's* shirt on 外，同义语有 keep *one's* hair (头发) on，有时还说 keep *one's* wig (假发) on，但在美国不通行。◇ be patient

lose *one's* **shirt** [ˌlu(ː)z ～ ˈʃəːrt] [话] **输得精光** 直译为"连衬衫都丢了"，这当然是一种夸张的表达法。与汉语"输得精光"一样，指在赛马或其他赌博中把所带的钱全都输掉了。也有时指由于进行大的投资，把自己的全部财产赔光了。不论在哪一种场合使用，你都需要适当打折扣地去听，因为美国人喜欢夸大，对事情往往言过其实。 *A: How did you do at the races? B: I lost my shirt.* 甲：你去赌赛马成绩如何? 乙：我输个精光。*My uncle was a wealthy man until he lost his shirt on the stock market.* 我叔父原是个有钱人，后来在股票市场上赔光了。◇ lose all *one's* money (on gambling, investment, etc.)

shiv

a shiv [ə ˈʃɪ(ː)v] [话] **匕首** 把刀作为武器使用时对刀的称呼。主要为黑社会用语。特别常指"弹簧刀"。 a shiv artist 是"经常以匕首为武器的人"，即"使用匕首的歹徒"。 *You'd better stay away from that guy. He always carries a shiv. [He's a shiv artist.]* 你最好别沾那个家伙的边儿。他总带着匕首[他是一个使用匕首的歹徒]。在 hobo (流浪汉) 用语中，这一表达法还可以表示"剃刀"的意思，但一般不通行。另外，过去也可以拼写为 chiv，现在几乎完全见不到了。◇ a knife

shoe

know where the shoe pinches [ˌnou ˌhwe(ː)rðə ˈʃuːˈpɪntʃəz] [口] **知道问题的所在** 这一表达法的来源很早，出典是希腊历史学家普卢塔克(Plutarch, 46?–120?)的名著《比较列传》(*Parallel Lives*)中所写的一段故事：有一个罗马人的妻子温柔、美貌，不论从哪个角度来看，都令人感到十分满意。可是，这个罗马人却跟她离了婚。当朋友们指责他的时候，他拿出一双新鞋来说："我穿上这双鞋，你们大概不会知道我的脚的哪一块儿疼吧。"这里的 pinch 是"(鞋) 夹脚"。本条条头直译为"知道鞋的哪儿夹脚"。转作比喻使用，表示"知道问题的所在"的意思。*When a man is suffering in life it's very difficult to give him advice, because only he knows where the shoe pinches.* 当一个人对人生感到苦恼的时候，你很难向他提供参考意见，因为只有他自己知道问题的所在。*There's no need to look for the source of the problem. I already know where the shoe pinches. It's just that I don't know what to do about it.* 没有必要去找问题的根源。我已经知道毛病出在什么地方，只是不知道如何处理而已。*The leaders we choose for this organization must be men of experience who already know where the shoe pinches and will not flinch at every difficult situation they meet.* 我们为这个组织选择的领导者必须是富有经验的人，他们已经知道问题的所在，而且在遇到每一个困难时都不退缩。也有省略动词 know 的时候。*Where the shoe pinches is money. We just don't have enough.* 关键在于钱。我们就是钱不够。下面的例句是对这一表达法的活用。*If you insist on marrying that girl, I can't stop you. But don't come running to me when the shoe starts pinching.* 如果你非要跟那个姑娘结婚不可，我不能阻拦你。不过，如果发生问题的时候，可不要跑来找我啊。◇ know where the difficulty [problem] lies / know where the difficulties [problems] lie

the shoe is on the other foot [ðəˈʃuː ˌɪzɔnðɪ ˌʌðərˈfu(ː)t] [口] **情况完全不同了** 直译为"把鞋穿错了脚"。当然可以按照字面意义使用，比如指一个人喝醉了酒，把左脚的鞋穿到右脚上，把右脚的鞋穿到左脚上的状态。但通常使用其比喻的意义。*He was my superior officer in the army, but now the shoe is on the other foot.* 在军队里的时候，他是我的长官，但是现在，情况完全不同了。*They treat us like dogs now, but wait until after the revolution. The shoe will be on the other foot.* 现在，他们把我们象狗一样对待，但是等着瞧吧，革命以后，情况就会完全不同啦。另外，请读者注意这一表达法与 turn the TABLES (on *someone*) 的被动语态 the tables are turned 之间的差异。the tables are turned 是"局势已经被扭转过来了"的意思。也就是说，the shoe is on the other foot 的重点是陈述"过去与现在情况完全不同了"这一客观事实，而 the tables are turned 的重点是陈述由于情况完全不同而产生的新的力量对比关系。例如最初的一个例句，如果使用 the tables are turned 而改换成 He was my superior officer in the army, but now the tables are turned. 那就不仅是陈述"情况完全不同了"这一事实，首先表现出来的是"这回我可处于有利的地位了"的意思，并含有"现在是我的天下了。过去你给我苦头吃，如今该我治治你啦。"的意味。如以上所述，the shoe is on the other foot 一般用于表示"过去与现在情况已经完全不同"的意思，但偶尔也有如下的用法：*A poet like yourself can take all the time you want in order to perfect your style, but with us newspaper reporters, the shoe is on the other foot. We have to sacrifice style for speed.* 象你这样的诗人愿意用多少时间去完善自己的风格都可以，但是对于我们新闻记者来说，情况就完全不同了，我们必须为速度牺牲风格。另外，在英国，这一表达法可以用 boot 代替 shoe，用 leg 代替 foot，但在美国只能用 shoe 和 foot。◇ the situation is reversed

wait for the other shoe to drop [ˌweɪt fəðɪ ˌʌðər ˈʃuːdə ˌdrɑ(ː)p] [口] **等待挨整** 直

译为“等待另一只鞋掉下来”。这是在欧美人生活中常有的情况：一楼的一个人正躺下睡觉，不一会儿，正上方二楼的一个人也要上床，他先脱下一只鞋，叭哒一声扔到地板上。这时一楼的人正要进入梦乡，听到声音之后完全清醒过来。他只好等待另一只鞋扔下的声音过后再睡。可是左等右等，还听不见楼上的鞋声。明知非有这一声音不可，可又迟迟不响，这个人内心的焦急程度不言而喻。把这种情况用语言表达出来，就是 wait for the other shoe to drop。作为比喻，表示“在发生一次祸事之后，预料还要发生第二次祸事时的惴惴不安的等待心情”。 *The boss hit the ceiling the other day when he found a mistake in the contract, but he didn't realize then that I was responsible. Now I'm waiting for the other shoe to drop.* 前几天，总经理发现合同中有一处错误，曾经大发雷霆，但是，当时他没有注意到那是我的责任。现在，我只好等待另一场暴风雨临头了。◇ wait for the second blow (that is almost sure to follow)

shoes

fill *someone's* **shoes** [.fil ～ 'ʃu:z] [口] **堪当重任** 直译为“填满他人的鞋”，但这一表达法完全作为比喻使用。*someone's* shoes 是“前任的地位、职务、责任等”，fill 是“有足够的条件接替”的意思。本条最初的构思是：能力大的人(这里指前任)穿的鞋大，接替的人不仅是把脚伸进那双大鞋中去 (→ step into *someone's* SHOES)，而且要完全填满那双大鞋，不在里面晃晃荡荡。因此，本条与 step into *someone's* shoes 不同，经常含有“要问能力如何”的意味。 *After Professor Hopkins died, there was no one to fill his shoes.* 霍普金斯教授去世之后，没有一个人堪继他的重任。*If the first-string quarterback gets hurt, we have another who can fill his shoes.* 如果作为正式队员的四分卫受伤，我们有能够接替他的人。*Alfred stepped into his father's shoes as president last year, but he hasn't yet been able to fill them.* 阿尔弗雷德去年继承他父亲的职务当上了总经理，但是至今尚未能堪当重任。也有时可以见到这样的例子：*I'll fill your shoes until you get back from your vacation.* 在你休假回来之前，我来代理你的工作。这只是很轻松地表示“代替工作”的意思，与 fill in for *someone* 混同，严格地说是使用错了。上面这一例句的正确说法应该是 I'll fill in for you until ～. ◇ sufficiently perform *one's* [*someone's*] responsibilities

be in *someone's* **shoes** [ɪn '～ .ʃu:z] [话] **处于某人的境地** 直译为“穿上某人的鞋”。这一表达法是把他人的“立场”、“境遇”等比喻为“鞋”。但是，尽管意思是“处于某人的境地”，本条并非强调理解对方的苦衷或者对对方表示同情，在这一点上，请不要与 put *oneself* in *someone's* SHOES (设身处地为他人着想)混同起来。其用法主要有二。其一是表达这样的意思：“如果自己处于某人的地位，一定怎样怎样”。 *If I were in his shoes, I'd resign.* 如果我是他，我一定辞职不干了。另一个用法是表示愿望，句型为：I would like to be [I wish I were] in *someone's* shoes. 例如：*I'd like to be [I wish I were] in Fred's shoes. He gets to kiss Sally three times in the school play.* 我真希望我是弗雷德，他在学校排演的剧目中能吻萨莉三次呀。如果是否定句，一般的句型是 I wouldn't want [like] to be in ～.或者 I'm glad I'm not in～. 例如：*I wouldn't want to be [I'm glad I'm not] in Wylie's shoes. He has to give a talk in English to a group of American businessmen.* 我不愿意[我庆幸没有]干怀利那个角色，他必须去跟一群美国商人用英语讲话。 ◇ be in *someone's* position

put *oneself* **in** *someone's* **shoes** [.put ～ ɪn'～ 'ʃu:z] [口] **设身处地为他人着想** 这一表达法是把他人的“境遇”、“处境”比喻为鞋，整个意思是“把自己的身子放在某人的境地”，强调理解对方和同情对方。请读者特别注意：千万不要与理解对方、同情对方毫无关系的 be in *someone's* SHOES 混同起来。*Mrs. Jones is a* *very selfish woman. She doesn't seem able to put herself in other people's shoes.* 琼斯夫人是一个非常自私的女人。她似乎就是不能设身处地为别人着想。如这一例句所示,大多用否定句。但也常常使用命令式。*Put yourself in Ralph's shoes. You wouldn't laugh at his sleeping in class if you thought about how hard he has to work to pay the medical bills for his sick mother.* 请你设身处地为拉尔夫想一想。他母亲有病,为了付医药费,他必须拼命地去干活。如果你想到这一点,就不会讪笑他在上课的时候打盹了。◇ think of how it would feel [be] to be in *someone's* position

step into *someone's* **shoes** [ˌstepɪntə ~ ˈʃuːz] [口] **继任** 直译为"把脚伸进他人的鞋里"。但是,这里的 shoes 作比喻使用,指"前任的位置、职务等"。*When the president died, there were many people who wanted to step into his shoes.* 总经理死后,许多人都想接替他的位置。如这一例句所示,这一表达法一般用于"接替死亡或退休者的位置"的场合,但并不限定如此。*If the first-string quarterback gets hurt, we have another who can step into his shoes.* 如果作为正式队员的四分卫受了伤,我们有人能够顶替他。另外,step into *someone's* shoes 不能按照其字面意义"穿错他人的鞋"使用,因为美国人不象日本人那样进屋就脱鞋,在实际上很难有穿错鞋的情况。万一在某种特殊情况下真穿错了鞋,可以这样说:*Oh, I'm sorry. I stepped into your shoes by mistake.* 哎呀,真对不起,我错穿你的鞋啦。→ fill *someone's* SHOES ◇ take *someone's* place

shoestring

live on a shoestring [ˌlɪvɔnə ˈʃuːstrɪŋ] [口] **生活贫困** 直译为"依靠一根鞋带 (a shoestring) 生活"。意思是"这一根鞋带如果断了,一切就全完了",形容由于缺钱,生活非常困难。据说,这一表达法的来源是:旧时,有一些贫穷的小贩常常沿街卖鞋带以维持最低的生计。*After my father died, we found ourselves living on a shoestring.* 我父亲死后,我们不得不过贫困的生活。即使不算贫困,能达到一般生活水平的人,为了夸大自己的感受,也常使用本条。*With two sons in college, we're being forced to live on a shoestring.* 我家有两个儿子上大学,所以不得不过紧日子。→ operate on a SHOESTRING ◇ live a very impoverished life

operate on a shoestring [ˈɑpəˌreɪdɔnə ˈʃuːˌstrɪŋ] [口] **缺乏资金,勉强维持** 直译为"依靠一根鞋带经营"。意思是:公司以很少的资金周转,惨淡经营。*This company operated on a shoestring for many years.* 这个公司以很少的资金惨淡经营了好多年。也可以构成 operate a company [enterprise, etc.] on a shoestring 的句型,作及物动词使用。特别是在这一场合,常用同义词 run 代替 operate。*He is operating [running] that company on a shoestring.* 他以很少的资金经营着那个公司。另外有 start (a company, enterprise, etc.) on a shoestring 的表达法,也经常使用。这是"在开办时资金很少"的意思,如果译成"周转资金很少"就不贴切了。*Mr. Butler started that company on a shoestring.* 巴特勒先生以很少的资金开办了那家公司。*Henry Ford started on a shoestring.* 亨利·福特几乎是白手起家。"以极少资金惨淡经营的企业"叫做 a shoestring operation。*A number of shoestring operations went under during the recent business slump.* 最近生意萧条,许多资金短缺的企业都倒闭了。→ live on a SHOESTRING ◇ do business with very little working capital

a shoestring operation [ə ˈʃu(ː)strɪŋ ˌɑpeˈreɪʃən] [口] **以极少资金惨淡经营的企业** → operate on a SHOESTRING

start on a shoestring [ˌstɑrdɔnə ˈʃuːˌstrɪŋ] [口] **以极少的资金开办企业** → operate on a SHOESTRING

shoo-in

a shoo-in [ə ˈʃuːˌɪ(ː)n] [话] **十拿九稳的取胜者** shoo 是象声词,为撵鸡时发出的

"嘘、嘘"声。也可以当动词用,说 shoo the chickens (嘘、嘘地赶鸡)。 shoo in 原作动词使用,是"双方串通进行假比赛"的意思。最初的构思是:"嘘、嘘地追赶着,使它跑个第一"。a horse that is shooed in 是"在假比赛中获胜的马"。但是,现在已经不使用这一意义,专用于表示在比赛或选举中的"必胜无疑者"。"假比赛"的意味完全消失了。*The Republican candidate is a shoo-in.* 那个共和党候选人十拿九稳会取胜。如这一例句所示,动词一般使用 be 动词。 *Of course he won. That horse was a shoo-in from the word go.* 当然他赢啦。从一开头,那匹马是十拿九稳获胜的。*I didn't expect our candidate to be a shoo-in, but I was surprised that the election was so close.* 我虽然并没有认为我党的候选人会稳操胜券,但是对手获得的选票与我们的如此不相上下却使我大吃一惊啊。这一表达法也可以单指比赛、选举等的结果,表示"取得压倒性的胜利"的意思。*It was a shoo-in. Our candidate won eighty-five percent of the vote.* 我们取得了压倒性的胜利啦。我党的候选人赢得 85% 的选票。*It'll be a shoo-in. That horse'll win going away.* 那肯定是个压倒性的胜利。那匹马一定能够迅速领先的。 *Don't expect this game to be a shoo-in. We're gonna hafta work hard to win it.* 不要认为这次比赛能取得压倒性的胜利。如果打算赢,我们非拼命干不可。◇ a sure [an easy] winner / an easy race [contest, etc.]

shoot

shoot [ˈʃuːt] [话] **质问** → FIREaway

Shoot. [ˈʃuːt] [话] **(表示轻度的后悔、失望等)咳!** → SHUCKS.

shoot the works → WORKS

shooter

a square shooter [ə ˈskweːr ˈʃu(ː)dər] [话] **老实人** → a straight SHOOTER

a straight shooter [ə ˈstreɪt ˈʃu(ː)dər] [话] **正直的人** 直译为"照直打枪的人",指无论在一般交往中还是业务关系中都没有不正言行的人,在这一意义上,也可以说 an honest person (诚实的人)。不过,a straight shooter 含有一种积极的意味,即除了诚实的本性外,还采取积极的行动。这种人不论对于什么事情都直言不讳,哪怕在追求自己利益的过程中,也极力避免有损于他人的行动。*If anything goes wrong with his plan, he'll be sure to tell you. He's a straight shooter.* 如果他的计划出了什么问题,他肯定会告诉你的。他是一个正直的人。另有一个说法 a square shooter, 同义。 ◇ an honest and straightforward person

shooting

a shooting iron → IRON

shop

(like) a bull in a china shop → BULL

a head shop [ə ˈhe(ː)d.ʃɑ(ː)p] [话] **幻觉用品商店** → an acid HEAD

shop talk [ˈʃɑ(ː)p .tɔ(ː)k] [口] **在非工作时间所谈的关于工作上的话** → talk SHOP

talk shop [.tɔ(ː)k ˈʃɑ(ː)p] [口] **谈论工作的事情** 直译为"讲自己商店的事",转义为"讲自己工作的事"。*I'm getting tired of dating Jim. He spends most of the time talking shop.* 我讨厌跟吉姆约会。他大部分时间都是谈自己工作上的事。*After dinner, the women went out into the garden while their husbands sat in the living room talking shop.* 晚饭以后,女人们都到花园里去了,她们的丈夫则坐在起居室里闲聊工作上的事情。*Promise me you won't talk shop with out guests at the restaurant tonight, dear.* 请你答应我,亲爱的,今天晚上在餐厅里不跟客人们谈工作上的事情。有时指"专业上的事情"。*Prime Ministers of the two countries met privately for over an hour to talk shop.* 两国首相为了讨论相互间的各种问题,私下会晤一个多小时。*Those professors are all nuclear scientists. It's impossible to understand them when they start talking shop.* 那些教授全是核科学家。当他们开始谈论专业时,你连一句也听不懂。*I know you are proud of your job as a hit man for the Mafia, dear, but you frighten our guests when you talk* *shop.* 亲爱的,我知道你对当黑手党的杀手这一工作感到自豪,不过,如果你谈自己的工作情况,会把我们的客人们吓坏的呀。shop talk [ˈʃɑ(ː)p ˌtɔ(ː)k] 是名词,意思为"在非工作时间所谈的关于工作上的话"。*That's enough shop talk. Let's forget about work and just enjoy ourselves.* 关于工作上的话,就到此为止吧。咱们把工作的事情忘掉,痛痛快快玩一阵子吧。◇ talk about *one's* work

shoplifter

a shoplifter [ə ˈʃɑ(ː)pˌlɪftər] [口] **在商店里偷东西的人** lift 原是"拿起"的意思,但在俚语中为"偷"(rob)的同义语。因此,a shoplifter 换句话说就是 shop robber (商店扒手)。shoplifter 是"在商店里偷东西的人",这种人的行为叫 shoplifting。*Most shoplifters these days are young people and ordinary housewives.* 最近,在商店里偷东西的人绝大多数是青年人和一般家庭妇女。*She was caught shoplifting.* 她在商店里偷东西时被抓住了。◇ a person who steals from store counters

short

give short shrift (to *someone* [*something*]) → SHRIFT

make short shrift of *something* [ˌmeɪk ˌʃort ˈʃrɪftəv ～] [口] **简单处理** → give short SHRIFT (to *someone* [*something*])

make short work of *something* [*someone*] → WORK

short-sighted

short-sighted[1] [ˈʃortˈsaɪdəd] [口] **目光短浅** a short-sighted person 是"目光短浅的人"。*He's short-sighted.* 他这个人目光短浅。有时与 NEAR-SIGHTED 相同,是"近视的"的意思,但在这一场合,第二音节的重音减弱,作 [ˈʃortˌsaɪdəd]。反义语"有先见之明"的英语为 far-sighted (→ FAR-SIGHTED[2])。*Short-sighted people cannot be expected to exhibit effective leadership.* 鼠目寸光的人没有可能显示出有效的领导作用。除指人而外,还可以形容 policy, plans, thinking 等。*These are extremely short-sighted plans.* 这是一些目光极为短浅的计划。另外,short-sighted 也可以不加连字符,作 shortsighted。◇ (*someone*) lacking the ability to see and plan ahead / (*something*) based on narrow, shortterm considerations

short-sighted[2] [ˈʃortˌsaɪdəd] [口] **近视的** → NEAR-SIGHTED

shot

a big shot [ə ˈbɪg ˌʃɑ(ː)t] [话] **要人** a shot 是"枪炮发射的子弹"。a big shot 是由 a big GUN 发展而来的表达法,是"要人"、"有权势的人"的意思,在口语中使用的范围很广,可指政界、实业界、社交界、黑社会各式各样的有头有脸的人物,甚至在对并非 big shot 的人说话时,也可以用这一表达法打招呼,其中含有诙谐或讽刺的味道。例如:*Hi, big shot. What's new?* 嘿,大人物,你好啊? *What's your problem, big shot?* 大人物,你在唠叨什么哪? 下面是一般用例:*Mr. Deeds is a big shot in Washington political circles.* 迪兹先生是华盛顿政界的一位要人。*The big shots of gambling gathered in Las Vegas.* 赌博界的头头脑脑都聚集到拉斯韦加斯了。*You think you're a big shot, don't you?* 你认为自己是个了不起的人物吧? big shot 中间可以加连字符,作为定语形容词使用。例如:*He's a big-shot gambler.* 他是一个大赌棍。*I have to entertain a big-shot guest tonight.* 今天晚上我必须招待一位重要的客人。在作为形容词使用的场合,也经常含有冷淡的或轻蔑的意味。*Frank used to be a friend of mine. Now he's become a big-shot TV actor.* 弗兰克过去是我的朋友。现在,人家已经变成电视上的大演员啦。◇ an important [influential] person

by a long shot [baɪə ˈlɔːŋ ˌʃɑ(ː)t] [话] **绝对地** a long shot 原来可能是"长距离的射击 (命中率小)"的意思。但在这一表达法中,应该解释为"由于偏离目标过远,着弹点与靶子之间的距离很长"。按照字面意义的用例:*Fred missed the target by a long shot.* 弗雷德偏离目标太远了。作为比喻使用时，基本的意思是“离得太远”亦即“相差悬殊”。主要用于否定句，表示“绝对(不)”、“决(不)”、“坚决(不)”等意思。这是在断定一件事的时候使用的强调的表达法。大多与形容词的比较级或最高级一起使用。*This is a pretty good steak, but it's not the best by a long shot.* 这是一份相当不错的牛排，但绝对不是最好的啊。*Betty isn't the prettiest girl in our class by a long shot.* 贝蒂绝对不是我们班里最好看的姑娘。*Ben's not the stronger of the two by a long shot.* 在那两个人中间，本决不是强的一方。在议论中，当坚决否定对方的话时，也可以使用于肯定句。*I don't care what you say, I say Betty is the prettiest girl in our class by a long shot.* 我不管你怎么说，依我来讲，贝蒂绝对是我们班上最漂亮的姑娘。在某种情况下，只用以表示“特别”、“格外”的意味。*A: This is the coldest day we've had this year. B: Yes, it is—by a long shot.* 甲：这是今年以来最冷的一天啦。乙：是的，今天格外冷。◇ by far

like a shot [.laɪkə 'ʃɑ(:)t] [话] **象颗子弹一样** 这里的 shot 是“从枪里发射出去的子弹”。本条习用语表示“嗖的一下”的速度之快，常用于形容一个人突然飞奔出去的样子。*As soon as the bell rang for the lunch break, Jimmy was out of the door like a shot.* 午休的铃声一响，吉米便象子弹一样冲出门去了。be off like a shot 是最常使用的句型。*When Kim heard that his expectant wife had gone to the hospital, he was off like a shot.* 当金听说他那怀孕的妻子已经进入医院的时候，他象颗发射出去的子弹一样飞奔去了。*The eager-beaver employee received his orders and was off like a shot.* 那个非常卖力气的雇员接到命令之后，象子弹一样飞奔了出去。同义的表达法还有 in a flash，在以上的例句中均可任意代换。但是，与 be off like a shot 等值的说法是 be gone in a flash。◇ in an instant

a long shot [ə 'lɔ:ŋ .ʃɑ(:)t] [口] **几乎没有成功的希望** 原为赛马用语，指“获胜可能性极小的马”。*Mr. Whiterock put his money on a long shot.* 怀特罗克先生把赌注押在一匹冷门的马上了。一般用于“几乎不可能成功”的场合。但是，a long shot 另外还有“高尔夫、篮球等远距离击球、投球”的意思，应该注意上下文，不要与本条的表达法混同。*The American golfer's weakness on long shots made him a long shot to win the tournament.* 那个美国高尔夫选手不善于长距离击球，使得他在比赛中没有什么取胜的希望。*I knew our plan was a long shot, but if it had succeeded we'd have been fixed for life.* 我知道咱们的计划几乎没有成功的希望，但是万一成功了，咱们就一辈子过舒服日子啦。*It's a long shot, but if you study hard enough you just might get into Harvard University.* 虽然成功的希望极少，但是，如果你真拼命用功，也有进哈佛大学的可能性啊。 除了明知不成而要拼命去干一下试试的重大事情而外，也有用于一些无关紧要的事情的场合。例如：*It's a long shot, but he may be at home tonight. Let's call and find out.* 他晚上不大可能在家，但是今天晚上说不定在。咱们打个电话问问看。有时用 take 构成 take a long shot 的表达法，意思是“尝试一下几乎没有成功希望的事情”。 *People who always play it safe never succeed big. Once in a while you have to take a long shot.* 始终小心谨慎的人决不会有大的成功。有时候要去尝试一下希望不大的事情。这一表达法除以上所讲而外，还有电影中的“远景”的意思。◇ a horse [player, plan, idea, etc.] with little chance (of winning, succeeding, etc.)

a mug shot [ə 'mʌ(:)g .ʃɑ(:)t] [话] **相貌照片** a MUG 是“大杯(如啤酒杯之类)”的意思，但是在这里指 face (脸)。由于古时常模拟人的脸形制做大杯，所以在俚语中便以 mug 表示“面孔”的意思。shot 为 snapshot ['snæ(:)p.ʃɑ(:)t] (快照)的缩略。*Do you have a mug shot of the murder suspect on file?* 你的档案中有那个杀人嫌疑犯的相貌照片吗？*Take a mug shot of this guy.* 把这个家伙的相貌拍照下来！ 如以上的例句所示，一般用于"犯人或者嫌疑犯相貌照片"的场合。进一步发展,也有时戏指汽车驾驶证、护照等所用的半身照片。*I have to get some mug shots for my new passport.* 我领新护照,需要拍几张半身相片。又指在一般 snapshot 中照得太不象样、简直类似"通缉犯"的照片。*Is this you? What a beautiful mug shot.* 这是你吗?作为通缉犯的照片,倒是够合适的啦。◇ a (full-face) photo

a parting shot [ə ˌpɑrdɪŋ ˈʃɑːt] [口] **临走时丢下的气恼话** 本来的意思是"在往后撤退时放的最后一枪",也就是俗话所说"黄鼠狼最后的一屁"。*The captain was hit by a parting shot from the enemy.* 敌人退却时放的最后一枪把上尉打中了。转用于表示"在争论、吵架时临走丢下的一句气恼话"的意思。"*—And don't you forget it!" With that parting shot, Bela stormed out of the room.* "你记住好啦!"贝拉丢下这么一句话,气冲冲地从屋子里走出去了。*I couldn't resist a parting shot:"I'm sure you'll be happy, now that you have both my wife and my money."* 我忍不住一腔怒火,丢下这样一句话:"你霸占了我的老婆和我的钱财,肯定会幸福的啦!"*I tried to get in a parting shot, but he shut the door before I could get it out.* 我打算留下最后一句气话,可是没等我说出口,他就把门关上了。give (*someone*) a parting shot (向某人说最后一句气恼话) 也是一个习用语。*From the doorway, Neil gave a parting shot. "And I won't be back."* 尼尔在门口丢下了一句气恼话:"我再也不来啦!"◇ a final (sharp) word before parting

a shot in the arm [əˌʃɑtnðɪ ˈɑ(ː)rm] [口] **最好的促进因素** shot 是"注射"。这一表达法可以按照字面意义使用,例如:*The doctor gave me a shot in the arm.* 医生在我的胳膊上注射了一针。作为比喻,指"使精神或自信得到恢复的东西"。具体形象是:由于有病或受到震惊而身体衰弱的人,打一针马上就回复了元气。有人译为"强心剂",也很不坏。常有与动词 be 一起使用的情况。但在这一场合是"对……的促进因素"的意思,所以后边大多要接 ～ for *someone* [*something*]。*The news of the enemy retreat was a shot in the arm for the bone-weary troops.* 对于精疲力竭的部队来说,敌人退却的消息是一针最好的强心剂。常用 big 加强语气。*That order was a big shot in the arm for our company.* 那批订货对我们公司起了很大的促进作用。常用 give *someone* [*something*] a shot in the arm 的形式表示"给予促进作用"的意思。*Sam's home run gave our team a shot in the arm.* 萨姆的本垒打给我们的棒球队一个很好的促进。*I was discouraged about my chances of passing the final exam, but my teacher's words of encouragement gave me a shot in the arm.* 我对于是否能通过期终考试已经失去信心,可是,老师鼓励我的话使我又振作起来了。从受到"促进作用"的方面来讲,不是用 be given a ～的句型,大多是用 get a shot in the arm 的表达法。*The dollar got a shot in the arm from America's new economic policy.* 美元的坚挺是受到美国新经济政策的推动。◇ a stimulus

a shot in the dark [ɔ ˌʃɑtnðə ˈdɑ(ː)rk] [口] **瞎猜** 直译为"在黑暗中打枪"。因为看不见目标,只能是"瞎打"。为了调整语气,几乎在所有的场合添加 just, only, a mere 等。*A: How did you know the answer? B: I didn't. It was just a shot in the dark.* 甲:你怎么知道答案了呢?乙:我不知道,只是瞎猜罢了。*My comment was just a shot in the dark, but I sensed from her expression that it had struck home.* 我的话只不过是瞎猜着说的,但是从她的表情看来,却正中了要害啊。加上动词 take,是"瞎蒙"的意思。*I didn't know the answer, but I decided I had nothing to lose by taking a shot in the dark.* 我不知道答案,但是我想我瞎蒙一通儿也没有什么损失。◇ (make) a random guess

shotgun

a shotgun marriage [ə ˈʃɑ(ː)t.gʌ(ː)n ˈmæ(ː)rɪdʒ] [口] **因使女方怀孕而不得已结婚** → a shotgun WEDDING

a shotgun wedding → WEDDING

shots

call *one's* **shots** [.kɔ(ː)l ～ ˈʃɑ(ː)ts] [话] **预先说明** 原为台球用语,意思是"预先宣布哪个球打进哪个口袋"。这里的 shot 是"打台球",call 是"宣布"。*In some games of pool, you are required to call your shots.* 在某几种台球打法中,需要预先讲清哪个球进哪个口袋。转作一般使用,表示"预先说明自己的意图"的意思。*Babe Ruth would sometimes call his shots by pointing at the stands with his bat before hitting a home run.* 巴贝·鲁思在进行本垒打之前,往往用他的球棒指着看台做预告。*We will have to prepare several strategies for defending our client since we can't expect the prosecution to call its shots in advance.* 我们为了替委托人辩护,必须准备几套作战方案,因为检查人员不可能预先把他们的想法告诉我们。*We never know in advance what the boss is planning. He never calls his shots.* 我们在事前从来不知道老板的计划。他绝对不把自己的想法预先告诉别人。◇ indicate in advance what *one* is planning to do

call the shots [.kɔ(ː)lðə ˈʃɑ(ː)ts] [话] **有发号施令的权力** 原为军事用语,意思是"下达大炮往哪里射击的命令"。shots 是"一发一发的大炮射击",call 是"指示、命令"。后来泛指"有发号施令的权力"。在大炮射击的场合,指示发炮的不限于长官,根据情况,普通一兵也可能受命承担这个任务。因此,在比喻的场合,也不问地位的高低或身份的贵贱,常用于表示"有发号施令的实际权力"的意思。*You're calling the shots. Just tell us what you want us to do and we'll do it.* 你掌握着大权。你要我们做什么,我们就去做什么。*Mr. Smith is the president, but from observing the executive director's overbearing attitude it is clear who calls the shots.* 史密斯先生是总经理,但是,从业务经理的那种傲慢态度来看,谁掌握着发号施令的权力是很清楚的。在强调的场合加 all。*If you want me to serve as your leader, I shall insist on calling all the shots.* 你们如果要我给你们当领导人,我可要求全部的指挥权呀。◇ give the orders

shoulder

give it to *someone* **straight from the shoulder** [.gɪvɪtːə ～ ˈstreɪtfrəm ðə ˈʃouldər] [话] **开诚布公地讲** → give it to *someone* STRAIGHT

give *someone* **the cold shoulder** [.gɪv ～ðə ˈkould ˈʃouldər] [口] **采取冷淡的态度** 这里的 shoulder 是"牛等连前腿的肩肉"的意思。因此,所谓 cold shoulder 就是"凉了的肩肉"。古时有这样的风俗习惯:在招待贵客时,飨以美味佳肴;对于行商和乞丐,则给"凉了的肩肉"吃。这就是 give *someone* the cold shoulder 具有"采取冷淡态度"意味的来源。但是,一般的美国人不知道这一来源,他们认为这一表达法所以表示"采取冷淡的态度",是因为在这种时候,人们往往把肩膀突然一耸,显出不高兴的神情。一般在日常会话中,当说 give *someone* the cold shoulder 的时候,既可以指上面所讲的表示冷淡的动作本身,也可以单指"采取冷淡的态度"这一比喻意义。*I've tried to become friendly with Phil, but he's always giving me the cold shoulder.* 我极力想跟菲尔成为好朋友,但是他总是对我采取冷淡的态度,不理不睬。*Though I'd met Mr. Frosty several times before, for some reason when I spoke to him yesterday he gave me the cold shoulder.* 我以前跟弗罗斯提先生见过几次面,可是当我昨天跟他说话的时候,不知为什么,他对我采取很冷淡的态度。"遭到冷遇"可以说 be given the cold shoulder,但一般是使用 get the cold shoulder (from *someone*)。*Ray wants to have a date with Susan, but every time he approaches her, he gets the cold shoulder.* 雷希望跟苏珊定期约会,但是每当他找她商量这个问题的时候,他都遭到了白眼。把 cold 与 shoulder 用连字符连起来,能以 cold-shoulder *someone* 的形式作为动词使用,意思与 give *someone* the cold shoulder 相同。*Hey, don't cold-shoulder me like that. We'll never settle our differences if we don't talk about them.* 喂,你不要象那样对我不理不睬呀! 我们如果不谈开,永远也解决不了相互之间的分歧啊。◇ exhibit a cold attitude toward *someone*

have a chip on *one's* **shoulder** → CHIP

put *one's* **shoulder to the wheel** [ˌput ~ ˈʃouldər təðə ˈhwiːl] [口] **拿出真正的干劲** 直译为"把肩膀放在车轮上"。这一表达法来自把陷入泥塘的马车向外推的情景。*The driver got out of the mired-down wagon and put his shoulder to the wheel.* 车夫从陷入泥塘的马车上下来,用肩膀抵住车轮往前推。随着时代的发展,当年的"马车"已经变成各式各样的交通工具了。但是,直至今日,只要是有 wheel 的交通工具,仍可用本条条头的旧有意义。*All right, you guys! Shoulders to the wheel! We can get this car started if we get it up to speed.* 好啦,伙计们! 加劲推哟! 这辆车只要一动,我们就能开走了。作为比喻,用以表示"拿出真正的干劲"、"拼命卖力气"的意思。例如: *We can finish this work on time if everyone will put his shoulder to the wheel.* 如果每个人都拿出真正的干劲,我们就能够按时完成这个工作。*Finals are only two weeks off. I've really got to start putting my shoulder to the wheel.* 离期末考试只有两个星期了。我必须认真努力复习功课啦。*Carl's a first-class salesman. When he decides to put his shoulder to the wheel, he can sell sand to an Arab.* 卡尔是个第一流的推销员。当他决心大卖力气的时候,他能够把沙子推销到阿拉伯人手里。◇ concentrate *one's* efforts

shoulders

have a head on *one's* **shoulders** → HEAD

rub shoulders (with *someone*) [ˌrʌbˈʃouldərz] [口] **在社交场所相互应酬** → rub ELBOWS (with *someone*)

shouting

be all over but the shouting [ˈɔː ˈlouvər bətðə ˈʃaudɪŋ] [话] **大局已定** 直译为"除了欢呼声,一切都结束了"。这是来源于体育运动的表达法。比赛还没有完,但是胜败已经确定无疑,只听到观众一阵又一阵的欢呼声。这一表达法的意思就是:"胜败已成定局,剩下的只有欢呼声了"。*When Stanford made still another touchdown, it was all over but the shouting.* 当斯坦福队又来一个触地得分球的时候,这场橄榄球赛的胜败已经定局了。这一表达法也常应用于体育运动之外的"竞争"。*It was a hard-fought election, but after the number three candidate stepped down in favor of the front-runner, it was all over but the shouting.* 选举的竞争非常激烈,但是,当第三位候选人自动退出、转而支持第一位候选人时,大局便定下来了。如以上的例句所示,在一般的情况下,只作"大局已定"解释就可以了。但是,如果上下文是以传达当时的实际情况为重点(例如体育比赛的实况转播),当然应该保留 shouting (欢呼声) 的原来意义。例如说: *Tech has made another touchdown! Well, it's all over but the shouting.* 工大又触地得分! 现在胜败已定,全场一片欢呼声。另外,也可以用 cheering [yelling] 来代替 shouting,而讲 be all over but the cheering [yelling]。◇ the outcome (of the game, etc.) is (virtually) decided

show

give the show away [ˌgɪvðə ˈʃou əˌweɪ] [口] **泄露秘密** the show 原来的意思为文娱节目的"情节或内容"。本条条头直译为"情节究竟是怎样开展的呢? 揭穿 (give away) 其中的秘密"。可以按照字面意义使用,例如: *I don't like people's giving the show away by telling me the ending of a movie before I see it.* 我不喜欢那种爱讲故事内容的人,在我还没看电影之前就把影片的结局告诉我。这里的 the show 指影片的"梗概",但在一般情况下,the show 泛指"秘密"。 *Don't tell my little sister about the surprise party. She's sure to give the show away.* 不要把搞突然袭击式晚会的事情告诉我妹妹。她肯定会泄露秘密的。 *This coat is a surprise for my wife. Don't deliver it to my home or you'll give the show away.* 我打算把这件外衣突然送给我的妻子,给她一个意外。请不要送到我家里,否则就会泄露秘密啦。 *Our rivals are obviously onto our plans. Which one of you gave the show away?* 我们的竞争对手显然已经发觉我们的计划。你们之中是谁泄的密? 强调时说 the whole [entire] show。 *Despite our attempts to keep our plans secret from the union, the boss's careless words gave the whole show away.* 尽管我们试图不让工会知道我们的计划,可是老板说话不留神,把秘密全都给泄漏出去了。◇ reveal *one's* intentions [plan(s)] ((加强语气用 whole, entire → all of))

It (all) goes to show you (that ～). [ˌɪt ˈgouztə ˈʃoujə / ˌɪˈdɔːl ˈgouztə ～] [话] **显而易见** 这里的 you 与 one 等同,为非人称的 you。本条直译为"事实证明了 (某种事情)",经常含有"只要根据常识判断就可以明白"的意味。 *You were cheated out of twenty dollars? Well, it (all) goes to show you that you shouldn't be too friendly with strangers.* 你被人骗去了二十美元吗? 是啊,显而易见,你不该跟陌生人太近乎啦。all 为加强语气,有时可用 just 代替。 *You say your fiancée ran off with another man? It just goes to show you. Never trust a beautiful woman.* 你说你的未婚妻跟别的男人跑啦? 那是明摆着的事情。美人永远是靠不住的啊。that ～以后的从句有时省略 you,例如: *The reason that we didn't succeed was that the committee was too large. It all goes to show that too many cooks spoil the broth.* 我们所以失败,就是因为委员会的规模太大了。显而易见,厨师多了烧坏汤嘛。下面为主语并非 It 而是具体事项的场合的例句: *Norman's book's becoming a best seller all goes to show that success doesn't necessarily require talent.* 诺曼的著作变成了一部畅销书,显而易见,成功并不一定非有天才不可啊。◇ *One* should have known (that ～). / *Something* clearly demonstrates that ～.

run the show [ˌrʌnðə ˈʃou] [话] **操纵** 这里的 show 本来是"主持演出"(杂技等文艺节目) 的意思。 *You may be the director, but I run the show. Don't you forget it.* 你可能是经理,但是我主持演出。你不要忘了这一点。转作比喻,广泛用以表示"操纵"某一机关、地方等等的意思。 *A cabinet minister is not as powerful as you may think. It's really the bureaucrats who run the show.* 内阁成员并没有你想象的那么大权力。实权操在官僚们的手中。 *It won't do any good to talk to my mother. My father runs the show at my house.* 跟我母亲谈没有什么用处。我家由我父亲当家作主。有时用 this 或者 that 代替定冠词 the。 *I don't mind if you make minor decisions when I'm not here, but just don't forget who's running this show.* 当我不在的时候,你可以对一些细小的问题做决定,但是千万不要忘记谁是这一摊儿的主管人。下一例句中 the whole show 的 whole 是为加强语气而增添的。 *I'll admit that Mary's a hard worker, but whenever you ask her to do anything she always tries to run the whole show.* 我承认玛丽是一位勤勤恳恳的工作人员,但是当你委托她做什么事情的时候,她总是企图独揽大权。◇ have charge / hold the power / (try to) take charge

steal the show [ˌsti(ː)lðə ˈʃou] [话] **配角倒比主角红** 这里的 show 是"演剧"或"杂技"的意思。直译为"偷戏",也就是"配角压过主角"。可以按照这一意义使用,例如: *The new actress who played the star's maid stole the show.* 给明星配戏演使唤丫头的那个新女演员竟把明星压过去了。后来进一步发展,就不局限于演戏,而用于表示"喧宾夺主"的一般意思了。 *I can never hope to impress my dates* *if I take them to my home. My little sister, who's prettier and livelier than I am, always steals the show.* 如果我把约会对象带到自己家里来，就不可能给人留下良好的印象。我的妹妹比我又漂亮又活泼，她总是喧宾夺主。*"He's a good private eye," said the inspector. "As long as he can solve this case, who cares if he steals the show?"* "他是一个很好的私人侦探，"巡官说："只要他能够破这个案子，他比警察出风头也算不了什么。"也有令人意想不到的"黑马"博得好评的场合。*An unseeded tennis player stole the show at Wimbledon this year.* 在今年的英国网球公开赛中，一个非种子选手大出风头了。有时与配角或者"黑马"毫无关系，只用于表示"博得喝彩"、"独享声名"或者"得到极大好评"的意思。*A Polish entry stole the show at the Cannes Film Festival.* 在戛纳电影节中，一部波兰的参赛作品得到极大的好评。*American Motors' new compact stole the show at the auto exhibition.* 在汽车展览会中，美国汽车公司的新产品小型客车博得极大的好评。*All the singers were very good, but Joan stole the show.* 所有的歌手都很不错，不过，乔安娜独享了声名。也可以讲 steal *someone's* show。*Be quiet. You're stealing my show.* 安静！你们不要喧宾夺主啊。*The big three U.S. auto firms have had their show stolen by Japanese car manufacturers.* 美国三大汽车公司的声誉已经被日本汽车制造厂压过去了。◇ get most of the attention [plaudits]

shrift

give short shrift (to *someone* [*something*]) [ˌgɪv ˌʃɔrt ˈʃrɪ(ː)ft] [口] **采取冷漠的态度** shrift 原为天主教用语，指"对神父的忏悔"或者"在忏悔后，神父给与的赦免"，也可以兼有两方面的意思。在囚犯被处死刑之前，要进行极简短的忏悔仪式，所以称之为 short shrift。现在，shrift 一词的本来意义已经无人使用，在英语中只保留了 short shrift 的形式，而且仅能用于比喻。*Charles lends money freely, but he gives short shrift to people looking for handouts.* 查理可以很爽快地把钱借给别人，但是他对于乞求施舍的人抱以冷漠的态度。常用 pretty, fairly 等副词修饰。*I don't know if he'll help us or not. He gave me pretty short shrift when I talked to him yesterday.* 我不知道他是否肯帮助咱们。当我昨天向他讲的时候，他对我相当的冷淡。下面是"对于事物冷淡"的例子。*Most reviewers have given fairly short shrift to that author's new book.* 绝大多数评论家对那位作者的新著采取非常冷漠的态度。*Our dog gives short shrift to bones without any meat on them.* 我家的狗对于不带一点肉的骨头连看也不看一眼。可以用 get 代替 give，而讲 get short shrift (from *someone*)，意思是"受人冷眼相待"。*My explanation that the driver in front backed into my car got short shrift from the police.* 我向警察报告说前边的司机往后倒车撞了我的车，却受到他的冷眼相待。如果讲 make short shrift of *something*，则是"简单处理"或"草草了事"的意思。*The hungry workers made short shrift of the meal.* 饥饿的工人们转眼之间就把饭菜一扫而光。◇ treat *someone* [*something*] in an abrupt [unsympathetic] manner / be (very) cold to *someone* / largely ignore *something*

make short shrift of *something* [ˌmeɪk ˌʃɔrt ˌʃrɪftəv ～] [口] **简单处理** → give short SHRIFT (to *someone* [*something*])

shrinking

a shrinking violet → VIOLET

Shucks

Shucks. [ˈʃʌks] [话] **糟糕！** 原意"玉米的皮"，转义"一文不值的东西"。be not worth shucks 是"毫无价值"。*This old car isn't worth shucks.* 这辆老破车没有一点用场。但是，在作感叹词使用的场合，与本来的意义毫无关系。在感到弄错什么事情的时候，或者灰心丧气的时候，以极轻快的口吻使用这一表达法。*Shucks. I forgot to buy a newspaper.* 糟糕！我忘记买报纸啦。女性也常把它挂在口头上。*Oh, shucks. I bought the wrong size.* 哎呀，糟糕！我买错号啦。*Aw, shucks. Why can't I go, Mom?* 唉，糟糕！妈妈，为什么我不能去呀？同样的表达法有 Shoot. 意思、用法完全一样。但与 Shucks.不同，孩子们很少使用。另外，Shucks. 还有一个完全不同的意义，即在谦逊时讲的"哪里，哪里"。人们在感到不好意思的时候常讲这句话，其中包含着纯朴和直爽的意味。比如当有人夸奖说"你头脑真不错呀"的时候，往往这样回答：*Shucks, everybody knows that.* 哪里哪里，这种事情谁都知道啊。*A: You were so brave to save my boy from drowning! B: Aw, shucks, it wasn't anything.* 甲：你把我的男孩从水里救上来，真太勇敢啦。乙：哦，哪里哪里，这算不了什么事。

shut

put up or shut up → PUT

Shut up. [ˌʃʌˈdʌ(ː)p] [话] **住嘴！** → SHADDAP! / PIPE down. / DRY up.

shut-eye

get some shut-eye [ˌgetsəm ˈʃʌˌdaɪ] [话] **睡觉** shut-eye 为"闭眼睛"。本条条头为 sleep (睡眠) 的轻松表达法。在许多的场合与 go to bed 是相同的。但是，get some shut-eye 与 get some sleep 同样，不一定非"上床去睡"不可，"和衣而卧"也可以，在椅子上坐着"睡着了"也可以 (→ SLEEP)。get some sleep 常用于否定的场合，例如说：*I didn't get any sleep last night.* 昨天夜里我一点也没有睡觉 [或一点也没有睡着觉]。然而，不知什么原因，get some shut-eye 几乎完全不用否定式。*Well, tomorrow's a big day. We'd better get some shut-eye.* 啊，明天是个重大的日子。咱们赶快睡下为好。◇ get some sleep

shutterbug

a shutterbug [ə ˈʃʌdərˌbʌ(ː)g] [话] **摄影迷** 把这个词分解开，就是 shutter + bug。shutter 当然就是照相机上的"快门"。这里的 bug 不是"虫子"，而在口语中为"热衷于某种事情的人"的意思(→ a FIREBUG)。*Mr. Jones is a real shutterbug.* 琼斯先生真是一位摄影迷。*The Americans are world- famous shutterbugs.* 美国人喜欢照相，是世界上出了名的。有时说 a camera bug。◇ a camera enthusiast

shuttle

an air shuttle [ə ˈneːr ˌʃʌtl] [口] **区间飞机** a shuttle 原来的意思是"织机的梭子"，过去别无他解。但是现在，人们广泛使用这个词表示"定期往返两地之间 (的交通工具)"。例如 a shuttle bus 是指"车站与机场之间的公共汽车"、"机场与飞机之间的公共汽车"、"铁路不通时联结两个车站的公共汽车"等。a shuttle plane 则是"联结两个城市的短途班机"的意思。一般常用 air shuttle，而较少使用 shuttle plane。在讲 air shuttle 的时候，也可以用于直升机，因此意思比较宽广。air shuttle 的特点与一般城市的公共汽车或上下班火车一样，用不着预订机票，登机前或登机后买票，或者使用月票，可以称之为"上下班飞机"。大多每小时有一次班机起飞。如果想乘坐的话，可以这样询问：*Is there an air shuttle from Boston to New York?* 有从波士顿到纽约的区间飞机吗？又如，你到了 Washington 之后，人家问 How did you come? (你怎么来的？)。你如果回答说 I took the air shuttle from New York. (我从纽约乘区间飞机来的)，这就洋味十足了。另外，连接两个邻近机场的"换乘用"班机也叫做 air shuttle。在这一场合，大多是直升机。*I took the air shuttle between San Francisco and Oakland airports.* 我乘坐了旧金山与奥克兰两机场之间的班机。◇ an aircraft which flies constant round trips (between nearby locations)

a shuttle bus [ə ˈʃʌtl ˌbʌs] [口] **区间车** → an air SHUTTLE

a shuttle plane [ə ˈʃʌtl ˌpleɪn] [口] **区间飞机** → an air SHUTTLE

sick

be sick [ˈsɪ(ː)k] [口] **呕吐** → lose *one's* DINNER

be sick and tired of *something* [ˌsɪkən'taɪrdəv ~] [口] **厌烦透了** 请比较下面三个例句。*I'm tired of your complaining.* 你的牢骚我听腻啦。*I'm sick of your complaining.* 你的牢骚让我很厌烦。*I'm sick and tired of your complaining.* 你的牢骚我厌烦透了。"厌烦"的程度按照 be tired of→be sick of→ be sick and tired of 的顺序越来越强。sick 是"身体不舒服",加上 of 后是"很厌烦"的意思。*I'm sick and tired of having to take care of your brother just because he refuses to go out and find a job.* 你弟弟不肯出去找工作,就得我来照顾他,真让我厌烦透了。*The Liberals were defeated because the people were sick and tired of having to pay such high taxes.* 自由党人在选举中惨败,因为老百姓对于要纳那么多的税款厌烦透了。be FED up (with *something*) 可以认为与 be sick and tired of 同义,在以上的例句中,皆可用它代替本条,如果仔细分析,则本条的"厌烦"心情比较强烈。◇ have had (just about) enough of *something*

be sick at heart → HEART

side

the flip side [ðə 'flɪpˌsaɪd] [话] **唱片的背面** 动词 flip 通常是"轻抛"、"翻动"的意思,在这里作为形容词使用。主要是青年人、流行音乐唱片节目播音员爱用这一表达法。*There's also a good number on the flip side of that record.* 那张唱片背面还有一首好听的歌曲哪。◇ the other side (of the record)

get up on the wrong side of the bed [geˌdʌpɒnðə ˌrɔ(ː)ŋ 'saɪdəðə 'be(ː)d] [话] **早晨起来就心不顺** → get out of BED on the wrong side

The grass is always greener on the other side. [ðə 'græ(ː)səz ˌɔːlweɪz 'griːnər ɔnðɪˌʌðər 'saɪd] [谚] **花儿总是人家的红** → The GRASS is always greener on the other side of the fence.

know which side *one's* **bread is buttered on** → BREAD

on the safe side [ɔ(ː)nðə 'seɪf ˌsaɪd] [口] **小心谨慎** → play it SAFE

side against *someone* [ˌsaɪd ə'genst ~] [口] **敌对** → SIDE with *someone*

side with *someone* ['saɪd wɪð ~] [口] **拥护** take SIDES 是与本条意思相同的表达法,但二者的用法迥然不同。take sides 从时间来说是"一时的",从态度来说是"积极的",而本条习用语既可以用于"一时的"、"积极的"的场合,也可以用于"长期的"、"消极的"的场合。另外还有一点不同,take sides 含有"从感情上袒护"这样一种主观的意思,而本条习用语则是"有理性的"、"有算计的",毫无主观的意味在内。例如,人们常说 I decided to side with that group. (我决定拥护那一派。) 由于 decide(经过冷静考虑后决定)是一个表示理性行为的动词,如果用英语说 I decided to take sides with that group. 就不妥当了。*Japan sided with Germany against the Allies in World War II.* 在第二次世界大战中,日本支持德国对抗同盟国。本条习用语的反义表达法为 side against *someone*,意思是"敌对"。*My brother sided against me in the argument with my uncle.* 当我与叔父发生争论的时候,我弟弟站到叔父的一边了。*The strike wasn't successful because many of the employees sided against the union.* 罢工没有成功,因为大多数雇工不站在工会的一边。◇ join forces with [against] *someone*

the wrong side of the tracks [ðə ˌrɔ(ː)ŋ ˌsaɪdəvðə 'træ(ː)ks] [口] **贫苦阶层(住区)** 直译为"铁路那边"。这一表达法来源于美国人的一种偏见:"凡是住在铁路内侧的人都相当有钱,受过良好教育;凡是住在铁路外侧的都是穷人,以及不干正经事的人们。"旧时在美国的乡村小镇,实际上正是这样一种格局,一条铁路线 (railroad tracks)把它划分成两个居民区。"铁路那边"既指贫穷阶层,又指他们所居住的"贫民窟"。当然,在资本主义社会里,在"贫穷"中还包含着"下贱"的意味。*Alan was hard-working and honest, but most girls didn't want to date him because he was born on the wrong side of the tracks.* 艾伦工作勤恳,为人正直，但是，由于他出身于贫苦阶级，大多数姑娘都不愿意跟他搞对象。*I don't care if she does live on what you call the wrong side of the tracks. She's my friend and I won't have you talking about her that way.* 我不在乎她是否住在你所称为的贫民区。她是我的朋友，我不允许你以那种态度谈论她。*Unless you've experienced it personally, you can't know how hard life can be when you're from the wrong side of the tracks.* 除非你亲身经历，否则你就不可能知道对于贫苦阶层出身的人们来说，人生是多么艰辛。从本条习用语又演绎出 the right side of the tracks 的表达法，意思是“铁路这边”，指“有教养的阶层”以及“规矩人住的地区”。但是，这一表达法不象 the wrong side of the tracks 那样普遍流行。*In most small towns, it's difficult to get ahead unless you're from the right side of the tracks.* 在大多数的小镇中，如果你不出生于有教养的阶层，就很难有好的出路。也有象下面这样的活用方式：*Mrs. Snooty will never have anything to do with a person until she learns which side of the tracks he is from.* 斯努提夫人不弄清一个人究竟出身于什么阶层，她决不跟那个人打任何交道。◇ ((on→in)) the less respectable part of town / the lower echelons of society

sides

take sides [ˌteɪk ˈsaɪdz] [口] **袒护** 直译为“取一边”。尽管是“取一边”(两边中的一边)，但 side 经常要用复数。这与 I like airplanes.（我喜欢飞机。）的用法一样，在泛指一种东西时可用复数形式。冷眼一看，take sides 好象与 SIDE with *someone* 同义，但两者之间的微妙意味有所不同。也就是说，take sides 常含有“积极支持”的意思，另外还包括“一时感情冲动”或者“轻率鲁莽”之类的味道。*I don't like him. He's always taking sides.* 我不喜欢他。他总爱袒护什么人。*I think it best not to take sides on this question.* 关于这个问题，我认为最好不要偏向哪一边。*Never take sides in another's family argument.* 在别人家发生争吵的时候，千万不要去袒护哪一边啊。但在应用于自己的行为时，不受上面的释义的限制。*Why do you criticize me for taking sides?* 我支持一边，你为什么要说三道四呢？另外，take sides with *someone* 和 take sides against *someone* 也是定型的表达法。前者是““拥护”，后者是“敌对”。*That guy always takes sides with whoever he thinks is the strongest.* 那个家伙认为哪个人最强壮，他就站在哪个人一边。*They are no special friends of mine, but still I didn't expect them to take sides against me.* 他们不是与我特别要好的朋友，但是我并没有预料到他们会支持别人与我作对。◇ favor [support] one side against the other / favor [support] *someone* / favor [support] the other side against *someone*

sidewalk

a sidewalk superintendent → SUPERINTENDENT

sieve

have a memory like a sieve [ˌhævə ˌmeməri laɪkə ˈsɪ(ː)v] [话] **记性太差** 直译为“有象筛子(sieve)一样的记忆力”。这就是说，即便装到脑袋里，也会从漏洞中哗哗地掉出去。*I'm simply no good at learning languages. I've got a memory like a sieve.* 我学外语简直不行。我的记性太差啦。如这一例句所示，这一表达法在学习、工作等方面使用的场合最多，但也可以用于日常生活中的事情，例如说：*Joe has probably forgotten our appointment. That guy has a memory like a sieve.* 乔大概已经忘掉我们的约会了。那个家伙的记性太差啦。同义的表达法有 have a head [mind] like a sieve。反义表达法为 have a memory like an ELEPHANT / have a mind like a SPONGE。◇ can't remember anything

sight

Out of sight, out of mind. [ˌaudəv ˈsaɪt ˌaudəv ˈmaɪnd] [谚] **久别情日疏** 直译为“离开视线，也就离开心头”。古希腊诗人荷马(Homer)的名言。这里的“情”

主要指男女间的爱情。*They say that absence makes the heart grow fonder, but if you ask me it's more often a case of out of sight, out of mind.* 俗话说"久别情愈切",但是,我认为"久别情日疏"的具体情况更多得多啊。*While I was away, my girl friend started going with another boy. I guess the old saying is right. "Out of sight, out of mind."* 当我不在的时候,我的女朋友开始跟别的小伙子交往了。古语说得对,"久别情日疏"嘛。◇ Someone one does not see often is soon forgotten.

be a sight for sore eyes [ə ˌsaɪtfər ˈsoːraɪz] [话] **久别重逢,欣喜若狂** 直译为"对于疼痛的眼睛是好看的风景"。这一表达法原来的构思是这样: The sight of you [it] is so pleasant that it would heal sore eyes. (见到你[它]是如此高兴,简直可以治好疼痛的眼睛。)也就是把与人相会或者见到某种事物比喻为"有效的眼药"了。在与友人久别重逢的时候最常使用这一表达法。*Well, well. If you aren't a sight for sore eyes. I haven't seen you in a coon's age.* 哎呀,与你相会真高兴极啦。我很久很久没有见到你了。下面是应用于物的例子。*After I had wandered about lost in the mountains for three days, the little village was a sight for sore eyes.* 我在山中迷了路,当流浪三天之后见到一个小村庄时,我简直欣喜若狂。在下一个例句中,讲的是经常碰见的人。*Seeing you two young people back together again is a sight for these sore old eyes.* 我见到你们两个年轻人和好如初,我这一颗衰老之心也乐开了花。在这里 a sight 指的是"两个人形影不离的样子",当然不能说是"久别重逢"了。◇ be a very welcome sight

sights

raise *one's* **sights** [ˌreɪz ~ ˈsaɪts] [口] **提高目标** 这里的 sights 是"大炮的瞄准器"。raise *one's* sights 是"调高瞄准器"的意思。例如,在军队里可以这样说: *Raise your sights! The shells are falling short!* 调高瞄准器! 炮弹没有射中目标! 这一表达法转作比喻使用。*William had been planning to go to the state university, but later he decided to raise his sights and try for Harvard.* 威廉原来打算进州立大学,后来他又提高目标,要考哈佛大学啦。下面是"提高预计的标准"的意思。*The foundation raised its sights from two million to three million dollars as the goal of its fund-raising campaign.* 基金会把捐款活动的目标从二百万美元提高到了三百万美元。set *one's* sights higher 与本条条头同义。◇ decide to aim higher / decide to try for a more difficult goal

set *one's* **sights higher** [ˌset~ ˌsaɪts ˈhaɪr] [口] **提高目标** → raise *one's* SIGHTS

set *one's* **sights on** (*doing*) *something* [ˌset ~ ˈsaɪ ˌtsɔn ~] [口] **对准重大目标** sights 是"枪炮的瞄准器"。set *one's* sights on *something* 是"瞄准某物"。*John set his sights on the bear's neck.* 约翰的枪瞄准了熊的脖子。但是,这一表达法很少按照字面意义使用,一般都是作为比喻,表示"对准重大的或困难的目标"的意思。*Ralph set his sights on (getting) a law degree from Stanford.* 拉尔夫的目标是在斯坦福大学获得法学学位。*He set his sights on (winning) the new girl in school.* 他把新来的女生作为追求的对象了。在日常生活中使用的具有"用枪瞄准"意思的表达法为 take a bead on *something* [ˌteɪkə ˈbiːˌdɔn ~]。bead 是"(枪的)圆形准星"的意思。*He took a bead on the target.* 他瞄准了靶子。但是,这一表达法与 set *one's* sights on 不同,不能使用比喻的意义。◇ decide to try to get [win] *something*

silent

(as) silent as the grave → GRAVE

silk

make a silk purse out of a sow's ear → PURSE

silly

a silly billy → BILLY

silver

be born with a silver spoon in *one's* **mouth** → SPOON

Every cloud has a silver lining. → CLOUD

Simon

a Simon Legree [ə 'saɪmən lə'griː] [口] **冷酷无情的老板、上司、老师等** 来源于斯托夫人 (Harriet Beecher Stowe) 的名著《汤姆叔叔的小屋》(*Uncle Tom's Cabin*) 中所写的奴隶贩子的名字。在形容公司老板对待职工、学校教师对待学生、军队长官对待士兵要求严格而达到冷酷无情的程度时使用。 *I like my job, but my boss is a Simon Legree.* 我的工作挺可心，但是我的老板是一个冷酷无情的家伙。常用 real 加强语气。 *My math teacher is a real Simon Legree. He gives us a test every week.* 我们的数学老师实在太厉害了。他每星期都考我们一回。也可以用 a slave driver (奴隶总管) 表示同样的意义。 *Our department head is a real slave driver.* 我们的部长简直象个奴隶总管一样。◇ an unmerciful taskmaster ((a real → really a))

simpleton

a simpleton [ə 'sɪmpltən] [口] **傻瓜** 从字面上看，是"头脑简单 (simple) 的人"的意思。在实际上，也用于表示"智能低的人"。但是，这一表达法大多是指"由于没有文化和经验，因而缺乏知识、常识以及风度的人"，特别是指"容易吃亏上当的人"。含有"对这种人只能宽大处理，发火也没有用"的意味。比 a SAP 或者 a BOOB 生硬一些，但可用于同样的场合。 *Surely you're not such a simpleton as to believe that.* 你大概不会傻到相信那种事情的程度吧。→ a DUMBHEAD ◇ a stupid person

sin

(as) ugly as sin [ə 'zʌgliəz 'sɪ(ː)n] [口] **相貌奇丑** 直译为"象罪恶一样难看"。这一表达法一般用于人，有时也形容动物。 *Mr. Smith is a very nice man, but he's as ugly as sin.* 史密斯先生是一个很好的人，但是相貌奇丑。如这一例句所示，在就人而言的时候，专形容"脸"，但用于动物的场合，一般指"整个的体形"。 *Prince may be as ugly as sin, but he's a wonderful hunting dog.* 普林斯的长相也许很难看，但它可是一只神奇的猎犬呀。◇ extremely ugly

single

a single [ə 'sɪŋgl] [口] **(棒球) 一垒打** → a FOUR-BAGGER

sink

everything but the kitchen sink [ˌevriθɪŋ bətðə ˌkɪtʃən 'sɪŋk] [话] **所有的一切** 直译为"除了厨房洗涤池(kitchen sink) 而外的每件东西"。这一表达法来源不明，主要与 take, carry away, steal, bring, lose 等动词一起使用。最初的构思可能是这样："虽然要把家中的一切设备拿走，但是厨房洗涤池是被固定住的东西，既不容易拿，也没有拿走的价值。因此，只把厨房洗涤池留下，拿走其他的一切东西。在实质上，是拿走了所有的一切。"下一例句是典型的用法之一。 *Thieves broke into the warehouse and carried away everything but the kitchen sink.* 窃贼们破门进入了仓库，把所有的一切全都拿走了。在翻译的时候，千万不要译成"只留下了厨房洗涤池"。有时本条与 take, carry away, steal 等意思完全不同的动词搭配使用。 *This insurance is very complete. It covers everything but the kitchen sink.* 这种保险是非常周全的，它包括所有的一切。当用戏谑的口吻强调"不论什么东西"这句话时，可以讲 everything including the kitchen sink (每种东西，包括厨房洗涤池在内)。 *Whenever my wife goes shopping, she buys everything including the kitchen sink.* 每当我妻子去买东西的时候，她是见着什么买什么。顺便提一下：与这一表达法构思相同的习用语有 everything that isn't nailed down (所有没有用钉子钉牢的东西)，同样可以译为"不论什么东西"，但只能与 take, carry away, steal 等动词一起使用。◇ everything (possible)

sinker

hook, line and sinker → HOOK

sins

One's **sins will find** *one* **out.** [～ˈsɪ(ː)nz-wəl ˌfaɪnd ～ˈaut] [口] **只要做错事情,必然招来恶果** 直译为"一个人的罪恶将会把这个人找出来"。这一表达法的出典是《圣经·旧约》中的《民数记》(Numbers)第 32 章 23 节: But if ye will not do so, ye have sinned against the Lord: and be sure your sin will find you out. (倘若你们不这样行,就得罪耶和华,要知道你们的罪必追上你们。)在宗教的观念中,sin 的意思是"破坏上帝戒律的罪行"。但是,在本条习用语的一般用法中,这种意义几乎完全消失,仅指"不良的事情"或者"荒唐的事情"。因此,本条条头的整个意思是:"只要做了不良的或者荒唐的事情,不管你逃到哪里去,总有一天会找到你,使你受到相应的惩罚。"这与中国人"恶有恶报"以及"不是不报,时辰未到"的观念有共通之处,但没有那样严重,一般含有"从本人看起来,所干的事情并没有什么了不起"的意味。另外,在《圣经》中,sin 是单数形式,但在日常会话中,一般要说 sins。*That guy's been cheating on his wife with many different women. Someday his sins will find him out.* 那个家伙瞒着他的老婆,跟许多别的女人乱搞。早晚有一天他会吃不了兜着走的。*If our country continues to spend more money than it takes in, there will come a day when our sins will find us out.* 如果我们国家继续大把花钱,入不敷出,早晚有一天会产生恶果。这一表达法也可以应用于身体或者健康状况。*You shouldn't work so hard. Your body can take only so much punishment, then your sins will find you out.* 你不要那么拼命地干活。你的体力有一定的限度,如果超过限度,早晚有一天要累垮的。有时用于表示"由于过去行为不当,现在要承受恶果"的情况。*We've had to borrow heavily over the past year in order to stay in business, but I'm afraid our sins have finally found us out. We're bankrupt.* 为了继续营业,我们去年不得不借大量的钱,但是,很遗憾,我们终于到了该尝苦果的时候了。我们公司已经破产啦。◇ *One* will (eventually) have to pay dearly (for *one's* misdeeds [behavior, lack of prudence, etc.])

sister

a big sister [ə ˈbɪg ˈsɪstər] [口] **姐姐** 在会话中,特别是儿童和青少年,一般不用 older [elder] sister,而用 big sister。这是一个习用的表达法,与"姐姐"的年龄大小无关。它比 older [elder] sister 的说法更富有人情味。虽然用的是 big 一词,但与本人实际身体的大小也毫无关系,因此,象下面这句话也是很自然的: *Helen's big sister is smaller than she is.* 海伦的姐姐比海伦瘦小。*A: I wish I had a big sister like yours. B: You can have mine if you want.* 甲:我真希望有一个象你姐姐那样的姐姐啊。乙:如果你想要的话,就把我姐姐让给你好啦。同样,在会话中常使用的是 a little sister,而不是 a younger sister。*My little sister has three children.* 我妹妹有三个孩子。◇ an older sister

a little sister [ə ˈlɪdl ˈsɪstər] [口] **妹妹** → a big SISTER

sit

sit around (*doing* [and *do*] *something*) [ˌsɪdəˈraund] [话] **闲呆着** 在日常会话中经常使用,小说中也经常出现。直译为"这儿坐坐,那儿坐坐"。实际上也有人这样翻译,但大多不够贴切。不错,在许多场合,sit around 的确有"正在坐着"的意思,但是这一表达法所表示的是"什么有益的事情也不干,只是游手好闲地度过大好时光"的状态或者态度,从本质上说,坐着也好,不坐着也无所谓。另外,主语可以是一个人,也可以是很多人。*I wish I could find a job. I get tired of sitting around doing nothing all day.* 我希望能找到一个工作。整天无所事事地闲呆着,我已经腻味了。常用 just 加强语气。*Don't just sit around. Do something!* 别老是闲呆着。干点什么事情! *It's foolish just to sit around waiting for help that may never come.* 只是闲呆着,等待根本不可指望的支援,那是很愚蠢的事情啊。*Most days we just sit around and chew the rag.* 我们大多数的日子只是呆着胡侃一阵。*A: What are you doing now? B: Nothing. Just sitting around.* 甲:你现在干什么哪? 乙:什么也没干。只是闲呆着。*We were sitting around listening to records when there was a loud knock at the door.* 我们正闲着没事听唱片,忽然有人使劲地敲门。◇ take *one's* leisure

sit up and take notice (of *something* [*someone*]) → NOTICE

sitting

be sitting pretty → PRETTY

situation

a ticklish situation [ə ˈtɪklɪʃ ˈsɪtʃuˈeɪʃən] [口] **一发千钧** 一般来说,ticklish 是"怕痒"的意思,在这里的意思是"如果胡乱去摸,就会大动起来,千万注意",也就是"必须慎重对待"。凡是不安定的、只要处理不当就会变得无法控制的situation,常常用 ticklish 形容,并构成习用语。*With both countries threatening to attack if negotiations broke down, it was a ticklish situation.* 两国都在威胁说:如果谈判不成,就要开始进攻。局势正处于千钧一发的状态。*It was a ticklish situation. If either side realized that I was trying to help the other, my life would be worth nothing.* 情况正是千钧一发。如果任何一方了解到我正试图帮助对方,我的命就玩儿完啦。同样,在些微的失误或失言就会造成重大后果的场合,除 situation 外,也可以把 ticklish 加在 job, business, question, position 等名词的前头。*Defusing a time bomb is a ticklish job.* 卸除定时炸弹的引信是一件需要特别加小心的工作。*Trying to get the Arabs and Israelis to agree on anything is a ticklish business.* 要使阿拉伯人与以色列人在任何一个问题上达成协议,都是令人大伤脑筋的事情。*The Prime Minister hesitated to express himself on the ticklish question of beef imports.* 首相对于牛肉进口这一敏感的问题迟迟不表示自己的意见。*I'm in a very ticklish position.* 我处于一个非常微妙的地位。◇ a situation requiring great care [delicacy]

a touch-and-go situation [ə ˌtʌtʃən.gou ˌsɪtʃuˈeɪʃən] [口] **一触即发的危险局势** → be TOUCH and go

six

give *something* **the deep six** [ˌgɪv ~ ðə ˌdi(ː)pˈsɪ(ː)ks] [话] **抛弃(某物)** → DEEP-SIX *something*

be six of one and half a dozen of the other [ˌsɪksəv ˈwʌnən ˌhæ(ː)fə ˌdʌzənə ˈðʌ(ː)ðər] [口] **相差无几** 直译为"一边是 6,一边是 12 的一半",也就是"结果相同"。一般英汉词典常把这一表达法译成"五十步笑百步"、"半斤八两"等,但是,它实际上并不含有"两者都没有什么了不起"的轻蔑意味,只是强调"差不多"而已,务请读者注意。*A: Would you rather go to Harvard or Columbia? B: I don't know. It's six of one and half a dozen of the other as far as I'm concerned.* 甲:你想进哈佛大学还是哥伦比亚大学? 乙:不知道。对于我来说,进哪一所都一样。*I've listened to the arguments of both men and I still don't know which one is at fault. It sounds like six of one and half a dozen of the other to me.* 我听了两个人的辩论,但是我还是没有弄清哪一方的论点站不住脚。据我看,二者没有什么差别啊。*There were reasons why I should go, but on the other hand there seemed to be just as many why I shouldn't. It was a case of six of one and half a dozen of the other.* 我有一些应该去的理由,但是不应该去的理由似乎也同样多。这是一个不分轩轾的问题。◇ there is [being] really no difference

six-gun

a six-gun [ə ˈsɪks.gʌ(ː)n] [话] **六响左轮** → a SIX-SHOOTER

six-shooter

a six-shooter [ə ˈsɪks.ʃu(ː)dər] [话] **六响左轮** 特指牛仔使用的六连发马枪,也是一

般手枪的戏称。 *Almost all cowboys used to carry six-shooters.* 几乎所有的牛仔都经常携带六响左轮。又称 a six-gun ['sɪks.gʌ(:)n]。◇ a six-shot revolver / a pistol

skeleton

a family skeleton [ə ˌfæməli 'skelətən] [口] **严格保密的家丑** → a SKELETON in the closet

a skeleton in the closet [ə 'skelətənɪnðə 'klɑːzət] [口] **决不外扬的家丑** 直译为"壁橱里的骷髅"。这一表达法是从如下的构思产生的:"某人被杀,尸体被藏到壁橱里了"。在实际使用的场合,一般也是应用于家庭内部的事情。*The way the Joneses avoid all conversation concerning Mr. Jones' younger brother leads me to suspect a skeleton in the closet.* 琼斯一家都极力避免谈论琼斯先生的弟弟,我怀疑他们一定有不愿外扬的家丑。*Many old families have a number of skeletons in their closets which they are loath to discuss.* 许多旧世家都有他们一系列避口不谈的家丑。closet 的前边有时加 family。*Don't say anything about my uncle's marrying a bar girl. My mother considers that a skeleton in the family closet.* 关于我叔叔与一个酒吧女郎结婚的事情,你一个字也不要提。我母亲认为那是不可外扬的家丑。也讲 a family skeleton。 *Now that we are to be married, I'll tell you about our family skeleton. My brother is actually only my half-brother, having been born secretly to a maid that used to work for my family.* 现在我们要结婚了,我把我们家的家丑告诉你。我的弟弟实际上跟我同父异母,他是我家一个女仆的私生子。另外,英国英语不用 closet,而用 cupboard,但在美国英语中决不使用后者。◇ a (scandalous) family secret

skies

praise *someone* [*something*] **to the skies** (for *something*) ['preɪz ~ təðə 'skaɪz] [口] **极力称赞** 直译为"称赞 (praise) 到天上 (to the skies)",与汉语俗话"捧上了天"的说法相同。但"捧上了天"含有贬义,本条习用语一般为褒义,在翻译时要注意。 *The President praised his staff to the skies for securing passage of the bill.* 由于总统的部下能使法案得到通过,总统对他们大加赞扬。*The principal, very happy that so many graduates had succeeded in entering first-rate universities, praised his teachers to the skies.* 校长见到许许多多毕业生都考取了一流大学,他非常高兴,对本校的老师们极力称赞。*Every one of the guests praised the hostess's cooking to the skies.* 客人们交口称赞女主人的烹调妙技。◇ give *someone* [*something*] unlimited praise

skin

Beauty is only skin deep. → BEAUTY

by the skin of *one's* **teeth** [ˌbaɪðə ˌskɪnəv ~ 'tiːθ] [话] **险些没有……** 这一表达法的出典是《圣经 · 旧约》中的《约伯记》(Job) 第 19 章 20 节。有些英语词典作 with the skin ~,这来源于《钦定本英文圣经》(King James Bible, 1611 年) 的译文 I am escaped with the skin of my teeth. 属于陈词滥调,现在无人使用。最近的《圣经》作 I have escaped by the skin of my teeth. 这是现代化的文章。这一表达法虽然很古老,但是现在仍然生动活泼,人们经常使用。*They escaped the burning building by the skin of their teeth.* 他们险些没有逃出失火的楼房。常用 just 加强语气。*We made the train just by the skin of our teeth.* 我们差一点没赶上火车。这一表达法应用在"时间"的场合最多 (意思为"差一点没赶上……"),但是也用于与时间没关系的事情,仅表示"勉勉强强"的意思。例如: *George passed English by the skin of his teeth.* 乔治考英语勉勉强强及了格。◇ barely ((放在主要动词前边))

be drenched to the skin [ˌdrentʃt(:)əðə 'skɪn] [口] **衣服被雨淋透了** 字面意义为"直到皮肤完全淋湿了"。只能用于穿着

衣服被雨淋的场合。*Having been caught in a sudden shower, we were drenched to the skin.* 我们遇到阵雨，衣服全都湿透了。◇ be wet clear to the skin / *one's* clothes are thoroughly wet

get under *someone's* **skin**[①] [ˌgedˈʌndər ～ ˈskɪ(ː)n] [话] **触怒** 这一表达法有完全不同的两个意义，其一是“触怒”，另一个是“入迷”，后一意义说明见下一条目。一个表示“不愉快”，一个表示“愉快（至少对本人来说）”，乍看起来，这两个意义大相径庭，但是，如果对这句英语溯本求源，就会了解两者出于一根。也就是说，按照字面意义，get under *one's* skin 是“有什么东西进入皮肤里了”。假如是刺儿、尘土之类令人不舒服的东西进入皮肤，当然会“激怒”；相反，如果是自己喜欢的、感到舒服的东西进入皮肤，就会“心花怒放”了。究竟是哪个意义，只能根据上下文进行判断。例如：That music gets under my skin. 如果只说这么一句，就无法判断说话人的真正意思是“那种音乐刺耳”还是“那种音乐悦耳”。“触怒”于人的东西有语言、说话方式、态度（神情）、人本身、笑声等等，范围极广。下面两个例句分别是语言和说话方式使人不高兴的场合。*Several things she said got under his skin.* 在她所说的话中，有几句使他很不高兴。*It's not her words, it's the way she says them that gets under my skin.* 使我恼火的并不是她的话，而是她的说话方式。在下一例句中，弄不清指的是人品、态度还是言语。*I don't consider myself a sensitive person, but that guy has a knack for getting under my skin.* 我不认为自己是一个神经过敏的人，但是，我一见那个家伙就憋不住生气。下面是指声音的场合。*That raucous laugh of his is getting under my skin.* 他那刺耳的笑声使我心里不住冒火。也常使用 let ～ get under *one's* skin 的形式。*You mustn't let Ann's criticism get under your skin.* 你不必为安的批评恼火啊。◇ irritate *someone*

get under *someone's* **skin**[②] [ˌgedˈʌndər ～ ˈskɪ(ː)n] [话] **入迷** 这一表达法大多使用上一条①的意思，但也常用本条②的意思。在②的场合，有“渗入皮肤中”的感觉，常伴有“在不知不觉之间”的意思。*I can't forget Jeanne. She's gotten under my skin.* 我不能忘掉珍妮。她已经走入我的心扉了。*I had planned to leave China after a year or two, but now I'm afraid it's too late. I've let this country get under my skin.* 我本来打算呆上一、二年就离开中国，但是现在可能为时已晚了。我已经迷上了这个国家。另有 have *someone* under *one's* skin 的表达法，一般应用于男女关系。*I've got you under my skin.* 你已经使我心醉神迷了。*Maybe it's unwise to marry Gene, but I can't help myself. I have him under my skin.* 也许同吉恩结婚不是一件聪明的事情，但是我已经身不由己啦。我迷上他了。◇ captivate *someone*

have a thick skin [ˌhævə ˌθɪk ˈskɪ(ː)n] [口] **脸憨皮厚** → THICK-SKINNED

have a thin skin [ˌhævə ˌθɪn ˈskɪ(ː)n] [口] **脸嫩皮薄** → THIN-SKINNED

have *someone* **under** *one's* **skin** [ˌhæv ～ ˌʌndər ～ ˈskɪ(ː)n] [话] **被某人迷住** → get under *someone's* SKIN[②]

jump out of *one's* **skin** [ˌdʒʌmˌpaudəv～ ˈskɪ(ː)n] [话] **吓一大跳** 直译为“从自己的皮肤里跳出来”。这是一个非常夸张的说法，在被吓得心惊肉跳的时候经常使用。有些英汉词典译成“惊喜若狂”，其实这一表达法只能在“惊”的场合使用。有时又作 leap out of *one's* skin，不过，在会话中多用 jump out ～。*The sound of the door banging shut in the deserted house made me jump out of my skin.* 在无人居住的破房子里，门砰的一声关上了，这声音把我吓了一大跳。常加 almost 或 nearly 调整语气，意思完全不变。例如：*When the car behind me backfired, I almost jumped out of my skin.* 当我后边的汽车发生逆火的时候，我被吓了一大跳。*I opened the door and nearly jumped out of my skin. There stood a man I had thought was dead for many years.* 我打开门，被吓了好大一跳。门里站着的那个人，我本来以为他

死了好多年了。◇ jump (with surprise [fright]) ((不加 almost, nearly))

be no skin off *someone's* **back** [nou ˌskɪn-ˌə(ː)f ˈ~ˌbæ(ː)k] [话] **无关痛痒** 直译为"不会剥去某人背上的皮"。这一表达法的来源是：古时，在惩罚水手时，用鞭子抽其后背，直到皮开肉绽的程度。最初的构思是："因为与事情毫无瓜葛，不会被抽开后背的皮"。*Why should he care whether I join the army and get killed or not? It's no skin off his back one way or the other.* 他怎么会关心我是否参军、会不会在战场上被打死呢？这完全无关他的痛痒啊。*I think you're a fool to marry her, but if you want to lead a miserable life, it's no skin off my back.* 我认为你要跟她结婚，实在太愚蠢了。不过，如果你愿意去过不幸的生活，那与我又有何干呢？另有 be no skin off *someone's* nose 的说法，也常使用。实际上就是把 back 改成了 nose(鼻子)，构思是"由于跌倒而碰破了鼻子的皮"。*Go ahead. Squander your money if you want. It's no skin off my nose.* 请随君便吧。你想挥霍你的钱财，那你就挥霍好啦。这与我无关痛痒啊。除 back 或 nose 外，有时用 elbow (肘)代换。*Do what you want. Either way it's no skin off my elbow.* 你想干什么就干什么吧。无论怎么样，也不关我的痛痒啊。有时使用 be 动词以外的动词。*So he was driving my car when he ran into somebody. So what? That doesn't mean any skin off my back.* 他撞人的时候，开的的确是我的汽车。可是，那又怎样呢？车是我的，但不能由此推论撞人也与我有干系呀。◇ be no concern of *someone's*

be no skin off *someone's* **elbow** [nou ˌskɪn ˌɔ(ː)f ˈ~ˌelbou] [话] **与某人没有干系** → be no SKIN off *someone's* back

be no skin off *someone's* **nose** [nou ˌskɪn-ˌɔ(ː)f ˈ~ˌnouz] [话] **不关某人的痛痒** → be no SKIN off *someone's* back

be only skin and bones [ˌounli ˌskɪnən-ˈbounz] [口] **只剩下皮包骨了** 指骨瘦如柴的人或者动物而言。*When the miners emerged from the ground two weeks after the cave-in, they were only skin and bones.* 在冒顶两个星期之后，当采煤工人从井下出来的时候，他们只剩下皮包骨了。这一表达法一般用 only，但也有时用 just, mere, nothing but 等。*That dog must be sick. It's just skin and bones.* 那条狗一定有病，它只剩下皮包骨啦。*You should eat more. You're nothing but skin and bones.* 你必须多吃点啦。你只剩下皮和骨头，连一点儿肉也没有了。→ a bag of BONES ◇ be extremely thin

save *one's* **own skin** [ˌseɪv ~ˈounˈskɪ(ː)n] [话] **保全自己** 直译为"救自己的皮肤"，意思是"别叫人家剥了皮"，亦即"保全自己"。这里的 skin 是"身体"或"生命"的意思。*When the fire broke out, everyone began pushing and shoving, desperate to save their own skins.* 当火灾发生的时候，每个人都连推带搡，拼命逃生。如此例所示，这一表达法含有"只顾自己"的意味。*I don't trust Barry. When the shooting starts, I'm sure he'll run off and leave us. He won't think about anything but saving his own skin.* 我不信任巴里。枪声一响，他就会扔下我们，逃之夭夭。他除了自己逃命而外，什么也不会考虑的啊。这一表达法不一定直接与"生命"挂钩，也可以用作比喻。*I had nothing to do with their cheating on the exam. She only accused me in order to save her own skin.* 他们在考试中作弊，这事与我不沾边儿。她只是为了开脱自己才指责我的呀。下一例句中的 sweet skin 的 sweet 是强调用语，具有"宝贵的"、"贵重的"的意味。*When the embezzlement came to light, Larry went to the police in hopes of saving his own sweet skin.* 当盗用公款的事情被发觉以后，拉利到警察局投案自首，希望保全自己。有时用 save *one's* own neck 表示同样的意义。◇ save *one's* own life / protect *oneself*

skin *someone* **alive** [ˌskɪn~əˈlaɪv] [话] **活剥某人的皮** 对于动物，可以按照字面意义使用，讲"活剥它的皮"。对于人，当然是比喻的用法，常带有威胁或警告的意思。*If the teacher catches you cheating, she'll skin you alive.* 如果老师抓住你考

试作弊，她会活剥你的皮的。这是严厉叱责的意思。*When the boss discovered we had sneaked out to a baseball game, he practically skinned us alive.* 当老板发现我们偷偷溜出去看棒球比赛的时候，他简直活剥了我们的皮哟。特别是在大人愤怒地威胁孩子的时候，这一表达法不仅含有叱责的意思，而且包括有体罚的可能性。因此，在受威胁的一方来说，就不仅是受口头的叱责，一般怀有"不知如何被惩处"的恐怖心情。*If I catch you snitching cookies again, I'll skin you alive.* 如果我再抓住你偷饼干吃，我要活剥你的皮。*You kids just try stealing apples from this store once more. I'll skin you alive.* 你们这些小鬼，再从我这商店偷一回苹果试试看！我会活剥你们的皮。从"活剥对方的皮"这一构思进一步发展，这一表达法还用于表示"把对方彻底打垮"或"使对方一败涂地"的意思。*A: Do you think you'll beat the opposing team? B: Yes, we'll skin them alive.* 甲：你认为你们队会击败对手吗？乙：是的，我们会把他们打得一败涂地。*The Pittsburgh Steelers skinned the Dallas Cowboys alive in the Pro-Bowl game.* 在职业保龄球比赛中，达拉斯牛仔队被匹兹堡钢铁工人队打得个落花流水。◇ reprimand [punish] *someone* severely / beat *someone* by a big score

skinny-dipping

go skinny-dipping [ˌgou ˈskɪniˌdɪpən] [话] **裸体游泳** skinny 一般作"瘦得皮包骨"解，但在这里的意思是"只有皮肤(skin)"，也就是"一丝不挂"。dipping 是"浸渍"。go skinny-dipping 直译为"去裸体游泳"，但这一表达法并不一定含有"去"的意味。例如说 Let's go skinny-dipping in the lake. 根据上下文，可能是"咱们到湖里裸体游泳去吧"的意思，也可能是"咱们在湖里裸体游泳吧"的意思。也有动词 skinny-dip，但很少使用。*When we were kids, we used to go skinny-dipping in the river.* 我们小的时候，常在河里裸体游泳。如果把这句话改为 ~ we used to skinny-dip in the river. 在语法上毫无错误，然而极少有人这样说。另外，作为动名词使用，例如说 I don't like skinny-dipping. (我不喜欢裸体游泳。) 这在语法上也没有错误，但并非习用的说法。如果讲流畅的英语，应为 I don't like to go skinny-dipping. ◇ go swimming in the nude

skip

skip work [a meeting] [ˌskɪpˈwə(ː)rk / ˌskɪpə ˈmiːdɪŋ] [口] **逃避工作[会议]** → GOOF off

skirt

a skirt [ə ˈskə(ː)rt] [俗] **青年女子** 这一表达法的来源是女性穿的 skirt (裙子)。这与中国旧时用"裙钗"一词指女子是同样的构思。因为是把女子看作"物"，所以只有男人使用这一表达法。虽然不算下流话，女性当然并不喜欢如此被称呼。大多指"青年女子"或"妙龄女郎"。*There are a lot of good-looking skirts among the new freshmen this year.* 在今年新入学的大学一年级生中，有很多好看的姑娘。*This is a stag party. No skirts allowed.* 此为男子集会，女性不得参加。*Who's that skirt Joe's squiring?* 乔带来的那个女子是谁呀？a skirt chaser 的意思是"专门追逐女性的人"。*That guy is a real skirt chaser. He runs after every pretty girl he sees.* 那家伙真是一个好色之徒，他见一个漂亮的姑娘就追一个。这一表达法又作 a woman chaser。◇ a girl / a (young) woman

a skirt chaser [ə ˈskə(ː)rt.tʃeɪsər] [俗] **专门追逐女性的人** → a SKIRT

skivvies

skivvies [ˈskɪvi(ː)z] [俗] **男子内衣** 与 underwear (内衣) 同义。一般为 T 恤衫 (T- Shirt)类和所谓短裤 (shorts)的总称。单数形式 a skivvy 或 a skivvy shirt 指"T 恤衫式内衣"，略嫌陈腐。但在美国海军中，现在仍用 skivvy 一词指称他们的制服中的 undershirt。*When Jane came in, Mike was still in his skivvies.* 当简走进屋里的时候，麦克还只穿着内衣。*He bought two sets of skivvies.* 他买了两套内衣。这一表达法有时仅指"短

裤”，但经常用复数形式。*Hey, Rick, can you lend me a clean pair of skivvies?* 喂，里克，你能借给我一条干净的短裤吗？顺便讲一下：在英国英语中，skivvy 是“女佣人”的蔑称，美国人不用此义。◇ underwear

sky

out of a clear blue sky [ˌaudəvə ˈklɪ(ː)r ˈbluː ˈskaɪ] [口] **意想不到** 直译为“从一个明亮的、蓝色的天空出来”，意思是“没有任何预兆，突如其来”。表示“突然地”、“意想不到地”，比 suddenly 一词更为强烈。*It came to me out of a clear blue sky.* 我忽然想起这件事来。就在这一例句中，也含有“过去完全没有考虑到”这样一种“突如其来”的意味。为了加强语气，常与 suddenly 一起使用。*Suddenly, out of a clear blue sky, an old friend from Denmark appeared on my doorstep.* 突然，一位丹麦老朋友意想不到地出现在我家的门前。大多与表示“说”的动词（如 ask, say, tell 之类）搭配。*Out of a clear blue sky, he asked me for a thousand dollars.* 他突如其来地向我要一千美元。有时在这一表达法前面加 from，而讲 from out of a clear blue sky，意思相同。也可以象 (from) out of a clear [blue] sky 这样，或是省略 blue，或是省略 clear，但极罕见。另有类似的表达法 out of [from] the blue（这里的 blue 为名词，诗歌用语，指“晴空”），意思和用法均与本条大致相同，只是语气稍弱一些。*We were discussing the weather when, out of the blue, he asked me to marry him.* 我们俩正在谈论天气，他突然向我求婚了。◇ (suddenly and) unexpectedly

Reach for the sky. [ˈri(ː)tʃ fəðə ˈskaɪ] [话] **举起手来！** reach for ～是“伸手去取……”，所以本条习用语直译为“把手伸出去取天空”，亦即“把手高高地举起来”的意思。*Reach for the sky or I'll shoot.* 举起手来，要不我开枪啦。有时省略，只说 Reach.例如：*Reach! I got you covered.* 举起手来！我的枪对准你啦。◇ Put your hands up. / Hands up.

sky juice → JUICE

sky's

the sky's the limit [ðəˈskaɪz ðəˈlɪmɪt] [口] **无限制** 直译为“天空是限度”，因为天空没有边际，所以这一表达法的意思是“没有界限”。在应用于金钱时，常表示“金钱的数额没有上限”。*You can bet any amount you want. The sky's the limit.* 你愿意下多少赌金都可以，没有限制。*We made a little money this time, but this is peanuts compared with what we can really do. Stick with me and the sky's the limit.* 咱们这一次赚了一点儿钱，但是与咱们实际能够赚的钱相比，不过九牛一毛而已。你跟我合作，不知会赚多么多哪。这一表达法还应用于晋升、发迹以及人生的前景等，范围非常广阔。*If you come to work for us, the sky's the limit. With talent and hard work, you can even become president some day.* 如果你来我们这里工作，前途不可限量啊。依靠能力和苦干，你将来都有可能当上总经理。*When I was young, I felt that the sky was the limit. Now I realize that the dreams of my youth were just that—only dreams.* 当我年轻的时候，我觉得人生的美景是无限的。现在我明白了自己青春时代的美梦只不过是美梦而已。◇ there's no limit (to what *someone* can do)

slammer

the slammer [ðə ˈslæːmər] [话] **拘留所** → the CLINK

slave

a slave driver [ə ˈsleɪv ˌdraɪvər] [口] **拿人当牛马一般对待的老板、上司、教员等** → a SIMON LEGREE

sleep

get some sleep [ˌgetsəm ˈsliːp] [口] **睡觉** → SLEEP

go to sleep [ˌgoudə ˈsliːp] [口] **睡觉** → SLEEP

sleep [ˈsliːp] [口] **睡觉** 相当于汉语“睡觉”的英语，除 sleep 外，常说的有 go to bed, go to sleep, get some sleep 等。从翻译

的角度来说，一概可以译成“睡觉”，但是这些英语的用法相互各有一些差异。首先是 go to bed，用不着说，这是“到床上去”的意思。 *Well, let's go to bed.* 好啦，咱们睡觉吧。这句话的含意是：“咱们现在换上睡衣，上床休息好吗？”如果把这句话改成 Let's sleep. 或者 Let's go to sleep.那是“咱们合上眼睛睡吧”的意思。Let's sleep. 或者 Let's go to sleep. 是已经换好睡衣上床就寝，而且一边躺着一边闲聊之后才使用的语言。 get some sleep 在以上两种情况下均可使用，另外，在没有床而“睡觉”的场合也可以使用。从意义上讲，比 go to bed 或者 go to sleep 更为积极，它强调“睡觉的必要性”。 *We have to get up at five o'clock tomorrow morning, you know. We'd better get some sleep.* 你要知道，咱们明天早晨五点钟必须起床。咱们最好马上睡觉。 *I was up all night last night studying. I've really got to get some sleep to-night.* 我昨天学习了一夜。今天晚上我可非睡觉不可啦。否定式 not get any [much] sleep 是在“本想睡觉，但由于某种原因(如身体有病、心里有事、有工作或应酬等)而未能就寝或入睡”的情况下使用的表达法。 *I didn't get any sleep last night. I had to play mahjongg with the boss until daybreak.* 昨天我一夜没睡，因为我不得不陪老板打麻将一直打到天明。 *With the neighbor's dog barking like that, I didn't get much sleep last night.* 由于邻居的狗那样狂吠，我昨天夜里就没睡多少觉。另外，get some sleep 的轻松说法为 get some SHUT-EYE。

sleeve

have an ace up *one's* **sleeve** → ACE

have something up *one's* **sleeve** [ˌhæv ˈsʌmθɪŋ ˌʌp ～ ˈsliːv] [口] **有所图谋** 有 have [keep] a card up *one's* sleeve 这样一个表达法，意思是“把一张扑克牌藏在袖子里”。这是在玩扑克牌时的一种不正当行为。 *He had a card up his sleeve.* 他把一张牌藏在袖子里啦。把这一表达法中的 a card 改换成 something，就构成本条条头的英语，直译为“袖子里藏着某种东西”。something 总是指“坏主意”。这一表达法专用作比喻，意味着“心怀叵测”、“搞阴谋诡计”。 *I don't trust that guy. He's always got something up his sleeve.* 我不信任那个家伙。他总搞阴谋诡计。 *The American military suspected that Japan might have something up her sleeve, but was obviously unprepared for a strike against Pearl Harbor.* 美军感觉到日本大概有什么阴谋诡计，但是对于日本偷袭珍珠港显然没有准备。常用 some trick 代替 something。例如：*I knew he must have some trick up his sleeve, but what it was I couldn't fathom.* 我知道他肯定有阴谋诡计，但是我摸不透究竟是什么坏主意。如果谈到自己有什么点子时，一般不用 something 或 some trick，而要用 a few tricks 或者 a few cards 等。因为自己“企图”的内容用不着去猜测，当然就不能用 something 或 some trick 了。 *Don't worry. I haven't lost yet. I still have a few tricks [cards] up my sleeve.* 不必担心。我还没有输。我还有一点妙计啊。下面的例句是疑问句的形式。*I don't like that look in your eye, Tom. What have you got up your sleeve?* 汤姆，我不喜欢你那个眼神儿。你在打什么坏主意哪？以上各例句中的动词全是 have，不过有时可以用 keep。但是，keep 有“另有心计，以备万一”的意味。 *Paul's offer seems straightforward enough, but we'd better be careful. He may be keeping something up his sleeve.* 保罗的建议似乎十分真诚，但是咱们还是加点小心为好。他也许别有心计哪。另外，如果把 something 改换为 an ace，而讲 have an ACEup *one's* sleeve (→)，那就是“手中握有王牌”的意思了。◇ have some secret plan

laugh up *one's* **sleeve** (at *someone* [*something*]) [ˌlæ(ː)ˌfʌp ～ ˈsliːv] [口] **暗笑** sleeve 是“袖子”，up *one's* sleeve 是“向着袖子里边”，加上 laugh，就是“向着袖子里边笑”的意思了。这是从 16 世纪下半叶就有的一个古老的表达法。当时，绅士们的上衣袖口很宽，他们在嘲笑

别人的时候，总是把脸藏到袖口里去笑。本条习用语即来源于此。这与中国京剧中的旦角在笑时往往用衣袖掩上嘴一样。现在，西服已经改变为窄袖，因此这一表达法就具有了“窃笑”、“暗笑”、“偷偷地笑”的意味。*George listens very courteously to everything I have to say, but I always have the feeling that he's laughing up his sleeve at me all the while.* 每当我说什么话的时候，乔治总是必恭必敬地听着，但是我始终有这样一种感觉：他虽然在听我的话，心里却不住地暗暗笑我。这是当着对方的面“心中暗笑”。也有与对方不在一起而“暗暗嘲笑”的场合，例如：*After Carter became President, Frenchmen stopped laughing up their sleeves at American policy. They started laughing out loud.* 自从卡特当总统之后，法国人不再暗笑美国的政策了。他们开始哈哈大笑了。另外，laugh up *one's*sleeve 的 up 有时用 in 代替，在这一场合，“嘲笑”的程度有减弱的倾向。*Don't just sit there laughing in your sleeve. If you think you can come up with a better idea than mine, let's hear it.* 你不要光坐在那里偷偷的笑呀。如果你认为你能够有比我更好的主意，让我们来听一听嘛。◇ be secretly amused

wear *one's* **heart on** *one's* **sleeve** → HEART

slew

a slew [ə 'slu:] [话] **许许多多** 与 slay(杀)的过去式拼法相同，但这一 slew 实际上来源于爱尔兰语 *sluagh*(意思是“许多”。发音与 slew 大致相同)。两者形同而意义完全不同，千万不要弄混。例如：*Jack slew a slew of giants.* 这句话的意思是：*Jack killed a lot of giants.* 杰克杀死了许多的巨大的动物。*I've got a slew of homework.* 我有大量的家庭作业。如以上的例句所示，一般用单数形式，但是，如果以强调的语气来讲，也可以用复数形式：*I've get slews of homework.* 我有大批大批的家庭作业啊。这句话与添加 whole 而讲 I've a whole slew of homework. 几乎完全一样，表示“堆积如山”的意思。有时拼写作 slue。◇ a lot

slew-foot

slew-foot ['slu:,fut] [口] **两脚往外撇** → PIGEON-TOED

slicker

a city slicker [ə 'sɪdi 'slɪkər] [口] **城里老油子** 农村居民对城市人的蔑称。slicker 是由形容词 slick (口齿伶俐的、狡猾的)加 -er 构成的名词，因而含有“他们总要欺骗乡下人，不可不加小心”的意味。*When our son went to New York, he was cheated out of his money by a city slicker.* 当我家的儿子去纽约的时候，他的钱被一个城里老油子骗走了。*When the railroad was put through our town, the place was suddenly swarming with city slickers out to make a quick buck.* 当我们的小镇通了铁路的时候，城里的老油子们突然蜂拥而至，企图在这里马上捞到一笔钱。反义语为 a country HICK。◇ a sly, city-bred fellow

slim

be slim pickings → PICKINGS

sling

sling hash → HASH

slip

a Freudian slip [ə 'frɔɪdiən 'slɪp] [口] **下意识泄露动机、愿望等的失言或笔误** Freudian 是“弗洛伊德的”或“弗洛伊德精神分析法的”。slip 是“滑脱(舌头或钢笔)”的意思。因此，如果在你的心里考虑 a Freudian slip 的后边是省略了 of the tongue 或者 of the pen，对这一表达法就容易理解了。这一表达法的来源是：弗洛伊德认为人们所以会把并没有想说或想写的东西错误地说了或写了出来，乃是下意识的欲望或思想的表现。举例来讲，如果有一个男子见到一个正给婴儿吃奶的年轻美貌的母亲，本来想对她说 You certainly have a lovely baby. (你的宝宝真可爱。)结果却说成了 You certainly have a lovely breast. (你的乳房真可爱。)这就是由于对 lovely breast 的意识比对 lovely baby 的意识强烈，结果走了嘴 (a slip of the tongue),

犯了 a Freudian slip 的过错。*Skippy made a Freudian slip when he told my secretary he wanted to give her a massage. He meant to say he wanted to give her a message.* 斯基皮下意识地说走了嘴。他本来要对我的女秘书说：他想告诉她一个信息 *(message)*，结果却说成了：他想给她按摩 *(massage)*。"失言"的人常有立即纠正自己的用语的情况，而听的人也常用这一表达法去回敬那个说错话的人。在这一场合，Freudian slip 的意思与"真心话"、"老实话"相近。例如：*A: Darling, don't be angry. You know how much I abhor you—I mean, adore you. B: Talk about a Freudian slip!* 甲：亲爱的，你别生气。你要知道，我是多么讨厌 *(abhor)* 你——不不，我是说多么热爱 *(adore)* 你。乙：到底把真心话吐出来啦！下面是"笔误"的例子。"*He is a bear." was a Freudian slip. He meant to write "He is a dear."* "他很粗鲁 *(bear)*"是下意识的笔误。他本来是要写"他很可爱 *(dear)*"。◇ inadvertently saying what *one* is really thinking ((make ～ → inadvertently say ～))

give *someone* **the slip** [.gɪv ～ðə 'slɪ(:)p] [话] **甩开某人** 这里的 slip 可以认为是 slip away from *someone* (从某人身边偷偷逃走) 中的 slip 的名词用法，意思是"趁对方一不留神而溜之大吉"。这一表达法的使用范围极广，如本来约定好了的约会却不赴约的场合，有人钉梢而把此人甩掉的场合，对方纠缠不休而自己巧妙逃避的场合，等等。*Ben promised to meet us at his lawyer's office over two hours ago. It looks like he's given us the slip.* 本约定在他的律师的事务所与我们会面，时间已经过两个多钟头了。看起来，他是把我们涮啦。*We've got to get to the meeting place on time. If we don't, Marcello will think we've given him the slip and gone back to America.* 我们必须准时到达约定会面的场所。如果我们不这样，马塞洛就会认为我们甩开他回美国了。*The man I'm sitting with isn't my date. He's just some stranger who's trying to make time with me. I'll give him the slip and meet you out front at ten o'clock.* 跟我坐在一起的男人并不是我约会的人。他只是个陌生人，死皮赖脸地缠着我。我会摆脱他的纠缠，十点钟在门口与你相会。也常用于表示"巧妙地逃开钉梢者的眼睛"，亦即与 shake *someone* (甩开某人) 的意思相同。*I followed him for over an hour before he finally gave me the slip in a crowded department store.* 我跟踪他一个多小时，最后他在挤满了人的百货店里把我甩掉了。也可以说 give *someone* the shake，常能代换 give *someone* the slip，但使用频率没有本条习用语高。◇ get away from *someone* / leave *someone*

let *something* [*someone*] **slip through** *one's* **fingers** → FINGERS

make a slip of the tongue [.meɪkə .slɪpəvðə 'tʌ(:)ŋ] [口] **走嘴** 在漫不经心地说出不该说的话的场合常常使用。"不该说的话"包括伤害对方的话、使对方恼怒的话、不得公开的秘密，以及暴露秘密的话，等等。*My wife is mad at me because I made a simple slip of the tongue. I meant to say "I adore you," but I said "I abhor you."* 由于我说话走了嘴，我的妻子对我大为恼火。我本来要说"我喜爱 *(adore)* 你"，但是说成了"我讨厌 *(abhor)* 你"。a slip 有时用 that slip 的形式。*They would never have found out about our plan if you hadn't made that slip of the tongue.* 如果你不是象那样随口乱说，他们决不会发觉咱们的计划啊。也有与 make 以外的词搭配使用的情况。*I'm sorry I hurt your feelings. It was only a slip of the tongue.* 我伤害了你的感情，向你道歉。我是一时说走了嘴。*The suspect convicted himself with a slip of the tongue. He said "I didn't kill her," even though no one had told him the murdered person was a woman.* 嫌疑犯由于说走了嘴而承认了自己的罪行。本来没有任何人告诉他被杀害的是一个女人，而他却说"我没有杀害她"。◇ inadvertently use the wrong word(s) [say the wrong thing]((不加 simple 等))

slippery

(as) slippery as an eel → EEL

slot

a slot machine [ə 'slɑ(ː)t mə,ʃiːn] [口] **吃角子老虎** → a one-armed BANDIT

slow

(as) slow as Christmas → CHRISTMAS

slue

a slue [ə 'sluː] [话] **许多** → a slew

slue-foot

slue-foot ['sluː,fut] [口] **外八字脚** → PIGEON-TOED

sly

on the sly [,ɔ(ː)nðə 'slaɪ] [话] **偷偷地** sly 是"狡猾的"。本条习用语最初的构思是:"很狡猾地躲开他人的眼睛"。*I just found out that my boy friend has been dating Alice on the sly.* 我刚刚发现我的男朋友偷偷地与艾丽丝约会啦。不仅用于象这样"偷偷地"干坏事的场合,也可以用于只是由于怕人家知道或者害臊而"偷偷地"干的场合。这一表达法与 secretly 一样,与事情本身的善恶无关,使用范围很广。*Because my father objects to my dating Tom, we have to meet on the sly.* 由于我父亲反对我跟汤姆约会,所以我们只好偷偷地见面。*Afraid that his comic- book- loving friends would laugh at him, Sam began reading great works of literature on the sly.* 萨姆害怕那些爱看连环漫画的朋友们笑他,偷偷地开始阅读著名的文学作品。◇ secretly

(as) sly as a fox → FOX

smackers

smackers ['smækərz] [话] **美元** → CLAMS

small

be small potatoes [,smɔːl pə'teɪdəz] [话] **规模小;等级低;没有什么了不起** → be small BEER

small beer

small beer ['smɔːl 'bɪːr] [话] **微不足道** → be small BEER

smart

get smart (with *someone*) [,get 'smɑ(ː)rt] [话] **口出狂言** → get WISE (with *someone*)

a smart aleck [ə 'smɑ(ː)r,dælɪk] [话] **狂妄自大的人** → a wise GUY

smash

smash *something* **up** [,smæ(ː)ʃ ~ 'ʌ(ː)p] [口] **打碎** → BANG *something* up

smile

not crack a smile [nɑt ,krækə 'smaɪl] [话] **没有一丝笑容** 直译为"不使微笑出裂缝"。最初的构思是:"不使脸上绽出微笑"。有时说:*The little boy finally cracked a smile.* 那个小男孩终于绽出了微笑。但一般用于否定句,讲:*The little boy didn't crack a smile.* 那个小男孩不曾有一点笑容。也常使用 without cracking a smile 的形式。*George tells jokes without cracking a smile.* 乔治在讲笑话的时候,自己没有一点笑容。◇ not smile (even a bit)

smoke

Holy smoke! ['houli'smouk] [话] **哎呀,天哪!** → Holy cow!

Watch *someone's* **smoke.** ['wɑtʃ ~ 'smouk] [话] **且看多么麻利快** 直译为"瞧着某人做事[干活]的速度快得冒烟了"。这一表达法是用机械以猛烈的速度旋转,就会发热冒"烟"作为比喻。从漫画上常常可以见到,在飞速奔跑的人或车的背后,画烟状的图形表示速度感。本条习用语的构思与此相同。一般用命令式。*Our daughter Joan hates to wash dishes, but offer her a dollar and watch her smoke.* 我们的女儿琼非常讨厌刷盘子,但是,如果说给她一美元,你就瞧她干得多么麻利快吧。常以 just 加强语气。*I can fix this in a jiffy. Just watch my smoke.* 这个东西我马上就能修好。你瞧我多么麻利快吧。在讲"人火速乘车走"的时候,用 dust(尘沙)代替 smoke,而说 Watch *someone's* dust. 以形容走的速度之快。*So you think I can't go there and back in thirty minutes?*

Just watch my dust. 你认为我用半个钟头不能到那里又赶回来吗？你瞧我往返多么快吧！ ◇ Watch how fast *someone* can do it.

Where there's smoke there's fire. [ˌhwer ðərzˈsmouk ðərzˈfaɪr] [谚] **无风不起浪** 直译为"有烟的地方就有火"。*There's probably nothing to the accusations against the candidate, but you know how most voters are. They tend to believe that where there's smoke there's fire.* 对于那位候选人的指控大概没有任何根据。不过，你是知道的，大多数选举人总爱相信"无风不起浪"这句格言。在 there's 与 fire 之间可以插入 at least some 之类的修饰语。*I don't take all these rumors at face value, but where there's smoke there's at least some fire.* 我并不完全相信所有这些流言，但是也不能一点风没有就起浪吧。另外，there's fire 可以变形为 there's got to be fire。*I think Fred's sold us down the river. You've seen how extremely nervous he is tonight. That's not like him. If you ask me, where there's smoke there's got to be fire.* 我认为弗雷德已经把我们出卖了。你们已经看到他今天晚上是多么坐立不安啦。这不象他往常的样子啊。叫我说，没做亏心事，不会坐不稳站不安。*Don't let Chuck kid you when he says that he and Nancy mean nothing to each other. You saw the way they were looking at each other tonight. Where there's smoke there's fire.* 查克说他与南希之间没什么关系，你别听他的瞎话啦。你今天晚上看见他们眉目传情的样子了。如果没有关系，就不会有那种眼神啦。如以上的例句所示，这句英文谚语的应用范围很广，在翻译时可以根据上下文灵活处理，不必拘泥于"无风不起浪"这几个字。另外，在英语词典中常收录有 There's no smoke without fire. 或者 No smoke without fire. 这与本条条头是同一谚语的不同形式，但主要用于英国，在美国是很难听到的。◇ If there is a rumor [an indication, evidence, etc.], there must be some truth behind it.

smooch

smooch [ˈsmu(ː)tʃ] [话] **亲吻** 象声词。从幼儿的天真的亲吻到情侣的热烈的接吻，使用范围很广。*The child smooched her grandmother on the cheek.* 小女孩在祖母的面颊上吻了一下。*A disheveled young couple who had been smooching in the back seat emerged from the car.* 一对在车后座上接吻的青年男女，头发凌乱、衣服不整地走下了汽车。也可以作名词使用。*Give Daddy a smooch.* 亲爸爸一下。另外有 a smooching party 的说法，指几对青年男女聚集在一起，享受接吻的快乐。在这一场合，smooch 完全是"接吻"的意思，决没有下流的意思。因此，在任何人面前都可以安心使用。◇ kiss

snake

snake eyes → EYES

a snake in the grass [ə ˈsneɪkɪnðə ˈgræːs] [话] **①隐患；②假仁假义的家伙** 直译为"草丛里的蛇"，指"在草丛里藏着的毒蛇"。这是一个历史相当悠久的表达法。罗马诗人维吉尔 (Virgil, 70—19 B. C.)的《牧歌》(*Eclogues*) 中有一句是 *Latet anguis in herba.* 把这句拉丁文直译成英语，则为 A snake lurks in the grass. (一条蛇潜伏在草丛中。)本条习用语即来源于此。原来表示①的意思，例如：*It seems a good plan, but there may be a snake in the grass somewhere.* 这似乎是一个很好的计划，但是也许有预想不到的危险。后来进一步发展为②的意思，现在主要使用②的意思。②是指从外表或行动看不出来、但与他打交道后，早晚会欺骗你或者背叛你的人。*I thought he was a friend of mine. I'll never trust that snake in the grass again.* 我本来以为他是我的朋友哪。我再也不信任那个吃里爬外的家伙啦。◇ ① an unforeseen danger / ② a deceitful [treacherous] person

snap

a snap course → COURSE

snappy

make it snappy [ˌmeɪkɪt ˈsnæ(ː)pi(ː)] [话] **赶快** 这里的 snappy 为拟态词,意思是"麻利"。因此,整个条头的意思是"赶紧干"、"赶快干"。常在催促他人的时候使用。虽然与 hurry 同样是"赶紧",但比 hurry 使用范围窄,一般用于表示"赶紧准备好"或"赶紧把事情或工作搞完",而不用于在到什么地方去的时候表示"赶紧抬腿走"。例如: *If we don't make it snappy, we won't make it to the movies on time.* 咱们不赶快,就要误了电影的开演时间啦。这句话不是在去看电影的途中说的,而是在准备出去看电影的时候说的。如果是在途中,一般要说 If we don't hurry ～. 顺便讲一下:这里的 hurry 也可以用 hurry up,但是 hurry up 的意思是把现在的步伐加快,即"更快一些",所以两者使用的场合尽管一样,在意义上还是有一点儿差异。另外, make it snappy 为男性用语,在用命令式的时候显得粗暴一些。*A cup of coffee. And make it snappy.* 来杯咖啡。赶快! *Make it snappy or I'll leave without you.* 快点儿!要不我扔下你走啦。*A: Wait, Daddy. I have to go to the bathroom. B: All right, but make it snappy.* 甲:等一下,爸爸。我得去一趟厕所。乙:好吧。不过,要快! ◇ hurry

sneeze

be nothing to sneeze at [ˌnʌθəntə ˈsniːzæ(ː)t] [话] **不可轻视** 直译为"不是打喷嚏 (sneeze) 的对象"。乍看起来,令人莫明其妙。但是,如果把这里的 sneeze 作为 sneer (嘲笑) 来考虑,意思就容易明白了。这一表达法主要用于金钱、机会等。 *I'd take the job if I were you. A thousand dollars a month is nothing to sneeze at.* 如果我是你的话,我就去干那个工作。每月一千美元,这不可轻视呀。*I realize you don't want to sell your house, but I think you should reconsider. An offer like that is nothing to sneeze at.* 我知道你不愿意卖你的房子,不过我认为你应该重新考虑一下。人家出的那个价钱,不可不掂量掂量啊。*I know you don't like politics, but, no matter how you look at it, a chance to work in the governor's office is nothing to sneeze at.* 我知道你不喜欢政治,不过,无论你的看法如何,有机会到州长手下工作可是非同小可啊。此外,可以用普通的否定词 not 代替本条中表示否定的 nothing, 而说 (be) not to be sneezed at。但是,这一说法有些生硬的感觉,因此不如本条条头那样为人们广泛使用。◇ be not to be disparaged / be something worthy of consideration

sneezed

not to be sneezed at [ˌnɑtəbi ˈsniːz ˌdæ(ː)t] [口] **值得重视** → be nothing to SNEEZE at

snitch

snitch on *someone* [ˈsnɪ(ː)ˌtʃɔ(ː)n ～] [话] **告密** → TELL on *someone*

snow

do a snow job (on *someone*) → JOB

give *someone* **a snow job** [ˌɡɪv ～ə ˈsnou ˌdʒɑːb] [话] **用花言巧语骗人** → do a snow JOB (on *someone*)

snow *someone* [ˈsnou ～] [话] **用花言巧语使人上圈套** → do a snow JOB (on *someone*)

(as) white as snow [əz ˈhwaɪdəz ˈsnou] [口] **雪白** 这是强调 white 的一个最常用的表达法。 *The new detergent got the sheets as white as snow.* 新的洗涤剂把床单洗得雪白。如果进一步强调,加 new-fallen(刚降下的)一词。 *The little puppy was as white as new-fallen snow.* 那只小狗象新下的雪一样白。另外,在警察与黑社会用语中,用这一表达法来强调 innocent(无辜),即"清白"的意思。 *You can't pin this rap on me. I'm as white as snow.* 你不能把这个罪名强加在我身上。我是清白无辜的啊。这种用法是由 I'm clean. (我是无辜的。) 发展而来,不能只说 I'm white. 务请读者注意。◇ pure white

So

So what? → WHAT

soap

no soap ['nou 'soup] [话] **不行** 18 世纪的英国喜剧作家富特 (Samuel Foote) 在他的作品中最早使用这一表达法,其本身没有任何意义。*I tried to make it go, but it's no soap. The battery must be dead.* 我打算把它开动,但是不行。一定是蓄电池没有电啦。如这一例句所示,可以在句子当中使用。但是,一般来说,单独使用 no soap 的时候居多。*No soap. He refuses to meet you.* 不行。他不肯见你。*No soap. We can't find her anywhere.* 不行。我们到哪儿也找不到她。no DICE 是同样的习用语,但用法略有不同。no soap 只指事情不顺利、不成功,达不到目的的"不行",而 no dice 除这一意义外,在表示"拒绝"时讲"不行"的场合也可以使用。因此,在下一例句中,如果换成 no soap,就有点儿不自然了。*No dice. I'm not going to help you.* 不行。我不能去帮助你。◇ (it is) no use [futile]

a soap opera → OPERA

wash *someone's* **mouth out with soap** → MOUTH

sob

a sob story → STORY

sober

(as) sober as a judge → JUDGE

social

a social butterfly → BUTTERFLY

a social climber → CLIMBER

soft-soap

soft-soap *someone* (into [out of] <*doing*> *something*) ['sɔ(:)ft'soup~] [话] **用甜言蜜语哄骗** soft-soap 是 soft soap(甜言蜜语) 的动词形式。有时用名词形式,例如: *Please spare me the soft soap. I'm not going to grant your request.* 请不要对我来甜言蜜语啦。我不会同意你的要求。但一般来说,要加连字符作为动词使用。*Don't try to soft-soap me. I'm not going to tell you the answer, and that's final.* 不要用甜言蜜语来哄我。我不会告诉你答案的,再罗嗦也没有用。soft-soap *someone* into (*doing*) *something* 是"用拍马屁的方式使某人干什么事"。*Jack hopes to soft-soap the boss into (giving him) a raise.* 杰克希望用拍老板马屁的方式让老板给他增加工资。也有 soft-soap *someone* out of (*doing*) *something* 的说法,意思是"用拍马屁的方式使某人停止做某事"或者"用花言巧语把某人的财物骗走"。*I hear he soft-soaped the boss out of transferring him.* 我听说他拍老板的马屁,结果老板没有把他调走。*The con man was a specialist in soft-soaping old ladies out of their savings.* 那个骗子手专门用花言巧语骗走老太太们的存款。◇ cajole *someone*

soldier

a dead soldier [ə 'de(:)d 'souldʒər] [话] **空酒瓶子** 直译为"阵亡的士兵"。这是个比喻的说法:因为人们喝酒的时候,总把空了的酒瓶子横放着,那样子很象阵亡士兵在战场上的尸体。不管是威士忌、啤酒、葡萄酒、白兰地还是中国白干,只要是装过酒精饮料的空瓶子,都可以用这一表达法来称呼。*Three hours after we had started drinking, the table was covered with dead soldiers.* 我们喝酒喝了三个小时之后,桌子上满是空瓶子了。虽然从具体形象来讲,在我们的头脑里出现的是横放着的空瓶子,但在使用本条时,并不一定非是横放着的空瓶子不可,立着的也行。*"This one's a dead soldier. Let's order another bottle," said Beau as he signaled to the waiter.* 博一边向服务员打手势,一边说:"这一瓶喝光了。咱们再叫一瓶吧。"有时又称 a dead MARINE。◇ an empty whiskey [beer, wine, brandy, etc.] bottle

somebody

(a) somebody [(ə) 'sʌm.bɑdi] [话] **大人物** 作为代词,是"某人"的意思;但作为名词,则是"有头有脸的人物"的意思了。一般不加冠词,有时伴有不定冠词。*I plan to be somebody someday.* 我计划将来成为一个大人物。*I can't stand that guy. He's always trying to act as if he were somebody.* 我对那个家伙无法忍

受。他一举一动都要摆大人物的神气。*I don't know who that man is, but from the reporters surrounding him he is obviously a somebody.* 我不知道那个人是谁，但是从许多记者把他围住来看，他显然是一位重要人物啦。◇ an important person

someplace

get someplace ['get ˌsʌmpleɪs] [话] **发迹** → go PLACES

something

something fierce → FIERCE

somewhere

get somewhere ['get ˌsʌmhwe(:)r] [话] **发迹** → go PLACES

song

for a song [fɔrə 'sɔ:ŋ] [话] **以极低的价钱** 直译为"用一只歌交换"。关于这一表达法的来源，有一种说法是：旧时，有一些流浪的艺人常到酒吧间或一般饭馆，请客人点播歌曲，以非常低廉的价格卖唱。但在现代美国人的观念中，这一表达法的含义是：东西极为便宜，简直不用出钱，只给唱一支歌就行了。不管语源如何，这一习用语都是"价钱极为便宜"的意味的夸张表现。用汉语来说，就是"跟白给一样"。*Brad's car is practically new, but he says that if someone will pay cash he's willing to let it go for a song.* 布雷德的小汽车跟新的一样，但是他说如果有人付现款，他愿意以极低的价格抛出去。如这一例句所示，在会话中常与 let it go (抛出) 搭配使用。当然也可以用其他动词 (如 sell, buy, get 等) 导入。*Because I had to move on such short notice, I was forced to sell my house for a song.* 因为我突然必须搬家，不得不以极低的价钱把我的房子卖了。*I got these rare old books for a song at a small secondhand bookstore.* 我在一家小的旧书店里，以很便宜的价格得到了这几本珍贵的旧书。◇ very cheaply

give *someone* **a song and dance** (about *something*) [ˌgɪv ~ə 'sɔ(:)ŋ ən'dæ(:)nts] [口] **废话连篇** 在旧时的轻松喜剧中，歌舞演员常常在表演中间夹杂着漫谈式的闲聊。这种闲聊大多是胡诌八扯，毫无新鲜味道，使听的人感到极为沉闷。本条习用语即来源于此。人们称这类胡诌八扯的演员为 a song-and-dance artist，所以本条习用语便具有"絮絮叨叨讲老一套毫无意义的话"这一比喻的意味。*When I asked Jack to repay the money he owes me, he gave me a song and dance about his uncle's hospital bills.* 当我向杰克索还他借我的钱的时候，他废话连篇，讲他叔父住医院的费用。如这一例句所示，本条习用语大多用于找借口或进行辩解的场合。有时用 some, the same old 等代替 a song and dance 中的冠词 a。*Ben's impossible. Now he's over there in the corner giving a girl some song and dance about being a New York radio announcer.* 本这个人讨厌极啦。现在，他在那边的角落里正对一个姑娘胡诌八扯，说他是纽约广播电台的播音员。*Every time I ask my boss for a raise, he gives me the same old song and dance business is bad; he's too busy to talk about it now; he'll think about it; et cetera, et cetera.* 每次我向老板要求增加工资，他总是那一套遁词，什么生意不好啦；现在他太忙没时间谈这个问题啦；容他考虑考虑再说啦；如此等等，等等。get a [some, the same old, etc.] song and dance (about *something*)是"受到他人的推托"。*Whenever I ask my husband to take me out to dinner, I just get a song and dance—about his being too tired.* 每当我要求丈夫带我到外边吃晚饭时，他总是推说他太累了，去不了。a [an old, etc.] song and dance 可以单独使用，也可以与其他动词搭配。*A: What did Ben say when you asked him to help us? B: Same old song and dance. He's too busy.* 甲：你去求本帮助我们的时候，他说什么？乙：还是那老一套推托的话。说他太忙。*When you've finished your song and dance, I have a few words I'd like to say.* 等你说完了你那些废话之后，我也有几句话想讲一讲。◇ give *someone's* a lot of nonsense [a string of excuses]

soon

if *one* **never sees** *someone* **again it'll be too soon** → SEES

would (just) as soon *do something***as** *do something* [(wu)d(ˌdʒʌst) əzˌsu(ː)n ˈ~əz ˈ~] [话] **干这个与干那个没有什么好恶之分** → *Someone* would just as soon *do something* as LOOK at you.

soph

a soph [ə ˈsɑ(ː)f] [话] **大学二年级学生** a sophomore 的缩略。有时也指"高中二年级学生",但主要是大学生用语。*I'll be a soph next year.* 我明年就上大二了。复数形式是 sophs [ˈsɑ(ː)fs]。*Bill and Mary are sophs.* 比尔和玛丽是大学二年级学生。→ a FROSH ◇ a second-year (college) student

sore

be sore (at *someone*) [ˈso(ː)r] [话] **恼怒** be sore 一般用于"肉体疼痛"的场合。但在日常会话中,常指"精神疼痛",即表示"生气"、"恼火"、"发怒"的意思。除 be sore 外,还有 feel [get] sore 等表达法。*My girl is sore at me for breaking our date last night.* 由于昨天晚上我失约了,我的女朋友大为恼火。*I can't help feeling sore at Louise for breaking her promise.* 由于路易丝违约,我抑制不住一腔的怒火。*Don't get sore. I didn't mean to break the dish.* 别生气啊。我不是故意打破盘子的。◇ (be) angry

a sore loser [ə ˌso(ː)r ˈluːzər] [话] **一输了就恼火的心胸狭窄的人** → a SOREHEAD

stick out like a sore thumb → THUMB

sorehead

a sorehead [ə ˈsoːrˌhe(ː)d] [话] **爱发脾气的人** 形容词 sore 是"一碰就疼的",此外还有"恼怒的"、"气冲冲的"的意思。条头 sorehead 中的 sore 属于后者。在会话中,千万要听清楚,不要把 a sore head [ˌso(ː)r ˈheːd] (疼痛的头) 与 a sorehead 弄混。不过,从语源上讲,两者并非毫无关系。有这样的人,只要稍微一碰他的"疼痛的头" (a sore head),他就会恼火,说出不满意的话。因此,就把这种"爱发脾气的人"称之为 a sorehead 了。在这种爱发脾气的人当中,本条习用语大多是指"如果对方有一点小小的过失或调皮,就唠唠叨叨没完没了的人"。*Lyle is a sorehead who gripes at every little thing that happens to him.* 莱尔是一个爱发脾气的人,不论碰到什么芝麻大的小事,他都唠叨个没完。*Don't be such a sorehead. I apologized, didn't I?* 不要那样老发脾气嘛。我不是认错了吗?另外,在体育运动或各种游戏中,这一表达法主要指"总挑对手的毛病而不干脆认输的人"。常用 real 加强语气。*That guy is a real sorehead. Every time he loses at mahjongg, he complains that somebody cheated him.* 那个家伙真是一个爱发脾气的人。每当他打麻将输了的时候,他都抱怨有人搞鬼。在体育运动或游戏的场合,也可以用 a sore loser 或 a sorehead loser 表示同样的意思。*Don't be such a sore loser. I beat you fair and square.* 你不要那样死不认输嘛。我是正大光明地打败了你的。◇ an easily offended person / easily offended ((such a → so))

a sorehead loser [ə ˌso(ː)rˌhe(ː)d ˈluːzər] [话] **死不认输的人** → a SOREHEAD

sorrows

drown *one's* **sorrows** (in *drink*) [ˌdraun ~ ˈsɑroz] [话] **以酒浇愁** → drown *one's* TROUBLES (in *drink*)

so-so

so-so [ˈsouˌsou] [口] **还凑合** "不特别好,也不特别坏"的意思。*A: How's business these days? B: So-so.* 甲:最近生意如何?乙:还凑合。*The dinner was only so-so, but we had a good time at the dance afterwards.* 晚饭只是过得去而已,但是我们在饭后跳舞,玩得很快活。*Nurse: How do you feel today? Patient: So-so.* 护士:你今天感觉怎么样?病人:还可以。*My son's grades have improved lately, but they're still only so-so.* 最近我儿子的成绩有所提高,不过依然是平平而已。也可以作为形容词直接放在名词

的前边。*After seeing our team's so-so performance last night, I'd say they don't have much chance to win the championship.* 从昨天晚上我们队的平平的战况来看，依我说，没有多大夺冠的机会。又讲 fair to middling，以上各例句均可代入。◇ not so good, not so bad / (very) average

soul-searching

soul-searching [ˈsoul.sə(ː)rtʃɪŋ] [口] **仔细考虑** search *one's* HEART (深深问自己的心) 的名词化是 heart-searching。但是，不知为什么，人们几乎不用 heart-searching，而以本条的 soul-searching 来代替。不过，从意义上来讲，本条习用语要比 search *one's* heart 用于含义更深刻的场合。一般把它译作"自我分析"，但这种译法不够全面，因为它不单是 self-analysis，从下面的例句就可以看出，实际上含有"伤脑筋"或"费时间"的沉重的意味。动词用 do，有时用 engage in，随后总是添加 much 或者 a lot of。例如：*It was obvious that the President had done much soul-searching in preparation for his speech on energy.* 总统在起草关于能源问题的演说稿时，显然是经过深思熟虑的。*I did a lot of soul-searching before I decided that I had to expose the murderer, even though it was my own brother.* 我左思右想，终于下决心揭发杀人犯，哪怕那是我的亲弟兄。也可以当作形容词使用，例如：*I spent many soul-searching hours trying to decide whether I could continue working for a company that used such dirty tactics against the union.* 一个公司竟用那样卑鄙的手段对待工会，我仔细考虑了很长时间究竟是否继续在那里工作。◇ examining of *one's* conscience [deepest motivations]

sound

safe and sound → SAFE

sound *someone* out [ˌsaund ～ ˈaut] [口] **试探** sound 是"测量深度"的意思。sound out 是由此而来的比喻说法，意思是"通过询问的方式，试探对方的意见、想法、心情等"。表示"关于(某一问题)"的意义的前置词，一般用 on 或者 about。*I'll sound him out about coming to work for us.* 我去试探试探他有没有到我们这里来工作的意图。*We'd better sound Frank out on this before mentioning it to his father.* 关于这件事情，我们在向弗兰克的父亲讲之前，最好先试探一下他本人的意见。有很多英华词典注明"用间接方式询问，或用暗示方法试探"，如果是这个意思，一般是讲 FEEL *someone* out 或者 put out a FEELER。sound out 并不限定"间接地"或"拐弯抹角地"，向对方直截了当地提出质问也可以，而且可以说，后者才是这一表达法的一般用法。从意义上讲，这一表达法与 ask 相近。当然，如果代入 *someone* 处的不是代词或简短的人名，则采取 sound out *someone* 的形式。*Always sound out the department head before taking anything up with the president.* 不管什么事情，在上交总经理之前，一定要先去试探部长的意见。*The students sounded out the principal about having a party after the track meet.* 学生们询问校长在开完运动会之后可不可以举行一次晚会。有时可以不用 *someone*，而用 *something*，但在这一场合，代入 *something* 处的词也必须是表示人的"意向"、"感情"之类的词。*We'd better sound out his receptiveness to the idea before making any definite plans.* 在确定任何最后的方案之前，我们最好是征求一下他的意见。在十年以前，只用动词 sound 就表达本条习用语的意思，但是自从 find 要加上 out 作 find out 表示"找到"的意思之后，现在 sound out 也依样画葫芦，成为普遍的表达法了。◇ ask someone his feelings (about something) / get someone's views

soup

be duck soup [ˈdʌkˌsuːp] [话] **易如反掌** 使用方法如下：*A: Do you think you can do it? B: Sure. It'll be duck soup.* 甲：你认为你干得了吗？乙：当然啦。易如反掌。*A: Was it a tough exam? B: Naw. It was duck soup.* 甲：考试题目很难吗？乙：不不，易如反掌。be duck soup 的字面意义为"是鸭汤"，本条习用语为什么会有"易如反掌"、"轻而易举"、"不费吹灰之力"的意义，不明。这是一个非常轻松的表达法，一般指事情"很容易"。也可以用否定式，例如：*It's not really difficult, but it's not exactly duck soup, either.* 那件事并不非常难，但也不是轻而易举。除了经常用于"事情"之外，偶尔也有应用于"人"的时候。在这一场合，指"好说话的对方"或"容易对付的敌人"。*A: Did you talk him into it? B: No problem. He was duck soup.* 甲：你已经说服他了吗？乙：没费什么劲。他很好说话。*All the challengers so far have been duck soup for the champ.* 到现在为止，所有的挑战者都不是冠军的对手。◇ be very easy / be very easy to handle

Too many cooks spoil the soup. [ˌtu(ː)ˌmeni ˈkuks ˌspɔɪlðə ˈsuːp] [谚] **厨师太多烧坏汤** → Too many COOKS spoil the broth.

sour

sour grapes → GRAPES

southpaw

a southpaw [ə ˈsauθˌpɔː] [话] **左撇子** → a LEFTY

sow's

make a silk purse out of a sow's ear → PURSE

spaced

be spaced out [ˌspeɪˈstaut] [话] **反应迟钝或头脑失常** space out 是"拉开距离"的意思，be spaced out 就是"被拉开距离"。*The trees in the garden were spaced out to prevent blocking the view.* 为了不挡住风景，庭院里的树在栽种时拉开了距离。这个 be spaced out 转义指吸毒后的"恍惚"状态。也就是说，由于麻醉品的影响，"脑细胞间的距离拉开了"。在使用这一意义的时候，be spaced out 的后边常加 on drugs。*Most of the people at the party were spaced out on drugs.* 出席社交晚会的人，大部分由于吸毒而精神恍惚了。后来，这个 be spaced out 又进一步发展，被用于表示虽然没有吸毒但仿佛吸毒一样的状态，即"反应迟钝"或"头脑失常"的意思。常用 really 加强语气。*That guy is really spaced out. He makes good grades in school, but when you try to carry on an ordinary conversation with him, he just sits and stares blankly at you.* 那个家伙的确是头脑失常。他在学校里成绩很不错，但是，当你想跟他随便谈谈的时候，他只是坐在那里茫然地望着你。*The new boy in our class is really spaced out. He'll agree with you one minute and then disagree with you on the same point the next.* 我们班里新来的男生简直头脑失灵。他刚刚表示赞成你所说的事情，转眼之间，他又说不赞成了。spaced-out 可作定语使用。*I had a date with a spaced-out blond last night.* 昨天晚上我与一个反应有点儿迟钝的金发美人约会了。按照"因吸毒而精神恍惚"或者"头脑失常"的意义使用 be spaced out，这是比较近的事情，特别是青年人喜欢这一表达法。◇ be out of touch with reality

spaced-out

spaced-out [ˈspeɪstˈaut] [话] **反应迟钝的或头脑失常的** → be SPACED out

spade

call a spade a spade [ˌkɔ(ː)lə ˈspeɪdə ˈspeɪd] [口] **实事求是地说** 这一习用语的来源很早。罗马帝国时代有一句拉丁文的格言是：*Ficus ficus, ligonem ligonem vocat.* 到了 16 世纪，英国人把它译为 Call a fig a fig and a spade a spade.（把无花果叫做无花果，把铲子叫做铲子。）后来缩略为 Call a spade a spade. 被人们普遍使用。原来的意思是"如果是 spade(铲子) 的话，就不要改用

其他的名称,说清楚是 spade 好啦"。换句话说,就是"不要拐弯抹角,痛痛快快地说"。 *I know he's your brother, but don't say he just borrowed the money from the company—it's clear that he embezzled it. For your own good you've got to call a spade a spade.* 我知道他是你的弟弟,但是,他决不是从公司借了钱,他是盗用了公司的资金——这是明明白白的事情。为了你自己好,你必须实事求是地说啊。 *You may say she doesn't necessarily respect the truth, but I believe in calling a spade a spade. If you ask me, she's an out-and-out liar.* 你也许说她没有必要尊重事实,但是我认为应该实事求是。如果叫我说,她是一个彻头彻尾的说谎大王。 *Authors used to use dashes and omit the so-called four-letter words. Nowadays they rather tend to call a spade a spade.* 过去作家们常用破折号来省略所谓的"四字母粗俗下流词",现在,他们反倒有照直说出粗话的倾向了。◇ say what *one* actually means

spanking

spanking new → NEW

sparks

a sparks [ə'spa(:)rks] [话] **(船上的)无线电技术员** 本条习用语来源于:在拍发电报的时候,机器上冒 sparks (电花)。虽然是复数形式,却当作单数使用。特指船上的无线电技术员,但在这一场合,一般要加定冠词。 *Who's the sparks on this ship?* 这条船上的无线电技术员是谁啊? *Hi, Sparks. Any important messages today?* 啊,无线电技术员先生! 今天有什么重要电报吗? 如这一例句所示,也常用作无线电技术员的爱称。◇ a (ship's) radio operator

sparrowgrass

sparrowgrass ['spærə,græ:s] [话] **芦笋** 直译为"麻雀草",但这种植物并不存在。在不熟悉 asparagus 的地方,把它误听为 sparrow | grass,于是产生了这一表达法。现在仍为地方方言,但用在标准语中,有时也用作戏谑语。 *Mike loves sparrowgrass salad.* 迈克喜欢芦笋沙拉。◇ asparagus

spec

a spec sheet → SHEET

special

a Saturday night special [ə ,sæ(:)dərdi ,naɪt 'spe(:)ʃəl] [口] **周末专用品(小口径手枪)** 美国很久以来,每到星期六的夜里,犯罪或暴力事件猛增。在这种场合,人们最广泛使用的是口径 22~23 毫米的小型手枪。虽然说是小型,但没有迪林格式袖珍手枪(derringer)那么小。其价钱很便宜,在市镇的枪械商店或通过邮购,都很容易弄到。另外,这种枪既不要起牌照,也用不着登记号码,只要不在上面留下指纹,使完把它一扔,使用者的踪迹很难被发现。因此,犯罪分子都把这种手枪当作至宝。相反,从捉拿或取缔者的角度来看,这种手枪乃是世界上最令人头疼的东西。密歇根州底特律市的警察们曾为这种手枪夜不安枕,他们特别奉送它 Saturday night special 的称号。这就是本条条头的来源。 *There are many people who feel that fewer murders would be committed in America if it were not for the ready availability of Saturday night specials.* 在美国,有许多人感觉到:如果不是人们能轻易弄到小口径手枪,杀人案件一定会少得多。 *Even law-abiding citizens in America keep Saturday night specials in their homes for protection against burglars.* 在美国,甚至守法良民的家中都有小口径手枪,以防备盗贼。◇ a cheap, small-bore pistol

specs

specs ['spe(:)ks] [话] **眼镜** spectacles 的缩略。一般来说,在表示"眼镜"一义的英语中,使用最多的是 glasses (eyeglasses 的缩略),但本条的 specs 也经常为人们使用。 *I left my specs at the office.* 我把眼镜忘到办公室了。spectacles 和 eyeglasses 主要是上年纪的人使用,年轻人如果使用,就有"老气横秋"的感觉。当然,在只说 glasses 而可能与"玻璃杯"一解混同的特殊场合,青年人也说 eyeglasses。最近，specs 日益陈旧，不过，由于这一表达法比 glasses 轻松，它还有很大的存在意义。◇ glasses

spectacle

make a spectacle of *oneself* (by *doing something*) [ˌmeɪkə ˈspektəkələv ~] [口] **当众出丑** → make an EXHIBITION of *oneself* (by *doing something*)

spick-and-span

spick-and-span [ˈspɪkənˈspæːn] [口] **干净漂亮** 最初是 14 世纪左右，造船工们使用的 span-new (崭新的)一词。当时，span 是"碎木片"的意思。span-new 是"象砍下来的碎木片一样新"，也就是"崭新"。到了 16 世纪，大概是受同义的荷兰语 *spiksplinter nieuw* (*spik* 与英语 spike 同样是"大钉"，*splinter* 是"细长木片"的意思)的影响，span-new 的强调表达法 spick-and-span-new 开始流行起来。到了 17 世纪，又开始出现脱落 new 的倾向，产生现在这样 spick-and-span 的形式。有时又去掉 k，而构成 spic-and-span。到此时为止，仍保有"崭新"的意义。但是没过多久，这一意义逐渐消失，在现代，主要用以表示"(象新的物品一样)干净漂亮"的意思了。这是一个广泛使用的表达法，它可以形容住宅、房间、厨房、桌子、衣服、车子、甚至孩子们的脸等等，所以在翻译的时候也可以适当变化。*His apartment is always spick-and-span.* 他的房间总是干干净净，一尘不染。*She always keeps her kitchen spick-and-span.* 她总是把厨房收拾得干干净净，非常整洁。*The children left for the party, their clothes all spick-and-span.* 孩子们全都穿着整洁的衣服去参加晚会了。如以上的例句所示，本条条头大多当作表语使用。在这一场合，特别是在英国英语中，拼写时可以去掉连字符。下面的例句是当作定语使用的场合。*He drove up in an old but spick-and-span car.* 他开一辆虽然旧了但是擦得雪亮的汽车来了。另外，前边所讲的最古老的形式 span-new，在美国某些地方的方言中依然存在，并保持原来的意义。◇ spotlessly clean

spilt

cry over spilt milk → MILK

spin

go (out) for a spin (in *something*) [ˌgou(ˌaut)fərə ˈspɪ(ː)n] [话] **兜风** 所乘的只限于汽车、汽艇、小型飞机等有发动机的交通工具。通常用于毫无目的地、只是乘坐取乐的场合。如加 out，仅为调整语调，意义上没有变化。*C'mon. Let's go for a spin.* 走，咱们兜风去。*We often go (out) for a spin through the country on Sunday afternoons.* 我们在星期日的午后，经常到乡下去兜风。*Ted has invited us to go for a spin in his father's plane.* 特德邀请我们乘他父亲的飞机去兜风。也可以说 take a spin。*Let's take a spin in the motorboat.* 咱们乘汽艇去兜风吧。在说"带着某人去兜风"的场合，很少用 take *someone* and go for a spin，一般都讲 take *someone* (out) for a spin。*Jim took Mary (out) for a spin in his new car.* 吉姆带着玛丽乘他的新汽车去兜风。如果正在行进中，则说 be out for a spin。*A: Where are you headed? B: Nowhere in particular. We're just out for a spin.* 甲：你们到哪儿去？乙：没有固定地方。我们只是兜风。◇ go for a short drive [flight, etc.]

play spin the bottle → BOTTLE

take a spin (in *something*) [ˌteɪkə ˈspɪ(ː)n] [话] **兜风** → go (out) for a SPIN (in *something*)

take *someone* **(out) for a spin** [ˌteɪk ~ (ˌaut)fərə ˈspɪ(ː)n] [话] **带着某人去兜风** → go (out) for a SPIN (in *something*)

spinach

spinach [ˈspɪnɪtʃ] [话] **金钱** → BREAD

spine

chill *someone's* **spine** [ˌtʃɪl ~ ˈspaɪn] [口] **使人感到脊梁骨都发凉** → SPINE-CHILLING

make *someone's* **spine tingle** [ˌmeɪk ~ ˈspaɪn ˌtɪŋgl] [口] **使人心情激动** → SPINE-TINGLING

spine-chilling

spine-chilling ['spaɪn'tʃɪlɪŋ] [口] **令人毛骨悚然的** 直译为"使人脊梁骨都发凉的"。通常指由于恐惧而产生的感情。不要与 SPINE-TINGLING 混同。 *We went to a spine-chilling movie about Dracula.* 我们去看了一部令人毛骨悚然的描写吸血鬼的影片。*It was spine-chilling to see the bodies of the mass-murder victims on TV.* 电视里大屠杀中被害者的尸体的镜头,真令人毛骨悚然啊。*Spending the night in that old haunted house was a spine-chilling experience.* 在那所闹鬼的老房子里过夜,真让人有了所谓"毛骨悚然"的经验啊。另外有 chill *someone's* spine 的说法,表示"使人感到脊梁骨都发凉"的意思。 *The terrible sight chilled my spine.* 看了那可怕的情景,我感到脊梁骨都发凉了。◇ scary / frightening

spine-tingling

spine-tingling ['spaɪn'tɪŋglɪŋ] [口] **令人心情激动的** 直译为"使人脊梁骨不住跳动的"。千万注意:它与表示恐怖感情的 SPINE-CHILLING 用法不同。 *We had a spine-tingling ride up the mountain in Tom's new sports car.* 我们乘着汤姆的新赛车一直开到山顶上,真是开心极啦。*My first ride in a small airplane was a spine-tingling experience.* 我第一次乘坐小型飞机的时候,心情无比激动。*It was spine-tingling to see the stadium filled with thousands of athletes from many countries.* 看到体育场里聚集了几千名各国运动员,实在令人兴奋极了。make *someone's* spine tingle 是"使人心情激动"。 *The beautiful view from the top of Mt. Taishan made my spine tingle.* 从泰山顶上看到的美景,使我的心情激动不已。◇ thrilling / exciting

spirit

The spirit is willing, but the flesh is weak. [ðə 'spɪrɪdɪzwɪlɪŋ ˌbʌtðə 'fleʃɪzwiːk] [口] **虽然心愿意,但是志不坚** 出典为《圣经·新约》中的《马太福音》(Matthew)第26章41节: Watch and pray that you may not enter into temptation; the spirit indeed is willing, but the flesh is weak. (总要警醒祷告,免得入了迷惑;你们心灵固然愿意,肉体却软弱了。)这是在最后的晚餐以后,耶稣来到客西马尼这个地方进行祷告,向那些睡着了的弟子们讲的话。因为这一表达法的含义是"虽然有干的心愿(the spirit is willing),但是身体没有力量(the flesh is weak)",所以一般在辩解的时候使用。 *A: You'd be healthier if you'd get up early every morning and go jogging. B: Well, the spirit is willing, but the flesh is weak.* 甲:如果你每天早晨早点起来做慢跑锻炼,你的身体一定会更健康的。乙:是呀,我心里愿意,就是坚持不了啊。有时可以添加《圣经》原典中有的 indeed 一词。 *I'm sorry I haven't written to you for so long. The spirit is indeed willing, but the flesh is weak.* 久未问候,实在抱歉。本来早想写信,始终没能动笔。*Every time I scold my son for playing tennis to the neglect of his homework he promises to do better, but soon he falls into his old ways again. It's a matter of the spirit is willing but the flesh is weak.* 每当我批评儿子忽视家庭作业而贪玩网球的时候,他总是答应要改,但是没有几天,他又依然我行我素了。这就是人们常说的"虽然心愿意,但是志不坚"啊。 *A: You shouldn't drink so much. You know the doctor said it wasn't good for you. B: I know, I know. It's not that the spirit isn't willing, it's just that the flesh is weak.* 甲:你不应该喝那么多酒啊。你知道,医生说过那对你身体不好。乙:我知道,我知道。我不是不想戒酒,只是办不到啊。有时可以省去条头的后半,只说 The spirit is willing. 例如: *Sorry I haven't gotten around to helping you. The spirit is willing and all that, you know, but ....* 真对不起,我抽不出时间去帮助你。心里虽然愿意,可是,你知道……。◇ *One's* intentions are good, but *one's* will is weak.

spirits

give *someone's* **spirits a lift** [ˌgɪv ～ ˈspɪrəts əˈlɪ(ː)ft] [口] **使精神振奋** → give *someone* a LIFT

splash

make a splash [ˌmeɪkə ˈsplæ(ː)ʃ] [口] **引起哄动** splash 原为象声词，指水的泼溅声或拍激声。*The frog made a splash when it dove into the old pond.* 青蛙跳入古老的池塘时，扑通一声发出溅水的声音。作为比喻，在干了引起世人注目的特殊事情时使用。但是，这种特殊事情不是指"为非作歹"或者"私奔"，一般是指受社会称赞的事情。*The new director's first movie made quite a splash.* 那位新导演所拍的第一部影片引起很大的哄动。把这句话说成 The new director made quite a splash with his first movie. 意思也完全一样。这就是说，"人"或"物"哪一个都可以是主语。quite 是强调用语，也可以用 real，但一般惯用的是 quite。*The new doctor and his beautiful wife made quite a splash when they moved to the quiet little community.* 当新来的医生和他的美貌的妻子移居平静的小社区时，引起很大的哄动。这种哄动一般只是昙花一现，转瞬即逝的，但也可能维持一定的时期，例如：*At one time the miniskirt made a real splash in the fashion world.* 在时装界里，超短裙大大流行了一阵子。*Sarah was determined to make a splash in New York society.* 萨拉下定决心在纽约的社交界大出风头。有些英汉词典注明这一表达法中的动词 make 可与 cut 通用，这大概是由于把 make a splash 与 cut a swath 弄混了的缘故。一般不用 cut a splash 的说法，因为这一说法的意思是"用刀咔地一声把水切开"，很可笑。→ cut a SWATH (through *something* [*someone*]) ◇ create a sensation

spliced

get spliced [ˌget ˈsplaɪst] [话] **结婚** splice 是"捻接（绳子等）"，"拼接（木板等）"的意思。加上 get，就是"被接上了"。这一表达法原为方言，后来在标准语中也作为戏谑语使用。*We've decided to get spliced in June.* 我们定于六月结婚。◇ get married

spoke

put a spoke in *someone's* **wheel** [ˌpudə ˈspoukən ～ ˌhwiːl] [口] **破坏他人的计划** 关于这一表达法的来源，有好几种说法。其中最可相信的说法是：古时，赶马车的人在下陡坡的时候，把预先准备好的 spoke(辐条) 插在车轮中，作为煞车。另一说法是：英国人把荷兰语 *spaak*(棒子) 误听为 spoke，因此，本条条头的原意为"把棒子插到车轮里"。第三种说法是：本条条头最初的意思是"为他人效劳，把辐条插到车轮里"，根据是在 19 世纪的某些文章中，这一表达法有用于良好意思的例句。由于可以引证的资料过少，在三个说法中，最后这一说法的可靠性最低。*That guy must enjoy other people's misery. Every time we plan something, he tries to put a spoke in our wheel.* 那个家伙一定最爱看别人倒霉。每当我们计划干什么事情的时候，他都从中作梗。*That company is trying to expand into our territory. We've got to find some way to put a spoke in their wheel.* 那个公司企图把他们的势力打进我们的地盘。我们必须想方设法破坏他们的计划。关于"破坏"的具体内容，不外是 ruin（摧毁）或者是 plow down（阻挠）。put a spoke in *someone's* wheel 也是同样。当然，在许多场合，听的人分不清说话者的含义是"摧毁"还是"阻挠"。在下一个例句中，显然是 ruin 的意思。*The weather put a spoke in the wheel of our picnic plans.* 恶劣的天气摧毁了我们去郊外野餐的计划。在下面的例句中作 slow down 解释比较适当。*The conservative party is forever searching for ways to put a spoke in the wheel of progress.* 保守党始终在寻求阻挠进步的手段。◇ hinder *someone's* plans [progress]

sponge

have a mind like a sponge [ˌhævə ˌmaɪndlaɪkə ˈspʌ(ː)ndʒ] [话] **头脑灵活，吸收得快** mind 是"头脑"的意思。本条条头直译为"有一个象海绵一样的头

脑”。最初的构思是:“在接受新事物的时候,就象海绵吸水一样快,马上就印人头脑中”。这一表达法包含两方面的意义,一是“记得快”,一是“碰到什么都吸收进去”。一般为褒义,但也含有如下的意味:不管好的坏的都往里边吸收。总之指“好奇心胜”,所以多用于孩子们身上。*Most small children are very quick to learn. They have minds like sponges.* 大多数小孩子的记性非常好。他们头脑灵活,吸收力强。*Ralph remembers practically everything he reads. He has a mind like a sponge.* 拉尔夫对于他所读过的东西几乎全都记得住。他头脑灵活,吸收力强。*My son used to have a mind like a sponge, and consequently did well in all his subjects. Recently, however, he seems to have lost interest in his studies.* 我的儿子一向头脑灵活,吸收得快,结果各门功课的成绩全都不错。可是最近,他似乎对于学习失去兴趣了。◇ absorb things very quickly

a sponge [ə ˈspʌ(:)ndʒ] [话] **厚着脸皮勒索别人的人** → SPONGE (*something*) off *someone*

sponge (*something*) **off** *someone* [ˈspʌ(:)ndʒ ˌɔ:f ~ / ˌspʌndʒ˛~ɔ(:)f ˈ~] [话] **厚着脸皮勒索别人** 最初的构思是:sponge (海绵) 是能够大量往里吸水的东西。本条条头的意思是:抓住别人的“善良”、“亲切”、“友情”或者“弱点”,而把别人的钱“吸了去”。次数不是“一回”,一般是指“长期地”。*You're always sponging off me. Don't you ever have any money of your own?* 你总是厚着脸皮向我勒索钱。你就从来没有过自己的钱吗? *Don't worry about the budget for our party. I can always sponge a few dollars off my father.* 关于我们举办晚会的预算,用不着发愁。我从我父亲手里总能挤出一些美元来的。这一表达法也常指“食客”而言。*Why don't you go out and look for a job? Don't you think you've been sponging off us long enough?* 你为什么不出去找找工作呢? 你不认为在我们家白吃白喝太久了吗? 有时用 on 代替 off,而讲 sponge on *someone*,意思不变。*That guy must think I'm a money tree. Every time I turn around he's sponging on me again.* 那个家伙一定认为我是一株摇钱树了。他一而再、再而三地厚着脸皮来勒索我。在亲密的朋友之间使用这一表达法时,意思就没有“勒索”那样严重,而是“暂借一下”的意思。*Can I sponge a couple dollars off you, Tom? I want to get some cigarettes.* 汤姆,你可以借给我两美元吗? 我想买盒烟。可以认为,说这句话的人不是“勒索”,而是准备还的。a sponge 为名词,意思是“厚着脸皮勒索别人的人”或者“象寄生虫一样的人”。*That guy's a real sponge. He's always bumming money from someone.* 那个家伙完全是一个寄生虫。他总是厚着脸皮向别人要钱花。◇ cadge (*something*) from *someone*

sponge on *someone* [ˈspʌ(:)ndʒ ˌɔ(:)n ~] [话] **厚着脸皮勒索别人** → SPONGE (*something*) off *someone*

throw in the sponge [ˌθrouɪnðə ˈspʌ(:)ndʒ] [口] **认输** → throw in the TOWEL

spoon

be born with a silver spoon in *one's* **mouth** [ˌborn wɪðə ˌsɪlvər ˈspu:nɪn ~ˌmauθ] [口] **生于富贵之家** 直译为“生下来的时候,嘴里叼着银匙子”。当然指出生于有钱的人家,但不仅仅如此,另外还含有在教育、环境等各个方面都处于优越地位的意味。这一表达法应用于比社会一般人受到各种独特的恩泽的人。*Charles was born with a silver spoon in his mouth. He's never had to do a lick of work in his life.* 查尔斯生于富贵之家。他一辈子从来不需要去干什么工作。*I've had to work hard for everything I've got— including my education. I wasn't born with a silver spoon in my mouth, you know.* 我现在所得到的一切,包括我所受的教育在内,都是靠拼命劳动得来的。你知道,我不是生于富贵之家呀。◇ be born into extremely favorable circumstances

a greasy spoon [ə ˌgri:zi ˈspu:n] [话] **廉价饭馆** 规模很小,最多不过一个便餐柜台

和两三张桌子。大多指"现炸现卖的小饭铺"。这一表达法含有如下的意思:"设备简陋,卖的食品也不怎么好吃,不过价钱便宜,而且速度快"。给客人用的匙子常常洗不干净,带有油污,因此称为 greasy spoon (油污的匙子)。*When I was a bachelor I often ate at a local greasy spoon.* 当我还是单身汉的时候,我常在附近的一家廉价饭馆吃饭。*We didn't have much time to eat, so Joe and I dropped in at a greasy spoon.* 我们没有很多吃饭的时间,因此我和乔就顺便进了一家廉价饭馆吃饭。另外,有时以 greasy-spoon 的形式作为形容词使用。这是对餐厅表示轻蔑时的用语,与餐厅规模的大小没有关系。*I'll never eat in that greasy-spoon restaurant again.* 我决不再到那家肮脏的餐厅吃饭啦。◇ a cheap (little) eating place

spot

hit the spot (with *someone*) [ˌhɪtðə ˈspɑ(ː)t] [话] **正中下怀** 这一表达法主要是在谈到食物或饮料的时候使用。这里的 spot 是"身心双方都在寻求的东西"的意思。整个条头的意思是:恰恰击中 (hit)这种东西。在夏日炎炎似火烧的时候,咕嘟一下喝上一杯冷啤酒,人们常说:*Ahhh, that hits the spot!* 啊!痛快极啦!这句话直译就是:"冷啤酒正中下怀"。*I'm very thirsty. A cold glass of lemonade would hit the spot right now.* 我渴极啦。现在要能喝上一杯冰镇柠檬汽水多痛快啊。*A hot cup of tea always hits the spot on a cold day.* 在寒冷的日子,喝上一杯热茶总是很舒服的事情。在讲"实在好吃极啦"、"再好也没有啦"的时候,常用 really 加强语气。*I don't usually eat desserts, but your apple pie really hit the spot with me tonight.* 我平常不吃甜食,但是今天晚上你烙的苹果馅饼实在好吃极啦,大饱我的口福。在饮食以外的场合,有时也使用这一表达法。*I'd like to listen to some music. A little Brahms would hit the spot tonight.* 我很想听一点音乐。今天晚上奏几首勃拉姆斯的作品,就正合我意了。◇ ((不加 with *someone*)) be delicious / be perfect

be in a spot [ɪnə ˈspɑ(ː)t] [口] **陷入困境** 这里的 spot 是"困难的境地"的意思。从小小的困难直到极大的困难,这一表达法的使用范围很广。因此,往往用加形容词的方法来示明困难的程度。*Joe is in a spot. If he doesn't finish his term paper by tomorrow, there is a good chance that he might flunk the course.* 乔陷入困境了。如果他到明天完不成期末论文,这门课程就多半要不及格了。在加强语气的场合,常用 tight, bad, tough 等形容词。*I was in a tight spot. The road had come to a dead-end and my pursuers were less than one minute behind me.* 当时我的情况非常危急。路到了尽头,原来是个死胡同,而在我身后追赶的人离我还不到一分钟的距离。相反,在减弱语气时,则常用 a bit of, somewhat of 等。*I'm in a bit of a spot. Can you lend me some money till Friday?* 我手头有一点困难。你能借给我点儿钱吗?星期五还你。在表示"使人处于困难境地"的意思时,常用 put *someone* in a spot 的说法。这一说法与 put *someone* on the SPOT 不同,它不包含"如果不善于应付就会丢丑"的意思。*My wife's losing our train tickets put us in a spot.* 我的妻子把火车票丢了,使我们处于困难的境地。◇ be in a difficult position ((强调的场合用 tight 等 → very))

a night spot [ə ˈnaɪtˌspɑ(ː)t] [话] **夜总会** 这里的 spot 是"场所"的意思。本条条头指男男女女在夜里喝酒、跳舞、甚至吃饭的娱乐场所,包括夜间俱乐部 (night club)、卡巴莱 (cabaret)以及大型酒吧。*He's very well known in the top night spots in Hollywood.* 他在好莱坞的一流夜总会里是一位大名鼎鼎的人物。*I know a nice little night spot in Greenwich Village.* 我知道格林威治村有一家规模不大但是极好的夜总会。◇ a night club

on the spot[1] [ɔnðə ˈspɑ(ː)t] [口] **当即** 这一表达法与汉语的"当即"同样,除了场所的因素外,还包括时间的意味。根据上下文，有时强调“当时”，也有时强调“现场”。*The boss was so angry over Ned's mistake that he fired him on the spot.* 老板对于内德的失误极为恼火，当即把他解雇了。*The automobile fair was very successful. We sold all our new cars on the spot.* 汽车展销会非常成功。我们当即把所生产的新车全都卖光了。一些英汉词典常把这一表达法译作“用现金”，不确切。*I paid for it on the spot.* 我当即付了钱。在这一例句中，究竟付的是现金还是支票，那是另外的问题。*Mr. Moneybags must be a very rich man. He offered to buy our house for twice what it is worth and then took out his checkbook and paid for it on the spot.* “钱包”先生一定是个大富翁。他要按市价的两倍购买我家的住宅，然后取出支票簿，当即付了款。这一表达法也可添加连字符，在名词(词组)的前边使用。*The crash victims received on-the-spot medical attention.* 交通事故中的负伤者当即得到了应急治疗。◇ right there [away]

on the spot② [ɔnðə 'spɑ(:)t] [口] **在现场** the spot 的意思是“非特定的场所”乃至“现在大家谈论的场所”。多用于工作，指在一定时间内停留的现场或现地。*I'm in charge of machine repair at our factory. Whenever there is a major breakdown, I have to be on the spot twenty-four hours a day.* 在我们工厂里，我负责修理机器。每当发生大故障的时候，我必须一天 24 小时在现场。*As our company's representative in Manila, Johnny has been our man on the spot for over two years now.* 琼尼是我们公司驻马尼拉的代表，在那里已经两年多了。◇ there / on the scene

put *someone* **in a spot** [.put ～ ɪnə 'spɑ(:)t] [口] **使人处于困难境地** → be in a SPOT

put *someone* **on the spot** [.put ～ ɔnðə 'spɑ(:)t] [口] **使人感到非常尴尬** 有人把本条条头译作“进退维谷”，但是，在被人追赶而无处可逃的场合，不能使用它。本条习用语的意思是“使人处于尴尬的局面”，一般用于既不能采取紧急对策、也无法加以补救的场合，例如在众目睽睽之下出丑，只有难为情而已。*Not having prepared adequately, the boss's tough questions put me on the spot.* 由于没有足够的准备，老板的尖锐的质问使我感到非常尴尬。*George hadn't studied the problem adequately, so he was put on the spot when the chairman suddenly asked him to stand up and explain it in the meeting.* 乔治没有对那个问题进行充分的研究，因此在会议中，当主席突然叫他站起来加以说明的时候，他陷入了尴尬的局面。*The newspaper's disclosure that the Prime Minister may have accepted a bribe put the government on the spot.* 报纸揭露首相可能有受贿行为，这使政府陷入了尴尬的局面。另外，在作为黑社会用语使用的场合，这一表达法又有“决定干掉某人”的意味，但在一般会话中不通用。有时使用 be 动词，有如下的说法：*Please help me. I'm on the spot.* 请帮我一下。我正在为难呢。但在这一场合，一般说 be in a SPOT。◇ put *someone* in a very uncomfortable position

spots

hit the high spots [.hɪtðə 'haɪ.spɑ(:)ts] [话] **看重要的地方；讲要点** 直译为“击中高的场所”。这里的“高”，根据上下文，为“重要”或“最有趣味”的意思。*We spent a week in Europe hitting the high spots.* 我们在欧洲度过了一个星期，参观了主要的名胜。可以象这样说，但大多要加上 only 或 just。*You won't have time to see all of Beijing, so we'll just hit the high spots.* 你没有时间逛遍北京城，所以咱们只选几处主要名胜看看吧。*It was only a half-hour lecture, so the speaker just hit the high spots.* 讲演只有半个钟头的时间，所以讲演者只谈了几个要点。*Please listen carefully. I have time enough only to hit the high spots.* 请大家注意听。我的时间只够讲几个要点。◇ see the most important [interesting] places / talk about [mention] the most important points

spread

spread it on thick [ˌspredɪdɔ(ː)n ˈθɪ(ː)k] [话] **大肆吹嘘或奉承** spread ~ on thick 是"厚厚地抹上一层(黄油)"的意思。 it 在这里指"在想说服对方的时候,或者为了达到某种目的而竭力博得对方好感的时候,所讲的言过其实的话"。*When the boss starts bragging about the company to outsiders, he really spreads it on thick.* 当老板开始对外界人士夸耀自己的公司的时候,他大吹了一阵牛皮。如这一例句所示,这一表达法可以只表示"夸大其词"的意味。但是,在大多的场合,是用以表示"为了达到目的而向对方大拍马屁"的情况。 *Don't take what he says seriously. He's just spreading it on thick because he wants you to help him.* 他说的话你不必当真去听。他只是由于想叫你帮忙才大肆阿谀奉承的。*Don't spread it on too thick. He doesn't care for flattery.* 不必过于吹吹拍拍。他不喜欢阿谀奉承那一套。另外,常用 lay 代替 spread,而讲 lay it on thick。特别是在用 really 加强语气的时候,有省略 thick 的情况。 *When Jack starts flattering someone, he really lays it on.* 当杰克开始奉承某个人的时候,他那马屁拍得实在叫人肉麻。在讲 lay it on 的时候,为了进一步加强语气,常用 with a trowel [ˈtrauəl] (意思是"用泥瓦匠的抹子")来代替 real 或 thick。这一说法具有"用抹子厚厚地抹上一层泥"的意味。*Did he use flattery? He laid it on with a trowel!* 他说奉承话了吗?他那马屁拍得叫人肉麻极啦! ◇ exaggerate / use a lot of flattery

spree

go on a spree [ˌgouɔ(ː)nə ˈspriː] [口] **痛饮** 意思是"与朋友一起,跑到各处去饮酒狂欢"。这一表达法与 go on a BINGE 不同,充满轻松的感觉,经常具有欢乐的气氛。*My husband doesn't go out often in the evenings, but once in a while he likes to go on a spree with his friends.* 我丈夫很少在晚间出去,但是有的时候他喜欢跟朋友们到处去饮酒作乐。go on a spree 一般作"痛饮"解,也可以说 ~ drinking spree。*We went on a drinking spree last night for the first time in a long while.* 昨天晚上我们出去痛饮一番,好长时间没有这样取乐了。另外,与酒没有关系,也可以用于"痛快地干某种事情"的意味。在这一场合,和加 drinking 一样,一般要在 spree 的前边加上表示内容的形容词。 *Once in a while my wife goes on a shopping spree.* 我的妻子有时出去痛痛快快买一阵东西。*The Giants went on a hitting spree in the bottom of the ninth inning and won the game 10 to 9.* 巨人队在第九回合的下半局连续进攻,结果以 10 比 9 取胜了。*After the recession, the whole country went on a building spree.* 在经济萧条过去之后,全国掀起了建筑的热潮。◇ go out drinking and partying / enjoy a time [period] of unrestrained ~

spring

be no spring chicken → CHICKEN

spud

a spud [ə ˈspʌ(ː)d] [话] **土豆** 原指掘土豆时使用的 a narrow spade (窄而长的铲子)。 *Peel these spuds for me, will you?* 把这些土豆的皮给我削掉好不好? ◇ a potato

spurs

win *one's* **spurs** (as a *something*) [ˌwɪn ~ ˈspəːrz] [口] **受到赏识** 直译为"得到马刺"。古时,在因立大功而被授予"骑士"勋位的时候,会得到一个金的马刺。这就是本条习用语的来源。历史悠久,已见于中古英语。基本意思是"自己的能力得到承认",但用于两种场合:一是"同事、同业、上司承认你够得上一个成员",一是范围更广一些,自己的能力"得到社会的承认",亦即"成名"。*Though he didn't become famous till many years later, he first won his spurs as a young reporter for The Washington Post.* 虽然他在许多年以后才成名,但是在《华盛顿邮报》当青年记者时就已经受人赏识了。*I won my spurs as a sailor working on an old freighter plying between San Francisco and Hong Kong.* 我是在往返于旧金山与香港之间的老式货轮上成为一名正式水手的。*The boss doesn't consider an employee to have won his spurs until he has made at least a million dollars in sales within one year.* 如果在一年之内销售额达不到一百万美元，总经理就不承认这个人是有足够资格的工作人员。*George had won his spurs as a stock broker before going into the hotel business.* 乔治在开始经营旅馆之前，是一个有足够能力的股票经纪人。以下各例句用以表示更广泛的"得到社会公认"、"在社会上成名"、"著名"的意思。*There are many good young translators who have not yet won their spurs simply because they haven't been fortunate enough to translate a best seller.* 有许多优秀的青年翻译工作者，只因为他们没得到翻译一部畅销书的幸运机会，依然不为世人所知。*She had acted in many movies before she finally won her spurs with the public at large.* 她演过许多影片之后，才得到广大群众的赏识。spurs 可以加形容词。*He won his literary spurs by writing an historical novel about the War Between the States.* 他由于写南北战争的历史小说而享有文名。◇ gain recognition [acceptance] (as a *something*) / become full-fledged [a full-fledged *something*]

square

call it square [ˌkɔ(:)lət ˈskweːr] [话] **算作两清** 这里的 square 是"借贷两清的"、"谁也不欠谁的"的意思，与 even 大致相同。 *Here's the ten dollars I owe you. Now we're square.* 这是我借你的十美元。现在，咱们两清啦。如果是象这样用 be square，那就是指实际上把借的钱一分不差地还清了。但是，如果用 call it square 的话，那就不同了，它指的是：有时在实际上借的一方占点儿便宜，有时不清楚哪一方占点儿便宜，总之，大家不算细帐，不斤斤计较得失，双方"算作两清"，把旧帐"一笔勾销"。 *If you don't have the ten dollars you owe me, give me eight-fifty and we'll call it square.* 如果你手里没有十美元，你还给我 8.5 美元就行，咱们算作两清啦。除象这样用于金钱的借贷关系外，还有如下的比喻用法。 *You saved my life once and now I've saved your son's. Now we can call it square. The next time I see you I'm going to kill you.* 你救过我一次命，现在我救了你儿子的命。咱们如今可以算作两清啦。等下次我见到你，我可要杀掉你。 *Let's not go through life hurting each other like this. Why don't we call it square and be friends?* 咱们别象这样一辈子互相伤害吧？为什么咱们不尽弃前嫌、言归于好呢？另外，可以用 even 代替 square，而讲 call it even，例如：*I bought the tickets and she paid for the dinner, so we decided to call it even.* 我花买票的钱，她付吃饭的钱，这样我们就算作两清啦。 square 多少有一些轻松的意味。不过，在所有上面的例句中，square 与 even 均可相互代换。◇ consider *someone's* [our] debts cleared

a square meal → MEAL

a square shooter [əˈskweːr ˈʃu(:)dər] [话] **正直的人** → a straight SHOOTER

squares

three squares a day [ˌθriː ˌskwe(:)rzə ˈdeɪ] [话] **一天三顿饱饭** → a square MEAL

squaw

***one's* squaw** [～ˈskwɔː] [俗] **老婆** squaw 本来是"美洲印第安人女子"的意思。*Three squaws were washing clothes in the river.* 三个印第安女人在河里洗衣服。在 squaw 一词前边加上 *one's*，就成为"妻子"的意思，但大多用以表示说话者本人的"老婆"。一般为戏谑语。在某种情况下，又是不受听者欢迎的俚语。因此，如果不是非常亲密的朋友，千万不可说 How's your squaw? (你老婆好吗?) 之类的话。 *My squaw says she wants me to take her to a dance tonight. I sure hope she doesn't mean a war dance.* 我的老婆说，她希望我今天晚上带她去跳舞。我实在希望她所指的不是"出征舞"啊。顺便讲一下：a war dance 是过去印

第安人在出去打仗之前所跳的舞蹈。squaw 有时又是"女人"的轻蔑语，相当于汉语的"娘儿们"。 *Fishing is a man's sport. I refuse to take along any squaws.* 钓鱼是一项男子的体育活动。我绝对不带娘儿们去。◇ *one's* wife

squeak

have a narrow squeak [ˌhævə ˌnærə ˈskwiːk] [话] **九死一生** → have a close SHAVE

squeal

squeal on *someone* [ˈskwiː ˌlɔ(ː)n ~] [话] **告密** squeal 的字面意义为"尖声呼叫"。在黑社会用语中，指"向警察告发某人的犯法行为"。在描绘盗匪的电影和情节小说的影响下，这一表达法与 RAT on *someone* 同样为广大群众所熟知。但它又与 rat on *someone* 有所不同，只是盗匪们的专用语，几乎不能作为一般用语使用。另外，本条条头的"告密"主要指"背叛同伙"或"出卖同伙"。*Squeal on me and you're dead.* 你要向警察告密，我就要你的命。*Me? Squeal on you, boss? That's ridiculous!* 你说我出卖你这位首领？这太滑稽可笑啦。在说"向什么人密告什么事"的时候，与 rat on *someone* 同样，一般的词序是 squeal on *someone* to *someone* for [about] *something*。 *He squealed on me to the cops for that bank heist.* 他向警察告发我抢银行的事。有时省略 on *someone* 的部分。*Who squealed?* 谁向警察告密啦？ "向警察出卖同伙的人"叫做 a squealer。 *Give that squealer a wooden kimono.* 把那个告密者干掉！◇ inform (the police) on *someone*

squealer

a squealer [ə ˈskwi(ː)lər] [话] **向警察出卖同伙的人** → SQUEAL on *someone*

squeeze

put the squeeze on *someone* [ˌputðə ˈskwiːzɔ(ː)n ~] [话] **对某人施加压力** 过去，squeeze 一词专用于表示 extortion (敲诈勒索)、graft(受贿)等"榨取金钱的事情"。因此，put the squeeze on *someone* 也只用于表示"以金钱为目的而施加压力"的意味。但是现在，这一表达法也可以用于与金钱毫无关系而施加压力的场合。 *He's putting the squeeze on me. If I don't do as he says, he'll tell my wife about my "business trips."* 他在对我施加压力。如果我不照他的话去做，他就向我的妻子揭露我"出差"的秘密。从这一例句也可以看出，本条习用语经常含有"抓住对方的小辫子"的意味。只要一琢磨，你就会体察这里的"出差"的葫芦里卖的是什么药了。*The police discovered that a former colleague was putting the squeeze on the Prime Minister for fifty thousand dollars a year.* 警察发现首相的一个过去的同事在威胁首相，要他每年赠送五万美元。一看便可知道，这位首相过去有见不得人的丑事。类似的表达法有 put the SCREWS on *someone*，请注意两者的不同。◇ pressure *someone* (into *doing something*) / intimidate *someone* (out of *something*)

squire

squire *someone* (to *something*) [ˈskwaɪr ~] [口] **男性带着女性前去或前来** a squire 是古法语 *esquier*(持盾者)传入中古英语后形成的新词，意思为"骑士的随从"。现在作为及物动词使用，指"男性陪伴女性出席舞会以及其他正式的社交集会"。这一习用语原来有些陈腐，相当生硬，但在日常会话中，人们以半开玩笑的口吻用它来表示"带搞对象的女性前去或前来"的意思，已经是司空见惯了。*Who are you squiring to the dance next week?* 你带谁去参加下个星期的舞会呀？ *Great party, isn't it? Are you squiring anyone tonight?* 真是美妙的社交晚会呀！今天晚上你带女朋友来吗？不仅限于正式的"社交集会"，只要是以娱乐和消遣为目的的场所，不管哪里都可以。例如说：*I can't make it tonight. I'm squiring my wife to the movies.* 今天晚上不行。我要带妻子去看电影。◇ escort *someone*

stab

have a stab at (*doing*) *something* [ˌhævə

'stæ:bət ~] [话] **试一下看** → take a STAB at (*doing*) *something*

take a stab at (*doing*) *something* [ˌteɪkə 'stæ:bət ~] [话] **试一下看** 直译为"用刀去刺"。*He took a stab at me [the shark] with a knife.* 他用一把刀刺我[那条鲨鱼]。作为比喻,stab 是"尝试"的意思。整个条头则为"试一下看"的意思。如果是现在时或将来时,一般含有"究竟能不能行,自已没有把握"的韵味。*I think I'll take a stab at this crossword puzzle.* 我想试猜一下这个纵横填字谜。如果是过去时,大多含有"没有成功"或"立即死了心"的意味,因此如下一例句所示,采取 *someone* took a stab at ~, but ~的句型。*I took a stab at learning French year before last, but it was a waste of time.* 前年我曾尝试去学法语,但是白搭了时间。有时说 have a stab at (*doing*) *something*,意思相同。另外,*something* 处可代入 it,例如:*Well, I'll take a stab at it.* 好,我试一下看。请读者注意:在这一场合,it 的发音由 [ət] 变为 [æt]。 → take a CRACK at (*doing*) *something* ◇ try (*doing*) *something*

stack

blow *one's* **stack** [ˌblou ~ 'stæ(:)k] [话] **勃然大怒** → blow *one's* TOP

stacked

play against a stacked deck [ˌpleɪ əˌgenstə ˌstæk:'de(:)k] [口] **预先做了手脚,你去参加必输** → play with a stacked DECK

play with a stacked deck → DECK

be well stacked [ˌwel'stæ(:)kt] [话] **体态优美** stack 是"堆积"。条头直译为"堆积得很好",指女性的体态丰满和匀称。*Talk about (being) well stacked! You should see her in a bikini!* 你要讲体态优美,应该去看她穿三点式泳装的线条! 如此例所示,这是男性使用的俚语。用正统的表达法来说,就是 have a good figure。*I'll admit that she's well stacked, but she has a face that would stop a clock.* 我承认她的身材长得很不错,可是她的脸却难看极了。在强调体态优美的程度时,用 really 替换 well。*The boss's new secretary is really stacked.* 老板的新秘书真是体态优美啊。也可以用连字符连接起来,形成 well-stacked,作定语使用。*Leon showed up at the party last night with a well-stacked blond.* 利昂带着一个体态轻盈的金发美人出席了昨天的社交晚会。◇ have a good figure

staff

the staff of life [ðə 'stæ(:)fəv 'laɪf] [口] **面包** staff 原义为"棍棒"。life 是"生命"。西方主食面包呈长条的棒形,因而谐意为"生命的支柱",自古就有如下的说法:*Bread is the staff of life.* 面包是生命的支柱。后来,the staff of life 一语也可以用于面包以外的东西,例如说:*Rice is the staff of life.* 大米是生命的支柱。*Buffalo meat was the plains Indians' staff of life.* 野牛肉曾经是平原印第安人生命的支柱。the staff of life 本是由古语 Bread is the staff of life 而来,自从单独使用之后,除"生命的支柱"的本义外,又转义为 bread 本身,这是一个比较文雅的说法。*Have you got any of the staff of life? I'm starving.* 你有面包吗? 我饿了。一般来说,the staff of life 是不可数名词。但是在表示一块面包的"块"的概念时,可以成为可数名词。*Jake produced a staff of life and cut off two slices.* 杰克取出一块面包,切下了两片。如前所述,这一表达法的本来意思为"面包、大米等成为生命的支柱的主食"。后来,如下面的例句所示,这一意义又引申为"某人或某些人特别喜好的饮食"。这是一种夸张的说法,大多带有诙谐的意味。在这一场合,the staff of life 的 the 大多改为 *one's*。*To Stu, beer is the staff of life.* 对于司徒来说,啤酒是他的命根子。*Chocolate ice cream is our children's staff of life.* 我们家的孩子们顶喜欢巧克力冰淇淋。◇ bread

stag

go stag [ˌgou 'stæ(:)g] [口] **不带女伴参加社交集会** → a STAG

a stag [ə 'stæ(:)g] [口] **不带女伴参加社交集会的男子** 这一表达法的来源是:stag (雄鹿) 有单独活动的习性。本条习用语指一个去参加通常是成双成对出席的社交集会的男子。*About half the men at the party were stags.* 参加晚会的男子有一半左右没带女伴。"(男子) 不带女伴参加社交集会"在英语中说 go stag。*Paul couldn't find a date so he's going stag.* 保罗找不到女伴,只好只身参加社交晚会了。最近,可能受妇女解放运动的影响,有时用 stag 一词表示"不带男伴的女性"的意思,但这种说法不太通用。◇ (a man [boy]) without a date

a stag line → LINE

stag or drag ['stæ(:)gər 'dræ:g] [话] **带伴侣与否均可** 直译为"可以不带伴侣 (stag),也可以硬拖 (drag)伴侣前来参加社交集会"。stag (不带女伴参加社交集会的男子) 原为专指男性的用语,但是,stag or drag 在邀请女性时也可以使用。也就是说,女性单独一个人出席也行。虽然大多用于舞会,其他社交集会均可使用。这是青年人举办社交集会时的口头禅。*I'm having a party at my house tonight. Come stag or drag.* 今天晚上在我家里举行社交集会,请来参加。带伴侣与否均可。如这一例句所示,这一表达法大多与 come 一起使用,但也常采取 It's (going to be) stag or drag. 的形式。主要为口语,但在高中或大学的舞会海报上也常有"Stag or Drag"的字样。◇ with or without a date

a stag party → PARTY

stage

get stage fright → FRIGHT

set the stage (for *something*) [ˌsetðə 'steɪdʒ] [口] **做准备工作** 原意"布置舞台"。*Tom is in charge of setting the stage for the new play.* 汤姆负责新上演的话剧的舞台布景。作为比喻使用时,以人为主语,表示"做准备工作"的意思。例如:*Humphrey set the stage for holding the dance party by securing the principal's permission.* 汉弗莱得到校长的许可,做了举行舞会的准备工作。*Mr. Sohritz actually created the company, but it was Dudley's hard work that set the stage.* 索利茨先生的确是公司的创办人,但是辛辛苦苦进行筹备工作的则是达德利。也可以用人以外的东西当作主语,但在这一场合,本条习用语具有"打基础"、"创造机会"等意味。*The breakdown in negotiations between the union and management set the stage for a renewed outbreak of strikes.* 劳资谈判的破裂促发了再度罢工的热潮。*Though the economic hardships of the German people facilitated Hitler's rise to power, it was the treaty conditions forced upon Germany at the end of World War I that set the stage.* 虽然德国人民的经济困难使希特勒轻而易举地上了台,但是为他当政创造条件的乃是第一次世界大战结束时对德和约的条款。the stage is set (for *something*) 的最初构思是"舞台已经布置好了",比喻意义为"万事俱备"。*The stage is set. All you have to do is to go and tell him who you are.* 一切都准备好了。你只要去告诉他你是谁就行啦。*If he agrees to cooperate, the stage will be set for us to take over the company.* 如果他同意合作,我们接管那个公司就算万事俱备了。◇ make it possible (to *do something*) / make possible (the *something*) / lay the foundation (for *something*)

stagger

stagger the imagination [ˌstæ(:)gərðɪ əˌmædʒə'neɪʃən] [口] **令人晕头转向** → boggle the MIND

stakes

pull up stakes [puˌlʌp 'steɪks] [话] **搬走** 这里的 stake 是"搭帐篷的支柱"。pull up 是"拔"。整个条头的意思是"拔桩子"。如果一时出去,可以不动帐篷,但是,如果不打算再回来,那就要把帐篷整理好,准备到别的地方去。在折叠帐篷之前,首先必须拔桩子。这就是本条习用语的来源。用于迁居、搬家的场合,经常含有"不再回来"的意味。*We're thinking of pulling up stakes and moving to California.* 我们想搬到加州去。*If you're looking for Mr. Foster, you're too late. He doesn't live here anymore. He* *pulled up stakes about a month ago.* 如果你是找福斯特先生,你来得太晚啦。他已不住在这儿啦。他搬走一个来月了。*You can't pull up stakes just like that. Where will you go? How will you live?* 你不能那样说搬走就搬走呀。你到哪儿去?你怎么生活呢?在从隐蔽的地方逃走的场合,也可以使用这一表达法。*When the police arrived at the suspect's apartment, they found he had already pulled up stakes and fled.* 当警察到达嫌疑犯所住的公寓房间时,他们发现他已经离开那里,逃之夭夭了。◇ conclude *one's* affairs (and leave) / leave

stand

stand out like a sore thumb [ˌstænˈdaut laɪkə ˌso(ː)r ˈθʌ(ː)m] [话] **特别引人注目** → stick out like a sore THUMB

stand *someone* **up** [ˌstæ(ː)*d* ～ˈʌ(ː)p] [话] **失约** 直译为"使人一直站在那儿"。用以表示"不去赴约,让人久等"的意思。这一表达法不能按照字面解释为"使人站起来",千万不要弄错。*I was supposed to have a date with Doris but she stood me up.* 我跟多丽丝定好了约会,但是她把我涮了。如这一例句所示,用于男女之间的"失约"的场合最多,但并不限定于此。*I don't know why I bother to make appointments with that guy. He's always standing me up.* 我不知道为什么偏偏要去约见那个家伙。他一向是失约的啊。在无论怎么等待而对方始终都不来的时候,人们常自言自语地讲:*It looks like I've [you've] been stood up.* 看起来,我[你]是挨涮啦。◇ not show up (for a date [an appointment] with *someone*)

stand up to *someone* [ˌstæ(ː)nˈdʌptə ～] [口] **大胆对抗** 与主语相比,*someone* 是强者。因此,这一表达法具有"不畏强暴,寸步不让"的意味。*You were very brave to stand up to the boss like that.* 你象那样对抗老板,真是太勇敢啦。*Jimmy is the only one in our class who can stand up to that bully.* 在我们班里,只有吉米一个人敢于对抗那个横行霸道的家伙。*Life would be easier for Jane if she would only stand up to her husband once in a while.* 简只要偶尔跟她的丈夫顶几句嘴,她的日子会过得更舒服些。*If England and France had stood up to Nazi Germany sooner, there might not have been a Second World War.* 如果英法两国早一些时候大胆对抗纳粹德国,第二次世界大战也许就不会发生。◇ oppose [confront] *someone*

star

hitch *one's* **wagon to a star** → WAGON

stars

see stars [ˌsiːˈstɑːrs] [话] **眼睛冒金星** 在头部遭到打击的时候,人眼经常看到"金星"。由于这种原因,在漫画中表示头部挨打时,常常在脑袋周围画上几颗星星。*I hit my head so hard on the door lintel that I saw stars.* 我的头部在门梁上重重地撞了一下,撞得我眼睛直冒金星。*The blow on his head made Jack see stars.* 杰克当头挨了一击,眼睛直冒金星。也可以利用这一 see stars 编成下面这样的趣谈:*A: I saw stars at noon today. B: That's impossible. How could you see stars in the daytime? A: I fell out of a tree and landed on my head.* 甲:今天中午我看到星星啦。乙:那不可能。你怎么会在白天看到星星哪?甲:我从树上掉下来,脑袋先着地了。◇ (become) dizzy

thank *one's* **lucky stars** (that ～) [ˌθæŋk ～ˌlʌki ˈstɑ(ː)rz] [话] **感到万幸** 直译为"感谢给自己带来幸运的星宿"。这一表达法可能来自占星术。意思是:不是由于自己的能力,也不是依靠努力,而是因为 luck (幸运),偶然得到非常好的结果,这要感谢上天的恩泽。常常省略 that。*Don't complain about the hospital bills. You should thank your lucky stars (that) you weren't killed in the accident.* 不要抱怨医院开的帐单吧。你没

有死于事故,就应该感到万幸啦。*When I see what a fat shrew Joyce has become, I thank my lucky stars that I decided not to marry her.* 当我见到乔伊斯已经变成一个又肥又胖的泼妇的时候,我感到自己不同她结婚实在是万分侥幸了。*My grade wasn't so hot, but that was a tough test. I thank my lucky stars I was able to pass it at all.* 我的分数不很理想,但是那次考试非常难,我能够及格就已经感到万幸了。有时可以省略 lucky。*You can thank your stars that you weren't asleep when the fire broke out.* 你真是福星高照,在起火的时候还没有睡着。◇ be very lucky

start

get off to a flying start [ˌgeˈdɔ(ː)ftuə ˌflaiiŋ ˈstɑ(ː)rt] [口] **开门红** 在快艇或汽车比赛时,必须先使全部参赛的快艇或汽车达到一定的速度,才能起跑。这种用"助跑方式"的起跑,在英语中叫做 a flying start。*The yachts approached the line in preparation for a flying start.* 各快艇向起跑线接近了,准备助跑方式的起跑。后来应用于一般的竞争或比赛,表示"比他人抢先一步的有利的开端"的意思。含有"使用了助跑方式"的意味。get off 是"出发"。整个条头直译是"以有利的开端出发"。如以下的例句所示,在体育运动、工作以及其他方面广泛使用。*Our team got off to a flying start by winning our first two games by lopsided scores.* 我们队来个开门红,以一边倒的比分赢了最初两局。*Our new company got off a flying start with three big orders during the first week of business.* 我们新成立的公司来了个开门红,在开始营业的头一个星期内就得到了三笔大宗订货。*The city bond's drive to build a new school got off to a flying start when several wealthy citizens signed up for large subscriptions.* 本市为新建一所学校而发起的捐献运动,由于几位有钱的市民认捐而来了个开门红。也可以用 be 动词,作 be off to a flying start。*She's off to a flying start in her new job as a furniture buyer.* 她在当家俱采购员的新工作岗位上,一开始就非常顺利。*I don't know if we can get everyone to go along with our plan or not, but if we can get the bureau chief's approval we'll be off to a flying start.* 我不晓得全局工作人员是否能够支持咱们的计划,但是,如果能够得到局长的批准,我们就有一个良好的开端了。在游泳比赛或赛跑时,如果发令枪未响之前就开始行动,在英语中说 jumping the gun,而不能用 flying 或 flying start 表达这种意思 (→ jump the GUN)。◇ get off to a successful beginning / begin successfully

state

Something is rotten in the state of Denmark. → DENMARK

stateside

stateside [ˈsteɪtˌsaɪd] [俗] **(去、在)美国** 原为美军用语。字面意义为"(海洋的)合众国一侧"(the <United> States' side <of the ocean>)。这是从外边看美国的说法,一般为不住在美国的人或者居住在国外的美国人口头使用。美国境内的一般公民几乎无人使用这一表达法。虽然并无恶意,但是格调不高。有些美国人听到外国人用这个词就感到厌烦。这一表达法的特点是不用前置词。用法与副词 there 相同,在翻译成汉语时,要根据上下文补充个"去"、"到"或者"在"字。*He went stateside.* 他去美国了。*He's stateside now.* 他现今在美国。*I bought it stateside.* 那是我在美国买的。第一个字母可以大写,作 Stateside。◇ to [in, etc.] America

station

a filling station [ə ˈfɪlɪŋ ˌsteɪʃən] [口] **加油站** 直译为"把汽车油箱灌满的车站"。*Is there a filling station near here?* 这附近有加油站吗? *Let's get some gas at the next filling station.* 咱们在下一个加油站加点油吧。又称 service station 或 a gas(oline) station。但请读者注意:不能说 gasoline station。◇ a service station

a gas station [ə ˈgæ(ː)s ˌsteɪʃən] [话] **加油**

站 → a filling STATION

a service station [ə 'sɔːrvəs ˌsteɪʃən] [口] **加油站** → a filling STATION

stay-at-home

a stay-at-home [ə 'steɪət.houm] [口] **不喜欢外出的人** → a STICK-IN-THE-MUD

stead

go in *someone's* stead [ˌgouɪn ～'ste(:)d] [口] **代替他人前去** → stand *someone* in good STEAD

stand *someone* in good stead [ˌstæ(:)d ～ ɪn.gud'ste(:)d] [口] **对某人很有用处(如知识、能力、经验等)** **stand** *someone* 是"使某人站立", in good stead 是"在良好的场所"。在现代, stead 是"代替"的意思, 如说 go in *someone's* stead (代替他人前去)。但在古时, 此词是"场所"的意思。从 homestead, bedstead 等名词中, 如今仍可看出这一意义的余痕。homestead 原意为"有 home 的场所", 现在一般指"住宅(包括附属的房屋及周围的土地)"。bedstead 原意为"铺垫子的场所", 现在作"床架"解, 也可以指"床"本身。从语源来讲, stand *someone* in good stead 的意思是"使某人站在好的场所", 作为比喻使用时, 表示"使某人处于有利的地位"、"把某人放在好的位置上"的意思。*I took a job with a construction company during my summer vacation, knowing that the experience would stand me in good stead after I graduated.* 在暑假中, 我到一家建筑公司去工作, 因为我认为在我毕业之后, 这种经验对我一定很有用处啊。*Col. Bellan May says that his ability to speak German stood him in good stead when he was captured during the war.* 贝兰·梅上校说他在战争中被俘虏的时候, 他由于能讲德语而得到很大好处。◇ be very useful (to *someone*)

steady

go steady (with *someone*) [ˌgou 'ste(:)di] [口] **只与确定的异性交往** steady 是"稳定不变"的意思。把这个词用在男女关系上, 如果说 go steady, 那就是"不东找一个西找一个, 只与一个人交往"的意思。这一表达法本来所反映的是学生生活中的男女交往的方式, 因而主要是大学生和高中学生们使用。在一般成年人听来, 多少有些幼稚的味道。*Jack and Jill have been going steady (with each other) for over a year.* 杰克与吉尔固定交往已经一年多了。*Parents often try to discourage their children from going steady.* 家长们往往试图劝阻他们的孩子跟固定的异性交往。*Let's go steady.* 咱们确定关系吧!"确定的异性朋友"本身叫做 *one's* steady。*Fred will never ask you for a date. He's Barbara's steady.* 弗雷德决不会找你约会的。他是巴巴拉的固定对象。顺便提一下: 人们常用 play the FIELD 作为 go steady 的反义惯用语。◇ date only one person [each other]

***one's* steady** [～'ste(:)di] [话] **确定的异性朋友** → go STEADY

steal

be a steal [ə 'stiːl] [话] **价钱便宜极了, 跟白给一样** 在谈商品价格时的用语, 意思是"跟偷来的东西一样便宜"。"买主"可以使用, 例如: *I wasn't planning to buy a dress like this, but it was such a steal that I couldn't resist.* 我本来没打算买象这样的衣服, 但是价钱便宜极了, 跟白给一样, 我就不能不买啦。"卖主"也可以使用, 例如: *Let me sell you one of these watches. They're a real steal.* 这种表卖给你一只吧。价钱便宜极了, 简直跟白给一样。再举一个例子: *At a hundred dollars, that camera is a steal.* 如果是一百美元, 那架照相机实在太便宜啦。在采取 be a steal at ～这一句型的时候, at ～处常添加 price (价钱)。例如说: *Why don't you buy that house? It's a steal at that price.* 你为什么不买那所房子? 要的价钱实在便宜极啦。◇ be a bargain

steam

blow off steam [ˌblou.ɔ(:)f 'stiːm] [话] **发泄郁闷的心情或过剩的精力** → let off STEAM

get up steam [ge.dʌp 'stiːm] [口] **振奋起**

来 → pick up STEAM

let off steam [leˌdɔ(:)f ˈstiːm] [话] **发泄郁闷的心情或过剩的精力** 本来的意思是“放掉多余的蒸气”。*I like the sound of the old locomotives letting [blowing] off steam.* 我喜欢听旧式火车头放蒸汽的声音。这是按字面意义的用法。转作比喻使用,首先是用于“发泄怒气、不满等”的场合。发泄的对象一般是人,例如:*We could hear Nolan in his office letting off steam to his secretary.* 我们听到诺兰在他的办公室里拿他的秘书撒气。也有时用以表示“一个人大声叫嚷”。*A: What's Charlie shouting about? B: Oh, don't mind him. He's just letting off steam.* 甲:查理在叫嚷什么哪? 乙:哦,你甭理他。他只是在发泄郁闷的心情。steam 的前边可以加 little 或者 some。*I don't know whether these letters I write to my congressman do any good or not, but it's a good way to let off a little steam.* 我不知道给我们选区的议员写的这些信是否能有点效果,不过这倒是发泄一下不满的好方法。下面是用以表示“发泄过多的精力”的例句。*I go to the tennis courts whenever I feel like letting off some steam.* 当我想要发泄一些过剩的精力时,我就到网球场去。*The children were so rowdy today that I sent them to the park to let off some steam.* 今天孩子们吵闹得太厉害,所以我打发他们到公园去发泄过剩的精力去了。一般用 let off ~,但有时用 blow off ~,二者意思相同,也可以互相置换,但后一说法不大用于“发泄精力”的场合。*A: Did I hear Tim threaten to resign? B: Yes. But he didn't really mean it. He was just blowing off steam.* 甲:听说蒂姆叫嚷要辞职不干了,真的吗? 乙:是的。不过,他并不是真心辞职。他只是发泄一下不满而已。◇ give vent to *one's* frustrations [emotions]

lose steam [ˌlu(:)z ˈstiːm] [口] **势头低落** → pick up STEAM

pick up steam [pɪˌkʌp ˈstiːm] [口] **势头增大** 原意为“蒸气机车提高发动机的转数,从而加快速度”。pick up 是动词,相当于“加快速度”(pick up speed)中的“加快”。以下例句中 pick up steam 的 steam 均可用 speed 代换,但是 steam 一词除“速度”外还有“力量强大”的意味。*The engine is picking up steam.* 发动机在加大力量。*After leaving the harbor, the boat picked up steam.* 汽船驶出港口以后,加快了速度。这两句话都是按照原意的用法。作为比喻使用时,则表示“势头增大”的意思。*The women's lib movement began picking up steam in the late 1960's.* 20 世纪 60 年代后半期,妇女解放运动开始活跃起来了。这句话的意思是:妇女解放运动过去已经有所活动,到了这时候,势头增大了。*When spring came, the Allied Army's drive for Berlin picked up steam.* 当春天来临时,盟军进攻柏林的势头增大了。*The presidential campaign is beginning to pick up steam.* 竞选总统运动的势头开始增大了。与此有关的表达法有 get up steam, lose steam, run out of steam。它们都是表示蒸气机运动的状态。兹按运动的顺序排列如下 (括号内是原意): get up steam (为了开动引擎而烧蒸气) → pick up steam → lose steam (减低速度) → run out of steam (停止)。按照字面意义,用法分别如下: *It takes about two hours for a ship that big to get up steam.* 象那样大的一只船,需要制造两个来小时的蒸汽才能开动。*One of the boilers blew up and the ship began losing steam.* 由于一个锅炉爆炸,那只船开始减低速度了。*Quick! More fuel! The engine's running out of steam.* 快! 多加燃料! 发动机要停下啦。作为比喻使用的场合,get up steam 的意思是“得到能够开始活动的力量”。*We hope to get up enough steam to begin our campaign in April.* 我们希望得到足够的力量,以便在四月开始我们的竞选运动。如这一例句所示,可以用于肯定句,但大多是在否定句中使用。*Our movement never got up enough steam to be effective.* 我们的运动始终没有足够的力量有效地开展起来。lose steam 是“势头衰退”的意思。*The Democratic candidate's campaign ap-*

pears to be losing steam. 民主党人竞选运动的势头似乎在衰退。*The recession has caused the union's drive for higher wages to lose a lot of steam.* 由于经济萧条，工会要求提高工资的活动大大失去了势头。run out of steam 是"力量衰竭"的意思。*Napoleon's drive to conquer Russia ran out of steam at Moscow.* 拿破仑征服俄国时，进军到莫斯科便力量衰竭了。*The Democratic candidate's campaign appears to be running out of steam.* 民主党人的竞选运动似乎日落西山了。◇ gain momentum

run out of steam [rʌn.audəv ˈstiːm] [口] **力量衰竭** → pick up STEAM

steel

have a mind like a steel trap → TRAP

steer

a bum steer [ə ˈbʌ(:)m ˈstɪːr] [话] **靠不住的消息** bum 原为名词，意思是"流浪者"(→ BUM *something* <off *someone*>)。转用作形容词，意思是"不中用的"、"无价值的"、"不可靠的"。steer 是"掌舵(船)"或"驾驶(汽车)"，与汉语的"舵手"同样，有"确定方向"的意思；后来成为俚语，用以表示"使人确定方向的忠告、情报等"的意味。因此，a bum steer 指"信不得的忠告"或"靠不住的消息"。有时是故意使对方迷失方向，也有时不是如此。究竟属于哪种情况，只能根据上下文来判断。*I'm tired of that guy's bum steers.* 我对那个家伙的道听途说已经腻味透啦。这一表达法可以象这样单独使用，但在大多数场合是使用如下两个惯用句型：give *someone* a bum steer (向某人讲靠不住的消息) 和 get a bum steer (from *someone*) (从某人那儿听到靠不住的消息)。*That guy gave me a bum steer when he told me this was a cheap restaurant.* 那个家伙告诉我说这个餐厅价格便宜，完全是瞎说八道。*I'm sorry I gave you a bum steer. I thought it was true at the time.* 很抱歉，我对你讲了一个不可靠的消息。当时我认为是真的呢。*I'm always getting bum steers from that guy. He probably even lies to his own mother.* 我总是从那个家伙的嘴里听到一些靠不住的消息。他大概对自己的亲娘也是谎话连篇的。◇ wrong information [advice]

steer clear of *someone* [*something*] [.stɪ(:)r ˈklɪ(:)rəv ~] [口] **避开** steer 具有"驾驶(汽车)"、"掌舵(船)"、"操纵"的意味。clear of ~是"躲避……"。*You'd better steer clear of those rocks. A number of boats have been wrecked there.* 你掌舵可要躲开那些岩石。有许多船在那里失事了。从这字面意义进一步发展，也经常作为比喻使用。*I'd advise you to steer clear of that guy. He spells trouble.* 我劝你对那个家伙敬而远之。他总制造麻烦。*In conversing with Mr. Stumper, you'd better steer clear of politics and religion.* 你与斯坦泼先生谈话的时候，以避开政治和宗教的话题为宜。*Although I've been dating Jim for almost three years now, he seems determined to steer clear of marriage.* 我跟吉姆谈情说爱现在已经快三年了，而他似乎坚决不和我结婚。◇ avoid *someone* [*something*]

step

step on it [ˈste.pɔ(:)nət] [话] **赶快** → step on the GAS

watch *one's* **step** [.wɑtʃ ~ ˈste(:)p] [口] **当心** step 是"脚踩的地方"(where *one* steps)。本条条头直译为"注意脚底下"。美国公共汽车的车门处有 Watch your step. (当心脚下)的标牌。*Watch your step. This road is full of cow pies.* 当心脚底下。这条路上到处是牛粪。转作比喻使用，例如：*Watch your step, friend. I'm the type who doesn't care to have strange men talking to my girl.* 喂，你要当心点！我可不是能够容忍陌生男子与我的女朋友谈话的那种人啊。*Harry'd better watch his step. Those new friends of his could get him into trouble.* 哈里当心点为妙。他的那些新朋友很可能给他带来麻烦。*Our company got into financial difficulty by not watching its step when it started its Middle East operations.* 我们公司由于在中东开始营业时

未加小心，结果发生了财政困难。step 的后边常用 with ～接续。*You'd better watch your step with Mr. Ladder. He gets very angry when anyone tries to give him unsolicited advice.* 你和莱德先生打交道时，可要多加小心。谁要是主动地向他提出忠告，他会大发脾气的。另外，在英国英语中，动词除 watch 外，还常用 mind，但在美国口语中极少这种情况。◇ be careful

sterner

be made of sterner stuff → STUFF

Stetson

a Stetson [ə ˈstetsən] [口] **牛仔帽** 19 世纪后半叶，美国有一家叫做 John B. Stetson 的制帽公司推出一种帽檐很宽而两侧略往上卷的、男子用的大顶毡帽。本条条头即指的是这种帽子。由于结实和实用，从美国西部开荒时代起，牛仔们就喜欢戴。后来，不论任何公司制造的这种帽子，一概称为 a Stetson (偶尔也称为 a John B.)。*Many men in the American west still wear Stetsons.* 在美国西部，许多男子仍然戴牛仔帽。又称 a Stetson hat。有时全用小写字母，作 stetson (hat)。◇ a cowboy hat

stew

stew in *one's* **own juice** → JUICE

stick

a cancer stick [ə ˈkæ(ː)ntsər ˌstɪk] [话] **(一支) 纸烟** 直译为"得癌症的棒"。与 a coffin NAIL 同样，是一种戏谑语。来源是：人们认为纸烟是引起 lung cancer (肺癌) 的主要祸首。*How many cancer sticks do you smoke a day?* 你一天吸多少支纸烟啊？◇ a cigarette

the carrot and the stick → CARROT

get on the stick [ge.dɔ(ː)nðə ˈstɪ(ː)k] [话] **加油干** 从字面上反映出的具体形象是：人用全身倚靠一根立着的棍棒。语源出典不明。*That guy's been goofing off a lot lately. He's gonna get fired if he doesn't get on the stick.* 那个家伙最近老是游手好闲。如果他不加油干，就要被解雇啦。在催促他人的时候也常用这一表达法，意思是"别磨蹭啦！"，"别慢条斯理地啦！"*If you're going with us, you'd better get on the stick.* 如果你要跟我们一起走，最好是快一点儿。*Get on the stick, you guys. We've got to get this work finished.* 伙计们，加油干呀！这个活儿我们非干完不可。另有 stay on the stick 的说法，意思是"始终干劲十足"或"始终精神旺盛"。*The boss isn't exactly a slave driver, but he expects his men to stay on the stick.* 老板并不是一个拿人当奴隶使用的人，但是他要求部下始终精神饱满，干劲十足。也可以用 be 代替 stay，而讲 be on the stick。*Cal's a model employee. He's always on the stick.* 卡尔是一个模范工作人员。他总是干劲十足。◇ become more alert and active / start working harder / get busy

a joy stick [ə ˈdʒɔɪ ˌstɪk] [话] **飞机的操纵杆** 这里的 joy 意思是"开飞机的乐趣"。本条条头的来源是：第一次世界大战时期，飞行员们为了强调驾驶飞机的乐趣，称"操纵杆(control lever)"为"快活棒(joy stick)"。专指滑翔机或小型飞机使用的棒形操纵杆。*A glider is very simple to fly. All it has is two foot pedals and a joy stick.* 驾驶滑翔机是非常简单的，只有两个脚踏板和一个操纵杆而已。*The pilot pulled back on the joy stick, and the plane came out of its dive.* 飞行员把操纵杆向后一拉，飞机从俯冲姿势恢复了正常。*When the pilot fainted, I reached over his shoulder and grabbed the joy stick.* 当飞行员昏过去的时候，我从他的肩头伸过手去，抓住了操纵杆。现在，不仅用于飞机，也可以用于一般机械类的棒形操纵杆。*The machine is operated by manipulating this joy stick.* 那台机器是用这一操纵杆开动的。又，最近还称带麻醉药的纸烟为 joy stick，意思为"吸了就快乐的小棒"。*Customs found twenty joy sticks in the youth's bag.* 海关在那个青年人的旅行袋里查获二十支带麻醉药的纸烟。另外，在英国英语中，把 joy stick 作为 penis 的隐语使用，但在美国英语中没有此义。◇ a control stick [lever]

be on the stick [ɔ(:)nðə ˈstɪ(:)k] [话] **干劲十足** → get on the STICK

stay on the stick [ˌsteɪɔ(:)nðə ˈstɪ(:)k] [话] **始终干劲十足** → get on the STICK

stick *someone* (with *something*) [ˈstɪk ~] [话] **强加于人** 首先看一下例句: *That shop that fixed my TV stuck me with a bill for two hundred dollars.* 那家商店给我修理了电视机,结果硬要二百美元。这是"不正当地多要钱"的例子。*That used-car dealer tried to stick me with a lemon.* 那家经营旧汽车的商店打算硬卖给我一辆有毛病的汽车。这是"往外塞劣质商品"的例子。不管是哪一个例子, stick *someone* 总有"把不正当的事物强加于人"的意思。从被强加者方面来说,则带有"上当"、"受骗"的悔恨心情。*We never deal with that distributor. He'll stick you every chance he gets.* 我们决不跟那个批发商做生意。他只要有机会就会欺骗你。只凭这句话,我们弄不清是"开花帐多算钱"还是"以次品充好货",或者两方面的情况全有,尽管如此,"以不正当的方法骗人"这一意思是一清二楚的。另外, stick 有按本条的释义使用被动语态的时候,例如说 *The last time I ate in that restaurant, I was stuck with an outrageous bill.* 上次我在那家饭馆吃饭,在开帐的时候他们很很敲了我的竹杠。值得注意的是:这一 be stuck with ~的句型往往会形成意义相当不同的另一表达法 be STUCK with (*doing*) *something* (→)。◇ foist *something* on *someone* / cheat *someone*

stick around [ˌstɪkə ˈraund] [话] **呆在那里** 这里的 stick 是"不离开", around 是"在那里"。在大多的场合,"呆在那里"即使是有目的,也没有什么了不起的事情。如果是非常严重的情况,就不能使用这一表达法,它一般含有"无所事事"的意味。*Why not stick around for two or three more days? I'll introduce you to some interesting people.* 再多呆两三天不好吗?我给你介绍几个有趣的人。*Stick around if you want to see some fun. Dingly put a snake in the sergeant's bed.* 如果你想看有趣的事情,可以呆在这儿呀。丁利给中士的床上放了一条蛇。*A: Going home now? B: No, I think I'll stick around a little longer.* 甲:现在回家吗?乙:不,我想在这儿多呆一会儿。在这句话里,乙并没有什么明确的目的。如果把 stick around 改成其他说法,意思与之最接近的是 stay (here [there])。不过,在以上各例句中,若将 stick around 换成 stay (here),就会失去"无所事事"的轻松味道。另有一个表达法 hang around (闲呆着) 与 stick around 相似,在大多的场合可以换用,但这一表达法用于完全没有目的或极少怀有目的的场合。◇ stay here [there]

stick by *someone* [ˌstɪkbaɪ ˈ~ / ˌstɪkˈbaɪ ~] [口] **忠于某人** 直译为"贴在某人身边"。虽然说是"贴",并不是指在肉体上,而是在精神上。把这意义引申,就是"不管发生什么事情也不丢开某人"的意思了。*I owe a lot for my success to my wife. She has stuck by me through thick and thin.* 对于我的成功,我的妻子有很大的功劳。她始终对我忠贞不渝。*I'd like to thank all of my friends for sticking by me during my period of difficulty.* 我感谢在我困难时期始终信任我的一切朋友们。这一表达法本身并没有"积极采取行动"的意味。*I don't care if the police do say you're guilty. I'll stick by you.* 即使警察说你有罪,我也不在乎。我仍然忠于你啊。在这一例句中,说话人并不是要去证明对方无罪,只是在吐露自己的眷恋情怀而已。◇ continue to support [back] *someone*

Stick 'em up. [ˈstɪkəˈmʌp] [话] **举起手来!** stick up 是"向上突出"。'em 是 them 的缩略,在这里指"两只手"。这是一个轻松的表达法,说话人一边拿枪威胁对方,一边这样讲。*Stick 'em up! One false move and you're dead.* 举起手来!你乱动一下,就要你的命。象这样的台词,在描绘强盗的影片、西部影剧以及儿童们的牛仔游戏中,是常常可以听到的。另有 Reach for the SKY 与之同义。顺便提一下:由 Stick 'em up. 派生出来的 stick *someone* [*someplace*] up 也是一个习用句型,意思是"强盗持枪袭击某人”。 *A robber stuck me [the bank] up.* 一个持枪匪徒袭击了我[银行]。在一般的口语中,还用 hold *someone* [*someplace*] up 表示同一的意义。这两种表达法的名词形式分别为 a stickup, a holdup,意思当然是“持枪打劫”了。*There was a stickup [holdup] at Mr. Smith's store yesterday.* 昨天,史密斯先生的商店遭到持枪匪徒的抢劫。◇ Raise your hands (over your head).

stick it out [ˌstɪkɪˈdaut] [话] **忍耐到底** 与 hold out (坚持到底) 不同,本条条头经常表示精神上的紧张状态。*The settlers were unable to hold out against the Indian attack.* 拓荒者们抵抗不住印第安人的进攻了。以下是 stick it out 的用例。*I know you don't like school, but you'll be graduating in another six months. Surely you can stick it out that long.* 我知道你不喜欢上学,但是再有六个月你就毕业啦。你一定能够忍耐到那个时候的。*I hope the snow melts soon. I don't know how much longer I can stick it out in this mountain cabin.* 我希望雪马上融化才好。我不知道自己在这山间小屋里还能忍耐多久。*I've got to get transferred back to the home office soon. I just can't stick it out in this hick town any longer.* 我非赶快调回总公司不可啦。在这个小乡镇里,我简直再也忍耐不下去了。◇ endure it

stick out like a sore thumb → THUMB

stick *someone* [*someplace*] **up** [ˌstɪk ～ ˈʌ(ː)p] [话] **强盗持枪袭击某人** → STICK ʼem up.

stick up for *someone* [ˌstɪkˈʌpfər ～] [话] **挺身为某人辩护** 这一表达法的意义包含着三个要素:一是“自己挺身而出”,二是“用口头辩论”,三是“站在处于不利境遇的人一边”。虽然简单地讲是“辩护”,但与 defend 等词截然不同。*Faith is a good friend. She sticks up for me even when she knows I'm wrong.* 费思是一位很好的朋友。甚至在知道我错了的时候,她仍挺身而出为我辩护。*I don't know why you always stick up for that guy. He isn't worth it.* 我不知道你为什么老是替那个家伙辩护。他不值得你那样做。如这一例句所示,本条习用语一般用于日常生活琐事,“在法庭上进行辩护”的场合不能使用。◇ (step forward and orally) defend *someone*

stick with *someone* [ˌstɪkwɪð ˈ～ / ˌstɪk ˈwɪð ～] [话] **跟着走** stick together 是“携手”或“团结”的意思。本条条头则具“追随”的意味。*Let the others go that way if they want to. You stick with me*[ˌstɪkwɪð ˈmiː]. *I know a short cut.* 别人愿意走那条路,就叫他们走去吧。你跟我来,我知道一条近道。这是按照字面意义,表示实际上跟着别人走路。也可以用作比喻,表示“追随某人”。例如: *Stick with me and you'll succeed in a big way.* 你跟着我,一定会取得巨大的成功。*His employees are very faithful. They stuck with him* [ˌstʌk ˈwɪðəm] *during the depression even though he often couldn't pay their salaries.* 他那个公司的工作人员非常忠实。在经济萧条的时候,他往往付不出工资,即便这样,他们还是追随着他。◇ stay with *someone*

stick with *something* [ˌstɪkwɪð ˈ～] [话] **照旧不变** 这一表达法与 STICK with it 近似,但在意思上有微妙的差异。这一点有注意的必要。stick with it 是尽管感到厌烦或必须吃苦也“坚持”,最后的抉择只有干或不干而已。本条条头与此不同,它在干之中有选择的余地,用于讲“我比较喜欢 *something*”的场合。因此,它比 stick with it 具有积极的姿态。例如在轮盘赌时说: *I'll stick with red.* 我还是押红的。这句话表示这个赌徒“我不喜欢黑的而喜欢红的”的强烈意志。*No whiskey for me, thanks. I'll stick with beer.* 谢谢,别给我倒威士忌。我照旧喝啤酒。*Lots of the guys are buying cars now that they're out of college, but I'm going to stick with my motorcycle a while longer.* 现在有许多青年刚从大学毕业就买汽车,但是我在一时之间照旧骑我的摩托。选择的余地不仅是二者居其一,也有从两个以上当中选取一个的场合,例如说: *For a while I had thought of changing my major to either English or* *math, but then I decided to stick with geology after all.* 我曾经一度考虑主修英语或者数学，但是后来决定仍旧研读地质学了。有时，stick with *something* 也与 stick with it 同样用于表示“坚持不懈”的意味。 *He stuck with his studies until he finally passed the entrance exam.* 他坚持不懈地用功，直至最后考上了大学。◇ continue with *something* / persevere with *something*

stick with it [ˌstɪk ˈwɪðɪt] [话] **坚持不懈** stick 的第一个意义是“粘住”。这一表达法的具体形象是“粘住了，离不开”。用于如下的场合：对“练习”、“工作”、“问题”、“谈判”等等需要有耐性的事情，本人虽然厌烦或者感到劳累，仍然坚持不懈地去搞。汉语成语叫做“锲而不舍”。*Alice hated to practice, but she stuck with it until she became a good piano player.* 艾丽丝讨厌练琴，但是在她成为一个优秀的钢琴师之前，她一直坚持不懈。*Many's the time my brother became disgusted with his job and thought of quitting, but he stuck with it. Now he's president of the company.* 我哥哥讨厌他的工作，曾经多次想要辞职，但是他一直坚持下来了。现在，他是公司的总经理。stick with it 本身就有“一直坚持到底”的意味，但是为了使这一意味更加明显，往往增添 to the end 或者 a little longer。 *That's a tough problem, but stick with it a little longer. I sure you'll get the answer.* 那是一个很难的问题，但是，你再坚持搞一下看。我相信你会得到答案的。stick to it 也表示同一的意思，但是一般用 with 而不用 to。另外，在极少的场合，不是用 it，而采取 stick with *something* [ˌstɪkwɪð ˈ～] 的形式。◇ persevere

stick-in-the-mud

a stick-in-the-mud [ə ˈstɪkɪnðə ˌmʌ(ː)d] [话] **老古董** 最初的构思是：象蛙一样留在泥(mud)中，到春天也不出来。由此引申，用以表示“不接受新事物的人”。例如：*You may say that my husband and I are stick-in-the-muds, but we don't believe in the free sex movement.* 你可以说我的丈夫和我是不接受新事物的老古董，但是我们不赞成性自由运动。*Don't be a stick-in-the-mud, Bob. What's wrong with making a little money under the table once in a while?* 别那么死心眼儿，鲍勃。偶尔捞点儿好处费又有什么不好啊？为了加强语气，可以增添 old。*If the boss weren't such an old stick-in-the-mud, our company could have expanded to twice its present size long ago.* 如果老板不是那样一个不开窍的老古董，我们公司早就比现在的规模扩大一倍啦。有时不是作为名词、而是作为形容词使用，表示“陈腐落后”的意思。例如：*I wouldn't vote for a stick-in-the-mud party like that if it were the last party on earth.* 我绝对不投那样一个陈腐的、落后于时代的政党的票，哪怕地球上只剩下它这一个政党。*You'll never get anywhere in this modern world if you don't get rid of your old stick-in-the-mud ideas.* 你如果不放弃你那些陈腐落后的旧思想，你在现代社会中是绝对不会得到成功的。有时由于具体形象相似，人们把这一表达法与 a stay-at-home (不喜欢出门的人) 混同起来，如说 *My husband is such a stick-in-the-mud. He'd rather stay home and watch a cowboy movie on TV than go out to a new musical.* 我的丈夫是一个最不喜欢出门的人。他宁愿呆在家里看电视中描写牛仔的影片，也不出去看新上演的歌舞剧。◇ (an) old-fashioned and unadventurous (person)

stickler

a stickler [ə ˈstɪklər] [口] **难题** 这一表达法虽然是“困难问题”的意思，但含有“特别”或“极端”的意味。*Help me translate this sentence, will you? It's a stickler.* 帮我翻译这个句子好吗？这个句子太难啦。这里也可以使用 It's difficult. 但反映不出“太”的意思。常用 real 加强语气。 *The question of how to overcome the nation's balance of payments problem is a real stickler.* 如何处理国际收支问题的确是一个极为困难的问题。冠词如果

用 the,则是“其中最困难的问题”的意思。*Diagnosis of the disease is not difficult. It's the cure that's the stickler.* 诊断这种病并不难。最大的难题是治疗方法。*A: How did the murderer ever get into the room? B: That's the stickler.* 甲:杀人犯是怎样进入屋子的?乙:这是难题中的难题啊。◇(不加 real) extremely difficult / the most difficult problem [question]

be a stickler (for *something*) [ə 'stɪklər] [口] **吹毛求疵的人** stickler 是动词 stickle (吹毛求疵) 的名词形式。但是,现在几乎没有人使用 stickle 这一动词了。*Be sure to introduce the ladies first at the company reception. The boss is a stickler for ceremony.* 在公司的招待会上,一定要先介绍女性。老板对于礼仪是个爱吹毛求疵的人。强调的场合加 real。*I don't mind a messy room, but my roommate is a real stickler for neatness.* 屋子脏了我并不在意,但是与我同屋住的人却对整洁程度挑剔得实在厉害。*You'd better not be late for English class. The professor is a real stickler for punctuality.* 上英语课的时候,你最好不要迟到。那位教授对于严守时间的问题总是唠叨个没完。也可以把 for 换成 when it comes to。*When it comes to table manners, my wife is a real stickler.* 关于用餐的礼仪,我的妻子实在是爱吹毛求疵。也可单独使用 stickler,例如:*Sticklers for rules are generally not very popular.* 对实施规章制度要求太严格的人总是不大受人欢迎。◇ be very strict [particular] (about *something*)

sticks

the sticks [ðə 'stɪ(:)ks] [话] 穷乡僻壤 → the BOONIES

stick-to-it-iveness

stick-to-it-iveness [ˌstɪk'tu:ədəvnəs] [口] **顽强精神** 原为 stick to it(坚持到底),加 -ive 后构成形容词,即 stick-to-it-ive [ˌstɪk'tu:ədəv]。再加 -ness 构成名词,就是本条条头的英语。形容词 stick-to-it-ive 仅在极少的场合使用。*He's a stick-to-it-ive person.* 他是一个顽强的人。与此相反,名词形式 stick-to-it-iveness 却是日常能够不断听到的表达法,其用法如下:*To be a good salesman you have to have a lot of stick-to-it-iveness.* 要当一个优秀的推销员,你必须有十分的顽强精神。*The most important requirement in mastering a foreign language is stick-to-it-iveness.* 要掌握一门外国语,最重要的必备条件是顽强精神。◇ perseverance

stickum

stickum ['stɪkəm] [话] **粘贴剂** stick them 的缩略 (这里的 stick 是“贴”)。按 stick 'em 的发音拼写而成。用作浆糊、胶水、骨胶、快速粘接剂等能把东西粘在一起的粘性物质的总称,是轻松的表达法。*Let me use some of your stickum.* 借给我粘贴剂用一下。*This stamp doesn't have any stickum on it.* 这张邮票上没有一点粘贴剂啊。◇ glue

stickup

a stickup [ə 'stɪˌkʌ(:)p] [话] **持枪抢匪** → STICK 'em up.

sticky-fingered

sticky-fingered ['stɪki'fɪŋgərd] [话] **手不老实** → have sticky FINGERS

stiff

stiff ['stɪ(:)f] [话] **喝醉了** 一般来说,stiff 是“坚硬的”(如 stiff paper 为“硬纸”)或“强烈的”(如 stiff wind 为“强风”)的意思。也有按照本条条头的意义使用的情况。17 世纪左右,开始用于表示“有酒量”,而把“有海量的人”、“能大量喝酒者”称为 a stiff drinker。后来进一步发展,遂产生了现在的“喝醉了”的意思。虽然是形容词,但不能用于名词之前,只作表语使用。如说:*He is stiff.* 他喝醉了。*I got stiff last night.* 我昨天夜里喝醉了。*We left the car in town. Everybody was so stiff that no one could drive.* 我们把汽车放在镇里了。每个人都酩酊大醉,没有一个能开车啦。◇ drunk

stinking

stinking drunk → DRUNK
stinking rich → RICH

stinko

stinko [ˈstɪŋkou] [话] **酩酊大醉** 这是把 stinking DRUNK (酩酊大醉) 中的 stinking 与 BLOTTO (烂醉如泥) 结合在一起的表达法。一般作表语使用。*Don't give him another drink. He's already stinko.* 不要再给他酒喝啦。他已经酩酊大醉了。◇ very drunk

stir

go stir crazy [ˌgou ˈstəːr ˌkreɪzɪ] [话] **因长期坐牢而发疯** → in [out of] STIR

in [out of] stir [ˌɪn / ˌaudə ˈstəːr] [话] **在[出]监狱** 人们认为 stir 一词源出盎格鲁撒克逊语的 styr (惩罚),勉强译作"监狱"。虽然说是"监狱",但与 prison (监狱) 等不同,它完全不指牢房的建筑物本身,而意味着"监狱中的生活"。因此,不加冠词,在使用时一般采取 in stir 的形式,有时采取反义的 out of stir 的表达法。*Patonelli was in stir for fifteen years.* 帕托奈利坐了 15 年牢。*Joe will soon be getting out of stir.* 乔不久就要出狱了。stir crazy 也是习用语,意思为"因长期坐牢而发疯"。这是个形容词短语,例如说: *Everybody gets a little stir crazy after a year or so in this place.* 在这个地方呆上一年左右,任何人都会有点儿精神失常。特别是与 go 结合在一起,又构成 go stir crazy 这样一个习用语。*He went stir crazy and they put him in the prison hospital.* 他由于长期坐牢而发疯了,已经被送入监狱的医院。但这一习用语并不限于"监狱",也可以转用于表示"因长期困在一个地方而发疯"的场合。*The boredom of our stay in the snowed-in mountain cabin made us all feel a little stir crazy.* 我们呆在被雪封住的山中小屋里无聊透顶,这简直使我们全都感到有点儿发疯了。*After a few weeks in the hospital, I began to go stir crazy.* 在医院里住了几个星期之后,我开始发疯了。◇ in [out of] prison

stitches

have *someone* **in stitches** [ˌhæv ~ ɪnˈstɪtʃəz] [口] **令人笑破肚皮** 在这里,stitches 的字面意义为"用针缝的缝儿"。原指做盲肠手术之后在下腹部用针缝的缝儿,后转义为"在动的时候或笑的时候针缝儿发疼",又进一步转义为"在急跑的时候感到侧腹疼痛"。因此,have *someone* in stitches 直译应为"使某人笑得肚皮发疼"。使用范围很广,除滑稽的动作、语言以及笑话外,还应用于滑稽的电影、戏剧等。*George's takeoff on the principal's way of talking had them in stitches.* 乔治滑稽地模仿校长的说话方式,使他们笑破了肚皮。*Our physics teacher's story of his boy's dog's antics had us in stitches.* 我们的物理老师讲他儿子饲养的狗的滑稽动作,使我们大家笑破了肚皮。*Jerry's jokes had me in stitches.* 杰里讲的笑话使我笑破了肚皮。*The movie had us all in stitches.* 那个影片使我们全都笑破了肚皮。另有 be in stitches (笑破肚皮) 和 keep *someone* in stitches (使人一直笑得肚皮疼) 的表达法。*On hearing the details of the episode, we were all in stitches.* 在倾听事情的详细情况时,我们全都笑破了肚皮。*The play kept us in stitches from beginning to end.* 那出戏从头到尾一直叫我们笑得肚皮疼。◇ make *someone* laugh uproariously

stock

lock, stock and barrel → LOCK

stomach

one's **eyes are bigger than** *one's* **stomach** → EYES

have butterflies in *one's* **stomach** → BUTTERFLIES

turn *someone's* **stomach** [ˌtə(ː)rn ~ ˈstʌmək] [口] **使人作呕或生气** 具体形象是"把胃使劲地拧"。这一表达法来源于:人们一见到死尸之类令人难受的东西,就会产生反胃的感觉。*The sight of the dead dog in the street turned my stomach.* 我在街上见到一只死狗,感到非常恶心。作为比喻,在表达非常不愉快的心情的同时,还含有恼怒的成分。

It turns my stomach to think of how the taxpayers' hard-earned money is being wasted. 我一想到纳税人辛辛苦苦挣来的钱被人浪费的情况,就感到生气。*The way that guy plays up to the teacher turns my stomach.* 我一见了那个家伙向老师拍马屁的样子就感到恶心。也有以人为主语的时候。*I refuse to be in the same room with that woman. She turns my stomach.* 我决不跟那个女人在一个房间里。她简直是令人作呕。◇ make *someone* (feel) sick / disgust *someone*

stone

kill two birds with one stone → BIRDS

leave no stone unturned [ˌli(ː)v ˌnouˈstou ˌnʌnˈtəːrnd] [口] **为寻求某种东西而用尽一切手段** 语源很古,来自公元前 477 年的一个故事。希腊的将军波利克拉特斯战胜了波斯的将军,但是他找不到藏金银财宝的场所。因此,他前往以解答困难问题驰名的特尔斐的阿波罗神庙,请求指示金银财宝所在的地方,当即得到这样的回答:"Leave no stone unturned."(把所有的石头都翻过来。)他照这样去做了,并终于找到了金银财宝。自那时起,千百年来人们都用这句话表示在寻找某种东西时尽到最大努力、采取一切手段的意思。几乎所有的词典都释义为"用尽一切手段",人们也按照这个解释使用,但是,这一解释只限于有"寻找"这一目的的文字或口语。其实,即使看起来与"寻找"无关的场合,如果你仔细分析,基本上还是具有"努力寻找达到目的的方法"的意味,也可以使用本条条头。例如说:*The President left no stone unturned in trying to accomplish peace in the Middle East.* 总统千方百计谋求中东的和平。这句话如果换个说法,就是 ~ in trying to find a way to accomplish ~ (……竭力寻求一种方法来达到……)了。*The police left no stone unturned in their search for the missing child.* 警察为了寻找失踪的儿童使用了一切手段。*Ralph is an aggressive salesman. When looking for new customers, he leaves no stone unturned.* 拉尔夫是一位积极进取的推销员。他在寻求新顾客方面用尽一切手段。*Medical researchers are leaving no stone unturned in their efforts to discover a cure for cancer.* 医学研究工作者们在为发现治疗癌症方法的努力中用尽了一切手段。另有一个变形是 There isn't a stone ~. 例如说:*I've got to save the company. There isn't a stone I'll leave unturned (in searching for a way to save the company).* 我必须挽救公司。我要用尽一切手段(寻求挽救公司的办法)。◇ do everything possible

stoned

stoned [ˈstoᵘnd] [话] **烂醉如泥** stoned 的原意为"被群众围住,往身上投石头"。转义"喝多了酒,不省人事"(就象被群众的石块砸昏过去一样)。*Stu was stoned last night.* 昨天晚上,司徒烂醉如泥。如这一例句所示,专作表语使用。在强调时常加 completely, 如说:*He's completely stoned.* 他酩酊大醉,完全不省人事了。主要与 be 动词一起使用,如果不用 be 而代之以 get 的话,则是"痛饮买醉"的意思。*Let's get stoned.* 咱们痛饮一番,来个一醉方休吧。◇ completely drunk

stone's

be within a stone's throw of *someplace* → THROW

stools

fall between two stools [ˌfɔ(ː)l bəˌtwi(ː)n ˈtu(ː)ˈstuːlz] [口] **鸡飞蛋打** stool 是"凳子"。本条条头的意思是:"由于想要坐两个凳子,结果一个也没有坐上而把屁股掉到两个凳子之间了"。正如汉语俗语"鸡飞蛋打"一样,由于既要鸡又要蛋,结果一样也捞不到手,双双落空。*The candidate fell between two stools when he entered both the presidential and senatorial election races.* 那位候选人既参加总统竞选,又参加参议院议员竞选,结果鸡飞蛋打,两头落空了。◇ (try for two things at once and) succeed at achieving neither objective

stops

pull out all the stops [.pu'lau.dɔːlðə 'stɑ(:)ps] [口] **全力以赴** 直译为"把风琴的所有音栓都拉出来",也就是"使音量达到最大的程度"。*The organist pulled out all the stops and filled the hall with music.* 风琴演奏者拉起所有的音栓,使琴音响彻整个的大厅。也可以转作比喻使用。*We're going to have to pull out all the stops if we are to finish this project by the deadline.* 我们要想到期完成这项计划,就必须全力以赴。*When Gloria gives a party she really pulls out all the stops, doesn't she.* 当格罗莉亚举行社交晚会的时候,她可是竭尽全力要把它办好呀。如以下的例句所示,这一表达法常伴有"to+不定式"或者"in+(动)名词"。*The Olympic Committee pulled out all the stops to make the Olympic Games a success.* 奥林匹克委员会竭尽全力去使奥运会开得成功。*The police are pulling out all the stops in their attempt to track down the kidnappers.* 警察在全力以赴,试图跟踪捉拿绑架犯们。*America pulled out all the stops in celebrating its bicentennial.* 美国竭尽全力盛大庆祝建国二百周年。◇ spare no effort (or expense)

store

a dime store [ə 'daɪm .sto(:)r] [话] **大众百货店** → a FIVE-AND-TEN

a ten-cent store [ə .ten'sent .sto(:)r] [口] **大众百货店** → a FIVE-AND-TEN

stories

spread stories (about *someone* [*something*]) [.spred 'sto(:)riz] [话] **散布谣言** 直译为"传播编造的故事",一般带有"恶意中伤"的意味。*Jane has been spreading stories about you.* 简散布关于你的谣言啦。*That guy has been spreading stories about how I made money by cheating people.* 那个家伙散布谣言,说我怎样靠骗人发了财。*If you don't stop spreading stories about my family, you'll be sorry.* 如果你不停止散布关于我的家庭的谣言,你一定会后悔的。*You'd better not believe what that guy says. He's always going around spreading stories.* 你最好别相信那小子的话。他总是到处散布谣言。当两三个朋友站在那儿闲聊的时候,另一个熟人来了,大家寒暄一番。在这一场合,有时用诙谐的口吻使用本条习用语。*A: I've just been spreading stories about you. B: Ha, ha. Nothing good, I hope. I've got too many fans already.* 甲:我正讲关于你的闲话哪。乙:哈哈。但愿不是什么好话。热烈拥护我的人已经太多啦。◇ spread (unfounded) rumors

storm

take *someone* [*something*] **by storm** [.teɪk ～.baɪ 'stɔ(:)rm] [口] **一下子使人迷上** 这里的 storm 是"象暴风雨那样突然袭击"的意思。本条条头直译为"用突然袭击的方式夺取……"。*The troops took the fort by storm.* 军队以突然袭击的方式攻占了城堡。作为比喻,是"使人很快地、狂热地入迷"的意思,在谈到绘画、音乐、文学等艺术方面的事情时经常使用。*This artist's paintings are very forceful. They don't grow on you little by little; they take you by storm.* 这位画家的作品给人的印象非常深刻。他的画不是使人逐渐地喜欢起来,而是一下子就叫你入迷。*The Beatles first visited America in 1964 and took the country by storm.* 甲壳虫乐队于 1964 年第一次访问美国,立即使美国人民为之倾倒。*When Gone With the Wind was first published, it took everyone by storm. All people talked about for months was Scarlett O'Hara.* 当《飘》首次出版的时候,立即使所有的读者大为倾倒。一连多少个月,大家谈论的话题全都是斯卡列特·奥哈拉。有时以人为主语。*Tyrone has a powerful personality. He doesn't try to win you to his side by logic; he rushes up to you, overwhelms you with his charm and wit, and proceeds to take you by storm.* 蒂龙具有很强的个性。他不是试着用逻辑把你征服到他的一边;他向你猛冲过来,用他的魅力和机智把

你压倒，然后一下子夺得你的心。下面的例子虽然是比喻用法，但仍有一半原来的意味，也就是说包含着“随心所欲”和“心醉神迷”两方面的意思。*Leonard Cornpone was a financial genius who took the business community by storm.* 伦纳德·康朋是一位金融天才，他一下子就使整个商界对他刮目相看了。◇ (quickly) captivate *someone* [*something*] / make a forceful impression on *someone* [*something*]

weather the storm [ˈweðər ðə ˈstɔ(:)rm] [口] **渡过难关** 这里的 weather 当然是动词，是“渡过恶劣的气候”、“在暴风雨中平安无事”的意思。本条条头直译为“渡过暴风雨”，作为比喻使用时，是“渡过难关”的意思。可以按照字面意义使用，例如：*When the typhoon struck, we were afraid our ship might not be able to weather the storm.* 当热带风暴袭来的时候，我们生怕我们的船经受不住狂风暴雨。下面是比喻的用例：*The recent recession was long and severe. Many companies failed to weather the storm.* 最近这次经济萧条时间长且严重。许多公司未能渡过难关。◇ survive the crisis

story

a cock-and-bull story [ə ˈkɑkənˈbu(:)l ˌsto(:)ri] [口] **荒诞无稽的故事** 直译为“雄鸡和公牛的故事”。出典不明，但这一表达法的来源很早，大概是根据有 cock 和 bull 出现的童话、寓言之类而来。在使用这一表达法时，即使说话的人是认真讲给对方听的，而且所讲的事情又是真实的，从听者来说，总感到“荒诞无稽，象神话一般”。*That's a cock-and-bull story if I ever heard one.* 我从来也没有听过这样荒诞无稽的故事。*Don't ask him how he got the name Jonathan Appleseed unless you want to hear some cock-and-bull story about his ancestors.* 如果你不想听他讲关于他的祖先的一些荒诞无稽的故事，千万不要问他为什么取“乔纳森苹果佬”这样一个怪名字。常常用以指对方的辩解或借口。在这一场合，惯用 give *someone* a cock-and-bull story 的形式。*I asked him why he was late and he gave me a cock-and-bull story about being stopped by a UFO.* 我问他为什么迟到，他对我编造了一套他被飞碟挡住的荒诞无稽的故事。◇ an absurd [improbable] story

a sob story [ə ˈsɑ:b ˌsto(:)ri] [话] **诉苦** sob 是“啜泣”。本条条头直译为“感伤的故事”，亦即“催人泪下的故事”。故事的内容有时是胡编乱造，也有时是夸大其词。常在辩解或找借口时使用。“向人诉苦”是 give *someone* a sob story。*When I asked Tom for the money he owed me, he gave me some sob story about losing his pay envelope.* 当我找汤姆讨还他向我借的钱的时候，他竟向我哀哀诉苦，说是他把装着工资的信封丢掉了。*The next time you're late for work, don't give me any of your sob stories about sitting up all night with a sick friend or something.* 下次你上班迟到的时候，不要再向我装出可怜相，说什么为了看护生病的朋友整夜没有睡觉之类的诉苦话啦。自古以来，sob story 就是商人售货的有力武器之一，所谓的“哭诉战术”。*My wife bought a lot of things she didn't need, simply because some salesman gave her a long sob story about his sick kids.* 我的妻子只是由于有一个推销员向她不断诉苦，说他家的孩子病了等等，就买了一大堆她并不需要的东西。get a sob story (from *someone*) 是“听人诉苦”。*We asked our landlord for a paint job, but all we got was a sob story about high taxes and inflation.* 我们去请房东把房屋再给油漆一下，可是只听到他向我们哀哀诉苦，说收税多了，通货膨胀等等。这一表达法偶尔用于表示“令人流泪的影片、戏剧、小说等”的意思，但在这一场合，一般讲 a TEAR-JERKER。*My wife enjoyed that movie. She likes sob stories.* 我的妻子欣赏那个影片。她喜欢哭鼻子的玩意儿。◇ a pathetic story / a tearful harangue

a tall story [ə ˈtɔ:l ˈsto(:)ri] [口] **大吹牛皮** 这里的 tall 是“夸大的”。本条条头直译为“怎么考虑也不可能有的故事”。“小小的夸张”、“稍微吹一点牛”,都不能用 tall story 来形容。*Don't believe what Ashford says. He's always ready to pull your leg with a tall story.* 不要相信阿什福德所说的话吧。他总是要用大吹牛皮的方式来愚弄你的。*Talk about a tall story! Tom told me that his aunt and uncle are so fat that when they went to Europe they had to ride in three different airplanes!* 你瞧这牛皮吹得有多大!汤姆告诉我说,他的婶母和叔父太胖了,当他随着他们去欧洲的时候,只好分别乘坐三架不同的飞机!美国人喜欢讲笑话是有名的;现在有 tall story 爱好者协会,对特别有趣的 tall-story teller 给予奖赏。在会上发表的 tall story 举例如下:*A: They say that people who live on that mountain are so big that they use baseball bats for toothpicks. B: That's not such a tall story. The people who live on the next mountain do the same thing, only they use oak trees for bats.* 甲:据说那座山上的居民身材极大,他们用打棒球的球棒当牙签。乙:这牛皮吹得还不够大。邻近一座山的居民也用球棒剔牙,只不过他们的球棒是用整个栎树的树干制成的。story 也可以用 tale 代替。*My grandfather is full of tall tales of the Old West.* 我的祖父有一肚子关于旧时西部的令人无法相信的逸话。◇ an unbelievably exaggerated story / an unbelievable story

to make a long story short [tə͵meɪkə ͵lɔ(ː)ŋ ͵stori ˈʃɔ(ː)rt] [话] **长话短说** 在把冗长的讲话或说明截短的场合,以及自己注意到讲话过长而马上进入结论的场合使用。这一表达法的意思是“总起来说”、“归根到底”、“简而言之”。*To make a long story short, despite all my efforts I failed the entrance exam.* 长话短说,虽然我尽了最大的努力,但是没有考上大学。*To make a long story short, I finally recovered the money I had left in the taxi.* 长话短说,我丢到出租汽车里的钱终于找回来了。另有 to cut a long story short 的说法,意思相同。◇ to omit the details

What's the story (on *something* [*someone*])? [͵hwʌtsðə ˈsto(ː)ri] [话] **怎么样啦?** 原为新闻记者或报纸编辑用语。story 是“关于某一事件的消息”,前边加上 What's the 之后,就是“某一事件的发展情况如何?”的意思。*What's the story on the Middle East situation today? Does our correspondent there say there'll be war?* 中东的局势现在怎么样啦?我们的驻当地记者有关于可能打仗的来电吗?后来进一步发展,一般人也使用起来了。*What's the story on those books I ordered? It's been over a month now.* 我订购的那些书怎么样啦?现在已经一个多月了。这一表达法主要用于询问“某事或某人”(on~)在那以后的情况。*What's the story on Mr. Clark? Did he say he'd come this week?* 克拉克先生怎么样啦?他说这个星期来吗?下一个例句是不加 on *something* 的形式。*What's the story? Have you nailed down that new contract?* 那以后怎么样啦?那个新合同你已经签订了吗?有时也可以用于与以前没有关系的事情。*What's the story on those papers you left on my desk?* 你放在我办公桌上的那些文件是怎么回事?*What's the story on this house? Is it for sale?* 这房子怎么回事?是出售的吗?◇ What is the news (on *something* [*someone*])? / Tell me about *something* [*someone*].

straight

give it to *someone* **straight** [͵gɪvɪtːə ~ ˈstreɪt] [话] **说实话** it 指 the facts(事实),straight 是“笔直地”。因此,本条条头直译应为“毫不歪曲地给予事实”。*Give it to me straight, doctor. Have I got cancer?* 大夫,请对我讲实话。我得癌症了吗?*I'll give it to you straight, Ralph. I don't love you anymore. I want a divorce.* 拉尔夫,我跟你开诚布公地说吧。我不再爱你了。我要离婚。有时加 from the shoulder,意思不变。*Don't try to spare my feelings. Give it to me straight from* *the shoulder*. 别怕伤害我的感情。请直截了当地说吧。◇ tell *someone* frankly

give *someone* **the straight goods** → GOODS

go straight [ˌgou ˈstreɪt] [话] **改恶从善** 直译当然是"照直走"。作为比喻,经常表示犯罪分子"改恶从善"的意思。"犯法"、"作恶"的英语是 be crooked, 而 crooked 的原意是"弯曲的"。go straight 这一表达法最初的构思就是"把那种 crooked 的状态矫正过来,成为笔直的样子"。但是,没有 be straight 这样的说法。 *When Lou got out of prison he was determined to go straight, but he turned crooked again when he found he couldn't get a decent job.* 当卢出狱的时候,他下定决心改恶从善,重新做人,但是当他发现自己找不到适当工作的时候,他又去为非作歹了。另外,go straight 的反义习用语为 turn CROOKED。◇ become an honest citizen

keep a straight face → FACE

set *someone* **straight** (on *something*) [ˌset ~ ˈstreɪt] [口] **纠正错误的想法** set 是"置放",straight 是"在正确的方向"。本条条头直译为"把某人摆到正确的方向"。在具体叙述纠正的"内容"时,用 on *something* 接续。例如: *Let me set you straight on one thing. I don't care if you are my brother, I will not have you coming in here giving orders to my employees.* 有一件事情我要纠正你的错误想法。你虽然是我的亲哥哥,但是我决不容许你来到这儿对我的雇员指手划脚。不过,也常有省略的情况。 *Set me straight if I'm wrong, but it seems to me that three people would be enough to handle this project.* 如果我错了,请指正。不过,在我看来,执行这个计划有三个人就足够了。 *Tom appears to be acting on a mistaken assumption. You'd better set him straight in a hurry.* 汤姆的行动似乎建立在一个错误的假定上了。你要赶快纠正他才好。 *Jack seemed to think that I'd be happy to lend him the money for the down payment. I set him straight on that right quick.* 杰克似乎认为我愿意借给他钱去付定金,我立即打破了他的如意算盘。◇ correct *someone's* mistaken thinking

a straight shooter → SHOOTER

straighten

straighten up and fly right [ˌstreɪtˈnʌpən ˌflaɪ ˈraɪt] [话] **改邪归正** 这一表达法是用飞机的飞行方式比喻人的生活态度或做法。straighten up 是"使飞机恢复水平姿势",也有"改正态度或做法"的意思,如说: *Straighten up and act your age.* 年纪不小了,应该规矩点啦。fly right 在这里是"正确驾驶,一直向前飞行"。本条条头的整个意思是:"纠正过去的错误姿势,使飞机的机体处于水平状态,并且正确驾驶,一直向前飞去"。 *He's been goofing off a lot in the office lately. If he doesn't straighten up and fly right, he's gonna get fired.* 他近来在公司里老是消极混泡。如果他不改邪归正,那是会被开除的啊。 *You'd better straighten up and fly right. Otherwise, you're not going to be able to graduate from high school.* 你还是改邪归正为好。要不然,你就不能从高中毕业啦。这一表达法也可以应用于男女关系。 *It appears that Phil has stopped running around with other women. After his wife threatened him with divorce, he must've decided to straighten up and fly right.* 菲尔似乎不再绕着别的女人的屁股转啦。自从他的妻子威胁要和他离婚之后,他一定是下决心改邪归正了。在 fly right 的前边有时加 start, 例如: *I was quite a hellion when I was young. But the first time I was arrested it threw a scare into me, and I decided that I had better straighten up and start flying right.* 我年轻的时候经常胡作非为。但是,第一次被捕把我吓坏了,我想还是开始改邪归正为好。◇ change *one's* ways [attitude] and behave as *one* should [and do as is expected of *one*]

straw

catch at a straw [ˌkætʃədə ˈstrɔː] [话] **怀着连稻草都要抓一把的侥幸心理** 这一表

达法来源于大家熟知的谚语: A drowning man will catch at a straw. (溺水者有根稻草也要抓一把。) catch at ~是"哪怕是……也要抓一把"的意思,溺水者拼命挣扎的状态由这个 at 活现出来。如果只说"抓稻草",英语是 catch a straw, 用不着 at。 "*Your father's plane exploded in flames over enemy territory,*" *said the officer.* "*But,*" *said Jim, catching at a straw,* "*No one actually saw him die, did they?*" 军官说:"你父亲乘的飞机在敌境上空爆炸烧毁了。""但是,"吉姆怀着连稻草都要抓一把的侥幸心理说:"没有任何人当场看到他死吧?"这一表达法经常使用复数,作 catch at straws。*Don't worry about the detective and all his nosy questions. He can't pin anything on us. He's just catching at straws.* 你不必在意那个侦探和他所提出的一切讨厌的问题。他无法把任何罪名强加在咱们身上。他只是象一个快淹死的人,连稻草也抓一把而已。也可以用 grasp 或 clutch 代替 catch。"*Maybe they made a mistake —maybe they put my number in the wrong place. or maybe I made a mistake — maybe I'm remembering the wrong number,*" *I thought desperately as I stared at the entrance exam results. But I knew deep inside I was only grasping at straws.* "也许是他们搞错了,把我的号码写错了地方;或者,也许是我搞错了,记错了自己的号码。"我望着大学发榜结果,无可奈何地想着。但是我心里深知,这只是一种有稻草也要抓一把的侥幸心理而已。"*But you said you'd be back,*" *she sobbed, clutching at straws, as he turned to walk away.* "*Yes, but not to see you,*" *he answered harshly.* "*You may as well face it. We're finished.*" 当他转过身去要走的时候,她怀着抓把稻草的心情,啜泣着说:"不过,你说过你要回来的啊。""是说过。然而不是为了看你。"他冷酷地回答说:"你要正视这一点。咱们之间的关系已经结束啦。" ◇ grasp at a forlorn hope / make a last desperate effort

clutch at a straw [.klʌtʃədə 'strɔː] [话] **怀着万一的侥幸心理** → catch at a STRAW

grasp at a straw [.græ(ː)spədə 'strɔː] [话] **怀着万一的侥幸心情** → catch at a STRAW

be the last straw [ðə 'læ(ː)'sːtrɔː] [口] **使人忍无可忍** 这一表达法含有气愤的心情,意思是说:过去已经忍耐许多次了,这回实在太不象话,叫人忍无可忍了。来源于古谚: It is the last straw that breaks the camel's back. (最后添加的一根稻草会压断骆驼的脊背。) 所谓 the last straw, 就是指骆驼的负荷已经达到最后的限度,如果再给它加上一点儿负荷,哪怕是一根稻草那么轻的东西,它的脊背也会被压断的。*I've put up with your missing so many deadlines because your work is so good, but this is the last straw. You'll get no more work from me.* 由于你的工作做得不错,所以你多次误期,我都迁就了。但是,现在我已经忍无可忍了,我不再交给你任何工作。当然,在谈到过去的事情的场合,不能公式化地译为"现在已经忍无可忍"。*He'd never been a very good driver. I'd refrained from firing him because of his family, but drinking on the job was absolutely the last straw.* 他从来就不是一个很好的司机。由于考虑到他的家庭情况,我一直没有解雇他。但是,他居然在工作中喝酒,我就绝对不再容忍了。*I knew he was lazy, but when I discovered that he was crooked as well, that was the last straw.* 我过去知道他很懒,但是当我发现他又是一个邪恶的家伙的时候,就对他忍无可忍了。由于忍无可忍,或者不给与工作,或者是解雇、开除,总之是采取决定性的甚至最致命的措施。即使达不到这一步,只是提出过去未曾有过的严格条件,也可以使用本条习用语。例如: *This is the last straw. Either you return the money to me within the week or our friendship is over.* 真叫人忍无可忍啦。要么你在一个星期之内还我钱,要么咱们就算绝交。又有如下的变形。*My wife was obviously upset. She set the drinks in front of me and my guests as if she were the proverbial camel showing* *off the last straw.* 我的妻子显然是生气啦。她把饮料放到我和我的客人们面前时，就好象谚语中的骆驼一样，显示出再也忍受不了的神情。→ the STRAW that broke the camel's back ◇ *one* can no longer tolerate the situation / be something *one* cannot tolerate

a **a straw in the wind** [ə ˌstrɔ(:)ɪnðə 'wɪ(:)nd] [口] **苗头** 直译为"风中的一根稻草"。英国法律学家和政治家约翰·塞尔登(John Selden)的秘书把他的言论集成《餐桌谈话》(*Table Talk*, 1689 年)一书，其中有这样一段话：Take a straw and throw it up into the air—you may see by that which way the wind blows. (你拿一根稻草，把它往空中扔，这样你就可以看出风往哪边吹了。)一般认为，这就是本条习用语的出处。指"隐隐约约的、不大清楚的征兆"，可以用于"好苗头"，也可以用于"坏苗头"。*The boss hadn't mentioned anything about a promotion, but his jovial mood when he took me out to dinner I looked on optimistically as a straw in the wind.* 老板丝毫没有提到晋级的事情，但是，从他带我出去吃饭时的愉快表情来看，我乐观地估计是这方面的好苗头。straw 也可以加-s 用作复数。*Though the citizens were not yet in the mood for revolution, their increasing grumblings about heavy taxes and low wages could be seen as straws in the wind.* 虽然老百姓还没想起来闹革命，但是他们对租税重和工资低日益不满，可以看作是闹革命的苗头。straw 的前边可以加形容词。*The government insisted that there would be no depression, but productivity was falling and unemployment was slowly increasing. Both of these were ominous straws in the wind.* 政府硬说不会出现经济萧条，但是生产率在下降，失业逐渐增多。这两项都是不详的苗头啊。如以上的例句所示，这一表达法一般用于比较重大的事情，至于"打喷嚏是感冒的征兆"之类的话，要用 a sign，说 A sneeze is a sign of catching cold。a straw vote 是由本条条头派生出来的表达法，意思是"非正式投票或调查"。在欧·亨利(O. Henry)的小说里有这样一句话：A straw vote only shows which way the hot air blows. 这是对塞尔登的名言的模仿，意思是"先作调查，只能表明政客的讲话毫无内容"。*The newspaper conducted a straw vote to test the strength of the parties in the coming election.* 为了衡量各政党在即将举行的选举中的力量，报纸作了非正式的调查。*The club president asked for a straw vote to get an idea of how many members would be interested in having a picnic.* 俱乐部主任为了掌握愿意举行野餐的会员人数，要求大家表示自己的意见。→ see which way the WIND blows ◇ a sign of (possible) future developments

the straw that broke the camel's back [ðə'strɔ:ðət,brokðə'kæ(:)məlz ˌbæ(:)k] [口] **最后致命的一击** 这一表达法源出古谚 It is the last straw that breaks the camel's back. (最后添加的一根稻草会压断骆驼的脊背。)也就是说，人不断地往骆驼背上增加负荷，本来已经达到了承重的极限，而他仍然往上加，在这时候，哪怕是加一根稻草那样轻的东西，骆驼的脊背也会被压断。这一表达法大多用过去时。*The workers had endured long hours, low pay, high prices and state- controlled unions for many years, but when the government announced another rise in the price of meat, that was the straw that broke the camel's back. Workers went out on strike all across the nation.* 多年以来，工人们一直忍受着长时间劳动、低工资、高物价和由国家控制工会，但是，当政府宣布再一次提高肉价的时候，这成了最后致命的一击。工人们在全国掀起了大罢工。这是"忍耐"超过限度的例句。下面是"失意"或"灰心"超过限度的场合。*The young man became progressively discouraged as year by year he failed to get into the university of his choice, but his failure this year to pass into even the entrance exam of an "easy" university was the straw that broke the camel's back. He walked* *out the next day and threw himself in front of a train.* 那个青年人一年又一年考不上他所志愿的大学，因此便越来越灰心了。可是，今年他连一所"容易"大学也没有考上，这给了他最后致命的一击。第二天，他走出家门，卧轨自杀了。也可以应用于身体健康的状况。*My husband was never very healthy, but he never complained about having to work long hours for his company. The doctor says that his recently having to work on Sundays as well was the straw that broke the camel's back.* 我的丈夫一向身体欠佳，可是为了公司加班加点，他从来也没有怨言。据医生说，他最近连星期日也必须加班，这可是最后致命的一击了。下一例句是变形的表达法，不使用 the straw。*The company struggled along for many years, getting by somehow in spite of a debt of millions of dollar, but when the inflation squeeze forced it to borrow one million more, the interest payments finally surpassed company profits and the camel's back was broken.* 公司一直奋斗了很多年，尽管欠下几百万美元的债，总算勉强维持下来了。可是由于恶性通货膨胀，它不得不又借了一百万美元，结果偿付利息的金额竟超过了公司的利润，使它受到最后致命的一击。→ be the last STRAW ◇ the final [decisive] blow

a straw vote [ə ˈstrɔː ˈvout] [口] **非正式的投票或调查** → a STRAWin the wind

straws

draw straws (to see *something*) [.drɔː ˈstrɔːz] [口] **抓阄儿** draw 是"抽"，straw 是"稻草"。古时有用长短不同的稻草"抽签"的习俗。现在，除稻草外，可以使用牙签、纸片、纸绳、小木棍等种种不同的代用品，只要与"抽稻草"的方式相同，一概叫做 draw straws。*Let's draw straws to see who goes first.* 咱们抓阄儿决定谁先去吧。*We decided by drawing straws.* 我们用抓阄儿的方式决定了。*In case of a tie, the winner will be decided by drawing straws.* 在打成平局的场合，胜者将由抓阄儿来决定。◇ draw lots (with straws [matchsticks, etc.])

stream

change horses in the middle of the stream → HORSES

street

the man in the street → MAN

be on easy street [.ɔ(ː) ˈniːziː .stri(ː)t] [话] **过舒服日子** easy street 是"安乐街"。这一表达法最初的构思是："只要住在安乐街上，就会过富裕生活"。当然要有钱，但是这一表达法更强调的是"日子过得舒服"。*If this venture is successful, we'll be on easy street.* 如果这次事业成功，我们以后就过舒服日子了。动词有时用 live。*George has been living on easy street ever since his latest book became a best seller.* 乔治自从他的新作成为畅销书之后，过上舒服的日子了。*Big-time lawyers like that all live on easy street.* 象那样赫赫有名的律师，全都过着舒服的日子。put *someone* on easy street 是"使某人过上舒服日子"。*His latest book has put him on easy street.* 他最近的著作使他过上了舒服的日子。e 和 s 两个字母可以大写，作 Easy Street。*You told me if I'd work with you I'd soon be on Easy Street. Well, I've worked with you for five years now, and I'm still living in a one-room apartment.* 你跟我说过，如果我随你工作，很快就会过上舒服日子。好啦，到现在我已经随你工作五年了，而我还住在公寓的一个小房间里啊。◇ be very well off (financially)

stride

hit *one's* **stride** [.hɪt ~ ˈstraɪd] [口] **达到最佳水平** 原为赛马用语。*The favorite hit its stride at the third turn and began moving up through the pack.* 最有希望获胜的那匹马在第三圈达到最佳水平，开始甩开马群向前奔了。这是本来的用法。这里的 hit 是"达到 (某一水平)"的意味。*one's* stride 系指 *one's* best stride (自已最大的步子)。整个条头的意思是"马的步子达到了最大的跨度"。后来进一步作为比喻使用，有时表示"从一开始就竭尽全力,好容易才达到最佳水平",有时表示"在开始的时候故意节省精力,过一阶段才进入正常状态"。大多讲的是人,但从下面的例句可以看出,并不以此为限。*The Giants are behind in the pennant race this year because they didn't hit their stride until the middle of the season.* 巨人队在今年的锦标赛中处于落后地位,因为直到赛季中期他们才打出最高的水平。*If you think the boss is angry now, wait till he hits his stride.* 如果你以为老板刚才是发怒了,那你就等着瞧吧,他还远远没有达到最高的水平哪。在加强语气或者调整语调的时候,常添加 really。*I usually start working at eight, but I don't really hit my stride until the middle of the morning.* 我平常是八点钟上班,但是在十点钟以前不真卖力气。动词有时用 reach, get into, get back into 等代替 hit,但是这些都是变形,不象 hit 那样普遍使用。*The midnight shift often doesn't reach its stride for about an hour or so.* 夜班往往过一个多小时才正常工作。*Hal is amazingly good bridge player. Once he gets into his stride he often sweeps the board.* 哈尔是一位异常出色的桥牌选手。一旦发挥最佳水平,他往往赢得全部赌注。在使用 get (back) into ～的场合,常省略代入 *one's* 的词。例如: *After the New Year, it takes our office a week or more to get back into (its) stride.* 新年以后,我们公司要过一个星期或者更多一点时间才会正常营业。反义语有 be off [out of] (*one's*) stride 或者 put *someone* off [out of] (*his*) stride,意思分别是"达不到最佳水平"和"使某人失去常态"。*I've been off (my) stride all week.* 我这个星期一直没有劲头儿。*The hecklers put the Prime Minister off (his) stride.* 在大会上公开捣乱的分子们使首相失去了常态。如以上的例句所示,在应用于人的场合,一般使用 off 而不使用 out of,而物的场合则恰恰相反。*The series of railway strikes has put the city out of (its) stride.* 铁路工人不断的罢工,使城市失去了正常的机能。◇ attain *one's* normal pace / reach *one's* normal level of performance

be off [out of] (*one's*) **stride** [ˌɔ(ː)f / ˌaudəv ˈstraɪd] [口] **达不到最佳水平** → hit *one's* STRIDE

put *someone* **off [out of]** (*his*) **stride** [ˌput ～ ˌɔ(ː)f / ˌaudəv ˈstraɪd] [口] **使某人失去常态** → hit *one's* STRIDE

take *something* **in** (*one's*) **stride** [ˌteɪk ～ ɪnˈstraɪd] [口] **冷静地去承受** 直译为"把某种东西拿到自己的大步子中"。原为乘马用语,这里的 stride 是"马的最有效率的步伐"。本条条头的整个意思是"越过各种障碍,stride 仍然不乱,按一定的速度继续向前跑"。*In a steeplechase, a horse must take all the obstacles in its stride.* 在越野赛马中,马必须保持一定的速度,越过所有的障碍物。作为比喻使用时,表示"不管遇到多大的困难也毫不动摇,冷静地去承受"的意思。一般来说,不仅表示"承受",而更含有"克服困难向前迈进"的意味。*She is a very strong woman. The death of her husband, her loss of income, her son's accident—she took them all in stride.* 她是一个非常坚强的女人。丈夫死了,财源断绝了,儿子发生事故了——所有这一切,她都很镇静地承受住了。如这一例句所示,大多省略 *one's*。为了调整语调,也有添加 *one's* 的情况,例如: *They are a stoic people. They have learned to take wars, famine and inflation all in (their) stride.* 那是一个善于吃苦的民族。他们学会了如何冷静地承受战争、饥馑和通货膨胀的苦痛。*My husband is a very kind man, but I often have difficulty taking his crude manners in stride.* 我的丈夫是一个非常和蔼的人,可是对于他那粗鲁的举止,我往往难以忍受啊。在下一例句中,就不仅是"冷静地去承受"的意味,应该更进一步解释为"很轻松地处理"为好。*He's a very bright boy. No matter how hard an exam, he just takes it in (his) stride.* 这个男孩子头脑非常好。不管考试的题目多么难,他都能毫不费力地解答出来。有时与意志的坚强或者突出的能力毫无关系,仅用这一表达法表示"习以为常"的意味。*Because of government policy, we aren't always able to get spare parts or new machinery. Over the years we have come to take breakdowns in (our) stride.* 由于政府的政策,我们长期不能弄到零件或者新机器了。经过若干年,我们对机器的故障已经习以为常了。相当于 *something* 的部分不限定是从客观上看"不好"的事情。也有下面这样的情况: *The rock singer destroyed himself with drugs. It seems he was unable to take his sudden rise to fame in stride.* 那个摇滚乐歌手因吸毒毁了自己。他似乎未能经受住突然成名的考验。◇ accept *something* calmly [as part of the normal course of events] / not allow *something* to upset *one* / deal with *something* as part of the normal course of activity

string

harp on the same (old) string [ˌhɑ(ː)rpɔn-ðə ˈseɪm ˈstrɪ(ː)ŋ / ～ˈseɪˌmouldˈstrɪ(ː)ŋ] [口] **老调重弹** harp 是"弹竖琴"。本条条头整体直译为"在演奏竖琴时,老是弹同一根弦"。也就是说,永远只发出同样的声音。常在唠唠叨叨地不断倾诉不平不满的场合使用。*Every time I meet Seth, he harps on the same string—that factionalist quarrel is ruining the company.* 我每次见到塞思,他都老调重弹,说什么宗派斗争正使公司遭到毁灭。常用 that string, 意思是"那种老调"。*Lou told you he can't get along with his boss? Is he still harping on that string?* 卢告诉你说他跟他的老板合不来吗?他还在弹那个老调吗?这一表达法也可以用于与不平不满没有关系的事情。下面是讲唠唠叨叨不断提出要求的例子。在添加 old 的场合,语气稍强。*I know you want to go to Hawaii on our vacation, and I said I would think about it. Do you have to keep harping on the same old string?* 我知道你希望咱们俩去夏威夷休假,我也说过我一定考虑这件事情。你干吗老是唠叨这件事没完呢?有时用 subject (话题)代替 string。*Do you have to keep harping on that subject? You sound like a broken record.* 你对那件事非翻来复去说个没完不可吗?你简直象一张破唱片啦。除 string, subject 而外,还有如下的说法: *Mrs. Highnose is always harping on how much money her husband makes.* 大鼻子太太总是唠唠叨叨讲她的丈夫赚了多少多少钱。◇ talk [write] (continually) about the same subject [about that, about ～]

have *someone* (dancing) on a string [ˌhæv ～ (ˌdæ(ː)ntsɪŋ) ɔnə ˈstrɪ(ː)ŋ] [话] **抓住某人弱点,任意摆布** have *someone* on a string 直译为"把某人用小绳拴上"。加上 dancing,就成为"牵着小绳使某人跳舞"了。一般认为这一表达法来源于偶人戏的表演,实际上是出自耍猴儿的动作。另外,这一表达法中加与不加 dancing 一词,意义没有大的差别,只是加上以后语气要强一些,有"任意操纵"的意思。不论加与不加 dancing,都常以 really 进行强调。*Until I get that letter back, he'll have me on a string.* 在取回那封信之前,他会任意摆布我的。*Mr. Stromboli really had us on a string. There's nothing we can do but follow his orders.* 斯特隆波利先生完全抓住我们的弱点啦。我们没有别的办法,对他只好唯命是从。*My grandfather has me dancing on a string, and the only way I can get off it is to give up my inheritance.* 我对祖父是唯命是听,我只有放弃财产继承权才能改变这种状况。*Helen really has Dick dancing on a string. He'll do practically anything she asks.* 迪克完全受海伦的摆布。实际上,她叫他干什么,他就干什么。动词有用 keep 代替 have 的时候,意思是"一直任意摆布或操纵"。*The gang boss kept his underlings all dancing on a string by holding evidence that would send them all to jail.* 匪帮的头目由于掌握着能把众匪徒送进监狱的证据,一直任意地摆布他们。这一 keep *someone* on a string 在应用于男女关系时,大多失去"利用对方迷恋的弱点任意加以摆布"的积极性质,而具有"用不即不离的手法使对方抱有

幻想"的意味。与 STRING *someone* along 的表达法近似。*Laura kept Floyd on a string for over a year before she threw him over for someone else.* 劳拉一直勾搭着弗洛伊德,过了一年多才甩掉他,跟另一个男的去了。*I don't believe they really intend to sign a contract with us. They're just keeping us on a string while they wait for a better offer from some other company.* 我不相信他们真心实意想要跟咱们签合同。他们只是在等待别的什么公司提出更好的条件的期间,给我们一剂宽心丸儿吃而已。◇ have *someone* completely under *one's* control

string *someone* **along** [ˌstrɪŋ ~ əˈlɔːŋ] [口] **挑逗他人抱幻想** 语源是:人们常提着一根小绳,挑逗小猫不住地追赶。这一表达法首先令人联想到的是男女关系。典型的事例是:自己不想跟现在交往的朋友结婚,可是又舍不得放手,于是就假装自己有结婚的心愿,象用小绳逗弄小猫一样,一直保持与对方的关系。当然,这一表达法不仅限于结婚问题,高中生在谈到与异性交往的事情时也常常使用。由于是一种有意识的行为,在万一发生问题时,当事人不能不负道义上的责任。*Georgia will never marry Tom. She's just stringing him along until someone she likes better shows up.* 乔治娅绝对不会跟汤姆结婚的。她只是在自己更喜欢的男人出现之前,不即不离地逗弄汤姆玩儿而已。*Although George had no serious intentions toward Sally, he kept stringing her along for more than a year before she finally gave up.* 虽然乔治对于萨莉并不真心实意,但是他在一年多的时间内一直吊她的胃口,直到她死了心为止。*Why don't you give up on Louise? She'll never give you a date. She's just stringing you along.* 你对路易丝为什么不断了念头?她绝对不会跟你约会的啊。她只是玩弄你的感情哪。当然也可以用于男女关系以外的事情,例如:*Let's not turn him down right away. Let's string him along for a while. If he gets impatient, maybe he'll come up with a better offer.* 咱们不要马上回绝他,先吊吊他的胃口再说。如果他忍耐不住,也许会提出更好的条件来啊。也有应用于自己身上的场合,例如:*Do I really have what it takes to become a novelist? Or am I just stringing myself along?* 我果真有成为一个小说家的才能吗?或者说,我只是在自己骗自己?◇ keep *someone* (temporarily) interested (for *one's* own amusement [*one's* own ends]) / (artfully) show enough interest to keep *someone* in a state of anticipation / deceive *oneself*

a string bean → BEAN

string *someone* **up** [ˌstrɪŋ~ˈʌ(ː)p] [话] **把人吊起来** string 本来是"细绳"或"鞋带",在这里指"大粗绳子"。本条条头直译为"把人吊上去"。具体形象如同西部影片中的私刑那样,把绳子套到人的脖子上,然后将绳子的终端搭到树枝上再往下拉,被处私刑的人的身体便吊了起来。如果使用其他方法把人吊死,也可以说 string *someone* up。这是西部影片中常常出现的一个习用语。*The crowd dragged the culprit from the jail and strung him up.* 群众把犯人从牢房里拖出来并把他吊死了。◇ hang *someone*

strings

pull strings [ˌpu(ː)l ˈstrɪ(ː)ŋz] [口] **走后门** 本来的意思是"在偶人戏中拉小绳使偶人活动"。*Puppets are made to work by pulling strings.* 木偶是被用拉绳的方式进行表演的。作为比喻,除用于表示"走后门"的意思外,还有"幕后操纵"的意味。例如:You have to pull strings if you want to get anything done in this town. 这句话一般解释为"在这个小镇里,如果你想做点什么事情,非走后门不可。"但是,如果根据上下文为黑手党即将引退的头子对他的继任者所说的话,那就可以理解为"在这个小镇里,如果你想做点什么事情,不进行幕后活动是不行的啊。"究竟如何解释,只能根据上下文来判断。不过,这一表达法多用于表示前一种意思。*During the war my father often had to pull strings in order to get* *enough rice for us to eat.* 在战争期间，我父亲为了使我们一家有足够的大米吃，常常必须去走后门。在 pull 与 strings 之间有时加 a few 或者 some。*Jack is going to pull a few strings to see if he can't get me a management position in his company.* 杰克正在走几个后门，看看能不能在他那个公司里给我谋到一个经营部门的位子。如果在 strings 的前边加上定冠词 the，作 pull the strings，那意思就明确了，是"幕后操纵"。*He's the man who pulls the strings around here.* 在这一带，他是个在幕后进行操纵的人物。主语绝大部分是"人"，但也有时是人以外的东西，例如：*It's money that pulls the strings around here.* 在这一带，最有势力的东西是金钱。可以用 wires 代替 strings 而讲 pull wires，意义和用法完全一样。*He's been pulling all kinds of wires to try to get transferred back to the home office.* 他为了要调回总公司，利用了各方面的人事关系。"走后门的人"或"政界的后台老板"在英语中是 a wirepuller。也可以说 stringpuller，但极罕见。*That senator is one of the most notorious wirepullers in the American government.* 那个参议员是美国政界名声最臭的黑后台之一。在这一场合，wirepuller 前边的形容词如果不是 notorious 而是 powerful 的话，那就是"势力最大的黑后台"的意思了。◇ use *one's* connections [influence]

be tied to *one's* **mother's apron strings** [.taɪdtə ~ .mʌðərz 'eɪprən .strɪ(:)ŋz] [话] **受着母亲的支配** 直译为"被绑在母亲的围裙带上"。这一表达法的来源是：幼小的孩子自己什么也干不了，总是贴在母亲身边，一刻也不离开。按本来的意义用法如下：*Children at that age are usually tied to their mother's apron strings.* 那么大的小孩子一般是离不开母亲的。从这一意义进一步发展，便用以指在心理上离不开母亲的男性。含有"言听计从"的意味。大多伴有 still (仍然) 一词。*I don't want to marry a man that's still tied to his mother's apron strings.* 我不愿意跟一个至今还离不开娘的男子结婚。从这一表达法又进一步发展，人们用 wife 代替 mother，构成 be tied to *one's* wife's apron strings，这就是现代中国流行的所谓"气管炎"(妻管严)了。*When we invited Jack to go bowling with us, he called home first before accepting. I hadn't realized that he was so tied to his wife's apron strings.* 当我们约杰克一起去玩保龄球的时候，他在应允之前先给家里打了电话。我过去不知道他是这样一个"气管炎"啊。有时也可以采取 have *someone* tied to *one's* apron strings 的形式，意思为"使人言听计从"、"任自己的意思摆布"。*My husband's mother still has him tied to her apron strings.* 我的丈夫至今还掌握在他妈的手心里。◇ be completely dependent on *one's* mother [under the control of *one's* wife]

strip

a drag strip [ə 'dræ(:)g .strɪp] [口] **减重短程高速汽车道** → a drag RACE

stroke

a stroke of luck [ə .stroukəv 'lʌ(:)k] [口] **意外的幸运** → have the devil's own LUCK

strong

(as) strong as an ox → OX

stubborn

(as) stubborn as a mule → MULE

stuck

get stuck (on *something*) [get 'stʌ(:)k] [话] **卡壳** → be STUCK (on *something*)

be stuck (on *something*) ['stʌ(:)k] [话] **卡住了** 这里的 stuck 是及物动词 stick (粘住)的过去分词。be stuck 是"被粘住，动不了"，也就是"碰到麻烦问题了，就象车轮陷入泥塘里一样，进也进不得，退也退不得"。*I'm stuck on my income tax form. It's too hard for me to figure out.* 我被所得税报告单卡住了。太难，我怎么也弄不明白。*These math problems are all really tough. I'm already stuck on the second one.* 这些数学习题

实在难。第二道题就把我卡住了。下面是不加 on *something* 的例子。*I'm completely stuck. I just can't figure this problem out.* 我一筹莫展啦。这道题我怎么也解答不出来。也可以用 get 代替 be,而讲 get stuck on *something*(卡壳)。*I got stuck on my English homework last night and couldn't finish.* 昨天晚上我做英语家庭作业,遇到难题卡了壳,没有能够做完。*The meeting took longer than expected because we got stuck on the question of whether to increase the company's capital next year.* 会议比预定的时间拖长了,因为我们在讨论来年是否增加公司资本的问题上卡了壳。另有 be [get] bogged down (on *something*) (陷入泥沼) 的说法,大致与本条条头同义,以上各例句皆可用它来代换。◇ have reached an impasse (on *something*)

be stuck on *oneself* [ˈstʌ.kɔ(ː)n ~] [话] **自负** → be STUCK on *someone*

be stuck on *someone* [ˈstʌ.kɔ(ː)n ~] [话] **迷恋(异性)** 这里的 stuck 是及物动词 stick (粘上) 的过去分词。因此, be stuck on *someone* 就是"(思想) 粘到某人身上离不开了",也就是"只想某人的事情"。这一表达法主要是高中生或大学生使用,语感不如 be in love with *someone* 深刻,语调很轻松。常用 really 加强语气。*Tom is really stuck on Mary. He can't think of anything else.* 汤姆真是迷上玛丽啦。他别的事情全不放在心上。*I used to always play the field, but after two or three dates with Suzie Goodenough, I was stuck on her.* 我过去一向跟许多女人谈情说爱,可是自从与苏吉·古迪纳夫约会两三次之后,我已经完全迷恋上她了。*I had met Rick only casually two or three times, but, before I knew it, I was stuck on him.* 我只是平平淡淡地跟里克会过两三次面,但是在不知不觉之间,我已经迷上他了。*Only one look, and Romeo and Juliet were stuck on each other.* 罗密欧与朱丽叶是一见钟情。尽管认真程度有所不同,可以说 be stuck on *someone* 与 be in love with *someone* 相等,而 get stuck on *someone* 则与 fall in love with *someone* 相等。*Talk about fickle! Pastey gets stuck on practically every pretty face that comes around.* 要讲朝三暮四,帕斯提可算到家啦。实际上,只要一有漂亮的脸蛋儿出现,他就会为之神魂颠倒了。但是,如果 on 的后边是接续 *oneself*,而作 be stuck on *oneself*,那是"自负"的意思。*Everybody would like Mr. Narcissus more if he weren't so stuck on himself.* 纳西苏斯先生如果不是那样自负,每个人都会更喜欢他。→ be STUCK (on *something*) ◇ be in love with *someone*

be stuck up [.stʌˈkʌ(ː)p] [话] **骄傲自满** 这里的 stuck 为及物动词 stick (作"伸出"解) 的过去分词。按字面意义, be stuck up 是"向上伸出"。也就是说,这一表达法的具体形象是 (*One's* nose) is stuck up (in the air.),含义为"装模作样,把鼻子向上翘得高高的"。不过,这一表达法并不按照字面意义用以表示"向上翘鼻子"的意味,经常以人为主语,专作比喻使用。例如: *I had always thought that Mary was stuck up, but once I got to know her I realized that she was only shy.* 我过去一直认为玛丽骄傲自满,但是自从我了解她以后,明白了她只是怕羞而已。*That guy is so stuck up he probably won't even talk to his own mother unless she makes an appointment in advance.* 那个家伙实在太自高自大了,恐怕他的亲生母亲不事先跟他约好时间地点,他也不肯与她谈话。如果用连字符接成 stuck-up,即可做定语。*I've never met such a stuck-up boy in my life.* 我有生以来还没遇到过如此骄傲自满的男子。◇ be conceited

be stuck with (*doing*) *something* [ˈstʌk-wɪð ~] [话] **不得不担当某种任务** 意思是:"碰到讨厌的事情了,脱不开身"。*I was stuck with being committee chairman because no one else wanted the job.* 我不得不担任委员会主席的职务,因为谁也不愿意干这个差事。*I was foolish enough to volunteer for the job of collecting donations in our office two years* *ago, and I'm still stuck with it.* 两年前，我非常愚蠢，自愿在我们公司从事征集捐款的工作，现在仍然不得脱身。一般使用 be stuck 的形式，但也有用其他动词代替 be 的情况。*Everyone hurried out of the restaurant and left me stuck with the bill.* 大家都匆忙地走出餐厅，只剩下我一个人不得不付帐了。◇ be unable to avoid (*doing*) *something*

student

a grad student [ə 'græːd ˌstjudənt] [话] **大学研究生院学生** 学生用语，为 a graduate student 的缩略。如果只说 a grad，那是"毕业生"，与本条条头的意思完全不同，请注意。*My big brother's a grad student at Podunk University.* 我哥哥是波敦克大学的研究生。→ a GRAD / an UNDERGRAD ◇ a graduate student

stuff

know *one's* **stuff** [ˌnou ～'stʌ(ː)f] [话] **精通** → know *one's* ONIONS

be made of sterner stuff [ˌmeɪdəv'stə(ː)rnər 'stʌ(ː)f] [口] **有骨气** 出典：莎士比亚《尤里乌斯·凯撒》(*Julius Caesar*) 第三幕第二场有名的场面——马克·安东尼在凯撒的葬礼上的演说：(Friends, Romans, countrymen, lend me your ears. I have come to bury Caesar, not to praise him .....) Brutus says he [Caesar] was ambitious, but .... When the poor have cried, Caesar has wept. Ambition should be made of sterner stuff. (朋友们，罗马人，同胞们，请听我讲几句话吧。我是来埋葬凯撒的，不是来颂扬他的……) 布鲁图说他[凯撒]有野心，但是……当贫穷的人们哭的时候，凯撒也掉泪了。野心应该是用更坚硬的材料制成的啊。sterner 是 stern(坚硬的)的比较级，本条条头的字面意义为"用更坚硬的东西制成的"。主语是"人"，所以意思是"人的性格、思想等方面，是由 sterner stuff 制作出来的"。这一表达法用于表示"在严峻的时刻具有积极斗争的精神"或者"绝对不想退让"，亦即汉语所说的"有坚强的斗志"或"骨头硬"。*I refuse to pretend not to notice while you spend all our money on another woman. I'm made of sterner stuff than that.* 你把我们所有的钱都花在另外的女人的身上，我决不充耳不闻。我不是那种没骨气的人啊。如这一例句所示，这一表达法在使用时一定要与其他事物作比较，后边接续 than ～。但是，省略 than ～这一部分的情况居多。*I was surprised that Tom gave in so quickly to their demands. I had thought he was made of sterner stuff.* 汤姆居然那么迅速地屈服于他们的要求，使我大吃一惊。我一直认为他是很有骨气的人哪。*After three years of severe drought, many farmers had given up and fled to the cities, but old Mr. Brown was made of sterner stuff. He was determined to stay and fight to the end to save his farm.* 在一连三年的严重干旱之后，许多农民都失去了希望，跑到城里去了，但是老布朗先生却是一个硬骨头。他决心不走，奋斗到底，维护他的农场。这一表达法不仅用于严重的情况，也可以用于象下面这样轻松的谈话：*If you want to walk home in all this rain, more power to you. You're made of sterner stuff than I. I'm going to take a taxi.* 在这样的滂沱大雨中，如果你愿意徒步走回家去，那就加油吧。我没有你那样的骨气，只好叫辆出租汽车走啦。◇ be of a stronger disposition (than that)

stuffed

be stuffed to the gills → GILLS

stump

go on the stump [ˌgouɔnðə 'stʌmp] [口] **出去进行竞选活动** → take the STUMP

stump *someplace* ['stʌmp ～] [口] **到某地进行竞选活动** → take the STUMP

take the stump [ˌteɪkðə 'stʌmp] [口] **走上讲坛** stump 是"树桩"。本条条头直译为"站到树桩上"。美国在拓荒时代，利用树桩作为讲坛发表演说，故产生这一表达法。又作 take to the stump，这一说法有"到处游说"的意思。例如：*The ex-President took to the stump to support his party's new candidate.* 前总统为了支援本党新的总统候选人，到处去进行竞选演说。不过,请读者注意:根据上下文,take the stump 也可能具有"到处游说"的意味。例如说: *The first candidate spoke so long that by the time the second speaker took the stump, everyone was getting restless.* 第一个候选人讲话的时间过长,等第二个发言人走上讲坛的时候,全场的人都开始骚动起来了。在这句话里,肯定应该作"走上讲坛"解。*Every four years, many candidates take the stump with dreams of becoming President.* 每隔四年,许多候选人都走上讲坛,梦想当上总统。在这句话里,根据前言后语,就有可能是"到处游说"的意思。 *She was one of the first people to take the stump for women's rights.* 她是为提高妇女权利而走上讲坛的先驱者之一。从这一表达法引申,也可以把 stump 作为动词使用,表示"到处游说"的意思。*With elections only a few weeks off, all the candidates are busily stumping their districts.* 只剩下三两个星期就要选举了,所有的候选人都忙着在他们的选举区进行竞选活动。也可以说 go on the stump,但只作"出去进行竞选活动"解,特别是在"为了支援××"一类的文句中使用。*Concerned over growing Republican government interference in the private sector, Haigan went on the stump for the minority party.* 由于共和党政府日益干涉私营企业,黑根为了支持在野政党,到处奔走,进行竞选活动。◇ begin to speak / go on (political) speaking tours / make speeches ((for ~ → in support of ~))

style

cramp *someone's* **style** [ˌkræ(:)mp ˈstaɪl] [话] **使人感到不舒畅** cramp 是"限制"、"拘束"的意思。style 是"一个人最熟悉的或最喜好的方法、做法、样式"的意思。这是一个表示"不随人愿"的轻松的说法,在并没有 style 那样郑重其事的含义之中,也具有一种幽默情调。*I became a free- lance reporter because having to write for a single newspaper cramped my style.* 由于只能给一家报纸写稿,心情很不舒畅,我就当自由撰写的记者了。*I don't want to get married. Having a wife and children would cramp my style.* 我不想结婚。有妻子儿女防碍我自由自在地生活。*I didn't like the army. All those rules cramped my style.* 我不喜欢军队的生活。所有那些规章制度都与我的生活节奏不合。◇ make it difficult for *someone* to indulge in *his* own style of working [living, etc.] / be too confining

sucker

a sucker① [ə ˈsʌ(:)kər] [话] **容易上当的人** sucker 的原义是"吸吮者"、"吃奶者"。后来进一步发展,具有种种不同的意味。在口语中,绝大多数场合是用以表示"容易上当的人"的意思。具体形象是:"一给他看香甜的东西,他马上就用嘴去嘬"。这一表达法与 a PUSHOVER 不同,经常带有"幼稚"、"无知"、"缺乏人情世故"、"想法天真"、"人太老实"等批判性的意味。 *I was a sucker to believe her.* 我居然相信她,真太傻啦。 *A sucker and his money are soon parted.* 为人太老实,金钱守不住。 *I refused to work for that kind of pay. I'm not that much of a sucker.* 给那么一点工资,我才不干呢。我可不是爱吃亏上当的傻瓜。有时用于命令句。 *Don't be a sucker. If you lend him that much money you'll never see it again.* 不要上当受骗。如果你借给他那么多的钱,你就绝对不会再要回来啦。如果从对方的角度看,sucker 则是"容易欺骗的笨蛋"。美国有过一个叫做 Barnum and Bailey 的大型杂技团,团长巴纳姆 (P.T. Barnum) 曾经在谈论观众时说过这样一句有名的话: "There's a sucker born every minute." ("每分钟都有一个容易欺骗的笨蛋出生。") be a sucker for *something* 也是一个定型的说法,意思是"对某种事情容易上当的人"。 *A: Why did you give him the money? B: I guess I'm just a sucker for a hard-luck story.* 甲:你为什么给他钱呀? 乙:我这种人一听到别人哀哀诉苦,就会上当受骗的。◇ (a) gullible (person) / a dupe

a sucker[②] [ə ˈsʌ(:)kər] [口] **棒糖** 在口语中，sucker 一词除 a SUCKER①的意义外，也常用于表示"棒棒糖"的意思。当然，主要是儿童们使用。这一表达法也是由"吸吮者"的原义发展而来。实际上，是一种带棒的圆球形的或者平板形的糖。一般直径 3～4 厘米，也有更大一些的。过去多用球形，最近采取动物之类的图案，制成平形。 *Suckers come in two shapes, round and flat.* 棒棒糖有两种形状，一是圆形，一是平形。 *Jimmy's favorite sucker is cherry.* 吉米最喜欢的是樱桃棒糖。能够吸吮一天的特大棒棒糖叫做 an all-day sucker。 *Tommy's so slow he can make an all-day sucker last two days.* 汤米是一个动作非常缓慢的孩子，一根特大的棒棒糖他能吃上两天。sucker 是美国英语，在英国英语中，"棒糖"叫做 a lollipop [ˈlɔlɪˌpɔp]。美国也使用 lollipop [ˈlɑ(:)liˌpɑp]，但毕竟用 sucker 的人居多。 *I bought the children some lollipops.* 我给孩子们买了一些棒棒糖。英美都有拼写为 lollypop 的情况。◇ (hard) candy on a stick

be a sucker for *something* [ə ˈsʌ(:)kərfər ～] [话] **对某种事情容易上当的人** → a SUCKER①

suds

suds [ˈsʌ(:)dz] [话] **啤酒** suds 本来是"肥皂泡"的意思。严格地讲，此词也指"肥皂液"本身，而实际上也有这样使用的情况。但在现代的感觉中，一般用 soapy water 表示"肥皂液"，而用 suds 表示"泡"。下一例句反映了两者的区别： *The maid spilled a bucket of soapy water and the kitchen floor was covered with suds.* 女仆弄翻了一桶肥皂液，厨房的地面上满是肥皂泡了。suds 转义"啤酒"，这是一个轻松的说法。只要你把"肥皂液"+"泡"的具体形象跟"啤酒"的具体形象联系在一起，自然就会明白两者形象的近似之处了。 *We'll need a lot of suds for the party tonight.* 今天晚上举行社交晚会，我们需要大量的啤酒。顺便提一下：刮胡子用的"皂沫"不叫 suds，而是 lather [ˈlæðər]。也就是说，虽然同是"肥皂的泡沫"，suds 大，为"泡"；lather 小，为"沫"。◇ beer

suit

follow suit [ˌfɑlə ˈsu:t] [口] **仿效他人** 这里的 suit 是扑克牌中 spades (黑桃)、hearts (红桃)、diamonds (方块)、clubs (梅花)等 13 张一组花式的"一组牌"。follow suit 在扑克游戏中是"别人出什么花式的牌，你就紧跟着出同样花式的牌"的意思。 *In this game, you must follow suit. If you can't, you may play any card you like.* 在这种打法中，你必须跟着前边的人出同样花式的牌。如果你没有同样的牌可出，你愿意出哪一张就出哪一张。这一表达法转作比喻使用，与汉语俗语"照猫画虎"、"照葫芦画瓢"、"照方抓药"等大致相同。 *When the major oil companies raised their prices, all the other companies followed suit.* 当几家大石油公司涨价的时候，其他各公司也都随着涨价了。 *America decided to boycott the Olympic Games, anticipating that other countries would follow suit.* 美国预料其他一些国家会群起效尤，就决定抵制奥运会了。 *When the guest of honor mistakenly drank from the finger bowl, in order to save him embarrassment all the other guests followed suit.* 当主宾误把洗手指碗中的水当酒喝了的时候，为了不使他难为情，所有其他的客人也都照样画葫芦，喝起洗手指碗中的水了。如以上的例句所示，这一表达法大多在许多人进行仿效的场合使用，但也有用于只是一个人"照猫画虎"的时候。 *I'm not familiar with Chinese customs, so I'll just watch what you do and follow suit.* 我不熟悉中国的风俗习惯，所以，我看你怎么做我就怎么做吧。◇ do the same (thing)

in *one's* **birthday suit** [ɪn ～ ˈbə(:)rθˌdeɪ ˌsu(:)t] [话] **光着身子** *one's* birthday suit 直译为"出生时的服装"，也就是"一丝不挂"的意思。这一表达法多作戏谑语。 *She was lying on the beach in her birthday suit.* 她光着身子躺在沙滩上。也有不用 in 而用 wearing 的表达法。 *He was wearing nothing but his birthday* suit. 他光着身子,什么也没有穿。◇ in the nude / naked

suit *someone* **down to the ground** → GROUND

a union suit [ə ˈju(ː)njən ˌsu(ː)t] [口] **男子上下连身的长内衣** → long JOHNS

summer

(an) Indian summer [(ə ˌn)ɪndɪən ˈsʌmər] [口] **小阳春** → an Indian GIVER

sun

every *something* [*someone*] **under the sun** [ˌevri ～ ˌʌndərðə ˈsʌ(ː)n] [口] **所有的一切** 夸张的表达法。直译为"太阳底下的一切",换句话说就是"地球上的一切"。*A worldwide nuclear war would destroy almost every man, woman and child under the sun.* 世界性的核战争,会毁灭几乎所有的男人、女人和儿童。这是按字面意义使用的例子。但是,这一表达法大多用于强调数目的众多,有"这样那样的"、"种种不同的"的意思。例如: *I studied every subject under the sun before I finally settled on geology.* 我在最后决定研究地质学之前,曾经读了好多好多的课程。这句话的意思决不是指"大学中的所有课程",而是指"这样那样好些种学科"。下面两个例子也是同样。*I tried every way under the sun to persuade him to come, but it was no use.* 我千方百计劝他前来,可是毫无效果。*He'll give you every excuse under the sun before he finally agrees to help you.* 他会先找种种的借口来推辞,最后才会答应帮助你。*Not having met for so long, we stayed up all night discussing everything under the sun.* 由于好久好久没见面了,我们互倾心曲,足足谈了一整夜。如果不加 every 而单独使用 under the sun,一般是按字面意义解释为"全世界的"或者"普天之下"。*I'm a country boy. I wouldn't live in New York if it were the most beautiful city under the sun.* 我是乡下人。即使纽约是全世界最美丽的城市,我也不愿意居住。*The Chinese are often said to work harder than any other people under the sun.* 人们常常称道中国人比世界上其他任何民族都更为勤劳。*Mrs. Fruitly makes the most delicious pies under the sun.* 弗鲁特利太太制作的馅饼是世界上最香的。此外有 where [why] under the sun 的形式,用于表示强调。*Where under the sun did you get a crazy hat like that?* 你究竟从什么地方弄来了那样一顶古里古怪的帽子呀? *Why under the sun didn't you tell me?* 你究竟为什么没有告诉我哪? under the sun 的意义和用法大致与 in the world 相同,几乎在所有的场合可以代换使用。◇ every *someone* [*something*] in existence [imaginable]

make hay while the sun shines → HAY

Sunday

a Sunday driver → DRIVER

Sundays

a month of Sundays [ə ˌmʌnθəv ˈsʌndi(ː)z] [话] **很长时间** 直译为"一个月的星期日",换言之就是"包含有三十个星期日的那么长时间",也就是约七个月的时间。这只是比喻的数字,无需一一计算。总之,这一表达法是强调"很长时间",既可以表示"很长时间没有如何如何",也可以表示"做某种事情需要很长时间"。*I haven't seen Charlie for a month of Sundays.* 我有很长时间没有见到查理了。*It always takes that committee a month of Sundays to decide anything.* 那个委员会不论决定什么事情,都需要很长的时间。关于这一表达法的来源,有一种并没有成为定论的说法是:旧时,人们认为星期日是一个星期中最长和最无聊的日子,把三十个(一个月)这样的日子连接起来,时间之长不言而喻。这就是人们最初的构思。◇ a very long time

superintendent

a sidewalk superintendent [ə ˈsaɪdˌwɔ(ː)k ˌsupərɪnˈtendənt] [口] **大厦修建、维修或拆除现场的参观者** 直译为"站在马路人行道上的工地监督者"。戏谑语。美国的建筑公司常在建筑工地的围墙上开许多了望孔,并且用心周到,在了望孔上边还有大字书写的 For Sidewalk Superintendents (供施工参观者用)的横幅。*Good weather always brings out a lot of sidewalk superintendents.* 如果天气好，总有很多的人参观施工。◇ a person who stops to watch work in progress at a building construction [repair, demolition] site

Suppose

Suppose I [you, we] *do something.* [sə'pouz ˌaɪ / ˌju(:) / ˌwi(:) ~] [话] **这样做怎么样?** 请先比较一下下面的两个例句。① *Suppose you try it and it doesn't work?* ② *Suppose you try it. I'm sure you'll succeed.* 两句都是用 suppose 开头，但是意思不一样。①是本来的用法，即先假定某种情况，而问"你怎么样"。全句的意思是："你做一下试试，要不顺手呢?"言外含有 What will you do then? (然后你怎么办?)的意味。②是"建议"。全句的意思是："你试一下如何? 我认为你一定能成功。"用 suppose 开头的句子，大多是 ②的用法。一个句子究竟是①的意义还是 ②的意义，要根据上下文进行判断。suppose 后边接续的代名词可以是第一人称或者第二人称。在第一人称的场合，一般总是"建议"，例如：*Suppose I talk to him. Maybe he'll give me the information.* 让我去跟他谈谈如何? 他也许会把那个信息透露给我的。在 we, you 的场合，可以是比 Let's ~ 轻快一些的"建议"，例如：*Suppose we go to a movie tonight. There's a good one on at the Rialto.* 今天晚上咱们去看电影如何? 丽都影院正演一个好片子哪。但是，有时不是"建议"，而是间接的"命令"，例如 *Suppose you tell me why you got home so late last night.* 你告诉我吧，昨天夜里你为什么回来那么晚呀? 在这一场合，语气虽然是温柔的，但言外却含有相当严厉的责难。*A: I wonder why the Joneses are so angry with us. B: Suppose you tell me.* 甲：不知道为什么琼斯一家对咱们那么恼火呀? 乙：这一点你大概比我清楚吧。◇ What do you think of the idea of my [our] *doing something*? / Let's *do something*. / I want you to *do something*. / (You) *do something*. / You should know that much better than I.

suspense

keep *someone* **in suspense** [ˌki(:)p ~ ɪn ˌsʌ'spe(:)nts] [口] **令人提心吊胆** 这里的 suspense 意味着一种无着无落的、不知命运如何的"紧张状态"。本条习用语经常在"不知此后怎样"的紧张情况下使用。造成紧张的原因有种种的不同，如不安、期待、惊险等等，但是，不论是哪种原因，都能使用本条条头的句型。*Don't keep us in suspense! Did you get the job or not?* 不要叫我们提溜着一颗心呀! 你到底得到没得到那份工作呀? *Expectations of a major earthquake in the very near future kept everyone in suspense.* 据预测，最近的将来会发生一次大地震，这使每个人都提心吊胆。*The prince's refusal to announce his wedding plans kept the whole nation in suspense.* 由于王子拒绝宣布他的结婚计划，这使得全国人民焦急不安。带有悬念的惊险影片或电视节目，也经常使用这一表达法。*The movie kept us in suspense from beginning to end.* 那个影片从头到尾一直使我们提心吊胆。◇ keep *someone* waiting (excitedly [anxiously]) (to find out what happened [what would happen, what the answer is, etc.])

swan

(as) graceful as a swan [əz 'greɪsfələzə 'swɑ:n] [口] **非常优美** 最初的构思是"象天鹅一样优美"，但不仅用于女子或舞蹈演员，也广泛用于男性、动物、交通工具等。*I love to watch Jane dance. She's as graceful as a swan.* 我很爱看简的舞蹈。她的舞姿优美极了。*Mary is as graceful as a swan in everything she does.* 玛丽不管干什么事情，姿态都非常优美。*Scott is usually rather clumsy, but when he gets on the high diving board he becomes graceful as a swan.* 斯科特平时比较笨拙，可是当他一走上高高的跳水台的时候，他的姿态就变得非常优美

了。也可以把 (as) gracefully as a swan 作为副词短语使用。*We thought the plane was going to crash, but just as it neared the ground it pulled out as gracefully as a swan.* 我们以为那架飞机要坠毁了,可是正当它接近地面的时候,又以非常优美的姿态掉头凌空了。◇ extremely graceful

swarming

be swarming with *people* [*something*] ['swɔ(:)rmɪŋ wɪð ~] [口] **群集** 动词 swarm 的意思是"成群蠕动",从语感上讲,近似拟态词"咕咕容容"。下面用 with ~的形式表示这一动作的主体。例如: *The roads in August swarm with hitchhikers.* 在八月,公路上拥满了免费搭车的人们。在实际会话中,为了强调这种动作,绝大多数的场合是象本条条头所示那样,用进行时来表达。另外,由于这一表达法的性质是群体,因而 with 后面的名词一般为复数形式。*The garden is swarming with mosquitoes.* 庭院里蚊子成团。*Lebanon seems to be swarming with terrorists.* 黎巴嫩境内似乎有大批的恐怖分子在活动。*We heard a whistle blow, and before we knew it, the place was swarming with cops.* 我们刚听到警笛声,没等明白是怎么回事,周围就已经布满了警察。根据以上所讲,乍看起来,这一表达法与 be LOUSY with *something* [*people*] 很相似,但是 be swarming with 自有它的特点,即不仅表示"多",而且表示"动"。因此,with 后边的名词一般是生物或者以动为前提的东西(如汽车等),即使不属于这两种范围,也必须是在当时当地能出现"动态"的事物。例如说: *Our minds were swarming with ideas about how to spend our summer vacation.* 我们的心里盘算着各种各样关于怎样过暑假的计划。另有大致同义的表达法 be teeming with,但在会话中大多使用 be swarming with。◇ be teeming with [full of, overflowing with] *people* [*something*]

swath

cut a swath (through *something* [*someone*]) [ˌkʌdə 'swɑ(:)θ] [口] **引起群众注目** a swath 指用大镰刀割牧草时留下的一条痕迹或者用园圃刈草机刈草坪时留下的刈幅。*This new lawn mower cuts a wider swath than the old one.* 这台新园圃刈草机所开的刈幅比那台旧的宽。也可以用于"刈幅"以外的事情,但具体形象是相同的。例如: *The tornado cut a wide swath of destruction through the city.* 龙卷风穿过城市,留下很宽一条破坏的痕迹。*The machine gun cut a swath through the charging soldiers.* 在机关枪的扫射下,冲锋的士兵一个接一个倒了下来。这就是说,虽然 cut a swath 的原义是"把草割倒,形成一个很宽的道路",也可以引申为"当一个显著的人物来到大批群众之中的时候,人们向两侧后退,中间出现一条很宽的道路"。因此,这一表达法就被用于表示"引起群众注目"的意思了。*A man with money and a personality like his cuts a swath wherever he goes.* 他既有钱,又有突出的个性,所以不论走到哪里,都很引人注目。*The movie star and his entourage cut a wide swath through our little town.* 在我们的小镇里,那位电影明星和他的随行人员大大引起群众的注目。除 wide 外,也常用 quite 加强语气。*The handsome new boy has been cutting quite a swath through the girls in our school.* 那个新来的男生十分英俊,引起我校女生们特别的注目。◇ attract a lot of attention (in *something* [among *someone*])

sweat

no sweat [ˌnou 'swe(:)t] [话] **没问题** 新的表达法。原来的构思是:"做那件事情,连汗都不用出"。男子常常使用。它包含着两个方面的意思:一方面是"很简单",一方面是"请不必担心"。*A: Can you lend me that much money? B: No sweat. I'll have it ready for you by tomorrow.* 甲:你能借给我那么多的钱吗? 乙:没问题。我在明天以前就给你准备好。*A: I've got to be at the station in thirty minutes. B: No sweat. I know a road that'll get us there in half that time.*

甲：我必须在三十分钟以内到达车站。乙：没问题。我知道一条捷径，咱们用一半时间就可以到达了。根据上下文，这一表达法的意义有贴近“很简单”的场合，也有贴近“请不必担心”的场合。常用 at all 或者 really 加强语气。*A job like this is no sweat at all. I'll be finished in ten minutes.* 这类工作实在太简单啦。我十分钟以内就能搞完。*It may look difficult but it's really no sweat.* 看起来可能很难，实际上非常简单。以上两个例子是以“简单”为重点，下面的例子则是强调“请不必担心”。*There's no sweat about taking an exam like that if you just keep up your daily homework.* 对于那种测验，只要你每天认真完成家庭作业，就用不着担心。◇ (that's) no problem

sweet

a sweet tooth → TOOTH

sweet-talk

sweet-talk *someone* (into [out of] <*doing*> *something*) [ˈswi(ː)ˈtɔ(ː)k ~] [话] **用甜言蜜语哄人** sweet-talk 乃是 sweet talk (甜言蜜语) 的动词形式。*Save your sweet talk. It won't work on me.* 把你的甜言蜜语收起来吧。那一套对我不起作用。如这一例句所示，有时使用名词词组的形式，但一般加连字符，当动词使用。直译为“讲甜言蜜语”，实际上这是一个比较轻松的表达法，接近“恭维”、“奉承”、“说好听的话”等意思。正确的解释是：“为了使对方按照自己的意图办事，用温柔的语气说话以博得对方的欢心”。*There is no use trying to sweet-talk me. The answer is no, no, a thousand times no! I'm not going to give you a date.* 你试图用甜言蜜语哄我，那没有用。回答是不，不，一千个不！我绝对不同你约会。sweet-talk *someone* into (*doing*) *something* 是“用甜言蜜语哄人去干某事”的意思。*I let my wife sweet-talk me into buying her a fur coat.* 我的妻子用甜言蜜语哄我，终于使我给她买了一件毛皮上衣。*Tom is trying to sweet-talk the boss into (giving him) a fat pay raise.* 汤姆竭力巴结老板，想使老板多给他增加工资。也有 sweet-talk *someone* out of (*doing*) *something* 的说法，意思是“用甜言蜜语哄人不去干某事”。*I'll try to sweet-talk her out of going.* 我要用甜言蜜语哄她不要去。*Be careful of Mr. Honeylips. He can sweet-talk a starving baby out of its bottle.* 你对甜嘴唇先生可要当心啊。他连饥饿的婴儿叼着的奶瓶子都能哄骗走。◇ wheedle *someone*

swine

cast pearls before swine → PEARLS

swing

get into the swing of things [geˌdɪntəðə ˈswɪŋəv ˌθɪ(ː)ŋz] [话] **适应环境** swing 是“摆动、振动”，things 是“周围的事物、各种活动、情况”的意思。这一表达法最初的构思是：“周围的情况象钟摆一样有一定的节奏，要使自己的节奏与环境的节奏合拍”。换句话说，就是“熟悉环境，适应环境”。*I enjoyed my new life in America, but somehow I just couldn't seem to get into the swing of things.* 我喜欢我在美国的新生活，但是，不知为什么，似乎总有不能适应环境的感觉。*New employees are usually allowed a few months to get into the swing of things before they are given any serious responsibilities.* 新来的工作人员在担负重要工作任务之前，公司总是给与几个月适应环境的预备期。有时用 be 动词代替 get，前置词也随之改为 in。当然，这是表示“正在适应”的状态。*I needn't have worried about my new life at school. I was in the swing of things before I knew it.* 我对于学校的新生活有过不必要的忧虑。其实，在不知不觉之间，我就逐步适

应环境了。也可以用其他名词取代 things, 句型为 get into the swing of *something*。例如: *I had difficulty getting into the swing of life in America.* 我费很大劲才适应了美国生活。◇ adapt to the rhythm of the activity there [here]

be in full swing [ɪn'fu(:)l 'swɪ(:)ŋ] [口] **达到高潮** 这一表达法给人的具体形象是: 秋千在以最大的幅度飘荡。可以用于"工作"、"社交晚会"、以及各种各样的活动, 使用范围极广。因此, 根据上下文, 可以有种种不同的译法, 如: "正在高潮"、"上了轨道"、"达到全盛"等等。有时说 be going (at) full swing, 同义。在这一场合, "活跃"的形象更加明显, 因此常在下面两个类型的例句中使用。*Business is very good now. All our factories are in [are going (at)] full swing.* 现在生意非常兴隆。我们所有的工厂都在百分之百地开工。*By the time we arrived, the party was in [was going (at)] full swing.* 我们到达的时候, 社交晚会正在高潮。*China and America have started a new cultural exchange program, but it won't be in full swing until next year.* 中国和美国开始执行一个新的文化交流计划, 但是明年才能步入正轨。也可以用 get into full swing 的形式, 这是"充分活动起来"的意思。*Business won't get into full swing until next month when the new president has been selected.* 在下月选出新董事长之前, 公司的营业是不会全面展开的。◇ be fully activated / be at the height of activity

take a swing (at *something*) [ˌteɪkə 'swɪ(:)ŋ ~] [口] **挥动(球棒等)** 最普通的用法是: "挥动球棒去打球", 即 *something* = the ball。但在不打球而"空抡"的场合, 也使用这一表达法。因此, 如果说 *Give me the bat. I'd like to take a few swings.* 这句话的意思可能是"把球棒给我。我想打几下球。"也可能是"把球棒给我。我想抡几下看。"另外, 在有球存在的场合, 本条习用语也只是"挥动(球棒)"的意味, 与挥动后是否打中球毫无关系。*I took a big swing at the ball and missed completely.* 我对着球猛力一挥, 球棒却完全落空了。*The number three batter took a terrific swing and sent the ball into the left-field stands.* 三号击球员猛地一击, 把球打到左外场的位置了。*The golfer took a careful swing and drove the ball straight down the fairway.* 高尔夫球运动员很谨慎地一击, 把球一直送入平坦的球道了。take a swing (at *something*) 中的 *something* 有时不是球, 而是人类以外的生物。在这一场合, 可以认为与 take a SWING at *someone* (→) 大致相同。*Instead of running away, the old lady took a swing at the bear with her broom.* 老太太见到熊没有逃跑, 而是挥动扫帚去打它。又有 have a swing (at *something*)的说法。*Let me have a few swings at the ball.* 让我用球棒击几下球吧。除 have 外, 可以使用 get。在这一场合, 增添了"挥动得很如意"的意味。*I can't seem to get a good swing at the ball today.* 今天这球, 我打得实在不顺手啊。take [have] a swing (at *something*) 从"挥动"转义为"试试看"。*You can't get the engine started? Here, let me take a swing at it.* 你发动不了引擎吗? 来, 让我试试看。但在表示这一意义时, 一般都使用 take a CRACK at (*doing*) *something* (→)的表达法。◇ hit (hard, carefully, etc.) at [try to hit] *something*

take a swing at *someone* [ˌteɪkə 'swɪŋət ~] [口] **殴打某人** 一般是"swing 胳膊, 用拳头打"的意思。有时指"用东西(棍棒之类)打", 但在这一场合, 大多在句子中示明使用什么东西。又, 在许多情况下, 是指"虽然挥动了拳头, 但是没有击中对方"。例如说 *He took a swing at* *me, but he missed.* 这句话的意思当然是他挥动拳头打我，但是没有打中。不过，即使没有 but 以下的部分，言外也有“没有打中”的意思（在这一点上，与 try to hit *someone* 相同）。*When the drunk took a swing at Joe, Joe just stepped back and laughed.* 当醉汉向乔挥动拳头的时候，乔只是向后退了一步，哈哈大笑了。*He took a swing at me with a club, but I ducked and hit him in the solar plexus.* 他抡起球棒来打我，但是我立即闪开了，并且照他的心窝儿打了一拳。也有用于“打中对方”的场合，但是在句子中对这一点必须有明确的交待。*He took a swing at me and clipped me on the chin.* 他抡起拳头，猛击到我的下巴上了。“得到 take a swing 的机会”的英语表达是 get a swing at *someone*。*I couldn't get a swing at him because he kept dodging from side to side.* 他总是左闪右闪，因而我没有得到狠揍他一下的机会。→ take a SWING (at *something*) ◇ try to hit *someone*

switch

be asleep at the switch [ə.sli(ː)pətðə ˈswɪ(ː)tʃ] [话] **玩忽职守** 这里的 switch 指“铁路的道岔扳子”、“转辙器”。这一表达法的原义为“在铁路扳道岔值班时睡着了”。只要了解这一点，就容易掌握它的比喻意义了。*The train wrecked because the dispatcher was asleep at the switch.* 火车因为调度员上班时睡着而脱了轨。这是按照字面意义的解释。但这句话也可以按照比喻意义，解释为“由于调度员玩忽职守，火车脱了轨”。这一表达法作为比喻，用于“自己应该做的事情而懒得去做”的场合。*We lost that hand because I was asleep at the switch and didn't catch my partner's signals.* 由于我一时疏忽，没有领会伙伴的信号，我们输掉了那手牌。*The lookout was asleep at the switch and didn't see the suspect leave the apartment.* 监视哨玩忽职守，没有看见嫌疑犯从公寓走出去。一般使用 be 动词，但也有用 fall 的时候。*Don't fall asleep at the switch. We've got to take advantage of every opportunity.* 不要总是楞着呀！我们必须利用每一个机会。catch *someone* asleep at the switch 是“出乎意料之外”的意思。*The sudden plunge in stock prices caught Al asleep at the switch, and he lost almost half his investment.* 股票价格的突然暴跌出乎阿尔的意料之外，这使他损失了几乎投资额的一半。*We had thought the contract was in the bag, but a competitor's sudden move caught us asleep at the switch and we lost it.* 我们本来以为那个合同已经十拿九稳是我们的，但是出乎意料之外，一个竞争对手突然活动起来，把我们的生意抢走了。◇ be not alert

catch *someone* asleep at the switch [ˌkætʃ ～ə.sli(ː)pətðə ˈswɪ(ː)tʃ] [话] **出乎意料之外** → be asleep at the SWITCH

fall asleep at the switch [ˌfɔ(ː)l ə.sli(ː)pətðə ˈswɪ(ː)tʃ] [话] **玩忽职守** → be asleep at the SWITCH

swoop

at one fell swoop [ət ˈwʌ(ː)n ˈfe(ː)l ˈswuːp] [口] **一下子(抢走、毁坏)** 出典：莎士比亚悲剧《麦克佩斯》(*Macbeth*)第四幕第三场。麦克达甫听到麦克佩斯把自己的所有妻子全都杀掉了，这样讲：O hell-kite! All? What! all my pretty chickens and their dam at one fell swoop?（哦，凶残的恶魔！全部？哎呀，你是说把我那些可爱的小鸡和母鸡一下子都宰了吗？）本条条头中的 fell 与 fall 的过去式不是一个语源，在莎士比亚时代，fell 用以表示“极端残酷”、“凶暴”的意味。现在已成废词，仅在本条习用语中使用。swoop 的意思是“猛禽急降下攫取猎物”、“突然袭击”。*The hawk plunged* *from the sky and took both rabbits at one fell swoop.* 老鹰从空中猛冲下来，一下子把两只兔子都叼走了。后来，这一表达法就被人们广泛使用，表示"一下子(抢走等)"的意思。*The tornado destroyed most of the city at one fell swoop.* 龙卷风一下子毁灭了大半个城市。*When the reactionaries took over the government, the people were deprived at one fell swoop of their rights, liberty and property.* 当反动派上台的时候，人民的权利、自由和财产一下子都被剥夺了。*The FBN cartel was secretly buying up shares of the company, planning to take it over at one fell swoop.* FBN 卡特尔偷偷购买那个公司的股票，计划一口将它吞并。如以上的例句所示，这一表达法原本是"一下子(袭击)"的意思，但在另一方面，又产生了下面这样的使用方法。*The guests all arrived at [in] one fell swoop.* 客人们一下子全都来了。*When the stock market suddenly rose, he recovered all his losses at [in] one fell swoop.* 当股票市场突然坚挺的时候，他一下子把所有的损失全都捞回来了。也就是说，在这里不是"一下子袭击"，而是"一齐"、"一总"的意思。严格地讲，这都属于误用的范围，不过现在已经非常普及，人们对此已司空见惯了。另外，如上面的例句所示，前置词一般用 at，但是，特别是在误用而又一般化的场合，大多使用 in 或 with 等。◇ all at once / with once blow

sword

a two-edged sword [ə ˌtu(:)ˌedʒ*d* ˈso(:)rd] [口] **两刃的利剑** 出典：《圣经 · 新约》中的《启示录》(Revelation)第 1 章 16 节：... in his right hand he held seven stars, from his mouth issued a sharp two-edged sword, and his face was like the sun shining in full strength. (他右手拿着七星；从他口中出来一把两刃的利剑；面貌如同烈日放光。) 这一表达法最初的构思是："因为两面有刃，在砍对手的时候，自己也会受伤"。一般用于表示"对自己有有利的一面，但是反过来也有不利的一面"的意思。比较起来，强调不利因素的场合要多一些。*The argument he used to justify his position proved to be a two-edged sword which ultimately led to his own defeat.* 他用以证明自己立场正确的论点，结果却成为导致他自己败北的两刃的利剑了。*Money is a two-edged sword. It can be used for either good or evil.* 金钱是两刃的利剑。既可以用于行善，也可以用于作恶。*Nuclear weapons are a two-edged sword. The more of them a nation builds to protect itself from its enemies, the greater the danger that they will bring about an all-out war.* 核武器是一把两刃的利剑。一个国家为了防御敌人所制造的核武器越多，它们引起全面战争的危险性越大。这一表达法也用于表示"人所讲的话有表面意义和内涵意义两个方面"，也就是"在他人看来，有善意和恶意两个方面"。大多指恭维、奉承之类的话。*Her tongue is a two-edged sword. Many of the nice things she says about people include cutting remarks about someone else.* 她的舌头是两刃的利剑。当她大肆称赞某一个人的时候，她的话里大多含有贬低另一个人的意思。*Most of his compliments tend to be two-edged swords. You shouldn't take them at face value.* 他的赞美之辞大多是两刃的利剑。你不要信以为真啊。也有用 argument [compliment, etc.] 代替 sword 的场合，例如说：*That's a two-edged argument [compliment].* 那种论点[称赞]是两刃的利剑。◇ (a) two-sided (*something*) / two aspects [sides] ((be 动词 → have))

swords

be at swords' points (with *someone* over *something*) → POINTS

cross swords (with *someone*) [ˌkrɔˈsːɔ(ː)rdz] [口] **交锋;争论** 这一表达法来源于古代用决斗解决问题的风俗。现在,在历史影片还可以听到按字面意义使用的对白,例如: *He is a skillful duelist. No one dares cross swords with him.* 他是一个技艺高强的决斗者,没有一个人敢和他交锋。但是,在现代会话中,这个 swords 变成了 words 的意思,"宝剑交锋"变成了"舌剑交锋",也就是专用于比喻了。使用范围很广,从"脸红脖子粗的争吵"一直到"学者们的冷静讨论"。不论哪一种场合,这一表达法都含有"坚持自己立场,彻底驳倒对方"的意味。*Don't ever try to cross swords with the principal. One teacher who tried it last year is out of work now.* 千万不要跟校长发生口角。去年有一位教师跟他争论,至今还失业哪。*Those two brothers are forever crossing swords over money matters.* 他们弟兄俩总是为钱的事情争吵。不限于"口角"、"吵嘴",也常用于较高知识水平的争论,把语言比做利剑,即汉语成语所说的"唇枪舌剑"。*The courtroom was packed. Everyone wanted to see the nation's two top lawyers cross swords.* 法庭里挤满了人。每个人都想看看全国最著名的两位律师的舌剑唇枪。◇ argue [quarrel, debate, etc.]

T

T

to a T [ˌtuə ˈtiː] [话] **正合适** 这里的 T 是设计人员等所使用的 T-square (丁字尺) 的 T,有时拼写作 tee。一般与动词 fit 或者 suit 一起使用,但与 suit *someone* down to the GROUND 中的 down to the ground (正合口味)不同,可以用于"口味"以外的事情。另外,与动词 fit 一起使用和与动词 suit 一起使用,意味也有所不同。例如说: *The dress fits her to a T.* 那件衣服对她正合适。这句话是指"尺寸合适",也就是从客观上看"很合身"。如果讲 *The dress suits her to a T.*从他人的眼光看,这是"她的那件衣服跟她的身材、年龄、身份等等非常协调"的意思;从她本人来看,则是"正合自己口味"的意思。*I don't know if the man I saw was the one you are locking for, but your description fits him to a T.* 我不知道我看见的那个男子是不是你在搜索的人,只是他的特征与你所讲的一模一样。*In light of your qualifications, this job suits you to a T.* 按照你的资格,这个工作对你正合适。*My new job is hard, but the hours suit me to a T.* 我的新工作很累人,但是时间对我很合适。有时也可以象下面这样使用: *You say he used insulting language while treating them very kindly? That's George to a T.* 你说他待人非常宽厚,可是出言不逊吗? 乔治正是那样一个人呀! ◇ perfectly / exactly

table

drink *someone* **under the table** [ˌdrɪŋk ~ ˌʌndərðə ˈteɪbl] [话] **灌醉** 具体形象是:"对方 (= *someone*) 已经醉倒桌子底下,而自己(=主语)饮了同样多的酒却安如泰山"。*He tried to drink me under the table.* 他曾打算把我灌醉。在这一场合,意思也是:"他跟我喝同样数量的酒,而企图使我喝醉"。有时 *someone* 为复数。*Joe drank us all under the table last night.* 昨天晚上乔把我们大家都灌醉了。这一表达法前面加上 can,意思不是"能够把某人灌醉",而是"比某人酒量大",语调很轻松。*He can drink me under the table.* 他的酒量比我的大。也有 drink *oneself* under the table 这样的反身用法,意思是"自己灌醉自己"。*He drank himself under the table.* 他喝得烂醉如泥了。也可以用 be 动词而讲 be under the table, 这一表达法与 be completely drunk 同义。*Stu is already under the table.* 司徒已经完全喝醉了。◇ outdrink *someone*

tables

turn the tables (on *someone*) [ˌtə(ː)rnðə ˈteɪblz] [口] **扭转局势** 字面意义为"转动桌子"。这一表达法的来源是:古时,在下国际象棋的时候,如果一方过强,连连取胜,为了使比赛更加有趣,习惯上是在下至中途的时候,把桌子旋转 180 度,使强者和弱者分别走对方的棋。"把强与弱、优与劣掉换位置",当然就成为"扭转局势"的意味了。从有关政治、经济、国际形势等的大块文章起,直至语调轻松的日常会话,使用范围极广。*When George Bush threatened to make war, the Iraqian government turned the tables by holding Americans in hostage.* 当乔治·布什威胁要打仗时,伊拉克扣留美国人作人质,使局势有所变化。下面的例句讲的是大学对抗赛的前哨战。*We were planning to steal the opposing team's mascot before the game, but they turned the tables on us by stealing ours first.* 我们计划在比赛之前去偷对方的吉祥物,但是偷鸡不成蚀把米,他们倒先把我们的吉祥物偷走了。也常使用被动语态 The tables are turned. (形势向相反的方向发展。)在这一场合,重点在于因立场反转而产生的新的力量对比关系。根据上下文,轻则具有"天翻地覆,好不痛快!"的意思,重则具有"过去把我整得好苦,现在该我狠狠整你啦!"的意思。*When I was a struggling young businessman you refused to lend me money, but now that I am president of a flourishing company and you have gone bankrupt, the tables are turned.* 在我初出茅庐为做生意而奋斗的时候,你拒绝借给我钱;但是如今我是一家生意兴隆的公司的总经理,而你已经破产了。咱们俩的地位翻过来啦。◇ reverse the situation

tabs

keep tabs on *something* [*someone*] [ˌki(ː)p ˈtæːbzɔ(ː)n ~] [话] **掌握情况、内容、动向等** 这里的 tab 大概来源于 tablet (笔记用纸)。本条条头的字面意义是"写在 tablet 上"或"做记录"。如果用单数,讲 keep (a) tab on ~,一般的解释是:"经过仔细计算,写到帐簿上"。例如: *My job is to keep (a) tab on daily sales.* 我的工作是仔细核算每天的货款收入,记到帐上。如果使用复数,作 keep tabs on daily sales, 那意思是"掌握每天货款收入的大致情况"。这一表达法含有"为了管理或监督"或者是"为了取缔"的意味。*It's difficult for the immigration service to keep tabs on the activities of all the foreigners in the country.* 移民局很难掌握住在国内的所有外国人的动态。tabs 的前边有时加形容词 close [closer] 等。*I'm going to have to keep closer tabs on how much I spend.* 我对我究竟用多少钱,必须掌握得更准确一些。*He may not be the culprit, but we'd better keep tabs on him anyway.* 他也许不是罪犯,但是我们无论如何以掌握他的情况为好。如这一例句所示,常用于"人的活动情况"。*It's difficult for a teacher to keep tabs on all his students throughout the year.* 一个教师很难掌握他的全部学生在整个年度的活动情况。*Mrs. Yates hired a private detective in order to keep tabs on her husband's nocturnal wanderings.* 耶茨太太为了掌握她丈夫夜里活动的情况,雇了一名私人侦探。常添加 try, 采取 try to keep tabs on 的形式。*I try to keep tabs on all the new developments in my field.* 我试图掌握自己专业的一切新的发展情况。◇ maintain a (continued) watch on *something* [*someone*] / keep *oneself* informed about *something* [*someone*]

tack

(as) sharp as a tack [əz ˈʃɑ(ː)rpəzə ˈtæ(ː)k] [话] **非常敏锐** tack 是"图钉",因此,本条条头直译为"象图钉一样尖锐"。"尖锐"二字的意义非常广泛,在这一表达法中所指的是"头脑理解得快"、"思想敏捷"。*Jimmy is as sharp as a tack. You never have to tell him anything more than once.* 吉米的头脑非常敏锐。不管告诉他什么事情,永远不必说第二回。*My wife always seems to know when I'm lying. She's sharp as a tack.* 我每次撒谎,我的妻子似乎马上就能明白。她的头脑非常敏锐。另外,类似的表达法有 (as) sharp as a needle [knife]等。这些表达法虽然在英美都使用,但请读者注意它们之间的差异。首先讲 (as) sharp as a tack, 这主要是美国英语,在物理上"尖锐"的场合(如说"铅笔头象针一样尖")很少使用。其次,(as) sharp as a needle 在美国只用于表示物理上的"尖锐",但在英国主要使用"头脑敏捷"这一比喻意义。至于 (as) sharp as a knife, 不论在美国或英国,使人联想到的首先是物理的意义。根据上下文也可能有"头脑灵活"的意味,但不是定型的用法。顺便讲一下:有些词典把 (as) sharp as a steel trap 也列为 (as) sharp as a tack 的同义语,但这一表达法乃是 have a mind like a steel TRAP 的讹误,一般是不使用的。◇ extremely perceptive

try another tack [ˌtraɪ əˌnʌðər ˈtæ(ː)k] [口] **采取别的方法试试看** a tack 原为海上用语,指"(船逆风行驶、曲折前进时的)一个航向"。比喻意味是"方针"、"做法"。*Since no amount of punishment or threat seemed to make the boy study, his parents decided to try another tack.* 由于

不论如何惩罚或者恫吓,似乎都没有能够使那个男孩认真学习,他的父母决定采取别的方法试试看了。*Our present advertising campaign doesn't seem to be very effective. We'd better try another tack.* 我们现在的宣传活动似乎没有多大效果。最好采取别的方法试试看。也可以采取 try a different [new] tack 的形式,意思一样。*If logic doesn't move him, try a different tack. Appeal to his sympathy.* 如果讲道理他无动于衷,就采取别的方法试试看,看能不能引起他的同情。*We've tried for over a month to get him to meet with us with no results. Let's try a new tack.* 我们试图使他与咱们见面已经一个多月了,毫无成果。咱们采取别的办法吧。◇ try a different method [approach]

tacks

get down to brass tacks [get.dauntə ˈbræ(ː)ˈstæ(ː)ks] [话] **言归正传** 本条条头直译为"下到黄铜的图钉那里"。关于语源,有如下的说法:过去,在美国的 general store (西部影片中常出现的杂货铺)里,为了量所售布匹的长度,柜台上每隔一码都按上黄铜的图钉(brass tacks)。女顾客往往一边说东道西,一边用目测方式估计布匹的尺寸。这时,店主就说:Let's get down to brass tacks. (咱们放到黄铜图钉上吧!)意思是:"光用嘴说并不能了解布匹的尺寸,不如把闲话收起来,赶快实际量一下吧。"这一表达法包含着两方面的意义:①不要总地谈论,谈各个具体的细节;②谈正题,亦即最主要的核心。有时偏重于一方面。大多应用于表示这样的意思:"抽象的话(或者不大重要的话)到此为止吧,咱们谈具体的(或者正题的)吧。" *Our meetings are largely a waste of time. We always talk for hours about ideas and theories without ever getting down to brass tacks.* 我们的会议大多是白浪费时间。我们总是用好几个小时空谈设想和理论,从来不讨论实质性的问题。*I believe we have talked enough about the general outline of the plan. Now let's get down to brass tacks.* 据我看,咱们对于这个计划的总的纲领已经谈得够多的了。现在言归正传,谈具体的细节吧。*So much for the type of work you will be doing in our company. Next let's get down to brass tacks concerning the conditions of your employment.* 关于你在我们公司里担任哪一类工作的问题,就谈到这里吧。下面,咱们谈一谈聘用你的具体条件。这一表达法也用于表示"前边没有总论或闲话,直接进入正题(或具体问题)"的意思。*Let's skip the formalities and immediately get down to brass tacks.* 咱们免除客套,马上言归正传吧。又作 come down to brass tacks, 但在这一场合,主语不是"人",一般是"话题本身"。*Everyone is for improving the welfare system, but when it comes down to brass tacks, no one is willing to provide any more money.* 人人赞成改进福利制度,但是一谈到具体问题,谁也不愿意再多出一分钱。意思是:"谁也不愿意再多纳税"。◇ get [come] down to important matters [the details, the matter to be discussed, the central point, etc.]

tail

can't make head or tail of *something* → HEAD

in two shakes of a lamb's tail → SHAKES

tail *someone* [ˈteɪl ～] [口] **钉梢** → SHADOW *someone*

turn tail [.tə(ː)rn ˈteɪl] [口] **夹着尾巴逃走** tail 是"尾巴"、"屁股",亦即"身体的后部"的意思。turn 是"转向"、"朝向"的意思。这一表达法直译为"把后背转向敌人",含有"胆小"、"卑怯"的意味。*Noel's a coward. He turned tail as soon as he saw us coming.* 诺埃尔是个胆小鬼。一见我们来,就夹着尾巴逃走啦。*The bully turned tail as soon as my big brother appeared.* 我哥哥刚一露面,那个欺侮人的孩子就夹着尾巴逃走了。*Why should I back down from my position? I'm not going to turn tail just because a few critics have attacked my book.* 为什么我必须放弃自己的主张呢?我决不因为少数批评家攻击我的著作就退缩不前。如下

面的例句所示,这一表达法常与 and run (跑)搭配使用。当然,在象上面那样单独使用 turn tail 的时候,也含有“逃走”的意味。*When the lion turned up, the hyenas turned tail and ran.* 当狮子出现时,那些鬣狗就夹着尾巴逃走了。还有一个名词 a turntail [ˈtə(ː)rn.teɪl] (胆小鬼),但人们不大使用。*I'll have nothing more to do with that turntail. At the first sign of danger, he ran off and left me.* 我再也不跟那个胆小鬼打交道啦。只要一见到有危险的苗头,他就把我丢下逃走了。◇ run away / make a cowardly retreat

with *one's* **tail between** *one's* **legs** [wɪð ~ˈteɪl bəˌtwi(ː)n ~ˈle(ː)gz] [口] **夹着尾巴** 原指狗夹起尾巴逃走的样子。*It appeared to be a fierce dog, but when the boys began to throw rocks at it, it ran away with its tail between its legs.* 那条狗的样子很凶猛,但是当男孩子们开始向它扔石头的时候,它夹着尾巴逃走了。这一意义进一步发展,也可以作为比喻应用于人。在大多数场合与具有“逃跑”意味的动词一起使用。*When the bully saw we weren't afraid of him, he ran off with his tail between his legs.* 那个爱欺侮人的小流氓见到我们并不害怕他,就夹着尾巴逃走了。*The landlord demands that I move, but I'm not going to slink off with my tail between my legs just because he has hired some fancy lawyer.* 房东要求我搬家,但是,我决不因为他雇用了一个相当不错的律师就乖乖地走人。*The opposing team had bragged that they would win hands down, but we sent them home with their tails between their legs.* 对方的球队曾经吹牛说他们不费吹灰之力就可以取胜,但是我们把他们打得落花流水,叫他们夹着尾巴回家了。◇ like a coward / timidly / utterly defeated

take

take a lot of doing → DOING

take *someone* **down a notch** [ˌteɪk ~ ˈdaunə ˌnɑ(ː)tʃ] [话] **挫某人的傲气** → take *someone* down a PEG

take *someone* **down a peg** → PEG

take *someone* **for** *something* [ˌteɪk ~ fər ˈ~] [话] **从某人处骗走某物** take ~ for ~是“确信××是××”或“误认为××是××”的意思,例如说: *What do you take me for, a fool?* 你认为我是什么呢? 一个大傻瓜? 在大多的场合是这样使用。但是,另外也可以用来表示“从某人处骗走某物”的意味。*That crooked gambler took me for a hundred dollars.* 那个不老实的赌棍从我手里骗去了一百美元。*Be careful when choosing a contractor. Some unscrupulous builders will take you for all you're worth.* 在选择承包商的时候可要多加小心。有些品质恶劣的建筑业者会骗走你所有的财产。被动语态有 be taken for *something* 和 get taken for *something* 两种形式。*A: How much was he [did he get] taken for? B: Ten thousand yuan.* 甲:他被人骗走了多少钱? 乙:一万元。另外,在使用被动语态时,可以省略 for *something*。但是,请读者注意:即便在这种场合,也并非仅仅是“受骗”的意思,依然包含着“被人骗走某物”的意味。*I'm afraid you've been taken by one of the oldest con games in the books.* 很遗憾,你上了一个最司空见惯的骗局的当了。与这一表达法相对的是 be taken in,这是“中他人之计”或“被甜言蜜语所欺骗”的意思,不涉及是否骗走什么东西的问题。→ TAKE *someone* in ◇ *swindle someone* out of *something*

take *someone* **in** [ˌteɪk ~ ˈɪ(ː)n] [话] **用计策或花言巧语等欺骗他人** take *someone* in 有两大类意义:一是“把流离失所的人请到自己家里投宿和招待”,一是本条条头的中文释义。例如: *Our neighbors were kind enough to take us in when we lost our home in the fire.* 当我家失火,房子被烧掉的时候,邻居们非常好,请我们到他们家里居住,百般关怀。在这一场合,take *someone* in 就不是“欺骗”的意思。*They took us in completely with their smooth talk and manners.* 他们的圆滑口才和文雅态度完全把我们欺骗住了。在这一场合,take *someone* in 显然是“用计策或花言巧语进行欺骗、引人上当”。另外，第二种意义的 take *someone* in 多用被动语态。当然，“欺骗或引人上当”的手段，在这种情况下，一般来说，仍然是“计策”或“花言巧语”。*I realize now how foolish I was to give him the money, but I was completely taken in by his apparent sincerity.* 我现在明白过来，我把钱交给他是多么愚蠢，可是，他那表面上的诚实态度完全将我欺骗住了。*My wife was taken in by the smooth line of a professional con artist.* 我的妻子被一个骗人老手的花言巧语骗了。除 be taken in by *something* [*someone*] 外，还有 get taken in by *something* [*someone*] 的表达法。例如：*Bill is so naïve I'm afraid for him to go to New York by himself. He's sure to get taken in by some gold digger [some gold digger's hard-luck story].* 比尔过于天真，叫他一个人去纽约，我实在担心。他肯定会上某个用色相诱骗男子的女人的当［上某个女骗子编造的不幸身世的瞎话的当］。◇ deceive *someone*

take it or leave it [ˈteɪ.kɪdər ˈliːvɪt] [话] **接受还是不接受，二者必须择一** 直译“是拿它还是放下它”，意思为“对于别人提出的条件，是接受还是不接受，二者必须择一”，强调没有商量的余地。*The job is for six days a week. I'm sorry but I'll have to ask you to take it or leave it. I can't offer you better conditions than the other workers have.* 那个工作是一星期上六天班。很抱歉，我必须向你问一下干还是不干。我不能给你比其他工作人员更优越的条件。*If it should come to a choice between take it or leave it, I've decided to leave it.* 如果必须在接受与不接受之间选择其一的话，我是决定放弃的。*Five hundred dollars is my final offer. Take it or leave it.* 五百美元是我最后的出价。行与不行，由你决定。*This is the only house we have left for sale. You'll have to take it or leave it.* 我们出售的房子只剩下这一所了。买与不买，由你决定。可以加连字符构成 take-it-or-leave-it，当形容词使用。*I'm really up a tree. It's a take-it-or-leave-it proposition, but I can't afford to take it and I can't afford to leave it.* 我真是进退维谷啊。那是一个接受与否必须两者择一的提议，但是，我既没有接受的力量，又不能拒绝。◇ accept it as is [without further negotiation] or else reject it / be satisfied with this one or none

take it out on *someone* [ˌteɪkɪˈdauˌdɔ(ː)n ～] [口] **拿别人撒气** 这里的 it 泛指“恼怒”、“灰心丧气”、“欲望得不到满足”等。本条的意思是“迁怒于没有直接关系的人”。*someone* 多指一个撒气的对象，但不限定人数，多少人都可以。*Don't take it out on me because you failed the exam. It's your own fault that you didn't study.* 你没有考及格，别拿我撒气呀。你没用功，那是你自己的过错。*I know you're angry, but don't take it out on the children. If you have to take it out on someone, take it out on me. I can take it. The children can't.* 我知道你在恼火，但是别拿孩子们撒气呀。如果你必须迁怒于人，你就拿我撒气好啦。我能忍受，孩子们忍受不了。如果后边加上 ～ by *doing something*，意思是“采取某种行动来撒气”。*When my mother got angry with my father, she took it out on me by not letting me go to the movies.* 当我母亲对我父亲恼火的时候，她就拿我撒气，不准我去看电影。撒气的对象有时不是“人”，而是“物”。*Whenever my husband is angry, he takes it out on an old punching bag he keeps in the garage.* 每当我丈夫恼怒的时候，他总是拿他挂在汽车库里练习拳击用的旧吊袋撒气。*When my grandfather is feeling upset, he takes it out on the weeds in his garden.* 当我祖父感到不顺心的时候，他就凶猛地去薅园圃中的杂草。也可以用 *one's* frustration(s), *one's* anger 等代替 it，例如：*Traffic accidents often occur because people take their frustrations out on other drivers.* 交通事故往往是由于有人失意而迁怒其他开车者才发生的。*Our company has a special room where employees can go and take their pent-up emotions out on a life-size image of the* *boss*. 我们公司专设一个摆着与总经理真人一样大小的塑像的房间,工作人员可以去那儿向塑像倾泻自己的满腔郁愤。*He's always taking out his anger on whoever happens to be nearby*. 每当他恼怒的时候,谁在他的身边他就拿谁撒气。◇ vent *one's* frustration [anger, emotions, etc.] (indiscriminately) on *someone*

take *something* **out of** *someone's* **hands** [ˌteɪk ～ˌaudəv ～ˈhæːndz] [口] **剥夺某人的领导权、职务等** → take *something* [*someone*] off *someone's* HANDS / be out of *someone's* HANDS

to take out [tə ˌteɪ ˈkaut] [话] **带走的** → to GO

taken

be quite taken with *someone* [*something*] [ˌkwaɪˈtːeɪkən wɪð ～] [口] **非常喜欢(某人或某物)** 如果用英语说"被人捉住",那是 be taken by。例如:*He was taken by the enemy*. 他被敌人捉住了。象条头那样,把这个 by 改成 with,作为比喻使用,意思就是"被……的魅力捉住"→"迷恋于某人或某物"→"喜欢上……"。在使用比喻意义的时候,前置词有时也可以用 by,但用 with 的情况占绝大多数。*George is quite taken with the girl he met last week*. 乔治一下子被上星期遇见的那个姑娘迷住了。如这一例句所示,本条条头一般用于"一见倾心"、"一听到就喜欢上"等场合。很少用于"逐渐入迷"的场合。*I was quite taken with his idea at first, but after further consideration, I don't believe it would be very practical*. 最初我非常喜欢他的方案,可是经过仔细考虑之后,我认为这个方案没有很大的实用价值。◇ be very attracted to *someone* [*something*]

takeoff

do a takeoff on *something* [*someone*] [ˌduə ˈteɪˌkɔ(ː)fɔn ～] [话] **学样逗笑** takeoff 的字面意义是"起飞"。本条最初的构思为"从某一台基 takeoff [ˌteɪˈkɔːf] (离开陆地)"。在这里指"脱离真人真事而夸大趣味的行为"。takeoff 是把 take off into a flight of fancy (脱离现实,进入空想) 中的动词 take off 转成了名词。这一表达法一般在模仿动作、说话腔调等惹人发笑的场合使用,为日常会话中经常出现的口语。*The boss walked in just as Jack was doing a takeoff on the way he runs a meeting*. 杰克正在模仿老板主持会议的神情逗人发笑的时候,老板走进来了。do an imitation of ～只是"学样",不管是否有趣;本条条头除了"有趣"之外,还含有"讽刺"的意味。*After the serious play was over, Mel did a takeoff on Mark Antony's famous speech from Shakespeare's Julius Caesar*. 在严肃的演剧终了之后,梅尔模仿在莎翁《尤里乌斯·凯撒》中出场的马克·安东尼的著名演说,逗人发笑。也常单独使用 takeoff。例如:*Don Quixote was intended as a takeoff on the Spanish nobility of the day*.《堂·吉诃德》一书的目的在于讽刺当时西班牙的贵族阶级。*The record started with a takeoff on one of President Reagan's speeches*. 那个唱片的开头部分是对里根总统一次演说的模仿。*Tom's takeoff on the president's speech had us in stitches*. 汤姆模仿总经理的讲话,使大家笑破肚皮。◇ parody *something* [*someone*] / do a parody of *something* [*someone*]

tale

an old wives' tale [ə ˌnould̩ˈwaɪvz ˌteɪl] [口] **无稽之谈** 自古就有的表达法。在 1525 年出版的《圣经》第一个英译本中就有 old wives' tales 一语,1611 年的《钦定本英文圣经》改作 old wives' fables, 见《提摩太前书》(First Timothy) 第 4 章 7 节: But refuse profane and old wives' fables. (只是要弃绝那世俗的言语,和老妇荒渺的话。) wives 当然是 wife 的复数形式。在古时, wife 是"女人"的意思,现在还保留着 a fishwife (卖鱼妇)、alewife (酒馆女老板)之类的名词。因此,本条整体直译为"老女人们所讲的故事"。多指自古以来的迷信传说,含有"不科学"、"不合理"、"不可靠"的意味。*You don't really believe that there is such* *a thing as the abominable snowman, do you? That's just an old wives' tale.* 你并不真相信有雪人这样一种动物,是吧?那只不过是无稽之谈而已。*The saying "Lightning never strikes twice in the same place" is a dangerous old wives' tale that has brought death to many people.* "雷永远不在同一地方打第二次"这一谚语是很危险的迷信,许多人为此丧生。*Our minister said that when he was young, he looked on the Bible as just a collection of old wives' tales.* 我们的牧师说,当他年轻的时候,他认为《圣经》只不过是一本迷信传说的合集而已。用某种植物叶子治伤口的民间疗法,也常被认为是 old wives' tale 之一。*Modern medicine is learning that many of the traditional cures that were once considered old wives' tales actually work.* 现代医学认识到:在一度被认为无稽之谈的传统治疗方法中,有许多疗法实际上很有效果。在许多场合,old wives' tale 可以与 superstition 互换使用。但是,尽管两者都作"迷信"解释,而 superstition 往往和"符咒"、"妖术"、"怪诞的故事"纠缠在一起,而且或多或少给人一种社会的甚至心理上的压力,觉得"如果不遵从或不相信,就会大祸临头"。因此,关于"完全不可靠的说法",如果使用 superstition 就不恰当了。下面的例句就是这样:*Surely you don't believe that wet pine wood will burn. That's just an old wives' tale.* 你一定不会相信松木湿了也能燃烧的说法吧。那完是无稽之谈。◇ a superstition / an old story of dubious truth

a tall tale [ə 'tɔ:l 'teɪl] [口] **吹牛** → a tall STORY

tales

tell tales out of school [.tel 'teɪlz audəv 'sku:l] [话] **泄露内部秘密** tell tales 的字面意义为"讲故事",也可以用于表示"背后说坏话"、"告密"等意味。后边加上 out of school,直译为"孩子们在校外讲学校的丑闻"。这就是本条习用语最初的构思。但在实际上,成年人使用它的场合倒比孩子们多。*The section chief was indicted for taking bribes because one of his assistants told tales out of school.* 由于一个助手泄露了内情,科长因受贿而被起诉了。*When Ralph mentioned some confidential business matters to a newspaperman, his boss called him on the carpet for telling tales out of school.* 当拉尔夫向一个新闻记者讲了一些业务上的机密的时候,老板因为他泄露内情而狠狠斥责他一顿。*Don't let Carl in on this. He's famous for telling tales out of school.* 不要让卡尔知道这件事情。他是以泄密而出名的人。◇ reveal inside secrets

talk

back talk ['bæ(:)k.tɔ(:)k] [话] **顶嘴** → TALK back (to *someone*)

shop talk ['ʃɑ(:)p .tɔ(:)k] [口] **工作上的话** → talk SHOP

Talk about (a) *something*! ['tɔ: ka.baut / kə.baudə '~] [话] **多么……!** Talk about a beautiful woman! 这句话不是"你谈谈美丽的女人!"的意思,而是"多么美丽的女人啊!"的意思。这是 Talk about a beautiful woman, look at that! (要讲美女的话,你瞧那个人!)的缩略。在会话中也可以有后半句,但一般采取简短的形式。例如:*Talk about a fancy price!* 多么高的价钱啊! 如果 *something* 是不可数名词,当然要省去 a 了。*Talk about crummy food!* 多么糟糕的饭食啊! *Talk about power!* 多么大的马力啊! *Talk about homework!* 多么大量的家庭作业啊! ◇ What (a) *something*!

talk back (to *someone*) [.tɔ(:)k'bæ(:)k] [口] **顶嘴** 一般用于晚辈对长辈、孩子对父母、部下对上级,不仅是"回话",而且是"用言语顶撞"的意思。*Our father never allowed us to talk back.* 父亲绝对不允许我们顶嘴。*Don't talk back to your mother!* 不许对你母亲顶嘴! *You'd better not talk back to the judge. He'll throw the book at you.* 你最好不要顶撞那个法官。他会判你最重的刑的。把词序倒换一下,构成名词词组 back talk (顶嘴)。在这一场合,不限于晚辈的"顶嘴",也用于同辈的争吵。*You'll do as I say! And* *none of your back talk.* 你要照我说的去做！不要废话！ *Any more back talk from you and you'll wake up in the hospital.* 你若是再顶一句嘴，我就叫你在医院里醒过来。give *someone* back talk 也是"对某人顶嘴"的意思，如果是肯定句，一般在 back talk 的前面加 a lot of 或 some；如果是否定句，加 any 或 any more。例如：*He gave me a lot of back talk, so I hit him.* 他向我不住地顶嘴，所以我揍了他。*Don't give me any back talk or your punishment will be worse.* 不许向我顶一句嘴，否则加重处罚你。◇ make impertinent replies

talk down to *someone*[ˌtɔ(:)k ˈdauntə ～] [口] **以轻蔑的态度讲话** *That guy's attitude makes me mad. He's always talking down to me.* 那个家伙的态度真叫我恼火。他总是以轻蔑的口吻对我讲话。*A successful politician knows he should never talk down to people.* 一个成功的政治家懂得他绝对不得用轻蔑的态度对人讲话。*People won't like you if they sense you are talking down to them.* 如果人们发觉你在用轻蔑的态度对他们讲话，他们是不会喜欢你的。◇ speak condescendingly to *someone*

be the talk of the town [ðə ˈtɔːkəvðə ˈtaun] [口] **弄得满城风雨** talk 是"谈话的资料"。town 可以指纽约、北京一类的都市，也可以指边远的小镇。*Their engagement is the talk of the town.* 他们俩的订婚弄得满城风雨。*Paul, who only graduated from college last year, has been the talk of the town ever since he won the competition to design the new city hall.* 保罗去年才从大学毕业，自从他在新市政厅设计竞赛中获胜以来，成了全城的著名人物。也有明确指出 town 的名称的情况，例如：*Angela's new Broadway play is the talk of the town in New York now.* 安吉拉在百老汇新上演的剧本，现在成为纽约全市的话题。◇ be the subject of everyone's conversation

tall

a tall order → ORDER

a tall story → STORY

a tall tale [ə ˈtɔːl ˈteɪl] [口] **吹牛** → a tall STORY

tank

a tank town → TOWN

tanning

give *someone* **a tanning** [ˌgɪv ～ ə ˈtæ(:)nɪŋ] [话] **体罚** → tan *someone's* HIDE

tap

have *someone* **on tap** (for *something*) [ˌhæv ～ ɔ(:)nˈtæ(:)p] [话] **准备了人** → have *something* on TAP (for *something*)

have *something* **on tap (for** *something*) [ˌhæv ～ɔ(:)nˈtæ(:)p] [话] **准备了应用东西** tap 与 faucet [ˈfɔ(:)sət], spigot [ˈspɪgət] 等同义，是"龙头"的意思。tap water [ˈtæpˌwɔdər] 直译为"从龙头出来的水"，即"自来水"。在酒馆或饭馆常有写着 "Beer on Tap" 的牌子，直译为"拧桶上的龙头就出来的啤酒"，即"有生啤酒"的意思。因此，条头的 have *something* on tap 的字面意义为"只要一拧龙头，马上就会出来某种东西"，作为比喻，就是"准备了应用东西"的意思。*We have some good dance music on tap for the party tonight.* 我们已经为今天的社交晚会准备了一些很好的舞曲。在应用于人的时候，可采取 have *someone* on tap 的形式，意思是"准备了人"。*We have an interesting speaker on tap for next week's meeting.* 我们已经为下个星期的会议准备了一位能引起兴趣的讲演者。特别是在讲"人"的场合，常在表示"准备万一"的意味的文句中使用。*Just in case our regular typist can't handle the load, we have two extra typists on tap for tomorrow's work.* 万一我们的正式打字员担负不了那么重的任务，我们已经为明天的工作准备了另外两名打字员。另外，be on tap for *something* 也是一个句型，以 have *something* [*someone*] on tap 中的 *something* [*someone*] 为主语。意思有时与 have *something* [*someone*] on tap 完全相同，但一般来说，两者之间有细微的差别。也就是说，have *something* [*someone*] on tap 是“准备好了”,而这一习用语则是“已经预定”。*There's a meeting on tap for tomorrow.* 明天预定开一个会。*What's on tap for next week?* 下星期预定干什么呀?下面是以人为主语的例子。*Who's on tap for tomorrow's program?* 明天的节目预定由谁上场?◇ have *something* [*someone*] ready [scheduled] / be scheduled

be on tap (for *something*) [ɔ(:)nˈtæ(:)p] [话] **预定** → have *something* on TAP (for *something*)

tape

Scotch tape [ˈskɑ(:)tʃ ˈteɪp] [口] **苏格兰胶带** 商品名称。但是,美国人对不论什么牌子的 cellophane tape [ˌseləˌfeɪn ˈteɪp] (透明胶带)都一概称之为 Scotch tape。*May I borrow your Scotch tape?* 你的苏格兰胶带可以借给我吗?两个词之间加上连字符即为动词,意思是“用透明胶带粘贴”。在这一场合,S 多改成小写 s。*Jim scotch-taped the poster to the wall.* 吉姆用透明胶带把海报贴到墙上。◇ cellophane tape

tar

a tar [ə ˈtɑ(:)r] [话] **水手** → a GOB

taste

acquire a taste for *something* [əˌkwaɪrə ˈteɪstfər ~] [口] **养成嗜好** → an acquired TASTE

an acquired taste [ənə ˌkwaɪrdˈteɪst] [口] **后天养成的嗜好** 上边一条习用语 acquire a taste for *something* 是“养成嗜好”的意思。*Lynn has recently acquired a taste for brandy.* 林恩最近养成了对白兰地酒的嗜好。把这条习用语改成过去分词+名词的形式,就是本条的 acquired taste。acquire (学到手)一词含有“一步一步体会”的意味。*Most people don't care for strong-smelling preserved bean curd at first. It's an acquired taste.* 大多数人最初不喜欢臭豆腐。吃臭豆腐是逐步养成的习惯。*One has to listen to that composer's music quite a bit before he comes to like it. It's definitely an acquired taste.* 那个作曲家的音乐作品,你必须听过许多次才会喜欢它。耳朵不听惯,绝对体会不到它的妙处。◇ something one must learn to like

give *someone* **a taste of** *his* **own medicine** → MEDICINE

leave a bad taste in *someone's* **mouth** [ˌli(:)və ˌbæ(:)dˈteɪstən ~ ˌmauθ] [口] **留下不良的印象** 可以按照字面意义使用,例如:*The medicine left a bad taste in my mouth.* 那药在我的嘴里留下了苦味。在这一场合,也可以讲 have a bad aftertaste [ˈæ:ftərˌteɪst]。*This coffee has a bad aftertaste.* 这种咖啡余味不佳。作为比喻,在直接体会到令人心里难受的滋味时使用。*The child's rudeness to his grandfather left a bad taste in everyone's mouth.* 那个孩子对于他祖父的蛮横无礼的态度,给每个人都留下了很坏的印象。*The man's cursing his daughter left a bad taste in my mouth.* 听到那个男人在咒骂他的女儿,我感到很不舒服。*That book left a bad taste in my mouth.* 那本书没有给我留下好印象。*Many people like pornographic films, but they always leave a bad taste in my mouth.* 许多人喜欢黄色影片,但是我看了之后,总是感到令人作呕。可以用 unpleasant 代替 bad,在这一场合,印象不佳的程度降低了一些。*Her attitude left an unpleasant taste in my mouth.* 她的态度使我不愉快。与此相反,如果说 leave a nasty taste in *someone's* mouth, 就比 bad taste 的感觉强烈得多。*Seeing the men indiscriminately killing the seals left a nasty taste in my mouth.* 见到人们任意打死海豹,我感到无比的愤慨。另外有 ~ in the mouth 的说法,但比 ~ in *someone's* mouth 生硬,在日常会话中很少使用。◇ disgust *someone* / give *someone* a disgusted feeling

tat

give *someone* **tit for tat** → TIT

tattle

tattle on *someone* [ˈtæ(:)dəˌlɔ(:)n ~] **告发** → TELL on *someone*

tattletale

a tattletale [ə ˈtæ(ː)dl.teɪl] [话] **搬弄是非的人** → TELL on *someone*

tattletale gray → GRAY

tax

a tax dodge → DODGE

tea

be *someone's* **cup of tea** → CUP

teach

I'll teach *someone* **to** *do something*. [ˈaɪl .ti(ː)tʃ ~tə ~] [话] **他胆敢这样做，我要好好教训教训他** 直译为"我要教给某人去做某事"。实际上也可以按照字面意义使用，例如：*I'll teach you to swim.* 我来教你游泳。但是，大多是反语用法。*Wait'll I catch you. I'll teach you to steal my marbles.* 你等着瞧吧！你胆敢偷我的玻璃球，我要好好教训教训你。*I'll teach you to get smart with me.* 你胆敢对我口出不逊，我要好好教训教训你。*Father: Where is Jimmy? I'll teach him to disobey me.* 父亲：吉米在哪儿？他胆敢不听我的话，我要好好教训教训他。也可以不采取上面的反语用法，而在 to 的前边加 not，作 I'll teach *someone* not to *do something*.（我要教训某人不去做某事。）以上的例句均可换用这一表达法。在实质上，两种表达法的意义完全一样。但是，反语用法富有口语味，语调既轻松而又有力。而加 not 则显得很呆板。再有，可以用 learn 代替 teach。在莎士比亚时代，曾用 learn 表示 teach 的意味，现代方言中仍保留着这一用法。使用 learn 比使用 teach 更显得轻松一些。*I'll learn ya to tell the teacher on me.* 你敢把我的事情告诉老师，看我好好教训教训你。This'll [That'll] teach *someone* (to *do something*). 也是一个惯用句型。用 This 作主语，是在向对方进行惩治之前或正在进行惩治的时候所讲的话。用 That 作主语，则是进行惩治之后的言语。*This'll teach him to put a frog in my bed.* 他胆敢把青蛙放在我的床上，现在叫他尝尝这样干的后果吧。*There. That'll teach you to get smart with me.* 怎么样？你胆敢对我出口不逊，现在尝到什么滋味了吧？助动词除 will 外，还可以用 ought to, should 等。*That ought to teach you.* 现在你该明白是什么滋味了吧。◇ I'll make *someone* suffer for *doing something*.

tear

cause wear and tear (on *something* [*someone*]) [.kɔ(ː)z ˈweːrən'teːr] [口] **造成消耗** → save WEAR and tear (on *something* [*someone*])

save wear and tear → WEAR

tear-jerker

a tear-jerker [ə ˈtɪ(ː)r.dʒərkər] [话] **使人流泪的戏剧、电影、电视片** 直译为"把眼泪(tear)一下子猛拉出来(jerk)的东西"。*Most housewives like tear-jerkers. That's why TV soap operas are so popular.* 绝大多数家庭妇女喜欢催人泪下的节目。这就是电视中肥皂剧大受欢迎的原因。*The play was such a tear-jerker that the audience was soon afloat in a sea of handkerchiefs.* 那出戏令人深为感动，刚开演不久，观众就纷纷用手帕拭泪了。常用 real 加强语气。*The movie Love Story was a real tear-jerker.*《爱情的故事》的确是一部催人泪下的影片。◇ a maudlin drama [movie, story, etc.]

tears

bore *someone* **to tears** [.bo(ː)r ~ təˈtɪːrz] [口] **使某人厌烦得要死** 最初的构思是：由于太闷得慌，直打呵欠流眼泪。与 bore *someone* to death 完全同义。*The pay is good, but he says the work bores him to tears.* 虽然工资很高，但是他说那个工作使他厌烦得要死。*Mathematics bores me to tears.* 数学使我厌烦得要死。在下面的例句中，"腻味"的意味比较强。*You bore me to tears. If you dislike what you're doing so much, why in the world don't you change jobs?* 你真让我腻味。你如果那么讨厌现在所干的事情，为什么不变换一下工作呢？也常使用 be bored to tears 的形式。*By the end of our stay in the* *country, we were all bored to tears.* 我们在乡下居住的最后阶段，大家全都憋闷得要死了。◇ completely bore *someone*

crocodile tears [ˈkrɑkəˌdaɪl ˌtɪ(ː)rz] [口] **鳄鱼的眼泪** 本条条头来源于如下的传说：古代埃及尼罗河附近有一些 crocodiles (鳄鱼)，它们为了吸引行人而发悲声、流眼泪，当它们吃那些闻声前来的行人时，依然在流眼泪。所以"鳄鱼的眼泪"表示"假慈悲"的意思。*That widow wet a lot of handkerchiefs over her dead husband, but it was apparently all crocodile tears. He'd been dead less than one month when she married again.* 自从丈夫死了以后，那个寡妇哭湿了许多条手帕。但是，显而易见，那都是鳄鱼的眼泪。丈夫死后还不到一个月，她就改嫁了。有时不拘泥于字面的"泪"字，只表示"表面的悲哀"的意味。*She keeps saying how sorry she is that I didn't pass the entrance exam, but they're just crocodile tears.* 她一直在说她为我没有考上大学感到非常难过，不过，那只是表面上的同情而已。另外，也有 weep crocodile tears (掉鳄鱼眼泪)这样的说法，但一般惯用 shed crocodile tears 一语。*Many crocodile tears are shed at funerals of rich old men.* 在富翁们下葬时，人们会流许多鳄鱼的眼泪。◇ false tears / insincere sorrow

tee

tee *someone* **off** [ˌtiː～ˈɔːf] [话] **使人生气** 美国的下流话中有 piss *someone* off 的说法，直译为"冲某人撒尿"，意思是"使人生气"。为了委婉一些，就改为 pee *someone* off。而只将 piss (小便)换成 PEE(撒尿，男性用语)还不能登大雅之堂，就又改用与 pee 合辙押韵的 tee 了，这就是本条条头。当然，这个 tee 本身并没有特定的意义。本条习用语的意思只是"使人生气"，语气不太强烈，一般不能用于"怒发冲冠"或"满腔怒火"的场合。*The guy's attitude tees me off.* 那个家伙的态度让我生气。*It tees me off the way some people park in the middle of the street.* 我对某些人在马路中间停车的作法感到很不愉快。常用 really 加强语气。*I guess I really teed Mary off by not taking her to the dance last night.* 昨天晚上我没带玛丽去跳舞，我想她一定挺生我的气。也常用被动语态 be teed off (at *someone* [*something*])。*I'm teed off. You should have told me you'd decided not to come.* 我生气了。你决定不来，应该通知我一声啊。*Ted was teed off at us for waking him up in the middle of the night.* 特德由于我们半夜把他叫起来而生我们的气了。*You're not still teed off at me about yesterday, are you?* 你不再为昨天的事情生我的气了吧？*I'm teed off at the way they treated us.* 我是在为他们对待我们的方式生气。get teed off (at *someone* [*something*])是"有气"的意思。*I get teed off at people who bring their yowling kids to the movies.* 我对那些把乱哭乱叫的孩子带来看电影的人有气。*Tim finally got teed off at our constant teasing.* 我们经常不断地取笑蒂姆，他终于生气了。◇ make *someone* angry

tee off on *someone* (for *something*) [ˌtiːˈɔːfɔ(ː)n ～] [话] **痛斥** tee off 是高尔夫球运动用语，意思是"从球座上发球"。*Tim teed off with a three-hundred-yard drive straight down the fairway.* 蒂姆从球座上发球，猛抽一下，球沿着平坦的球道一直跑了三百码远。由"用力猛抽"的意思转为比喻，就变成了"严厉斥责"或"狠狠批评"。*The chief teed off on us for not finishing the work on time.* 由于没有按时完成工作，头儿把我们狠狠批评了一顿。这一表达法虽然是在"恼火"或"发脾气"的场合使用，但只能是"上级对下级"、"长辈对晚辈"，不能逆行。至于"痛斥的理由"，常在 for *something* 部分叙明。*My father teed off on me for spending so much money yesterday.* 因为我昨天花钱太多，我父亲严厉地申斥了我。*The teacher teed off on me for forgetting my homework twice in a row.* 由于连续两次忘记做家庭作业，老师狠狠地批评了我。on 的后边大多用 *someone*，但在表示"猛烈指责"的

意思时，也可以讲 tee off on *something*。例如：*The chairman of the Socialist Party teed off on the Japanese government's new tax plan.* 社会党委员长猛烈指责日本政府的新税制方案。*The mayor teed off on the police department's laxness in cracking down on drunken driving.* 市长猛烈指责警察局不认真取缔酒后开车。另外，如果用 with 代替 on，构成 tee off (*something*) with *something* 的形式，比喻意义是"从……开始"(begin <*something*> with ～)，务请注意。*We'll tee off the convention with a welcome party.* 这次大会先举行一个欢迎晚会。◇ berate / vigorously attack

tee off on *something* [ˌtiːˈɔːfɔ(ː)n ～] [话] **猛烈指责** → / TEE off on *someone* (for *something*)

tee off (*something*) **with** *something* [ˌtiːˈɔːf wɪð ～] [话] **从……开始** → TEE off on *someone* (for *something*)

to a tee [ˌtuə ˈtiː] [话] **正合适** → to a T

teeming

be teeming with *people* [*something*] [ˈtiːmɪŋ wɪð ～] [口] **人山人海** → be SWARMING with *people* [*something*]

teeth

armed to the teeth (with *something*) [ˌɑrmdtəðə ˈtiːθ] [口] **全副武装** 直译为"武装到牙齿"，这是强调 armed 的表达法。大多与 be 动词一起使用。*The soldiers were armed to the teeth.* 士兵们已经全副武装了。也常用于军队以外的场合。*The man was armed to the teeth. He had a rifle on his shoulder, a pistol in one hand, and a knife stuck in his belt.* 那个人全副武装。他的肩上背着步枪，一只手里拿着手枪，腰带上还别着一把匕首。有时不是指真的武器。而是把一些东西比喻为某人的武器，本条习用语也应用于以这种"武器"武装起来的场合。*The students came armed to the teeth with dictionaries, reference books, notebooks, pencils, etc.* 学生们全副武装，带着词典、参考书、笔记本、铅笔等等上学来了。另外，可以用 to the teeth 与其他过去时动词结合，强调"达到极点"，如 fed up to the teeth (腻味透了), dressed to the teeth (打扮得花枝招展)等。但这些词句太陈腐，会话中极少使用。◇ carrying an abundance of weapons [*something*]

by the skin of *one's* **teeth** → SKIN

cut *one's* **teeth on** *something* [ˌkʌt ～ ˈtiːθɔ(ː)n ～] [口] **由某种事情开始锻炼** cut a tooth 是"出牙"的意思。*The baby is cutting a tooth.* 那个婴儿出了一颗牙。当婴儿刚出牙的时候，大人常让他们嘴里含块橡皮或塑料。本条条头 cut *one's* teeth on *something* 就是"在初出牙时嚼某种东西"的意思，亦即"用某种东西促使出牙"。*The baby is cutting its teeth on a rubber toy.* 那个婴儿刚刚出牙，嘴里嚼着橡皮玩具。转作比喻使用，意思是"在从事某种工作之前，最初经过了什么锻炼"。*A number of today's novelists cut their teeth on newspaper work.* 当今的许多小说家都是新闻记者出身。*It isn't hard to operate. I cut my teeth on a machine like that.* 操作并不难。我最初用的就是那种机器。*The winning driver said that he cut his teeth on motorcycles before graduating to racing cars.* 据获胜的驾驶员说，他是首先骑摩托车训练，进一步才驾驶赛车的。◇ gain *one's* initial experience in [on, with] *something*

lie in *one's* **teeth** [ˌlaɪ ɪn～ˈtiːθ] [话] **弥天大谎** 一般指带有恶意的、从个人利益出发的谎言。*Bill is lying in his teeth. I never stole his money.* 比尔完全是在说谎。我绝对没有偷他的钱。*I don't believe it. You're lying in your teeth.* 我不相信。你所说的完全是谎话。*That man was lying in his teeth when he said I met him in New York last week. I've never been to New York in my life.* 那个人说上个星期我在纽约遇见他了，真是睁着眼睛说瞎话。我这辈子还没去过纽约哪。◇ knowingly tell a complete lie

be like pulling hen's teeth [laɪk ˌpulən ˈhe(ː)nzˌtiːθ] [话] **极为困难** 直译为"象

拔母鸡的牙一样”。因为母鸡根本没有牙,无从拔起,所以这一习用语似乎表示“不可能的事情”。但在实际使用的时候,不是指不管怎样努力也办不到的事情,而是指虽然非常费劲但是仍有一线希望的事情。例如: *It's like pulling hen's teeth to make anything grow in this poor soil.* 在这种贫瘠的土壤中,无论栽培什么作物都是很不容易生长的。这就是说,虽然“不容易生长”,却有生长的可能性。 *George is a real clam. Getting information out of him is like pulling hen's teeth.* 乔治真是一个守口如瓶的人。要想从他嘴里得到情报,比登天还难。言外之意是:尽管非常费劲,还是可能使乔治张口的。 *My husband is a stick-in-the-mud if there ever was one. It's like pulling hen's teeth to get him to take me out anywhere.* 我丈夫是一个最不喜欢出门的人。要想叫他带我到什么地方去,那简直比登天还难。 *Getting that guy to work is like pulling hen's teeth.* 要叫那个家伙干活,实在太困难了。◇ be extremely difficult

(as) scarce as hen's teeth [əz ˌskersəz ˈhe(:)nzˌti:θ] [话] **极少** 字面意义为“象母鸡的牙一样稀少”。这是强调“少”的夸张说法。 *Good secretaries are scarce as hen's teeth these days.* 最近,好的秘书打着灯笼也没处找。 *During the war, chocolate became as scarce as hen's teeth.* 在战争期间,巧克力变成非常稀罕的东西了。 *It would appear that completely honest politicians are becoming as scarce as hen's teeth.* 看起来,绝对诚实的政治家越来越如凤毛麟角了。◇ extremely scarce

set *someone's* **teeth on edge** [ˌset ~ ˈti:θɔ(:)ˌne:dʒ] [口] **使人不愉快** 本条习用语源出《圣经·旧约》中的《以西结书》(Ezekiel)第18章2节: The fathers have eaten sour grapes, and the children's teeth are set on edge. (父亲吃了酸葡萄,儿子的牙酸倒了。)以前曾把 edge 作为动词使用,而有 edge the teeth 的表达法,与本条同义,但到现代已不通行。动词 edge 原义“研磨”, edge the teeth 是“用锉锉牙”,作为比喻,就是“使人产生象锉牙那样的难受感觉”。后来,又将 edge 当作名词使用,产生了 set *someone's* teeth on edge 这一表达法。前者被时代淘汰,只剩下后者存留至今。“使人不愉快”的主体通常是气味、声音、人的态度或行为。动词偶尔用 put 代替 set,而讲 put *someone's* teeth on edge。 *I like the sour taste of lemon juice, but it sets my teeth on edge.* 我喜欢柠檬汁的酸味,但是它使我倒牙。 *Fingernails scraping a blackboard always set my teeth on edge.* 我听到用手指甲刮黑板的声音就感到很不舒服。 *Greta's whiney voice sets my teeth on edge.* 格里塔的响鼻子的声音使我感到很不舒服。 *Paul's affected mannerisms tend to set people's teeth on edge.* 保罗的装模作样的神情容易使人感到讨厌。另有一个句型相似的表达法,即用 nerves (神经)代替 teeth, 作 set *someone's* NERVES on edge。◇ give *someone* feelings of nervous irritation / greatly irritate *someone*

tell

Don't tell me (that) ~ [ˌdounˈtelmi (ðət) ~] [话] **不会吧!** 字面意义为“不要告诉我 (那个)”。例如说: *Don't tell me how to do it. I know better than you.* 用不着告诉我怎么做。我比你更熟悉。但是,如果后边承接的是由 that 引导的从句 (有时省略 that),则多半具有“不会吧?”、“未必吧?”、“不至于吧?”的意味。 *With gas prices this high, don't tell me (that) you're going to buy a Cadillac!* 汽油的价钱这么高,你不会去买一辆卡迪拉克牌轿车吧? *Today's the day you promised to take me dancing. Don't tell me (that) you've forgotten!* 你答应过今天带我去跳舞。总不会忘记吧! *Don't tell me (that) the railroad's going to raise its fares again!* 铁路不至于又要涨票价吧! 如以上的例句所示,本条习用语是在不相信他人会有某种行为或意图的时候使用,此外,也有应用于自己的行为的场合。 *Oh, oh. Don't tell me I forgot to bring my wallet.* 哎呀呀! 我不会忘带钱

包吧? ◇ Surely *one* [*something*, *someone*] is [has] not ～.

(can) tell [(kən)ˈte(ː)l] [口] **凭着视觉、听觉、嗅觉、味觉、触觉知道** tell 一词主要有两种意义:一是"告诉",二是"知道"。在前一场合,原则上伴有间接宾语,如:*Can you tell me what time it is?* 你能告诉我现在是什么时间吗?因此,如果没有间接宾语,基本上就是"知道"的意味。至于知道的方式,必须通过"五感"之一、之几或者全部。例如说:*Can you tell what time it is?* 你知道现在几点钟吗?这句话的意思并不是要求对方估量或推测,而是在对面有挂钟、坐钟之类,由于说话人视力差或者正处于难以观看的位置,才询问对方是否看得清楚。这是"凭着视觉知道"的场合。下面再举一个例子: *A: Who is that coming down the road? B: I don't know. It's too dark. I can't tell.* 甲:从马路那边走来的是谁啊?乙:我不晓得。天太黑了,我看不清。tell 一词在表示"知道"意味的场合,一般与 can, can't 或同类的词结合使用。以下按"听觉"、"嗅觉"、"味觉"、"触觉"的顺序各举一例: *I could tell who it was by the sound of his voice.* 一听他的声音,我就知道那是谁了。*A: How can you tell it's rotten? B: You can tell by the smell.* 甲:你怎么能知道它腐烂了呢?乙:一闻气味就知道啦。*The pie was delicious, but I couldn't quite tell what flavor it was.* 那馅饼很香,但是我说不清它是什么味道。*This is cheap material. You can tell by the feel.* 这是便宜的布料,一摸就能知道。在用"五感"区别两个以上的事物时,也可以使用这一表达法。*They're identical twins. It's difficult to tell one from the other.* 他们是一卵双胞,很难区别谁是谁。*Those two singers sound so much alike that I never can tell them apart.* 那两个歌手的声音太相似了,我怎么也分不清。下面是"用感官观察不出来"的例子: *A: Why do you think she got so angry? B: I dunno. There's no telling with a woman like that.* 甲:你认为她为什么那么恼怒?乙:我不知道。象那种女人,你根本无法理解。最后,举一个动用"五感"的例子: *After rubbing the object with his fingers and studying it carefully from all angles, he put it to his ear and shook it. Then he smelled it and put it to his tongue. But try as he might, he couldn't tell what it was.* 他先用手指去触摸,并从各个角度去仔细观察;又把它放到耳边去摇晃;然后用鼻子闻,用舌头舔。但是,无论怎样,他都未能知道那是一种什么东西。◇ discern (*something* [which is which]) / identify (*someone* [*something*]) / know

tell *someone* **off** (for *something*) [ˌte(ː)l ～ ˈɔːf] [话] **责备** 在对方言行失度而自己忍不住愤怒时使用。SCOLD *someone* (for *something*)通常是对下级或晚辈使用,本条习用语一般用于对同辈甚至长辈。*The cop told me off for crossing the street against the light.* 我因为过马路闯了红灯,被警察申斥了一顿。*I'm going to tell that fellow off. He's been talking ever since the concert started.* 我要去说说那个家伙。音乐会开始后,他一直喋喋不休。◇ berate [censure] *someone*

tell on *someone* [ˈte ˌlɔ(ː)n ～] [口] **告发** 主要是高中生以下的孩子们使用。*If you do that, I'll tell on you.* 如果你干那个,我就揭发你。"向谁告发"一般不讲 tell on *someone* to *someone*, 而用 tell *someone* on *someone* 的形式。*Jimmy told my mother on me.* 吉米向我母亲告发了我。如果加上告发的具体事实,语序是 tell *someone* on *someone* for *something*。*I'm going to tell the teacher on you for pulling my hair.* 你薅我的头发,我要去告诉老师。也常说 snitch on [ˈsnɪ(ː)ˌtʃɔ(ː)n] *someone*, 意思一样。还有 tattle on [ˈtæːdəˌlɔ(ː)n] *someone* 的说法,不过使用频率比 tell 或 snitch 低。在使用 snitch 和 tattle 的场合,语序与 tell on *someone* 不同,必须是 snitch [tattle] on *someone* to *someone* for *something*。*Lucy snitched on me to Granny for eating the cookies.* 露西向奶奶告发了我吃曲奇饼干的事情。有时,成年人之间也以半开玩笑的口吻使用这一表达法。*You wouldn't tell the boss on me [snitch*

<*tattle*> *on me to the boss], would you?* 你不会去向老板揭发我吧? 有时省略 on *someone*。 *Don't worry. I won't tell [snitch, tattle].* 甭担心。我不会告发的。另外,在孩子们中间,把"搬弄是非的人"、"爱去告密的人"叫做 a tattletale ['tæ(:)dl.teɪl] (又称 a tattler ['tæːdələr],但很少使用)。*I don't like Charlie. He's a tattletale.* 我不喜欢查理。他是一个爱告密的人。◇ report *someone* (to *someone* for *something*)

temper

lose *one's* **temper** (with *someone* over *something*) [.lu(:)z ~ 'tempər] [口] **动肝火** temper 是"心平气和"的意思。lose (失去)"心平气和",就是"发怒"了。*She's very quick to lose her temper.* 她非常容易动肝火。*I lost my temper with her last night.* 昨天晚上我对她发脾气了。发脾气的对象如果是 *something*,前置词大多用 over。根据上下文,也可以用 because of。*You shouldn't lose your temper over [because of] a little thing like that.* 你不必为了那样一点小事动肝火啊。又,如果是放在句子的最后,大多不用 over,而用 about。*It's nothing to lose your temper about.* 你没有什么可发火的呀。◇ get angry

ten

ten to one ['te(:)ntə 'wʌ(:)n] [话] **十拿九稳** → DOLLARS to doughnuts

ten-cent

a ten-cent store [ə .ten'sent .sto(:)r] [口] **大众百货店** → a FIVE-AND-TEN

ten-gallon

a ten-gallon hat → HAT

ten-spot

a ten-spot [ə 'te(:)n .spɑt] [话] **十美元的钞票** 相当轻松的用语。直译为"十个斑点"。*Can you lend me a ten-spot?* 你能借给我十美元吗? 有时指扑克牌的"10"或台球的"10 号球",但使用频率极低。◇ a ten-dollar bill

tenterhooks

be on tenterhooks [ɔ(:)n'tentər.huks] [口] **提心吊胆** tenter 是"绷布架",语源同 tent (帐篷),古时 tent 一词意思是"纸糊的东西"。tenterhook 是"往 tenter 上绷布用的挂钩"。但是,这是家庭织布时代的用语,现在只能在本条习用语中使用。条头直译为"正挂在绷布钩上"。专作比喻使用。*We were all on tenterhooks, waiting for news of the missing plane.* 我们大家都提心吊胆地等待失踪飞机的消息。这是把人的心情比做绷紧了的布。*I was on tenterhooks all day, wondering whether the answer would be good or bad.* 我整天焦急不安,不晓得是否能得到满意的答复。*Having been on tenterhooks so long, everyone almost jumped out of his skin when the telephone suddenly rang.* 大家心情紧张的时间过长了,当电话的铃声突然响起的时候,几乎人人都被吓了一大跳。也常使用 keep *someone* on tenterhooks,意思是"使人心情紧张"。*Don't keep us on tenterhooks. Tell us what happened.* 不要让我们着急嘛。快告诉我们发生了什么事情。*The movie kept us on tenterhooks from beginning to end.* 那部影片从头到尾一直使我们心情紧张。*It'd be wiser not to give him your answer right away. Keep him on tenterhooks for a while.* 你不马上回答他可能更明智一些。叫他心里先打一会儿鼓再说。◇ be in a state of anxiety [excitement]

test

make up a test [.meɪ 'kʌpə 'te(:)st] [口] **补考** → a MAKE-UP

a make-up test [ə 'meikʌp .test] [口] **补考** → a MAKE-UP

a pop test [ə 'pɑp 'te(:)st] [话] **突击考试** → a pop QUIZ

tether

be at the end of *one's* **tether** → END

thank

I'll thank you to *do something*. [.aɪl'θæ(:)ŋkjudə ~] [话] **你这样做好不好?** 反语。有讽刺意味。直译为"如果

你这样做，我很感谢”。但实际上并非表示谢意，而是一种毫不客气的、非常冷淡的说法。语调也很强硬，接近于吵嘴。*I'll thank you to stop smoking*. 你停止抽烟好不好？可以说，在口气上越和蔼，表明讨厌对方的心情越强烈。上了年纪的妇女爱用这一表达法。*I'll thank you to be a little more polite*. 你稍微规矩一点好不好？*I'll thank you to get out of my seat*. 这是我的位子，你躲开好不好？男性也有时讲：*I'll thank you not to step on my foot*.你别踩我的脚好不好？但在这一场合，大多采取 How about ～ing ～? 的形式。这也是一个口气强硬的说法，大有动武的架势。*How about getting out of my seat?* 你从我的坐位上走开怎么样？偶尔不是反语用法，而是按照 I'll thank you ～. 的字面意义使用。*I'll thank you for the salt, please*. 请给我拿一下盐好吗？但是，这不是日常会话。一般要说：*Would you pass (me) the salt, please?* 把盐递给我好吗？◇ ((讽刺地)) Please *do something*. / I'd appreciate your *doing something*.

that

that's that [ˌðæ(ː)ts ˈðæːt / ˈðæːts ˈðæːt] [话] **全完啦** 直译为“那个就是那个”。在使用现在时的时候，不是 that is that, 一般作 that's that。大多用于不再抱有希望的场合，表示“已经完啦！”、“没戏唱啦！”或者“已经没办法啦！”的意思。“*Well, I guess that's that,*” *he sighed as he watched the last of his stake being raked off the gambling table*. 他一边看着自己最后的赌注从赌桌上被人搂走，一边叹息着说：“哎，一切全完啦。”*Alice turned down my proposal. She said she liked me, but .... Then she kissed me on the cheek, and that was that*. 艾丽丝拒绝了我的求婚。她说她喜欢我，不过…… 然后，她在我的颊上吻了一下，这出戏算收场了。*If you absolutely refuse to help me, I guess that's that. I'll have to try to do it alone*. 如果你坚决不肯帮助我，我想再求你也没有用了。我只好一个人试着去干啦。也可以用 that seems to be that 的形式，意思是“大概差不多了吧”。例如，主持会议的人说：*Well, that seems to be that. If no one has any questions, the meeting is closed*. 现在，大概差不多了吧。如果没有人提什么问题，会议到此结束。除以上的一些用法外，人们还常用这一表达法强调在拒绝某件事情时态度是多么坚决。意思是：“不论你说什么，也是绝对不行”。*You can talk till you're blue in the face, but you won't persuade me. I'm not going, and that's that*. 你就是一直谈到舌敝唇焦，也甭想说服我。我说不去，就是不去。*I'm tired of his treating me like a slave. I won't put up with it any longer and that's that*. 他拿我当奴隶对待，我已经厌烦透了。今后我绝对不再忍耐啦。◇ that's the end of it / that's all [final]

theory

one's **pet theory** [～ˌpetˈθɪ(ː)ri] [口] **一贯主张** → *one's* pet PEEVE

there

have *someone* **there** → HAVE

look here and there (for *something* [*someone*]) [ˌluk ˈhɪrənˈðe(ː)r] [口] **到处搜索** → look HIGH and low (for *something* [*someone*])

be neither here nor there → HERE

be not all there [ˌnɑˌdɔːlˈðe(ː)r] [话] **神志失常** 字面意义为“不是全都在那儿”。*The members aren't all there yet*. 人员还没有到齐。在这一场合，既然说 all, 主语必须是复数形式。但是，在指一个人的时候，也可以用 be not all there。例如：*He is not all there*. 直译为“他不是整个都在那儿”，也就是“缺点什么”。这是 crazy (精神不正常) 的委婉说法。*When I told them that I was able to read people's minds, they looked at me as if I weren't all there*. 当我告诉他们说我能够看透人们的心思的时候，他们用仿佛我神志失常的眼光看我。*Close your mouth, son. People will think you're not all there*. 儿子，你闭上嘴吧！人们会认为你是个傻瓜哪。如果有若干这种“缺点什么”的人凑在一起，当然可以构成复

数形式的主语，如说：*They aren't all there.* 他们的神志不正常。在这一场合，be not all there 虽然也是用复数主语，但与本条开头所讲的字面意义有所不同。换句话说，根据具体情况，There are not all there. 既可以是“他们不是全体到齐”的意思，也可以是“他们的神志不正常”的意思。*If you tell Jane that, she'll think we're not all there.* 如果你把那种事情告诉简，她会认为咱们神志失常了。从以上的例句可以看到，be not all there 一般用否定式，但有时也这样讲：*That guy is always doing the craziest things. I sometimes wonder if he's all there.* 那个家伙总是在干最荒唐的事情。我有时怀疑他的神志是否正常。◇ be a little crazy

thermos

a thermos bottle → BOTTLE

thick

lay it on (thick) [ˌleɪəˈdɔːn / ˌleɪədɔ(ː)nˈθɪ(ː)k] [话] **言过其实；过分吹捧** → SPREAD it on thick

spread it on thick → SPREAD

through thick and thin [ˌθru(ː)ˈθɪkənˈθɪ(ː)n] [口] **有甘也有苦** 这是一个很古老的习用语，在莎士比亚时代以前就已经使用。thick 原与 thicket (草丛)同义，thin 原意为“开阔地”。本条的字面意义为“穿过草丛和开阔地”，也就是“有时要披荆斩棘，非常辛苦；有时走开阔地，其乐融融”。如果读者的脑子里能浮现出这样的画面，就容易理解这一表达法的含义了。有些美国人不知道本条习用语的来源，他们把 thick 当作“富有的时候”，把 thin 当作“贫穷的时候”，而将本条条头解释为“有富的时候也有穷的时候”，结果也是一样。*We've been through thick and thin together.* 我们一向是同甘苦，共患难。如这一例句所示，本条习用语常用于回顾过去的场合。也有时把重点放在 thick 上，表示“总算跨过了艰难险阻”的感慨心情。*I've brought this company through thick and thin for over twenty years.* 二十多年以来，我跨过无数的艰难险阻，总算把这个公司维持下来了。◇ through good times and bad (times)

thick-headed

thick-headed [ˈθɪkˌhedɪd] [口] **头脑迟钝** 条头的本义不是“头部厚”，而是“头骨厚”，任何事情进入脑子都需要很长时间。*I've never seen such a thick-headed person.* 我从来没有见过如此头脑迟钝的人。如此例所示，可以作为定语使用，但主要是用作表语。*Don't be so thick-headed. Don't you see that they're only trying to trick you?* 你头脑不要那样迟钝呀。你没看出来他们只是打算骗你吗？ *Dick is too thick-headed to see that Jane is in love with him.* 迪克的头脑过于迟钝，竟看不出简爱上他了。*I guess I'm just thick-headed. The teacher explained this math problem to me twice and I still don't understand it.* 我的头脑实在太迟钝了。这道数学题老师向我讲解了两次，我还是没有弄明白。与本条意义相似的用法有 dense, thick-skulled, thick-witted, dim-witted 等。在会话中最常用的是 thick-headed 和 dense。◇ slow to understand

thick-skinned

thick-skinned [ˈθɪkˈskɪ(ː)nd] [口] **感觉迟钝或胸怀宽阔** 字面意义为“皮肤厚的”，如说：*The rhinoceros is a thick-skinned animal.* 犀牛是一种皮肤厚的动物。作为比喻，指感觉迟钝或者胸怀宽阔。有的词典译为“脸皮厚”，但这个词本身并没有“厚颜无耻”之类的坏意思。既有在对人恼怒时使用它的场合，也有在对人赞美时使用的场合。也就是说，根据上下文，它既可以表示好的意味，也可以表示坏的意味。*Thick-skinned people are not easily offended by what other people say about them.* 胸怀宽阔的人听了别人的闲言碎语是不会轻易恼怒的。*Don't worry. Jim never loses his cool. He is so thick-skinned that he probably wouldn't take offense even if the whole town was against him.* 不必担心。吉姆永远不会失去他的冷静。他的胸怀非常宽阔，哪怕全城的人都起来反对他，他大概也不会生气的。*It's no use trying to make Karl angry. He is unbelievably thick-skinned.* 你想使卡尔发怒，那是白费劲。他感觉迟钝达到了令人难以相信的程度。除了最常使用的 be thick-skinned 这一习用语外，人们还常使用 have a thick skin, *someone's* skin is thick 等表达法。*I sure wish I had a thick skin like Jane's. Nothing ever seems to hurt her feelings.* 我多么希望有简那样宽大的胸怀呀。不论发生什么事情，似乎都伤害不了她的感情。*Don't worry about hurting Ralph's feelings. His skin is an inch thick.* 你甭担心伤害拉尔夫的感情。他的皮有一英寸厚。*New Yorkers are noted for their thick skins.* 纽约人以感觉迟钝出名。反义语是 THIN-SKINNED。◇ impervious to criticism [slights, taunts, etc.]

thick-skulled

thick-skulled [ˈθɪkˈskʌ(:)ld] [口] **头脑迟钝** → THICK-HEADED

thick-witted

thick-witted [ˈθɪk ˌwɪdɪd] [口] **头脑迟钝** → THICK-HEADED

thin

disappear into thin air [dɪsəˌpɪr ɪntə ˌθɪnˈeːr] [口] **忽然消失** → vanish into thin AIR

out of thin air → AIR

through thick and thin → THICK

vanish into thin air → AIR

thing

do *one's* **(own) thing** [ˈdu(:) ～ (ˌoun) ˈθɪ(:)ŋ] [话] **做自己喜好的事情** *one's* (own) thing 是"某人(自己)喜好的事情"，包含有"适合"他去做的意味。这是青年人爱用的一个轻松的表达法。*I'm not interested in making a lot of money. I just want to do my thing and be left alone by the world.* 我没有发大财的兴趣。我只希望去干自己喜欢的事情，世人别来打扰我。大多作 *one's* own thing, own 使语气加强。*But I don't want to follow in your footsteps, Dad. Can't you just let me do my own thing?* 但是，爸爸，我不愿意继承你的事业。你不能允许我干自己喜欢的事情吗？*Now that you're working in a company, you can't expect to continue doing your own thing. You've got to follow orders.* 你既然在一家公司工作，就不能象过去一样去干自己喜欢的事情。你必须服从命令啊。还有一个 be *one's* thing 的说法，即用 be 动词代替 do，而且去掉 own。这也是个习用语。但是，这一习用语中的 *one's* thing 既表示"某人喜欢的事情"，也同样表示"对某人适合的事情"。究竟在一个句子里突出哪一种意义，必须根据上下文来判断。*For the last time, I'm not going back to school. Painting is my thing and I'm going to do it.* 我最后再讲一遍，我决心不回学校了。绘画适合我的个性。我要沿着这条路走。*Collecting old coins is Rob's thing. He spends all his spare time at it.* 罗布喜欢收集古钱。他的业余时间全都用在这上面了。◇ do what *one* wants to do / do as *one* likes

have a thing about *something* [ˌhævə ˈθɪ(:)ŋəˌbaut ～] [话] **不知为什么非常讨厌或喜好** 意思是"对于某件事抱有难以陈述的感情"，亦即"怀有偏见"。*Floyd has a thing about girls with long hair. Maybe he was frightened by a long-haired witch when he was a kid.* 不知为什么，弗洛伊德非常讨厌长发女郎。可能他小的时候被长头发的巫婆吓坏了。下边例句的前半部分与此完全相同，但是意思却恰恰相反。*Floyd has a thing about girls with long hair. He won't even date a short-haired girl.* 不知为什么，弗洛伊德非常喜欢长发女郎。他甚至不跟短发的姑娘约会。究竟是"讨厌"还是"喜欢"，必须根据上下文来决定。不过，用于表示"讨厌"的场合比较多。*Ruth has a thing about flying. She absolutely refuses to go anywhere by airplane.* 鲁丝不知为什么非常讨厌飞机。她不论到什么地方去，都绝对不乘飞机。本条习用语的重点是非常片面的感情，与感情的强弱没有直接关系。但是，在实际使用时，绝大多数是表示“极讨厌”或“极喜欢”的意思。*As long as you work for this newspaper, you'd better keep your style terse. The editor has a thing about long, rambling sentences.* 只要你在这家报社工作，文字务必力求简短。主编最讨厌冗长的、松散的句子。*Prof. Jones has a thing about papers being handed in late. If one is even ten minutes past the deadline, he won't accept it.* 琼斯教授最讨厌学生迟交论文。一到了截止期限，哪怕过十分钟他都不收。◇ have strong feelings about *something* / dislike [like] *something*

if it's the last thing *one* **does** [ˌɪfɪtsðə ˈlæ(ː)stˈθɪŋ ~ ˈdʌːz] [话] **无论如何** 这里的 if 与 even if (即使) 相同。实际上，在强调的时候，也用 even if 代替 if。本条直译为“即使那是某人做的最后的事情”，也就是说，“哪怕牺牲性命，成为活在世上所做的最后一件事情”，充满“无论如何也要去干”的心情。*I'm going to get even with that guy if it's the last thing I do.* 我无论如何也要向那个家伙报仇。*He's failed the entrance exam twice already, but he's not giving up. He says he's going to get into that university if it's the last thing he does.* 他两次考大学都名落孙山，但是他并不死心。他说，无论如何他也要进那所大学。*A: The fish aren't biting. Let's go home. B: No, I'm going to catch a fish today if it's the last thing I do.* 甲：鱼不咬钩。咱们回去吧。乙：不。今天我无论如何也要钓上一条鱼来。◇ no matter how long it takes

not know the first thing about *something* [nɑtˌnou ðəˌfərstˈθɪŋ əˌbaut ~] [口] **一窍不通** 这里的 *something* 指“需要知识的东西”或“有内容的东西”。本条直译为“关于某种事物，连初步知识(the first thing) 都不懂”。*I wish I could help you fix your car, but I'm afraid I don't know the first thing about engines.* 我倒愿意帮你修理你的汽车，不过，很遗憾，我对于发动机可是一窍不通啊。*When we got married, my wife didn't know the first thing about cooking.* 当我们结婚的时候，我的妻子对于烹饪是一窍不通。*How do you expect to become a translator? You don't know the first thing about foreign languages.* 你怎么认为自己能成为一个翻译家呢？你对外语一窍不通啊。◇ not know anything at all about *something*

thingabob

a thingabob [ə ˈθɪŋəˌbɑːb] [话] **一个什么东西** → a THINGAMABOB

thingamabob

a thingamabob [ə ˈθɪŋəməˌbɑːb] [话] **一个什么东西** 对于一种东西的名称，在叫不出、一时想不起来、避讳说或者嫌说起来麻烦的时候，使用这一表达法代替。在英国，可以象大致同义的 a WHATCHAMACALLIT 一样指“一个叫什么的人”，但在美国只用于指物。*What does this thingamabob do?* 这玩意儿是干什么的？*He pushed a little thingamabob on the desk and all the doors swung shut.* 他用手一按桌子上的一个小玩意儿，所有的门都啪的一声关上了。*See that stick-like thingamabob there? If you pull that, the wheels go down.* 你看见那儿的好象一根棍子的东西了吧？如果你一拉它，轮子就往下落。以上是：东西有名称，但由于某种原因，嘴里不直接说出来。有的东西根本就没有名称，人们不知道怎样称呼，这时也可以使用这一表达法。*The flying saucer was covered with bright thingamabobs that looked like orange tennis balls.* 飞碟表面有闪闪发光的东西，看起来象是一些桔红色的网球。也可以把 thingamabob 拼写为 thingumabob，发音相同。又有脱落 ma 的 thingabob [ˈθɪŋəˌbɑːb]和脱落 a 的 thingumbob [ˈθɪŋəmˌbɑːb]的形式。更正确地讲，thingumbob 是始祖，后来经过种种变化，到现在，使用 thingamabob 的人最多。从构造上讲，是 thing + -umbob，但只有 thing 的部分有意义，而 -umbob 则是没有意义的词尾。另有 thingamajig 和 thingumajig (发音均为 [ˈθɪŋəməˌdʒɪ(ː)g])，同义。在英语中，这一类的表达法非常丰富，如代表机械类的 gadget [ˈgæ(:)dʒət] 或 gismo [ˈgɪ(:)zˌmou], 意味着"小摆饰"、"小玩意儿"的 doohickey [ˈdu:ˌhɪki] 或 doodad [ˈdu(:)ˌdæ(:)d] 等, 用法同前。◇ a thing

thingamajig

a thingamajig [ə ˈθɪŋəməˌdʒɪ(:)g] [话] **一件什么东西** → a THINGAMABOB

thingumbob

a thingumbob [ə ˈθɪŋəmˌbɑ:b] [话] **一件什么东西** → a THINGAMABOB

think

have another think coming [hævə ˌnʌðər ˌθɪŋˈk:ʌmɪŋ] [话] **大错特错** think 本来是动词, 在这里变为名词使用。have ～ coming 是"最近有……来临"的意思, 如 *I have a raise coming.* 我的工资最近要提高。本条直译为"最近有另外的想法来临"。乍听起来很难理解, 但在英语中, 这是一个毫不客气的、直截了当的表达法。*If he thinks I'd marry him, he has another think coming.* 如果他认为我会跟他结婚, 那就大错特错了。*If you think I'll go along with your crazy ideas, you've got another think coming.* 如果你以为我赞成你的疯狂的想法, 那就大错特错了。有时用 guess 代替 think, 而讲 have another guess coming。◇ be entirely wrong

think a lot of *someone* [*something*] [ˌθɪŋkə ˈlɑ(:)dəv～] [口] **(对人)敬爱; (对物)珍视** 本条的意思是"对某人或某物评价很高, 而且非常喜欢"。如果望文生义, 解释为"对某人或某物想得很多", 那就与英语的原意相差十万八千里了。"对……想得很多"一般说 think a lot about ～。*He thinks a lot about his students.* 他经常考虑学生们的事情。如果省略 a lot, 而讲 think of ～, 那只是"想……"的意思。think a lot of ～则具有"尊重"和"喜爱"两方面的意思。*I don't know if Jack is actually in love with Mary, but he seems to think a lot of her.* 我不知道杰克是否真的爱上了玛丽, 但是他似乎已经拜倒在她的石榴裙下了。*My husband thinks a lot of those old books.* 我的丈夫珍视那些旧书。*Though I don't care for Jim, I think a lot of his ideas.* 虽然我不喜欢吉姆, 但是我认为他的一些想法很有价值。*Though he will never admit it, Ted really thinks a lot of his big brother.* 虽然特德绝对不会承认这一点, 但是实际上他很尊崇自己的哥哥。在用 so 加强语气的场合以及在否定句中, a lot 一般改用 much。*Why do you think so much of that dog?* 为什么你那么珍视那条狗呢? *I don't think much of anyone who would treat his friends that way.* 我不喜欢象那样对待自己朋友的人。*I'm sorry to have to say it, but I don't think much of your friend Bob.* 很抱歉, 我不得不说我很讨厌你的朋友鲍勃。*The people don't seem to think very much of the President's foreign policy.* 人民似乎对总统的外交政策评价不很高。◇ like *someone* [*something*] very much / have a lot of respect for *someone* [*something*]

think better of *doing something* [ˌθɪŋk ˈbedərəv～] [口] **改变主意** 字面意义为"对做某件事情更好地思索"。乍看起来似乎是"做某事比较好", 实际上恰恰相反。本条最初的构思是: "本来打算做某件事情, 现在要更好地考虑"。后来进一步发展, 则变成"经过认真考虑、研究、观察, 结果不干了"的意味, 也就是"改变了原来的主意"。*After I had driven the old car for a while, I began to think better of buying it.* 我试开了一会儿那辆旧汽车, 开始改变主意, 打算不买它了。*When I saw Jim's behavior, I thought better of dating him.* 当我见到吉姆的举止动作的时候, 我改变主意, 打算不跟他约会了。又, think better of 的后边有时接 it 等代词, 从表面上来看, 很象下一条 THINK better of *something* [*someone*] 的句型。但是, 如果那个代词所代的是动名词, 仍然是本条条头的意思。*I had planned to enter that university, but after visiting the campus I thought better of it.* 我曾经计划入那所大学, 但是在参观校园之后, 我改变主意, 不打算到那里去上学了。这句话中的 it 所代的是 entering that university。*I was tempted to forget my* *studies and go to a movie tonight, but then I thought better of it.* 我本想今天晚上抛开书本去看电影,可是随后改变主意,不去了。这里的 it 是 forgetting my studies and going to a movie 的意思。如果 think better of 的后边不是接的动名词,而是一般的名词或代词,则是下一条 think better of *something* [*someone*] 的含义。◇ change *one's* mind (about *doing something*)

think better of *something* [*someone*] [ˌθɪŋk ˈbedərəv~] [口] **改变看法,觉得没有所想的那么坏** 本条习用语与带有动名词的 THINK better of *doing something* 不同,它的字面意义是"对于印象不佳的物或人,改变了看法,认为比较好"。把下面的例句与前一条的例句比较一下,就会明白这两条的差异了。本条中的 *something* 或 *someone* 处多用代词。*After I had driven the old car for a while, I began to think better of it.* 我试开了一会儿那辆旧汽车,我开始觉得它没有所想象的那么破。*When I saw Jim's behavior, I thought better of him.* 当我见到吉姆的举止动作的时候,我改变看法,认为他不那么坏了。*I had never particularly liked that university, but after visiting the campus I thought better of it.* 我从来没有特别喜欢过那所大学,但是在参观校园之后,我对它颇有好感了。◇ (come to) have a better opinion of *something* [*someone*]

thinking

put on *one's* **thinking cap** → CAP

thin-skinned

thin-skinned [ˈθɪnˈskɪ(ː)nd] [口] **神经过敏** 可以按照字面意义使用,例如:*Thin- skinned oranges are usually sweeter.* 一般来说,柑橘的皮越薄越甜。但多作比喻使用,而且只用于人。由于 thin-skinned 的人大多很难相处,所以与 THICK-SKINNED(胸怀宽阔) 不同,这一表达法经常含有贬意。例如:*Thin-skinned people are easily offended by what other people say about them.* 神经过敏的人一听到别人谈论他们的话就容易动怒。*You shouldn't be so thin- skinned. I'm sure Susan didn't mean to hurt you by speaking so frankly.* 你不要那么神经过敏。我敢肯定,苏珊那么坦率地讲话并没有伤害你的意图。此外,也常用 have a thin skin, *someone's* skin is thin 等形式。*I never dreamed that Luke had such a thin skin.* 我做梦也没有想到卢克是那样一个神经过敏的人。*Mark wouldn't make a good politician. His skin is too thin.* 马克不会成为优秀的政治家。他太爱神经过敏了。◇ overly sensitive to criticism [slights, taunts, etc.]

third

give *someone* **the third degree** → DEGREE

Thomas

a doubting Thomas [ə ˌdaudɪŋ ˈtɑ(ː)məs] [口] **多疑的人** 来自《圣经》的习用语之一。见《圣经·新约》中的《约翰福音》(John) 第 20 章 24～29 节。Thomas (多马) 是耶稣的十二使徒之一。当耶稣已经出现在他面前的时候,他还说,我不看见他手上的钉痕,不摸到他肋旁的枪迹,决不相信耶稣的复活。因此,Thomas 一词就成了"多疑的人"的代称。*You're just a doubting Thomas. You won't believe anything I tell you.* 你真是一个多疑的人啊。我告诉你什么事情你都不相信。*Dick is a doubting Thomas. It'll be difficult to convince him unless we show him proof.* 迪克是一个多疑的人。我们不拿出证据来,是很难说服他的。◇ a perpetual doubter

thought

on second thought [ɔ(ː)n ˈsekənd ˌθɔ(ː)t] [口] **经过重新考虑** → have second THOUGHTS (about *something*)

thoughts

give *someone* **second thoughts** (about *something*) [ˌgɪv ~ ˌsekənd ˈθɔːts] [口] **使某人重新考虑** → have second THOUGHTS (about *something*)

have second thoughts (about *something*) [ˌhæv ˌsekənd ˈθɔːts] [口] **重新考虑** 直译为"对某件事有第二种想法",亦即"重新

考虑"、"另打主意"。*Upon observing Jim's behavior, I began to have second thoughts about accepting his invitation to the dance.* 我观察吉姆的行为之后，开始重新考虑是否应该去参加他的舞会了。*For a while I was planning to follow my father's wishes and study law, but now I'm having second thoughts.* 我曾一度打算按照父亲的愿望学习法律，但是现在我在另打主意了。也有 make *someone* have second thoughts 的说法，意思是"使某人重新考虑"。*My brother's marital troubles are making me have second thoughts about getting married.* 我哥哥的婚姻纠纷使我重新考虑自己是否结婚的问题。与此同义的表达法有 give *someone* second thoughts。*The threatening weather gave us second thoughts about starting on our hike today.* 今天阴云密布，使我们重新考虑是否前去远足了。on second thought 也是习用语，意为"经过重新考虑"，但常有"还是……"的意思。*Would you mail these letters for me? —No, wait. On second thought, I think I'll do it myself.* 你能代我把这几封信寄出去吗？——不，等一等。还是我自己寄去吧。*I felt perhaps I should speak to her at once, but on second thought I decided to wait.* 我曾觉得也许我应该马上对她讲，但转而一想，还是决定等一等。另外，在英国英语中，thought 可以是复数，而讲 on second thoughts，但在美国口语里它常作单数，加 -s 反倒刺耳了。◇ wonder if *one* (really) should (*do something*) / think again

A penny for your thoughts. → PENNY

threads

a set of threads [ə ˌsetə'θreːdz] [话] **一套西服** 特指男性成套的西服，包括上衣和裤子。threads 是"线"，条头直译为"一套线"。相当轻松的表达法。*That's a nice set of threads you're wearing. Did you just get them?* 你穿的这套西服真不错呀。刚买的吗？◇ a suit / clothes

three-bagger

a three-bagger [ə 'θriː'bæːgər] [话] **(棒球) 三垒打** → a FOUR-BAGGER

three-time

a three-time loser [ə 'θriː ˌtaɪm 'luːzər] [话] **坐过三次牢的人** → a two-time LOSER

throat

cut *one's* own throat [ˌkʌt ~ ˌoun 'θrout] [口] **自己坑害自己** 直译为"自己抹自己的脖子"。*He cut his own throat with a knife.* 他用刀抹了自己的脖子。这是按照字面意义的用法。以下是作为比喻使用的例子。汉语这类说法很多，如"自寻死路"、"自取灭亡"、"自掘坟墓"、"自招灾祸"、"自找麻烦"等等，在翻译时可以斟酌使用。*I never refuse anyone's business simply because I don't like him. That'd just be cutting my own throat.* 我决不因为讨厌对方而拒绝跟他做生意，因为那将是自己坑害自己。*Bob was hoping to get a promotion this year, but he cut his own throat by losing his temper and quarreling with the president.* 鲍勃本来指望今年得到提升，但是由于发脾气，跟总经理吵嘴，自己断送了大好的前程。◇ hurt *one's* own interests / ruin *one's* own chances / undercut *one's* own position

feel a lump in *one's* throat → LUMP

jump down *someone's* throat (for *something*) [ˌdʒʌmp.daun ~ 'θrout] [话] **不分青红皂白地严厉训斥** 字面意义为"跳进某人的喉咙"。具体形象是："当对方打算说什么，正张开嘴的时候，斥责的声音向他的嗓子眼儿飞进去"。因此，多用于不听"说明"、"解释"的场合。主语当然是长辈或上级，至少是平等身份的人。*My mother is always jumping down my throat for not cleaning up my room.* 我一不打扫自己的房间，母亲就劈头盖脸地申斥我一顿。*Now wait a minute. Let me finish before you jump down my throat.* 等一等，你先别大嚷大叫，容我把话说完。*I won't have you jumping down my throat every time I do something you don't like.* 你不要在我做你不喜欢的事情的时候，总是唠唠叨叨指责个没完。常用 really 加强语气。*The boss really* *jumped down Ted's throat for missing the meeting.* 由于特德没有出席会议，老板不分青红皂白地狠狠训斥了他一大顿。◇ berate [get angry with] *someone*

ram *something* **down** *someone's* **throat** [ˌræ(ː)m ~ ˌdaun ~ ˈθrout] [话] **强加于人** 直译为"硬把某物塞到某人的喉咙里"。*That guy is forever trying to ram his opinions down other people's throats.* 那个家伙总是想把自己的意见强加于他人。*He is going to accept my conditions even if I have to ram them down his throat.* 哪怕必须动用强迫的手段，也要使他接受我的条件。另外，动词使用 ram (塞入)的场合最多，但也可以换用同义词 shove, cram, force, push, thrust 等。不过，在会话中很少使用 thrust，因为它使句子显得很生硬。◇ force *something* upon *someone*

throats

be at each other's throats (over *something*) [əˌdi(ː)ˌtʃʌðəz ˈθrouts] [口] **吵架** 字面意义为"相互在咬对方的喉颈"。这是大打出手的样子。但在实际上，最多不过是吵起来，一般不包括斗殴在内。*Those two guys are always at each other's throats over something.* 那两个家伙总是为了某件事情吵起来。*It's sad to see two brothers at each other's throats over their father's money.* 见到弟兄二人为了父亲的遗产相互争吵，实在可悲。*Break it up, you guys. Do you always have to be at each other's throats?* 你们两个家伙停火吧！你们非得永远相互争吵不可吗？*Tom and Jerry are never in the same room more than five minutes before they are at each other's throats. They've been enemies ever since they broke up as business partners.* 汤姆和杰里在一个房间里呆不到五分钟就会争吵起来。自从他们不再合伙搞生意之后，就成为仇人了。◇ be quarreling (with each other)

through

through and through [ˈθru(ː)ənˈθruː] [口] **完完全全** through (通过)的强调表达法，但是它的意思并不是"完全穿过去"，而是"彻头彻尾"。一般用于强调令人不愉快的事态，特别是多与形容词 wet (湿的)结合在一起。但并不限定如此。*I'm wet through and through.* 我被雨淋透了。*Someone left the windows open, and the pillows are wet through and through.* 有人没关窗户，枕头全都被雨淋透了。以下是未与 wet 结合的用例。*Politics in that country are rotten through and through.* 那个国家的政治已经腐败透了。*My father would never be happy living in the city. He's a farmer through and through.* 我父亲住在城里也决不会感到幸福。他是一个地地道道的农民。大家从以上的例句也可以断定，through and through 绝对不是"从中穿过去"的意思。因此，在你要讲"子弹完全从他的身体中穿过去了"的时候，不能说 The bullet went through and through his body. 正确的译文是 The bullet went completely through his body. ◇ completely ((放在被修饰语的前边)) / *Someone* will be a ~ till *he* dies.

throw

throw a race [game, etc.] [ˌθrouəˈreɪs / ˈgeɪm] [口 **搞假比赛故意输掉** 原为赛马用语。指在体育比赛或竞赛中选手有意识输掉的行为。切勿按字面意义解释为"放弃比赛或竞赛"。*The jockey was accused of throwing a race last year.* 那位职业赛马骑师被指责去年比赛时故意输掉。因为本条习用语大多用于特定的竞赛，所以也常用定冠词，作 the race。*The champion driver was under pressure to throw the race.* 最优秀的驾驶选手受到要他在比赛中故意输掉的压力。可以用 game 或者 match, fight, bout 等代替 race。*A stranger told me that if I didn't throw the game I'd never see my son alive again.* 一个陌生人告诉我说，如果我不在竞赛中故意输掉，就不会再见到我儿子活着的姿态了。*I'm sure Rod didn't lose intentionally. He would never throw a match.* 我敢肯定，罗德不是故意输掉的。他决不会故意输掉

比赛的。*The champ did so poorly that people wondered if he weren't being paid to throw the fight [bout].* 冠军在比赛中表现得太差劲了，人们怀疑他是否因得到钱而故意输掉的。◇ deliberately lose a race [game, match, etc.]

throw *someone* **over** (for *someone*) [ˌθrou~ˈouvər] [话] **抛弃情人或朋友** 一般用于有了新欢而抛弃旧情人的场合。例如：*Harriet threw Tom over.* 哈丽特抛弃了汤姆。在应用于男女关系时，常在后边接续 for *someone* (所换的新人)。本条整个的意思是："抛弃某人，换了……"。*A: I thought you were still dating Deldee. B: No, She threw me over for some new guy.* 甲：我以为你还跟戴尔迪搞对象哪。乙：不，她甩了我，又跟别的小伙子交朋友了。*You may have me dancing on a string, baby, but just don't try to throw me over. Not unless you want a nice new wooden kimono.* 你可以任意操纵我，宝贝儿，但是可不要打算把我甩掉。除非你想要一副漂亮的新棺材。这一表达法首先令人联想到"男女关系"，但也有仅仅表示"抛弃(人)"的场合，例如：*You can't throw me over like this. We've been friends too long.* 你不能象这样抛弃我。咱们已经是多年的老朋友了。*When Jim became rich, he threw his old friends over and started running with a new crowd.* 吉姆发财之后，抛弃了旧友，开始与一帮新认识的人交往了。◇ jilt *someone* / abandon *someone*

throw up [ˌθrouˈʌ(ː)p] [口] **呕吐(吃下的东西)** → lose *one's* DINNER

be within a stone's throw of *someplace* [ˌwɪðɪnə ˈstounz ˈθrouəv ~] [口] **距离不远** 字面意义为"扔块石头能达到的地方"，强调距离很近，与实际上扔块石头是否能达到无关。这一表达法有三个基本形式：①A is within a stone's throw of B. ②A is only a stone's throw from B. ③It's only a stone's throw from A to B [to A from B]. 全都是"A 与 B 距离很近"的意思。条头虽然以①的形式为代表，但三者均为人们所常用。②、③的 only 是加强语气。另外还用 just 或 merely。这两种形式一般添加 only 或 just，而①的形式恰恰相反，大多不加这类的词。*There are many good eating places within a stone's throw of her apartment.* 在她的公寓附近，有许多很好的小吃店。*His house is just a stone's throw from where we live.* 他的家离我们的住处近极了。*It's just a stone's throw from Beijing to Tianjin.* 北京与天津距离很近。在②的场合，有时省略 from B，例如：*His house is just a stone's throw. Why don't we walk?* 他家很近，咱们步行去吧？也有时换用 away，例如：*Compared to the distance from China to America, Japan is only a stone's throw away.* 与中国和美国之间的距离相比，日本只不过是一水之隔而已。◇ be very near [not very far from] *someplace*

thumb

have a green thumb [ˌhævə ˈgriːn ˈθʌ(ː)m] [口] **有高超的种植才能** green thumb 的字面意义为"绿色的拇指"。作为比喻，意味着"有培育花木、蔬菜等植物的才能"。*Mr. White has a green thumb. His garden is always beautiful.* 怀特先生有搞园艺的本领。他家的庭院总是很美的。*I wish I had a green thumb like you. I can never get anything to grow.* 我但愿有你那样搞园艺的才能。我种什么都不生长。以上两例是用于"园艺"，也可以用于"栽培大田作物"，例如：*A farmer has to have not only lots of land but a green thumb as well.* 一个农民光有大量土地不行，他还必须有高超的种地本领。有时用 have 以外的动词。*It takes [You need] a green thumb to grow cabbages as large as that.* 要培育出那么大个的元白菜，必须有高超的种植才能。◇ have a talent for making things grow

have *someone* **under** *one's* **thumb** [ˌhæv ~ ˌʌndər ~ ˈθʌ(ː)m] [口] **把某人捏在手心里** 直译为"把某人按在拇指下边"。含有"随时可以碾死他"的意味。本条习用语用于对某人具有决定性的影响的场合。*Mr. Stokes is a big man in this town. He's even got the mayor under* *his thumb.* 斯托克斯先生是本城的大亨。连市长都捏在他的手心里。也常用于掌握对方弱点的场合。*The sergeant had had the second lieutenant under his thumb ever since he learned of the lieutenant's past.* 军士自从了解少尉的历史之后,就把他捏在自己的手心里了。be under *someone's* thumb 的形式是"受某人支配"的意思。*He's under my [his wife's] thumb.* 他受我[他的妻子]的支配。◇ have *someone* under *one's* control [influence]

stick out like a sore thumb [ˌstɪ'kaut laɪkə ˌso(:)r 'θʌ(:)m] [话] **特别扎眼** stick out 是"显著";sore thumb 是"受伤的拇指"。这一表达法的来源是:拇指受伤要比其他任何手指受伤都更惹人注目。它强调"不美好的事物特别显眼"的意思。*The dilapidated old house stuck out like a sore thumb among the other, modern houses on the street.* 那座荒废失修的老房子在大街上其他现代化的房屋中间显得特别扎眼。*If you want to be inconspicuous, you'd better shave off your beard. It makes you stick out like a sore thumb.* 如果你不想引人注目,最好是把你的络腮胡子刮去。那太扎眼啦。不仅用于有形的东西,也可以这样讲:*When I first arrived in America, my accent stuck out like a sore thumb.* 当我初到美国的时候,我的口音特别引人注目。有时用 stand out 代替 stick out,意思不变。也可以说 stick out a mile,大致同义。◇ be very noticeable

thumb *one's* **nose at** *someone* [ˌθʌm ～ 'nouzət ～] [口] **嗤之以鼻** → thumb *one's* NOSE at *something*

thumb *one's* **nose at** *something* → NOSE

thumbs

be all thumbs [ˌɔ:l 'θʌ(:)mz] [口] **笨手笨脚** 直译为"全都是拇指 (thumb)"。这当然不会灵巧了。*When it comes to driving a car, I'm all thumbs.* 要讲开汽车,我简直笨透了。这是泛指动作不灵活。但一般用于表示"指头不能随意动作"的意思。有时指"生来如此"或者"不熟练"。例如:*Paul has always been all thumbs.* 保罗生来就笨手笨脚。*I've just begun to learn to knit, so I'm still all thumbs.* 我刚开始学织东西,因此手还不大听用。另外,也常用于表示由于着急或紧张而手不听用的情况。*Billy tried to fix the broken vase before his mother came home, but he was all thumbs.* 比利打算在母亲回来前把打坏的花瓶修理好,可他的手完全不听使唤了。可以用 become 代替 be,如 *Whenever I'm tense I become all thumbs.* 我一紧张,手脚就不灵了。◇ lack dexterity / be very clumsy

turn thumbs down on *something* [ˌtə(:)rn 'θʌ(:)mz'daunɔn ～] [口] **不赞成** 这一表达法来源于古罗马的一种风俗:在角斗场上,皇帝如果对失败的斗士翘起拇指,那意味着叫他活下去,如果把拇指的指尖向下,那意味着"杀"。现在,"把拇指的指尖向下"则表示不赞成某一提议或者拒绝某一要求。*My husband turned thumbs down on our building a new house.* 我丈夫不赞成我们建一座新房子。*Dad turned thumbs down on my using the car.* 爸爸没允许我用汽车。有用 to 代替 on 的情况,但极罕见。◇ not agree to *something*

twiddle *one's* **thumbs** [ˌtwɪdl ～ 'θʌ(:)mz] [口] **无所事事** 本来指"两个拇指互相捻弄"的动作。英美等国的人在闲极无聊或者焦急不安的时候常有这样捻弄拇指的习惯。*When the boss starts to twiddle his thumbs, you'd better watch out. It means he's beginning to get impatient.* 当老板开始捻弄拇指的时候,你可要多加小心。那表明他又开始焦躁不安了。转作比喻使用,表示"无所事事"、"闲度时光"的意思。在这一场合,并不伴有捻弄拇指的动作。*Those guys just sit around twiddling their thumbs while we do all the work.* 当我们拼命工作的时候,那些家伙竟坐在那里闲呆着。本条习用语常用于表示"无所事事地等待着"的状态。有时句子中并没有表示"等待"的文字,但是实际上含有这样的意味。*I'm going to call him again. I'm tired of twiddling my thumbs waiting for an answer.* 我再给他打一次电话看看。我白白在这里等待回话，实在腻味透了。*Because of bad weather, we had to spend six hours twiddling our thumbs at the airport.* 由于天气恶劣，我们不得不在机场白白蹲了六个小时。*You can sit around and twiddle your thumbs if you want to. I'm going to find out what's going on.* 你愿意四平八稳地闲呆着，那随你的便。我得出去看看外面的情况如何了。◇ do nothing

tick

be (as) full as a tick [əz ˈfuləzə ˈtɪ(:)k] [话] **肚皮都要胀破了** tick 学名"蜱"，俗称"壁虱"。本条直译为"象吸了血的壁虱那样，肚子鼓得圆圆的"。转义"吃得极饱"。*A: Would you like something more to eat? B: Thank you, but I couldn't eat another bite. I'm as full as a tick.* 甲：你还喜欢吃点什么吗？乙：谢谢，但是我再也吃不下去了，我的肚皮都要胀破啦。这一习用语不但没有使人从 tick 一词产生肮脏的感觉，反倒是强调 be full 的一种令人忍俊不禁的表现。*After the big Christmas dinner, we were all as full as ticks.* 在圣诞节的盛大晚宴之后，我们的肚皮都要胀破了。as ～ as 中的前一个 as 在会话中常因语调关系而省略。*No wonder Jack is so fat. He always eats until he's full as a tick.* 无怪乎杰克那么胖，他总是吃到快撑破肚皮才算罢休。◇ be completely full [satiated]

what makes *someone* tick [ˌhwʌtˌmeɪks ～ ˈtɪ(:)k] [话] **一个人的主要动机** tick 是"钟表嘀嗒嘀嗒响"。使钟表嘀嗒嘀嗒响的是发条，那么使人活动的东西是什么呢？这一习用语是把人比做钟表，所谓"使人嘀嗒嘀嗒响的东西"系指人的基本想法，亦即动机。因为是"基本想法"，所以这一表达法不能用于一时的冲动或心血来潮。而且，一般是在不大了解某人的动机是什么的场合使用。*The latest biography of Abraham Lincoln isn't very good. Even when you've finished reading it, you still feel you're not sure what made him tick.* 最近出版的关于林肯的传记写得不太好。你把整本书读完了，还觉得摸不清林肯活动的主要动机是什么。*Sometimes I wonder what makes that guy tick. He often demands high fees for his work, but at other times he'll do the same work for practically nothing.* 有时候，我对那个家伙的内心活动感到莫名其妙。他对于自己的工作往往要求很高的报酬，但是有时做同样的工作，他又等于连一分钱也不要。本条习用语可以应用于人以外的事物，在这一场合，当然不是"基本想法"，而是"主要动力"的意思。*There are few men today who really know what makes the world tick.* 现在很少有人真正了解世界运转的主要动力是什么。◇ what motivates *someone* / how *someone's* mind works

what makes *something* tick [ˌhwʌtˌmeɪks ～ ˈtɪ(:)k] [话] **主要动力** → what makes *someone* TICK

ticker

a ticker [ə ˈtɪkər] [话] **心脏** ticker 是"滴嗒滴嗒 (tick-tock) 响的东西"。tick-tock 一般使人联想到钟表，但 ticker 却不是钟表，而是指"人的心脏"的一种轻松说法。主要是男性用语。*The doc says I've got a bad ticker.* 大夫说我有心脏病。◇ a heart

tickled

be tickled pink → PINK

ticklish

a ticklish situation → SITUATION

tide

turn the tide [ˌtə(:)rnðə ˈtaɪd] [口] **扭转局势** tide 是"潮"或"潮流"。本条字面意义为"改变潮流"。但是，加上 suddenly 一类的词就产生了速度感，便具有"把局势一下子扭转过来"的意义了。*We were losing badly, but Jake's four-run homer in the seventh inning suddenly turned the tide and we won by a wide margin.* 我们原来输得很惨，但是在第七回合，杰克的本垒打连得四分，把局势一下子扭转过来，反败为大胜了。这是 turn the tide 与 suddenly 或 completely 一起使用的情况。如果只是本条条头的话，则与变

化的速度或势头无关,因此仅能译作"扭转局势"。*The company was on the verge of bankruptcy, but our desperate effort to improve sales finally, little by little, began to turn the tide.* 公司曾濒临破产的边缘,但由于我们拼命努力增加销售额,终于使局势一点一点地开始扭转过来了。*The Battle of Midway turned the tide of the Pacific War.* 中途岛战役改变了太平洋战争的局势。*The Confederate Army fought bravely but was unable to turn the tide against the better-equipped Yankees.* 南部联军作战勇敢,但是在与装备较好的北军对阵中未能扭转局势。◇ reverse the situation / change [reverse] the course of events [of the war, etc.]

tie

tie *someone* **down** [ˌtaɪ~ ˈdaun] [口] **捆住手脚** 可以按照字面意义使用,如: *The little people tied Gulliver down.* 小人们把格列佛捆绑起来了。作为比喻使用时,捆绑所用的东西不是"绳子",而是"规章"、"工作"、"家务"、"义务"以及"某种情况"等。经过捆绑之后,任何事情都不能做。本条与 tie *someone's* HANDS 表面上相似,但用法有所不同,务请读者注意。tie *someone's* hands 不是五花大绑,而是捆住一个地方,使其达不到某一种目的。tie *someone* down 则多用于五花大绑,使人完全不能行动的场合。两者均常用被动语态。*We are tied down by a lot of rules that prevent us from doing our work properly.* 我们受一大套规章制度的束缚,根本不能正常进行我们的工作。*I'm so tied down by housework that I don't get out much these days.* 由于家务缠身,我最近几乎不能出门。另外,在实际上"身体不能动弹"的场合,有时不是被绳子捆住,而是被"炮火"封住。*Enemy gunfire tied the soldiers down on the beach.* 敌人的炮火使得士兵们在海边上动不得身了。◇ prevent *someone* from acting freely

tie one on → ONE

tie *someone* **up** [ˌtaɪ ~ ˈʌ(:)p] [话] **使某人动不了窝儿** → be TIED up (with *something*)

tied

be fit to be tied → FIT

be tied up (with *something*) [ˌtaɪˈdʌ(:)p] [话] **由于忙而脱不开身** 意思是:就象手脚都被绳子捆住 (tied up) 一样,由于工作忙、有约会等等,腾不出身来。*The meeting is going to tie me up all today.* 今天开会,我一整天都动不了窝儿。如这一例句所示,可以用主动语态,但一般是用被动语态。*I'm tied up right now. Ask him to call back after lunch.* 我现在正忙得脱不开身。叫他下午再来电话吧。*I'm tied up with a previous appointment this afternoon. How about tomorrow?* 今天下午我已经有约会了,没有空儿。明天如何? ◇ be busy

tight

sit tight [ˌsɪˈt:aɪt] [话] **耐心等待** 字面意义为"好好地坐下",实际上与坐或不坐没有直接关系。例如: *Let's just sit tight and see what our opponents will do next.* 我们不要动,只瞧着敌方下一步怎么办好啦。根据上下文,sit 一词可能真是坐着,也可能作为比喻表示"安安静静,一动不动",两种解释全说得通。但是,一般来说,这一表达法总是用于"为了弄清楚事情怎样发展而耐心观望"的场合。*I'm sure they saw our signal. All we have to do is sit tight and wait for help to arrive.* 他们一定看见咱们的信号啦。我们所要做的只是安下心来,等待前来营救而已。*It would be a mistake to show your hand too soon. Just sit tight. They'll come back sooner or later with a better offer, I'm sure.* 千万不要过早摊牌。一定要耐心等待。我敢肯定,他们迟早会回来出更高价钱的。也可以用极轻松的语调说: *Sit tight. I'll be right back.* 你乖乖地等着。我马上就回来。*Maybe he's waiting for us on the other side of the station. You sit tight. I'll go and see if I can find him.* 他也许在车站的另一面等我们哪。你在这里呆着,我去看看他在不在。◇ be patient / wait (patiently) /

(you) wait here

time

beat *someone's* **time** (with *someone*) [ˌbi(ː)t ~ ˈtaɪm] [话] **勾搭别人的女朋友**这里的 time 是 make TIME with *someone* (→)的 time。beat 是"抢在前头"。本条原意是"抢在对方前头向着目标前进"。所谓"目标",当然指"女性"。因此,除特殊情况外,主语总是"男性"。*You'd better watch out. I hear Stu is beating your time with Sally.* 你最好是当心点儿。我听说司徒去勾搭你的萨莉了。这是 20 世纪 30 年代开始流行的表达法,高中生、大学生等年轻人使用。*You stay away from my girl. If I see you trying to beat my time, you'll be sorry.* 你不要靠近我的女朋友。如果你胆敢去勾搭她,我会叫你后悔的。*I wish I could trust Frances more, but it seems that whenever my back is turned, some other guy starts beating my time.* 我很愿意对弗兰西斯更信任一些,但是,只要我一转脸儿,似乎就有别的人勾搭她。◇ become more intimate with *someone* than *someone* (is) / get overly friendly [intimate] (with *someone*)

bide *one's* **time** [ˌbaɪd ~ ˈtaɪm] [口] **等待良好的机会** bide 是书面语言,与 wait 同义。但是,bide *one's* time 却是口头用语。意思是"等待有利时机的到来",经常含有"从容不迫"的意味。换句话说,不是瞪着眼到处找机会,而是坐观形势发展,任其自然。*Conditions are not yet favorable for us to make our move. We will just have to bide our time.* 我们还没有开始行动的有利条件,只能静候良好的时机了。*I longed for revenge, but I knew I couldn't be impatient. If I bided my time, an opportunity was sure to come.* 我曾渴望报仇雪恨,但是我知道不能够急躁。只要我耐心等待,好机会必然会到来的。*Rhett Butler realized that if he asked Scarlett to marry him too soon she would make a fool of him, so he decided to bide his time.* 雷特·巴特勒认识到:如果他急着向斯卡利特求婚,她一定会作弄他,因此,他决定耐心等待好机会来临了。◇ wait for a (more) favorable opportunity

the big time [ðə ˈbɪg ˌtaɪm] [话] **第一流** 这里的 time 并没有时间的意思。勉强翻译,可以说是"等级"、"标准"、"水平"。加个 big,就是在某一领域"出类拔萃"的意思。但不包含善恶的观念,如说"论电影,好莱坞是世界之最(第一流)","论犯罪,黑手党堪称冠军(第一流)"。the big time 在商业、体育运动、音乐等各种领域里都可以应用,其中包含着"大家公认"的意思。这是一个非常轻松的说法。*Of all the hundreds of professional music groups playing, very few manage to hit the big time.* 在当前经常演出的几百个职业乐团中,只有极少数能努力成为第一流的乐团。*Bill's outstanding business acumen and forceful personality soon brought him into the big time as an executive in a large electronics company.* 由于具有杰出的商业头脑和坚强个性,比尔很快就成为一家大的电子公司的首脑人物了。下面是应用于强盗集团的例子。*If we succeed in this heist, we'll be in the big time.* 如果这次抢劫成功,我们在哥儿们中就露脸了。big-time 是形容词,也可以应用于不同的领域,意思是"有名的,杰出的,重要的,一流的"。*June's brother is on a big-time television show in New York.* 琼的哥哥在纽约的一部很有名的电视剧中出场了。*People don't like those big-time politicians in Washington telling them what to do.* 美国人不喜欢华盛顿的那些大政客们对他们指手划脚。*Her father is a big-time executive or something in some trading company.* 她的父亲是某个贸易公司的大经理什么的。*Biff's ambition is to become a big-time baseball player.* 比弗梦想成为一个著名的棒球运动员。◇ the top circles

chow time [ˈtʃau ˌtaɪm] [话] **开饭时间** *I always get hungry before chow time.* 我总是不到开饭时间肚子就饿了。*Let's go. It's chow time.* 咱们走吧,到开饭时间啦。有时连成一个词,写作 chow-time。

→ CHOW ◇ mealtime / time to eat

every time *one* **turns around** [ˌevri ˌtaɪm ～ ˌtə(ː)rnzə ˈraund] [话] **经常不断地** 直译为“每当自己转身的时候”。因为一个人每天不知道要转多少次身，所以本条习用语意味着“老是……”、“总是……”、“没完没了”，多少带有不耐烦的心情。*I'm sorry, Billy, but I can't be taking you to the movies every time I turn around.* 对不起，比利，我不能一天到晚老带你去看电影啊。*Jack said that every time he turns around, his wife wants him to buy her a new dress.* 据杰克说，他的妻子经常不断地叫他给买新衣服。也可以用 forever 表示同样的意味，但是此词与 every time *one* turns around 不同，经常与进行时一起使用，而且放在动词的前边。如上边两个例句用 forever 要这样讲：～ I can't be forever taking you to the movies. / Jack said that his wife is forever wanting him to ～. ◇ always ((用法与 forever 同))

(I'm telling you) for the last time [(ˌaɪmˈtelənjə) fərðə ˈlæ(ː)sːˈtaɪm] [话] **我跟你说过多少回啦?** 首先比较一下使用 for the last time 的下列两个句子。*I saw her for the last time on April the fifteenth.* 我最后一次见到她是在 4 月 15 日。*For the last time, we're not buying a new car.* 这句话不是“这是最后一次，我们再也不买新汽车了。”的意思，而是“跟你说过多少次啦? 我说不买新汽车就是不买。”也就是说，可以认为在 For 的前边省略了 I'm telling you。这个 for the last time 是强调它后面语句的表达法，直译是“我说这句话是最后一次了”。在表示“过去已经说过多次，现在不愿意再费唇舌”的意思时使用。含有“忍无可忍”的意味，亦即“跟你说多少次啦，还不明白?”、“怎么说你才会明白哪?” *I'm telling you for the last time, stop pestering me with your stupid questions.* 我跟你说过多少次啦? 别再拿你那些愚蠢的问题来烦我啦。*For the last time, I'm not interested in going to the beach this Sunday.* 跟你说过多少次啦? 我下星期日不想去海边，说不去就是不去。◇ How many times do I have to tell you? / I'm tired of telling you

have a time [ˌhævə ˈtaɪm] [话] **遇到很大困难** 字面意义为“有一个时间”，实际上是“有一个吃苦的时间”。一般用于表示“遇到很大困难”或“弄得狼狈不堪”的意思。*I had a time with this problem today.* 今天在解这道习题时我遇到很大困难。大多加副词 quite 或 real 等。*I had quite a time with the children today.* 今天我被孩子们弄得真够受的。*The company had quite a time during the oil shock.* 在石油危机期间，公司曾经遇到极大的困难。*We had a real time getting home from the airport last night.* 昨天晚上从机场回家的时候，我们被弄得狼狈不堪。有时，“有一个时间”是“有一段愉快的时间”的意思。在这一场合，必须加 quite 或 real。反过来说，如果不带 quite 或 real，就不能作“有一段愉快的时间”解释。*My parents had quite a time in Hawaii this summer. They swam every day and made many new friends.* 今年夏天我的父母在夏威夷度过了非常愉快的时光。他们每天游泳，并且交了好多新朋友。这一段话是由两个句子组成，根据第二个句子就可以判断出前一句的 have quite a time 是“有一段愉快的时间”。如果没有 They swam ～以下的叙述，就难以判断在夏威夷究竟是“狼狈不堪”还是“愉快已极”了。→ have the TIME of *one's* life ◇ have a (very) difficult time

have the time of *one's* **life** [ˌhævðə ˈtaɪməv ～ ˈlaɪf] [话] **度过无比快乐的时光** 这是强调 have a good time (有一个快乐的时光)的表达法。the time of *one's* life 可以认为是 the best time of *one's* life 省略了其中的 best 一词，字面意义为“一生最美好的时光”。为惯用语。*I had the time of my life at the Mardi Gras in New Orleans.* 我在新奥尔良度过狂欢节的最后一天，实在快乐极了。*My parents wrote that they are having the time of their lives in Europe this summer.* 我的父母来信说，他们今年夏天在欧洲度过无比快乐的时光。*The children always* *have the time of their lives when they visit their grandparents' home.* 孩子们到了祖父母家里,总是有无比快乐的时光。有时作反语使用,意思是"费了很大的劲",大有"经过千辛万苦"的意味。*I had the time of my life trying to get this thing through customs.* 我费了九牛二虎之力才使这东西通过了海关。在这一场合,可以认为是强调 have a TIME 的说法。◇ have a wonderful time

have time on *one's* **hands** [ˌhæv ˈtaɪmɔn ~ ˌhæ(ː)ndz] [口] **有充分的时间** → have *something* on *one's* HANDS

have time to kill [ˌhæv ˈtaɪm təˈkɪ(ː)l] [口] **还有空余时间** → kill TIME

in the nick of time → NICK

It's high time *someone did something.* [ˌɪts ˈhaɪ ˈtaɪm ~] [口] **现在是应该采取行动的时候了** 有"为时已晚"的意味。这里的 high 不是"高",而与 high summer (盛夏)和 the high Middle Ages (中世纪最盛期)中的 high 相同,是"全盛(时期)"的意思。如果采取条头 It's high time *someone did something.* 的形式,那就不是表示"全盛(时期)",而带有"稍微晚了一点儿"的感觉。请注意:永远要用 *someone did something* 这样的过去式。另外,在讲"为时已晚"的时候,可以指以年为单位的长时间,也可以指以分为单位的短时间。请看下边的例句:*It's high time the government did something about the employment problem.* 政府应该着手解决失业问题了。*Your brother has been living with us for two months now without working. It's high time he found a job.* 你弟弟游手好闲,在咱们家里已经住两个月了。现在他应该去找个工作啦。*It's almost ten o'clock. It's high time you started studying.* 快到十点钟了,你应该开始学习啦。*It's high time we left. If we don't hurry, we'll be late.* 我们应该动身了。如果不快点儿,我们就要迟误啦。◇ It's time to stop dallying and *do something.*

kill time [ˌkɪlˈtaɪm] [口] **消磨时间** 直译为"杀时间",意思是"在要干某种事情之前,打发走剩余的时间"。一般是在下一步行动之前无所事事的场合使用。*Since I arrived an hour early, I killed time by taking a walk in a nearby park.* 因为早到了一小时,我到附近的公园里散步消磨时间。*A: Are you busy now? B: No, I'm just killing time until the meeting.* 甲:你现在忙吗? 乙:不忙。我等着开会,正在消磨时间哪。也常用 have time to kill 的说法,意思是"在下一步行动之前有闲工夫"。*Having some time to kill, I dropped in at a bookstore.* 因为还有一点闲工夫,我顺便走进一家书店。*You don't have any time to kill. Your exam starts in only thirty minutes.* 你没有一点儿闲工夫了。只剩三十分钟考试就开始啦。*Our son always wants to kill time even when he doesn't have any time to kill.* 我家的儿子甚至在没有任何闲工夫的时候也要消磨时间。可以用表示时间单位的名词 hour, day 等代替 time。*We have three hours to kill until the train leaves. Let's go to a movie.* 到开车时间还有三个钟头,咱们去看电影吧。◇ beguile the time

Long time no see. [ˈlɔ(ː)ŋ ˈtaɪm ˌnouˈsiː] [话] **久违久违** 正式说法应该是 I've not seen you for a long time. 本条习用语原为在美国的外籍人士的笨拙说法,不合英语语法。后来成为通用的寒暄话,带诙谐意味,在亲密无间的伙伴们之间使用。第二次世界大战期间大为流行,后来稍见衰微,但至今仍然常常入耳。*Hey, Clint, long time no see. Where in the world have you been keeping yourself?* 嘿,克林特,好久不见啦。你究竟藏到哪儿去了? ◇ It's been a long time (since I've seen you).

make good time [ˌmeɪkˌgudˈtaɪm] [口] **顺利前进** 一般用于汽车,但有时也用于其他交通工具或步行者。原形是不加 good 的 make time,但现在大多使用 make good time 的形式。*We made good time on the freeway. [We made time on the freeway.]* 我们在高速公路上开车很顺利。make time 本是"腾出时间"亦即"从从容容"的意思。如果"顺利前进",当然就会"从从容容"了。虽然是讲"顺利前进",但与速度并没有直接关系。"顺利前进"的意味是"按预定的时间到达某一地点"。因此,虽然在个别路段开车缓慢,但总的来说仍保持预期的速度,这就可以讲 make good time;在大城市中心的行车高峰时间,哪怕时速平均只有二十公里,也可以说 make good time。 *We made good time until about two hours out of Dallas, then we ran into a snowstorm.* 我们从达拉斯开车出来,顺利前进约两个小时,然后就遇见暴风雪了。 *The tangle of vines and undergrowth in the forest prevented the hikers from making very good time.* 在森林中,爬藤和草丛的缠绕使徒步远足的人们不能很顺利地前进。good 有时用比较级。 *We'll make better time once we get out of the city.* 只要我们出了城,就会更顺利地往前开了。good 的反义语是 poor。 *We made poor time over the narrow country roads.* 因为乡村的公路很窄,我们未能顺利地开车前进。但是,这句话一般仍然是运用 make good time 的否定形式来表达: *We didn't make very good time over the narrow country roads.* 另外,可以用 excellent, great 等形容词代替 good。 *We made excellent [great] time until our plane ran into a strong head wind.* 我们的飞机在遇到强烈的顶头风之前,一直非常顺利地飞行。以上全是讲交通工具或步行者"顺利前进"的例子,但有时也可以用以表示"工作顺利进行"的意思。 *Yesterday the work didn't go very smoothly, but today we're making pretty good time.* 昨天,工作进展不很顺利,但是今天我们却是一帆风顺了。◇ maintain satisfactory speed

make time with *someone* [.meɪk 'taɪmwɪð ~] [话] **与女人亲热** make time 有 make good TIME(顺利前进)(→) 的意味。本条习用语基本上是由 make good time 发展开来,原来的意思是"与某人的关系顺利进展"。最初只用于勾搭别人的老婆或者情人的场合,如说: *You'd better keep an eye on Ralph. I hear he's been making time with your girl.* 你注意一下拉尔夫为妙。我听说他在跟你的女朋友眉来眼去哪。现在不以此为限,应用较广泛。不过,究竟"热乎"到什么程度,只能由上下文来定。 *You'd better not try to make time with me. My husband's a professional wrestler.* 你最好别打算跟我调情。我丈夫是一个职业拳击师。这只是口头勾搭的程度。 *Brian was in the back seat of the car making time with his girl friend.* 布赖恩在汽车的后排座上与他的女朋友亲热。这就可能深了一步,难免搂搂抱抱了。 *You made time with Molly at the dance last night? That's nothing to brag about. Anybody can do that.* 昨天晚上在舞会上,你跟莫莉亲热了一番吗?那没什么可吹嘘的。任何人都能做到这点。 *Steve is out in the kitchen making time with that cute maid.* 史蒂夫跑到厨房里,在跟那个漂亮的女仆调情呢。◇ court [get overly friendly with, get intimate with, get amorous with, hug and kiss, etc.] *someone*

not give *someone* **the time of day** [nɑt .gɪv ~ ðə'taɪməv 'deɪ] [口] **连看都不看一眼** the time of day 原是"寒暄"的意思。条头的整个意思原是"不向某人问候"(→ pass the TIME of day)。指由于厌恶、轻蔑、繁忙而完全无视某人的存在的态度。 *Since Maria became famous, she doesn't give her old friends the time of day.* 自从玛丽亚成名以后,她对老朋友连看都不看一眼。这是使用 don't 的形式。一般采取 wouldn't 或者 won't 的形式,例如: *I tried to apologize for having ruined his plans, but he wouldn't give me the time of day.* 我打算为我毁了他的计划的事向他道歉,但是他连看都不看我一眼。在强调时可以加 even。 *You'd better have an introduction if you want to talk with Mr. Lerner. Otherwise he probably won't even give you the time of day.* 你如果想跟勒纳先生谈话,最好有人为你引见。否则的话,他很可能连看都不看你一眼。 *Me, date Fensterwald? You must have rocks in your head. I wouldn't even give that creep the time of day.* 你说我跟芬斯特瓦尔德搞对象?你的头脑一定出毛病了。我对那样讨厌的

家伙根本就不理睬。◇ not (even) speak to *someone*

pass the time of day (with *someone*) [ˌpæ(ː)sðə ˈtaɪməˈdeɪ] [口] **闲聊天儿** 旧时，除 Good morning. 和 Good afternoon. 外，人们也常讲 Good time of day. 因此，便把"互相问候"说成 pass the time of day。后来，the time of day 失去"问候"的意思，而被解释为"一天里的某一段时间"。pass 也从"相互"的意思转成了"度过"。现在，本条习用语已经不是表示"相互问候"，而是表示"大家闲聊天儿，悠然自得地度过一段时间"。往往是指在碰到他人的时候，经过寒暄之后，站着闲聊一阵子，但并不限定如此。如果前往朋友的住宅或办公室，闲谈天气、气候、商情、相互的近况等"不着边际的日常琐事"，也叫做 pass the time of day。*People were standing here and there passing the time of day.* 人们这一团那一伙地站着聊大天儿。*John and I are old friends. He often drops by my office for an hour or so just to pass the time of day.* 约翰跟我是老朋友。他常顺便来到我的办公室，闲聊上一个来钟头再走。*I was sitting in my living room passing the time of day with Mrs. Brown when suddenly a strange man walked in.* 我正坐在起居室里跟布朗太太闲聊天儿，忽然一个陌生的男子走了进来。*A: Excuse me. Am I interrupting an important conference? B: Not at all. We were just passing the time of day.* 甲：请原谅。是不是我打扰了你们重要的会谈？乙：一点也不。我们只是在闲聊天儿。另外，使用 the time of day 的习用语还有 not give *someone* the TIME of day。◇ engage in casual conversation

play for time [ˌpleɪfər ˈtaɪm] [话] **故意拖延时间** 直译为"为了得到时间而玩各种把戏"。在为了使事情向有利于自己的方向发展而找某种理由故意拖延时间的场合使用。*There was absolutely no reason why they couldn't have signed the contract right away. They were only playing for time in hopes of making a better deal elsewhere.* 他们绝对没有不立即签订合同的理由。他们只是故意拖延时间，指望从别处搞到更好的交易。*Knowing that the police would arrive shortly, I played for time by telling the burglar that I couldn't find my wife's jewelry.* 我知道警察马上就会到来，所以故意拖延时间，告诉强盗我找不到妻子的宝石。◇ use delaying tactics

time hangs heavy on *someone's* **hands** [ˌtaɪm ˌhæŋz ˈhevɪən ~ ˈhæːndz] [话] **时间过得太沉闷了** 字面意义为"时间在某人手中很沉重地往下坠"，亦即"时间成为沉重的负担"。*Time hung heavy on our hands during the long winter we spent in the Antarctic.* 在南极度过漫长的冬天的时候，我们感到实在沉闷极了。*A person with imagination never finds time hanging heavy on his hands.* 一个想象力丰富的人永远不会感到时间过得沉闷。*With time hanging heavy on my hands, I decided to build a sailboat.* 由于时间过得太无聊，我决心建造一只帆船了。也可以用 too 来加强语气，例如：*Many young people get into trouble because, with no household chores and little homework, time hangs too heavy on their hands.* 许多青少年所以惹事生非，是因为不但没有家务缠身，又少有家庭作业，时间过得太沉闷了。另有类似的表达法 have time on *one's* hands，但远远没有条头的英语语气强烈（→ have *something* on *one's* HANDS）。◇ *someone* has (much) more time than *he* knows how to use

Time is of the essence. [ˈtaɪmɪzəvðə ˈesənts] [口] **时间最宝贵** → be of the ESSENCE

tin

have a tin ear → EAR

a tin lizzie [ə ˌtɪnˈlɪzi] [话] **破旧小汽车** → a FLIVVER

tip

be on the tip of *someone's* **tongue** [ɔnðə ˌtɪpəv ~ ˈtʌ(ː)ŋ] [口] **在舌头尖上** 有两种用法：①表示"话已经到了嘴边上，可是想不起来了"。②表示"话已经到嘴边

上,差一点没说出来”,即汉语的“话到舌尖留半句”的意思。有些英汉词典只列入②的意义,但一般美国人首先联想到的则是①的意义。在实际上,当你遇到这一习用语时,如果不根据上下文,就无法判断是 ①还是 ②的意思。请比较下面两个例句。*Her name was on the tip of my tongue, but for the life of me I couldn't recall it.* 她的名字就在我的嘴边上,可是我无论如何也想不起来了。*His name was on the tip of my tongue, but I refrained from saying it just in time.* 他的名字已经到了我的嘴边上,我差一点没说出来。乍看起来,句型相似,但是,头一句当然是①的用法,后一句则是②的用法。常用 right 加强语气,例如:*Oh, why can't I remember it! It's right on the tip of my tongue!* 哎呀,我怎么会记不得呀! 就在我的嘴边上嘛! 如以上的例句所示,使用 be 动词的场合最多,但有时采取 have *something* on the tip of *one's* tongue 的形式,意思相同。*A: Do you know the answer to the riddle, Jane? B: Wait! Don't tell me. I have it right on the tip of my tongue.* 甲:简,你知道这条谜语的谜底吗? 乙:等一下! 别告诉我。就在我的嘴边上了。◇ be just on the edge of *someone's* memory / (*someone*) almost said *something*

the tip of the iceberg [ðə ˌtɪpəðə ˈaɪsˌbəːrg] [口] **冰山的一角** iceberg 是“浮在海洋里的巨大的冰山”。tip 指“冰山伸出海面的部分”。可以按照字面意义使用。*From the ship we could see only the tip of the iceberg.* 我们从船上只能看见冰山的一角。大多用作比喻,意思是“表面上的事物,整体中的一小部分”。*The vocal dissatisfaction accompanying the dispatch of US troops to the Middle East constitutes only the tip of the iceberg.* 人们对美国派兵中东地区的不满声浪只不过是冰山的一角而已。◇ one small part of the whole

tired

be dead tired [ˈdeːd ˈtaɪrd] [口] **累得要死** → be dead on *one's* FEET

be sick and tired of *something* → SICK

tit

give *someone* **tit for tat** [ˌgɪv ～ ˈtɪtfər-ˈtæ(ː)t] [口] **一报还一报** 按字面讲是“你给我 tat,我还你 tit”。这是一个自古以来就有的表达法,16 世纪英国就已经使用。关于语源,一说系由 tip for tap (tip 和 tap 都是“轻打”的意思)转来,一说系出自法语 *tant pour tant* (*tant* 等于英语的 much, *pour* 等于英语的 for),但两说均非定论。不管来源如何,总是“你给我一下子,我马上还你一下子”的意味。不过语调比较轻松,不能用于“报仇雪恨”之类严重的场合。*Jimmy hit me, so I just gave him tit for tat.* 吉米打了我,而我只是一报还一报呀。*He pulled my hair so I gave him tit for tat by throwing water on him.* 他拉我的头发,所以我一报还一报,向他身上泼水。可用 return 代替 give。*She hasn't returned the book I lent her so I'm not going to give her back her umbrella. I believe in returning tit for tat.* 她不归还我借给她的书,所以我也不归还她的伞。我信奉一报还一报的原则。*Charles has a quick mind. I often try to tease him but he always returns tit for tat.* 查尔斯的脑子来得快。我常想戏弄他,可是他总是立即还去。有时用 be tit for tat 的形式。*He didn't speak to me so I didn't speak to him. It was tit for tat.* 他没有跟我说话,所以我也没有对他说话。这叫一报还一报呀。◇ give the equivalent in retaliation

toast

propose a toast [prəˌpouzə ˈtoust] [口] **带头干杯** → BOTTOMS up.

(as) warm as toast [əz ˈwɔ(ː)rməz ˈtoust] [口] **暖烘烘的** 最初的构思是“象烤面包片(toast) 一样热乎”。这一习用语只用于在寒冷的时候令人感到格外温暖和舒服的衣服、床铺、房间等,不能用于天气或气候。*In my new overcoat, I felt warm as toast.* 穿上我的新大衣,我感到身上暖烘烘的。*The hot-water bottle in the bed made my feet as warm as toast.* 床上的热水袋使我的脚暖烘烘的。*We* *lit the stove and soon the room was as warm as toast.* 我们点起了火炉，房间里很快就温暖如春了。◇ comfortably warm

toes

keep *someone* **on** *his* **toes** [ˌki(:)p ~ ɔn ~ ˈtouz] [口] **使某人精神紧张** → be on *one's* TOES

be on *one's* **toes** [ɔn ~ ˈtouz] [口] **保持警惕** toes 是"脚尖"。on *one's* toes 是"用脚尖站着"的意思。转作比喻使用，表示一种积极的姿态，即"保持警惕，以便随时能够应付变化的局势"。*You have to be on your toes in this class. The prof likes to give pop quizzes.* 你上这门课必须保持警惕。老师喜欢搞突然袭击式的测验。*Don't worry about Jim's missing a chance for a sale. He's always on his toes.* 甭担心吉姆会错过一个推销的机会。他永远不会疏忽大意的。可以用 stay 或 keep 代替 be 动词，而讲 stay [keep] on *one's* toes。*The competition in this business is very stiff. You always have to stay on your toes.* 这种生意中的竞争非常激烈。你随时都得保持警惕。也可以说 keep *someone* on *his* toes，意思是"使某人保持警惕"或"使某人精神紧张"。*Our boss is a dynamic leader. His energy and new ideas always keep us on our toes.* 我们的老板是一位坚强的领导人。他精力充沛，又不断有新的点子，使我们的精神永远处于紧张的状态。◇ be alert

step on *someone's* **toes** [ˌstepɔ(:)n ~ ˈtouz] [口] **由于言行过分而侵犯他人的势力范围** 字面意义为"踩他人的脚尖"。*Ow! You stepped on my toes!* 喔唷！你踩我的脚啦！作为比喻，这里的 toes 系指"人站立的地方"，亦即"某人的势力范围或主管单位"。条头的整个意思是"把脚伸进他人的领地"或"有越权行动"。常应用于工作。*I hope I didn't step on your toes when I suggested at the meeting that your section draw up the report.* 我在会议上提议由你们科起草报告书，请不要认为侵犯了你们科的职权才好。*The ministries of the government have to move very carefully in order to avoid stepping on each other's toes.* 政府各部在行动中必须特别谨慎，努力避免发生相互越权的事情。*If you want to transfer one of your men to another department, even temporarily, you'd best do it through the personnel office. Otherwise, they'll accuse you of stepping on their toes.* 如果你想把自己的一个部下调到其他科室，哪怕是临时的，最好还是通过人事科。否则的话，他们会指责你越权。偶尔用于表示"伤害他人的感情"(offend *someone*) 的意思。*Because of the diversity of people attending the meeting, each speaker had to pick his words with care in order not to step on anyone's toes.* 因为有各种各样的人参加会议，每个发言的人都必须慎重选择自己的词句，以免伤害任何人的感情。在极少的场合以 tread 代替 step，但有点生硬的感觉。*Most partnerships that break up do so because the partners find themselves treading on each other's toes.* 合营公司所以垮台，大多是由于合伙人互相争权夺利。◇ trespass on *someone's* area of authority

turn up *one's* **toes** [ˌtə(:)r ˈnʌp ~ ˈtouz] [话] **死** 原来的习用语为 turn up *one's* toes to the daisies (直译：使自己的脚指朝向雏菊)，现在省略了 to the daisies 这一部分。这一习用语当然是一种轻松的说法，所以这样讲，是因为在坟墓上往往生长着雏菊。*Grandpa turned up his toes at the ripe old age of ninety.* 爷爷在九十高寿时去世了。*Your hamster is going to turn up his toes if you don't feed him right.* 如果你不好好喂它，你的仓鼠就要死掉啦。→ be pushing up DAISIES ◇ die

togs

togs [ˈtɑ(:)gz] [话] **衣服** 来源于 toga (古罗马人穿的白色外衣) 一词。可以用于表示一般的衣服，如说：*Those are nice looking togs you're wearing tonight.* 你今天晚上穿的衣服很好看啊。但大多指具有特定用途的服装，如 golf togs (高尔夫球服)，riding togs (骑马服)，tennis togs

(网球服)等,以及这些服装的附属品(长筒靴、围巾、帽子等)。在这一场合,发音作 [ˈ~ ˌtɑːgz]。*Jane bought new ski togs this year.* 简今年买了新的滑雪服。◇ clothes / ~wear

told

all told [ˈɔːl ˈtould] [口] **全部** told 当然是 tell 的过去分词。tell 除"说"一义外,还有"数"的意思。条头中的 told 是后者。现在,除了在 all told 之类的习用语中以外,几乎完全不用这一意义了。all told 直译为"把所有的都数过"。因此,*All told, there were about thirty-five people at the party.* 这句话只能译作"出席社交晚会的总共有 35 人左右。"而不能误译为"大家说,出席社交晚会的有 35 人左右。"这是因为:tell 在用"说"一义时,必须有间接宾语。另外,至少在日常会话中,如果 all 与 everyone 或 everybody 同义,就几乎不可能成为主语。在上面的例句中,假若要表示"大家说"的意思,可以改写为 Everyone told me that there were ~. 或者 Everyone said that there were ~. 一般来说,all told 不是放在句子前端就是放在句子末尾。*I've got twenty-three dollars all told.* 我身上总共有 23 美元。◇ altogether

Tom

every Tom, Dick and Harry [ˌevri ˈtɑːm ˈdɪkən ˈhæ(ː)ri] [口] **不论张三李四,有一个算一个** 这一习用语是用英美常见的一般男人名字并列而成。在使用时,大多怀有轻视广大群众的心情。Tom, Dick 和 Harry 虽然都是男人名字,说话时可以包括女性。但完全是女人的场合不能使用。*It's no wonder the roads are crowded. Every Tom, Dick and Harry thinks he has to have a car these days.* 道路拥挤是不足为奇的。最近,不论张三李四都认为自己必须有一辆小汽车。也可以讲 every last man and his wife。◇ everybody

tome

a weighty tome [ə ˈweɪdi ˈtoum] [口] **艰深的著作** weighty 是 weight 的形容词,意思是"沉重的"。tome 是"书",特别指"学术巨著"。weighty tome 有时指"巨大而沉重的书本",但一般来讲不是这个意思,它所指的是"内容分量重"。通常使用轻松的、开玩笑的口吻,极少严肃认真的意味。*Harold takes himself to be a real egghead, doesn't he. He's always reading some unfathomable weighty tome.* 哈罗德装腔作势,大摆知识分子的架子。他总是在读高深莫测的堂皇巨著。weighty 的比较级为 weightier,最高级为 weightiest。*That guy will never be a scholar. The weightiest tome he's ever read is Action Comics.* 那个家伙绝对成不了一个学者。他所读过的最艰深的著作是《战斗连环漫画》。◇ a difficult book

Tommy

a Tommy gun → GUN

ton

like a ton of bricks → BRICKS

tone-deaf

be tone-deaf [ˈtoun.deːf] [口] **音盲** → have a tin EAR

tongs

go at *something* **hammer and tongs** → HAMMER

tongue

the cat has *someone's* **tongue** → CAT

find *one's* **tongue** [ˌfaɪnd ~ ˈtʌ(ː)ŋ] [口] **张口结舌以后好容易能说话了** 直译为"找到自己的舌头",意思是"在由于惊恐、羞臊等而 lose *one's* TONGUE(直译"失去自己的舌头",即"张口结舌")之后,精神恢复正常,又把不知跑到哪里去了的舌头找到,能说话了"。*At first he was so surprised to see her that he lost his tongue, but after he found it again he began to ask one question after another.* 在最初见到她的时候,他大吃一惊,张口结舌,但是,当他稳定下来能够说话以后,就开始象连珠炮似地问这问那了。*I wanted to explain, but by the time I found my tongue she had hung up.* 我想解释一下,可是当我在张口结舌之后好容易能说出

话的时候,她已经把电话挂上了。多用于否定句。*The offer they were making me was almost too good to be true. I opened my mouth to speak but couldn't seem to find my tongue.* 他们提供给我的条件太好了,几乎达到令人不能相信的程度。我张开嘴要说话,可是舌头似乎完全不顶用了。*When my father told me that he had arranged for me to study abroad for a year, I was so surprised I had difficulty in finding my tongue.* 当我父亲告诉我说他已经安排我去国外留学一年的时候,我感到非常意外,好半天说不出话来。如以上的例句所示,一般用于吃惊的场合,但偶尔也用于害臊的场合。*I want to ask her to marry me, but every time we are alone I have difficulty in finding my tongue.* 我想向她求婚,但是每当我们俩单独在一起的时候,我总是感到难以启齿。◇ regain *one's* ability to speak / speak (freely)

have a sharp tongue [ˌhævə ˈʃɑ(ː)rp ˈtʌ(ː)ŋ] [口] **尖酸刻薄** 直译为"有一个锐利的舌头"。*Jane is a nice girl, but she has a sharp tongue when angered.* 简是一个很好的姑娘,但是一生起气来,嘴很刻薄。在下一例句中指"尖酸刻薄的人"。*Old Mr. Gruff may have a kind heart, but he certainly has the sharpest tongue in town.* 格拉夫老先生的内心也许很慈善,但是他的嘴肯定是全镇最尖酸刻薄的。可以用 control, use 等动词代替 have。*If Wanda ever hopes to get married, she'll have to learn to control her sharp tongue.* 如果旺达希望结婚的话,她必须学会控制自己刻薄的嘴巴。也可以采取 with a sharp tongue 的形式。*There's nothing more unpleasant than a sour old woman with a sharp tongue.* 再没有比尖酸刻薄的、令人讨厌的老太婆更使人不愉快的了。◇ speak sharply ((sharpest→ sharper than anyone))

hold *one's* **tongue** [ˌhould ~ ˈtʌ(ː)ŋ] [口] **保持沉默** 字面意义为"控制自己的舌头"。*Hold your tongue. You will speak when spoken to and not before.* 你别出声。有人向你说话的时候,你再张嘴好了。*I had an impulse to blurt out the whole truth, but I knew it would hurt many people so I held my tongue.* 我真想把真实情况都抖搂出来,但是我知道这会伤害许多人,所以我保持沉默了。tongue 的前面有时加形容词。*Hold your stupid tongue! Everything you say only makes it worse for us!* 闭上你那张笨嘴!你多说一句,只会使我们的情况更糟。◇ keep quiet ((stupid→, you fool))

keep a civil tongue in *one's* **head** [ˌki(ː)pə ˌsɪvəlˈtʌ(ː)ŋˌɪn ~ ˌhe(ː)d] [口] **说话彬彬有礼** 这里的 civil 是 polite (有礼貌)的意思。条头直译为"在头脑里准备一个文明的舌头"。"*How can we talk with you old hens clucking so loud?*" "你们这些老婆子吵吵嚷嚷,我们简直无法跟你们谈话呀!"那些"老婆子"可能针锋相对地回答说:"*I'll thank you to keep a civil tongue in your head, young man!*" "小伙子,请你说话客气点儿!"一般用于父母、老师、上司等长辈教训或批评孩子们或年轻人的场合。所谓 civil tongue 包含着"遣词造句"和"谈话内容"这两方面的意义,因此,即便口头客气,如果说话的内容并不文明,就不能算为 civil. *Young people don't have any manners these days. None of them knows how to keep a civil tongue in his head.* 现在的年轻人没有任何礼貌,他们全都不晓得怎样说话客客气气。*If you had kept a civil tongue in your head, your teacher probably wouldn't have punished you just for being late.* 如果你说话彬彬有礼,你们的老师就不会仅仅为了迟到而惩罚你了。也可以直接用作命令句,例如: *A: Why didn't you call me as you promised? B: I was busy. You aren't the only busy man around here, you know. A: Keep a civil tongue in your head!* 甲:你约定给我打电话,为什么没有打呀? 乙:我当时很忙。你要知道,你在这里并不是唯一的大忙人啊。甲:你说话客气点儿! ◇ speak (more) politely

lose *one's* **tongue** [ˌlu(ː)z ~ ˈtʌ(ː)ŋ] [口] **张口结舌** 原来的构思是:由于"失掉舌头"

而"说不出话来"。如果是大人对孩子讲，常用的说法是 the CAT has *someone's* tongue。本条习用语是成年人之间使用。*The stranger's question surprised me so, that I temporarily lost my tongue.* 陌生人的询问使我大吃一惊，一时之间连话都说不出来了。这是以"惊恐"为原因的场合。也有因"害臊"而张口结舌的场合，例如：*I want to ask her to marry me, but every time we're alone I lose my tongue.* 我很想向她求婚，但是每当我们单独在一起的时候，我的舌头就不好使了。又用于受窘的场合。*Speak up! Have you lost your tongue?* 你倒说呀！难到舌头不好使了吗？*I asked you what you did with the money. Surely you haven't lost your tongue.* 我是问你用那钱干什么了？你还没哑巴吧。◇ lose *one's* ability to speak (freely) / can't speak [talk]

make a slip of the tongue → SLIP

be on the tip of *someone's* **tongue** → TIP

a tongue twister → TWISTER

tongue-lashing

give *someone* **a tongue-lashing** (for *something*) [ˌgɪv ～ ə ˈtʌŋˌlæ(ː)ʃɪŋ] [口] **严厉申斥** 字面意义为"用舌头鞭打某人"。在斥责他人失误、过错或不履行义务的场合使用。*The math teacher gave her charges a tongue-lashing for not turning in their homework on time.* 数学老师因为学生们没有按时交家庭作业而狠狠训斥了他们一顿。在强调严厉程度时添加 severe (严厉的)一词，作 give *someone* a severe tongue-lashing。*When Charles returned from his business trip a day late, he was given a severe tongue-lashing by the head of his department.* 查尔斯因为出差晚回来一天，被他们的部长狠狠批评了一大顿。另有一个把本条条头倒转过来的说法，作 tongue-lash *someone*，但几乎无人使用。◇ scold harshly

tongue-tied

be tongue-tied [ˈtʌŋˌtaɪd] [口] **舌头不好使了** 字面意义为"舌头被捆上了"。一般指在失去冷静时发生的一时说不出话来的现象。有时是找不到所要说的话，有时虽然明白该说什么话但是堵在嗓子眼里一时倾吐不出来。*He's not stupid. He was just tongue-tied.* 他并不是一个傻瓜。他只不过没能说出话来罢了。如果用 get [become] 代替 be 动词，意思是"不能启齿"。*I want to ask Doris for a date, but every time I meet her I get tongue-tied.* 我很想跟多丽丝约会，但是每当见到她的时候，我就感到无法启齿。*I got a poor grade in public speaking because whenever I stood up in front of the class I became tongue-tied.* 我的公开演讲的分数很差，因为每当我站在全班同学的面前，我就结结巴巴讲不出什么来了。也有 leave *someone* tongue-tied 的说法，意思是"令人瞠目结舌"。*The boss's announcement that he was doubling my salary left me tongue-tied.* 老板宣布把我的工资提高一倍，令我瞠目结舌。tongue-tied 也可以作为定语使用。*At the time, I was only a tongue-tied youth of sixteen.* 那时，我只是一个连话都说不好的 16 岁的少年。◇ can't express *oneself* fluently

tonsure

take the tonsure [ˌteɪkðə ˈtɑ(ː)nʃər] [口] **就任圣职** tonsure 是"削发"。古时，要想成为天主教的 monk (修士)，就必须剃去头发。*St. Francis of Assisi was twenty-four years old when he took the tonsure.* 阿西西的圣弗朗西斯是在 24 岁削发成为修士的。在现代，即便当神甫也不必削发，所以这一习用语只表示"就任圣职"的意思。*William has decided to give up his law practice and take the tonsure.* 威廉决心放弃当律师而去就任圣职了。新教根本就没有"削发"的习惯，所以在讲新教徒而使用本条习用语的时候，就带有诙谐的味道。*The minister of the Methodist church says he had wanted to take the tonsure ever since he could remember.* 卫理公会教会的牧师说，自从他能够记事儿那一天起，他就想削发出家。在新教中，"就任圣职"一般讲 become a minister 或者 enter the ministry

(都是"当牧师"的意思),没有滑稽的意味。顺便提一下,take the tonsure 只用于男性,女性要用 take the veil,因为当修女时要蒙上面纱。*Since Mother Teresa took the veil, she has devoted her life to the poor.* 特雷萨修女院长自从就任圣职以来,就把自己献给了穷苦的人们。另外,在中译英的时候,如果讲佛教的"出家",可以用 take the tonsure 一语。◇ become a priest [minister]

too

have one too many → ONE

toodle-oo

toodle-oo ['tudə'lu:] [话] **拜拜(再见)** 主要是女性用语。有时男性以女性的腔调戏用。*I'll see you tomorrow. Toodle-oo.* 明天见。拜拜。另外,有时作为动词"去"、"回去"的意味使用。*I've got to toodle-oo before it gets too late.* 我必须在天不太晚的时候回去。◇ bye-bye

tooth

as eye for an eye and a tooth for a tooth → EYE

fight (*someone* [*something*]) **tooth and nail** [ˌfaɪt 'tu(:)θə'n:eɪl] [口] **拼命斗争** 直译为"用牙 (tooth) 和爪 (nail) 斗",也就是"又咬又挠,拼死斗争"。首先令人想到的是弱小动物斗争的形象。*The cat fought the German shepherd tooth and nail.* 那只猫连咬带挠,拼命与德国牧羊狗斗争。fight 后边往往不接宾语,一般用 to *do something* 的形式继续,例如:*The cat fought tooth and nail to escape from the German shepherd.* 那只猫为了逃脱德国牧羊狗,又咬又挠,拼命斗争。作为比喻,当然也是用于"弱者拼命抵抗"的场合。*The union fought tooth and nail to have the members who had been fired reinstated.* 工会为了使被解雇的工人恢复工作,拼命进行斗争。*The small shop owners are fighting the supermarket chain tooth and nail to prevent it from locating a store in their neighborhood.* 小商店的店主们为了阻止超级市场在他们的邻近地区设立联号,正拼命进行斗争。*The opposition parties fought tooth and nail to block passage of the bill.* 各在野政党为了阻止那个法案的通过而拼命斗争。也有可以按照字面意义解释的场合。*The woman fought tooth and nail to escape from the man who had attacked her.* 那个女人为了逃开袭击她的男子,又咬又挠,拼命反抗。另外,使用的动词以 fight 为最多,但偶尔也用 oppose, defend, go at, struggle 等。◇ fight with every means available

be long in the tooth [ˌlɔ(:)ŋɪnðə 'tu:θ] [话] **上了年纪** 直译为"牙很长"。来源是:马每增加一岁,牙床就萎缩一些,因此,马的岁数越大,牙显得越长。*I'm long in the tooth and short on brains, otherwise I have no problems.* 我年纪大,脑子有些迟钝,没有别的什么毛病。常与 too, a bit, rather 等副词一起使用。*That actor is a bit long in the tooth for romantic roles.* 那个演员演风流小生的角色,年纪有点太大了。*I'm afraid I'm rather long in the tooth to think of getting married now.* 现在考虑结婚,恐怕我已经年纪太大了啊。get long in the tooth 也表示"上了年纪"的意思。*I'm getting too long in the tooth for this kind of job.* 我干这种工作年纪已经太大了。◇ be old

a sweet tooth [ə 'swi(:)ˌt:u(:)θ] [口] **爱吃甜的** 直译为"甜的牙",指"对甜东西的需求"。最常使用的形式是 have a sweet tooth (喜欢吃甜的东西)。*I've always had a sweet tooth.* 我一向喜欢吃甜的东西。常用 terrible 加强语气。*My sister has a terrible sweet tooth.* 我妹妹极爱吃甜的东西。acquire [get] a sweet tooth 是"对甜的东西爱好起来", get rid of [lose] *one's* sweet tooth 是"不再爱吃甜的东西"。*I've acquired a sweet tooth since I stopped smoking.* 自从戒烟以后,我开始爱吃甜的东西了。*If I could get rid of my sweet tooth, maybe I could lose some weight.* 如果我能停止吃甜的东西,我的体重也许会减轻一些。◇ a craving for sweet things

tootsie

a tootsie [ə 'tutsi] [话] **脚丫儿** 相当于 foot

的幼儿用语 footsie,把它更进一步童稚化,就是本条条头的说法。*Mommy, I hurt my tootsie.* 妈妈,我把我的脚丫儿弄痛了。这一习用语主要是儿童使用,但成年人有时用于开玩笑的场合。*Let me warm my tootsies by the stove.* 请让我在炉子边上烤烤脚丫儿吧。play tootsie 为 play FOOTSIE 的变形,是情侣不使周围的人注意而在桌子底下相互“碰脚”的意思。*Even today grandpa and grandma like to play tootsie under the card table.* 直到现在,爷爷和奶奶在打扑克的时候还常常在桌子底下碰脚丫儿呢。有时拼写作 a tootsy。◇ a foot

top

blow *one's* **top** [.blou ～ 'tɑ(:)p] [话] **勃然大怒** 这里的 top 是 top of *one's* head (头顶)。条头的字面意义为“吹跑脑袋的顶部”,恼怒的程度可想而知。最初的构思是:“由于恼怒,脑袋一下子爆炸了”。*When my father learned that I had smashed a fender on the car, he blew his top.* 当我父亲知道我撞坏了汽车的一个挡泥板的时候,他勃然大怒了。*If the boss finds out about this, he'll blow his top.* 如果老板发现了这个,他一定会勃然大怒的。偶尔使用这一表达法表示“头脑出毛病”的意思。*Jack was acting so strangely that we thought he must have blown his top.* 杰克的行动太奇怪了,我们以为他的头脑一定出了毛病啦。另外有 blow *one's* stack, blow [bust] a gasket, blow a fuse 等说法,也是“勃然大怒”。但是,它们没有象 top 那样有“头脑”出毛病的意味。stack 是“烟囱”,如: *Don't blow your stack. I said I was sorry, didn't I?* 你不要大发脾气啦。我不是道歉赔不是了吗? 特别是 gasket (密封垫)和 fuse (保险丝)的场合,与 be going to 或者 be about to 一起使用,常有“不断积累的怒气终于爆发”、“找岔儿发泄一腔怒火”的意思。*You should have seen Lew's face when he saw me with his girl. I thought he was going to blow [bust] a gasket.* 你真该瞧瞧卢在看到我带着他的女朋友时的脸色。我想,他气得都要爆炸了。*When the old man saw the broken fence, he was speechless with anger. We were afraid he was about to blow a fuse.* 当那老人看到篱笆被弄坏了的时候,他气得连一句话也没有说。我们生怕他大发雷霆。◇ get very [so] angry / lose *one's* mind

shout at the top of *one's* **lungs** [.ʃaudətðə 'tɑ(:)pəv ～ 'lʌ(:)ŋz] [口] **用尽量大的声音喊叫** lung 是“肺”,但在这里指 lung power(发音的能力)。条头直译为“在发音的能力的顶端(top) 叫喊”。这是强调 loudly 的说法,在表示“用尽力量使自己的声音达到极限”的时候使用。条头的动词是以 shout 为代表,可以换用 scream, yell, call 等。*The children were playing and screaming at the top of their lungs.* 孩子们在游戏,他们放开嗓门喊叫。*The student meetings are so noisy that the speaker has to shout at the top of his lungs in order to be heard.* 学生大会嘈杂极了,发言人为了使大家听到,不得不尽量大声喊叫。lungs 可用 voice 代换,意义和用法完全相同。*Didn't you hear me call you? I was yelling at the top of my voice.* 你没听到我叫你吗? 我是用最大的声音叫喊的呀。◇ shout very loudly [in a very loud voice]

shout at the top of *one's* **voice** [.ʃaudətðə 'tɑ(:)pəv ～ 'vɔɪs] [口] **用尽量大的声音喊叫** → shout at the TOP of *one's* lungs

sleep like a top [.sli(:)plaɪkə 'tɑ(:)p] [话] **熟睡** top 是“陀螺”。A top sleeps. 指“陀螺飞速旋转好象定在一点不动”的状态。条头 sleep like a top 直译为“象陀螺一样睡觉”,也就是“睡得一直很顺利,儿乎连身也不翻”、“睡得很香”、“熟睡”的意思。*I slept like a top last night.* 我昨天夜里睡得很香。*He's upstairs, sleeping like a top.* 他在楼上,正睡得香着呢。◇ sleep very well

talk off the top of *one's* **head**[.tɔ(:).kɔ(:)f-ðə 'tɑpəv ～ 'he(:)d] [话] **说话不经过大脑** 指不经过深思熟虑的发言,有“灵机一动,随口便说”的意味。*You should take what George says with a grain of salt. He's always talking off the top of* *his head.* 乔治所说的话，你决不可全信。他总是灵机一动，随口就讲。有时更具体一些，不是指"灵机一动"，而是指 without being sure of the facts (不了解实际情况)。*I'm only talking off the top of my head, but I don't' think our company's production capacity is large enough to process such an order.* 我不大了解实际情况，不过，我认为咱们公司的生产能力不够大，完不成那样一批订货。◇ talk before thinking carefully / talk without being sure of the facts

a top kick → KICK

torch

carry a torch for *someone* [ˈkeriə ˈto(ː)rtʃ fər ～] [话] **单相思** 这里的 torch (火炬) 指 torch of love (爱情的火炬)，即"热爱的火焰"。条头的整个意思是"心里继续燃烧着对某人热爱的火焰"。carry 比 hold 具有更强烈的"不断持续"的意味，表示"一点也不死心，始终等待对方能够接受自己的爱情"。*Meg has been carrying a torch for Paul for almost two years.* 梅格对保罗单恋已经将近两年了。一度相恋，而在被甩之后一直思念对方的场合，也常使用这一习用语。又，a torch 亦可作 the torch。*Dick is still carrying the torch for his ex fiancée.* 迪克依然怀恋他过去的未婚妻。a 和 the 虽然经常可以相互代换，但是在双方过去曾经互相热爱的场合，大多用 the。有时也可以用于并非"一头热"的场合。不过，这是极个别的情况，如：*Despite their long separation, they're still carrying the torch for each other.* 他们虽然分离已久，但是依然相互爱恋。◇ nurture a one-sided love

toss

toss of *a drink* [ˌtɔː ˈsɔːf ～] [话] **一口喝干** → KNOCK back *a drink*

total

total *a vehicle* [ˈtoudl ～] [话] **完全摧毁 (某种交通工具)** 动词 total 一般是"合计"的意思，但在这里为 totally wreck (完全破坏)的略语。totally wreck 是与 partially wreck (部分破坏)相对而言，指"破坏到完全无法修理的程度"。大多应用于汽车，也可以应用于摩托车、小型飞机、汽艇等。一般用于作为主语的人毁坏自己驾驶着的交通工具的场合。He has totaled three cars. 这句话的意思不是"他在一次交通事故中完全撞坏了三辆汽车"，而是"他已经毁坏了他驾驶过的三辆汽车"。*Hank totaled his car last night, but miraculously he wasn't hurt.* 汉克昨天夜里把自己驾驶的汽车完全撞坏了，可是他本人奇迹般地没有受一点伤。常用被动语态，在这一场合当然与何人驾驶无关了。*Two cars and a motorcycle were totaled in that accident.* 在那次交通事故中，有两辆小汽车和一辆摩托车被完全撞坏了。◇ totally [completely] wreck *a vehicle*

totem

(the) low man on the totem pole → MAN

touch

have the Midas touch [ˌhævðə ˈmaɪdəs ˈtʌ(ː)tʃ] [口] **有生财的技能或运气** Midas 见于希腊神话，为弗里吉亚 (Phrygia) 的一位国王。神人赐给他一种力量，任何东西只要他的手一碰就会变成黄金。本条的意思是"具有象米达斯那样用手一碰，那东西就会变成黄金的力量"。作为比喻，表示"不论干什么都会有金钱滚滚而来"的意味，不仅指有发财的秘诀，也可以指有来钱的运气。*Sid Lucker has the Midas touch. Every enterprise he takes part in is highly profitable.* 锡德·勒克不论干什么生意都会发大财。凡是他参加的企业全有高额的利润。有时讲 have the King Midas touch。*You let Tom buy lottery tickets for you. He has the King Midas touch.* 你叫汤姆替你去买彩票。他的手气特别好，干什么都赢钱。还有一个从条头派生的习用语是 everything *one* touches turns to gold (只要手一触，物物皆成金)，同义。*Dudley's family is very rich. Apparently everything his father touches turns to gold.* 达德利家非常有钱。看起来，他的父亲不论干什么都发大财啊。*I've never* *seen such a lucky guy. Everything he touches turns to gold.* 我从来没有见过那样一个幸运的人。他不论干什么都发大财。◇ make money at whatever *one* attempts

lose *one's* **touch** [ˌlu(:)z ~ ˈtʌ(:)tʃ] [口] **技能衰退** touch 本来的意思是"技巧"、"诀窍"、"手腕"。lose 是"忘掉"。*I used to be an expert safecracker, but after so many years in stir I've lost my touch.* 我过去是撬盗保险箱的专家,但是,由于住监狱的年头太多,竟把这种技术忘掉了。转作比喻,为人们广泛使用。*None of that author's recent books have sold well. I think he's lost his touch.* 那位作家的最近几本著作销路全都不佳。据我看,他的文笔已经不行了。*That's the third girl who's turned me down for a date this month. I must be losing my touch.* 在这个月里,她是第三个拒绝跟我约会的姑娘。我的本事一定是不灵了。*The reason the company is going downhill is that the boss is getting too old. He's lost his touch.* 公司在走下坡路的原因是总经理年纪太大,能力不行了。另有 regain *one's* touch 的说法。regain 是"恢复"的意思。*If a painter has been away from his easel a long time, it's difficult for him to regain his touch.* 如果一个画家长期离开他的画架,就很难恢复往日的技能。◇ lose *one's* ability [finesse]

regain *one's* **touch** [rəˌgeɪn ~ ˈtʌ(:)tʃ] [口] **恢复技能** → lose *one's* TOUCH

be touch and go [ˈtʌ(:)tʃənˈgou] [口] **万分危险** touch and go 原是海上专门用语,指"船从狭窄的或过浅的水道小心翼翼地开过去"。*The pilot had to take the ship touch and go through the narrow mouth of the channel.* 领航员不得不引导海轮小心翼翼地穿过航道的狭窄入口。也就是说,touch and go 表示"时刻注意别撞到两岸或触到水底"的微妙感觉。作为比喻,广泛用于表示"万分危险"或者"千钧一发"的状态。*We were lucky to win. It was touch and go until the final minute of the game.* 我们侥幸获胜了。直到比赛的最后一分钟,还龙争虎斗难分胜负呢。*If we can reach the border, we'll be safe. Until then it'll be touch and go.* 如果能到达国境线,我们就安全了。在到达之前,还是万分危险的。常常使用 pretty much, rather 等调整语调。例如: *A: Will he live, doctor? B: I can't say yet. It's still pretty much [rather] touch and go.* 甲:大夫,他的命能保住吗? 乙:我还说不准。他还远远没有脱离危险期哪。a touch-and-go situation 也是习用语,意思是"千钧一发的形势"。显然,把 touch and go 用连字符连接起来,就可以作为定语形容词使用了。*It's still too early to celebrate. True, the worst of the recession is over, but our company is still in a very touch-and-go situation.* 现在兴高采烈,为时还太早啊。不错,经济衰退最糟糕的阶段已经过去了,但是我们公司还处在万分危险的状态。◇ very uncertain [risky]

tough

be a tough nut to crack → NUT

towel

throw in the towel [ˌθrouɪnðə ˈtauəl] [口] **认输** 字面意义为"扔进毛巾",在拳击比赛中,当教练员看到自己的运动员必输无疑时,就将白色毛巾扔进比赛场,表示"认输"。也可以用 sponge [ˈspʌ(:)ndʒ](海绵)代替 towel。*The challenger's manager threw in the towel [sponge].* 挑战者的经纪人把毛巾[海绵]扔进了拳击比赛场。常转作比喻使用,在这一场合,towel 也全可以用 sponge 代换。*The Democratic Party's presidential candidate, feeling that he no longer had any chance of being elected, finally threw in the towel.* 民主党的总统候选人感到他再也没有任何当选的机会,终于承认败北了。*After fighting against poor business conditions for over a year, the ABC Company finally threw in the towel and declared bankruptcy.* ABC 公司在不景气的情况下奋斗了一年多,终于放弃一切希望,宣告破产了。*I'll never throw in the towel.* 我决不会认输。◇ admit defeat

towering

be in a towering rage → RAGE

town

go to town (on *something*) [ˌgoudə 'taun] [话] **劲头十足** 字面意义为"到城里去"。语源似乎是这样:在老早以前,美国农民很少到城里去游逛。如果偶然有这样的机会,他们就赶紧干完农活,精神百倍地前往。作为比喻,表示劲头十足地从事某种活动的样子,包括工作的样子、说话的样子、吃饭的样子等等,使用的范围极广。常用 really 加强语气。*Tom spends a lot of time goofing off around the office, but once he starts to work, he really goes to town.* 汤姆在办公室里有很大一部分时间消极混泡,但是,他一旦开始干活,那劲头真是十足啊。*They're going to town on that building, aren't they. At this rate, it'll be finished before the end of the year.* 他们修建那座大楼,可真是干劲十足。照这样子,年底以前就可以竣工。*If you ask Fred about his trip to Paris, he doesn't have much to say about the cathedrals or art museums, but when he starts describing the girls, he really goes to town.* 如果你问起弗雷德他在巴黎旅游的情况,关于大教堂或美术馆,他只是三言两语,一带而过,但是当他开始讲到姑娘的时候,那劲头可就十足了。下面的例句是表示"在比赛中,一鼓作气乘胜前进"。*The school baseball team is really going to town this year. We've won all our games so far by lopsided scores.* 学校的棒球队今年简直是势如破竹。迄今的所有比赛,我们都取得了一面倒的胜利。下面是表示"在社会上一帆风顺,取得巨大成功"的例子。*George didn't show much promise in college, but as soon as he graduated, he went to town in a big way. Now he's an executive in a leading corporation.* 乔治在大学时没有什么突出的地方,可刚一毕业他就大露头角,现在已经是某大企业的经理了。也可以表示"大吃"或"狼吞虎咽"的意味。*The children went to town on the ice cream.* 孩子们大口大口地吃冰淇淋。*The cat went to town on the fish.* 那只猫大口大口地吃鱼。◇ work [talk, win, eat *something*, etc.] (practically) nonstop [(very) fast] / demonstrate a lot of strength and energy

a man about town → a MAN-ABOUT-TOWN

a one-horse town [ə ˌwʌnˌho(:)rs 'taun] [话] **荒凉的小镇** 在汽车流行之前的时代产生的习用语。直译为"只有一匹马的小镇",形容某一城镇的简陋和荒凉。实际上多指很小的城镇,但这一表达法与城镇的规模无关,有时从说话人的主观来讲,几十万人的大城市也被看作荒凉的小镇。*He grew up in some one-horse town in New York.* 他是在纽约州某一个荒凉的小镇长大的。*Because of the flood, we had to put up in a little place in Texas. It was a real one-horse town.* 由于洪水泛滥,我们不得不在得克萨斯州的一个小地方住下来。那是一个非常荒凉的小镇。*What say we clear out of this one-horse town?* 咱们离开这个荒凉的小镇好不好? *To a real New Yorker, San Francisco is just a one-horse town.* 对于一个地地道道的纽约人来说,旧金山只不过是个荒凉小镇而已。也可以把这一习用语中的 one-horse 提出来,放在别的名词前边,表示"小小的"、"二流的"、"贫弱的"等意味。*He works for some one-horse trading company.* 他在某一家二流的贸易公司工作。◇ a dull country town

paint the town red [ˌpeɪntðə ˌtaun 're(:)d] [话] **到繁华地区痛饮一番** 字面意义为"把市镇漆成红色"。这是有百年以上历史的美国英语,语源有两种说法:(一)印第安人到美国西部的城镇点火,烧得通红;(二)牛仔们赶了几个月牛,好容易到达城镇,首先前往 red-light district(红灯区)热闹一番。作为比喻,是从一个酒馆到一个酒馆开怀痛饮的意思,所以第二个说法可能是正确的。*After delivering the cattle to the railroad after two or three months on the trail, the cowboys were ready to paint the town red.* 经过两三个月的长途跋涉,在把牛送到铁路上之后，牛仔们准备到繁华地区开怀痛饮一番了。常与 go out and ～连接使用。*Bob went out and painted the town red with a couple of old college friends last night.* 鲍勃昨天晚上与大学时代的两个老朋友到闹市区开怀痛饮了一番。*Gil flunked out of college his first year. Having more money than brains, he spent most of his nights painting the town red.* 吉尔上了一年大学，就由于考试不及格而被勒令退学了。他脑子少而钱挺多，几乎每天晚间都去繁华地区痛饮一番。如以上的例句所示，这一表达法大多用于"闹闹哄哄"的场合，但并不限定如此。比如在下边的丈夫与妻子的会话中，就只是"两个人出去喝点酒"的意思，并没有"狂欢"的意味：*I finally got my promotion. Let's celebrate by painting the town red tonight.* 我终于得到晋升了。今天晚上咱们出去走走，喝点酒庆祝一番吧。另外，有时省略 red，意思不变。◇ go out and carouse

be the talk of the town → TALK

a tank town [ə 'tæ(:)ŋk ˌtaun] [话] **偏僻的小镇** 这里的 tank 指"铁路线上为蒸气机车供水的水塔"。本条习用语可以按照字面意义使用，如：*The train stopped at a tank town to take on water.* 火车为了上水，停在一个有水塔的小镇了。转用于日常会话，表示"连个车站都没有，火车只是为了上水才在那里停下的那么偏僻的、简陋的小镇"。*We passed through a series of tank towns.* 我们穿过了一系列偏僻的小镇。*I wouldn't want to live in a tank town like that.* 我可不愿意住在那样一个偏僻的小镇。◇ a dull country town

toy

toy with theidea of *doing something* → IDEA

traces

kick over the traces [kɪˌkovərðə 'treɪsəz] [口] **摆脱束缚** traces 是"排子车、马车上的挽绳"。kick over 是"踢翻"。当一匹马被套上挽绳从事重劳动的时候，大概也有累急了的情况。因此，本条习用语可以按照字面意义使用：*The horse kicked over the traces and ran off.* 那匹马把挽绳踢翻，跑掉了。转用于人，也是指由于难以忍受而摆脱羁绊的情况。*Tired of living with a nagging wife, Ned kicked over the traces and ran off with another woman.* 内德已经厌倦了与哓哓不休的妻子生活在一起，就摆脱羁绊，跟另一个女人私奔了。*I'm fed up with working in this company from 9 to 5 six days a week. If I had the capital, I'd kick over the traces and become independent.* 在这个公司里，一个星期上六天班，每天从上午九点直到下午五点，我已经腻味透了。如果我有资本的话，我要摆脱枷锁，独立经营。*As soon as Hugh was old enough, he kicked over the traces and ran off to join the navy.* 休刚一达到规定年龄就离开家庭参加海军去了。◇ break loose (from the restrictions on *one's* freedom)

track

gain the inside track (for *something*) [ˌgeɪnðɪ 'ɪnˌsaid'træ(:)k] [话] **占据有利地位** → have the inside TRACK (for *something*)

have the inside track (for *something*) [ˌhævðɪ 'ɪnˌsaɪd'træ(:)k] [话] **处于有利地位** 本来的意思是"占内圈跑道"，如说：*As the cars approach the starting line, number 13 has the inside track.* 当所有参赛的汽车齐集起跑线的时候，13 号占内圈跑道。内圈跑道被称为"便宜跑道"，占这一跑道就会有利于参赛的选手，因此，have the inside track 作为比喻是"处于有利地位"的意思。在另外有竞争者而比较谁的地位有利的场合使用。*The contract is still up for grabs, but if we can get an introduction from Mr. Heeky we'll have an inside track.* 那项合同还没有签订，人人都有到手的机会，但是，如果我们能够得到希吉先生的介绍，我们就会处于有利的地位了。*Alf has the inside track for the job because he graduated from a top university.* 阿尔夫是一流大学的毕业生，所以在争取那个

工作时处于有利的地位。*Many women would like to marry the handsome crown prince, but so far no one seems to have the inside track.* 许多女子都想嫁给英俊的王储，可是到现在为止，似乎还没有一个人处于有利的地位。有时用 gain, put (*someone*) 等动词代替 have。*We have too many rivals. We've got to do something to gain the inside track.* 我们的竞争对手太多了。我们为了占据有利地位，非做点工作不可啦。*The President has agreed to endorse our candidate. This'll put us on the inside track.* 总统已经同意支持我们的候选人了。这会使我们处于有利的地位。◇ be in an advantageous position (to *do something*)

keep track (of *something* [*someone*]) [ˌki(:)p ˈtræ(:)k] [口] **掌握情况** 这里的 track 原是"动物的足迹"、"猎物通过的道路"的意思。本条习用语的基本意义是"顺着足迹或道路一直追下去"。在使用时，表示"认真掌握人或事物的情况"、"仔细分析这些情况并存储到脑子里"以及"牢牢记住"的意味。可以应用于金钱的运转、比赛的记录、人们的活动等等，范围很广。*The boss makes us keep track of every cent we spend.* 老板要求我们对我们所花的每一分钱都要掌握它的来龙去脉。*The score changes so fast it's hard to keep track (of it).* 得分记录变化太快了，很难一一记住。*Jay has his fingers in so many pies that it's impossible to keep track of all his activities.* 杰伊插手的事情太多了，很难掌握他的全部活动情况。*It's hard to keep track of all the new popular songs these days.* 最近有很多新流行歌曲，很难把它们全都记住。*We'll have to keep track of the time so that we won't be late getting back home.* 为了不晚回家，我们必须掌握时间。以下是应用于"人"的例子。*I try to keep track of all my old college classmates.* 我打算掌握我在大学时代的全部同班同学毕业后的情况。下面两个例句的重点是"在头脑中分析和整理"。*He has so many girl friends it's hard to keep track (of them).* 他的女朋友过多，简直分不清谁是谁了。*How do you ever manage to keep track of all those professional baseball players? I never can remember who plays for what team.* 你对于所有那些职业棒球选手怎么会记得一清二楚啊？我连谁是哪个队的选手都记不得。◇ keep count (of *something*) / follow (the ins and outs) of *something* / keep *oneself* informed (about *something* [*someone*])

lose track (of *something* [*someone*]) [ˌlu(:)z ˈtræ(:)k] [口] **已经不了解情况** track 原是"动物的足迹"、"猎物通过的道路"的意思。lose 是"失去"。*They lost track of the wounded bear at the river.* 他们在河边失去了受伤的熊的足迹。也可以用于人表示同样的意味。*The police followed the suspect as far as Chicago. There they lost track of him.* 警察跟踪嫌疑犯，一直到达芝加哥。在那里，他们却失去了他的踪影。转作比喻，同样广泛使用。*I've lost track of developments in my field since I retired.* 自从退休以后，我对于自己专业的发展情况已经不大了解了。*I've lost track of many of my old college classmates.* 我对于许多大学同班同学毕业后的情况都不了解。*A: How much money have you spent so far? B: I dunno. I've lost track.* 甲：到现在为止，你已花了多少钱？乙：不知道。我已不记得了。*It's easy to lose track of the days when you're on vacation.* 人在假期间很容易失去时间观念。◇ fail to keep *oneself* informed (about *something* [*someone*]) / fail to follow (the ins and outs of) *something* / lose count (of *something*)

put *someone* **on the inside track** (for *something*) [ˌput ～ ɔnðɪˈɪnˌsaɪdˈtræ(:)k] [话] **使某人处于有利的地位** → have the inside TRACK (for *something*)

throw *someone* **off the track** (by *doing something*) [ˌθrou～ ˌɔ(:)fðə ˈtræ(:)k] [口] **摆脱某人的追踪** → throw *someone* off the SCENT (by *doing something*)

tracks

make tracks [ˌmeɪkˈtræ(:)ks] [话] **赶紧走** 字面意义为"做出足迹"。最初的构思

是:在软地面上留下的足迹,快跑的脚印要比慢走的脚印鲜明。在使用时,主要有三种形式:① make tracks for *someplace*,意思是"赶紧向某处走"。*As soon as I heard about my little brother's accident, I made tracks for home.* 我一听说弟弟出了意外,就赶紧回家了。② make tracks out of *someplace* 是"赶紧从某处逃走"。*someplace* 处大多代入 here 或 there。*When we saw the lion coming, we made tracks out of there.* 当我们见到狮子走过来的时候,就赶紧从那儿逃走了。③ make tracks (后面不接前置词短语),有仅表示"赶紧走"的情况,但主要用于表示"赶紧逃走"的意味。*There's the sheriff! Let's make tracks!* 保安官来了!咱们赶紧逃走吧! ◇ hurry (toward [away (from)]) / get out of here fast

the wrong side of the tracks → SIDE

train

a gravy train [ə ˈgreɪvi ˌtreɪn] [话] **美差** gravy 是"肉汁",在这里有"香蜜"的意思。本条的构思是:"只要搭乘运载香蜜的 train (列车),就可以尝到甜头"。*This job is a gravy train. The company is very small, but the pay is good and the hours are unbelievably short.* 这份工作是个美差事。公司规模虽然很小,但是工资高,上班时间少到令人难以相信的程度。*This company is not a gravy train. If you are not satisfied with your salary, you may quit any time you please.* 这个公司没有什么油水。如果你对工资不满意,随时可以辞职。*Take it from an old pro, young feller. Driving a cab in New York ain't no gravy train.* 小伙子,你听一下老行家的劝告吧。在纽约开出租汽车不是一个美差事。可以加上 get on (乘),讲 get on the gravy train (干上美差),意思是"大有油水"。*Using inside information concerning large government contracts, the lawyer got on the gravy train by buying stocks before the contracts were publicly announced.* 那个律师利用政府将要大批订货的内部消息,在合同正式公布之前收购股票,发了大财。◇ an easy way [place] to make a lot of money

trap

a flea trap [ə ˈfliː ˌtræ(ː)p] [话] **简陋的小客栈** 原来的构思是"整个旅舍就跟跳蚤捕捉器一样"。这是一个强调廉价客栈的肮脏的表达法。实际上也可以按照字面意义使用,如:*That hotel is a real flea trap.* 那家旅馆简直象一个跳蚤捕捉器。比喻用法:*I refuse to stay in this flea trap another single night.* 我决不在这家简陋的小客栈再住一夜了。◇ a cheap (dirty) hotel

have a mind like a steel trap [ˌhævə ˈmaɪndlaɪkə ˌstiːlˈtræ(ː)p] [口] **头脑灵活** steel trap 是为了捕熊等野兽而用钢铁制作的机关,非常灵敏,只要野兽一陷入这种机关,门会很迅速地关闭。因此,人们用它来形容领会得快、一听就忘不了、头脑十分灵活的人。*Ted would make a good lawyer. He has a mind like a steel trap.* 特德可以成为一名很好的律师。他的头脑非常灵活。*You don't have to explain anything to Susan more than once. She's got a mind like a steel trap.* 不管什么事情,对苏珊用不着讲第二回。她的头脑灵敏极了。*Be careful what you say in front of their representative. He has a mind like a steel trap. If you even hint at our plans, he'll soon get the complete picture.* 在他们的代表面前,你说话可要多加小心。他的头脑非常敏锐。如果你对咱们的计划稍微有点暗示,他立即就会窥其全豹了。◇ have an extremely sharp mind

one's **trap** [~ ˈtræ(ː)p] [话] **口** a trap 有"陷阱"、"夹子"、"圈套"等意味,但在轻松的会话中常指"人的口"。不过,这个"口"主要表示"多嘴多舌的口"。*Shut your trap!* 闭上你的嘴! 这是不许人再说话的意思。*Keep your trap shut.* 你不要吭气。这是叫人保持沉默或者"不要对别人讲"的意思。*I should have kept my trap shut.* 我不吭气就好啦。*Open your trap once more, I'll paste you one.* 你再敢吭一声,我就狠狠揍你一巴掌!

◇ *one's* mouth

treat

trick or treat → TRICK

tree

bark up the wrong tree [.bɑ(ː)r.kʌpðə 'rɔ(ː)ŋ 'triː] [话] **弄错目标** 本条的字面意义为"对着错误的树向上狂吠"。黑夜里,在猎浣熊的时候,猎犬把猎物追到一棵树上,可是猎物又从那一棵树转移到别的树上去了。猎犬不知道这一情况,对着原来那棵树狂吠。因为那棵树上已经没有猎物,所以说是"错误的树"。这就是本条习用语的来源。后来专作比喻使用,一般用进行时。*We may be barking up the wrong tree. This substance may turn out not to be a cure for cancer after all.* 我们也许弄错了目标。这种物质可能对癌症没有任何疗效。*If you think I'm going to help you again, you're barking up the wrong tree.* 如果你以为我还会去帮助你,那你可领会错了。*You're barking up the wrong tree. My son didn't break your window. He's been at home all day.* 你找错人啦。我的儿子没有打破你的窗户玻璃。他一整天没有出屋了。◇ direct *one's* inquiries [efforts, complaints, etc.] in the wrong direction / be quite wrong

be lit up like a Christmas tree [.lɪ'dʌplaɪkə 'krɪsmə.striː] [话] **喝醉之后非常高兴** be lit up (醉得很痛快)的原义是"闪闪发光",因此下接 like a Christmas tree (象圣诞树一样),构成了本条习用语。可以单独使用 be lit up,加上 like ~之后,进一步增强了"兴高采烈"的意味。be drunk 也是"喝醉"的意思,但是既可能酒后闹事,也可能"借酒浇愁愁更愁",而 be lit up like a Christmas tree 就不同了,至少说他本人高兴得不得了。*Mr. Bigdrinker was lit up like a Christmas tree at the party last night.* 在昨天的社交晚会上,大酒徒先生喝醉之后高兴极了。还可以用 all 加强语气。*Stu is really asking for trouble. He came to work yesterday all lit up like a Christmas tree.* 司徒真是自找麻烦。昨天喝得大醉,手舞足蹈地前来上班。有时条头与喝醉的本人高兴与否无关,仅用于强调他酩酊大醉的状态,如:*The driver of the wrecked car was lit up like a Christmas tree.* 那个撞坏汽车的司机醉得象一滩泥。◇ be gloriously [very] drunk

be up a tree [.ʌpə 'triː] [话] **非常难办** 条头的来源是:袋鼠被狗追急了,就跳上树去。由于袋鼠在树上一动也不能动,所以人们就常用这一表达法形容非常受窘的状态。*I'm up a tree. I've got a date to take Mary to a concert tonight, but I've lost the tickets.* 我现在陷入窘境了。今天晚上我约好带玛丽去听音乐会,但是我把票丢了。*We're up a tree. The guest speaker for tonight's meeting just called to say he's sick and can't make it.* 我们陷入窘境了。今天晚上会议的特邀演讲人刚刚来电话,说他有病不能出席了。除 be 动词外,有时使用 leave 或 have。*The bank's refusal to lend us any more money has left us up a tree.* 银行拒绝再向我们贷款,使我们陷入极大的困境。*The prosecutor's shrewd questions very quickly had the defendant up a tree.* 在检查官的巧妙提问之下,被告很快就无言可答了。◇ be in a very awkward [difficult] position [situation]

trees

can't see the forest for the trees [.kæ(ː)nt .si(ː)ðə'fɔ(ː)rəst fərðə'triːz] [口] **只见树木不见森林** → can't see the WOODS for the trees

can't see the woods for the trees → WOODS

trey

a trey [ə 'treɪ] [话] **扑克牌的 3** 拉丁语的 3 是 *trēs*,传入中古法语作 *treis*,又由中古法语传入中古英语,拼写为 trey。在掷骰子或玩西洋骨牌 (dominoes) 时也使用此词。但是,一般美国人讲 trey,首先想到的是扑克牌中的 3。在扑克牌游戏中,trey 与 three 同样频繁地为人们所使用。*Jill played a trey on my deuce.* 吉尔出张 3 压我的 2。◇ a three

trick

do the trick [.du(:)ðə 'trɪk] [口] **用点手段达到目的** 有人一见到本条条头,也许首先认为是"恶作剧"的意思,这大概与 play a trick 弄混了。另外一点也请读者注意,条头的 trick 前面总是用定冠词。这一 trick 的意思是"用简单的手段或方法取得的效果"。do the trick 的意思是"略施小计就达到所期望的目标"。*A: The cabbie refuses to take us there. B: Offer him an extra twenty dollars. That ought to do the trick.* 甲:出租汽车司机不肯把我们送到那个地方。乙:多给他加二十美元。那他就会干了。*I don't have a screw driver, but this ruler should do the trick.* 我没带螺丝刀,但是这把尺子就能顶用。*You don't have to kill him. A tap on the head will do the trick.* 你没有必要动刀动枪去杀他。只要一敲他的脑壳就万事大吉了。另有 turn the trick 的说法,即把动词 do 变成 turn,从而增加了"经过种种努力,最后 (达到目的)"的意味。*The boss wasn't inclined to accept our plan at first. I think it was our enthusiasm that turned the trick.* 老板最初没有采纳我们的计划的意思。我认为是我们的热忱终于打动了他的心。◇ answer the purpose / be effective

trick or treat ['trɪ(:)kər'tri:t] [口] **要恶作剧还是给点心** 美国有一种风俗,在 10 月 31 日万圣日前夕(Halloween),戴上假面具又经过化装的孩子们(从儿童到中学生都可以)成群结队到附近的人家挨户去要点心。在这样的时候,孩子们的嘴里总是念叨着 trick or treat 这一习用语。trick 是"恶作剧",treat 是"送给孩子的小礼物",大多是一般点心。本条条头的整个意思是:"不给点心,我们就搞恶作剧啦!" *"Trick or treat! Trick or treat!" shouted the children when Mrs. Smith opened the front door.* 当史密斯太太打开房门的时候,孩子们喊道:"要恶作剧还是给点心?要恶作剧还是给点心?"在孩子们前来的时候,一般都是给点心或水果,但也有讨厌孩子、什么也不给的人家。在这种时候,孩子们所搞的 trick 都是小小的恶作剧,例如用肥皂在窗户玻璃上写字等。trick or treat 不仅是喊叫的口号,而且表示这种行动本身。也就是说,人们可以讲 go [come] for trick or treat(去或来搞要恶作剧或是给点心的活动)。*Tonight is Halloween. Are you going out for trick or treat with us?* 今天晚上是万圣日前夕。你跟我们一起出去搞要恶作剧还是给点心的活动吗? *I'm sure there'll be some children coming for trick or treat tonight. I think I'll bake some cookies for them.* 今天晚上肯定有一些孩子来搞要恶作剧还是给点心的活动。我想烤些曲奇饼给他们预备着。go [come] for trick or treat 还有 go [come] tricking or treating 的形式。*That old Mr. Jones never gives us anything when we go tricking or treating at his house, so we always soap his car windows.* 当我们到琼斯先生家去搞要恶作剧还是给点心时,那老头儿绝对不给我们任何东西。因此,我们总是在他的汽车窗子上用肥皂乱涂一阵。◇ Give us a treat or we'll play a trick on you. / asking for Halloween treats

turn the trick [.tə(:)rnðə 'trɪk] [口] **经过种种努力,最后达到目的** → do the TRICK

trig

trig ['trɪ(:)g] [话] **三角** trigonometry [.trɪgə'nɑ(:)mətri] 的缩略。大学和高中学生用语。*My roommate is crazy. He says he loves trig.* 与我住同一房间的同学头脑挺古怪。他说他喜欢三角。◇ trigonometry

trigger

be quick on the trigger [.kwɪkɔ(:)nðə 'trɪgər] [话] **反应迅速** → be too quick on the TRIGGER

be slow on the trigger [.slouɔ(:)nðə 'trɪgər] [话] **遇事迟钝** → be too quick on the TRIGGER

be too quick on the trigger [.tu(:) .kwɪkɔ(:)nðə 'trɪgər] [话] **反应过快** 字面意义为"过早地扣扳机 (trigger)",亦即"开枪过早"。*An innocent man died because the policeman was too quick on the trigger.* 由于那个警察开枪过早,一个无辜的男子被打死了。作为比喻使

用，表示“慌手慌脚，性子过急，不分青红皂白”的意思。*That guy is too quick on the trigger. He's always hurting people by jumping to unfounded conclusions.* 那个家伙性子太急。他总是马上跳到毫无根据的结论，因而伤害他人的感情。常用 so 代替 too。*Don't be so quick on the trigger. You haven't heard his side of the story yet. Maybe it wasn't his fault.* 不要急于下结论。你还没听他这方面的陈述哪。也许并不是他的过错。*You've got to learn not to be so quick on the trigger. Always be sure of your facts before you act.* 你必须学会稳扎稳打，不要慌手慌脚。永远要先弄清事实，然后再采取行动。如果不加 too [so] 而只是 be quick on the trigger，就不一定是“性子急”的意思，根据上下文，有时与 be quick on the DRAW 大致同义。be quick on the draw 的字面意义为“拔枪快”，比喻意义为“头脑敏捷”，因此是褒义语。例如：*I lost an opportunity for a big sale because I wan't quick enough on the trigger.* 由于我的头脑反应不够快，白白失掉了一大批订货。与此相反，be too [so] quick on the trigger 则是“过早地扣扳机”，或是误杀无辜，或是造成不必要的杀伤，因此一般含有贬义。反义的习用语是 be slow [too slow] on the trigger，字面意义为“扣扳机慢[过慢]”，比喻意义为“遇事迟钝”，根据上下文，有时是“谨慎”或“过于谨慎”的意味。*You'd have more friends if you were a little slower on the trigger.* 如果你稍微谨慎一些，你会有更多的朋友的。◇ react too quickly

trip

an ego trip [ə ˈniːˌgou ˌtrɪp] [话] **洋洋自得** 条头没有很长历史，最近才大为流行。ego 本是“自我”的意思，在这里可作“自尊心”解。trip 本来是“旅行”，但在这里与吸毒使用的 trip (吸毒后产生的幻觉)相同，有“因充满 ego 而飘飘然”的意味，也就是汉语的“洋洋得意”或“洋洋自得”。*That candidate knows he doesn't have a chance of winning the election. He's just on an ego trip.* 那个候选人知道自己没有当选的可能性。他只是名利熏心，自鸣得意而已。这句话的含意是：这位“候选人”尽管没有一点当选的希望，但是由于自己的名字与其他有名望的候选人并列在一起，所以心满意足，洋洋自得。*I enjoyed going to New York with the boss and being entertained by all those big-time industrialists. It was quite an ego trip.* 我有幸陪老板去纽约，又受到所有那些大实业家的款待，真是够得意的啊。*I can't stand that guy when he gets on one of his ego trips about how he's going to enter Harvard University and join the Finance Ministry.* 当那个家伙吹嘘说他要进哈佛大学求学，然后进财政部工作的时候，那种洋洋得意的样子实在叫我受不了。*I wonder what it's like to be a big star and have everyone on the street recognize you. It must be some big ego trip.* 当一个大明星，走到街上人人都认识你—我不知道这会是一种什么滋味，肯定令人十分得意的。ego 和 trip 的中间加连字符，构成动词 ego-trip，意思是“由于出足风头而自鸣得意”。*How in the world does the governor ever get any work done? He's always ego-tripping around the state kissing babies and making speeches.* 州长究竟什么时候正经干工作呀？他总是在州里到处游逛，一会儿吻吻婴儿，一会儿讲个话，神气得了不得。还有一个不大常用的名词 ego-tripper，意思是“自命不凡的人”，含有贬义。*Every time our meetings are televised, that ego-tripper tries to hog the cameras.* 每当我们的会议上电视的时候，那个自命不凡的人总试图独占镜头。◇ boosting [a boost to] *one's* ego / a self-glorifying fantasy / an ego-inflating experience

triple

a triple [ə ˈtrɪpl] [口] **三垒打** → a FOUR-BAGGER

triple-date

triple-date [ˈtrɪpl ˈdeɪt] [口] **三对男女一起约会** → DOUBLE-DATE

trooper

swear like a trooper [ˌswe(ː)r laɪkə ˈtruːpər] [话] **满嘴脏话** 这里的 swear 是"讲 damn, goddamn, hell, son of a bitch, fuck 等等不堪入耳的下流话"。trooper 在现代英语中指 state trooper (州警察), 原义是"骑兵",过去骑兵大概以"满嘴脏话"闻名。*In order to be accepted by his fellow laborers, Henry found he had to learn to swear like a trooper.* 为了与一起干活的人们打成一片,亨利发现他必须学会满嘴讲下流话。*The sergeant swears like a trooper at his men.* 军士长对于他的部下满嘴是脏话。*She pretends to be a lady, but you should hear her when she gets angry. She swears like a trooper.* 她装扮成贵妇人的样子,但是你听听她在恼火时说些什么。她满嘴全是脏话。◇ curse unrestrainedly

trouble

ask for trouble [ˌæskfər ˈtrʌbl] [话] **自找麻烦** 字面意义为"祈求麻烦"。主要用进行时。常用 really 加强语气。*Anyone who drives on the freeway with worn-out tires is asking for trouble.* 如果用已经磨损了的轮胎在高速公路上行驶,那是自找苦吃。往往用于表示忠告,意思是"那样做会出麻烦,应该适可而止"。*The boss has warned us that he's going to start firing inefficient workers. You're just asking for trouble by coming in late every morning.* 老板已经警告我们,他要开始解雇不称职的工作人员。你这样每天早晨迟到,简直是自找麻烦。男人之间吵架的时候常讲这一习用语。*A: I said you've got the ugliest face I've ever seen. B: You're really asking for trouble, aren't you.* 甲:我是说,我从来没见过象你那样丑陋的嘴脸。乙:你是不是想找麻烦了! 相似的表达法有 ask for it, 从语法上讲可以代入以上三个例句,恰当得很。但是,换上 ask for it 以后,语气增强了。这是因为 ask for trouble 仅指"招来麻烦",trouble 也泛指一般的灾祸;如果象 ask for it 这样使用 it,则是指明灾祸的具体内容,从而有更加切实的感觉。在上边的三个例句中,换上 ask for it 之后,第一句的"自找苦吃"须改译为"自己找死";第二句的"自找麻烦"须改译为"自找开除";第三句的"想找麻烦"须改译为"找揍"。在谈到过去的事情时,大多是使用 ask for it, 这是因为既然是过去的事情,"灾祸"的内容已经一清二楚,那就没有再用 ask for trouble 这样暧昧的词句来表达的必要。以代词 it 取代 trouble, 从心理上讲,也是极其自然的事情。*A: Why did you hit him? B: He asked for it, so I just gave it to him.* 甲:你为什么打他? 乙:他干了要挨打的事情,所以我才给他一巴掌。顺便讲一下:与 ask for trouble 同义的表达法有 look for trouble, 但不能讲 look for it。◇ risk calamity

look for trouble [ˌlukfər ˈtrʌbl] [话] **招灾惹祸** → ask for TROUBLE

troubled

fish in troubled waters → WATERS

pour oil on troubled waters → OIL

troubles

drown *one's* **troubles** (in *drink*) [ˌdraun ~ ˈtrʌblz] [话] **借酒浇愁** 借用酒的力量来忘却烦恼,这在哪个国家都是如此。人们希望通过喝酒,哪怕在一时之间把自己的愁事忘掉也好。本条的字面意义为"把自己的 troubles 浸到酒里淹死"。括号中 in *drink* 的部分,有时直接用 in drink, 有时代入 wine, whiskey, brandy 等酒类的具体名称。*You've got to face up to life. You can't forever be trying to drown your troubles in drink.* 你必须正视人生。你不能总是借酒浇愁。*I've found it's a great mistake to try to drown your troubles in wine. I've got a terrible hangover this morning.* 我发觉借酒浇愁是一个很大的错误。今天早晨我头痛恶心得非常厉害。也常有把 in *drink* 部分省略的情况。如: *I'm fed up with everything. I think I'll go out and drown my troubles tonight.* 我对一切事情都厌烦透了。我想今天晚上出去借酒浇一浇我的愁。*There's not enough whiskey in the whole world to drown all my troubles.* 要想消除我的一切烦恼,全世界的威士忌

都不够用。有时用 sorrows (悲伤), woes (苦恼)等代替 troubles。*Old man Clayton has been drowning his sorrows in liquor ever since his family was killed in an automobile accident.* 克莱顿老人自全家人死于一场车祸后,一直借酒浇愁。◇ forget *one's* troubles [sorrows, etc.] by drinking [getting drunk] / make *someone* forget *his* troubles [sorrows, etc.]

trowel

lay it on with a trowel [ˌleɪˌdɔ(ː)n wɪðə ˈtrauəl] [话] **夸大其词;大肆吹捧** → SPREAD it on thick

true

be too good to be true → GOOD

trumpet

blow *one's* own trumpet [ˌblou ～ ˌoun ˈtrʌmpət] [话] **自我赞赏** 本条来源于:古时,国王入城的时候,要吹喇叭表示颂扬。条头字面意义为"吹自己的喇叭"。最初的构思是"自己所带的喇叭本来是为颂扬别人使用的,结果却为颂扬自己而吹了"。有时也可以译为"自吹自擂"。*I don't trust that guy. He's always blowing his own trumpet.* 我不信任那个家伙。他总是自我赞赏。*I don't want to blow my own trumpet, but this is not a bad piece of work.* 我不是自吹自擂,这个活儿干得可不坏呀。*If you blow your own trumpet so often, no one else will blow it for you.* 如果你总那么自我陶醉,别的人就不会称赞你了。另外,因为 trumpet 是 horn (铜管乐器)的一种,所以也可以讲 blow *one's* own horn, 有时又作 toot *one's* own horn。还有一个表达法是 sing *one's* own praises (→ sing *someone's* PRAISES <for *something*>)。◇ praise *oneself*

try

give *something* a try [ˌgɪv ～ ə ˈtraɪ] [口] **试试看** 与 have a TRY(at *something*) 相同,用于表示"不知能不能行,试一下看"的意思。*It looks difficult, but I'll give it a try anyway.* 看起来很难,不过,无论如何我要试一下看。另外,也常用于表示"试试看某种游戏或工作是否有意思"、"试试看机器是否正常运转"等意味。*I'd like to give tennis a try.* 我想打网球,看看有意思没有。*The machine should be OK now. Let's give it a try.* 机器现在应该好使了,我们开动一下试试吧。◇ try *something* (to see if *one* can do it [if it's interesting, if it works, etc.])

give it the old college try [ˌgɪvɪtðɪ ˈoulː-ˈkɑlədʒ ˈtraɪ] [话] **全力以赴** the old college try 直译为"大学时代的老一套的尝试",意思是"在大学时代,无论是对功课还是对体育运动,都竭尽所有的力量了"。条头的最初构思是:"大学生对一切事物都充满热情,拿出十足的干劲"。言外有"乍看起来也许根本不行"的意味。另外,在文字上虽然是 old college, 但除步入社会的大学生外,在校的大学生以及高、初中学生均可使用。*We have one minute to go ninety yards to score or we lose the game. Let's give it the old college try.* 如果要得分,我们每分钟必须前进九十码。否则,我们就要输掉这场比赛了。咱们全力以赴吧。*I don't think I can pass my exams, but I'm going to give it the old college try.* 我认为我在考试中不会及格,不过我要全力以赴。也可以用 her 代替 it, 而讲 give her the old college try。但是, her 一词在书写时一般用省略形式 'er, 在会话时总是不发 h 音。*We may not be able to make the deadline, but we'll give 'er the old college try.* 我们也许到最后期限仍完不成,但是我们要全力以赴。如以上的例句所示,一般使用 give it ～或 give her ～的句型,但有时讲 make the old college try, 同义。例如:*I made the old college try but it didn't work.* 我用尽所有的力量,但是还是不行。◇ try *one's* best / do *one's* utmost

have a try (at <*doing*> *something*) [ˌhævə ˈtraɪ(ət ～)] [口] **试一下** try 是"试试"的意思。本条基本上与 take a CRACK at (*doing*) *something* 和 take a STAB at (*doing*) *something* 同义,但是既无前者的积极因素,也无后者的消极因素,可以说是完全折中的表达法。与 try (*doing*) *something* 大体相同，但大多表示"试一下"或"稍微试试"的意思。*I think I'd like to have a try at playing tennis.* 我想试一下打网球。*That looks like fun. Let me have a try at it.* 那玩意儿看起来很有意思。让我也试一下看。又，如果根据上下文，宾语十分清楚，可以省略 at 以下部分，如：*Shall I have a try?* 我能试一下吗？*Let me have a try.* 让我试一试。另外，如果 *something* 处代人 it，它的发音由 [ət] 转为 [æt]，务请注意。→ give *something* a TRY / try *one's* HAND at (*doing*) *something* ◇ try (*doing*) *something*

try *something* **out** [ˌtraɪ ～ ˈaut] [口] **试验效果、能力、性能等** → TRY out for *something*

try out for *something* [ˌtraɪ ˈautfər～] [口] **参加选拔考试** try *something* 是"试试看"。*He tried translating.* 他试着进行翻译。try *something* out 是"试验效果、能力、性能等"。*He tried the new formula out.* 他试验了新的配方。因此，条头的 try out for *something* 乃是"试试自己的能力，看能否通过选拔考试"的意思。特别用于体育队、乐团 (the band, the orchestra, the glee club, the choral club, the choir)、剧团等。*Jim is going to try out for the baseball team.* 吉姆要参加棒球队的选拔考试。*If you practice hard, you'll be good enough to try out for the band next year.* 如果你刻苦练习，明年就可以参加乐团的选拔考试。顺便讲一下：一般来说，选拔考试是一个人一个人地进行，所以称为 a try-out。如果是"选拔大会"，当然有很多人参加，每人要进行一次 try-out，所以在这一场合，一般用复数形式 try-outs。*The drama club is holding try-outs for the new play this afternoon.* 今天下午，戏剧俱乐部开选拔大会，选拔排演新戏的演员。另外，单数形式 try-out 常用于表示"机器的试车"、"戏剧的试演"等意思。*The new machine is to be given a try-out today.* 新机器准备今天试车。→ GO out for *something* ◇ enter the trials to become a member of *something*

try-out

a try-out [ə ˈtraɪˌaut] [口] **试车；试演** → TRY out for *something*

try-outs

try-outs [ˈtraɪˌauts] [口] **选拔大会** → TRY out for *something*

tub

a tub of blubber → BLUBBER

a tub of lard → LARD

Tubby

Tubby [ˈtʌ(ː)bi] [俗] **大胖子** → FATSO

tube

a boob tube [ə ˈbuːb ˌtjuːb] [话] **电视机** a BOOB 是"笨蛋"、"蠢人"。tube 是"管子"，在这里指"阴极射线管"。条头直译为"给愚人预备的阴极射线管"。最初的构思是："电视节目一般都很低级，喜欢看的全是愚人"。这是一个对电视机的轻蔑称呼，也有时不含轻蔑的意味，仅是戏称。*Watching television will rot your mind. I don't even own a boob tube.* 看电视会腐蚀你的心灵。我根本就不要电视机。*Anything good on the boob tube tonight?* 今天晚上电视里有什么好节目吗？◇ a television (set)

tucker

tucker *someone* **out** [ˌtʌkər ～ ˈaut] [话] **弄得筋疲力尽** 语源是：tuck (折起) +后缀 -er (表示"屡次"的意思)。out 是强调的副词，意思是"完全地"。*The hike tuckered me out.* 远足把我弄得筋疲力尽了。这是主动语态。但是，一般多用被动语态，如：*Let's quit. I'm tuckered out.* 咱们停下来吧。我已经筋疲力尽了。这是不加任何修饰语的用法。不过，大多是用 all, PLUMB, completely 等加强语气。*After swimming all afternoon, I was all tuckered out.* 整个下午一直游泳，现在我已经累得完全不行了。另有 leave *someone* all [plumb, etc.] tuckered out，形式略有改变，意思相同。*Playing with the kids left me plumb tuckered out.* 跟孩子们一起玩，把我累得筋疲力竭。另外，tucker 一词有点方言的味道，特别是与方言色彩浓厚的 PLUMB(→) 一起使用、

再加上方言腔的时候，戏谑的气氛就十足了。意思和 be ALL in, be beat 等一样，而语感却有些不同。◇ exhaust *someone*

tuckered

be (all) tuckered out [(ˌɔːl) ˌtʌkər ˈdaut] [话] **已经筋疲力竭** → TUCKER *someone* out

tumble

give *someone* **a tumble** [ˌgɪv ～ ə ˈtʌ(ː)mbl] [话] **给某人满意的答复** tumble 是"翻跟头"。give *someone* a tumble 的意思是"在异性引诱时，给他翻个跟头"，也就是"表示同意"。但是，大多用否定句。*I've been trying to make time with Mary for I don't know how long, but she just won't give me a tumble.* 我打算跟玛丽交朋友，已经不知道向她讲了多长时间了，可是她就是不给我满意的答复。*Aw, c'mon, baby. Give me a tumble, won't you?* 喂，来呀，小宝贝儿。你答应我好吗？*Rhett had to wait many years before Scarlett finally gave him a tumble.* 雷特一直等待了很多年，斯卡利特才给他满意的答复。以上讲的是相互认识的男女之间的情况。但是，这一表达法也可以用于萍水相逢的男女之间的关系，强调"不屑一顾"、"连看也不看一眼"的意味。*I tried to talk to more than ten different girls on the beach, but none of them would give me a tumble.* 我在海滩上试着去和十几个不同的姑娘攀谈，没有一个人理我。有时用于男女关系以外的事情，如：*I tried to get a job, but after people learned that I was an ex-con no one would give me a tumble.* 我曾去找工作，但是他们了解我蹲过牢房以后，没有一个人理睬我。◇ give *someone* a sign of encouragement

tummy

a tummy dimple → DIMPLE

tune

call the tune [ˌkɔːlðə ˈtjuːn] [口] **有决定权** 英国有这样一个谚语：He who pays the piper calls the tune.（谁付吹笛钱，谁有点曲权。）本条习用语就是由这一谚语的后半部分构成的。前半部分里边的 pay the PIPER(→) 也同样是习用语。旧时，在英国的 bar（酒吧）和 inn（一层卖酒的小旅馆）中，常有流动的吹笛人前来，由客人点曲，客人随着笛声或歌或舞。每当这种时候，"向吹笛者付钱的人" (He who pays the piper) 有"点曲" (calls the tune)的权利。后来，这一谚语作为比喻广泛使用起来了。首先举一个按谚语原形使用的例子。*Once the government starts paying subsidies to private schools, it always begins to try to assert its control over them. After all, he who pays the piper calls the tune.* 政府一旦开始向私立学校发补助金，它必然要坚持对那些学校的监督权。总而言之，谁付吹笛钱，谁有点曲权嘛。下面是活用原形的例子。*I don't think we should let Mr. Bigman invest so much money in our company. If we let him pay that much to the piper, he's naturally going to want to help call the tune.* 我认为，我们不应该让毕格曼先生向我们的公司投入那么多的资本。如果我们让他付太多的吹笛钱，他当然想要得到一定的点曲权了。最后，是单独使用 call the tune 的例子。*Bill has taken his father's place as company president, but I suspect his father is still calling the tune.* 比尔已经接替他的父亲当了公司的董事长，不过，我觉得实权仍然在当老子的手心里。*Though still with vast influence, America is no longer able to call the tune in Western Europe.* 美国对西欧仍然发生巨大的影响，但是已经不可能再在那里发号施令了。◇ give the orders

can't carry a tune [ˌkæ(ː)nt ˌke(ː)riə ˈtjuːn] [口] **由于是音盲而不能歌唱** → have a tin EAR

change *one's* **tune** [ˌtʃeɪndʒ～ ˈtjuːn] [口] **改变态度** 直译为"改变曲调"。转作比喻，tune 指"所说的话"。因此，这一习用语的精确释义为"改变说法"。*Though the manager of the inn greeted our group very heartily, when he found that we didn't have any money he very quickly* *changed his tune.* 那家客店的老板虽然非常热情地欢迎我们这帮人，但是，当他知道我们连一分钱都没有的时候，他的态度马上就改变了。有象这样用于从“热情”变到“冷淡”的场合，但是主要是用于表示态度从“傲慢”变到“谦恭”。*At first very haughty, the man, upon learning that my friend was rich, quickly changed his tune.* 那个人最初非常傲慢，但是听说我的朋友很有钱之后，他马上改变了态度。*Tell George that if he doesn't cooperate we'll boycott the meeting. That'll make him change his tune.* 你告诉乔治，如果他不合作，我们就拒绝参加会议。这样就会使他改变态度啦。*June used to be very critical of the way we raised our children, but when she became a mother herself she began to change her tune.* 琼对我们抚育孩子的方式一向吹毛求疵，但是她当了母亲之后，就开始改变她的腔调了。*You treat me like a kid now, but just you wait. I'm going to be a big man some day. You'll change your tune then.* 你现在总是把我当成小孩子，但是，你等着好啦。我总有一天会成为雄赳赳的大男子汉的。到那时候，你的态度就会改变了。另有一个说法是 (begin to) sing a different [another] tune, 同义。◇ change *one's* attitude

He who pays the piper calls the tune. [ˈhiːhu ˌpeɪzðə ˈpaɪpər ˌkɔ(ː)lzðə ˈtʃuːn] [谚] **谁付吹笛钱，谁有点曲权** → pay the PIPER / call the TUNE

(begin to) sing a different [another] tune [(bəˌgɪntə) ˌsɪŋə ˌdɪfərənˈtʃuːn / ˌnʌðərˈtʃuːn] [口] **改变态度或看法** → change *one's* TUNE

tunnel

see the light at the end of the tunnel → LIGHT

turkey

quit (*something*) cold turkey [ˌkwɪt ˈkould ˈtərki] [话] **一下子戒掉(毒品、烟酒等不良嗜好)** 来源：突然停止 (quit) 服用毒品，就会发生戒毒症状，浑身起鸡皮疙瘩。cold turkey 是“冷的火鸡(那样的皮肤)”。本条习用语本来的意思是：“宁愿忍受全身起鸡皮疙瘩之苦，也一下子戒掉毒品。”后来不仅限于毒品，在一下子戒掉各种恶习(吸烟、饮酒等)的时候广泛使用。*It's almost impossible to quit heroin cold turkey.* 一下子戒掉海洛因几乎不可能。代入 *something* 处的词，如 heroin, drinking, smoking 等，如果上下文已经交待清楚，可以省略。*A.A. is an organization to help alcoholics quit cold turkey.* 嗜酒者互诫协会是帮助酒徒一下子戒除恶习的组织。cold turkey 也有与 quit 以外的动词一起使用的情况。*A: Have you quit smoking? B: Yeah. I kicked the habit cold turkey.* 甲：你戒烟了吗？乙：是的，我一下子戒掉了这个恶习。如以上的例句所示，这一表达法一般用于“对健康有害的恶习”，但偶尔也用于其他方面的恶习。在这一场合，多带有半开玩笑的性质。*I've decided to quit gambling cold turkey.* 我决定戒赌了。→ kick the HABIT ◇ quit suddenly [abruptly] / stop taking heroin [drinking, smoking, etc.] without a tapering off period

talk turkey [ˌtɔ(ː)k ˈtəːrki] [话] **打开天窗说亮话** 语源不明，但有这样一种说法：过去，美国的一个印第安人与一个白人同去狩猎，他们猎得一些火鸡和乌鸦。在分猎物的时候，白人首先说：“我拿一只火鸡，你拿一只乌鸦。”然后又分，白人还说：“我拿一只火鸡，你拿一只乌鸦。”如此这般，他一直是拿火鸡。结果，那个印第安人提出抗议说：You always talk turkey. Now I talk turkey. (你总说火鸡。这回我说火鸡。)据说，从那以后，人们就用“说火鸡”来表示“明白说”、“干脆说”或“坦率说”的意思了。这一说法没有多大历史根据，但作为故事倒很有趣。本条习用语的使用范围相当广，包括“不再转弯抹角，干脆说清楚”，“不再隐瞒，合盘托出”，“不再支吾搪塞，坦白交代”等各种意味。*We've been beating around the bush with each other long enough. It's time we started talking turkey.* 咱们彼此兜圈子的时间已经够长的了。现在该坦率地交换一下意见了。*I met with Mr. Smith last night in order to try to find out what was really on his mind, but I couldn't get him to talk turkey.* 昨天晚上我会见史密斯先生，打算探听一下他的真正意图，可是我没能使他开诚布公地讲出来。*I knew when she refused to look me in the eye that she wasn't talking turkey.* 当她不肯直视我的眼睛时，我就知道她并没有讲真话。*If that guy doesn't talk turkey, I'm going to make him eat crow!* 如果那个家伙不说老实话，我就给他点儿颜色看看！*Let's talk turkey a moment, John. I have some serious questions I think you can answer.* 约翰，咱们坦率地谈一下吧。我有几个重要的问题，我想你是能够回答的。◇ speak frankly [plainly and honestly]

turn

do *someone* **a bad turn** [.du(:) ~ ə.bæ(:)dˈtə:rn] [口] **对别人做坏事** → do *someone* a good TURN

do *someone* **a good turn** [.du(:) ~ ə.gudˈtə:rn] [口] **对别人做好事** turn 是“对待别人的行为”。本条直译为“向某人做好的行为”。*I've done that guy several good turns, but he never seems to remember it when I need his help.* 我帮过那小子好几次，可是当我需要他来帮忙的时候，他似乎一点也不记得我的好处。*Thank you for helping me. I hope I'll be able to do you a good turn someday.* 谢谢你帮助我。我希望将来有报答你的一天。do *someone* a good turn 的后边添上 by+动名词，则表示 good turn 的具体内容。*I wish I could do something for her. She did me a good turn by helping me get a job last year.* 我愿意有机会为她效劳。去年我找工作的时候，她曾帮了我很大的忙。do *someone* a good turn 的反义语为 do *someone* a bad turn (对别人做坏事)，论使用频率，后者远远不如前者。*You did me a bad turn when you told the boss I could type. Now he has me typing his letters whenever his secretary is sick.* 你告诉老板说我会打字，这可是对我做了一件坏事。现在，每当他的秘书请病假的时候，他就叫我给他打信件。◇ do *someone* a favor / help *someone*

make *someone* **turn over in** *his* **grave** →GRAVE

One good turn deserves another. [ˈwʌn .gudˈtə:rn də.zə:rvz əˈnʌðər] [谚] **好事应有好报** deserve 是“应该受到”、“应该得到”、“值得”的意思。*He deserves to be promoted.* 他应该得到提升。*He deserves to be punished.* 他应该受到惩罚。从以上的例句可以看出，这个动词既能用于好的事情，也能用于坏的事情。本条条头直译为“一个好的行为当然值得得到另一个好的行为”。这里的 turn 是 deed (行为) 的意思，两者也可以代换使用。不过，本条是一个谚语，固定使用 turn。*A: Thank you for helping me. B: Don't mention it. You helped me out the other day, and one good turn deserves another.* 甲：感谢你帮助我。乙：不要客气。前几天你帮助过我，这叫做投桃报李嘛。这是在对方表示谢意的时候向对方讲的。下面的例句是在对方感到不过意的时候而向对方讲的话。*A: You needn't bother taking me home. B: It's no bother. Besides, you lent me your class notes, and one good turn deserves another.* 甲：你不必送我回家，那太麻烦你了。乙：没什么麻烦的。再说，你还把课堂笔记借给了我，你的好意应该得到报答。◇ One favor [good deed] should be repaid with another.

speak out of turn [.spi(:)kaudəvˈtə:rn] [口] **说话太过火了** turn 是“顺序”。out of turn 是“乱了顺序”。因此，speak out of turn 的字面意义为“打乱先后顺序的讲话”。*Terry is speaking out of turn. He's supposed to come after the next speaker.* 特里的发言乱了顺序，他是排在下一位讲演者的后边的。后来进一步发展，speak out of turn 作为比喻使用，就从“打乱先后次序”转成“打乱上下次序”(不顾地位、身份、权限、立场)，亦即“说话过火”，有时等于汉语“乱弹琴”。You spoke out of turn. You should have let the ambassador make those remarks. 这句话可以按照字面意义理解为"你真乱弹琴。你应该让大使先发言啊。"但也可以按照比喻意义理解为"你真乱弹琴。你应该尊重大使,让他发言啊。"下面是比喻的用例。*I'm sorry I spoke out of turn yesterday, chief. I should have controlled my temper.* 老板,真对不起,昨天我说话太过火了。我应该控制我的脾气。*The boss is still angry with you for speaking out of turn at last week's meeting.* 你在上个星期的会议中发言失当,老板还生你的气哪。*You spoke out of turn when you criticized Prof. Wiggly's methods of teaching.* 你批评威格里教授的教学法,实在太放肆了。有时可以用于"打乱上下关系"以外的场合,例如在对等关系中表示"失礼"的意味。*I may be speaking out of turn, but I think you're a beautiful woman.* 我说这话也许很冒昧,可我认为你是一位美丽的女子。◇ speak inappropriately [indiscriminately]

turn in [ˌtə(ː)rˈnɪ(ː)n] [话] **夜里上床睡觉** turn in 原是农业用语,意思为"将表层的土以及肥料翻入地下"。后来转义为"把自己卷到毯子里",再进一步变成了不及物动词短语。*I think I'll turn in.* 我想我该上床睡觉了。*My husband never turns in before twelve o'clock.* 我丈夫从来不在十二点以前上床睡觉。◇ go to bed

turn to (and *do something*) [ˈtəːrnˈtuː] [口] **着手工作、学习等** turn to *something* [*someone*] 一般有如下的意义: turn to the wall (转过身去面向墙壁); turn to an encyclopedia (去查百科全书); turn to a friend (去求朋友帮助) 等。如果 to 以下不接名词,则多半是条头的释义。特别是在会话中,带有"鼓足干劲"、"精神十足"、"锐不可当"的意思。*Okay, you guys, turn to!* 喂,伙计们,铆劲儿干吧! 如果另有词句接在后边,一般采取如下的形式: turn to and +动词。*We all turned to and cleaned the whole house before Mother returned home.* 我们全都着手打扫卫生,在母亲回来以前把整个屋子弄得干干净净。*Doris finally turned to and studied for her test.* 多丽丝终于鼓起劲来,埋头准备考试了。*If we all turn to, we can finish this work today.* 如果我们大家鼓足干劲,这个工作今天能够干完。◇ begin working (energetically) / apply *oneself* (diligently)

turnabout

Turnabout is fair play. [ˌtə(ː)rnəˈbauts ˌfeːrˈpleɪ] [话] **一报还一报** 直译为"互相交替是公平的"。可以在已经报复之后使用,也可以在要求进行报复的时候使用。*You hit me first! Turnabout's fair play!* 你先打过我啦! 一报还一报嘛! *Let me bat now. Turnabout's fair play.* 现在该我打你了,一报还一报。这句英语一般是儿童使用,但成年人也有使用的时候。*They shouldn't complain about our selling in their territory. Turnabout is fair play.* 他们不应当抱怨我们侵占他们的销售地盘。一报还一报嘛。◇ It is only fair to let *someone* have *his* turn, too.

turnpike

a turnpike [ə ˈtə(ː)rnˌpaɪk] [口] **收费高速公路** → a HIGHWAY

turns

every time *one* **turns around** → TIME

turntail

a turntail [ə ˈtə(ː)rnˌteɪl] [口] **胆小鬼** → turn TAIL

turtle

turn turtle [ˌtə(ː)rnˈtəːrdl] [口] **翻车; 翻船** 最初的构想为 turtle (龟)翻身的样子。如果用英语解释,就是 turn over like a turtle (象龟那样翻过来)。*The car skidded on the wet pavement and turned turtle in the ditch.* 汽车在湿了的路面上打滑,翻到明沟里去了。◇ turn upside down

twister

a tongue twister [ə ˈtʌŋ ˌtwɪstər] [口] **绕口令** 字面意义为"使舌头运转不灵的东西"。英语的绕口令大多是集合第一个字母 (辅音) 相同的词构成一个完整的有意义的语句。*A: What's your favorite tongue twister? B: I like " She sells seashells by the seashore." A: That's old hat. I prefer " Shy Sarah saw six Swiss wrist watches." Or how about "The sixth sheik's sixth sheep's sick"?* 甲：你最喜欢的绕口令是什么？乙：我喜欢 *She sells seashells by the seashore* [ˈʃi(ː)selz ˈsi(ː)-ˌʃelz baɪðə ˈsi(ː)ˌʃo(ː)r]。甲：那都老掉牙了。我喜欢 *Shy Sarah saw six Swiss wrist watches* [ˈʃaɪ ˈseːrə ˌsɔ(ː) ˈsɪks ˈswɪs ˈrɪst ˌwɑ(ː)tʃəz]。或者 *The sixth sheik's sixth sheep's sick.* [ðə ˌsɪksθ ˈʃi(ː)ks ˌsɪksθ ˈʃi(ː)ps ˈsɪk]. 你看怎么样？tongue twister 一般是为游戏用而编造出来的东西。另有一种由 1～2 个字构成的词，并非特意编造，但是很难发音，一般称之为 a JAWBREAKER。有时，人们对 jawbreaker 也称呼为 tongue twister。*The full scientific name of DNA is a real tongue twister: deoxyribonucleic acid.* DNA 的正式科学名称简直是个绕口令，叫 *deoxyribonucleic acid* [ˌdi(ː)ˈɑksɪˈraɪbou.njuːkˈ-liːɪk ˈæsɪd] (脱氧核糖核酸)。◇ a sentence [phrase] that is hard to say fast

a twister [ə ˈtwɪstər] [话] **大龙卷风** 直译为"卷自己的东西"。*A huge, black twister was moving toward the town.* 巨大的、黑色的龙卷风向城镇刮来了。◇ a tornado

two

do number two [ˌdu(ː) ˌnʌmbər ˈtuː] [话] 拉屎 → GRUNT

two-bagger

a two-bagger [ə ˈtuːˈbæːgər] [话] **二垒打** → a FOUR-BAGGER

two-edged

a two-edged sword → SWORD

two-spot

a two-spot [ə ˈtuː ˌspɑt] [话] **两美元的钞票** 直译为"有两个斑点的东西"。相当轻松的用语。*I think I'll bet this two-spot on Apple Knocker in the next race.* 下次赛马，我想把这张两美元钞票押在"乡巴佬"身上。有时表示"扑克牌的 2"、"骰子的 2 点"、"台球的 2 号球"等意味，但比指金钱的场合少。◇ a two-dollar bill

two-time

two-time *someone* (with *someone*) [ˈtu(ː) ˌtaɪm ～] [话] **朝三暮四** two-time 指"男女关系上，本来已经有确定的对象，而又与其他异性交往或私通"的情况。但很少用于夫妇关系，一般用于情侣、学生间的固定朋友(→ go STEADY <with *someone*>) 的关系。*Bill's steady has been two-timing him behind his back.* 比尔的女朋友背着他跟别人勾搭上了。*If Joe thinks he can get away with two-timing me, he has another think coming.* 如果乔认为他背着我胡搞也不要紧，那他就打错主意了。"two-time 的人"在英语中叫做 a two-timer。*Mary claims that men are all low-down two-timers.* 玛丽断定说，一切男子都是卑鄙的朝三暮四的人。另外，也可以这样说：*Rudy's wife found out that he had been two-timing her with his secretary.* 鲁迪的妻子发现他背着她跟他的女秘书私通。然而，在夫妇关系方面，如果讲到"男人有外遇"或"女方不贞洁"的时候，一般说 cheat on *someone*。*Les discovered that his wife had been cheating on him.* 莱斯发现他的妻子对他不忠。◇ (secretly) date [go out with] someone else [*someone*]

a two-time loser → LOSER

two-timer

a two-timer [ə ˈtuːˌtaɪmər] [话] **朝三暮四的人** → TWO-TIME *someone* (with *someone*)

U

ugly

(as) ugly as sin → SIN
an ugly customer → CUSTOMER

uh-huh

uh-huh [ˌʌ(ː)ˈhʌ] [话] **嗯** yes 的轻松说法，与 YEAH 的意思相似。这里的[ʌ]带有鼻音。 *A: Are you going? B: Uh-huh. (I'm going.)* 甲：你去吗？ 乙：嗯。（我去。） 在打电话的时候，如果说 uh-huh...uh-huh，那是“我听明白了”的意思。这一表达法与 I see... I see 类似，但 I see 语调比较硬，使用率很低。如果把头一个音节拉长，第二个音节发音稍重，作 [ˌʌːˈhʌ]，则表示怀疑或否定对方所说的话，大致等于汉语的“哼”。 *Jack: I'd really like to take you to the movies, but I'm going to be very busy tonight. Jill: Uh-huh! You mean you're going to be busy with another girl, don't you?* 杰克：我的确想带你去看电影，不过，我今天晚上太忙。吉尔：哼！你的意思是说，你忙着陪别的姑娘去玩，是吧？ ◇ yes

uh-uh

uh-uh [ˈʌˌʌ] [话] **不！** → HUH-UH

ump

an ump [əˈnʌ(ː)mp] [话] **裁判** an umpire [ˈʌmˌpaɪr] 的缩略。多指棒球的裁判，但也可以用于足球、网球等。 *Who's going to be the ump?* 谁给当裁判？ *Funk's unc is a National League ump.* 芬克的叔叔是全国棒球联盟的裁判。在称呼比赛中的裁判时也常使用。 *Hey, ump! You need glasses!* 喂，裁判！你需要戴眼镜啦！ ◇ an umpire

umpteen

umpteen [ˈʌmpˈtiːn] [话] **多得数不过来** 形容词。虽然可以当表语使用，但习惯上总是放在名词的前边。强调数目之多。 *I've told her umpteen times and still she doesn't remember.* 我告诉她不知有多少次了，她还是记不住。 *I can give you umpteen reasons why it won't work.* 究竟为什么不行，我可以给你列出数不尽的理由来。 *It was a big party. There must have been umpteen people there.* 那是一次盛大的社交晚会，一定来了很多很多人。以上是单独使用 umpteen 强调数目之多的例子。也可以把它加在数词的前边起同样的作用，如 umpteen thousand（几万，几十万那么多），umpteen million（几百万，几千万那么多）。 *Stop complaining. There are umpteen million people in the world who I'm sure would be happy to exchange their life for yours.* 你不要发牢骚啦。我敢肯定，世界上会有千千万万人愿意与你换一下生活处境。umpteenth 可以当序数词使用。 *For the umpteenth time, stop bothering me while I'm working!* 我告诉你千百遍了，在我工作的时候不要打扰我！ ◇ any number of / many dozens of

unbowed

bloody but unbowed → BLOODY

Unc

Unc [ˈʌ(ː)ŋk] [话] **伯伯、叔叔** uncle [ˈʌŋkl] 一词去掉 -le 构成。主要是与自己的伯父、叔父对话时用作爱称。 *Could you lend me your car tomorrow, Unc?* 叔叔，你明天能把汽车借给我一用吗？第一个字母小写，可作为普通名词使用。 *His unc's very rich.* 他的叔父很有钱。不过，这种用法极罕见。 ◇ Uncle

uncle

cry uncle [ˌkraɪ ˈʌŋkl] [话] **认输** → say UNCLE

I'll be a monkey's uncle. [ˈaɪlbiə ˈmʌŋki ˈzʌŋkl] [话] **吓了一大跳** → I'll be HORNSWOGGLED.

say uncle [ˌseɪ ˈʌŋkl] [话] **认输** 直译为"叫叔叔"。男孩子交起手来（有时是真打架，有时是闹着玩）的时候，常使用这一表达法。一般是把对方按在底下的男孩子用命令的口气说："Say uncle!"（认输吧！），只要对方的孩子不说"Uncle! Uncle!"（输了！输了！），得胜的一方就拧他胳膊，胳肢他，弄疼他，继续不断进攻，直到他认输为止。上面的对话在英语中大致等于"Give up?" "I give up! I give up!"有时，成年人也把条头作为比喻使用。*We're going to undersell on this product until all our competitors say uncle.* 我们要以比别人低的价格出售这种产品，直到所有的竞争对手都告饶为止。另外，也有时用 cry 代替 say，而讲 cry uncle。◇ give up

Uncle Sam [ˌʌŋkl ˈsæːm] [话] **山姆大叔** 这是美国人日常对自己国家及本国政府的昵称。所谓"山姆大叔"是把美国及美国政府拟人化了。1812 年战争的时候，美国政府发给军队的肉装在木桶里，桶上写着 U.S.的字样。那种肉是由商人 Samuel Wilson 加工的，他的绰号叫做 Uncle Sam。桶上的 U. S.本来是 the United States 的缩略，但是在不知不觉之间，人们却戏谑地用它来表示 Uncle Sam 的意思了。时过境迁，Samuel Wilson 这个人逐渐被大家忘掉，因此，美国人就都认为 Uncle Sam = the United States 了。Uncle Sam 在漫画中的形象是：一个又瘦又高的白胡子老头儿，穿黑色燕尾服和带有白条纹与红条纹的裤子，大礼帽的帽带上有几颗用直线勾成的星星。这个形象最初见于 1869 年出版的 *Harper's Magazine*（《哈泼斯杂志》，月刊）。*Uncle Sam seems to be having a lot of trade problems these days.* 山姆大叔最近似乎被贸易问题弄得焦头烂额。*It's true I have a good salary, but Uncle Sam gets most of it.* 我的工资的确很高，但是大部分都叫山姆大叔拿去了（即所得税高的意思）。另外，有的词典将 Uncle Sam 释义为"典型的美国人"，请读者注意，根本不能这样使用。◇ the United States (government)

undergrad

an undergrad [ə ˈnʌndər.græːd] [话] **大学本科生** 大学生用语，an undergraduate student 的缩略。与研究生相对而言。*A: Are you a graduate student? B: No, I'm still an undergrad.* 甲：你是研究生吗？乙：不，我现在还是本科生。也可以称为 an undergraduate [ə ˌnʌndərˈgræːdʒuət]。另外，与 an undergrad 相对的"研究生"不叫 a GRAD，而是 a grad STUDENT。◇ an undergraduate student

underwear

long- handle underwear [ˈlɔ(ː)ŋ ˌhændl ˈʌndərwer] [话] **男子用上下连身的长内衣** → long JOHNS

undies

undies [ˈʌndi(ː)z] [话] **妇女儿童的内衣** 女性用语。特指三角裤衩。词的构成：underwear 的第一音节 +表示"小"的后缀-ie+ 复数的-s。一件内衣也用复数。*I have to buy some new undies.* 我必须买新内衣了。◇ (ladies' [children's]) underwear

union

a union suit [ə ˈju(ː)njən ˌsu(ː)t] [口] **男子用上下连身的长内衣** → long JOHNS

united

present a united front [prəˌzentə juˌnaɪdəd ˈfrʌ(ː)nt] [口] **结成统一战线** → close RANKS (with *someone*)

unlisted

an unlisted number → NUMBER

unwashed

the great unwashed [ðə ˌgreɪˌdʌnˈwɑːʃt] [话] **广大群众** 按字面意义，unwashed 是"没有洗的"。从语法上讲，the +形容词可以成为集合名词，如 the poor 是"穷苦的人们"。the+过去分词也起同样的作用。如 underprivileged（贫困的、没有社会地位的）加上 the，成为 the underprivileged 之后，就是"贫苦阶层”。同样，the unwashed 表示“没有文化的人民群众”。great 在这里是表示“多数的”、“数不尽的”的意味的形容词。*George believes that no government can succeed if it does not consider the opinions of the great unwashed.* 乔治认为，如果不考虑广大群众的意见，任何政府也不会成功。有时省略 great，也有时 great 的 g 和 unwashed 的 u 用大写字母。*That guy will never take the bus. He seems to think he's too good to rub shoulders with the (great) unwashed.* 那个家伙绝对不坐公共汽车。他似乎认为自己比广大群众高出一头，不能与他们摩肩接踵。*The government seems increasingly to believe that it has to make all of the decisions for the Great Unwashed.* 政府似乎越来越相信，它在做任何决定时都必须考虑广大群众的利益。◇ the (hordes of) common people

up

be on the up and up [ɔ(:)nðɪ ˌʌpəˈnʌ(:)p] [话] **正直** 任何英语词典都有两个解释，一是“正直 (诚实)”，一是“向上 (顺利)”。但前者是美国英语，后者是英国英语，请勿混同。例如：*Don't be afraid to take a job with that organization. They're very much on the up and up.* 用不着担心到那个协会去工作。那是一个很可靠的机构。如果这句话是英国英语，后半句要改译为“那是一个蒸蒸日上的机构”。*He seems to be on the up and up, but we'd better check his story out just to be sure.* 他似乎是一个正直的人，但是对他所讲的情况还是核实一番为好。*She may very well prove to be on the up and up, but it pays to be careful. This burg is full of gold diggers, you know.* 她这个人可能是很正直的，但是以小心谨慎为妙。你要知道，这个城里到处是以色相诱骗男人钱财的女子啊。如以上的例句所示，一般是指“人品”而言。但也有如下的用法：*I'm sure his story is on the up and up. I've known his family for many years.* 他的话肯定是真实的。我跟他的家庭交往多年了。有时加连字符，写作 on the up-and-up。◇ honest / trustworthy

be up and about [around] [ˌʌpənəˈbaut / ˌʌpənəˈraund] [话] **起床后活动** 如果只用 be up，意思是“不是在躺着”，既可以指“从床上起身”，也可以指“离开床走动”。本条习用语则指离开床后进行活动的状态。*You can call me anytime after six in the morning. I'm usually up and about by then.* 在早上六点钟以后，你什么时候给我打电话都可以。一般来说，到那时候我已经起床活动了。可以用 around 代替 about，意思一样，而且在任何句子里都能互相代换。不过，比较起来，人们多愿使用 about。*My grandfather suffers from insomnia. He's often still up and around at two or three in the morning.* 我的祖父患有失眠症。他往往在早晨两三点钟还没有上床就寝。常用这一习用语表示病人见好能够下床走动的意思。但在这一场合，about [around]不仅指“室内”，也可以指“到外边走走”。*He's up but not really about yet.* 他的病见好，能下床了，但是还不能任意走动呢。*Fortunately, his injury isn't serious. The doctor says he should be up and around by next week.* 幸好他的伤势不严重。据医生说，他到下个星期就可以下床走动了。*Don't worry about me. I'm sure it's just a cold. I'll be up and about in no time.* 请不必为我担心。我只是感冒罢了，马上就会好起来的。◇ be awake and moving about

upchuck

upchuck˙ [ˈʌpˌtʃʌk] [话] **呕吐食物** → lose *one's* DINNER

upper

gain the upper hand → HAND

lose the upper hand [ˌlu(:)zðɪ ˌʌpərˈhæ:nd] [口] **处于不利的地位** → gain the upper HAND

upstairs

kick *someone* upstairs [ˌkɪk ～ˌʌpˈstɛ:rz] [话] **明升暗降** 直译为“把某人踢到楼上去”。既然是 kick，对被踢者来说，当然

不是一件愉快的事情。用现在的流行话来讲,就是"让他靠边站"了。踢的对象是"不顶用的人"、"捣乱的人"、"讨厌的人"等等。 *After the president became too old to run the company, the board of directors kicked him upstairs to the position of board chairman.* 总经理年纪太大,已经无力经营公司,董事会把他明升暗降,让他当董事长了。 *When Mr. Green proved ineffective as head of the sales department, they kicked him upstairs.* 当他们看到格林先生没有当营业部部长的能力时,就把他明升暗降了。kick *someone* downstairs (把某人踢到楼下去) 的意思是 demote *someone* (降某人的职),这一表达法不象 upstairs 那样常用。 *Mr. Kibler complained so loudly about having nothing to do that they kicked him downstairs and put him to work again.* 基布勒先生大嚷大叫地抱怨他无事可做,因此,他被降职之后又恢复了工作。 ◇ promote *someone* out of the way

uptake

be quick on the uptake [ˌkwɪkɔ(ː)nðɪ ˈʌpˌteɪk] [话] **领会得快** uptake 的字面意义为"拾起"。"拾起"什么呢? 是"对方所要说的话"。所谓"拾起对方所要说的话",就是"领会"、"吸收"、"理解"的意思。因此,be quick on the uptake 为"领会[吸收、理解]得快"。 *I'm sure Jean understood the importance of what you told her. She's very quick on the uptake.* 琼一定理解了你告诉她的话的重要性。她的头脑领会得非常快。 *Be careful what you say around Ben. He's very quick on the uptake.* 在本的跟前你说话可要多加小心。他的头脑非常敏锐。 *Betty is a very pleasant girl to be with—pleasing to look at and quick on the uptake.* 跟贝蒂这样一个姑娘在一起,实在令人愉快。她不但长的好看,理解力也很强。反义语为 be slow on the uptake, 意思当然是"领会得慢"。 *I'm sorry if I seem slow on the uptake, but I don't understand the reason for your objection to my plan.* 我头脑有些迟钝,请多原谅。不过,我不理解你反对我的计划的理由。 ◇ have a quick mind

be slow on the uptake [ˌslouɔ(ː)nðɪ ˈʌpˌteɪk] [话] **领会得慢** → be quick on the UPTAKE

uptight

be uptight [ˌʌpˈtaɪt] [话] **紧张** 比较新的习用语。与 HANG loose 反义,指"肩头用力"的状态。 *I was so uptight at my job interview I could hardly talk.* 在就业面谈的时候我非常紧张,几乎连话都说不出来了。 *Just hang loose. You can't establish good rapport with your customers if you're too uptight.* 要轻松自如。你如果过于紧张,就不可能与顾客搞好关系。以上是表示直接紧张的场合。下面四个例句是表示"发愁"、"不安"或者"一本正经"。在极少的情况下,也可以表示"恼怒"。使用的范围虽然很广,表示的意义似乎很多,但是这些意义却有一个共同之处,那就是全都表达内心的"紧张"状态。 *So what if she turns you down? There's no need to be so uptight about it. Girls like her are a dime a dozen.* 她拒绝你的求婚,那又有什么了不起啊? 用不着为这件事那么发愁。象她那样的姑娘有的是,很容易找。 *Why are you so uptight about a little thing like that? It's nothing to worry about really.* 对那样芝麻大的小事,你为什么那么忐忑不安呢? 实际上一点也不必担心啊。 *Most government bureaucrats tend to be uptight. They're very difficult to rap with.* 大多数官僚都是一本正经,人们很难跟他们自由而坦率地谈话。 *Westerners often feel that Japanese society as a whole is too uptight.* 西方人往往感到整个日本社会过于拘谨了。get uptight 是"紧张起来",与 be uptight 同样,用于表示种种不同的意味。 *I meant what I said as just a little friendly advice. There's no need to get uptight about it.* 我所说的话只是想站在朋友的立场给你一个小小的忠告,你用不着火冒三丈呀。 *People who get uptight every time the market goes down shouldn't speculate* *in stocks.* 每当行情低落就提心吊胆的人,不应该去搞股票投机生意。此外,uptight 还表示"好极了"(特别是在寒暄中)或者"经济困难"的意思。这样使用的人全都是青年。 *A: How're ya doin'? B: Uptight, man. Uptight.* 甲:你好吗?乙:好极了,哥儿们。好极了。*After I lost my job, things got pretty uptight.* 我自从失业以后,经济上非常困难。uptight 也可以放在名词前边,作为定语使用。但在这一场合,大多是"死板"的意思。 *It's difficult to make friends with an uptight guy like that.* 跟他那样一个死板的家伙交朋友很难。*I don't want to work for an uptight outfit like that bank.* 我不愿意到一个象那家银行似的死气沉沉的单位去工作。◇ be nervous [upset, stiff-mannered]

V

veil

take the veil [ˌteɪkðə ˈveɪl] [口] **当修女** → take the TONSURE

veins

have ice water in *one's* **veins** → WATER

vengeance

with a vengeance [ˌwɪðə ˈvendʒənts] [口] **以猛烈的劲头** vengeance 是"复仇"。但是,with a vengeance 却不是"为了复仇"或"胸中燃烧着复仇的烈火"的意思。也可以说本来有这种意味,不过经过逐渐的演变,到了现代,已经从"象胸中燃烧着的复仇烈火那样猛烈"变成单纯的"以猛烈的劲头"、"剧烈地"、"激烈地"了。至少说,为了容易理解,可以这样考虑。在使用时,根据具体情况,偶尔也有符合原来的意思的场合,如:*He attacked his brother's killer with a vengeance.* 他怀着复仇的心情,猛烈袭击杀死他弟弟的凶手。但是,本条习用语广泛用于与"复仇"毫无关系的事情。*The old man was obviously half starved. He attacked the meal with a vengeance.* 老头儿显然饿得要死了,他向饭食猛扑过去。*All along the front line, enemy shells began raining down with a vengeance.* 在整个前线,敌人的炮弹开始象暴雨似地向下落。*When Gordon realized that he might not graduate, he began to study with a vengeance.* 戈登了解到他可能毕不了业的时候,就开始拼命用功了。如上所述,with a vengeance 一般不能表达"为了复仇"或"胸中燃烧着复仇的烈火"的意思,如果想要表达这种意思,在英语中要用 out of vengeance, in revenge [rəˈvendʒ], with vengeance in *one's* heart 等。◇ with great force [vigor, speed, diligence, etc.]

vest

play *one's* **cards close to the vest** → CARDS

play it close to the vest [ˌpleɪ ɪt ˌkloustəðə ˈve(ː)st] [口] **极力保守秘密** → play *one's* CARDS close to the vest

vet

a vet[①] [ə ˈve(ː)t] [话] **兽医** a veterinarian [ˈə ˌvetərəˈnerɪən] 的缩略。*I've got to take my dog to the vet.* 我必须带我的狗到兽医那儿去了。◇ a veterinarian

a vet[②] [ə ˈve(ː)t] [话] **退伍军人** a veteran [ˈvetərən] 的缩略。*Dick's dad is a World War II vet.* 迪克的爸爸是第二次世界大战的退伍兵。*Charles is a vet, but he never saw any action.* 查尔斯当过兵,但是从来没打过仗。◇ a veteran

view

take a dim view of *something* [ˌteɪkə ˌdɪm ˈvju(ː)əv ～] [口] **不乐意;不赞同** 直译为"持有暗淡的看法"。所谓"暗淡的",意思是"否定的"或"悲观的"。换句话说,take a dim view of *something* = take a pessimistic view of *something*(持有悲观的看法)。*Henry takes a dim view of human nature.* 亨利对于人性持有悲观的看法。这是按照原义的用法。但一般来说,这一习用语的语调比较轻松,只用于表示"怏怏不乐"的意思。这种"怏怏不乐"主要出现在"内心并不赞成,但表面又不能反对"或者"即使反对也毫无用处"的场合。*Most parents take a dim view of their children's dating too young.* 绝大多数当父母的都对他们的子女过早搞对象不太高兴。*I'm afraid my wife will take a dim view of my going abroad without her.* 我不带妻子出国,她对这件事一定会怏怏不乐的。*The villagers take a dim view of all the city people coming to bathe in their ocean.* 城里人大

批前来洗海水浴，村民们感到很不高兴。*The ruling party took a dim view of the opposition party's tax revision proposal.* 执政党对反对党提出的税制修正案大为不悦。*I take a dim view of your working so late every night.* 你每天夜里工作到那么晚，我心里很不高兴啊。◇ be not very happy about *something*

vine

a clinging vine [ə ˌklɪŋɪŋ ˈvaɪn] [口] **依赖男子的女人** 指"象绕在树上(clinging)的爬藤 (vine)一样总挎着男人胳膊"的女子。 *Every time we invite Bill to dinner, he shows up with one of his clinging vines.* 我们每次请比尔来吃饭的时候，他总是带着一位贴在身上撒娇的女人。*A: I've decided to marry Joanne. B: What? That clinging vine?* 甲：我已经决定跟乔安妮结婚了。乙：什么？跟那个贴在男人身上撒娇的姑娘？如以上的例句所示，这一习用语大多用于未婚的女性，但也有时用于已婚者，表示"依赖丈夫的女人"的意思。不过，在用于未婚者时，意思是"贴在身上"；在用于已婚者时，意思是"不能独立自主，一切依靠男人"。从常识上来说，在已经结婚之后还一天到晚贴在丈夫身上撒娇的女人也是很少见的。*Why don't you do something by yourself for a change? When I married you I didn't realize you were such a clinging vine.* 你为什么不改变一下，依靠自己去做点什么事情呢？当我跟你结婚的时候，我不知道你是这样一个没有独立能力的女人。可以作为形容词使用，但只限于 the clinging-vine type 一语。*Some men seem to prefer the clinging-vine type.* 有些男人似乎喜欢贴在身上撒娇这一类型的女子。◇ an excessively dependent girl [woman]

die on the vine [ˌdaɪɔ(ː)nðə ˈvaɪn] [口] **希望破灭；计划落空** → wither on the VINE

wither on the vine [ˌwɪðərɔ(ː)nðə ˈvaɪn] [口] **希望破灭；计划落空** 直译为"在蔓上枯萎"。*For lack of water, the grapes withered on the vine.* 由于缺水，葡萄在蔓上枯萎了。转作比喻使用，指计划落空、希望破灭等。至于落空或破灭的原因，多半是由于缺少援助、支持、资金以及良好的环境等。 *For lack of popular support, the city's plan to build a new bridge withered on the vine.* 由于缺少群众的支持，建造一座新桥的城市计划落空了。*As the recession deepened, all my hopes of starting my own business withered on the vine.* 由于经济衰退的日益严重，我想创办自己的公司的一切希望全都破灭了。另有一个说法是 die on the vine (直译为"在蔓上死去")。 *When that country's Prime Minister refused to accept our compromise offer, hopes for a peaceful settlement died on the vine.* 当那个国家的首相拒绝接受我们的妥协方案的时候，和平解决的希望完全破灭了。◇ come to nothing

violet

a shrinking violet [ə ˌʃrɪŋkɪŋ ˈvaɪələt] [口] **畏首畏尾的人** 字面意义为"正在发蔫的紫罗兰"。紫罗兰在背阴的地方或其他植物的叶荫下边悄悄地开花，因此成为 modesty (谦虚) 的象征。过去，仅 violet 一个词就意味着"腼腆的人"，现在必须添加 shrinking。*George has a very good mind. He would rise fast in the world if he weren't such a shrinking violet.* 乔治的头脑非常聪明。如果他不是那样一个畏首畏尾的人，在社会上早就出人头地了。如这一例句所示，一般用于成年人。*Thank you for inviting my wife as well, but I don't think she will want to come with us. She's something of a shrinking violet.* 非常感谢你也邀请我的妻子。但是，我想她是不会愿意前来的。她是一个不爱出头露面的人。*Don't be such a shrinking violet, Barbro. Why don't you accept Fred's invitation to the dance?* 巴布罗，不要那么腼腼腆腆嘛。你为什么不接受弗雷德的约请前去参加舞会呢？◇ a shy person ((something of a → a somewhat)) / shy ((such a → so / something of a → somewhat))

V.I.P.

a V.I.P. [ə'viː ˌaɪ 'piː] [话] **大人物** 仅取 very important person (非常重要的人) 中每一个单词的第一个字母构成的表达法。务请注意:发音不是 ['vɪp],必须是 ['vi ˌaɪ 'piː]。 *I gotta entertain a V.I.P. tonight.* 今天晚上我必须接待一位大人物。也可以写作 VIP。*This room is reserved for visiting VIP's.* 这个房间是给来访的大人物留用的。◇ a dignitary

visiting

a visiting fireman → FIREMAN

voice

shout at the top of ***one's*** **voice** [ˌʃaudətðə 'tɑ(ː)pəv ~ 'vɔɪs] [口] **放声大叫** → shout at the TOP of *one's* lungs

vomit

vomit ['vɑ(ː)mət] [口] **呕吐食物** → lose *one's* DINNER

vote

a straw vote [ə 'strɔː 'vout] [口] **非正式投票或调查** → a STRAW in the wind

wad

shoot *one's* **wad** [ˌʃu(ː)t ~ ˈwɑːd] [话] **用尽了所有力量** wad 指"纸、胶皮之类软的东西的一团"。由于成叠的钞票常用皮筋缠上,所以 wad 又有"一捆钞票"以及"一大笔钱"的意味。条头原义为"挥金如土"。*It was foolish of you to shoot your wad on one throw of the dice.* 你是真够愚蠢的,掷一下骰子就把所有的钱全输光了。后来进一步发展,一般用于表示"用尽了所有力量"的意思。这是一个轻松的现代习用语。*I think that director has shot his wad. He hasn't made a good movie for many years.* 我认为那位导演已经江郎才尽了。他很多年都没有拍出一部好片子了。*You'd better take me out of the game for a while, coach. I shot my wad on that last touchdown drive.* 教练,你最好叫我下场休息一会儿。在刚才触地得分时,我用尽了所有力气,一点劲儿都没有了。根据上下文,大多表示"已经用尽力气,再也不行了"的意味。"*I've shot my wad,*" *said the old man.* "*I've given the world my best, but now I have nothing left to give. I'm content to die.*" "我已经不行了,"那位老人说,"我对社会竭尽自己的所能,现在已经毫无余力了。我死也心满意足啦。"另有 shoot *one's* BOLT 的说法,同义,几乎在所有的场合都可以与本条互换使用。但在正式书写时,只能用 shoot *one's* bolt。◇ use up [expend] (all [most of]) *one's* resources [energy, energies, etc.] / be a force of the past

wagon

a crash wagon [ə ˈkræ(ː)ʃ ˌwæ(ː)gən] [话] **飞机场急救车** crash 的意思是"碰撞"、"飞机坠毁"。wagon 原义是"四轮马车",现在广泛作为俚语使用,指一切四轮车。本条条头指从电视新闻节目或电影中常常可以见到的那种飞机场急救车,在飞机发生故障临时着陆时使用。*A crash wagon was standing by when the damaged plane landed.* 当受损飞机着陆的时候,一辆急救车已经守候在那里。◇ a crash truck

fix *someone's* **wagon** [ˌfɪks ˈ~ ˌwæːgən] [话] **使人陷入困难境地** wagon 是美国一般家庭都有的儿童用四轮自行车。本条条头的最初构思是:孩子的 wagon 坏了,闹着要爸爸给修理。爸爸很有自信,就开始修理起来。可是等修理完一试验,却更加不好用了。第三者见到孩子在那里哇哇哭,就问道:"宝宝怎么啦?"那个孩子说:"爸爸修理我的车了(意思是不修理倒好,越修理越坏)。"fix 本义为"修理",在这里却完全相反,是"毁坏"的意思。因此,作为比喻,fix *someone's* wagon 使用于表示"使人受窘"、"使人受到严重损害"的意思。当然也可以按照字面意义使用,如:*The little boy begged his father to fix his wagon.* 小男孩央告他的父亲给他修理自行车。这根据上下文就可以判断,丝毫不成问题。*You fixed my wagon when you told the boss I skipped out and went to the baseball game yesterday afternoon.* 你向老板说昨天下午我从公司溜出去看棒球比赛,使我倒了大霉。这一例句讲的是"有意去做"的情况。但也有"并非有意如此"的场合,例如:*My husband really fixed our wagon when he lost his pay envelop. We had to give up our long- awaited summer vacation.* 我的丈夫把工资袋丢掉了,实在使我们窘极啦。我们不得不放弃了期待已久的暑期休假。本条条头也常带有威胁的口吻,表示一定要报一箭之仇的心情。*If he tries to interfere. I'll fix his wagon.* 如果他胆敢捣乱,我决不饶他。在"我决不饶他"之后,如果说明具体措施,大多是接续 I'll ~的形式,如: *I'll sue him for breach of promise.* 我要控诉他违反契约。因为儿童的 wagon 一般漆成红色,所以在强调的时候,人们常讲 fix *someone's* little red wagon。◇ cause *someone* a hard time / make things difficult for *someone*

hitch *one's* **wagon to a star** [.hɪtʃ ~ 'wæ(:)gən tuə.stɑ:r] [口] **怀有大志** 字面意义为"把自己的马车拴到一颗星上"。出典: R.W.爱默生 (Ralph Waldo Emerson)1870 年出版的《社会与孤独》(*Society and Solitude*)。其中有这样一句话: It is wise for man "in every instance of his labor, to hitch his wagon to a star, and see his chores done by the gods themselves." (对于人来说,聪明的办法是"在他的劳动的每一个步骤,都把自己的马车拴到一颗星上[意思是借助大自然的力量],并且看着神本身[指大自然本身]替他干一切日常琐事"。) 本条条头现在的用法与爱默生的原话有所不同。爱默生的意思是:"只要借助星(指大自然)的力量,任何事情都办得到"。现在已经完全失去"借助大自然的力量"的意味,仅表示"只要怀有大志,就会无坚不摧,无敌不克"了。一般用于以拼搏的精神向伟大目标迈进的场合。*When I was young, I dreamed of hitching my wagon to a star and becoming a great scientist or political leader.* 当我年轻的时候,我曾心怀大志,梦想当一位伟大的科学家或政治领袖。*It is fine to hitch your wagon to a star, but that alone is not enough. Without hard work to match, you'll find your wagon forever stuck in the mud of everyday life.* 胸怀大志是一件很好的事情,但是光有大志是不够的。如果不加上艰苦的努力,理想就必定陷入日常生活的泥沼。有时用 the stars 代替 a star。*Most people are satisfied with life's small successes, but the man who is daring enough to hitch his wagon to the stars finds that the sky is no limit.* 大多数人只满足于人生中的一些小小的成功,但是怀有大志的人却看到前途是无可限量的。◇ have great [noble] ambitions

be of the wagon [.ɔ(:)fðə 'wæ:gən] [话] **开酒戒** → be on the WAGON

be on the wagon [.ɔ(:)nðə 'wæ:gən] [话] **戒酒** 原作 be on the water wagon。water wagon 是行军时随身带的"水车"。因此, be on the water wagon 是"只喝水,不饮酒"的意思。现在,一般省略 water 一词。*No beer for me, please. I'm on the wagon.* 请不要给我啤酒。我戒酒了。*Al has been on the wagon ever since he joined Alcoholics Anonymous.* 阿尔自从参加嗜酒者互诫协会以后,一直不喝酒。除 be 动词外,也用 go, climb, jump, hop 等动词。如果用 go,意思只是"戒酒"。如果用 climb,则是"相当苦痛地戒酒"。如果用 hop 或 jump,是"轻而易举地戒酒"的意思。*I went on the wagon last month when my doctor told me I had a bad liver.* 由于医生说我的肝脏有病,我从上个月就戒酒了。put *someone* on the wagon 是"命令某人戒酒",主语大多是医生。*My doctor put me on the wagon last month.* 我的医生上个月命令我戒酒了。be on the wagon 进一步发展,又产生了它的反义语 be off the wagon,意思是"开酒戒"。*I've been off the wagon ever since my doctor gave me a clean bill of health.* 自从医生给我开了健康证明书以后,我就开了酒戒。与 on the wagon 的场合同样,除 be 动词外,也可以使用 get, climb, jump, hop 等动词。*It's hard to climb on the wagon but very easy to hop off again.* 戒酒非常不易,开戒却很容易。还常用动词 fall。fall 是"滑落", fall off the wagon 则有"不由得开了酒戒"的意味。*A. A. members cooperate in encouraging one another not to fall of the wagon.* 嗜酒者互诫协会的会员们互相勉励不要意志薄弱重开酒戒。◇ be not drinking

a paddy wagon [ə 'pædi .wæ(:)gən] [话] **囚车** Paddy 是爱尔兰语,为男子名 Padraig (英语作 Patrick) 的昵称。现在成为对一切爱尔兰男子的昵称。因为纽约的警察中有很多人是爱尔兰后裔,所以 paddy 一词有"警察"的意味。wagon 原义"四轮马车",现在也可以指汽车,在这里主要指把犯人运到警察局或拘留所时使用的囚车。*Since the two drunks wouldn't stop fighting, the policeman decided he had no choice but to call the paddy wagon.* 由于两个醉鬼不停止斗殴,警察无奈,只好呼叫囚车了。如这一例句所示,冠词用 the 的时候比用 a 的时候多。囚车又称 a Black Maria [ə ˌblæk məˈraɪə]。以上的两个名称都是相当于 a patrol wagon 的轻松说法。◇ a patrol wagon

a patrol wagan [ə ˈpətroul ˌwæ(:)gən] [口] **囚车** → a paddy WAGON

a rubberneck wagon [ə ˈrʌbərˌnek ˌwæ(:)gən] [话] **旅游车** → RUBBERNECK at *something*

Wait

Wait up. [ˌweɪdˈʌ(:)p] [话] **站下等等我!** 向先走的人呼喊时的用语。这是 *Wait* until I [we] catch *up* with you.的省略。*Wait up. I want to tell you something.* 你站下等等我!我有话对你说。*Hey! Wait up!* 喂!站下等等我!也有在非祈使句中使用的情况,如:*I called to you many times. Why didn't you wait up?* 我向你喊叫许多声了。为什么你不站下等我呢?但是,这种用法是很少的。为了表达同样的意思,一般是讲 Why didn't you wait for me? 另外,也偶尔说 Wait up for me [us]. 但在加 for ~ 的场合,一般是去掉 up 而只说 Wait for me [us]. ◇ Wait (for me [us]).

wait

wait up (for *someone*) [ˈweɪˈdʌ(:)p] [口] **不睡觉等待** 本条与前一条 WAIT up. (站下等等我!)的意思不同,指一直不上床睡觉,等待夜里很晚才回家的亲人。*I'll be late getting home tonight. Don't wait up.* 今天夜里我很晚才回家。你先睡好了,不必等我。*My husband waited up for Tim until twelve o'clock last night.* 昨天夜里,我丈夫一直等蒂姆到十二点才上床睡觉。◇ stay up [awake] waiting for *someone*

walk

the cock of the walk → COCK

walk all over *someone* [ˌwɔ(:) ˌkɔ(:) ˈlouvər ~] [话] **任意欺负** 直译为"在某人身上绕着圈走"。意思是"任意地践踏、侮辱、欺负",很容易理解。*Helen is so timid that she lets her husband walk all over her.* 海伦太怯懦了,使得她丈夫任意地欺负她。如这一例句所示,本条习用语用于无视对方的存在或对方的心情而为所欲为的场合。*Don't show that guy any weakness. He'll try to walk all over you.* 千万不要向那个家伙显示出任何的弱点。否则,他会骑在你的脖子上拉屎的。*If you think you can walk all over me, you've got another think coming.* 如果你以为可以骑在我的脖子上撒尿,那你就大错特错了。也可以用在体育运动方面,表示"彻底击败"的意思,如:*The Giants walked all over the Dodgers in last night's game.* 在昨天晚上的比赛中,巨人队彻底击败了诡计队。另外有从本条衍生出来的 use *someone* for a DOORMAT,也是习用语。◇ treat *someone* however *one* likes

walking

get *one's* **walking papers** [ˌget ~ ˈwɔːkɪŋ ˌpeɪpərz] [话] **被开除** → give *someone his* walking PAPERS

give *someone his* **walking papers** → PAPERS

wall

beat *one's* **head against a brick wall** → HEAD

drive *someone* **to the wall** [ˌdraɪv ~ təðə ˈwɔːl] [口] **逼得走投无路** drive 是"驱赶"。*The police dog finally drove me to the wall. There was no escape.* 警犬终于把我追到一面墙前,弄得我无处可逃了。这是按字面意义的用法。但是,作比喻使用的场合居多。*The price war instituted by our competitor finally drove our small company to the wall.* 我们的对手搞价格战,使得我们这个小公司走投无路了。*Unfortunately, some young people contemplate suicide because their parents' desire for them to succeed has driven them to the wall.* 不幸的是,由于父母望子成龙,有些青年被逼得走投无

路而企图自杀。*Driven to the wall by his cousin's threats to go to the police, Rubin decided that murder was the only way out.* 由于表兄威胁说要去报告警察，鲁宾被逼得走投无路，他心里想：除了把他杀掉，就没有第二条路可走。另有一个说法是把 drive 换成 push，作 push *someone* to the wall，意思不是"追赶到墙前"，而是"推到墙前"。但在作为比喻使用时，与用 drive 的说法完全是一样的意思，只不过使用率略低一些。*I'm a desperate man. Don't try to push me to the wall or someone will get hurt.* 我是一个亡命徒。别把我逼得走头无路，否则有人会遭殃的。◇ force *someone* into a hopeless [desperate] position [situation]

drive *someone* **up the wall** [ˌdraɪv ～ˌʌpðə ˈwɔːl] [话] **使人心烦意乱** 直译为"把人逼得要爬上墙"，这是对内心焦躁不安状态的夸大表现。*Turn down the volume of the radio, will you? The noise is driving me up the wall.* 你把收音机的音量放小点儿好吗？那么大的声响吵得我心烦意乱。*I don't want to go to the movies with Jack and Jill. They drive me up the wall with their constant billing and cooing.* 我不愿跟杰克和吉尔一道看电影。他们老是喁喁私语，弄得我心烦意乱。◇ make *someone* very nervous and irritable

go over the wall [ˌgouˌovər ðə ˈwɔːl] [话] **越狱潜逃** 字面意义是"越墙而走"，但本条完全是比喻说法，囚犯的任何逃走方法均可以应用。*I heard that three prisoners went over the wall last night at Folsom Prison.* 我听说昨天夜里有三个囚犯从福尔索姆监狱逃走了。◇ escape from prison

the handwriting on the wall → HANDWRITING

have *one's* **back to the wall** → BACK

push *someone* **to the wall** [ˌpuʃ ～ təðə ˈwɔːl] [口] **逼得走投无路** → drive *someone* to the WALL

wallflower

a wallflower [ə ˈwɔːlˌflauər] [口] **在舞会中无人邀请跳舞的女子** 直译为"壁花"。在开跳舞会的时候，没有男性来邀请伴舞的女子，始终靠墙站着，就象装饰 wall 的 flower 一样，故名。*No one invited me to the prom, so I'm not going. I don't want to be a wallflower.* 没有人来约我参加学校的舞会，所以我不去。我不愿去当壁花。*I'm too shy to ask for a date. I usually end up dancing with all the wallflowers.* 我这个人太腼腆，不好意思向女人请求约会。我总是凑合着跟那些壁花跳舞。"壁花"一般是女性，但有时也戏指男人。*Hi, Tom. Why aren't you dancing? Are you a wallflower tonight?* 喂，汤姆，你为什么不跳舞？今天晚上你是壁花吗？◇ (a girl who) just stand(s) around waiting to be invited to dance

wanna

wanna [ˈwɑnə] [话] **想要……** want to 的音变，也就是将 want to 按日常会话中的发音拼写而成。在漫画或小说的对话部分常可以看到。*A: Ya wanna go* [jəˌwɑnə ˈgou]? *B: No, I don't wanna* [ˈno ədəˈwɑnə]. 甲：你想去吗？乙：不，我不想去。顺便讲一下：want 与不定冠词结合为 want a(n) ～时，发音也是 [ˈwɑnə]，但不能按发音拼写为 wanna，仍然要写为 want a(n)。例如：*A: You want an apple* [jəˈwɑnə ˈnæpl]? *B: No, I want a drink* [ˈnouəˌw ɑnə ˈdrɪŋk]. 甲：你想要个苹果吗？乙：不，我想要一杯酒。◇ want to

war

All's fair in love and war. → LOVE

warm

be warm [ˈwɔ(ː)rm] [话] **接近目标** 原为儿童游戏用语。美国人一听到这一说法，首先想到的也是儿童游戏。例如儿童们玩"寻宝物"时说：*You're warm ... You're getting warmer ... Now you're getting hot.* 你快找到了……更接近了……现在就在你的手头了。但本条应用范围很广，从猜谜语的场合直到讲科学家的发现。*The mathematician hadn't found the right equation yet, but he felt he was getting warmer day by day.* 那位数学家还没有找到正确的方程式，但是他感到已经日益接近它了。*A: Is that the right answer? B: No, but you're warm.* 甲：那是正确的答案吗？乙：不是，但是你已经距它不远了。*The detective's questions so far were just shots in the dark, but he realized from the look on the suspect's face that he was getting warm.* 到目前为止，侦探提出的问题全是试探性的，没有一定目标，但是从嫌疑犯的面部表情来看，他明白自己已经快击中要害了。与 warm 相对，最近又出现了 be cold (远离目标) 的说法。*A: Am I getting warmer now? B: Yes, you're very warm.... No, now you're getting colder .... Now you're really cold.* 甲：我现在接近目标吗？乙：是的，你已经很接近了……不，现在越来越远了……现在已经相差十万八千里啦。◇ be close

(as) warm as toast → TOAST

warpath

go on the warpath (against *someone* [*something*]) [ˌgouɔnðə ˈwɔ(ː)rˌpæ(ː)θ] [口] **由于满腔怒火而采取坚决的态度** → take the WARPATH (against *someone* [*something*])

be on the warpath [ɔnðə ˈwɔ(ː)rˌpæ(ː)θ] [口] **怒气冲天** warpath 直译为"战争的小道"，原是"美国印第安人前去打仗时通过的小路"。因此, be on the warpath 本来的意思是"走在战争的小道上"，亦即"印第安人前去打仗"。在描写美国西部生活的影剧中，常有这样的台词: *You'd better take your family to the fort. The Indians are on the warpath.* 你把家眷带到堡垒里边去比较安全。印第安人前来叫阵了。印第安人在作战时经常是怒气冲冲，因此，本条条头就成为表示"勃然大怒"的习用语了。*Be sure to be at work on time tomorrow, everybody. The boss is on the warpath because so many people have been punching in late recently.* 大家明天一定要按时上班。最近晚点打出勤卡的人太多了，老板非常恼火。*Ned's girl friend is on the warpath because she saw him with another girl last night.* 内德的女朋友怒气冲冲，因为她看见内德昨天晚上跟另一个姑娘在一起。在这一例句中，因为明确指出愤怒的对象，所以能用 be out for *someone's* SCALP 替换。另有 be on the warpath against ～的形式，意思与 take the WARPATH (against *someone* [*something*]) (→)一样。◇ be very angry

take the warpath (against *someone* [*something*]) [ˌteɪkðə ˈwɔ(ː)rˌpæ(ː)θ] [口] **采取坚决打击的态度** 本来的意思是"印第安人出征"，现今还可常在西部影剧中听到这样的台词 (→ be on the WARPATH)。作为比喻，在情况不断恶化，令人终于忍无可忍，只好"披挂上阵"的场合使用。一般是在"上阵"之前已经准备好一定的对策或计划，"采取坚决打击的态度"的对象大多为复数。*The police, having gotten so much flak over the recent increase in traffic accidents, have taken the warpath against reckless drivers.* 由于最近交通事故不断增加，警察受到很多的责难，他们对乱开车的司机采取了坚决打击的态度。*The principal has finally taken the warpath against cheating on exams.* 校长终于对在考试中作弊的行为采取了坚决打击的态度。也可以说 go on the warpath。*The government went on the warpath against drug traffickers.* 政府对贩卖毒品的人采取了坚决打击的态度。◇ take strong steps

wash

come out in the wash [kʌˌmautnðə ˈwɑːʃ] [口] **自然而然地解决** 字面意义为"衣服脏了，只要用水一洗就会干净的"。*You needn't try to get those spots off that dress now. They'll come out in the wash.* 你现在不必设法把那件衣服上的污点去掉。只要用水一洗，它们自然而然地就会掉了。用作比喻，表示"当前的问题自然而然地会得到解决"的意思。*I never try to solve every little problem that arises at the office. Most of them come out in the wash.* 我从来不试图去解决办公室里发生的每个小问题。它们大部分是会自然而然地得到解决的。常用 all 加强语气。*I'll admit that the situation doesn't look too bright now, but don't* *worry. It'll all come out in the wash.* 我承认现在的情况的确不太妙，不过，用不着担心。一切问题都会自然而然得到解决的。*We made a few mistakes, but fortunately they all came out in the wash.* 我们犯了一点点错误，但是，幸运的是，这些错误全都自然而然地纠正了过来。如以上的例句所示，come out in the wash 一般用于表示"自然而然地得到解决"的意思。但是，它还可以表示另外一种意味，即："对于当前的疑难问题，不久就会自见分晓"。这一场合也是"洗"，不过不是"去污"，而是从所洗的衣服口袋里"掉出东西来"。可以按照字面意义使用，如：*You must have forgotten to empty your pockets. These tickets came out in the wash.* 你一定是忘记把衣服口袋里的东西掏出来了。在洗的时候，这几张票掉出来了。作为比喻，用例如下：*The answers will all come out in the wash.* 答案全都会自见分晓的。*I was unable to fathom the reasons for his behavior, but I wasn't worried. I was fairly sure they would eventually come out in the wash.* 我没能弄清他为什么采取那样的行动，但是我并不感到烦恼。我确信，他的动机是会自动显露出来的。◇ be resolved [become clear] during the natural course of events

not wash [nɑt ˈwɑːʃ] [话] **理由站不住脚** 字面意义为"衣服掉色或走样儿，不耐水洗"。*This fabric won't wash. It isn't color-fast.* 这种纤维不耐水洗，容易掉色。用作比喻，是指"言论"、"事情"等经不起检查，只要一追究就破绽百出。*His story is plausible enough on the surface, but I doubt if it'll wash.* 他的话从表面上看好象很有道理，但是我认为它未必站得住脚。从英语的句型来说，这是肯定句。但本条条头用肯定句可以说是例外，一般都是用否定句。*Your alibi doesn't wash, Al. Three people say they saw you at the scene of the crime.* 阿尔，你说你不在犯罪现场，这站不住脚。有三个人讲，他们看见你在犯罪现场了。常加 just 增强语气，有"无论怎么说"的意思。*The stereotype of the Chinese as Sick Man of East Asia just doesn't wash any more.* 不管怎么讲，把中国人看做东亚病夫的旧观念再也站不住脚了。*I'm sorry, but your story just doesn't wash. You'll have to come up with a better explanation than that if you want to convince me.* 非常遗憾，你讲的话怎么也不合情理。如果你想说服我，你必须考虑如何更好地解释一下才行。not wash with me 也是一个习用语，意思是"我不听那一套"。*That guy's so-called bravery just won't wash with me. He's a coward and always was one.* 那个家伙号称勇敢，不论怎么说，我也不信那一套。他是个胆小鬼，而且一向如此。*You'll have to think of a better excuse than that. That one just won't wash with me.* 你应该想出一个更好的辩解的理由。不管怎么讲，你那个理由在我跟前站不住脚。本条习用语原为英国英语，美国人使用它是晚近的事情。◇ not stand up under examination / be not convincing (to *someone*)

wash out (of *flight school*) [ˌwɑ(ː)ˈʃaut] [话] **在航空学校因成绩不佳而退学** → FLUNK out (of *school*)

washed

be all washed up [ˈɔːl ˌwɑːʃˈtʌ(ː)p] [话] **完全不行了** be washed up 的意思是"被冲到海岸上"。*The exhausted sailor was washed up on the shore.* 那个筋疲力竭的水手被冲到海岸上了。从"一个人筋疲力竭而被冲到海岸上"这一具体形象出发，就产生了比喻的意义："干某种事情的时代已经一去不复返了"。*That guy is washed up.* 那个家伙已经日暮途穷了。可以象这样按照本条条头的原形作为比喻使用，但一般要加强调的副词 all。如：*As a writer, I'm all washed up. My powers of concentration are gone.* 作为一个作家，我已经完全不行了。我再也没能力聚精会神地写作。*The champ tried to make a comeback, but it was clear from the first round that he was all washed up.* 那位拳击冠军企图东山再起。但是从第一个回合就显示得很清楚，他已经完全不灵了。有时用 completely 代替 all。特别是在否定句中,一般均用 completely,也可以说它是构成否定式的一个成份。*I may be getting old, but I'm not completely washed up yet.* 我也许年纪大了,但是我并没完全不中用啊。◇ be no longer any good / be finished [through] (as a *something*)

WASP

a WASP [ə ˈwɑ(:)sp] [口] **祖先是英国新教徒的美国人** 小写的 wasp 是"黄蜂"。如果写成 WASP (有时作 Wasp),则为 White Anglo-Saxon Protestant 的缩略,直译为"白人盎格鲁—撒克逊新教徒"。这是对支持美国权势集团 (the Establishment)的大、中资产阶级的白人的蔑称。*Some people say America has too many WASPs.* 有些人说:在美国,祖先是英国新教徒的白人太多了。◇ a white Anglo-Saxon Protestant

watcher

a clock watcher [ə ˈklɑ(:)kˌwɑtʃər] [口] **老是看钟表等下班的工作人员** clock watcher 直译为"一直盯着时钟的人"。这种人在上班的时候,一会儿翻弄文件,一会儿看墙上的钟,到整十二点,他说"该吃饭啦",到下午五点,他说"该回家啦"。他们的哲学是"不迟到、不告假、不干活"。美国的公司里常有这一类人的踪迹。*Hal always appears to be busy, but actually he's a notorious clock watcher.* 哈尔永远是很忙的样子,但是实际上,他是一个著名的混泡专家。当然不仅是对公司职员,对任何单位的工作人员都可以使用这一表达法,有时还可以用在学生身上。*Clock watchers can never make top grades.* 在上课时间总看钟表等下课的学生决不可能有好分数。◇ a person who thinks more about the time than his work

water

Blood is thicker than water. → BLOOD

come hell or high water → HELL

go through hell and high water → HELL

have ice water in *one's* veins [ˌhæv ˈaɪsˌwɔ(:)dərɪn ~ veɪnz] [口] **具有超人的胆量** 直译为"血管里流着冰水"。这一习用语强调遇事毫不惊慌、冷静沉着的样子。*That guy isn't afraid of anything. He's got ice water in his veins.* 那个家伙天不怕地不怕,他具有超人的胆量。*Captain Nemo has ice water in his veins. He walked right up to the alien creature and started talking to it.* 尼莫船长具有超人的胆量。他向那个不知是什么的动物一直走去,并且开始对它讲话。在极少的场合,用于表示"残酷无情"的意味,即所谓的"冷血动物"。*That guy makes no bones about killing people's pets. He must have ice water in his veins.* 那个家伙毫不犹豫地杀死别人的爱畜。他一定是个冷血动物。◇ have unbelievably strong nerves / be extremely unfeeling

be in hot water [ɪn ˌhɑt ˈwɔ(:)dər] [话] **处于困境** 自 16 世纪初就有的古老的说法。有人说语源是:古时,每当有小偷、强盗闯入家门时,人们就从窗户往他们身上浇热水。但这一说法不可信。本条的意义与 be in trouble 大致相同。*I'm in a bit of hot water. Can you help bail me out?* 我现在有点陷入困境了。你能拉我一把吗? *Jack was often in hot water when he was young, but he always managed to get out of it somehow.* 杰克年轻的时候经常处于困境,不过,他总是设法摆脱。常用 be in hot water with *someone* 的形式,意思是"与某人的关系很糟糕",近似 be in DUTCH with *someone*。*Please don't ask me to help you cheat on the exam. I'm in a lot of hot water with the prof as it is.* 请不要叫我帮你在考试中作弊。我跟教授的关系已经很糟糕了。*I'm afraid our son is in hot water with the police for getting drunk and hitting an officer.* 我们的儿子喝醉酒,殴打一名警官,恐怕跟警察当局发生了很大麻烦。另有 get in(to) hot water (陷入困境) 和 put *someone* in hot water (使人陷入困境) 的形式。*You'd better be sure to have receipts to match your expenses. You don't want to get into hot water with the tax office.* 你最好是妥善

保存你所花的钱的收据。你不想跟税务局发生纠葛吧。*The governor's slip of the tongue about plans to raise taxes put him in hot water with the voters.* 州长走嘴泄露了增税计划，这使他搞糟了与选民之间的关系。◇ be in trouble

keep *one's* **head above water** → HEAD

be like a fish out of water → FISH

(roll off *someone***) like water off a duck's back** [(ˌrouˌlɔ(ː)f ～) ˌlaɪkˈwɔdərɔ(ː)fəˈdʌkˌsbæ(ː)k] [话] **满不在乎** 字面意义为"就象往鸭子的背上 (duck's back) 浇水一样"，水不能浸透鸭子的羽毛，全都流了下去。用作比喻，形容对他人的指责或批评毫不介意或恬不知耻的样子。*Jack doesn't care what people say. Criticism rolls off him like water off a duck's back.* 不管别人说什么，杰克都不往心里去。他对于批评是满不在乎的。*You can't make Sam angry. Insults roll off him like water off a duck's back.* 你没办法使萨姆动怒。他对侮辱也满不在乎。*That guy is hopeless. All my admonitions are like water off a duck's back.* 那个家伙已经不可救药。我的一切警告都被他当作耳边风。◇ have absolutely no effect (on *someone*)

not hold water [nɑt ˌhouldˈwɔ(ː)dər] [口] **不合情理** hold water 的字面意义为"容器不漏水"。转义为"议论、谈话等有条有理"。*It seems like a reasonable argument, but will it hold water in a court of law?* 这个论点好象很合理，不知道在法庭上能不能讲得通？这是肯定式。但在实际会话中，用否定式的场合占绝大多数。*I think I see your point, but your argument doesn't hold water.* 我想我已经明白你要说什么了，不过你的论点站不住脚。*Economists are beginning to realize that Keynesian theories don't necessarily hold water.* 经济学家们开始认识到凯恩斯学派的理论不一定行得通。*That accusation won't hold water. Everyone knows that I've never even met your wife.* 那种指责不合情理。所有的人都知道，我跟你老婆连面也没有见过。常用 just 加强语气。*I'm afraid I can't accept that excuse. It just doesn't hold water.* 很遗憾，我不能相信那种辩解。那完全站不住脚啊。◇ be not logical [reasonable, provable]

of the first water [əvðə ˈfəːrstˈwɔːdər] [口] **第一流的** 旧时，阿拉伯的珠宝商人把钻石比做水，并根据透明度把钻石分为三个等级，称为"第一水"、"第二水"和"第三水"。本条条头的英语是阿拉伯语的直译，直至 19 世纪中叶，英国的珠宝商人广泛使用 a diamond of the first water (一级钻石)、a diamond of the second water(二级钻石)、a diamond of the third water(三级钻石)的粗略分类法。此后，这些专门行话逐渐消失，只剩下了一个 of the first water，广泛用于表示"第一流的"、"头等的"、"最佳的"等意味。因为条头现在不仅用于宝石，所以下一例句就不能按区别钻石等级的专门术语来翻译成"第一水的"。*This is a diamond of the first water.* 这是一颗质量极好的钻石。在讲人时，用法如下：*He is a gentleman of the first water.* 他是位第一流的绅士。*We were sorry when Jacob quit the firm. He was a salesman of the first water.* 雅各布辞去公司的职务时，我们感到很遗憾。他本是一位最优秀的推销员。也可以应用于小说之类。*As mysteries, Agatha Christie's novels are of the first water.* 作为侦探小说，阿加萨·克里斯蒂的作品是第一流的。相反，在谈到不好的情况时，也常用本条习用语来强调糟糕的严重程度。"第一流的"坏当然是"最坏"、"最差"、"最糟糕"的意思了。*I realize only too well now that what I did was a mistake of the first water.* 现在我才深切地体会到我所犯的错误是最严重的。*If he thinks that, then he's a boob of the first water.* 如果他那样想，那他可是天字第一号的大傻瓜了。在会话中也常听见 a joke of the first water 的说法，称赞的时候不能使用。*He'll never be elected. His whole platform is a joke of the first water.* 他绝对不会当选。他的选举纲领完全是胡说八道。◇ of the highest quality / first-class ((在名词前)) / of the worst kind

pour cold water on *something* (by *doing something*) [ˌpo(ː)r ˌkould ˈwɔ(ː)dərɔn～] [话] **泼冷水** → throw cold WATER on *something* (by *doing something*)

running water [ˈrʌnɪŋ ˈwɔːdər] [口] **自来水** 字面意义为"流水",指"河川的流水"。但美国人一谈到 running water, 普遍理解为"自来水"。如说: *Many houses in this area still don't have running water.* 在这个地区,许多人家还没有装自来水。这是与 city [town] water (城市上水道)表示同样的意味。然而,严密地讲, running water 的含义比较广。只要是用管子引入室内而拧开龙头出的水,哪怕是从院内井中泵出的水,也一概称为 running water。*Does your weekend home have running water?* 你的周末别墅有自来水吗? *Our house has hot and cold running water.* 我们家的水管子有热水和冷水。◇ water available through indoor pipes

take to *something* **like a duck to water** → DUCK

throw cold water on *something* (by *doing something*) [ˌθrouˌkould ˈwɔ(ː)dərɔn ～] [话] **泼冷水** 可以按照字面意义使用,如: *He threw cold water on the red-hot stove.* 他往烧得通红的火炉上泼了凉水。转作比喻,用于对计划、思考、希望等"泼冷水"。*Dad threw cold water on our plan to go on a picnic by refusing to let us use the car.* 爸爸不允许我们用小汽车,给我们出去郊游的计划泼了冷水。*Inflation has thrown cold water on the editor's hopes of increasing the size of the newspaper.* 通货膨胀使主编增加报纸篇幅的希望幻灭了。也可以用 pour 代替 throw。*Our club meetings go much more smoothly when Sally isn't there. She tries to pour cold water on practically every suggestion that comes up.* 当萨莉不在的时候,我们俱乐部的会议开得非常顺利。她几乎对于每一个提案都要泼冷水。◇ ruin [discourage] *something*

tread water [ˌtred ˈwɔːdər] [话] **裹足不前** 原义"踩水"或"立泳"。常这样使用: *In order to pass life-saving, you must be able to tread water for at least thirty minutes.* 要取得水上救生员的资格,你必须能够立泳至少三十分钟。转作比喻使用,表示"降低速度,停止活动"。多用于经济或企业经营方面。*The stock market is sluggish now because the big investors are treading water until they see how the economic situation will develop.* 股票市场现在很萧条,因为大投资家在观望经济发展的趋势,裹足不前。*Most manufacturers are only treading water, waiting for the recession to end.* 绝大多数工厂主都裹足不前,等待萧条时期过去再说。◇ ((不加 only)) withhold action / be in a state of suspended action

water over the dam [ˈwɔ(ː)dərˌovərðə ˈdæːm] [口] **无可挽回** 字面意义为"水漫过堤坝"。作为比喻, water 指"人有生以来经历的事情", dam 指"今日"。乍看起来,好象与 WATER under the bridge 相似,但请读者注意两者的不同。本条的 water over the dam 原义很清楚:"水漫过堤坝之后,再也不能返回原来的地方"。换句话说,"人生有如流水,过了今日,今日就永不复还"。多用 that's (all) water over the dam 的形式,意思是"(一切)成为过去,已经无可挽回"。*I realize now that it would have been better to have done it differently, but that's water over the dam.* 我现在认识到,如果采取另外一种办法就好了。但是,时过境迁,已经无可挽回。*Stop talking about what you could have done to avoid the accident. That's all water over the dam.* 你不要再说你如果怎样做就能避免那次事故了。一切都成为过去,已无可挽回啦。◇ something that can't be changed

water under the bridge [ˈwɔ(ː)dər ˌʌndərðə ˈbrɪːdʒ] [口] **已经过去的种种事情** 字面意义为"桥下的流水"。本条是把人生比做流水, water 指"一生中过去的事情", bridge 指"自己今日的立足点"。原来的意思是:"站在今日这座桥上,回首一生中流逝的事情"。There has been a lot of water under the bridge since ～. 或 A lot of water has gone [passed] under the bridge since ～. 是常用的句型，换个说法就是：Many things have happened since ～.（自从……以后，发生了许许多多的事情。）特别是在感叹"回首前尘不忍看"的时候，常使用这一表达法。*It'll soon be fifteen years since I graduated from college. There's been a lot of water under the bridge since then.* 我从大学毕业以后，转眼快十五年了。在这期间，可发生了不少事情啊。*It's been almost a year since I broke up with Jim. There's been too much water under the bridge since then for us to ever make up again.* 我跟吉姆离异已经快一年了。在这期间，我经历了过多的事情，使我们不会破镜重圆了。在下一个例句中，重点不是"发生的事情多"，而是"过去的时间长"。*How've you been, George? A lot of water has gone under the bridge since we last met.* 乔治，你好吗？自从上次相会以后，咱们好久没有见面了。但是，即使在这一场合，也含有"如果聊一聊各人的种种情况，一定非常有趣"的韵味，也就是说，本来的意思基本上没有改变。另外，本条与 WATER over the dam (→)有相似之处，最近美国人也有时弄混。严格地讲，两者的用法不同，务请读者注意。◇ (have been a lot of [too many, etc.]) things (that) have happened

You can lead a horse to water, but you can't make him drink. → HORSE

Waterloo

meet *one's* **Waterloo** [ˌmi(ː)t ～ ˈwɔ(ː)dərˌluː] [口] **惨败** Waterloo (滑铁卢)是拿破仑被威灵顿将军击败的战场。拿破仑由于这次败北而被流放圣赫勒纳岛。本条直译为"遇见自己的滑铁卢"。自从滑铁卢战役(1815年)以后，这句话就具有"彻底失败，再也站不起来"的意味。*The Democratic candidate met his Waterloo at the hands of an obscure Republican rival.* 民主党候选人惨败于一个名不经传的共和党竞争者的手下了。也可以用于戏谑。*Sid claimed that he would never fall in love, but when he was introduced to Sally he knew he had met his Waterloo.* 锡德声称他绝不会坠入情网，但自从结识萨莉后，他知道自己已经兵败滑铁卢了。另有 be *someone's* Waterloo 的句型，如 *Watergate was President Nixon's Waterloo.* 水门事件是尼克松总统的滑铁卢之战（尼克松总统因水门事件而一败涂地）。有时字头小写，作 waterloo。◇ meet a crushing defeat

be *someone's* **Waterloo** [～ ˈwɔ(ː)dərˌluː] [口] **一败涂地** → meet *one's* WATERLOO

waters

fish in troubled waters [ˌfɪʃ ɪnˈtrʌbld ˈwɔːdərz] [口] **混水摸鱼** 本条来源是：自古以来，钓鱼人都知道在海上有点风浪的时候，鱼容易上钩。fish 原义"垂钓"，在这里指"趁机谋利"。troubled waters 是16世纪开始出现的成语，原义"内心的混乱状态"，在本条中指"他人的不幸、困难、混乱等"。本条习用语使用于乘人之危谋取私利的场合。表面上与"趁火打劫"相似，但使用范围比较广。而在实际上到火灾现场偷或抢东西的场合，却不能使用这一表达法。*We mustn't let him know that there is a difference of opinion among us. He likes to fish in troubled waters.* 我们不能让他知道我们之间有意见分歧。他喜欢混水摸鱼。*As soon as George learned that Mary was against the plan, he immediately came to fish in troubled waters.* 刚一听说玛丽反对那个计划，乔治马上就来混水摸鱼了。*Don't follow that guy's advice. He's always fishing in troubled waters.* 别听那个家伙的建议。他一向是混水摸鱼。不仅限于个人，也可以应用于公司、机关、团体或国家。*That country is good at fishing in the troubled waters of the Middle East.* 那个国家善于在中东的纷乱中混水摸鱼。◇ take advantage of troubled conditions (for *one's* own gain)

pour oil on troubled waters → OIL

Still waters run deep. [ˈstɪ(ː)l ˈwɔːdərz ˌrʌndiːp] [谚] **大智若愚** 原义为"水流平静的江河深"。在这里，still waters 指"沉默寡言的人"，含有"很少表示自己的思想感情"的意思。run deep 原义"河

深”，在这里指“深思熟虑”，有时指“蕴藏很深的感情”。正如“大智若愚”这个汉语成语一样，本条习用语大多表示好的意味。但实际上与好、坏无关，既可以表示“神机妙算”，也可以表示“包藏祸心”。*A: The man is a fool. Every time I ask him a question he just stares at me. B: That doesn't really prove anything. Still waters run deep, you know.* 甲：那个人是个傻瓜。每当我问他什么事情的时候，他总是直勾勾地看着我。乙：光凭这一点，并不能下任何结论。成语说得好，大智若愚嘛。*I think the boss would respect your opinions more if you didn't talk so much. It isn't necessarily true that still waters run deep, but most people seem to believe it.* 我认为，如果你不那样喋喋不休，老板也许会更尊重你的意见。大智若愚这个说法不一定正确，但是大多数人似乎相信它。下面的例句不是讲思想深，而是讲感情深。*Elaine was such a quiet girl, but then I should have known that still waters run deep. It wasn't until after we were married that I realized what depths of emotion she was capable of.* 伊莱恩是一个非常文静的姑娘，但是在那个时候我忘记了“静水河深”这句谚语。直到我们结婚以后，我才了解她是一个多么富有感情的人。下边的例句表示“奸诈”甚至”心怀叵测”的意味。*I wouldn't trust Farley too far if I were you. A quiet man like him seems harmless enough, but remember, still waters often run deep.* 如果我是你的话，我不会过分地信任法利。象他那样温和的人似乎对人绝对无害，但是你要记住，不言不语的人往往有一肚子的坏主意。◇ Quiet people are (often) profound thinkers [capable of great emotion].

waver

a flag waver [ə ˈflæːg ˌweɪvər] [话] **沙文主义者** 直译为“摇旗的人”。这里的 flag 指 national flag (国旗)。本条习用语大多用于表示“摇旗呐喊”之类的轻蔑意味。*Joseph is a real flag waver. He thinks we should send troops into any country that refuses to sell us oil cheaply.* 约瑟夫是个不折不扣的沙文主义者。他认为凡是拒绝廉价卖给我们石油的国家，我们就应当派兵前去。有时不指人，而指宣传沙文主义的书籍、戏剧、电影、诗歌等等。*Most of the movies produced during the war were simply flag wavers.* 战争期间制作的影片绝大部分不过是宣传沙文主义的东西而已。◇ (an) overly patriotic (person [movie, etc.])

waves

make waves [ˌmeɪ ˈkweɪvz] [话] **兴风作浪** 条头的构思与汉语相同，即以某种不必要的动作使原来平静的事物陷入混乱的状态。*One of the first things you have to learn if you want to be a successful bureaucrat is not to make waves.* 如果你想官运亨通，首先应该牢记的事情之一就是不要兴风作浪。*We had just about completed the delicate negotiations when Mr. Storm started making waves by complaining about some of the conditions.* 我们正要结束那次棘手的谈判的时候，斯托姆先生开始兴风作浪，表示不同意其中的几个条款。一般来说，兴风作浪并不是故意而为，但也有例外的用法，如：*If you want to make yourself heard by your parents, you've got to make a few waves.* 如果你想要父母倾听一下自己的意见，那你非兴点风作点浪不可。◇ disturb normal procedures / create problems / raise a commotion

way

get under way [gedˌʌndər ˈweɪ] [口] **出发** 现代英语的 way 来源于盎格鲁—撒克逊人古时使用过的日耳曼语 *wegan*(等于 move 或 carry)，具有“move 之路”的意味。盎格鲁—撒克逊人使用的荷兰语又照搬 *wegan* 的派生词 *weg*，构成了 *onder weg*。这是个海上交通用语，意思是“(起锚后)在 move”，亦即“航行中”。这个 *onder weg* 又改译为英语，便是 under way。在英语中，原来也是表示“航行中”的海上用语，后来人们才作为比喻广泛使用。最常用的形式乃是 get under way ("走上航路"→"出发"、"开始")。本来意义的用例: *The ship got under way at one o'clock.* 船在一点钟启航了。下面是比喻的用例: *If everyone is ready, let's get under way.* 如果大家都准备好了,咱们就出发吧。*Though independence was declared in 1776, America didn't really get under way as a nation until Washington took office as the first President in 1789.* 虽然在 1776 年就发表了独立宣言,但是直到 1789 年华盛顿就任第一届总统,美国才真正开始成为一个国家。*When I arrived at the front, an enemy attack was just getting under way.* 当我到达前线的时候,正赶上敌人开始进攻。其次,也常使用 be under way 的形式。它本来的意思是"船在动着",亦即"航行中"。*I could tell from the motion of the ship that we were already under way.* 通过震动,我知道船已经在航行中了。转义"正在进行中"。*Plans are under way to build a new city hospital.* 建造一所新的市立医院的计划正在进行中。常在 be 和 under way 之间添加 well 一词,表示"相当"的意思。*We got an early start and were well under way by the time the sun came up.* 我们早早启程,到太阳升起的时候,已经走了相当一段路程。*By the end of the first year, orders were pouring in and our new business was well under way.* 到第一年度末,订货源源而来,我们的新公司已经搞得相当不错了。在美国人写的文章中,往往不是 under way,而变成了 under weigh。从语源来说,这个 weigh 也是出自日耳曼语系的 *wegan* 一词,因此与 way 相通。但是按现在的用法,用 weigh 是错误的。这种误用之所以产生,大概是由于在海上用语中还有一个意思与本条条头相似的 weigh anchor (起锚→启航),而且 way 和 weigh 的发音又都是 ['weɪ],人们把二者弄混了。◇ start

go out of *one's* **way to** *do something* [gou ˌaudəv ~ 'weɪdə ~] [口] **特意或故意干某种事情** 直译为"为了干某种事情而离开自己走的路",也就是"绕远儿"。*There's no need for you to go out of your way to take me home. I can take a bus from here.* 你不必绕远儿送我回家。我从这里可以坐公共汽车。作为比喻,是"特意或故意干超出正常的事情"的意思。*Everyone went out of their way to be nice to the new student from China.* 大家对从中国来的新学生特别亲切。如这一例句所示,这一习用语常用于"出自善意"的场合,但也有恰恰相反,用于"出自恶意"的时候。另外,还可以用于跟善意或恶意毫无关系的情况。*I know you don't like Martha, but that doesn't mean you have to go out of your way to be rude to her.* 我知道你不喜欢马莎,但是那并不意味着你要特意对她采取粗暴无礼的态度。*Greg has a rotten temper, so I've always gone out of my way to avoid irritating him.* 格雷格的性情非常暴躁,因此,我总是注意不去刺激他。*Though his poems have never been very popular, for some reason the critics have always gone out of their way to praise them.* 虽然他的诗还不曾脍炙人口,不知为什么,批评家却总是有意加以赞扬。另有 go out of *one's* way for *someone* 的形式,意思是"特意为某人做某事"。*I don't mind helping her if it's convenient, but I'm certainly not going to go out of my way for her [to do it].* 方便的话,帮她一下也未为不可,但是我可不想特意为她效劳。◇ make a special effort to *do something*

have a way with *someone* [*something*] [ˌhævə 'weɪwɪð ~] [口] **善于应付人或物** 意思是:主语对于 with 后边的人或物有使其发挥所期待的作用的才能。这一习用语只用于表示良好的意思,总是用肯定句型。*Amy should make a wonderful teacher. She has a way with young children.* 艾米一定会成为一位优秀的教师。她善于应付幼小的儿童。*Let's get Phyllis to talk to the boss for us. She seems to have a way with him.* 让菲利斯代表我们去跟老板讲吧。她似乎很有跟老板打交道的本领。someone 处有时为 something,一般是"动物"。*Graham has a way with horses. Even the wildest ones* *soon respond to him.* 格雷厄姆善于应付马。哪怕是最狂暴的马,在他手里过不了多久就会变得听话了。也可以这样讲: *He has a way with computers.* 他善于使用电脑。但与其说这是本来意义的转用,勿宁说是例外。◇ have a talent for handling *someone* [*something*]

be in the family way [.ɪnðə 'fæməli 'weɪ] [话] **有身孕** 妇女怀孕的委婉说法。way 在这里是"风味"、"样子"的意味。本条直译为"有家庭风味了",亦即"快生孩子了"。在一般人的感觉中,仅有夫妇还不是完全的家庭,有了孩子才算是个 family。例如过去有一首题名《二人喝茶》("Tea for Two")的歌非常流行,其中就有这样一句: "We will raise a family, a boy for you a girl for me."(我们组织一个家庭吧,你要个儿子,我来个女儿。) *Mrs. Beeler appears to be in the family way.* 比勒夫人似乎有身孕啦。*I swear, every time you turn around that woman is in the family way again.* 不管你什么时候碰见那个女人,她肚子里肯定有孩子。可以省略 be 动词,也可以使用 be 动词以外的动词。*I hear that that boy put the Jones girl in the family way.* 我听说那个小伙子使琼斯家的姑娘怀孕了。*We thought she was only getting fatter, but when the doctor examined her, he found her in the family way.* 我们以为她只是发胖,但是医生对她一检查,发现她怀孕了。有时, the family 作 a family。*Mrs. Smith announced to her family that she was in a family way.* 史密斯太太对她的家人宣布她已经怀孕了。◇ be pregnant

No way. ['nou 'weɪ] [话] **没门儿** 这是比较新的口语。直译为"没有方法"。有两种含义。一是表示坚决拒绝,等于 Absolutely not! (绝对不成!)原意为"绝对没有说服我的方法 (way)",大多加惊叹号,作 No way! 用法如下: *A: Let's fly to New York for the weekend. B: No way! I'm scared to death of airplanes.* 甲:咱们周末坐飞机去纽约吧。乙:那可不行!我对于飞机怕得要死。*A: Can I go to the movies tonight, Mom? B: No way! You have to study for your test tomorrow.* 甲:妈妈,今天晚上我能去看电影吗? 乙:没门儿! 你明天考试,必须复习功课。*A: Lynn wonders if you'd lend him the money. B: No way! That guy never pays you back.* 甲:林恩问你能不能借给他点钱。乙:没门儿! 那个家伙是绝对不会还的。另一种含义是"办不到"、"不可能"。原意为"没有那样做的方法 (way)"。在这一场合,一般只强调没有可能性,不涉及意志或感情。在使用时比"没门儿!"的语气轻,大多不加惊叹号。与 It's impossible. 大致相同。*A: How about a game of golf tomorrow? B: No way. I'm loaded down with work.* 甲:明天比赛高尔夫球怎么样? 乙:办不到啊。我工作太忙,脱不开身。*A: Can't you fix this today? B: Now way. It requires a replacement part that I'll have to order.* 甲:这个你今天能修好吗?乙:不可能。它要换个零件,非去订购不可。◇ Absolutely not. / It's impossible.

pave the way (for *someone* to *do something*) [.peɪvðə 'weɪ] [口] **铺平道路** 条头整个意思是"为某人做某事铺平道路",即"使 for 后边的人容易前进"。*Bush's withdrawal from the race paved the way for Reagan to win the Republican nomination.* 布什退出竞选为里根赢得共和党的提名铺平了道路。*Tom had a motive for the murder too, you know. His brother's death paved the way for him to take over his father's company.* 你要知道,在那次谋杀案中,汤姆也有杀人的动机。他哥哥的死,为他接管他父亲的公司铺平了道路。有时省略 for 以下的部分。*It's true that we did most of the work on the project, but it was Mr. Nagel's patient negotiating that paved the way.* 的确,这项计划的绝大部分工作是我们干的,但是,内格尔先生的耐心谈判为我们铺平了道路。也常使用被动语态,如: *Thanks to your efforts, the way is now paved for us to proceed.* 由于你的努力,我们前进的道路现在已经铺平了。*Because of his uncle's offer of financial assistance, the way had been paved for*

Benny to attend college. 由于伯父的资助，本尼上大学的道路已经铺平了。另有 pave the way to *something* 的形式，常用于一般性的场合，如：*Education does not necessarily pave the way to happiness.* 受教育不一定能得到幸福。*The development of steam power paved the way to the industrial revolution.* 蒸气动力的发展为产业革命铺平了道路。◇ open the way / make it possible / lay the groundwork

rub *someone* **the wrong way** [ˌrʌb ~ ðəˈrɔ(ː)ŋ weɪ] [话] **使人恼火** 字面意义为"戗着抚摩某人"。如果把"某人"理解为"某人的神经"，自然就容易掌握原意了。主语总是"人"，或者人的"态度"、"言语行动"。*Frank may be a nice guy, but he always rubs me the wrong way.* 弗兰克也许是一个好青年，但他总惹我生气。*It's true that Ruby is a beautiful girl, but the way she talks tends to rub people the wrong way.* 鲁迪的确是一个美丽的姑娘，但是她的说话方式往往使人恼火。◇ irritate *someone*

see *one's* **way clear to** *doing something* [ˌsiː ~ˌweɪ ˈklɪ(ː)rtə ~] [话] **愿意去干某件事情** 字面意义为"看清自己去做某事的道路"。这是一个委婉的说法，实际用于表示"不可能"、"想不到"、"不愿意干"的意思。因此，大多构成否定句或疑问句。*I just couldn't see my way clear to deceiving an innocent girl like Felicia.* 我无论如何也不曾有欺骗象费利西娅那样一个单纯的姑娘的心思。*How he ever saw his way clear to making such an important decision on his own authority I'll never know!* 他怎么胆敢利用他的职权作出那样一个重要的决定，我完全无法理解！*I'm afraid I can't see my way clear to lending them the money unless they are willing to put up sufficient collateral.* 很遗憾，如果他们不愿意拿出足够的担保品，我是不可能借给他们钱的。也有用于肯定句的场合，如：*Talk to her a little more. I think she's finally beginning to see her way clear to accepting our proposal.* 再跟她谈一谈吧。我总觉得她已经开始愿意接受我们的建议了。也有省略 clear 的情况。*Do you think you could see your way (clear) to lending a poor man a dollar or two for a meal?* 你愿意借给这个可怜的人一两美元去吃顿饭吗？◇ bring *oneself* to *do something* / convince *oneself* that *one* should *do something*

see which way the wind blows → WIND

There's more than one way to skin a cat. [ðerz ˌmo(ː)rðən ˈwʌn ˈweɪdə ˌskɪnə ˈkæ(ː)t] [口] **另有办法** 直译为"剥猫皮的方法不止一个"。在表示"我另外有办法"的时候使用。过去有一部畅销书叫 *101 Ways to Skin a Cat*（《剥猫皮 101 法》），书名即由本条习用语而来。*If my father won't let me have the money, I'll get it some other way. I'll show him there's more than one way to skin a cat.* 如果我父亲不给我这笔钱，我也会从别的地方弄到手。我要叫他知道我的办法多得很。*None of the companies I called on showed any interest in my invention, but there's more than one way to skin a cat. I'll build it and market it myself.* 我访问了几家公司，它们没有一家对我的发明发生任何兴趣。但是，活人还能叫尿憋死？我要自己制造，自己销售。◇ there are (any number of) other ways to do it

weasel *one's* **way into** *something* [ˌwiːzəl ~ ˈweɪ ɪntə ~] [话] **用花言巧语钻进一般进不去的地方**→ a WEASEL

ways

cut both ways [ˌkʌ(ː)t ˌbouθ ˈweɪz] [口] **互有利弊** 直译为"两面都砍"，原意是"如果挥舞双刃的剑，可以砍到对方，但也可以伤害自己"。用于说明有好的一面也有坏的一面，有有利的一面也有不利的一面。*Most decisions, by their very nature, cut both ways. Seldom does any decision produce results that are only good.* 绝大多数的决定，从其根本性质来说，都是有利也有弊的。只产生良好结果的决定可以说绝无仅有。也常用于在议论中的论点或理由。*Unfortunately that ar-*

gument is a two-edged sword—it cuts both ways. It can be used against us as well as for us. 不幸的是，那个论点是双刃的剑，有利也有弊。既可以用来保卫我们，也可以被人用来对付我们。◇ have two sides

mend *one's* **ways** [ˌmend ~ ˈweɪz] [口] **改邪归正** mend 是"改正"。ways 在这里泛指"行为"、"生活作风"、"思想方法"等。*The boy is incorrigible. No matter what I say, he absolutely refuses to mend his ways.* 那个男孩子已经不可救药了。不管我怎样费尽唇舌，他也绝对不肯改邪归正。*Since the Justice Ministry has begun prosecuting government officials for bribery, many are beginning to realize that they are going to have to mend their ways.* 自从司法部开始追究政府官员的受贿问题以来，有许多人已经认识到他们必须端正态度了。◇ improve *one's* (moral) behavior

(there are) no two ways about it [(ˌðerər) ˌnou ˌtuː ˈweɪzə ˈbaudɪt] [话] **没有选择的余地** 字面意义为"关于那件事情，没有两个方法"，也就是"只有一个方法"。这一习用语含有"绝对地"的强烈意味。*I guess there're no two ways about it. We'll just have to go and take our medicine.* 我看没有选择的余地了。我们只能前去甘心受罚。*There are no two ways about it. Either you pay the money you owe me or I'll sue.* 没有选择的余地。你不还欠我的那笔钱，我就控告你。*The boss says there are no two ways about it—either finish the work by Wednesday or give up our vacation.* 老板说没有选择的余地，我们如果到星期三完不成任务，就得放弃我们的休假。*There are no two ways about it. Japan must secure a sufficient supply of oil.* 没有选择的余地，日本必须确保石油的充分供应。父母命令子女时常使用这一习用语，而且在这一场合大多省略 there are。*You are going to do your homework right now and no two ways about it.* 你马上开始做作业，没有二话可说。*You be home by ten o'clock, and no two ways about it!* 你必须十点以前回家，没有商量的余地。◇ there is [one has] no alternative

wayside

fall by the wayside [ˌfɔ(ː)l baɪðə ˈweɪˌsaɪd] [口] **由于困难而掉队** 字面意义为"倒在路边上"。*Only eight people finished the marathon. The rest, defeated by the August heat, fell by the wayside.* 在马拉松比赛中，只有八个人到达了终点。其余的人耐不住八月的炎热，都倒在路边上了。作为比喻，主要用于因不能克服困难而在中途放弃奋斗目标的场合。*Tom and Harry entered law school together, but the going was so difficult that Tom fell by the wayside before the first year was up.* 汤姆和哈里一起进了法学院，但是由于功课太难了，不到一年，汤姆就掉了队。本条习用语有与 drop out (of *something*) [ˌdrɑ(ː) ˈpaut] (退出)意义相同的时候，但是 drop out 的使用范围比较广，不只限于因为困难而掉队，也有仅仅由于厌烦而不干的场合。*Jules dropped out of the marathon after the first lap and went swimming.* 朱尔斯参加马拉松比赛，跑完一圈就退场去游泳了。*She found college boring and soon dropped out.* 她感到在大学里太无聊，不久就退学了。◇ give up / fail / quit

weak

(as) weak as a baby [ə ˈzwi(ː)kəzə ˈbeɪbi] [口] **一点力气都没有** → (as) weak as a KITTEN

(as) weak as a kitten → KITTEN

weaker

the weaker sex → SEX

wear

cause wear and tear (on *something* [*someone*]) [ˌkɔ(ː)z ˈweːrən ˈteːr] [口] **造成磨损** → save WEAR and tear (on *something* [*someone*])

save wear and tear (on *something* [*someone*]) [ˌseɪv ˈweːrənˈteːr] [口] **减轻磨损的程度** save 是"节省"; wear 是"消耗"; tear 是"撕裂"。tear 只是在这里与 wear 合辙

押韵,没有实际意义。*Driving at low speeds saves wear and tear on your engine.* 低速行驶可以减轻引擎磨损的程度。除用于机器、工具、零件等以外,还可以用于人的体力和精神,如: *Shopping early before the stores are crowded saves wear and tear.* 在商店还不拥挤的时候,早早地去买东西,可以减轻疲劳的程度。另外,特别是在谈到机械类的时候,有 save *something* from wear and tear (防止某物磨损) 的说法。*Banning this area from big trucks has done a lot to save the roads from wear and tear.* 这个区段禁止大卡车通行,防止了路面的严重磨损。反义语"造成磨损"的英语说法是 cause wear and tear (on *something* [*someone*])。*Small children with lots of energy cause wear and tear on parents' nerves.* 精力充沛的小孩子使父母格外劳神。◇ prevent *something* [*someone*] from becoming worn out

weasel

a weasel [ə 'wiːzəl] [口] **鬼鬼祟祟的家伙** weasel 是"鼬"。这种鼠很小,脚步很轻,到处乱跑。美国人对它有"鬼鬼祟祟"的印象。本条的原意就是"象鼬那样鬼鬼祟祟、到处乱转的人"。*Don't trust him. He's a weasel.* 不要信任他。他这个人诡计多端。*That guy is worse than a weasel. He's a dyed-in-the-wool snake in the grass.* 那个家伙岂止是诡计多端,他是个彻头彻尾的潜伏着的敌人。weasel 作为动词使用,可构成几个常用句型。第一个是 weasel *something* out of *someone* (用花言巧语向对方探听秘密)。*Rod tried to weasel your phone number out of me.* 罗德对我花言巧语,企图探听出你的电话号码。第二个是 weasel *one's* way into *something* (用花言巧语为手段,走进平常不准进入的场所)。*A newspaper reporter weaseled his way into the meeting.* 一个新闻记者用花言巧语为手段,混进了那次会议的会场。*something* 处不仅代人具体的场所,也有如下的用法: *Don't let him weasel his way into your confidence.* 不管他怎样甜言蜜语,你千万不要相信他。另有 WEASEL out of *something* (→)的说法。在黑社会和监狱的用语中,a weasel 是"告密者"的意思。因此,作为动词,weasel (on *someone*) 便是"告密"了。*Don't trust that guy. He's a weasel.* 不要相信那个家伙。他是一个告密者。*Somebody must've weaseled.* 一定有人告密了。*If you weasel on us, you're dead.* 如果你敢去告密,就要你的命。顺便讲一下:在黑社会用语中,weasel 与 rat 完全同义,不论是名词的场合或动词的场合,均可互相代换 (→ RAT on *someone*)。◇ (a) sneaky (person)

weasel (on *someone*) ['wiːzəl] [话] **告密** → a WEASEL

weasel out of *something* [ˌwiːzəl 'audəv~] [话] **用花言巧语逃避诺言、义务、责任等** weasel 作为名词有"奸滑"的意思,在作为动词使用时,仍然脱离不掉这一意思 (→ a WEASEL)。*I don't want to go to that dinner tonight. I wish there were some way I could weasel out of it.* 我今天晚上不想参加那个宴会。我希望找个巧妙的办法推托掉。*It sounds like that company is trying to weasel out of its contract with us.* 看起来,那个公司想用花言巧语来逃避跟我们订立的合同。*The responsibility is yours, and if you think you can weasel out of it, you've got another think coming.* 责任在你身上,如果你认为用花言巧语就能够逃避责任,那就大错特错了。◇ back [get, talk *one's* way] out of *something*

weasel *something* **out of** *someone* [ˌwiːzəl ~ 'audəv ~] [话] **用花言巧语向对方探听秘密** → a WEASEL

weasel *one's* **way into** *something* [ˌwiːzəl ~ 'weɪ ɪntə ~] [话] **用花言巧语为手段,走进平常不准进入的场所** → a WEASEL

a weasel word → WORD

weather

(as) changeable as the weather [əz 'tʃeɪndʒəbələzðə 'we(ː)ðər] [口] **变幻莫测** 直译是"象天气那样容易变化"。*Who knows how Mr. Henne will react to my suggestion? His moods are as* *changeable as the weather*. 谁知道亨先生对我的建议会有什么反响呢？他的情绪是变幻莫测的。*Sue seems to like me on one date and then turns very cool on the next. She's changeable as the weather*. 在这一次约会中，苏似乎很喜欢我，而在另一次约会时，她又冷若冰霜。她的态度变幻莫测。*Roy says he's going to quit his job, but I wouldn't bank on it. His decisions are as changeable as the weather*. 罗伊说他要辞去他的工作，但是我可不相信他的话。他总是三心二意，反复无常。◇ extremely changeable [unreliable]

be under the weather [ˌʌndərðə ˈwe(ː)ðər]

[口] **身体不舒服** 原意“晕船”。这里的 weather 等于 bad weather (坏天气)。in the weather (在坏天气中) 的意思是“正在甲板上”。under the weather (在坏天气下) 的意思是“由于晕船，必须从甲板上回到船舱里去”。这就是本条习用语的来源。在现代，主要用于表示“身体不舒服”的意思。当然，如今也可以这样说：*Because of the high waves, several of the passengers are under the weather today*. 由于风浪太大，今天有一些乘客晕船了。因为有说明情况的从句 Because of the high waves，所以读者可以立即明白 under the weather 是“晕船”的意思。但是，如果没有这样的从句，就不一定是“晕船”的意思了，很有可能是由于感冒而“身体不舒服”。例如：*Because of the flu epidemic, several of the passengers are under the weather today*. 因为发生流行性感冒，今天有一些乘客身体不舒服了。现代的主要用法举例如下：*My husband hasn't been to work this week. He's been under the weather since Sunday*. 我丈夫这个星期没有上班。从星期日起，他一直身体不舒服。*Jack's under the weather this morning with a bad cold*. 杰克今天早晨病了，伤风很严重。除 be 动词外，也可以用 feel 或 look。*I'm not going to stay home from work just because I feel a little under the weather*. 我不打算因为身体有一点不舒服就呆在家里不去上班。*You look a bit under the weather today*. 你今天看起来有点不舒服似的。也可以转用于表示“喝醉”的意思。*Jack was completely drunk, and Jim was [felt, looked] a good bit under the weather himself*. 杰克酩酊大醉了，吉姆本人也有了很大醉意［觉得很有醉意，看起来很有醉意］。◇ be not feeling well / be ill

wedded

wedded bliss → BLISS

wedding

a shotgun wedding [ə ˈʃɑ(ː)t ˌgʌ(ː)n ˈwedɪŋ]

[口] **强制结婚** 本条条头来源于这样一种风俗：一个男子使未婚的女子怀孕了，或者破坏了处女的贞操，女方的父亲大为愤怒，用猎枪 (shotgun) 相威胁，在治安法官 (a justice of the peace) 的见证下，强迫二人结婚。*When the old farmer found that the salesman had been intimate with his daughter, he threatened him with a shotgun wedding*. 当那个老农夫发现推销员跟他的女儿已经发生了不正当关系的时候，他用猎枪威胁他必须娶他的女儿。这是实际上动“猎枪”的例子。现在已经没有那种老式猎枪 (shotgun) 的影子了，因此，使用其他方法进行威胁的“强制结婚”也一概称之为 shotgun wedding。*Bill said he hadn't planned to marry her— that it was a shotgun wedding*. 比尔说，他并没有打算跟她结婚，他们是被强制结婚的。仅凭这句话的现有词句，看不出女方的爸爸是否真正动了“猎枪”。有时用 marriage 代替 wedding。*Since she couldn't get her father's permission to marry her boy friend, she tricked him into forcing a shotgun marriage by wearing a cushion under her dress*. 由于她父亲不允许她跟自己的男朋友结婚，她就使个花招，在衣服下边塞了一个坐垫，骗得她父亲强制他们结婚了。如上面的例句所示，shotgun wedding 用于表示“结婚”的场合最多，但有时又作为比喻，用于表示“被迫合并”的意味。*The merger between the two companies was obviously a shotgun wedding, forced on them by economic ne-*

cessity. 两个公司的合并显然是出于经济上的需要,不得已而为之的。◇ a forced marriage

week

knock *someone* **into the middle of next week** → MIDDLE

wee-wee

wee-wee [ˈwi(ː)ˌwiː] [话] **撒尿** → PEE-PEE

weigh

weigh on *someone's* **conscience** → CONSCIENCE

weigh on *someone's* **mind** → MIND

weight

pull *one's* **(own) weight** [ˌpul ～ (ˌoun) ˈweɪt] [口] **尽到自己的力量或责任** 字面意义为"用(自己)整个的体重去拖"。划船比赛用语。在划船的时候,必须使用全身的力量。*Jake was kicked off the rowing team for not pulling his weight in the last race.* 杰克在上次比赛中没有用全身的力量划船,因而被划船队开除了。在划船比赛中,哪怕是一个人不用劲,就得由全体选手来负担。作为比喻,一般也是用于集体或小组共同进行的工作。*Several people have been complaining that you haven't been pulling your weight on the sales team.* 有几个人抱怨说,你在推销小组中不大卖劲儿。如这一例句所示,用于否定句的时候最多。此外,也可以用于疑问句和假设句。*Anyone who doesn't pull his weight in this office will be fired.* 凡是在这个机关不竭力完成自己任务的人,一律开除。*What do you mean I haven't been pulling my weight! I work twice as hard as the rest of the people around here.* 你说我没有尽力完成我的任务,这话是什么意思?我比周围的人加倍努力干活儿啊。条头中的 own 原来没有,但为了语调轻松,常把它加上。*If everyone would start pulling his own weight around here, we'd get a lot more work done.* 如果这里的每一个人都能尽力完成自己的任务,我们还会干出更多的工作哪。◇ do *one's* (own) share of the work / carry *one's* (own) share of the responsibility

throw *one's* **weight around** [ˌθrou ～ ˈweɪdəˌraund] [口] **滥用权力** *one's* weight 的字面意义为"自己的体重"。本条直译为"到处投掷自己的重量",也就是"大逞威风,用整个身子去撞对方"的意味。作为比喻,主要用于表示"滥用自己的权力"。根据上下文,*one's* weight 除"权力"外,还可以意味着"职权"、"头衔"、"地位"、"权威"等等。*Lasting peace might be possible if the big powers would just stop throwing their weight around.* 只要各大国不向周围世界炫耀自己的威力,永久的和平也许是可能的。*This office has gotten too small for my needs. I think I'll throw my weight around a bit and see if I can't get a larger one.* 这间办公室太小,已经不够用了。我想稍微利用一些自己的职权,看看能否弄到一间大一点的。*Mr. Feather tried to throw his weight around by threatening to have me fired, but I just told him to go to the devil.* 费瑟先生仗势欺人,说要解雇我,但是我告诉他随他的便好啦。*The senator threw his weight around in hopes of intimidating the school authorities into admitting his daughter.* 那个参议员摆出他的头衔,企图威胁学校当局允许他的女儿入学。常有泛指"装腔作势"、"大摆架子"、"神气十足"的情况。*Don't be so timid. If you want to get things done, you've got to learn to throw your weight around.* 你不要那么缩手缩脚。如果你想要完成工作任务,就必须学会怎样显出你的威风来。*Don't try to throw your weight around with me. I can crush you anytime I please.* 你不要想对我装腔作势。不管什么时候,我都可以把你打翻在地。*Don't pay any attention to him. He just likes to throw his weight around.* 根本不用理会他。他只是喜欢摆摆架子而已。◇ brandish *one's* influence [authority, title]

weighty

a weighty tome → TOME

welcome

put out the welcome mat (for *someone*) → MAT

wear out *one's* **welcome** [ˌweˈraut ～ ˈwe(ː)lkəm] [口] **因呆得太久或去得太频繁而不再受人欢迎** wear out 是"由于长时间或多次使用而磨损"。welcome 是"欢迎"。本条的意思是"最初是受人欢迎的，但是时间一长，人家的欢迎就会逐渐磨损，亦即不再受人欢迎"。*Though Joe and Mary were happy to see me when I arrived, after a week I somehow began to feel that I had worn out my welcome.* 虽然在我刚来的时候，乔和玛丽都很高兴见到我，但是过了一个星期之后，我开始感觉到在别人家住得太久已经不再受欢迎了。*You mustn't go to play at Jimmy's so often. You'll wear out your welcome.* 你不要老是到吉米家里去玩。时间一长就不受欢迎啦。*I really must go home now before I wear out my welcome.* 我现在的确该回家了，否则呆得太久不受欢迎了。◇ become no longer welcome

well

be all very well [ˈɔːl ˌveri ˈwe(ː)l] [话] **好倒很好，不过……** → be all WELL and good

be all well and good [ˈɔːl ˌwelən ˈgu(ː)d] [话] **那倒不错，可是……** 反语用法。因此，一般要在后边接 but ～，例如：*It's all well and good for you to quit your job, but what do you intend to do for a living?* 你辞掉工作倒是不错，不过你今后打算怎么过活呢？*If you want to go bar-hopping with your friends every night that's all well and good, but don't expect me to be waiting quietly for you when you get home.* 如果你愿意每天夜里与你的朋友们出入酒吧，那倒也不坏，不过，当你回家的时候，你不要指望我会安安静静地等你。有时为了缓和语气，省略 and good，只讲 be all very well。*It's all very well for you to say you want a raise, but are you prepared to work harder to get it?* 你说希望增加工资，这也不错，不过，你准备多卖点劲儿以对得起增加的工资吗？◇ (it [that]) is your [*someone's*] decision (and I will not object) / it is easy enough

well-heeled

well-heeled [ˈwe(ː)l ˈhi(ː)ld] [话] **富有的** → be well HEELED

well-stacked

well-stacked [ˈwe(ː)lˈstæ(ː)kt] [话] **迷人的** → be well STACKED

Western

Western civ [ˌwestərn ˈsɪːv] [话] **西方文化(大学课程)** 美国各大学一年级的必修课程之一。civ 为学生用语，是 civilization [ˌsɪvələˈzeɪʃən]的缩略。*I hear they may make Western civ and elective next year.* 我听说西方文化明年也许成为选修课了。◇ Western civilization

wet

be all wet [ˌɔːl ˈwe(ː)t] [话] **(意见、想法、看法等)完全错误** 直译为"完全湿了"。可以按照字面意义使用，如：*You're all wet. If you don't change your clothes, you'll catch cold.* 你完全湿透了。如果你不换衣服，会伤风的。究竟是按照字面解释还是按照条头的译文解释，只能根据上下文来判断。本条是一个相当轻松的习用语。*When Columbus claimed the world was round, people thought he was all wet.* 当哥伦布声称地球是圆的的时候，人们以为他的想法是完全错误的。*If you think I would marry a man like you, you're all wet.* 如果你以为我会跟你这样的男人结婚，那就大错特错了。◇ be completely mistaken

throw a wet blanket on *something* → BLANKET

be wet behind the ears → EARS

a wet blanket → BLANKET

whaddya

whaddya [ˈhwʌdəjə] [话] **你如何？** what do you 的音变，亦即按 what do you 在日常会话中的发音写出，常见于漫画、小说的会话部分。*Hi, Joe. Whaddya say?* 喂，乔，你说怎么样？ *Whaddya say we go to the movies?* 你说，咱们去看电影如何？ *Well, whaddya know! If it isn't*

Frank Smith! 哎呀，我当是谁呢！原来是弗兰克·史密斯呀！*Whaddya think of this idea?* 你认为这个主意如何？*Whaddya mean you aren't going?* 你说不去，这是怎么回事？◇ what do you

whaddyacallit

a whaddyacallit [ə 'hwʌdəjə,kɔːlət] [话] **不知叫什么的东西** → a WHATCHAMACALLIT

what

give *someone* **what for** (for *something*) [,gɪv ~ ,hwʌt'fo(ː)r] [话] **严厉叱责** what for (为什么)怎么会有"叱责"的意思呢？语源可能是把 What (in the world did you do a fool think like that) for! (你究竟为什么干出那样愚蠢的事情！)的中间部分抽掉，将 what 与 for 凑在一起，使其代表整句话的意义。give *someone* 是"把这句话给与某人"，意思是"对某人讲"。*Jerry's girl gave him what for for forgetting about their date last night.* 杰里由于忘记了昨天晚上的约会，被他的女朋友狠训了一顿。这句话里的 what for for ~ [,hwʌt'fo(ː)r fər ~] 可能令人产生异样的感觉，但是没有两个 for 就不能文通理顺，这一点要请读者注意。在进一步强调时，添加 really。*When we broke Mr. Grouch's window, he really gave us what for.* 当我们打破格劳什先生的窗户玻璃时，我们被他狠狠地申斥了一大顿。另有一个说法是 give *someone* hell (for *something*)，意思和用法均大致相同 (→ CATCH it <from *someone* for *something*>)。不管对于什么人都可以安心使用 give *someone* what for 这一习用语，但是 give *someone* hell 就不同了，有些人把它当作"下流话"，因此，美国人往往根据时间、地点、场合有意识地用 give *someone* what for 作为 give *someone* hell 的委婉说法。◇ berate *someone* roundly

have what it takes (to *do something*) [,hæv ,hwʌdɪ't:eɪks] [话] **具备必要的条件** 由 it takes *something* to *do something* (做某事需要某种条件)这一句型演化而来。例如：*It takes talent to be an actor like that.* 当那样一个演员需要有天才。在这一场合，可以象条头的说法那样，用 what 表示"必要的天才"。但是，本条习用语几乎全部用否定句或疑问句，如：*Sarah is a beautiful woman, but she doesn't have what it takes to be a first-rate actress.* 萨拉是个美丽的女人，然而她不具备成为一流演员的必要条件。萨拉必要的东西实际上是"天才"，但在这句话里并不明确指出。因此，本条习用语是一种含蓄的说法，富有余味。*War is hell, Lieutenant. It's not enough just to be rich and handsome. You've got to have what it takes.* 中尉，战争是非常残酷的啊。光是有钱，长相英俊，那不顶用。你必须具备当军人的条件。这里指的是"勇敢"和"作战能力"。*I haven't got what it takes to kill a man.* 我不是一个能去杀人的材料。*Bill wants to work with us. Do you think he's got what it takes?* 比尔想要跟咱们一起干。你以为他干得了吗？不仅限于"人"，有时应用于"物"。*The group's music was good, but it just didn't have what it takes to attract large audiences.* 那个乐团演奏的乐曲很不错，但是缺少吸引广大听众的必要因素。*I haven't got what it takes to buy a house like that.* 我没有买那样一所房子的必要条件。这里的"必要条件"显然指的是"钱"。◇ have the ability [(the) courage, the money, sex appeal, etc.]

So what? [,sou 'hwɑ(ː)t] [话] **那又怎么样？** 在受别人质问或者责难的时候，往往会反唇相讥说"那又怎么样？"意思是："那为什么不行？""那有什么了不起！"在英语中，每当这一场合，用 So what? 的人最多。*A: You've been getting home awfully late recently. B: So what? Can't I enjoy myself if I want to?* 甲：最近，你回家非常晚啊。乙：那又怎么样？如果我想痛快一下，就不能玩玩去吗？*O. K. I admit it. I'm a couple of days behind schedule in my work. So what?* 对，我承认这一点。我的工作是迟误了两三天。但是，那又怎么样啊？往往有这样一种句型：开头用 so 概括对方质问或责难的主旨，然后再以 So what?回击。*So I take a drink once in a while, so what?* 不错，我有时候喝上一杯。但是，那又怎么样啊？ 当进行质问或责难的人不同意对方辩解的理由时，也可以用 So what? 表示“那算不上什么理由”的意思。*A: I couldn't meet you last night because my car broke down. B: So what? You could've at least called me, couldn't you?* 甲：我昨晚没能与你相见是因为我的汽车出毛病了。乙：那算什么理由呢？ 你至少应该给我打个电话呀，是吧？ 另外，So what? 还有如下用法：*A: I told him you were busy, so .... B: So what?* 甲：我告诉他说你很忙，所以……。乙：所以什么？ 这就是在对方说到 so ...而停顿下来的时候，听话的人用 So what? 承接 so，或作为插话，或表示催促对方往下说。◇ What does it [that] matter?

What do you say I [we] *do something*? [ˌhwʌdəjə ˈseɪ ˌaɪ / ˌwi(ː) ～] [话] **我[我们]做……，你看如何？** → WHAT say I [we] *do something*?

What gives? [ˌhwʌt ˈgɪːvz] [话] **发生了什么事？** 与 WHAT'S cooking? 相同，大多是在注意到周围的气氛有变化或者谈话的内容离了谱的时候，用于轻声的询问。*"What gives?" Joe asked his mother as he overheard strange voices coming from the living room.* “发生了什么事？”乔听到从起居室传来陌生人的讲话声，就向他的母亲问道。又如，当警察到达出事现场的时候，也常用这一习用语询问早已在那儿的警察。*A: What gives? B: It's a murder.* 甲：出啥事啦？ 乙：杀人案。有时后边加 with ～，如 *What gives with the books? I thought we were going drinking tonight.* 那些书又怎么啦？ 我原以为今天晚上我们该出去喝酒啦。另外，还可以作为很随便的寒暄语，在这一点上与 WHAT'S cooking?, WHAT'S new? 相似。如：*"Hi Joe. What gives?" "Nothing much."* “喂，乔，你好吗？”“外甥打灯笼，照旧。”◇ What's happening [happened]?

What say I [we] *doing something*? [ˈhwʌt ˈseɪ ˌaɪ / ˌwi(ː) ～] [话] **我[我们]做……如何？** 正式说法是 What would you say to (the idea of) my [our] *doing something*? 本条可以认为是这一说法的变形。*What say I pay him in advance?* 我向他预先付款如何？ *What say we take in a movie or something tonight?* 今天晚上咱们去看个电影如何？ *What say you and I get married?* 你我结婚如何？ 有时加入 do you，作 What do you say I [we] ～? [ˌhwʌdəjə ˈseɪ ˌaɪ / ˌwi(ː) ～]，意思和用法完全相同。◇ How about (my [our]) *doing something*?

whatchamacallit

a whatchamacallit [ə ˈhwʌtʃəməˌkɔːlət] [话] **不知叫什么的东西** 根据日常会话的发音，把 what you may call it 拼写成一个词。在不知道东西的名字、忘记某种东西的名字、避讳某种东西的名字或者认为说出名字对方也不了解的场合使用。*What's this whatchamacallit here?* 这儿那个叫不出名字的东西是什么？ *Hand me that whatchamacallit, will you?* 把那个叫不出名字的东西拿给我好吗？ 也有如下的用法：*Linda fell down and bruised her whatchamacallit.* 琳达摔倒了，跌伤了她的那个什么部分。这是不肯露骨地讲屁股或下腹部而一语带过去。在用复数时，与普通名词一样，只加个 -s 就可以。*What do you call these little whatchamacallits?* 这些不知名的小玩意儿，你管它们叫什么？ 在这一场合，也有时给由 what-you-may-call-them 构成的 whatchamacallem 加个 -s，作 whatchamacallems [ˈhwʌtʃəməˌkɔːləmz]。在已经是复数形式的名词后边又加上表示复数的 -s 好象很不合理，但是人们习以为常，也只得如此。有时词尾是 -ums，拼写作 whatchamacallums。*Hand me those whatchamacallums, will you?* 把那些我叫不出名字的东西拿给我好吗？ 有时指人的姓氏。在这一场合，第一个字母大写，作 Whatchamacallit。*I saw Doris Whatchamacallit yesterday.* 昨天我看见那个不知道她姓什么的多丽丝了。在表示人的姓氏的这类用语中还有 Whatchamacallim [ˈhwʌtʃəməˌkɔːləm],

What's-his [her]-name ['hwʌtsəz.neɪm / 'hwʌtsər.neɪm]等等。Whatchamacallim 是将 what you may call him 按照发音拼写而成，对男女均可使用。有时在指女性时说 What-you-may-call-her→What-chamacaller ['hwʌtʃəmə.kɔːlər]，但是，即使是女性，一般也用 Whatchamacallim。Whatchamacallim 也象 Whatchamacallem [-callum]那样，可以把词尾拼写为 -em [-um]。*His roommate is Dick Whatchamacallum.* 与他同屋住的叫迪克，不知姓什么。复数形式也是加 -s，但一般写作 -callems 或者 -callums。*Didn't you use to live next door to the Whatchamacallems?* 你跟那个姓什么来着的一家人没住过邻居吗？What's-his [her] -name 只有单数形式。*I met Judy What's-her-name today.* 今天我遇见了不知姓什么的叫做朱迪的女人。往往用 whaddyacallit ['hwʌdəjə .kɔːlət]代替 whatchamacallit，这一说法由 What do you call it? 而来，它也象 whatchamacallit 一样，词尾要按照所指的对象和单复数变化，形成 whaddyacallits, whaddyacallim, whaddyacaller, whaddyacallems 等。此外还有 whatsis ['hwʌtsəs], whozis ['huːzəs] 的说法，系按照 What's this? Who's this? 的发音拼写而成。两者一般均用于"物"，whozis 也极少用于"人"。*In order to turn the machine on, you turn this little whatsis [whozis].* 你要开动机器，就拧这个不知叫什么名字的小东西。◇ a thing

what's

What's cooking? [.hwʌts 'ku(:)kən] [话] **发生了什么事？** 原意是：锅里正在烹调 (cook) 什么东西，可是，不知道究竟是哪样美味佳肴。这一习用语多用于询问周围发生了什么事或者有什么样的计划。意义与 What's happening?, WHAT'S going on?, WHAT'S up?, WHAT gives? 等完全相同。如果问"正在做什么菜"，绝对不用 What's cooking?，一般是说 What's for dinner? (今天吃什么菜?)。再有，这一习用语还可以代替寒暄语，语调极轻松。*Hi, Frank. What's cooking?* 喂，弗兰克。怎么样？在这一场合，与 WHAT gives?, WHAT'S new? 等大致相同。*"What's cooking?" Joe asked, seeing his mother, father and brother gathered in the kitchen.* 乔见到他的母亲、父亲和哥哥聚集在厨房里，就问："发生了什么事？"◇ What's happening?

What's going on? [.hwʌts .gouə 'nɔːn] [话] **出什么事了？** 意思与 What's happening?, WHAT'S cooking? , WHAT gives?, WHAT'S up? 等大致相同，但语气相当强烈。例如：*"Hey, what's going on?" yelled Mr. Franklin as he was grabbed from behind by a stranger.* 当富兰克林先生被一个陌生人从背后抓住时，他大声喊道："喂，干什么？"这是一种很严厉的口吻。*"What's going on, I wonder?" Joe said to his brother as two police cars went by them at high speed.* 当两辆警车从他们身边疾驰而过的时候，乔对他的哥哥说："不知出什么事了？" ◇ What's happening?

What's new? [.hwʌts'njuː] [话] **你好吗？** 原意"最近社会上有什么新鲜事吗？"。实际上是很轻松的寒暄语，往往与 How are you? 和 How are you doing (these days)? 的意思一样。*Hi, what's new?* 嘿，你好吗？ *A: What's new? B: Nothing much. What's new with you?* 甲：怎么样？ 乙：照旧。你怎么样啊？ ◇ How are things with you?

What's up? [.hwʌ'tsʌ(:)p] [话] **怎么啦？** 与 WHAT'S cooking?, WHAT'S going on?, WHAT gives? 等大致相同，意思是"怎么啦？"、"发生什么事了？"。字面意义为"什么上去了？"，实际却是"什么起来了？"的意思。也就是说，这一习用语本来是 What's come up?，后来省略掉其中的 come 又把 What has 的缩略形式 What's 当作了 What is 的缩略形式。*"What's up?" said Charlie when he saw his friend Joe watching a crowd of people. "Search me, I just got here myself,"* "怎么啦？"查理看见他的朋友乔在观望着一群人，就对乔说。"不晓得，我也是刚来到这儿啊。" *A: I hear you were looking for me. What's up? B: Nothing* *much. I just wanted to get your opinion on this.* 甲：我听说你找过我。怎么啦？乙：没什么。我只是想听听你对这个问题的意见而已。◇ What's happened [happening]? / What is it?

whatsis

a whatsis [ə 'hwʌtsəs] [话] **说不出名字的东西** → a WHATCHAMACALLIT

wheat

separate the wheat from the chaff ['sepəˌreɪtðə 'hwi(:)t frəmðə 'tʃæ:f] [口] **分清有益的和无益的** 直译为"把小麦 (wheat) 从谷壳 (chaff) 中挑选出来"，也就是"选出有益之物"的意思。*So many books have been written about economic theory that it's difficult to separate the wheat from the chaff.* 关于经济理论的著作有如汗牛充栋，很难分清哪一本有用和哪一本没有用。*The mayor's office receives many suggestions on how to improve the city's environment. It's my job to separate the wheat from the chaff.* 市长办公室收到许多关于如何改进城市环境的建议，我的工作就是分清哪些建议有用和哪些建议没有用处。*Some of Ben's ideas are very good, but he's always talking off the top of his head. You have to be careful to separate the wheat from the chaff.* 本的意见有一些是很好的，不过，他总是灵机一动就要说出来。你必须注意分清哪些有用哪些没用。→ separate the SHEEP from the goats ◇ separate the useful from the useless

whee

Whee! ['hwi:(:)] [话] **哇呀!** ((儿童们表示愉快、兴奋时的叫声))主要是孩子们使用，如果成年人使用的话，一般有滑稽之感。*Whee! A whole week's vacation from school!* 哇呀！学校放假整整一个星期！*Whee! A bike! Thank you, Daddy! It's just what I wanted!* 哇呀！自行车！谢谢你，爸爸！这正是我求之不得的东西！*Father: Suppose we go to the zoo today? Children: Whee! Let's go!* 父亲：咱们今天去动物园好吗？孩子们：哇呀！去，去！*"Whee!" screamed the children as the roller coaster started down again.* 当游园的滑行列车又向下驶的时候，孩子们高兴得"哇呀！哇呀！"地喊叫起来了。◇ Hooray! / What fun!

wheel

a big wheel [ə ˌbɪg 'hwi:l] [话] **大亨** 这一习用语是把公司、团体等比做机器，而机器则有各式各样的 wheel，如嵌齿轮(cog wheel)，偏心轮 (eccentric wheel)，飞轮 (fly wheel)等。轮子越大，作用也越大。这就是本条原来的构思。*The big wheels of industry are showing dissatisfaction with the President's policy.* 实业界的大亨们对总统的政策表示不满。*Ernest thinks he's a big wheel in campus politics but actually he's only a small cog.* 欧内斯特认为他在大学内的政治活动中是一个举足轻重的人物，但是实际上他只不过是个小小的螺丝钉而已。往往省略 big，只用 wheel。*Mr. Handle is a wheel in the auto industry.* 汉德尔先生是汽车工业界的大亨。◇ an important [influential] person

put a spoke in *someone's* **wheel** → SPOKE

put *one's* **shoulder to the wheel** → SHOULDER

when

Say when. ['seɪ 'hwe(:)n] [话] **够了请说一声** 在给对方的杯子里倒饮料(酒、茶等)时的用语，一边倒一边说。为了容易理解，可以认为它是 Say when you want me to stop pouring. (当你想叫我停止倒的时候，请说一声。)的省略形式。*A: Say when. B: That's enough.* 甲：够了请说一声。乙：这足够了。在回答时，本来应该说 That's enough. 或者 That's plenty, thanks. (够了，谢谢。)但人们往往只用一个 When.表示"够了"的意味。在最初这样使用的时候，可能有一种新鲜的、幽默的感觉，然而现在已经成为陈词滥调，平平凡凡了。另外，除斟酒倒茶之类外，又转用于给别人往盘子里拨食物的时候或者给别人的汽车加油的时候。*A: I'll serve your plate. Please say when. B: When! When!—That's too much!* 甲：我给你往盘子里拨菜。够了请说一声。

乙:够了!够了!太多啦!如以上的例句所示,一般用祈使句,但并不限定如此。*Start filling the tank. I'll say when.* 请开始往水箱里上水。上够了,我告诉你。◇ Say when to stop.

where

tell *someone* **where to get off** [ˌtel ~ ˌhwerdə ˌgedˈɔːf] [话] **忍耐不住一腔怒火** get off 的字面意义为从交通工具上"下来"(如下车、下船),在这里是"停止"的意味。本条条头的整个意思是"告诉某人在什么地方下去",也就是"告诉某人停止令人恼火的言行"。这是在对某人的言行(一般是连续多次)已经忍无可忍而怒吼"适可而止吧!"的时候的用语。但可以按照字面意义使用,如: *The conductor told me where to get off.* 公共汽车的售票员告诉我应该在哪一站下车。这句话意思很明显,不会与其他混淆。但下一个例句就会发生歧义: *After I had changed my destination for the third time, the conductor finally told me where to get off.* 这句话不能理解为"告诉我应该在哪一站下车",正确的意思是"在我第三次改变前往地点的时候,公共汽车的售票员终于忍不住他的一腔怒火了。"总之,千万要注意上下文,避免搞错。*I'm going to tell that guy where to get off. I'm tired of his thinking he can order me around.* 我要告诉那个家伙应该适可而止。他认为可以随便支配我,这我已经不能忍耐了。◇ (get fed up and) speak angrily

Where does *someone* **get off** *doing something?* → GET

whew

Whew! [ˈhjuː / ˈhwuː / ˈhuː] [话] **唷!** 象声词。表示安心、惊异、不快等,使用范围很广,因此在翻译时可以根据上下文适当变换,不要墨守"唷"一个字。在下边的两个例句中,Whew! 是在脱险之后表示安心的声音。*Whew! That was close! He almost saw us.* 唷!真危险啊!差一点儿没叫他看见咱们。*Whew! Another inch and that car would have hit me!* 唷!只差一英寸那辆汽车就撞上我啦!下面的两个例句表示惊叹。*Whew! Look at all that money.* 嘿!你瞧那么多的钱!*Whew! What a beautiful scene!* 哎呀!多么美丽的景色啊!在筋疲力竭的时候也可以使用。*Whew! I'm beat. Let's take a rest.* 哎哟!我累极了。咱们休息一下吧。下面是在遇到令人不快的事物时发出的声音。*Whew! What a terrible smell.* 唷!多么难闻的气味!Whew! 有时作 Phew! [ˈfjuː], 又在极少的场合用 Phoo! [ˈfuː]。两者的用法与 Whew! 完全一样。

whirlybird

a whirlybird [ə ˈhwə(ː)rliˌbə(ː)rd] [话] **直升机** 构成方法: 动词 whirl (旋转) 加 -y 变成形容词,然后再加上 bird(鸟)。直译为"旋转的鸟"。*Have you ever ridden in a whirlybird?* 你坐过直升机吗? *Jack is a whirlybird pilot.* 杰克是一个直升机驾驶员。也可以写作 whirly-bird 或 whirly bird。又称 a CHOPPER, an EGGBEATER。◇ a helicopter

whiskers

the cat's whiskers [ðə ˌkæ(ː)ts ˈhwɪskərz] [话] **了不起的东西或人** → the cat's MEOW

whiskey

bootleg whiskey [ˈbu(ː)tˌle(ː)g ˈhwɪski] [口] **私酿的威士忌** bootleg 是"靴统"。旧时,一些美国人把禁止进口的东西或者私酿的酒放在高统靴子里偷偷运输。本条习用语即由此而来。动词 bootleg 是"私制、私运、私卖"的意思,本来并不限定用于威士忌,但现在主要是在讲威士忌的时候使用。私造、私运、私卖的人叫做 a bootlegger。如果省略 whiskey,只说 bootleg,也表示"私酿的酒"的意思。顺便讲一下: MOONSHINE 或者 white LIGHTNING 也是"私酿的酒",但一般指"玉米威士忌",而 bootleg whiskey 则可以用于任何种类的威士忌。*Investigators caught three men hauling bootleg whiskey.* 侦探们抓住了三个贩运私酿威士忌的人。◇ illegal whiskey

whistle

blow the whistle on *someone* [*something*] (for *something*) [ˌblouðə ˈhwɪsəlɔ(ː)n ～] [口] **警告、禁止** 源出体育比赛，裁判员在进行警告或者制止犯规的时候，要吹哨子。一般用于取缔不良现象的场合。*The tax office blew the whistle on our company for constantly overrunning our entertainment account.* 税务局警告我们公司，不得经常超额支出交际费。*The school finally blew the whistle on students' cutting class.* 学校终于发出警告，不准学生任意旷课。有时只用于表示"使人停止"的意思。*The government blew the whistle on the latest space project.* 政府取消了最近的航天计划。有时不是"吹哨子"的本人进行禁止，而是把同事或同伙所做的坏事汇报给上司、警察、当局等，请他们取缔或逮捕。*Officer O'Malley blew the whistle on three of his fellow officers for taking bribes.* 奥马利警官把三个同事受贿的情况汇报给了上级。◇ (give warning and) stop *someone* (from *doing something*)

wet *one's* **whistle** [ˌwet ～ ˈhwɪsl] [话] **喝一杯** whistle 是"哨子"，这里指"喉咙"，因此，本条条头直译为"润嗓子"。"润"的手段一般是用威士忌等酒类饮料。*Let's stop in that bar over there and wet our whistles.* 我们到那边的酒吧间去坐坐，喝上一杯吧。*Would you like to wet your whistle before we eat?* 咱们吃饭前先喝上一杯好吗？但是，也可以用于不是"酒"的场合，如：*There was an old man sitting at the counter, wetting his whistle with a bottle of pop.* 有个老头儿坐在柜台那儿喝汽水。如这一例句所示，"用某种饮料(润嗓子)"一般用 with ～，但也可用 on ～。◇ have a drink / drink ((不加 with 或 on))

whistle in the dark → DARK

white

bleed *someone* **white** [ˌbliːd ～ ˈhwaɪt] [口] **榨取个精光** bleed 是"使流血"，white 是"把血吸干使达到发白的程度"。*Never borrow money from a loan shark. He'll bleed you white.* 绝对不要向放高利贷的人借钱。他会把你榨个精光。*My wife is bleeding me white with her spendthrift ways.* 我的老婆挥霍无度，把我挤个精光。*In past wars, the conquering nation often bled the loser white by forcing it to pay high reparations.* 在过去的战争中，战胜国往往勒索大量赔款，把战败国榨个精光。*Dishonesty among politicians is bleeding the government white.* 政客们的不廉使得国家民穷财尽。如以上的例句所示，几乎在所有的场合，"榨取"的东西都是"金钱"，但也有极少数的例外。*Growing high-yield crops without sufficient fertilizer will bleed the soil white.* 栽培高产作物而不施足够的肥料，只能使土壤的养分消耗净尽。◇ take all *someone's* money

in black and white → BLACK

(as) white as a ghost [əz ˈhwaɪdəzə ˈgoust] [话] **吓得脸色煞白** → (as) white as a SHEET

(as) white as a sheet → SHEET

(as) white as snow → SNOW

a white elephant → ELEPHANT

a white lie → LIE

white lightning → LIGHTNING

white mule → MULE

whole

go (the) whole hog → HOG

whop

a belly whop [ə ˈbeliˌhwɑ(ː)p] [话] **胸腹先着水的笨拙跳水动作** → a belly FLOP

whozis

a whozis [ə ˈhuːzəs] [话] **不知叫什么的东西** → a WHATCHAMACALLIT

why

Why don't I [you,we] *do something*? [ˌhwaɪ ˌdountaɪ / ˌdountʃu / ˌdounwi ～] [话] **我[你、我们]这样做如何？** 直译为"我[你、我们]为什么不做某事呢？"在形式上是疑问句，实际上不是向对方质问"为什么？"，而是提出建议的一种表达法，不能用于第三人称。首先在以 I 为主语的场合，条头用法如下：*Why don't I go? I know the way much better than you.* 我去如何？我对道路比你熟悉得多。*Why*

don't I tell Graham that you're sick? 我告诉格雷厄姆说你病了如何？下边是以 we 为主语的场合。*Why don't we eat out for a change?* 咱们到外边去吃一顿，换换口味如何？*The weather's so bad. Why don't we just stay home and watch TV?* 天气太坏了，咱们就在家里呆着看电视好吗？下边是以 you 为主语的场合。*Why don't you go with us? There's plenty of room.* 你跟我们一起去如何？车里有你坐的位子。*Why don't you go jump in the lake?* 你走开行不行？◇ Perhaps I [we] should *do something*. / Let's *do something*. / Won't you *do something*? / (You) *do something*.

wide

give *someone* [*something*] **(a) wide berth** → BERTH

a wide place in the road → PLACE

wife

every last man and his wife [ˌevri ˈlæːstˈmæ(ː)nənhɪz ˈwaɪf] [口] **不论谁，有一个算一个** → every TOM, Dick and Harry

wiggle

get a wiggle on [ˌgedə ˈwɪgəˌlɔːn] [话] **赶快干或走** get on 与 put on 相同，是"穿上"的意思。wiggle 是"全身或部分身体扭动"，而 get a wiggle on 的 wiggle 则又增添了"迅速"、"麻利"的意味。大多用于如下的场合：为了按期完成任务，赶快干；在外出前，赶快做准备工作；在前往目的地的路途上，由于怕迟误而赶快走，等等。*If we don't get a wiggle on, we won't make the deadline [train].* 如果我们不赶快干[走]，就赶不上截止期限[火车]了。父母对子女用本条习用语时，常用命令式。*Get a wiggle on! You'll be late for school!* 赶快！你上学要迟到啦！get a MOVE on 大致同义。◇ hurry (up)

wild

sow (*one's*) **wild oats** → OATS

be wild about *something* [*someone*] [ˈwaɪl dəˌbaut ～] [话] **狂热爱好** → be CRAZY about *something* [*someone*]

Wild

Wild horses couldn't drag it from me. → HORSES

wildfire

spread like wildfire [ˌspred laɪk ˈwaɪldˌfaɪr] [口] **迅速传开(流言、消息)** spread 是"传播"。wildfire 原指"在帆船时代的海战中向敌船放火时使用的易燃化合物"，现在指"一点起来就扑不灭的野火、山林之火等"。但是，此词不能单独使用，只用于本条条头 spread like wildfire 之类的习用语。在谈到山林火灾时，可以按照字面意义使用，讲 *The flames spread like wildfire.* 转眼之间星星之火已呈燎原之势了。不过，人们不说 The fire is spreading like wildfire. 可能由于语感不佳，极力避免与 fire 一词搭配。也可以转作比喻使用。*When the President suddenly canceled all his appointments for the next three days, the rumor spread like wildfire that he had had a heart attack.* 当总统突然取消了此后三天的一切预先安排的活动时，关于他心脏病发作的流言马上传开了。*News of the cholera outbreak spread like wildfire.* 发生霍乱的消息迅速传开了。除流言、消息外，还可以用于传染病。*The disease spread through the slums of the city like wildfire.* 这种病转瞬之间在全市的贫民区中传播开了。◇ spread very quickly

wild-goose

a wild-goose chase → CHASE

will

cut *someone* **out of** *one's* **will** [ˌkʌt ～ ˌaudəv ～ ˈwɪ(ː)l] [口] **分文遗产也不给某人** → cut *someone* off without a CENT

willies

give *someone* **the willies** [ˌgɪv ～ ðəˈwɪliːz] [话] **使人不安** 20 世纪初开始流行。willies 一词表示不安的状态。"使人不安"的内容很广泛，包括"令人毛骨悚然"、"令人心惊肉跳"、"令人非常着急"等等。一般使用时，语气不太强烈。

I hope Ralph calls soon to let us know whether he succeeded or not. All this waiting is giving me the willies. 我盼望拉尔夫早点来电话告诉我们他成功了没有。老这么等待,使我心里着急。*Mr. Conrad is a very nice man, but the way he stares silently into space for hours on end gives people the willies.* 康拉德先生是一个很好的人,但是他一连几小时默默地凝望天空的样子可真令人有点害怕。*I know there's no such thing as a haunted house, but still that old abandoned mansion in our neighborhood gives me the willies every time I pass by it.* 我知道世界上并没有什么闹鬼的房子,但是每当我从附近久无人居住的宅第门口经过的时候,总还是有些毛骨悚然。*The way George would walk along the top of the wall behind his house always gave his mother the willies.* 乔治的母亲看到他在房后的墙头上行走的样子,总有点心惊肉跳。*Stop walking around the room like that. You're giving me the willies.* 你不要在房间里来回乱转啦。这使我神经紧张。get the willies 是"感到不安"。*I get the willies whenever I'm with someone who gestures with both hands while he is driving.* 每当我乘汽车,遇到用两只手打手势的驾驶者时,我心里就感到不安。*Now, Mother, don't start getting the willies just because Lynn is a little late coming home.* 哎呀,妈妈,你不必为林恩稍微晚回家一会儿就那么着急啊。◇ make *someone* nervous

win

win (*someone*) **going away** → GOING

wind

get *one's* **second wind** [ˌget ~ ˌsekənd-ˈwɪ(ː)nd] [口] **恢复元气** second wind 的意思是"在运动时呼吸急促,运动停止后,又恢复了平静的呼吸"。条头的整个意思是"恢复元气"。如果更精确地来讲,不是"通过休息恢复元气",而是"在运动之间逐渐恢复元气"。*Not having played tennis for a long time, I was exhausted after the first three games. Then, however, I got my second wind and went on to win the set.* 我很久没有打网球了,所以在打完前三盘的时候已经筋疲力尽,不过,随后我恢复了元气,拿下了这一局。*The first hour of mountain climbing is always the hardest. But don't worry, in a little while you'll begin to get your second wind.* 登山的最初一小时永远是最累的。不过不要担心,过不多久你就会开始恢复元气了。如以上两个例句所示,本条习用语首先令人想到的就是在运动中"急促的呼吸平静下来"的样子。但是,也可以作为比喻使用,与呼吸没有直接关系,表示"恢复精神"或"恢复常态"的意思。在这一场合,仍然是"在行动中恢复"。*The first few days after the summer vacation seemed to drag by very slowly, but then I began to get my second wind and started to enjoy my studies.* 暑假终了后的最初几天仿佛过得非常慢,但是此后我开始振作精神,享受学习的乐趣了。*Just when everyone thought the speaker was about to conclude his talk, he seemed to get his second wind and continued to speak for almost another hour.* 正当每个听众都以为发言人马上要结束他的讲话的时候,他好象鼓起劲儿来,又继续说了一个来小时。◇ regain *one's* energy [stride]

get wind of *something* [ˌget ˈwɪndəv ~] [口] **听到风声** 本条条头来源于:野生动物通过风可以嗅出周围的情况。*The deer, getting wind of the hunter, escaped in the opposite direction.* 鹿嗅出有猎人到来,就向相反的方向逃走了。作为比喻,大多用于说话者有害怕泄露出去的秘密的场合。*Don't mention this plan to anyone. If our competitors get wind of it, we'll lose our advantage.* 这个计划不要对任何人讲。如果我们的竞争对手听到风声,我们就会失去优势。*The teacher has somehow gotten wind of our plan to cut class.* 不知为什么,老师已经耳闻我们逃课的计划了。*Mum's the word. We don't want Mom to get wind of where we are taking her for her birthday dinner.* 不许声张。我们不想叫妈妈查觉在她生日

那一天我们请她到什么地方去吃饭。◇ hear about *something*

sail close to the wind [ˌseɪl ˌkloustəðə ˈwɪ(:)nd] [口] **言行几乎越轨** 原是海上用语,意思是"使船头切风行驶,稍一不慎,就会造成逆帆"。这是一种危险的行驶方法,需要有高超的技术。这里的 close 是 at a close angle (与风的方向成锐角)的意思。*That ship is sailing dangerously close to the wind.* 那只船冒着危险,切风行驶。这是按照字面意义的用法。转作比喻,绝大多数用于表示"言语行动几乎超越道德、法律、礼仪的常轨"。*He may not be really dishonest, but he usually sails pretty close to the wind.* 他可能不是一个真正不诚实的人,但只是经常跟骗子手相差无几。如这一例句所示,close 的前面一般要加副词。除 pretty 外,另外可以加 too, very, fairly, a bit, awfully 等。*That's sailing too close to the wind for me. If the authorities get wind of our activities, they could raise all kinds of difficulties.* 那对我来说,实在太冒风险了。如果当局听到我们活动的风声,准会大找我们的麻烦。*That director doesn't exactly make pornographic movies, but he sails very close to the wind.* 那个导演并不制作十足的黄色影片,但是他已经贴近这类影片的边缘了。*You may not have really insulted her, but you were sailing awfully close to the wind.* 你也许没有真正侮辱她,但是你所说的话几乎和侮辱她一样啊。除以上的各种用法外,有时还应用于"金钱"、"经济"。*I don't think we should attempt such a large project on our present budget. That's sailing too close to the wind.* 我认为,以我们现在的预算,不要搞那么大的规划。那太冒风险啦。*We were forced to sail close to the wind for many years until my writings began to sell well.* 在我的作品开始畅销以前,我们家不得不过了许多年的紧日子。有时用 near 代替 close,作 sail near to the wind,但这是英国英语。◇ come close (to it) / adopt [be on] a dangerous course / live [be] in near poverty [bankruptcy]

see which way the wind blows [ˌsi(:) ˌhwɪtʃ ˌweɪðə ˈwɪnd,blouz] [口] **静观事情的演变** 直译为"看风往哪边吹"。which way the wind blows (风吹的方向) 指"事情的演变"、"动向"、"形势"。see (看)有"了解"、"掌握"的意味。本条条头源出英国法学家和政治家塞尔登 (John Selden, 1584–1654)的一句话: Take a straw and throw it up into the air—you may see by that which way the wind blows. (拿一根稻草并往空中扔去,你可以看到风向哪一边吹。) a STRAW in the wind (预兆)一语也来源于此。*Would there be war? There were so many conflicting straws in the wind that it was difficult to see which way the wind was blowing.* 会发生战争吗? 相互矛盾的预兆太多了,很难判明事态演变的方向。在下一例句中,which 以下的部分大致等于"形势"。*It's too early to take a stand yet. Let's wait a little to see which way the wind blows.* 现在确定立场还太早。咱们且等一下,看看形势再说。有时用 how 或 where 代替 which way,意思不变。*The way my girl was cozying up to Bob, it was only too easy to see how the wind was blowing.* 从我的女朋友拼命巴结鲍勃的样子来看,今后事态的发展已经是洞若观火了。动词也不仅用 see,还可以根据上下文适当地改用 know, can [be able to] tell, find out, discover 等。*We won't know [be able to tell, be able to discern] which way the wind is blowing on the oil situation until after the next OPEC meeting.* 不等到石油输出国组织的下一次会议开完,我们摸不清石油问题的发展情况。*I know you're anxious to be transferred back to the home office. When I get back I'll sound out the boss and try to find out [discover] which way the wind is blowing.* 我知道你急欲调回总公司。我回去以后,一定向总经理探询一下,看看他的意思如何。也可以利用"风吹的 direction(方向)"来讲俏皮话,如: *Now that my greatest rival had been transferred and my own mentor had become president, the wind was finally blowing in my* direction. 现在，我最大的竞争对手已经调走了，我的直接领导又当了总经理，春风终于向我吹来。◇ discern how things develop [the situation develops]

a straw in the wind → STRAW

take the wind out of *someone's* **sails** [ˌteɪkðə ˈwɪ(ː)nˌdaudəv ～ ˈseɪlz] [口] **由于摧毁他人的企图、想法、计划等而使他人意气消沉** 直译为"从某人的帆上夺走风"。这是用船帆突然失去风力的样子来比喻人的心理状态。下面的例句是典型的用法。*The news that another company had already secured the translation rights to the book took the wind out of the publisher's sails.* 那家出版社听说另外一家公司已经取得该书的翻译权，不禁大失所望。本条条头原意"为了阻止敌船的活动，而行驶到敌船的上风，把风挡住，使它吹不到敌船的帆上"，这是古时海战常用的战术。作为比喻，用于表示"在别人想干什么的时候或者正顺利进行什么事情的时候，突然前来破坏捣乱，使别人大为扫兴"的意思。不仅是有意识如此，有时这种"破坏捣乱"是由形势造成的。一般含有"突然"的意味。另外，本条习用语虽然包括"破坏捣乱"和"使人扫兴"两方面的意思，但在具体的句子中，大多是偏重于一方面。例如，以下两个例句是强调"破坏捣乱"的事实因素。*Foreign competition has taken the wind out of the sails of the U. S. automobile industry.* 由于外国的竞争，美国的汽车工业已经不如过去那样兴旺了。*The sudden appearance of the new witness for the prosecution took the wind out of the sails of the defense.* 由于原告一方突然出现新的证人，使得被告一方的企图完全落空了。以下的三个例句侧重心理因素。但是，根据事实因素严重程度的不同，心理因素也是从"有点扫兴"直到"垂头丧气"，种种不一。*Betty's demonstration that his first two conclusions were false certainly took the wind out of Tim's sails in a hurry.* 贝蒂证明蒂姆最初下的两个结论都是错误的，使得蒂姆马上就垂头丧气了。*Why don't you tell him that if he two-times you just once more, you're through. That should take the wind out of his sails.* 你告诉他如果他再乱搞男女关系，你就跟他告吹如何？这样一来，他就会老实下来了。*Tell him we know who is supplying him with money. That should take some wind out of his sails.* 你告诉他，我们知道是谁在供给他钱。这样一来，就会使他不那么气焰嚣张了。另外有 have the wind taken out of *one's* sails 的形式。*Business was pretty good until we had the wind taken out of our sails by the drop in the value of the dollar.* 在美元贬值使我们的投机完全落空之前，我们的生意本来是很兴隆的。◇ put a sudden end to [(quickly) destroy] *someone's* enthusiasm [momentum, aims, plans, overbearing attitude, etc.]

three sheets to the wind → SHEETS

windbag

a windbag [ə ˈwɪndˌbæːg] [话] **饶舌的人** 原为英国英语，意思是"风笛的皮口袋"。但美国人的理解是"除了空气外，什么也出不来的口袋"。这种饶舌的人总是自以为了不起，而且大腹便便的胖子居多。当然也不限定如此。*John is such a windbag. He can talk for hours at a time without saying anything.* 约翰是一个饶舌大王。他能够一连好几个小时滔滔不断地讲毫无内容的废话。*Don't tell me you've invited that windbag for dinner!* 你不会约请那个令人讨厌的饶舌大王来家里吃晚饭吧！常用 real 加强语气。*The last speaker was a real windbag. By the end of his talk we were all bored to tears.* 最后的发言人是个真正的饶舌大王。到他讲完话的时候，我们全都烦得要死了。◇ a talkative bore

window

a bay window [ə ˈbeɪ ˈwɪndə] [话] **大肚皮** 字面意义为"凸窗"。*The east side of the living room is a curving bay window.* 起居室的东墙有一面弧形的凸窗。凸窗使人联想到人的大肚子。*Anybody who eats well is bound to get a bag window.* 凡是吃得太好的人，必然落得一个大肚

皮。因为大肚皮的形状也象 pot (壶),所以又称 a potbelly['pɑt.beli]。◇ a fat paunch

winds

throw [fling, cast] *something* **to the winds** [.θrou / .flɪŋ / .kæ(:)st ~ təðə 'wɪ(:)ndz] [口] **把……抛到九霄云外** → throw CAUTION to the winds

Windy

the Windy City [ðə 'wɪndi 'sɪdi] [口] **芝加哥市** 字面意义为"多风之城",因为 Chicago(芝加哥)位于密歇根湖畔,经常有风从湖面吹来。*We spent three days in the Windy City on the way to New York.* 我们前去纽约的途中,在芝加哥市停留了三天。另外,请读者注意:Chicago 的发音不是 ['ʃkɑŋo],而是 [ʃə'kɑgou]。◇ Chicago

wing

take *someone* **under** *one's* **wing** [.teɪk ~ ʌndər ~ 'wɪ(:)ŋ] [口] **庇护** wing 是"翅膀"。最初的构思是:"照顾弱者,就象母鸡用翅膀保护雏鸡一样"。*The government has announced that it will take ten thousand refugees under its wing.* 政府已经宣布要庇护一万名难民。*My aunt is always taking stray cats under her wing.* 我的婶母总是庇护野猫。有时,"庇护"的内容包括"亲自教导"或"言传身教"。*Bill probably wouldn't have made it through graduate school if Professor Thompson hadn't taken him under his wing.* 比尔如果不是受汤普森教授的亲自指导,大概不可能从研究院毕业。◇ look after *someone* / give personal guidance to *someone*

wings

clip *someone's* **wings** (by *doing something*) [.klɪp ~ 'wɪ(:)ŋz] [话] **制约** 字面意义为"剪短鸟翅膀"。*Jack clipped his pet owl's wings so that it couldn't fly away.* 杰克剪短他饲养的猫头鹰的翅膀,使它不能飞走。转作比喻使用,表示"对于行为不妥或过分的人进行约束"的意思。*Jack spent so much of his time entertaining clients that the department head clipped his wings by cutting back on his entertainment account.* 杰克在招待客户方面花费的时间太多了,部长用削减他的交际费的手段对他进行制约。*George used to go out almost every night, but his father clipped his wings by refusing to let him use the car.* 乔治从前几乎每天夜里都要出去,但是他父亲不准他再使用汽车,对他进行了制约。*If the Allies had clipped Hitler's wings in the early stages of his political career, there might not have been a Second World War.* 如果同盟国在希特勒政治活动的初期阶段对他进行制约,也许就不会发生第二次世界大战。*The new road law has clipped the wings of drunken drivers.* 新道路法制约了酒后开车的人们。◇ restrain *someone's* activities

earn *one's* **wings** [.ə(:)rn ~ 'wɪ(:)ŋz] [口] **能够胜任** 这里的 wings 原为军队用语,指"空军徽章"。这种徽章取展翅(wings)的鸟形图案,正式名称为 aviation badge。航空兵完成一定的飞行训练,被授予这种徽章。*I earned my wings at Pensacola Naval Air Station in Florida.* 我在弗罗里达州的彭萨科拉海军航空基地获得了空军徽章。一个人获得空军徽章之后,到什么地方都有充当飞行员的资格。实际上,美国民航飞行员大多来自空军,他们是在服兵役期间取得驾驶飞机的资格的。一般人取得飞行员的资格虽然也可以说 earn *one's* wings,但毕竟这是军队用语,所以通常要用 get *one's* pilot's license。作为比喻,本条习用语的意思是 prove *oneself* responsible [reliable, able, mature],亦即与 win *one's* SPURS 大致同义。下边两个例句是用于工作的场合。*The boss thinks you've finally earned your wings. He's going to put you in charge of the next project.* 老板认为你终于能够胜任工作了,下一项计划打算叫你负责。*Bill's a veteran dictionary editor who earned his wings helping to compile the third edition of Webster's New International.* 比尔是一位老资格的词典编辑,他因为参加编

纂《韦氏新国际词典》第三版而取得独立工作的能力。也可以应用于驾驶技术，如：*Please let me drive the car to San Francisco with my friends, Dad. Haven't I earned my wings by driving for three years now without an accident?* 爸爸，请允许我驾驶汽车与朋友们一起去旧金山吧。我已经开车三年没有发生事故，该够格了吧。有时用 get 代替 earn，如：*That race driver got his wings driving in small, country stock-car races.* 在乡村的小型的汽车竞赛中，那个赛车选手达到了应有的水平。◇ prove *oneself* responsible [reliable] / prove [demonstrate] *one's* ability [maturity] / gain *one's* experience

get *one's* **wings** [ˌget ~ ˈwɪ(ː)ŋz] [话] **工作、技术等达到应有的水平** → earn *one's* WINGS

test *one's* **wings** [ˌtest ~ ˈwɪ(ː)ŋz] [口] **试验自己的力量** → try *one's* WINGS

try *one's* **wings** [ˌtraɪ ~ ˈwɪ(ː)ŋz] [口] **试一试自己的能力** 直译为"试验自己的翅膀"，指小鸟尝试一下自己能不能独立飞翔。*The fledgling eagle tried its wings too soon and fell to the ground.* 那只雏雕过早地试飞，结果摔到地面上了。这是按照字面意义的使用方法。下面的例句是比喻用法，但在造句方面与上边的例句完全一样。*The fledgling socialist party tried its wings too soon and was decisively defeated at the polls.* 社会党羽毛未丰就想试一下自己的力量，结果在大选中彻底败北了。在比喻用法中，一般也包含"单独去干"的意味。*I worked as a newspaperman for many years before I got up sufficient nerve to try my wings as a novelist.* 在我有足够的勇气去试一下自己当小说家的能力之前，我当了好多年的新闻记者。*I know you want me to stay and work in your office, Dad, but please let me go to New York. I'd like to try my wings further afield.* 爸爸，我知道你希望我留在你的公司里工作，但是，请你允许我去纽约吧。我喜欢在更广阔的天地里单独去干，试一试自己的能力。有时用 test 代替 try，意思不变。*After two years as an attorney's assistant, the young lawyer felt ready to test his wings on a case of his own.* 那位年轻的律师在当了两年律师助手之后，觉得自己已经可以独立办案试一下自己的身手了。◇ test *one's* strength [abilities]

wink

not sleep a wink [nɑt ˌsli(ː)pə ˈwɪŋk] [话] **连个盹也没打** → not bat an EYE

winks

grab forty winks [ˌgræ(ː)b ˌfo(ː)rdi ˈwɪŋks] [话] **小睡片刻** grab 是"抓"。forty winks 直译为"眨四十次眼"。整个条头意思是"稍微睡一会儿"。在这里，grab 含有"抓时间"或"忙里偷闲"的意味。*Hold all calls for me, Miss Jones. I'm going to grab forty winks on the couch in my office.* 琼斯小姐，你替我接所有的电话。我要在办公室的长沙发上稍微睡一会儿。*I think I'll eat early so I can grab forty winks before the meeting.* 我想早点吃饭，以便能在开会之前小睡片刻。*During a break in the all-night session, a few of the negotiators were grabbing forty winks at their seats.* 在通宵会议的休息时间中，有几个参加谈判的人坐在自己的席位上打盹。动词一般用 grab，但有时也可以使用 snatch, catch, get 等。*I feel better now. I managed to snatch forty winks while I was waiting.* 现在我感到精神多啦。我在等待的时候，设法眯了一会儿。◇ take a short nap / nap

wino

a wino [ə ˈwaɪˌnou] [话] **酒鬼、醉鬼** 特指身无分文又无职业、专喝廉价酒、喝醉了不论什么地方都可以倒下的酒徒。所喝的大多是便宜的葡萄酒或威士忌，但不限定如此，只要是酒类，不管哪一种都可以。wino 是去掉 wine (葡萄酒)的 -e 而添个 -o 构成的。复数为 winos [ˈwaɪˌnouz]。这是个轻松的说法，按照条头的释义，一般指男性。*An unshaved wino with a filthy, tattered coat was lying on the sidewalk.* 有一个满脸胡子、穿着又脏又破的上衣的醉鬼躺在便道上。有时戏指 an alcoholic (嗜酒者)。*The boss's wife is a wino.* 老板的太太是个酒鬼。又,同伴之间常用这一习用语开玩笑。*That's your third martini. You're getting to be a real wino, aren't you?* 你已经在喝第三杯马丁尼鸡尾酒了。看起来,你要成为真正的酒鬼啦。◇ a drunk

wire

down to the wire [ˌdauntəðə ˈwaɪr] [口] **直至最后一秒钟** wire 原指"赛马时在终点线上空拉着的铁丝"。down to the wire 是"一直达到铁丝的地方",亦即"直至终点"。*The two leading horses were neck and neck all the way down to the wire.* 领先的两匹马互不相让,一直竞争到终点。转作比喻时也往往强调 all the way (路上一直不停)。*The two countries struggled for a compromise all the way down to the wire.* 两个国家一直在努力寻求一个折中方案。如果与 be coming 或 be getting 结合到一起,则是"接近期限"的意味。*The election campaign is coming down to the wire with no candidate holding a decisive lead.* 竞选运动已经快收场了,没有一个候选人占有绝对优势。*We're getting down to the wire on this project. We'll have to pick up speed if we're going to finish in time.* 这项设计已经快到期限了。如果我们打算按期完成,就必须加快速度。◇ to the finish / until the very last moment / to the [an] end

wires

pull wires [ˌpu(:)l ˈwaɪrz] [口] **走后门** → pull STRINGS

wise

get wise (to *something* [*someone*]) [ˌget ˈwaɪz] [话] **发觉** 直译为"对某事或某人聪明起来"。本条条头原意是"因为发觉了对方的秘密或企图,所以能够巧妙地采取应付的手段"。其中经常含有发觉者与被发觉者之间利害冲突的概念。也就是说,从发觉者方面来看,"如果不知道,就会受损失";从被发觉者来看,"如果被人知道,就大为不利"。一般用于很不容易发觉的秘密、阴谋、企图等。*If the cops get wise to our scheme, we're done for.* 如果警察发觉咱们的计划,咱们就完蛋了。*It was a long time before I got wise to the fact that my boss had no intention of promoting me.* 我了解到老板并没有提升我的意图已经是很久以后的事情了。get wise to *someone* 不是"发觉人的存在",仍然是"发觉人的秘密、阴谋等"的意思。*Mum's the word. If he ever gets wise to us, there'll be the devil to pay.* 千万不要对别人讲。如果他发觉我们的计划,那就糟糕了。*Bob often called in sick in order to go to a baseball game until the boss got wise and told him he had to have a doctor's certificate each time he was sick.* 鲍勃为了去看棒球比赛,经常来电话告病假。老板终于觉察出来,就告诉鲍勃说:每次告病假必须有医生的诊断书。可以用 be 动词代替 get; 讲 be wise to *something* [*someone*] (注意到本人应该知道的事情),用法与 be onto *someone's* GAME 大致相同。*You may as well give up. I'm wise to your little game.* 你还是认输吧。我已经明白你的鬼把戏了。*It seems he was wise to you from the beginning. He was only pretending ignorance in hopes of finding out how much you knew.* 他好象从一开始就发觉你的企图了。他只是假装不知道,打算探明你究竟知道多少。另有 WISE up (to *something* [*someone*]) 的说法,也是用于"发觉"如果不知道就对自己不利的事情的场合。但是其重点在于"发觉"这两个字本身,而不在于对方被发觉后是否处境困难。◇ become aware (of *something* [*someone's something*])

get wise (with *someone*) [ˌget ˈwaɪz] [话] **说大话** get wise 的字面意义为"聪明起来"。*Just because people get older doesn't necessarily mean they get wiser.* 人越老并不一定越聪明。往往转用于表示"故作聪明,说东道西"、"针小棒大,兴风作雨"或者"目无长上,夸夸其谈"等意义。*You'd better not try to get wise with Professor Wilson. He's a stickler for* *proper behavior.* 你在威尔逊教授面前，最好不要说狂妄的话。他对行为举止要求得非常严格。*Don't get wise, young man. Just answer my question in plain and simple language.* 年轻人，不要口出狂言。对于我提出的问题，你用清楚而简单的话回答就行了。另外，get smart 也是"说大话"的意思，但比说 get wise 的语调稍微轻松一点儿。*Don't get smart with me or I'll pin your ears back.* 别跟我说大话，否则我会狠揍你一顿。◇ become impudent

put *someone* **wise** (to *something* [*someone*]) [ˌput ～ ˈwaɪz] [话] **使人知道对他有利害关系的事情** 直译为"使某人聪明"。意思不仅仅是"使人了解"，而且是告知某人对他有直接利害关系的事情，他得不到这一情报就会受到损失。*I felt very grateful to Mr. Norris until my friends put me wise to the fact that he was actually cheating me.* 在我的朋友们告知我诺里斯先生实际上是在欺骗我之前，我对他是非常感激的。如这一例句所示，本条习用语一般用于当事者不了解事实或者当事者处于很难了解事实的状况的场合。另外，to *something* 大多属于"秘密"性质，但这只是因为此类文句居多，本条习用语本身并没有"秘密"的意味。*The guy didn't show up for our appointment. Someone must have put him wise to our plan.* 那个家伙没有来赴约。一定有人把我们的计划透漏给他了。*It looks as if our plan to bilk Mr. Steed isn't going to work. Somebody has put him wise to us.* 看起来，我们向斯蒂德先生骗钱的计划很不顺利啊。准是有人已经把我们的底细告诉他了。"使人知道"的手段并不限于用嘴，也可以用"神色"、"姿态"等。*Lois's nervousness put Jack wise to the fact that she was not there to see him of her own free will.* 杰克从洛伊丝坐立不安的样子明白了她并不是自愿前来看他的。如以上的例句所示，是用在 wise 后边加 to *something* [*someone*] 的方式来表示"使人知道的事情或情况"，但也有省略这一部分的场合。*I didn't realize at first that something strange was going on. It was Bela's being dressed as a doctor that put me wise.* 最初我没有感到有什么奇怪的。而贝拉扮作医生，才使我省悟过来。◇ make *someone* aware (of *something* [*someone's something*])

a wise guy → GUY

wise *someone* **up** (to *something* [*someone*]) [ˌwaɪz ～ ˈʌ(ː)p] [话] **使某人注意到他所应该知道的事情** → WISE up (to *something* [*someone*])

wise up (to *something* [*someone*]) [ˌwaɪ ˈzʌ(ː)p] [话] **注意到自己应该知道的事情** 本条条头与 get WISE (to *something* [*someone*]) (发觉)似乎意思相同，实际上两者之间有若干的差异。get wise 的重点在于"利害关系"，本条的重点则是"注意到"这几个字本身。因此，get wise 的场合一般伴有 to *something*，而本条条头则多省略这一部分。例如：If the cops wise up to our scheme, we're done for. 与 If the cops get wise to our scheme, we're done for. 这两种说法全都是"如果警察发觉咱们的计划，咱们就完蛋了。"的意思，但就英语来说，后一个说法比较自然。前者的重点是"警察发觉"，而后者的重点则是"咱们完蛋了"。*Don't beat your brains out for this outfit. Wise up. They're not going to give you any medals for working harder than you have to.* 不必为这样一个公司卖命。赶快清醒吧。你就是怎样额外多干，也没有人给你发勋章啊。*Jack isn't very sharp, is he. He never wised up to the fact that we were only pulling his leg.* 杰克的头脑不很灵敏。他完全没有注意到我们只是在耍弄他。*You'd better be careful. Joe's going to wise up to you one of these days. Then you'll be sorry.* 你小心一点好。用不了几天，乔就会注意到你所干的勾当。到那时候，后悔就晚啦。有时把 wise 作及物动词使用，而讲 wise *someone* up (to *something*) (使某人注意到他所应该知道的事情)。*You'd better wise him up. He's going to lose his job if he doesn't get on the stick.* 你提醒他一下为好。他如果不卖力气，就会丢掉自己的工作了。*The* *incident wised me up to the fact that they were out to cheat me.* 那件事情使我注意到他们是要欺骗我。◇ become aware (of *something* [*someone's something*])

wiseacre

a wiseacre [ə ˈwaɪ.zeɪkər] [口] **不知天高地厚、狂妄自大的人** → a wise GUY

with

get with it [.get ˈwɪ(:)ðɪt] [话] **鼓起干劲** 这里的 it 泛指"应该做的事情"。本条条头的字面意义为"在感情上与 it 在一起",意思是"集中精神",常含有"不要磨磨蹭蹭"的意味。*If I don't get with it, I won't finish my homework in time.* 如果我不加把劲儿,我就不能按时完成我的家庭作业了。*C'mon, let's get with it. The party starts at seven and we're not half ready yet.* 来,咱们加把劲儿。晚会在七点钟开始,我们连一半还没有准备好哪。*Stop goofing off and get with it.* 不要偷懒,加劲干吧。也可以用 be 动词代替 get 而讲 be with it,但在这一场合,主要是用于否定句,表示"心不在焉"或"精神不能集中"的意思。*Something's wrong with me today. I'm just not with it.* 我今天有点儿不对头,精神就是不能集中。另外,根据上下文,it 可以泛指"时代"。get [be] with it 是"顺应新潮流"、"接受新事物"的意思。在这一场合,get with it 大多用祈使句。主要是青年人使用,比条头的释义更具有轻松的感觉。*Get with it, Glen. You're behind the times.* 格伦,要顺应新潮流呀!你落后于时代啦。*Get with it. Nobody bowls anymore. Tennis is the game nowadays.* 要接受新事物呀!现在没有人再玩保龄球了。时兴的是网球。在使用这一意义时,也可以换成 be 动词,而讲 be with it。常用 really 加强语气。*I like that rock group. They're really with it.* 我喜欢那个摇滚乐队。他们的确够新潮的。*Archie is really with it in that new set of duds of his.* 阿尔奇穿上他那套新衣服,可真够时髦的。◇ get busy [to work] / Don't be old-fashioned.

be with *someone* [ˈwɪð .~] [话] **理解某人所说的话** 原意"与某人在一起",人们最常使用这一意义。*I was with him yesterday.* 昨天我曾和他在一起。从这一意义进一步发展,便是"跟着他走"即"赞成"的意思。*Are you with me or against me?* 你对我的意见是赞成呢还是反对?更进一步,就用于表示"理解"的意味了。*I'm sorry, I'm not quite with you. Would you repeat that last part again?* 对不起,你的话我没有十分理解。最后的部分可以再说一遍吗?在使用这一意义的时候,现在时占绝对多数。*The difference between "say" and "talk" is that "say" requires content while "talk" does not. Are you with me?* 英语的 say 与 talk 的不同点是:say 要求有所说的具体内容,而 talk 并不如此。你理解了吗? *Is everyone with me on what I've said so far?* 到此为止,大家都理解我所说的话了吗?另外,如果对别人所说的话当场反问而说 I wasn't with you. 大多表示"刚才心到别处去了,没有和你在一起"亦即"心不在焉"的意思。*I'm sorry, I wasn't with you. What were you saying?* 对不起,我失神了。你说什么来着?◇ understand / follow *someone* [what *someone* said]

wits

keep *one's* **wits about** *one* [.ki(:)p ~ ˈwɪtsə.baut ~] [口] **头脑冷静,保持警惕** wits 是"思考能力"、"智慧"的意思,在这里特别指"冷静的判断力"、"高度的警觉性"、"丝毫也不麻痹大意"。本条直译为"始终把冷静的判断力或高度的警觉性保持在自己的身边"。*If you want to make money in the commodities market, you must keep your wits about you.* 如果你想在商品市场上赚钱,必须头脑冷静,保持警惕。但实际上,并不限定"冷静"与"警惕"的意味永远保持各一半的比例,根据具体情况,大多是把重点放在二者中的一方。*I'll admit we appear to be trapped, but let's keep our wits about us. There may be a way out of this yet.* 看起来,我们似乎是进入圈套了,但是要保持冷静,也许还会有脱逃的方法。在这句话里，“冷静”是重点；但在下一个例句中，重点乃是“警惕”。*In this game you've really got to keep your wits about you. One slip will allow your opponent to make a very big score.* 在这一局里，你可要加倍警惕。只要有一点失误，就会使对方赢得极多的分数。除用 keep 外，还有 have *one's* wits about *one* 的说法。在使用 keep 的时候，显得紧张；在使用 have 的时候，态度比较从容。*The boss says that if he'd only had his wits about him at the time, he wouldn't have turned down such a good offer.* 老板说，如果他当时不是粗心大意，他是不会拒绝人家提出的那么好的条件的。*A man in a dangerous job like that has to have his wits about him.* 干那种危险工作的人，是一点儿也大意不得的。在上面两个例句中，前者是反省，后者是一般性论述，都没有紧张的感觉，因此，在这种场合多用 have。当然可以把 have 都换成 keep，只不过换成 keep 以后就带来了比较紧张的感觉。◇ stay calm (and think clearly)

live by *one's* **wits** [.lɪvbaɪ ~ 'wɪts] [口] **没有固定职业，凭动脑筋吃饭** 直译为“靠自己的智慧生活”。意思是：“不找安定的职业或固定的工作，每天凭着要自己的小聪明混日子”。大多用于靠临时打工吃饭的场合。总之，这是一种不受时间与规章制度束缚的超社会的生活方式。*Carl ran away from home at the age of twelve and lived by his wits on the streets of the city.* 卡尔十二岁时就从家里逃走了，在城市的大街上靠自己的小聪明吃饭。*Despite his good education, he apparently has no desire to hold a steady job. He'd rather travel from country to country, living only by his wits and whatever fortune might bring him.* 虽然他受过很好的教育，但是他显然不愿意干固定的工作。他似乎喜欢周游列国，只依靠小聪明和碰运气生活下去。也有与是否从事固定的工作毫无关系，象下面例句这样的用法：*Dodging enemy patrols and securing what extra food we could from native villages, we lived by our wits in the jungle for over half a year.* 我们巧妙地躲开敌人的巡逻队，竭力从当地的村庄弄到尽可能多的食品，依靠自己的聪明智慧，在那个深山老林中生活了半年多。偶尔用 make *one's* living by *one's* wits 的说法。*She was forced by the death of her husband and a lack of education to make her living by her wits.* 丈夫死了，自己又没受过教育，她不得不依靠自己的机智过活。◇ live (on [in, etc.] *someplace*) by depending (only) on *one's* native intelligence

wits'

be at *one's* **wits' end** → END

wives'

an old wives' tale → TALE

wolf

keep the wolf from the door [.ki(:)pðə 'wulf:rəmðə .do(:)r] [口] **免于饥饿** 直译为“让狼不接近家门口”。原意是：“人吃不上饭，身体软弱，狼就会来骚扰，因此必须吃饱”。*Many in the poorer nations of the world die every year because they are unable to keep the wolf from the door.* 在世界上贫穷的国家中，每年有许多人由于吃不上饭而被饿死。*During the Great Depression, people were happy to have any kind of work that would help to keep the wolf from the door.* 在大萧条时期，只要能混上饭吃，人们不管什么工作都愿意做。以上是实际上“免于饥饿”的场合。除此而外，还常用作比喻，很轻松地表示“生活过得去”的意思。在这一场合，始终以本人的生活水平为基准，因此不必以贫困的状态为前提。*I'm going to have to find another job. With six children, I barely make enough in my present job to keep the wolf from the door.* 我必须另找一个工作了。我有六个孩子，现在的工作只够糊口而已。如果生活水平已经相当高的人使用这一习用语，当然会有夸大其词的意思了。*Hy Awnhogg turned down their offer of a hundred thousand dollars a year as being hardly enough to keep the wolf from the* *door.* 人家给海·奥恩霍格每年十万美元的薪金,他因为那只够勉强维持吃饭而没有接受。◇ obtain enough food / keep from starving

a wolf [ə ˈwu(ː)lf] [话] **色鬼** 指见了女人就追逐的下贱男子。他们只把女人当作色情的对象,因此遭到女人的白眼。*Don't you dare speak to me, you wolf!* 你不要来跟我搭话,你这个色鬼! *I wouldn't give that guy the time of day. He's the biggest wolf in school.* 我对那个男生连看也不看一眼。他是全校最大的色鬼,见了女的就追。*A pack of the town wolves were hanging around on the street corner, whistling at all the girls that went by.* 城里的一伙色鬼聚集在大街的拐角上,凡是有姑娘走过,他们就吹口哨起哄。*How dare you paw me like that! I thought you were a nice boy, but you're just like all the others—a wolf in sheep's clothing.* 你怎么敢这样来碰我! 我还以为你是个有教养的人哪,原来你跟所有的其他男人一样,是个披着羊皮的豺狼。→ a WOLF in sheep's clothing ◇ a girl hunter

a wolf in sheep's clothing [ə ˈwulf ɪn.ʃiːps ˈklouðɪŋ] [口] **披着羊皮的豺狼** 源出《圣经·新约》中的《马太福音》(Matthew)第 7 章 15 节: Beware of false prophets, who come to you in sheep's clothing but inwardly are ravenous wolves. (你们要防备假先知;他们到你们这里来,外面披着羊皮,里面却是残暴的狼。)用法如下: *The man that said he would help us turned out to be a wolf in sheep's clothing who was only out for our money.* 那个说要帮助咱们的人,原来是个披着羊皮的豺狼,他只是为咱们的钱而来。*I'd be careful of that boy if I were you. He seems nice enough, but I've heard that he's actually a wolf in sheep's clothing.* 我如果是你,我一定对那个小伙子多加小心。他看起来非常好,但我听说他实际上是一个披着羊皮的豺狼。◇ a seemingly innocent person with ulterior motives

woman

the little woman [ðə .lɪdl ˈwumən] [话] **老婆** 请注意:一定要加 the。戏谑语,只在男性亲密朋友之间使用。这里的 little 没有特定意义,如果勉强解释,它具有"可爱的"、"应该爱护的"的意味。*I promised the little woman to be home early tonight.* 我答应我老婆今天晚上早回家。有时也用以表示"你太太"。*How's the little woman?* 你太太好吗? ◇ *one's* wife

make an honest woman of *someone* [.meɪkə ˈnɑ(ː)nəst ˈwumənəv ～] [话] **与发生关系的女人正式结婚** honest 过去是"守贞操的"的意味。因此,条头直译为"使某女子成为一个守贞操的人"。不结婚就与男人发生关系,当然不能算守贞操,所以"使守贞操"云云的意思就是跟发生关系的女人正式结婚,使她成为名正言顺的夫人。*I'm in a bit of a fix. Martha's pregnant and she insists that I make an honest woman of her.* 我有点儿陷入窘境了。马莎怀孕了,逼着我跟她正式结婚。给多年同居的女人办理正式结婚手续,也可以使用这一习用语。*He was getting on in years, and, after reading up on the inheritance laws, he decided he had better make an honest woman of the old girl.* 他的岁数大了,在仔细阅读遗产法之后,认为与同居多年的女伴正式结婚比较好。*If you refuse to make an honest woman of me, we're through. I'll raise the baby by myself.* 如果你不肯跟我正式结婚,咱们就一刀两断。孩子由我自己养育成人。◇ marry *someone*

a woman chaser [ə ˈwumən .tʃeɪsər] [话] **专门追逐女性的男子** → a SKIRT

a woman of the world [ə .wumənəvðə ˈwəːrld] [口] **视野广阔、知识丰富、善于应酬的女人** → a MAN of the world

wood

knock on wood [.nɑ(ː).kɔ(ː)n ˈwu(ː)d] [话] **敲木头祝愿万事如意** 一般英语词典收录的不是 knock on wood,而是 touch wood。意思虽然相同,但 touch wood 为英国英语,美国人并不使用。knock on wood 的字面意义为"敲木头"。不管

桌子也好,柱子也好,只要原材料是木头的东西,什么都可以。当然,天然的树木也行。关于语源,则有种种的说法。其一是:如果谈到未来的事情表示乐观,谈到过去的成绩表示自满,复仇女神 Nemesis (涅墨西斯) 就会嫉妒,从中作梗。只要敲一敲或摸一摸木头,便能解除女神的祸患。据说,本条习用语即由这一古老的传说而来。但是,一般的美国人意识不到它的出典,只是带着半开玩笑的心情,敲敲木头来祝愿万事如意而已。*"I feel certain I'll pass my entrance exam next week," said Mason, as he knocked on wood.* 梅森一边敲着木头一边说:"我觉得下个星期的入学考试我一定能及格。" *My grandfather claims he's going to live to be a hundred, but he always knocks on wood when he says it.* 我的祖父声称他要活到一百岁,但是每当他说这话的时候,总是敲木头进行祷告。*"I've never been sick a day in my life," he said, knocking on wood.* 他一边敲着木头祝愿,一边说:"我这一生中,从来没有生过一天病。"不只在自己说话时敲木头,当他人说话时也可以敲木头。*When the Treasury Secretary announced that the inflation rate should soon drop, the President smiled wryly and knocked on the arm of his chair.* 当财政部长宣布说通货膨胀率即将下降的时候,总统苦笑着,敲了敲椅子的扶手。关于祝愿的方式,实际上有三种:一是只"敲木头";二是一边"敲木头"一边说 knock on wood;三是没有动作,仅是口头上说"敲木头"。*I'm sure China won't have big earthquake soon—knock on wood.* 我敢肯定中国最近不会发生大地震——敲木头(祝愿万事如意)。这句话可以表示说话的人实际上敲手边的木头,也可以表示只是口头上这样说说而已。

wooden

a wooden kimono [ə ˌwudnkə'mounə] [话] **棺材** → a wooden OVERCOAT

a wooden overcoat → OVER-COAT

woods

(like) a babe in the woods → BABE

can't see the woods for the trees [ˌkæ(ː)nt ˌsi(ː)ðə'wu(ː)dz fərðə'triːz] [口] **只见树木不见森林** 自古就有的说法。来源于 1546 年英国人约翰·海伍德 (John Heywood)所编《格言集》(*Proverbs*)中如下的一条:One cannot see the wood for the trees. (人只注意树木就看不见森林。)意思是"人只注意部分就看不见全体。"在英国,表示"森林"的 wood 为单数,但在美国英语中只能用复数形式 woods。常用 forest 代替 woods,意思完全相同。*Many students fail to master English because, bogged down in a morass of grammatical details, they can't see the woods for the trees.* 许多学生未能把英语学到手,因为他们陷入了语法细则的泥沼,只见树木不见森林。*The former president was often accused of not evolving a comprehensive foreign policy because he couldn't see the forest for the trees.* 前任总统常常受到这样的指责:由于他只见树木不见森林,未能开展全方位的外交政策。*Kyle's reports are too detailed. You have a hard time seeing the woods for the trees.* 凯尔的报告书过于详细了。很难拨开树木看见森林。这个例句是把 can't see 变换了一个说法。在下面的例句中这一说法变化更大一点:*A good manager is interested only in the forest. He should leave the trees to his assistants.* 一个优秀的经理只抓重要环节。他应当把具体事务交给自己的助手。◇ can't grasp the overall picture [situation] for [because of] (*one's* attention being distracted by) all the details

a neck of the woods → NECK

be not out of the woods [nɑˌdaudəðə 'wu(ː)dz] [口] **不能安枕无忧** *The hunter hasn't come out of the woods yet.* 猎人还没有从森林中出来。如这一例句所示,如果使用 be 动词以外的动词,out of the woods 只能按照字面意义解释。但是,如果使用 be 动词的话,那就几乎完全是比喻说法了。woods 指"困难"、"危险"等。条头整个的意思是"没有摆脱困难或危险"。这一习用语一般用否定式,只是偶尔地用肯定式,如:*I had thought* *that we would be out of the woods by now.* 我原以为咱们现在该安枕无忧了。常加 still, yet, until 等副词,表示"还不能安枕无忧"的意味。*Although we had somehow made it to the shore without drowning, we still weren't out of the woods. A cold wind was blowing and we were miles from the nearest house.* 虽然我们好歹没有淹死,总算爬到了岸边,可是我们还不能安枕无忧。寒风在刮,我们距离最近的人家还有好几英里远哪。*I've passed English, but I won't be out of the woods until after the math exam on Friday.* 我的英语已经及格了,但是在星期五的数学考试没有过去之前,我还不能安枕无忧。*The worst of the recession is over, but we're still not completely out of the woods yet.* 萧条的最坏阶段已经过去了,但是我们还不能完全安枕无忧。如这一例句所示,常用 completely 或 entirely 加强语气。另外,也有不加 -s 而作 ~ out of the wood 的情况,但这是英国英语,在美国英语中不能使用。◇ be unable to relax

wool

pull the wool over *someone's* **eyes** [ˌpulðə ˈwu(:)louvər ～ ˌaɪz] [口] **蒙蔽、欺骗** 这里的 wool 是"古时男子所戴假发上的羊毛"。在旧俚语中,wool 是 hair 的意思,本条习用语过去也曾用 hair 代替 wool。整个条头的意思是"把某人假发的羊毛往下拉到他的眼睛上",虽然说是美国英语,在英国英语中也常使用。后来又从"使眼睛看不见"的意思一转,广泛用于表示"蒙蔽"和"以某种口实欺骗"的意味。*The defendant sought to pull the wool over the jury's eyes by claiming that the bribe was a political contribution.* 被告声称贿赂是政治捐款,企图用这种口实欺骗陪审团。在要叙明欺骗手段的场合,大多后面接续 by *doing something*,也有时用 with *something*。*When I demanded that Jack pay me the money he owed me, he tried to pull the wood over my eyes with some sob story about his wife being sick in the hospital.* 当我要求杰克把他借我的钱还给我的时候,他说老婆生病住院,企图用诉苦方式蒙混过关。*If you think you can pull the wool over my eyes with such an absurd story, you are sadly mistaken.* 如果你认为能用那种荒唐故事欺骗我,那你可是大错特错了。*The suspect pulled the wool over the eyes of the police by buying a plane ticket for Paris, and then he escaped by boat.* 嫌疑犯为了欺骗警察,买了一张去巴黎的飞机票,然后坐船逃走了。◇ deceive *someone*

word

as good as *one's* **word** [əz ˌgudəz ～ ˈwəːrd] [口] **守信用的** 这里的 *one's* word 不单是"人所讲的话",跟说 I gave my word. (=I promised.) 这句话时的 word 一样,是"诺言"的意思。a man as good as his word 是"守信用的人"。*You can trust Mr. Harris. He's always as good as his word.* 你可以信任哈里斯先生。他永远是守信用的。*He promised us he would be there on time. And sure enough, as good as his word, he was waiting for us when we arrived.* 他跟我们约定按时到达那里。果不其然,当我们去了的时候,他已经在等我们了。有些词典收录 as good as *one's* promise, 说它是本条条头的同义语,但是,这既不是一个习用语,实际上也极少使用。◇ faithful to *one's* promise(s)

a four-letter word [ə ˌfourledər ˈwəːrd] [口] **四字母粗俗下流词** 英语的粗俗下流词大多由四个字母构成。four-letter word 的概念比较广,既包括 fuck, cunt, dick 之类有关"性"的猥词,也包括 shit, piss, fart 之类有关"排泄"的粗词。总起来讲,是令人感到不快的、人们认为应该避讳的一些词。有关宗教的一些词,如 damn, hell, Christ 等,如果脱离本来的意义,单用于"强调"时,也是广义的 four-letter word。这类词一般指由四个字母构成的单音节词,但也有 Christ, prick 等例外。讨厌用 four-letter word 的美国人非常多。*Four-letter words were absolutely taboo in American movies until Clark Gable shocked moviegoers* *with his use of "damn" in the last scene of Gone With the Wind.* 在克拉克·盖博于《飘》的最后一景中使用 *damn* 一词令电影观众大惊失色之前，四字母粗俗下流词是美国电影界绝对禁忌的东西。*It's not very pleasant to be around him, Half his conversation seems to consist of four-letter words.* 跟他在一起非常不愉快。他的谈话有一半是粗俗下流的。*Most magazines for men depend on nudie pictures and four-letter words to maintain their circulations.* 专供男性阅读的杂志，大多是靠裸体照片和粗俗下流的文字维持发行册数。下面的例句当然是开玩笑的用法。*That guy is so lazy that he thinks "work" is a four-letter word.* 那个家伙太懒了，他认为 *work*（工作）是个四字母粗俗下流词。◇ a curse word / a dirty word

from the word go [frəmðə ˌwə(:)rd ˈgou] [话] **从一开始** go 是喊叫声，相当于"开始!"或"走!"本条条头直译为"从 go 这个词起"，这是强调 from the beginning [start] 的说法。这一习用语为轻松的口语，很少见于文字。*What's the matter with you? You've been against this plan from the word go, haven't you.* 你是怎么啦？你从一开始就反对这个计划啊。*Anne never liked me from the word go.* 安妮压根儿就不喜欢我。如以上的例句所示，大多用于否定句。*He's man who can take a good idea and make it work right from the word go.* 他这个人只要有好办法，马上就会把它付诸行动。这句话里的 right 是用以强调 from the word go 的副词。有时 go 加引号。*We are now living in an age of ferment and change, where people feel from the word "go" that anything that can happen probably will.* 我们现在生活于一个动荡与变革的时代，人们从一开始就感觉到任何有可能发生的事情都会发生。◇ from the very beginning

give (*someone*) *one's* **word** [ˌgɪv ~ ˈwəːrd] [口] **许诺** → as good as *one's* WORD

hang on *someone's* **every word** [ˌhæŋɔn ~ ˌevri ˈwəːrd] [口] **全神贯注听每一个字** 字面意义为"抓住他人讲话的每一个字不放"。有时作 hang on *someone's* words，但 every word 更能反映出"每一个字都不漏掉"的意思。*Prof. Green's lecture was so interesting that the audience hung on his every word.* 格林教授的讲座实在有意思极了，听众全神贯注，生怕漏掉一个字。◇ listen very avidly (to what *someone* is saying)

have a word with *someone* (about *something*) [ˌhævə ˈwəːrd wɪð ~] [口] **与某人商量一下** → have WORDS (with *someone* over *something*)

mum's the word → MUM'S

not breathe a word (to anyone) [nɑt ˌbriːðə ˈwəːrd (tu ˈe(:)niˌwʌn)] [话] **一个字也不吐露** 指不向任何人泄露秘密。这是强调 not tell (anyone) 的说法。*A: Don't tell anyone. It's a secret. B: Oh, no. I won't breathe a word.* 甲：不要对任何人讲。这是秘密。乙：不不，我决不吐露一个字。*Your secret is safe with me. I won't breathe a word to anyone.* 你的秘密在我身上是保险的。我决不向任何人吐露一个字。*Jane promised not to breathe a word of our talk to anyone.* 简保证不把咱们的谈话泄露给任何一个人。◇ never tell (anyone)

put in a good word (to *someone*) **for** *someone* [*something*] [ˌpudɪnə ˌgud ˈwəːrd fər ~] [话] **美言** 直译为"替某人说句好话"。*A: Do you think Sally will give me a date? B: I dunno. But I'll put in a good word for you when I see her.* 甲：你以为萨莉会答应我的约会吗？乙：我不晓得。不过，当我见到她的时候，我为你美言几句。*I've applied to Mr. Smith for a job. Will you put in a good word to him for me?* 我已经向史密斯先生申请得到一份工作了。你愿意在他面前为我美言几句吗？*I'll put in a good word for your plan.* 我会推荐你的计划。另外，有时省略 good，只讲 put in a word ~，意思不变。◇ say something good (to *someone*) in support of *someone* [*something*]

take *someone* **at** *his* **word** [ˌteɪk ~ ət ~ ˈwəːrd] [口] **相信某人的话** 直译为"按照

某人的言语来判断他”。换句话说就是“相信他不会撒谎”,亦即“相信他的人品”。因此,虽然条头的译文是“相信某人的话”,但是严密地讲,信赖的直接对象并不是“言语”,而是“人品”。在这一点上,与 take *someone's* WORD for it 不大一样。请比较下面的两句话。*You can take her at her word.* 她的话是信得过的。*You can take her word for it.* 关于这件事,你可以相信她的话。虽然都是相信她的“话”,但前者的重点是“人品”。*Why shouldn't I take him at his word? He's never lied to me yet.* 我为什么不应该相信他的话呢?他还从来没有对我说过谎呀。*You've got to learn not to take people at their word. You'll get cheated almost every time.* 你要懂得不能完全听信别人的话,不然十有八九要上当的。*When Jack promised to marry me I took him at his word. But after a month or so, he left me for another woman.* 当杰克说一定跟我结婚的时候,我信以为真了。那知道刚过一个来月,他就丢开我跟另一个女人搞上了。◇ believe what [everything] *someone* says / believe *someone*

take *someone's* **word for it** [ˌteɪk ～ ˈwəːrd ˌforɪt] [口] **相信某人所说的话** it 指“所说的事情”。另一习用语 take *someone* at *his* WORD (相信某人的话)与本条极相似,但该条的重点是相信说话人的“人品”,即“他说的话不会错”,而本条条头是只相信说话人所讲的这一件“事情”,即说话人在讲别的事情时是否撒谎不得而知。常用祈使句。*Take my word for it. Someday Ronald's going to be a big success.* 相信我的话吧。早晚有一天罗纳德是会取得巨大成功的。如此例所示,常用于表示“管保没错儿”的意思。*There'll be another war in the Middle East before the year is out. Take my word for it.* 不出今年,中东还得发生战争。我的话管保没错儿。*Don't take my word for it. Ask Sally. She'll tell you the same thing.* 你不相信我的话,就去问萨莉。她告诉你的准跟我的一样。*You shouldn't have taken his word for it. You should have called the office and checked.* 你不该相信他所说的话。你应当向公司打个电话核实一下。You can take my word for it. 是“我敢打保票。”的意思。*Don't worry. It's not going to rain tomorrow. You can take my word for it.* 不必发愁。明天下不了雨。我敢打保票。也可以用 that 代替 it,强调“没错儿”或“一定”的意思。*He'll show up. You can take my word for that.* 他会露面的。管保没错儿。◇ You can be sure of it. / accept what *someone* says

be unable to get a word in edgeways [ʌˌneɪbl təˌgedə ˌwə(ː)rdɪn ˈe(ː)dʒˌweɪz] [口] **没有插嘴的余地** 指“对方滔滔不绝地讲话”的样子。对方可以是一个人,也可以是复数。另外,be unable to 可以换用 be impossible to, can't, can hardly 等形式,edgeways 则常以同义的 edgewise [ˈe(ː)dʒˌwaɪz] (从旁边)来代替。*Mr. Mum apparently wanted to say something, but he was unable to get a word in edgeways.* 马姆先生显然想要说点什么,但是没有他插嘴的余地。*Mrs. Gosse is quite a chatterbox. When she is talking, it's impossible to get a word in edgeways.* 戈斯太太是一个大话匣子。当她高谈阔论的时候,别人没有插嘴的余地。*With everyone talking at once, I couldn't get a word in edgewise.* 一时之间人人都在讲话,没有我插嘴的余地。*When my mother-in-law is talking, it's no use ever trying to get a word in edgewise.* 当我婆婆讲话的时候,要想插嘴,根本没门儿。◇ be unable to enter the conversation [interrupt *someone's* monologue]

a weasel word [ə ˈwiːzəl ˌwəːrd] [口] **模棱两可的话** 字面意义为“鼬的话”。1900 年 S. 查普林 (Stewart Chaplin)在《世纪杂志》(*Century Magazine*)上最初使用。1916 年罗斯福在演说中使用后遂脍炙人口。*In 1916, Theodore Roosevelt attacked Woodrow Wilson's call for "Universal Voluntary Training" by calling "voluntary" a weasel word. You can have "universal training" or you can have "voluntary training", but you can't have *both, he said. When used together, "voluntary" is a weasel word which sucks all the meaning out of the term "universal".* 1916年,西奥多·罗斯福攻击伍德罗·威尔逊号召的"全国普遍志愿训练"中的"志愿"二字模棱两可。他说,你可以说"全国普遍训练",也可以说"志愿训练",但是不能合而为一。如果两者并用,则"志愿"二字就会把"全国普遍"一词的概念吸收净尽而使整体的意义暧昧不明了。*Most politicians appear to be adept at using weasel words.* 大多数政治家似乎都善于使用模棱两可的词句。这是指含含糊糊的、令人摸不清到底要说什么的词句。本条习用语有时不是指"暧昧的话",而是指"假话"或"欺人之谈"。*I'm sick and tired of your weasel words! Can't you just say yes or no?* 我对你那套和稀泥的话已经腻味透了。你不能脆脆快快说行或是不行吗?也可以使用形容词 weasel-worded (使用暧昧词句的)。*I just got another weasel- worded letter from that guy who owes me a thousand dollars.* 那个家伙欠我一千元美金,刚才我又收到他来的一封打马虎眼的信。◇ an equivocal [evasive] word

words

Actions speak louder than words. → ACTIONS

be at a loss for words [ədə ˌlɔːs fərˈwəːrdz] [口] **不知说什么好** → be at a LOSS

eat *one's* **words** [ˌi(ː)t ～ ˈwəːrdz] [口] **收回前言** 字面意义为"吃自己的话",即"取消以前说过的话"。请读者注意:千万不要望文生义,误译为"食言","食言"是 go back on *one's* word。本条条头前边一般加用 make, force, have to [ˈhæftə] 等,表示"不得不取消"的意思。另外,"收回前言"不仅是"订正不符合事实的谬说",往往包括"撤消侮辱或批评他人的讲话"。*If you make too definite a statement at this point, you may later end up having to eat your words.* 如果你在这个节骨眼儿上讲过于肯定的话,将来你很可能不得不收回前言。*The people who said that Reagan would never be elected President were forced to eat their words when he came through with flying colors.* 有些人说里根绝对不能当选为总统,当他大获全胜的时候,那些人不得不收回自己的前言。*So Harry said I was afraid of him, did he? I'll make him eat his words.* 哈里是说我害怕他吗?我会叫他把这话收回去的。*Sally called me stupid, but I'll make her eat her words. I'll show her I can make better grades than she can.* 萨莉管我叫傻瓜,但是我会叫她把这话再咽回去的。我要叫她看看我能取得比她更好的成绩。◇ take back what *one* has said

hang on *someone's* **words** [ˌhæŋən ～ ˈwəːrdz] [口] **倾听他人的讲话** → hang on *someone's* every WORD

have words(with *someone* over *something*) [ˌhæv ˈwəːrdz] [口] **争论** *We had words last night, so today we're not speaking.* 我们昨天晚上发生了口角,所以今天两个人不过话。*I had words with Charlene last night over whose turn it was to wash the dishes.* 昨天晚上我跟查伦争论该轮到谁刷盘子了。*Jack and Jill had words over which one spilled the pail of water.* 杰克和吉尔为谁弄洒了那桶水吵了起来。如以上的例句所示,have words 与 have an argument (争吵)的意思大致相同。但是,如果我们说 have a word 或者 have a few words,那就是"谈一谈"、"听听意见"、"商量商量"的意思了。在这一场合,不能省略 with *someone*。另外,后面不是接续 over *something*,而是用 about [concerning] *something*。*I'm going to have a word [few words] with that guy. He never keeps his promises.* 我想跟那个家伙谈一谈。他老不守信用。*Why don't you have a word with Bill? He knows all about it.* 你向比尔打听一下如何?他对这件事清楚得很。*I'll have a few words with him about that tomorrow.* 明天我跟他商量一下那个问题。◇ have a quarrel / argue

not mince (*one's*) **words** (with *someone*) [nɑt ˌmɪnts ˈwəːrdz] [口] **直言不讳** mince 是"切碎"。因此, not mince words 是

"不把话切碎",也就是"想说什么就冲口而出,不吞吞吐吐"。特别用于发怒或进行批评的场合。另外,在日常会话中,省略 one's 的时候居多。*After what has happened, I'm not going to mince words with you. You're a fool and a buffoon and I won't have you working for me anymore.* 既然发生了这种情况,我就要打开窗子说亮话了。你又蠢又笨,我再也不要你在我这儿干活了。*Jay is not one to mince words. He often hurts people's feelings by telling them exactly what he thinks.* 杰伊是一个直言不讳的人,怎么想就怎么说,为此他往往伤害他人的感情。*My husband doesn't like to mince his words. He prefers to call a spade a spade.* 我丈夫喜欢直言不讳,有啥说啥。◇ speak bluntly (to *someone*)

put words into *someone's* **mouth** [ˌput-ˈwəːrdz ɪntə ～ ˌmauθ] [口] **硬说某人讲过他实际上并没有说的话** 字面意义为"把话塞到某人的嘴里"。在日常会话中,into 常改为 in。"硬说某人讲过什么话"大多是"故意地",但也有时是"碰巧造成这样的后果"。*Don't pay any attention to what Stu says. He's always putting words into people's mouths.* 司徒所说的话,你一句也不要去听。别人并没有那样说,而他总是说人家讲过。这个例句中的 he 可能是"故意造谣",但也可能只是一个听着风便是雨的冒失鬼。自己的话被歪曲了的人往往这样说: *That's not what I said. Don't start putting words in my mouth.* 我没有说过那种话。不要把那话强加在我的头上。也有在要讲某件事情的时候用这一习用语作为开场白的情况,语气很轻松: *I hope I'm not putting words into his mouth, but I think John disagrees with this plan.* 约翰并没有说过这样的话,不过我认为,他不赞成这个计划。其次,本条习用语的原意是"把话塞到某人的嘴里",因此人们也用它来表示"教别人怎样讲"的意味。在一个句子里,它究竟是表示哪一种意义,主要是根据上下文来判断。请比较下面两个用例。*Someone is putting words into Joan's mouth. She's not the kind of person to say a terrible thing like that.* 有人无事生非,编造琼说的话。她不是能说那样可怕的事情的人。*Someone is putting words into Joan's mouth. She's not sharp enough to think of that idea herself.* 有人在教琼怎样讲。她本人的头脑还没有那么机灵,想不出那个主意来。附带说一句:在某些词典中只有第二个释义,其实,使用条头的释义的时候比较多。◇ attribute to *someone* words that *he* didn't say

take the words out of *someone's* **mouth** [ˌteɪkðə ˈwəːrdzaudəv ～ˈmauθ] [话] **说出某人心里要讲的话** 字面意义为"先从某人嘴里取出他要说的话"。words 的前边所以加 the,是指从嘴里就要冒出来的"那句话"。这个 the 不能省略。*I was going to suggest going to a movie when Lois took the words out of my mouth.* 我正要提议去看电影,洛伊丝把这话先说出来了。在实际上想要说而未说的场合,当然可以用本条习用语。此外,在自己还完全没有考虑到的场合,如果对方提出什么建议,自己觉得"正中下怀"的时候,也常使用这一习用语。特别是往往与加强语气的 right 一起使用。*A: Let's have a drink. B: You took the words right out of my mouth.* 甲:咱们喝一杯去吧。乙:简直是正中下怀啊! 另外,有一个形式上相反的说法为 put WORDS into *someone's* mouth, 二者在意义上并无关系。◇ say the same thing *someone* was about to say

weigh *one's* **words** [ˌweɪ ～ ˈwəːrdz] [口] **斟酌词句** 字面意义为"称词句的重量",指在发言时掂量每个词语的意味。*You must learn to weigh your words when speaking to important clients.* 你必须学会在对重要客户讲话时字斟句酌。*The President answered the question slowly, weighing his words.* 总统字斟句酌,慢条斯理地回答那个问题。常用 (very) carefully 或 with (great) care 加强语气。*In explaining to the parents their child's chances of recovery, the doctor weighed his words with (great) care.* 医生在向孩子的父母说明那个孩子康复的

可能性时，非常谨慎地斟酌自己的语句。◇ take care in selecting the words *one* uses ((with (great) care → take great care ~))

work

be all in a day's work [ˌɔː lɪnə ˈdeɪ ˈzwə(ː)rk] [话] **那是应该做的事情** 字面意义为“所有的只是一天工作中的一部分”，也就是“并非特别辛苦的事情”、“那只是分内的事情”的意思。*I don't like night duty, but when you work in a hospital as I do, you learn to consider it to be all in a day's work.* 我不喜欢上夜班。但是，既然象我这样在医院里工作，就得认为上夜班是应该应分的事情了。这种“应分的事”不仅限于规定的任务。*I don't mind staying after school to help my students. It's all in a day's work.* 放学以后留下来辅导学生，我一点也不觉得苦。这是我应该做的事情。除工作以外也广泛使用，特别是当有人表示感谢的时候，常用本条习用语来回答。*A: Thank you for returning my lost pocketbook. B: There's no need to thank me. It's all in a day's work.* 甲：谢谢你把捡到的钱包归还给我。乙：不用谢。这是应该做的事情。有时把 a day's work 改成 the day's work，而讲 be all in the day's work。◇ be just part of *one's* job / be just what anyone would do

have *one's* **work cut out for** *one* [ˌhæv ~ ˈwə(ː)rkːəˈdautfər ~] [话] **要吃很大的苦头** 字面意义为“由别人裁剪自己的工作”。如果不知道本条习用语是由西服店的工作方法而来，会感到莫名其妙。原来，所谓“由别人裁剪自己的工作”，是从“由别人裁剪西服的衣料”这一原意而来。因为是由别人裁剪，说不定裁成什么驴样马样。尽管如此，自己还得耐着性子去缝。于是，作为比喻使用时，本条习用语就有了“要吃很大的苦头”的意思。一般用于表示“今后麻烦多着呢”的意思，例如：*Any student who hopes to enter that university has his work cut out for him.* 凡是希望进那所大学的学生，肩上的担子可不轻啊。*Mary has a terrible temper. The man who marries her will have his work cut out for him.* 玛丽的脾气非常暴躁。谁要跟她结婚，是要吃很大的苦头的。*We have our work cut out for us if we're to finish this project by the end of the month.* 如果要求月底以前完成这个计划，那实在够我们呛的。也可以用没有 for *one* 的句型，但极罕见。◇ face a difficult task

make quick work of *something* [*someone*] [ˌmeɪk ˈkwɪk ˈwə(ː)rkəv ~] [话] **轻而易举** → make short WORK of *something* [*someone*]

make short work of *something* [*someone*] [ˌmeɪk ˈʃɔrt ˈwə(ː)rkəv ~] [话] **不费吹灰之力** 直译为“对某事或某人做短的工作 (short work)”，指“对事情，轻快地、麻利地干完”，“对人，很容易地一下子打垮”。“事情”的内容包括学习、工作、体育运动、议论、吵架、吃饭等等，范围很广。*Li made short work of the English test.* 李不费吹灰之力就答好了英语的试卷。*The professor made short work of my argument.* 教授三言两语就驳倒了我的论点。在讲食物的时候，“不费吹灰之力”就是“转眼之间就吃掉了”的意思。*The girls made short work of the cake.* 女孩子们转眼之间就把蛋糕吃光了。下边是“对人不费吹灰之力”的例子：*The champion will make short work of the challenger.* 冠军将会不费吹灰之力击败挑战者。有时用 quick (快) 代替 short，而讲 make quick work of *something* [*someone*] ◇ dispose of *something* [*someone*] quickly

a work addict [ə ˈwəːrˌkæ(ː)dɪkt] [口] **工作迷** → a WORKAHOLIC

work *someone* **over** [ˌwə(ː)rk ~ ˈouvər] [话] **狠狠收拾某人** over 有“在全身各处”的意思。直译为“在某人的全身各处工作一下”，意思是“对某人全身狠狠收拾一顿，或是踢，或是打，或是拧，使其感到痛苦”。*The men worked him over until he was almost unconscious, but he still refused to tell where the money was hidden.* 那些家伙狠狠地收拾他，几乎使他昏了过去，尽管如此，他还是不讲钱藏在了什

么地方。*If he doesn't come across with the information, work him over until he does.* 如果他不给送来情报，就狠狠收拾他，直到送来为止。*The gang worked over all the storekeepers who refused to pay "protection money."* 黑帮分子把所有拒绝交纳"保护费"的店主都狠狠收拾了一顿。另有一个用法是把 work over 改成名词形式，作 give *someone* a working over。在这一场合，多以形容词 good 加强语气。*The reporter still hasn't learned his lesson. We'd better give him another good working over.* 那个记者还没有接受教训。我们最好是再狠狠地收拾他一顿。◇ beat *someone* (thoroughly)

workaholic

a workaholic [ə ˌwə(:)rkəˈhɔ(:)lɪk] [口] **有工作瘾头的人** 一个新名词，由 work (工作) 与 alcoholic (酒精中毒者) 结合而成。指不做点什么事情心里就难受、一有空闲便焦躁不安的人，这种人很象有酒瘾的人似的。*My father was a workaholic. He never made time to play with us kids.* 我父亲有工作的瘾头。他连一点时间也不腾出来跟我们孩子们玩儿。有时使用 an addict (有瘾的人)，而讲 a work addict。◇ a compulsive worker

working

give *someone* **a working over** [ˌgɪv ～ ə ˌwə(:)rkɪˈnouvər] [话] **狠狠地收拾某人** → WORK *someone* over

works

give *someone* **the works** [ˌgɪv ～ ðə ˈwə(:)rks] [话] **狠狠地整某人** → the WORKS

gum up the works [ˌgʌmˈʌpðə ˈwə(:)rks] [话] **把计划、工作等搞糟** 这里的 gum 是"用树脂之类的东西将某物粘住"。works 是"机械的装置"。条头直译为"把机械装置抹上粘的东西"。可以按照字面意义使用，如：*This clock doesn't run. Someone spilled some resin or something in it and gummed up the works.* 这个钟不走了。有人弄进去树脂之类的东西，把里边的机件都粘住了。转作比喻使用，表示"毁坏"的意思，用于"计划"、"工作"等。*I was going to take my family to the beach today, but my wife gummed up the works by inviting my in-laws for dinner.* 今天我本要带领全家去海滨，可是我的妻子邀请她的父母前来吃晚饭，把整个计划打乱了。*Don't mention our talk to anyone for the time being. You'll gum up the works if you tell the wrong person.* 我们刚才的谈话你不要对任何人讲。如果你告诉不适当的人，就会把事情搞糟了。可以使用 things 代替 works，而讲 gum things up。也可以既不用 works 也不用 things，只讲 gum *something* up 或者 gum up *something*。不论采取哪种形式，意思不变。*We decided not to include Simon in our plans. He's always gumming things up with his bonehead mistakes.* 我们决定不叫西蒙参加我们的计划。他一向爱犯愚蠢的错误，把事情搞糟。*It's a good plan. I hope Harold doesn't gum it up.* 那是一个很好的计划。我希望哈罗德不把它搞糟。主语一般是"人"，但也有不是如此的场合。*The weather gummed up our plans for a picnic today.* 坏天气使今天我们出去野游的计划告吹了。◇ ruin everything

shoot the works [ˌʃu(:)tðə ˈwə(:)rks] [话] **豁出去** the works 是"所有的一切"。本条直译为"把所有的一切射出去"，也就是"一下子都用光"的意味。用于不惜一切金钱或力量、也不考虑这样做的后果的场合。*Let's shoot the works and have caviar, lobster and champagne for dinner.* 咱们豁出去吧，晚餐要吃鱼子酱、大虾，喝香槟酒。但是，特别是在谈到"钱"的场合，虽然说是"孤注一掷"，倒不一定指"倾囊中所有"，而是指"不考虑钱多钱少的问题"。*We usually go camping near home for our vacation, but this year we decided to shoot the works and go to Europe.* 我们放假的时候总是到离家近的地方野营，但是今年决定不惜金钱前往欧洲去旅行了。有时表示"盛大举行"的意味。常用 really 加强语气。*The Joneses really shot the works on their* *son's wedding reception.* 琼斯夫妇为儿子结婚举行的招待会的确是够盛大的。以下是无论什么"全都豁出去"的用例。*With ammunition getting low, the captain decided to shoot the works in an attempt to break through the enemy blockade.* 弹药越来越少,上尉决心不顾一切牺牲突破敌人的封锁线。*In hopes of getting out of its financial bind in one fell swoop, the company has decided to shoot the works on this one project.* 公司决定把一切人力物力都投入这一个计划,以期一下子摆脱经济上的困难。*Though his engine was seriously overheating, the race driver knew he had no choice but to throw caution to the winds and shoot the works if he hoped to win.* 虽然发动机过热,但是那个赛车选手知道:如果他希望获胜,那就没有别的选择,只能豁出一切,拼搏到底。◇ spare no expense [effort] / use all *one's* remaining resources [power]

the works [ðə ˈwə(ː)rks] [话] **全套** 指"一包在内",例如去理发店的时候,如果说 *I'll have the works.* 这是指包括所有的项目,除理发外,还要洗头、刮脸、修指甲、按摩等。假如是把汽车开进加油站,说同样一句话,那意思当然是指除加油而外,还要检修车、注润滑油、洗车等。*Gimme a hamburger with the works.* 给我来一盘汉堡牛排,全套。这里的"全套"指汉堡牛排所有附带的东西,如番茄酱、洋葱、芥末、泡菜等。*A: What benefits did you ask for when you applied for the job? B: Saturdays off, two weeks' paid vacation, full unemployment and health benefits—the works.* 甲:当你应聘去干那个工作的时候,你提出了什么条件啦? 乙:星期六不上班;每年两个星期休假,其间工资照付;失业保险;健康保险;总之,一应俱全。另外,在带有 the works 的习用语中,特别应该注意的是 give *someone* the works 和 get the works (from *someone*)。这两种说法虽然也都可以用于"服务"、"物品"、"待遇"等,但是一般来说,前一说法用于表示"狠狠地整人",后一说法用于表示"挨人狠狠地整一顿"的意味。*Give him the works, but don't kill him. We don't want a murder rap on our hands.* 狠狠地收拾收拾他,但是不要杀死他。我们不愿意落下个杀人的罪名。"收拾"大多是使用"暴力",但也有时只是用"口头"。*I really got the works from the chief for not coming to work yesterday.* 我昨天没来上班,被科长狠狠地训斥了一大顿。在以上两个例句中,works 照样含有"全套"的意味:前者表示"用全套的暴力行为",后者表示"用全套的批评词句"。◇ everything / all the accessories / the complete treatment

world

come down in the world [kʌm ˈdaunənðə ˌwəːrld] [口] **没落** 这里的 world 是"人间"的意思。条头直译为"在人间往下掉",指有地位、名声、财产的人失掉这些东西,至于"往下掉"到什么程度,要根据上下文决定。在表示"没落"的程度时,常加副词 a bit, somewhat, completely 等。在使用 completely 的场合,有"彻底垮台"的意味。*Mr. Redding has come down in the world since he was forced to resign as cabinet minister because of a scandal.* 雷丁先生因丑闻而被迫辞去内阁部长职务以后,弄得身败名裂。*From what I hear, Lowman has come down in the world a bit since we last met.* 我听说,自从我们上次会面以后,洛曼有点儿走下坡路。*The Lostrocks family used to be very wealthy, but they've come completely down in the world since the family business went bankrupt.* 罗思托洛克斯家过去非常有钱,但是自从他家的生意破产之后,就一贫如洗了。反义语为 come up in the WORLD。◇ fall in status

come up in the world [ˌkʌˈmʌpənðə ˌwəːrld] [口] **发迹** 直译为"在人间往上升"。意思与 rise in the WORLD 大致相同,但 come up in the world 的使用范围窄。也就是说,rise in the world 常用于一般性的谈论,而本条条头总是具体陈述某一特定人物。主要是回顾过去,而讲"比那个时候 come up 了",因此,构成完成时的句子的情况居多。常用 really 或 certainly 加强语气。*Elliott had really come up in the world the last time I saw him.* 上次我见到埃利奥特的时候，他已经非常出息了。下边的例句是讲未来的事情。这是假定在未来的某个时刻来回顾现在的情况。*I'm sure you'll have come up in the world when next we meet.* 我确信在我们下次见面的时候，你一定飞黄腾达了。本条习用语除"发迹"外，根据上下文，还有类似"一步登天"的意思。*Mr. Jones appears to have come up in the world since his oldest son married the boss's daughter.* 自从他的长子与老板的女儿结婚以后，琼斯先生的社会地位似乎突然上升了。也可以用于国家、机关或团体。*Labor unions have certainly come up in the world in the past eighty years.* 在过去的八十年间，工会的地位大大提高了。反义语为 come down in the WORLD。◇ rise in status / improve *one's* position in life [in the world]

be dead to the world [ˈde(ː)d təðə ˈwəːrld] [话] **酣睡** 字面意义为"对外部世界死去了"，这是表示熟睡状态的习用语。*Ben studied till three o'clock this morning. Now he's upstairs dead to the world.* 本复习功课一直到今天早晨三点钟。现在他在楼上睡大觉呢。有时用于表示"完全失去知觉"的意味。*You were dead to the world for two hours after that brick hit you on the head.* 在那块砖头打中你的头部之后，你有两个钟头完全失去了知觉。另外，条头过去可以用于"酩酊大醉"的场合，现在不再表示这一意义了。◇ be sound asleep / be completely unconscious

have the world at *one's* **feet** [ˌhævðə ˈwəːrldət ～ˈfiːt] [口] **受群众爱戴** 直译为"世界在自己的脚下"。虽然可以用于以武力征服的场合，但本条习用语的基本意思是"大家匍伏在自己的脚下称颂"，也就是受到群众的拥护或爱戴。因为周围全是捧场的人们，自己不论干什么都会如愿以偿。*If your book becomes a best-seller, you'll have the world at your feet. Then you'll be able to write anything you want.* 如果你的著作成为一本畅销书，你就会受到人们的爱戴。这样一来，你想写什么便能写什么了。强调的时候可以用 all the world, 但一般均用 the whole world。*When the victorious Caesar returned to Rome, he had the whole world at his feet.* 当战胜者凯撒回到罗马的时候，他受到全体人民的爱戴。也可以使用 with the world at *one's* feet 或 the whole world is at *one's* feet 的形式。*Sally never dreamed that someday she would be a great star with the world at her feet.* 萨莉做梦也没有想到她有一天会成为一个人们崇拜的大明星。*Ten years ago the whole world was at my feet. Now I'm just a penniless has-been.* 十年前，我曾受到整个社会的赞颂。现在呢，我是个一文不名的落魄人。本条习用语偶尔用于表示"前途远大"的意思 (→ have the WORLD before *one*)。◇ be lionized by the world

have the world before *one* [ˌhævðə wəːrld bəˈfo(ː)r ～] [口] **有远大的前途** 直译为"世界在眼前"，意思是"世界正在眼前展开"，指前途无量。*You are young and you have the world before you. You must make the best of your opportunities.* 你年轻，有远大的前途。你必须最大限度地利用自己的机会。强调的场合说 the whole (wide) world 或者 all the world。*Only twenty years ago I was a student and felt I had the whole world before me. Now I'm already worrying about retirement.* 仅仅二十年前，我还是个大学生，觉得自己的前途非常远大。而今呢，我已为退休而发愁了。另外，也可以使用 with the world before *one*, the world is before *one* 的形式，意思相同。*When you are young with all the world [and all the world is] before you, you feel you are able to accomplish anything.* 人在年轻的时候，由于前程远大，总觉得任何事情都能够完成。◇ have the many possibilities of the future to choose and experience

in the world [ɪnðə ˈwəːrld] [口] **世界上；到底、究竟** → every *something* [*someone*] under the SUN

a man of the world → MAN

be out of this world [ˈaudəv ˌðɪs ˈwəːrld] [话] **出类拔萃** 字面意义为"离开这个世界"，意思是"简直超出世界上的一切东西"。*The food at that restaurant is out of this world.* 那家餐厅的食品与众不同。*Isn't Jill's gown out of this world?* 吉尔的礼服简直再漂亮也没有了，是吧？有时含有讽刺性质，表示"脱离现实"、"不合情理"的意味。*That's not a bad house, but the price they are asking for it is out of this world.* 那所房子倒不坏，不过他们要的价钱也太出类拔萃了。◇ be really wonderful [delicious, beautiful, etc.] / be extremely unrealistic

rise in the world [ˌraɪzənðə ˈwərld] [口] **社会地位上升** 具有同样意味的 come up in the WORLD 通常讲特定的人，并以过去的水准进行回顾，因而大多使用完成时。本条没有这样的限制，一般广泛使用。come up ～全部可以换用 rise ～，反过来则不一定行得通。在下面的头两个例句中，说话者如果不是已经飞黄腾达的老前辈，使用 come up ～就不相宜。*You have to study hard and work hard if you hope to rise in the world.* 如果你希望发迹，就必须刻苦学习和拼命工作。*Through hard work, Elliott quickly rose in the world, and within ten years was president of his own company.* 埃利奥特由于拼命工作，很快就飞黄腾达起来，仅仅十年就当上了本公司的总经理。也可以应用于国家、机关、团体。常用 far 加强语气。*China has risen far in the world since the end of 1970's.* 自从70年代末起，中国突飞猛进地发展起来了。◇ become a success (in life) / rise in status / improve *one's* position in life [in the world] ((far → vastly <improve>))

set the world on fire [ˌsetðə ˈwəːrld-ɔ(ː)nˌfaɪr] [口] **轰动世界** 这是一个夸大的说法，直译为"点把火烧整个世界"。一般用于不断发表杰作、做出突出成绩、从而"引起巨大反响"的场合。至于"巨大反响"的内容，从"令人刮目相看"直到"涌现狂热信徒"，范围极广。*I don't want to set the world of fire. I'm satisfied just to be an ordinary wage earner.* 我不想轰动世界。我只当一名领工资吃饭的人就心满意足了。*Jarvis is a competent novelist, but hardly one to set the world on fire.* 贾维斯是一个很有才气的小说家，但是还不足以轰动世界。如以上的例句所示，大多构成否定句，但并不限定如此。*Stick with me and we'll set the world on fire. We'll be the greatest dancing team in the country.* 你要跟我在一起，咱们就会轰动社会，咱们将是全国最佳的双人舞搭当。◇ (do something to) excite the world [the world's imagination] / make a great reputation for *oneself*

a woman of the world [ə ˌwumənəvðə ˈwəːrld] [口] **很有见识的女子** → a MAN of the world

worm

The early bird catches the worm. → BIRD

worse

go from bad to worse → BAD

worst

put *one's* worst foot forward [ˌput ～ ˌwə(ː)rst ˌfut ˈfɔːrwərd] [话] **给人留下最坏的印象** → put *one's* best FOOT forward

worth

be not worth the paper it's written on → PAPER

***one's* two cents worth** → CENTS

would

would (just) as soon *do something* as *do something* [(wu)d (ˌdʒʌst) əzˌsu(ː)n ˈ～ əz ˈ～] [话] **做这个也可以，做那个也可以，没有好恶的不同** → *Someone* would just as soon *do something* as LOOK at you.

would-be

a would-be *something* [ə ˈwudˌbiː ～] [口] **①想要成为某种人物的人；②自认为是某种人物；③有意采取的行动或怀着好意去做某事的人** ①是 a person who hopes to become a ～的意思。*Hollywood is full of young, would-be actresses who dream of being famous someday.* 好莱坞充满了年轻的、想当女演员的、梦想将来有一天成名的人。*Would-be poets must work very hard studying and practicing many styles of poetry.* 有志当诗人的人必须刻苦学习和努力尝试多种诗歌的风格。②是 a person who (mistakenly) thinks he is a ～的意思。*Be careful of who you go into business with. The world is full of would-be businessmen who don't know the first thing about business.* 你对于跟你一道做生意的人要加小心。社会上到处都是自认为是生意人的家伙，他们连做生意的最起码知识都没有。*Jack is a would-be wit whose jokes all fall flat.* 杰克自认为是幽默大师，他的笑话却总是平淡无奇。在使用这一意义时，可以把"事物"或"场所"人格化。*I wouldn't eat in that would-be restaurant again, even if I were starving.* 哪怕我挨饿，也决不到那家美其名为饭店的地方吃饭。③是 an act which is intended to be (a) ～的意思。*Would-be kindnesses often cause great inconvenience to the recipient.* 本来出于好意的行动，往往给对方造成很大的麻烦。在这一意义时，主语如果是"人"，便为 a well-intentioned person who tries (but fails) to be a ～的意思。*My three-year-old daughter is mother's would-be helper.* 我三岁的女儿自动地去帮助母亲干活。另外，也有这样的场合：究竟按①、②、③的哪一个意义来解释，必须根据前后关系来判断。*Publishing companies receive manuscripts from hundreds of would-be authors every year.* 出版公司每年要收到成千百部有志当作家［自认为是作家］的人们送来的书稿。◇ ① (a person) hopeful of becoming a *something* ② (a person who) mistakenly thinks of himself [herself] as a *something* (but～) / an imitation *something* ③ an act that is intended to be (a) *something* / (a well-intentioned person who) tries to be (a) *something*

wow

Wow! ['wau] [话] **哇！**((表示惊叹)) *Wow! I can't believe it! I've won ten thousand yuan!* 哇！简直令人难以相信！我中了一万元奖券！本条条头是表示极度惊异的用语，在 GOLLY, GEE, GOSH, 等许多同类的感叹词中，是最强烈的表达法。在使用时不拘年龄、性别，但根据上下文，略有幼稚的意味。*Wow! Look at that! A helicopter flying upside down.* 哇！你瞧！一架直升飞机整个翻过来飞。*Wow! A year in Paris! Do you really mean it, Dad?!* 哇！到巴黎呆一年！这是真的吗，爸爸?! *You sat next to Paul Newman at the concert? Wow!* 在音乐会中，你是坐在保罗·纽曼旁边了吗？哇！本条条头可以原封不动地作为动词使用，构成 wow *someone* 的形式，意思是"使人惊叹"、"使观众等热烈赞扬"。*The comedian wowed the audience with his seemingly endless string of oneliners.* 那个喜剧演员以他那似乎没完没了的一连串小笑话博得听众热烈的赞扬。*You'll wow all the boys with that low-cut gown.* 你穿那件低领口的衣服会使所有的青年男子神魂颠倒的。

wow *someone* ['wau ～] [话] **使人惊叹** → Wow!

write

be nothing to write home about → HOME

be something to write home about [ˌsʌ-mtə ˌraɪt 'hou m əˌbaut] [话] **好得了不得** → be nothing to write HOME about

Y

ya

ya [jə] [话] **你** 把非重音的 you 按发音拼写而成。在漫画、小说中的会话部分经常见到。*Ya hungry?* 你饿吗? *Ya aren't goin', are ya?* 你不去吧? *Are ya afraid to go in?* 你害怕走进去吗? ◇ you

yeah

yeah ['je(:)ə] [话] **嗯** 与 yes 相当的轻松的回答用语。主要对伙伴或晚辈使用。过去绝对禁止对长上使用,现在大有放宽尺度的倾向。不过,如果使用得不好,就会令人感到缺乏礼貌,伤害他人的自尊心。因此,这个用语不能说是对任何人都通用。*A: Seen Jim lately? B: Yeah. Saw him last week.* 甲:最近见到吉姆了吗? 乙:嗯。上星期见到他了。有时作 yeh ['je:],很不礼貌。◇ yes

yeh

yeh ['je:] [俗] **嗯** → YEAH

yelling

be all over but the yelling ['ɔ: 'louvər bətðə 'jelɪŋ] [话] **大局已定** → be all over but the SHOUTING

yep

yep ['je(:)p] [话] **嗯** yes 的轻松说法,可以认为是把 YEAH 的语气进一步加强。发音时是把 yes 的尾音上挑,略微加重,将 [s] 换成 [p]。但要注意:[p] 是闭锁音,最后双唇合拢,不能张开。在回答时,比使用 yeah 更干脆。例如说 *Yeah, I'm going.* 嗯,我去。根据声调,可能含有"虽然我不大想去……"的意思。如果说 *Yep, I'm going.* 则多多少少含有"我一定去"的意思。又如,一位父亲说 *Yeah, that's my boy.* 嗯,那是我的男孩子。假若不注意说话的声调或前后关系,就不了解这位父亲对自己的儿子究竟有何想法。如果他说 *Yep, that's my boy.* 则大多含有"没错,那是我的儿子,够好的吧?"的意思。yep 的反义词为 NOPE,在干脆否定时使用。◇ yes

yokel

a yokel [ə'joukl] [口] **乡巴佬** → a country HICK / a country BUMPKIN

yo-yo

a yo-yo [ə 'jou.jou] [话] **笨蛋** 原为玩具名。作为商品名的 yo-yo 开头字头大写,作 Yo-Yo, 现在一般都是小写。*Danny is very good with a yo-yo.* 丹尼玩"摇摇"玩得非常好。*The plane hit some rough air and started going up and down like a yo-yo.* 飞机撞到了强气流,开始象"摇摇"一样上下摆动。可以把"人"比做"摇摇",这样说: *You yo-yo. That's not the way to do it.* 你这个笨蛋。不是那样干。为什么用"摇摇"表示"笨蛋"的意思,来源不详。主要是青年人使用,语气相当轻松。男女均可使用,但一般用于男性身上。*I was walking down the street in New York when some yo-yo stops me and asks me which subway to take for Disneyland.* 当我正在纽约的大街上漫步的时候,一个笨蛋拦住了我,问我去迪斯尼乐园要乘哪一条地铁。顺便提一下:在这一例句中,没有遵循时态一致的原则,这是会话体裁的特征。在想要描写生动的场合,用现在时比较传神。*A: I hear the Loser brothers have opened a consulting office. B: Those yo-yos? They wouldn't know how to tell a lawyer how to get to court.* 甲:我听说洛塞弟兄开了一个咨询公司。乙:那两个笨蛋吗? 他们连律师去法院走哪条路都说不清楚。◇ a stupid [an incompetent] person

yummy

yummy ['jʌmi] [话] **好吃** 在品尝食物觉得很香的时候,嘴唇和舌头一边动着一边发出 yum 或者 yum-yum 的声音,这是个象声词,表示好吃的意思。本条条头是形容词的形式。主要使用者为妇女儿童。*These are yummy pickles.* 这泡菜很好吃。*That cake looks yummy.* 那个蛋糕看样子一定好吃。比较级为 yummier,最高级为 yummiest。*We had the yummiest meal at that restaurant.* 我们在那家餐厅吃了一顿极好吃的饭。除"好吃"的意思外,有时表示"好看"。*What a yummy color!* 多么好看的颜色啊! *That's a yummy dress she's wearing.* 她穿的那件衣服真好看。◇ delicious / beautiful

Z

Z

from A to Z → A

zillion

a zillion [ə ˈzɪljən] [话] **无限大的数目** → a JILLION

zip

zip [ˈzɪ(:)p] [话] **(体育比赛)零分** zip 一词一般有"尖啸声"、"活力"、"精力"等意思。 *Cars were zipping by on the highway.* 汽车一辆接一辆在公路上飞驰而过。 *I don't have any zip today. Maybe I'm catching a cold.* 我今天一点儿精神都没有，可能是感冒啦。 *That author's stories are interesting, but his style doesn't have any zip.* 那位作家写的小说很有趣，但是笔下没有一点儿魄力。此外，在许多场合又表示"数字的零"的意味。 *A: How much cash have you got on you? B: Zip.* 甲：你带着多少现金？乙：一分也没有。在 20 世纪初，zip 是学生的俚语，意思是考试的"零分"。最近又开始复活，特别指体育比赛的"零分"。在电视等的体育节目中，常有这样的解说：*At halftime, the score was still zip to zip.* 上半时终了，比分仍然是零比零。 *The final score was eleven to zip.* 最后比分是 11 比 0。会话举例：*A: What's the score? B: Three to zip.* 甲：比分是多少？乙：3 比 0。◇ none / nothing

a zip code → CODE

z's

catch some z's [ˌkætʃsəm ˈziːz] [话] **睡觉** → grab some z's

grab some z's [ˌgræ(:)bsəm ˈziːz] [话] **睡觉** grab 是"抓取"的意思。z's 是 z 的复数形式。美国的漫画常用连串的 z-z-z-z 表示 snore (打呼噜)。因此，特别是在青年人中间，就用 grab some z's 表示"睡觉"。这是一个相当轻松的说法，不论"夜里睡"还是"白天睡"，全都可以使用。但是，grab 一词是具有积极意愿的行为，所以本条习用语一般用于主动去就寝的场合，在"并没有睡觉的打算而昏昏沉沉入睡"的场合是很少使用的。*I've gotta get up early in the morning. I'm gonna grab some z's.* 明天早晨我必须早起。我要睡觉去啦。 *I work till late at night, so I always grab some z's after lunch if I can.* 我夜里工作到很晚，因此只要有可能，我总是在午饭之后睡上一觉。动词可以用 catch 代替 grab; some z's 可以用 a few z's 或 a couple of z's 等代替。 *Dick often catches a few z's on his way to work on the train.* 迪克经常在坐火车去上班的途中打个盹儿。◇ sleep

索引

B

C

D

E

F

G

H

I

L

M

N

O

P

Q

R

S

T

U

V

W

Y

Z